DESIGNING WITH PROGRAMMABLE ARRAY LOGIC

Acknowledgements

The following employees of Monolithic Memories made contributions to this 2nd edition of the PAL APPLICATION HANDBOOK. Specific technical contributions are sited on line two of the PAL DESIGN SPECIFICATION.

Product Planning and Applications Department

Ehud Gordon, Applications Engineer
Saeed Kazmi, PAL Product Marketing Engineer
Nadia Sachs, Senior Applications Engineer
Shlomo Waser, Manager, Product Planning and Applications

Sales

Bernard Brafman, District Sales Manager (Northern California)
Harry Hughes, Field Applications Engineer (Northern Europe)
Dick Jones, District Sales Manager (Illinois)
Vincent Leclerc, Field Applications Engineer (Southern Europe)
Brad Mitchell, Field Applications Engineer (South East)
Willy Voldan, Field Applications Engineer (Central Europe)
Mike Volpigno, Field Applications Engineer (East Coast)

Graphics

Adamson & Walton, Graphic Designers (Mountain View)

To these individuals we extend our gratitude,

John Birkner, Monolithic Memories Fellow
Vincent Coli, Applications Engineer

DESIGNING WITH PROGRAMMABLE ARRAY LOGIC

by the Technical Staff of
Monolithic Memories, Inc.

SECOND EDITION

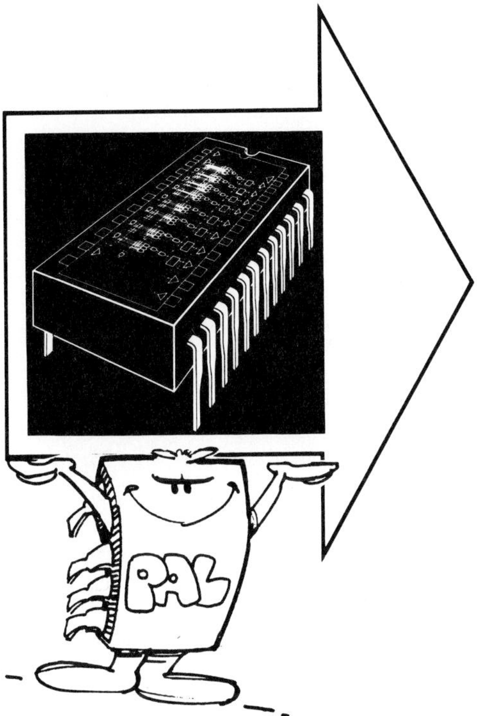

McGraw-Hill Book Company

New York St. Louis San Francisco Auckland
Bogotá Hamburg Johannesburg London
Madrid Mexico Montreal New Delhi
Panama Paris São Paulo Singapore
Sydney Tokyo Toronto

Monolithic Memories MMI

1234567890 DOC DOC 89876543

ISBN 0-07-042723-2

The editors for this book were Harry H. Helms and Ruth L. Weine.

Printed and bound by R. R. Donnelley & Sons Company.

Table of Contents

The PAL™ Concept

Monolithic Memories' family of PAL devices gives designers a powerful tool with unique capabilities for use in new and existing logic designs. The PAL saves time and money by solving many of the system partitioning and interface problems brought about by increases in semiconductor device technology.

Rapid advances in large scale integration technology have led to larger and larger standard logic functions; single I.C.s now perform functions that formerly required complete circuit cards. While LSI offers many advantages, advances have been made at the expense of device flexibility. Most LSI devices still require large numbers of SSI/MSI devices for interfacing with user systems. Designers are still forced to turn to random logic for many applications.

The designer is confronted with another problem when a low to medium complexity product is designed. Often the function is well defined and could derive significant benefits from fabrication as an integrated circuit. However, the design cycle for a custom circuit is long and the costs can be very high. This makes the risk significant enough to deter most users. The technology to support maximum flexibility combined with fast turn around on custom logic has simply not been available. Monolithic Memories offers the programmable solution.

The PAL family offers a fresh approach to using fuse programmable logic. PALs are a conceptually unified group of devices which combine programmable flexibility with high speed and an extensive selection of interface options. PALs can lower inventory, cut design cycles and provide high complexity with maximum flexibility. These features, combined with lower package count and high reliability, truly make the PAL a circuit designer's best friend.

The PAL—Teaching Old PROMs New Tricks

MMI developed the modern PROM and introduced many of the architectures and techniques now regarded as industry standards. As the world's largest PROM manufacturer, MMI has the proven technology and high volume production capability required to manufacture and support the PAL.

The PAL is an extension of the fusible link technology pioneered by Monolithic Memories for use in bi-polar PROMs. The fusible link PROM first gave the digital systems designer the power to "write on silicon." In a few seconds he was able to transform a blank PROM from a general purpose device into one containing a custom algorithm, microprogram, or Boolean transfer function. This opened up new horizons for the use of PROMs in computer control stores, character generators, data storage tables and many other applications. The wide acceptance of this technology is clearly demonstrated by today's multi-million dollar PROM market.

The key to the PROM's success is that it allows the designer to quickly and easily customize the chip to fit his unique requirements. The PAL extends this programmable flexibility by utilizing proven fusible link technology to implement logic functions. Using PALs the designer can quickly and effectively implement custom logic varying in complexity from random gates to complex arithmetic functions.

ANDs and ORs

The PAL implements the familiar sum of products logic by using a programmable AND array whose output terms feed a fixed OR array. Since the sum of products form can express any Boolean transfer function, the PAL's uses are only limited by the number of terms available in the AND - OR arrays. PALs come in different sizes to allow for effective logic optimization.

Figure 1 shows the basic PAL structure for a two input, one output logic segment. The general logic equation for this segment is

$$\text{Output} = (I_1+\overline{f_1})(\overline{I_1}+\overline{f_2})(I_2+\overline{f_3})(\overline{I_2}+\overline{f_4}) + (I_1+\overline{f_5})(\overline{I_1}+\overline{f_6})(I_2+\overline{f_7})(\overline{I_2}+\overline{f_8})$$

where the "f" terms represent the state of the fusible links in the PAL's AND array. An unblown link represents a logic 1. Thus,

fuse blown, $f = 0$

fuse intact, $f = 1$

An unprogrammed PAL has all fuses intact.

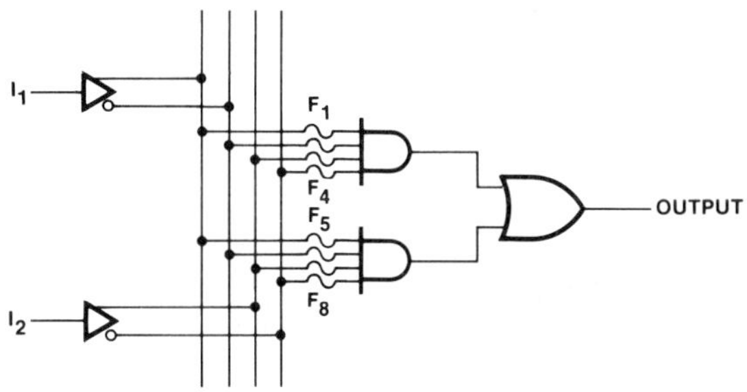

Figure 1

PAL Notation

Logic equations, while convenient for small functions, rapidly become cumbersome in large systems. To reduce possible confusion, complex logic networks are generally defined by logic diagrams and truth tables. Figure 2 shows the logic convention adopted to keep PAL logic easy to understand and use. In the figure, an "x" represents an intact fuse used to perform the logic AND function. (Note: the input terms on the common line with the x's are not connected together.) The logic symbology shown in Figure 2 has been informally adopted by integrated circuit manufacturers because it clearly establishes a one-to-one correspondence between the chip layout and the logic diagram. It also allows the logic diagram and truth table to be combined into a compact and easy to read form, thereby serving as a convenient shorthand for PALs. The two input - one output example from Figure 1 redrawn using the new logic convention is shown in Figure 3.

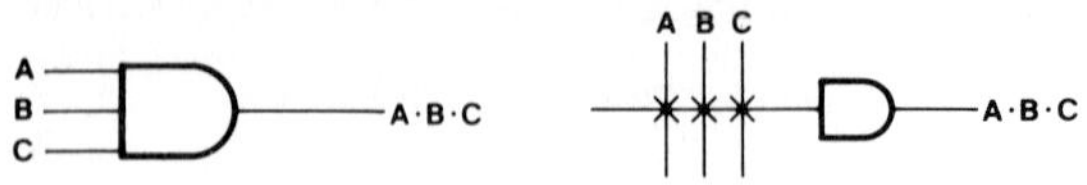

Figure 2

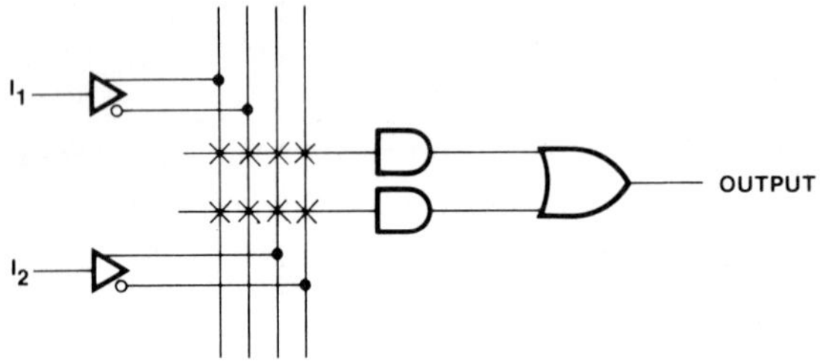

Figure 3

As a simple PAL example, consider the implementation of the transfer function:

$$\text{Output} = I_1\overline{I_2} + \overline{I_1}I_2$$

The normal combinatorial logic diagram for this function is shown in figure 4, with the PAL logic equivalent shown in figure 5.

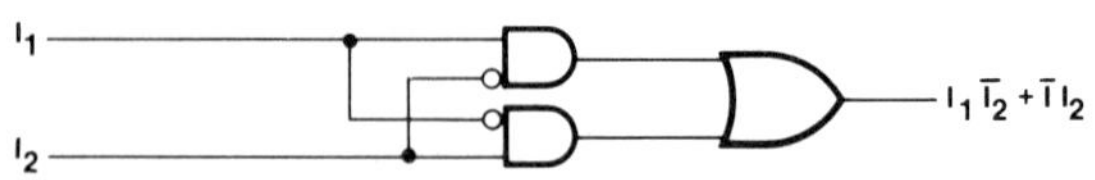

Figure 4

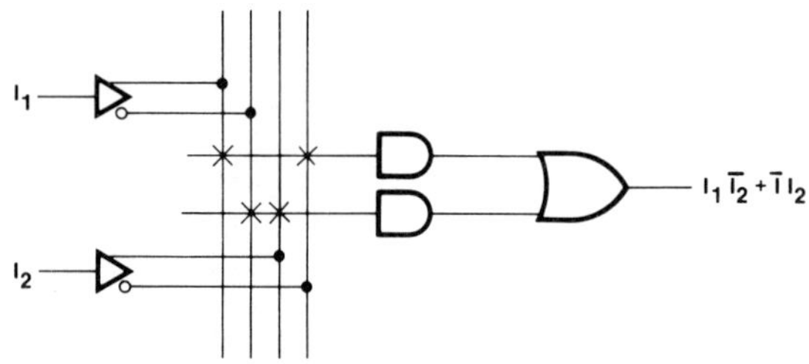

Figure 5

Using this logic convention it is now possible to compare the PAL structure to the structure of the more familiar PROM and PLA. The basic logic structure of a PROM consists of a fixed AND array whose outputs feed a programmable OR array (figure 6). PROMs are low-cost, easy to program, and available in a variety of sizes and organizations. They are most commonly used to store computer programs and data. In these applications the fixed input is a computer memory address; the output is the contents of that memory location.

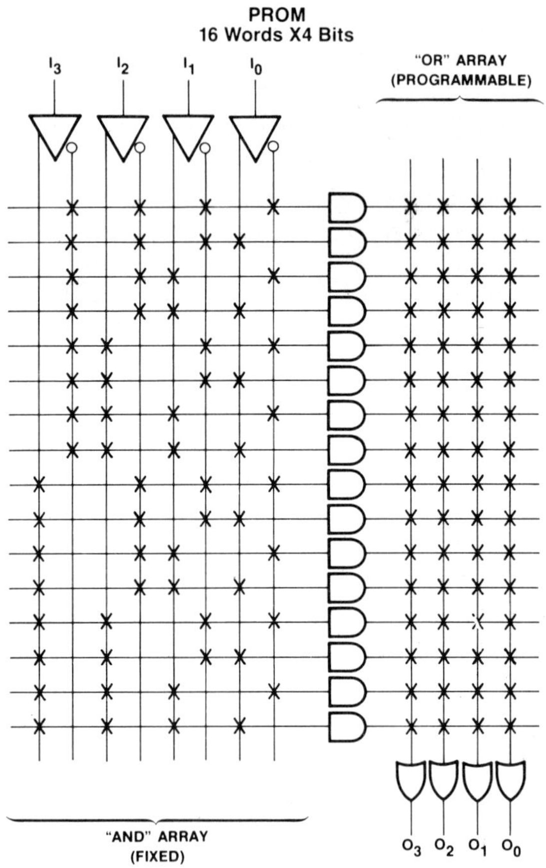

Figure 6

The basic logic structure of the PLA consists of a programmable AND array whose outputs feed a programmable OR array (Figure 7). Since the designer has complete control over all inputs and outputs, the PLA provides the ultimate flexibility for implementing logic functions. They are used in a wide variety of applications. However, this generality makes PLAs expensive, quite formidable to understand, and costly to program (they require special programmers).

The basic logic structure of the PAL, as mentioned earlier, consists of a programmable AND array whose outputs feed a fixed OR array (Figure 8). The PAL combines much of the flexibility of the PLA with the low cost and easy programmability of the PROM. Table 1 summarizes the characteristics of the PROM, PLA, and PAL logic families.

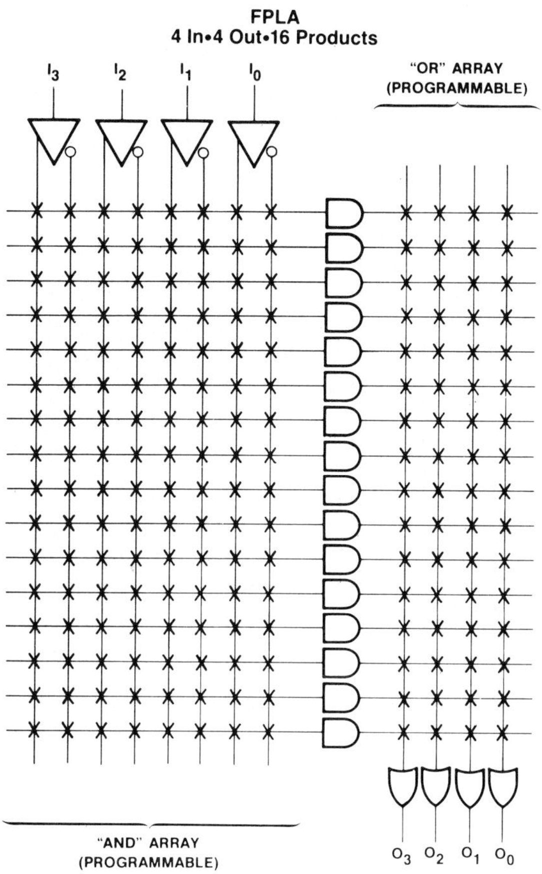

Figure 7

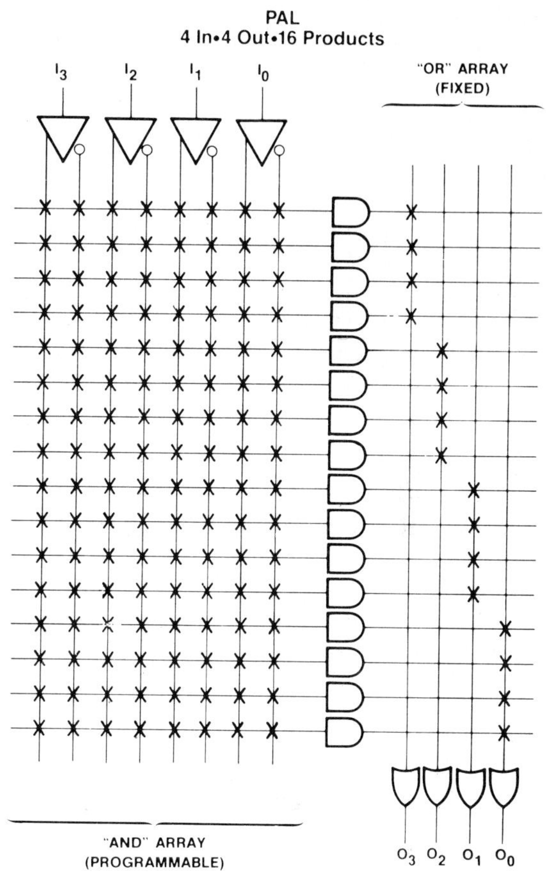

Figure 8

	AND	OR	OUTPUT OPTIONS
PROM	Fixed	Prog	TS, OC
FPLA	Prog	Prog	TS, OC, Fusible Polarity
FPGA	Prog	None	TS, OC, Fusible Polarity
FPLS	Prog	Prog	TS, Registered Feedback, I/O
PAL	Prog	Fixed	TS, Registered Feedback, I/O

Table 1

PAL Input/Output/Function/Performance Chart

PART NUMBER	INPUT	OUTPUT	PROGRAMMABLE I/O'S	FEEDBACK REGISTER	OUTPUT POLARITY	FUNCTIONS	PERFORMANCE			
							STD	A	-2	-4
PAL10H8	10	8			AND-OR	AND-OR Gate Array	X		X	
PAL12H6	12	6			AND-OR	AND-OR Gate Array	X		X	
PAL14H4	14	4			AND-OR	AND-OR Gate Array	X		X	
PAL16H2	16	2			AND-OR	AND-OR Gate Array	X		X	
PAL16C1	16	2			BOTH[1]	AND-OR Gate Array	X		X	
PAL20C1	20	2			BOTH[1]	AND-OR Gate Array	X			
PAL10L8	10	8			AND-NOR	AND-OR Invert Gate Array	X		X	
PAL12L6	12	6			AND-NOR	AND-OR Invert Gate Array	X		X	
PAL14L4	14	4			AND-NOR	AND-OR Invert Gate Array	X		X	
PAL16L2	16	2			AND-NOR	AND-OR Invert Gate Array	X		X	
PAL12L10	12	10			AND-NOR	AND-OR Invert Gate Array	X			
PAL14L8	14	8			AND-NOR	AND-OR Invert Gate Array	X			
PAL16L6	16	6			AND-NOR	AND-OR Invert Gate Array	X			
PAL18L4	18	4			AND-NOR	AND-OR Invert Gate Array	X			
PAL20L2	20	2			AND-NOR	AND-OR Invert Gate Array	X			
PAL16L8	10	2	6		AND-NOR	AND-OR Invert Gate Array	X	X	X	X
PAL20L10	12	2	8		AND-NOR	AND-OR Invert Gate Array	X			
PAL16R8	8	8		8	AND-NOR	AND-OR Invert Array w/Reg's	X	X	X	X
PAL16R6	8	6	2	6	AND-NOR	AND-OR Invert Array w/Reg's	X	X	X	X
PAL16R4	8	4	4	4	AND-NOR	AND-OR Invert Array w/Reg's	X	X	X	X
PAL20X10	10	10		10	AND-NOR	AND-OR-XOR Invert w/Reg's	X			
PAL20X8	10	8	2	8	AND-NOR	AND-OR-XOR Invert w/Reg's	X			
PAL20X4	10	4	6	4	AND-NOR	AND-OR-XOR Invert w/Reg's	X			
PAL16X4	8	4	4	4	AND-NOR	AND-OR-XOR Invert w/Reg's	X			
PAL16A4	8	4	4	4	AND-NOR	AND-CARRY-OR-XOR Invert w/Reg's	X			

[1] Simultaneous AND-OR and AND-NOR outputs

Table 2

PALs For Every Task

The members of the PAL family and their characteristics are summarized in Table 2. They are designed to cover the spectrum of logic functions at reduced cost and lower package count. This allows the designer to select the PAL that best fits his application. PALs come in the following basic configurations:

Gate Arrays

PAL gate arrays are available in sizes from 12x10 (12 input terms, 10 output terms) to 20x2, with both active high and active low output configurations available (figure 9). This wide variety of input/output formats allows the PAL to replace many different sized blocks of combinatorial logic with single packages.

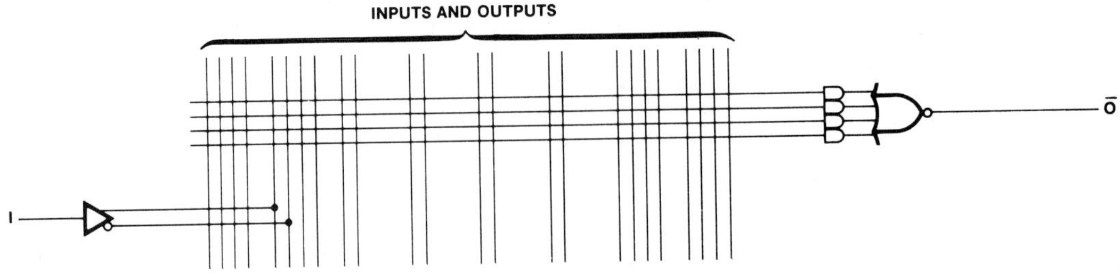

Figure 9

Programmable I/O

A feature of the high-end members of the PAL family is programmable input/output. This allows the product terms to directly control the outputs of the PAL (Figure 10). One product term is used to enable the three-state buffer, which in turn gates the summation term to the output pin. The output is also fed back into the PAL array as an input. Thus the PAL drives the I/O pin when the three-state gate is enabled; the I/O pin is an input to the PAL array when the three-state gate is disabled. This feature can be used to allocate available pins for I/O functions or to provide bi-directional output pins for operations such as shifting and rotating serial data.

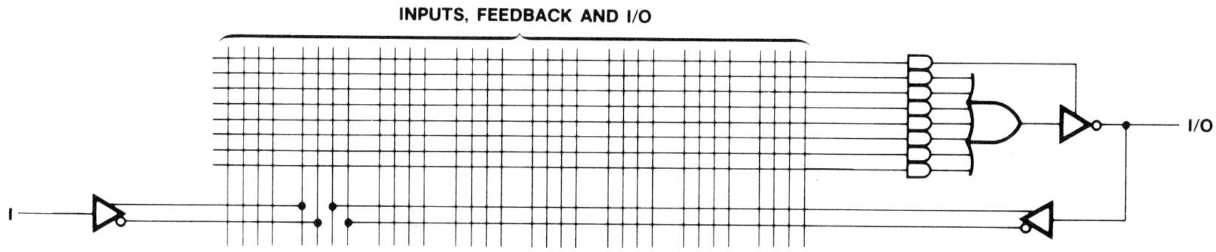

Figure 10

Registered Outputs with Feedback

Another feature of the high end members of the PAL family is registered data outputs with registered feedback. Each product term is stored into a D-type output flip-flop on the rising edge of the system clock (Figure 11). The Q output of the flip-flop can then be gated to the output pin by enabling the active low three-state buffer.

In addition to being available for transmission, the Q output is fed back into the PAL array as an input term. This feedback allows the PAL to "remember" the previous state, and it can alter its function based upon that state. This allows the designer to configure the PAL as a state sequencer which can be programmed to execute such elementary functions as count up, count down, skip, shift, and branch. These functions can be executed by the registered PAL at rates of up to 20 MHz.

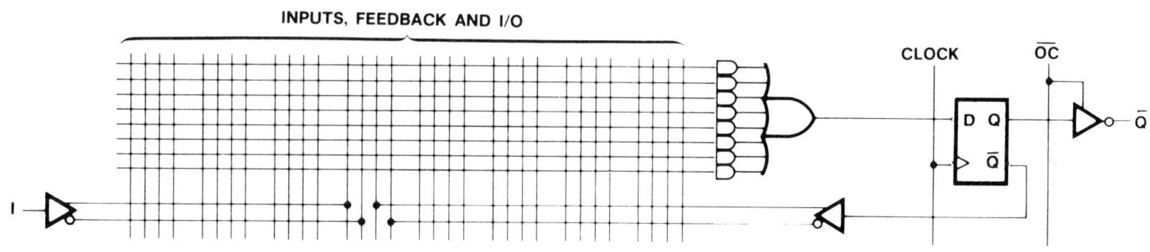

Figure 11

XOR PALs

These PALs feature an exclusive OR function. The sum of products is segmented into two sums which are then exclusive ORed (XOR) at the input of the D-type flip-flop (Figure 12). All of the features of the Registered PALs are included in the XOR PALs. The XOR function provides an easy implementation of the HOLD operation used in counters and other state sequencers.

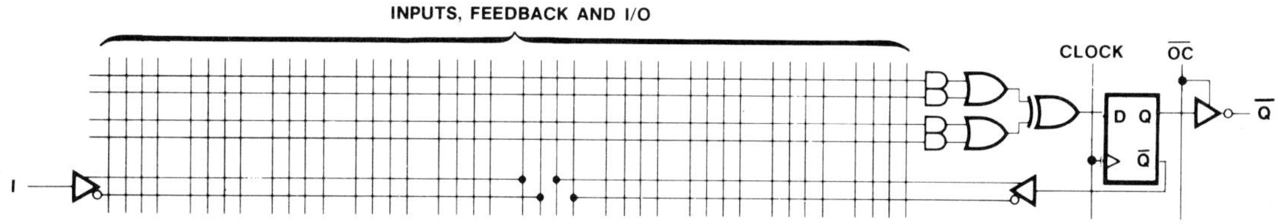

Figure 12

Arithmetic Gated Feedback

The arithmetic functions (add, subtract, greater than, and less than) are implemented by addition of gated feedback to the features of the XOR PALs. The XOR at the input of the D-type flip-flop allows carrys from previous operations to be XORed with two variable sums generated by the PAL array. The flip-flop Q output is fed back to be gated with input terms A (Figure 13). This gated feedback provides any one of the 16 possible Boolean combinations which are mapped in the Karnaugh map (Figure 15). Figure 14 shows how the PAL array can be programmed to perform these 16 operations. These features provide for versatile operations on two variables and facilitate the parallel generation of carrys necessary for fast arithmetic operations.

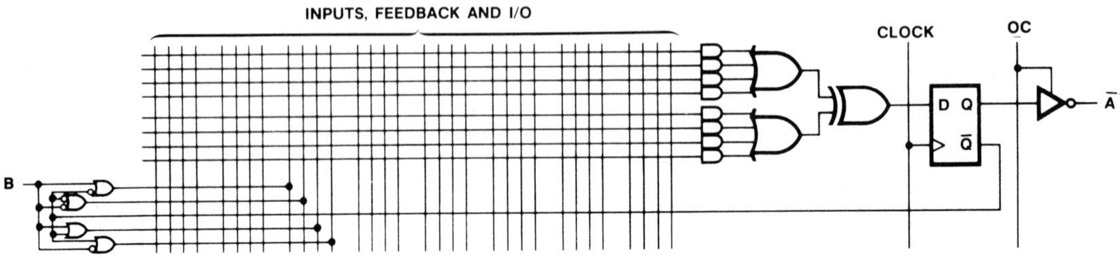

Figure 13

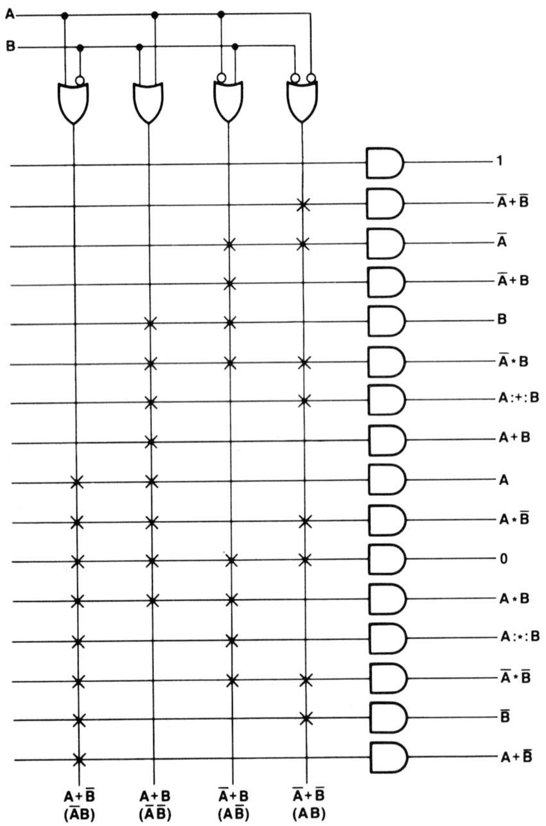

Figure 14

(Ā + B), (Ā + B̄) / (A + B̄), (A + B)

	--	-x	xx	x-
--	1	Ā+B̄	Ā	Ā+B
-x	A+B	A:+:B	Ā•B	B
xx	A	A•B̄	0	A•B
x-	A+B̄	B̄	Ā•B̄	A:•:B

Figure 15

It should now be clear that the PAL family can replace most Small-Scale Integrated Logic (SSI) logic in use today, thereby lowering product cost and giving the designer even greater flexibility in implementing logic functions.

PAL Programming

PALs can be programmed in most standard PROM programmers with the addition of a PAL personality card. The PAL appears to the programmer as a PROM. During programming half of the PAL outputs are selected for programming while the other outputs and the inputs are used for addressing. The outputs are then switched to program the other locations. Verification uses the same procedure with the programming lines held in a low state.

PALASM (PAL Assembler)

PALASM is the software used to define, simulate, build, and test PALs. PALASM accepts the PAL Design Specification as an input file. It verifies the design against an optional function table and generates the fuse plot which is used to program the PALs. PALASM is available upon request in many source code media and is documented in the PAL Design Concepts section.

HALs (Hard Array Logic)

The HAL family is the mask programmed version of a PAL. The HAL is to a PAL just as a ROM is to a PROM. A standard wafer is fabricated to the 6th mask. Then a custom metal mask is used to fabricate Aluminum links for a HAL instead of the programmable Ti-W fuse array used in a PAL.

The HAL is a cost-effective solution for large quantities and is unique in that it is a gate array with a programmable prototype.

HMSI (HAL Medium Scale Integration)

The HMSI family is derived from the PAL using HAL technology. These devices perform predetermined functions which are not available in the existing TTL family. Because they are produced in volume, the user receives the benefit of volume pricing. HMSI PAL designs are given in the Applications section with their 74LS number in line 2 of the PAL design Specification.

PAL Technology

PALs are manufactured using the proven TTL Schottky bipolar Ti-W fuse process to make fusible-link PROMs. An NPN emitter follower array forms the programmable AND array. PNP inputs provide high-impedance inputs (0.25 mA max) to the array. All outputs are standard TTL drivers with internal active pull-up transistors. Typical PAL propagation delay time is 25 ns, and all PALs are packaged in space saving 20-pin and 24-pin SKINNYDIP™.

PAL Data Security

The circuitry used for programming and logic verification can be used at any time to determine the logic pattern stored in the PAL array. For security, the PAL has a "last fuse" which can be blown to disable the verification logic. This provides a significant deterrent to potential copiers, and it can be used to effectively protect proprietary designs.

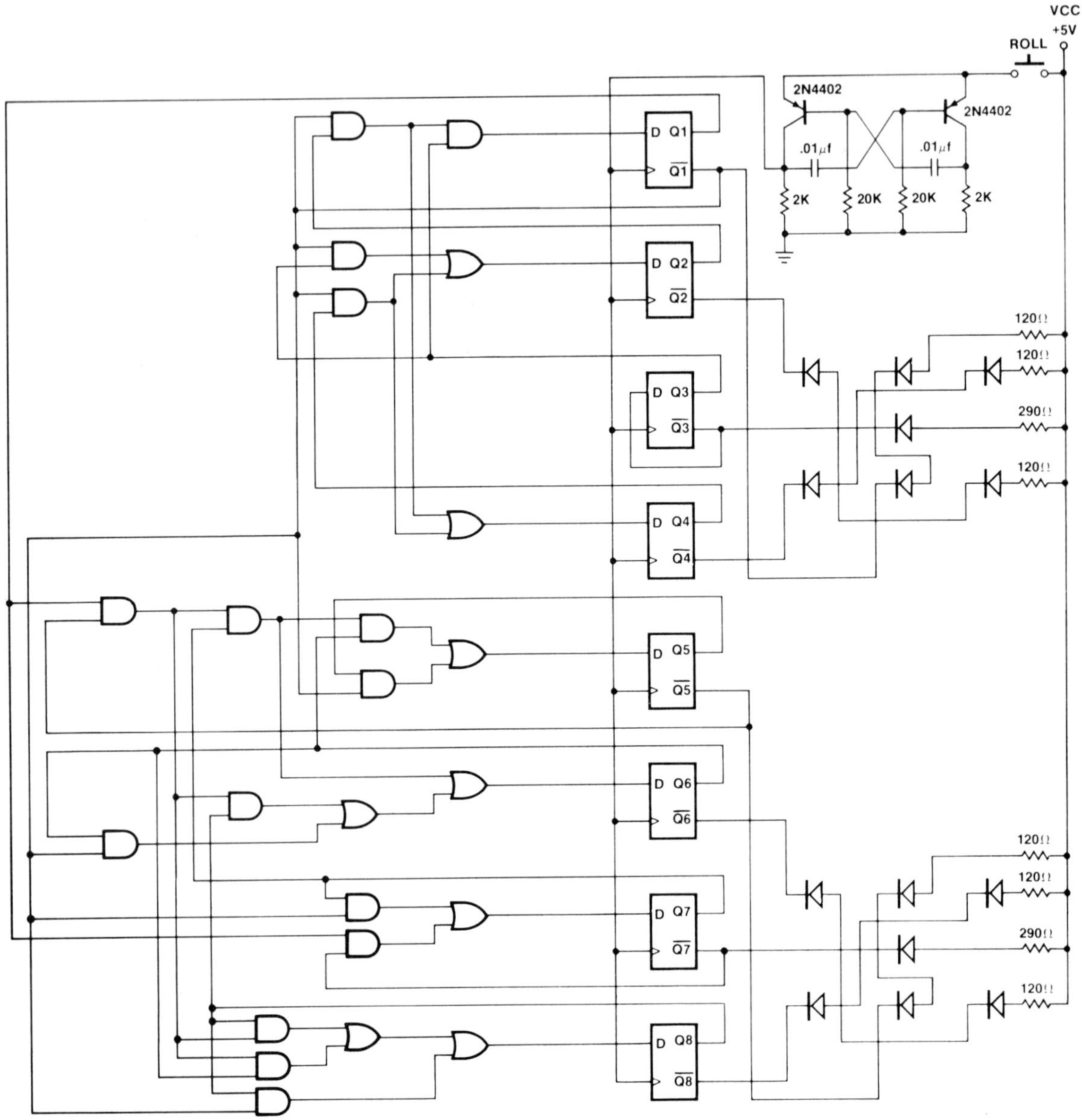
VCC
+5V
ROLL
2N4402
2N4402
.01μf
.01μf
2K
20K
20K
2K
D Q1
Q1
D Q2
Q2
D Q3
Q3
D Q4
Q4
D Q5
Q5
D Q6
Q6
D Q7
Q7
D Q8
Q8
120Ω
120Ω
290Ω
120Ω
120Ω
120Ω
290Ω
120Ω

Figure 16

PAL Part Numbers

The PAL part number is unique in that the part number code also defines the part's logic operation. The PAL parts code system is shown in Figure 17. For example, a PAL14L4CN would be a 14 input term, 4 output term, active-low PAL with a commercial temperature range packaged in a 20-pin plastic dip.

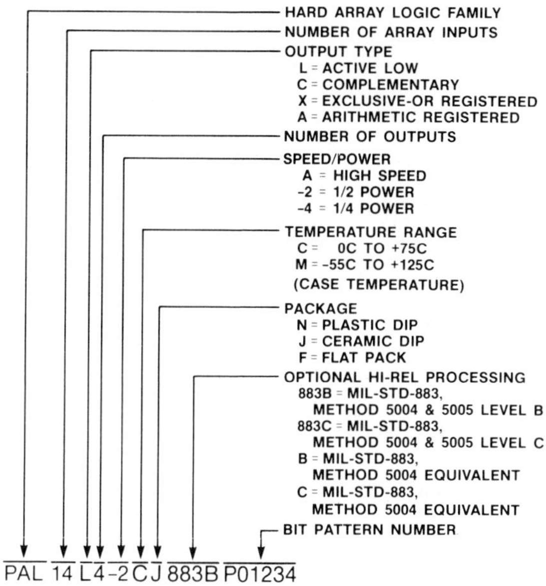

Figure 17

PAL Logic Symbols

The logic symbols for each of the individual PAL devices gives a concise functional description of that PAL's logic function. This symbol makes a convenient reference when selecting the PAL that best fits a specific application. Figure 18 shows the logic symbol for a PAL10H8 gate array.

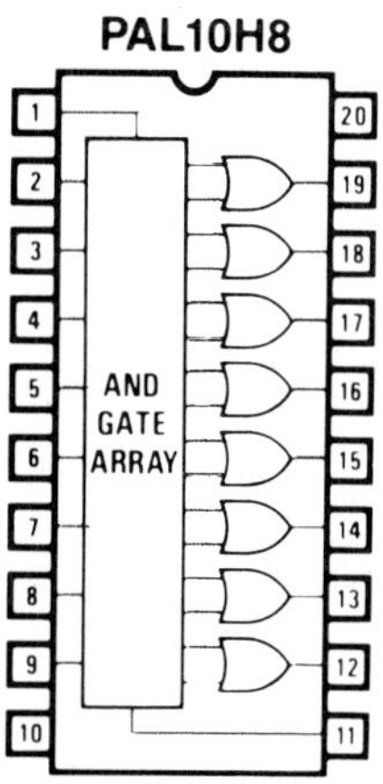

Figure 18

A PAL Example

As an example of how the PAL enables the designer to reduce costs and simplify logic design, consider the design of a simple, high-volume consumer product: an electronic dice game. This type of product will be produced in extremely high volume, so it is essential that every possible production cost be minimized.

The electronic dice game is simply constructed using a free running oscillator whose output is used to drive two asynchronous modulo six counters. When the user "rolls" the dice (presses a button), the current state of the counters is decoded and latched into a display resembling the pattern seen on an ordinary pair of dice.

A conventional logic diagram for the dice game is shown in Figure 16. (A detailed logic derivation is shown in the PAL applications section of this handbook). It is implemented using standard TTL, SSI and MSI parts, with a total I.C. count of eight: six quad gate packages and two quad D-latches. Looks like a nice, clean logic design, right? Wrong!!

PAL Goes to the Casino

A brief examination of Figure 16 reveals two basic facts: first, the circuit contains mostly simple, combinatorial logic, and second, it uses a clocked state transition sequence. Remembering that the PAL family contains ample provision for these features, the PAL catalog is consulted. The PAL16R8 has all the required functions, and the entire logic content of the circuit can be programmed into a single PAL shown in Figure 19.

In this example, the PAL effected an eight to one package count reduction and a significant cost savings. This is typical of the power and cost effective performance that the PAL family brings to logic design.

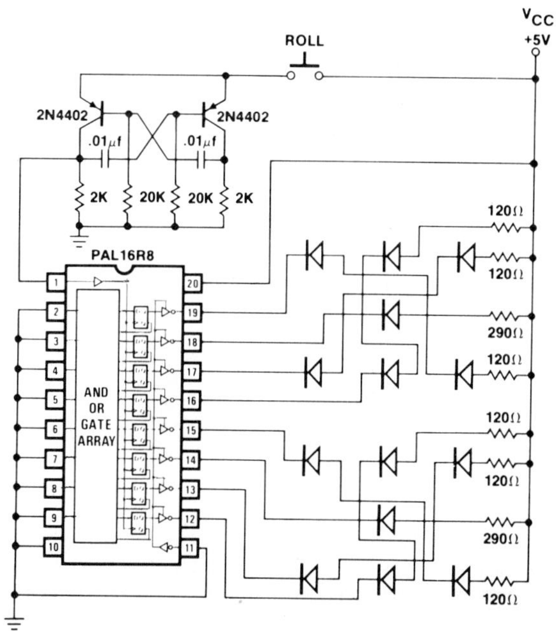

Figure 19

Advantages of Using PALs

The PAL has a unique place in the world of logic design. Not only does it offer many advantages over conventional logic, it also provides many features not found anywhere else. The PAL family:

- Programmable replacement for conventional TTL logic.
- Reduces IC inventories substantially and simplifies their control.
- Reduces chip count by at least 4 to 1.
- Expedites and simplifies prototyping and board layout.
- Saves space with 20-pin and 24-pin Skinny DIP packages.
- High speed: 25ns typical propagation delay.
- Programmed on standard PROM programmers.
- Programmable three-state outputs.
- Special feature eliminates possibility of copying by competitors.

All of these features combine together to lower product development costs and increase product cost effectiveness. The bottom line is that PALs save money.

Direct Logic Replacement

In both new and existing designs the PAL can be used to replace various logic functions. This allows the designer to optimize a circuit in many ways never before possible. The PAL is particularly effective when used to provide interfaces required by many LSI functions. PAL flexibility combined with LSI function density makes a powerful team.

Design Flexibility

The PAL offers the systems logic designer a whole new world of options. Until now, the decision on logic system implementation was usually between SSI/MSI logic functions on one hand and microprocessors on the other. In many cases the function required is too awkward to implement the first way and too simple to justify the second. Now the PAL offers the designer high functional density, high speed, and low cost. Even better, PALs come in a variety of sizes and functions, thereby further increasing the designer's options.

Space Efficiency

By allowing designers to replace many simple logic functions with single packages, the PAL allows more compact P.C. board layouts. The PAL's space saving 20-pin "skinny dip" helps to further reduce board area while simplifying board layout and fabrication. This means that many multi-card systems can now be reduced to one or two cards, and that can make the difference between a profitable success or an expensive disaster.

Smaller Inventory

The PAL family can be used to replace up to 90% of the conventional TTL family with just 25 parts. This considerably lowers both shelving and inventory cataloging requirements. Even better, small custom modifications to the standard functions are easy for PAL users, not so easy for standard TTL users.

High Speed

The PAL family runs faster or equal to the best of bipolar logic circuits. This makes the PAL the ideal choice for most logical operations or control sequence which requires a medium complexity and high speed. Also, in many microcomputer systems, the PAL can be used to handle high speed data interfaces that are not feasible for the microprocessor alone. This can be used to significantly extend the capabilities of the low-cost, low-speed NMOS microprocessors into areas formerly requiring high-cost bipolar microprocessors.

Easy Programming

The members of the PAL family can be quickly and easily programmed using standard PROM programmers. This allows designers to use PALs with a minimum investment in special equipment. Many types of programmable logic, such as the FPLA, require an expensive, dedicated programmer.

Secure Data

The PAL verification logic can be completely disabled by blowing out a special "last link." This prevents the unauthorized copying of valuable data, and makes the PAL perfect for use in any application where data integrity must be carefully guarded.

Summary

The 25 member PAL family of logic devices offers logic designers new options in the implementation of sequential and combinatorial logic designs. The family is fast, compact, flexible, and easy to use in both new and existing designs. It promises to reduce costs in most areas of design and production with a corresponding increase in product profitability.

A Great Performer!

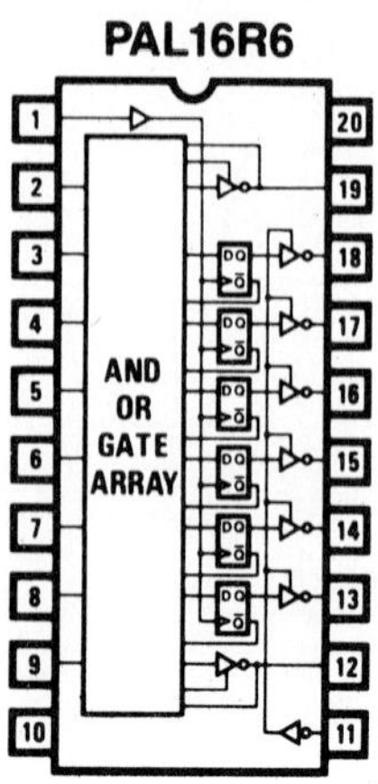

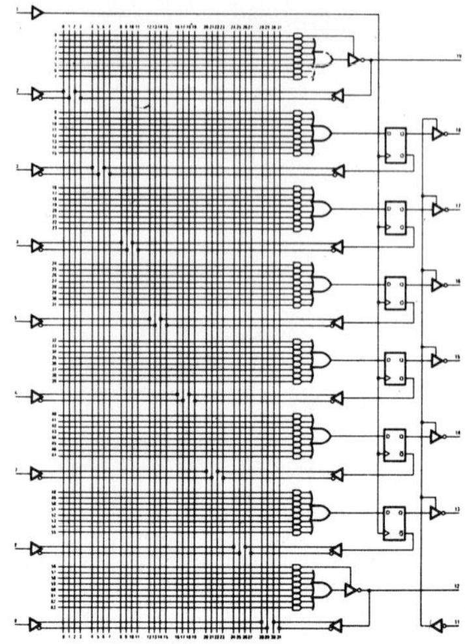

PAL16R6 Logic Symbols

PAL16R6 Logic Diagram

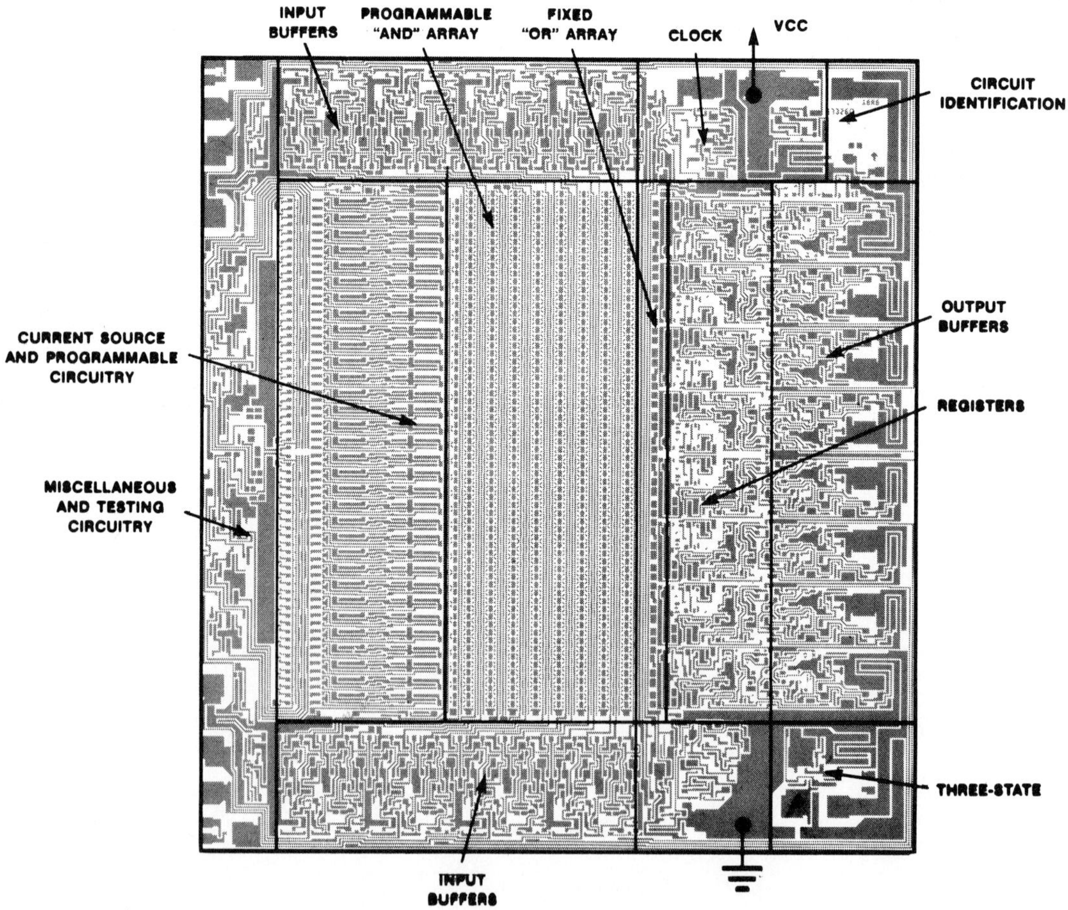

PAL16R6 Metalization

PAL
PAL
PAL

FAMILY PORTRAIT

25 PALs - count 'em!

PAL Logic Symbols

Active High PALs

PAL10H8

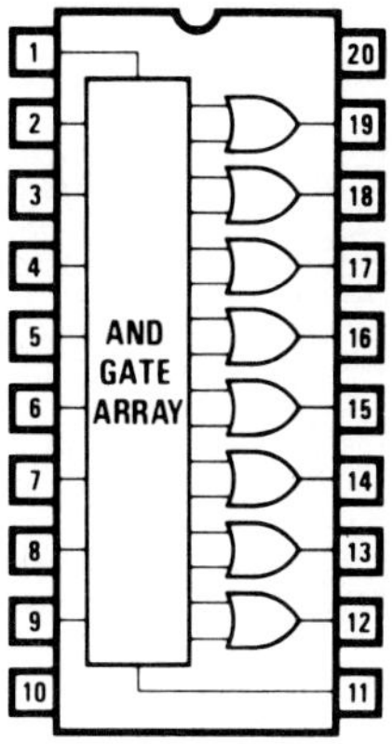

OCTAL 10 INPUT
AND-OR GATE ARRAY

PAL12H6

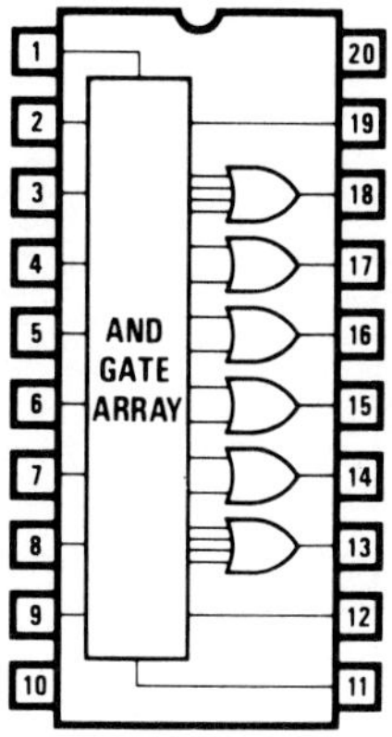

HEX 12 INPUT
AND-OR GATE ARRAY

PAL14H4

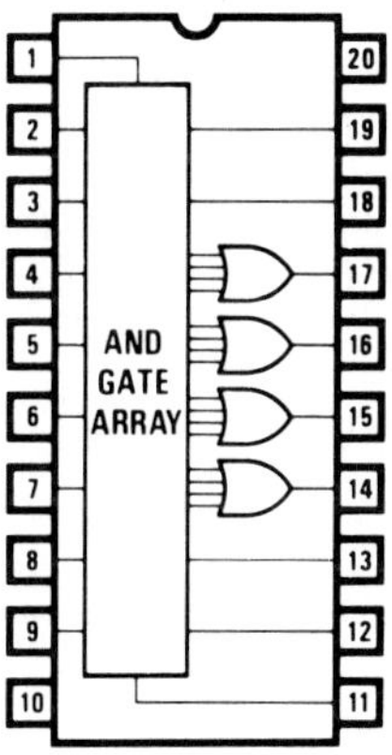

QUAD 14 INPUT
AND-OR GATE ARRAY

PAL16H2

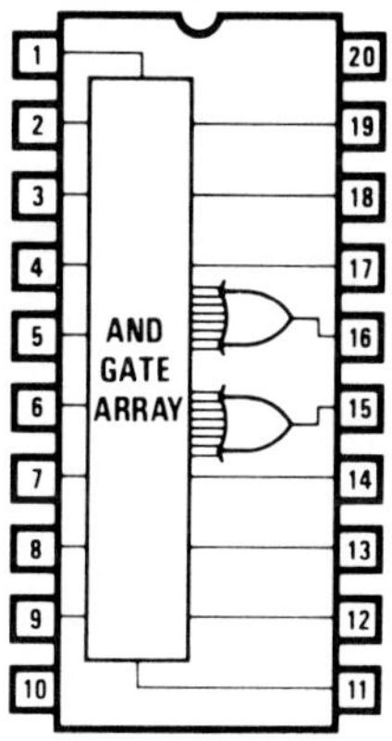

DUAL 16 INPUT
AND-OR GATE ARRAY

PAL Logic Symbols

PALs With Complementary Output

PAL16C1

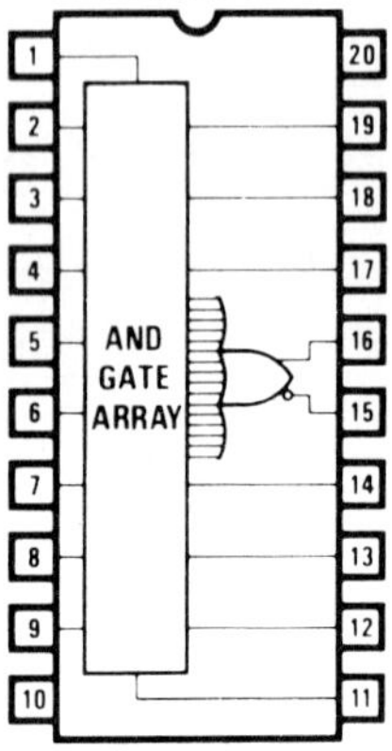

16 INPUT
AND-OR AND-OR-INVERT GATE ARRAY

PAL20C1

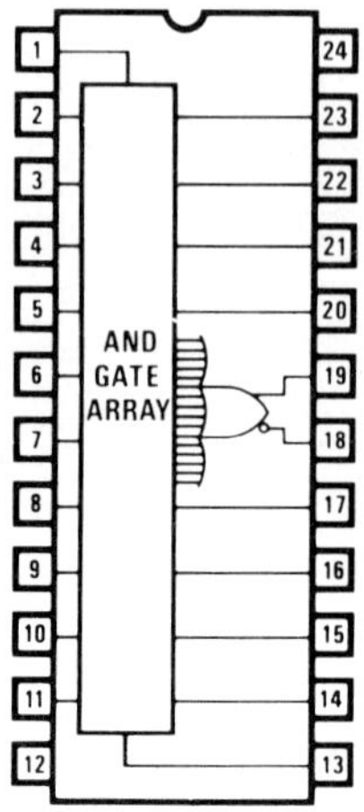

20 INPUT
AND-OR AND-OR-INVERT GATE ARRAY

Active Low PALs

PAL10L8

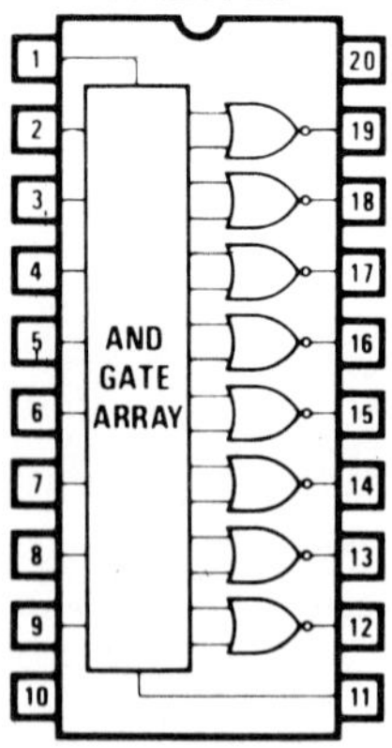

OCTAL 10 INPUT
AND-OR-INVERT GATE ARRAY

PAL12L6

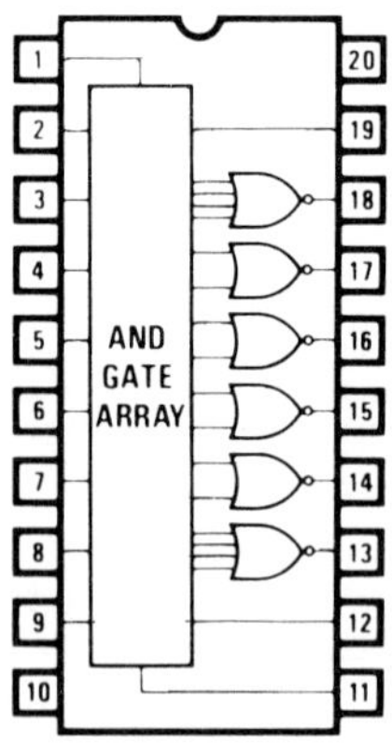

HEX 12 INPUT
AND-OR-INVERT GATE ARRAY

PAL14L4

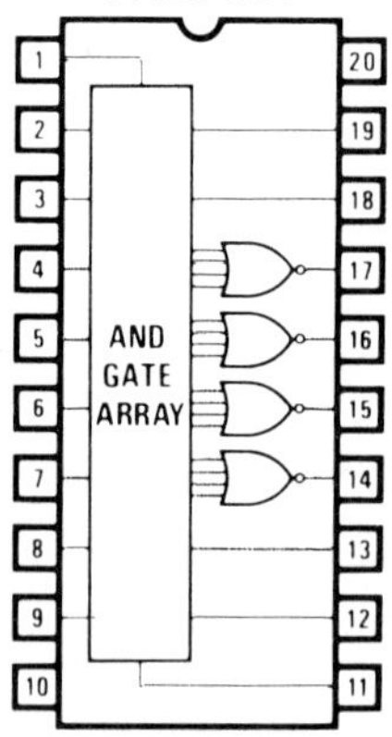

QUAD 14 INPUT
AND-OR-INVERT GATE ARRAY

PAL16L2

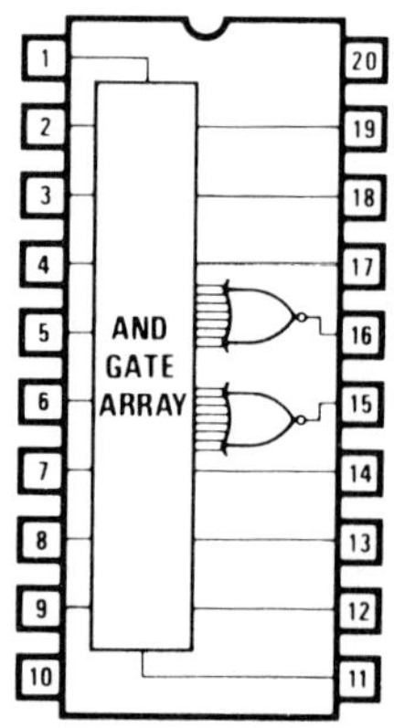

DUAL 16-INPUT
AND-OR-INVERT GATE ARRAY

PAL Logic Symbols

More Active Low PALs

PAL12L10

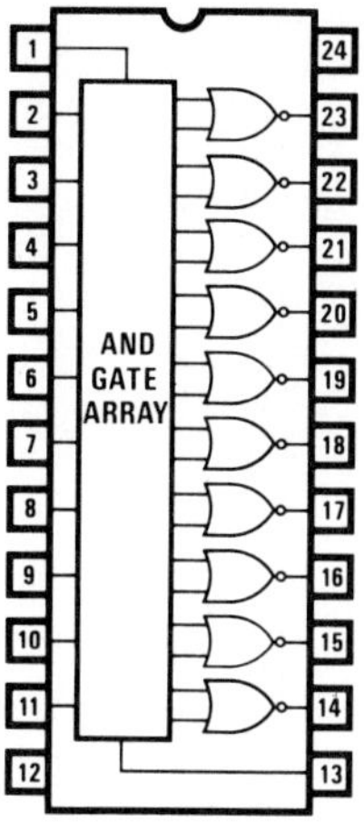

DECA 12 INPUT
AND-OR-INVERT GATE ARRAY

PAL14L8

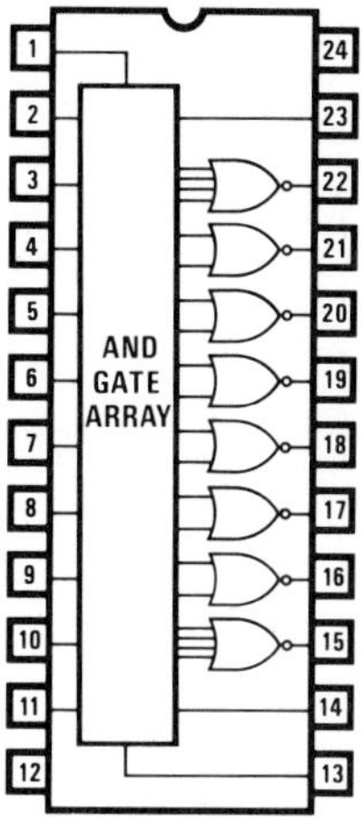

OCTAL 14 INPUT
AND-OR-INVERT GATE ARRAY

PAL16L6

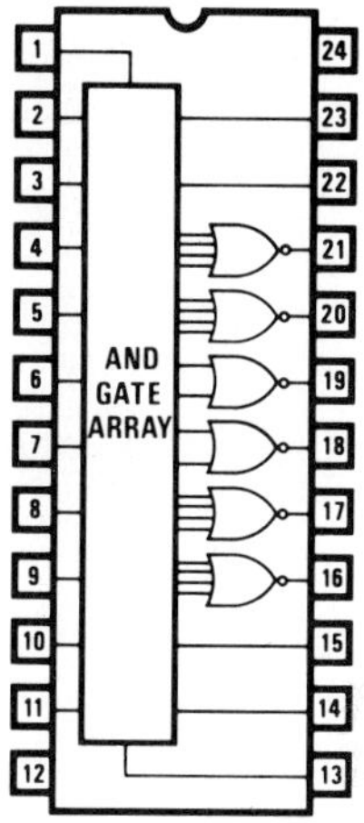

HEX 16 INPUT
AND-OR-INVERT GATE ARRAY

PAL18L4

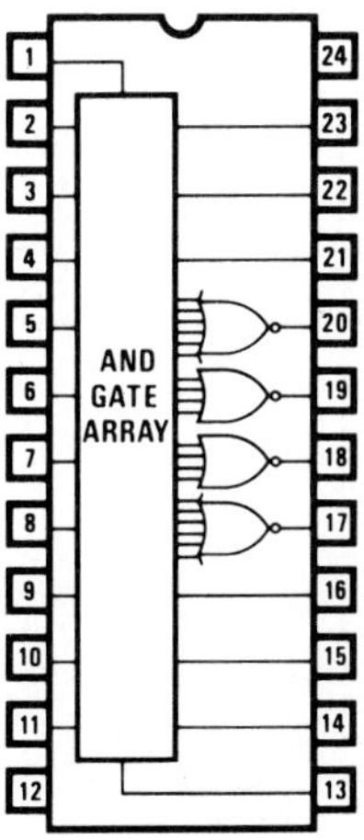

QUAD 18 INPUT
AND-OR-INVERT GATE ARRAY

PAL20L2

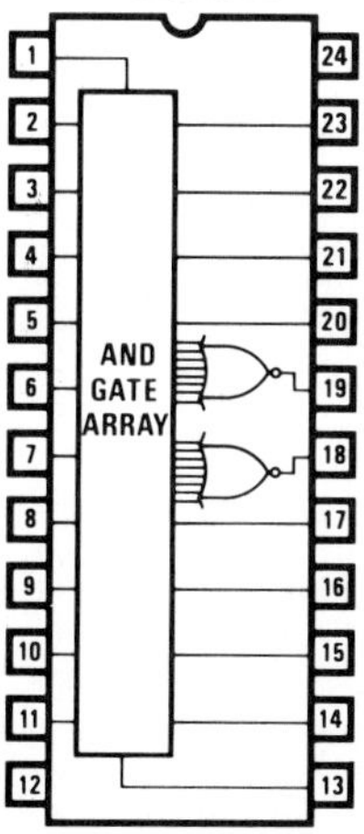

DUAL 20 INPUT
AND-OR-INVERT GATE ARRAY

PAL Logic Symbols

PALs With Feedback

PAL16L8

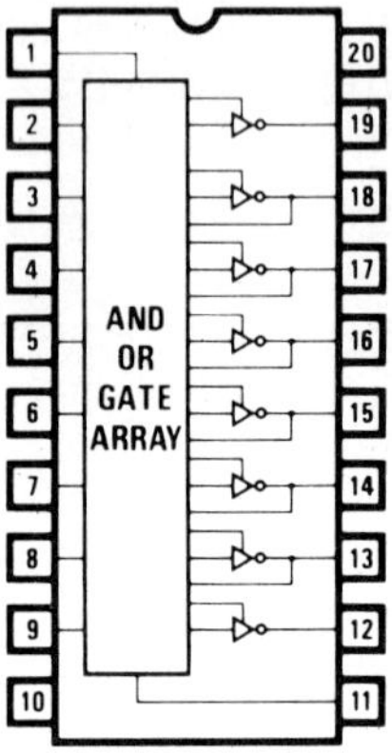

OCTAL 16 INPUT
AND-OR-INVERT GATE ARRAY

PAL20L10

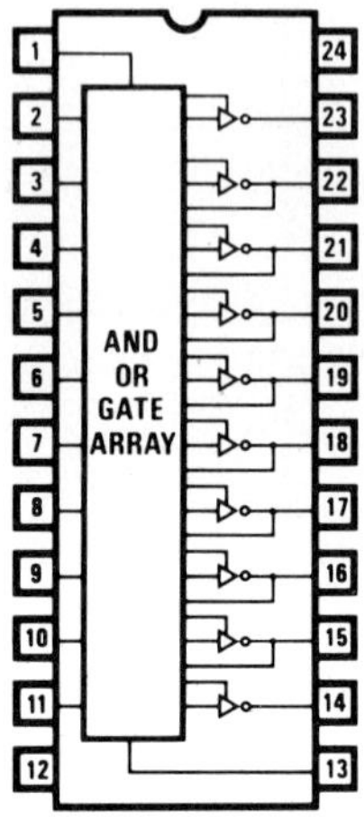

DECA 20 INPUT
AND-OR-INVERT GATE ARRAY

PALs With Registered Outputs

PAL16R8

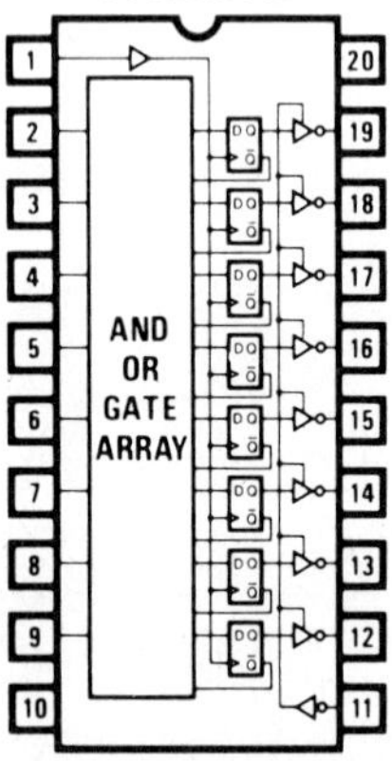

OCTAL 16 INPUT REGISTERED
AND-OR GATE ARRAY

PAL16R6

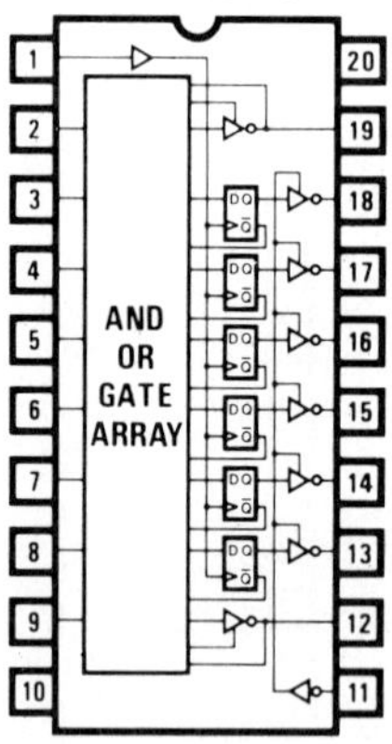

HEX 16 INPUT REGISTERED
AND-OR GATE ARRAY

PAL16R4

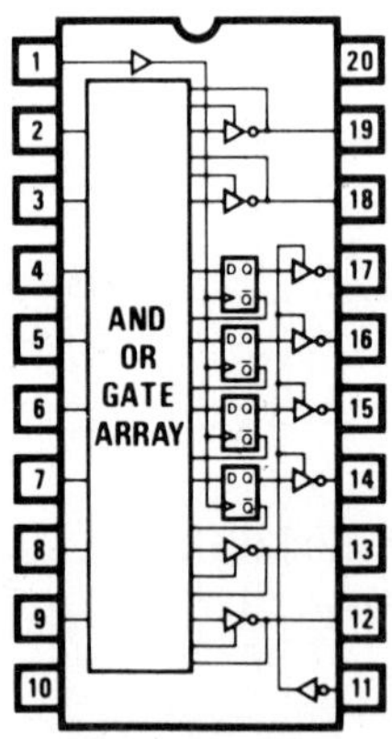

QUAD 16 INPUT REGISTERED
AND-OR GATE ARRAY

PAL Logic Symbols

PALs With Exclusive OR

PAL20X10

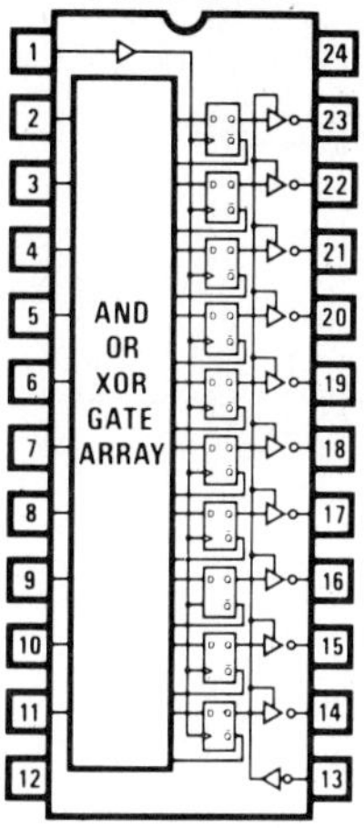

DECA 20 INPUT REGISTERED
AND-OR-XOR GATE ARRAY

PAL20X8

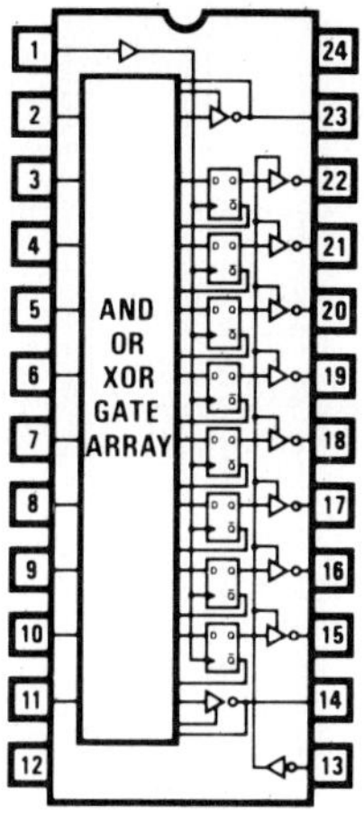

OCTAL 20 INPUT REGISTERED
AND-OR-XOR GATE ARRAY

PAL20X4

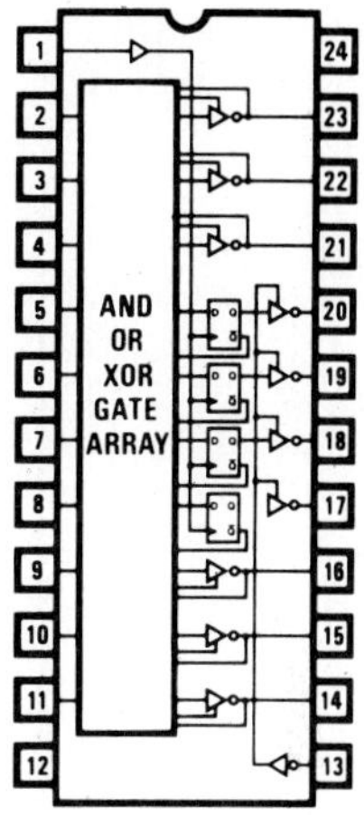

QUAD 20 INPUT REGISTERED
AND-OR-XOR GATE ARRAY

PALs With Arithmetic Gated Feedback

PAL16X4

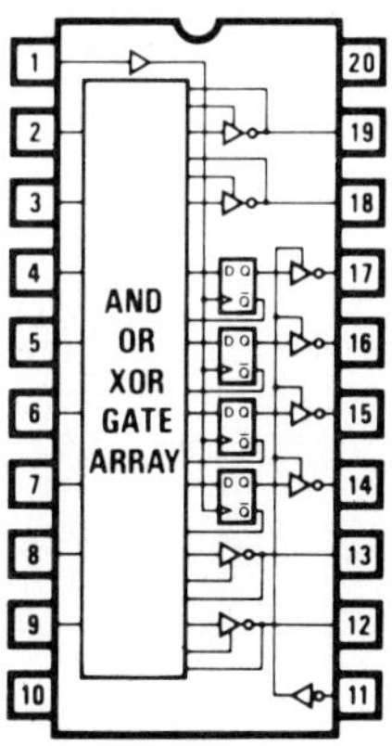

QUAD 16 INPUT REGISTERED
AND-OR-XOR GATE ARRAY

PAL16A4

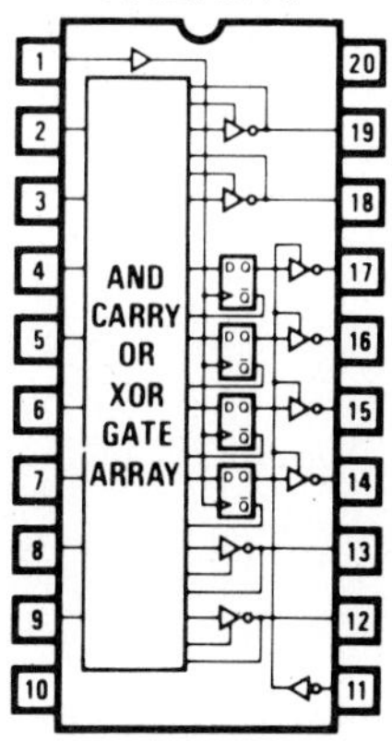

QUAD 16 INPUT REGISTERED
AND-CARRY-OR-XOR GATE ARRAY

Logic Diagram PAL10H8

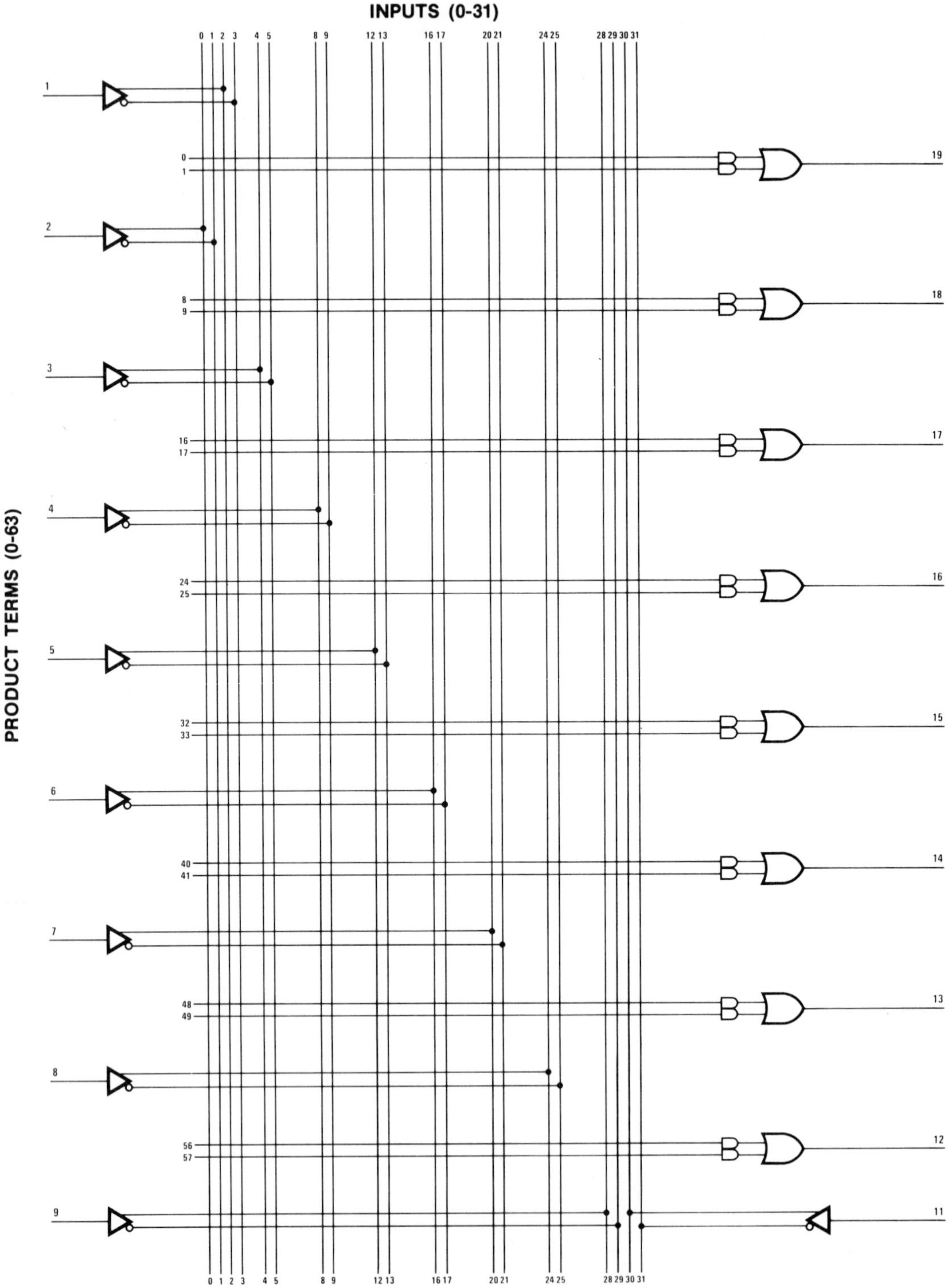

Logic Diagram PAL12H6

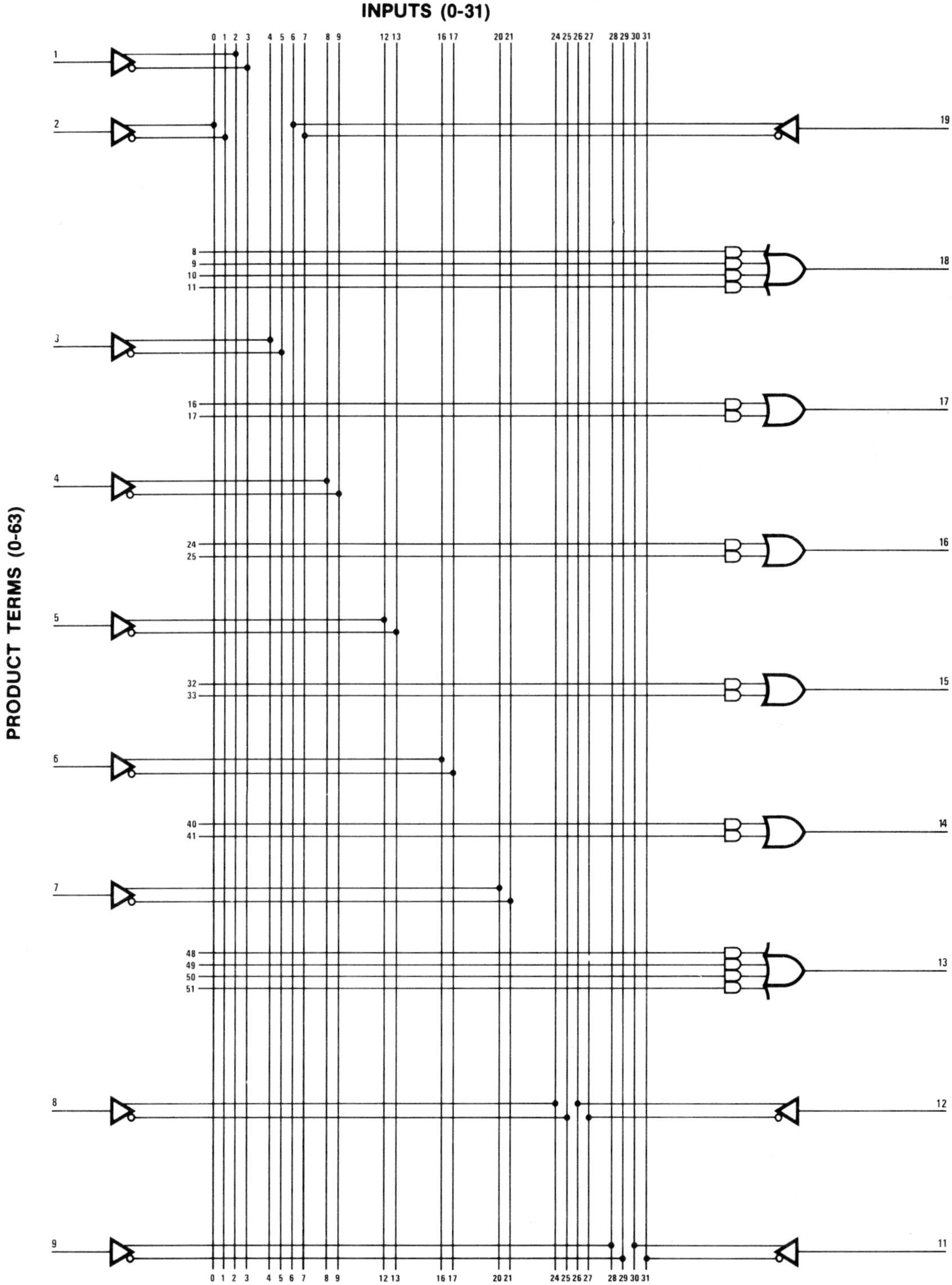

Logic Diagram PAL14H4

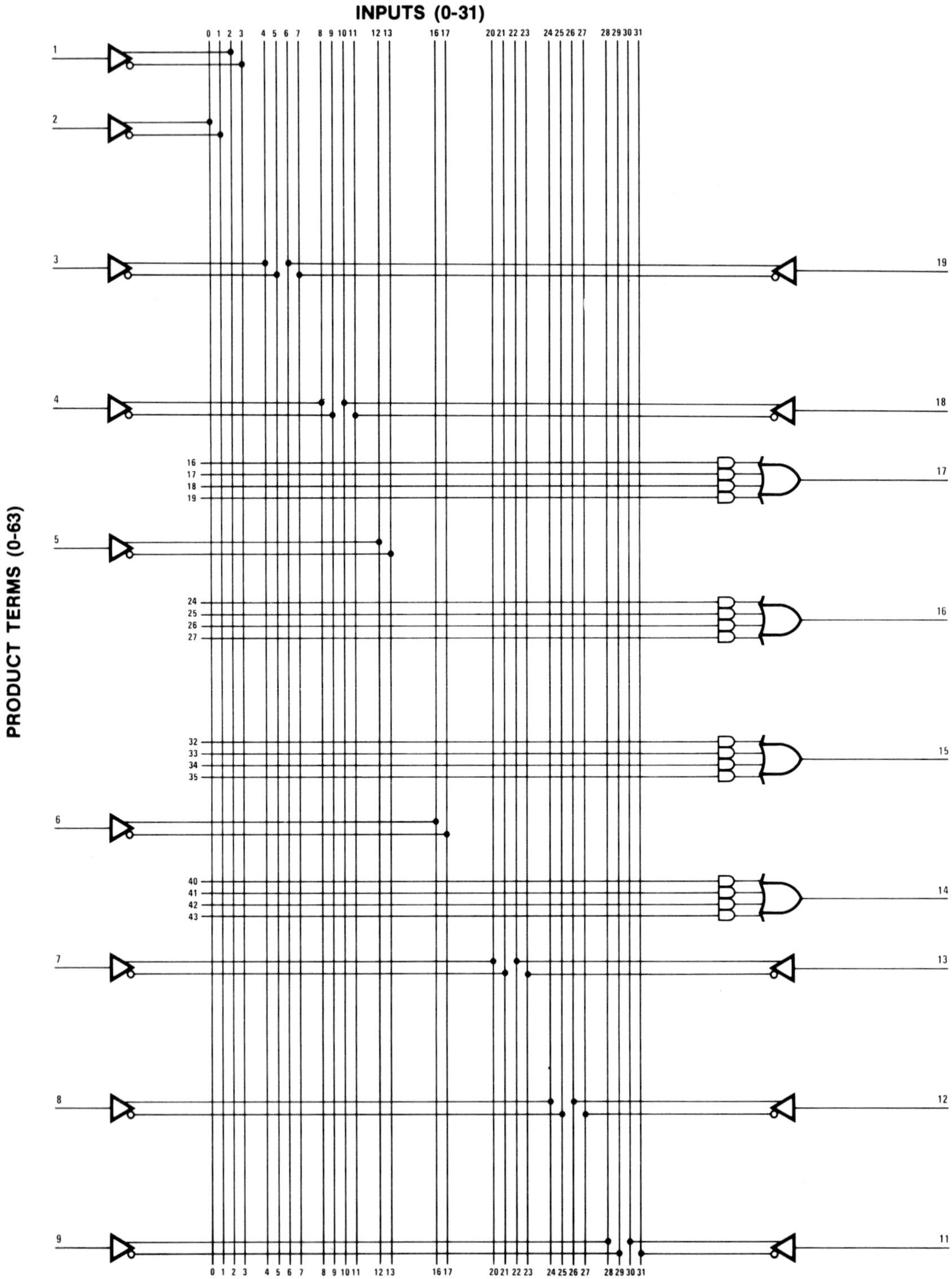

Logic Diagram PAL16H2

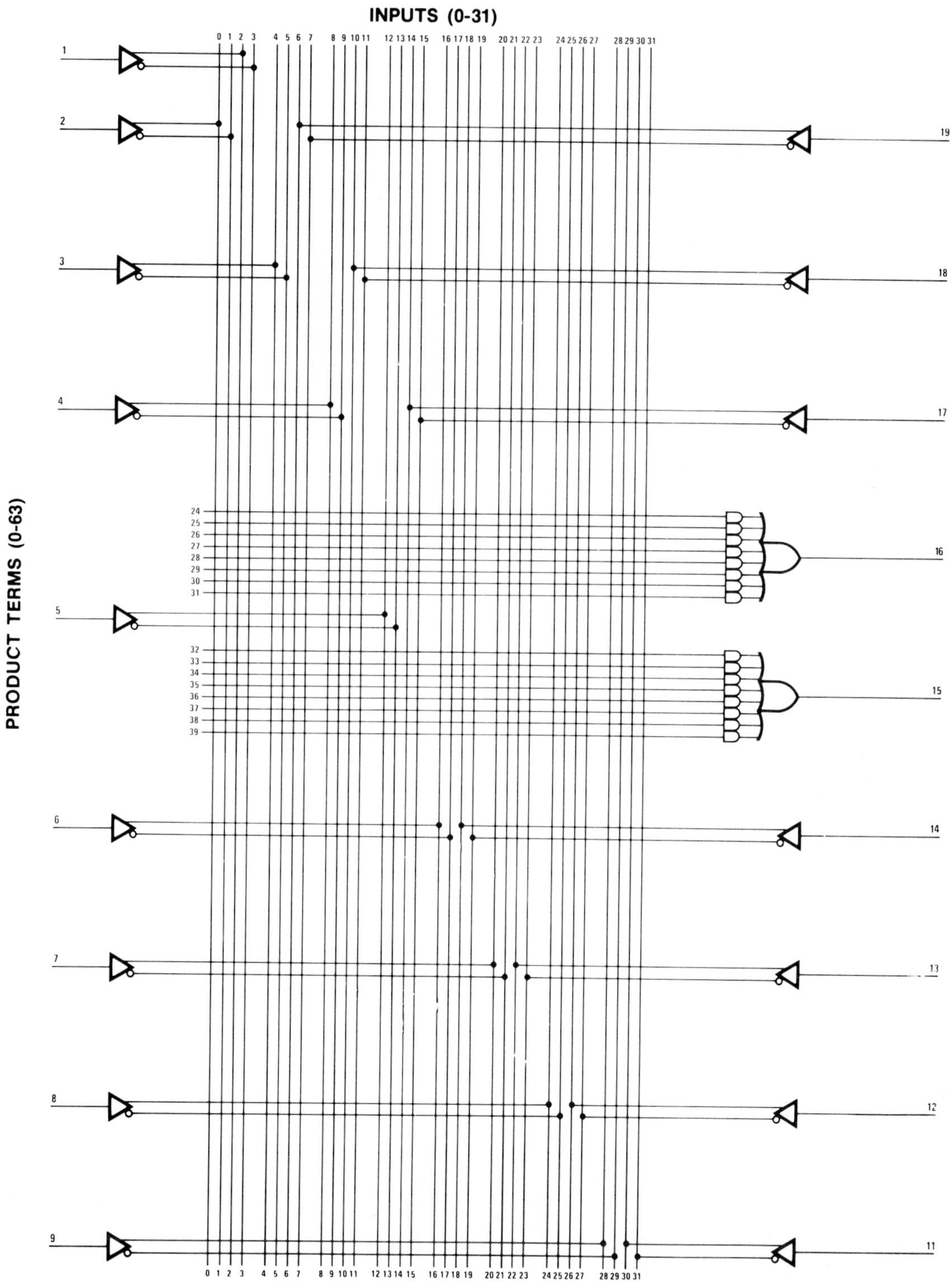

Logic Diagram PAL16C1

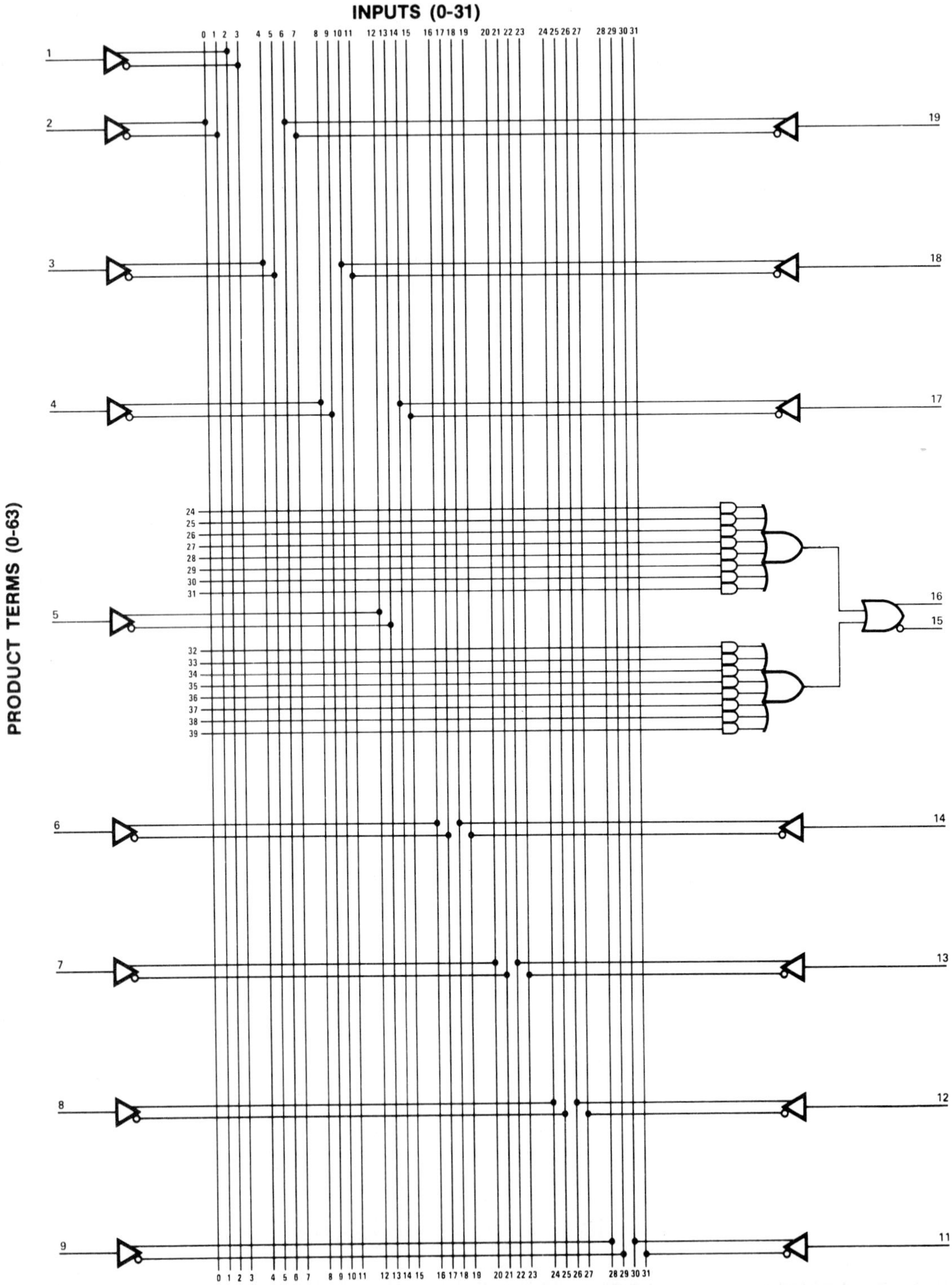

Logic Diagram PAL20C1

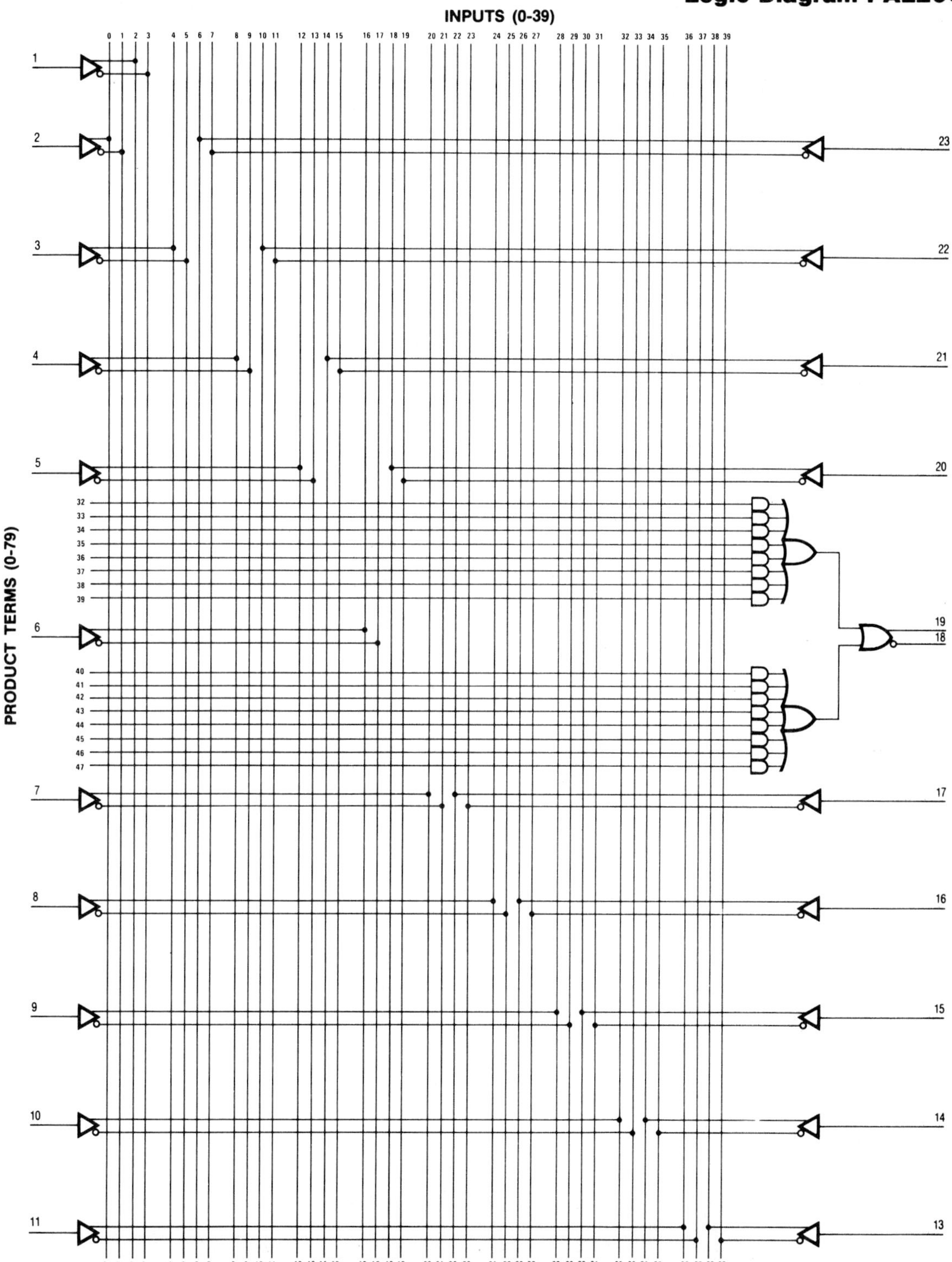

Logic Diagram PAL10L8

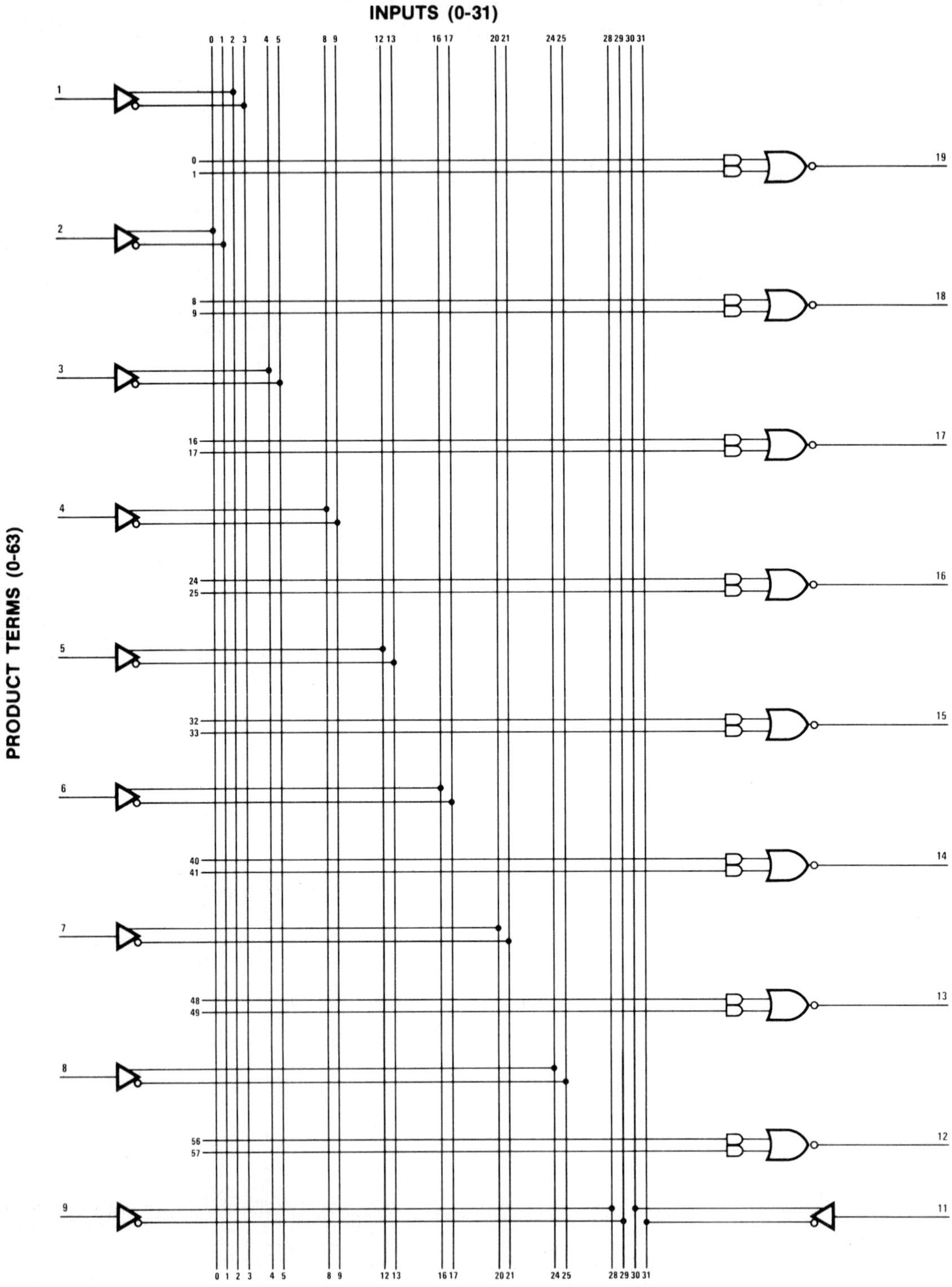

Logic Diagram PAL12L6

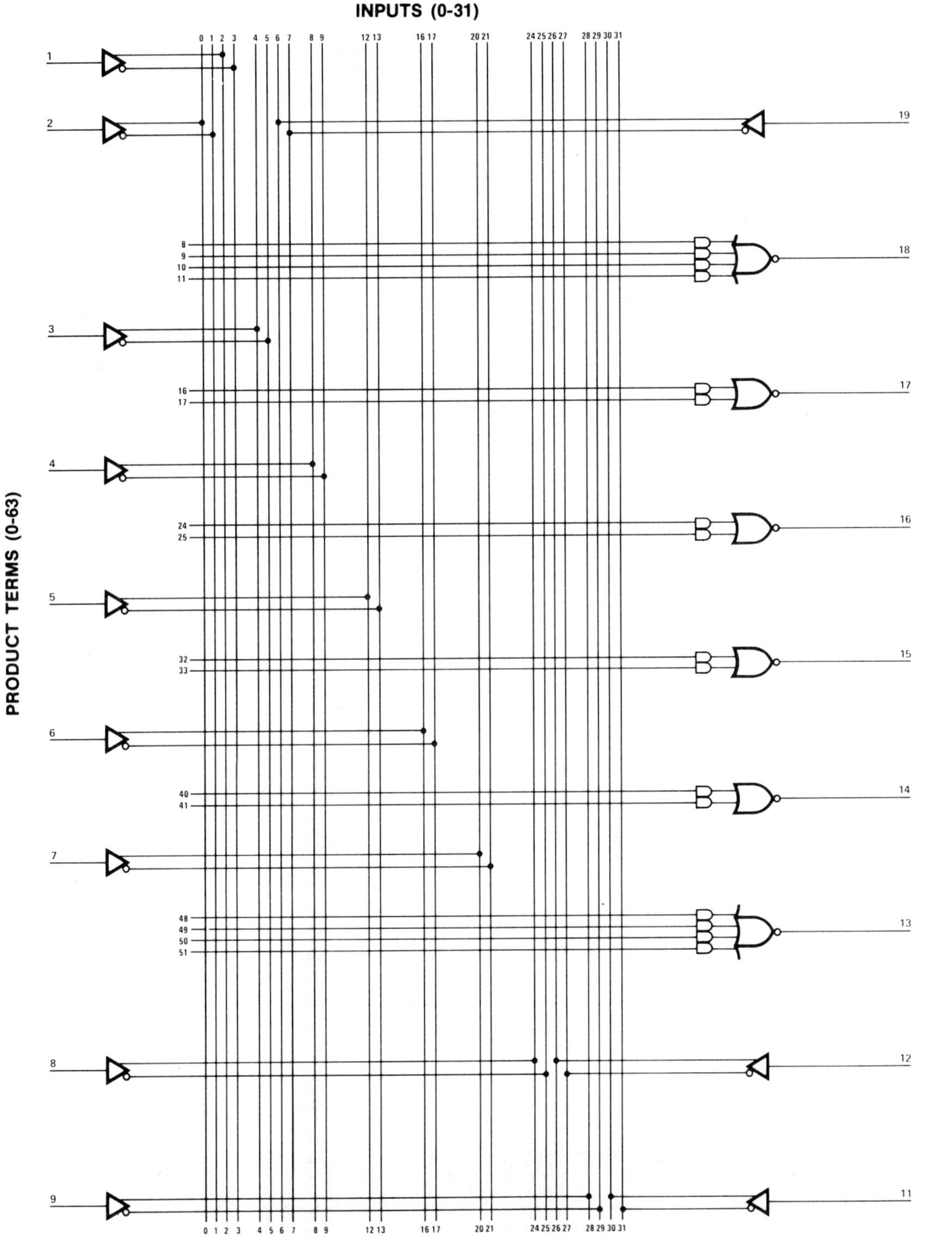

Logic Diagram PAL14L4

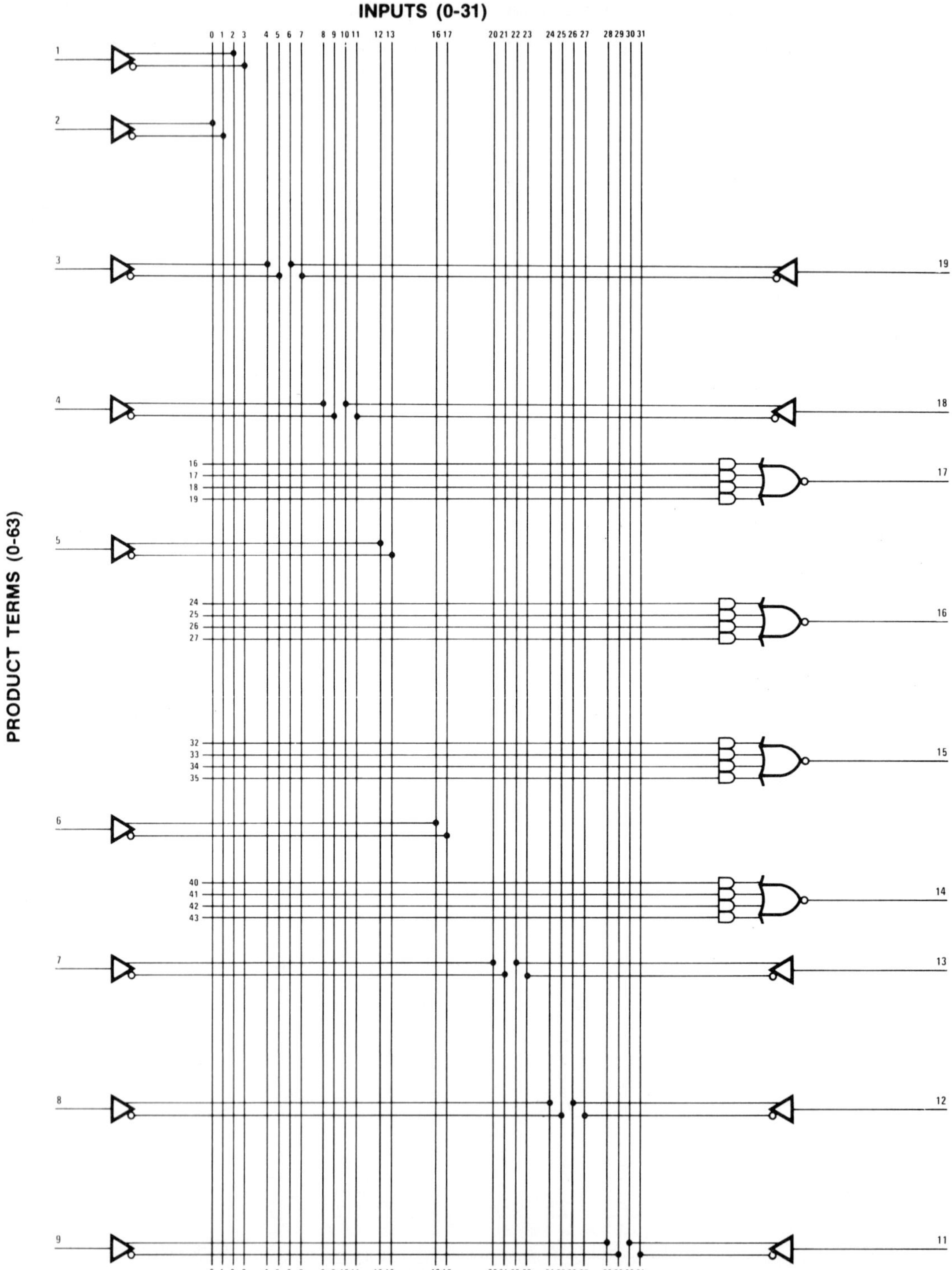

Logic Diagram PAL16L2

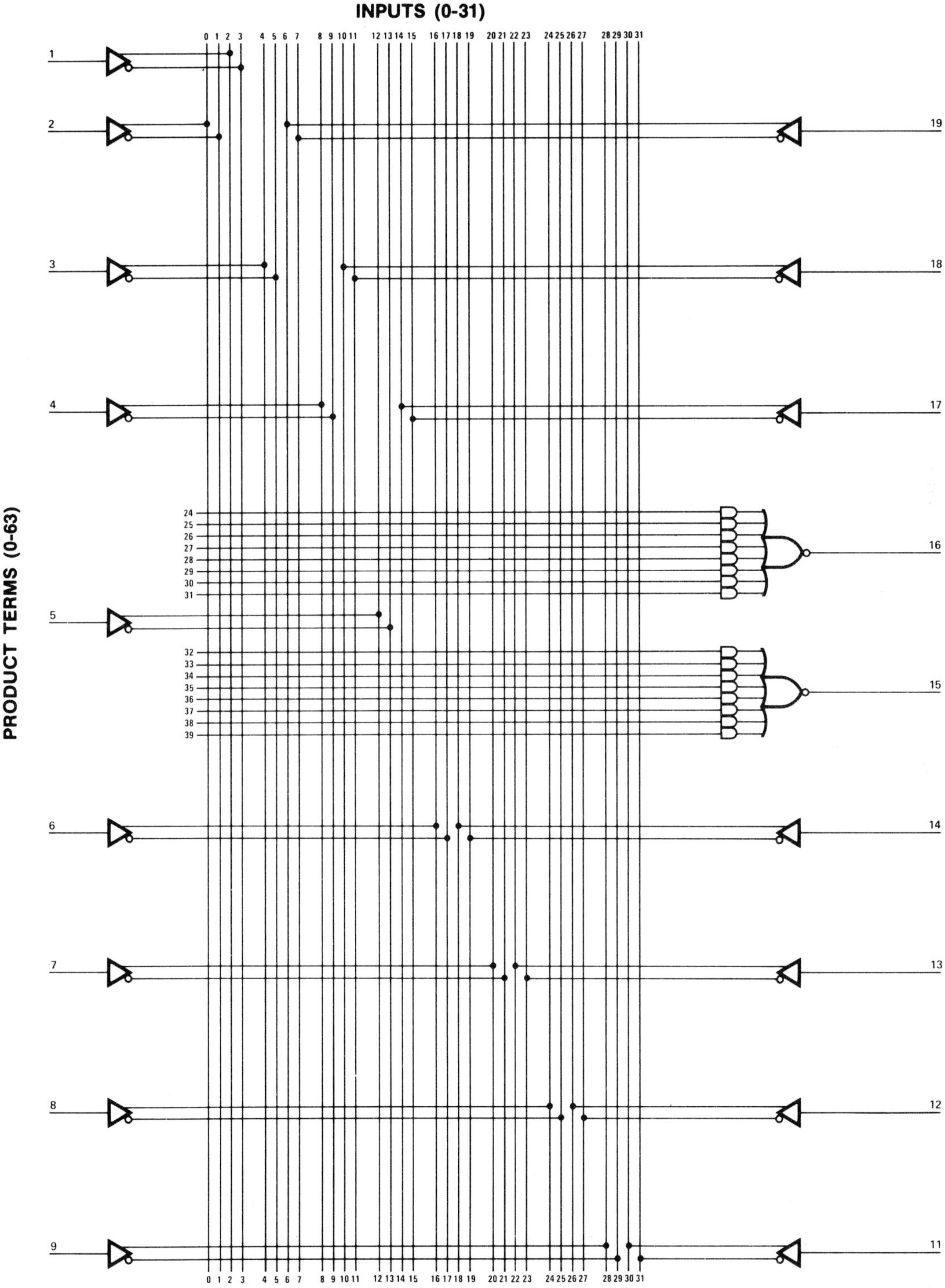

Logic Diagram PAL12L10

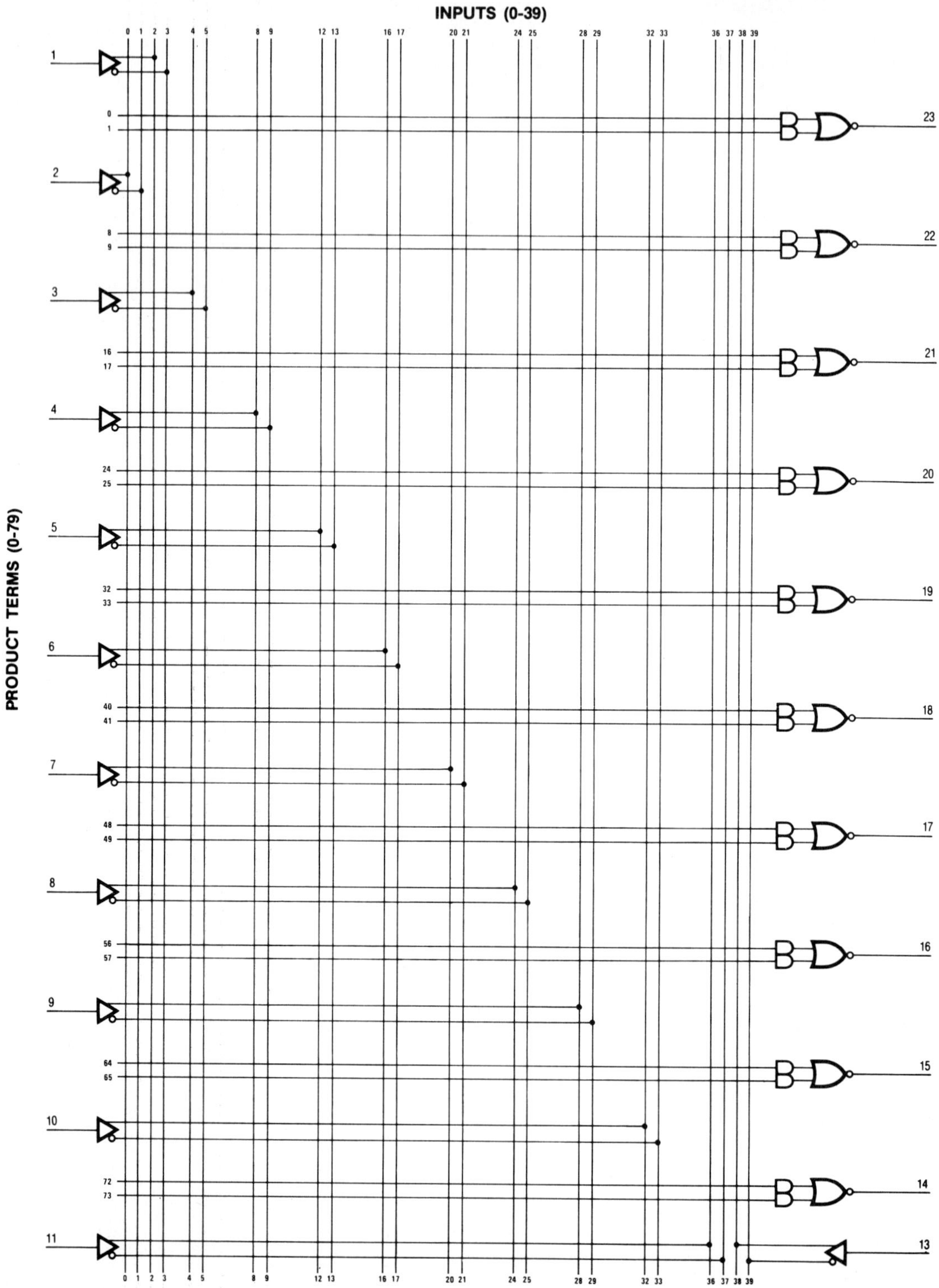

Logic Diagram PAL14L8

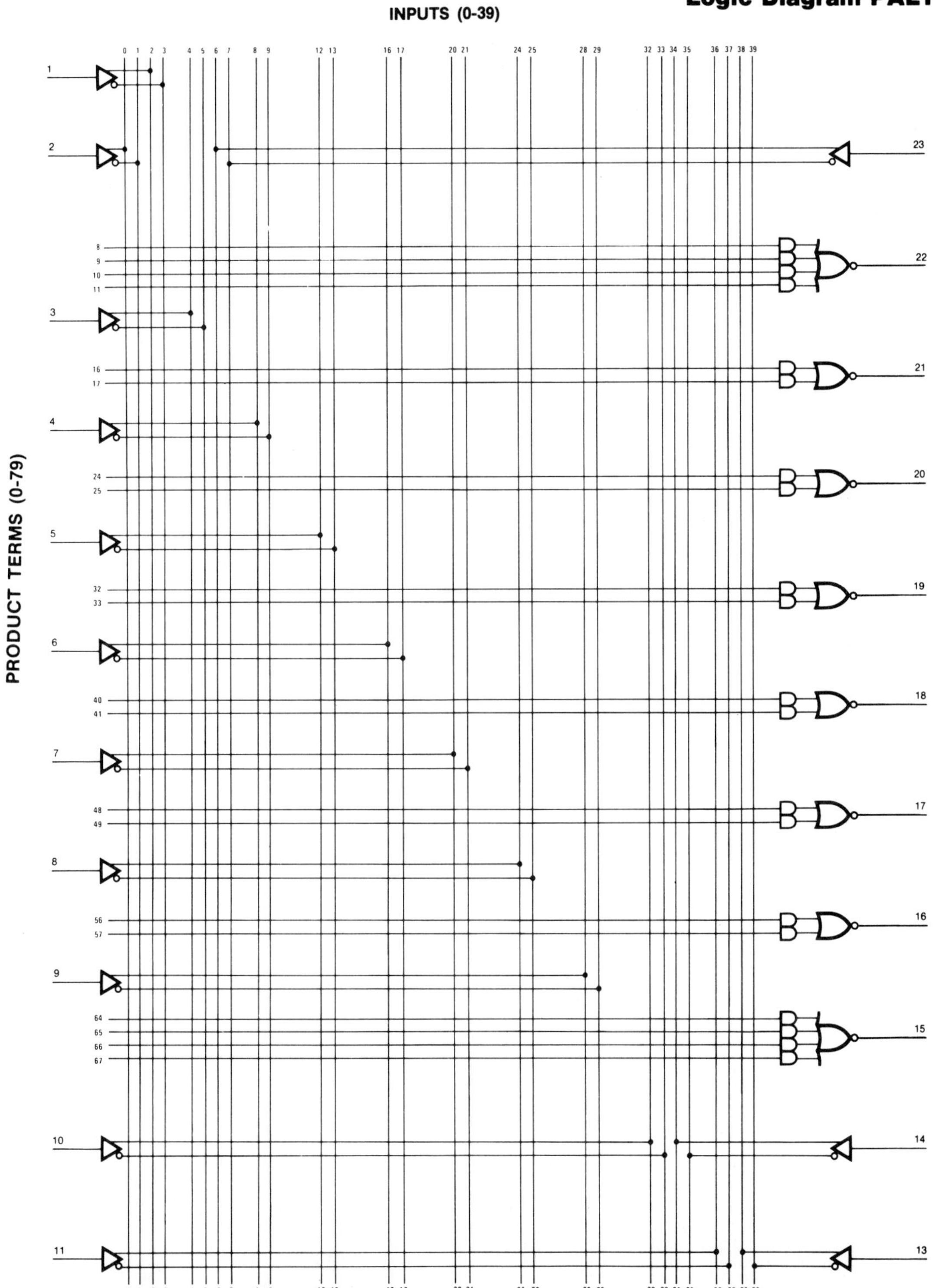

Logic Diagram PAL16L6

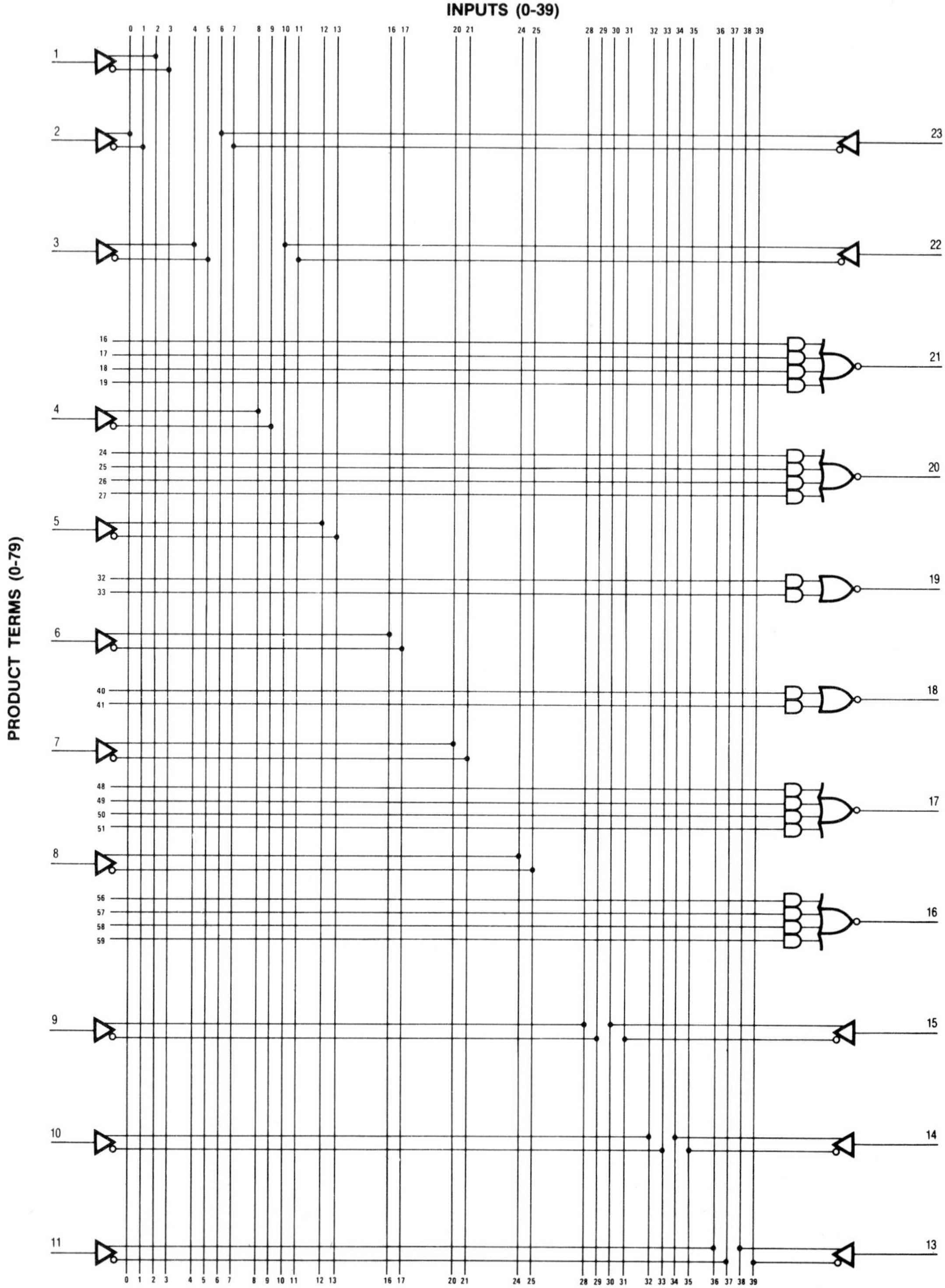

Logic Diagram PAL18L4

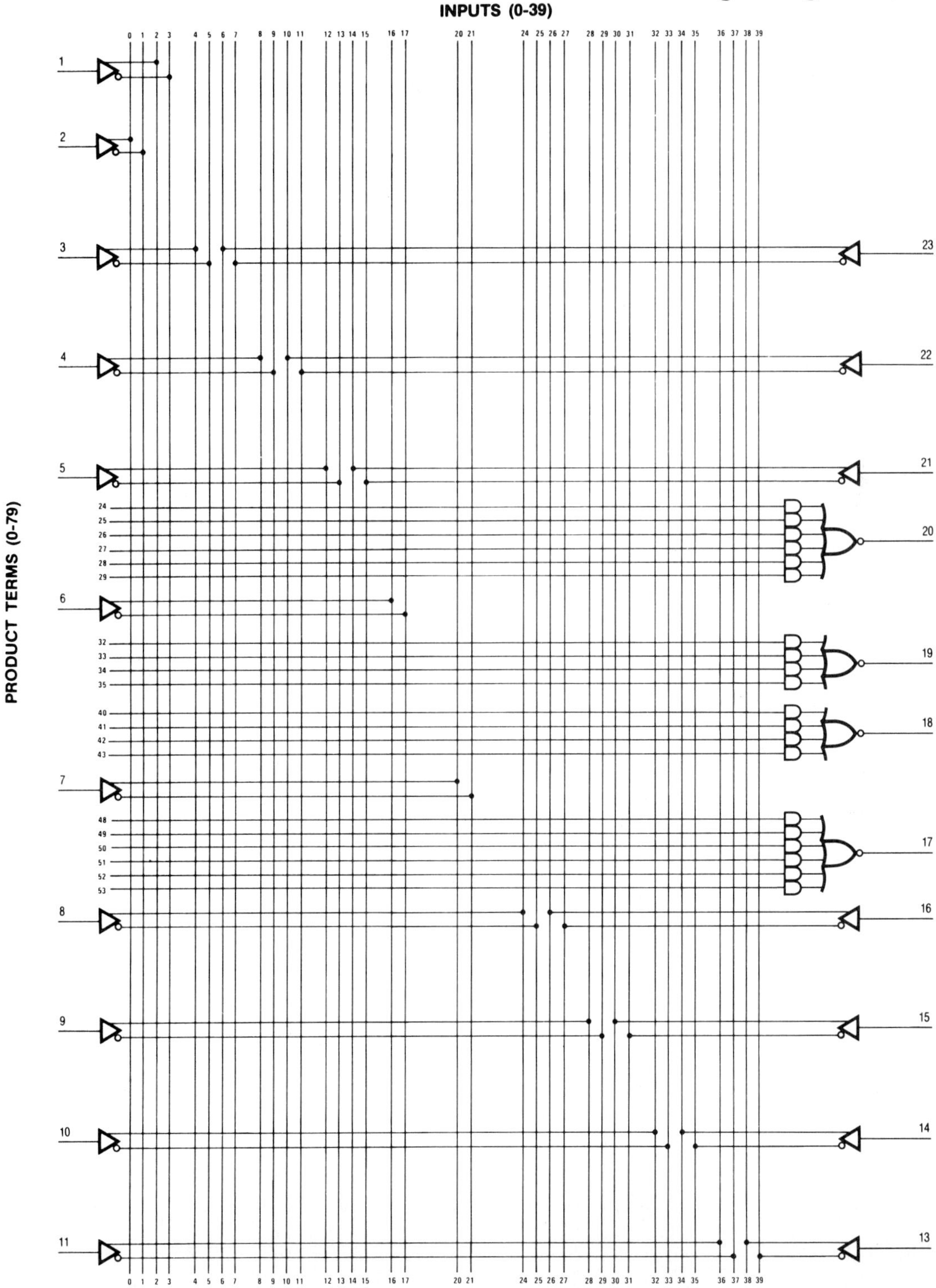

Logic Diagram PAL20L2

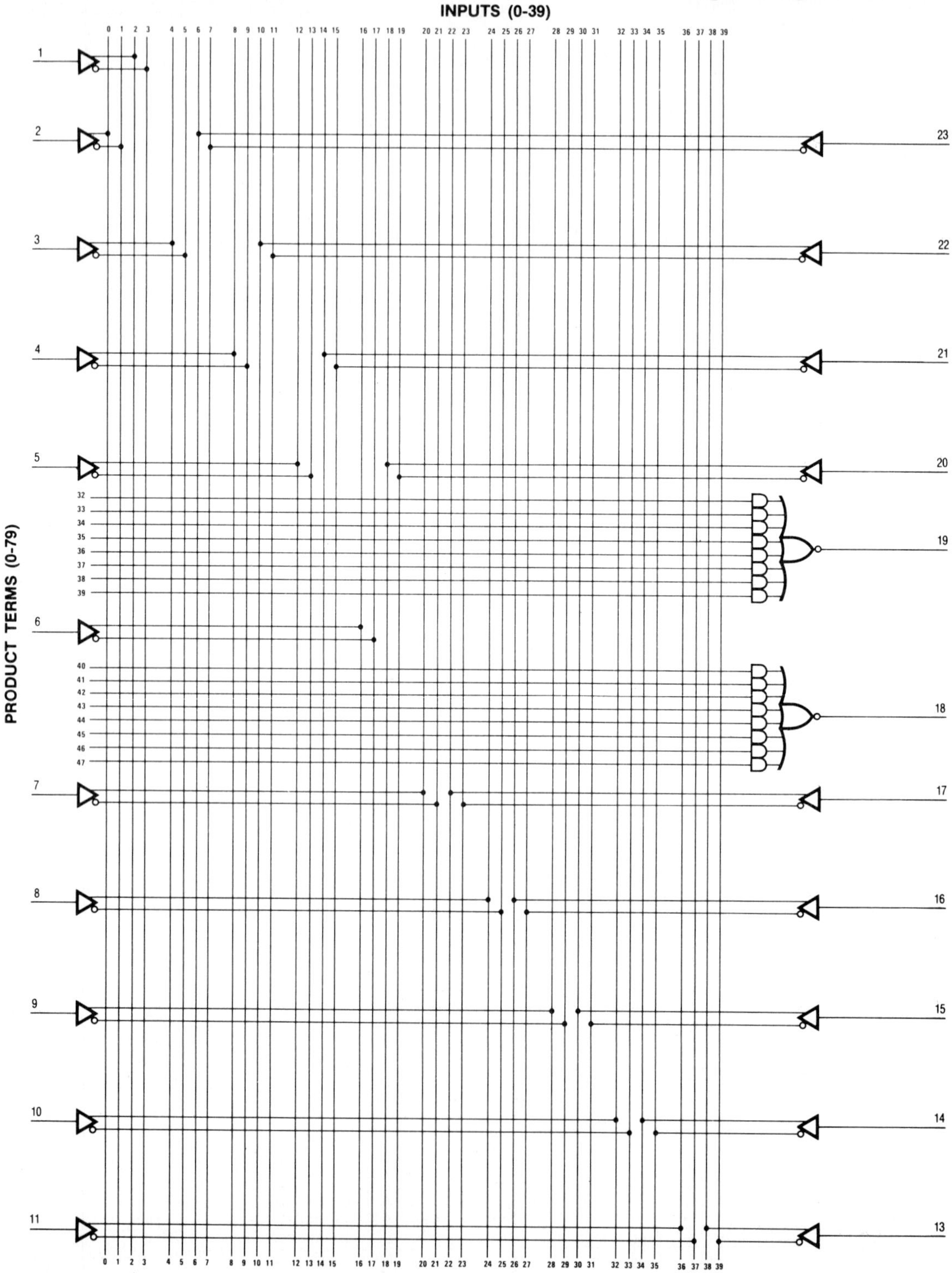

Logic Diagram PAL16L8

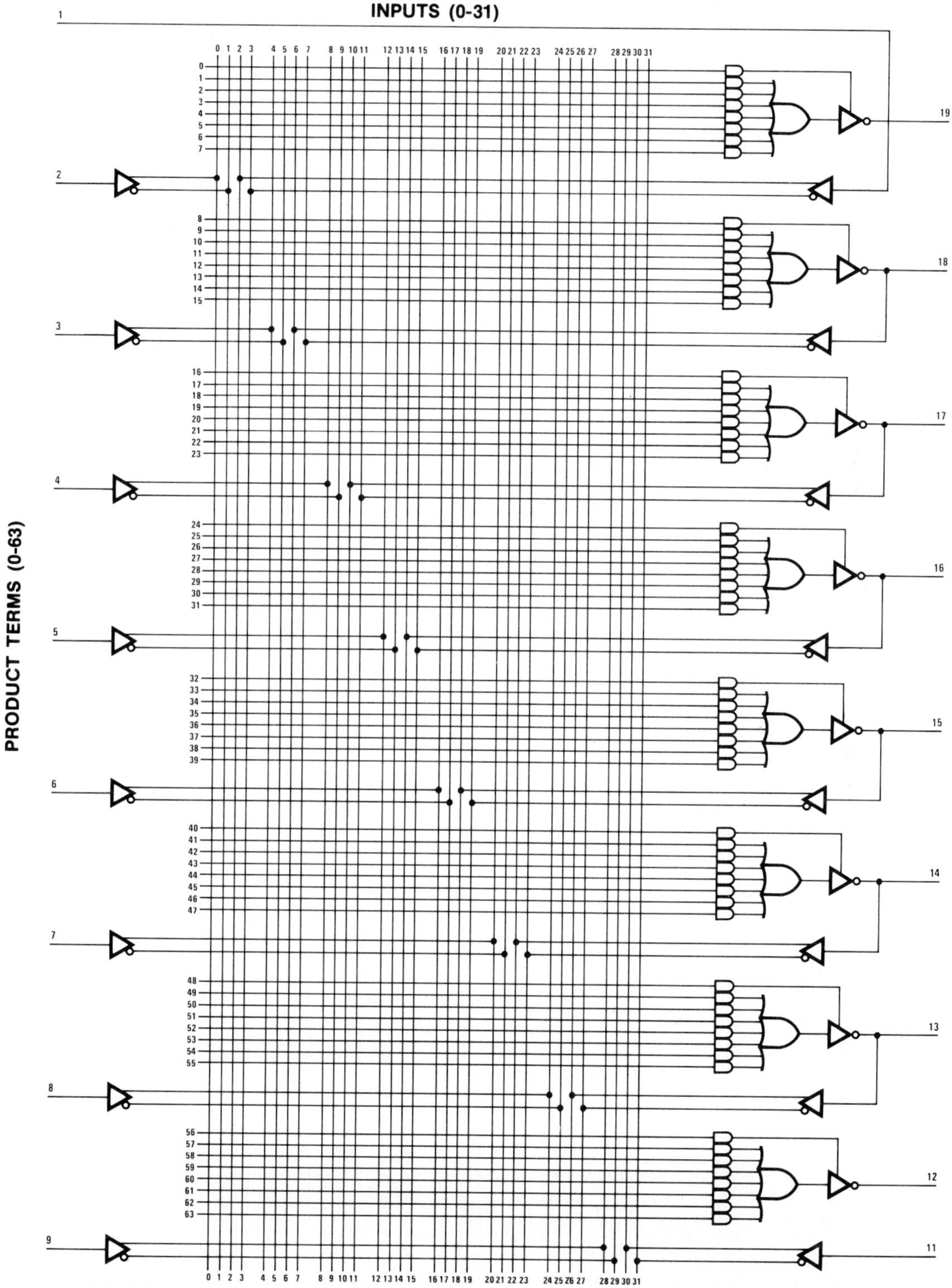

Logic Diagram PAL20L10

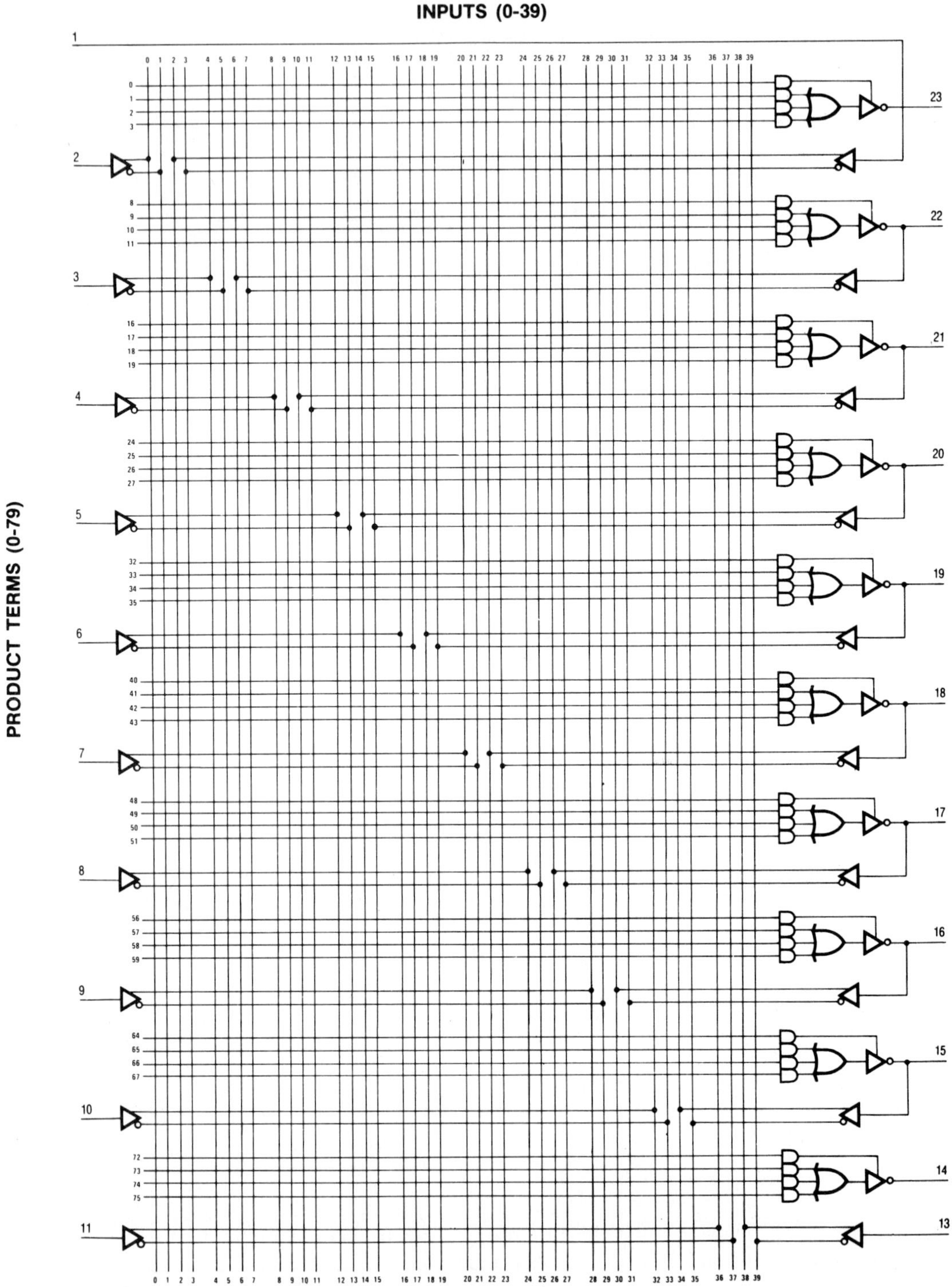

Logic Diagram PAL16R8

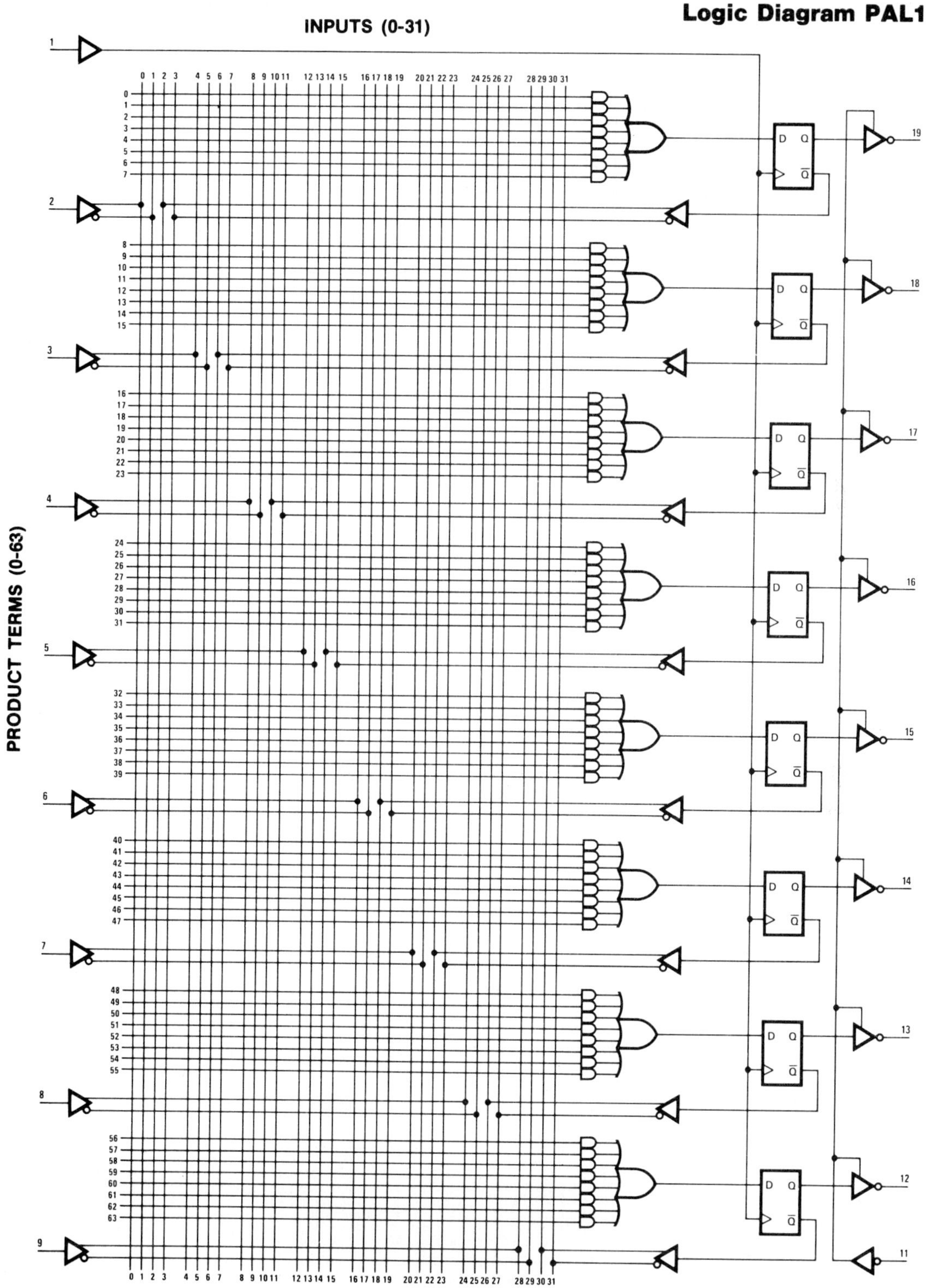

Logic Diagram PAL16R6

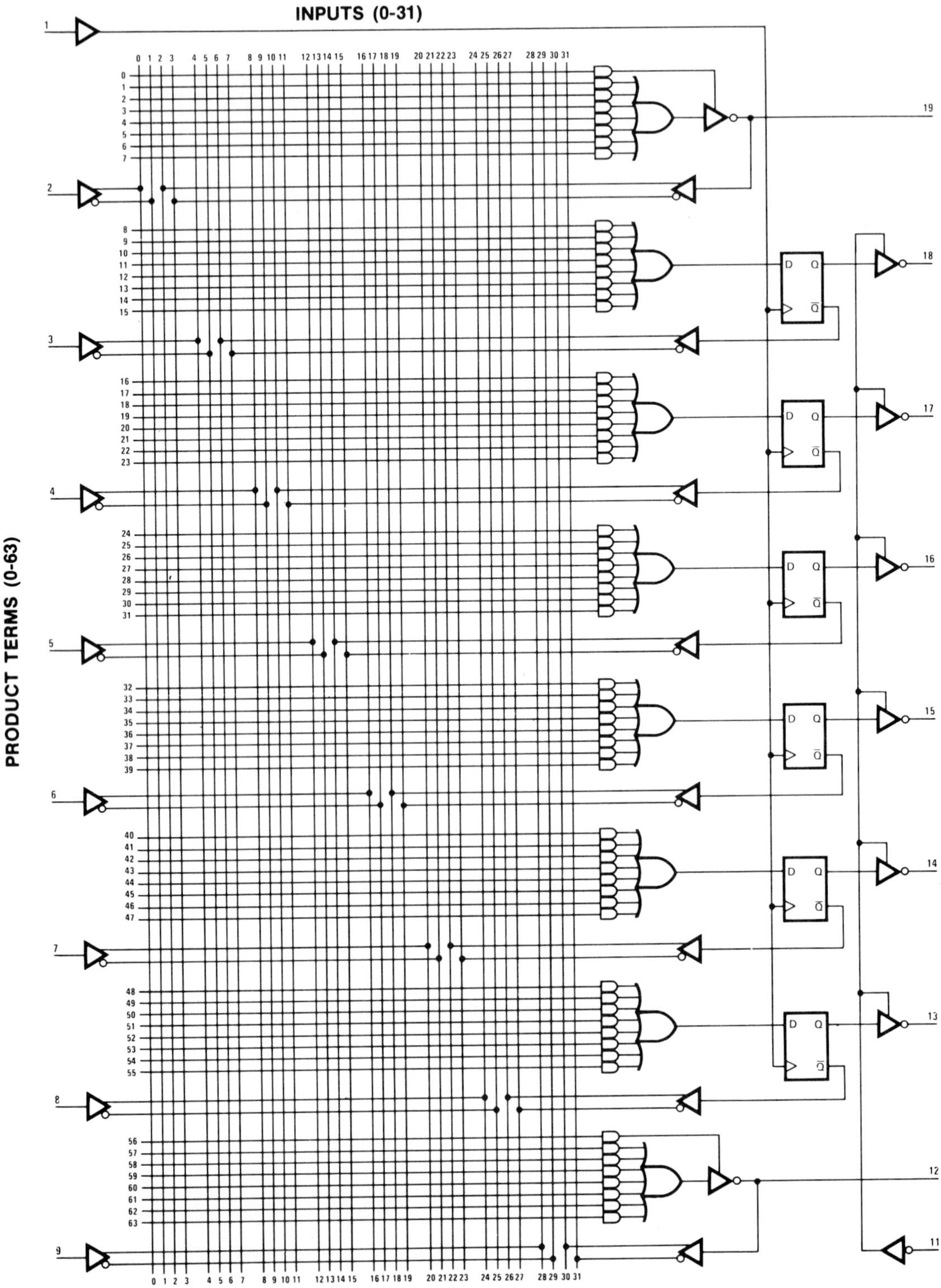

Logic Diagram PAL16R4

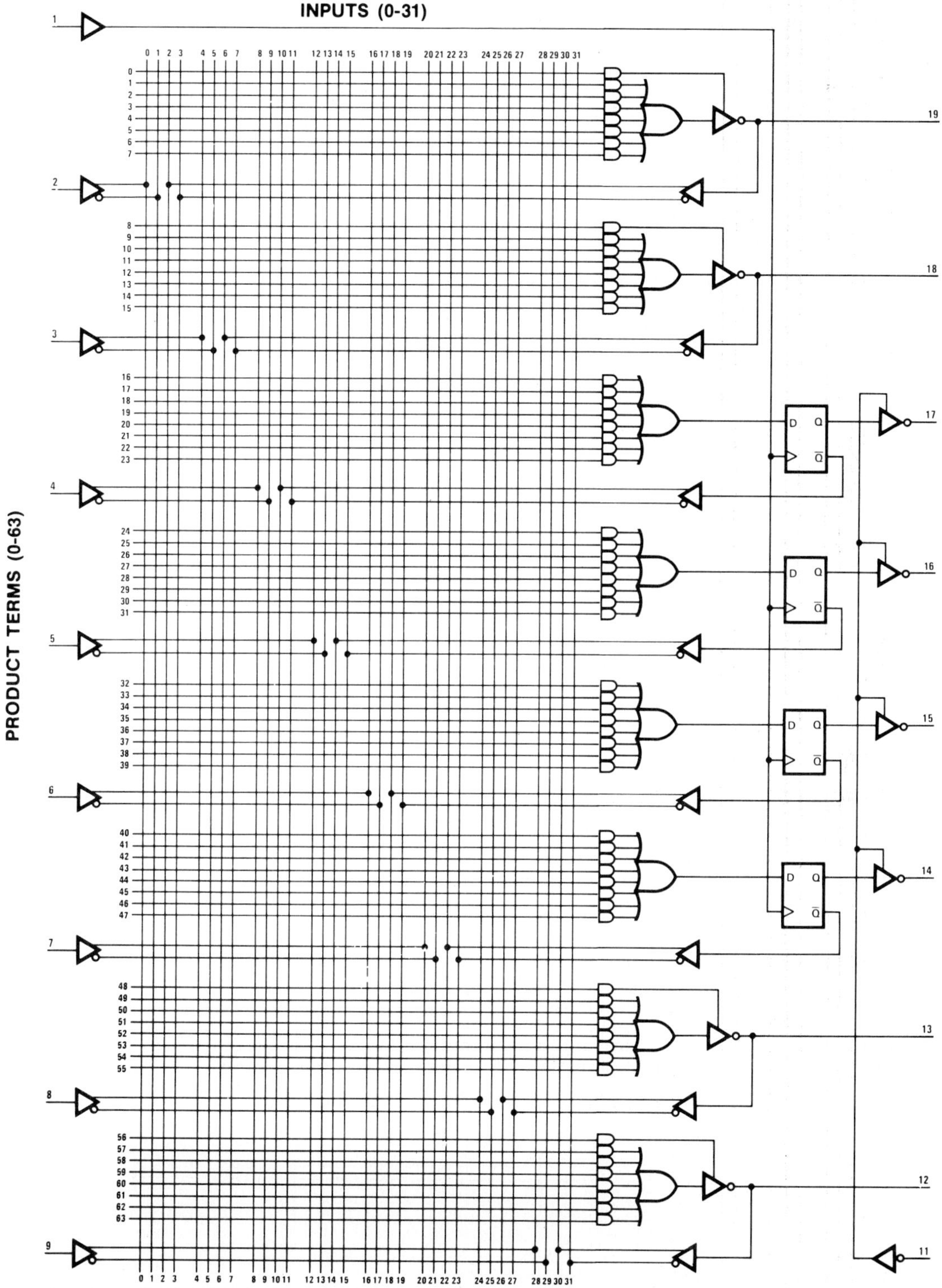

Logic Diagram PAL20X10

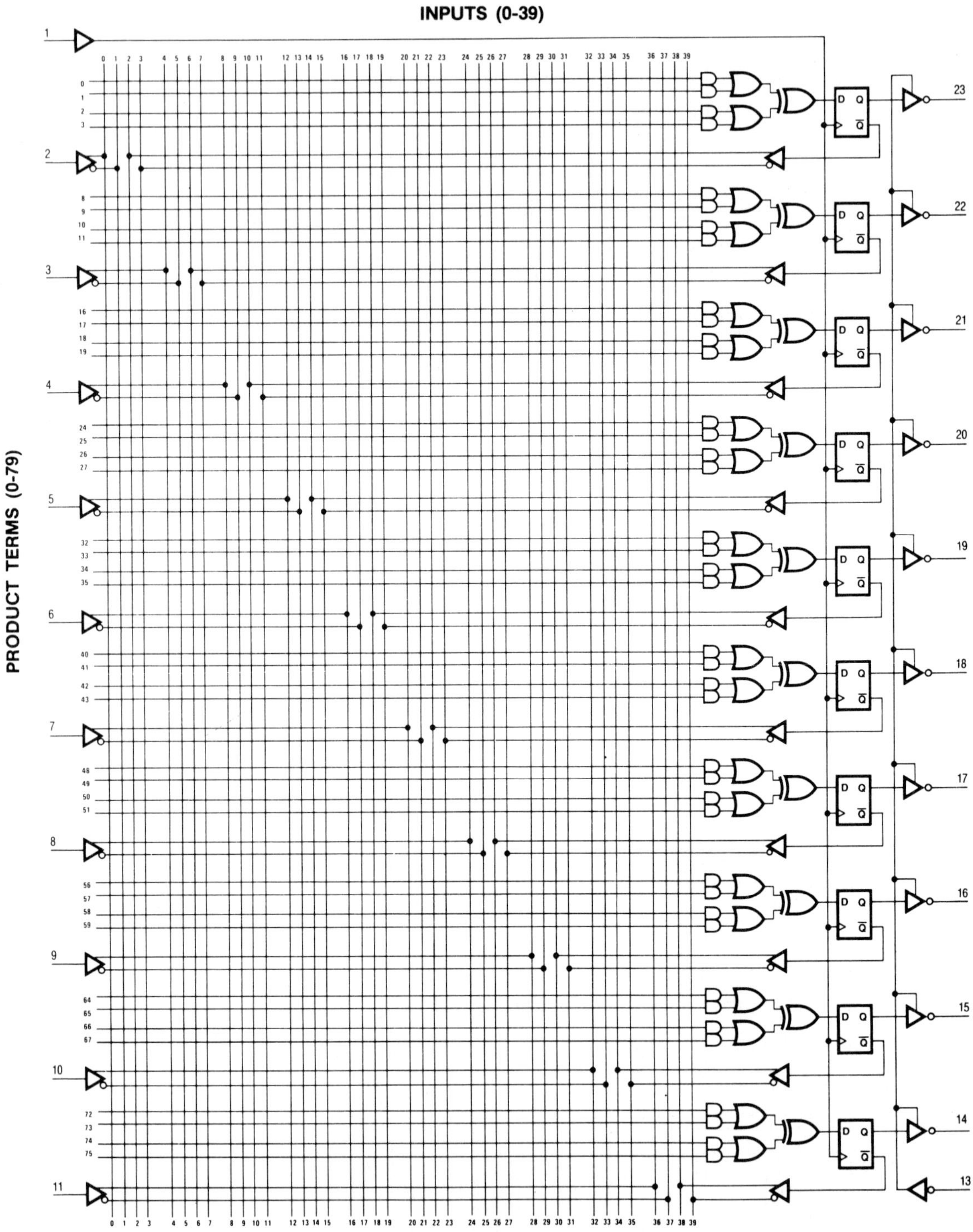

Logic Diagram PAL20X8

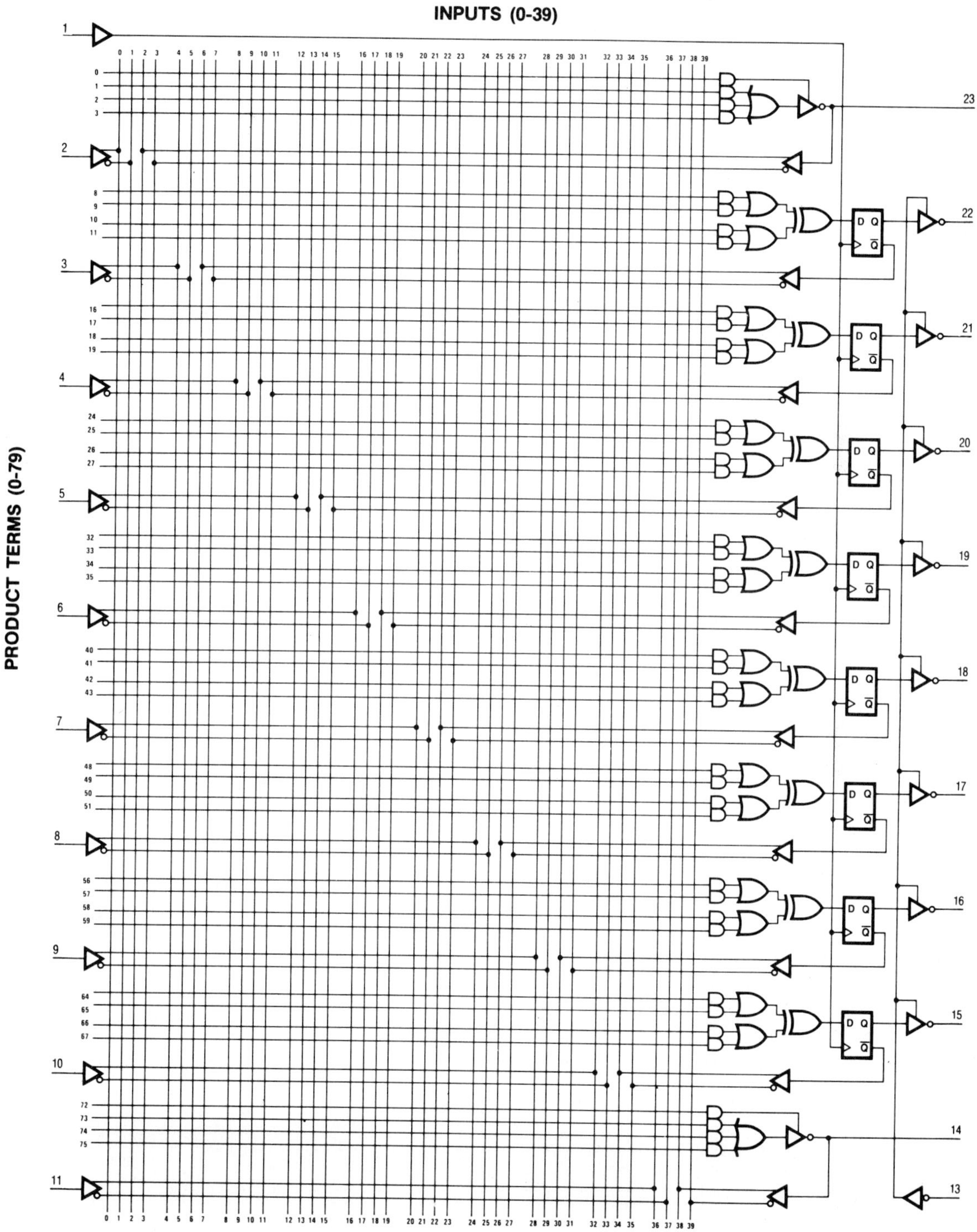

Logic Diagram PAL20X4

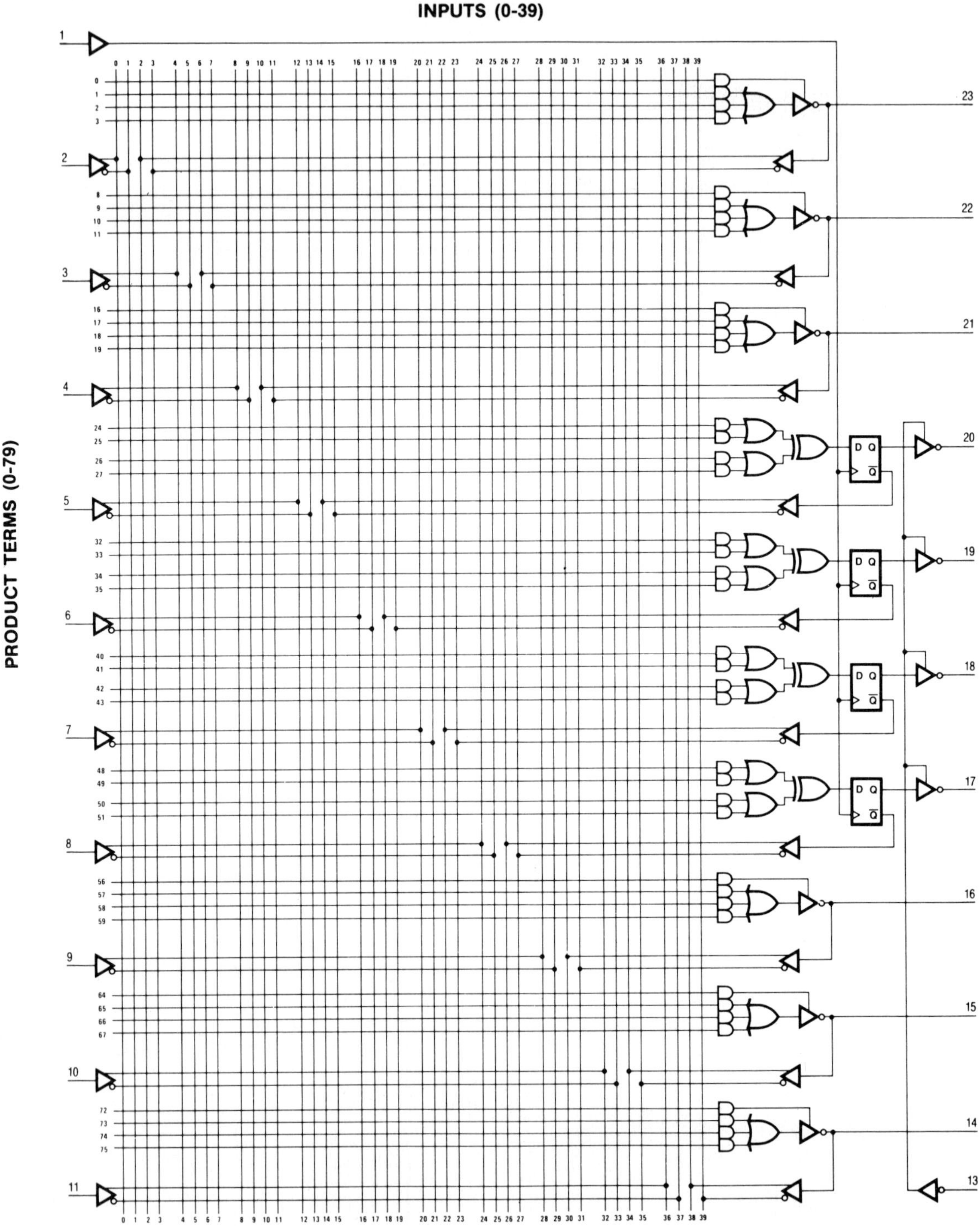

Logic Diagram PAL16X4

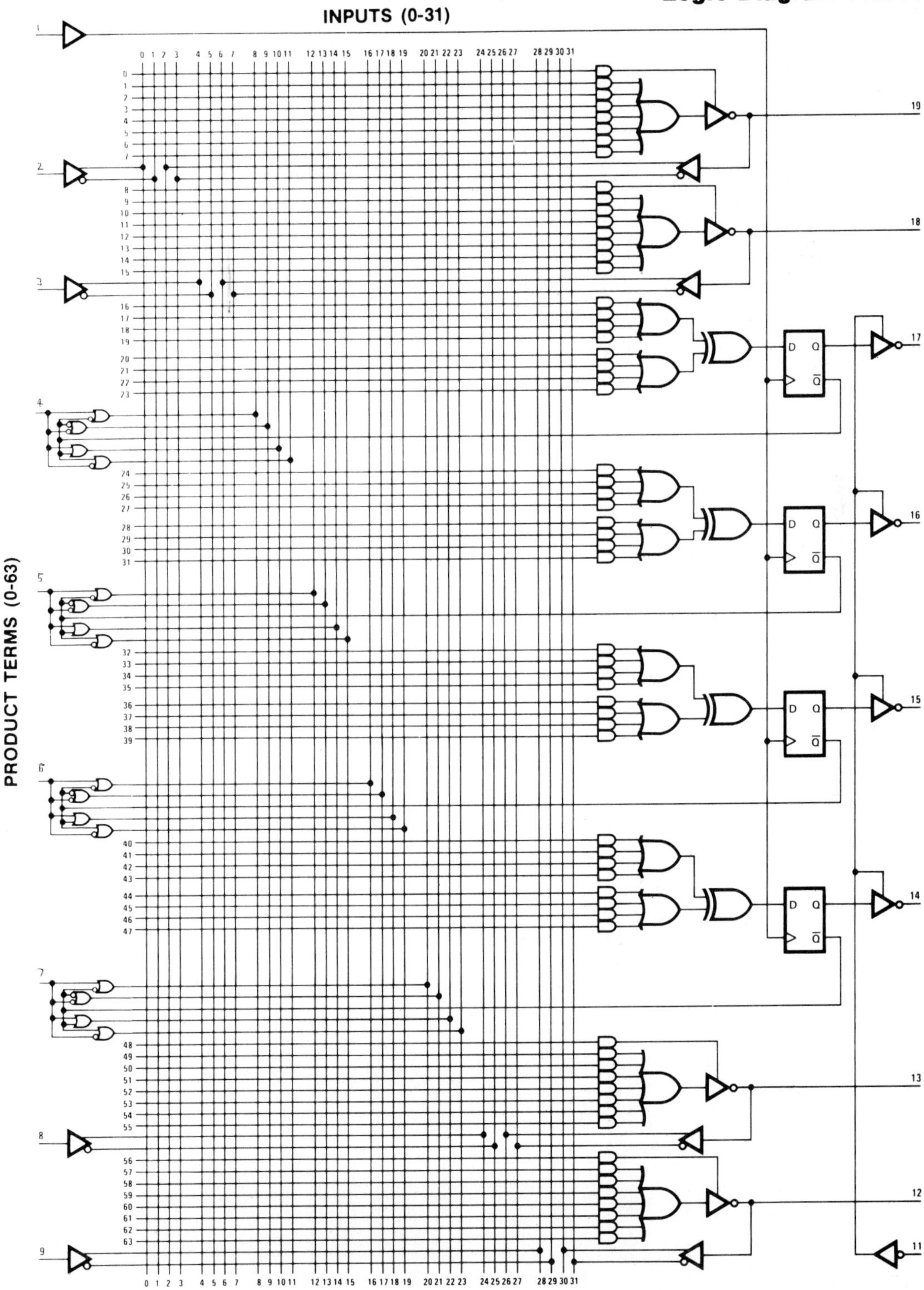

Logic Diagram PAL16A4

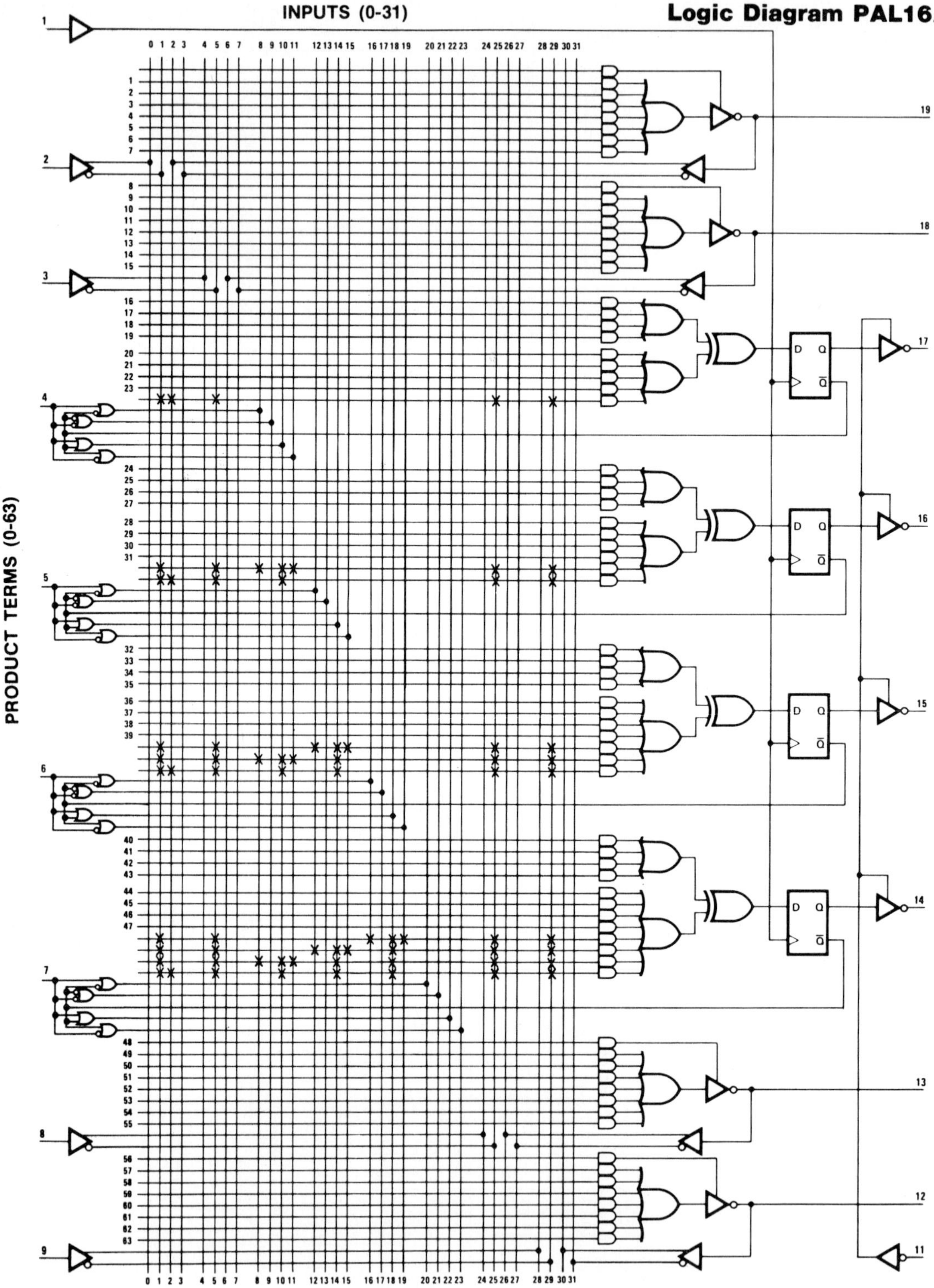

Selecting the Right PAL

The 25-member PAL Family offers a wide range of complexity to choose from. Starting with the PAL10H8 (10 inputs, 8 active high outputs), the first 15 PALs can replace random SSI gate functions by at least a 4 to 1 chip count reduction. With a variety of input/output pin ratios and Active High or Active Low outputs, this group, described as combinatorial, is designed to provide the Low Power Schottky (LS) fan-out and fan-in characteristics of 8 mA output sink (I_{OL}) for totem-pole outputs and 0.25 mA input loading (I_{IL}).

The rest of the PAL family provides the additional features of three-state outputs, programmable I/O pins, registered outputs with feedback, Exclusive OR operator, and arithmetic gated feedback.

The three-state outputs drive the standard LS output sink of 24 mA (I_{OL}) providing bus-driving capabilities.

The programmable I/O pins, allow individual product terms to directly control output data flow. The control logic can be used to either gate product terms out of the three-state buffer or to route data into the product term matrix. This bi-directional capability can be used to implement shift and rotate functions as well as programmable allocation of input and output pins.

The registered outputs allow individual product sums to be clocked into the internal D flip-flops on the rising edge of the clock. The stored data can then be gated to the output buffer by enabling the three-state buffer. The true or complement of the data can also be fed back into the array. This facilitates the construction of state machines in a single chip.

The Exclusive OR operator allows for easy implementation of the HOLD function needed in counters and other state sequencers.

The arithmetic gated feedback allows for any of the 16 possible Boolean operations to be performed between the feedback and input pin. This provides arithmetic and logic operations. A provision for carry propagation required for fast arithmetic operations is also available.

In all PALs unused inputs should be tied to either V_{CC} or GND. The series resistor required for unused inputs on standard TTL is NOT required for PALs, thus using less parts.

Defining the Pinout

The first step in designing a PAL is selecting the pinout. The example shown below (Figure 1) shows a method for circling a section of conveniently drawn logic to define a boundary for a PAL function. This boundary will dictate a specific number of input pins and output pins. For this example, 8 inputs and 6 outputs are required, well within the capability of the PAL10L8. Assignment of inputs and outputs to specific pins can now be done using the PAL Logic Symbol as shown below.

NOTE: This pinout can later be changed to suit printed circuit board.

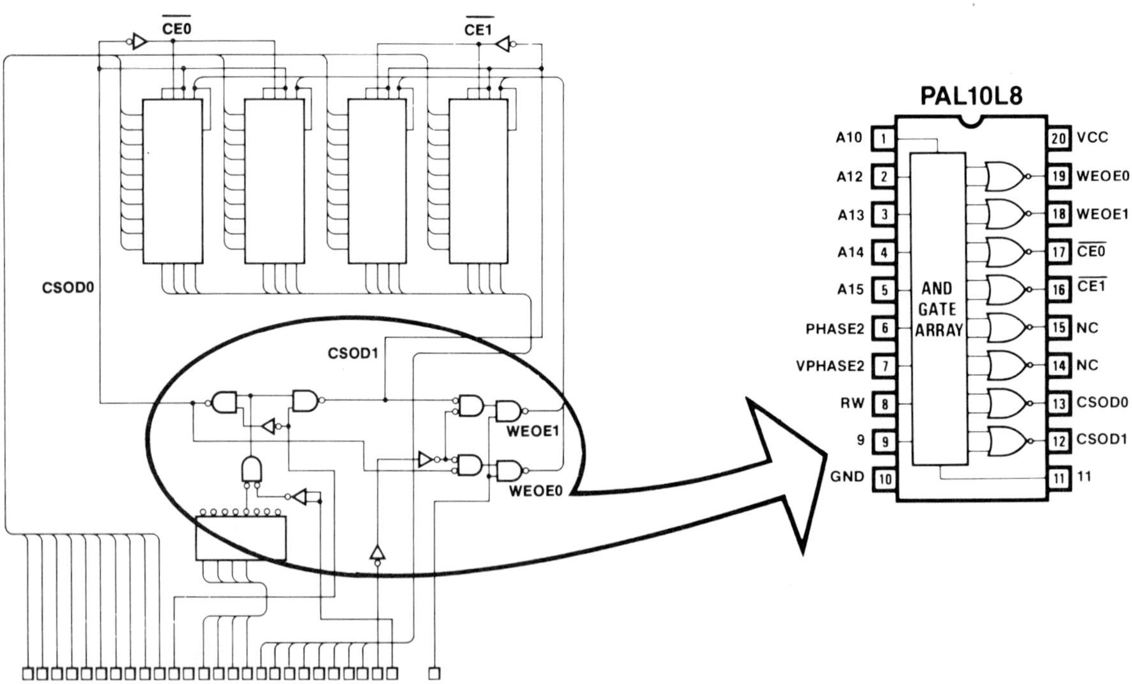

Figure 1. Using PAL to replace random logic in 6800 Microprocessor Bus

Specifying the Design

The next step is to write the Boolean logic equations (in sum of products form) which will transform the inputs into the desired outputs. These explicit logic equations specify the design precisely. They are easily simulated and edited.

Since PALs have predominately active low outputs, it may be necessary to apply DeMorgan's Law to change the output polarity of an equation when implementing it in a PAL. DeMorgan's Law states that the inverse or complement of any Boolean expression can be found by successively applying the following theorems:

$$\overline{(X + Y)} = \overline{X} * \overline{Y} \quad \text{and} \quad \overline{(X * Y)} = \overline{X} + \overline{Y}$$

Examples of equations written with active high and active low outputs are shown in the following table:

ACTIVE HIGH OUTPUT	ACTIVE LOW OUTPUT
$O = \overline{I1}$	$\overline{O} = I1$
$O = \overline{I1} \cdot \overline{I2}$	$\overline{O} = I1 + I2$
$O = I1 + \overline{I2}$	$\overline{O} = \overline{I1} \cdot I2$
$O = I1 + \overline{I2} \cdot I3$	$\overline{O} = \overline{I1} \cdot I2 + \overline{I1} \cdot \overline{I3}$
O = I1 :+: I2	$\overline{O}$ = I1 :*: I2

Some designers may prefer to consult the PAL Logic Diagram before writing the equations. The basic method is simply to choose the appropriate logic diagram, label the corresponding pin names, and mark the fuse interconnections needed to implement the desired logic transform function.

Fuses left intact are indicated on the logic diagram by an "X" at the intersection of the input line and the AND gate product line. A blown fuse is not marked. The PAL Logic Diagrams are provided with no fuses marked, allowing the designer to use the diagram as a coding form. Actually, the unprogrammed PAL is shipped with all Xs (all fuses) intact.

The Boolean logic equations can then be read directly from the logic diagram.

Design Verification and Documentation

An optional FUNCTION TABLE and DESCRIPTION may be included. The FUNCTION TABLE serves the dual purpose of documenting and verifying the design (using the PALASM simulator). The device operation and application are described in the DESCRIPTION.

Phantom Fuses

Phantom fuse locations are those locations where a fuse does not exist. Unprogrammed PALs with phantom fuse locations appear to a PROM programmer as being partially programmed. Since the PROM programmer will expect to verify all possible fuse locations, the PAL programming format must provide the expected pattern to verify non-existent fuse nodes. PALASM and PAL programmers tweek the fuse plot for the phantom fuses automatically so these nodes will be treated properly when verified. The following PALs have phantom fuses:

PAL10H8	PAL10L8	PAL12L10
PAL12H6	PAL12L6	PAL14L8
PAL14H4	PAL14L4	PAL16L6
PAL16H2	PAL16L2	PAL18L4
	PAL16C1	PAL20L2
		PAL20C1

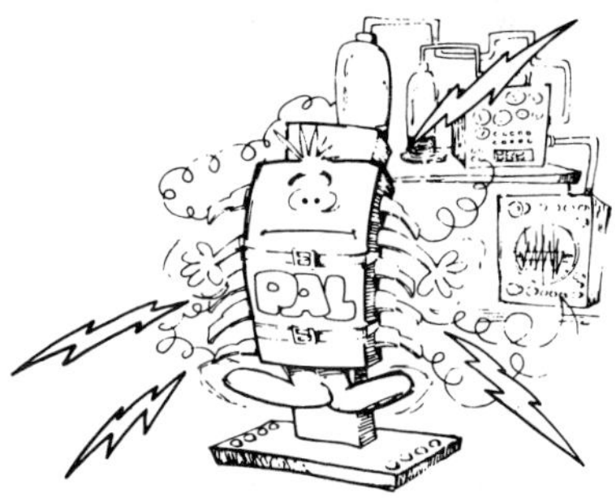

PALASM

PALASM is the key tool used in automating the process of "designing your own chip." PALASM is a FORTRAN IV program which assembles the PAL Design Specification translating the logic equation to a PAL fuse pattern. The fuse pattern may be generated in a format compatible with either a PAL or a PROM programmer.

PALASM also contains a simulator which exercises the Function Table vectors in the logic equations. Inconsistencies between the vectors and the equations are reported as errors. The simulator also translates the Function Table vectors to a set of universal test vectors which may be used for functional testing after the device is fabricated.

PALASM source code is available to users on the following pages. Other source code media is available upon request.

PAL Design Specification

The PAL Design Specification is the input file used with PALASM. It is also the recommended data sheet format for describing the function of a PAL once it has acquired the unique personality of a particular fuse pattern. The format for the PAL Design Specification as shown on the opposite page is:

Line 1 PAL part number left justified followed by PAL DESIGN SPECIFICATION

Line 2 User's part number followed by originator's name and the date

Line 3 Device application name

Line 4 User's company name, city, state

Line 5 **Pin List.**
The pin list is a sequence of symbolic names separated by one or more spaces on one or more lines in order of the device pin numbers. Each symbolic name is unique (except for unused pins which may have the same name.) All pins including power and ground must be named. Names may use any printable character except the operator: "=:*+/()". The prefix "/", may be used to logically complement the name.

Line m **Equations.**
The transfer function of the device is expressed in the following three forms:

1. SYMBOL = EXPRESSION
2. IF (PRODUCT) SYMBOL = EXPRESSION
3. SYMBOL: = EXPRESSION

The following terms are used to construct the equations:

SYMBOL	Pin name with optional prefix, "/".
PRODUCT	A sequence of SYMBOLS separated by the AND operator, "*".
IF	Conditional equality, when the PRODUCT is logically true. Otherwise, high impedance (high-Z).
EXPRESSION	A sequence of SYMBOLS separated by operators.

OPERATORS (in hierarchy of evaluation)

;	Comment follows
/	Complement, prefix to a pin name.
*	AND (product)
+	OR (sum)
:+:	XOR (exclusive OR)
:*:	XNOR (exclusive NOR)
( )	Conditional three-state (IF STATEMENT) or fixed symbol
=	Equality
:=	Replaced by after the low to high transition of the clock.

Line n **Function Table.** (optional)
The function table begins with the keyword, "FUNCTION TABLE." It is followed by a pin list which may be in a different order and polarity from the pin list in Line 5. VCC and GND cannot be listed. The pin list is followed by a dashed line; e.g., ----------- (length optional), which in turn is followed by a list of vectors, one vector per line. One state must be specified for each pin name and optionally separated by spaces. A vector is a sequence of states listed in the same order as the pin list and followed by an optional comment. The vector list is followed by another dashed line.

Definition of Function Table States:

H	HIGH LEVEL
L	LOW LEVEL
X	IRRELEVANT
C	TRANSITION FROM LOW TO HIGH LEVEL
Z	OFF (HIGH IMPEDANCE)

Line o **Description.** (Optional if following Function Table).
This section begins with the keyword, "DESCRIPTION." The device operation and application are described here.

```
PAL10L8                                          PAL DESIGN SPECIFICATION 1
P00123                                             VINCENT COLI 07/08/81 2
EXAMPLE                                                                  3
MMI SUNNYVALE, CALIFORNIA                                                4
A B C NC NC NC NC NC NC GND NC NC NC NC NC NC NC /F NC VCC               5


F = A*B + C      ;A AND B OR C                                           m


FUNCTION TABLE                                                           n

A B C F

;ABC F  COMMENT
-------------------------
 LLL L  ALL LOWS
 LHL L  TEST AND GATE LOW
 HLL L  TEST AND GATE LOW
 HHL H  TEST AND GATE
 XXH H  TEST OR GATE HIGH
-------------------------


DESCRIPTION                                                              o

THIS EXAMPLE ILLUSTRATES THE FORMAT OF THE PAL DESIGN SPECIFICATION.
```

PAL DESIGN SPECIFICATION

```
EXAMPLE

 1 000XXXXXXXXXXXXXXHX1
 2 010XXXXXXXXXXXXXXHX1
 3 100XXXXXXXXXXXXXXHX1
 4 110XXXXXXXXXXXXXXLX1
 5 XX1XXXXXXXXXXXXXXLX1

PASS SIMULATION
```

FUNCTION TABLE SIMULATION

```
EXAMPLE

               11 1111 1111 2222 2222 2233
   0123 4567 8901 2345 6789 0123 4567 8901


 8 X-X- --   --   --   --   --   --   ---- A*B
 9 ---- X-   --   --   --   --   --   ---- C

LEGEND:  X : FUSE NOT BLOWN (L,N,0)   - : FUSE BLOWN   (H,P,1)

NUMBER OF FUSES BLOWN =   61
```

BRIEF FUSE PLOT

PAL Legend

Constants

LOW (L)	NEGATIVE (N)	ZERO (0)	GND	FALSE	×	FUSE NOT BLOWN
HIGH (H)	POSITIVE (P)	ONE (1)	V_{CC}	TRUE	–	FUSE BLOWN

Operators
(IN HIERARCHY OF EVALUATION)

```
;    COMMENT FOLLOWS
/    COMPLEMENT, PREFIX TO A PIN NAME
*    AND (PRODUCT)
+    OR (SUM)
:+:  XOR (EXCLUSIVE OR)
:*:  XNOR (EXCLUSIVE NOR)
( )  CONDITIONAL THREE-STATE (IF STATEMENT) OR FIXED SYMBOL
 =   EQUALITY
:=   REPLACED BY AFTER THE LOW TO HIGH TRANSITION OF THE CLOCK
```

Equations

Standard $\dot{O}_1 = I_1 \overline{I_2} + \overline{I_1} I_2$ PALASM `O1 = I1*/I2 + /I1*I2`

Function Table States

H = HIGH LEVEL C = TRANSITION FROM LOW TO HIGH
L = LOW LEVEL Z = OFF (HIGH IMPEDANCE)
X = IRRELEVANT

Test Conditions

H = TEST HIGH 1 = DRIVE HIGH C = DRIVE INPUT FROM LOW TO HIGH
L = TEST LOW 0 = DRIVE LOW Z = TEST FOR HIGH IMPEDANCE
X = IRRELEVANT

Conventional Symbology

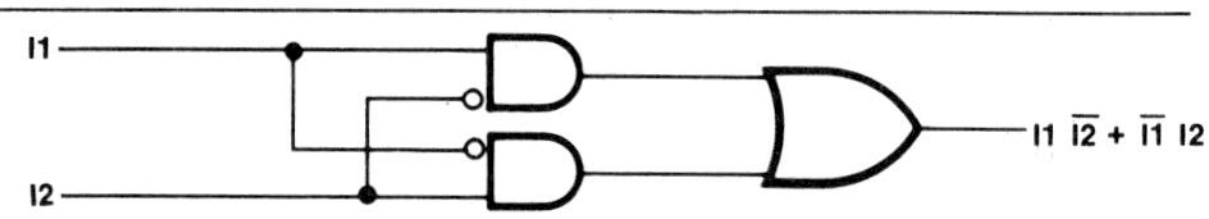

PAL Symbology

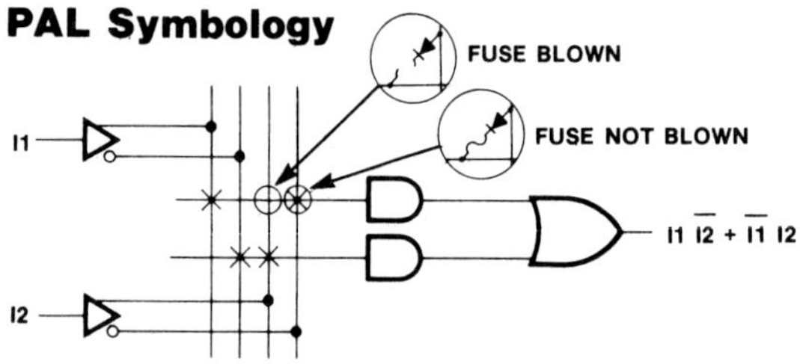

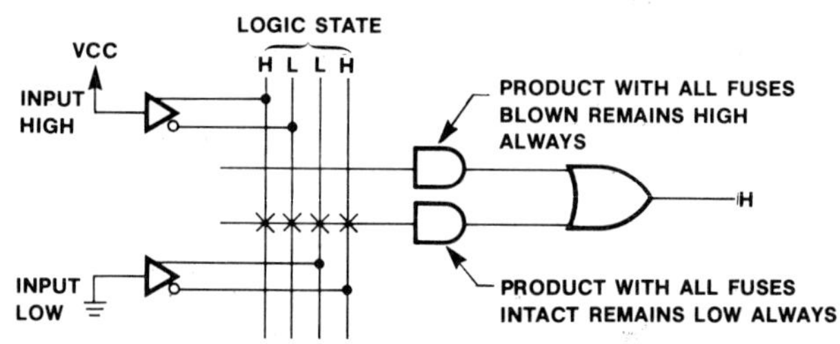

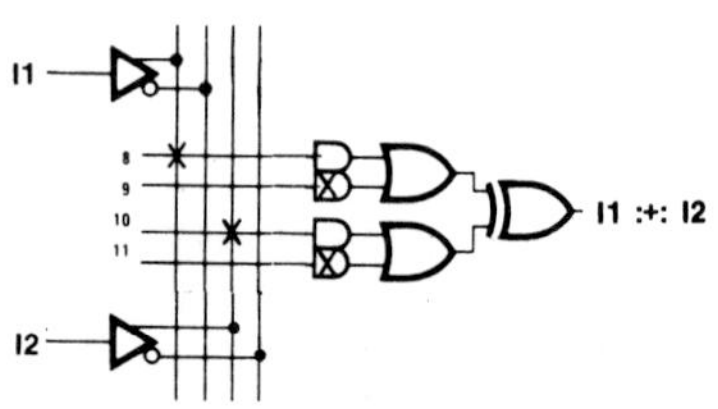

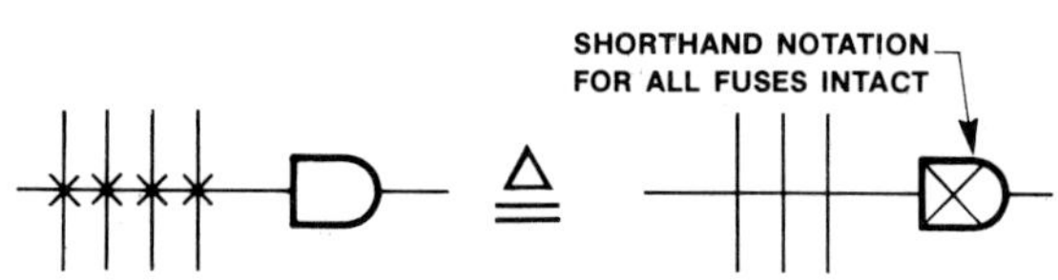

PAL Logic Diagram

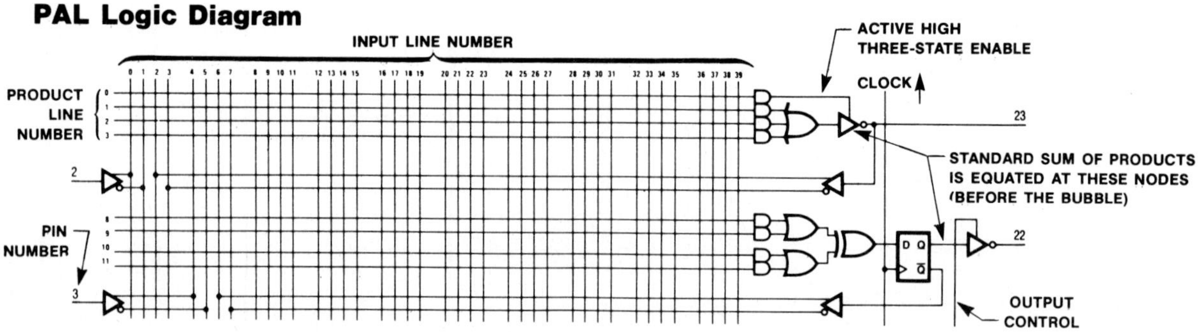

PALASM Flow Chart (Main Program)

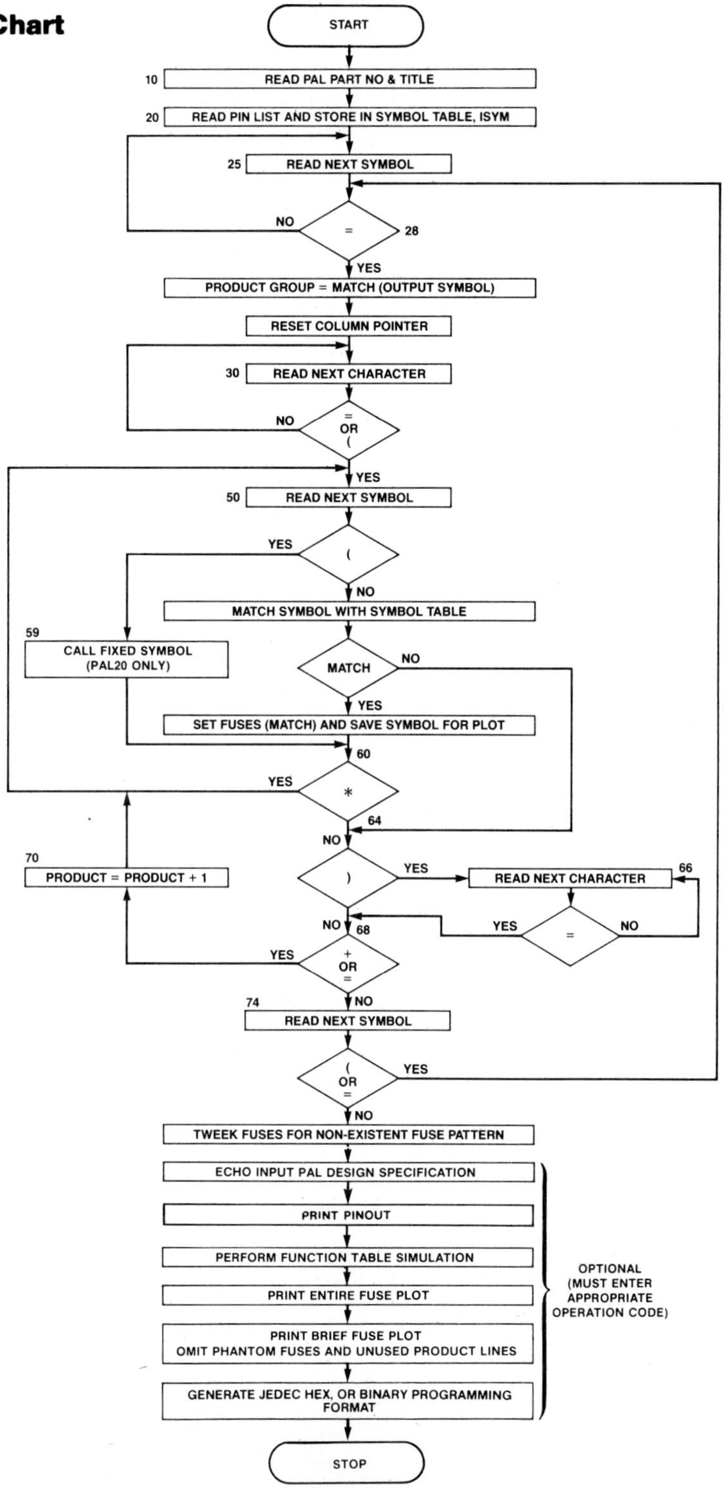

†A SPECIAL DATA I/O FORMAT IS PROVIDED FOR SERIES 24 PALs.

PALASM Flow Chart (Simulator)

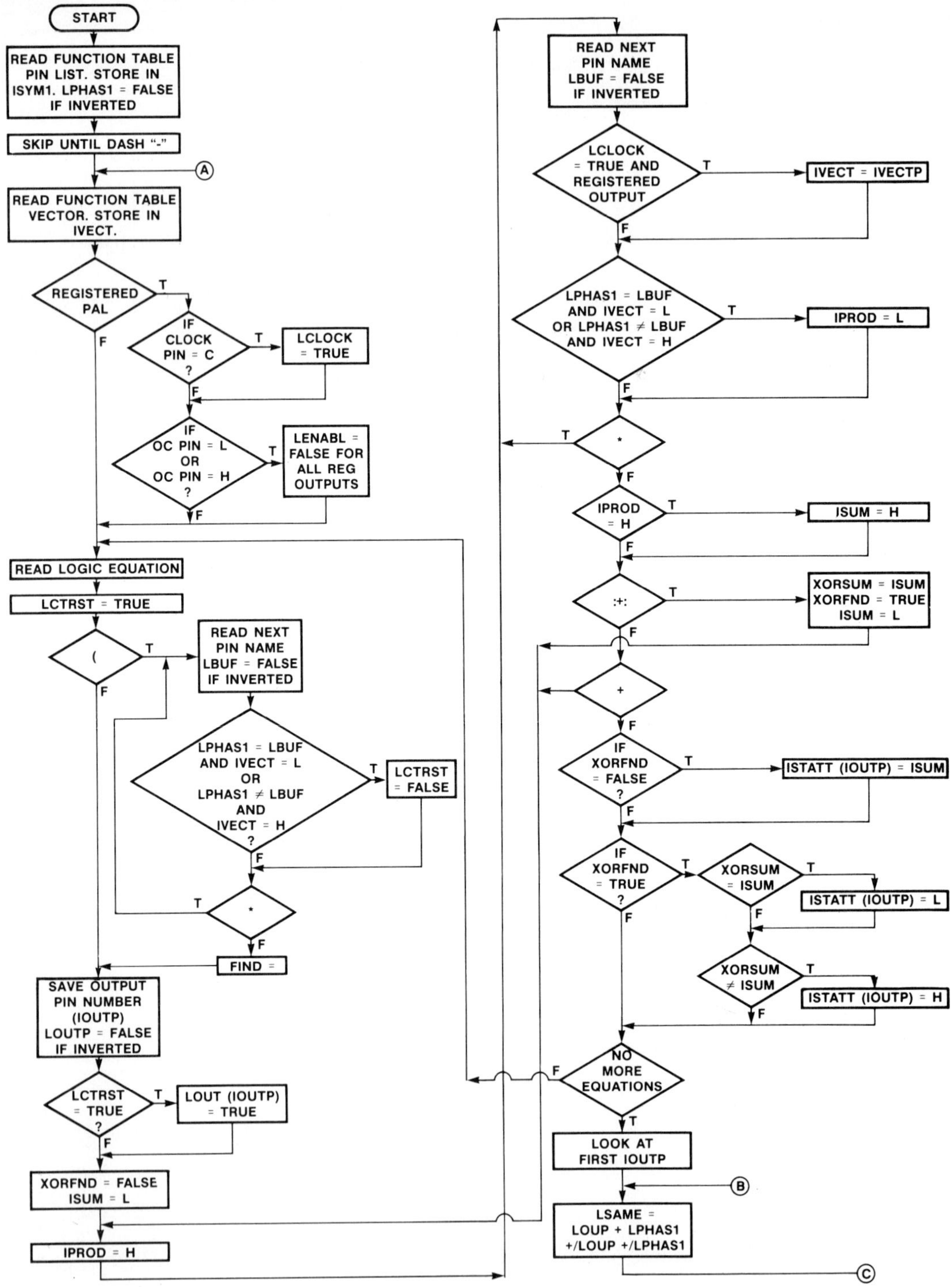

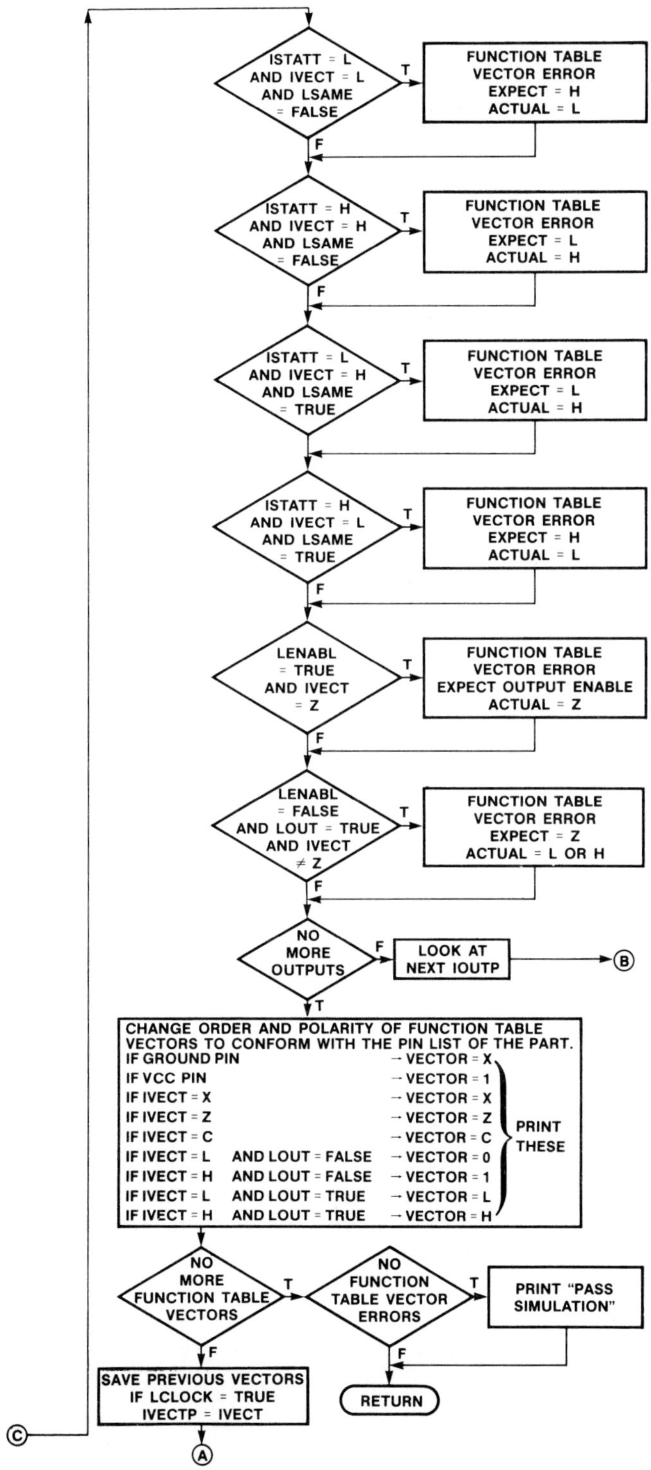
ISTATT = L
AND IVECT = L
AND LSAME
= FALSE
FUNCTION TABLE
VECTOR ERROR
EXPECT = H
ACTUAL = L
ISTATT = H
AND IVECT = H
AND LSAME
= FALSE
FUNCTION TABLE
VECTOR ERROR
EXPECT = L
ACTUAL = H
ISTATT = L
AND IVECT = H
AND LSAME
= TRUE
FUNCTION TABLE
VECTOR ERROR
EXPECT = L
ACTUAL = H
ISTATT = H
AND IVECT = L
AND LSAME
= TRUE
FUNCTION TABLE
VECTOR ERROR
EXPECT = H
ACTUAL = L
LENABL
= TRUE
AND IVECT
= Z
FUNCTION TABLE
VECTOR ERROR
EXPECT OUTPUT ENABLE
ACTUAL = Z
LENABL
= FALSE
AND LOUT = TRUE
AND IVECT
≠ Z
FUNCTION TABLE
VECTOR ERROR
EXPECT = Z
ACTUAL = L OR H
NO
MORE
OUTPUTS
LOOK AT
NEXT IOUTP
B
CHANGE ORDER AND POLARITY OF FUNCTION TABLE
VECTORS TO CONFORM WITH THE PIN LIST OF THE PART.
IF GROUND PIN → VECTOR = X
IF VCC PIN → VECTOR = 1
IF IVECT = X → VECTOR = X
IF IVECT = Z → VECTOR = Z
IF IVECT = C → VECTOR = C
IF IVECT = L AND LOUT = FALSE → VECTOR = 0
IF IVECT = H AND LOUT = FALSE → VECTOR = 1
IF IVECT = L AND LOUT = TRUE → VECTOR = L
IF IVECT = H AND LOUT = TRUE → VECTOR = H
PRINT
THESE
NO
MORE
FUNCTION TABLE
VECTORS
NO
FUNCTION
TABLE VECTOR
ERRORS
PRINT "PASS
SIMULATION"
SAVE PREVIOUS VECTORS
IF LCLOCK = TRUE
IVECTP = IVECT
RETURN
C
A
T
F

```
C***PALASM20**PALASM20**PALASM20**PALASM20**PALASM20**PALASM20**PALASM20*
C
C  P A L A S M  2 0  -  TRANSLATES SYMBOLIC EQUATIONS INTO PAL OBJECT
C                       CODE FORMATTED FOR DIRECT INPUT TO STANDARD
C                       PROM AND PAL PROGRAMMERS.
C
C                       INPUT:       PAL DESIGN SPECIFICATION ASSIGNED
C                                    TO RPD(1).  OPERATION CODES ARE
C                                    ASSIGNED TO ROP(5).
C
C                       OUTPUT:      ECHO, SIMULATION, AND FUSE PATTERN
C                                    ARE ASSIGNED TO POF(6).  JEDEC, HEX,
C                                    AND BINARY PROGRAMMING FORMATS ARE
C                                    ASSIGNED TO PDF(6).  PROMPTS AND
C                                    ERROR MESSAGES ARE ASSIGNED TO
C                                    PMS(6).
C
C                       PART NUMBER: THE PAL PART NUMBER MUST APPEAR
C                                    IN COLUMN ONE OF LINE ONE.
C
C                       PIN LIST:    20 SYMBOLIC PIN NAMES MUST APPEAR
C                                    STARTING ON LINE FIVE.
C
C                       EQUATIONS:   STARTING FIRST LINE AFTER THE
C                                    PIN LIST IN THE FOLLOWING FORMS:
C
C                                       A = B*C + D
C
C                                       A := B*C + D
C
C                                       IF( A*B )  C = D + E
C
C                                       A2 := (A1:*:B1)  + /C
C
C                                    ALL CHARACTERS FOLLOWING ';' ARE
C                                    IGNORED UNTIL THE NEXT LINE.
C
C                                    BLANKS ARE IGNORED.
C
C                       OPERATORS:   ( IN HIERARCHY OF EVALUATION )
C
C                                     ;    COMMENT FOLLOWS
C                                     /    COMPLEMENT
C                                     *    AND (PRODUCT)
C                                     +    OR (SUM)
C                                    :+:   XOR (EXCLUSIVE OR)
C                                    :*:   XNOR (EXCLUSIVE NOR)
C                                    ( )   CONDITIONAL THREE-STATE
C                                          OR FIXED SYMBOL
C                                     =    EQUALITY
C                                    :=    REPLACED BY (AFTER CLOCK)
C
C                       FIXED SYMBOLS
C                       FOR PAL16X4
C                       AND PAL16A4
```

```
C                          ONLY:         (AN+/BN)     WHERE N = 0,1,2,3
C                                        (AN+BN)      FOR OUTPUT PINS
C                                        (AN)         17,16,15,14, RESP
C                                        (/AN+/BN)    A IS OUTPUT
C                                        (/BN)        B IS INPUT
C                                        (AN:+:BN)
C                                        (AN*/BN)
C                                        (/AN+BN)
C                                        (AN:*:BN)
C                                        (BN)
C                                        (AN*BN)
C                                        (/AN)
C                                        (/AN*/BN)
C                                        (/AN*BN)
C
C                          FUNCTION      L, H, X, Z, AND C ARE VALID
C                            TABLE:      FUNCTION TABLE VECTOR ENTRIES.
C
C                          REFERENCE:    A COMPLETE USERS GUIDE TO
C                                        DESIGNING WITH PALS USING PALASM
C                                        IS PROVIDED IN THE MONOLITHIC
C                                        MEMORIES PAL HANDBOOK.
C
C                          SUBROUTINES:  INITLZ,GETSYM,INCR,MATCH,FIXSYM,
C                                        IXLATE,ECHO,CAT,PINOUT,PLOT,TWEEK,
C                                        BINR,PLOTF,SUMCHK,HEX,SLIP,FANTOM,
C                                        IODC2,IODC4,TEST,FIXTST
C
C                          REV LEVEL:    VERSION 1.5  (11/15/82)
C
C                          AUTHORS:      JOHN BIRKNER AND VINCENT COLI
C                                        FAULT TESTING BY IMTIYAZ BENGALI
C                                        MONOLITHIC MEMORIES INC.
C                                        1165 EAST ARQUES AVENUE
C                                        SUNNYVALE, CALIFORNIA 94043
C                                        (408) 739-3535
C
C                          FINE PRINT:   MONOLITHIC MEMORIES TAKES NO
C                                        RESPONSIBILITY FOR THE OPERATION
C                                        OR MAINTENANCE OF THIS PROGRAM.
C                                        THE SOURCE CODE AS PRINTED HERE
C                                        PRODUCED THE OBJECT CODE OF THE
C                                        EXAMPLES IN THE APPLICATIONS
C                                        SECTION ON A VAX/VMS 11/780
C                                        COMPUTER WITH FORTRAN 77 AND A
C                                        NATIONAL CSS IBM SYSTEM/370
C                                        WITH FORTRAN IV (LEVEL G).
C
C**********************************************************************
C
C
C**********************************************************************
C
C
C     MAIN PROGRAM
C
```

```
      IMPLICIT INTEGER (A-Z)
      INTEGER IPAL(4),REST(73),PATNUM(80),TITLE(80),COMP(80),
     1        ISYM(8,20),IBUF(8,20)
      LOGICAL LBLANK,LLEFT,LAND,LOR,LSLASH,LEQUAL,LRIGHT,LXOR,LXNOR,
     1        LFIX,LFIRST,LMATCH,LFUSES(32,64),LPHASE(20),LBUF(20),
     2        LPROD(80),LSAME,LACT,LOPERR,LINP,LPRD,LERR,LSA11,LSA01
      CHARACTER BEL
      COMMON  LBLANK,LLEFT,LAND,LOR,LSLASH,LEQUAL,LRIGHT,LXOR,LXNOR
      COMMON /PGE/ IPAGE(80,200)
      COMMON /LFUSES/LFUSES
      COMMON /LUNIT/ PMS,POF,PDF
      COMMON /FTEST/ IFUNCT,IDESC,IEND
      DATA E/'E'/,O/'O'/,T/'T'/,P/'P'/,B/'B'/,H/'H'/,S/'S'/,L/'L'/,
     1     N/'N'/,C/'C'/,Q/'Q'/,U/'U'/,F/'F'/,R/'R'/,A/'A'/,I/'I'/,
     2     J/'J'/
      DATA BB/'B'/,CC/'C'/,DD/'D'/,EE/'E'/,FF/'F'/,II/'I'/,JJ/'J'/,
     1     NN/'N'/,OO/'O'/,PP/'P'/,RR/'R'/,SS/'S'/,TT/'T'/,UU/'U'/
      DATA BEL/007/
C
C
C     ASSIGNMENT OF DATA SET REFERENCES
C     RPD - PAL DESIGN SPECIFICATION (INPUT)
C     ROC - OPERATION CODE (INPUT)
C     POF - ECHO, PINOUT, TEST, AND PLOT (OUTPUT)
C     PDF - JEDEC, HEX, AND BINARY PROGRAMMING FORMATS (OUTPUT)
C     PMS - PROMPTS AND ERROR MESSAGES (OUTPUT)
      WRITE(6,3)
    3 FORMAT(/,' 20-PIN PALASM VERSION 1.5')
      WRITE(6,1)
    1 FORMAT(/,' WHAT IS THE LOGICAL UNIT NUMBER FOR OUTPUT(6)?: '$)
      READ(5,2) LUN
    2 FORMAT(I4)
      RPD=1
      ROC=5
      POF=LUN
      PDF=LUN
      PMS=LUN
      IFUNCT=0
      IDESC=0
C     INITIALIZE LSAME AND LACT TO FALSE (ACTIVE HIGH/LOW ERROR)
      LSAME=.FALSE.
      LACT=.FALSE.
C     INITIALIZE LOPERR TO FALSE (OUTPUT PIN ERROR)
      LOPERR=.FALSE.
C     INITIALIZE LINP TO FALSE (INPUT PIN ERROR)
      LINP=.FALSE.
C     INITIALIZE LPRD TO FALSE (PRODUCT LINE ERROR)
      LPRD=.FALSE.
C     READ IN FIRST 4 LINES OF THE PAL DESIGN SPECIFICATION
      READ(RPD,10) IPAL,INOAI,IOT,INOO,REST,PATNUM,TITLE,COMP
   10 FORMAT(4A1,A1,A1,A1,73A1,/,80A1,/,80A1,/,80A1)
C     READ IN PIN LIST (LINE 5) THROUGH THE END OF THE PAL DESIGN
C      SPECIFICATION
      DO 15 J=1,200
          READ(RPD,11,END=16) (IPAGE(I,J),I=1,80)
   11     FORMAT(80A1)
```

```
C      CHECK FOR 'FUNCTION TABLE' AND SAVE ITS LINE NUMBER
       IF(      IFUNCT.EQ.0  .AND.IPAGE(1,J).EQ.FF.AND.
     1      IPAGE(2,J).EQ.UU.AND.IPAGE(3,J).EQ.NN.AND.
     2      IPAGE(4,J).EQ.CC.AND.IPAGE(5,J).EQ.TT.AND.
     3      IPAGE(6,J).EQ.II.AND.IPAGE(7,J).EQ.OO.AND.
     4      IPAGE(8,J).EQ.NN.AND.IPAGE(10,J).EQ.TT.AND.
     5      IPAGE(12,J).EQ.BB.AND.IPAGE(14,J).EQ.EE ) IFUNCT=J
C      CHECK FOR 'DESCRIPTION' AND SAVE ITS LINE NUMBER
       IF(      IDESC.EQ.0  .AND.IPAGE(1,J).EQ.DD.AND.
     1      IPAGE(2,J).EQ.EE.AND.IPAGE(3,J).EQ.SS.AND.
     2      IPAGE(4,J).EQ.CC.AND.IPAGE(5,J).EQ.RR.AND.
     3      IPAGE(6,J).EQ.II.AND.IPAGE(7,J).EQ.PP.AND.
     4      IPAGE(8,J).EQ.TT.AND.IPAGE(9,J).EQ.II.AND.
     5      IPAGE(10,J).EQ.OO.AND.IPAGE(11,J).EQ.NN ) IDESC=J
   15  CONTINUE
C      SAVE THE LAST LINE NUMBER OF THE PAL DESIGN SPECIFICATION
   16  IEND=J-1
       CALL INITLZ(INOAI,IOT,INOO,ITYPE,LFUSES,IC,IL,IBLOW,LFIX,IPCTR)
       ILE=IL+1
C      PRINT ERROR MESSAGE FOR INVALID PAL PART TYPE
       IF(ITYPE.NE.0) GO TO 17
           WRITE(PMS,18) IPAL,INOAI,IOT,INOO
   18      FORMAT(/,' PAL PART TYPE ',4A1,A1,A1,A1,' IS INCORRECT')
           CALL EXIT
C      GET 20 PIN NAMES
   17  DO 20 J=1,20
   20      CALL GETSYM(LPHASE,ISYM,J,IC,IL,LFIX)
           IF(.NOT.(LEQUAL.OR.LLEFT.OR.LAND.OR.LOR.OR.LRIGHT)) GO TO 24
               WRITE(PMS,23)
   23          FORMAT(/,' LESS THAN 20 PIN NAMES IN PIN LIST')
               CALL EXIT
   24  ILE=IL
C      BYPASS FUSE PLOT ASSEMBLY IF HAL (H IN COLUMN 1, LINE 1)
       IF( IPAL(1).EQ.H ) GO TO 108
   25  CALL GETSYM(LBUF,IBUF,1,IC,IL,LFIX)
   28      IF(.NOT.LEQUAL) GO TO 25
           COUNT=0
           ILL=IL
           CALL MATCH(IMATCH,IBUF,ISYM)
           IF( IMATCH.EQ.0 ) GO TO 100
           IPRD=IMATCH
C          CHECK FOR VALID POLARITY
           LSAME = ( (      LPHASE(IMATCH)).AND.(      LBUF(1)).OR.
     1               (.NOT.LPHASE(IMATCH)).AND.(.NOT.LBUF(1)) )
           IF( IOT.EQ.H.AND.(.NOT.LSAME) )                  LACT=.TRUE.
           IF( (.NOT.(IOT.EQ.H.OR.IOT.EQ.C)).AND.(LSAME) ) LACT=.TRUE.
C          CHECK FOR VALID OUTPUT PIN
           IF( (ITYPE.EQ.1.OR.ITYPE.EQ.5.OR.ITYPE.EQ.6).AND.IOT.NE.A.
     1     AND.(IMATCH.LT.12.OR.IMATCH.GT.19) ) LOPERR=.TRUE.
           IF(  ITYPE.EQ.2.AND.(IMATCH.LT.13.OR.IMATCH.GT.18) )
     1                                          LOPERR=.TRUE.
           IF(  ITYPE.EQ.3.AND.(IMATCH.LT.14.OR.IMATCH.GT.17) )
     1                                          LOPERR=.TRUE.
           IF(  ITYPE.EQ.4.AND.(IMATCH.LT.15.OR.IMATCH.GT.16) )
     1                                          LOPERR=.TRUE.
           IF( (LACT).OR.(LOPERR) ) GO TO 100
```

```
      I88PRO=(19-IMATCH)*8 + 1
C     START PAL16C1 ON PRODUCT LINE 24 (I88PRO=25)
      IF(IOT.EQ.C) I88PRO=25
      IC=0
30      CALL INCR(IC,IL,LFIX)
        IF( .NOT.(LEQUAL.OR.LLEFT) ) GO TO 30
        LPROD(I88PRO)=.TRUE.
        IF( (.NOT.LLEFT).AND.(REST(3).NE.PP) ) CALL SLIP(LFUSES,
     1     I88PRO,INOAI,IOT,INOO,IBLOW)
      DO 70 I8PRO=1,16
          COUNT = COUNT + 1
          IF( (LXOR).AND.I8PRO.NE.5 ) GO TO 70
          IPROD = I88PRO + I8PRO - 1
          LPROD(IPROD)=.TRUE.
          LFIRST=.TRUE.
50          ILL=IL
            CALL GETSYM(LBUF,IBUF,1,IC,IL,LFIX)
          IF( (ITYPE.EQ.1.OR.ITYPE.EQ.2.AND.IPRD.GT.13
     1        .AND.IPRD.LT.18).AND.COUNT.GT.2 ) LPRD=.TRUE.
          IF( (ITYPE.EQ.3.OR.ITYPE.EQ.2.AND.(IPRD.EQ.13.OR.
     1        IPRD.EQ.18)).AND.COUNT.GT.4 ) LPRD=.TRUE.
          IF( IOT.NE.A.AND.IOT.NE.C.AND.COUNT.GT.8 ) LPRD=.TRUE.
          IF( .NOT.LPRD ) GO TO 69
          IF(IL.NE.IFUNCT.AND.IL.NE.IDESC) ILL=IL
          IPROD = IPROD - 1
          GO TO 118
69          IF(LFIX) GO TO 59
            CALL MATCH(IMATCH,IBUF,ISYM)
C           CHECK FOR INVALID INPUT PIN
            IF( ITYPE.EQ.1.AND.(IMATCH.GE.12.AND.IMATCH.LE.19) )
     1          LINP=.TRUE.
            IF( ITYPE.EQ.2.AND.(IMATCH.GE.13.AND.IMATCH.LE.18) )
     1          LINP=.TRUE.
            IF( ITYPE.EQ.3.AND.(IMATCH.GE.14.AND.IMATCH.LE.17) )
     1          LINP=.TRUE.
            IF( ITYPE.EQ.4.AND.(IMATCH.EQ.15.OR.IMATCH.EQ.16) )
     1          LINP=.TRUE.
            IF( ITYPE.EQ.5.AND.(IMATCH.EQ.12.OR.IMATCH.EQ.19) )
     1          LINP=.TRUE.
            IF( ITYPE.EQ.6.AND.(IMATCH.EQ.1.OR.IMATCH.EQ.11) )
     1          LINP=.TRUE.
            ILL=IL
            IF(LINP) GO TO 100
            IF( IMATCH.EQ.0 ) GO TO 100
            IF( IMATCH.EQ.10.OR.IMATCH.EQ.99 ) GO TO 64
            IF(.NOT.LFIRST) GO TO 58
                LFIRST=.FALSE.
                DO 56 I=1,32
                    IBLOW = IBLOW + 1
56                  LFUSES(I,IPROD)=.TRUE.
58          CALL IXLATE(IINPUT,IMATCH,LPHASE,LBUF,ITYPE)
            IF(IINPUT.LE.0) GO TO 60
            IBLOW = IBLOW - 1
            LFUSES(IINPUT,IPROD)=.FALSE.
            CALL PLOT(LBUF,IBUF,LFUSES,IPROD,TITLE,.FALSE.,ITYPE,
     1             LPROD,IOP,IBLOW,IPCTR)
```

```
              GO TO 60
   59         CALL FIXSYM(LBUF,IBUF,IC,IL,LFIRST,LFUSES,IBLOW,
     1                     IPROD,LFIX)
   60         IF(LAND) GO TO 50
   64       IF(.NOT.LRIGHT) GO TO 68
   66         CALL INCR(IC,IL,LFIX)
              IF(.NOT.LEQUAL)  GO TO 66
   68       IF( .NOT.(LOR.OR.LEQUAL) ) GO TO 74
   70       CONTINUE
   74     ILL=IL
          CALL GETSYM(LBUF,IBUF,1,IC,IL,LFIX)
          IF(LLEFT.OR.LEQUAL) GO TO 28
  100 IF( ILL.EQ.IFUNCT.OR.ILL.EQ.IDESC ) GO TO 102
C     PRINT AN ERROR MESSAGE IF UNRECOGNIZABLE SYMBOL
      ILERR=ILL+4
      WRITE(PMS,99) BEL
   99 FORMAT(' ',A1)
      WRITE(PMS,101) (IBUF(I,1),I=1,8),ILERR,(IPAGE(I,ILL),I=1,80)
  101 FORMAT(/,' ERROR SYMBOL = ',8A1,'      IN LINE NUMBER ',I3,
     1      /,' ',80A1)
C     PRINT AN ERROR MESSAGE FOR ACTIVE HIGH/LOW PART
      IF( (LACT).AND.(      LSAME).AND.(.NOT.LOPERR) )
     1          WRITE(PMS,103) IPAL,INOAI,IOT,INOO
  103 FORMAT(' OUTPUT MUST BE INVERTED SINCE ',4A1,A1,A1,A1,
     1       ' IS AN ACTIVE LOW DEVICE')
      IF( (LACT).AND.(.NOT.LSAME).AND.(.NOT.LOPERR) )
     1          WRITE(PMS,109) IPAL,INOAI,IOT,INOO
  109 FORMAT(' OUTPUT CANNOT BE INVERTED SINCE ',4A1,A1,A1,A1,
     1       ' IS AN ACTIVE HIGH DEVICE')
C     PRINT AN ERROR MESSAGE FOR AN INVALID OUTPUT PIN
      IF( (LOPERR).AND.IMATCH.NE.0 )
     1          WRITE(PMS,105) IMATCH,IPAL,INOAI,IOT,INOO
  105 FORMAT(' THIS PIN NUMBER ',I2,' IS AN INVALID OUTPUT PIN',
     1       ' FOR ',4A1,A1,A1,A1)
C     PRINT AN ERROR MESSAGE FOR AN INVALID INPUT PIN
      IF(LINP) WRITE(PMS,115) IMATCH,IPAL,INOAI,IOT,INOO
  115 FORMAT(' THIS PIN NUMBER ',I2,' IS AN INVALID INPUT PIN',
     1       ' FOR ',4A1,A1,A1,A1)
C     PRINT AN ERROR MESSAGE FOR INVALID PRODUCT LINE
  118 ILERR=ILL+4
      IF(LPRD) WRITE(PMS,119)
     1 (ISYM(I,IPRD),I=1,8),IPRD,ILERR,(IPAGE(I,ILL),I=1,80)
  119 FORMAT(/,' OUTPUT PIN NAME = ',8A1,'  OUTPUT PIN NUMBER = ',I2,
     1      /,' MINTERM IN LINE NUMBER ',I3,/,' ',80A1)
      IF( LPRD.AND.COUNT.LT.8 )
     1          WRITE(PMS,116) IPROD,IPAL,INOAI,IOT,INOO
  116 FORMAT(' THIS PRODUCT LINE NUMBER ',I2,' IS NOT VALID',
     1       ' FOR ',4A1,A1,A1,A1)
      IF( LPRD.AND.COUNT.GT.8 )
     1          WRITE(PMS,117) IPAL,INOAI,IOT,INOO
  117 FORMAT(' MAXIUM OF 8 PRODUCT LINES ARE VALID FOR ',4A1,A1,A1,A1,
     1     /,' TOO MANY MINTERMS ARE SPECIFIED IN THIS EQUATION')
      CALL EXIT
  102 IF(ITYPE.LE.4) CALL TWEEK(ITYPE,IOT,LFUSES)
  108 WRITE(6,106)
  106 FORMAT(/,' OPERATION CODES:')
```

```
      WRITE(6,107)
  107 FORMAT(/,' E=ECHO INPUT  O=PINOUT  T=SIMULATE  F=FAULT TEST',
     1       /,' P=PLOT  B=BRIEF  J=JEDEC FORMAT  H=HEX  S=SHORT'.
     2       /,' L=BHLF  N=BNPF  C=CATALOG  Q=QUIT')
      WRITE(6,110)
  110 FORMAT(/,' ENTER OPERATION CODE: ',$)
      READ(ROC,120) IOP
  120 FORMAT(A1)
C     CALL IODC2
      IF(POF.NE.6) WRITE(POF,125)
  125 FORMAT('1')
      IF(IOP.EQ.E) CALL ECHO(IPAL,INOAI,IOT,INOO,REST,PATNUM,TITLE,
     1                       COMP)
      IF(IOP.EQ.O) CALL PINOUT(IPAL,INOAI,IOT,INOO,TITLE)
      IF(IOP.EQ.T) CALL TEST(LPHASE,LBUF,TITLE,IC,IL,ILE,ISYM,IBUF,
     1                       ITYPE,INOO,LFIX,IPCTR,LERR,ISAF,IPCTR1,
     2                       .FALSE.,.FALSE.)
C     INITIALIZING THE TOTAL FAULTS. CALLING FOR SA1/SA0 TEST
      ISAF=0
      IF(IOP.EQ.F) GO TO 200
      IF(IOP.EQ.JJ) CALL PLOTF
  135 IF(IOP.EQ.P) CALL PLOT(LBUF,IBUF,LFUSES,IPROD,TITLE,.TRUE.,ITYPE,
     1                       LPROD,IOP,IBLOW,IPCTR0)
      IF(IOP.EQ.B) CALL PLOT(LBUF,IBUF,LFUSES,IPROD,TITLE,.TRUE.,ITYPE,
     1                       LPROD,IOP,IBLOW,IPCTR0)
      IF(IOP.EQ.H) CALL HEX(LFUSES,H)
      IF(IOP.EQ.S) CALL HEX(LFUSES,S)
      IF(IOP.EQ.L) CALL BINR(LFUSES,H,L)
      IF(IOP.EQ.N) CALL BINR(LFUSES,P,N)
      IF(IOP.EQ.C) CALL CAT
C     CALL IODC4
      IF(IOP.NE.Q ) GO TO 108
      CALL EXIT
C     SETTING THE PARAMETERS FOR SA1/SA0 TESTS
  200 IPCTR=0
      CALL TEST(LPHASE,LBUF,TITLE,IC,IL,ILE,ISYM,IBUF,ITYPE,
     1          INOO,IFIX,IPCTR,LERR,ISAF,IPCTR1,.FALSE.,.FALSE.)
      IPCTR0=IPCTR
C     LOOPING FOR SA1 TEST
      DO 210 IPCTR1=1,IPCTR0
      LSA11=.TRUE.
      CALL TEST(LPHASE,LBUF,TITLE,IC,IL,ILE,ISYM,IBUF,ITYPE,
     1          INOO,IFIX,IPCTR,LERR,ISAF,IPCTR1,LSA11,.FALSE.)
  210 CONTINUE
      ISA1=ISAF
C     LOOPING FOR SA0 TEST
      DO 215 IPCTR1=1,IPCTR0
      LSA01=.TRUE.
      CALL TEST(LPHASE,LBUF,TITLE,IC,IL,ILE,ISYM,IBUF,ITYPE,
     1          INOO,IFIX,IPCTR,LERR,ISAF,IPCTR1,.FALSE.,LSA01)
  215 CONTINUE
      ISA0=ISAF-ISA1
      IFAULT=(ISAF*100)/(IPCTR0*2)
      WRITE(POF,220) ISA1
  220 FORMAT(/,' NUMBER OF STUCK AT ONE (SA1)  FAULTS ARE ='I3)
      WRITE(POF,225) ISA0
```

```
  225 FORMAT(/,' NUMBER OF STUCK AT ZERO (SA0) FAULTS ARE ='I3)
      WRITE(POF,230) IFAULT
  230 FORMAT(/,' PRODUCT  TERM   COVERAGE                    ='I4,'%',/)
      GO TO 135
      END
C
C***********************************************************************
C
      SUBROUTINE INITLZ(INOAI,IOT,INOO,ITYPE,LFUSES,IC,IL,IBLOW,LFIX,
     1                  IPCTR)
C     THIS SUBROUTINE INITIALIZES VARIABLES AND MATCHES PAL PART
C     NUMBER WITH ITYPE
      IMPLICIT INTEGER (A-Z)
      LOGICAL LBLANK,LLEFT,LAND,LOR,LSLASH,LEQUAL,LRIGHT,LXOR,LXNOR,
     1        LFIX,LFUSES(32,64)
      COMMON  LBLANK,LLEFT,LAND,LOR,LSLASH,LEQUAL,LRIGHT,LXOR,LXNOR
      COMMON /PGE/ IPAGE(80,200)
      DATA H/'H'/,L/'L'/,C/'C'/,R/'R'/,X/'X'/,A/'A'/,
     1     I0/'0'/,I2/'2'/,I4/'4'/,I6/'6'/,I8/'8'/
C     INITIALIZE LFUSES ARRAY (FUSE ARRAY)
      DO 20 J=1,64
         DO 20 I=1,32
   20       LFUSES(I,J)=.FALSE.
C     INITIALIZE IBLOW (NUMBER OF FUSES BLOWN)
      IBLOW=0
C     INITIALIZE IPCTR (NUMBER OF PRODUCT TERMS)
      IPCTR=0
C     INITIALIZE IC AND IL (COLUMN AND LINE POINTERS)
      IC=0
      IL=1
C     INITIALIZE ITYPE (PAL PART TYPE)
      ITYPE=0
C     ITYPE IS ASSIGNED THE FOLLOWING VALUES FOR THESE PAL TYPES:
C          PAL10H8,PAL10L8                          ITYPE=1
C          PAL12H6,PAL12L6                          ITYPE=2
C          PAL14H4,PAL14L4                          ITYPE=3
C          PAL16H2,PAL16L2,PAL16C1                  ITYPE=4
C          PAL16L8                                  ITYPE=5
C          PAL16R4,PAL16R6,PAL16R8,PAL16X4,PAL16A4  ITYPE=6
C     DETERMINE ITYPE
      IF(  INOAI.EQ.I0 )                            ITYPE=1
      IF(  INOAI.EQ.I2 )                            ITYPE=2
      IF(  INOAI.EQ.I4 )                            ITYPE=3
      IF( (INOAI.EQ.I6) )                           ITYPE=4
      IF( (INOAI.EQ.I6).AND.(INOO.EQ.I8) )          ITYPE=5
      IF( (IOT.EQ.R).OR.(IOT.EQ.X).OR.(IOT.EQ.A) )  ITYPE=6
      IF( .NOT.(IOT.EQ.H.OR.IOT.EQ.L.OR.IOT.EQ.C
     1      .OR.IOT.EQ.R.OR.IOT.EQ.X.OR.IOT.EQ.A) ) ITYPE=0
      CALL INCR(IC,IL,LFIX)
      RETURN
      END
C
C***********************************************************************
C
      SUBROUTINE GETSYM(LPHASE,ISYM,J,IC,IL,LFIX)
C     THIS SUBROUTINE GETS THE PIN NAME, / IF COMPLEMENT LOGIC, AND
```

```
C      THE FOLLOWING OPERATION SYMBOL IF ANY
      IMPLICIT INTEGER (A-Z)
      INTEGER ISYM(8,20)
      LOGICAL LBLANK,LLEFT,LAND,LOR,LSLASH,LEQUAL,LRIGHT,LXOR,LXNOR,
     1        LFIX,LPHASE(20)
      COMMON  LBLANK,LLEFT,LAND,LOR,LSLASH,LEQUAL,LRIGHT,LXOR,LXNOR
      COMMON /PGE/ IPAGE(80,200)
      DATA IBLANK/' '/
      LFIX=.FALSE.
      IF( .NOT.(LLEFT.OR.LAND.OR.LOR.OR.LEQUAL.OR.LRIGHT) ) GO TO 10
      CALL INCR(IC,IL,LFIX)
      IF(LLEFT) GO TO 60
   10 LPHASE(J)=( .NOT.LSLASH )
      IF(LPHASE(J)) GO TO 15
      CALL INCR(IC,IL,LFIX)
   15 DO 20 I=1,8
   20     ISYM(I,J)=IBLANK
   25 DO 30 I=1,7
   30     ISYM(I,J)=ISYM(I+1,J)
      ISYM(8,J)=IPAGE(IC,IL)
      CALL INCR(IC,IL,LFIX)
      IF( LLEFT.OR.LBLANK.OR.LAND.OR.LOR.OR.LRIGHT.OR.LEQUAL ) RETURN
      GO TO 25
   60 LFIX=.TRUE.
      RETURN
      END
C
C***********************************************************************
C
      SUBROUTINE INCR(IC,IL,LFIX)
C     THIS SUBROUTINE INCREMENTS COLUMN AND LINE POINTERS
C      BLANKS AND CHARACTERS AFTER ';' ARE IGNORED
      IMPLICIT INTEGER (A-Z)
      LOGICAL LBLANK,LLEFT,LAND,LOR,LSLASH,LEQUAL,LRIGHT,LXOR,LXNOR,
     1        LFIX,LX1
      COMMON  LBLANK,LLEFT,LAND,LOR,LSLASH,LEQUAL,LRIGHT,LXOR,LXNOR
      COMMON /PGE/ IPAGE(80,200)
      COMMON /LUNIT/ PMS,POF,PDF
      DATA IBLANK/' '/,ILEFT/'('/,IAND/'*'/,IOR/'+'/,COMENT/';'/,
     1     ISLASH/'/'/,IEQUAL/'='/,IRIGHT/')'/,ICOLON/':'/
      LBLANK=.FALSE.
      LXOR=.FALSE.
      LXNOR=.FALSE.
      LX1=.FALSE.
      LRIGHT=.FALSE.
   10 IC=IC+1
      IF(IC .LE.79 .AND. IPAGE(IC,IL).NE.COMENT) GO TO 30
      IL=IL+1
      IF(IL.LE.200) GO TO 20
          WRITE(PMS,15)
   15     FORMAT(/,' SOURCE FILE EXCEEDS 200 LINES OR MISSING',
     1            ' DESCRIPTION OR FUNCTION TABLE KEY WORD')
          CALL EXIT
   20 IC=0
      GO TO 10
   30 IF( IPAGE(IC,IL).EQ.ICOLON.AND.(LFIX) ) RETURN
```

```
      IF( IPAGE(IC,IL).NE.IBLANK ) GO TO 31
          LBLANK=.TRUE.
          GO TO 10
   31 IF( IPAGE(IC,IL).NE.ICOLON ) GO TO 32
      IF( (LXOR).OR.(LXNOR) )  GO TO 33
      LX1=.TRUE.
      GO TO 10
   33 IF(LXOR)  LOR=.TRUE.
      IF(LXNOR) LAND=.TRUE.
      RETURN
   32 IF( .NOT.(LX1.AND.(IPAGE(IC,IL).EQ.IOR.OR.IPAGE(IC,IL).EQ.IAND)) )
     1     GO TO 34
      IF( IPAGE(IC,IL).EQ.IOR  ) LXOR=.TRUE.
      IF( IPAGE(IC,IL).EQ.IAND ) LXNOR=.TRUE.
      GO TO 10
   34 LLEFT =( IPAGE(IC,IL).EQ.ILEFT  )
      LAND  =( IPAGE(IC,IL).EQ.IAND   )
      LOR   =( IPAGE(IC,IL).EQ. IOR   )
      LSLASH=( IPAGE(IC,IL).EQ.ISLASH )
      LEQUAL=( IPAGE(IC,IL).EQ.IEQUAL )
      LRIGHT=( IPAGE(IC,IL).EQ.IRIGHT )
      RETURN
      END
C
C***********************************************************************
C
      SUBROUTINE MATCH(IMATCH,IBUF,ISYM)
C     THIS SUBROUTINE FINDS A MATCH BETWEEN THE PIN NAME IN THE EQUATION
C      AND THE PIN NAME IN THE PIN LIST OR FUNCTION TABLE PIN LIST
      IMPLICIT INTEGER (A-Z)
      INTEGER IBUF(8,20),ISYM(8,20)
      LOGICAL LMATCH
      DATA C/'C'/,A/'A'/,R/'R'/,Y/'Y'/
      IMATCH=0
      DO 20 J=1,20
          LMATCH=.TRUE.
          DO 10 I=1,8
   10         LMATCH=LMATCH.AND.(IBUF(I,1).EQ.ISYM(I,J))
          IF(LMATCH) IMATCH=J
   20     CONTINUE
C     MATCH CARRY WHICH IS FOUND IN THE PAL16A4
      IF( IBUF(3,1).EQ.C.AND.IBUF(4,1).EQ.A.AND.IBUF(5,1).EQ.R.AND.
     1    IBUF(6,1).EQ.R.AND.IBUF(7,1).EQ.Y ) IMATCH=99
      RETURN
      END
C
C***********************************************************************
C
      SUBROUTINE IXLATE(IINPUT,IMATCH,LPHASE,LBUF,ITYPE)
C     THIS SUBROUTINE FINDS A MATCH BETWEEN THE INPUT PIN NUMBER AND
C      THE INPUT LINE NUMBER FOR A SPECIFIC PAL.  ADD 1 TO THE INPUT
C      LINE NUMBER IF THE PIN IS A COMPLEMENT
      IMPLICIT INTEGER (A-Z)
      INTEGER ITABLE(20,6)
      LOGICAL LPHASE(20),LBUF(20)
      DATA    ITABLE/
```

```
     1   3, 1, 5, 9,13,17,21,25,29,-10,31,-1,-1,-1,-1,-1,-1,-1,-1,-20,
     2   3, 1, 5, 9,13,17,21,25,29,-10,31,27,-1,-1,-1,-1,-1,-1, 7,-20,
     3   3, 1, 5, 9,13,17,21,25,29,-10,31,27,23,-1,-1,-1,-1,11, 7,-20,
     4   3, 1, 5, 9,13,17,21,25,29,-10,31,27,23,19,-1,-1,15,11, 7,-20,
     5   3, 1, 5, 9,13,17,21,25,29,-10,31,-1,27,23,19,15,11, 7,-1,-20,
     6  -1, 1, 5, 9,13,17,21,25,29,-10,-1,31,27,23,19,15,11, 7, 3,-20/
      IINPUT=0
      IBUBL=0
      IF(((     LPHASE(IMATCH)).AND.(.NOT.LBUF(1))).OR.
     1   ((.NOT.LPHASE(IMATCH)).AND.(     LBUF(1)))) IBUBL=1
      IF( ITABLE(IMATCH,ITYPE).GT.0 ) IINPUT=ITABLE(IMATCH,ITYPE)+IBUBL
      RETURN
      END
C
C***********************************************************************
C
      SUBROUTINE FIXSYM(LBUF,IBUF,IC,IL,LFIRST,LFUSES,IBLOW,IPROD,LFIX)
C     THIS SUBROUTINE EVALUATES THE FIXED SYMBOLS FOUND IN THE
C      PAL16X4 AND PAL16A4
      IMPLICIT INTEGER (A-Z)
      LOGICAL LBUF(20),LFUSES(32,64),LFIRST,LMATCH,LFIX
      INTEGER IBUF(8,20),TITLE(80),FIXBUF(8),TABLE(5,14)
      COMMON /PGE/ IPAGE(80,200)
      DATA A/'A'/,B/'B'/,ISLASH/'/'/,IOR/'+'/,IBLANK/' '/,IRIGHT/')'/,
     1        IAND/'*'/,N/'N'/,Q/'Q'/,N0/'0'/,N1/'1'/,N2/'2'/,N3/'3'/,
     2      ICOLON/':'/,
     3        TABLE      /      ' ','A','+','/','B',' ',' ','A','+','B',
     4      ' ',' ',' ',' ','A','/','A','+','/','B',' ',' ',' ','/','B',
     5      'A',':','+',':','B',' ','A','*','/','B',' ','/','A','+','B',
     6      'A',':','*',':','B',' ',' ',' ',' ','B',' ',' ','A','*','B',
     7      ' ',' ',' ','/','A','/','A','*','/','B',' ','/','A','*','B'/
      IINPUT=0
      DO 20 I=1,8
          IBUF(I,1)=IBLANK
   20     FIXBUF(I)=IBLANK
   21 CALL INCR(IC,IL,LFIX)
      I=IPAGE(IC,IL)
      IF(I.EQ.IRIGHT) GO TO 40
      IF(I.EQ.N0) IINPUT=8
      IF(I.EQ.N1) IINPUT=12
      IF(I.EQ.N2) IINPUT=16
      IF(I.EQ.N3) IINPUT=20
      DO 24 J=1,7
   24     IBUF(J,1)=IBUF(J+1,1)
      IBUF(8,1)=I
      IF(.NOT. ( (I.EQ.A).OR.(I.EQ.B).OR.(I.EQ.ISLASH).OR.(I.EQ.IOR)
     1       .OR.(I.EQ.IAND).OR.(I.EQ.ICOLON) ) )  GO TO 21
      DO 30 I=1,4
   30     FIXBUF(I)=FIXBUF(I+1)
      FIXBUF(5)=IPAGE(IC,IL)
      GO TO 21
   40 IMATCH=0
      DO 60 J=1,14
          LMATCH=.TRUE.
          DO 50 I=1,5
   50         LMATCH=LMATCH .AND. ( FIXBUF(I).EQ.TABLE(I,J) )
```

```
   60      IF(LMATCH) IMATCH=J
      IF(IMATCH.EQ.0) GO TO 100
      IF(.NOT.LFIRST) GO TO 85
           LFIRST=.FALSE.
           DO 80 I=1,32
                LFUSES(I,IPROD)=.TRUE.
   80           IBLOW = IBLOW + 1
   85 DO 90 I=1,4
           IF( (IMATCH-7).LE.0 ) GO TO 90
           ISUM1=IINPUT+I
           LFUSES(ISUM1,IPROD)=.FALSE.
           IBLOW = IBLOW - 1
           IMATCH=IMATCH-8
   90 IMATCH=IMATCH+IMATCH
      LBUF(1)=.TRUE.
      CALL PLOT(LBUF,IBUF,LFUSES,IPROD,TITLE,.FALSE.,ITYPE,
     1          LPROD,IOP,IBLOW,IPCTR)
  100 LFIX=.FALSE.
      CALL INCR(IC,IL,LFIX)
      RETURN
      END
C
C***********************************************************************
C
      SUBROUTINE ECHO(IPAL,INOAI,IOT,INOO,REST,PATNUM,TITLE,COMP)
C     THIS SUBROUTINE PRINTS THE PAL DESIGN SPECIFICATION INPUT FILE
      IMPLICIT INTEGER (A-Z)
      INTEGER IPAL(4),REST(73),PATNUM(80),TITLE(80),COMP(80)
      COMMON /PGE/ IPAGE(80,200)
      COMMON /LUNIT/ PMS,POF,PDF
      COMMON /FTEST/ IFUNCT,IDESC,IEND
      DATA IBLANK/' '/
      WRITE(POF,5) IPAL,INOAI,IOT,INOO,REST,PATNUM,TITLE,COMP
    5 FORMAT(/,' ',4A1,A1,A1,A1,73A1,/,' ',80A1,/,' ',80A1,/,' ',80A1)
      DO 20 IL=1,IEND
           IC=81
   10      IC=IC-1
           IF( IPAGE(IC,IL).EQ.IBLANK.AND.IC.GT.1 ) GO TO 10
           WRITE(POF,15) (IPAGE(I,IL),I=1,IC)
   15      FORMAT(' ',80A1)
   20 CONTINUE
      RETURN
      END
C
C***********************************************************************
C
      SUBROUTINE CAT
C     THIS SUBROUTINE PRINTS THE PALASM CATOLOG
      IMPLICIT INTEGER (A-Z)
      COMMON /LUNIT/ PMS,POF,PDF
      WRITE(PMS,10)
   10 FORMAT(/,' 20-PIN PALASM VERSION 1.5')
      WRITE(PMS,20)
   20 FORMAT(/,' THIS PALASM AIDS THE USER IN THE DESIGN AND',
     1         ' PROGRAMMING OF THE',/,' SERIES 20 PAL FAMILY.  THE',
     2         ' FOLLOWING OPTIONS ARE PROVIDED:',
```

```
     3      //,'    ECHO (E)     - PRINTS THE PAL DESIGN',
     4          ' SPECIFICATION',
     5      //,'    PINOUT (O)   - PRINTS THE PINOUT OF THE PAL',
     6      //,'    SIMULATE (T) - EXERCISES THE FUNCTION TABLE',
     7          ' VECTORS IN THE LOGIC',/,'                     ',
     8          ' EQUATIONS AND GENERATES TEST VECTORS',
     9      //,'    FAULT (F)    - PERFORMS FAULT TESTING',
     A      //,'    PLOT (P)     - PRINTS THE ENTIRE FUSE PLOT')
      WRITE(PMS,30)
   30 FORMAT(/,'    BRIEF (B)    - PRINTS ONLY THE USED PRODUCT LINES',
     1          ' OF THE FUSE PLOT',/,'                     PHANTOM',
     2          ' FUSES ARE OMITTED',
     3      //,'    JEDEC (J)    - GENERATES JEDEC PROGRAMMING FORMAT',
     4      //,'    HEX (H)      - GENERATES HEX PROGRAMMING FORMAT',
     5      //,'    SHORT (S)    - GENERATES HEX PROGRAMMING FORMAT',
     6      //,'    BHLF (L)     - GENERATES BHLF PROGRAMMING FORMAT',
     7      //,'    BNPF (N)     - GENERATES BNPF PROGRAMMING FORMAT',
     8      //,'    CATALOG (C)  - PRINTS THE PALASM CATALOG',
     9      //,'    QUIT (Q)     - EXIT PALASM')
      RETURN
      END
C
C***********************************************************************
C
      SUBROUTINE PINOUT(IPAL,INOAI,IOT,INOO,TITLE)
C     THIS SUBROUTINE PRINTS THE PINOUT OF THE PAL
      IMPLICIT INTEGER (A-Z)
      INTEGER IPAL(4),TITLE(80),PIN(12,20),IIN(7,2)
      COMMON /PGE/ IPAGE(80,200)
      COMMON /LUNIT/ PMS,POF,PDF
      DATA IBLANK/' '/,ISTAR/'*'/
      DO 10 J=1,20
          DO 5 I=1,12
    5         PIN(I,J)=IBLANK
   10 CONTINUE
   15 DO 25 J=1,2
          DO 20 I=1,7
   20         IIN(I,J)=IBLANK
   25 CONTINUE
      IIN(2,1)=IPAL(1)
      IIN(4,1)=IPAL(2)
      IIN(6,1)=IPAL(3)
      IIN(1,2)=IPAL(4)
      IIN(3,2)=INOAI
      IIN(5,2)=IOT
      IIN(7,2)=INOO
      J=0
      IL=0
   30 IC=0
      IL=IL+1
   35 IC=IC+1
   40 IF( IC.GT.80 ) GO TO 30
      IF( IPAGE(IC,IL).EQ.IBLANK ) GO TO 35
      J=J+1
      IF(J.GT.20) GO TO 60
      DO 55 I=1,12
```

```
        PIN(I,J)=IPAGE(IC,IL)
        IC=IC+1
        IF( IC.GT.80 ) GO TO 40
        IF( IPAGE(IC,IL).EQ.IBLANK ) GO TO 40
   55 CONTINUE
   60 DO 75 J=1,10
        II=0
   65   II=II+1
        IF(II.EQ.13) GO TO 75
        IF( PIN(II,J).NE.IBLANK ) GO TO 65
        I=13
   70   I=I-1
        II=II-1
        PIN(I,J)=PIN(II,J)
        PIN(II,J)=IBLANK
        IF(II.NE.1) GO TO 70
   75 CONTINUE
      WRITE(POF,76) TITLE
   76 FORMAT(/,' ',80A1)
      WRITE(POF,78) ISTAR,ISTAR,ISTAR,ISTAR,ISTAR,ISTAR,ISTAR,ISTAR,
     1              ISTAR,ISTAR,ISTAR,ISTAR,ISTAR,ISTAR,ISTAR,ISTAR,
     2              ISTAR,ISTAR,ISTAR,ISTAR,ISTAR,ISTAR,ISTAR,ISTAR,
     3              ISTAR,ISTAR,ISTAR,ISTAR,ISTAR,ISTAR,ISTAR,ISTAR
   78 FORMAT(/,' ',18X,14A1,3X,14A1,
     1       /,' ',18X,A1,13X,A1,1X,A1,13X,A1)
      JJ=20
      DO 88 J=1,10
        WRITE(POF,80) ISTAR,ISTAR,ISTAR,ISTAR,ISTAR,ISTAR,ISTAR,ISTAR
   80   FORMAT(' ',15X,4A1,29X,4A1)
        WRITE(POF,81) (PIN(I,J),I=1,12),ISTAR,J,ISTAR,
     1       (IIN(I,1),I=1,7),ISTAR,JJ,ISTAR,(PIN(I,JJ),I=1,12)
   81   FORMAT(' ',12A1,3X,A1,I2,A1,11X,7A1,11X,A1,I2,A1,3X,12A1)
        WRITE(POF,82) ISTAR,ISTAR,ISTAR,ISTAR,ISTAR,ISTAR,ISTAR,ISTAR
   82   FORMAT(' ',15X,4A1,29X,4A1)
        WRITE(POF,84) ISTAR,(IIN(I,2),I=1,7),ISTAR
   84   FORMAT(' ',18X,A1,11X,7A1,11X,A1)
        DO 86 II=1,2
            DO 85 I=1,7
   85           IIN(I,II)=IBLANK
   86   CONTINUE
        JJ=JJ-1
   88 CONTINUE
      WRITE(POF,90) ISTAR,ISTAR,ISTAR,ISTAR,ISTAR,ISTAR,ISTAR,ISTAR,
     1              ISTAR,ISTAR,ISTAR,ISTAR,ISTAR,ISTAR,ISTAR,ISTAR,
     2              ISTAR,ISTAR,ISTAR,ISTAR,ISTAR,ISTAR,ISTAR,ISTAR,
     3              ISTAR,ISTAR,ISTAR,ISTAR,ISTAR,ISTAR,ISTAR
   90 FORMAT(' ',18X,31A1)
      RETURN
      END
C
C***********************************************************************
C
      SUBROUTINE PLOT(LBUF,IBUF,LFUSES,IPROD,TITLE,LDUMP,ITYPE,
     1                LPROD,IOP,IBLOW,IPCTR0)
C     THIS THIS SUBROUTINE PRODUCES THE FUSE PLOT
      IMPLICIT INTEGER (A-Z)
```

```
      INTEGER IBUF(8,20),IOUT(64),ISAVE(64,32),TITLE(80)
      LOGICAL LBUF(20),LFUSES(32,64),LDUMP,LPROD(80)
      COMMON /LUNIT/ PMS,POF,PDF
      DATA ISAVE/2048*' '/,IAND/'*'/,IOR/'+'/,ISLASH/'/'/,
     1     IDASH/'-'/,X/'X'/,IBLANK/' '/,P/'P'/,B/'B'/,
     2     HIFANT/'O'/
      IF(LDUMP) GO TO 60
      IF(ISAVE(IPROD,1).NE.IBLANK) RETURN
      IF( LBUF(1) ) GO TO 5
      DO 30 J=1,31
   30     ISAVE(IPROD,J)=ISAVE(IPROD,J+1)
      ISAVE(IPROD,32)=ISLASH
    5 DO 20 I=1,8
          IF( ISAVE(IPROD,1).NE.IBLANK ) RETURN
           IF( IBUF(I,1).EQ.IBLANK ) GO TO 20
           DO 10 J=1,31
   10          ISAVE(IPROD,J)=ISAVE(IPROD,J+1)
           ISAVE(IPROD,32)=IBUF(I,1)
   20      CONTINUE
      IF(ISAVE(IPROD,1).NE.IBLANK) RETURN
   40 DO 50 J=1,31
   50      ISAVE(IPROD,J)=ISAVE(IPROD,J+1)
      ISAVE(IPROD,32)=IAND
      RETURN
C     PRINT FUSE PLOT
   60 WRITE(POF,62) TITLE
   62 FORMAT(/,' ',80A1,//,
     1 '                11 1111 1111 2222 2222 2233',/,
     2 '     0123 4567 8901 2345 6789 0123 4567 8901',/)
      DO 100 I88PRO=1,57,8
          DO 94 I8PRO=1,8
              IPROD=I88PRO+I8PRO-1
              ISAVE(IPROD,32)=IBLANK
              DO 70 I=1,32
                  IF( ISAVE(IPROD,1).NE.IBLANK ) GO TO 70
                  DO 65 J=1,31
                      ISAVE(IPROD,J)=ISAVE(IPROD,J+1)
   65                 CONTINUE
                  ISAVE(IPROD,32)=IBLANK
   70         CONTINUE
              DO 80 I=1,32
                  IOUT(I)=X
                  IF( LFUSES(I,IPROD) ) IOUT(I)=IDASH
                  IOUT(I+32)=ISAVE(IPROD,I)
   80         CONTINUE
              IF(ITYPE.LE.4) CALL FANTOM(ITYPE,IOUT,IPROD,I8PRO)
              IPROD=IPROD-1
              DO 85 J=1,32
                  IF( IOP.EQ.B.AND.IOUT(J).EQ.HIFANT ) IOUT(J)=IBLANK
   85         CONTINUE
              IF( (IOP.EQ.P).OR.(IOP.EQ.B.AND.(LPROD(IPROD+1))) )
     1        WRITE(POF,90) IPROD,IOUT
   90         FORMAT(' ',I2,8(' ',4A1),' ',32A1)
   94         CONTINUE
          WRITE(POF,96)
   96     FORMAT(1X)
```

```
 100      CONTINUE
      WRITE(POF,110)
 110  FORMAT(/,
     1' LEGEND:  X : FUSE NOT BLOWN (L,N,0)    - : FUSE BLOWN   (H,P,1)')
      IF( IOP.EQ.P.AND.ITYPE.LE.4 ) WRITE(POF,111)
 111  FORMAT(
     1'          0 : PHANTOM FUSE   (L,N,0)    O : PHANTOM FUSE (H,P,1)')
      WRITE(POF,112) IBLOW
 112  FORMAT(/,' NUMBER OF FUSES BLOWN = ',I4)
      RETURN
      END
C
C***********************************************************************
C
      SUBROUTINE PLOTF
C     THIS SUBROUTINE GENERATES THE JEDEC PROGRAMMING FORMAT OUTPUT
C      COMPATIBILE WITH THE DATA I/O PROGRAMMABLE LOGIC PAK (PLDS)
      IMPLICIT INTEGER (A-Z)
      LOGICAL LFUSES (32,64)
      INTEGER IPBUF(32),ZERO,ONE
      INTEGER ISUM(4),IADR,STX,ETX,IDEC(4),IPT,IINP,J1,J2
      INTEGER IDECIO(4),ISUMV(4),ISUMIO(4),BUFIO(32)
      COMMON  /LUNIT/ PMS,POF,PDF
      COMMON  /IPT/ IPT
      COMMON  /LFUSES/ LFUSES
      COMMON  /SUM/ ISUM,IDEC,IPBUF,BUFIO
      DATA ZERO/'0'/, ONE/'1'/
      IADR=0
      STX=2
      ETX=3
      ISUM(2)=0
      ISUM(4)=230
      WRITE(PDF,10) STX
  10  FORMAT(' ',A1,'*F0*')
      DO 300 IPT=1,64
         DO 50  IINP=1,32
            IF(LFUSES(IINP,IPT)) IPBUF(IINP)=ONE
            IF(.NOT.(LFUSES(IINP,IPT))) IPBUF(IINP)=ZERO
  50        CONTINUE
         IF(LFUSES(1,IPT)) GO TO 100
         IF(.NOT.LFUSES(2,IPT)) GO TO 250
 100     IDEC(4)=IADR
         DO 150 J=1,3
            J1=5-J
            J2=4-J
            IDEC(J2)=IDEC(J1)/10
            IDEC(J1)=IDEC(J1)-10*IDEC(J2)
            IDECIO(J1)=ICONV(IDEC(J1))
 150     CONTINUE
         IDECIO(1)=ICONV(IDEC(1))
         CALL SUMCHK
         WRITE(PDF,201)IDECIO,IPBUF
 201     FORMAT(' L',4A1,' ',8(4A1,' '),'*')
 250     IADR=IADR+32
 300  CONTINUE
      ISUMIO(1)=ICONV(ISUM(2)/16)
```

```
      ISUM(2)=MOD(ISUM(2),16)
      ISUMIO(2)=ICONV(ISUM(2))
      ISUMIO(3)=ICONV(ISUM(4)/16)
      ISUM(4)=MOD(ISUM(4),16)
      ISUMIO(4)=ICONV(ISUM(4))
      WRITE(PDF,400) ETX,ISUMIO
  400 FORMAT(' *',A1,4A1,'*',/)
      RETURN
      END
C
C***********************************************************************
C
      SUBROUTINE SUMCHK
C     THIS SUBROUTINE CALCULATES THE SUMCHECK FOR THE JEDEC
C      PROGRAMMING FORMAT
      IMPLICIT INTEGER (A-Z)
      LOGICAL LFUSES(32,64)
      INTEGER IPBUF(32), BUFIO(32)
      INTEGER ISUM(4),IDEC(4)
      COMMON /IPT/ IPT
      COMMON /LFUSES/ LFUSES
      COMMON /SUM/ ISUM,IDEC,IPBUF,BUFIO
      DO 50 J=1,32
         IF(LFUSES(J,IPT)) BUFIO(J)=49
         IF(.NOT.LFUSES(J,IPT)) BUFIO(J)=48
         ISUM(4)=ISUM(4)+BUFIO(J)
         IF(ISUM(4).GE.256) ISUM(2)=ISUM(2)+1
         ISUM(4)=MOD(ISUM(4),256)
   50 CONTINUE
      DO 100 J=1,4
         ISUM(4)=ISUM(4)+IDEC(J)+48
         IF(ISUM(4).GE.256) ISUM(2)=ISUM(2)+1
         ISUM(4)=MOD(ISUM(4),256)
  100 CONTINUE
      ISUM(4)=ISUM(4)+173
      ISUM(2)=ISUM(2)+1
      IF(ISUM(4).GE.256) ISUM(2)=ISUM(2)+1
      ISUM(4)=MOD(ISUM(4),256)
      RETURN
      END
C
C***********************************************************************
C
      INTEGER FUNCTION ICONV(K)
C     THIS INTEGER FUNCTION CONVERTS DECIMAL INTO ASCII CODE FOR THE
C      JEDEC PROGRAMMING FORMAT
      IMPLICIT INTEGER (A-Z)
      DATA A/'0'/,B/'1'/,C/'2'/,D/'3'/,E/'4'/,F/'5'/,G/'6'/,H/'7'/,
     1     I/'8'/,J/'9'/,X/'A'/,L/'B'/,M/'C'/,N/'D'/,O/'E'/,P/'F'/
      IF(K.EQ.0) ICONV=A
      IF(K.EQ.1) ICONV=B
      IF(K.EQ.2) ICONV=C
      IF(K.EQ.3) ICONV=D
      IF(K.EQ.4) ICONV=E
      IF(K.EQ.5) ICONV=F
      IF(K.EQ.6) ICONV=G
```

```
      IF(K.EQ.7)  ICONV=H
      IF(K.EQ.8)  ICONV=I
      IF(K.EQ.9)  ICONV=J
      IF(K.EQ.10) ICONV=X
      IF(K.EQ.11) ICONV=L
      IF(K.EQ.12) ICONV=M
      IF(K.EQ.13) ICONV=N
      IF(K.EQ.14) ICONV=O
      IF(K.EQ.15) ICONV=P
      RETURN
      END
C
C***********************************************************************
C
      SUBROUTINE HEX(LFUSES,IOP)
C     THIS SUBROUTINE GENERATES HEX PROGRAMMING FORMATS
      IMPLICIT INTEGER (A-Z)
      INTEGER ZTABLE(16),ITEMP(64),ZCSUM(4)
      LOGICAL LFUSES(32,64)
      CHARACTER SOH,STX,ETX,BEL
      COMMON /LUNIT/ PMS,POF,PDF
      DATA H/'H'/,S/'S'/,IBLANK/' '/,
     1    ZTABLE/'0','1','2','3','4','5','6','7',
     2           '8','9','A','B','C','D','E','F'/
      DATA SOH/001/,STX/002/,ETX/003/,BEL/007/
      CSUM=0
      IF(IOP.EQ.H) WRITE(PDF,10)
   10 FORMAT(//,'                                                    .',//)
C***** NOTE: SOME PROM PROGRAMMERS NEED A START CHARACTER.
C*****       THIS PROGRAM OUTPUTS AN STX FOR THE DATA I/O MODEL 9
C*****         (USE SOH FOR MODEL 5)
      WRITE(PDF,5) BEL,BEL,BEL,BEL,BEL,BEL,BEL,STX,SOH
    5 FORMAT(' ',9A1)
      DO 40 I=1,33,32
      INC=I-1
        DO 40 IPROD=1,7,2
          DO 20 J=1,2
              DO 20 IINPUT=1,32
              IHEX=0
              ISUM2=IPROD + J-1 + INC
              IF(LFUSES(IINPUT,ISUM2 +  0 )) IHEX=IHEX+1
              IF(LFUSES(IINPUT,ISUM2 +  8 )) IHEX=IHEX+2
              IF(LFUSES(IINPUT,ISUM2 + 16 )) IHEX=IHEX+4
              IF(LFUSES(IINPUT,ISUM2 + 24 )) IHEX=IHEX+8
              CSUM=CSUM+IHEX
              ISUMX=IINPUT+(32*(J-1))
   20         ITEMP(ISUMX)=ZTABLE(IHEX+1)
          IF(IOP.EQ.H) WRITE(PDF,30) ITEMP
   30     FORMAT(' ',32(A1,' '),'.',/,' ',32(A1,' '),'.')
   40     IF(IOP.EQ.S) WRITE(PDF,50) ITEMP
   50     FORMAT(' ',64A1)
      IF(IOP.EQ.H) WRITE(PDF,70)
   70 FORMAT(' ',//,'                                                    .',//)
      WRITE(PDF,80) ETX
   80 FORMAT(' ',A1)
C     CONVERT DECIMAL CHECK SUM INTO HEX CHECK SUM
```

```
      DO 85 I=1,4
           ZTEMP=CSUM-16*(CSUM/16)
           ZCSUM(5-I)=ZTABLE(ZTEMP+1)
           CSUM=CSUM/16
   85 CONTINUE
      IF(ZCSUM(1).EQ.ZTABLE(1)) ZCSUM(1)=IBLANK
      WRITE(PMS,90) ZCSUM(1),ZCSUM(2),ZCSUM(3),ZCSUM(4)
   90 FORMAT(/' HEX CHECK SUM = ',4A1)
      RETURN
      END
C
C***********************************************************************
C
      SUBROUTINE TWEEK(ITYPE,IOT,LFUSES)
C     THIS SUBROUTINE TWEEKS LFUSES (THE PROGRAMMING FUSE PLOT)
C      FOR HIGH AND LOW PHANTOM FUSES
      IMPLICIT INTEGER (A-Z)
      LOGICAL LFUSES(32,64)
      DATA L/'L'/,C/'C'/
      IF(ITYPE.GE.4) GO TO 20
      DO 10 IPROD=1,64
          LFUSES(15,IPROD)=.TRUE.
          LFUSES(16,IPROD)=.TRUE.
          LFUSES(19,IPROD)=.TRUE.
          LFUSES(20,IPROD)=.TRUE.
          IF(ITYPE.GE.3) GO TO 10
          LFUSES(11,IPROD)=.TRUE.
          LFUSES(12,IPROD)=.TRUE.
          LFUSES(23,IPROD)=.TRUE.
          LFUSES(24,IPROD)=.TRUE.
          IF(ITYPE.GE.2) GO TO 10
          LFUSES( 7,IPROD)=.TRUE.
          LFUSES( 8,IPROD)=.TRUE.
          LFUSES(27,IPROD)=.TRUE.
          LFUSES(28,IPROD)=.TRUE.
   10     CONTINUE
       DO 18 IINPUT=7,28
          DO 12 IPROD=1,57,8
              LFUSES(IINPUT,IPROD+4)=.FALSE.
              LFUSES(IINPUT,IPROD+5)=.FALSE.
              LFUSES(IINPUT,IPROD+6)=.FALSE.
   12         LFUSES(IINPUT,IPROD+7)=.FALSE.
          IF(ITYPE.GE.3) GO TO 18
          DO 14 IPROD=17,41,8
              LFUSES(IINPUT,IPROD+2)=.FALSE.
   14         LFUSES(IINPUT,IPROD+3)=.FALSE.
          IF(ITYPE.GE.2) GO TO 18
          DO 16 IPROD=1,57,8
              LFUSES(IINPUT,IPROD+2)=.FALSE.
   16         LFUSES(IINPUT,IPROD+3)=.FALSE.
   18 CONTINUE
   20 IF( (ITYPE.EQ.1) .OR. ((ITYPE.EQ.4).AND.(IOT.EQ.L)) ) RETURN
      DO 99 IINPUT=1,32
          DO 30 IPROD=1,8
              LFUSES(IINPUT,IPROD+ 0)= (IOT.NE.L)
   30         IF(IOT.NE.C) LFUSES(IINPUT,IPROD+56)= (IOT.NE.L)
```

```
          IF(ITYPE.LE.2) GO TO 99
          DO 40 IPROD=1,8
              LFUSES(IINPUT,IPROD+ 8)= (IOT.NE.L)
   40         IF(IOT.NE.C) LFUSES(IINPUT,IPROD+48)= (IOT.NE.L)
          IF(ITYPE.LE.3) GO TO 99
          DO 50 IPROD=1,8
              LFUSES(IINPUT,IPROD+16)= (IOT.NE.L)
   50         IF(IOT.NE.C) LFUSES(IINPUT,IPROD+40)= (IOT.NE.L)
   99     CONTINUE
      RETURN
      END
C
C***********************************************************************
C
      SUBROUTINE BINR(LFUSES,H,L)
C     THIS SUBROUTINE GENERATES BINARY PROGRAMMING FORMATS
      IMPLICIT INTEGER (A-Z)
      INTEGER ITEMP(4,8)
      LOGICAL LFUSES(32,64)
      COMMON /LUNIT/ PMS,POF,PDF
      WRITE(PDF,10)
   10 FORMAT(//,'
      DO 20 I=1,33,32
      INC=I-1
        DO 20 IPROD=1,8
            DO 20 J=1,25,8
              DO 15 K=1,8
                IINPUT=J+K-1
                ITEMP(1,K)=L
                ITEMP(2,K)=L
                ITEMP(3,K)=L
                ITEMP(4,K)=L
                ISUM3=IPROD+INC
                IF(LFUSES(IINPUT,ISUM3 +  0 )) ITEMP(4,K)=H
                IF(LFUSES(IINPUT,ISUM3 +  8 )) ITEMP(3,K)=H
                IF(LFUSES(IINPUT,ISUM3 + 16 )) ITEMP(2,K)=H
                IF(LFUSES(IINPUT,ISUM3 + 24 )) ITEMP(1,K)=H
   15           CONTINUE
   20         WRITE(PDF,30) ITEMP
   30         FORMAT(' ',8('B',4A1,'F '))
      WRITE(PDF,10)
      RETURN
      END
C
C***********************************************************************
C
      SUBROUTINE SLIP(LFUSES,I88PRO,INOAI,IOT,INOO,IBLOW)
C     THIS SUBROUTINE WILL BLOW THE ENTIRE CONDITIONAL THREE-STATE
C      PRODUCT LINE WHEN 'IF(VCC)' CONDITION IS USED FOR THE
C      CORRESPONDING OUTPUT PIN
      IMPLICIT INTEGER (A-Z)
      LOGICAL LFUSES(32,64)
      DATA R/'R'/,I1/'1'/,I2/'2'/,I4/'4'/,I6/'6'/,I8/'8'/
      IF( (INOAI.NE.I6) .OR. (INOO.EQ.I1) .OR.  (INOO.EQ.I2) .OR.
     1    ( (IOT.EQ.R).AND.(INOO.EQ.I8) ) .OR.
     2    ( (I88PRO.GE. 9).AND.(I88PRO.LE.49).AND.(INOO.EQ.I6) ) .OR.
```

```
     3    ( (I88PRO.GE.17).AND.(I88PRO.LE.41).AND.(INOO.EQ.I4)) ) RETURN
      DO 10 I=1,32
      IBLOW = IBLOW + 1
   10 LFUSES(I,I88PRO) = .TRUE.
      I88PRO = I88PRO + 1
      RETURN
      END
C
C***********************************************************************
C
      SUBROUTINE FANTOM(ITYPE,IOUT,IPROD,I8PRO)
C     THIS SUBROUTINE UPDATES IOUT (THE PRINTED FUSE PLOT)
C      FOR HIGH AND LOW PHANTOM FUSES
      IMPLICIT INTEGER (A-Z)
      INTEGER IOUT(64)
      DATA X/'X'/,IDASH/'-'/,LOFANT/'0'/,HIFANT/'O'/
      DO 10 I=1,32
          IF( IOUT(I).EQ.IDASH ) IOUT(I)=HIFANT
          IF( IOUT(I).EQ.X )     IOUT(I)=LOFANT
   10 CONTINUE
      IF((ITYPE.EQ.4).AND.((IPROD.LE.24).OR.(IPROD.GE.41))) RETURN
      IF((ITYPE.EQ.3).AND.((IPROD.LE.16).OR.(IPROD.GE.45))) RETURN
      IF((ITYPE.EQ.2).AND.((IPROD.LE. 8).OR.(IPROD.GE.53))) RETURN
      IF((ITYPE.LE.3).AND.(I8PRO.GE.5)) RETURN
      IF((ITYPE.LE.2).AND.(IPROD.GE.19).AND.(IPROD.LE.48).AND.
     1   (I8PRO.GE.3)) RETURN
      IF((ITYPE.EQ.1).AND.(I8PRO.GE.3)) RETURN
      DO 50 I=1,32
        IF(((I.EQ.15).OR.(I.EQ.16).OR.(I.EQ.19).OR.(I.EQ.20)).AND.
     1   (ITYPE.LE.3)) GO TO 50
        IF(((I.EQ.11).OR.(I.EQ.12).OR.(I.EQ.23).OR.(I.EQ.24)).AND.
     1   (ITYPE.LE.2)) GO TO 50
        IF(((I.EQ. 7).OR.(I.EQ. 8).OR.(I.EQ.27).OR.(I.EQ.28)).AND.
     1   (ITYPE.LE.1)) GO TO 50
        IF( IOUT(I).EQ.HIFANT ) IOUT(I)=IDASH
        IF( IOUT(I).EQ.LOFANT ) IOUT(I)=X
   50 CONTINUE
      RETURN
      END
C
C***********************************************************************
C
      SUBROUTINE IODC2
C***** THIS ROUTINE IS OPTIONAL, IT MAY BE USED TO TURN PERIPHERALS ON
      IMPLICIT INTEGER (A-Z)
      CHARACTER BEL,DC2,ESC,FF,NUL
      COMMON /LUNIT/ PMS,POF,PDF
      DATA BEL/007/,DC2/022/
      WRITE(PDF,10) DC2,BEL
   10 FORMAT(' ',2A1)
      RETURN
      END
C
C***********************************************************************
C
      SUBROUTINE IODC4
```

```
C***** THIS ROUTINE IS OPTIONAL, IT MAY BE USED TO TURN PERIPHERALS OFF
      IMPLICIT INTEGER (A-Z)
      CHARACTER BEL,DC3,DC4
      COMMON /LUNIT/ PMS,POF,PDF
      DATA BEL/007/,DC3/023/,DC4/024/
      WRITE(PDF,10) BEL,DC3,DC4
   10 FORMAT(' ',3A1)
      RETURN
      END
C
C***********************************************************************
C
      SUBROUTINE TEST(LPHASE,LBUF,TITLE,IC,IL,ILE,ISYM,IBUF,ITYPE,
     1                INOO,LFIX,IPCTR,LERR,ISAF,IPCTR1,LSA11,LSA01)
C     THIS SUBROUTINE PERFORMS THE FUNCTION TABLE SIMULATION
C      AND GENERATES TEST VECTORS
      IMPLICIT INTEGER (A-Z)
      INTEGER ISYM(8,20),ISYM1(8,20),IBUF(8,20),IVECT(20),IVECTP(20),
     1        ISTATE(20),ISTATT(20),IPIN(20),TITLE(80),IPCTR
      LOGICAL LBLANK,LLEFT,LAND,LOR,LSLASH,LEQUAL,LRIGHT,LXOR,LXNOR,
     1        LFIX,LSAME,XORFND,LERR,LPHASE(20),LPHAS1(20),LBUF(20),
     2        LOUT(20),LOUTP(20),LCLOCK,LPTRST,LCTRST,LENABL(20),NREG,
     3        LSA11,LSA12,LSA01
      CHARACTER BEL
      COMMON  LBLANK,LLEFT,LAND,LOR,LSLASH,LEQUAL,LRIGHT,LXOR,LXNOR
      COMMON /PGE/ IPAGE(80,200)
      COMMON /LUNIT/ PMS,POF,PDF
      COMMON /FTEST/ IFUNCT,IDESC,IEND
      DATA IDASH/'-'/,L/'L'/,H/'H'/,X/'X'/,C/'C'/,Z/'Z'/,N0/'0'/,
     1     N1/'1'/,ERR/'?'/,IBLANK/' '/,COMENT/';'/,I4/'4'/,I6/'6'/,
     2     I8/'8'/
      DATA BEL/007/
C     PRINT AN ERROR MESSAGE IF NO FUNCTION TABLE IS SUPPLIED
      IF(IFUNCT.NE.0) GO TO 3
      WRITE(PMS,2)
    2 FORMAT(/,' FUNCTION TABLE MUST BE SUPPLIED IN ORDER TO PERFORM',
     1        ' SIMULATION')
      RETURN
C     PRINT TITLE
    3 IF((.NOT.LSA11).AND.(.NOT.LSA01)) WRITE(POF,4) TITLE
    4 FORMAT(/,' ',80A1,/)
C     INITIALIZE LERR (FUNCTION TABLE ERROR FLAG) TO NO ERROR
      LERR=.FALSE.
C     INITIALIZE NERR (NUMBER OF FUNCTION TABLE ERRORS) TO NO ERRORS
      NERR=0
C     INITIALIZE ITRST (THREE-STATE ENABLE FUNCTION TABLE PIN NUMBER)
      ITRST=0
C     SET THE STARTING POINT OF THE FUNCTION TABLE TO COLUMN 0
C     AND IFUNCT + 1
      IC=0
      IL=IFUNCT + 1
C     INITIALIZE SA1/SA0 PARAMETERS
      IPCTR3=0
      IEQN=0
      IPCTR=0
C     MAKE A DUMMY CALL TO INCR
```

```
      CALL INCR(IC,IL,LFIX)
C     GET THE FUNCTION TABLE PIN LIST (UP TO 18)
C      GO ONE MORE THAN MAX TO LOOK FOR DASHED LINE
      DO 10 I=1,19
      CALL GETSYM(LPHAS1,ISYM1,I,IC,IL,LFIX)
         DO 5 J=1,8
    5    IBUF(J,1)=ISYM1(J,I)
      IF(IBUF(8,1).EQ.IDASH) GO TO 12
      CALL MATCH(IMATCH,IBUF,ISYM)
      IF(IMATCH.NE.0) GO TO 7
      WRITE(PMS,6) (IBUF(J,1),J=1,8)
    6 FORMAT(/,' FUNCTION TABLE PIN LIST ERROR AT', 8A1)
      RETURN
    7 LOUT(I)=.FALSE.
      ISTATT(I)=X
      IVECTP(I)=X
C     IF APPROPIATE PAL TYPE, REMEMBER LOCATION OF CLOCK AND THREE-STATE
C      ENABLE PIN IN FUNCTION TABLE PIN LIST
      IF(ITYPE.NE.6) GO TO 10
      IF(IMATCH.EQ.1)  ICLOCK=I
      IF(IMATCH.EQ.11) ITRST=I
   10 IPIN(I)=IMATCH
C     ALL SIGNAL NAMES FOR THE FUNCTIONAL TEST HAVE BEEN READ IN
C      ADJUST COUNT
   12 IMAX=I-1
      NVECT=0
C
C*****START OF MAIN LOOP FOR SIMULATION*****
C
C     INITIALLY THERE ARE NO FAULTS. IPCTR2 IS THE POINTER FOR
C     TOTAL NUMBER OF PRODUCT TERMS. IEQN IS EQUATION COUNT.
C     IPCTR3 IS THE PRODUCT TERM POINTER IN A PARTICULAR EQN.
   90 IPCTR2=0
      IEQN=0
      IPCTR3=0
      LSA12=.FALSE.
      LSA02=.FALSE.
      NVECT=NVECT+1
      IC1=0
      IL1=ILE
C     GO PASSED COMMENT LINES
   23 IF(IPAGE(1,IL).NE.COMENT) GO TO 24
      IL=IL+1
      GO TO 23
   24 CONTINUE
C     GETS VECTORS FROM FUNCTION TABLE
      DO 20 I=1,IMAX
        IF(IPAGE(IC,IL).EQ.IBLANK) GO TO 21
        GO TO 22
   21   IC=IC+1
        IF(IPAGE(IC,IL).EQ.IBLANK) GO TO 21
   22   IVECT(I)=IPAGE(IC,IL)
        IC=IC+1
   20 CONTINUE
C     ADVANCE LINE COUNT TO SKIP FUNCTION TABLE COMMENTS
      IL=IL+1
```

```
      IC=1
      IF(IVECT(1).EQ.IDASH) GO TO 95
C     CHECK FOR VALID FUNCTION TABLE VALUES (L,H,X,Z,C)
      DO 11 I=1,IMAX
         IF( IVECT(I).EQ.L.OR.IVECT(I).EQ.H.OR.IVECT(I).EQ.X.OR.
     1       IVECT(I).EQ.Z.OR.IVECT(I).EQ.C) GO TO 11
         WRITE(PMS,8) IVECT(I),NVECT
    8    FORMAT(/,' ',A1,' IS NOT AN ALLOWED FUNCTION TABLE ENTRY',
     1                     ' IN VECTOR ',I3)
         RETURN
   11 CONTINUE
C     INITIALIZE CLOCK AND THREE-STATE ENABLE FLAGS
      LCLOCK=.FALSE.
      LCTRST=.TRUE.
      LPTRST=.TRUE.
      DO 13 I=1,IMAX
   13    LENABL(I)=.TRUE.
C     INITIALIZE NREG (NOT REGISTERED OUTPUT) TO FALSE
      NREG=.FALSE.
C     INITIALIZE ISTATE ARRAY TO ALL X'S
      DO 15 I=1,20
   15 ISTATE(I)=X
C     CHECK IF THIS PAL TYPE HAS REGISTERS
      IF(ITYPE.NE.6) GO TO 25
C     CHECK CLOCK AND THREE-STATE ENABLE PINS AND CHANGE FLAG IF NEEDED
      IF(IVECT(ICLOCK).EQ.C) LCLOCK=.TRUE.
      IF(ITRST.EQ.0) GO TO 25
      LSAME=( (      LPHASE(11)).AND.(      LPHAS1(ITRST)).OR.
     1        (.NOT.LPHASE(11)).AND.(.NOT.LPHAS1(ITRST)) )
      IF( IVECT(ITRST).EQ.L.AND.(.NOT.LSAME).OR.
     1    IVECT(ITRST).EQ.H.AND.(      LSAME) ) LPTRST=.FALSE.
      IF(LPTRST) GO TO 25
C     DISABLE REGISTERED OUTPUTS IF APPROPRIATE
      DO 46 I=1,IMAX
         J=IPIN(I)
         IF(J.EQ.14.OR.J.EQ.15.OR.J.EQ.16.OR.J.EQ.17) LENABL(I)=.FALSE.
         IF( INOO.EQ.I6.AND.(J.EQ.13.OR.J.EQ.18) )    LENABL(I)=.FALSE.
         IF( INOO.EQ.I8.AND.(J.EQ.12.OR.J.EQ.13
     1                  .OR.J.EQ.18.OR.J.EQ.19) )    LENABL(I)=.FALSE.
   46 CONTINUE
C
C*****SCAN THROUGH THE LOGIC EQUATIONS*****
C
C     MAKE A DUMMY CALL TO INCR
   25 CALL INCR(IC1,IL1,LFIX)
   26 CALL GETSYM(LBUF,IBUF,1,IC1,IL1,LFIX)
      IF(LLEFT) GO TO 29
   27 IF(.NOT.LEQUAL) GO TO 26
      IF(LEQUAL) IEQN=IEQN+1
C     EVALUATE CONDITIONAL THREE-STATE PRODUCT LINE
   29 IF(LEQUAL) GO TO 35
      NREG=.TRUE.
   33 CALL GETSYM(LBUF,IBUF,1,IC1,IL1,LFIX)
      CALL MATCH(IINP,IBUF,ISYM1)
C     CHECK FOR GND, VCC, /GND, OR /VCC IN CONDITIONAL THREE-STATE
C      PRODUCT LINE
```

```
      IF(IINP.NE.0) GO TO 32
      CALL MATCH(IMATCH,IBUF,ISYM)
      ILL=IL1
      IF( IINP.EQ.0.AND.IMATCH.NE.10.AND.IMATCH.NE.20 ) GO TO 100
      IF( IMATCH.EQ.10.AND.(LBUF(1)).OR.
     1    IMATCH.EQ.20.AND.(.NOT.LBUF(1)) ) LCTRST=.FALSE.
      GO TO 34
   32 ITEST=IVECT(IINP)
      IF(  ITEST.EQ.L.AND.(      LPHAS1(IINP)).AND.(      LBUF(1))
     1.OR. ITEST.EQ.H.AND.(      LPHAS1(IINP)).AND.(.NOT.LBUF(1))
     2.OR. ITEST.EQ.H.AND.(.NOT.LPHAS1(IINP)).AND.(      LBUF(1))
     3.OR. ITEST.EQ.L.AND.(.NOT.LPHAS1(IINP)).AND.(.NOT.LBUF(1))
     4  )  LCTRST=.FALSE.
      IF(ITEST.EQ.X.OR.ITEST.EQ.Z) LCTRST=.FALSE.
   34 IF(LAND) GO TO 33
      GO TO 27
C     EVALUATE THE LOGIC EQUATION
C     FIND THE PIN NUMBER OF THE OUTPUT VECTORS
   35  IPCTR3=0
      CALL MATCH(IOUTP,IBUF,ISYM1)
C     FLAG UNREGISTERED OUTPUTS
      CALL MATCH(IOUT,IBUF,ISYM)
      IF(ITYPE.LE.5) NREG=.TRUE.
      IF( (INOO.EQ.I4.OR.INOO.EQ.I6).AND.(IOUT.EQ.12.OR.IOUT.EQ.19) )
     1     NREG=.TRUE.
      IF( (INOO.EQ.I4).AND.(IOUT.EQ.13.OR.IOUT.EQ.18) ) NREG=.TRUE.
      ILL=IL1
      IF(IOUTP.EQ.0) GO TO 100
      IF(NREG) LENABL(IOUTP)=LCTRST
      LOUT(IOUTP)=.TRUE.
      IF( .NOT.LCTRST ) LOUT(IOUTP)=.FALSE.
      LCTRST=.TRUE.
      LOUTP(IOUTP)=LBUF(1)
C     DETERMINE PRODUCT TERM AND EVENTUALLY SUM FOR OUTPUT KEEPING
C      TRACK TO SEE IF AN XOR (EXCLUSIVE OR) HAS BEEN FOUND
      XORSUM=H
      XORFND=.FALSE.
      ISUM=L
   28 IPCTR2=IPCTR2+1
      IPCTR3=IPCTR3+1
      IPCTR=IPCTR+1
      IPROD=H
   30 ILL=IL1
      CALL GETSYM(LBUF,IBUF,1,IC1,IL1,LFIX)
      IF( .NOT.LFIX ) GO TO 39
C     EVALUATE THE FIXED SYMBOLS FOUND IN THE PAL16X4 AND PAL16A4
          LFIX=.FALSE.
          CALL FIXTST(LPHAS1,LBUF,IC1,IL1,ISYM,ISYM1,IBUF,
     1                IVECT,IVECTP,ITEST,LCLOCK,NREG,LFIX)
          IF(IPROD.EQ.H) IPROD=ITEST
          GO TO 38
   39 CALL MATCH(IINP,IBUF,ISYM1)
      IF(IINP.NE.0) GO TO 47
      CALL MATCH(IMATCH,IBUF,ISYM)
      IF(IMATCH.NE.10.AND.IMATCH.NE.20) GO TO 100
C     TWEEK FOR GND AND VCC IN PRODUCT LINE
```

```
      IF(IMATCH.EQ.10) ITEST=L
      IF(IMATCH.EQ.20) ITEST=H
      IINP=19
      LPHAS1(19)=.TRUE.
      GO TO 37
   47 ITEST=IVECT(IINP)
C     GET REGISTERED FEED BACK VALUES
      IF(NREG) GO TO 37
      CALL MATCH(IIFB,IBUF,ISYM)
      IF( (INOO.EQ.I4.OR.INOO.EQ.I6.OR.INOO.EQ.I8).AND.
     1    (IIFB.EQ.14.OR.IIFB.EQ.15.OR.IIFB.EQ.16.OR.IIFB.EQ.17) )
     2     ITEST=IVECTP(IINP)
      IF( (INOO.EQ.I6.OR.INOO.EQ.I8).AND.(IIFB.EQ.13.OR.IIFB.EQ.18) )
     1     ITEST=IVECTP(IINP)
      IF(  INOO.EQ.I8.AND.(IIFB.EQ.12.OR.IIFB.EQ.19) )
     1     ITEST=IVECTP(IINP)
   37 IF( ITEST.EQ.X.OR.ITEST.EQ.Z ) ITEST=L
      IF(  ITEST.EQ.L.AND.(      LPHAS1(IINP)).AND.(      LBUF(1))
     1.OR. ITEST.EQ.H.AND.(      LPHAS1(IINP)).AND.(.NOT.LBUF(1))
     2.OR. ITEST.EQ.H.AND.(.NOT.LPHAS1(IINP)).AND.(      LBUF(1))
     3.OR. ITEST.EQ.L.AND.(.NOT.LPHAS1(IINP)).AND.(.NOT.LBUF(1))
     4  )  IPROD=L
C     CHECK FOR A PARTICULAR PRODUCT TERM AND GO FOR SA1 TEST
      IF((IPCTR2.EQ.IPCTR1).AND.(LSA11))GO TO 110
   38 IF(LRIGHT) CALL INCR(IC1,IL1,LFIX)
      IF(LAND) GO TO 30
C     CHECK FOR A PARTICULAR PRODUCT TERM AND GO FOR SA0 TEST
      IF((IPCTR2.EQ.IPCTR1).AND.(LSA01))GO TO 120
  121 IF(ISUM.EQ.L.AND.IPROD.EQ.X) ISUM=X
      IF( (ISUM.NE.H).AND.IPROD.EQ.H ) ISUM=H
C     CHECK FOR XOR (EXCLUSIVE OR) AND SAVE INTERMEDIATE VALUE
      IF(.NOT.LXOR) GO TO 31
      XORSUM=ISUM
      XORFND=.TRUE.
      ISUM=L
      GO TO 28
   31 IF(LOR) GO TO 28
      IPCTR3=0
C     IF END OF EQUATION HAS BEEN FOUND, DETERMINE FINAL SUM AND SAVE IT
      IF(.NOT.XORFND)     ISTATT(IOUTP)=ISUM
      IF( (XORFND).AND.((ISUM.EQ.L.AND.XORSUM.EQ.L).OR.
     1                  (ISUM.EQ.H.AND.XORSUM.EQ.H)) ) ISTATT(IOUTP)=L
      IF( (XORFND).AND.((ISUM.EQ.H.AND.XORSUM.EQ.L).OR.
     1                  (ISUM.EQ.L.AND.XORSUM.EQ.H)) ) ISTATT(IOUTP)=H
      IF( (XORFND).AND. (ISUM.EQ.X.OR. XORSUM.EQ.X) )  ISTATT(IOUTP)=X
C     REGISTER DOES NOT CHANGE STATE IF NO CLOCK PULSE IS RECEIVED
      IF( (LCLOCK).OR.(NREG) ) GO TO 36
      LSAME = ( (      LOUTP(IOUTP)).AND.(      LPHAS1(IOUTP)).OR.
     1          (.NOT.LOUTP(IOUTP)).AND.(.NOT.LPHAS1(IOUTP)) )
      IF( IVECTP(IOUTP).EQ.L.AND.(      LSAME) ) ISTATT(IOUTP)=L
      IF( IVECTP(IOUTP).EQ.H.AND.(      LSAME) ) ISTATT(IOUTP)=H
      IF( IVECTP(IOUTP).EQ.L.AND.(.NOT.LSAME) ) ISTATT(IOUTP)=H
      IF( IVECTP(IOUTP).EQ.H.AND.(.NOT.LSAME) ) ISTATT(IOUTP)=L
   36 NREG=.FALSE.
C     CHECK IF ALL EQUATIONS HAVE BEEN PROCESSED BY COMPARING CURRENT
C      LINE NUMBER WITH FUNCTION TABLE LINE NUMBER
```

```
      IF(IDESC.NE.0.AND.IL1.LT.IFUNCT.AND.IL1.LT.IDESC.OR.
     1   IDESC.EQ.0.AND.IL1.LT.IFUNCT) GO TO 27
C     DETERMINE OUTPUT LOGIC VALUES
C      COMPARE OUTPUTS TO SEE IF VECTOR AGREES WITH RESULTS
      DO 50 I=1,IMAX
      IF( .NOT.LOUT(I) ) GO TO 50
      IF( ISTATT(I).EQ.X.AND.IVECT(I).EQ.X ) GO TO 50
      LSAME = ( (      LOUTP(I)).AND.(      LPHAS1(I)).OR.
     1          (.NOT.LOUTP(I)).AND.(.NOT.LPHAS1(I)) )
      IMESS=40
      IF(ISTATT(I).EQ.L.AND.IVECT(I).EQ.L.AND.(.NOT.LSAME)) IMESS=41
      IF(ISTATT(I).EQ.H.AND.IVECT(I).EQ.H.AND.(.NOT.LSAME)) IMESS=42
      IF(ISTATT(I).EQ.L.AND.IVECT(I).EQ.H.AND.(      LSAME)) IMESS=42
      IF(ISTATT(I).EQ.H.AND.IVECT(I).EQ.L.AND.(      LSAME)) IMESS=41
      IF( (      LENABL(I)).AND.IVECT(I).EQ.Z )              IMESS=43
      IF( (.NOT.LENABL(I)).AND.(LOUT(I)).AND.IVECT(I).NE.Z) IMESS=44
      IF(IMESS.NE.40) LERR=.TRUE.
C     IF NO FAULTS GO FOR NEXT VECTOR ELSE GET OUT OF SIMULATION
C      AND START SIMULATION FOR THE NEXT PRODUCT TERM.
      IF((.NOT.LERR).AND.((LSA11).OR.(LSA01))) GO TO 50
      IF((LERR).AND.((LSA11).OR.(LSA01))) GO TO 115
      IF(IMESS.EQ.41) WRITE(PMS,41) NVECT,(ISYM1(J,I),J=1,8)
   41 FORMAT(/,' FUNCTION TABLE ERROR IN VECTOR',I3,'  PIN =',8A1,
     1        '  EXPECT = H  ACTUAL = L')
      IF(IMESS.EQ.42) WRITE(PMS,42) NVECT,(ISYM1(J,I),J=1,8)
   42 FORMAT(/,' FUNCTION TABLE ERROR IN VECTOR',I3,'  PIN =',8A1,
     1        '  EXPECT = L  ACTUAL = H')
      IF(IMESS.EQ.43) WRITE(PMS,43) NVECT,(ISYM1(J,I),J=1,8)
   43 FORMAT(/,' FUNCTION TABLE ERROR IN VECTOR',I3,'  PIN =',8A1,
     1       /,'  EXPECT  = OUTPUT ENABLE  ACTUAL = Z')
      IF(IMESS.EQ.44) WRITE(PMS,44) NVECT,(ISYM1(J,I),J=1,8),IVECT(I)
   44 FORMAT(/,' FUNCTION TABLE ERROR IN VECTOR',I3,'  PIN =',8A1,
     1        '  EXPECT = Z  ACTUAL = ',A1)
      IF( (IMESS.NE.40).AND.(PMS.EQ.6) ) WRITE(PMS,45) BEL
   45 FORMAT(' ',A1)
      IF(IMESS.NE.40) IVECT(I)=ERR
      IF(IMESS.NE.40) NERR=NERR+1
   50 CONTINUE
C     CHANGE THE ORDER OF VECTORS FROM THE ORDER OF APPEARANCE IN THE
C      FUNCTION TABLE TO THAT OF THE PIN LIST AND TWEEK FOR OUTPUT
      DO 65 I=1,20
         DO 55 J=1,IMAX
         IF(IPIN(J).NE.I) GO TO 55
         IF( IVECT(J).EQ.L.OR.IVECT(J).EQ.H ) GO TO 51
         ISTATE(I)=IVECT(J)
         GO TO 65
   51    LSAME=( (      LPHASE(I)).AND.(      LPHAS1(J)).OR.
     1           (.NOT.LPHASE(I)).AND.(.NOT.LPHAS1(J)) )
         IF( INOO.EQ.N1.AND.(I.EQ.15.OR.I.EQ.16) )  LOUT(J)=.TRUE.
         IF( (.NOT.LOUT(J)).AND.(      LSAME).AND.
     1         IVECT(J).EQ.L )                      ISTATE(I)=N0
         IF( (.NOT.LOUT(J)).AND.(      LSAME).AND.
     1         IVECT(J).EQ.H )                      ISTATE(I)=N1
         IF( (.NOT.LOUT(J)).AND.(.NOT.LSAME).AND.
     1         IVECT(J).EQ.L )                      ISTATE(I)=N1
         IF( (.NOT.LOUT(J)).AND.(.NOT.LSAME).AND.
```

```
     1          IVECT(J).EQ.H )                           ISTATE(I)=N0
        IF( (      LOUT(J)).AND.(      LSAME).AND.
     1          IVECT(J).EQ.L.AND.(      LENABL(J)) ) ISTATE(I)=L
        IF( (      LOUT(J)).AND.(      LSAME).AND.
     1          IVECT(J).EQ.H.AND.(      LENABL(J)) ) ISTATE(I)=H
        IF( (      LOUT(J)).AND.(.NOT.LSAME).AND.
     1          IVECT(J).EQ.L.AND.(      LENABL(J)) ) ISTATE(I)=H
        IF( (      LOUT(J)).AND.(.NOT.LSAME).AND.
     1          IVECT(J).EQ.H.AND.(      LENABL(J)) ) ISTATE(I)=L
        IF( IVECT(J).EQ.ERR )                         ISTATE(I)=ERR
        GO TO 65
   55 CONTINUE
C     SAVE PRESENT VECTORS FOR FEED BACK USED WITH NEXT SET OF VECTORS
C      IF CLOCK PULSE AND NOT Z (HI-Z IS ASYNCHRONOUS)
   65 IF( (LCLOCK).AND.IVECT(J).NE.Z ) IVECTP(J)=IVECT(J)
C     ASSIGN X TO GROUND PIN AND 1 TO VCC PIN
      ISTATE(10)=X
      ISTATE(20)=N1
C     PRINT TEST VECTORS
      IF((.NOT.LSA11).AND.(.NOT.LSA01))WRITE(POF,60)
     1 NVECT,(ISTATE(I),I=1,20)
   60 FORMAT(' ',I3,' ',20A1)
      GO TO 90
C     TERMINATE SIMULATION
   95 IF((.NOT.LERR).AND.(LSA11))WRITE(POF,150) IPCTR4,IEQN1
  150 FORMAT(' ',' PRODUCT: ',I3,' OF ','EQUATION.',I3,
     1 ' UNTESTED(SA1)FAULT')
      IF((.NOT.LERR).AND.(LSA01)) WRITE(POF,155) IPCTR4,IEQN1
  155 FORMAT(' ',' PRODUCT: ',I3,' OF ','EQUATION.',I3,
     1 ' UNTESTED(SA0)FAULT')
      IF((.NOT.LERR).AND.((.NOT.LSA11).AND.(.NOT.LSA01))) WRITE(POF,67)
   67 FORMAT(/,' PASS SIMULATION')
      IPCTR=IPCTR/(NVECT-1)
      IF((      LERR).AND.((.NOT.LSA11).AND.(.NOT.LSA01)))
     1WRITE(POF,68) NERR
   68 FORMAT(/,' NUMBER OF FUNCTION TABLE ERRORS =',I3)
      RETURN
C     PRINT AN ERROR MESSAGE FOR AN UNDEFINED PIN NAME
  100 ILERR=ILL+4
      WRITE(PMS,101) (IBUF(I,1),I=1,8),ILERR,(IPAGE(I,ILL),I=1,80)
  101 FORMAT(/,' ERROR SYMBOL = ',8A1,'       IN LINE NUMBER ',I3,
     1       /,' ',80A1,/,' THIS PIN NAME IS NOT DEFINED IN THE',
     2                    ' FUNCTION TABLE PIN LIST')
      RETURN
C     THE PRODUCT TERM IS PULLED HIGH AND THE PRODUCT NUMBER
C     AND EQN NUMBER IS REMEMBERED
  110 IPROD=H
      LSA12=.TRUE.
      IEQN1=IEQN
      IPCTR4=IPCTR3
      GO TO 38
C     THE PRODUCT TERM IS TESTED FOR SA0 FAULT AND ALSO REMEMBERED
  120 IPROD=L
      LSA02=.TRUE.
      IEQN1=IEQN
      IPCTR4=IPCTR3
```

```
      GO TO 121
C     IF NO FAULT THEN NEXT PRODUCT TERM
  115 ISAF=ISAF+1
      LERR=.FALSE.
      RETURN
      END
C
C***********************************************************************
C
      SUBROUTINE FIXTST(LPHAS1,LBUF,IC1,IL1,ISYM,ISYM1,IBUF,
     1                  IVECT,IVECTP,ITEST,LCLOCK,NREG,LFIX)
C     THIS SUBROUTINE EVALUATES THE FIXED SYMBOLS FOUND IN THE
C      PAL16X4 AND PAL16A4 FOR THE FUNCTION TABLE
      IMPLICIT INTEGER (A-Z)
      INTEGER ISYM(8,20),ISYM1(8,20),IBUF(8,20),IVECT(20),IVECTP(20)
      LOGICAL LBLANK,LLEFT,LAND,LOR,LSLASH,LEQUAL,LRIGHT,LXOR,LXNOR,
     1        LFIX,LPHAS1(20),LBUF(20),LCLOCK,NREG,TOR,TXOR,TXNOR,TAND,
     2        LPHASA,LPHASB
      COMMON  LBLANK,LLEFT,LAND,LOR,LSLASH,LEQUAL,LRIGHT,LXOR,LXNOR
      COMMON /PGE/ IPAGE(80,200)
      DATA L/'L'/,H/'H'/,X/'X'/,Z/'Z'/
C     GET OUTPUT PIN AN (WHERE N=0,1,2,3)
      CALL GETSYM(LBUF,IBUF,1,IC1,IL1,LFIX)
      CALL MATCH(IINP,IBUF,ISYM1)
      ITESTA=IVECT(IINP)
      LPHASA = ( (      LBUF(1)).AND.(      LPHAS1(IINP)).OR.
     1          (.NOT.LBUF(1)).AND.(.NOT.LPHAS1(IINP)) )
C     GET REGISTERED FEED BACK VALUES
      IF(NREG) GO TO 5
      CALL MATCH(IIFB,IBUF,ISYM)
      IF( IIFB.EQ.14.OR.IIFB.EQ.15.OR.IIFB.EQ.16.OR.IIFB.EQ.17 )
     1    ITESTA=IVECTP(IINP)
    5 IF( (.NOT.LPHASA).AND.ITESTA.EQ.L ) GO TO 10
      IF( (.NOT.LPHASA).AND.ITESTA.EQ.H ) GO TO 15
      GO TO 20
   10 ITESTA=H
      GO TO 20
   15 ITESTA=L
   20 IF( .NOT.LRIGHT ) GO TO 25
           ITEST=ITESTA
           RETURN
C     SAVE THE FIXED SYMBOL OPERATORS
   25 TOR   = (LOR.AND.(.NOT.LXOR))
      TXOR  = (LXOR)
      TXNOR = (LXNOR)
      TAND  = (LAND.AND.(.NOT.LXNOR))
C     GET INPUT BN (WHERE N=0,1,2,3)
      CALL GETSYM(LBUF,IBUF,1,IC1,IL1,LFIX)
      CALL MATCH(IINP,IBUF,ISYM1)
      ITESTB=IVECT(IINP)
      LPHASB = ( (      LBUF(1)).AND.(      LPHAS1(IINP)).OR.
     1          (.NOT.LBUF(1)).AND.(.NOT.LPHAS1(IINP)) )
      IF( (.NOT.LPHASB).AND.ITESTB.EQ.L ) GO TO 30
      IF( (.NOT.LPHASB).AND.ITESTB.EQ.H ) GO TO 35
      GO TO 40
   30 ITESTB=H
```

```
      GO TO 40
   35 ITESTB=L
C     EVALUATE THE FIXED SYMBOL EXPRESSION
   40 ITEST=L
      IF(    (TOR).AND.(ITESTA.EQ.H.OR. ITESTB.EQ.H) )       ITEST=H
      IF(   (TXOR).AND.((ITESTA.EQ.H.AND.ITESTB.NE.H).OR.
     1                 (ITESTA.NE.H.AND.ITESTB.EQ.H) ))      ITEST=H
      IF( (TXNOR).AND.((ITESTA.EQ.ITESTB).OR.
     1                 (ITESTA.EQ.X.OR.ITESTB.EQ.X) ))       ITEST=H
      IF(   (TAND).AND.(ITESTA.NE.L.AND.ITESTB.NE.L) )       ITEST=H
      IF( (ITESTA.EQ.X.OR.ITESTA.EQ.Z).AND.(ITESTB.EQ.X) ) ITEST=X
      RETURN
      END
```

```
C**PALASM24**PALASM24**PALASM24**PALASM24**PALASM24**PALASM24**PALASM24*
C
C  P A L A S M  2 4  -  TRANSLATES SYMBOLIC EQUATIONS INTO PAL OBJECT
C                       CODE FORMATTED FOR DIRECT INPUT TO STANDARD
C                       PROM AND PAL PROGRAMMERS.
C
C                       INPUT:        PAL DESIGN SPECIFICATION ASSIGNED
C                                     TO RPD(1).  OPERATION CODES ARE
C                                     ASSIGNED TO ROP(5).
C
C                       OUTPUT:       ECHO, SIMULATION, AND FUSE PATTERN
C                                     ARE ASSIGNED TO POF(6).  JEDEC, HEX,
C                                     AND BINARY PROGRAMMING FORMATS ARE
C                                     ASSIGNED TO PDF(6).  PROMPTS AND
C                                     ERROR MESSAGES ARE ASSIGNED TO
C                                     PMS(6).
C
C                       PART NUMBER:  THE PAL PART NUMBER MUST APPEAR
C                                     IN COLUMN ONE OF LINE ONE.
C
C                       PIN LIST:     24 SYMBOLIC PIN NAMES MUST APPEAR
C                                     STARTING ON LINE FIVE.
C
C                       EQUATIONS:    STARTING FIRST LINE AFTER THE
C                                     PIN LIST IN THE FOLLOWING FORMS:
C
C                                        A = B*C + D
C
C                                        A := B*C + D
C
C                                        IF( A*B )  C = D + E
C
C                                     ALL CHARACTERS FOLLOWING ';' ARE
C                                     IGNORED UNTIL THE NEXT LINE.
C
C                                     BLANKS ARE IGNORED.
C
C                       OPERATORS:    ( IN HIERARCHY OF EVALUATION )
C
C                                      ;     COMMENT FOLLOWS
C                                      /     COMPLEMENT
C                                      *     AND (PRODUCT)
C                                      +     OR (SUM)
C                                     :+:    XOR (EXCLUSIVE OR)
C                                     ( )    CONDITIONAL THREE-STATE
C                                      =     EQUALITY
C                                     :=     REPLACED BY (AFTER CLOCK)
C
C                       FUNCTION      L, H, X, Z, AND C ARE VALID
C                         TABLE:      FUNCTION TABLE VECTOR ENTRIES.
C
C                       REFERENCE:    A COMPLETE USERS GUIDE TO
C                                     DESIGNING WITH PALS USING PALASM
C                                     IS PROVIDED IN THE MONOLITHIC
C                                     MEMORIES PAL HANDBOOK.
```

```
C
C                       SUBROUTINES: INITLZ,GETSYM,INCR,MATCH,IXLATE,
C                                    ECHO,CAT,PINOUT,PLOT,PLOTF,HEX,
C                                    SUMCHK,TWEEK,BINR,SLIP,FANTOM,
C                                    IODC2,IODC4,TEST
C
C                       REV LEVEL:   VERSION 1.5  (11/15/82)
C
C                       AUTHORS:     JOHN BIRKNER AND VINCENT COLI
C                                    FAULT TESTING BY IMTIYAZ BENGALI
C                                    MONOLITHIC MEMORIES INC.
C                                    1165 EAST ARQUES AVENUE
C                                    SUNNYVALE, CALIFORNIA 94043
C                                    (408) 739-3535
C
C                       FINE PRINT:  MONOLITHIC MEMORIES TAKES NO
C                                    RESPONSIBILITY FOR THE OPERATION
C                                    OR MAINTENANCE OF THIS PROGRAM.
C                                    THE SOURCE CODE AS PRINTED HERE
C                                    PRODUCED THE OBJECT CODE OF THE
C                                    EXAMPLES IN THE APPLICATIONS
C                                    SECTION ON A VAX/VMS 11/780
C                                    COMPUTER WITH FORTRAN 77 AND A
C                                    NATIONAL CSS IBM SYSTEM/370
C                                    WITH FORTRAN IV (LEVEL G).
C
C***********************************************************************
C
C
C***********************************************************************
C
C
C     MAIN PROGRAM
C
      IMPLICIT INTEGER (A-Z)
      INTEGER IPAL(3),INAME(5),REST(72),PATNUM(80),TITLE(80),COMP(80),
     1        ISYM(8,24),IBUF(8,24),JPROD(80)
      LOGICAL LBLANK,LLEFT,LAND,LOR,LSLASH,LEQUAL,LRIGHT,LXOR,LFIRST,
     1        LMATCH,LFUSES(40,80),LPHASE(24),LBUF(24),LPROD(80),
     2        LSAME,LACT,LOPERR,LINP,LERR,LSA11,LSA01
      CHARACTER BEL
      COMMON  LBLANK,LLEFT,LAND,LOR,LSLASH,LEQUAL,LRIGHT,LXOR
      COMMON /PGE/ IPAGE(80,200)
      COMMON /LFUSES/LFUSES
      COMMON /FTEST/ IFUNCT,IDESC,IEND
      COMMON /LUNIT/ PMS,POF,PDF
      DATA E/'E'/,O/'O'/,T/'T'/,P/'P'/,B/'B'/,D/'D'/,H/'H'/,S/'S'/,
     1     L/'L'/,N/'N'/,C/'C'/,Q/'Q'/,U/'U'/,F/'F'/,Y/'Y'/
      DATA BB/'B'/,CC/'C'/,DD/'D'/,EE/'E'/,FF/'F'/,II/'I'/,NN/'N'/,
     1     OO/'O'/,PP/'P'/,RR/'R'/,SS/'S'/,TT/'T'/,UU/'U'/,JJ/'J'/
      DATA BEL/007/
C
C
C     ASSIGNMENT OF DATA SET REFERENCES
C     RPD - PAL DESIGN SPECIFICATION (INPUT)
C     ROC - OPERATION CODE (INPUT)
```

```
C       POF - ECHO, PINOUT, TEST, AND PLOT (OUTPUT)
C       PDF - JEDEC, HEX, AND BINARY PROGRAMMING FORMATS (OUTPUT)
C       PMS - PROMPTS AND ERROR MESSAGES (OUTPUT)
        WRITE(6,3)
      3 FORMAT(/,' 24-PIN PALASM VERSION 1.5')
        WRITE(6,1)
      1 FORMAT(/,' WHAT IS THE LOGICAL UNIT NUMBER FOR OUTPUT(6)?: '$)
        READ(5,2) LUN
      2 FORMAT(I4)
        RPD=1
        ROC=5
        POF=LUN
        PDF=LUN
        PMS=LUN
        IFUNCT=0
        IDESC=0
C       INITIALIZE LSAME AND LACT TO FALSE (ACTIVE HIGH/LOW ERROR)
        LSAME=.FALSE.
        LACT=.FALSE.
C       INITIALIZE LOPERR TO FALSE (OUTPUT PIN ERROR)
        LOPERR=.FALSE.
C       READ IN FIRST 4 LINES OF PAL DESIGN SPECIFICATION
        READ(RPD,10) IPAL,INAME,REST,PATNUM,TITLE,COMP
     10 FORMAT(3A1,5A1,72A1,/,80A1,/,80A1,/,80A1)
C       READ IN PIN LIST (LINE 5) THROUGH THE END OF THE PAL DESIGN
C        SPECIFICATION
        DO 15 J=1,200
            READ(RPD,11,END=16) (IPAGE(I,J),I=1,80)
     11     FORMAT(80A1)
C           CHECK FOR 'FUNCTION TABLE' AND SAVE ITS LINE NUMBER
            IF(      IFUNCT.EQ.0 .AND.IPAGE(1,J).EQ.FF.AND.
      1         IPAGE(2,J).EQ.UU.AND.IPAGE(3,J).EQ.NN.AND.
      2         IPAGE(4,J).EQ.CC.AND.IPAGE(5,J).EQ.TT.AND.
      3         IPAGE(6,J).EQ.II.AND.IPAGE(7,J).EQ.OO.AND.
      4         IPAGE(8,J).EQ.NN.AND.IPAGE(10,J).EQ.TT.AND.
      5         IPAGE(12,J).EQ.BB.AND.IPAGE(14,J).EQ.EE ) IFUNCT=J
C           CHECK FOR 'DESCRIPTION' AND SAVE ITS LINE NUMBER
            IF(       IDESC.EQ.0 .AND.IPAGE(1,J).EQ.DD.AND.
      1         IPAGE(2,J).EQ.EE.AND.IPAGE(3,J).EQ.SS.AND.
      2         IPAGE(4,J).EQ.CC.AND.IPAGE(5,J).EQ.RR.AND.
      3         IPAGE(6,J).EQ.II.AND.IPAGE(7,J).EQ.PP.AND.
      4         IPAGE(8,J).EQ.TT.AND.IPAGE(9,J).EQ.II.AND.
      5         IPAGE(10,J).EQ.OO.AND.IPAGE(11,J).EQ.NN ) IDESC=J
     15 CONTINUE
C       SAVE THE LAST LINE NUMBER OF THE PAL DESIGN SPECIFICATION
     16 IEND=J-1
        CALL INITLZ(INAME,ITYPE,LFUSES,IC,IL,IBLOW,IPCTR)
C       PRINT ERROR MESSAGE FOR INVALID PAL PART TYPE
        IF(ITYPE.NE.0) GO TO 17
        WRITE(PMS,18) IPAL,INAME
     18 FORMAT(/,' PAL PART TYPE ',3A1,5A1,' IS INCORRECT')
        CALL EXIT
C       GET 24 PIN NAMES
     17 DO 20 J=1,24
     20     CALL GETSYM(LPHASE,ISYM,J,IC,IL)
            IF(.NOT.(LEQUAL.OR.LLEFT.OR.LAND.OR.LOR.OR.LRIGHT)) GO TO 24
```

```
              WRITE(PMS,23)
   23         FORMAT(/, ' LESS THAN 24 PIN NAMES IN PIN LIST')
              CALL EXIT
   24 ILE=IL
C     BYPASS FUSE PLOT ASSEMBLY IF HAL (H IN LINE 1, COLUMN 1)
      IF( IPAL(1).EQ.H ) GO TO 108
   25 CALL GETSYM(LBUF,IBUF,1,IC,IL)
   28     IF(.NOT.LEQUAL) GO TO 25
          ILL=IL
          CALL MATCH(IMATCH,IBUF,ISYM)
          IF( IMATCH.EQ.0 ) GO TO 100
C         CHECK FOR VALID POLARITY (ACTIVE LOW)
          LSAME = ( (      LPHASE(IMATCH)).AND.(      LBUF(1)).OR.
     1                (.NOT.LPHASE(IMATCH)).AND.(.NOT.LBUF(1)) )
          IF( ITYPE.NE.6.AND.(LSAME) ) LACT=.TRUE.
C         CHECK FOR VALID OUTPUT PIN
   29     IF( (ITYPE.EQ.1.OR.ITYPE.EQ.7.OR.ITYPE.EQ.8.OR.ITYPE.EQ.9.OR.
     1          ITYPE.EQ.10).AND.(IMATCH.LT.14.OR.IMATCH.GT.23) )
     2          LOPERR=.TRUE.
          IF( (ITYPE.EQ.2.OR.ITYPE.EQ.11.OR.ITYPE.EQ.12.OR.ITYPE.EQ.13
     1          .OR.ITYPE.EQ.14).AND.(IMATCH.LT.15.OR.IMATCH.GT.22) )
     2          LOPERR=.TRUE.
          IF(   ITYPE.EQ.3.AND.(IMATCH.LT.16.OR.IMATCH.GT.21) )
     1          LOPERR=.TRUE.
          IF(   ITYPE.EQ.4.AND.(IMATCH.LT.17.OR.IMATCH.GT.20) )
     1          LOPERR=.TRUE.
          IF( (ITYPE.EQ.5.OR.ITYPE.EQ.6).AND.
     1         (IMATCH.LT.18.OR.IMATCH.GT.19) ) LOPERR=.TRUE.
          IF( (LACT).OR.(LOPERR) ) GO TO 100
          I88PRO=(23-IMATCH)*8 + 1
C         START PAL20C1 ON PRODUCT LINE 32 (I88PRO=33)
          IF(INAME(3).EQ.C) I88PRO=33
          IC=0
   30       CALL INCR(IC,IL)
            IF( .NOT.(LEQUAL.OR.LLEFT) ) GO TO 30
            LPROD(I88PRO)=.TRUE.
            IF(.NOT.LLEFT) CALL SLIP(LFUSES,I88PRO,ITYPE,IBLOW)
          DO 70 I8PRO=1,16
              IF( (LXOR).AND.I8PRO.NE.3 ) GO TO 70
              IPROD = I88PRO + I8PRO - 1
              LPROD(IPROD)=.TRUE.
              LFIRST=.TRUE.
   50           ILL=IL
                CALL GETSYM(LBUF,IBUF,1,IC,IL)
                CALL MATCH(IMATCH,IBUF,ISYM)
C               CHECK FOR INVALID INPUT PIN
                IF( ITYPE.EQ.1.AND.(IMATCH.GE.14.AND.IMATCH.LE.23) )
     1              LINP=.TRUE.
                IF( ITYPE.EQ.2.AND.(IMATCH.GE.15.AND.IMATCH.LE.22) )
     1              LINP=.TRUE.
                IF( ITYPE.EQ.3.AND.(IMATCH.GE.16.AND.IMATCH.LE.21) )
     1              LINP=.TRUE.
                IF( ITYPE.EQ.4.AND.(IMATCH.GE.17.AND.IMATCH.LE.20) )
     1              LINP=.TRUE.
                IF( ITYPE.EQ.5.AND.(IMATCH.EQ.18.OR.IMATCH.EQ.19) )
     1              LINP=.TRUE.
```

```
              IF( ITYPE.EQ.6.AND.(IMATCH.EQ.18.OR.IMATCH.EQ.19) )
     1            LINP=.TRUE.
              IF( ITYPE.EQ.7.AND.(IMATCH.EQ.14.OR.IMATCH.EQ.23) )
     1            LINP=.TRUE.
              IF( ITYPE.EQ.8..AND.(IMATCH.EQ.1.OR.IMATCH.EQ.13) )
     1            LINP=.TRUE.
              IF( ITYPE.EQ.9..AND.(IMATCH.EQ.1.OR.IMATCH.EQ.13) )
     1            LINP=.TRUE.
              IF( ITYPE.EQ.10..AND.(IMATCH.EQ.1.OR.IMATCH.EQ.13) )
     1            LINP=.TRUE.
              IF( ITYPE.EQ.11.AND.(IMATCH.EQ.15.OR.IMATCH.EQ.22) )
     1            LINP=.TRUE.
              IF( ITYPE.GE.12.AND.(IMATCH.EQ.1.OR.IMATCH.EQ.13) )
     1            LINP=.TRUE.
              ILL=IL
              IF(LINP) GO TO 100
              IF(IMATCH.EQ.0) GO TO 100
              IF(IMATCH.EQ.12) GO TO 64
              IF(.NOT.LFIRST) GO TO 58
                  LFIRST=.FALSE.
                  DO 56 I=1,40
                      IBLOW = IBLOW + 1
   56                 LFUSES(I,IPROD)=.TRUE.
   58         CALL IXLATE(IINPUT,LPHASE,IMATCH,LBUF,ITYPE)
              IF(IINPUT.LE.0) GO TO 60
              IBLOW = IBLOW - 1
              LFUSES(IINPUT,IPROD)=.FALSE.
              CALL PLOT(LBUF,IBUF,LFUSES,IPROD,TITLE,.FALSE.,ITYPE,
     1                  LPROD,IOP,IBLOW)
   60         IF(LAND) GO TO 50
   64         IF(.NOT.LRIGHT) GO TO 68
   66         CALL INCR(IC,IL)
              IF(.NOT.LEQUAL) GO TO 66
   68       IF( .NOT.(LOR.OR.LEQUAL) ) GO TO 74
   70       CONTINUE
   74     ILL=IL
          CALL GETSYM(LBUF,IBUF,1,IC,IL)
          IF(LLEFT.OR.LEQUAL) GO TO 28
  100 IF( ILL.EQ.IFUNCT.OR.ILL.EQ.IDESC.OR.ILL.EQ.IEND ) GO TO 102
C     PRINT AN ERROR MESSAGE FOR AN UNRECOGNIZABLE SYMBOL
      ILERR=ILL+4
      WRITE(PMS,99) BEL
   99 FORMAT(' ',A1)
      WRITE(PMS,101) (IBUF(I,1),I=1,8),ILERR,(IPAGE(I,ILL),I=1,80)
  101 FORMAT(/,' ERROR SYMBOL =  ',8A1,'      IN LINE NUMBER ',I3,
     1       /,' ',80A1)
C     PRINT AN ERROR MESSAGE FOR ACTIVE HIGH/LOW ERRORS
      IF( (LACT).AND.(.NOT.LOPERR) ) WRITE(PMS,103) IPAL,INAME
  103 FORMAT(' OUTPUT MUST BE INVERTED SINCE ',3A1,5A1,
     1       ' IS AN ACTIVE LOW DEVICE')
C     PRINT AN ERROR MESSAGE FOR AN INVALID OUTPUT PIN
      IF( (LOPERR).AND.IMATCH.NE.0 ) WRITE(PMS,105) IMATCH,IPAL,INAME
  105 FORMAT(' THIS PIN, NUMBER ',I2,' IS AN INVALID OUTPUT PIN',
     1       ' FOR ',3A1,5A1)
C     PRINT AN ERROR MESSAGE FOR AN INVALID INPUT PIN
      IF(LINP) WRITE(PMS,115) IMATCH,IPAL,INAME
```

```
  115 FORMAT(' THIS PIN NUMBER ',I2,' IS AN INVALID INPUT PIN',
     1       ' FOR ',3A1,5A1)
      CALL EXIT
  102 CALL TWEEK(ITYPE,LFUSES)
  108 WRITE(6,106)
  106 FORMAT(/,' OPERATION CODES:')
      WRITE(6,107)
  107 FORMAT(/,' E=ECHO INPUT  O=PINOUT  T=SIMULATE  F=FAULT TEST',
     2        /,' P=PLOT  B=BRIEF  J=JEDEC FORMAT  H=HEX  S=SHORT',
     3        /,' L=BHLF  N=BNPF  C=CATALOG  Q=QUIT')
      WRITE(6,110)
  110 FORMAT(/,' ENTER OPERATION CODE: ',$)
      READ(ROC,120) IOP
  120 FORMAT(A1)
C     CALL IODC2
      IF(POF.NE.6) WRITE(POF,125)
  125 FORMAT('1')
      IF(IOP.EQ.E) CALL ECHO(IPAL,INAME,REST,PATNUM,TITLE,COMP)
      IF(IOP.EQ.O) CALL PINOUT(IPAL,INAME,TITLE)
      IF(IOP.EQ.T) CALL TEST(LPHASE,LBUF,TITLE,IC,IL,ILE,ISYM,IBUF,
     1                  ITYPE,IPCTR,LERR,ISAF,IPCTR1,.FALSE.,.FALSE.)
      IF(IOP.EQ.JJ) CALL PLOTF
      ISAF=0
      IF(IOP.EQ.F) GO TO 200
  135 IF(IOP.EQ.P) CALL PLOT(LBUF,IBUF,LFUSES,IPROD,TITLE,.TRUE.,ITYPE,
     1                       LPROD,IOP,IBLOW,IPCTR0)
      IF(IOP.EQ.B) CALL PLOT(LBUF,IBUF,LFUSES,IPROD,TITLE,.TRUE.,ITYPE,
     1                       LPROD,IOP,IBLOW,IPCTR0)
      IF(IOP.EQ.H) CALL HEX(LFUSES,H)
      IF(IOP.EQ.S) CALL HEX(LFUSES,S)
      IF(IOP.EQ.L) CALL BINR(LFUSES,H,L)
      IF(IOP.EQ.N) CALL BINR(LFUSES,P,N)
      IF(IOP.EQ.C) CALL CAT
C     CALL IODC4
      IF(IOP.NE.Q ) GO TO 108
      CALL EXIT
C  SETTING THE PARAMETERS FOR THE SA0/SA1 TESTS
  200 IPCTR=0
      CALL TEST(LPHASE,LBUF,TITLE,IC,IL,ILE,ISYM,IBUF,ITYPE,IPCTR,
     1          LERR,ISAF,IPCTR1,.FALSE.,.FALSE.)
      IPCTR0=IPCTR
C  LOOPING FOR SA1 TEST
      DO 210 IPCTR1=1,IPCTR0
      LSA11=.TRUE.
      CALL TEST(LPHASE,LBUF,TITLE,IC,IL,ILE,ISYM,IBUF,ITYPE,IPCTR,
     1          LERR,ISAF,IPCTR1,LSA11,.FALSE.)
  210 CONTINUE
      ISA1=ISAF
C   LOOPING FOR SA0 TEST
      DO 215 IPCTR1=1,IPCTR0
      LSA01=.TRUE.
      CALL TEST(LPHASE,LBUF,TITILE,IC,IL,ILE,ISYM,IBUF,ITYPE,IPCTR,
     1          LERR,ISAF,IPCTR1,.FALSE.,LSA01)
  215 CONTINUE
      ISA0=ISAF-ISA1
      IFAULT=(ISAF*100)/(2*IPCTR0)
```

```
      WRITE(POF,220) ISA1
  220 FORMAT(/,' NUMBER OF STUCK AT ONE  (SA1) FAULTS ARE =',I3)
      WRITE(POF,225) ISA0
  225 FORMAT(/,' NUMBER OF STUCK AT ZERO (SA0) FAULTS ARE =',I3)
      WRITE(POF,230)IFAULT
  230 FORMAT(/,' PRODUCT   TERM   COVERAGE                 ='I4,'%',/)
      GO TO 135
      END
C
C***********************************************************************
C
      SUBROUTINE INITLZ(INAME,ITYPE,LFUSES,IC,IL,IBLOW,IPCTR)
C     THIS SUBROUTINE INITIALIZIES VARIABLES AND MATCHES PAL PART
C      NUMBER WITH ITYPE
      IMPLICIT INTEGER (A-Z)
      INTEGER INAME(5),INFO(6,14)
      LOGICAL LBLANK,LLEFT,LAND,LOR,LSLASH,LEQUAL,LRIGHT,LFUSES(40,80),
     1        LMATCH,LXOR
      COMMON  LBLANK,LLEFT,LAND,LOR,LSLASH,LEQUAL,LRIGHT,LXOR
      COMMON /PGE/ IPAGE(80,200)
      DATA INFO/
     1     '1','2','L','1','0',1,
     2     '1','4','L','8',' ',2,
     3     '1','6','L','6',' ',3,
     4     '1','8','L','4',' ',4,
     5     '2','0','L','2',' ',5,
     6     '2','0','C','1',' ',6,
     7     '2','0','L','1','0',7,
     8     '2','0','X','1','0',8,
     9     '2','0','X','8',' ',9,
     A     '2','0','X','4',' ',10,
     B     '2','0','L','8',' ',11,
     C     '2','0','R','8',' ',12,
     D     '2','0','R','6',' ',13,
     E     '2','0','R','4',' ',14/
C     INITIALIZE LFUSES ARRAY (FUSE ARRAY)
      DO 20 J=1,80
         DO 20 I=1,40
   20       LFUSES(I,J)=.FALSE.
C     INITIALIZE IBLOW (NUMBER OF FUSES BLOWN)
      IBLOW=0
      IPCTR=0
C     INITIALIZE IC AND IL (COLUMN AND LINE POINTERS)
      IC=0
      IL=1
C     INITIALIZE ITYPE (PAL PART TYPE)
      ITYPE=0
C     ITYPE IS ASSIGNED THE FOLLOWING VALUES FOR THESE PAL TYPES:
C     PAL12L10 =  1   PAL14L8  =  2   PAL16L6  =  3   PAL18L4  =  4
C     PAL20L2  =  5   PAL20C1  =  6   PAL20L10 =  7   PAL20X10 =  8
C     PAL20X8  =  9   PAL20X4  = 10   PAL20L8  = 11   PAL20R8  = 12
C     PAL20R6  = 13   PAL20R4  = 14
      DO 40 J=1,14
         LMATCH=.TRUE.
         DO 30 I=1,4
   30       IF(INAME(I).NE.INFO(I,J)) LMATCH=.FALSE.
```

```
            IF(LMATCH) ITYPE=INFO(6,J)
            IF (LMATCH) GO TO 50
   40 CONTINUE
      IF(ITYPE.EQ.0) RETURN
   50 CALL INCR(IC,IL)
      RETURN
      END
C
C***********************************************************************
C
      SUBROUTINE GETSYM(LPHASE,ISYM,J,IC,IL)
C     THIS SUBROUTINE GETS THE PIN NAME, / IF COMPLEMENT LOGIC, AND
C      THE FOLLOWING OPERATION SYMBOL IF ANY
      IMPLICIT INTEGER (A-Z)
      INTEGER ISYM(8,24)
      LOGICAL LBLANK,LLEFT,LAND,LOR,LSLASH,LEQUAL,LRIGHT,LXOR,LPHASE(24)
      COMMON  LBLANK,LLEFT,LAND,LOR,LSLASH,LEQUAL,LRIGHT,LXOR
      COMMON /PGE/ IPAGE(80,200)
      DATA IBLANK/' '/
      IF( .NOT.(LLEFT.OR.LAND.OR.LOR.OR.LEQUAL.OR.LRIGHT) )  GO TO 10
      CALL INCR(IC,IL)
   10 LPHASE(J)=(.NOT.LSLASH)
      IF(LPHASE(J)) GO TO 15
      CALL INCR(IC,IL)
   15 DO 20 I=1,8
   20     ISYM(I,J)=IBLANK
   25 DO 30 I=1,7
   30     ISYM(I,J)=ISYM(I+1,J)
      ISYM(8,J)=IPAGE(IC,IL)
      CALL INCR(IC,IL)
      IF( LLEFT.OR.LBLANK.OR.LAND.OR.LOR.OR.LRIGHT.OR.LEQUAL ) RETURN
      GO TO 25
      END
C
C***********************************************************************
C
      SUBROUTINE INCR(IC,IL)
C     THIS SUBROUTINE INCREMENTS COLUMN AND LINE POINTERS
C      BLANKS AND CHARACTERS AFTER ';' ARE IGNORED
      IMPLICIT INTEGER (A-Z)
      LOGICAL LBLANK,LLEFT,LAND,LOR,LSLASH,LEQUAL,LRIGHT,LXOR,LXOR1
      COMMON  LBLANK,LLEFT,LAND,LOR,LSLASH,LEQUAL,LRIGHT,LXOR
      COMMON /PGE/ IPAGE(80,200)
      COMMON /LUNIT/ PMS,POF,PDF
      DATA IBLANK/' '/,ILEFT/'('/,IAND/'*'/,IOR/'+'/,COMENT/';'/,
     1        ISLASH/'/'/,IEQUAL/'='/,IRIGHT/')'/,ICOLON/':'/
      LBLANK=.FALSE.
      LXOR=.FALSE.
      LXOR1=.FALSE.
   10 IC=IC+1
      IF( IC.LE.79.AND.IPAGE(IC,IL).NE.COMENT ) GO TO 30
      IL=IL+1
      IF(IL.LE.200) GO TO 20
          WRITE(PMS,15)
   15     FORMAT(/,' SOURCE FILE EXCEEDS 200 LINES OR MISSING',
     1             ' DESCRIPTION OR FUNCTION TABLE KEY WORD')
```

```
        CALL EXIT
   20 IC=0
      GO TO 10
   30 IF(IPAGE(IC,IL).NE.IBLANK) GO TO 31
      LBLANK=.TRUE.
      GO TO 10
   31 IF(IPAGE(IC,IL).NE.ICOLON) GO TO 32
      IF(LXOR) GO TO 33
      LXOR1=.TRUE.
      GO TO 10
   33 LOR=.TRUE.
      RETURN
   32 IF( .NOT.(IPAGE(IC,IL).EQ.IOR.AND.(LXOR1)) ) GO TO 34
      LXOR=.TRUE.
      GO TO 10
   34 LLEFT =(IPAGE(IC,IL).EQ.ILEFT)
      LAND  =(IPAGE(IC,IL).EQ.IAND)
      LOR   =(IPAGE(IC,IL).EQ.IOR)
      LSLASH=(IPAGE(IC,IL).EQ.ISLASH)
      LEQUAL=(IPAGE(IC,IL).EQ.IEQUAL)
      LRIGHT=(IPAGE(IC,IL).EQ.IRIGHT)
      RETURN
      END
C
C***********************************************************************
C
      SUBROUTINE MATCH(IMATCH,IBUF,ISYM)
C     THIS SUBROUTINE FINDS A MATCH BETWEEN THE PIN NAME IN THE EQUATION
C      AND THE PIN NAME IN THE PIN LIST OR FUNCTION TABLE PIN LIST
      IMPLICIT INTEGER (A-Z)
      INTEGER IBUF(8,24),ISYM(8,24)
      LOGICAL LMATCH
      IMATCH=0
      DO 20 J=1,24
          LMATCH=.TRUE.
          DO 10 I=1,8
   10         LMATCH=LMATCH.AND.(IBUF(I,1).EQ.ISYM(I,J))
          IF(LMATCH) IMATCH=J
   20     CONTINUE
      RETURN
      END
C
C***********************************************************************
C
      SUBROUTINE IXLATE(IINPUT,LPHASE,IMATCH,LBUF,ITYPE)
C     THIS SUBROUTINE FINDS A MATCH BETWEEN INPUT PIN NUMBER AND
C      THE INPUT LINE NUMBER FOR A SPECIFIC PAL.  ADD 1 TO THE INPUT
C      LINE NUMBER IF THE PIN IS A COMPLEMENT
      IMPLICIT INTEGER (A-Z)
      INTEGER ITABLE(24,14)
      LOGICAL LPHASE(24),LBUF(24)
      DATA    ITABLE/
     1 3,1,5,9,13,17,21,25,29,33,37,0,39, 0, 0, 0, 0, 0, 0, 0, 0,0,0,0,
     2 3,1,5,9,13,17,21,25,29,33,37,0,39,35, 0, 0, 0, 0, 0, 0, 0,7,0,
     3 3,1,5,9,13,17,21,25,29,33,37,0,39,35,31, 0, 0, 0, 0, 0, 0,11,7,0,
     4 3,1,5,9,13,17,21,25,29,33,37,0,39,35,31,27, 0, 0, 0, 0,15,11,7,0,
```

```
     5 3,1,5,9,13,17,21,25,29,33,37,0,39,35,31,27,23, 0, 0,19,15,11,7,0,
     6 3,1,5,9,13,17,21,25,29,33,37,0,39,35,31,27,23, 0, 0,19,15,11,7,0,
     7 3,1,5,9,13,17,21,25,29,33,37,0,39, 0,35,31,27,23,19,15,11, 7,0,0,
     8 0,1,5,9,13,17,21,25,29,33,37,0, 0,39,35,31,27,23,19,15,11, 7,3,0,
     9 0,1,5,9,13,17,21,25,29,33,37,0, 0,39,35,31,27,23,19,15,11, 7,3,0,
     A 0,1,5,9,13,17,21,25,29,33,37,0, 0,39,35,31,27,23,19,15,11, 7,3,0,
     B 3,1,5,9,13,17,21,25,29,33,37,0,39,35, 0,31,27,23,19,15,11, 0,7,0,
     C 0,1,5,9,13,17,21,25,29,33,37,0, 0,39,35,31,27,23,19,15,11, 7,3,0,
     D 0,1,5,9,13,17,21,25,29,33,37,0, 0,39,35,31,27,23,19,15,11, 7,3,0,
     E 0,1,5,9,13,17,21,25,29,33,37,0, 0,39,35,31,27,23,19,15,11, 7,3,0/
      IBUBL=0
      IF( ((      LPHASE(IMATCH)).AND.(.NOT.LBUF(1))).OR.
     1    ((.NOT.LPHASE(IMATCH)).AND.(      LBUF(1))) ) IBUBL=1
      IINPUT=ITABLE(IMATCH,ITYPE)+IBUBL
      RETURN
      END
C
C***********************************************************************
C
      SUBROUTINE ECHO(IPAL,INAME,REST,PATNUM,TITLE,COMP)
C     THIS SUBROUTINE PRINTS THE PAL DESIGN SPECIFICATION INPUT FILE
      IMPLICIT INTEGER (A-Z)
      INTEGER IPAL(3),INAME(5),REST(72),PATNUM(80),TITLE(80),COMP(80)
      COMMON /PGE/ IPAGE(80,200)
      COMMON /LUNIT/ PMS,POF,PDF
      COMMON /FTEST/ IFUNCT,IDESC,IEND
      DATA IBLANK/' '/
      WRITE(POF,5) IPAL,INAME,REST,PATNUM,TITLE,COMP
    5 FORMAT(/,' ',3A1,5A1,72A1,/,' ',80A1,/,' ',80A1,/,' ',80A1)
      DO 20 IL=1,IEND
          IC=81
   10     IC=IC-1
          IF( IPAGE(IC,IL).EQ.IBLANK.AND.IC.GT.1 ) GO TO 10
          WRITE(POF,15) (IPAGE(I,IL),I=1,IC)
   15     FORMAT(' ',80A1)
   20 CONTINUE
      RETURN
      END
C
C***********************************************************************
C
      SUBROUTINE CAT
C     THIS SUBROUTINE PRINTS THE PALASM CATALOG
      IMPLICIT INTEGER (A-Z)
      COMMON /LUNIT/ PMS,POF,PDF
      WRITE(PMS,10)
   10 FORMAT(/,' 24-PIN PALASM VERSION 1.5')
      WRITE(PMS,20)
   20 FORMAT(/,' THIS PALASM AIDS THE USER IN THE DESIGN AND',
     1        ' PROGRAMMING OF THE',/,' SERIES 24 PAL FAMILY.  THE',
     2        ' FOLLOWING OPTIONS ARE PROVIDED:',
     3      /,'    ECHO (E)      - PRINTS THE PAL DESIGN',
     4        ' SPECIFICATION',
     5     //,'    PINOUT (O)    - PRINTS THE PINOUT OF THE PAL',
     6     //,'    SIMULATE (T)  - EXERCISES THE FUNCTION TABLE',
     7        ' VECTORS IN THE LOGIC',/,'                    ',
```

```
     8          ' EQUATIONS AND GENERATES TEST VECTORS',
     9      //,'     FAULT (F)     - PERFORMS FAULT TESTING',
     A      //,'     PLOT (P)      - PRINTS THE ENTIRE FUSE PLOT')
      WRITE(PMS,30)
   30 FORMAT(/,'     BRIEF (B)     - PRINTS ONLY THE USED PRODUCT LINES',
     1          ' OF THE FUSE PLOT',/,'                        PHANTOM',
     2          ' FUSES ARE OMITTED',
     3      //,'     JEDEC (J)     - GENERATES JEDEC PROGRAMMING FORMAT',
     4      //,'     HEX (H)       - GENERATES HEX PROGRAMMING FORMAT',
     5      //,'     SHORT (S)     - GENERATES HEX PROGRAMMING FORMAT',
     6      //,'     BHLF (L)      - GENERATES BHLF PROGRAMMING FORMAT',
     7      //,'     BNPF (N)      - GENERATES BNPF PROGRAMMING FORMAT',
     8      //,'     CATALOG (C)   - PRINTS THE PALASM CATALOG',
     9      //,'     QUIT (Q)      - EXIT PALASM')
      RETURN
      END
C
C***********************************************************************
C
      SUBROUTINE PINOUT(IPAL,INAME,TITLE)
C     THIS SUBROUTINE PRINTS THE PINOUT OF THE PAL
      IMPLICIT INTEGER (A-Z)
      INTEGER IPAL(3),INAME(5),TITLE(80),PIN(12,24),IIN(8,2)
      COMMON /PGE/ IPAGE(80,200)
      COMMON /LUNIT/ PMS,POF,PDF
      DATA IBLANK/' '/,ISTAR/'*'/
      DO 10 J=1,24
          DO 5 I=1,12
    5         PIN(I,J)=IBLANK
   10 CONTINUE
   15 DO 25 J=1,2
          DO 20 I=1,8
   20         IIN(I,J)=IBLANK
   25 CONTINUE
      IIN(2,1)=IPAL(1)
      IIN(4,1)=IPAL(2)
      IIN(6,1)=IPAL(3)
      IIN(1,2)=INAME(1)
      IIN(3,2)=INAME(2)
      IIN(5,2)=INAME(3)
      IIN(7,2)=INAME(4)
      IIN(8,2)=INAME(5)
      J=0
      IL=0
   30 IC=0
      IL=IL+1
   35 IC=IC+1
   40 IF( IC.GT.80 ) GO TO 30
      IF( IPAGE(IC,IL).EQ.IBLANK ) GO TO 35
      J=J+1
      IF(J.GT.24) GO TO 60
      DO 55 I=1,12
          PIN(I,J)=IPAGE(IC,IL)
          IC=IC+1
          IF( IC.GT.80 ) GO TO 40
          IF( IPAGE(IC,IL).EQ.IBLANK ) GO TO 40
```

```
   55      CONTINUE
   60 DO 75 J=1,12
           II=0
   65      II=II+1
           IF(II.EQ.13) GO TO 75
           IF( PIN(II,J).NE.IBLANK ) GO TO 65
           I=13
   70      I=I-1
           II=II-1
           PIN(I,J)=PIN(II,J)
           PIN(II,J)=IBLANK
           IF(II.NE.1) GO TO 70
   75 CONTINUE
      WRITE(POF,76) TITLE
   76 FORMAT(/,' ',80A1)
      WRITE(POF,78) ISTAR,ISTAR,ISTAR,ISTAR,ISTAR,ISTAR,ISTAR,ISTAR,
     1              ISTAR,ISTAR,ISTAR,ISTAR,ISTAR,ISTAR,ISTAR,ISTAR,
     2              ISTAR,ISTAR,ISTAR,ISTAR,ISTAR,ISTAR,ISTAR,ISTAR,
     3              ISTAR,ISTAR,ISTAR,ISTAR,ISTAR,ISTAR,ISTAR,ISTAR
   78 FORMAT(/,' ',18X,14A1,3X,14A1,
     1       /,' ',18X,A1,13X,A1,1X,A1,13X,A1)
      JJ=24
      DO 88 J=1,12
           WRITE(POF,80) ISTAR,ISTAR,ISTAR,ISTAR,ISTAR,ISTAR,ISTAR,ISTAR
   80      FORMAT(' ',15X,4A1,29X,4A1)
           WRITE(POF,81) (PIN(I,J),I=1,12),ISTAR,J,ISTAR,
     1          (IIN(I,1),I=1,8),ISTAR,JJ,ISTAR,(PIN(I,JJ),I=1,12)
   81      FORMAT(' ',12A1,3X,A1,I2,A1,11X,8A1,10X,A1,I2,A1,3X,12A1)
           WRITE(POF,82) ISTAR,ISTAR,ISTAR,ISTAR,ISTAR,ISTAR,ISTAR,ISTAR
   82      FORMAT(' ',15X,4A1,29X,4A1)
           WRITE(POF,84) ISTAR,(IIN(I,2),I=1,8),ISTAR
   84      FORMAT(' ',18X,A1,11X,8A1,10X,A1)
           DO 86 II=1,2
               DO 85 I=1,8
   85              IIN(I,II)=IBLANK
   86      CONTINUE
           JJ=JJ-1
   88 CONTINUE
      WRITE(POF,90) ISTAR,ISTAR,ISTAR,ISTAR,ISTAR,ISTAR,ISTAR,ISTAR,
     1              ISTAR,ISTAR,ISTAR,ISTAR,ISTAR,ISTAR,ISTAR,ISTAR,
     2              ISTAR,ISTAR,ISTAR,ISTAR,ISTAR,ISTAR,ISTAR,ISTAR,
     3              ISTAR,ISTAR,ISTAR,ISTAR,ISTAR,ISTAR,ISTAR
   90 FORMAT(' ',18X,31A1)
      RETURN
      END
C
C***********************************************************************
C
      SUBROUTINE PLOT(LBUF,IBUF,LFUSES,IPROD,TITLE,LDUMP,ITYPE,LPROD,
     1                IOP,IBLOW)
C     THIS SUBROUTINE PRODUCES THE FUSE PLOT
      IMPLICIT INTEGER (A-Z)
      INTEGER IBUF(8,24),IOUT(64),ISAVE(80,40),TITLE(80),IDATA(40)
      LOGICAL LBUF(24),LFUSES(40,80),LDUMP,LPROD(80)
      CHARACTER STX,ETX
      COMMON /LUNIT/ PMS,POF,PDF
```

```
      DATA ISAVE/3200*' '/,IAND/'*'/,IOR/'+'/,ISLASH/'/'/,
     1     IDASH/'-'/,X/'X'/,IBLANK/' '/,P/'P'/,B/'B'/,
     2     D/'D'/,ZERO/'0'/,ONE/'1'/,FX/'0'/,FIDASH/'O'/
      DATA STX/002/,ETX/003/
      IF(LDUMP) GO TO 58
      IF(ISAVE(IPROD,1).NE.IBLANK) RETURN
      IF(LBUF(1)) GO TO 5
      DO 30 J=1,39
   30     ISAVE(IPROD,J)=ISAVE(IPROD,J+1)
      ISAVE(IPROD,40)=ISLASH
    5 DO 20 I=1,8
         IF( ISAVE(IPROD,1).NE.IBLANK ) RETURN
          IF( IBUF(I,1).EQ.IBLANK ) GO TO 20
          DO 10 J=1,39
   10         ISAVE(IPROD,J)=ISAVE(IPROD,J+1)
          ISAVE(IPROD,40)=IBUF(I,1)
   20     CONTINUE
      IF(ISAVE(IPROD,1).NE.IBLANK) RETURN
   40 DO 50 J=1,39
   50     ISAVE(IPROD,J)=ISAVE(IPROD,J+1)
      ISAVE(IPROD,40)=IAND
      RETURN
C     PRINT FUSE PLOT
   58 IF(IOP.EQ.D) GO TO 62
      WRITE(POF,61) TITLE
   61 FORMAT(/,' ',80A1,//,
     1 '                 11 1111 1111 2222 2222 2233 3333 3333',/,
     2 '    0123 4567 8901 2345 6789 0123 4567 8901 2345 6789',/)
      GO TO 64
C***** STX DETERMINES THE STARTING CHARACTER FOR DATA I/O FORMAT
   62 WRITE(PDF,63) STX
   63 FORMAT(' ',A1,'*L0000'/)
   64 DO 100 I88PRO=1,73,8
          DO 94 I8PRO=1,8
              IPROD=I88PRO+I8PRO-1
              ISAVE(IPROD,40)=IBLANK
              DO 70 I=1,40
                  IF( ISAVE(IPROD,1).NE.IBLANK ) GO TO 70
                  DO 65 J=1,39
   65                 ISAVE(IPROD,J)=ISAVE(IPROD,J+1)
                  ISAVE(IPROD,40)=IBLANK
   70             CONTINUE
              DO 75 I=1,24
                  IOUT(I+40)=ISAVE(IPROD,I)
   75         CONTINUE
              IF( ISAVE(IPROD,25).NE.IBLANK ) IOUT(64)=IDASH
              DO 80 I=1,40
                  IOUT(I)=X
                  IF(LFUSES(I,IPROD)) IOUT(I)=IDASH
   80         CONTINUE
              CALL FANTOM(ITYPE,IOP,IOUT,IPROD,I8PRO)
              IF(IOP.NE.D) GO TO 85
              K=0
   81         DO 82 I=1,40
                 IF((IOUT(I).EQ.FX).OR.(IOUT(I).EQ.FIDASH)) GO TO 82
                 K=K+1
```

```
                  IF(IOUT(I).EQ.X)      IDATA(K)=ZERO
                  IF(IOUT(I).EQ.IDASH) IDATA(K)=ONE
   82          CONTINUE
               DO 83 I=1,40
                  IF( (IOUT(I).EQ.X).OR.(IOUT(I).EQ.IDASH) ) GO TO 86
   83          CONTINUE
               GO TO 94
   86          WRITE(PDF,84) IDATA
   84          FORMAT(' ',40(A1,' '))
               GO TO 94
   85          IPROD=IPROD-1
               IF( (IOP.EQ.P).OR.(IOP.EQ.B.AND.(LPROD(IPROD+1))) )
     1         WRITE(POF,90) IPROD,IOUT
   90          FORMAT(' ',I2,10(' ',4A1),' ',24A1)
   94          CONTINUE
            WRITE(POF,96)
   96       FORMAT(1X)
  100       CONTINUE
        IF(IOP.NE.D) GO TO 105
        WRITE(PDF,101) ETX
  101 FORMAT(' ',A1)
        RETURN
  105 WRITE(POF,110)
  110 FORMAT(/,
     1' LEGEND:  X : FUSE NOT BLOWN (L,N,0)   - : FUSE BLOWN   (H,P,1)')
        IF(IOP.EQ.P) WRITE(POF,111)
  111 FORMAT(
     1'          0 : PHANTOM FUSE   (L,N,0)   O : PHANTOM FUSE (H,P,1)')
        WRITE(POF,112) IBLOW
  112 FORMAT(/,' NUMBER OF FUSES BLOW = ',I4)
        WRITE(POF,113)
  113 FORMAT(//)
        RETURN
        END
C
C***********************************************************************
C
      SUBROUTINE PLOTF
C     THIS SUBROUTINE GENERATES THE JEDEC PROGRAMMING FORMAT OUTPUT
C      COMPATIBLE WITH THE DATA I/O PROGRAMMABLE LOGIC PAK (PLDS)
      IMPLICIT INTEGER (A-Z)
      LOGICAL LFUSES(40,80)
      INTEGER IPBUF(40),ZERO,ONE
      INTEGER ISUM(4),IADR,STX,ETX,IDEC(4),IPT,IINP,J1,J2
      INTEGER IDECIO(4),ISUMV(4),ISUMIO(4),BUFIO(40)
      COMMON /LUNIT/PMS,POF,PDF
      COMMON /IPT/IPT
      COMMON /LFUSES/LFUSES
      COMMON /SUM/ISUM,IDEC,IPBUF,BUFIO
      DATA ZERO/'0'/,ONE/'1'/
      IADR=0
      STX=2
      ETX=3
      ISUM(2)=0
      ISUM(4)=230
      WRITE(PDF,10) STX
```

```
   10 FORMAT(' ',A1,'*F0*')
      DO 300 IPT=1,80
         DO 50 IINP=1,40
            IF(LFUSES(IINP,IPT)) IPBUF(IINP)=ONE
            IF(.NOT.(LFUSES(IINP,IPT))) IPBUF(IINP)=ZERO
   50    CONTINUE
         IF(LFUSES(1,IPT)) GO TO 100
         IF(.NOT.LFUSES(2,IPT)) GO TO 250
  100    IDEC(4)=IADR
         DO 150 J=1,3
            J1=5-J
            J2=4-J
            IDEC(J2)=IDEC(J1)/10
            IDEC(J1)=IDEC(J1)-10*IDEC(J2)
            IDECIO(J1)=ICONV(IDEC(J1))
  150    CONTINUE
         IDECIO(1)=ICONV(IDEC(1))
         CALL SUMCHK
         WRITE(PDF,201) IDECIO,IPBUF
  201    FORMAT(' L',4A1,' ',10(4A1,' '),'*')
  250    IADR=IADR+40
  300 CONTINUE
      ISUMIO(1)=ICONV(ISUM(2)/16)
      ISUM(2)=MOD(ISUM(2),16)
      ISUMIO(2)=ICONV(ISUM(2))
      ISUMIO(3)=ICONV(ISUM(4)/16)
      ISUM(4)=MOD(ISUM(4),16)
      ISUMIO(4)=ICONV(ISUM(4))
      WRITE(PDF,400) ETX,ISUMIO
  400 FORMAT(' *',A1,4A1,'*',/)
      RETURN
      END
C
C***********************************************************************
C
      SUBROUTINE SUMCHK
C     THIS SUBROUTINE GENERATES THE CHECK SUM FOR THE JEDEC
C      PROGRAMMING FORMAT
      IMPLICIT INTEGER(A-Z)
      LOGICAL LFUSES(40,80)
      INTEGER IPBUF(40), BUFIO(40)
      INTEGER ISUM(4), IDEC(4)
      COMMON /IPT/IPT
      COMMON /LFUSES/ LFUSES
      COMMON /SUM/ ISUM, IDEC,IPBUF,BUFIO
      DO 50 J=1,40
         IF(LFUSES(J,IPT)) BUFIO(J)=49
         IF(.NOT.LFUSES(J,IPT)) BUFIO(J)=48
         ISUM(4)=ISUM(4)+BUFIO(J)
         IF(ISUM(4).GE.256) ISUM(2)=ISUM(2)+1
         ISUM(4)=MOD(ISUM(4),256)
   50 CONTINUE
      DO 100 J=1,4
         ISUM(4)=ISUM(4)+IDEC(J)+48
         IF(ISUM(4).GE.256) ISUM(2)=ISUM(2)+1
         ISUM(4)=MOD(ISUM(4),256)
```

```
  100 CONTINUE
      ISUM(4)=ISUM(4)+173
      ISUM(2)=ISUM(2)+1
      IF(ISUM(4).GE.256) ISUM(2)=ISUM(2)+1
      ISUM(4)=MOD(ISUM(4),256)
      RETURN
      END
C
C***********************************************************************
C
      INTEGER FUNCTION ICONV(K)
C     THIS INTEGER FUNCTION CONVERTS DECIMAL INTO ASCII CODE FOR THE
C      JEDEC PROGRAMMING FORMAT
      IMPLICIT INTEGER (A-Z)
      DATA A/'0'/,B/'1'/,C/'2'/,D/'3'/,E/'4'/,F/'5'/,G/'6'/,H/'7'/,
     1     I/'8'/,J/'9'/,X/'A'/,L/'B'/,M/'C'/,N/'D'/,O/'E'/,P/'F'/
      IF(K.EQ.0) ICONV=A
      IF(K.EQ.1) ICONV=B
      IF(K.EQ.2) ICONV=C
      IF(K.EQ.3) ICONV=D
      IF(K.EQ.4) ICONV=E
      IF(K.EQ.5) ICONV=F
      IF(K.EQ.6) ICONV=G
      IF(K.EQ.7) ICONV=H
      IF(K.EQ.8) ICONV=I
      IF(K.EQ.9) ICONV=J
      IF(K.EQ.10)ICONV=X
      IF(K.EQ.11)ICONV=L
      IF(K.EQ.12)ICONV=M
      IF(K.EQ.13)ICONV=N
      IF(K.EQ.14)ICONV=O
      IF(K.EQ.15)ICONV=P
      RETURN
      END
C
C***********************************************************************
C
      SUBROUTINE HEX(LFUSES,IOP)
C     THIS SUBROUTINE GENERATES HEX PROGRAMMING FORMATS
      IMPLICIT INTEGER (A-Z)
      INTEGER ITEMP(80),ZTABL1(32),ZTABL2(16),ZCSUM(4)
      LOGICAL LFUSES(40,80)
      CHARACTER SOH,STX,ETX,BEL
      COMMON /LUNIT/PMS,POF,PDF
      DATA H/'H'/,S/'S'/,IBLANK/' '/,
     1     ZTABL1/'00','01','02','03','04','05','06','07',
     2            '08','09','0A','0B','0C','0D','0E','0F',
     3            '10','11','12','13','14','15','16','17',
     4            '18','19','1A','1B','1C','1D','1E','1F'/,
     5     ZTABL2/'0','1','2','3','4','5','6','7',
     6            '8','9','A','B','C','D','E','F'/
      DATA SOH/001/,STX/002/,ETX/003/,BEL/007/
      CSUM=0
      IF(IOP.EQ.H) WRITE(PDF,10)
   10 FORMAT(//,80(' '),//)
C***** NOTE: SOME PROM PROGRAMMERS NEED A START CHARACTER.
```

```
C*****        THIS PROGRAM OUTPUTS AN STX FOR THE DATA I/O MODEL 9
C*****          (USE SOH FOR MODEL 5)
      WRITE(PDF,5) BEL,BEL,BEL,BEL,BEL,BEL,BEL,STX,SOH
    5 FORMAT(' ',9A1)
      DO 40 I=1,41,40
      INC=I-1
        DO 40 IPROD=1,7,2
          DO 20 J=1,2
              DO 20 IINPUT=1,40
              IHEX=0
              ISUM2=IPROD + J-1 + INC
              IF(LFUSES(IINPUT,ISUM2 +  0 )) IHEX=IHEX+1
              IF(LFUSES(IINPUT,ISUM2 +  8 )) IHEX=IHEX+2
              IF(LFUSES(IINPUT,ISUM2 + 16 )) IHEX=IHEX+4
              IF(LFUSES(IINPUT,ISUM2 + 24 )) IHEX=IHEX+8
              IF(LFUSES(IINPUT,ISUM2 + 32 )) IHEX=IHEX+16
              CSUM=CSUM+IHEX
              ISUMX=IINPUT+(40*(J-1))
   20         ITEMP(ISUMX)=ZTABL1(IHEX+1)
           IF(IOP.EQ.H) WRITE(PDF,60) ITEMP
   60      FORMAT(4(' ',20(A2,' '),'.',/))
   40      IF(IOP.EQ.S) WRITE(PDF,61) ITEMP
   61      FORMAT(4(' ',20A2,'.',/))
      IF(IOP.EQ.H) WRITE(PDF,70)
   70 FORMAT(//,80(' '),//)
      WRITE(PDF,80) ETX
   80 FORMAT(' ',A1)
C     CONVERT DECIMAL CHECK SUM INTO HEX CHECK SUM
      DO 85 I=1,4
           ZTEMP=CSUM-16*(CSUM/16)
           ZCSUM(5-I)=ZTABL2(ZTEMP+1)
           CSUM=CSUM/16
   85 CONTINUE
      IF(ZCSUM(1).EQ.ZTABL2(1)) ZCSUM(1)=IBLANK
      WRITE(PMS,90) ZCSUM(1),ZCSUM(2),ZCSUM(3),ZCSUM(4)
   90 FORMAT(/,' HEX CHECK SUM = ',4A1)
      RETURN
      END
C
C***********************************************************************
C
      BLOCK DATA
      IMPLICIT INTEGER (A-Z)
      COMMON /BLK/ PR8X10(10,14),PROD8(8,11),PRODLN(40,7)
      DATA PR8X10/
     1      4, 4, 4, 4, 4, 4, 4, 4, 4, 4,
     2      3, 6, 5, 5, 5, 5, 5, 5, 6, 3,
     3      3, 3, 7, 7, 8, 8, 7, 7, 3, 3,
     4      3, 3, 3, 9,10,10, 9, 3, 3, 3,
     5      3, 3, 3, 3, 1, 1, 3, 3, 3, 3,
     6      2, 2, 2, 2, 1, 1, 3, 3, 3, 3,
     7     11,11,11,11,11,11,11,11,11,11,
     8     11,11,11,11,11,11,11,11,11,11,
     9     11,11,11,11,11,11,11,11,11,11,
     A     11,11,11,11,11,11,11,11,11,11,
     B      3, 1, 1, 1, 1, 1, 1, 1, 1, 3,
```

```
     C      3, 1, 1, 1, 1, 1, 1, 1, 1, 3,
     D      3, 1, 1, 1, 1, 1, 1, 1, 1, 3,
     E      3, 1, 1, 1, 1, 1, 1, 1, 1, 3/
      DATA PROD8/
     1     1,1,1,1,1,1,1,1,
     2     2,2,2,2,2,2,2,2,
     3     3,3,3,3,3,3,3,3,
     4     4,4,3,3,3,3,3,3,
     5     5,5,3,3,3,3,3,3,
     6     5,5,5,5,3,3,3,3,
     7     6,6,6,6,3,3,3,3,
     8     6,6,3,3,3,3,3,3,
     9     7,7,7,7,7,7,3,3,
     A     7,7,7,7,3,3,3,3,
     B     1,1,1,1,3,3,3,3/
      DATA PRODLN/
     1     40*1HX,
     2     40*1HP,
     3     40*1HN,
     4     6*1HX,2*1HP,2*1HX,2*1HP,2*1HX,2*1HP,2*1HX,
     4     2*1HP,2*1HX,2*1HP,2*1HX,2*1HP,2*1HX,2*1HP,
     4     2*1HX,2*1HP,4*1HX,
     5     10*1HX,2*1HP,2*1HX,2*1HP,2*1HX,2*1HP,2*1HX,
     5     2*1HP,2*1HX,2*1HP,2*1HX,2*1HP,8*1HX,
     6     14*1HX,2*1HP,2*1HX,2*1HP,2*1HX,2*1HP,2*1HX,
     6     2*1HP,12*1HX,
     7     18*1HX,2*1HP,2*1HX,2*1HP,16*1HX/
      END
C
C***********************************************************************
C
      SUBROUTINE TWEEK(ITYPE,LFUSES)
C     THIS SUBROUTINE TWEEKS LFUSES (THE PROGRAMMING FUSE PLOT)
C      FOR HIGH AND LOW PHANTOM FUSES
      IMPLICIT INTEGER (A-Z)
      LOGICAL LFUSES(40,80),LBLANK,LLEFT,LAND,LOR,LSLASH,
     1        LEQUAL,LRIGHT,LXOR
      COMMON  LBLANK,LLEFT,LAND,LOR,LSLASH,LEQUAL,LRIGHT,LXOR
      COMMON /BLK/ PR8X10(10,14),PROD8(8,11),PRODLN(40,7)
      DATA P/'P'/,N/'N'/
      FUSPTR=1
      DO 30 OUTPUT=1,10
         GRTYPE=PR8X10(OUTPUT,ITYPE)
         DO 30 PRLINE=1,8
            LNTYPE=PROD8(PRLINE,GRTYPE)
            DO 20 COL=1,40
               IF(PRODLN(COL,LNTYPE).EQ.P)
     1            LFUSES(COL,FUSPTR)=.TRUE.
               IF(PRODLN(COL,LNTYPE).EQ.N)
     1            LFUSES(COL,FUSPTR)=.FALSE.
   20       CONTINUE
            FUSPTR=FUSPTR+1
   30 CONTINUE
      RETURN
      END
C
```

```
C***********************************************************************
C
      SUBROUTINE BINR(LFUSES,H,L)
C     THIS SUBROUTINE GENERATES BINARY PROGRAMMING FORMATS
      IMPLICIT INTEGER (A-Z)
      INTEGER ITEMP(5,10)
      LOGICAL LFUSES(40,80)
      COMMON /LUNIT/ PMS,POF,PDF
      WRITE(PDF,10)
   10 FORMAT(//,'
      DO 20 I=1,41,40
      INC=I-1
        DO 20 IPROD=1,8
            DO 20 J=1,31,10
              DO 15 K=1,10
                IINPUT=J+K-1
                ITEMP(1,K)=L
                ITEMP(2,K)=L
                ITEMP(3,K)=L
                ITEMP(4,K)=L
                ITEMP(5,K)=L
                ISUM3=IPROD+INC
                IF(LFUSES(IINPUT,ISUM3 +  0 )) ITEMP(5,K)=H
                IF(LFUSES(IINPUT,ISUM3 +  8 )) ITEMP(4,K)=H
                IF(LFUSES(IINPUT,ISUM3 + 16 )) ITEMP(3,K)=H
                IF(LFUSES(IINPUT,ISUM3 + 24 )) ITEMP(2,K)=H
                IF(LFUSES(IINPUT,ISUM3 + 32 )) ITEMP(1,K)=H
   15           CONTINUE
   20         WRITE(PDF,30) ITEMP
   30         FORMAT(' ',10('B',5A1,'F '))
      WRITE(PDF,10)
      RETURN
      END
C
C***********************************************************************
C
      SUBROUTINE SLIP(LFUSES,I88PRO,ITYPE,IBLOW)
C     THIS SUBROUTINE WILL BLOW THE ENTIRE CONDITIONAL THREE-STATE
C      PRODUCT LINE WHEN 'IF(VCC)' CONDITION IS USED FOR THE
C      CORRESPONDING OUTPUT PIN
      IMPLICIT INTEGER (A-Z)
      INTEGER IENABL(10,14)
      LOGICAL LFUSES(40,80)
C     1=ENABLED OUTPUT.   0=ANYTHING ELSE FOR THAT OUTPUT
      DATA IENABL/
     1     0,0,0,0,0,0,0,0,0,0,
     2     0,0,0,0,0,0,0,0,0,0,
     3     0,0,0,0,0,0,0,0,0,0,
     4     0,0,0,0,0,0,0,0,0,0,
     5     0,0,0,0,0,0,0,0,0,0,
     6     0,0,0,0,0,0,0,0,0,0,
     7     1,1,1,1,1,1,1,1,1,1,
     8     0,0,0,0,0,0,0,0,0,0,
     9     1,0,0,0,0,0,0,0,0,1,
     A     1,1,1,0,0,0,0,1,1,1,
     B     0,1,1,1,1,1,1,1,1,0,
```

```
     C     0,0,0,0,0,0,0,0,0,0,
     D     0,1,0,0,0,0,0,0,1,0,
     E     0,1,1,0,0,0,0,1,1,0/
      IOUT=(I88PRO-1)/8+1
      IF(IENABL(IOUT,ITYPE).EQ.0) RETURN
      DO 10 I=1,40
      IBLOW = IBLOW + 1
   10 LFUSES(I,I88PRO) = .TRUE.
      I88PRO = I88PRO + 1
      RETURN
      END
C
C***********************************************************************
C
      SUBROUTINE FANTOM(ITYPE,IOP,IOUT,IPROD,I8PRO)
C     THIS SUBROUTINE UPDATES IOUT (THE PRINTED FUSE PLOT)
C      FOR HIGH AND LOW PHANTOM FUSES
      IMPLICIT INTEGER (A-Z)
      INTEGER IOUT(64)
      LOGICAL LBLANK,LLEFT,LAND,LOR,LSLASH,LEQUAL,LRIGHT,LXOR
      COMMON  LBLANK,LLEFT,LAND,LOR,LSLASH,LEQUAL,LRIGHT,LXOR
      COMMON /BLK/ PR8X10(10,14),PROD8(8,11),PRODLN(40,7)
      DATA B/'B'/,N/'N'/,P/'P'/,LOFANT/'0'/,HIFANT/'O'/,IBLANK/' '/
C     GET OUTPUT GROUPING
      OUTPUT=(IPROD-1)/8+1
      GRTYPE=PR8X10(OUTPUT,ITYPE)
      LNTYPE=PROD8(I8PRO,GRTYPE)
      DO 10 COL=1,40
         IF( PRODLN(COL,LNTYPE).EQ.P.AND.IOP.EQ.P ) IOUT(COL)=HIFANT
         IF( PRODLN(COL,LNTYPE).EQ.P.AND.IOP.EQ.B ) IOUT(COL)=IBLANK
         IF( PRODLN(COL,LNTYPE).EQ.N )              IOUT(COL)=LOFANT
   10 CONTINUE
      RETURN
      END
C
C***********************************************************************
C
      SUBROUTINE IODC2
C***** THIS ROUTINE IS OPTIONAL, IT MAY BE USED TO TURN PERIPHERALS ON
      IMPLICIT INTEGER (A-Z)
      CHARACTER BEL,DC2
      COMMON /LUNIT/ PMS,POF,PDF
      DATA BEL/007/,DC2/022/
      WRITE(PDF,10) DC2,BEL
   10 FORMAT(' ',2A1)
      RETURN
      END
C
C***********************************************************************
C
      SUBROUTINE IODC4
C***** THIS ROUTINE IS OPTIONAL, IT MAY BE USED TO TURN PERIPHERALS OFF
      IMPLICIT INTEGER (A-Z)
      CHARACTER BEL,DC3,DC4
      DATA BEL/007/,DC3/023/,DC4/024/
      WRITE(PDF,10) BEL,DC3,DC4
```

```
   10 FORMAT(' ',3A1)
      RETURN
      END
C
C***********************************************************************
C
      SUBROUTINE TEST(LPHASE,LBUF,TITLE,IC,IL,ILE,ISYM,IBUF,ITYPE,
     1                IPCTR,LERR,ISAF,IPCTR1,LSA11,LSA01)
C     THIS SUBROUTINE PERFORMS THE FUNCTION TABLE SIMULATION
C      AND GENERATES TEST VECTORS
      IMPLICIT INTEGER (A-Z)
      INTEGER ISYM(8,24),ISYM1(8,24),IBUF(8,24),IVECT(24),IVECTP(24),
     1        ISTATE(24),ISTATT(24),IPIN(24),TITLE(80),IPCTR
      LOGICAL LBLANK,LLEFT,LAND,LOR,LSLASH,LEQUAL,LRIGHT,LXOR,LSAME,
     1        XORFND,LERR,LPHASE(24),LPHAS1(24),LBUF(24),LOUT(24),
     2        LOUTP(24),LCLOCK,LPTRST,LCTRST,LENABL(24),NREG,
     3        LSA11,LSA12,LSA01,LSA02
      CHARACTER BEL
      COMMON  LBLANK,LLEFT,LAND,LOR,LSLASH,LEQUAL,LRIGHT,LXOR
      COMMON /PGE/ IPAGE(80,200)
      COMMON /LUNIT/ PMS,POF,PDF
      COMMON /FTEST/ IFUNCT,IDESC,IEND
      DATA IDASH/'-'/,L/'L'/,H/'H'/,X/'X'/,C/'C'/,Z/'Z'/,N0/'0'/,
     1     N1/'1'/,ERR/'?'/,IBLANK/' '/,COMENT/';'/
      DATA BEL/007/
C     PRINT AN ERROR MESSAGE IF NO FUNCTION TABLE IS SUPPLIED
      IF(IFUNCT.NE.0) GO TO 3
      WRITE(PMS,2)
    2 FORMAT(/,' FUNCTION TABLE MUST BE SUPPLIED IN ORDER TO PERFORM',
     1          ' SIMULATION')
      RETURN
C     PRINT TITLE
    3 IF((.NOT.LSA11).AND.(.NOT.LSA01)) WRITE(POF,4) TITLE
    4 FORMAT(/,' ',80A1,/)
C     INITIALIZE LERR (FUNCTION TABLE ERROR FLAG) TO NO ERROR
      LERR=.FALSE.
C     INITIALIZE NERR (NUMBER OF FUNCTION TABLE ERRORS) TO NO ERROR
      NERR=0
C     SET THE STARTING POINT OF THE FUNCTION TABLE TO COLUMN 0
C      AND IFUNCT + 1
      IC=0
      IL=IFUNCT + 1
C     INITIALISE SA1/SA0 PARAMETERS
      IPCTR3=0
      IEQN=0
      IPCTR=0
C     INITIALIZE ITRST (THREE-STATE ENABLE FUNCTION TABLE PIN NUMBER)
      ITRST=0
C     MAKE A DUMMY CALL TO INCR
      CALL INCR(IC,IL)
C     GET THE FUNCTION TABLE PIN LIST (UP TO 22)
C      GO ONE MORE THAN MAX TO LOOK FOR DASHED LINE
      DO 10 I=1,23
      CALL GETSYM(LPHAS1,ISYM1,I,IC,IL)
         DO 5 J=1,8
    5    IBUF(J,1)=ISYM1(J,I)
```

```
      IF(IBUF(8,1).EQ.IDASH) GO TO 12
      CALL MATCH(IMATCH,IBUF,ISYM)
      IF(IMATCH.NE.0) GO TO 7
      WRITE(PMS,6) (IBUF(J,1),J=1,8)
    6 FORMAT(/,' FUNCTION TABLE PIN LIST ERROR AT', 8A1)
      RETURN
    7 LOUT(I)=.FALSE.
      ISTATT(I)=X
      IVECTP(I)=X
C     IF APPROPIATE PAL TYPE, REMEMBER LOCATION OF CLOCK AND THREE-STATE
C      ENABLE PIN IN FUNCTION TABLE PIN LIST
      IF( .NOT.(ITYPE.EQ.8.OR.ITYPE.EQ.9.OR.ITYPE.EQ.10.OR.
     1          ITYPE.EQ.12.OR.ITYPE.EQ.13.OR.ITYPE.EQ.14) ) GO TO 10
      IF(IMATCH.EQ.1)  ICLOCK=I
      IF(IMATCH.EQ.13) ITRST=I
   10 IPIN(I)=IMATCH
C     ALL SIGNAL NAMES FOR THE FUNCTIONAL TEST HAVE BEEN READ IN
C      ADJUST COUNT
   12 IMAX=I-1
      NVECT=0
C
C*****START OF MAIN LOOP FOR SIMULATION*****
C
C
   90 IPCTR2=0
      IEQN=0
      IPCTR3=0
      LSA12=.FALSE.
      LSA02=.FALSE.
      NVECT=NVECT+1
      IC1=0
      IL1=ILE
C     GO PASSED COMMENT LINES
   23 IF(IPAGE(1,IL).NE.COMENT) GO TO 24
      IL=IL+1
      GO TO 23
   24 CONTINUE
C     GETS VECTORS FROM FUNCTION TABLE
      DO 20 I=1,IMAX
        IF(IPAGE(IC,IL).EQ.IBLANK) GO TO 21
        GO TO 22
   21   IC=IC+1
        IF(IPAGE(IC,IL).EQ.IBLANK) GO TO 21
   22   IVECT(I)=IPAGE(IC,IL)
        IC=IC+1
   20 CONTINUE
C     ADVANCE LINE COUNT TO SKIP FUNCTION TABLE COMMENTS
      IL=IL+1
      IC=1
      IF(IVECT(1).EQ.IDASH) GO TO 95
C     CHECK FOR VALID FUNCTION TABLE VALUES (L,H,X,Z,C)
      DO 11 I=1,IMAX
         IF( IVECT(I).EQ.L.OR.IVECT(I).EQ.H.OR.IVECT(I).EQ.X.OR.
     1         IVECT(I).EQ.Z.OR.IVECT(I).EQ.C) GO TO 11
         WRITE(PMS,8) IVECT(I),NVECT
    8    FORMAT(/,' ',A1,' IS NOT AN ALLOWED FUNCTION TABLE ENTRY',
```

```
     1                    ' IN VECTOR ',I3)
          RETURN
   11 CONTINUE
C     INITIALIZE CLOCK AND THREE-STATE ENABLE FLAGS
      LCLOCK=.FALSE.
      LCTRST=.TRUE.
      LPTRST=.TRUE.
      DO 13 I=1,IMAX
   13    LENABL(I)=.TRUE.
C     INITIALIZE NREG (NOT REGISTERED OUTPUT) TO FALSE
      NREG=.FALSE.
C     INITIALIZE ISTATE ARRAY TO ALL X'S
      DO 15 I=1,24
   15 ISTATE(I)=X
C     CHECK IF THIS PAL TYPE HAS REGISTERS
      IF( .NOT.(ITYPE.EQ.8.OR.ITYPE.EQ.9.OR.ITYPE.EQ.10.OR.
     1          ITYPE.EQ.12.OR.ITYPE.EQ.13.OR.ITYPE.EQ.14) ) GO TO 25
C     CHECK CLOCK AND THREE-STATE ENABLE PINS AND CHANGE FLAG IF NEEDED
      IF(IVECT(ICLOCK).EQ.C) LCLOCK=.TRUE.
      IF(ITRST.EQ.0) GO TO 25
      LSAME=( (     LPHASE(13)).AND.(     LPHAS1(ITRST)).OR.
     1        (.NOT.LPHASE(13)).AND.(.NOT.LPHAS1(ITRST)) )
      IF( IVECT(ITRST).EQ.L.AND.(.NOT.LSAME).OR.
     1    IVECT(ITRST).EQ.H.AND.(     LSAME) ) LPTRST=.FALSE.
      IF(LPTRST) GO TO 25
C     DISABLE REGISTERED OUTPUTS IF APPROPRIATE
      DO 46 I=1,IMAX
         J=IPIN(I)
         IF(J.EQ.17.OR.J.EQ.18.OR.J.EQ.19.OR.J.EQ.20) LENABL(I)=.FALSE.
         IF( (ITYPE.EQ.8.OR.ITYPE.EQ.9.OR.ITYPE.EQ.12.OR.
     1        ITYPE.EQ.13).AND.(J.EQ.16.OR.J.EQ.21) ) LENABL(I)=.FALSE.
         IF( (ITYPE.EQ.8.OR.ITYPE.EQ.9.OR.ITYPE.EQ.12).AND.
     1       (J.EQ.15.OR.J.EQ.22) )                   LENABL(I)=.FALSE.
         IF(  ITYPE.EQ.8.AND.(J.EQ.14.OR.J.EQ.23) )   LENABL(I)=.FALSE.
   46 CONTINUE
C
C*****SCAN THROUGH THE LOGIC EQUATIONS*****
C
C     MAKE A DUMMY CALL TO INCR
   25 CALL INCR(IC1,IL1)
   26 CALL GETSYM(LBUF,IBUF,1,IC1,IL1)
      IF(LLEFT) GO TO 29
   27 IF(.NOT.LEQUAL) GO TO 26
      IF(LEQUAL) IEQN=IEQN+1
C     EVALUATE CONDITIONAL THREE-STATE PRODUCT LINE
   29 IF(LEQUAL) GO TO 35
      NREG=.TRUE.
   33 CALL GETSYM(LBUF,IBUF,1,IC1,IL1)
      CALL MATCH(IINP,IBUF,ISYM1)
C     CHECK FOR GND, VCC, /GND, OR /VCC IN CONDITIONAL THREE-STATE
C     PRODUCT LINE
      IF(IINP.NE.0) GO TO 32
      CALL MATCH(IMATCH,IBUF,ISYM)
      ILL=IL1
      IF( IMATCH.EQ.12.AND.(LBUF(1)).OR.
     1    IMATCH.EQ.24.AND.(.NOT.LBUF(1)) ) LCTRST=.FALSE.
```

```
      IF( IINP.EQ.0.AND.IMATCH.NE.12.AND.IMATCH.NE.24 ) GO TO 100
      GO TO 34
   32 ITEST=IVECT(IINP)
      IF(  ITEST.EQ.L.AND.(      LPHAS1(IINP)).AND.(      LBUF(1))
     1.OR. ITEST.EQ.H.AND.(      LPHAS1(IINP)).AND.(.NOT.LBUF(1))
     2.OR. ITEST.EQ.H.AND.(.NOT.LPHAS1(IINP)).AND.(      LBUF(1))
     3.OR. ITEST.EQ.L.AND.(.NOT.LPHAS1(IINP)).AND.(.NOT.LBUF(1))
     4  )  LCTRST=.FALSE.
      IF(ITEST.EQ.X.OR.ITEST.EQ.Z) LCTRST=.FALSE.
   34 IF(LAND) GO TO 33
      GO TO 27
C
C     EVALUATE THE LOGIC EQUATION
C     FIND PIN NUMBER OF THE OUTPUT VECTORS
   35 IPCTR3=0
      CALL MATCH(IOUTP,IBUF,ISYM1)
C     FLAG FOR UNREGISTERED OUTPUTS
      CALL MATCH(IOUT,IBUF,ISYM)
      IF(ITYPE.LE.7.OR.ITYPE.EQ.11) NREG=.TRUE.
      IF( (ITYPE.EQ.9.OR.ITYPE.EQ.10).AND.(IOUT.EQ.14.OR.IOUT.EQ.23) )
     1      NREG=.TRUE.
      IF( (ITYPE.EQ.10.OR.ITYPE.EQ.13.OR.ITYPE.EQ.14).AND.
     1     (IOUT.EQ.15.OR.IOUT.EQ.22) ) NREG=.TRUE.
      IF( (ITYPE.EQ.10.OR.ITYPE.EQ.14).AND.(IOUT.EQ.16.OR.IOUT.EQ.21) )
     1      NREG=.TRUE.
      ILL=IL1
      IF(IOUTP.EQ.0) GO TO 100
      IF(NREG) LENABL(IOUTP)=LCTRST
      LOUT(IOUTP)=.TRUE.
      IF( .NOT.LCTRST ) LOUT(IOUTP)=.FALSE.
      LCTRST=.TRUE.
      LOUTP(IOUTP)=LBUF(1)
C     DETERMINE PRODUCT TERM AND EVENTUALLY SUM FOR OUTPUT KEEPING
C      TRACK TO SEE IF AN XOR (EXCLUSIVE OR) HAS BEEN FOUND
      XORSUM=H
      XORFND=.FALSE.
      ISUM=L
   28 IPCTR2=IPCTR2+1
      IPCTR3=IPCTR3+1
      IPCTR=IPCTR+1
      IPROD=H
   30 ILL=IL1
      CALL GETSYM(LBUF,IBUF,1,IC1,IL1)
      CALL MATCH(IINP,IBUF,ISYM1)
      IF(IINP.NE.0) GO TO 47
      CALL MATCH(IMATCH,IBUF,ISYM)
      IF(IMATCH.NE.12.AND.IMATCH.NE.24) GO TO 100
C     TWEEK FOR GND AND VCC IN PRODUCT LINE
      IF(IMATCH.EQ.12) ITEST=L
      IF(IMATCH.EQ.24) ITEST=H
      IINP=23
      LPHAS1(23)=.TRUE.
      GO TO 37
   47 ITEST=IVECT(IINP)
C     GET REGISTERED FEED BACK VALUES
      IF(NREG) GO TO 37
```

```
      CALL MATCH(IIFB,IBUF,ISYM)
      IF( (ITYPE.EQ.8.OR.ITYPE.EQ.9.OR.ITYPE.EQ.10.OR.ITYPE.EQ.12.OR.
     1      ITYPE.EQ.13.OR.ITYPE.EQ.14).AND.(IIFB.EQ.17.OR.IIFB.EQ.18.OR.
     2      IIFB.EQ.19.OR.IIFB.EQ.20) ) ITEST=IVECTP(IINP)
      IF( (ITYPE.EQ.8.OR.ITYPE.EQ.9.OR.ITYPE.EQ.12.OR.ITYPE.EQ.13).AND.
     1     (IIFB.EQ.16.OR.IIFB.EQ.21) ) ITEST=IVECTP(IINP)
      IF( (ITYPE.EQ.8.OR.ITYPE.EQ.9.OR.ITYPE.EQ.12).AND.
     1     (IIFB.EQ.15.OR.IIFB.EQ.22) ) ITEST=IVECTP(IINP)
      IF(  ITYPE.EQ.8.AND.(IIFB.EQ.14.OR.IIFB.EQ.23) )
     1                                 ITEST=IVECTP(IINP)
   37 IF(ITEST.EQ.X.OR.ITEST.EQ.Z) ITEST=L
      IF(  ITEST.EQ.L.AND.(      LPHAS1(IINP)).AND.(      LBUF(1))
     1.OR. ITEST.EQ.H.AND.(      LPHAS1(IINP)).AND.(.NOT.LBUF(1))
     2.OR. ITEST.EQ.H.AND.(.NOT.LPHAS1(IINP)).AND.(      LBUF(1))
     3.OR. ITEST.EQ.L.AND.(.NOT.LPHAS1(IINP)).AND.(.NOT.LBUF(1))
     4  )  IPROD=L
      IF((IPCTR2.EQ.IPCTR1).AND.(LSA11)) GO TO 110
   38 IF(LAND) GO TO 30
      IF ((IPCTR2.EQ.IPCTR1).AND.(LSA01)) GO TO 120
  121 IF(ISUM.EQ.L.AND.IPROD.EQ.X) ISUM=X
      IF( (ISUM.NE.H).AND.IPROD.EQ.H ) ISUM=H
C     CHECK FOR XOR (EXCLUSIVE OR) AND SAVE INTERMEDIATE VALUE
      IF(.NOT.LXOR) GO TO 31
      XORSUM=ISUM
      XORFND=.TRUE.
      ISUM=L
      GO TO 28
   31 IF(LOR) GO TO 28
      IPCTR3=0
C     IF END OF EQUATION HAS BEEN FOUND, DETERMINE FINAL SUM AND SAVE IT
      IF(.NOT.XORFND)    ISTATT(IOUTP)=ISUM
      IF( (XORFND).AND.((ISUM.EQ.L.AND.XORSUM.EQ.L).OR.
     1                  (ISUM.EQ.H.AND.XORSUM.EQ.H)) ) ISTATT(IOUTP)=L
      IF( (XORFND).AND.((ISUM.EQ.H.AND.XORSUM.EQ.L).OR.
     1                  (ISUM.EQ.L.AND.XORSUM.EQ.H)) ) ISTATT(IOUTP)=H
      IF( (XORFND).AND.  (ISUM.EQ.X.OR. XORSUM.EQ.X) )  ISTATT(IOUTP)=X
C     REGISTER DOES NOT CHANGE STATE IF NO CLOCK PULSE IS RECEIVED
      IF( (LCLOCK).OR.(NREG) ) GO TO 36
      LSAME = ( (      LOUTP(IOUTP)).AND.(      LPHAS1(IOUTP)).OR.
     1          (.NOT.LOUTP(IOUTP)).AND.(.NOT.LPHAS1(IOUTP)) )
      IF( IVECTP(IOUTP).EQ.L.AND.(      LSAME) ) ISTATT(IOUTP)=L
      IF( IVECTP(IOUTP).EQ.H.AND.(      LSAME) ) ISTATT(IOUTP)=H
      IF( IVECTP(IOUTP).EQ.L.AND.(.NOT.LSAME) ) ISTATT(IOUTP)=H
      IF( IVECTP(IOUTP).EQ.H.AND.(.NOT.LSAME) ) ISTATT(IOUTP)=L
   36 NREG=.FALSE.
C     CHECK IF ALL EQUATIONS HAVE BEEN PROCESSED BY COMPARING CURRENT
C      LINE NUMBER WITH FUNCTION TABLE LINE NUMBER
      IF(IDESC.NE.0.AND.IL1.LT.IFUNCT.AND.IL1.LT.IDESC.OR.
     1   IDESC.EQ.0.AND.IL1.LT.IFUNCT) GO TO 27
C     DETERMINE OUTPUT LOGIC VALUES
C      COMPARE OUTPUTS TO SEE IF VECTOR AGREES WITH RESULTS
      DO 50 I=1,IMAX
      IF(.NOT.LOUT(I)) GO TO 50
      IF(ISTATT(I).EQ.X.AND.IVECT(I).EQ.X) GO TO 50
      LSAME = ( (      LOUTP(I)).AND.(      LPHAS1(I)).OR.
     1          (.NOT.LOUTP(I)).AND.(.NOT.LPHAS1(I)) )
```

```
      IMESS=40
      IF(ISTATT(I).EQ.L.AND.IVECT(I).EQ.L.AND.(.NOT.LSAME))   IMESS=41
      IF(ISTATT(I).EQ.H.AND.IVECT(I).EQ.H.AND.(.NOT.LSAME))   IMESS=42
      IF(ISTATT(I).EQ.L.AND.IVECT(I).EQ.H.AND.(     LSAME))   IMESS=42
      IF(ISTATT(I).EQ.H.AND.IVECT(I).EQ.L.AND.(     LSAME))   IMESS=41
      IF( (      LENABL(I)).AND.IVECT(I).EQ.Z )               IMESS=43
      IF( (.NOT.LENABL(I)).AND.(LOUT(I)).AND.IVECT(I).NE.Z ) IMESS=44
      IF(IMESS.NE.40) LERR=.TRUE.
      IF((.NOT.LERR).AND.((LSA11).OR.(LSA01))) GO TO 50
      IF((LERR).AND.((LSA11).OR.(LSA01))) GO TO 115
      IF(IMESS.EQ.41) WRITE(PMS,41) NVECT,(ISYM1(J,I),J=1,8)
   41 FORMAT(/,' FUNCTION TABLE ERROR IN VECTOR',I3,'  PIN =',8A1,
     1         '  EXPECT = H  ACTUAL = L')
      IF(IMESS.EQ.42) WRITE(PMS,42) NVECT,(ISYM1(J,I),J=1,8)
   42 FORMAT(/,' FUNCTION TABLE ERROR IN VECTOR',I3,'  PIN =',8A1,
     1         '  EXPECT = L  ACTUAL = H')
      IF(IMESS.EQ.43) WRITE(PMS,43) NVECT,(ISYM1(J,I),J=1,8)
   43 FORMAT(/,' FUNCTION TABLE ERROR IN VECTOR',I3,'  PIN =',8A1,
     1       /,'  EXPECT  = OUTPUT ENABLE  ACTUAL = Z')
      IF(IMESS.EQ.44) WRITE(PMS,44) NVECT,(ISYM1(J,I),J=1,8),IVECT(I)
   44 FORMAT(/,' FUNCTION TABLE ERROR IN VECTOR',I3,'  PIN =',8A1,
     1         '  EXPECT = Z  ACTUAL = ',A1)
      IF( (IMESS.NE.40).AND.(PMS.EQ.6) ) WRITE(PMS,45) BEL
   45 FORMAT(' ',A1)
      IF(IMESS.NE.40) IVECT(I)=ERR
      IF(IMESS.NE.40) NERR=NERR+1
   50 CONTINUE
C     CHANGE THE ORDER OF VECTORS FROM THE ORDER OF APPEARANCE IN THE
C      FUNCTION TABLE TO THAT OF THE PIN LIST AND TWEEK FOR OUTPUT
      DO 65 I=1,24
         DO 55 J=1,IMAX
         IF(IPIN(J).NE.I) GO TO 55
         IF( IVECT(J).EQ.L.OR.IVECT(J).EQ.H ) GO TO 51
         ISTATE(I)=IVECT(J)
         GO TO 65
   51    LSAME=( (      LPHASE(I)).AND.(      LPHAS1(J)).OR.
     1           (.NOT.LPHASE(I)).AND.(.NOT.LPHAS1(J)) )
         IF( ITYPE.EQ.6.AND.(I.EQ.18.OR.I.EQ.19) )  LOUT(J)=.TRUE.
         IF( (.NOT.LOUT(J)).AND.(      LSAME).AND.
     1         IVECT(J).EQ.L )                      ISTATE(I)=N0
         IF( (.NOT.LOUT(J)).AND.(      LSAME).AND.
     1         IVECT(J).EQ.H )                      ISTATE(I)=N1
         IF( (.NOT.LOUT(J)).AND.(.NOT.LSAME).AND.
     1         IVECT(J).EQ.L )                      ISTATE(I)=N1
         IF( (.NOT.LOUT(J)).AND.(.NOT.LSAME).AND.
     1         IVECT(J).EQ.H )                      ISTATE(I)=N0
         IF( (      LOUT(J)).AND.(      LSAME).AND.
     1         IVECT(J).EQ.L.AND.(      LENABL(J)) ) ISTATE(I)=L
         IF( (      LOUT(J)).AND.(      LSAME).AND.
     1         IVECT(J).EQ.H.AND.(      LENABL(J)) ) ISTATE(I)=H
         IF( (      LOUT(J)).AND.(.NOT.LSAME).AND.
     1         IVECT(J).EQ.L.AND.(      LENABL(J)) ) ISTATE(I)=H
         IF( (      LOUT(J)).AND.(.NOT.LSAME).AND.
     1         IVECT(J).EQ.H.AND.(      LENABL(J)) ) ISTATE(I)=L
         IF( IVECT(J).EQ.ERR )                      ISTATE(I)=ERR
         GO TO 65
```

```
   55 CONTINUE
C     SAVE PRESENT VECTORS FOR FEED BACK USED WITH NEXT SET OF VECTORS
C      IF CLOCK PULSE AND NOT Z (HI-Z IS ASYNCHRONOUS)
   65 IF( (LCLOCK).AND.IVECT(J).NE.Z ) IVECTP(J)=IVECT(J)
C     ASSIGN X TO GROUND PIN AND 1 TO VCC PIN
      ISTATE(12)=X
      ISTATE(24)=N1
C     PRINT TEST VECTORS
      IF((.NOT.LSA11).AND.(.NOT.LSA01)) WRITE(POF,60) NVECT,
     1   (ISTATE(I),I=1,24)
   60 FORMAT(' ',I3,' ',24A1)
      GO TO 90
C     TERMINATE SIMULATION
   95 IF((.NOT.LERR).AND.(LSA11)) WRITE(POF,150) IPCTR4,IEQN1
  150 FORMAT(' ',' PRODUCT: ',I3,' OF ','EQUATION',I3,
     1 ' UNTESTED(SA1) FAULT')
      IF((.NOT.LERR).AND.(LSA01)) WRITE(POF,155) IPCTR4,IEQN1
  155 FORMAT(' ',' PRODUCT: ',I3,' OF ','EQUATION',I3,
     1 ' UNTESTED(SA0) FAULT')
      IF((.NOT.LERR).AND.((.NOT.LSA11).AND.(.NOT.LSA01))) WRITE(POF,67)
   67 FORMAT(/,' PASS SIMULATION')
      IPCTR=IPCTR/(NVECT-1)
      IF((      LERR).AND.((.NOT.LSA11).AND.(.NOT.LSA01)))
     1WRITE(POF,68) NERR
   68 FORMAT(/,' NUMBER OF FUNCTION TABLE ERRORS =',I3)
      RETURN
C     PRINT AN ERROR MESSAGE FOR AN UNDEFINED PIN NAME
  100 ILERR=ILL+4
      WRITE(PMS,101) (IBUF(I,1),I=1,8),ILERR,(IPAGE(I,ILL),I=1,80)
  101 FORMAT(/,' ERROR SYMBOL =  ',8A1,'       IN LINE NUMBER ',I3,
     1       /,' ',80A1,/,' THIS PIN NAME IS NOT DEFINED IN THE',
     2                    ' FUNCTION TABLE PIN LIST')
      RETURN
  110 IPROD=H
      LSA12=.TRUE.
      IEQN1=IEQN
      IPCTR4=IPCTR3
      GO TO 38
  120 IPROD=L
      LSA02=.TRUE.
      IEQN1=IEQN
      IPCTR4=IPCTR3
      GO TO   121
  115 ISAF=ISAF+1
      LERR=.FALSE.
      RETURN
      END
```

```
500 PRINTTAB(22)"PALASM-20 IN BASIC":PRINT:PRINT"REVISION LEVEL 2.15";
510 PRINTTAB(38)"01/16/80       DJ":PRINT
520 PRINT"WELCOME TO PALASM-20.  THE SOURCE CODE FOR THIS PROGRAM"
530 PRINT"WAS WRITTEN IN BASIC ON AN 8-BIT MICROCOMPUTER.  IT IS"
540 PRINT"INTENDED TO BE USED ON A DISK SYSTEM ONLY.  THE OUTPUTS"
550 PRINT"ARE DUMPED TO DISK FILES NAMED BY THE OPERATOR.  USE YOUR"
560 PRINT"STANDARD SYSTEM INSTRUCTIONS TO PRINT, LIST, OR ";
570 PRINT"DUMP TO AN":PRINT"RS232 PORT."
580 PRINT"":PRINT"PLEASE REFERE TO THE PAL INFORMATION BY MONOLITHIC"
590 PRINT"MEMORIES, INC. FOR ANY QUESTIONS REGARDING THE FORMAT OR"
600 PRINT"DESIGN SPECIFICATIONS AS USED BY THIS PROGRAM."
610 PRINT"":INPUT"PRESS <RETURN> TO CONTINUE...";A$
620 PRINT"":PRINT"     THIS PROGRAM CAN BE RUN IN EITHER THE"
630 PRINT"COMPILED OR INTERPRETED MODES.  THE ONLY DIFFERENCE"
640 PRINT"SHOULD BE THE SPEED OF OPERATION.":PRINT""
650 PRINT:PRINT"FINE PRINT:"
660 PRINT"THIS PROGRAM IS DISTRIBUTED ON AN 'AS IS' BASIS."
670 PRINT"IT WAS TRANSLATED FROM A FORTRAN IV PROGRAM"
680 PRINT"AND EVERY EFFORT WAS TAKEN TO INSURE ITS ACCURACY."
690 PRINT"HOWEVER, THE USER SHOULD ALSO VERIFY ITS ACCURACY"
700 PRINT"AND COMPLETENESS. ":PRINT"":PRINT""
710 PRINT:INPUT"PRESS <RETURN> TO BEGIN PROGRAM...";A$
1000 A$="":FORX%=1TO16:PRINT"":NEXT:CLEAR1000:DEFINTC,F,H,N,O,T,X,Y,Z
1010 DIMF(31,63):DEFSTRA,D,L,P:DIMA(15),P(21),L(50):C=0:X$="":A$=""
1020 X=0:PRINT"ENTER 1 TO CREATE PAL DESIGN SPECIFICATION FILE FROM KEYBOARD"
1030 PRINT"ENTER 2 TO READ EXISTING PAL DESIGN SPECIFICATION FILE  ";
1040 INPUTX:X=ABS(X):ONXGOTO1060,1130
1050 GOTO1000
1060 PRINT:PRINT:PRINT"ENTER DESIGN SPEC FILENAME (FILENAME/EXT:D)"
1070 PRINT"ENTER 'END' (WITHOUT QUOTES) AFTER LAST LINE."
1080 PRINT"FILENAME ? ";:LINEINPUTA$
1090 OPEN"O",1,A$
1100 LINEINPUTA$
1110 IFA$="END"THEN1120ELSEPRINT#1,A$:GOTO1100
1120 CLOSE:GOTO1000
1130 ONERRORGOTO2260
1140 PRINT:PRINT:PRINT"ENTER FILENAME (FILENAME/EXT.PASSWORD:D) TO BE ";
1150 PRINT"ASSEMBLED ?":LINEINPUTF$
1160 X=1:OPEN"I",1,F$
1170 INPUT#1,A:L(X)=A:X=X+1:PRINTA
1180 IFEOF(1)THEN1190ELSE1170
1190 CLOSE1:NL=X
1200 ONERRORGOTO0
2000      REM *** VERIFY PART NUMBER AND GET TYPE ***
2010 A=L(1):TY=0
2020 X=INSTR(A,"PAL")
2030 OT$=MID$(A,X+5,1):P=MID$(A,X+6,1):P3%=VAL(P)
2040 PN=MID$(A,X,7):P=LEFT$(PN,3):IFP<>"PAL"THENGOTO2090ELSEP=MID$(PN,4,4)
2050 IFP="10H8"ORP="10L8"THENTY=1ELSEIFP="12H6"ORP="12L6"THENTY=2
2060 IFP="14H4"ORP="14L4"THENTY=3
2070 IFP="16H2"ORP="16L2"ORP="16C1"THENTY=4ELSEIFP="16L8"THENTY=5
2080 IFP="16R4"ORP="16R6"ORP="16R8"THENTY=6ELSEIFP="16A4"ORP="16X4"THENTY=7
2090 IFTY=0THENGOSUB7210:PRINT"INVALID PART NUMBER":END
```

```
2200        REM *** VERIFY PIN LIST ***
2210 LC%=5:Y=1:ONERRORGOTO2250
2220 A=L(LC%)+" ":C=LEN(A$):FORX=1TOC
2230 P$=MID$(A,X,1):IFP<>" "THENP(Y)=P(Y)+P ELSEY=Y+1
2240 NEXT:IFY=21THEN2270ELSEIFY<21THENLC%=LC%+1:GOTO2220
2250 GOSUB7210:PRINT"INVALID PIN LIST":END
2260 RESUME1130
2270 IFP(10)<>"GND"THENPRINT"ERROR CORRECTED... PIN 10 IS NOW ´GND´":P(10)="GND"
2280 IFP(20)<>"VCC"THENPRINT"ERROR CORRECTED... PIN 20 IS NOW ´VCC´":P(20)="VCC"
2290 ONERRORGOTO0:GOSUB5000
2400        REM *** FIND OUTPUT IN EQUATION ***
2410 OU=0:IFTY>4THENNO=8ELSENO=P3%
2420 LC%=LC%+1:A=L(LC%):IFLC%>NLTHEN4010
2430 FC=0:FS=0:FR=0:AT="":DL=")/ "
2440 CE=INSTR(A,"="):IFCE=0THEN2420
2450 OU=OU+1:IFOU>NO THEN3290
2460 AL=LEFT$(A,CE-1):CT=LEN(A):CN=CE
2470 CN=CN-1:IFCN=0THENGOTO2500
2480 P=MID$(A,CN,1):IFP=" "THEN2470ELSEIFP=":"THENFR=1:GOTO2470
2490 P=MID$(A,CN,1):IFINSTR(DL,P)=0THENAT=P+AT:CN=CN-1:IFCN<>0THEN2490
2500 FORZ=12TO19:IFAT=P(Z)ORP(Z)=("/"+AT)THENGOSUB4710:GOTO2520ELSENEXT
2510 GOSUB7210:PRINT"OUTPUT UNDEFINED BY PIN LIST":PRINT"#",A;"--(";AT;")":END
2520 IFY=0THENGOSUB7210:PRINT"INVALID OUTPUT PIN":PRINT"#";A;"--(";AT;")":END
2530 IFY>100THENFR=1:Y=Y-100ELSEIFY<0THENFC=1:Y=-YELSEFS=1
2540 Y=Y-1:GOSUB4410
2550 Y1=Y+NP
2560 IF(FS=1 OR FR=1)AND INSTR(AL,")")<>0THEN2590
2570 IFFC=1ANDINSTR(AL,")")=0THENY=Y+1:CN=CE+1:GOSUB4410:GOTO3050
2580 IFFC=1THEN2710ELSECN=CE+1:GOTO3050
2590 GOSUB7210:PRINT"EQUATION INVALID FOR THIS OUTPUT TYPE"
2600 PRINT"#";A;" PIN =";ZO:END
2700        REM **** THREE-STATE ENABLE ONLY ****
2710 IFINSTR(AL,"VCC")<>0THENCN=CE+1:Y=Y+1:GOSUB4410:GOTO3050
2720 CN=INSTR(AL,"("):CT=INSTR(AL,")"):IFCN=0ORCT=0THEN2590
2730 A=AL:CN=CN+1:CT=CT-1
2740 IFINSTR(A,"+")<>0THENGOSUB7210:PRINT"INVALID CONDITIONAL STATEMENT"
2750 IFINSTR(A,"+")<>0THENPRINT"#";A:END
2760 DL="(:)+*":AT=""
2770 IFCN>CTTHENGOTO2810
2780 P=MID$(A,CN,1):IFP=" "THENCN=CN+1:GOTO2770
2790 IFINSTR(DL,P)=0THENAT=AT+P:IFCN<>CTTHENCN=CN+1:GOTO2770
2800 GOSUB3200:GOTO2760
2810 Y=Y+1:A=L(LC%):CN=CE+1:CT=LEN(A)
2820 GOSUB4410
2830 GOTO3050
3000        REM *** INPUT PROCESSING FOR SIMPLE OUTPUTS ***
3010 LC%=LC%+1:A=L(LC%):IFLC%>NLTHEN4010:REM** RE-ENTRY POINT **
3020 IFINSTR(A,"DESCRIPTION")<>0THEN4010
3025 IFINSTR(A,"FUNCTION TABLE")<>0THEN4010
3030 CT=LEN(A):CN=1
3040 IFINSTR(A,"=")<>0THEN2430
3050 DL="(:)+* ":AT=""
3060 IFCN>CTTHEN3010
```

```
3070 P=MID$(A,CN,1):IFP=" "THENCN=CN+1:GOTO3060
3080 IFP="+"ANDAT<>""THENGOSUB3210:Y=Y+1:IFY>Y1THEN3150ELSEGOSUB4410:GOTO3050
3090 IFP="+"ANDAT=""THENCN=CN+1:Y=Y+1:IFY>Y1THEN3150ELSEGOSUB4410:GOTO3060
3100 IFP="*"THENGOSUB3210:GOTO3050
3110 IFTY=7AND(P="(" OR P=":")THEN9000
3120 IFP="(" OR P=")" OR P=":"THEN2590
3130 AT=AT+P:CN=CN+1
3140 IFCT=CN-1ANDAT<>""THENGOSUB3210:GOTO3060ELSEGOTO3060
3150 GOSUB7210:PRINT"EXCESSIVE NUMBER OF TERMS FOR THIS OUTPUT"
3160 PRINT"MAXIMUM NUMBER OF TERMS IS";NP;"FOR OUTPUT PIN";ZO:END
3200     REM *** INPUT MATCH AND SET FUSE ***
3210 FORZ=1TO20
3220 IFAT=P(Z)THENGOSUB3310:X=X-1:GOTO3280
3230 IFAT="/"+P(Z)THENGOSUB3310:GOTO3280
3240 IFASC(P(Z))=47ANDAT=MID$(P(Z),2)THENGOSUB3310:GOTO3280
3250 NEXT
3260 GOSUB7210:PRINT"INPUT UNDEFINED BY PIN LIST"
3270 PRINT"#";L(LC%);"--(";AT;")":END
3280 F(X,Y)=0:NB=NB-1:CN=CN+1:RETURN
3290 GOSUB7210:PRINT"EXCESSIVE NUMBER OF EQUATIONS GIVEN."
3300 PRINT"ONLY THE FIRST";NO;" WILL BE ASSEMBLED.";GOTO4010
3310 GOSUB4510:IFX<>0THENRETURNELSEGOSUB7210:PRINT"INVALID INPUT PIN"
3320 PRINT"#";A;"--(";AT;")":END
4000     REM **** OPTION SELECT ****
4010 PRINT"ENTER OPTION AT THIS TIME:"
4020 PRINT"X = X-PLOT (OVERLAY TO LOGIC DIAGRAM)"
4030 PRINT"H = HEX (ASCII HEX PROGRAMMER FORMAT)"
4040 PRINT"N = BPNF (ASCII PROGRAMMER FORMAT)"
4050 PRINT"L = BHLF (ASCII PROGRAMMER FORMAT)"
4060 PRINT"Q = QUIT (END PROGRAM)"
4070 PRINT"":INPUT"OPTION ";A2
4080 IFA2="X"THENGOSUB6010:GOTO4010
4090 IFA2="H"THENGOSUB7010:GOTO4010
4100 IFA2="N"THEND0="N":D1="P":GOSUB8010:GOTO4010
4110 IFA2="L"THEND0="L":D1="H":GOSUB8010:GOTO4010
4120 IFA2="Q"THENENDELSE4010
4400     REM *** INITZL PROD LINE WITH BLOWN FUSES ***
4410 FORX=0TO31:IFF(X,Y)=0THENF(X,Y)=1:NB=NB+1
4420 NEXT:RETURNELSENEXT:RETURN
4500      REM **** INPUT TABLE FUNCTION ****
4510 IFZ>1ANDZ<10THENX=(Z-2)*4+1:RETURN
4520 IFZ=10ORZ=20THENX=0:RETURN
4530 IF(TY<6ANDZ=1) OR (TY>5ANDZ=19) THENX=3:RETURN
4540 IF(TY<6ANDZ=11)OR(TY>5ANDZ=12)THENX=31:RETURN
4550 IFTY=1THENX=0:RETURN
4560 IF(TY<5ANDZ=12)OR(TY>4ANDZ=13)THENX=27:RETURN
4570 IF(TY<5ANDZ=19)OR(TY>4ANDZ=18)THENX=7:RETURN
4580 IFTY=2THENX=0:RETURN
4590 IF(TY<5ANDZ=13)OR(TY>4ANDZ=14)THENX=23:RETURN
4600 IF(TY<5ANDZ=18)OR(TY>4ANDZ=17)THENX=11:RETURN
4610 IFTY=3THENX=0:RETURN
4620 IFZ=14OR(TY>4ANDZ=15)THENX=19:RETURN
4630 IFZ=17OR(TY>4ANDZ=16)THENX=15:RETURN
4640 X=0:RETURN
4700      REM **** OUTPUT TABLE FUNCTION ****
```

```
4710 Y=(19-Z)*8+1:NP=0:ZO=Z
4720 IFY>57ORY<1THENY=0:RETURN
4730 IFTY=1THENNP=2:RETURN
4740 IFTY>4THENNP=8
4750 IFRIGHT$(PN,2)="R8"THENY=Y+100:RETURN
4760 IFTY=5THENY=-Y:RETURN
4770 IFTY>4AND(Z=12ORZ=19)THENY=-Y:RETURN
4780 IFRIGHT$(PN,2)="R6"THENY=Y+100:RETURN
4790 IFTY>4AND(Z=13ORZ=18)THENY=-Y:RETURN
4800 IFTY>5THENY=Y+100:RETURN
4810 IFZ=12ORZ=19THENY=0:RETURN
4820 IFTY=2AND(Z=13ORZ=18)THENNP=4:RETURN
4830 IFTY=2THENNP=2:RETURN
4840 IFZ=13ORZ=18THENY=0:RETURN
4850 IFTY=3THENNP=4:RETURN
4860 IFZ=14ORZ=17THENY=0:RETURN
4870 IFRIGHT$(PN,2)="C1"THENY=25:NP=16:RETURN
4880 NP=8:RETURN
5000      REM  **** VIRGIN FUSE PATTERN INITIALIZATION ****
5010 NB=0:ONTYGOTO5020,5060,5160,5240,5320,5320,5320
5020 FORY=0TO63STEP8:FORX=0TO31:F(X,Y)=0:F(X,Y+1)=0:F(X,Y+2)=2:F(X,Y+3)=2
5030 F(X,Y+4)=2:F(X,Y+5)=2:F(X,Y+6)=2:F(X,Y+7)=2:NEXTX,Y
5040 FORY=0TO57STEP8:FORX=6TO27STEP4:F(X,Y)=3:F(X+1,Y)=3:F(X,Y+1)=3
5050 F(X+1,Y+1)=3:NEXTX,Y:RETURN
5060 IFOT$="L"THENC=2ELSEC=3
5070 FORY=0TO63STEP56:FORX=0TO31:GOSUB5340:NEXTX,Y
5080 FORY=8TO55STEP8:FORX=0TO31:F(X,Y)=0:F(X,Y+1)=0:F(X,Y+4)=2
5090 F(X,Y+5)=2:F(X,Y+6)=2:F(X,Y+7)=2:NEXTX,Y
5100 FORX=0TO31:F(X,10)=0:F(X,11)=0:F(X,50)=0:F(X,51)=0:NEXTX
5110 FORY=18TO43STEP8:FORX=0TO31:F(X,Y)=2:F(X,Y+1)=2:NEXTX,Y
5120 FORY=8TO49STEP8:FORX=10TO23STEP4:F(X,Y)=3:F(X,Y+1)=3
5130 F(X+1,Y)=3:F(X+1,Y+1)=3:NEXTX,Y
5140 FORY=10TO51STEP40:FORX=10TO23STEP4:F(X,Y)=3:F(X,Y+1)=3
5150 F(X+1,Y)=3:F(X+1,Y+1)=3:NEXTX,Y:RETURN
5160 IFOT$="L"THENC=2ELSEC=3
5170 FORY=0TO63STEP8:IFY=16THENY=48
5180 FORX=0TO31:GOSUB5340:NEXTX,Y
5190 FORY=16TO47STEP8:FORX=0TO31:F(X,Y)=0:F(X,Y+1)=0:F(X,Y+2)=0
5200 F(X,Y+3)=0:F(X,Y+4)=2:F(X,Y+5)=2:F(X,Y+6)=2:F(X,Y+7)=2:NEXTX,Y
5210 FORY=16TO43STEP2:FORX=14TO19STEP4:IFY=20THENY=24ELSEIFY=28THENY=32
5220 IFY=36THENY=40
5230 F(X,Y)=3:F(X,Y+1)=3:F(X+1,Y)=3:F(X+1,Y+1)=3:NEXTX,Y:RETURN
5240 IFOT$="L"THENC=2ELSEC=3
5250 FORY=0TO23STEP8:FORX=0TO31:F(X,Y)=C:F(X,Y+1)=C:F(X,Y+2)=C
5260 GOSUB5340:NEXTX,Y
5270 IFOT$="H"THENC=3ELSEC=2
5280 FORY=40TO63STEP8:FORX=0TO31:GOSUB5340:NEXTX,Y
5290 C=0
5300 FORY=24TO39STEP8:FORX=0TO31:GOSUB5340:NEXTX,Y
5310 RETURN
5320 C=0:FORY=0TO63STEP8:FORX=0TO31:GOSUB5340:NEXTX,Y
5330 RETURN
5340 F(X,Y)=C:F(X,Y+1)=C:F(X,Y+2)=C:F(X,Y+3)=C:F(X,Y+4)=C
5350 F(X,Y+5)=C:F(X,Y+6)=C:F(X,Y+7)=C:RETURN
6000      REM **** X-PLOT FUNCTION ****
```

```
6010 A1="                 11 1111 1111 2222 2222 2233"
6020 A2="   0123 4567 8901 2345 6789 0123 4567 8901"
6030 A3="X = FUSE INTACT   (L,N,0)         - = FUSE BLOWN     (H,P,1)"
6040 A4="0 = PHANTOM FUSE  (L,N,0)         O = PHANTOM FUSE  (H,P,1)"
6050 ONERRORGOTO6900
6060 PRINT"ENTER FILENAME (FILENAME/EXT.PASSWORD:D) FOR X-PLOT OUTPUT ? "
6070 LINEINPUTX$
6080 OPEN"O",1,X$
6090 C=0:A(0)="X":A(1)="-":A(2)="0":A(3)="O":CLS:PRINTL(3):PRINT""
6100 ONERRORGOTO0
6110 FORX=1TO4:PRINT#1,L(X):NEXTX
6120 PRINT#1,"":PRINT#1,"NUMBER OF FUSES BLOWN =";NB:PRINT#1,""
6130 PRINT:PRINT"NUMBER OF FUSES BLOWN =";NB:PRINT
6140 PRINT#1,A1:PRINT#1,A2:PRINT#1," "
6150 IFC=64THENPRINT#1," ":PRINT#1,A3:PRINT#1,A4:A1="":A3="":A4="":CLOSE:RETURN
6160 PRINT:PRINTA1:PRINTA2:PRINT
6170 FORY=0TO7:GOSUB6200:NEXTY
6180 PRINT#1," ":PRINT:PRINT"LEGAND:":PRINTA3:PRINTA4
6190 FORX=0TO800:NEXTX:CLS:GOTO6150
6200 A=" ":FORX=0TO31STEP4:A=A+A(F(X,C))+A(F(X+1,C))+A(F(X+2,C))+A(F(X+3,C))+"
"
6210 NEXTX:PRINTUSING"##";C;:PRINTA
6220 PRINT#1,USING"##";C;:PRINT#1,A$:C=C+1:RETURN
6900 GOSUB7210:PRINT"INVALID FILENAME":RESUME6050
7000      REM **** HEX FUNCTION ****
7010 A(0)="0":A(1)="1":A(2)="2":A(3)="3":A(4)="4":A(5)="5"
7020 A(6)="6":A(7)="7":A(8)="8":A(9)="9":A(10)="A":A(11)="B"
7030 A(12)="C":A(13)="D":A(14)="E":A(15)="F"
7040 ONERRORGOTO7200
7050 PRINT"ENTER FILENAME (FILENAME/EXT.PASSWORD:D) FOR HEX OUTPUT ? "
7060 LINEINPUTX$
7070 OPEN"O",1,X$
7080 ONERRORGOTO0
7100 PRINT:PRINT"NUMBER OF FUSES BLOWN =";NB:PRINT
7110 PRINT:PRINTL(3):PRINT:PRINT#1,CHR$(18);CHR$(07);CHR$(07)
7120 FORX=1TO4:PRINT#1,L(X):NEXTX
7130 PRINT#1,"":PRINT#1,"NUMBER OF FUSES BLOWN =";NB:PRINT#1,""
7140 PRINT#1,CHR$(01);CHR$(02);
7150 C=-1:FORY=0TO39:C=C+1:A="":IFY=8THENY=32
7160 FORX=0TO31
7170 H=(F(X,Y)AND1)+(2*(F(X,Y+8)AND1))+(4*(F(X,Y+16)AND1))+(8*(F(X,Y+24)AND1))
7180 PRINTA(H)+" ";:A=A+A(H)+" ":NEXTX:PRINT:PRINT#1,A:NEXTY
7190 PRINT#1,CHR$(20);CHR$(07):CLOSE:RETURN
7200 GOSUB7210:PRINT"INVALID FILENAME":RESUME7040
7210 PRINT"*** ERROR *** ... ":RETURN
8000     REM *** BHLF AND BPNF FUNCTIONS ***
8010 ONERRORGOTO8190
8020 PRINT"ENTER FILENAME (FILENAME/EXT.PASSWORD:D) FOR B";D1;D0;"F OUTPUT ? "
8030 LINEINPUTX$
8040 OPEN"O",1,X$
8050 ONERRORGOTO0
8060 PRINT:PRINTL(3):PRINT:PRINT#1,CHR$(18);CHR$(07);CHR$(07)
8070 FORX=1TO4:PRINT#1,L(X):NEXTX:PRINT#1,CHR$(01);CHR$(02)
8080 FORY=0TO39:IFY=8THENY=32
8090 FORX=0TO31
```

```
8100 PRINT"B";:PRINT#1,"B";
8110 C=24:GOSUB8170:C=16:GOSUB8170
8120 C=8:GOSUB8170:C=0:GOSUB8170
8130 PRINT"F ";:PRINT#1,"F ";
8140 IFX=7 ORX=15 ORX=23 ORX=31 THENPRINT"":PRINT#1," "
8150 NEXTX,Y
8160 PRINT:PRINT#1,CHR$(20);CHR$(07):CLOSE:RETURN
8170 IF(F(X,Y+C)AND1)=0THENPRINTD0;:PRINT#1,D0;:RETURN
8180 PRINTD1;:PRINT#1,D1;:RETURN
8190 GOSUB7210:PRINT"INVALID FILENAME":RESUME8010
9000      REM *** FOR 16A4 AND 16X4 PALS ONLY ***
9010 IFY<16ORY>47THEN2590
9020 IFP=":"THENA1=MID$(A,CN,3)ELSEGOTO9060
9030 IFA1=":+:"THENY=4*(INT((Y+4)/4)):GOSUB4410:CN=CN+3:GOTO3050
9040 IFA1=":*:"THENGOSUB7210:PRINT"´:*:´ IS USED INSIDE PARENTHESES ONLY":END
9050 GOSUB7210:PRINT"´";P;"´ IS INVALID AS USED IN:":PRINT"#";A:END
9060 N8=CN:N9=INSTR(CN,A,")"):IFN9=0THEN9050
9070 A1=MID$(A,N8,N9-N8+1)
9080 N=VAL(RIGHT$(A1,2)):IFN<0ORN>3THEN9090ELSE9100
9090 GOSUB7210:PRINT"INVALID EXPRESSION ´";A1;"´":END
9100 X=N*4+8
9110 N0=LEN(A1)-3:IFN0>6THEN9090
9120 ONN0GOTO9130,9150,9170,9180,9200,9250
9130 C=2:GOSUB9300:IFMID$(A1,2,1)="A"THENC=3ELSEC=0
9140 GOSUB9300:GOTO9290
9150 C=1:GOSUB9300:IFMID$(A1,3,1)="A"THENC=0ELSEC=3
9160 GOSUB9300:GOTO9290
9170 AT=A1:GOTO3260
9180 C=2:GOSUB9300:IFINSTR(A1,"+")<>0THEN9290
9190 C=0:GOSUB9300:C=3:GOSUB9300:GOTO9290
9200 IFINSTR(A1,"+B")<>0THENC=0:GOSUB9300:GOTO9290
9210 IFINSTR(A1,"+/")<>0THENC=3:GOSUB9300:GOTO9290
9220 C=1:GOSUB9300:C=2:GOSUB9300
9230 IFINSTR(A1,"*B")<>0THENC=0:GOSUB9300:GOTO9290
9240 C=3:GOSUB9300:GOTO9290
9250 IFINSTR(A1,"+/")<>0THENC=1:GOSUB9300:GOTO9290
9260 IFINSTR(A1,"+:")<>0THENC=1:GOSUB9300:C=2:GOSUB9300:GOTO9290
9270 C=0:GOSUB9300:C=3:GOSUB9300
9280 IFINSTR(A1,"*/")<>0THENC=1:GOSUB9300:GOTO9290
9290 CN=CN+N0+3:GOTO3050
9300 F(X+C,Y)=0:NB=NB-1:RETURN
```

Table of Contents

PAL Applications

Introduction to PAL Applications

The PAL family brings a unique flexibility to the field of logic design. Using PALs, designers can both replace conventional logic in existing products and optimize the design of new products. Previous sections discussed the PAL concept and provided information on the advantages gained and the techniques used when designing with PALs. This section shows PALs at work in applications ranging from simple logic gate replacement to complete system designs.

Each example is presented as a complete PAL design. The required logic function is described, the PAL that best solves the problem is selected, and the actual PAL logic implementation is shown. The PAL logic is shown as both the PAL design specification and the actual PALASM output for the PAL programmer. This makes the examples complete enough to serve as guides for designers using PALs in their own systems.

The PAL is a versatile device whose applications are practically unlimited. These applications examples, combined with the PAL design information contained in the rest of this book, will help designers to get the feel of PAL design procedures. With a little practice and study, PAL design will become a natural extension of the normal logic design process.

Basic Gates

PAL
TTL
TRASH

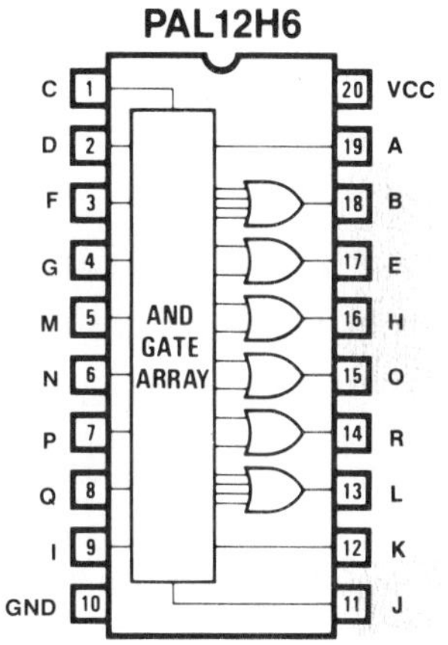
PAL12H6
C 1
D 2
F 3
G 4
M 5
N 6
P 7
Q 8
I 9
GND 10
20 VCC
19 A
18 B
17 E
16 H
15 O
14 R
13 L
12 K
11 J
AND
GATE
ARRAY

```
PAL12H6                                          PAL DESIGN SPECIFICATION
BGATES                                             VINCENT COLI 06/12/81
BASIC GATES
MMI SUNNYVALE, CALIFORNIA
C D F G M N P Q I GND J K L R O H E B A VCC
```

```
B = /A                  ;INVERTER
```

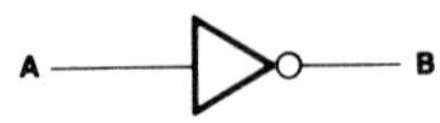


```
E = C*D                 ;AND GATE
```

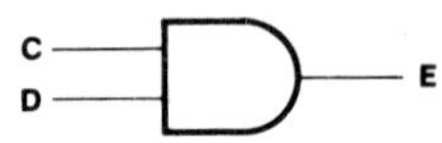

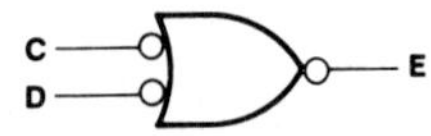


```
H = F + G               ;OR GATE
```

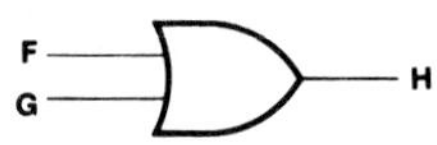

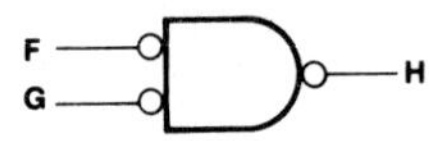


```
L = /I + /J + /K        ;NAND GATE
```

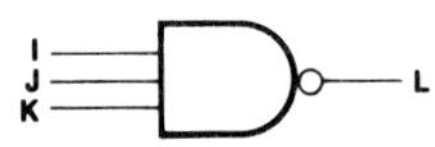

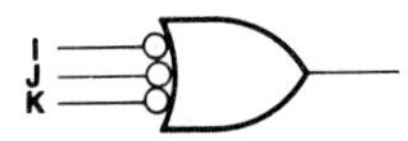


```
O = /M*/N               ;NOR GATE
```

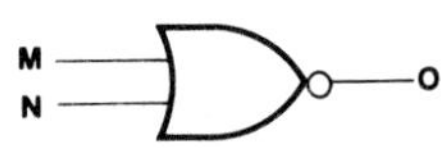

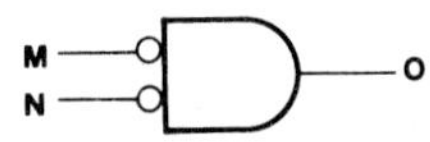


```
R = P*/Q + /P*Q         ;EXCLUSIVE OR GATE
```

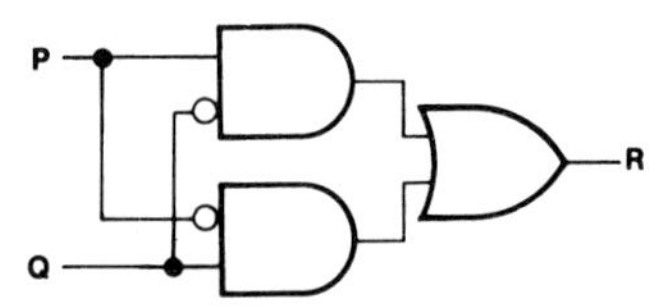

PAL12H6

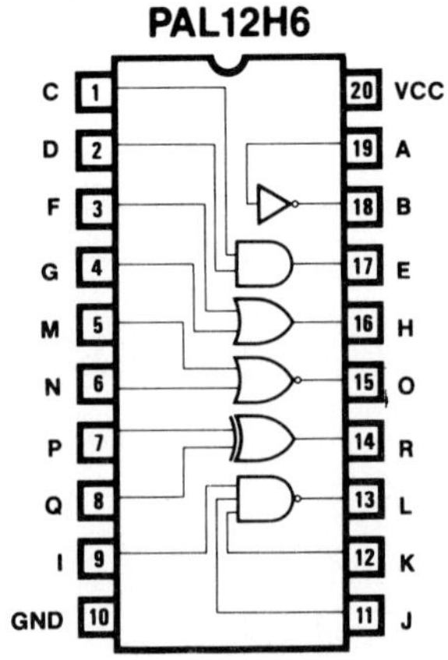

```
FUNCTION TABLE

A B C D E F G H I J K L M N O P Q R

;AB   CDE   FGH   IJKL   MNO   PQR    COMMENTS
------------------------------------------------------------
 LH   XXX   XXX   XXXX   XXX   XXX    TEST INVERTER
 HL   XXX   XXX   XXXX   XXX   XXX    TEST INVERTER
 XX   LLL   XXX   XXXX   XXX   XXX    TEST AND GATE
 XX   LHL   XXX   XXXX   XXX   XXX    TEST AND GATE
 XX   HLL   XXX   XXXX   XXX   XXX    TEST AND GATE
 XX   HHH   XXX   XXXX   XXX   XXX    TEST AND GATE
 XX   XXX   LLL   XXXX   XXX   XXX    TEST OR GATE
 XX   XXX   LHH   XXXX   XXX   XXX    TEST OR GATE
 XX   XXX   HLH   XXXX   XXX   XXX    TEST OR GATE
 XX   XXX   HHH   XXXX   XXX   XXX    TEST OR GATE
 XX   XXX   XXX   LLLH   XXX   XXX    TEST NAND GATE
 XX   XXX   XXX   LLHH   XXX   XXX    TEST NAND GATE
 XX   XXX   XXX   LHLH   XXX   XXX    TEST NAND GATE
 XX   XXX   XXX   HLLH   XXX   XXX    TEST NAND GATE
 XX   XXX   XXX   HHHL   XXX   XXX    TEST NAND GATE
 XX   XXX   XXX   XXXX   LLH   XXX    TEST NOR GATE
 XX   XXX   XXX   XXXX   LHL   XXX    TEST NOR GATE
 XX   XXX   XXX   XXXX   HLL   XXX    TEST NOR GATE
 XX   XXX   XXX   XXXX   HHL   XXX    TEST NOR GATE
 XX   XXX   XXX   XXXX   XXX   LLL    TEST EXCLUSIVE OR GATE
 XX   XXX   XXX   XXXX   XXX   LHH    TEST EXCLUSIVE OR GATE
 XX   XXX   XXX   XXXX   XXX   HLH    TEST EXCLUSIVE OR GATE
 XX   XXX   XXX   XXXX   XXX   HHL    TEST EXCLUSIVE OR GATE
------------------------------------------------------------


DESCRIPTION

THIS EXAMPLE ILLUSTRATES THE USE OF FUSIBLE LOGIC TO IMPLEMENT THE BASIC
GATES; INVERTER, AND GATE, OR GATE, NAND GATE, NOR GATE, AND EXCLUSIVE OR
GATE.

THE FUNCTION TABLE EXERCISES ALL INPUTS AND TESTS BASIC FUNCTION PERFORMANCE.
PALASM EXERCISES THE FUNCTION TABLE TO SIMULATE THE BASIC GATES.
```

```
BASIC GATES

 1 XXXXXXXXXXXXXXXXXH01
 2 XXXXXXXXXXXXXXXXXL11
 3 00XXXXXXXXXXXXXXLXX1
 4 01XXXXXXXXXXXXXXLXX1
 5 10XXXXXXXXXXXXXXLXX1
 6 11XXXXXXXXXXXXXXHXX1
 7 XX00XXXXXXXXXXXLXXX1
 8 XX01XXXXXXXXXXXHXXX1
 9 XX10XXXXXXXXXXXHXXX1
10 XX11XXXXXXXXXXXHXXX1
11 XXXXXXXX0X00HXXXXXX1
12 XXXXXXXX0X01HXXXXXX1
13 XXXXXXXX0X10HXXXXXX1
14 XXXXXXXX1X00HXXXXXX1
15 XXXXXXXX1X11LXXXXXX1
16 XXXX00XXXXXXXXHXXXX1
17 XXXX01XXXXXXXXLXXXX1
18 XXXX10XXXXXXXXLXXXX1
19 XXXX11XXXXXXXXLXXXX1
20 XXXXXX00XXXXXLXXXXX1
21 XXXXXX01XXXXXHXXXXX1
22 XXXXXX10XXXXXHXXXXX1
23 XXXXXX11XXXXXLXXXXX1

PASS SIMULATION


BASIC GATES

               11 1111 1111 2222 2222 2233
   0123 4567 8901 2345 6789 0123 4567 8901


 8 ---- ---X --   --   --   --   ---- ---- /A

16 X-X- ---- --   --   --   --   ---- ---- C*D

24 ---- X--- --   --   --   --   ---- ---- F
25 ---- ---- X-   --   --   --   ---- ---- G

32 ---- ---- --   -X   -X   --   ---- ---- /M*/N

40 ---- ---- --   --   --   X-   -X-- ---- P*/Q
41 ---- ---- --   --   --   -X   X--- ---- /P*Q

48 ---- ---- --   --   --   --   ---- -X-- /I
49 ---- ---- --   --   --   --   ---- ---X /J
50 ---- ---- --   --   --   --   ---X ---- /K


LEGEND:  X : FUSE NOT BLOWN (L,N,0)   - : FUSE BLOWN   (H,P,1)

NUMBER OF FUSES BLOWN =  306
```

Basic Gates

Logic Diagram PAL12H6

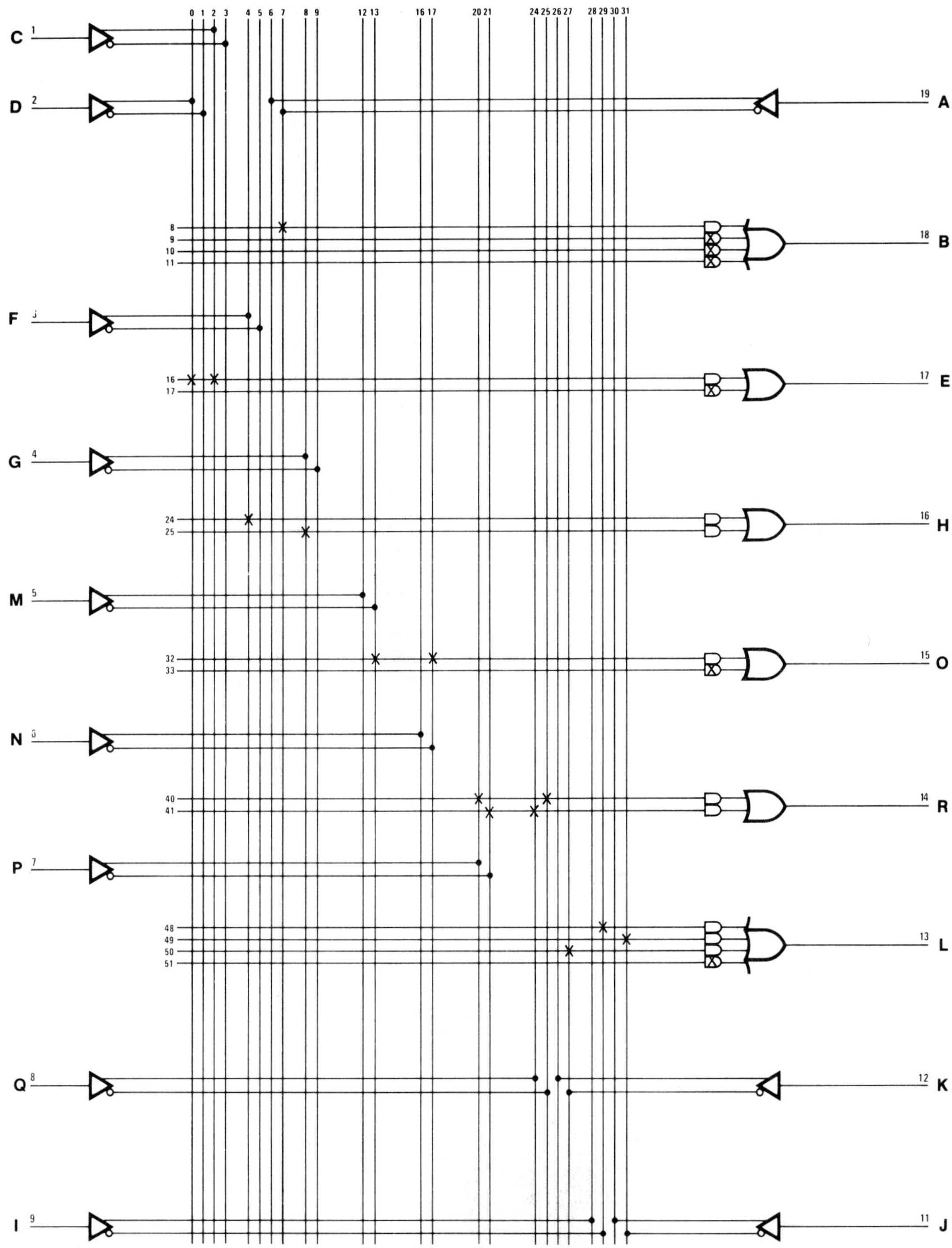

PAL
IMPORTANT,
NOTES

Basic Clocked Flip-Flops

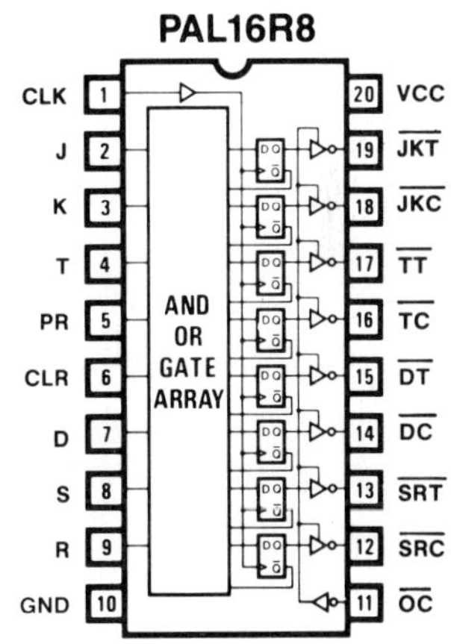

```
PAL16R8                                          PAL DESIGN SPECIFICATION
BFLIP                                              VINCENT COLI 07/19/81
BASIC CLOCKED FLIP-FLOPS
MMI SUNNYVALE, CALIFORNIA
CLK J K T PR CLR D S R GND
/OC /SRC /SRT /DC /DT /TC /TT /JKC /JKT VCC


JKT := J*/JKT*/CLR           ;J-K FLIP-FLOP (TRUE)
     + /K* JKT*/CLR          ;(JKT = Q)
     + PR                    ;PRESET Q

JKC := /J* K  */PR           ;J-K FLIP-FLOP (COMPLEMENT)
     + /J*/JKT*/PR           ;(JKC = /Q)
     + K* JKT*/PR            ;
     + CLR                   ;CLEAR /Q

TT  := T*/TT*/CLR            ;T FLIP-FLOP (TRUE)
     + /T* TT*/CLR           ;(TT = Q)
     + PR                    ;PRESET Q

TC  := /T*/TT*/PR            ;T FLIP-FLOP (COMPLEMENT)
     + T* TT*/PR             ;(TC = /Q)
     + CLR                   ;CLEAR /Q

DT  := D*/CLR                ;D FLIP-FLOP (TRUE) (DT = Q)
     + PR                    ;PRESET Q

DC  := /D*/PR                ;D FLIP-FLOP (COMPLEMENT) (DC = /Q)
     + CLR                   ;CLEAR /Q

SRT := S*      /CLR          ;SET-RESET FLIP-FLOP (TRUE)
     + /R* SRT*/CLR          ;(SRT = Q)
     + PR                    ;PRESET Q

SRC := /S* R  */PR           ;SET-RESET FLIP-FLOP (COMPLEMENT)
     + /S*/SRT*/PR           ;(SRC = /Q)
     + CLR                   ;CLEAR /Q
```

```
FUNCTION TABLE

CLK /OC PR CLR J K JKT JKC T TT TC D DT DC S R SRT SRC

;   CONTROL    J-K FLIP-FLOP  T FLIP-FLOP  D FLIP-FLOP  S-R FLIP-FLOP
; C  /          IN     OUT     IN    OUT     IN    OUT     IN     OUT
;LK OC PR CLR  J  K  Q   /Q    T   Q   /Q    D   Q   /Q    S  R  Q   /Q     COMMENT
-------------------------------------------------------------------------------------
 X  H  X  X    X  X  Z   Z     X   Z   Z     X   Z   Z     X  X  Z   Z      HI-Z
;
;   TEST J-K FLIP-FLOP
;
 C  L  L  H    X  X  L   H     X   X   X     X   X   X     X  X  X   X      CLEAR
 C  L  L  L    L  L  L   H     X   X   X     X   X   X     X  X  X   X
 C  L  L  L    L  H  L   H     X   X   X     X   X   X     X  X  X   X
 C  L  L  L    H  H  H   L     X   X   X     X   X   X     X  X  X   X      TOGGLE
 C  L  L  L    H  L  H   L     X   X   X     X   X   X     X  X  X   X
 C  L  L  L    L  L  H   L     X   X   X     X   X   X     X  X  X   X
 C  L  L  L    L  H  L   H     X   X   X     X   X   X     X  X  X   X
 C  L  H  L    X  X  H   L     X   X   X     X   X   X     X  X  X   X      PRESET
 C  L  L  L    H  H  L   H     X   X   X     X   X   X     X  X  X   X      TOGGLE
 C  L  L  L    H  L  H   L     X   X   X     X   X   X     X  X  X   X
;
;   TEST T FLIP-FLOP
;
 C  L  L  H    X  X  X   X     X   L   H     X   X   X     X  X  X   X      CLEAR
 C  L  L  L    X  X  X   X     L   L   H     X   X   X     X  X  X   X
 C  L  L  L    X  X  X   X     H   H   L     X   X   X     X  X  X   X      TOGGLE
 C  L  L  L    X  X  X   X     H   L   H     X   X   X     X  X  X   X      TOGGLE
 C  L  H  L    X  X  X   X     X   H   L     X   X   X     X  X  X   X      PRESET
;
;   TEST D FLIP-FLOP
;
 C  L  L  H    X  X  X   X     X   X   X     X   L   H     X  X  X   X      CLEAR
 C  L  L  L    X  X  X   X     X   X   X     L   L   H     X  X  X   X
 C  L  L  L    X  X  X   X     X   X   X     H   H   L     X  X  X   X
 C  L  L  L    X  X  X   X     X   X   X     L   L   H     X  X  X   X
 C  L  H  L    X  X  X   X     X   X   X     X   H   L     X  X  X   X      PRESET
;
;   TEST S-R FLIP-FLOP
;
 C  L  L  H    X  X  X   X     X   X   X     X   X   X     X  X  L   H      CLEAR
 C  L  L  L    X  X  X   X     X   X   X     X   X   X     L  L  L   H
 C  L  L  L    X  X  X   X     X   X   X     X   X   X     H  L  H   L      SET
 C  L  L  L    X  X  X   X     X   X   X     X   X   X     L  H  L   H      RESET
 C  L  L  L    X  X  X   X     X   X   X     X   X   X     L  H  L   H      HOLD
 C  L  H  L    X  X  X   X     X   X   X     X   X   X     X  X  H   L      PRESET
 C  L  L  L    X  X  X   X     X   X   X     X   X   X     L  L  H   L
 C  L  L  L    X  X  X   X     X   X   X     X   X   X     H  L  H   L
-------------------------------------------------------------------------------------
```

DESCRIPTION
THIS EXAMPLE ILLUSTRATES THE USE OF FUSIBLE LOGIC TO IMPLEMENT THE BASIC FLIP-FLOPS: J-K FLIP-FLOP, T FLIP-FLOP, D FLIP-FLOP, AND S-R FLIP-FLOP.

NEXT STATE TABLE FOR THE BASIC FLIP-FLOPS:

TYPE OF FLIP-FLOP	INPUT	Q = L		Q = H	
		Q+ = L	Q+ = H	Q+ = L	Q+ = H
J-K	J	L	H	X	X
	K	X	X	H	L
T	T	L	H	H	L
D	D	L	H	L	H
SET-RESET	S	L	H	L	X
	R	X	L	H	L

NOTE THAT A PAL16L8 MAY BE SUBSTITUTED FOR THIS DESIGN. THEN THE CLOCK INPUT (CLK) WOULD BE GATED WITH THE DATA INPUTS TO IMPLEMENT THE BASIC FLIP-FLOPS.

THE FUNCTION TABLE EXERCISES ALL INPUTS AND TESTS BASIC FUNCTION PERFORMANCE. PALASM EXERCISES THE FUNCTION TABLE TO SIMULATE THE BASIC CLOCKED FLIP-FLOPS.

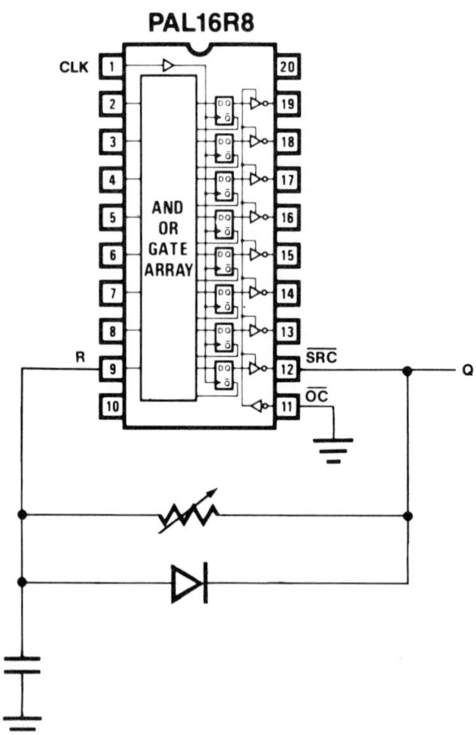

IMPLEMENTATION OF THE S-R FLIP-FLOP AS A DIVIDE-BY-N COUNTER

```
BASIC CLOCKED FLIP-FLOPS

 1 XXXXXXXXXX1ZZZZZZZZ1
 2 CXXX01XXXX0XXXXXXLH1
 3 C00X00XXXX0XXXXXXLH1
 4 C01X00XXXX0XXXXXXLH1
 5 C11X00XXXX0XXXXXXHL1
 6 C10X00XXXX0XXXXXXHL1
 7 C00X00XXXX0XXXXXXHL1
 8 C01X00XXXX0XXXXXXLH1
 9 CXXX10XXXX0XXXXXXHL1
10 C11X00XXXX0XXXXXXLH1
11 C10X00XXXX0XXXXXXHL1
12 CXXX01XXXX0XXXXLHXX1
13 CXX000XXXX0XXXXLHXX1
14 CXX100XXXX0XXXXHLXX1
15 CXX100XXXX0XXXXLHXX1
16 CXXX10XXXX0XXXXHLXX1
17 CXXX01XXXX0XXLHXXXX1
18 CXXX000XXX0XXLHXXXX1
19 CXXX001XXX0XXHLXXXX1
20 CXXX000XXX0XXLHXXXX1
21 CXXX10XXXX0XXHLXXXX1
22 CXXX01XXXX0LHXXXXXX1
23 CXXX00X00X0LHXXXXXX1
24 CXXX00X10X0HLXXXXXX1
25 CXXX00X01X0LHXXXXXX1
26 CXXX00X01X0LHXXXXXX1
27 CXXX10XXXX0HLXXXXXX1
28 CXXX00X00X0HLXXXXXX1
29 CXXX00X10X0HLXXXXXX1

PASS SIMULATION
```

```
BASIC CLOCKED FLIP-FLOPS

               11 1111 1111 2222 2222 2233
   0123 4567 8901 2345 6789 0123 4567 8901

 0 X-X- ---- ---- ---- -X-- ---- ---- ---- J*/JKT*/CLR
 1 ---X -X-- ---- ---- -X-- ---- ---- ---- /K*JKT*/CLR
 2 ---- ---- ---- X--- ---- ---- ---- ---- PR

 8 -X-- X--- ---- -X-- ---- ---- ---- ---- /J*K*/PR
 9 -XX- ---- ---- -X-- ---- ---- ---- ---- /J*/JKT*/PR
10 ---X X--- ---- -X-- ---- ---- ---- ---- K*JKT*/PR
11 ---- ---- ---- ---- X--- ---- ---- ---- CLR

16 ---- ---- X-X- ---- -X-- ---- ---- ---- T*/TT*/CLR
17 ---- ---- -X-X ---- -X-- ---- ---- ---- /T*TT*/CLR
18 ---- ---- ---- X--- ---- ---- ---- ---- PR

24 ---- ---- -XX- -X-- ---- ---- ---- ---- /T*/TT*/PR
25 ---- ---- X--X -X-- ---- ---- ---- ---- T*TT*/PR
26 ---- ---- ---- ---- X--- ---- ---- ---- CLR

32 ---- ---- ---- ---- -X-- X--- ---- ---- D*/CLR
33 ---- ---- ---- X--- ---- ---- ---- ---- PR

40 ---- ---- ---- -X-- ---- -X-- ---- ---- /D*/PR
41 ---- ---- ---- ---- X--- ---- ---- ---- CLR

48 ---- ---- ---- ---- -X-- ---- X--- ---- S*/CLR
49 ---- ---- ---- ---- -X-- ---- ---X -X-- /R*SRT*/CLR
50 ---- ---- ---- X--- ---- ---- ---- ---- PR

56 ---- ---- ---- -X-- ---- ---- -X-- X--- /S*R*/PR
57 ---- ---- ---- -X-- ---- ---- -XX- ---- /S*/SRT*/PR
58 ---- ---- ---- ---- X--- ---- ---- ---- CLR

LEGEND:  X : FUSE NOT BLOWN (L,N,0)   - : FUSE BLOWN   (H,P,1)

NUMBER OF FUSES BLOWN =  686
```

Basic Clocked Flip-Flops

Logic Diagram PAL16R8

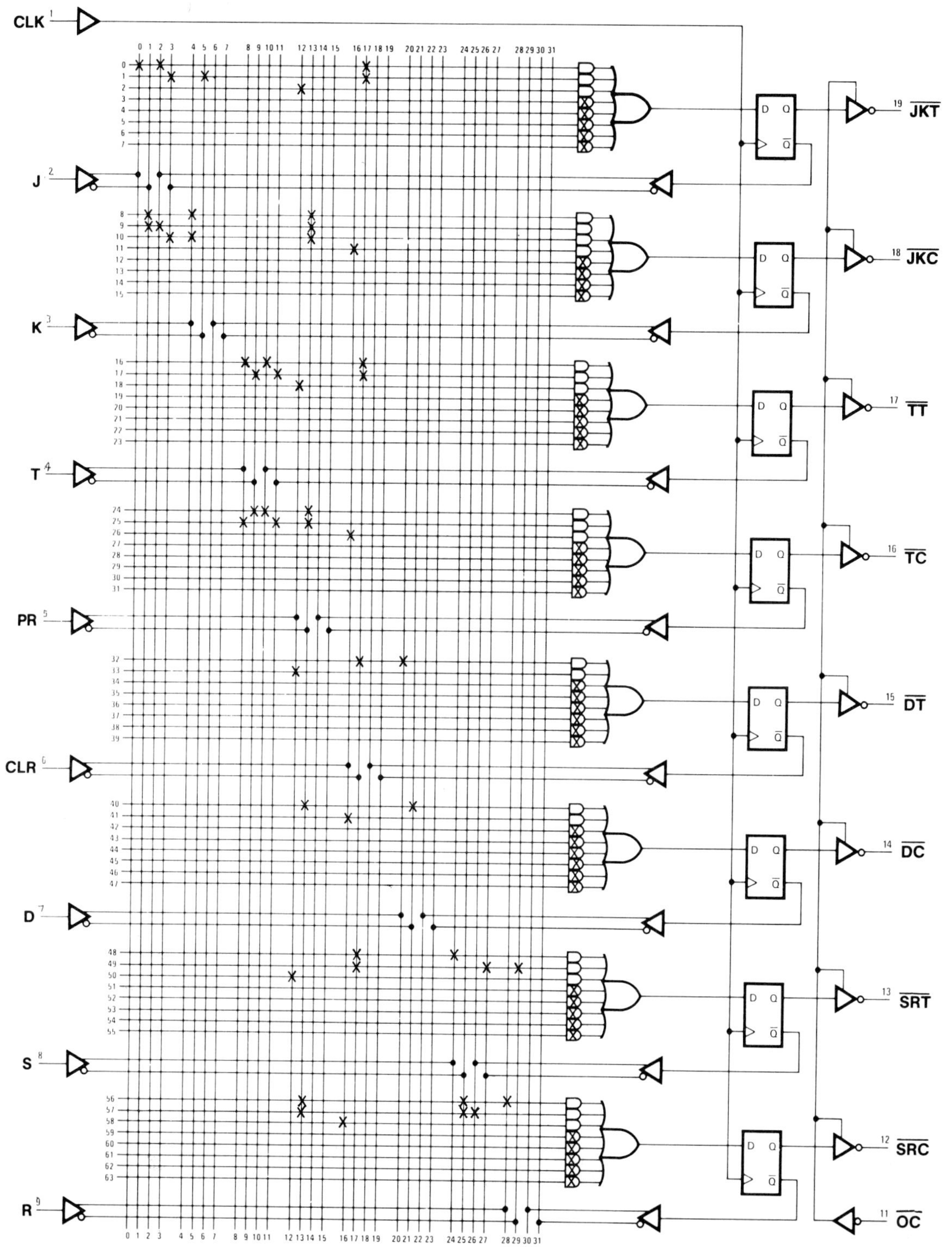

PAL
IMPORTANT NOTES

Memory Mapped I/O

PAL16L2

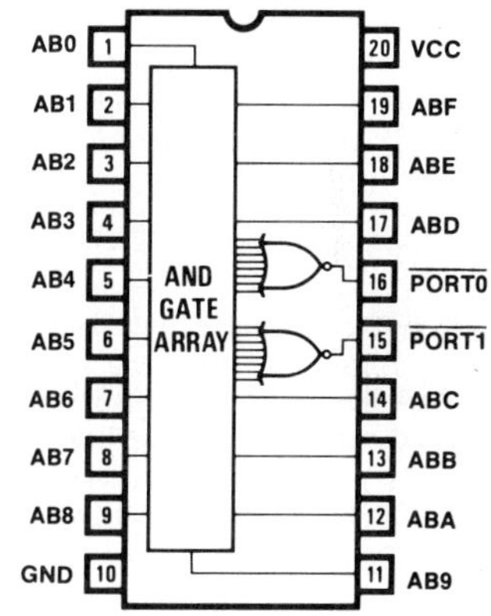

Memory Mapped I/O

Functional Description

Memory mapped I/O interfaces I/O devices to a computer by treating the device's physical address as a memory address. This removes the requirement for special I/O decoding and enhances the flexibility of the I/O system. The PAL provides a simple and direct method for implementing memory mapped I/O in mini and micro computer systems.

Circuit Operation

The circuits shown in Figure 1 are typical of those found in memory mapped I/O applications. The inputs to the decode logic are the system memory address lines, A0-AF. The logic compares the address on the memory bus with the programmed comparison address. When an address on the bus matches, the I/O port enable signal is set. This enable signal can then be used in conjunction with other system control signals to transfer data to and from the system data bus. Other examples in this applications section cover this I/O control decoding in more detail.

PAL Design

The PAL is used to monitor the system memory address bus. Typical microcomputers use a 16 bit address, so fully decoding the I/O addresses for two ports can be accomplished using the PAL 16L2. Partial decoding for a larger number of ports can be performed by other members of the PAL family.

The logic equations for the memory mapped I/O logic are as follows:

$$\text{PORT 0} = \overline{\text{AB0}} \cdot \overline{\text{AB1}} \cdot \overline{\text{AB2}} \cdot \text{AB3} \cdot \text{AB4} \cdot \text{AB5} \cdot \text{AB6} \cdot \overline{\text{AB7}} \cdot \text{AB8} \cdot \text{AB9} \cdot \text{ABA} \cdot \text{ABB} \cdot \text{ABC} \cdot \overline{\text{ABD}} \cdot \overline{\text{ABE}} \cdot \overline{\text{ABF}}$$

$$\text{PORT 1} = \text{AB0} \cdot \overline{\text{AB1}} \cdot \overline{\text{AB2}} \cdot \text{AB3} \cdot \text{AB4} \cdot \text{AB5} \cdot \text{AB6} \cdot \overline{\text{AB7}} \cdot \text{AB8} \cdot \text{AB9} \cdot \text{ABA} \cdot \text{ABB} \cdot \text{ABC} \cdot \overline{\text{ABD}} \cdot \overline{\text{ABE}} \cdot \overline{\text{ABF}}$$

The above example shows address decoding for memory locations 1F78 hex and 1F79 hex. Equation terms can be changed to accommodate any 16 bit address.

In operation, the PAL enable outputs will go high whenever one of the programmed addresses matches the address on the system memory address bus. Since the PAL fully decodes the address, any two I/O address may be used.

Conclusion

The PAL provides a single chip decoder for use in memory mapped I/O operations. This technique lowers interface parts counts and allows users an effective way to interface I/O devices to the microcomputer system.

PORT0 = 1F78

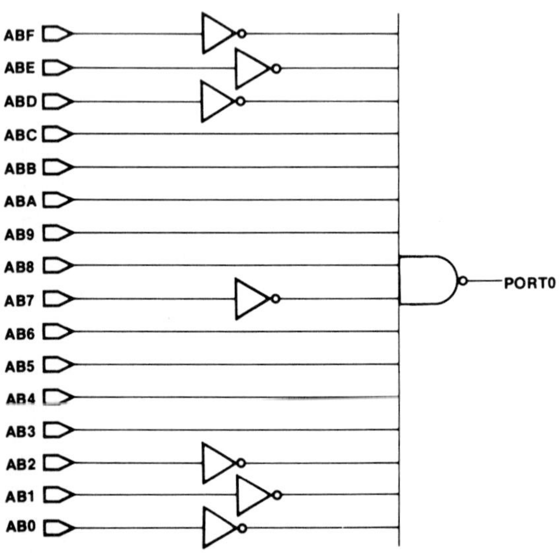

MEMORY MAPPED IO

PORT1 = 1F79

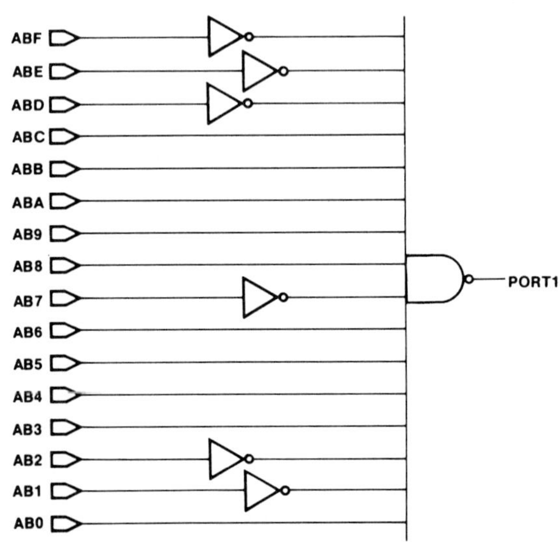

MEMORY MAPPED IO

```
PAL16L2                                          PAL DESIGN SPECIFICATION
MMAP                                             BIRKNER/COLI 06/29/81
MEMORY MAPPED I/O
MMI SUNNYVALE, CALIFORNIA
AB0 AB1 AB2 AB3 AB4 AB5 AB6 AB7 AB8 GND
AB9 ABA ABB ABC /PORT1 /PORT0 ABD ABE ABF VCC


PORT0 = /AB0*/AB1*/AB2* AB3* AB4* AB5* AB6*/AB7  ;SELECT PORT0
      *  AB8* AB9* ABA *ABB* ABC*/ABD*/ABE*/ABF  ;    (1F78)

PORT1 =  AB0*/AB1*/AB2* AB3* AB4* AB5* AB6*/AB7  ;SELECT PORT1
      *  AB8* AB9* ABA* ABB* ABC*/ABD*/ABE*/ABF  ;    (1F79)


FUNCTION TABLE

ABF ABE ABD ABC ABB ABA AB9 AB8 AB7 AB6 AB5 AB4 AB3 AB2 AB1 AB0 /PORT0 /PORT1

;---INPUTS AB----      ---OUTPUTS---
;FEDCBA9876543210      /PORT0 /PORT1     COMMENTS
-----------------------------------------------------------------------
 LLLLHHHHLHHHHLLL        H      H        TEST 0F78
 LLLHHHHLLHHHHLLL        H      H        TEST 1E78
 LLLHHHHHHHHHHLLL        H      H        TEST 1FF8
 LLLHHHHHLHHHLLLL        H      H        TEST 1F70
 LLLHHHHHLHHHHLLL        L      H        TEST 1F78
 LLLHHHHHLHHHHLLH        H      L        TEST 1F79
 LLLHHHHHLHHHHLHL        H      H        TEST 1F7A
 LLLHHHHHHHHHHLLH        H      H        TEST 1FF9
 LLLHHHHLLHHHHLLH        H      H        TEST 1E79
 LLHHHHHHLHHHHLLH        H      H        TEST 3F79
 LLLLLLLLLLLLLLLL        H      H        TEST ALL L'S
 HHHHHHHHHHHHHHHH        H      H        TEST ALL H'S
 LHLHLHLHLHLHLHLH        H      H        TEST ODD  CHECKERBOARD
 HLHLHLHLHLHLHLHL        H      H        TEST EVEN CHECKERBOARD
 LLHHLLHHLLHHLLHH        H      H        TEST ODD  DOUBLE CHECKERBOARD
 HHLLHHLLHHLLHHLL        H      H        TEST EVEN DOUBLE CHECKERBOARD
-----------------------------------------------------------------------


DESCRIPTION

THIS PAL PROVIDES A SINGLE CHIP DECODER FOR USE IN MEMORY MAPPED I/O
OPERATIONS.  EQUATION TERMS CAN BE CHANGED TO ACCOMODATE ANY 16-BIT
ADDRESS.

THE PAL WILL MONITOR THE SYSTEM MEMORY ADDRESS BUS AND DECODE THE
SPECIFIED MEMORY ADDRESS WORD (1F78,1F79) TO PRODUCE A PORT ENABLE
PIN FOR PORT0 AND PORT1.
```

```
MEMORY MAPPED I/O

 1 000111101X1110HH0001
 2 000111100X1111HH0001
 3 000111111X1111HH0001
 4 000011101X1111HH0001
 5 000111101X1111HL0001
 6 100111101X1111LH0001
 7 010111101X1111HH0001
 8 100111111X1111HH0001
 9 100111100X1111HH0001
10 100111101X1111HH1001
11 000000000X0000HH0001
12 111111111X1111HH1111
13 101010101X0101HH0101
14 010101010X1010HH1011
15 110011001X1001HH1001
16 001100110X0110HH0111

PASS SIMULATION
```

```
MEMORY MAPPED I/O

               11 1111 1111 2222 2222 2233
   0123 4567 8901 2345 6789 0123 4567 8901


24 -X-X -X-X X--X X--X X-X- X-X- -XX- X-X- /AB0*/AB1*/AB2*AB3*AB4*AB5*AB6-

32 -XX- -X-X X--X X--X X-X- X-X- -XX- X-X- AB0*/AB1*/AB2*AB3*AB4*AB5*AB6*-


LEGEND:  X : FUSE NOT BLOWN (L,N,0)   - : FUSE BLOWN   (H,P,1)

NUMBER OF FUSES BLOWN =   32
```

Memory Mapped I/O

Logic Diagram PAL16L2

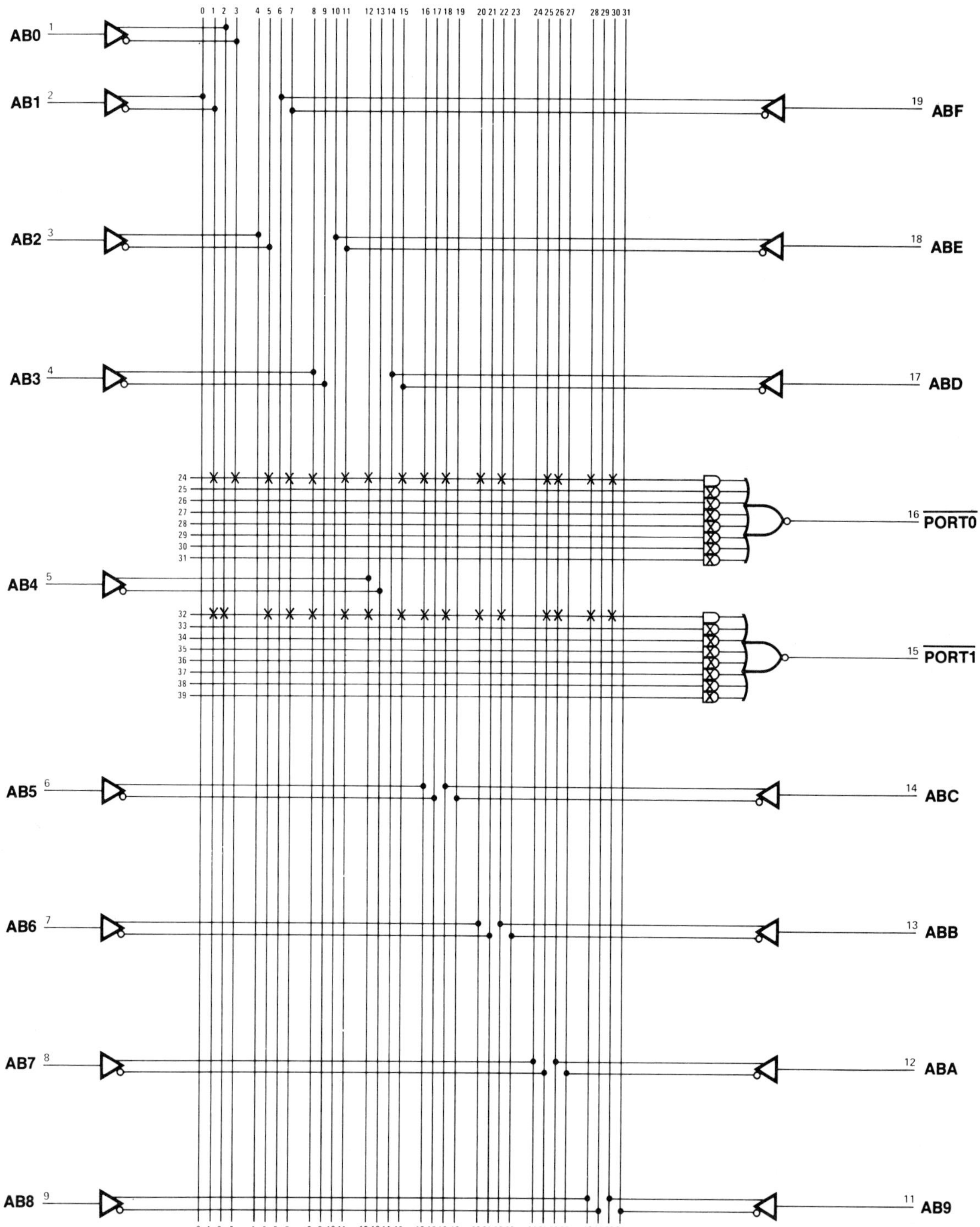

PAL
IMPORTANT NOTES

Memory Interface Logic for 6800 Microprocessor Bus

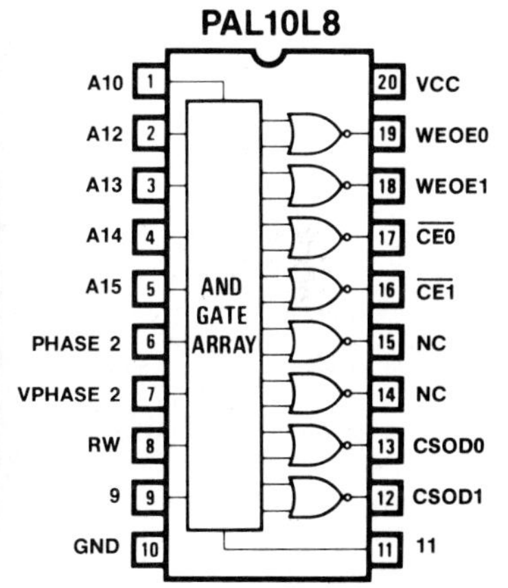

Memory Interface Logic for 6800 Microprocessor Bus

Logic Schematic

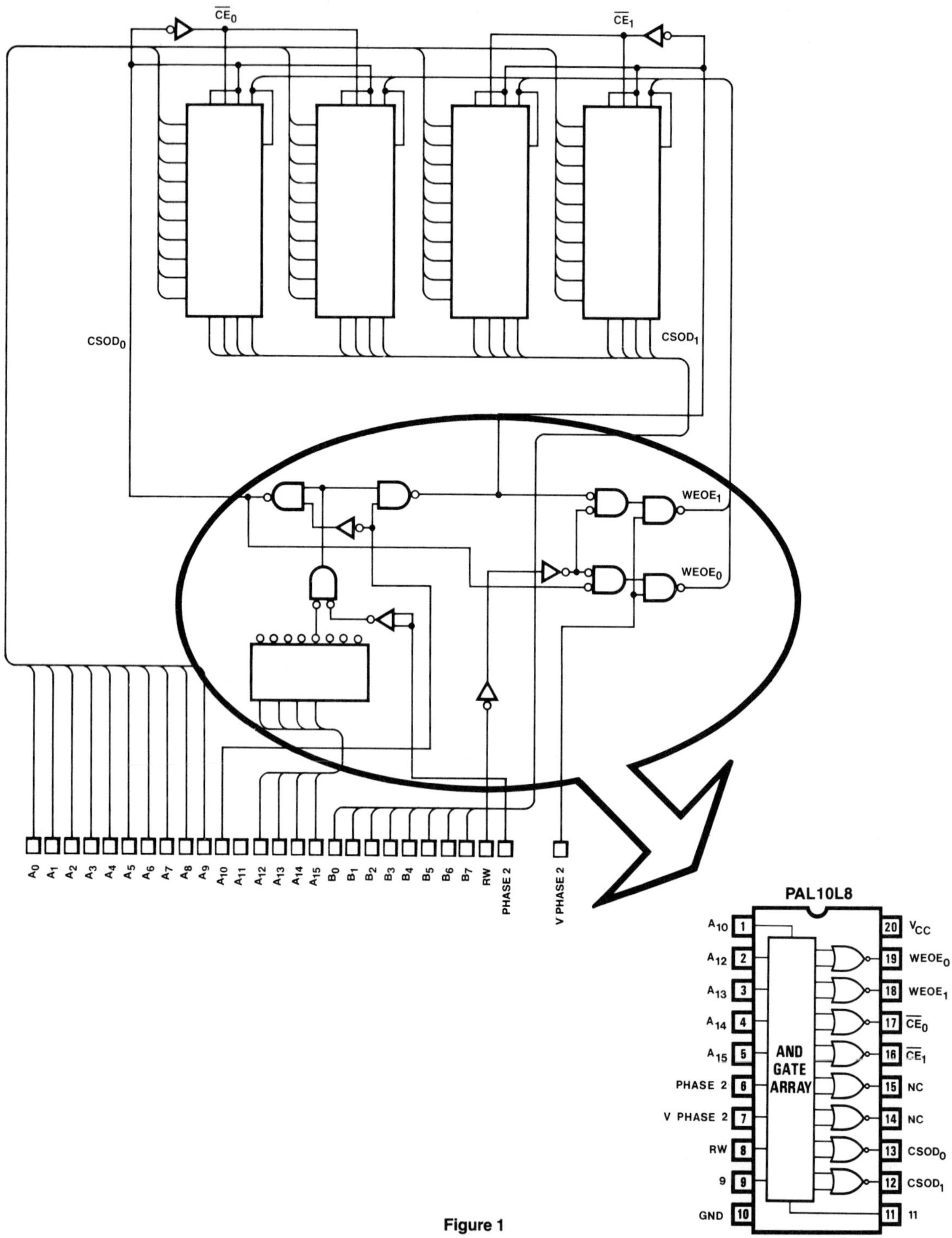

Figure 1

M6800 Memory Interface

Functional Description

The M6800 microprocessor is interfaced to memories by decoding the system memory address bus and several system control lines to generate the required memory control signals. This function is normally performed by combinatorial logic. In many applications, however, the PAL provides a more effective solution.

Circuit Operation

The logic schematic shown in Figure 1 is typical of most M6800 memory interfaces. The circuit shown is a 2048 x 8 bit static memory organized as four 1k x 4 bit RAM chips. The inputs to the RAM are the 10 memory address lines to select the individual memory location, the read/write line to determine whether data is to be read from or written into the memory, and the chip enable line to allow the device to perform the requested data transfer. Data to be written into the memory must be stable on the system data bus when the write signal is given. Data read from the memory will be placed on the data bus within one memory access time after the address has been decoded and the read signal given.

The circled area of combinatorial logic in Figure 1 is used to decode the 6800 address and control signals. Address bits 0-9 are routed directly to all four memory chips. Bit 10 is used to select whether chips 0 and 1 or chips 2 and 3 are to be selected. Bits 12-15 are connected to the A inputs of a digital comparator whose B inputs are jumpered to select the memory page address. If the memory is to be located from 0-800H (the first 2k page in the memory), all four comparator B inputs would be grounded. Then, whenever an address with bits 12-15 low appeared on the bus, a match would occur and the memory would be selected. Changing the jumpers allows the memory to be used anywhere in the 6800's address space or allows the use of multiple cards to construct a larger memory.

The read/write control logic for the memory is generated by decoding the read/write (R/W), phase 2 clock (Phase2), and valid memory address (Vphase2) system control lines. A logic high on the R/W line indicates a memory read; a logic high indicates a memory write.

The valid memory address line (Vphase2) is used to enable the address decoder output. When this enable occurs, the state of the address select and read/write logic is established. Then, when the phase 2 clock goes high, the memory transfer is performed. The relationship between the signals for both read and write operations is shown in Figure 2. (Consult 6800 data book for detailed design information.)

PAL Implementation

All of the combinatorial logic in the circled area of figure 1 can be replaced by a single PAL. This will lower system cost by reducing the device package count and lowering P.C. board area. The logic section has eight input terms and six output terms. Referring to the PAL family table it is seen that the PAL 10L8 fits the task nicely. The only tricky part of the transition from combinatorial logic to a PAL is encountered in the address decoding section. In the original circuit the decoder is jumpered with a match address for use during the address comparison. With the PAL, the address is programmed directly into the gate array.

The general logic equations for the decoder are as follows:

$$\overline{\mathrm{WEOE0}} = \overline{\mathrm{A10}} \cdot \overline{\mathrm{A12}} \cdot \overline{\mathrm{A13}} \cdot \mathrm{A14} \cdot \overline{\mathrm{A15}} \cdot \mathrm{PHASE2} \cdot \mathrm{VPHASE2} \cdot \overline{\mathrm{RW}}$$
$$\overline{\mathrm{WEOE1}} = \mathrm{A10} \cdot \overline{\mathrm{A12}} \cdot \overline{\mathrm{A13}} \cdot \mathrm{A14} \cdot \mathrm{A15} \cdot \mathrm{PHASE2} \cdot \mathrm{VPHASE2} \cdot \overline{\mathrm{RW}}$$
$$\mathrm{CSOD0} = \overline{\mathrm{A10}} \cdot \overline{\mathrm{A12}} \cdot \overline{\mathrm{A13}} \cdot \overline{\mathrm{A14}} \cdot \overline{\mathrm{A15}} \cdot \mathrm{PHASE2}$$
$$\mathrm{CSOD1} = \mathrm{A10} \cdot \overline{\mathrm{A12}} \cdot \overline{\mathrm{A13}} \cdot \mathrm{A14} \cdot \overline{\mathrm{A15}} \cdot \mathrm{PHASE2}$$
$$\mathrm{CE0} = \overline{\mathrm{CSOD0}}$$
$$\mathrm{CE1} = \overline{\mathrm{CSOD1}}$$

The above equations show the decoder set for page 0 (0-800H), but this could be easily changed by modifying the address terms. Note that the CE0 and CE1 terms can either be derived directly or by feeding the CSOD0 and CSOD1 terms back into the PAL as inputs.

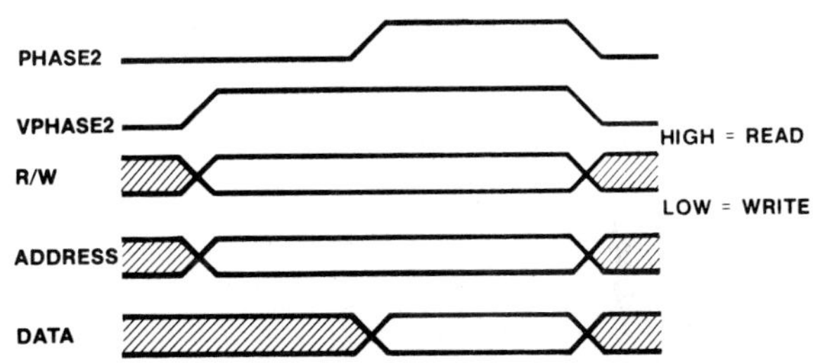

Figure 2

Conclusion

The PAL makes an effective direct logic replacement in many combinatorial logic applications. This can make both new and old designs more cost effective. In this example, the PAL both lowers package count and increases circuit reliability in a typical microcomputer memory application. These advantages can be easily extended to similar designs.

```
PAL10L8                                                PAL DESIGN SPECIFICATION
MIL                                                       BIRKNER/COLI 07/21/81
MEMORY INTERFACE LOGIC FOR 6800 MICROPROCESSOR BUS
MMI SUNNYVALE, CALIFORNIA
A10 A12 A13 A14 A15 PHASE2 VPHASE2 RW 9 GND
11 CSOD1 CSOD0 NC NC /CE1 /CE0 WEOE1 WEOE0 VCC


/WEOE0 = /A10*/A12*/A13* A14*/A15* PHASE2* VPHASE2*/RW ;DEC WRITE ENABLE CHIP 0

/WEOE1 =  A10*/A12*/A13* A14* A15* PHASE2* VPHASE2*/RW ;DEC WRITE ENABLE CHIP 1

/CSOD0 = /A10*/A12*/A13*/A14*/A15* PHASE2         ;DECODE OUTPUT DISABLE CHIP 0

/CSOD1 =  A10*/A12*/A13* A14*/A15* PHASE2         ;DECODE OUTPUT DISABLE CHIP 1

   CE0 = 9    ;ENABLE CHIP 0 (COMPLEMENT OF CSOD0)

   CE1 = 11   ;ENABLE CHIP 1 (COMPLEMENT OF CSOD1)


FUNCTION TABLE

A10 A12 A13 A14 A15 PHASE2 VPHASE2 RW 9 11 WEOE0 WEOE1 /CE0 /CE1 CSOD0 CSOD1

;ADD BUS
; 11111   PHASE R PINS  WRITE-ENABLE  CHIP-ENABLE  OUTPUT-DISABLE
; 02345   2  V2 W 9 11      0    1        0   1        0      1     COMMENTS
-------------------------------------------------------------------------------
  LLLHL   H  H  L H H       L    H        L   L        H      H     WRITE EN 0
  HLLHH   H  H  L H H       H    L        L   L        H      H     WRITE EN 1
  LLLLL   H  X  X L H       H    H        H   L        L      H     OUTPUT EN 0
  HLLHL   H  X  X H L       H    H        L   H        H      L     OUTPUT EN 1
  LLLHL   H  H  H H H       H    H        L   L        H      H     RW=H
  HLLHH   H  H  H H H       H    H        L   L        H      H     RW=H
  XXXXX   L  X  X H H       H    H        L   L        H      H     PHASE2=L
  LLLHL   H  L  L H H       H    H        L   L        H      H     VPHASE2=L
  HLLHH   H  L  L H H       H    H        L   L        H      H     VPHASE2=L
-------------------------------------------------------------------------------


DESCRIPTION

THIS DEVICE PROVIDES THE INTERFACE LOGIC BETWEEN A 6800 MICROPRESSOR BUS
AND FOUR STATIC 4k MEMORY CHIPS.  ADDRESS BUS (A), READ/WRITE (RW), PHASE 2
CLOCK (PHASE2), AND VALID MEMORY ADDRESS (VPHASE2) ARE DECODED TO PRODUCE
THE PROPER WRITE ENABLE (WEOE), CHIP ENABLE (CE), AND OUTPUT DISABLE (CSOD)
SIGNALS FOR MEMORY DATA TRANSFERS.

NOTE THAT /CE0 AND /CE1 ARE THE COMPLEMENTS OF CSOD0 AND CSOD1, RESPECTIVELY.
THESE FUNCTIONS ARE IMPLEMENTED BY THE EXTERNAL CONNECTIONS CSOD0 TO PIN 9 AND
CSOD1 TO PIN 11.
```

```
MEMORY INTERFACE LOGIC FOR 6800 MICROPROCESSOR BUS

 1 000101101X1HHXXLLHL1
 2 100111101X1HHXXLLLH1
 3 000001XX0X1HLXXLHHH1
 4 100101XX1X0LHXXHLHH1
 5 000101111X1HHXXLLHH1
 6 100111111X1HHXXLLHH1
 7 XXXXX0XX1X1HHXXLLHH1
 8 000101001X1HHXXLLHH1
 9 100111001X1HHXXLLHH1

PASS SIMULATION
```

```
MEMORY INTERFACE LOGIC FOR 6800 MICROPROCESSOR BUS

                11 1111 1111 2222 2222 2233
   0123 4567 8901 2345 6789 0123 4567 8901

 0 -X-X -X   X-   -X   X-   X-   -X   ---- /A10*/A12*/A13*A14*/A15*PHASE2-

 8 -XX- -X   X-   X-   X-   X-   -X   ---- A10*/A12*/A13*A14*A15*PHASE2*V-

16 ---- --   --   --   --   --   --   X--- 9

24 ---- --   --   --   --   --   --   --X- 11


48 -X-X -X   -X   -X   X-   --   --   ---- /A10*/A12*/A13*/A14*/A15*PHASE-

56 -XX- -X   X-   -X   X-   --   --   ---- A10*/A12*/A13*A14*/A15*PHASE2

LEGEND:  X : FUSE NOT BLOWN (L,N,0)   - : FUSE BLOWN   (H,P,1)

NUMBER OF FUSES BLOWN =  162
```

Memory Interface Logic for 6800 Microprocessor Bus **Logic Diagram PAL10L8**

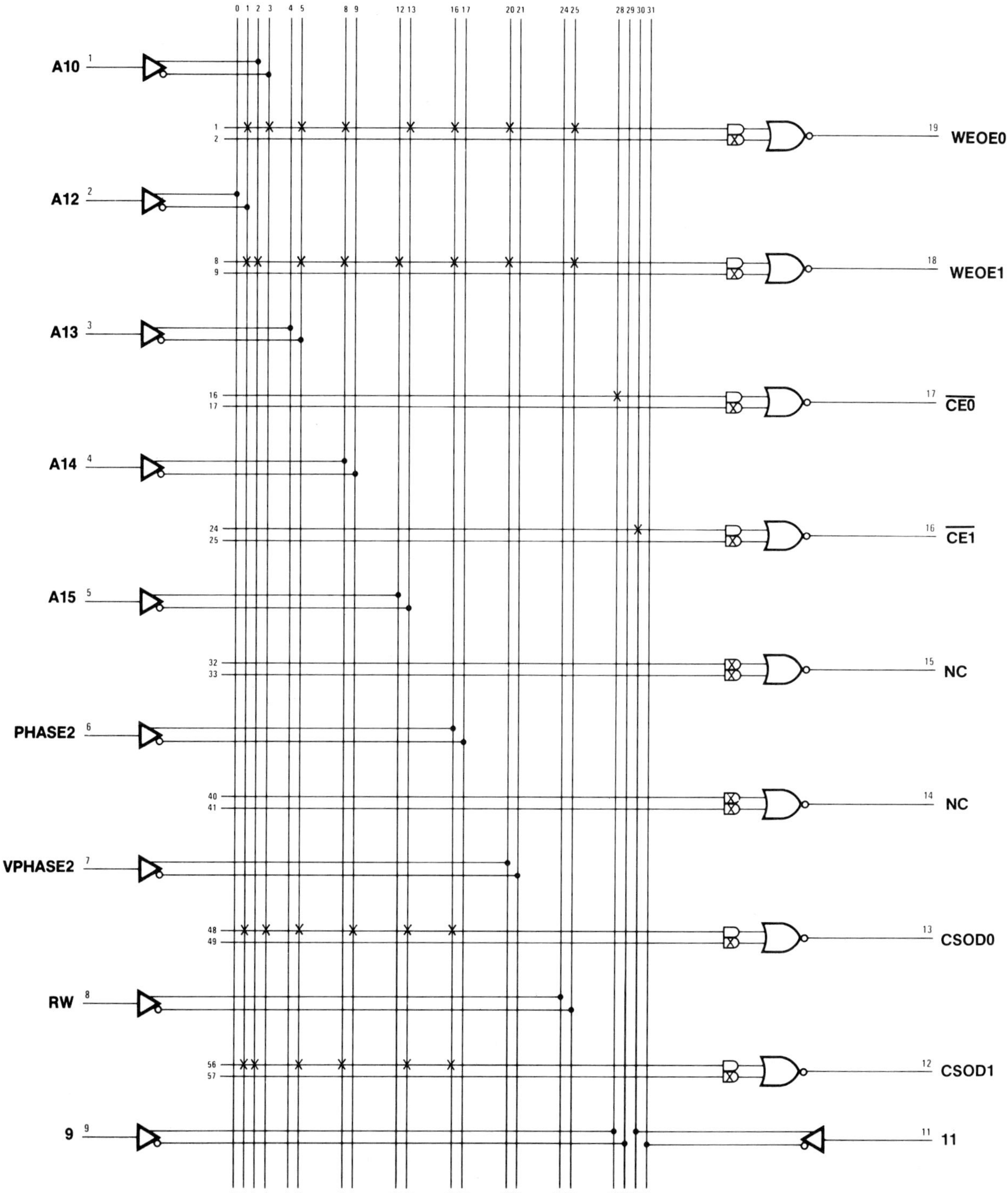

IMPORTANT,
NOTES
PAL

Video Logic

PAL20L10

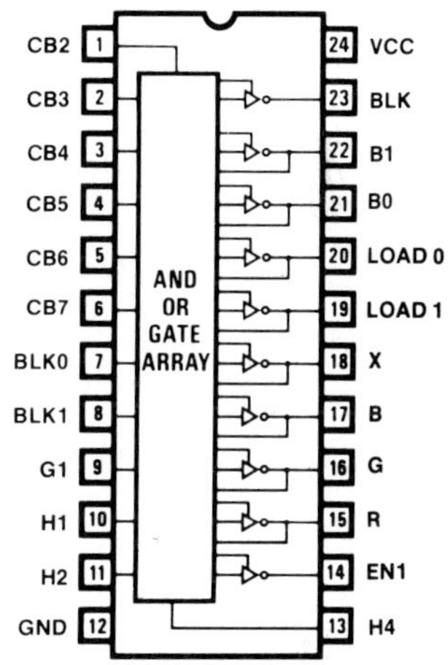

Functional Description

Many microcomputer systems use a CRT monitor or conventional television rather than a VDU perhaps because of cost reduction or because a color display is necessary.

The circuit diagram shows all of the TTL chips used on a video interface board.

The top portion is the color and blanking drive decoding and the lower is the enable logic for PROMs and registers containing driving data. The LS03s are open collector drivers and the two bank drive decoders are wire-ORed using 2kΩ resistors.

PAL Implementation

All of the logic can be put into one PAL20L10, also eliminating the pull-up resistors. This provides a dramatic reduction in component count and board size. The wire-OR configuration is an obvious candidate for PAL implementation, since the logic function /F = A * B + C * D is exactly in the PAL configuration.

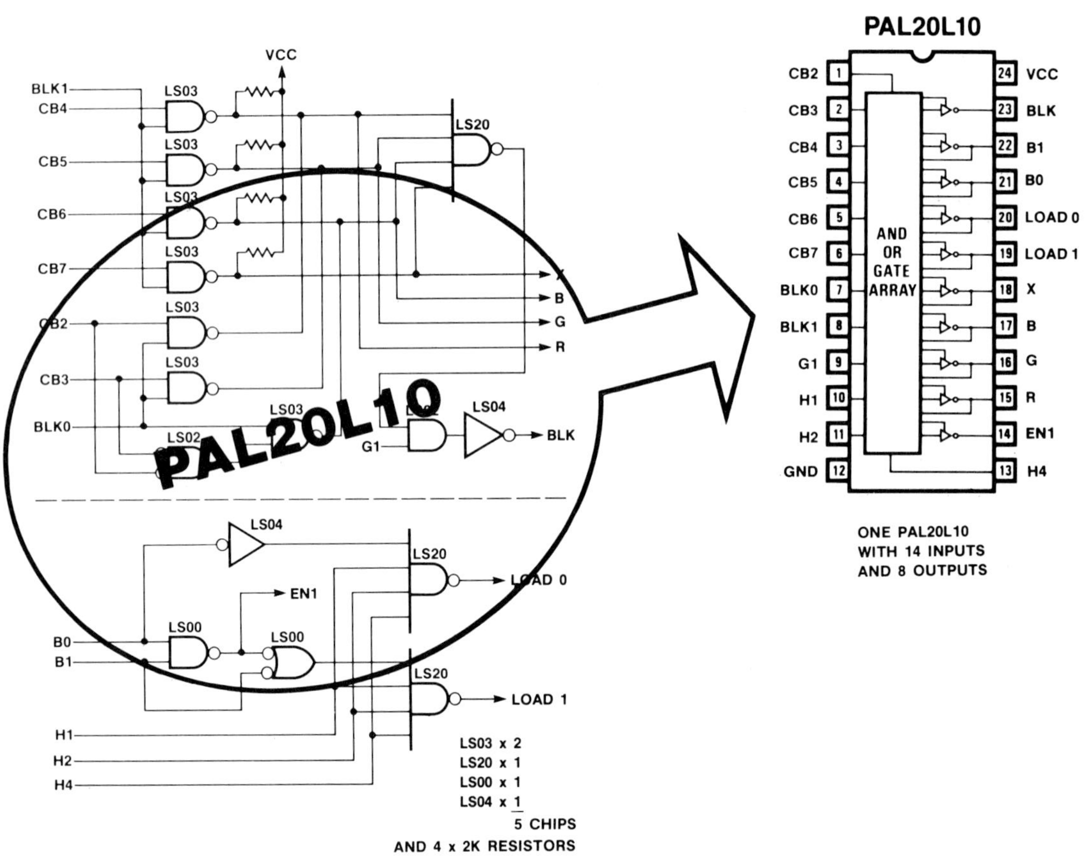

```
PAL20L10                                          PAL DESIGN SPECIFICATION
VIDLOG                                               HARRY HUGHES 02/18/81
VIDEO LOGIC
MMI ENGLAND
CB2 CB3 CB4 CB5 CB6 CB7 BLK0 BLK1 G1 H1 H2 GND
H4 EN1 R G B X LOAD1 LOAD0 B0 B1 BLK VCC

IF (VCC) /LOAD0 = /B0* H1* H2* H4

IF (VCC) /LOAD1 =  H1* H2* H4*/B1
                +  H1* H2* H4* B1* B0

IF (VCC) /EN1   =  B1* B0

IF (VCC) /R     =  CB4* BLK1
                +  CB2* BLK0

IF (VCC) /G     =  CB5* BLK1
                +  CB3* BLK0

IF (VCC) /B     =  CB6* BLK1
                + /CB2*/CB3* BLK0

IF (VCC) /X     =  CB7* BLK1

IF (VCC) /BLK   = /G1*/BLK1*/BLK0
                + /G1*/BLK0*/CB4*/CB5*/CB6*/CB7

FUNCTION TABLE

CB2 CB3 CB4 CB5 CB6 CB7 BLK0 BLK1 G1 H1 H2 H4 B1 B0 EN1 R G B X LOAD1 LOAD0 BLK

;CCCCCC   -BLANK-                 E
;BBBBBB   BLK BLK   G  HHH  BB   N    R G B X   LOAD    BLK     COMMENTS
;234567    0   1    1  124  10   1              1  0
-----------------------------------------------------------------------------
 XXXXXX    X   X    X  HHH  HL   X    X X X X   H  L     X      LOAD0
 XXXXXX    X   X    X  HHH  LL   X    X X X X   L  L     X      LOAD1
 XXXXXX    X   X    X  HHH  HH   L    X X X X   L  H     X      LOAD1
 XXXXXX    X   X    X  LLL  HH   L    X X X X   H  H     X      EN1
 XXHXXX    X   H    X  XXX  XX   X    L X X X   X  X     X      R
 HXXXXX    H   X    X  XXX  XX   X    L X X X   X  X     X      R
 XXXHXX    X   H    X  XXX  XX   X    X L X X   X  X     X      G
 XHXXXX    H   X    X  XXX  XX   X    X L X X   X  X     X      G
 XXXXHX    X   H    X  XXX  XX   X    X X L X   X  X     X      B
 LLXXXX    H   X    X  XXX  XX   X    X X L X   X  X     X      B
 XXXXXH    X   H    X  XXX  XX   X    X X X L   X  X     X      X
 XXXXXX    L   L    L  XXX  XX   X    X X X X   X  X     L      BLK
 XXLLLL    L   X    L  XXX  XX   X    X X X X   X  X     L      BLK
-----------------------------------------------------------------------------

DESCRIPTION
THIS PAL REPLACES ALL OF THE TTL LOGIC USED ON A VIDEO DRIVER BOARD (5 ICs)
TOGETHER WITH 4 PULL-UP RESISTORS.
```

```
VIDEO LOGIC

 1 XXXXXXXXX11X1XXXXXHL01X1
 2 XXXXXXXXX11X1XXXXXLL00X1
 3 XXXXXXXXX11X1LXXXXLH11X1
 4 XXXXXXXXX00X0LXXXXHH11X1
 5 XX1XXXX1XXXXXXLXXXXXXXX1
 6 1XXXXX1XXXXXXXLXXXXXXXX1
 7 XXX1XXX1XXXXXXXLXXXXXXX1
 8 X1XXXX1XXXXXXXXLXXXXXXX1
 9 XXXX1XX1XXXXXXXXLXXXXXX1
10 00XXXX1XXXXXXXXXLXXXXXX1
11 XXXXX1X1XXXXXXXXXLXXXXX1
12 XXXXXX000XXXXXXXXXXXXXL1
13 XX00000X0XXXXXXXXXXXXXL1

PASS SIMULATION

VIDEO LOGIC

                11 1111 1111 2222 2222 2233 3333 3333
   0123 4567 8901 2345 6789 0123 4567 8901 2345 6789

 0 ---- ---- ---- ---- ---- ---- ---- ---- ---- ----
 1 ---- ---- ---- ---- ---- -X-- -X-- -X-- ---- ---- /G1*/BLK1*/BLK0
 2 ---- -X-- -X-- -X-- -X-- -X-- ---- -X-- ---- ---- /G1*/BLK0*/CB4*/CB5*/CB-


24 ---- ---- ---- ---- ---- ---- ---- ---- ---- ----
25 ---- ---- ---X ---- ---- ---- ---- ---- X--- X-X- /B0*H1*H2*H4

32 ---- ---- ---- ---- ---- ---- ---- ---- ---- ----
33 ---- ---X ---- ---- ---- ---- ---- ---- X--- X-X- H1*H2*H4*/B1
34 ---- --X- --X- ---- ---- ---- ---- ---- X--- X-X- H1*H2*H4*B1*B0

40 ---- ---- ---- ---- ---- ---- ---- ---- ---- ----
41 ---- ---- ---- ---- X--- ---- X--- ---- ---- ---- CB7*BLK1

48 ---- ---- ---- ---- ---- ---- ---- ---- ---- ----
49 ---- ---- ---- X--- ---- ---- X--- ---- ---- ---- CB6*BLK1
50 -X-X ---- ---- ---- ---- X--- ---- ---- ---- ---- /CB2*/CB3*BLK0

56 ---- ---- ---- ---- ---- ---- ---- ---- ---- ----
57 ---- ---- X--- ---- ---- ---- X--- ---- ---- ---- CB5*BLK1
58 X--- ---- ---- ---- ---- X--- ---- ---- ---- ---- CB3*BLK0

64 ---- ---- ---- ---- ---- ---- ---- ---- ---- ----
65 ---- X--- ---- ---- ---- ---- X--- ---- ---- ---- CB4*BLK1
66 --X- ---- ---- ---- ---- X--- ---- ---- ---- ---- CB2*BLK0

72 ---- ---- ---- ---- ---- ---- ---- ---- ---- ----
73 ---- --X- --X- ---- ---- ---- ---- ---- ---- ---- B1*B0

LEGEND:  X : FUSE NOT BLOWN (L,N,0)   - : FUSE BLOWN   (H,P,1)

NUMBER OF FUSES BLOW =  801
```

Video Logic Replacement

Logic Diagram PAL20L10

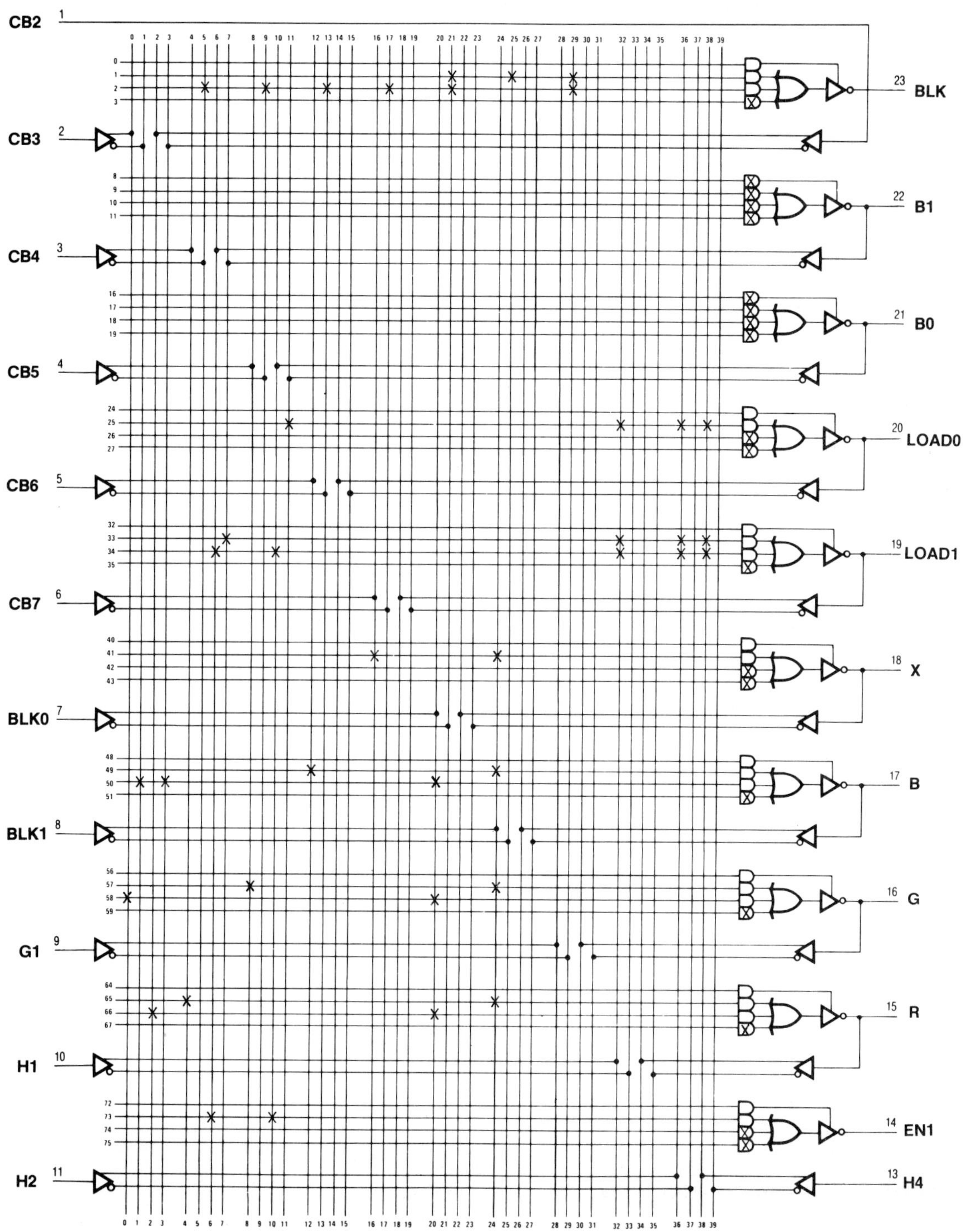

PAL
IMPORTANT,
NOTES

Binary to BCD Converter

PAL16R8

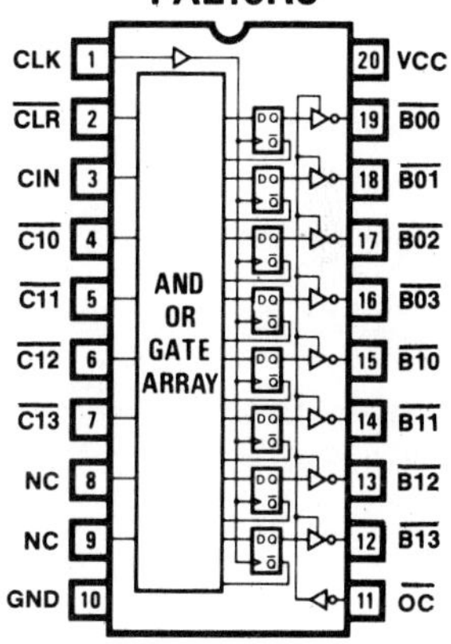

Serial Binary to Parallel BCD Conversion

The purpose of this circuit is to convert a serial stream of binary data into a parallel BCD representation as depicted by Figure 1.

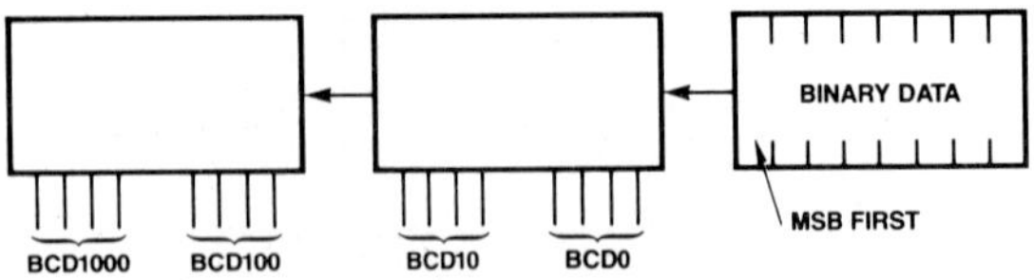

Figure 1. Conceptual Diagram of Binary to BCD Converter

Couleur's Technique (BIDEC)

In this conversion technique (Ref. 1), the input binary data is shifted left (starting with the MSB) into the BCD register. The beauty of this method is that after each clock pulse, the BCD output contains correct BCD representation for the "relative" binary data shifted so far. We illustrate the last statement in Figure 2.

Logic Design

The overall conversion problem can be segmented into four-bit binary blocks. Each block represents one BCD digit and is expandable by C_{IN} and C_{OUT}. The BCD building block, is shown in Figure 3 as a state machine.

The combinational network can be designed from a "next-state" truth table. The truth table can be constructed by observing that a left shift is a multiplication by 2, and a carryin adds 1 to the LSB.

In equation form:

BCD (next state): = 2∗ BCD (present state) + C_{IN}
Of course, if it were binary it will be simply,

$$Q_n := Q_{n-1}$$

However, BCD requires some corrections as will be shown shortly. For simplicity we analyze the three relevent cases:

a) BCD (present state): = 0 − 4
then BCD (next state): = 0 − 8 which are representable in BCD format

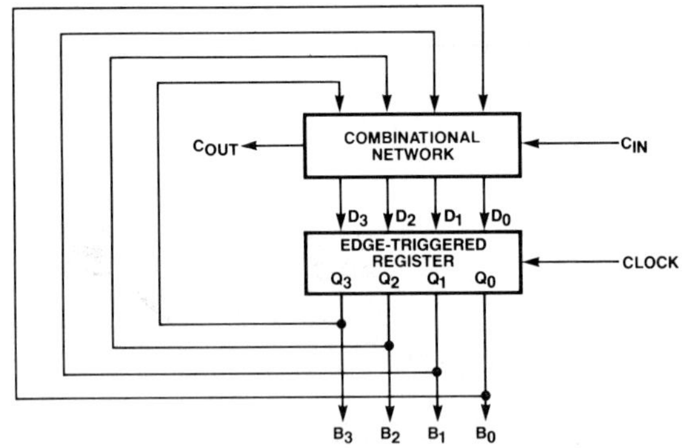

Figure 3, BCD Converter Building Block.

b) BCD (present state): = 5 − 9
then BCD (next state): = 10 − 18 which are not representable in one BCD digit, and a carry out is generated.
e.g. If BCD (present state): = 6
then BCD (next state): = 2 and C_{OUT} = 1

c) If C_{IN} = 1 then it is simply shifted into the LSB of the BCD digit (the old LSB was shifted left leaving a zero in its original position).
Thus, regardless of the BCD (present state) value, the following is true:

BO (next state): = C_{IN}

Truth Table

The preceding discussion is summarized by Tables 1 and 2.

PRESENT STATE B_3-B_0	NEXT STATE B_3-B_0	C_{OUT}
0-4	0-8	0
5-9	0-8	1
10-15	DON'T CARE	DON'T CARE

Table 1, General Truth Table.

n	PRESENT STATE B_3	B_2	B_1	B_0	NEXT STATE B_3	B_2	B_1	B_0	C_{OUT}
0	0	0	0	0	0	0	0	C_{IN}	
1	0	0	0	1	0	0	1	C_{IN}	0
2	0	0	1	0	0	1	0	C_{IN}	0
3	0	0	1	1	0	1	1	C_{IN}	0
4	0	1	0	0	1	0	0	C_{IN}	0
5	0	1	0	1	0	0	0	C_{IN}	1
6	0	1	1	0	0	0	1	C_{IN}	1
7	0	1	1	1	0	1	0	C_{IN}	1
8	1	0	0	0	0	1	1	C_{IN}	1
9	1	0	0	1	1	0	0	C_{IN}	1
10-15					X	X	X	X	X

Table 2: Detailed Truth Table.

												128	64	32	16	8	4	2	1	← RELATIVE WEIGHT BEFORE LAST SHIFT
												64	32	16	8	4	2	1		← RELATIVE WEIGHT BEFORE 7TH SHIFT
												32	16	8	4	2	1			← RELATIVE WEIGHT BEFORE 6TH SHIFT
												16	8	4	2	1				← RELATIVE WEIGHT BEFORE 5TH SHIFT
												8	4	2	1					← RELATIVE WEIGHT BEFORE 4TH SHIFT
												4	2	1						← RELATIVE WEIGHT BEFORE 3RD SHIFT
												2	1							← RELATIVE WEIGHT BEFORE 2ND SHIFT
CONVERSION REGISTER												1								← RELATIVE WEIGHT BEFORE 1ST SHIFT
10^2				10^1				10^0				1	0	0	1	0	0	0	0	← BINARY INPUT
											1	0	0	1	0	0	0	0		← 1 SHIFTED IN
										1	0	0	1	0	0	0	0			← 2 SHIFTED IN
									1	0	0	1	0	0	0	0				← 4 SHIFTED IN
								1	0	0	1	0	0	0	0					← 9 SHIFTED IN
							1	1	0	0	0	0	0	0						← 18 SHIFTED IN
						1	1	0	1	1	0	0	0							← 36 SHIFTED IN
					1	1	1	0	0	1	0	0								← 72 SHIFTED IN
			1	0	1	0	0	0	1	0	C									← 144 SHIFTED IN
1				4				4												

Figure 2: Tabular Representation of the Conversion Cycle.

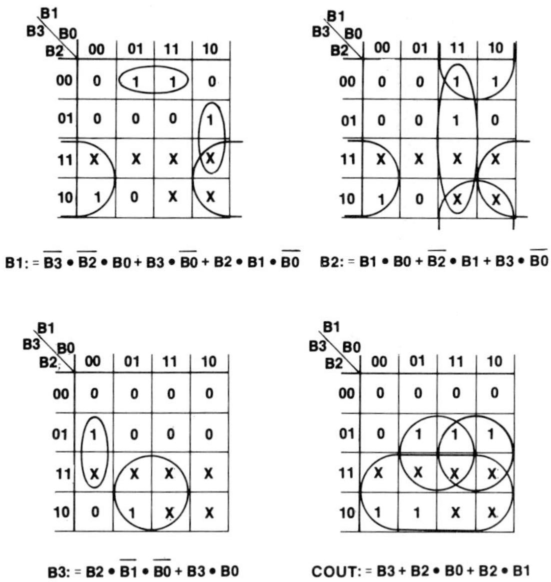

Figure 4. Karnaugh Maps

PAL Implementation

The PAL16R8 implements two BCD digits. One of the pins is assigned to the clear (CLR) function. The BCD conversion register must be initialized to zero before shifting of the binary input data is started. The eight output registers are assigned to the two BCD digits.

At this point, it seems that we are short of one output pin for the C_{OUT} in expanding to more BCD digits. However, the basic equations indicate that C_{OUT} is a function of the four preceding BCD bits. Therefore, by inputting these four bits to the next stage, the C_{OUT} is derived internally by the latter stage. A similar trick is used in each chip to cascade internally.

This expansion solution implies that in the least significant BCD stage the equation is:

$$(1)\ BO: = C_{IN}$$

whereas in later stages the equation is:

$$(2)\ BO: = C_{13} + C_{12} \bullet C_{10} + C_{12} \bullet C_{11}$$

where the C terms are driven by the corresponding B terms of a preceding stage. However, in order to have a universal solution, we OR the two equations. If the PAL is used as the least significant stage C_{10}, C_{11}, C_{12} and C_{13} are grounded and equation (1) holds. If the PAL is used as an intermediate stage, C_{IN} is grounded and equation (2) holds.

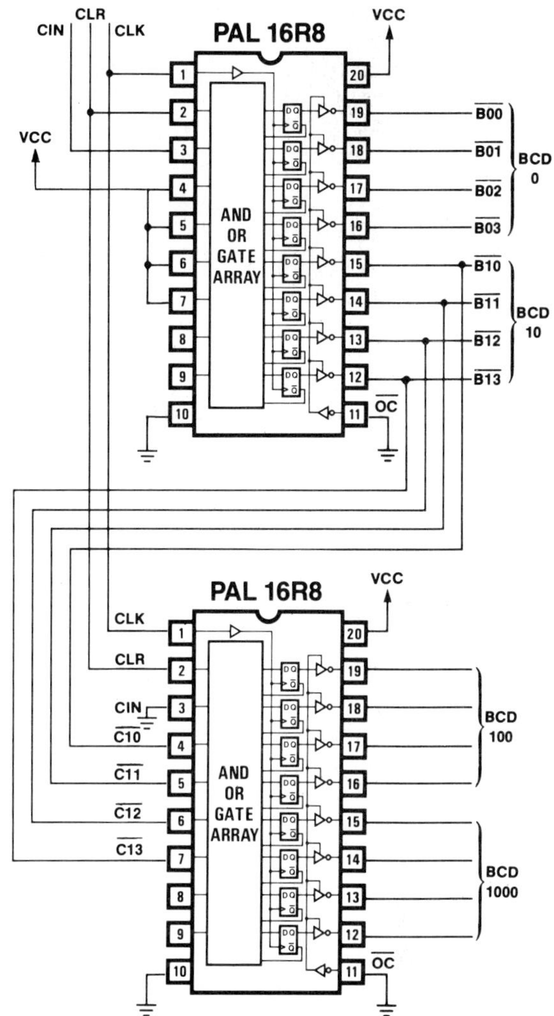

Figure 5. Logic Schematic

Summary

A similar algorithm was described in Ref. 2, where the two BCD digits were implemented with four ICs and could be clocked at 80 ns. Here we described one chip implementation that can be clocked at 60 ns.

References

1. *"Binary to BCD Conversion Techniques"* by B. MacDonald, EDN Dec. 1, 1969.
2. *"Special PROM Mode Effects Binary to BCD Converter"*, by D.M. Brockman, Electronics.

```
PAL16R8                                          PAL DESIGN SPECIFICATION
BBCD                                            S. WASER/V. COLI 09/14/81
BINARY TO BCD CONVERTER
MMI SUNNYVALE, CALIFORNIA
CLK /CLR CIN /C10 /C11 /C12 /C13 NC NC GND
/OC /B13 /B12 /B11 /B10 /B03 /B02 /B01 /B00 VCC


B00 := /CLR* CIN                          ;CONVERT B00 (LSB)
     + /CLR* C13
     + /CLR* C12* C10
     + /CLR* C12* C11

B01 := /CLR*/B03*/B02* B00                ;CONVERT B01
     + /CLR* B03*/B00
     + /CLR* B02* B01*/B00

B02 := /CLR* B01* B00                     ;CONVERT B02
     + /CLR*/B02* B01
     + /CLR* B03*/B00

B03 := /CLR* B02*/B01*/B00                ;CONVERT B03
     + /CLR* B03* B00

B10 := /CLR* B03                          ;CONVERT B10
     + /CLR* B02* B00
     + /CLR* B02* B01

B11 := /CLR*/B13*/B12* B10                ;CONVERT B11
     + /CLR* B13*/B10
     + /CLR* B12* B11*/B10

B12 := /CLR* B11* B10                     ;CONVERT B12
     + /CLR*/B12* B11
     + /CLR* B13*/B10

B13 := /CLR* B12*/B11*/B10                ;CONVERT B13 (MSB)
     + /CLR* B13* B10
```

```
FUNCTION TABLE

CIN C13 C12 C11 C10 /CLR CLK /OC B13 B12 B11 B10 B03 B02 B01 B00

;INPUTS   CONTROL   -OUTPUTS-
; CARRY    /          (BCD)
;C CCCC   C C /     BBBB BBBB
;I 1111   L L O     1111 0000
;N 3210   R K C     3210 3210      COMMENTS
-------------------------------------------------------------------------
 X XXXX   L C L     LLLL LLLL      CLEAR (0)
 H LLLL   H C L     LLLL LLLH      SERIAL INPUT A H (1)
 H LLLL   H C L     LLLL LLHH      SERIAL INPUT A H (3)
 L LLLL   H C L     LLLL LHHL      SERIAL INPUT A L (6)
 H LLLL   H C L     LLLH LLHH      SERIAL INPUT A H (13)
 X XXXX   L C L     LLLL LLLL      CLEAR (0)
 H LLLL   H C L     LLLL LLLH      SERIAL INPUT A H (1)
 L LLLL   H C L     LLLL LLHL      SERIAL INPUT A L (2)
 L LLLL   H C L     LLLL LHLL      SERIAL INPUT A L (4)
 L LLLL   H C L     LLLL HLLL      SERIAL INPUT A L (8)
 H LLLL   H C L     LLLH LHHH      SERIAL INPUT A H (17)
 L LLLL   H C L     LLHH LHLL      SERIAL INPUT A L (34)
 L LLLL   H C L     LHHL HLLL      SERIAL INPUT A L (68)
 X XXXX   L C L     LLLL LLLL      CLEAR (0)
 H LLLL   H C L     LLLL LLLH      SERIAL INPUT A H (1)
 L LLLL   H C L     LLLL LLHL      SERIAL INPUT A L (2)
 H LLLL   H C L     LLLL LHLH      SERIAL INPUT A H (5)
 H LLLL   H C L     LLLH LLLH      SERIAL INPUT A H (11)
 L LLLL   H C L     LLHL LLHL      SERIAL INPUT A L (22)
 H LLLL   H C L     LHLL LHLH      SERIAL INPUT A H (45)
 L LLLL   H C L     HLLH LLLL      SERIAL INPUT A L (90)
 X XXXX   L C L     LLLL LLLL      CLEAR REGISTERS TO TEST CASCADABILITY
 L HLLH   H C L     LLLL LLLH      SERIAL INPUT A L (178)  (TEST BCD 100, 1000)
 L LHHH   H C L     LLLL LLHH      SERIAL INPUT A L (360)  (TEST BCD 100, 1000)
 L LHHL   H C L     LLLL LHHH      SERIAL INPUT A L (720)  (TEST BCD 100, 1000)
 L LLHL   H C L     LLLH LHLL      SERIAL INPUT A L (1440) (TEST BCD 100, 1000)
 L LHLL   H C L     LLHL HLLL      SERIAL INPUT A L (2880) (TEST BCD 100, 1000)
 L HLLL   H C L     LHLH LHHH      SERIAL INPUT A L (5760) (TEST BCD 100, 1000)
 X XXXX   L C L     LLLL LLLL      CLEAR (0)
 H LLLL   H C L     LLLL LLLH      SERIAL INPUT A H (1)
 H LLLL   H C L     LLLL LLHH      SERIAL INPUT A H (3)
 H LLLL   H C L     LLLL LHHH      SERIAL INPUT A H (7)
 H LLLL   H C L     LLLH LHLH      SERIAL INPUT A H (15)
 H LLLL   H C L     LLHH LLLH      SERIAL INPUT A H (31)
 H LLLL   H C L     LHHL LLHH      SERIAL INPUT A H (63)
 X XXXX   L C L     LLLL LLLL      CLEAR REGISTERS TO TEST CASCADABILITY
 L LHHL   H C L     LLLL LLLH      SERIAL INPUT A H (127)  (TEST BCD 100, 1000)
 L LLHL   H C L     LLLL LLHL      SERIAL INPUT A H (255)  (TEST BCD 100, 1000)
 L LHLH   H C L     LLLL LHLH      SERIAL INPUT A H (511)  (TEST BCD 100, 1000)
 L LLLH   H C L     LLLH LLLL      SERIAL INPUT A H (1023) (TEST BCD 100, 1000)
 L LLHL   H C L     LLHL LLLL      SERIAL INPUT A H (2047) (TEST BCD 100, 1000)
 L LHLL   H C L     LHLL LLLL      SERIAL INPUT A H (4097) (TEST BCD 100, 1000)
 L HLLH   H C L     HLLL LLLH      SERIAL INPUT A H (8196) (TEST BCD 100, 1000)
 X XXXX   X X H     ZZZZ ZZZZ      TEST HI-Z
-------------------------------------------------------------------------
```

DESCRIPTION

THE FUNCTION OF THIS PAL IS TO CONVERT A SERIAL STREAM OF BINARY DATA INTO A PARALLEL BCD REPRESENTATION. AFTER EACH CLOCK PULSE, THE BCD OUTPUT CONTAINS THE CORRECT BCD REPRESENTATION FOR THE RELATIVE BINARY DATA SHIFTED SO FAR.

THE INPUT BINARY DATA IS SHIFTED LEFT (STARTING WITH THE MSB) INTO THE BCD REGISTER. THIS TECHNIQUE IS KNOWN AS COULEUR'S TECHNIQUE (BIDEC).

THE COMBITORIAL NETWORK IS DESIGNED FROM THE FOLLOWING NEXT-STATE TABLE:

PRESENT STATE B3-B0	NEXT STATE B3-B0	COUT
0-4	0-8	0
5-9	0-8	1
10-15	X	X

```
BINARY TO BCD CONVERTER

 1 C0XXXXXXXX0HHHHHHHH1
 2 C111111XXX0HHHHHHHL1
 3 C111111XXX0HHHHHHLL1
 4 C101111XXX0HHHHHLLH1
 5 C111111XXX0HHHLHHLL1
 6 C0XXXXXXXX0HHHHHHHH1
 7 C111111XXX0HHHHHHHL1
 8 C101111XXX0HHHHHHLH1
 9 C101111XXX0HHHHHLHH1
10 C101111XXX0HHHHLHHH1
11 C111111XXX0HHHLHLLL1
12 C101111XXX0HHLLHLHH1
13 C101111XXX0HLLHLHHH1
14 C0XXXXXXXX0HHHHHHHH1
15 C111111XXX0HHHHHHHL1
16 C101111XXX0HHHHHHLH1
17 C111111XXX0HHHHHLHL1
18 C111111XXX0HHHLHHHL1
19 C101111XXX0HHLHHHLH1
20 C111111XXX0HLHHHLHL1
21 C101111XXX0LHHLHHHH1
22 C0XXXXXXXX0HHHHHHHH1
23 C100110XXX0HHHHHHHL1
24 C100001XXX0HHHHHHLL1
25 C101001XXX0HHHHHLLL1
26 C101011XXX0HHHLHLHH1
27 C101101XXX0HHLHLHHH1
28 C101110XXX0HLHLHLLL1
29 C0XXXXXXXX0HHHHHHHH1
30 C111111XXX0HHHHHHHL1
31 C111111XXX0HHHHHHLL1
32 C111111XXX0HHHHHLLL1
33 C111111XXX0HHHLHLHL1
34 C111111XXX0HHLLHHHL1
35 C111111XXX0HLLHHHLL1
36 C0XXXXXXXX0HHHHHHHH1
37 C101001XXX0HHHHHHHL1
38 C101011XXX0HHHHHHLH1
39 C100101XXX0HHHHHLHL1
40 C100111XXX0HHHLHHHH1
41 C101011XXX0HHLHHHHH1
42 C101101XXX0HLHHHHHH1
43 C100110XXX0LHHHHHHL1
44 XXXXXXXXXX1ZZZZZZZZ1

PASS SIMULATION
```

```
BINARY TO BCD CONVERTER

               11 1111 1111 2222 2222 2233
   0123 4567 8901 2345 6789 0123 4567 8901

 0 X--- X--- ---- ---- ---- ---- ---- ---- /CLR*CIN
 1 X--- ---- ---- ---- ---- -X-- ---- ---- /CLR*C13
 2 X--- ---- -X-- ---- -X-- ---- ---- ---- /CLR*C12*C10
 3 X--- ---- ---- -X-- -X-- ---- ---- ---- /CLR*C12*C11

 8 X--X ---- --X- --X- ---- ---- ---- ---- /CLR*/B03*/B02*B00
 9 X-X- ---- ---- ---X ---- ---- ---- ---- /CLR*B03*/B00
10 X-X- ---X ---X ---- ---- ---- ---- ---- /CLR*B02*B01*/B00

16 X--X ---X ---- ---- ---- ---- ---- ---- /CLR*B01*B00
17 X--- ---X --X- ---- ---- ---- ---- ---- /CLR*/B02*B01
18 X-X- ---- ---- ---X ---- ---- ---- ---- /CLR*B03*/B00

24 X-X- --X- ---X ---- ---- ---- ---- ---- /CLR*B02*/B01*/B00
25 X--X ---- ---- ---X ---- ---- ---- ---- /CLR*B03*B00

32 X--- ---- ---- ---X ---- ---- ---- ---- /CLR*B03
33 X--X ---- ---X ---- ---- ---- ---- ---- /CLR*B02*B00
34 X--- ---X ---X ---- ---- ---- ---- ---- /CLR*B02*B01

40 X--- ---- ---- ---- ---X ---- --X- --X- /CLR*/B13*/B12*B10
41 X--- ---- ---- ---- --X- ---- ---- ---X /CLR*B13*/B10
42 X--- ---- ---- ---- --X- ---X ---X ---- /CLR*B12*B11*/B10

48 X--- ---- ---- ---- ---X ---X ---- ---- /CLR*B11*B10
49 X--- ---- ---- ---- ---- ---X --X- ---- /CLR*/B12*B11
50 X--- ---- ---- ---- --X- ---- ---- ---X /CLR*B13*/B10

56 X--- ---- ---- ---- --X- --X- ---X ---- /CLR*B12*/B11*/B10
57 X--- ---- ---- ---- ---X ---- ---- ---X /CLR*B13*B10


LEGEND:  X : FUSE NOT BLOWN (L,N,0)   - : FUSE BLOWN   (H,P,1)

NUMBER OF FUSES BLOWN =  664
```

Binary to BCD Converter

Logic Diagram PAL16R8

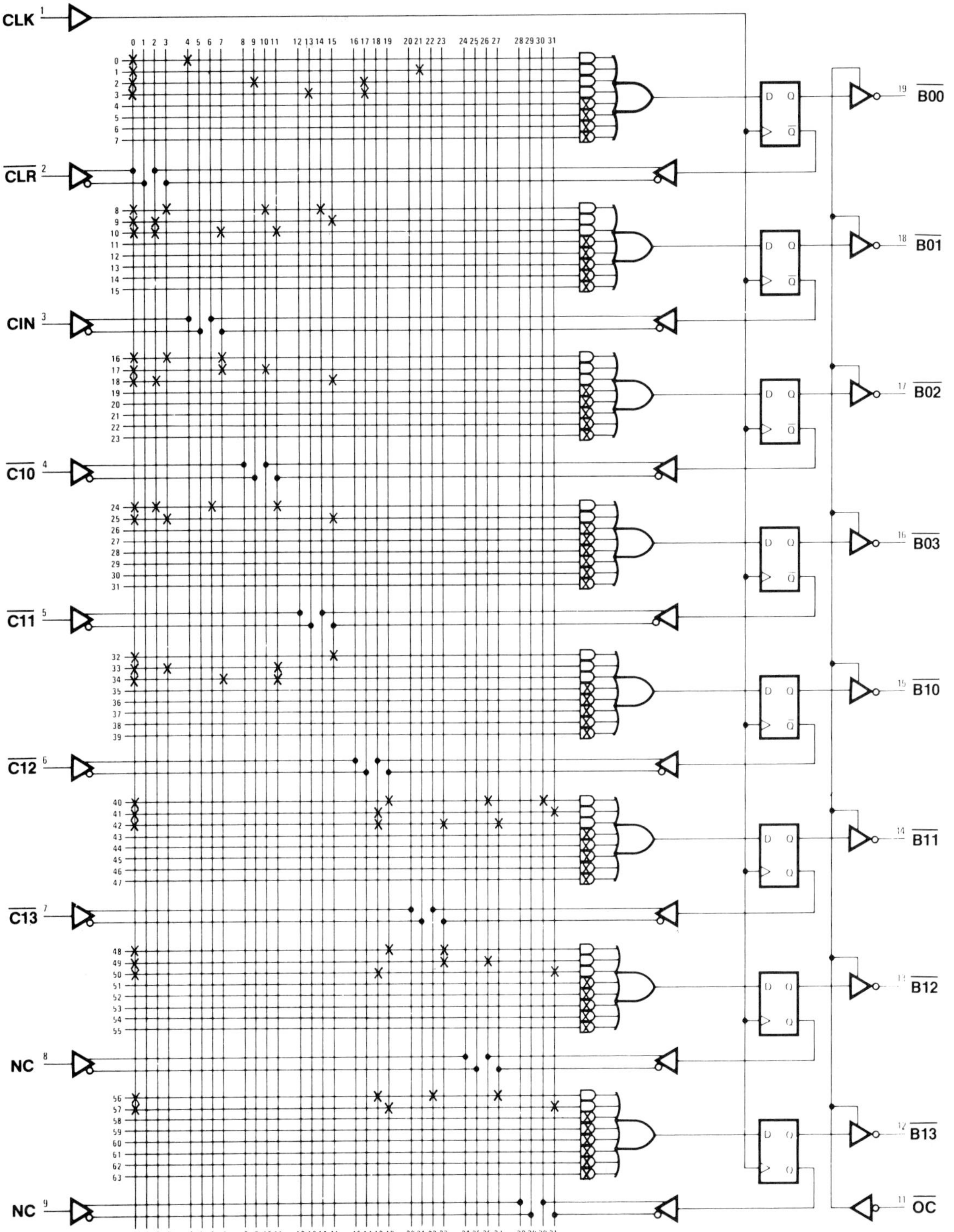

PAL
IMPORTANT,
NOTES

Deglitcher

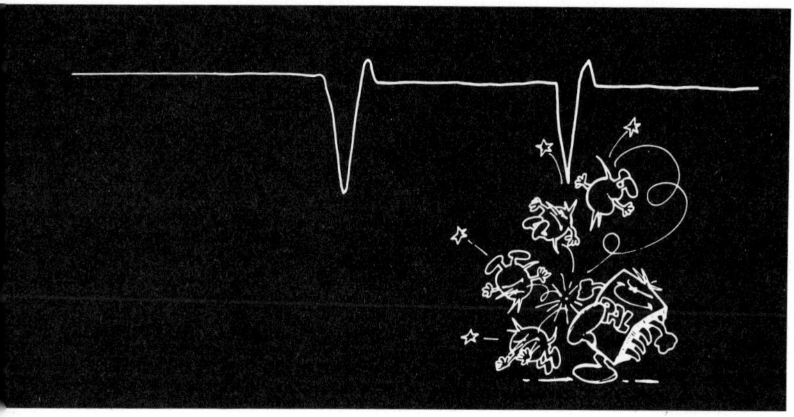

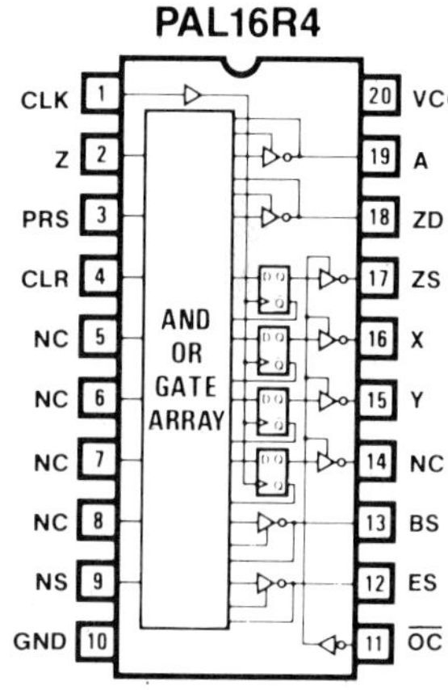
PAL16R4
CLK 1
Z 2
PRS 3
CLR 4
NC 5
NC 6
NC 7
NC 8
NS 9
GND 10
AND
OR
GATE
ARRAY
20 VCC
19 A
18 ZD
17 ZS
16 X
15 Y
14 NC
13 BS
12 ES
11 $\overline{OC}$

```
PAL16R4                                         PAL DESIGN SPECIFICATION
DEGL                                            VINCENT LECLERC 03/03/81
DEGLITCHER
MMI FRANCE
CLK Z PRS CLR NC NC NC NC NC GND /OC ES BS NC Y X ZS ZD A VCC


/ZS := /PRS*/Z
     +  CLR                           ;CLEAR

/X  := /PRS*/X*/Y
     + /PRS*/X   */ZS
     + /PRS*   /Y*/ZS
     +  CLR                           ;CLEAR

/Y  := /PRS*/ZS
     +  CLR                           ;CLEAR

IF(VCC) /BS =  X + /Y + /ZS           ;BEGINNING OF SIGNAL

IF(VCC) /ES = /X +  Y +  ZS           ;END OF SIGNAL

IF(VCC) /A  = /PRS*ZD*/BS*/ES
            + /PRS*ZD        */A
            + /PRS   * BS    */A
            + /PRS       * ES*/A
            +  CLR                    ;CLEAR

IF(VCC) /ZD = /PRS*/A* BS
            + /PRS*/A* ES
            + /PRS*/A*/ZD
            + /PRS*/BS*/ES*/ZD        ;Z DETECTED
            + CLR                     ;CLEAR


FUNCTION TABLE

CLK /OC Z PRS CLR X Y ZS BS ES ZD A   ;COMMENTS
----------------------------------------------------------
 C   L  X  L   H  L L  L  L  L  L L    CLEAR
 C   L  L  L   L  L L  L  L  L  L H    INITIAL STATE S00
 C   L  H  L   L  L L  H  L  L  L H    INPUT Z
 C   L  L  L   L  L H  L  L  L  L H    STATE S00 TO S01
 C   L  H  L   L  L L  H  L  L  L H    STATE S01 TO S00
 C   L  H  L   L  L H  H  H  L  H H    STATE S00 TO S01
 C   L  L  L   L  H H  L  L  L  H L    STATE S01 TO S11
 C   L  L  L   L  H L  L  L  H  H H    STATE S11 TO S10
 C   L  L  L   L  L L  L  L  L  L H    STATE S10 TO S00
 C   L  X  H   L  H H  H  L  L  H H    PRESET TEST
 X   H  X  X   X  Z Z  Z  X  X  X X    ENABLE TEST
----------------------------------------------------------
```

DESCRIPTION

THE SYSTEM DETECTS THE BEGINNING AND THE END OF A SIGNAL WHICH IS DISTURBED BY GLITCHES.

```
DEGLITCHER

 1 CX01XXXXXX0LLXLLLLL1
 2 C000XXXXXX0LLXLLLLH1
 3 C100XXXXXX0LLXLLHLH1
 4 C000XXXXXX0LLXHLLLH1
 5 C100XXXXXX0LLXLLHLH1
 6 C100XXXXXX0LHXHLHHH1
 7 C000XXXXXX0LLXHHLHL1
 8 C000XXXXXX0HLXLHLHH1
 9 C000XXXXXX0LLXLLLLH1
10 CX10XXXXXX0LLXHHHHH1
11 XXXXXXXXXX1XXXZZZXX1

PASS SIMULATION
```

DEGLITCHER

```
           11 1111 1111 2222 2222 2233
0123 4567 8901 2345 6789 0123 4567 8901

 0 ---- ---- ---- ---- ---- ---- ---- ----
 1 ---- -XX- ---- ---- ---- ---- ---X ---X /PRS*ZD*/BS*/ES
 2 ---X -XX- ---- ---- ---- ---- ---- ---- /PRS*ZD*/A
 3 ---X -X-- ---- ---- ---- ---- --X- ---- /PRS*BS*/A
 4 ---X -X-- ---- ---- ---- ---- ---- --X- /PRS*ES*/A
 5 ---- ---- X--- ---- ---- ---- ---- ---- CLR

 8 ---- ---- ---- ---- ---- ---- ---- ----
 9 ---X -X-- ---- ---- ---- ---- --X- ---- /PRS*/A*BS
10 ---X -X-- ---- ---- ---- ---- ---- --X- /PRS*/A*ES
11 ---X -X-X ---- ---- ---- ---- ---- ---- /PRS*/A*/ZD
12 ---- -X-X ---- ---- ---- ---- ---X ---X /PRS*/BS*/ES*/ZD
13 ---- ---- X--- ---- ---- ---- ---- ---- CLR

16 -X-- -X-- ---- ---- ---- ---- ---- ---- /PRS*/Z
17 ---- ---- X--- ---- ---- ---- ---- ---- CLR

24 ---- -X-- ---- ---X ---X ---- ---- ---- /PRS*/X*/Y
25 ---- -X-- ---X ---X ---- ---- ---- ---- /PRS*/X*/ZS
26 ---- -X-- ---X ---- ---X ---- ---- ---- /PRS*/Y*/ZS
27 ---- ---- X--- ---- ---- ---- ---- ---- CLR

32 ---- -X-- ---X ---- ---- ---- ---- ---- /PRS*/ZS
33 ---- ---- X--- ---- ---- ---- ---- ---- CLR


48 ---- ---- ---- ---- ---- ---- ---- ----
49 ---- ---- ---- --X- ---- ---- ---- ---- X
50 ---- ---- ---- ---- ---X ---- ---- ---- /Y
51 ---- ---- ---X ---- ---- ---- ---- ---- /ZS

56 ---- ---- ---- ---- ---- ---- ---- ----
57 ---- ---- ---- ---X ---- ---- ---- ---- /X
58 ---- ---- ---- ---- --X- ---- ---- ---- Y
59 ---- ---- --X- ---- ---- ---- ---- ---- ZS
```

LEGEND: X : FUSE NOT BLOWN (L,N,0)   - : FUSE BLOWN   (H,P,1)

NUMBER OF FUSES BLOWN = 846

Deglitcher

Logic Diagram PAL16R4

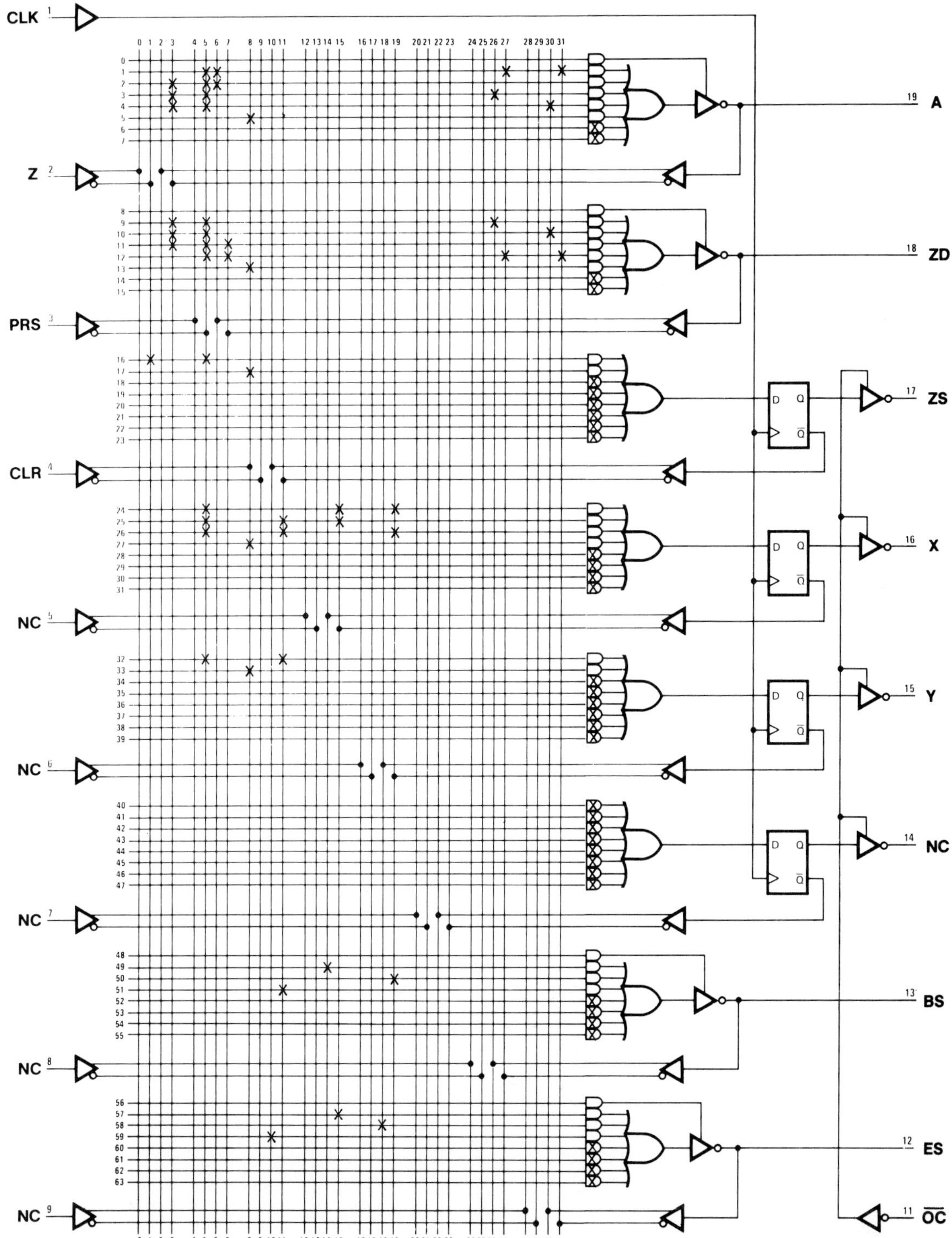

PAL
IMPORTANT, NOTES

Electronic Dice Game

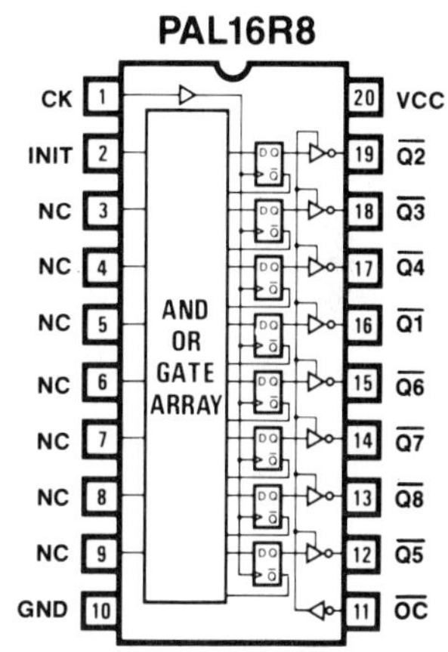

Logic Design Using Standard TTL

In one die, seven LEDs make up the display (Figure 1). Notice they can be connected such that only four lines are required to drive them. The LEDs are turned on when the appropriate line is driven low. Since there are four lines to be driven it is necessary to use four D-type flip-flops for each die. For reference the outputs of the flip-flops are labeled Q_1-Q_4 and the inputs are labeled D_1-D_4 (Figure 2). By using the inverting output of the Flip-Flop we can use positive logic in the design. That is, a logical "1" at a Q output represents an LED being turned on.

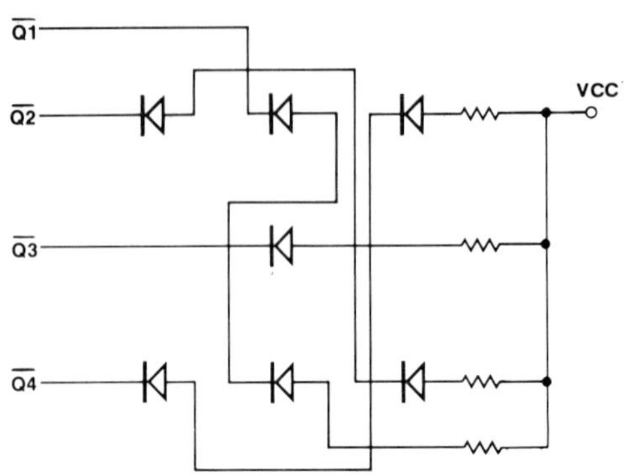

Figure 1

Looking at the Karnaugh Maps (Figure 3), it may be noticed that the simplest logic equations were not generated. This was to insure a path to a valid state from all invalid states.

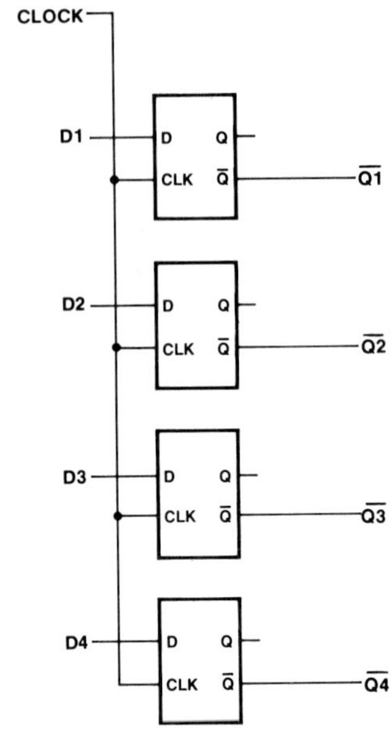

Figure 2

The present state of table 1 shows the preferred sequence in which the LEDs should turn on. The next state shows the conditions necessary to increment when clocked. From these two tables the Karnaugh Maps of Figure 3 were made. Using the Karnaugh Maps the following equations are obtained;

$$D_1 = \overline{Q_1}\, Q_2\, Q_3 \qquad D_2 = \overline{Q_1}\, Q_3 + \overline{Q_1}\, Q_4$$

$$D_3 = \overline{Q_3} \qquad D_4 = \overline{Q_1}\, Q_2 + \overline{Q_1}\, Q_4$$

These equations satisfy the requirements for one die. By substituting Q_5-Q_8 for Q_1-Q_4 and D_5-D_8 for D_1-D_4 we have the following equations;

$$D_5 = \overline{Q_5}\, Q_6\, Q_7 \qquad D_6 = \overline{Q_5}\, Q_7 + \overline{Q_5}\, Q_8$$

$$D_7 = \overline{Q_7} \qquad D_8 = \overline{Q_5}\,\overline{Q_7} + \overline{Q_5}\, Q_8$$

	PRESENT STATE				NEXT STATE			
STATE	Q_4	Q_3	Q_2	Q_1	D_4	D_3	D_2	D_1
1	0	1	0	0	0	0	1	0
2	0	0	1	0	1	1	0	0
3	1	1	0	0	1	0	1	0
4	1	0	1	0	1	1	1	0
5	1	1	1	0	1	0	1	1
6	1	0	1	1	0	1	0	0

Table 1

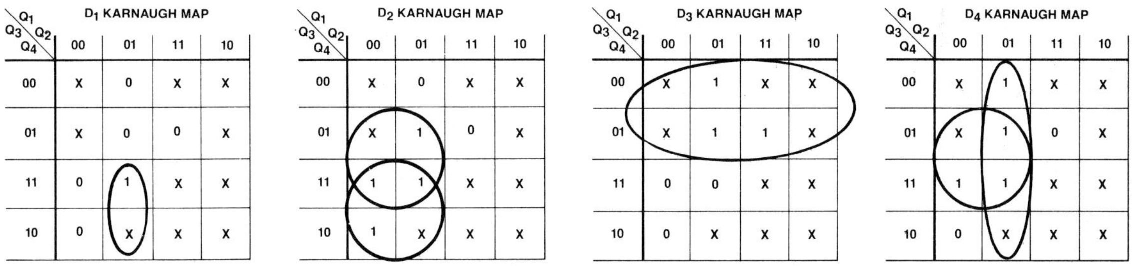

Note: X means Don't Care

Figure 3

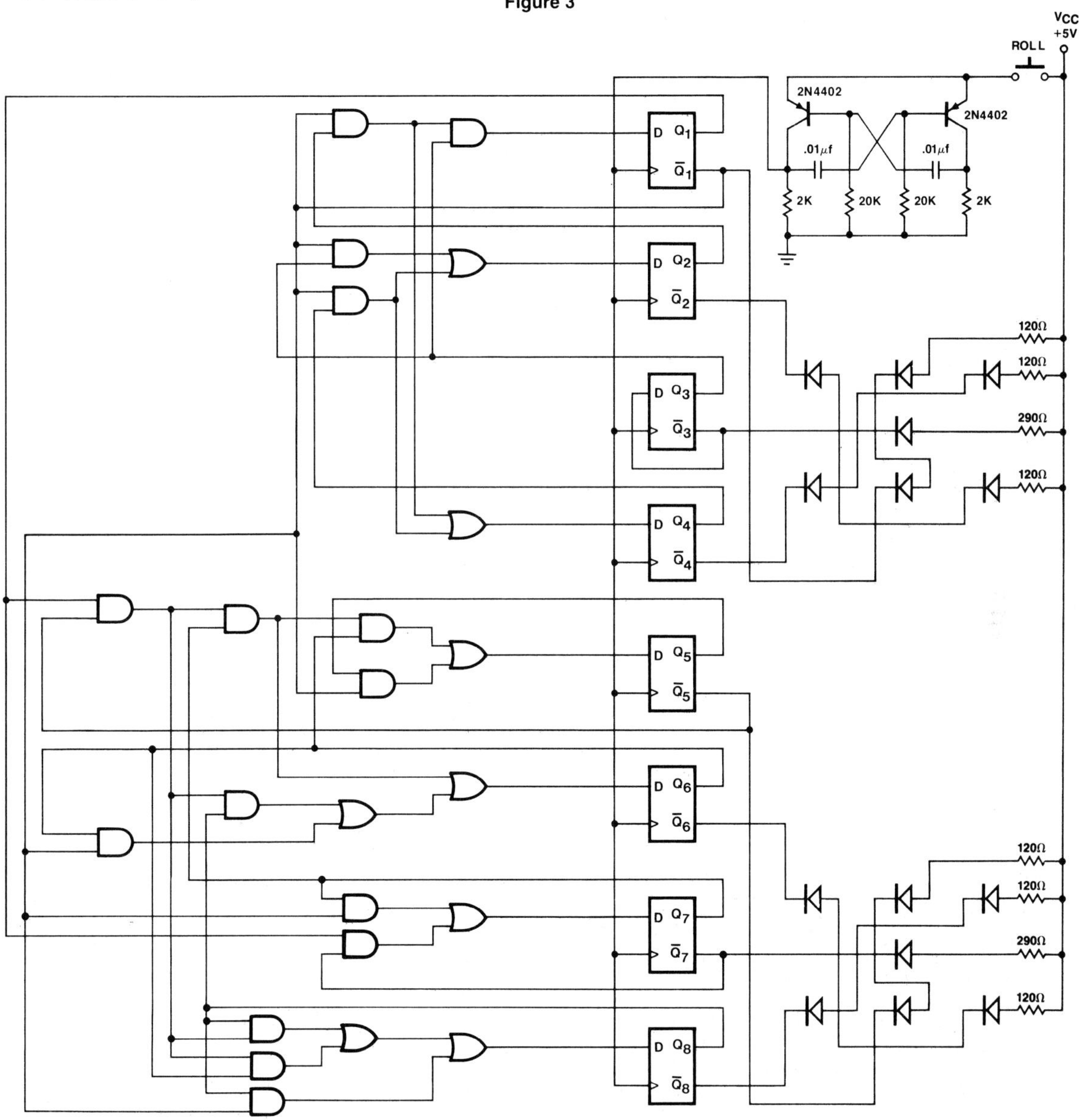

Figure 4

However, since this is a synchronous design the clocks of the two die are common. If the same equations are used for both die there will be only six different states. To get around this the first die is allowed to go through each of the six states incrementing with each clock. The second die is inhibited from incrementing except when the first die goes from the 6th state to the 1st state. At this time the second die is allowed to increment one time. Looking at the present state of table 1 it is noticed that whenever output Q_1 is high, the next clock should increment the second die. Whenever Q_1 is low the second die should remain the same. From this we now write all the equations.

$$D_1 = \overline{Q_1}\, Q_2\, Q_3$$
$$D_2 = \overline{Q_1}\, Q_3 + \overline{Q_1}\, Q_4$$
$$D_3 = \overline{Q_3}$$
$$D_4 = \overline{Q_1}\, Q_2 + \overline{Q_1}\, Q_4$$
$$D_5 = \overline{Q_1}\, Q_5 + Q_1\, \overline{Q_5}\, Q_6\, Q_7$$
$$D_6 = \overline{Q_1}\, Q_6 + Q_1\, \overline{Q_5}\, Q_7 + Q_1\, \overline{Q_5}\, Q_8$$
$$D_7 = \overline{Q_1}\, Q_7 + Q_1\, \overline{Q_7}$$
$$D_8 = \overline{Q_1}\, Q_8 + Q_1\, \overline{Q_5}\, Q_6 + Q_1\, \overline{Q_5}\, Q_8$$

From these equations the logic diagram can be drawn. (Figure 4)

Logic Design Using PALs

The design requires 8 registered outputs. Looking at the PAL Data Sheet we determine that a PAL16R8 best suits this application. The equations developed above can be used here without change. The PAL Design Specification shows the implementation of these equations. Note that the pinout is chosen to convenience PC board layout which is shown below.

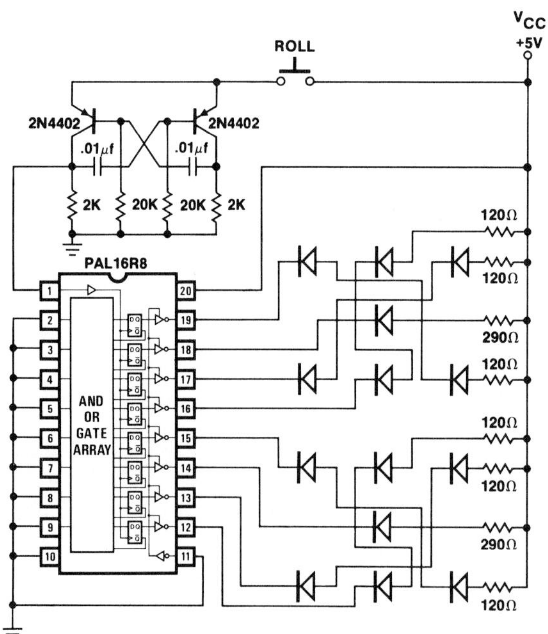

Applications

Rules for CRAPS

The following is a set of rules that apply whether you are playing in Las Vegas with dice or at home with a PAL.

The first roll is called the come-out and you win on a 7 or 11 or you "crap-out" on a 2 (snake eyes), 3 (ace caught a deuce) or 12 (box cars). If none of the above happens you will have rolled a number between 4 and 10. Mark this number well, you will need to roll it again to win. At this point no "crap" can hurt you, but unless you've programmed your PAL right, a seven can. Normal probabilities in 36 throws:

7 will appear	6 times
6	5
8	5
5	4
9	4
4	3
10	3
3	2
11	2
2	1
12	1

```
PAL16R8                                      PAL DESIGN SPECIFICATION
EDG                                              VETTER/COLI 07/06/81
ELECTRONIC DICE GAME
MMI SUNYVALE, CALIFORNIA
CK INIT NC NC NC NC NC NC NC GND
/OC /Q5 /Q8 /Q7 /Q6 /Q1 /Q4 /Q3 /Q2 VCC


Q1 :=  /Q1* Q2* Q3
    +   INIT

Q2 :=  /Q1* Q3*/INIT
    +  /Q1* Q4*/INIT

Q3 :=  /Q3*/INIT

Q4 :=  /Q1* Q2*/INIT
    +  /Q1* Q4*/INIT

Q5 :=  Q1*/Q5* Q6* Q7*/INIT
    + /Q1* Q5*/INIT

Q6 :=  Q1*/Q5* Q7*/INIT
    +  Q1*/Q5* Q8*/INIT
    + /Q1* Q6*/INIT

Q7 :=  Q1*/Q7*/INIT
    + /Q1* Q7*/INIT

Q8 :=  Q1*/Q5* Q6*/INIT
    +  Q1*/Q5* Q8*/INIT
    + /Q1* Q8*/INIT
```

```
FUNCTION TABLE

CK /OC INIT /Q1 /Q2 /Q3 /Q4 /Q5 /Q6 /Q7 /Q8

;-CONTROLS-     /OUTPUTS     COMMENTS
;C /            QQQQQQQQ    NUMBER DISPLAYED
;K OC  INIT     12345678    DIE 2  DIE 1
-----------------------------------------------
 C L    H       LHHHHHHH    INITIALIZE COUNTER
 C L    L       HHLHHHLH     1       1
 C L    L       HLHHHHLH     2       1
 C L    L       HHLLHHLH     3       1
 C L    L       HLHLHHLH     4       1
 C L    L       HLLLHHLH     5       1
 C L    L       LLHLHHLH     6       1
;
 C L    L       HHLHHLHH     1       2
 C L    L       HLHHHLHH     2       2
 C L    L       HHLLHLHH     3       2
 C L    L       HLHLHLHH     4       2
 C L    L       HLLLHLHH     5       2
 C L    L       LLHLHLHH     6       2
;
 C L    L       HHLHHHLL     1       3
 C L    L       HLHHHHLL     2       3
 C L    L       HHLLHHLL     3       3
 C L    L       HLHLHHLL     4       3
 C L    L       HLLLHHLL     5       3
 C L    L       LLHLHHLL     6       3
;
 C L    L       HHLHHLHL     1       4
 C L    L       HLHHHLHL     2       4
 C L    L       HHLLHLHL     3       4
 C L    L       HLHLHLHL     4       4
 C L    L       HLLLHLHL     5       4
 C L    L       LLHLHLHL     6       4
;
 C L    L       HHLHHLLL     1       5
 C L    L       HLHHHLLL     2       5
 C L    L       HHLLHLLL     3       5
 C L    L       HLHLHLLL     4       5
 C L    L       HLLLHLLL     5       5
 C L    L       LLHLHLLL     6       5
;
 C L    L       HHLHLLHL     1       6
 C L    L       HLHHLLHL     2       6
 C L    L       HHLLLLHL     3       6
 C L    L       HLHLLLHL     4       6
 C L    L       HLLLLLHL     5       6
 C L    L       LLHLLLHL     6       6
;
 C H    X       ZZZZZZZZ    TEST HI-Z
-----------------------------------------------
```

DESCRIPTION

THE DUAL MODULO-SIX COUNTER INCREMENTS ON THE RISING EDGE OF THE CLOCK (CK). THE THREE-STATE OUTPUTS ARE HIGH-Z WHEN THE OUTPUT CONTROL LINE (/OC) IS HIGH AND ENABLED WHEN THE OUTPUT CONTROL LINE (/OC) IS LOW.

THE "INIT" LINE IS NEEDED TO INITIALIZE THE COUNTER SO THAT THE FUNCTION TABLE SIMULATION COULD BE PERFORMED AND THE PART COULD BE TESTED AT THE TIME OF FABRICATION. THIS LINE AS WELL AS ALL OTHER UNUSED INPUTS SHOULD BE TIED TO GND.

THERE ARE 36 DIFFERENT STATES TO THE COUNT SEQUENCE. EACH STATE CORRESPONDS TO ONE OF THE NUMBER COMBINATIONS TO BE DISPLAYED ON THE DICE.

NOTE THAT THE PINOUT IS CHOSEN TO CONVENIENCE PC BOARD LAYOUT.

ELECTRONIC DICE GAME

```
 1 C1XXXXXXXX0HHHHLHHH1
 2 C0XXXXXXXX0HHLHHHLH1
 3 C0XXXXXXXX0HHLHHHHL1
 4 C0XXXXXXXX0HHLHHLLH1
 5 C0XXXXXXXX0HHLHHLHL1
 6 C0XXXXXXXX0HHLHHLLL1
 7 C0XXXXXXXX0HHLHLLHL1
 8 C0XXXXXXXX0HHHLHHLH1
 9 C0XXXXXXXX0HHHLHHHL1
10 C0XXXXXXXX0HHHLHLLH1
11 C0XXXXXXXX0HHHLHLHL1
12 C0XXXXXXXX0HHHLHLLL1
13 C0XXXXXXXX0HHHLLLHL1
14 C0XXXXXXXX0HLLHHHLH1
15 C0XXXXXXXX0HLLHHHHL1
16 C0XXXXXXXX0HLLHHLLH1
17 C0XXXXXXXX0HLLHHLHL1
18 C0XXXXXXXX0HLLHHLLL1
19 C0XXXXXXXX0HLLHLLHL1
20 C0XXXXXXXX0HLHLHHLH1
21 C0XXXXXXXX0HLHLHHHL1
22 C0XXXXXXXX0HLHLHLLH1
23 C0XXXXXXXX0HLHLHLHL1
24 C0XXXXXXXX0HLHLHLLL1
25 C0XXXXXXXX0HLHLLLHL1
26 C0XXXXXXXX0HLLLHHLH1
27 C0XXXXXXXX0HLLLHHHL1
28 C0XXXXXXXX0HLLLHLLH1
29 C0XXXXXXXX0HLLLHLHL1
30 C0XXXXXXXX0HLLLHLLL1
31 C0XXXXXXXX0HLLLLLHL1
32 C0XXXXXXXX0LLHLHHLH1
33 C0XXXXXXXX0LLHLHHHL1
34 C0XXXXXXXX0LLHLHLLH1
35 C0XXXXXXXX0LLHLHLHL1
36 C0XXXXXXXX0LLHLHLLL1
37 C0XXXXXXXX0LLHLLLHL1
38 CXXXXXXXXX1ZZZZZZZZ1
```

PASS SIMULATION

```
ELECTRONIC DICE GAME

                11 1111 1111 2222 2222 2233
   0123 4567 8901 2345 6789 0123 4567 8901

 0 -X-- ---X ---- --X- ---- ---- ---- ---- /Q1*Q3*/INIT
 1 -X-- ---- ---X --X- ---- ---- ---- ---- /Q1*Q4*/INIT

 8 -X-- --X- ---- ---- ---- ---- ---- ---- /Q3*/INIT

16 -X-X ---- ---- --X- ---- ---- ---- ---- /Q1*Q2*/INIT
17 -X-- ---- ---X --X- ---- ---- ---- ---- /Q1*Q4*/INIT

24 ---X ---X ---- --X- ---- ---- ---- ---- /Q1*Q2*Q3
25 X--- ---- ---- ---- ---- ---- ---- ---- INIT

32 -X-- ---- ---- ---X ---- ---X ---- --X- Q1*/Q5*Q7*/INIT
33 -X-- ---- ---- ---X ---- ---- ---X --X- Q1*/Q5*Q8*/INIT
34 -X-- ---- ---- --X- ---X ---- ---- ---- /Q1*Q6*/INIT

40 -X-- ---- ---- ---X ---- --X- ---- ---- Q1*/Q7*/INIT
41 -X-- ---- ---- --X- ---- ---X ---- ---- /Q1*Q7*/INIT

48 -X-- ---- ---- ---X ---X ---- ---- --X- Q1*/Q5*Q6*/INIT
49 -X-- ---- ---- ---X ---- ---- ---X --X- Q1*/Q5*Q8*/INIT
50 -X-- ---- ---- --X- ---- ---- ---X ---- /Q1*Q8*/INIT

56 -X-- ---- ---- ---X ---X ---X ---- --X- Q1*/Q5*Q6*Q7*/INIT
57 -X-- ---- ---- --X- ---- ---- ---- ---X /Q1*Q5*/INIT


LEGEND:  X : FUSE NOT BLOWN (L,N,0)   - : FUSE BLOWN   (H,P,1)

NUMBER OF FUSES BLOWN =  490
```

Electronic Dice Game

Logic Diagram PAL16R8

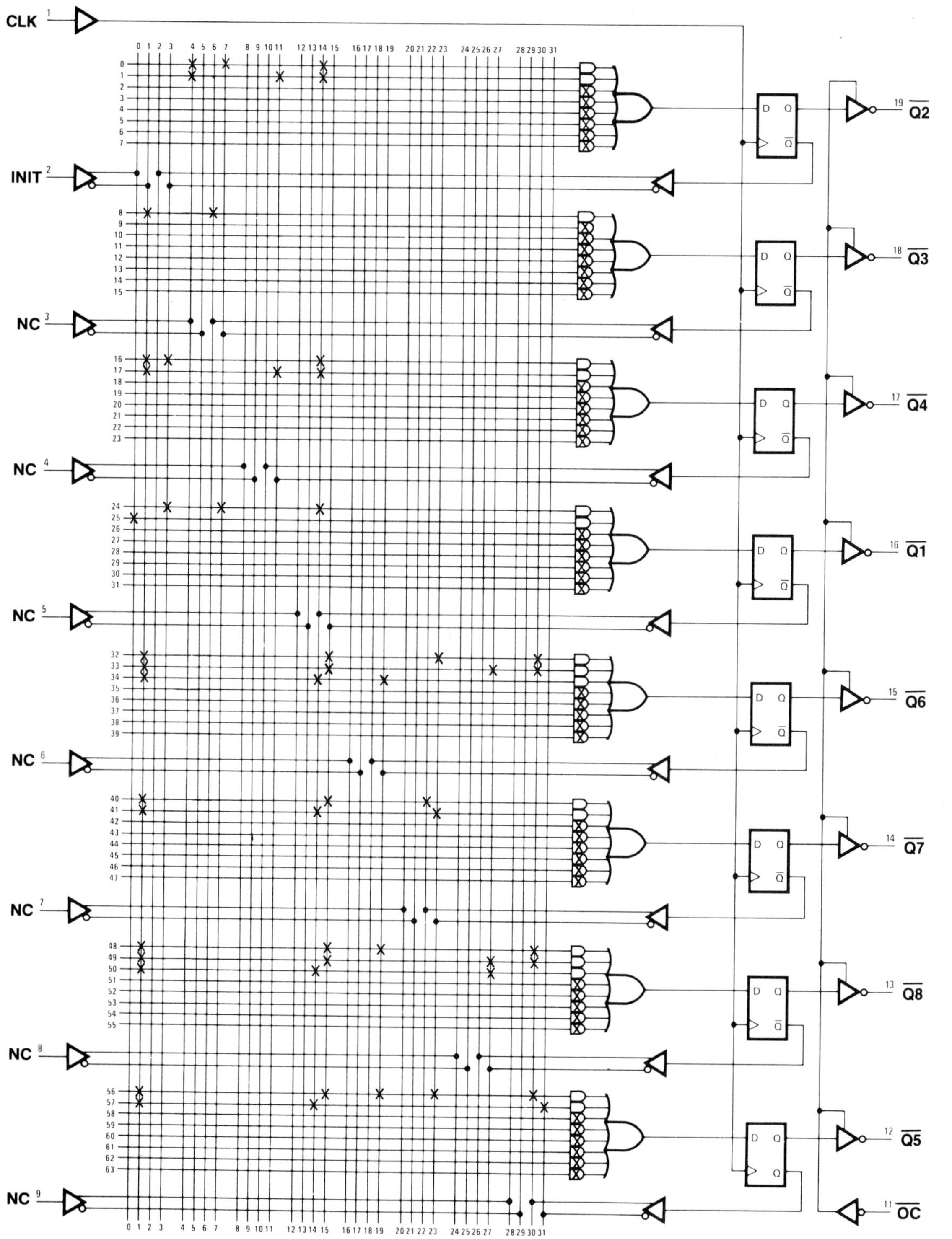

PAL
IMPORTANT
NOTES

9-Bit Register

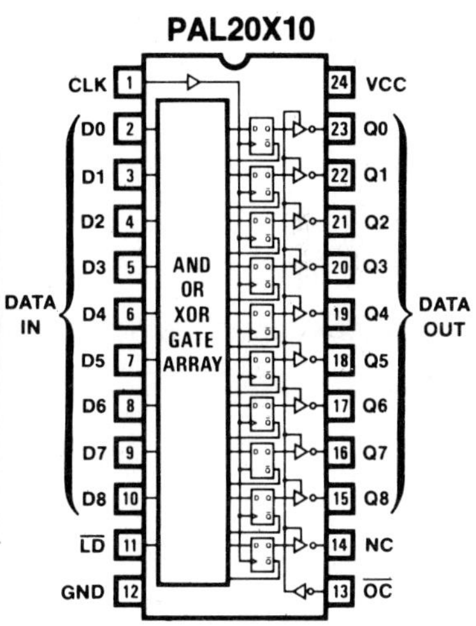

```
PAL20X10                                         PAL DESIGN SPECIFICATION
P8125                                              BIRKNER/COLI 07/19/81
9-BIT REGISTER
MMI SUNNYVALE, CALIFORNIA
CLK D0 D1 D2 D3 D4 D5 D6 D7 D8 /LD GND
/OC NC Q8 Q7 Q6 Q5 Q4 Q3 Q2 Q1  Q0 VCC


/Q0 := /Q0*/LD      ;HOLD Q0
     + /D0* LD      ;LOAD D0

/Q1 := /Q1*/LD      ;HOLD Q1
     + /D1* LD      ;LOAD D1

/Q2 := /Q2*/LD      ;HOLD Q2
     + /D2* LD      ;LOAD D2

/Q3 := /Q3*/LD      ;HOLD Q3
     + /D3* LD      ;LOAD D3

/Q4 := /Q4*/LD      ;HOLD Q4
     + /D4* LD      ;LOAD D4

/Q5 := /Q5*/LD      ;HOLD Q5
     + /D5* LD      ;LOAD D5

/Q6 := /Q6*/LD      ;HOLD Q6
     + /D6* LD      ;LOAD D6

/Q7 := /Q7*/LD      ;HOLD Q7
     + /D7* LD      ;LOAD D7

/Q8 := /Q8*/LD      ;HOLD Q8
     + /D8* LD      ;LOAD D8


FUNCTION TABLE

/OC CLK /LD D8 D7 D6 D5 D4 D3 D2 D1 D0 Q8 Q7 Q6 Q5 Q4 Q3 Q2 Q1 Q0

;/ C /    DATA IN     DATA OUT
;O L L   DDDDDDDDD   QQQQQQQQQ
;C K D   876543210   876543210     COMMENT
---------------------------------------------------------
 L C L   LLLLLLLLL   LLLLLLLLL     LOAD ALL ZEROS
 L C H   XXXXXXXXX   LLLLLLLLL     HOLD ALL ZEROS
 L C L   HHHHHHHHH   HHHHHHHHH     LOAD ALL ONES
 L C H   XXXXXXXXX   HHHHHHHHH     HOLD ALL ONES
 L C L   LHLHLHLHL   LHLHLHLHL     LOAD EVEN CHECKERBOARD
 L C H   XXXXXXXXX   LHLHLHLHL     HOLD EVEN CHECKERBOARD
 L C L   HLHLHLHLH   HLHLHLHLH     LOAD ODD  CHECKERBOARD
 L C H   XXXXXXXXX   HLHLHLHLH     HOLD ODD  CHECKERBOARD
 H X X   XXXXXXXXX   ZZZZZZZZZ     TEST HI-Z
---------------------------------------------------------
```

DESCRIPTION

THIS 9-BIT REGISTER LOADS THE DATA (D8-D0) ON THE RISING EDGE OF THE CLOCK (CLK) IF THE LOAD LINE (/LD) IS ASSERTED (LOW ON PIN 11) AND OTHERWISE HOLDS THE ORIGINAL VALUE.

THE 9-BIT ARCHITECTURE MAKES THIS REGISTER IDEAL FOR PARITY BUS INTERFACING IN MICROPROGRAMMED SYSTEMS.

THESE OPERATIONS ARE EXERCISED IN THE FUNCTION TABLE AND SUMMARIZED IN OPERATIONS TABLE:

/OC	CLK	/LD	D8-D0	Q8-Q0	OPERATION
H	X	X	X	Z	HI-Z
L	C	H	X	Q	HOLD
L	C	L	D	D	LOAD

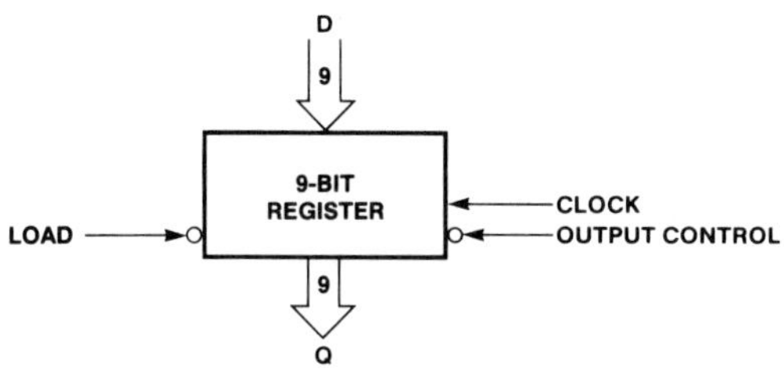

9-BIT REGISTER

```
1 C0000000000X0XLLLLLLLLL1
2 CXXXXXXXXX1X0XLLLLLLLLL1
3 C1111111110X0XHHHHHHHHH1
4 CXXXXXXXXX1X0XHHHHHHHHH1
5 C0101010100X0XLHLHLHLHL1
6 CXXXXXXXXX1X0XLHLHLHLHL1
7 C1010101010X0XHLHLHLHLH1
8 CXXXXXXXXX1X0XHLHLHLHLH1
9 XXXXXXXXXXXX1XZZZZZZZZZ1
```

PASS SIMULATION

9-BIT REGISTER

```
                 11 1111 1111 2222 2222 2233 3333 3333
   0123 4567 8901 2345 6789 0123 4567 8901 2345 6789

 0 ---X ---- ---- ---- ---- ---- ---- ---- ---- X--- /Q0*/LD
 1 -X-- ---- ---- ---- ---- ---- ---- ---- ---- -X-- /D0*LD

 8 ---- ---X ---- ---- ---- ---- ---- ---- ---- X--- /Q1*/LD
 9 ---- -X-- ---- ---- ---- ---- ---- ---- ---- -X-- /D1*LD

16 ---- ---- ---X ---- ---- ---- ---- ---- ---- X--- /Q2*/LD
17 ---- ---- -X-- ---- ---- ---- ---- ---- ---- -X-- /D2*LD

24 ---- ---- ---- ---X ---- ---- ---- ---- ---- X--- /Q3*/LD
25 ---- ---- ---- -X-- ---- ---- ---- ---- ---- -X-- /D3*LD

32 ---- ---- ---- ---- ---X ---- ---- ---- ---- X--- /Q4*/LD
33 ---- ---- ---- ---- -X-- ---- ---- ---- ---- -X-- /D4*LD

40 ---- ---- ---- ---- ---- ---X ---- ---- ---- X--- /Q5*/LD
41 ---- ---- ---- ---- ---- -X-- ---- ---- ---- -X-- /D5*LD

48 ---- ---- ---- ---- ---- ---- ---X ---- ---- X--- /Q6*/LD
49 ---- ---- ---- ---- ---- ---- -X-- ---- ---- -X-- /D6*LD

56 ---- ---- ---- ---- ---- ---- ---- ---X ---- X--- /Q7*/LD
57 ---- ---- ---- ---- ---- ---- ---- -X-- ---- -X-- /D7*LD

64 ---- ---- ---- ---- ---- ---- ---- ---- ---X X--- /Q8*/LD
65 ---- ---- ---- ---- ---- ---- ---- ---- -X-- -X-- /D8*LD


LEGEND:  X : FUSE NOT BLOWN (L,N,0)   - : FUSE BLOWN   (H,P,1)

NUMBER OF FUSES BLOW =  684
```

9-Bit Register

Logic Diagram PAL20X10

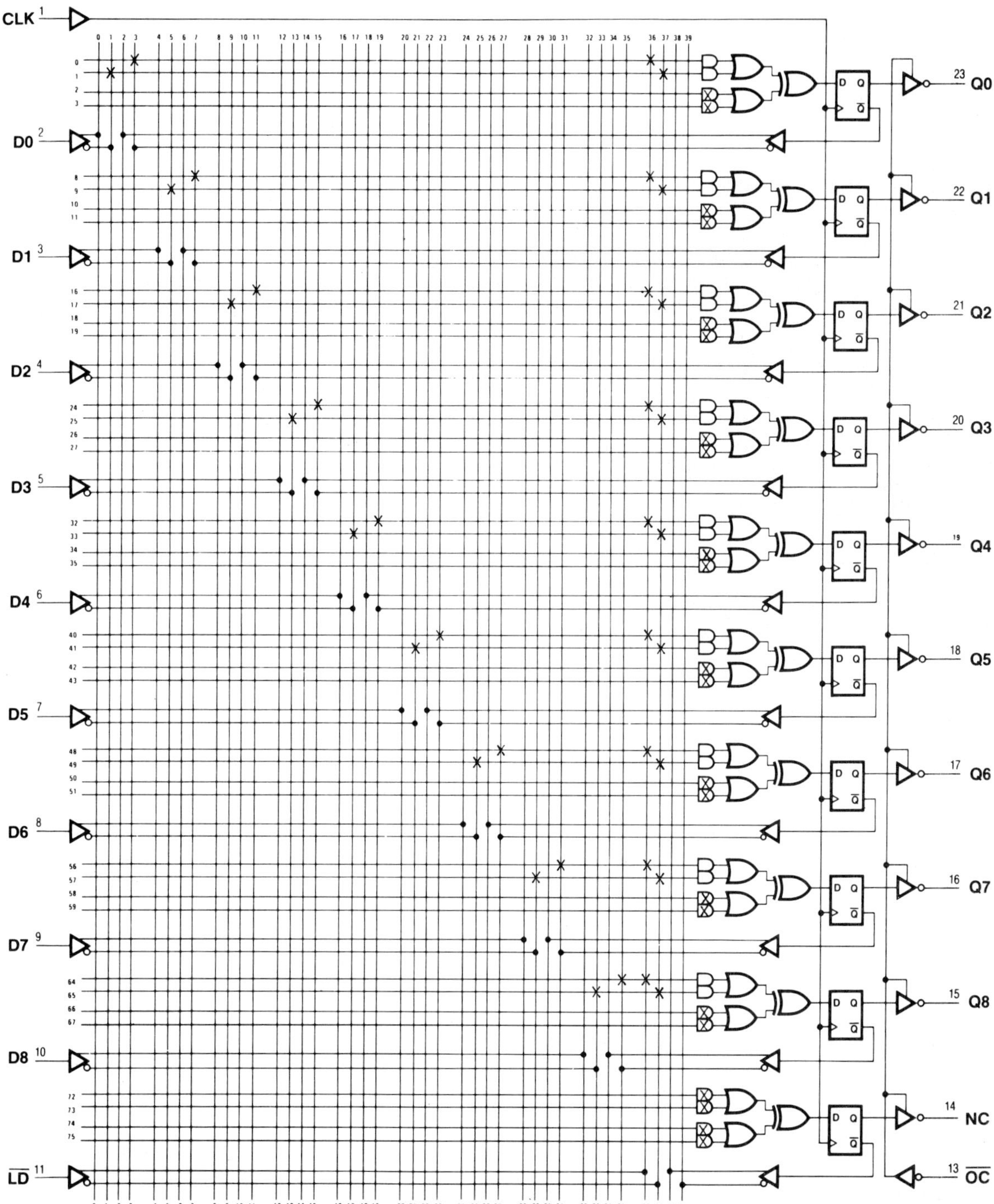

PAL
IMPORTANT,
NOTES

Multifunction Octal Register

PAL20X8

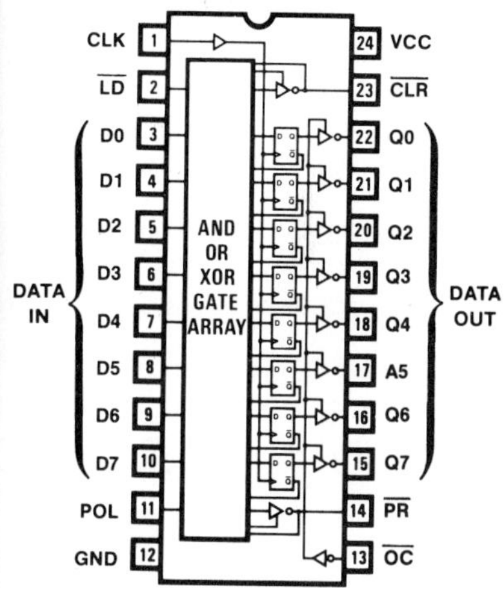

```
PAL20X8                                          PAL DESIGN SPECIFICATION
74LS380                                  BIRKNER/KAZMI/BLASCO 02/16/81
MULTIFUNCTION OCTAL REGISTER
MMI SUNNYVALE, CALIFORNIA
CLK /LD D0 D1 D2 D3 D4 D5 D6 D7  POL GND
/OC /PR Q7 Q6 Q5 Q4 Q3 Q2 Q1 Q0 /CLR VCC


/Q0 :=   CLR                                  ;CLEAR
     +  /CLR*/PR*/LD*/Q0                      ;HOLD
    :+: /CLR*/PR* LD* POL*/D0                 ;LOAD  D0 (TRUE)
     +  /CLR*/PR* LD*/POL* D0                 ;LOAD /D0 (COMP)

/Q1 :=   CLR                                  ;CLEAR
     +  /CLR*/PR*/LD*/Q1                      ;HOLD
    :+: /CLR*/PR* LD* POL*/D1                 ;LOAD  D1 (TRUE)
     +  /CLR*/PR* LD*/POL* D1                 ;LOAD /D1 (COMP)

/Q2 :=   CLR                                  ;CLEAR
     +  /CLR*/PR*/LD*/Q2                      ;HOLD
    :+: /CLR*/PR* LD* POL*/D2                 ;LOAD  D2 (TRUE)
     +  /CLR*/PR* LD*/POL* D2                 ;LOAD /D2 (COMP)

/Q3 :=   CLR                                  ;CLEAR
     +  /CLR*/PR*/LD*/Q3                      ;HOLD
    :+: /CLR*/PR* LD* POL*/D3                 ;LOAD  D3 (TRUE)
     +  /CLR*/PR* LD*/POL* D3                 ;LOAD /D3 (COMP)

/Q4 :=   CLR                                  ;CLEAR
     +  /CLR*/PR*/LD*/Q4                      ;HOLD
    :+: /CLR*/PR* LD* POL*/D4                 ;LOAD  D4 (TRUE)
     +  /CLR*/PR* LD*/POL* D4                 ;LOAD /D4 (COMP)

/Q5 :=   CLR                                  ;CLEAR
     +  /CLR*/PR*/LD*/Q5                      ;HOLD
    :+: /CLR*/PR* LD* POL*/D5                 ;LOAD  D5 (TRUE)
     +  /CLR*/PR* LD*/POL* D5                 ;LOAD /D5 (COMP)

/Q6 :=   CLR                                  ;CLEAR
     +  /CLR*/PR*/LD*/Q6                      ;HOLD
    :+: /CLR*/PR* LD* POL*/D6                 ;LOAD  D6 (TRUE)
     +  /CLR*/PR* LD*/POL* D6                 ;LOAD /D6 (COMP)

/Q7 :=   CLR                                  ;CLEAR
     +  /CLR*/PR*/LD*/Q7                      ;HOLD
    :+: /CLR*/PR* LD* POL*/D7                 ;LOAD  D7 (TRUE)
     +  /CLR*/PR* LD*/POL* D7                 ;LOAD /D7 (COMP)
```

```
FUNCTION TABLE

D7 D6 D5 D4 D3 D2 D1 D0 /CLR /PR /LD POL CLK /OC Q7 Q6 Q5 Q4 Q3 Q2 Q1 Q0

;  INPUTS            CONTROL             OUTPUTS    COMMENTS
; D7----D0  /CLR /PR /LD POL CLK /OC   Q7----Q0
--------------------------------------------------------------------------
;CLEAR AND PRESET TESTS
  HHHHHHHH    L    L    L    H    C    L    LLLLLLLL   CLEAR (OVERRIDES PRESET/LOAD)
  LLLLLLLL    H    L    L    H    C    L    HHHHHHHH   PRESET (OVERRIDES LOAD)
  LLLLLLLL    L    L    L    L    C    L    LLLLLLLL   CLEAR (POL=L)
  HHHHHHHH    H    L    L    L    C    L    HHHHHHHH   PRESET (POL=L)
;LOAD DATA - WALKING ZEROES (TRUE DATA)
  HHHHHHHL    H    H    L    H    C    L    HHHHHHHL   LOAD HEX(FE)
  HHHHHHLH    H    H    L    H    C    L    HHHHHHLH   LOAD HEX(FD)
  HHHHHLHH    H    H    L    H    C    L    HHHHHLHH   LOAD HEX(FB)
  HHHHLHHH    H    H    L    H    C    L    HHHHLHHH   LOAD HEX(F7)
  HHHLHHHH    H    H    L    H    C    L    HHHLHHHH   LOAD HEX(EF)
  HHLHHHHH    H    H    L    H    C    L    HHLHHHHH   LOAD HEX(DF)
  HLHHHHHH    H    H    L    H    C    L    HLHHHHHH   LOAD HEX(BF)
  LHHHHHHH    H    H    L    H    C    L    LHHHHHHH   LOAD HEX(7F)
  HHHHHHHH    H    H    L    H    C    L    HHHHHHHH   LOAD HEX(FF)
;LOAD DATA - WALKING ONES (TRUE DATA)
  LLLLLLLH    H    H    L    H    C    L    LLLLLLLH   LOAD HEX(01)
  LLLLLLHL    H    H    L    H    C    L    LLLLLLHL   LOAD HEX(02)
  LLLLLHLL    H    H    L    H    C    L    LLLLLHLL   LOAD HEX(04)
  LLLLHLLL    H    H    L    H    C    L    LLLLHLLL   LOAD HEX(08)
  LLLHLLLL    H    H    L    H    C    L    LLLHLLLL   LOAD HEX(10)
  LLHLLLLL    H    H    L    H    C    L    LLHLLLLL   LOAD HEX(20)
  LHLLLLLL    H    H    L    H    C    L    LHLLLLLL   LOAD HEX(40)
  HLLLLLLL    H    H    L    H    C    L    HLLLLLLL   LOAD HEX(80)
  LLLLLLLL    H    H    L    H    C    L    LLLLLLLL   LOAD HEX(00)
;LOAD DATA - WALKING ONES (COMP DATA) WITH HOLD TESTS
  LLLLLLLL    H    H    H    L    C    L    LLLLLLLL   HOLD
  LLLLLLLL    H    H    L    L    C    L    HHHHHHHH   LOAD HEX(00)  (COMP)
  LLLLLLLL    H    H    H    H    C    L    HHHHHHHH   HOLD
  LLLLLLLH    H    H    L    L    C    L    HHHHHHHL   LOAD HEX(01)  (COMP)
  LLLLLLLL    H    H    H    L    C    L    HHHHHHHL   HOLD
  LLLLLLHL    H    H    L    L    C    L    HHHHHHLH   LOAD HEX(02)  (COMP)
  HHHHHHHH    H    H    H    H    C    L    HHHHHHLH   HOLD
  LLLLLHLL    H    H    L    L    C    L    HHHHHLHH   LOAD HEX(04)  (COMP)
  LLLLLLLL    H    H    H    L    C    L    HHHHHLHH   HOLD
  LLLLHLLL    H    H    L    L    C    L    HHHHLHHH   LOAD HEX(80)  (COMP)
  HHHHHHHH    H    H    H    H    C    L    HHHHLHHH   HOLD
  LLLHLLLL    H    H    L    L    C    L    HHHLHHHH   LOAD HEX(10)  (COMP)
  LLLLLLLL    H    H    H    L    C    L    HHHLHHHH   HOLD
  LLHLLLLL    H    H    L    L    C    L    HHLHHHHH   LOAD HEX(20)  (COMP)
  HHHHHHHH    H    H    H    H    C    L    HHLHHHHH   HOLD
  LHLLLLLL    H    H    L    L    C    L    HLHHHHHH   LOAD HEX(40)  (COMP)
  LLLLLLLL    H    H    H    L    C    L    HLHHHHHH   HOLD
  HLLLLLLL    H    H    L    L    C    L    LHHHHHHH   LOAD HEX(80)  (COMP)
  HHHHHHHH    H    H    H    H    C    L    LHHHHHHH   HOLD
  LLLLLLLL    H    H    L    L    C    L    HHHHHHHH   LOAD HEX(00)  (COMP)
  XXXXXXXX    X    X    X    X    X    H    ZZZZZZZZ   TEST HI-Z
--------------------------------------------------------------------------
```

DESCRIPTION

THIS IS AN 8-BIT SYNCHRONOUS REGISTER WITH PARALLEL LOAD, LOAD COMPLEMENT, PRESET, CLEAR, AND HOLD CAPABILITIES. FOUR CONTROL INPUTS (/LD,POL,/CLR,/PR) PROVIDE ONE OF FOUR OPERATIONS WHICH OCCUR SYNCHRONOUSLY WITH THE CLOCK (CLK).

THE LOAD OPERATION LOADS THE INPUTS (D7-D0) INTO THE OUTPUT REGISTER (Q7-Q0), WHEN POL=H OR LOADS THE COMPLEMENT OF THE INPUTS WHEN POL=L. THE CLEAR (/CLR) OPERATION RESETS THE OUTPUT REGISTERS TO ALL LOWS. THE PRESET (/PR) OPERATION PRESETS THE OUTPUT REGISTERS TO ALL HIGHS. THE HOLD OPERATION HOLDS THE PREVIOUS VALUE REGARDLESS OF CLOCK TRANSITIONS.

CLEAR OVERRIDES PRESET, PRESET OVERRIDES LOAD, AND LOAD OVERRIDES HOLD.

THESE OPERATIONS ARE EXERCISED IN THE FUNCTION TABLE AND SUMMARIZED IN THE OPERATIONS TABLE:

/OC	CLK	/CLR	/PR	/LD	POL	D7-D0	Q7-Q0	OPERATION
H	X	X	X	X	X	X	Z	HI-Z
L	C	L	X	X	X	X	L	CLEAR
L	C	H	L	L	X	X	H	PRESET
L	C	H	H	H	X	X	Q	HOLD
L	C	H	H	L	H	D	D	LOAD TRUE
L	C	H	H	L	L	D	/D	LOAD COMP

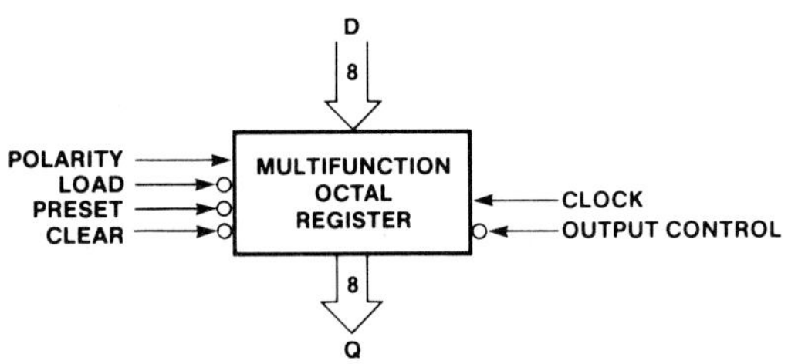

MULTIFUNCTION OCTAL REGISTER

```
 1 C0111111111X00LLLLLLLL01
 2 C0000000001X00HHHHHHHH11
 3 C0000000000X00LLLLLLLL01
 4 C0111111110X00HHHHHHHH11
 5 C0011111111X01HHHHHHHL11
 6 C0101111111X01HHHHHHLH11
 7 C0110111111X01HHHHHLHH11
 8 C0111011111X01HHHHLHHH11
 9 C0111101111X01HHHLHHHH11
10 C0111110111X01HHLHHHHH11
11 C0111111011X01HLHHHHHH11
12 C0111111101X01LHHHHHHH11
13 C0111111111X01HHHHHHHH11
14 C0100000001X01LLLLLLLH11
15 C0010000001X01LLLLLLHL11
16 C0001000001X01LLLLLHLL11
17 C0000100001X01LLLLHLLL11
18 C0000010001X01LLLHLLLL11
19 C0000001001X01LLHLLLLL11
20 C0000000101X01LHLLLLLL11
21 C0000000011X01HLLLLLLL11
22 C0000000001X01LLLLLLLL11
23 C1000000000X01LLLLLLLL11
24 C0000000000X01HHHHHHHH11
25 C1000000001X01HHHHHHHH11
26 C0100000000X01HHHHHHHL11
27 C1000000000X01HHHHHHHL11
28 C0010000000X01HHHHHHLH11
29 C1111111111X01HHHHHHLH11
30 C0001000000X01HHHHHLHH11
31 C1000000000X01HHHHHLHH11
32 C0000100000X01HHHHLHHH11
33 C1111111111X01HHHHLHHH11
34 C0000010000X01HHHLHHHH11
35 C1000000000X01HHHLHHHH11
36 C0000001000X01HHLHHHHH11
37 C1111111111X01HHLHHHHH11
38 C0000000100X01HLHHHHHH11
39 C1000000000X01HLHHHHHH11
40 C0000000010X01LHHHHHHH11
41 C1111111111X01LHHHHHHH11
42 C0000000000X01HHHHHHHH11
43 XXXXXXXXXXXX1XZZZZZZZZX1
```

PASS SIMULATION

```
MULTIFUNCTION OCTAL REGISTER

               11 1111 1111 2222 2222 2233 3333 3333
   0123 4567 8901 2345 6789 0123 4567 8901 2345 6789


  8 ---X ---- ---- ---- ---- ---- ---- ---- ---- ---- CLR
  9 X-X- ---X ---- ---- ---- ---- ---- ---- ---- --X- /CLR*/PR*/LD*/Q0
 10 -XX- -X-- ---- ---- ---- ---- ---- ---- ---- X-X- /CLR*/PR*LD*POL*/D0
 11 -XX- X--- ---- ---- ---- ---- ---- ---- ---- -XX- /CLR*/PR*LD*/POL*D0

 16 ---X ---- ---- ---- ---- ---- ---- ---- ---- ---- CLR
 17 X-X- ---- ---X ---- ---- ---- ---- ---- ---- --X- /CLR*/PR*/LD*/Q1
 18 -XX- ---- -X-- ---- ---- ---- ---- ---- ---- X-X- /CLR*/PR*LD*POL*/D1
 19 -XX- ---- X--- ---- ---- ---- ---- ---- ---- -XX- /CLR*/PR*LD*/POL*D1

 24 ---X ---- ---- ---- ---- ---- ---- ---- ---- ---- CLR
 25 X-X- ---- ---- ---X ---- ---- ---- ---- ---- --X- /CLR*/PR*/LD*/Q2
 26 -XX- ---- ---- -X-- ---- ---- ---- ---- ---- X-X- /CLR*/PR*LD*POL*/D2
 27 -XX- ---- ---- X--- ---- ---- ---- ---- ---- -XX- /CLR*/PR*LD*/POL*D2

 32 ---X ---- ---- ---- ---- ---- ---- ---- ---- ---- CLR
 33 X-X- ---- ---- ---- ---X ---- ---- ---- ---- --X- /CLR*/PR*/LD*/Q3
 34 -XX- ---- ---- ---- -X-- ---- ---- ---- ---- X-X- /CLR*/PR*LD*POL*/D3
 35 -XX- ---- ---- ---- X--- ---- ---- ---- ---- -XX- /CLR*/PR*LD*/POL*D3

 40 ---X ---- ---- ---- ---- ---- ---- ---- ---- ---- CLR
 41 X-X- ---- ---- ---- ---- ---X ---- ---- ---- --X- /CLR*/PR*/LD*/Q4
 42 -XX- ---- ---- ---- ---- -X-- ---- ---- ---- X-X- /CLR*/PR*LD*POL*/D4
 43 -XX- ---- ---- ---- ---- X--- ---- ---- ---- -XX- /CLR*/PR*LD*/POL*D4

 48 ---X ---- ---- ---- ---- ---- ---- ---- ---- ---- CLR
 49 X-X- ---- ---- ---- ---- ---- ---X ---- ---- --X- /CLR*/PR*/LD*/Q5
 50 -XX- ---- ---- ---- ---- ---- -X-- ---- ---- X-X- /CLR*/PR*LD*POL*/D5
 51 -XX- ---- ---- ---- ---- ---- X--- ---- ---- -XX- /CLR*/PR*LD*/POL*D5

 56 ---X ---- ---- ---- ---- ---- ---- ---- ---- ---- CLR
 57 X-X- ---- ---- ---- ---- ---- ---- ---X ---- --X- /CLR*/PR*/LD*/Q6
 58 -XX- ---- ---- ---- ---- ---- ---- -X-- ---- X-X- /CLR*/PR*LD*POL*/D6
 59 -XX- ---- ---- ---- ---- ---- ---- X--- ---- -XX- /CLR*/PR*LD*/POL*D6

 64 ---X ---- ---- ---- ---- ---- ---- ---- ---- ---- CLR
 65 X-X- ---- ---- ---- ---- ---- ---- ---- ---X --X- /CLR*/PR*/LD*/Q7
 66 -XX- ---- ---- ---- ---- ---- ---- ---- -X-- X-X- /CLR*/PR*LD*POL*/D7
 67 -XX- ---- ---- ---- ---- ---- ---- ---- X--- -XX- /CLR*/PR*LD*/POL*D7


LEGEND:  X : FUSE NOT BLOWN (L,N,0)   - : FUSE BLOWN   (H,P,1)

NUMBER OF FUSES BLOW = 1160
```

Multifunction Octal Register

Logic Diagram PAL20X 8

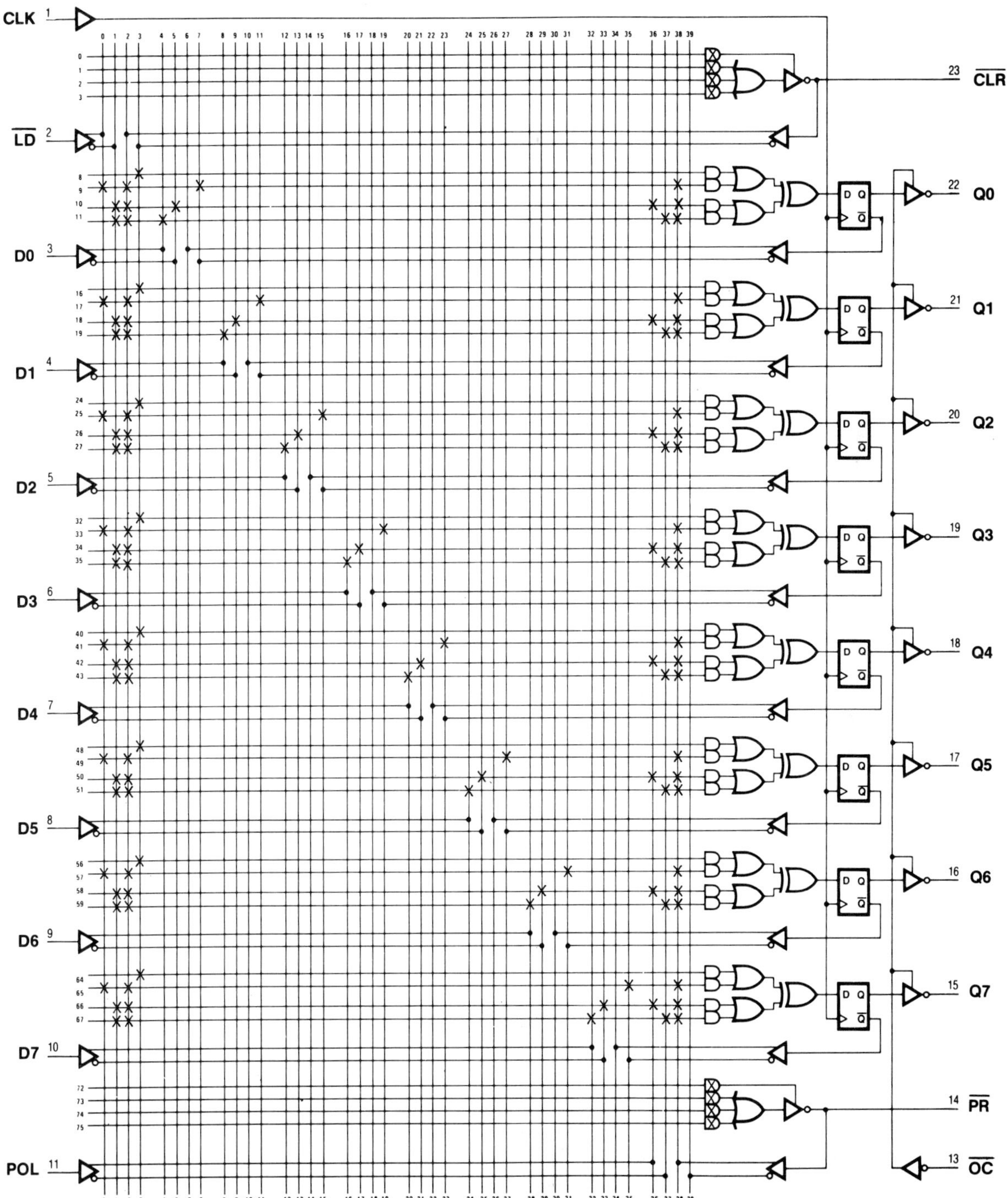

Application

16-Bit Register

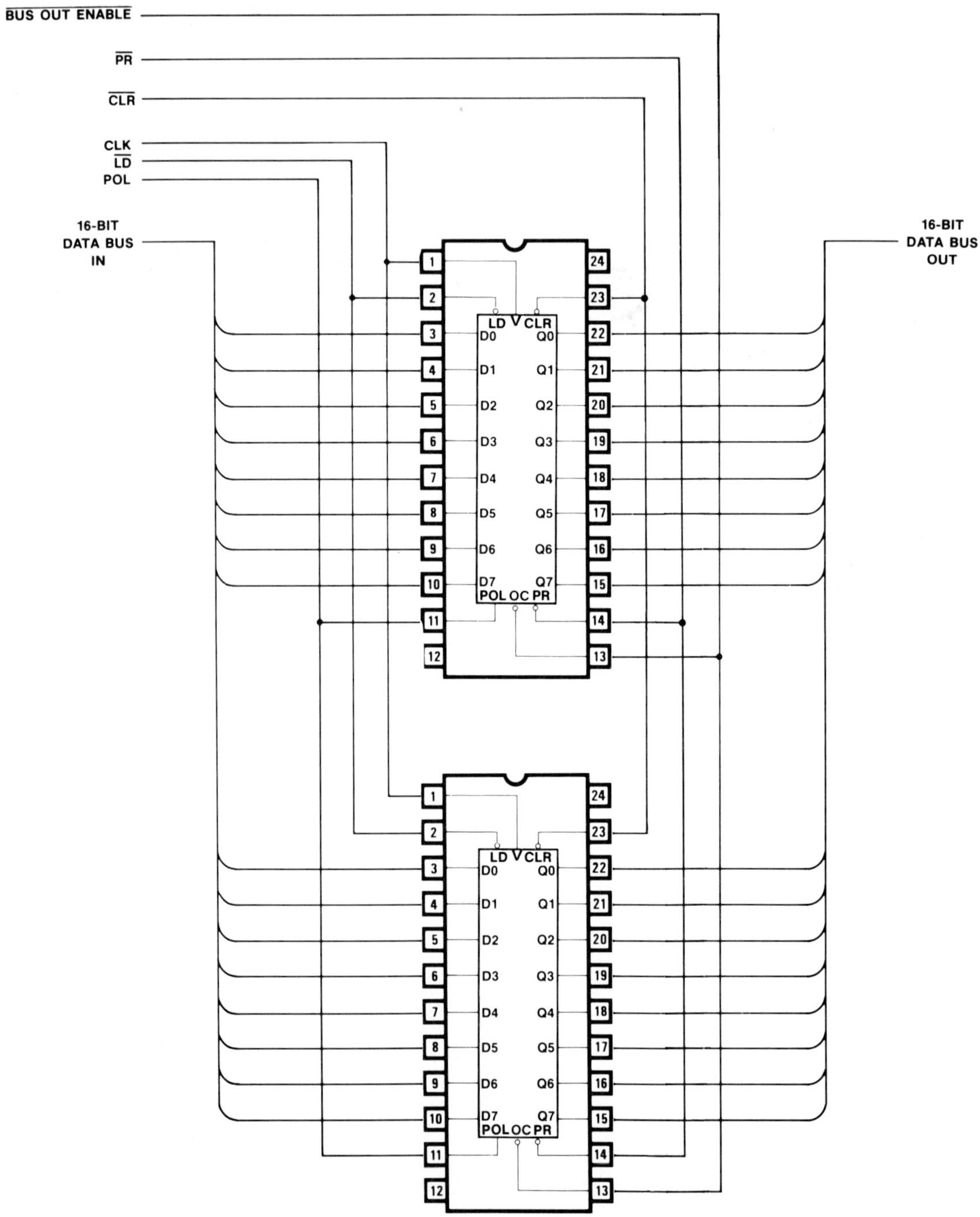

8-Bit I/O Priority Interrupt Encoder With Registers

PAL16R4

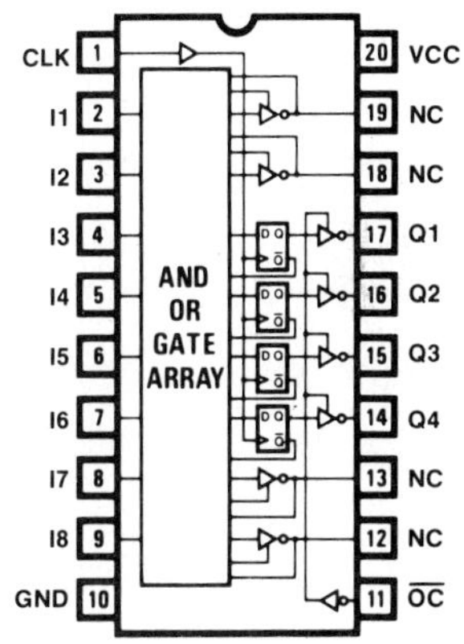

```
PAL16R4                                              PAL DESIGN SPECIFICATION
8BITENC                                                 VINCENT COLI 06/28/81
8-BIT I/O PRIORITY INTERRUPT ENCODER WITH REGISTERS
MMI SUNNYVALE, CALIFORNIA
CLK I1 I2 I3 I4 I5 I6 I7 I8 GND
/OC NC NC Q4 Q3 Q2 Q1 NC NC VCC


/Q1 := /I1* I2
     + /I1*/I2*/I3* I4
     + /I1*/I2*/I3*/I4*/I5* I6
     + /I1*/I2*/I3*/I4*/I5*/I6*/I7* I8

/Q2 := /I1*/I2* I3
     + /I1*/I2*/I3* I4
     + /I1*/I2*/I3*/I4*/I5*/I6* I7
     + /I1*/I2*/I3*/I4*/I5*/I6*/I7* I8

/Q3 := /I1*/I2*/I3*/I4* I5
     + /I1*/I2*/I3*/I4*/I5* I6
     + /I1*/I2*/I3*/I4*/I5*/I6* I7
     + /I1*/I2*/I3*/I4*/I5*/I6*/I7* I8

/Q4 := I1 + I2 + I3 + I4 + I5 + I6 + I7 + I8    ;INTERRUPT FLAG


FUNCTION TABLE

I8 I7 I6 I5 I4 I3 I2 I1 CLK /OC Q4 Q3 Q2 Q1

;-INPUTS-   CONTROL   OUTPUTS   COMMENTS
;IIIIIIII   CLK /OC    QQQQ
;87654321              4321
-----------------------------------------------------------------------
 LXXXXXXH    C   L      LHHH     I1 INTERRUPT (HIGHEST PRIORITY DEVICE)
 LXXXXXHL    C   L      LHHL     I2 INTERRUPT
 LXXXXHLL    C   L      LHLH     I3 INTERRUPT
 LXXXHLLL    C   L      LHLL     I4 INTERRUPT
 LXXHLLLL    C   L      LLHH     I5 INTERRUPT
 LXHLLLLL    C   L      LLHL     I6 INTERRUPT
 LHLLLLLL    C   L      LLLH     I7 INTERRUPT
 HLLLLLLL    C   L      LLLL     I8 INTERRUPT (LOWEST PRIORITY DEVICE)
 LLLLLLLL    C   L      HHHH     INTERRUPT FLAG
 XXXXXXXX    X   H      ZZZZ     TEST HI-Z
-----------------------------------------------------------------------
```

DESCRIPTION

THE I/O PRIORITY INTERRUPT ENCODER PRIORITIZES 8 I/O LINES (I1 THRU I8) PRODUCING 111 (Q3, Q2, AND Q1 RESPECTIVELY) FOR THE HIGHEST PRIORITY I/O DEVICE (I1) AND 000 FOR AN INTERRUPT FROM THE LOWEST PRIORITY I/O DEVICE (I8).

OUTPUT Q4 SERVES AS THE INTERRUPT FLAG AND GOES LOW WHEN ANY OF THE 8 I/O INPUTS GO HIGH.

THE PRIORITY INTERRUPT ENCODER REGISTERS ARE UPDATED ON THE RISING EDGE OF THE INTERRUPT CLOCK INPUT (CLK). THE 3-STATE OUTPUTS ARE HIGH-Z WHEN THE OUTPUT CONTROL LINE (/OC) IS LOW.

```
8-BIT I/O PRIORITY INTERRUPT ENCODER WITH REGISTERS

 1 C1XXXXXX0X0XXLHHHXX1
 2 C01XXXXX0X0XXLHHLXX1
 3 C001XXXX0X0XXLHLHXX1
 4 C0001XXX0X0XXLHLLXX1
 5 C00001XX0X0XXLLHHXX1
 6 C000001X0X0XXLLHLXX1
 7 C00000010X0XXLLLHXX1
 8 C00000001X0XXLLLLXX1
 9 C00000000X0XXHHHHXX1
10 XXXXXXXXXX1XXZZZZXX1

PASS SIMULATION
```

```
8-BIT I/O PRIORITY INTERRUPT ENCODER WITH REGISTERS

               11 1111 1111 2222 2222 2233
   0123 4567 8901 2345 6789 0123 4567 8901


16 -X-- X--- ---- ---- ---- ---- ---- ---- /I1*I2
17 -X-- -X-- -X-- X--- ---- ---- ---- ---- /I1*/I2*/I3*I4
18 -X-- -X-- -X-- -X-- -X-- X--- ---- ---- /I1*/I2*/I3*/I4*/I5*I6
19 -X-- -X-- -X-- -X-- -X-- -X-- -X-- X--- /I1*/I2*/I3*/I4*/I5*/I6*/I7*I8

24 -X-- -X-- X--- ---- ---- ---- ---- ---- /I1*/I2*I3
25 -X-- -X-- -X-- X--- ---- ---- ---- ---- /I1*/I2*/I3*I4
26 -X-- -X-- -X-- -X-- -X-- -X-- X--- ---- /I1*/I2*/I3*/I4*/I5*/I6*I7
27 -X-- -X-- -X-- -X-- -X-- -X-- -X-- X--- /I1*/I2*/I3*/I4*/I5*/I6*/I7*I8

32 -X-- -X-- -X-- -X-- X--- ---- ---- ---- /I1*/I2*/I3*/I4*I5
33 -X-- -X-- -X-- -X-- -X-- X--- ---- ---- /I1*/I2*/I3*/I4*/I5*I6
34 -X-- -X-- -X-- -X-- -X-- -X-- X--- ---- /I1*/I2*/I3*/I4*/I5*/I6*I7
35 -X-- -X-- -X-- -X-- -X-- -X-- -X-- X--- /I1*/I2*/I3*/I4*/I5*/I6*/I7*I8

40 X--- ---- ---- ---- ---- ---- ---- ---- I1
41 ---- X--- ---- ---- ---- ---- ---- ---- I2
42 ---- ---- X--- ---- ---- ---- ---- ---- I3
43 ---- ---- ---- X--- ---- ---- ---- ---- I4
44 ---- ---- ---- ---- X--- ---- ---- ---- I5
45 ---- ---- ---- ---- ---- X--- ---- ---- I6
46 ---- ---- ---- ---- ---- ---- X--- ---- I7
47 ---- ---- ---- ---- ---- ---- ---- X--- I8


LEGEND:  X : FUSE NOT BLOWN (L,N,0)   - : FUSE BLOWN   (H,P,1)

NUMBER OF FUSES BLOWN =  564
```

8-Bit I/O Priority Interrupt Encoder with Registers

Logic Diagram PAL16R4

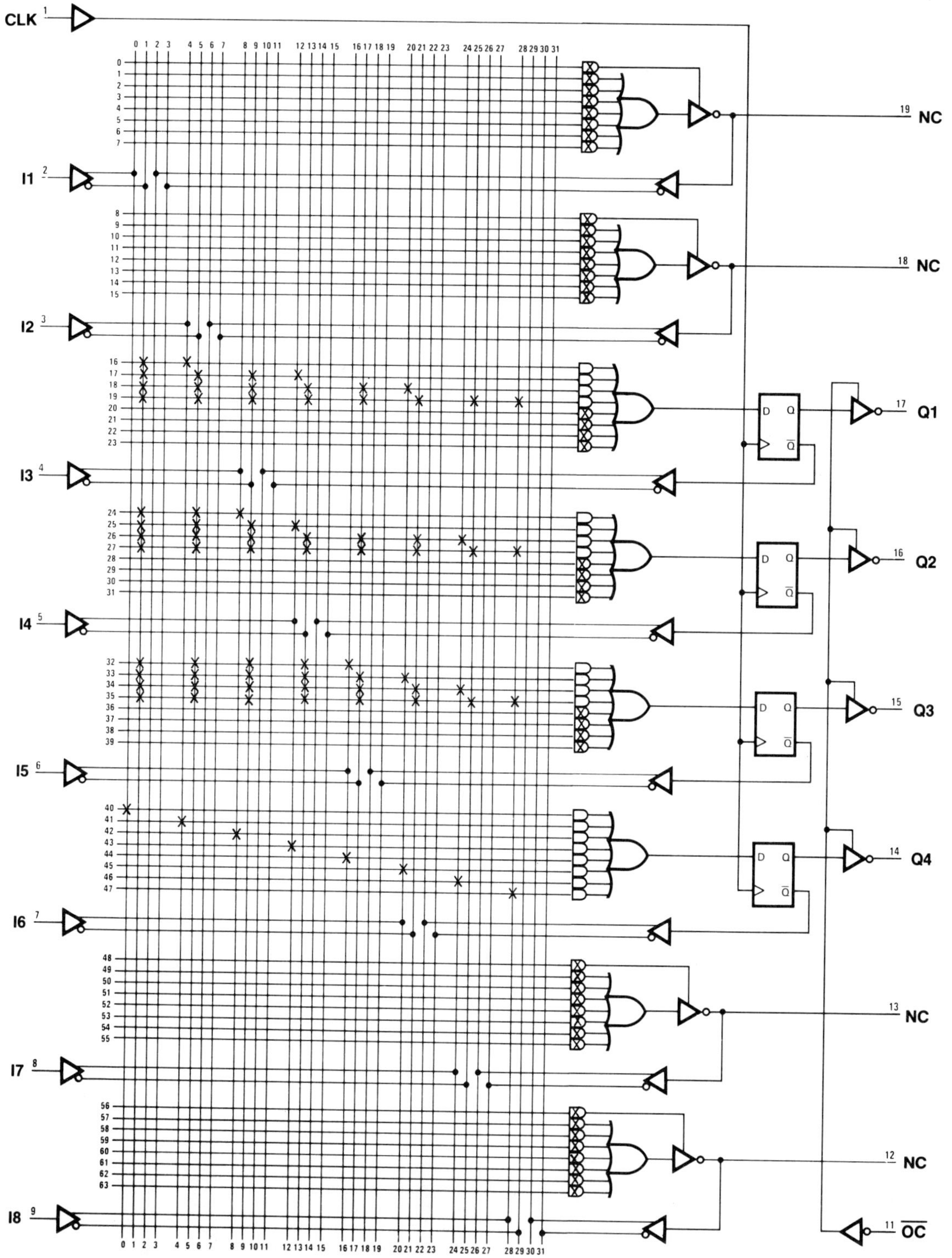

PAL
IMPORTANT,
NOTES

BCD/Hex Counter

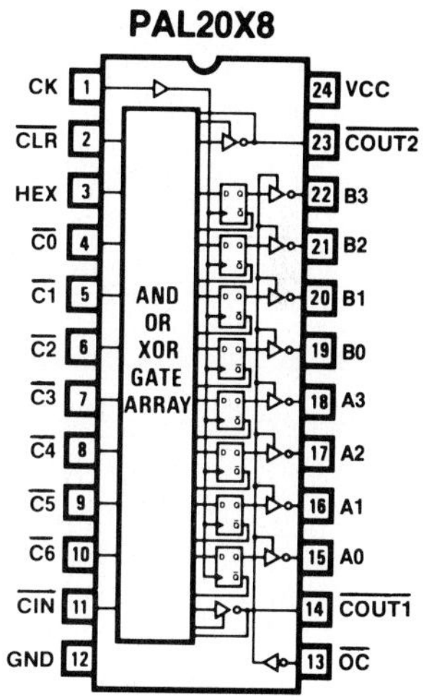

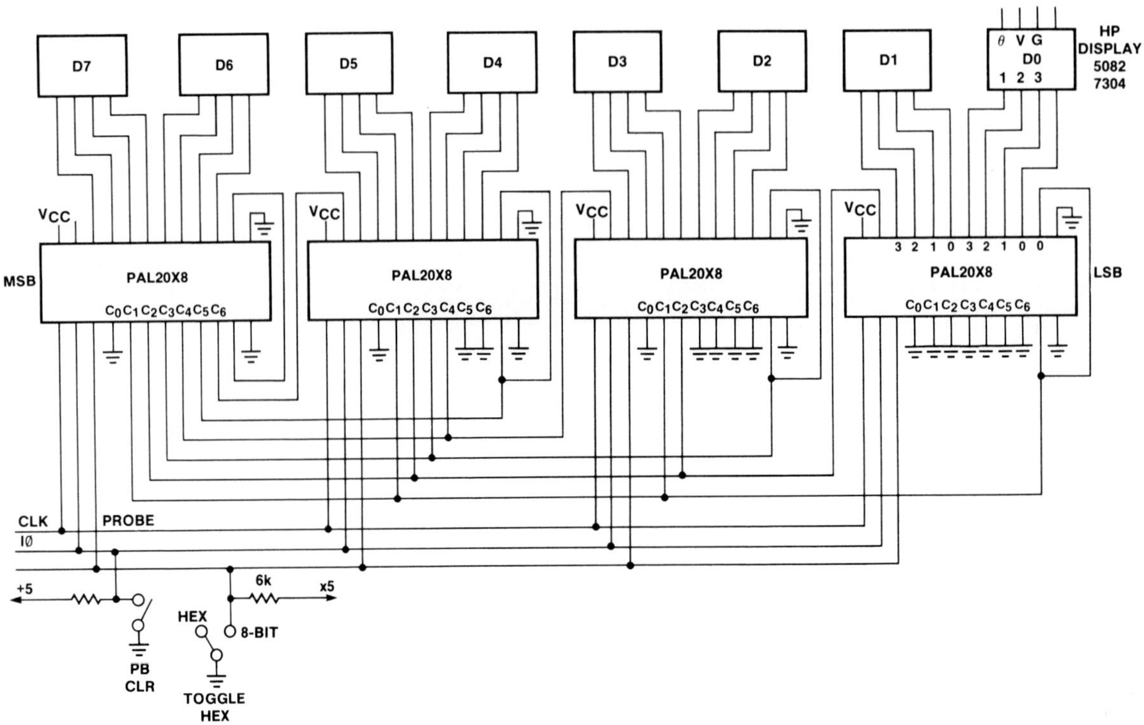
D7
D6
D5
D4
D3
D2
D1
θ V G
D0
1 2 3
HP
DISPLAY
5082
7304
VCC
MSB
PAL20X8
C0 C1 C2 C3 C4 C5 C6
3 2 1 0 3 2 1 0 0
LSB
CLK
PROBE
IØ
+5
6k
x5
HEX
8-BIT
PB
CLR
TOGGLE
HEX

```
PAL20X8                                               PAL DESIGN SPECIFICATION
BHEX                                                     SAEED KAZMI 04/28/81
BCD/HEX COUNTER
MMI  SUNNYVALE, CALIFORNIA
CK /CLR HEX /C0 /C1 /C2 /C3 /C4 /C5 /C6 /CIN GND
/OC /COUT1 A0 A1 A2 A3 B0 B1 B2 B3 /COUT2 VCC


IF (VCC) COUT2 = /CLR*B0*B1*B2*B3                      ;HEX COUNT CARRY OUT
               + /CLR* /HEX*B0*B3                      ;BCD COUNT CARRY OUT

/B3 :=  CLR                                            ;CLEAR
     + /CLR*/B3                                        ;HOLD, MSB OF STAGE 2
    :+:/CLR*C0*C1*C2*C3*C4*C5*C6*CIN*B0*B1*B2          ;INCREMENT
     + /CLR* /HEX*B0*B3                                ;CLEAR IF BCD & COUNT=9

/B2 :=  CLR
     + /CLR*/B2
    :+:/CLR*C0*C1*C2*C3*C4*C5*C6*CIN*B0*B1

/B1 :=  CLR
     + /CLR*/B1
    :+:/CLR*  HEX*C0*C1*C2*C3*C4*C5*C6*CIN*B0
     + /CLR* /HEX*C0*C1*C2*C3*C4*C5*C6*CIN*B0*/B3      ;CLEAR IF BCD & COUNT=9

/B0 :=  CLR
     + /CLR*/B0                                        ;HOLD, LSB OF STAGE 2
    :+:/CLR*C0*C1*C2*C3*C4*C5*C6*CIN

/A3 :=  CLR
     + /CLR*/A3                                        ;HOLD, MSB OF STAGE 1
    :+:/CLR*C0*C1*C2*C3*C4*C5*C6*A0*A1*A2
     + /CLR* /HEX*A0*A3                                ;CLEAR IF BCD & COUNT=9

/A2 :=  CLR
     + /CLR*/A2
    :+:/CLR*C0*C1*C2*C3*C4*C5*C6*A0*A1

/A1 :=  CLR
     + /CLR*/A1
    :+:/CLR*  HEX*C0*C1*C2*C3*C4*C5*C6*A0
     + /CLR* /HEX*C0*C1*C2*C3*C4*C5*C6*A0*/A3          ;CLEAR IF BCD & COUNT=9

/A0 :=  CLR
     + /CLR*/A0                                        ;HOLD, LSB OF STAGE 1
    :+:/CLR*C0*C1*C2*C3*C4*C5*C6

IF (VCC) COUT1 = /CLR* HEX*A0*A1*A2*A3                 ;HEX COUNT, INT. CARRY
               + /CLR*/HEX*A0*A3                       ;BCD COUNT, INT. CARRY
```

```
FUNCTION TABLE

HEX CLR CK OC C0 C1 C2 C3 C4 C5 C6
COUT2 B3 B2 B1 B0 COUT1 A3 A2 A1 A0 CIN

;H C C O C C C C C C C C B B B B C A A A A C
;E L K C 0 1 2 3 4 5 6 O 3 2 1 0 O 3 2 1 0 I
;X R                   U         U         N
;                      T         T
;                      2         1                    COMMENT
-----------------------------------------------------------------------
 X H C H L L L L L L L L L L L L L L L L L L       CLEAR
 X H C H H H H H H H H L L L L L L L L L L H       HOLD, HEX COUNT 00
 H L C H H H H H H H H L L L L H L L L L H H       HEX COUNT 11
 H L C H H H H H H H H L L L H L L L L H L H                 22
 H L C H H H H H H H H L L L H H L L L H H H                 33
 H L C H H H H H H H H L L H L L L L H L L H                 44
 H L C H H H H H H H H L L H L H L L H L H H                 55
 H L C H H H H H H H H L L H H L L L H H L H                 66
 H L C H H H H H H H H L L H H H L L H H H H                 77
 H L C H H H H H H H H L H L L L L H L L L H                 88
 H L C H H H H H H H H L H L L H L H L L H H                 99
 H L C H H H H H H H H L H L H L L H L H L H                 AA
 H L C H H H H H H H H L H L H H L H L H H H                 BB
 H L C H H H H H H H H L H H L L L H H L L H                 CC
 H L C H H H H H H H H L H H L H L H H L H H                 DD
 H L C H H H H H H H H L H H H L L H H H L H                 EE
 H L C H H H H H H H H H H H H H H H H H H H                 FF
 H L C H H H H H H H H L L L L L L L L L L H        BCD COUNT 00
 L L C H H H H H H H H L L L L H L L L L H H                 11
 L L C H H H H H H H H L L L H L L L L H L H                 22
 L L C H H H H H H H H L L L H H L L L H H H                 33
 L L C H H H H H H H H L L H L L L L H L L H                 44
 L L C H H H H H H H H L L H L H L L H L H H                 55
 L L C H H H H H H H H L L H H L L L H H L H                 66
 L L C H H H H H H H H L L H H H L L H H H H                 77
 L L C H H H H H H H H L H L L L L H L L L H                 88
 L L C H H H H H H H H H H L L H H H L L H H                 99
 L L C H H H H H H H H L L L L L L L L L L H                100
-----------------------------------------------------------------------
```

DESCRIPTION

FOUR IDENTICALLY PROGRAMMED PALS ARE USED TO DRIVE EIGHT OF HP'S NUMERIC AND HEX INDICATORS (5082-7340). EACH PAL CONSISTS OF TWO FOUR BIT COUNTERS. STAGE 1 IS THE LSB AND STAGE 2 IS THE MSB. CARRYOUT OF STAGE 1 IS CALLED INTERNAL CARRY (COUT1) AND IS FED EXTERNALLY TO STAGE 2. COUT2 IS FED INTO THE NEXT PAL. CARRYOUT AND INTERNAL CARRYS FROM THE LOWER PAL ARE CONNECTED TO ALL OF THE HIGHER PALS TO PERFORM THE CARRY LOOK AHEAD OPERATION.

THESE PALS HAVE TESTABILITY BUILT INTO THEM. COUT1 IS CONNECTED TO CIN EXTERNALLY AND CAN FORCE COUT1 TO GO HIGH, THUS STAGE 2 MAY START COUNTING AT THE SAME TIME AS STAGE 1 WHICH REDUCES THE NUMBER OF TEST VECTORS IN THE FUNCTION TABLE.

THIS COUNTER OPERATES AT 10 MHz AND CAN PERFORM THE FOLLOWING OPERATIONS:

HEX	CLR	OPERATION
X	H	CLEAR
L	L	COUNT BCD
H	L	COUNT HEX

BCD/HEX COUNTER

```
 1 C0X11111111X0HLLLLLLLLH1
 2 C0X00000000X0HLLLLLLLLH1
 3 C1100000000X0HHLLLHLLLH1
 4 C1100000000X0HLHLLLHLLH1
 5 C1100000000X0HHHLLHHLLH1
 6 C1100000000X0HLLHLLLHLH1
 7 C1100000000X0HHLHLHLHLH1
 8 C1100000000X0HLHHLLHHLH1
 9 C1100000000X0HHHHLHHHLH1
10 C1100000000X0HLLLHLLLHH1
11 C1100000000X0HHLLHHLLHH1
12 C1100000000X0HLHLHLHLHH1
13 C1100000000X0HHHLHHHLHH1
14 C1100000000X0HLLHHLLHHH1
15 C1100000000X0HHLHHHLHHH1
16 C1100000000X0HLHHHLHHHH1
17 C1100000000X0LHHHHHHHHL1
18 C1100000000X0HLLLLLLLLH1
19 C1000000000X0HHLLLHLLLH1
20 C1000000000X0HLHLLLHLLH1
21 C1000000000X0HHHLLHHLLH1
22 C1000000000X0HLLHLLLHLH1
23 C1000000000X0HHLHLHLHLH1
24 C1000000000X0HLHHLLHHLH1
25 C1000000000X0HHHHLHHHLH1
26 C1000000000X0HLLLHLLLHH1
27 C1000000000X0LHLLHHLLHL1
28 C1000000000X0HLLLLLLLLH1
```

PASS SIMULATION

```
BCD/HEX COUNTER

               11 1111 1111 2222 2222 2233 3333 3333
   0123 4567 8901 2345 6789 0123 4567 8901 2345 6789

 0 ---- ---- ---- ---- ---- ---- ---- ---- ---- ----
 1 X--- --X- --X- --X- --X- ---- ---- ---- ---- ---- /CLR*B0*B1*B2*B3
 2 X--- -XX- ---- ---- --X- ---- ---- ---- ---- ---- /CLR*/HEX*B0*B3

 8 -X-- ---- ---- ---- ---- ---- ---- ---- ---- ---- CLR
 9 X--- ---X ---- ---- ---- ---- ---- ---- ---- ---- /CLR*/B3
10 X--- ---- -XX- -XX- -XX- -X-- -X-- -X-- -X-- -X-- /CLR*C0*C1*C2*C3*C4*C5*-
11 X--- -XX- ---- ---- --X- ---- ---- ---- ---- ---- /CLR*/HEX*B0*B3

16 -X-- ---- ---- ---- ---- ---- ---- ---- ---- ---- CLR
17 X--- ---- ---X ---- ---- ---- ---- ---- ---- ---- /CLR*/B2
18 X--- ---- -X-- -XX- -XX- -X-- -X-- -X-- -X-- -X-- /CLR*C0*C1*C2*C3*C4*C5*-

24 -X-- ---- ---- ---- ---- ---- ---- ---- ---- ---- CLR
25 X--- ---- ---- ---X ---- ---- ---- ---- ---- ---- /CLR*/B1
26 X--- X--- -X-- -X-- -XX- -X-- -X-- -X-- -X-- -X-- /CLR*HEX*C0*C1*C2*C3*C4-
27 X--- -X-X -X-- -X-- -XX- -X-- -X-- -X-- -X-- -X-- /CLR*/HEX*C0*C1*C2*C3*C-

32 -X-- ---- ---- ---- ---- ---- ---- ---- ---- ---- CLR
33 X--- ---- ---- ---- ---X ---- ---- ---- ---- ---- /CLR*/B0
34 X--- ---- -X-- -X-- -X-- -X-- -X-- -X-- -X-- -X-- /CLR*C0*C1*C2*C3*C4*C5*-

40 -X-- ---- ---- ---- ---- ---- ---- ---- ---- ---- CLR
41 X--- ---- ---- ---- ---- ---X ---- ---- ---- ---- /CLR*/A3
42 X--- ---- -X-- -X-- -X-- -X-- -XX- -XX- -XX- ---- /CLR*C0*C1*C2*C3*C4*C5*-
43 X--- -X-- ---- ---- ---- --X- ---- ---- --X- ---- /CLR*/HEX*A0*A3

48 -X-- ---- ---- ---- ---- ---- ---- ---- ---- ---- CLR
49 X--- ---- ---- ---- ---- ---- ---X ---- ---- ---- /CLR*/A2
50 X--- ---- -X-- -X-- -X-- -X-- -X-- -XX- -XX- ---- /CLR*C0*C1*C2*C3*C4*C5*-

56 -X-- ---- ---- ---- ---- ---- ---- ---- ---- ---- CLR
57 X--- ---- ---- ---- ---- ---- ---- ---X ---- ---- /CLR*/A1
58 X--- X--- -X-- -X-- -X-- -X-- -X-- -X-- -XX- ---- /CLR*HEX*C0*C1*C2*C3*C4-
59 X--- -X-- -X-- -X-- -X-- -X-X -X-- -X-- -XX- ---- /CLR*/HEX*C0*C1*C2*C3*C-

64 -X-- ---- ---- ---- ---- ---- ---- ---- ---- ---- CLR
65 X--- ---- ---- ---- ---- ---- ---- ---- ---X ---- /CLR*/A0
66 X--- ---- -X-- -X-- -X-- -X-- -X-- -X-- -X-- ---- /CLR*C0*C1*C2*C3*C4*C5*-

72 ---- ---- ---- ---- ---- ---- ---- ---- ---- ----
73 X--- X--- ---- ---- ---- --X- --X- --X- --X- ---- /CLR*HEX*A0*A1*A2*A3
74 X--- -X-- ---- ---- ---- --X- ---- ---- --X- ---- /CLR*/HEX*A0*A3

LEGEND:  X : FUSE NOT BLOWN (L,N,0)   - : FUSE BLOWN   (H,P,1)

NUMBER OF FUSES BLOW = 1204
```

BCD/HEX Counter

Logic Diagram PAL20X8

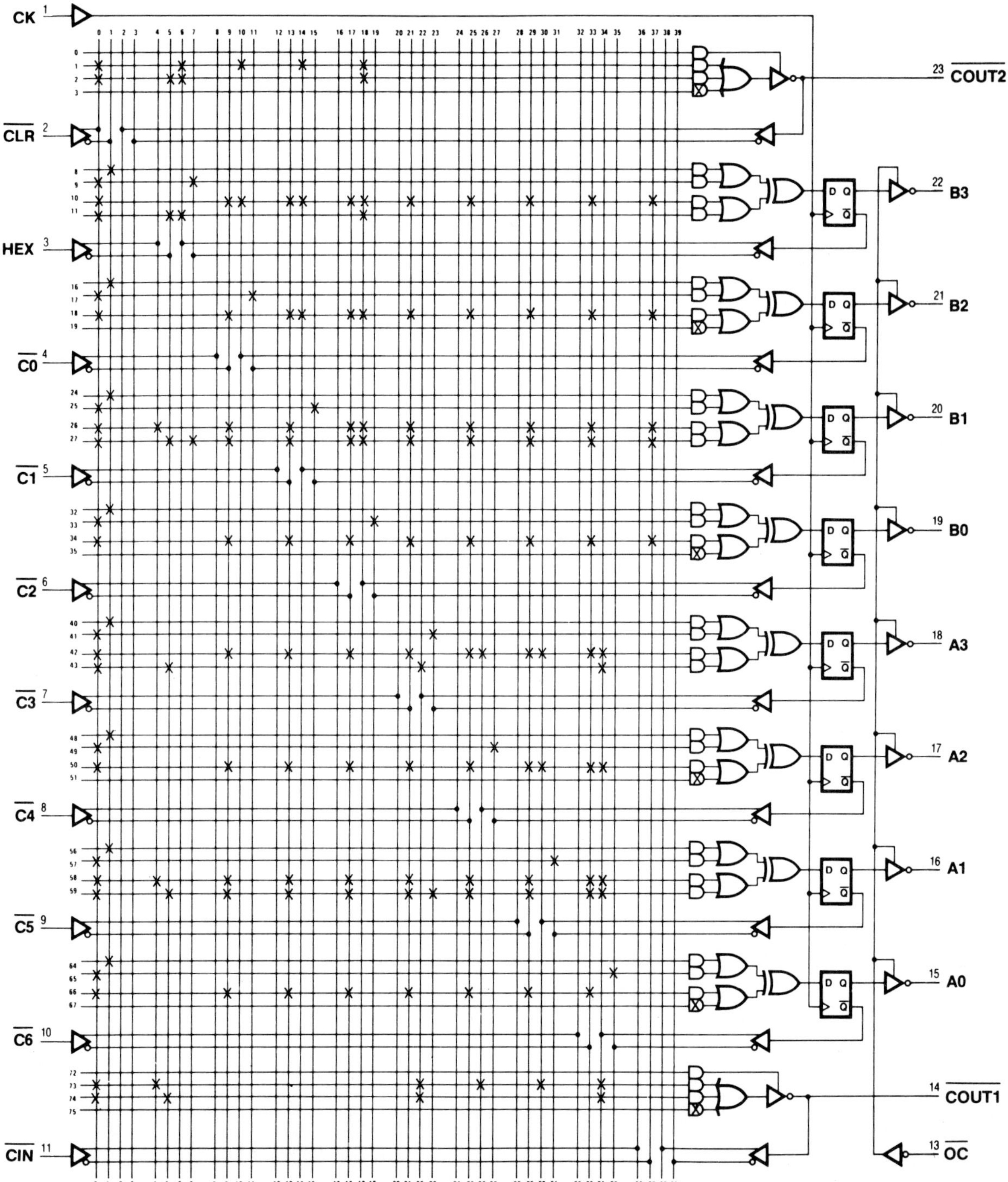

PAL
IMPORTANT, NOTES

64k Dynamic RAM Refresh Controller

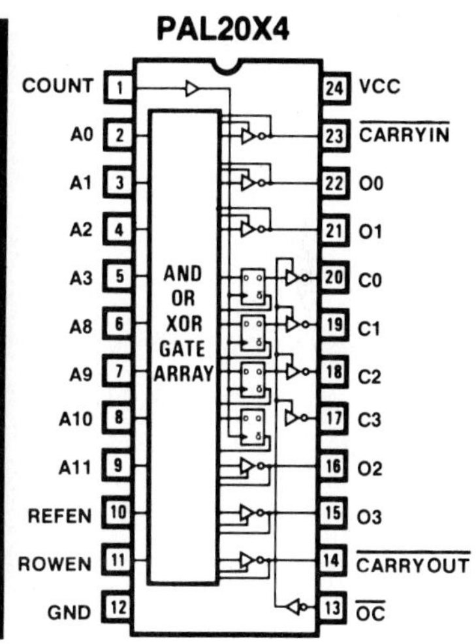

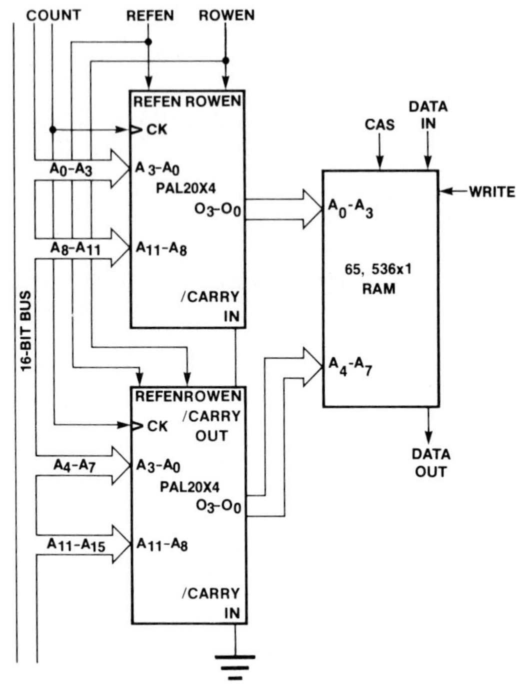
COUNT
REFEN
ROWEN
REFEN ROWEN
CK
A0-A3
A 3-A0
PAL20X4
O3-O0
A8-A11
A11-A8
/CARRY IN
16-BIT BUS
REFENROWEN
/CARRY OUT
A4-A7
A3-A0
PAL20X4
O3-O0
A11-A15
A11-A8
/CARRY IN
DATA IN
CAS
WRITE
A0-A3
65, 536x1 RAM
A4-A7
DATA OUT

```
PAL20X4                                              PAL DESIGN SPECIFICATION
DYNRAM                                               MIKE VOLPIGNO   07/15/81
64k DYNAMIC RAM REFRESH CONTROLLER
MMI FIELD APPLICATIONS ENGINEER NEWTON, MASSACHUSETTS
COUNT A0 A1 A2 A3 A8 A9 A10 A11 REFEN ROWEN GND
/OC /CARRYOUT O3 O2 C3 C2 C1 C0 O1 O0 /CARRYIN VCC


        /C0 :=  /C0                             ;INCR REF ADDRESS COUNTER
             +   REFEN*/ROWEN                   ;SET REF COUNTER
            :+:  CARRYIN                        ;INCR REF COUNTER
             +   REFEN*/ROWEN                   ;SET REF COUNTER

        /C1 :=  /C1                             ;INCR REF COUNTER
             +   REFEN*/ROWEN                   ;SET REF COUNTER
            :+:  CARRYIN* C0                    ;INCR REF COUNTER
             +   REFEN*/ROWEN                   ;SET REF COUNTER

        /C2 :=  /C2                             ;INCR REF COUNTER
             +   REFEN*/ROWEN                   ;SET REF COUNTER
            :+:  CARRYIN* C0* C1                ;INCR REF COUNTER
             +   REFEN*/ROWEN                   ;SET REF COUNTER

        /C3 :=  /C3                             ;INCR REF COUNTER
             +   REFEN*/ROWEN                   ;SET REF COUNTER
            :+:  CARRYIN* C0* C1* C2            ;INCR REF COUNTER
             +   REFEN*/ROWEN                   ;SET REF COUNTER

IF (VCC)   /O0 =  /A0*/REFEN* ROWEN             ;SELECT LOWER ADDRESS
               +  /A8*/REFEN*/ROWEN             ;SELECT UPPER ADDRESS
               +  /C0* REFEN* ROWEN             ;SELECT REFRESH ADDRESS

IF (VCC)   /O1 =  /A1*/REFEN* ROWEN             ;SELECT LOWER ADDRESS
               +  /A9*/REFEN*/ROWEN             ;SELECT UPPER ADDRESS
               +  /C1* REFEN* ROWEN             ;SELECT REFRESH ADDRESS

IF (VCC)   /O2 =  /A2* /REFEN* ROWEN            ;SELECT LOWER ADDRESS
               +  /A10*/REFEN*/ROWEN            ;SELECT UPPER ADDRESS
               +  /C2*  REFEN* ROWEN            ;SELECT REFRESH ADDRESS

IF (VCC)   /O3 =  /A3* /REFEN* ROWEN            ;SELECT LOWER ADDRESS
               +  /A11*/REFEN*/ROWEN            ;SELECT UPPER ADDRESS
               +  /C3*  REFEN* ROWEN            ;SELECT REFRESH ADDRESS

IF (VCC) CARRYOUT =  CARRYIN* C0* C1* C2* C3 ;CARRY OUT
```

```
FUNCTION TABLE

A0 A1 A2 A3 A8 A9 A10 A11 COUNT /OC REFEN ROWEN /CARRYIN /CARRYOUT
O3 O2 O1 O0 C3 C2 C1 C0

;--DATA-                          --CARRIES--
;AAAAAAAA   ----CONTROLS---         /      /
;      11   COU  /   REF  ROW    CARRY  CARRY   OOOO  CCCC
;32101098   NT   OC  EN   EN       IN    OUT    3210  3210     COMMENTS
-----------------------------------------------------------------------------
 XXXXXXXX    C   L    H    L        H      H    HHHH  HHHH     SET REF CNTR
 XXXXLLLL    C   L    L    L        H      H    LLLL  HHHH     UPPER ADDR LOW
 XXXXHHHH    C   L    L    L        H      H    HHHH  HHHH     UPPER ADDR HI
 LLLLXXXX    C   L    L    H        H      H    LLLL  HHHH     LOWER ADDR LOW
 HHHHLLLL    C   L    L    H        H      H    HHHH  HHHH     LOWER ADDR HI
 XXXXXXXX    C   L    H    H        L      H    LLLL  LLLL     INCR REF ADDR
 XXXXXXXX    C   L    H    H        L      H    LLLH  LLLH
 XXXXXXXX    C   L    H    H        L      H    LLHL  LLHL
 XXXXXXXX    C   L    H    H        L      H    LLHH  LLHH
 XXXXXXXX    C   L    H    H        L      H    LHLL  LHLL
 XXXXXXXX    C   L    H    H        L      H    LHLH  LHLH
 XXXXXXXX    C   L    H    H        L      H    LHHL  LHHL
 XXXXXXXX    C   L    H    H        L      H    LHHH  LHHH
 XXXXXXXX    C   L    H    H        L      H    HLLL  HLLL
 XXXXXXXX    C   L    H    H        L      H    HLLH  HLLH
 XXXXXXXX    C   L    H    H        L      H    HLHL  HLHL
 XXXXXXXX    C   L    H    H        L      H    HLHH  HLHH
 XXXXXXXX    C   L    H    H        L      H    HHLL  HHLL
 XXXXXXXX    C   L    H    H        L      H    HHLH  HHLH
 XXXXXXXX    C   L    H    H        L      H    HHHL  HHHL
 XXXXXXXX    C   L    H    H        L      L    HHHH  HHHH     CARRY OUT
 XXXXXXXX    X   H    X    X        X      X    XXXX  ZZZZ     TEST HI-Z
-----------------------------------------------------------------------------
```

DESCRIPTION

TWO IDENTICALLY PROGRAMMED PAL20X4 CAN PERFORM THE 64k DYNAMIC RAM REFRESH CONTROL FUNCTION.

EITHER COLUMN OR ROW ADDRESSES TO THE RAM ARE SELECTED DEPENDING ON ROW ENABLE (ROWEN).

AN ADDRESS COUNTER (C3-C0) IS SELECTED DURING REFRESH WHEN ROW ENABLE (ROWEN) IS HIGH.

THESE OPERATIONS ARE EXERCISED IN THE FUNCTION TABLE AND SUMMERIZED IN THE OPERATIONS TABLE:

/OC	COUNT	REFEN	ROWEN	O3-O0	OPERATION
H	X	X	X	Z	HI-Z
L	C	L	L	A3-A0	SELECT LOW ADDR BITS
L	C	L	H	A11-A8	SELECT UPPER ADDR BITS
L	C	H	H	C3-C0	SELECT REFRESH ADDR BITS
L	C	H	L	H	SET REFRESH COUNTER

```
64k DYNAMIC RAM REFRESH CONTROLLER

 1 CXXXXXXXX10X0HHHHHHHHH11
 2 CXXXX000000X0HLLHHHHLL11
 3 CXXXX111100X0HHHHHHHHH11
 4 C0000XXXX01X0HLLHHHHLL11
 5 C1111000001X0HHHHHHHHH11
 6 CXXXXXXXX11X0HLLLLLLLL01
 7 CXXXXXXXX11X0HLLLLLHLH01
 8 CXXXXXXXX11X0HLLLLHLHL01
 9 CXXXXXXXX11X0HLLLLHHHH01
10 CXXXXXXXX11X0HLHLHLLLL01
11 CXXXXXXXX11X0HLHLHLHLH01
12 CXXXXXXXX11X0HLHLHHLHL01
13 CXXXXXXXX11X0HLHLHHHHH01
14 CXXXXXXXX11X0HHLHLLLLL01
15 CXXXXXXXX11X0HHLHLLHLH01
16 CXXXXXXXX11X0HHLHLHLHL01
17 CXXXXXXXX11X0HHLHLHHHH01
18 CXXXXXXXX11X0HHHHHLLLL01
19 CXXXXXXXX11X0HHHHHLHLH01
20 CXXXXXXXX11X0HHHHHHLHL01
21 CXXXXXXXX11X0LHHHHHHHH01
22 XXXXXXXXXXXX1XXXZZZZXXX1

PASS SIMULATION
```

```
64k DYNAMIC RAM REFRESH CONTROLLER

                11 1111 1111 2222 2222 2233 3333 3333
   0123 4567 8901 2345 6789 0123 4567 8901 2345 6789


 8 ---- ---- ---- ---- ---- ---- ---- ---- ---- ----
 9 -X-- ---- ---- ---- ---- ---- ---- ---- -X-- X--- /A0*/REFEN*ROWEN
10 ---- ---- ---- ---- -X-- ---- ---- ---- -X-- -X-- /A8*/REFEN*/ROWEN
11 ---- ---- ---- ---X ---- ---- ---- ---- X--- X--- /C0*REFEN*ROWEN

16 ---- ---- ---- ---- ---- ---- ---- ---- ---- ----
17 ---- -X-- ---- ---- ---- ---- ---- ---- -X-- X--- /A1*/REFEN*ROWEN
18 ---- ---- ---- ---- ---- -X-- ---- ---- -X-- -X-- /A9*/REFEN*/ROWEN
19 ---- ---- ---- ---- ---X ---- ---- ---- X--- X--- /C1*REFEN*ROWEN

24 ---- ---- ---- ---X ---- ---- ---- ---- ---- ---- /C0
25 ---- ---- ---- ---- ---- ---- ---- ---- X--- -X-- REFEN*/ROWEN
26 ---X ---- ---- ---- ---- ---- ---- ---- ---- ---- CARRYIN
27 ---- ---- ---- ---- ---- ---- ---- ---- X--- -X-- REFEN*/ROWEN

32 ---- ---- ---- ---- ---X ---- ---- ---- ---- ---- /C1
33 ---- ---- ---- ---- ---- ---- ---- ---- X--- -X-- REFEN*/ROWEN
34 ---X ---- ---- --X- ---- ---- ---- ---- ---- ---- CARRYIN*C0
35 ---- ---- ---- ---- ---- ---- ---- ---- X--- -X-- REFEN*/ROWEN

40 ---- ---- ---- ---- ---- ---X ---- ---- ---- ---- /C2
41 ---- ---- ---- ---- ---- ---- ---- ---- X--- -X-- REFEN*/ROWEN
42 ---X ---- ---- --X- --X- ---- ---- ---- ---- ---- CARRYIN*C0*C1
43 ---- ---- ---- ---- ---- ---- ---- ---- X--- -X-- REFEN*/ROWEN

48 ---- ---- ---- ---- ---- ---- ---X ---- ---- ---- /C3
49 ---- ---- ---- ---- ---- ---- ---- ---- X--- -X-- REFEN*/ROWEN
50 ---X ---- ---- --X- --X- --X- ---- ---- ---- ---- CARRYIN*C0*C1*C2
51 ---- ---- ---- ---- ---- ---- ---- ---- X--- -X-- REFEN*/ROWEN

56 ---- ---- ---- ---- ---- ---- ---- ---- ---- ----
57 ---- ---- -X-- ---- ---- ---- ---- ---- -X-- X--- /A2*/REFEN*ROWEN
58 ---- ---- ---- ---- ---- ---- -X-- ---- -X-- -X-- /A10*/REFEN*/ROWEN
59 ---- ---- ---- ---- ---- ---X ---- ---- X--- X--- /C2*REFEN*ROWEN

64 ---- ---- ---- ---- ---- ---- ---- ---- ---- ----
65 ---- ---- ---- -X-- ---- ---- ---- ---- -X-- X--- /A3*/REFEN*ROWEN
66 ---- ---- ---- ---- ---- ---- ---- -X-- -X-- -X-- /A11*/REFEN*/ROWEN
67 ---- ---- ---- ---- ---- ---- ---X ---- X--- X--- /C3*REFEN*ROWEN

72 ---- ---- ---- ---- ---- ---- ---- ---- ---- ----
73 ---X ---- ---- --X- --X- --X- --X- ---- ---- ---- CARRYIN*C0*C1*C2*C3

LEGEND:  X : FUSE NOT BLOWN (L,N,0)   - : FUSE BLOWN   (H,P,1)

NUMBER OF FUSES BLOW = 1289
```

64k Dynamic RAM Refresh Controller

Logic Diagram PAL20X4

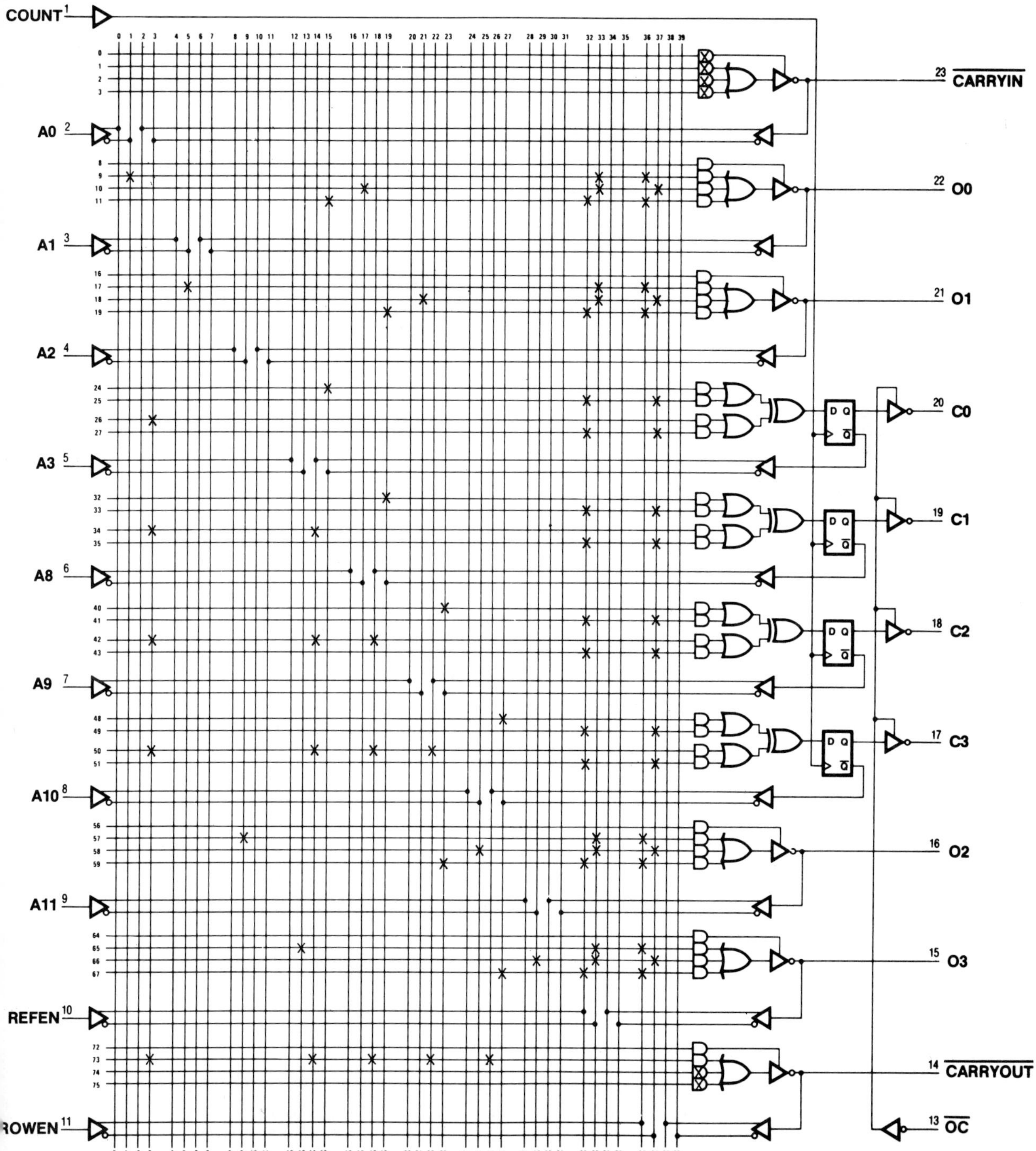

PAL
IMPORTANT NOTES

State Counter for Multiplier/Divider

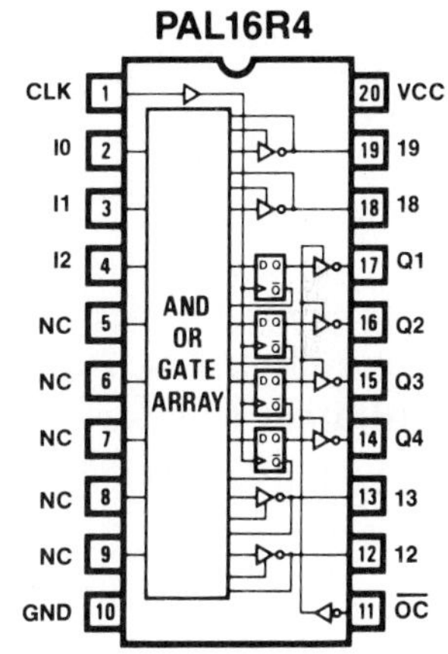

Transition Flow Chart Multiplier/Divider

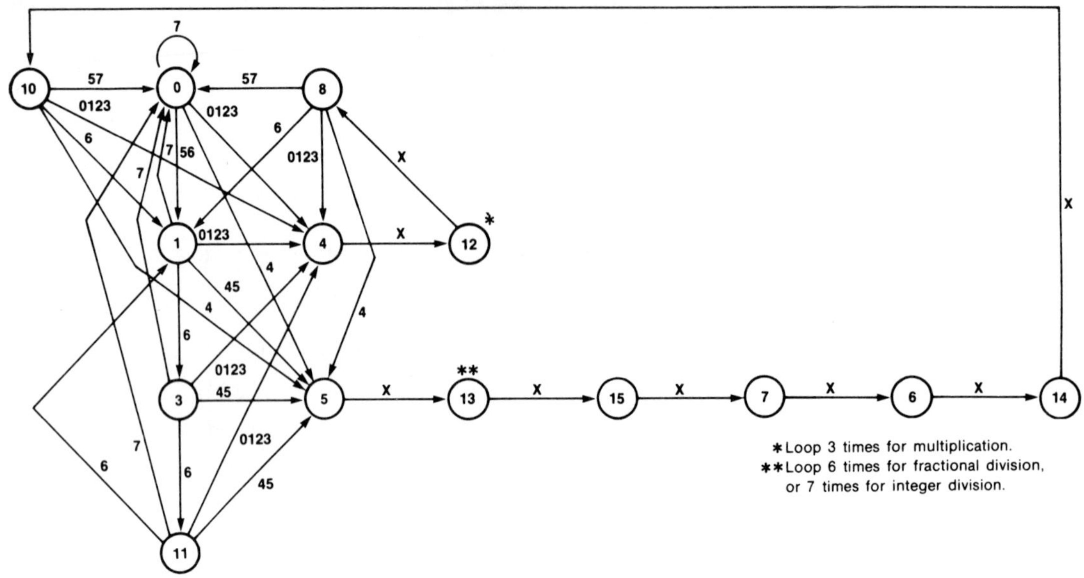

State Counter Using PAL16R4 for Multiplier/Divider

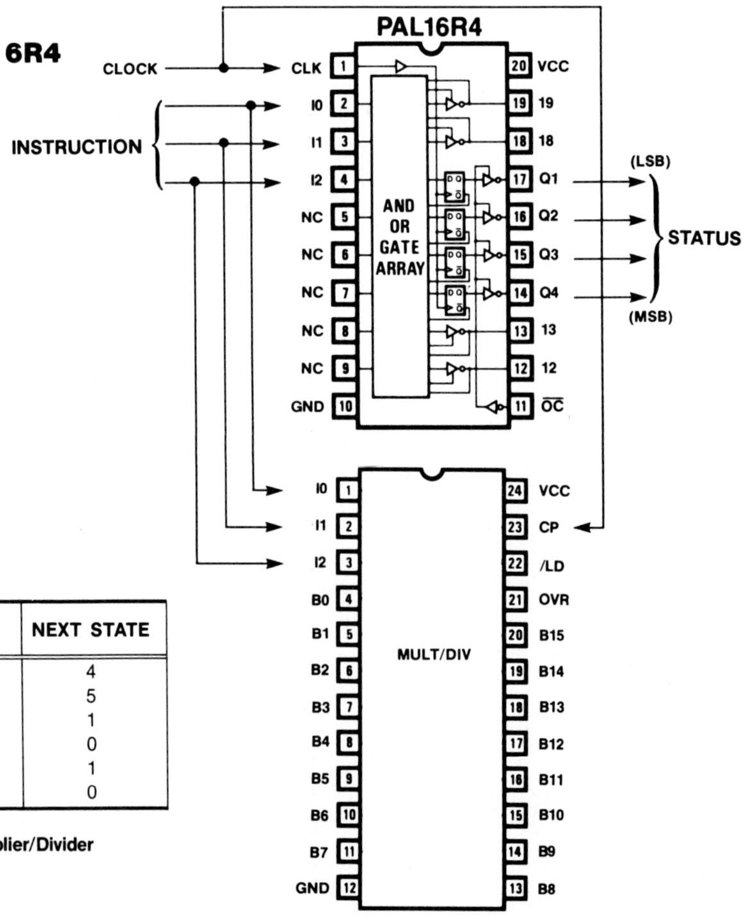

INSTRUCTION CODE	STARTING STATE	NEXT STATE
0, 1, 2, 3	0, 8, 10	4
4	0, 8, 10	5
5	0	1
5, 7	8, 10	0
6	0, 8, 10	1
7	0, 8, 10	0

Figure 1 Transition Table Multiplier/Divider

```
PAL16R4                                         PAL DESIGN SPECIFICATION
STCNT                                              WILLY VOLDAN 01/27/81
STATE COUNTER FOR MULTIPLIER/DIVIDER
MMI MUNICH GmbH
CLK I0 I1 I2 NC NC NC NC NC GND
/OC 12 13 Q4 Q3 Q2 Q1 18 19 VCC


IF(VCC) /19 =                 /I2*/I1*/I0
            +                 /I2*/I1* I0
            +                 /I2* I1*/I0
            +                 /I2* I1* I0

IF(VCC) /18 =  Q1* Q2* Q3*/Q4
            +  Q1* Q2* Q3* Q4
            +  Q1*/Q2* Q3*/Q4
            + /Q1* Q2* Q3* Q4
            + /Q1*/Q2* Q3* Q4
            + /Q1*/Q2* Q3*/Q4

      /Q4  :=  Q1* Q2*/Q3*/Q4
            +  Q1*/Q2*/Q3*/Q4
            + /Q1*/Q2* Q3* Q4* I2* I1*/I0
            +  Q1* Q2*/Q3* Q4
            + /Q1* Q2*/Q3* Q4
            +  Q1*/Q2*/Q3* Q4
            + /Q1* Q2*/Q3*/Q4

      /Q3  :=  19* 18
            +      18         * I2*/I1*/I0
            + /Q1* Q2* Q3* Q4* I2*/I1* I0
            + /Q1*/Q2* Q3* Q4* I2*/I1* I0
            + /Q1*/Q2* Q3*/Q4* I2*/I1* I0
            + /Q1*/Q2*/Q3* Q4
            + /Q1*/Q2*/Q3*/Q4
            + /13

      /Q2  := /Q1* Q2* Q3* Q4* I2* I1*/I0
            + /Q1*/Q2*/Q3* Q4
            + /Q1*/Q2*/Q3*/Q4
            +  Q1*/Q2*/Q3*/Q4
            + /Q1*/Q2* Q3* Q4* I2* I1*/I0
            +  Q1*/Q2*/Q3* Q4
            + /Q1* Q2*/Q3*/Q4

      /Q1  :=  Q1* Q2* Q3*/Q4* I2* I1*/I0
            +  Q1* Q2* Q3* Q4* I2*/I1* I0
            +  Q1* Q2* Q3* Q4* I2* I1*/I0
            +  Q1*/Q2* Q3*/Q4* I2* I1*/I0
            + /Q1*/Q2* Q3*/Q4* I2* I1*/I0
            + /Q1* Q2* Q3* Q4* I2* I1*/I0
            +      18         * I2*/I1*/I0
            +         /12
```

```
IF(VCC) /13 :=  Q1* Q2*/Q3* Q4
             + /Q1* Q2*/Q3* Q4
             +  Q1*/Q2*/Q3* Q4
             + /Q1* Q2*/Q3*/Q4

IF(VCC) /12 := /Q1* Q2* Q3* Q4* I2*/I1* I0
             + /Q1*/Q2* Q3* Q4* I2*/I1* I0
             + /Q1*/Q2* Q3*/Q4* I2*/I1* I0
             + /Q1*/Q2*/Q3*/Q4
             + /Q1*/Q2* Q3* Q4* I2* I1*/I0
             + /Q1* Q2*/Q3* Q4
             + /Q1* Q2*/Q3*/Q4
```

```
FUNCTION TABLE

/OC CLK I0 I1 I2 12 13 18 19 Q4 Q3 Q2 Q1

;           INST              STATE
;CONTROL    III    1 1 1 1    QQQQ
;/OC CLK    012    2 3 8 9    4321       COMMENTS
---------------------------------------------------
  L   C     HHL    X X X X    HHHH
  L   C     HLH    X X X X    HHHL
  L   C     LHH    X X X X    HHLL
  L   C     HHH    X X X X    HHHH
  L   C     HLH    X X X X    HHHL
  L   C     LHH    X X X X    HHLL
  L   C     HLH    L X X X    HLHL
  L   C     XXX    L L X X    LLHL
  L   C     XXX    X X X X    LHLH
  L   C     HLH    X H X X    HHHH
  H   X     XXX    X X X X    ZZZZ       DISABLED
---------------------------------------------------
```

DESCRIPTION

IN MANY SEQUENTIAL CIRCUITS IT IS DESIRABLE TO KNOW THE STATE OF THE SYSTEM. THIS PAL16R4 APPLICATION IS AN EXAMPLE OF A STATE COUNTER FOR THE MMI SEQUENTIAL MULTIPLIER/DIVIDER.

THE STATES ARE REPRESENTED BY A FOUR BIT COUNTER WHERE Q1 IS THE LEAST SIGNIFICANT BIT AND Q4 IS THE MOST SIGNIFICANT BIT.

THE NEXT-STATE OF THE COUNTER AND THE MULTIPLIER/DIVIDER IS A FUNCTION THE PRESENT STATE AND THE INSTRUCTION LINES I2-I0. FOR EXAMPLE IF THE MACHINE IS AT STATE 0 AND THE INSTRUCTION IS 0,1,2 OR 3 THEN THE NEXT STATE IS 4 (MULTIPLY INSTRUCTION), IF THE INSTRUCTION IS 5 (DIVIDE INSTRUCTION), ETC.

```
STATE COUNTER FOR MULTIPLIER/DIVIDER

 1 C110XXXXXX0XXHHHHXX1
 2 C101XXXXXX0XXHHHLXX1
 3 C011XXXXXX0XXHHLLXX1
 4 C111XXXXXX0XXHHHHXX1
 5 C101XXXXXX0XXHHHLXX1
 6 C011XXXXXX0XXHHLLXX1
 7 C101XXXXXX0LXHLHLXX1
 8 CXXXXXXXXX0LLLLHLXX1
 9 CXXXXXXXXX0XXLHLHXX1
10 C101XXXXXX0XHHHHHXX1
11 XXXXXXXXXX1XXZZZZXX1

PASS SIMULATION
```

```
STATE COUNTER FOR MULTIPLIER/DIVIDER

                11 1111 1111 2222 2222 2233
   0123 4567 8901 2345 6789 0123 4567 8901

 0 ---- ---- ---- ---- ---- ---- ---- ----
 1 -X-- -X-- -X-- ---- ---- ---- ---- ---- /I2*/I1*/I0
 2 X--- -X-- -X-- ---- ---- ---- ---- ---- /I2*/I1*I0
 3 -X-- X--- -X-- ---- ---- ---- ---- ---- /I2*I1*/I0
 4 X--- X--- -X-- ---- ---- ---- ---- ---- /I2*I1*I0

 8 ---- ---- ---- ---- ---- ---- ---- ----
 9 ---- ---- --X- --X- --X- ---X ---- ---- Q1*Q2*Q3*/Q4
10 ---- ---- --X- --X- --X- --X- ---- ---- Q1*Q2*Q3*Q4
11 ---- ---- --X- ---X --X- ---X ---- ---- Q1*/Q2*Q3*/Q4
12 ---- ---- ---X --X- --X- --X- ---- ---- /Q1*Q2*Q3*Q4
13 ---- ---- ---X ---X --X- --X- ---- ---- /Q1*/Q2*Q3*Q4
14 ---- ---- ---X ---X --X- ---X ---- ---- /Q1*/Q2*Q3*/Q4

16 -X-- X--- X-X- --X- --X- ---X ---- ---- Q1*Q2*Q3*/Q4*I2*I1*/I0
17 X--- -X-- X-X- --X- --X- --X- ---- ---- Q1*Q2*Q3*Q4*I2*/I1*I0
18 -X-- X--- X-X- --X- --X- --X- ---- ---- Q1*Q2*Q3*Q4*I2*I1*/I0
19 -X-- X--- X-X- ---X --X- ---X ---- ---- Q1*/Q2*Q3*/Q4*I2*I1*/I0
20 -X-- X--- X--X ---X --X- ---X ---- ---- /Q1*/Q2*Q3*/Q4*I2*I1*/I0
21 -X-- X--- X--X --X- --X- --X- ---- ---- /Q1*Q2*Q3*Q4*I2*I1*/I0
22 -X-- -XX- X--- ---- ---- ---- ---- ---- 18*I2*/I1*/I0
23 ---- ---- ---- ---- ---- ---- ---- ---X /12
```

```
STATE COUNTER FOR MULTIPLIER/DIVIDER (CONTINUED)

                11 1111 1111 2222 2222 2233
   0123 4567 8901 2345 6789 0123 4567 8901

24 -X-- X--- X--X --X- --X- --X- ---- ---- /Q1*Q2*Q3*Q4*I2*I1*/I0
25 ---- ---- ---X ---X ---X --X- ---- ---- /Q1*/Q2*/Q3*Q4
26 ---- ---- ---X ---X ---X ---X ---- ---- /Q1*/Q2*/Q3*/Q4
27 ---- ---- --X- ---X ---X ---X ---- ---- Q1*/Q2*/Q3*/Q4
28 -X-- X--- X--X ---X --X- --X- ---- ---- /Q1*/Q2*Q3*Q4*I2*I1*/I0
29 ---- ---- --X- ---X ---X --X- ---- ---- Q1*/Q2*/Q3*Q4
30 ---- ---- ---X --X- ---X ---X ---- ---- /Q1*Q2*/Q3*/Q4

32 --X- --X- ---- ---- ---- ---- ---- ---- 19*18
33 -X-- -XX- X--- ---- ---- ---- ---- ---- 18*I2*/I1*/I0
34 X--- -X-- X--X --X- --X- --X- ---- ---- /Q1*Q2*Q3*Q4*I2*/I1*I0
35 X--- -X-- X--X ---X --X- --X- ---- ---- /Q1*/Q2*Q3*Q4*I2*/I1*I0
36 X--- -X-- X--X ---X --X- ---X ---- ---- /Q1*/Q2*Q3*/Q4*I2*/I1*I0
37 ---- ---- ---X ---X ---X --X- ---- ---- /Q1*/Q2*/Q3*Q4
38 ---- ---- ---X ---X ---X ---X ---- ---- /Q1*/Q2*/Q3*/Q4
39 ---- ---- ---- ---- ---- ---- ---X ---- /13

40 ---- ---- --X- --X- ---X ---X ---- ---- Q1*Q2*/Q3*/Q4
41 ---- ---- --X- ---X ---X ---X ---- ---- Q1*/Q2*/Q3*/Q4
42 -X-- X--- X--X ---X --X- --X- ---- ---- /Q1*/Q2*Q3*Q4*I2*I1*/I0
43 ---- ---- --X- --X- ---X --X- ---- ---- Q1*Q2*/Q3*Q4
44 ---- ---- ---X --X- ---X --X- ---- ---- /Q1*Q2*/Q3*Q4
45 ---- ---- --X- ---X ---X --X- ---- ---- Q1*/Q2*/Q3*Q4
46 ---- ---- ---X --X- ---X ---X ---- ---- /Q1*Q2*/Q3*/Q4

48 ---- ---- ---- ---- ---- ---- ---- ----
49 ---- ---- --X- --X- ---X --X- ---- ---- Q1*Q2*/Q3*Q4
50 ---- ---- ---X --X- ---X --X- ---- ---- /Q1*Q2*/Q3*Q4
51 ---- ---- --X- ---X ---X --X- ---- ---- Q1*/Q2*/Q3*Q4
52 ---- ---- ---X --X- ---X ---X ---- ---- /Q1*Q2*/Q3*/Q4

56 ---- ---- ---- ---- ---- ---- ---- ----
57 X--- -X-- X--X --X- --X- --X- ---- ---- /Q1*Q2*Q3*Q4*I2*/I1*I0
58 X--- -X-- X--X ---X --X- --X- ---- ---- /Q1*/Q2*Q3*Q4*I2*/I1*I0
59 X--- -X-- X--X ---X --X- ---X ---- ---- /Q1*/Q2*Q3*/Q4*I2*/I1*I0
60 ---- ---- ---X ---X ---X ---X ---- ---- /Q1*/Q2*/Q3*/Q4
61 -X-- X--- X--X ---X --X- --X- ---- ---- /Q1*/Q2*Q3*Q4*I2*I1*/I0
62 ---- ---- ---X --X- ---X --X- ---- ---- /Q1*Q2*/Q3*Q4
63 ---- ---- ---X --X- ---X ---X ---- ---- /Q1*Q2*/Q3*/Q4

LEGEND:  X : FUSE NOT BLOWN (L,N,0)   - : FUSE BLOWN   (H,P,1)

NUMBER OF FUSES BLOWN = 1520
```

State Counter for Multiplier/Divider

Logic Diagram PAL16R4

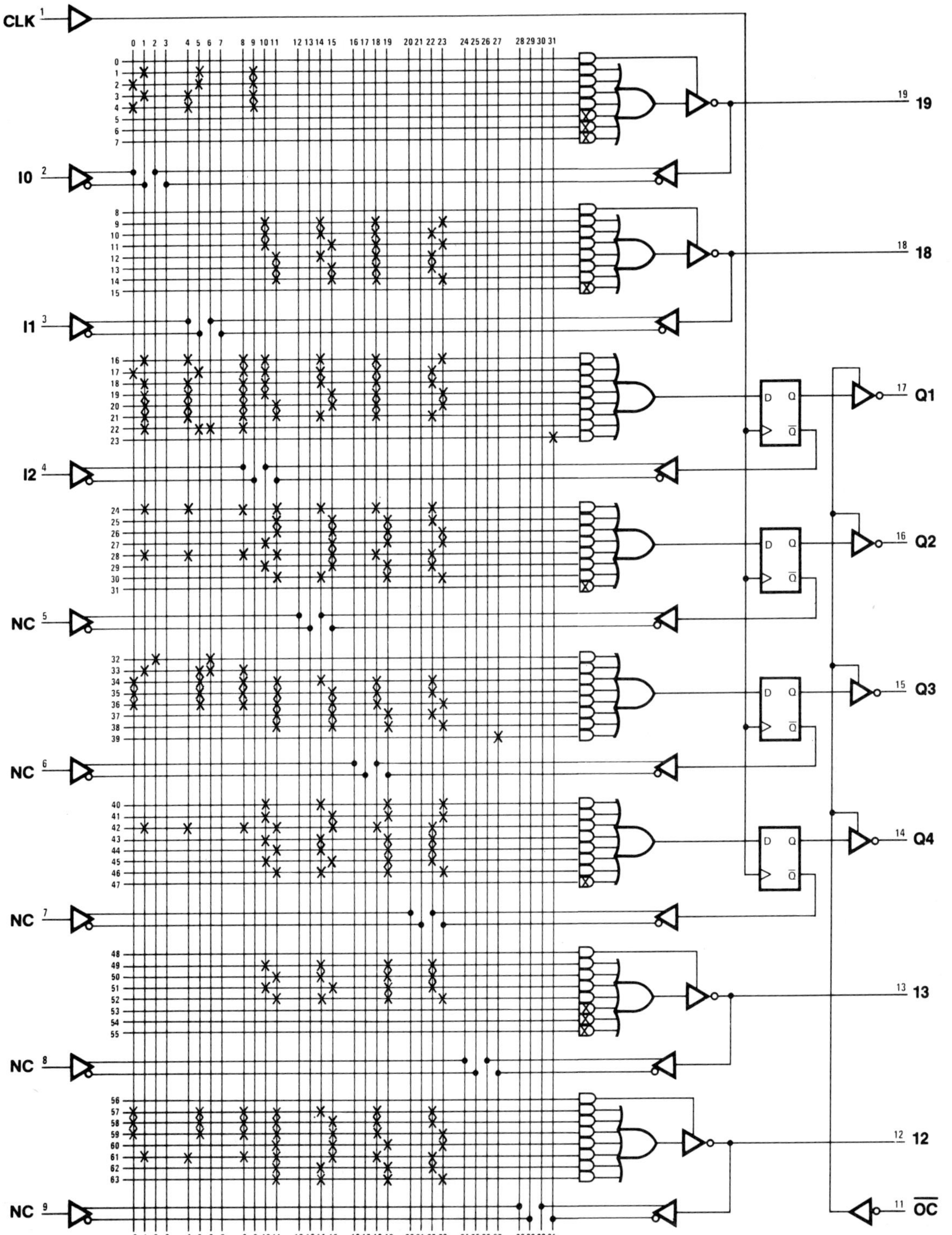

PAL
IMPORTANT,
NOTES

ALU/Accumulator

PAL16A4

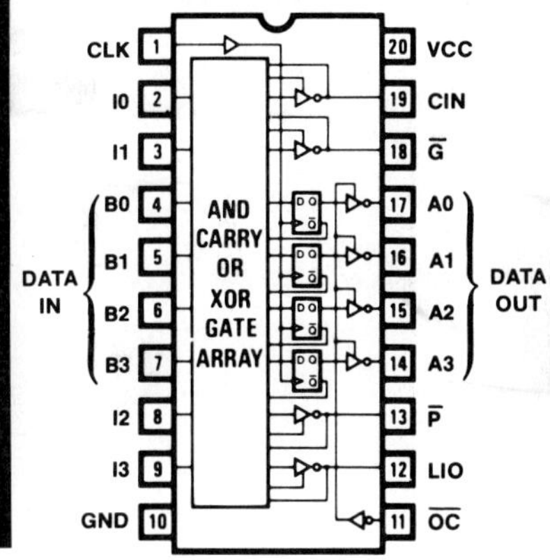

```
PAL16A4                                         PAL DESIGN SPECIFICATION
ALU                                               BIRKNER/COLI 07/15/81
ALU/ACCUMULATOR
MMI SUNNYVALE, CALIFORNIA
CLK I0  I1 B0 B1 B2 B3 I2 I3  GND
/OC LIO /P A3 A2 A1 A0 /G CIN VCC


CARRY0 .EQU   /I3*/I2*/I1*/I0 * CIN

CARRY1 .EQU   /I3*/I2*/I1*/I0 * (A0*B0)
            + /I3*/I2*/I1*/I0 * (A0+B0)*CIN

CARRY2 .EQU   /I3*/I2*/I1*/I0 * (A1*B1)
            + /I3*/I2*/I1*/I0 * (A1+B1)*(A0*B0)
            + /I3*/I2*/I1*/I0 * (A1+B1)*(A0+B0)*CIN

CARRY3 .EQU   /I3*/I2*/I1*/I0 * (A2*B2)
            + /I3*/I2*/I1*/I0 * (A2+B2)*(A1*B1)
            + /I3*/I2*/I1*/I0 * (A2+B2)*(A1+B1)*(A0*B0)
            + /I3*/I2*/I1*/I0 * (A2+B2)*(A1+B1)*(A0*B0)*CIN


/A0 :=  /I3*/I2*/I1*/I0*(A0:*:B0)    ;A0 PLUS B0
     +  /I3*/I2* I0*(/A0)            ;HOLD A0    (A0 AND)
     +  /I3*/I2* I1*(/B0)            ;LOAD B0    (  B0   )
     +  /I3* I2*/I1*/I0*(B0)         ;LOAD /B0
    :+: /I3* I2*/I1* I0*(/A0*/B0)    ;A0 OR B0
     +  /I3* I2* I1*/I0*/CIN         ;SHIFT LEFT A0
     +  /I3* I2* I1* I0*(/A1)        ;SHIFT RIGHT A0
     +   I3*(/A0)                    ;HOLD A0 (LSB)
     +   CARRY0                      ;A0 PLUS B0 PLUS 1

/A1 :=  /I3*/I2*/I1*/I0*(A1:*:B1)    ;A1 PLUS B1
     +  /I3*/I2* I0*(/A1)            ;HOLD A1    (A1 AND)
     +  /I3*/I2* I1*(/B1)            ;LOAD B1    (  B1   )
     +  /I3* I2*/I1*/I0*(B1)         ;LOAD /B1
    :+: /I3* I2*/I1* I0*(/A1*/B1)    ;A1 OR B1
     +  /I3* I2* I1*/I0*(/A0)        ;SHIFT LEFT A1
     +  /I3* I2* I1* I0*(/A2)        ;SHIFT RIGHT A1
     +   I3*(/A1)                    ;HOLD A1
     +   CARRY1                      ;A1 PLUS B1 PLUS 1

/A2 :=  /I3*/I2*/I1*/I0*(A2:*:B2)    ;A2 PLUS B2
     +  /I3*/I2* I0*(/A2)            ;HOLD A2    (A2 AND)
     +  /I3*/I2* I1*(/B2)            ;LOAD B2    (  B2   )
     +  /I3* I2*/I1*/I0*(B2)         ;LOAD /B2
    :+: /I3* I2*/I1* I0*(/A2*/B2)    ;A2 OR B2
     +  /I3* I2* I1*/I0*(/A1)        ;SHIFT LEFT A2
     +  /I3* I2* I1* I0*(/A3)        ;SHIFT RIGHT A2
     +   I3*(/A2)                    ;HOLD A2
     +   CARRY2                      ;A2 PLUS B2 PLUS 1
```

```
/A3 :=  /I3*/I2*/I1*/I0*(A3:*:B3)    ;A3 PLUS B3
     +  /I3*/I2* I0*(/A3)            ;HOLD A3    (A3 AND)
     +  /I3*/I2* I1*(/B3)            ;LOAD B3    (  B3  )
     +  /I3* I2*/I1*/I0*(B3)         ;LOAD /B3
    :+: /I3* I2*/I1* I0*(/A3*/B3)    ;A3 OR B3
     +  /I3* I2* I1*/I0*(/A2)        ;SHIFT LEFT A3
     +  /I3* I2* I1* I0*/LIO         ;SHIFT RIGHT A3
     +   I3*(/A3)                    ;HOLD A3 (MSB)
     +   CARRY3                      ;A3 PLUS B3 PLUS 1

IF(VCC)  G  =  /I3*/I2*/I1*/I0 * (A3*B3)
             +  /I3*/I2*/I1*/I0 * (A3+B3)*(A2*B2)
             +  /I3*/I2*/I1*/I0 * (A3+B3)*(A2+B2)*(A1*B1)
             +  /I3*/I2*/I1*/I0 * (A3+B3)*(A2+B2)*(A1+B1)*(A0*B0)

IF(VCC)  P  =  /I3*/I2*/I1*/I0 * (A3+B3)*(A2+B2)*(A1+B1)*(A0+B0)
             +  /I3*/I2*/I1* I0 * (/A3)*(/A2)*(/A1)*(/A0)
             +  /I3*/I2* I1*/I0 * (/B3)*(/B2)*(/B1)*(/B0)
             +  /I3*/I2* I1* I0 * (/A3+/B3)*(/A2+/B2)*(/A1+/B1)*(/A0+/B0)
             +  /I3* I2*/I1* I0 * (/A3*/B3)*(/A2*/B2)*(/A1*/B1)*(/A0*/B0)
             +  /I3* I2* I1*/I0 * (/A2)*(/A1)*(/A0)*/CIN
             +  /I3* I2* I1* I0 * /LIO*(/A3)*(/A2)*(/A1)

IF (/I3* I2* I1*/I0) /LIO = (/A3)    ;SHIFT LEFT OUT

IF (/I3* I2* I1* I0) /CIN = (/A0)    ;SHIFT RIGHT OUT
```

DESCRIPTION

THE ALU ACCUMULATOR LOADS THE A-REGISTER WITH ONE OF EIGHT OPERANDS ON THE RISING EDGE OF THE CLOCK. G AND P OUTPUT GENERATE AND PROPAGATE ON THE ADD INSTRUCTION. P OUTPUTS OP = ZERO ON INSTRUCTIONS 1,2,3,5,6,7.

OPERATIONS TABLE:

/OC	CLK	I3	I2	I1	I0	LIO	CIN	A3-A0	OPERATION	
H	X	X	X	X	X	X	X	Z	HI-Z	A =Z
L	C	L	L	L	L	X	L	A PLUS B	ADD	A:=A PLUS B
L	C	L	L	L	L	X	H	A PL B PL 1	ADD	A:=A PLUS B PLUS 1
L	C	L	L	L	H	X	X	A	HOLD	A:=A
L	C	L	L	H	L	X	X	B	LOAD	A:=B
L	C	L	L	H	H	X	X	A AND B	AND	A:=A*B
L	C	L	H	L	L	X	X	/B	LOAD COMP	A:=/B
L	C	L	H	L	H	X	X	A OR B	OR	A:=A+B
L	C	L	H	H	L	X	LI	SL(A)	SHIFT LEFT	
L	C	L	H	H	H	RI	X	SR(A)	SHIFT RIGHT	
L	C	H	X	X	X	X	X	A	HOLD	A:=A

```
ALU/ACCUMULATOR

               11 1111 1111 2222 2222 2233
   0123 4567 8901 2345 6789 0123 4567 8901

 0 X--- X--- ---- ---- ---- ---- X--- -X-- /I3*I2*I1*I0
 1 ---- ---- XX-- ---- ---- ---- ---- ---- /A0

 8 ---- ---- ---- ---- ---- ---- ---- ----
 9 -X-- -X-- ---- ---- ---- X-XX -X-- -X-- /I3*/I2*/I1*/I0*A3*B3
10 -X-- -X-- ---- ---- X-XX --X- -X-- -X-- /I3*/I2*/I1*/I0*A3+B3*A2*B2
11 -X-- -X-- ---- X-XX --X- --X- -X-- -X-- /I3*/I2*/I1*/I0*A3+B3*A2+B2*A1-
12 -X-- -X-- X-XX --X- --X- --X- -X-- -X-- /I3*/I2*/I1*/I0*A3+B3*A2+B2*A1-

16 -X-- -X-- X--X ---- ---- ---- -X-- -X-- /I3*/I2*/I1*/I0*A0:*:B0
17 X--- ---- XX-- ---- ---- ---- -X-- -X-- /I3*/I2*I0*/A0
18 ---- X--- -X-X ---- ---- ---- -X-- -X-- /I3*/I2*I1*/B0
19 -X-- -X-- X-X- ---- ---- ---- X--- -X-- /I3*I2*/I1*/I0*B0
20 X--- -X-- XX-X ---- ---- ---- X--- -X-- /I3*I2*/I1*I0*/A0*/B0
21 -X-X X--- ---- ---- ---- ---- X--- -X-- /I3*I2*I1*/I0*/CIN
22 X--- X--- ---- XX-- ---- ---- X--- -X-- /I3*I2*I1*I0*/A1
23 ---- ---- XX-- ---- ---- ---- ---- X--- I3*/A0

24 -X-- -X-- ---- X--X ---- ---- -X-- -X-- /I3*/I2*/I1*/I0*A1:*:B1
25 X--- ---- ---- XX-- ---- ---- -X-- -X-- /I3*/I2*I0*/A1
26 ---- X--- ---- -X-X ---- ---- -X-- -X-- /I3*/I2*I1*/B1
27 -X-- -X-- ---- X-X- ---- ---- X--- -X-- /I3*I2*/I1*/I0*B1
28 X--- -X-- ---- XX-X ---- ---- X--- -X-- /I3*I2*/I1*I0*/A1*/B1
29 -X-- X--- XX-- ---- ---- ---- X--- -X-- /I3*I2*I1*/I0*/A0
30 X--- X--- ---- ---- XX-- ---- X--- -X-- /I3*I2*I1*I0*/A2
31 ---- ---- ---- XX-- ---- ---- ---- X--- I3*/A1

32 -X-- -X-- ---- ---- X--X ---- -X-- -X-- /I3*/I2*/I1*/I0*A2:*:B2
33 X--- ---- ---- ---- XX-- ---- -X-- -X-- /I3*/I2*I0*/A2
34 ---- X--- ---- ---- -X-X ---- -X-- -X-- /I3*/I2*I1*/B2
35 -X-- -X-- ---- ---- X-X- ---- X--- -X-- /I3*I2*/I1*/I0*B2
36 X--- -X-- ---- ---- XX-X ---- X--- -X-- /I3*I2*/I1*I0*/A2*/B2
37 -X-- X--- ---- XX-- ---- ---- X--- -X-- /I3*I2*I1*/I0*/A1
38 X--- X--- ---- ---- ---- XX-- X--- -X-- /I3*I2*I1*I0*/A3
39 ---- ---- ---- ---- XX-- ---- ---- X--- I3*/A2

40 -X-- -X-- ---- ---- ---- X--X -X-- -X-- /I3*/I2*/I1*/I0*A3:*:B3
41 X--- ---- ---- ---- ---- XX-- -X-- -X-- /I3*/I2*I0*/A3
42 ---- X--- ---- ---- ---- -X-X -X-- -X-- /I3*/I2*I1*/B3
43 -X-- -X-- ---- ---- ---- X-X- X--- -X-- /I3*I2*/I1*/I0*B3
44 X--- -X-- ---- ---- ---- XX-X X--- -X-- /I3*I2*/I1*I0*/A3*/B3
45 -X-- X--- ---- ---- XX-- ---- X--- -X-- /I3*I2*I1*/I0*/A2
46 X--- X--- ---- ---- ---- ---- X--- -X-X /I3*I2*I1*I0*/LIO
47 ---- ---- ---- ---- ---- XX-- ---- X--- I3*/A3

48 ---- ---- ---- ---- ---- ---- ---- ----
49 -X-- -X-- --X- --X- --X- --X- -X-- -X-- /I3*/I2*/I1*/I0*A3+B3*A2+B2*A1-
50 X--- -X-- XX-- XX-- XX-- XX-- -X-- -X-- /I3*/I2*/I1*I0*/A3*/A2*/A1*/A0
51 -X-- X--- -X-X -X-X -X-X -X-X -X-- -X-- /I3*/I2*I1*/I0*/B3*/B2*/B1*/B0
52 X--- X--- -X-- -X-- -X-- -X-- -X-- -X-- /I3*/I2*I1*I0*/A3+/B3*/A2+/B2*-
53 X--- -X-- XX-X XX-X XX-X XX-X X--- -X-- /I3*I2*/I1*I0*/A3*/B3*/A2*/B2*-
54 -X-X X--- XX-- XX-- XX-- ---- X--- -X-- /I3*I2*I1*/I0*/A2*/A1*/A0*/CIN
55 X--- X--- ---- XX-- XX-- XX-- X--- -X-X /I3*I2*I1*I0*/LIO*/A3*/A2*/A1

56 -X-- X--- ---- ---- ---- ---- X--- -X-- /I3*I2*I1*/I0
57 ---- ---- ---- ---- ---- XX-- ---- ---- /A3
LEGEND:   X : FUSE NOT BLOWN (L,N,0)    - : FUSE BLOWN    (H,P,1)
NUMBER OF FUSES BLOWN = 1270
```

ALU/Accumulator

Logic Diagram PAL16A4

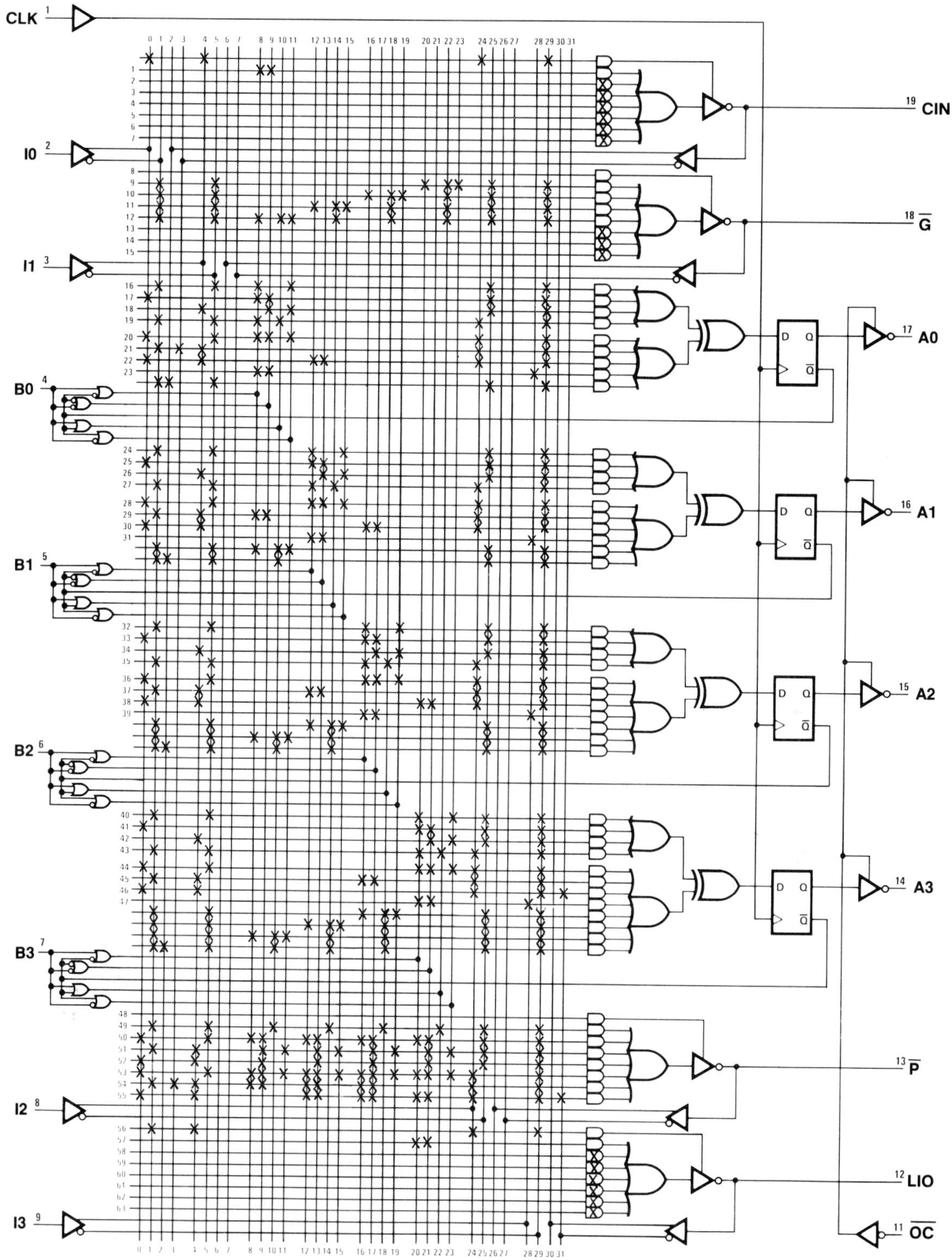

PAL
IMPORTANT,
NOTES

Stepper Motor Controller

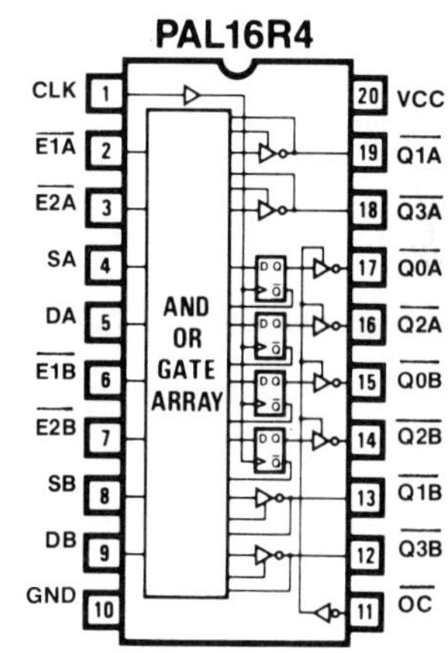

Functional Description

Stepper motors and linear actuators are used in a variety of applications requiring precise rotational and/or linear movement. Examples are printers, floppy disc drives, mechanical valves, etc. Stepper motors are two-phase permanent magnet motors which provide discrete angular movement every time the polarity of a winding is changed. In the case of linear actuators, the angular movement is converted to a linear movement via a load screw. In essence, they are dc motors without brushes, where the user provides commutation with external logic.

Circuit Operation

One type of drive circuit, unipolar drive, is shown in Figure 1 below. Two drive sequences are given in Tables 1A and 1B. Angular rotation is achieved by saturating the transistor drivers in the sequence shown in the appropriate table (full or half step). Now, assume the circuit of Figure 1 is connected to a stepper motor designed for 7.5° steps. By following the step sequence of Table 1A (full step), the shaft will rotate 7.5° each time the state is changed. If the sequence of Table 1B is followed, a 3.75° (half step) rotation will result for each change of state. For both step sequences, the direction can be reversed by stepping backwards through the table (step 4-3-2-1-4-etc.).

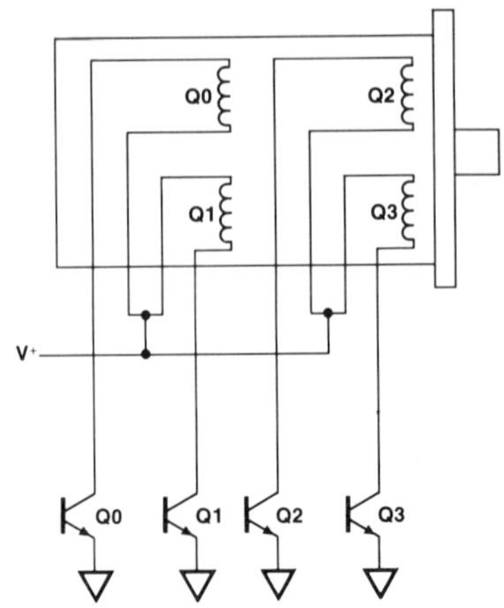

Figure 1

Table 1A
FULL STEP SEQUENCE

CLOCKWISE ROTATION (↓) — COUNTER-CLOCKWISE ROTATION (↑)

STEP	Q0	Q1	Q2	Q3
1	1	0	1	0
2	1	0	0	1
3	0	1	0	1
4	0	1	1	0
1	1	0	1	0

Table 1B
HALF STEP SEQUENCE

CLOCKWISE ROTATION (↓) — COUNTER-CLOCKWISE ROTATION (↑)

STEP	Q0	Q1	Q2	Q3
1	1	0	1	0
2	1	0	0	0
3	1	0	0	1
4	0	0	0	1
5	0	1	0	1
6	0	1	0	0
7	0	1	1	0
8	0	0	1	0
1	1	0	1	0

PAL Implementation

In this application, one PAL16R4 can be used to provide the logic levels required to drive two stepper motors in the full step mode. Due to the high current drive required (100-400 mA/phase), external inverting high current buffers would be used (ULN 2001 or equivalent). In the design, the following features are provided within the PAL:

- Enable/Disable inputs to enable stepping of either section. (/E inputs).
- Select clockwise or counter-clockwise rotation.
- Set the motor to logic state step 1.

A block diagram/pinout is shown in Figure 2.

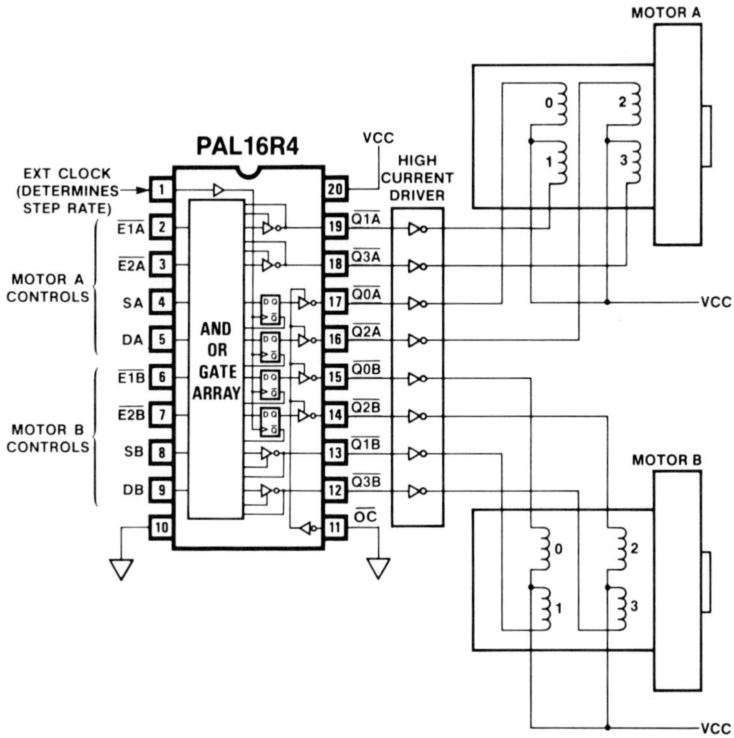

Figure 2

A function table for each motor control section is given below.

CLOCK	$\overline{E1}$	$\overline{E2}$	S	D	FUNCTION
X	1	X	X	X	Hold motor in current position
X	X	1	X	X	Hold motor in current position
↑	0	0	1	X	Set outputs to step 1 levels
↑	0	0	0	0	Step motor clockwise
↑	0	0	0	1	Step motor counter-clockwise

The full step sequence (Table 1A) can be simplified from 4 outputs to 2 outputs since Q1 = Q0 and Q3 = Q2. The sequences can then be expressed as follows:

	D = 0		D = 1	
STEP	Q0	Q2	Q0	Q2
1	1	1	1	1
2	1	0	0	1
3	0	0	0	0
4	0	1	1	0
1	1	1	1	1

$Q1 = \overline{Q0}$ $\quad$ $Q3 = \overline{Q2}$

when S = 1:

Q0 = 1 Q1 = 0 Q2 = 1 Q3 = 0

when E1 = 1 or E2 = 1

Q0 = q0 Q1 = q1 Q2 = q2 Q3 = q3

The step sequences can be converted to equations by use of a Karnaugh map.

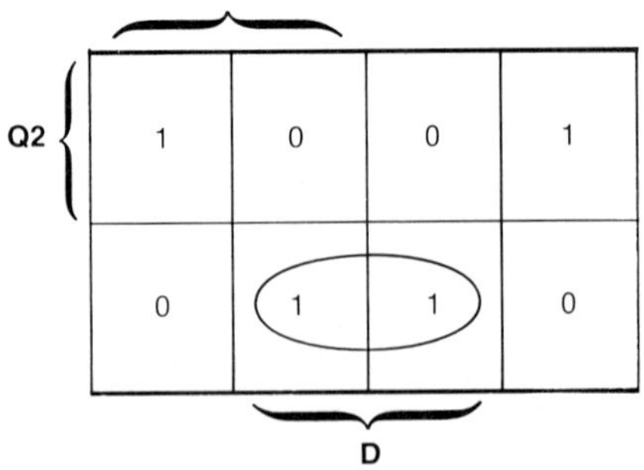

$Q0 = Q2 \cdot \overline{D} + \overline{Q2} \cdot D$

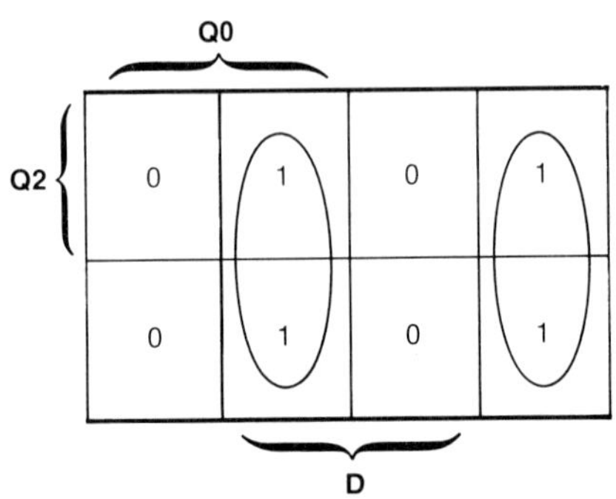

$Q2 = Q0 \cdot D + \overline{Q0} \cdot \overline{D}$

Factor in E1 and E2:

$Q0 = \overline{E1} \cdot \overline{E2} \cdot Q2 \cdot \overline{D} + \overline{E1} \cdot \overline{E2} \cdot \overline{Q2} \cdot \overline{D}$

$Q2 = \overline{E1} \cdot \overline{E2} \cdot Q0 \cdot D + \overline{E1} \cdot \overline{E2} \cdot \overline{Q0} \cdot \overline{D}$

Express the set function as an equation:

$Q0 = \overline{E1} \cdot E2 \cdot S$ $\qquad$ $Q2 = \overline{E1} \cdot \overline{E2} \cdot S$

Express the hold function (when E1 or E2 = 1)

$Q0 = q0 \cdot E1 + q0 \cdot E2$ $\quad$ $Q2 = q2 \cdot E1 + q2 \cdot E2$

Combining all the above:

$Q0 := \overline{E1} \cdot \overline{E2} \cdot S + Q0 \cdot E1 + Q0 \cdot E2 + \overline{E1} \cdot \overline{E2} \cdot Q2 \cdot \overline{D} + \overline{E1} \cdot \overline{E2} \cdot \overline{Q2} \cdot D$

$Q1 := Q0$

$Q2 := \overline{E1} \cdot \overline{E2} \cdot S + Q2 \cdot E1 + Q2 \cdot E2 + \overline{E1} \cdot \overline{E2} \cdot Q0 \cdot D + \overline{E1} \cdot \overline{E2} \cdot \overline{Q0} \cdot \overline{D}$

$Q3 := Q2$

Conclusion

Although this example could be used "as is" in a stepper motor application, the programmability of PAL's could allow for any desired modifications. Changes to the circuit might include:

1. Drive only one stepper motor, using a PAL16R6. The other flip-flops could be used as a programmable counter, allowing for different speed settings.
2. Drive only one stepper motor, using the extra inputs and outputs to handle other circuit functions.
3. Drive only one stepper motor, using a PAL16R6. The other flip-flops could be used as a 4-bit position counter.
4. The substitution of a PAL16R8, and another *inverting* buffer would allow the driving and control of four stepper motors.
5. Re-program for half-step operation.

```
PAL16R4                                               PAL DESIGN SPECIFICATION
SMC                                                      DAVE SACKETT 02/23/81
STEPPER MOTOR CONTROLLER
DEVOE COMPANY, INDIANAPOLIS, INDIANA
CLK /E1A /E2A SA DA /E1B /E2B SB DB GND
/OC /Q3B /Q1B /Q2B /Q0B /Q2A /Q0A /Q3A /Q1A VCC


Q0A :=  Q0A*/E1A                 ;HOLD IF NOT E1
     +  Q0A*/E2A                 ;HOLD IF NOT E2
     +  SA * E1A* E2A            ;STEP 1 IF SET
     + /Q2A* E1A* E2A* DA        ;LOAD /Q2A IF COUNTER-CLOCKWISE
     +  Q2A* E1A* E2A*/DA        ;LOAD  Q2A IF CLOCKWISE

IF (VCC) Q1A = /Q0A

Q2A :=  Q2A*/E1A                 ;HOLD IF NOT E1
     +  Q2A*/E2A                 ;HOLD IF NOT E2
     +  SA * E1A* E2A            ;STEP 1 IF SET
     +  Q0A* E1A* E2A* DA        ;LOAD  Q0A IF COUNTER-CLOCKWISE
     + /Q0A* E1A* E2A*/DA        ;LOAD /Q0A IF CLOCKWISE

IF (VCC) Q3A = /Q2A

Q0B :=  Q0B*/E1B                 ;HOLD IF NOT E1
     +  Q0B*/E2B                 ;HOLD IF NOT E2
     +  SB * E1B* E2B            ;STEP 1 IF SET
     + /Q2B* E1B* E2B* DB        ;LOAD /Q2B IF COUNTER-CLOCKWISE
     +  Q2B* E1B* E2B*/DB        ;LOAD  Q2B IF CLOCKWISE

IF (VCC) Q1B = /Q0B

Q2B :=  Q2B*/E1B                 ;HOLD IF NOT E1
     +  Q2B*/E2B                 ;HOLD IF NOT E2
     +  SB * E1B* E2B            ;STEP 1 IF SET
     +  Q0B* E1B* E2B* DB        ;LOAD  Q0B IF COUNTER-CLOCKWISE
     + /Q0B* E1B* E2B*/DB        ;LOAD /Q0B IF CLOCKWISE

IF (VCC) Q3B = /Q2B
```

```
FUNCTION TABLE

CLK /OC /E1A /E2A SA DA Q0A Q1A Q2A Q3A /E1B /E2B SB DB Q0B Q1B Q2B Q3B

;CHIP     STEPPER MOTOR A     STEPPER MOTOR B
;C  /      CONTROL  STEP       CONTROL  STEP
;L  O      E E S D  QQQQ       E E S D  QQQQ
;K  C      1 2 A A  0123       1 2 A A  0123       COMMENTS
---------------------------------------------------------------------
 C  L      L L H X  HLHL       L L H X  HLHL       SET TO STEP 1
 C  L      H H X X  HLHL       H H X X  HLHL       HOLD
 C  L      L L L L  HLLH       L L L H  LHHL       STEP A CW, B CCW
 C  L      L L L L  LHLH       L L L H  LHLH       STEP A CW, B CCW
 C  L      L L L L  LHHL       L L L H  HLLH       STEP A CW, B CCW
 C  L      L L L L  HLHL       L L L H  HLHL       STEP A CW, B CCW
 C  L      L L L L  HLLH       L L L H  LHHL       STEP A CW, B CCW
 C  L      L L L L  LHLH       L L L H  LHLH       STEP A CW, B CCW
 C  L      L L L H  HLLH       L L L L  LHHL       STEP A CCW, B CW
 C  L      H L L H  HLLH       H L L L  LHHL       HOLD
 C  L      L H L H  HLLH       L H L L  LHHL       HOLD
 C  L      L H H H  HLLH       L H H L  LHHL       HOLD
---------------------------------------------------------------------
```

DESCRIPTION

THIS PAL16R4 PROVIDES THE LOGIC LEVELS REQUIRED TO DRIVE TWO STEPPER MOTORS IN THE FULL STEP MODE.

THE FOLLOWING OPERATIONS MAY BE PERFORMED FOR EACH STEPPER MOTOR CONTROLLER INDIVIDUALLY:

CLK	/E1	/E2	S	D	OPERATION
X	H	X	X	X	HOLD MOTOR IN CURRENT POSITION
X	X	H	X	X	HOLD MOTOR IN CURRENT POSITION
C	L	L	H	X	SET OUTPUTS TO STEP 1 LEVELS
C	L	L	L	L	STEP MOTOR CLOCKWISE
C	L	L	L	H	STEP MOTOR COUNTER-CLOCKWISE

```
STEPPER MOTOR CONTROLLER

 1 C001X001XX0HHLLLLHH1
 2 C11XX11XXX0HHLLLLHH1
 3 C00000001X0HLLHHLLH1
 4 C00000001X0LLHHHHLL1
 5 C00000001X0LHHLLHHL1
 6 C00000001X0HHLLLLHH1
 7 C00000001X0HLLHHLLH1
 8 C00000001X0LLHHHHLL1
 9 C00010000X0HLLHHLLH1
10 C10011000X0HLLHHLLH1
11 C01010100X0HLLHHLLH1
12 C01110110X0HLLHHLLH1

PASS SIMULATION
```

```
STEPPER MOTOR CONTROLLER

               11 1111 1111 2222 2222 2233
   0123 4567 8901 2345 6789 0123 4567 8901

 0 ---- ---- ---- ---- ---- ---- ---- ----
 1 ---- ---- --X- ---- ---- ---- ---- ---- /Q0A

 8 ---- ---- ---- ---- ---- ---- ---- ----
 9 ---- ---- ---- --X- ---- ---- ---- ---- /Q2A

16 X--- ---- ---X ---- ---- ---- ---- ---- Q0A*/E1A
17 ---- X--- ---X ---- ---- ---- ---- ---- Q0A*/E2A
18 -X-- -X-- X--- ---- ---- ---- ---- ---- SA*E1A*E2A
19 -X-- -X-- ---- X-X- ---- ---- ---- ---- /Q2A*E1A*E2A*DA
20 -X-- -X-- ---- -X-X ---- ---- ---- ---- Q2A*E1A*E2A*/DA

24 X--- ---- ---- ---X ---- ---- ---- ---- Q2A*/E1A
25 ---- X--- ---- ---X ---- ---- ---- ---- Q2A*/E2A
26 -X-- -X-- X--- ---- ---- ---- ---- ---- SA*E1A*E2A
27 -X-- -X-- ---X X--- ---- ---- ---- ---- Q0A*E1A*E2A*DA
28 -X-- -X-- --X- -X-- ---- ---- ---- ---- /Q0A*E1A*E2A*/DA

32 ---- ---- ---- ---- X--X ---- ---- ---- Q0B*/E1B
33 ---- ---- ---- ---- ---X X--- ---- ---- Q0B*/E2B
34 ---- ---- ---- ---- -X-- -X-- X--- ---- SB*E1B*E2B
35 ---- ---- ---- ---- -X-- -XX- ---- X--- /Q2B*E1B*E2B*DB
36 ---- ---- ---- ---- -X-- -X-X ---- -X-- Q2B*E1B*E2B*/DB

40 ---- ---- ---- ---- X--- ---X ---- ---- Q2B*/E1B
41 ---- ---- ---- ---- ---- X--X ---- ---- Q2B*/E2B
42 ---- ---- ---- ---- -X-- -X-- X--- ---- SB*E1B*E2B
43 ---- ---- ---- ---- -X-X -X-- ---- X--- Q0B*E1B*E2B*DB
44 ---- ---- ---- ---- -XX- -X-- ---- -X-- /Q0B*E1B*E2B*/DB

48 ---- ---- ---- ---- ---- ---- ---- ----
49 ---- ---- ---- ---- --X- ---- ---- ---- /Q0B

56 ---- ---- ---- ---- ---- ---- ---- ----
57 ---- ---- ---- ---- ---- --X- ---- ---- /Q2B

LEGEND:   X : FUSE NOT BLOWN (L,N,0)    - : FUSE BLOWN   (H,P,1)

NUMBER OF FUSES BLOWN =  832
```

Stepper Motor Controller

Logic Diagram PAL16R4

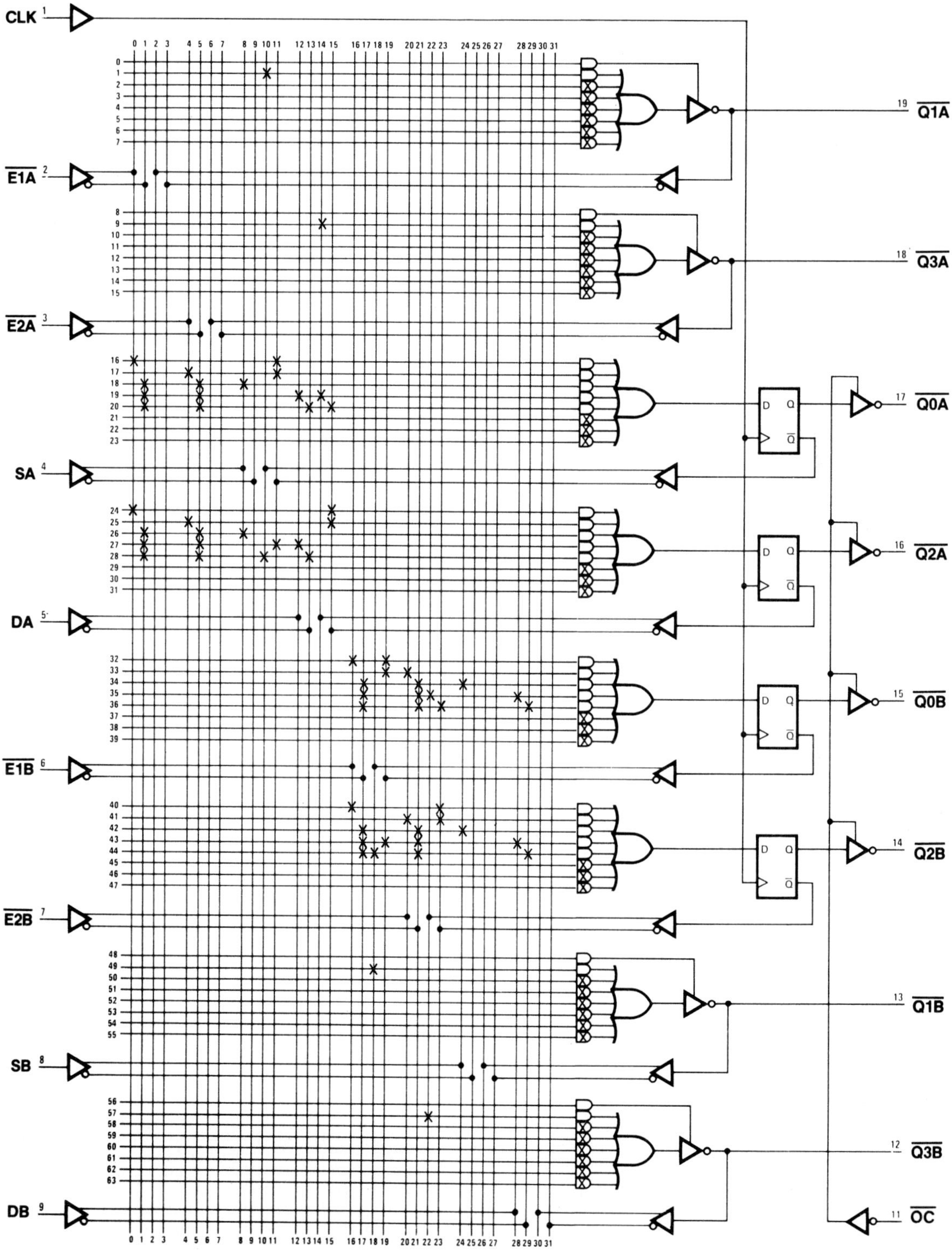

PAL
IMPORTANT, NOTES

Shaft Encoder

PAL16R4

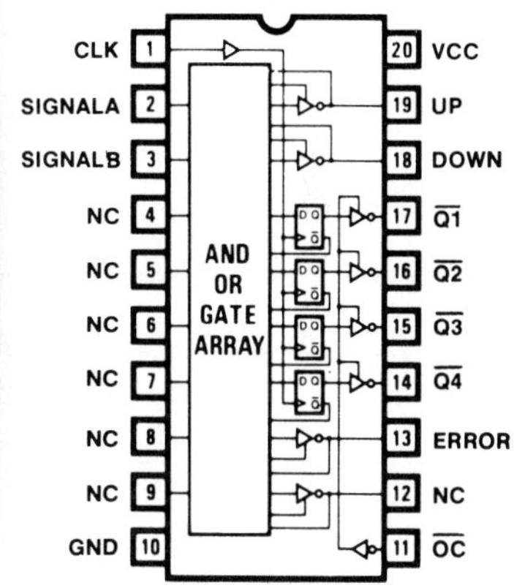

```
PAL16R4                                           PAL DESIGN SPECIFICATION
SHEN                                                 WILLY VOLDAN 03/03/81
SHAFT ENCODER
MMI MUNICH GmbH
CLK SIGNALA SIGNALB NC NC NC NC NC NC GND
/OC NC ERROR /Q4 /Q3 /Q2 /Q1 DOWN UP VCC


IF(VCC)    /UP =  Q1*/Q2*/SIGNALB
                + /Q1* Q2* SIGNALB
                +  Q3*/Q4* SIGNALA
                + /Q3* Q4*/SIGNALA

IF(VCC) /DOWN =  Q1*/Q2* SIGNALB
                + /Q1* Q2*/SIGNALB
                +  Q3*/Q4*/SIGNALA
                + /Q3* Q4* SIGNALA

Q1 := SIGNALA

Q2 := Q1

Q3 := SIGNALB

Q4 := Q3

IF(VCC) /ERROR = /Q1* Q2*/Q3* Q4
                 + /Q1* Q2* Q3*/Q4
                 +  Q1*/Q2*/Q3* Q4
                 +  Q1*/Q2* Q3*/Q4


FUNCTION TABLE

/OC CLK SIGNALA SIGNALB ERROR Q4 Q3 Q2 Q1 DOWN UP

;            SIGNAL              QQQQ
;/OC   CLK    A  B     ERROR   4321   DOWN   UP    COMMENTS
-----------------------------------------------------------
  L     C     H  L       H     XLLH    H     L      COUNT UP
  L     C     L  H       H     XHHL    H     L      COUNT UP
  L     C     H  H       H     XHLH    L     H      COUNT DOWN
  L     C     L  L       H     XLHL    L     H      COUNT DOWN
  L     C     H  H       H     LHXH    H     L      COUNT UP
  L     C     L  L       H     HLXL    H     L      COUNT UP
  L     C     L  H       H     LHXL    L     H      COUNT DOWN
  L     C     H  L       H     HLXH    L     H      COUNT DOWN
  L     C     L  H       L     LHHL    X     X      ERROR FLAG
  L     C     H  L       L     HLLH    X     X      ERROR FLAG
  H     X     X  X       X     ZZZZ    X     X      DISABLED
-----------------------------------------------------------
```

DESCRIPTION

THE PAL CONTROLS A 4-BIT UP/DOWN COUNTER WITH THE OUTPUTS "UP" AND "DOWN". (UP=H MEANS COUNT UP; DOWN=H MEANS COUNT DOWN)

THIS DESIGN WITH GLITCHLESS OUTPUTS WILL SERVE WELL IN ELECTRICALLY NOISY INDUSTRIAL ENVIRONMENTS.

THE PINNING AND THE OUTPUT POLARITY ARE GIVEN AS A FIRST PROPOSAL AND CAN BE CHANGED ACCORDING TO THE PC BOARD LAYOUT.

BLOCK DIAGRAM:

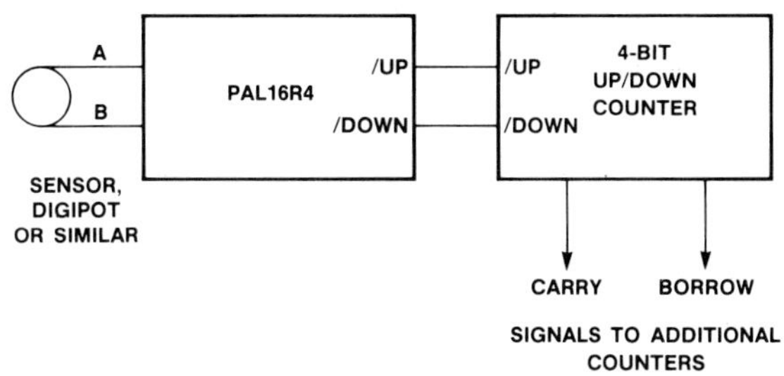


```
SHAFT ENCODER

 1 C10XXXXXXX0XHXHHLHL1
 2 C01XXXXXXX0XHXLLHHL1
 3 C11XXXXXXX0XHXLHLLH1
 4 C00XXXXXXX0XHXHLHLH1
 5 C11XXXXXXX0XHHLXLHL1
 6 C00XXXXXXX0XHLHXHHL1
 7 C01XXXXXXX0XHHLXHLH1
 8 C10XXXXXXX0XHLHXLLH1
 9 C01XXXXXXX0XLHLLHXX1
10 C10XXXXXXX0XLLHHLXX1
11 XXXXXXXXXX1XXZZZZXX1

PASS SIMULATION
```

```
SHAFT ENCODER

                 11 1111 1111 2222 2222 2233
   0123 4567 8901 2345 6789 0123 4567 8901

 0 ---- ---- ---- ---- ---- ---- ---- ----
 1 ---- -X-- ---X --X- ---- ---- ---- ---- Q1*/Q2*/SIGNALB
 2 ---- X--- --X- ---X ---- ---- ---- ---- /Q1*Q2*SIGNALB
 3 X--- ---- ---- ---- ---X --X- ---- ---- Q3*/Q4*SIGNALA
 4 -X-- ---- ---- ---- --X- ---X ---- ---- /Q3*Q4*/SIGNALA

 8 ---- ---- ---- ---- ---- ---- ---- ----
 9 ---- X--- ---X --X- ---- ---- ---- ---- Q1*/Q2*SIGNALB
10 ---- -X-- --X- ---X ---- ---- ---- ---- /Q1*Q2*/SIGNALB
11 -X-- ---- ---- ---- ---X --X- ---- ---- Q3*/Q4*/SIGNALA
12 X--- ---- ---- ---- --X- ---X ---- ---- /Q3*Q4*SIGNALA

16 X--- ---- ---- ---- ---- ---- ---- ---- SIGNALA

24 ---- ---- ---X ---- ---- ---- ---- ---- Q1

32 ---- X--- ---- ---- ---- ---- ---- ---- SIGNALB

40 ---- ---- ---- ---- ---X ---- ---- ---- Q3

48 ---- ---- ---- ---- ---- ---- ---- ----
49 ---- ---- --X- ---X --X- ---X ---- ---- /Q1*Q2*/Q3*Q4
50 ---- ---- --X- ---X ---X --X- ---- ---- /Q1*Q2*Q3*/Q4
51 ---- ---- ---X --X- --X- ---X ---- ---- Q1*/Q2*/Q3*Q4
52 ---- ---- ---X --X- ---X --X- ---- ---- Q1*/Q2*Q3*/Q4


LEGEND:  X : FUSE NOT BLOWN (L,N,0)    - : FUSE BLOWN   (H,P,1)

NUMBER OF FUSES BLOWN =  564
```

Shaft Encoder

Logic Diagram PAL16R4

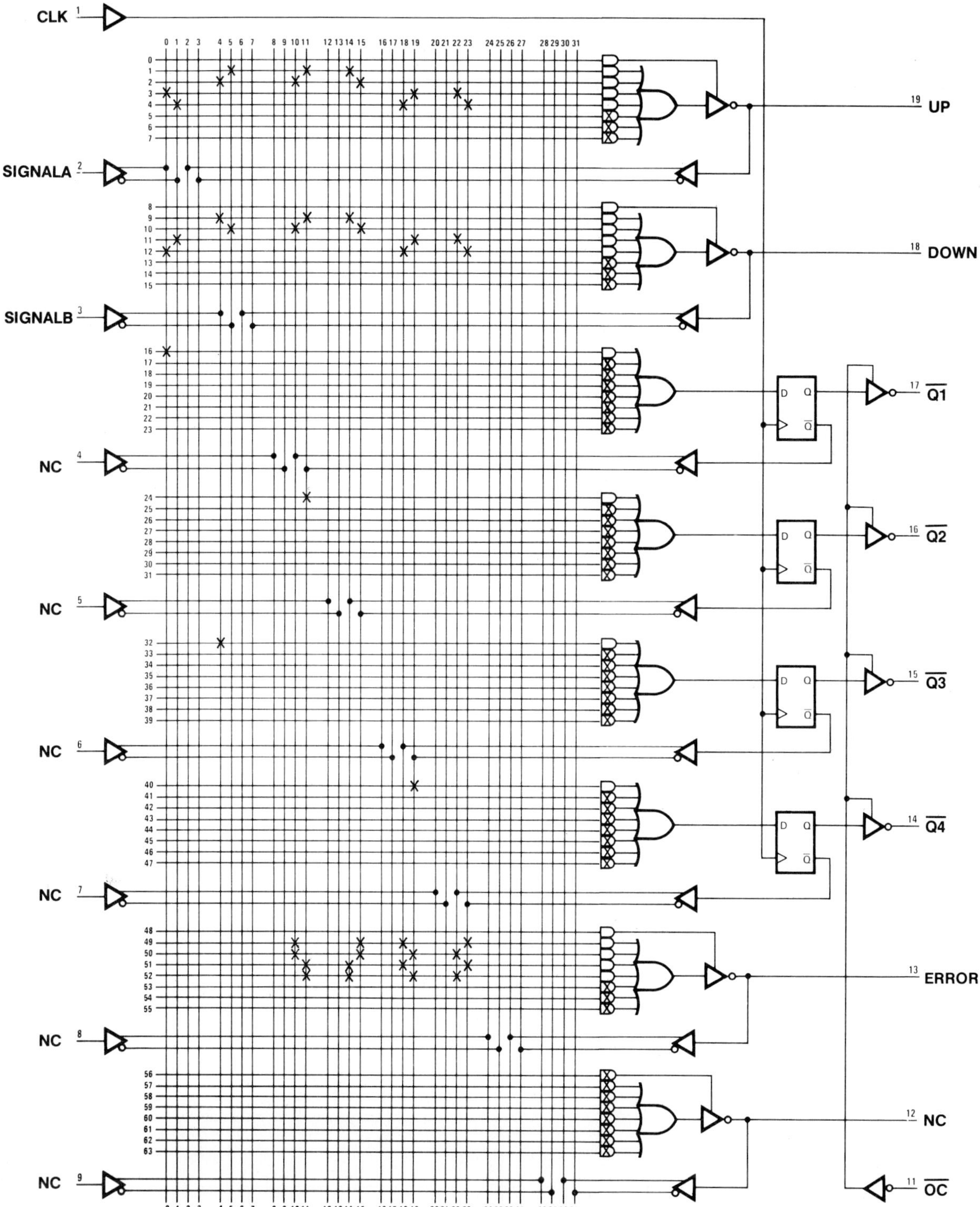

Truthtable:

SIGNAL A	SIGNAL B	Q1	Q1	Q3	Q4	COUNT
0	0	0	0	0	0	no change
0	↑	0	0	0	1	down
0	↓	0	0	1	0	up
0	1	0	0	1	1	no change
↑	0	0	1	0	0	up
↑	↑	0	1	0	1	error
↑	↓	0	1	1	0	error
↑	1	0	1	1	1	down
↓	0	1	0	0	0	down
↓	↓	1	0	0	1	error
↓	↓	1	0	1	0	error
↓	1	1	0	1	1	up
1	0	1	1	0	0	no change
1	↓	1	1	0	1	up
1	↓	1	1	1	0	down
1	1	1	1	1	1	no change

Quad 4:1 Mux

PAL18L4

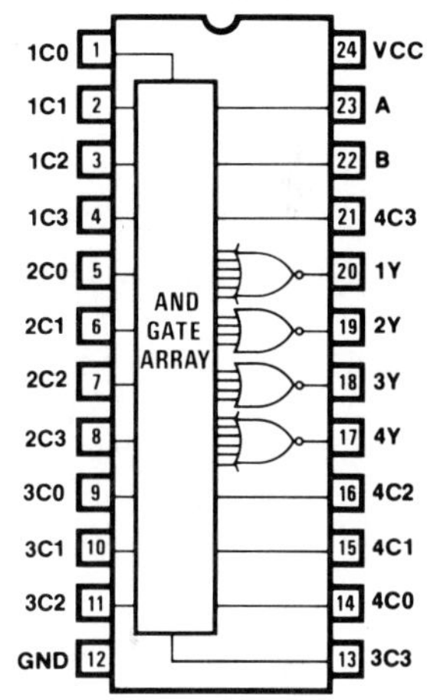

```
PAL18L4                                        PAL DESIGN SPECIFICATION
74LS453                                  BIRKNER/KAZMI/BLASCO 03/10/81
QUAD 4:1 MULTIPLEXER
MMI SUNNYVALE, CALIFORNIA
1C0 1C1 1C2 1C3 2C0 2C1 2C2 2C3 3C0 3C1 3C2 GND
3C3 4C0 4C1 4C2  4Y  3Y  2Y  1Y 4C3  B   A  VCC


/1Y  =  /B*/A * /1C0                          ;SELECT INPUT 1C0
     +  /B* A * /1C1                          ;SELECT INPUT 1C1
     +   B*/A * /1C2                          ;SELECT INPUT 1C2
     +   B* A * /1C3                          ;SELECT INPUT 1C3

/2Y  =  /B*/A * /2C0                          ;SELECT INPUT 2C0
     +  /B* A * /2C1                          ;SELECT INPUT 2C1
     +   B*/A * /2C2                          ;SELECT INPUT 2C2
     +   B* A * /2C3                          ;SELECT INPUT 2C3

/3Y  =  /B*/A * /3C0                          ;SELECT INPUT 3C0
     +  /B* A * /3C1                          ;SELECT INPUT 3C1
     +   B*/A * /3C2                          ;SELECT INPUT 3C2
     +   B* A * /3C3                          ;SELECT INPUT 3C3

/4Y  =  /B*/A * /4C0                          ;SELECT INPUT 4C0
     +  /B* A * /4C1                          ;SELECT INPUT 4C1
     +   B*/A * /4C2                          ;SELECT INPUT 4C2
     +   B* A * /4C3                          ;SELECT INPUT 4C3
```

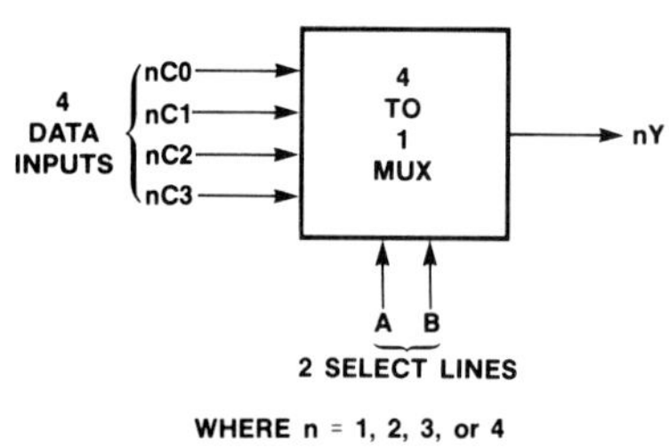

```
FUNCTION TABLE

B A 1C0 1C1 1C2 1C3 2C0 2C1 2C2 2C3 3C0 3C1 3C2 3C3 4C0 4C1 4C2 4C3 1Y 2Y 3Y 4Y

; SEL  --------INPUTS--------  --OUTPUTS--      COMMENTS
;       1C    2C    3C    4C
; B A  0123  0123  0123  0123  1Y 2Y 3Y 4Y
--------------------------------------------------------------
  L L  LHHH  HHHH  HHHH  HHHH  L  H  H  H       1C0=0
  L L  HHHH  LHHH  HHHH  HHHH  H  L  H  H       2C0=0
  L L  HHHH  HHHH  LHHH  HHHH  H  H  L  H       3C0=0
  L L  HHHH  HHHH  HHHH  LHHH  H  H  H  L       4C0=0
  L L  HLLL  LLLL  LLLL  LLLL  H  L  L  L       1C0=1
  L L  LLLL  HLLL  LLLL  LLLL  L  H  L  L       2C0=1
  L L  LLLL  LLLL  HLLL  LLLL  L  L  H  L       3C0=1
  L L  LLLL  LLLL  LLLL  HLLL  L  L  L  H       4C0=1
  L L  HHHH  HHHH  HHHH  HHHH  H  H  H  H       TOGGLE LINES
  L H  HLHH  HHHH  HHHH  HHHH  L  H  H  H       1C1=0
  L H  HHHH  HLHH  HHHH  HHHH  H  L  H  H       2C1=0
  L H  HHHH  HHHH  HLHH  HHHH  H  H  L  H       3C1=0
  L H  HHHH  HHHH  HHHH  HLHH  H  H  H  L       4C1=0
  L H  LHLL  LLLL  LLLL  LLLL  H  L  L  L       1C1=1
  L H  LLLL  LHLL  LLLL  LLLL  L  H  L  L       2C1=1
  L H  LLLL  LLLL  LHLL  LLLL  L  L  H  L       3C1=1
  L H  LLLL  LLLL  LLLL  LHLL  L  L  L  H       4C1=1
  L H  HHHH  HHHH  HHHH  HHHH  H  H  H  H       TOGGLE LINES
  H L  HHLH  HHHH  HHHH  HHHH  L  H  H  H       1C2=0
  H L  HHHH  HHLH  HHHH  HHHH  H  L  H  H       2C2=0
  H L  HHHH  HHHH  HHLH  HHHH  H  H  L  H       3C2=0
  H L  HHHH  HHHH  HHHH  HHLH  H  H  H  L       4C2=0
  H L  LLHL  LLLL  LLLL  LLLL  H  L  L  L       1C2=1
  H L  LLLL  LLHL  LLLL  LLLL  L  H  L  L       2C2=1
  H L  LLLL  LLLL  LLHL  LLLL  L  L  H  L       3C2=1
  H L  LLLL  LLLL  LLLL  LLHL  L  L  L  H       4C2=1
  H L  HHHH  HHHH  HHHH  HHHH  H  H  H  H       TOGGLE LINES
  H H  HHHL  HHHH  HHHH  HHHH  L  H  H  H       1C3=0
  H H  HHHH  HHHL  HHHH  HHHH  H  L  H  H       2C3=0
  H H  HHHH  HHHH  HHHL  HHHH  H  H  L  H       3C3=0
  H H  HHHH  HHHH  HHHH  HHHL  H  H  H  L       4C3=0
  H H  LLLH  LLLL  LLLL  LLLL  H  L  L  L       1C3=1
  H H  LLLL  LLLH  LLLL  LLLL  L  H  L  L       2C3=1
  H H  LLLL  LLLL  LLLH  LLLL  L  L  H  L       3C3=1
  H H  LLLL  LLLL  LLLL  LLLH  L  L  L  H       4C3=1
  H H  HHHH  HHHH  HHHH  HHHH  H  H  H  H       TOGGLE LINES
--------------------------------------------------------------
```

DESCRIPTION

THIS IS AN EXAMPLE OF A QUAD 4-TO-1 MULTIPLEXER USING A PAL18L4. SELECT LINES A,B ARE ENCODED IN BINARY, WITH A REPRESENTING THE LSB.

OPERATIONS TABLE:

INPUT SELECT B	A	OUTPUTS Y
L	L	C0
L	H	C1
H	L	C2
H	H	C3

```
QUAD 4:1 MULTIPLEXER

 1 01111111111X1111HHHL1001
 2 11110111111X1111HHLH1001
 3 11111111011X1111HLHH1001
 4 11111111111X1011LHHH1001
 5 10000000000X0000LLLH0001
 6 00001000000X0000LLHL0001
 7 00000000100X0000LHLL0001
 8 00000000000X0100HLLL0001
 9 11111111111X1111HHHH1001
10 10111111111X1111HHHL1011
11 11111011111X1111HHLH1011
12 11111111101X1111HLHH1011
13 11111111111X1101LHHH1011
14 01000000000X0000LLLH0011
15 00000100000X0000LLHL0011
16 00000000010X0000LHLL0011
17 00000000000X0010HLLL0011
18 11111111111X1111HHHH1011
19 11011111111X1111HHHL1101
20 11111101111X1111HHLH1101
21 11111111110X1111HLHH1101
22 11111111111X1110LHHH1101
23 00100000000X0000LLLH0101
24 00000010000X0000LLHL0101
25 00000000001X0000LHLL0101
26 00000000000X0001HLLL0101
27 11111111111X1111HHHH1101
28 11101111111X1111HHHL1111
29 11111110111X1111HHLH1111
30 11111111111X0111HLHH1111
31 11111111111X1111LHHH0111
32 00010000000X0000LLLH0111
33 00000001000X0000LLHL0111
34 00000000000X1000LHLL0111
35 00000000000X0000HLLL1111
36 11111111111X1111HHHH1111

PASS SIMULATION
```

QUAD 4:1 MULTIPLEXER

```
              11 1111 1111 2222 2222 2233 3333 3333
   0123 4567 8901 2345 6789 0123 4567 8901 2345 6789



24 ---X ---X ---X ---- --   --   ---- ---- ---- ---- /B*/A*/1C0
25 -X-- --X- ---X ---- --   --   ---- ---- ---- ---- /B*A*/1C1
26 ---- -X-X --X- ---- --   --   ---- ---- ---- ---- B*/A*/1C2
27 ---- --X- -XX- ---- --   --   ---- ---- ---- ---- B*A*/1C3

32 ---- ---X ---X -X-- --   --   ---- ---- ---- ---- /B*/A*/2C0
33 ---- --X- ---X ---- -X   --   ---- ---- ---- ---- /B*A*/2C1
34 ---- ---X --X- ---- --   -X   ---- ---- ---- ---- B*/A*/2C2
35 ---- --X- --X- ---- --   --   -X-- ---- ---- ---- B*A*/2C3

40 ---- ---X ---X ---- --   --   ---- -X-- ---- ---- /B*/A*/3C0
41 ---- --X- ---X ---- --   --   ---- ---- -X-- ---- /B*A*/3C1
42 ---- ---X --X- ---- --   --   ---- ---- ---- -X-- B*/A*/3C2
43 ---- --X- --X- ---- --   --   ---- ---- ---- ---X B*A*/3C3

48 ---- ---X ---X ---- --   --   ---- ---- ---X ---- /B*/A*/4C0
49 ---- --X- ---X ---- --   --   ---- ---X ---- ---- /B*A*/4C1
50 ---- ---X --X- ---- --   --   ---X ---- ---- ---- B*/A*/4C2
51 ---- --X- --X- ---X --   --   ---- ---- ---- ---- B*A*/4C3
```

LEGEND: X : FUSE NOT BLOWN (L,N,0)   - : FUSE BLOWN   (H,P,1)

NUMBER OF FUSES BLOW = 592

Quad 4:1 Multiplexer

Logic Diagram PAL18L4

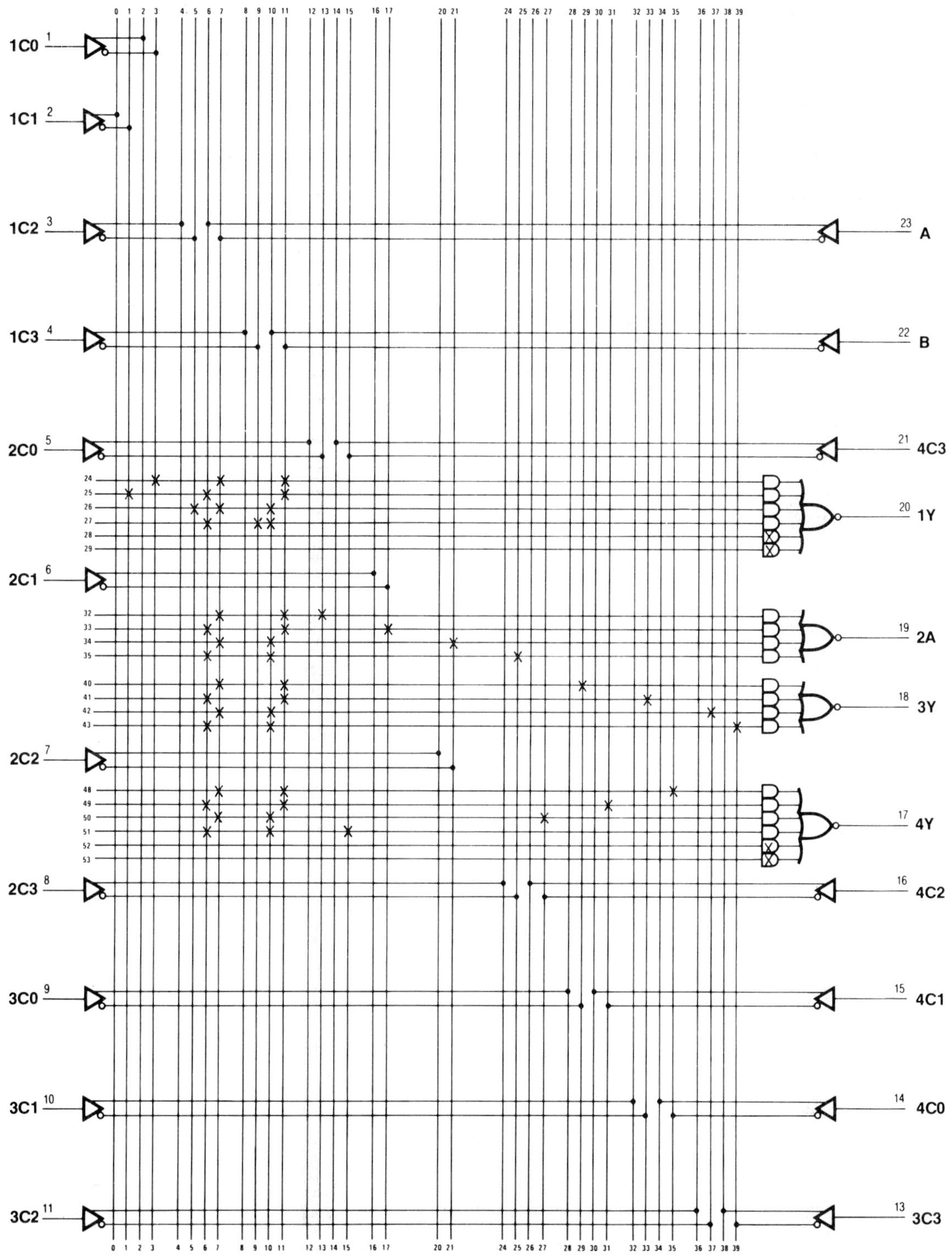

Application

4:1 Bus Select

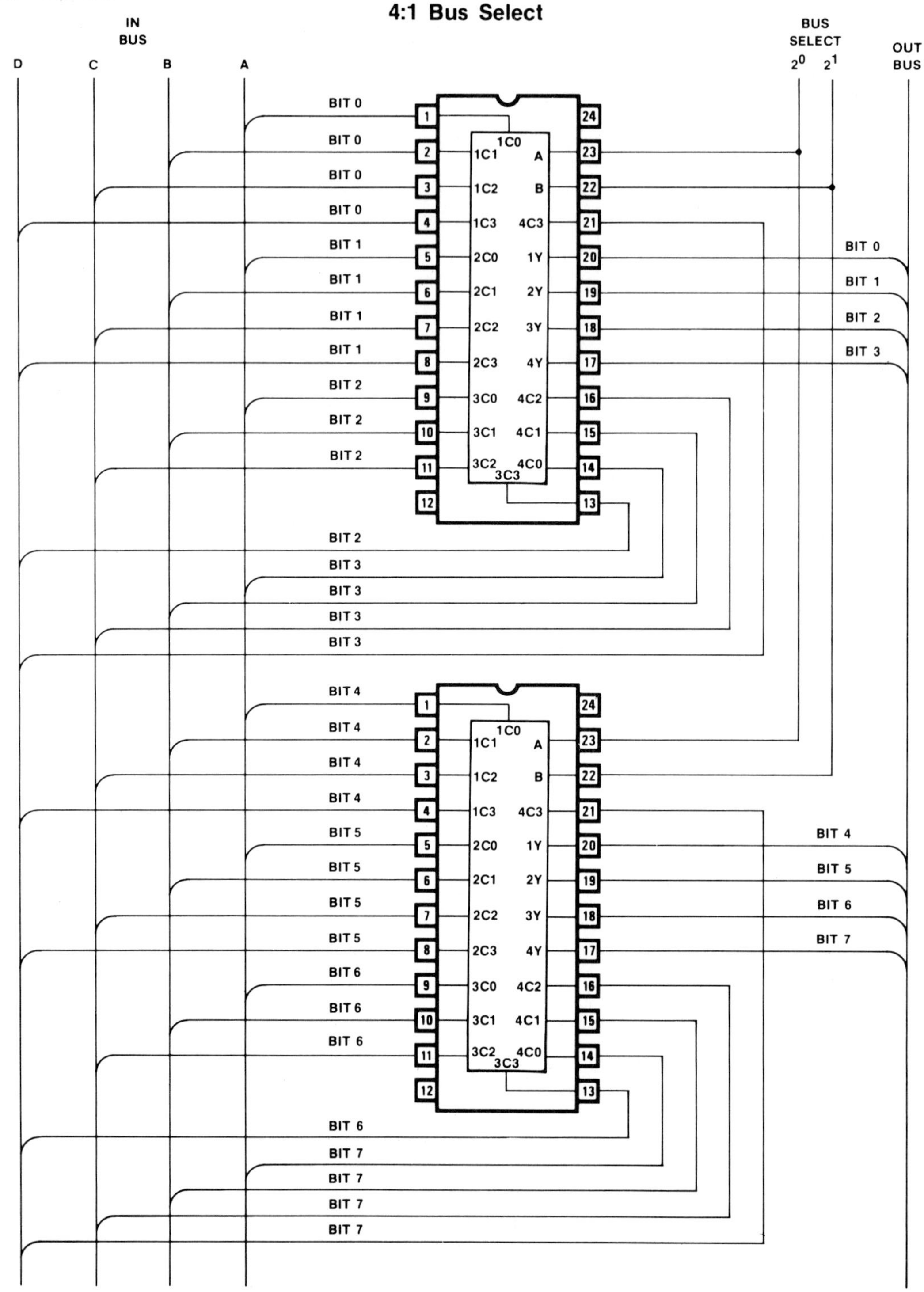

Dual 8:1 Mux

PAL20L2

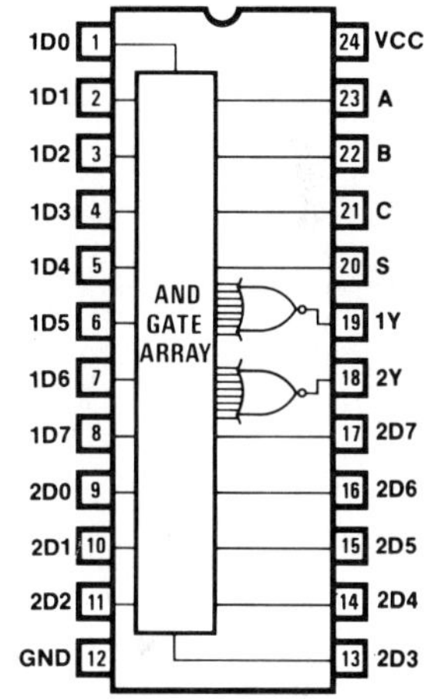

```
PAL20L2                                              PAL DESIGN SPECIFICATION
74LS451                                         BIRKNER/KAZMI/BLASCO 03/10/81
DUAL 8:1 MULTIPLEXER
MMI SUNNYVALE, CALIFORNIA
1D0 1D1 1D2 1D3 1D4 1D5 1D6 1D7 2D0 2D1 2D2 GND
2D3 2D4 2D5 2D6 2D7  2Y  1Y  S   C   B   A  VCC


/1Y  =  /S*/C*/B*/A * /1D0                    ;SELECT INPUT 1D0
     +  /S*/C*/B* A * /1D1                    ;SELECT INPUT 1D1
     +  /S*/C* B*/A * /1D2                    ;SELECT INPUT 1D2
     +  /S*/C* B* A * /1D3                    ;SELECT INPUT 1D3
     +  /S* C*/B*/A * /1D4                    ;SELECT INPUT 1D4
     +  /S* C*/B* A * /1D5                    ;SELECT INPUT 1D5
     +  /S* C* B*/A * /1D6                    ;SELECT INPUT 1D6
     +  /S* C* B* A * /1D7                    ;SELECT INPUT 1D7

/2Y  =  /S*/C*/B*/A * /2D0                    ;SELECT INPUT 2D0
     +  /S*/C*/B* A * /2D1                    ;SELECT INPUT 2D1
     +  /S*/C* B*/A * /2D2                    ;SELECT INPUT 2D2
     +  /S*/C* B* A * /2D3                    ;SELECT INPUT 2D3
     +  /S* C*/B*/A * /2D4                    ;SELECT INPUT 2D4
     +  /S* C*/B* A * /2D5                    ;SELECT INPUT 2D5
     +  /S* C* B*/A * /2D6                    ;SELECT INPUT 2D6
     +  /S* C* B* A * /2D7                    ;SELECT INPUT 2D7
```

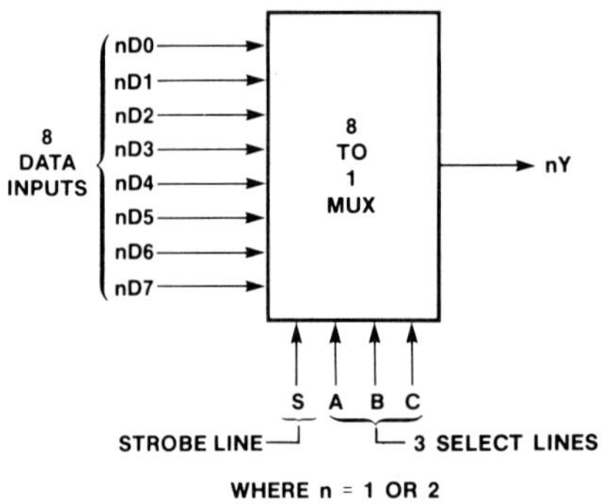

```
FUNCTION TABLE

C B A 1D0 1D1 1D2 1D3 1D4 1D5 1D6 1D7 2D0 2D1 2D2 2D3 2D4 2D5 2D6 2D7 S 1Y 2Y

;SELECT   INPUTS    INPUTS       OUTPUTS     COMMENTS
;          1D-        2D-
; C B A  01234567  01234567   S  1Y  2Y
------------------------------------------------------------------
  L L L  LHHHHHHH  LHHHHHHH   L   L   L      1D0=0 2D0=0
  L L L  HLLLLLLL  LHHHHHHH   L   H   L      1D0=1 2D0=0
  L L L  LHHHHHHH  HLLLLLLL   L   L   H      1D0=0 2D0=1
  L L L  HLLLLLLL  HLLLLLLL   L   H   H      1D0=1 2D0=1
  L L L  HHHHHHHH  HHHHHHHH   L   H   H      TOGGLE OTHER LINES
  L L H  HLHHHHHH  HLHHHHHH   L   L   L      1D1=0 2D1=0
  L L H  LHLLLLLL  HLHHHHHH   L   H   L      1D1=1 2D1=0
  L L H  HLHHHHHH  LHLLLLLL   L   L   H      1D1=0 2D1=1
  L L H  LHLLLLLL  LHLLLLLL   L   H   H      1D1=1 2D1=1
  L L H  HHHHHHHH  HHHHHHHH   L   H   H      TOGGLE OTHER LINES
  L H L  HHLHHHHH  HHLHHHHH   L   L   L      1D2=0 2D2=0
  L H L  LLHLLLLL  HHLHHHHH   L   H   L      1D2=1 2D2=0
  L H L  HHLHHHHH  LLHLLLLL   L   L   H      1D2=0 2D2=1
  L H L  LLHLLLLL  LLHLLLLL   L   H   H      1D2=1 2D2=1
  L H L  HHHHHHHH  HHHHHHHH   L   H   H      TOGGLE OTHER LINES
  L H H  HHHLHHHH  HHHLHHHH   L   L   L      1D3=0 2D3=0
  L H H  LLLHLLLL  HHHLHHHH   L   H   L      1D3=1 2D3=0
  L H H  HHHLHHHH  LLLHLLLL   L   L   H      1D3=0 2D3=1
  L H H  LLLHLLLL  LLLHLLLL   L   H   H      1D3=1 2D3=1
  L H H  HHHHHHHH  HHHHHHHH   L   H   H      TOGGLE OTHER LINES
  H L L  HHHHLHHH  HHHHLHHH   L   L   L      1D4=0 2D4=0
  H L L  LLLLHLLL  HHHHLHHH   L   H   L      1D4=1 2D4=0
  H L L  HHHHLHHH  LLLLHLLL   L   L   H      1D4=0 2D4=1
  H L L  LLLLHLLL  LLLLHLLL   L   H   H      1D4=1 2D4=1
  H L L  HHHHHHHH  HHHHHHHH   L   H   H      TOGGLE OTHER LINES
  H L H  HHHHHLHH  HHHHHLHH   L   L   L      1D5=0 2D5=0
  H L H  LLLLLHLL  HHHHHLHH   L   H   L      1D5=1 2D5=0
  H L H  HHHHHLHH  LLLLLHLL   L   L   H      1D5=0 2D5=1
  H L H  LLLLLHLL  LLLLLHLL   L   H   H      1D5=1 2D5=1
  H L H  HHHHHHHH  HHHHHHHH   L   H   H      TOGGLE OTHER LINES
  H H L  HHHHHHLH  HHHHHHLH   L   L   L      1D6=0 2D6=0
  H H L  LLLLLLHL  HHHHHHLH   L   H   L      1D6=1 2D6=0
  H H L  HHHHHHLH  LLLLLLHL   L   L   H      1D6=0 2D6=1
  H H L  LLLLLLHL  LLLLLLHL   L   H   H      1D6=1 2D6=1
  H H L  HHHHHHHH  HHHHHHHH   L   H   H      TOGGLE OTHER LINES
  H H H  HHHHHHHL  HHHHHHHL   L   L   L      1D7=0 2D7=0
  H H H  LLLLLLLH  HHHHHHHL   L   H   L      1D7=1 2D7=0
  H H H  HHHHHHHL  LLLLLLLH   L   L   H      1D7=0 2D7=1
  H H H  LLLLLLLH  LLLLLLLH   L   H   H      1D7=1 2D7=1
  H H H  HHHHHHHH  HHHHHHHH   L   H   H      TOGGLE OTHER LINES
  X X X  LLLLLLLL  LLLLLLLL   H   H   H      STROBE TEST 0
  X X X  HHHHHHHH  HHHHHHHH   H   H   H      STROBE TEST 1
------------------------------------------------------------------
```

DESCRIPTION

THIS IS AN EXAMPLE OF A DUAL 8-TO-1 MULTIPLEXER USING A PAL20L2. A STROBE LINE (S) IS PROVIDED TO GATE THE OUTPUTS OFF (Y=H) WHEN THE STROBE INPUT IS HIGH. THE SELECT LINES A,B,C ARE ENCODED IN BINARY, WITH A REPRESENTING THE LSB.

OPERATIONS TABLE:

-----INPUTS-----				OUTPUTS
SELECT			STROBE	
C	B	A	S	Y
X	X	X	H	H
L	L	L	L	D0
L	L	H	L	D1
L	H	L	L	D2
L	H	H	L	D3
H	L	L	L	D4
H	L	H	L	D5
H	H	L	L	D6
H	H	H	L	D7

Dual 8:1 Multiplexer

Logic Diagram PAL20L2

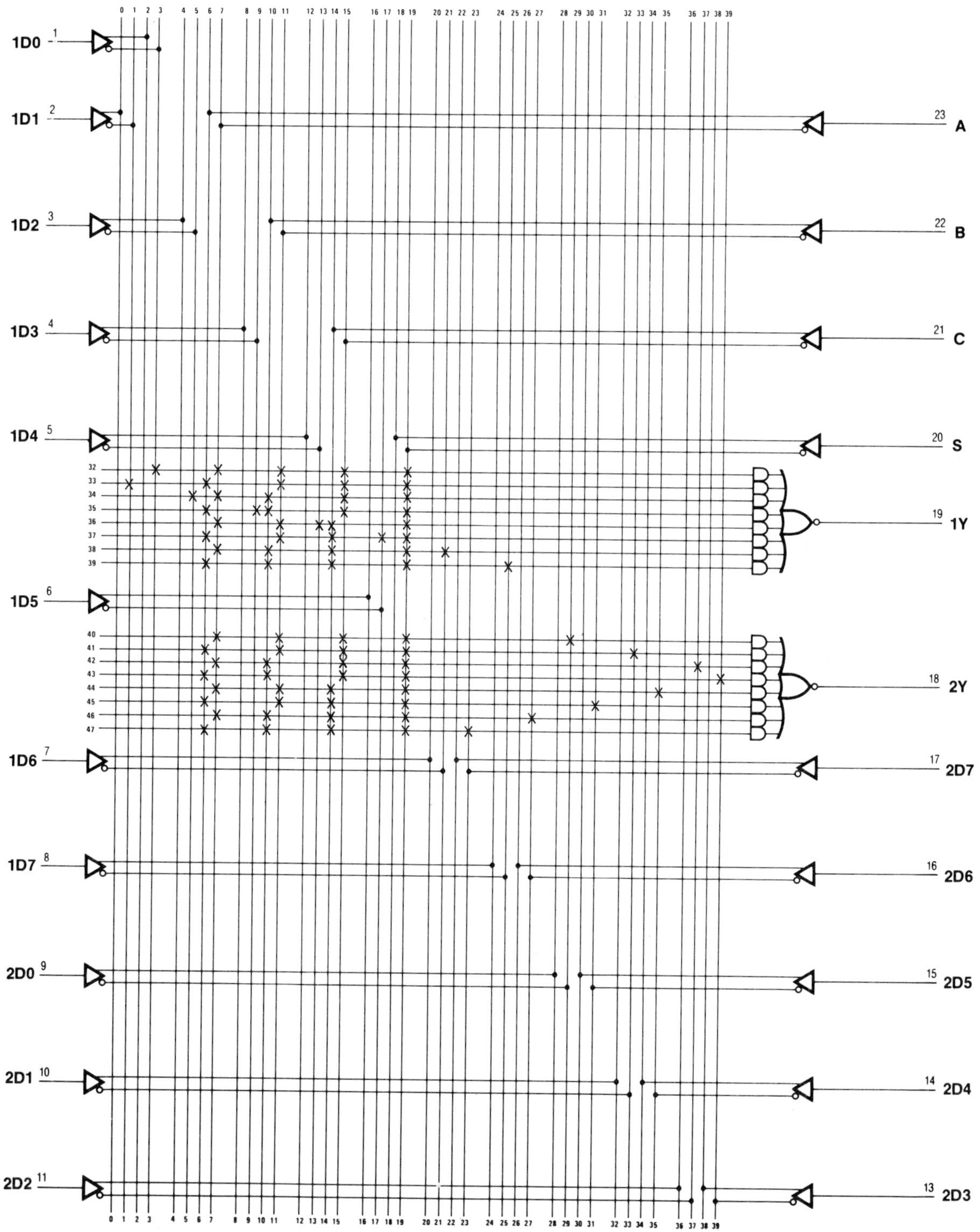

Application

8:1 Bus Select

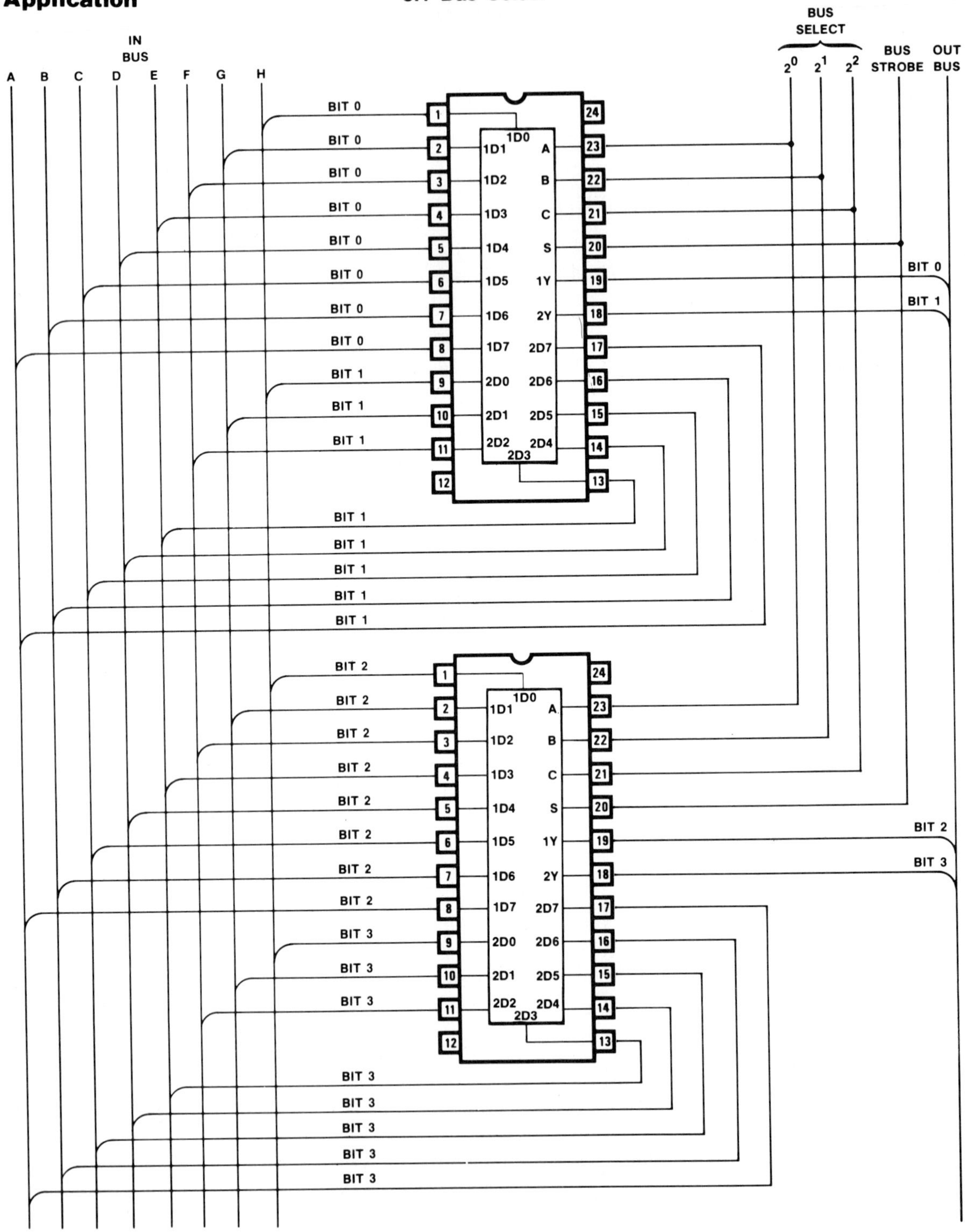

16:1 Mux

PAL20C1

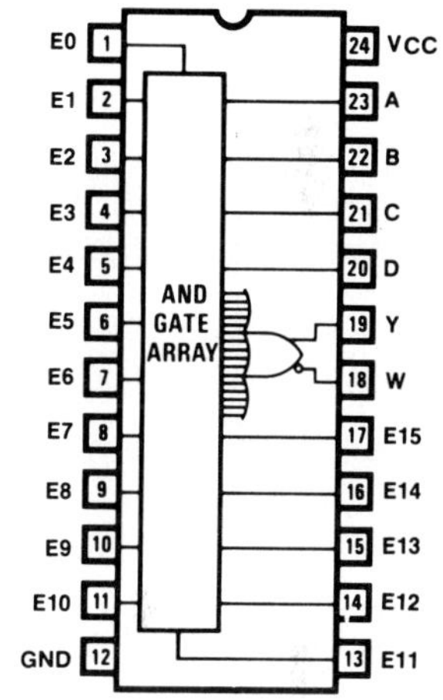

```
PAL20C1                                    PAL DESIGN SPECIFICATION
74LS450                                BIRKNER/KAZMI/BLASCO 02/19/81
16:1 MULTIPLEXER
MMI SUNNYVALE, CALIFORNIA
E0  E1  E2  E3  E4  E5  E6  E7  E8  E9  E10 GND
E11 E12 E13 E14 E15 W   Y   D   C   B    A  VCC

Y  =  /D*/C*/B*/A * E0                 ;SELECT INPUT E0
   +  /D*/C*/B* A * E1                 ;SELECT INPUT E1
   +  /D*/C* B*/A * E2                 ;SELECT INPUT E2
   +  /D*/C* B* A * E3                 ;SELECT INPUT E3
   +  /D* C*/B*/A * E4                 ;SELECT INPUT E4
   +  /D* C*/B* A * E5                 ;SELECT INPUT E5
   +  /D* C* B*/A * E6                 ;SELECT INPUT E6
   +  /D* C* B* A * E7                 ;SELECT INPUT E7
   +   D*/C*/B*/A * E8                 ;SELECT INPUT E8
   +   D*/C*/B* A * E9                 ;SELECT INPUT E9
   +   D*/C* B*/A * E10                ;SELECT INPUT E10
   +   D*/C* B* A * E11                ;SELECT INPUT E11
   +   D* C*/B*/A * E12                ;SELECT INPUT E12
   +   D* C*/B* A * E13                ;SELECT INPUT E13
   +   D* C* B*/A * E14                ;SELECT INPUT E14
   +   D* C* B* A * E15                ;SELECT INPUT E15
```

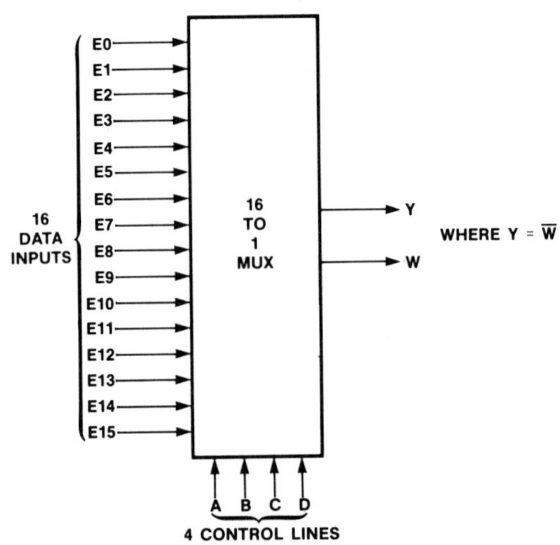

```
FUNCTION TABLE

D C B A E0 E1 E2 E3 E4 E5 E6 E7 E8 E9 E10 E11 E12 E13 E14 E15 Y W

;  SELECT   -----INPUTS-----  OUTPUTS   COMMENTS
;                     111111
; D C B A   0123456789012345   Y  W
-------------------------------------------------------------
  L L L L   LHHHHHHHHHHHHHHH   L  H     INPUT E0 = 0
  L L L L   HLLLLLLLLLLLLLLL   H  L     INPUT E0 = 1
  L L L L   HHHHHHHHHHHHHHHH   H  L     TOGGLE OTHER LINES
  L L L H   HLHHHHHHHHHHHHHH   L  H     INPUT E1 = 0
  L L L H   LHLLLLLLLLLLLLLL   H  L     INPUT E1 = 1
  L L L H   HHHHHHHHHHHHHHHH   H  L     TOGGLE OTHER LINES
  L L H L   HHLHHHHHHHHHHHHH   L  H     INPUT E2 = 0
  L L H L   LLHLLLLLLLLLLLLL   H  L     INPUT E2 = 1
  L L H L   HHHHHHHHHHHHHHHH   H  L     TOGGLE OTHER LINES
  L L H H   HHHLHHHHHHHHHHHH   L  H     INPUT E3 = 0
  L L H H   LLLHLLLLLLLLLLLL   H  L     INPUT E3 = 1
  L L H H   HHHHHHHHHHHHHHHH   H  L     TOGGLE OTHER LINES
  L H L L   HHHHLHHHHHHHHHHH   L  H     INPUT E4 = 0
  L H L L   LLLLHLLLLLLLLLLL   H  L     INPUT E4 = 1
  L H L L   HHHHHHHHHHHHHHHH   H  L     TOGGLE OTHER LINES
  L H L H   HHHHHLHHHHHHHHHH   L  H     INPUT E5 = 0
  L H L H   LLLLLHLLLLLLLLLL   H  L     INPUT E5 = 1
  L H L H   HHHHHHHHHHHHHHHH   H  L     TOGGLE OTHER LINES
  L H H L   HHHHHHLHHHHHHHHH   L  H     INPUT E6 = 0
  L H H L   LLLLLLHLLLLLLLLL   H  L     INPUT E6 = 1
  L H H L   HHHHHHHHHHHHHHHH   H  L     TOGGLE OTHER LINES
  L H H H   HHHHHHHLHHHHHHHH   L  H     INPUT E7 = 0
  L H H H   LLLLLLLHLLLLLLLL   H  L     INPUT E7 = 1
  L H H H   HHHHHHHHHHHHHHHH   H  L     TOGGLE OTHER LINES
  H L L L   HHHHHHHHLHHHHHHH   L  H     INPUT E8 = 0
  H L L L   LLLLLLLLHLLLLLLL   H  L     INPUT E8 = 1
  H L L L   HHHHHHHHHHHHHHHH   H  L     TOGGLE OTHER LINES
  H L L H   HHHHHHHHHLHHHHHH   L  H     INPUT E9 = 0
  H L L H   LLLLLLLLLHLLLLLL   H  L     INPUT E9 = 1
  H L L H   HHHHHHHHHHHHHHHH   H  L     TOGGLE OTHER LINES
  H L H L   HHHHHHHHHHLHHHHH   L  H     INPUT E10 = 0
  H L H L   LLLLLLLLLLHLLLLL   H  L     INPUT E10 = 1
  H L H L   HHHHHHHHHHHHHHHH   H  L     TOGGLE OTHER LINES
  H L H H   HHHHHHHHHHHLHHHH   L  H     INPUT E11 = 0
  H L H H   LLLLLLLLLLLHLLLL   H  L     INPUT E11 = 1
  H L H H   HHHHHHHHHHHHHHHH   H  L     TOGGLE OTHER LINES
  H H L L   HHHHHHHHHHHHLHHH   L  H     INPUT E12 = 0
  H H L L   LLLLLLLLLLLLHLLL   H  L     INPUT E12 = 1
  H H L L   HHHHHHHHHHHHHHHH   H  L     TOGGLE OTHER LINES
  H H L H   HHHHHHHHHHHHHLHH   L  H     INPUT E13 = 0
  H H L H   LLLLLLLLLLLLLHLL   H  L     INPUT E13 = 1
  H H L H   HHHHHHHHHHHHHHHH   H  L     TOGGLE OTHER LINES
  H H H L   HHHHHHHHHHHHHHLH   L  H     INPUT E14 = 0
  H H H L   LLLLLLLLLLLLLLHL   H  L     INPUT E14 = 1
  H H H L   HHHHHHHHHHHHHHHH   H  L     TOGGLE OTHER LINES
  H H H H   HHHHHHHHHHHHHHHL   L  H     INPUT E15 = 0
  H H H H   LLLLLLLLLLLLLLLH   H  L     INPUT E15 = 1
  H H H H   HHHHHHHHHHHHHHHH   H  L     TOGGLE OTHER LINES
-------------------------------------------------------------
```

DESCRIPTION

THIS IS AN EXAMPLE OF A 16-TO-1 MULTIPLEXER USING A PAL20C1. BOTH TRUE (Y) AND COMPLIMENT (W) OUTPUTS ARE PROVIDED. THE SELECT LINES A,B,C,D ARE ENCODED IN BINARY, WITH A REPRESENTING THE LSB AND D REPRESENTING THE MSB.

OPERATIONS TABLE:

INPUTS SELECT LINES				OUTPUTS	
D	C	B	A	W	Y
L	L	L	L	/E0	E0
L	L	L	H	/E1	E1
L	L	H	L	/E2	E2
L	L	H	H	/E3	E3
L	H	L	L	/E4	E4
L	H	L	H	/E5	E5
L	H	H	L	/E6	E6
L	H	H	H	/E7	E7
H	L	L	L	/E8	E8
H	L	L	H	/E9	E9
H	L	H	L	/E10	E10
H	L	H	H	/E11	E11
H	H	L	L	/E12	E12
H	H	L	H	/E13	E13
H	H	H	L	/E14	E14
H	H	H	H	/E15	E15

16:1 MULTIPLEXER

```
 1 01111111111X11111HL00001
 2 10000000000X00000LH00001
 3 11111111111X11111LH00001
 4 10111111111X11111HL00011
 5 01000000000X00000LH00011
 6 11111111111X11111LH00011
 7 11011111111X11111HL00101
 8 00100000000X00000LH00101
 9 11111111111X11111LH00101
10 11101111111X11111HL00111
11 00010000000X00000LH00111
12 11111111111X11111LH00111
13 11110111111X11111HL01001
14 00001000000X00000LH01001
15 11111111111X11111LH01001
16 11111011111X11111HL01011
17 00000100000X00000LH01011
18 11111111111X11111LH01011
19 11111101111X11111HL01101
20 00000010000X00000LH01101
21 11111111111X11111LH01101
22 11111110111X11111HL01111
23 00000001000X00000LH01111
24 11111111111X11111LH01111
25 11111111011X11111HL10001
26 00000000100X00000LH10001
27 11111111111X11111LH10001
28 11111111101X11111HL10011
29 00000000010X00000LH10011
30 11111111111X11111LH10011
31 11111111110X11111HL10101
32 00000000001X00000LH10101
33 11111111111X11111LH10101
34 11111111111X01111HL10111
35 00000000000X10000LH10111
36 11111111111X11111LH10111
37 11111111111X10111HL11001
38 00000000000X01000LH11001
39 11111111111X11111LH11001
40 11111111111X11011HL11011
41 00000000000X00100LH11011
42 11111111111X11111LH11011
43 11111111111X11101HL11101
44 00000000000X00010LH11101
45 11111111111X11111LH11101
46 11111111111X11110HL11111
47 00000000000X00001LH11111
48 11111111111X11111LH11111
```

PASS SIMULATION

16:1 MULTIPLEXER

```
               11 1111 1111 2222 2222 2233 3333 3333
     0123 4567 8901 2345 6789 0123 4567 8901 2345 6789



32 --X- ---X ---X ---X ---X ---- ---- ---- ---- ---- /D*/C*/B*/A*E0
33 X--- --X- ---X ---X ---X ---- ---- ---- ---- ---- /D*/C*/B*A*E1
34 ---- X--X --X- ---X ---X ---- ---- ---- ---- ---- /D*/C*B*/A*E2
35 ---- --X- X-X- ---X ---X ---- ---- ---- ---- ---- /D*/C*B*A*E3
36 ---- ---X ---X X-X- ---X ---- ---- ---- ---- ---- /D*C*/B*/A*E4
37 ---- --X- ---X --X- X--X ---- ---- ---- ---- ---- /D*C*/B*A*E5
38 ---- ---X --X- --X- ---X X--- ---- ---- ---- ---- /D*C*B*/A*E6
39 ---- --X- --X- --X- ---X ---- X--- ---- ---- ---- /D*C*B*A*E7

40 ---- ---X ---X ---X --X- ---- ---- X--- ---- ---- D*/C*/B*/A*E8
41 ---- --X- ---X ---X --X- ---- ---- ---- X--- ---- D*/C*/B*A*E9
42 ---- ---X --X- ---X --X- ---- ---- ---- ---- X--- D*/C*B*/A*E10
43 ---- --X- --X- ---X --X- ---- ---- ---- ---- --X- D*/C*B*A*E11
44 ---- ---X ---X --X- --X- ---- ---- ---- --X- ---- D*C*/B*/A*E12
45 ---- --X- ---X --X- --X- ---- ---- --X- ---- ---- D*C*/B*A*E13
46 ---- ---X --X- --X- --X- ---- --X- ---- ---- ---- D*C*B*/A*E14
47 ---- --X- --X- --X- --X- --X- ---- ---- ---- ---- D*C*B*A*E15
```

LEGEND: X : FUSE NOT BLOWN (L,N,0) - : FUSE BLOWN (H,P,1)

NUMBER OF FUSES BLOW = 560

16:1 Multiplexer

Logic Diagram PAL20C1

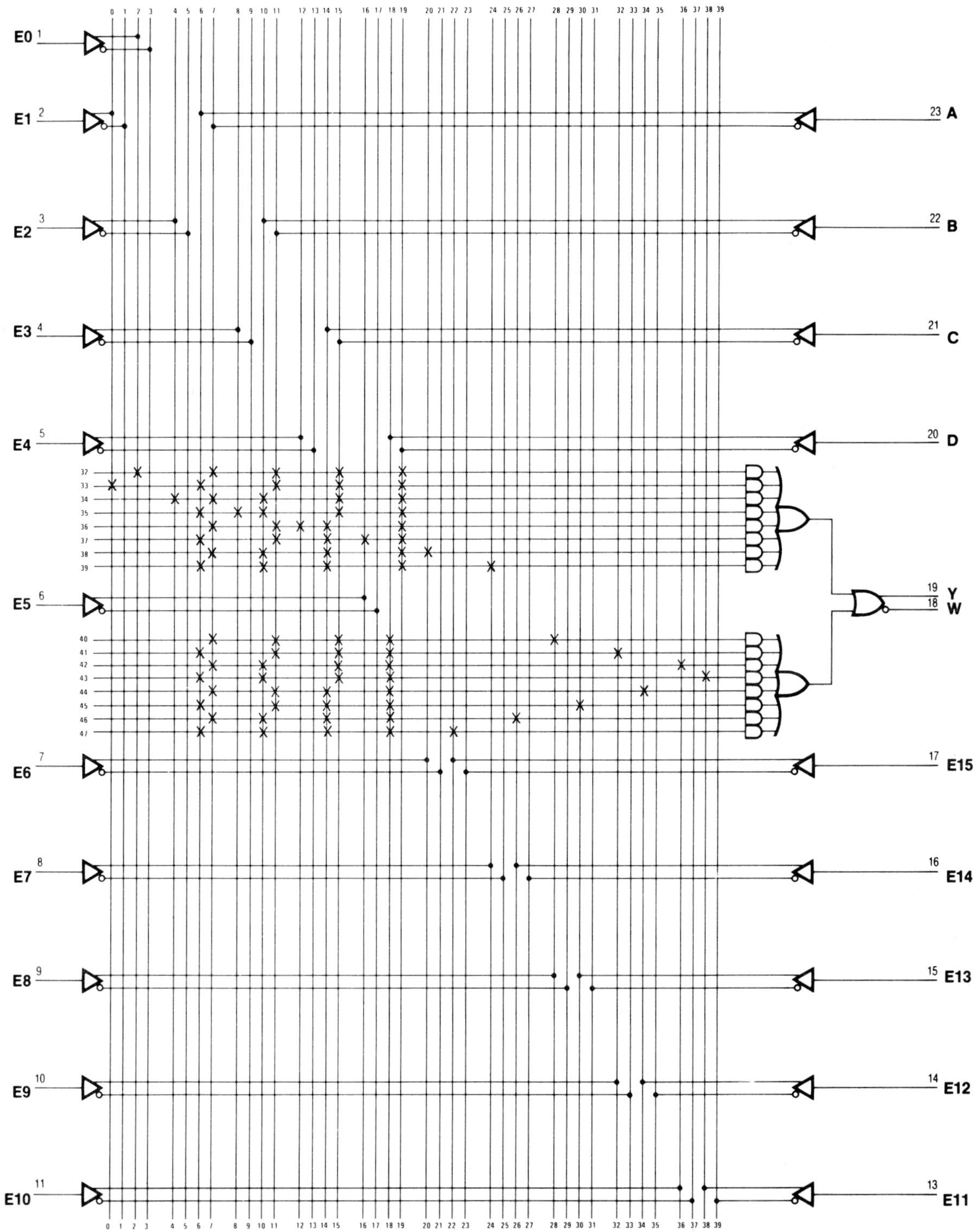

Application

Test Condition Mux

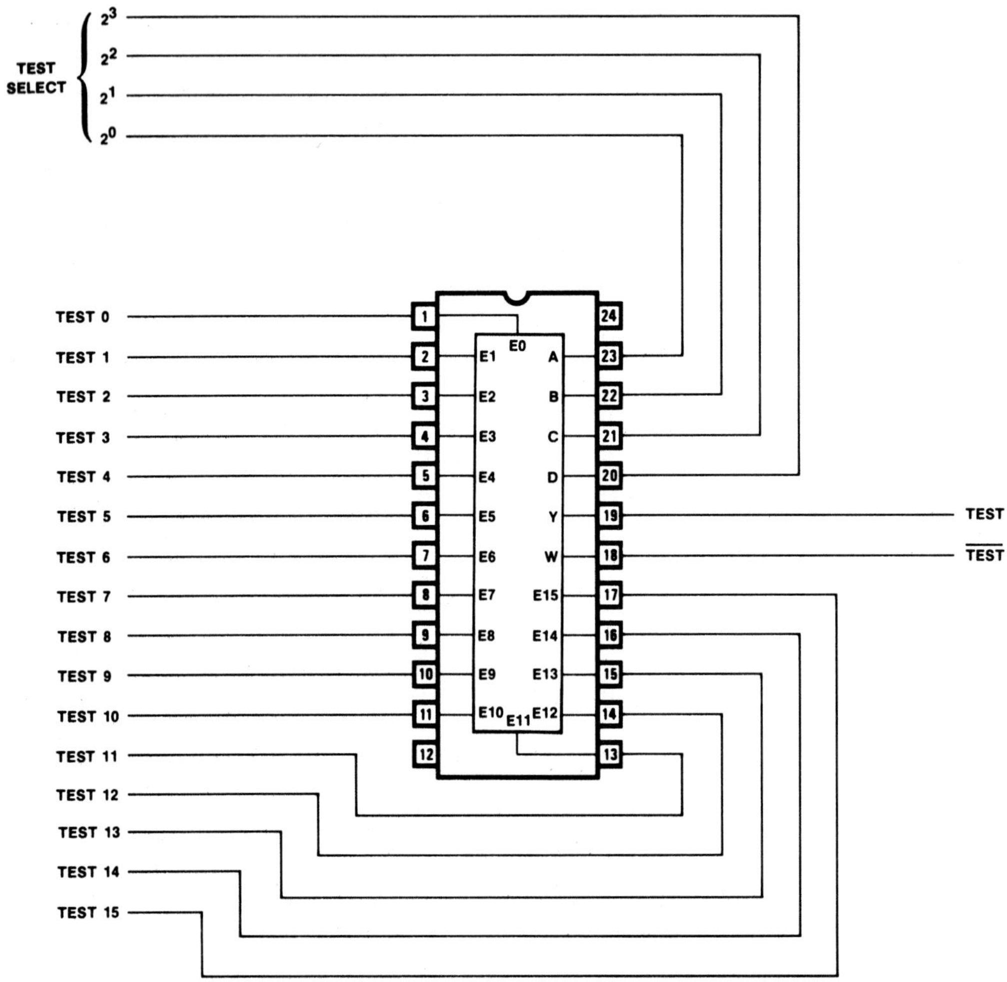

Octal Shift Register

PAL20X8

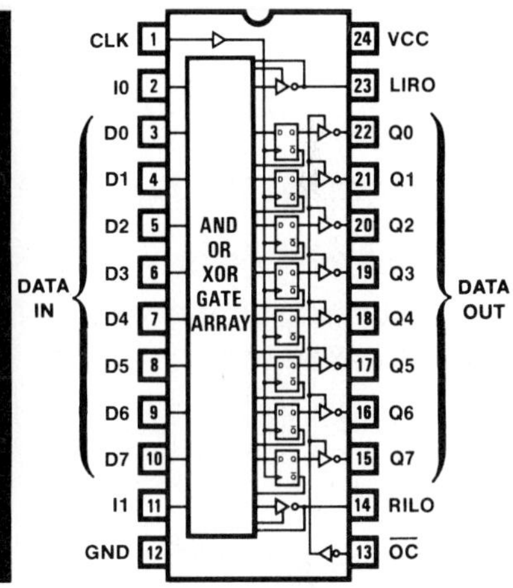

```
PAL20X8                                            PAL DESIGN SPECIFICATION
74LS498                                                UDI GORDON 02/20/81
OCTAL SHIFT REGISTER
MMI SUNNYVALE, CALIFORNIA
CLK  I0   D0 D1 D2 D3 D4 D5 D6 D7  I1  GND
/OC RILO Q7 Q6 Q5 Q4 Q3 Q2 Q1 Q0 LIRO VCC


/Q0 :=  /I1*/I0*/Q0                 ;HOLD Q0
     +  /I1* I0*/Q1                 ;SHIFT RIGHT
    :+:  I1*/I0*/LIRO               ;SHIFT LEFT
     +   I1* I0*/D0                 ;LOAD D0

/Q1 :=  /I1*/I0*/Q1                 ;HOLD Q1
     +  /I1* I0*/Q2                 ;SHIFT RIGHT
    :+:  I1*/I0*/Q0                 ;SHIFT LEFT
     +   I1* I0*/D1                 ;LOAD D1

/Q2 :=  /I1*/I0*/Q2                 ;HOLD Q2
     +  /I1* I0*/Q3                 ;SHIFT RIGHT
    :+:  I1*/I0*/Q1                 ;SHIFT LEFT
     +   I1* I0*/D2                 ;LOAD D2

/Q3 :=  /I1*/I0*/Q3                 ;HOLD Q3
     +  /I1* I0*/Q4                 ;SHIFT RIGHT
    :+:  I1*/I0*/Q2                 ;SHIFT LEFT
     +   I1* I0*/D3                 ;LOAD D3

/Q4 :=  /I1*/I0*/Q4                 ;HOLD Q4
     +  /I1* I0*/Q5                 ;SHIFT RIGHT
    :+:  I1*/I0*/Q3                 ;SHIFT LEFT
     +   I1* I0*/D4                 ;LOAD D4

/Q5 :=  /I1*/I0*/Q5                 ;HOLD Q5
     +  /I1* I0*/Q6                 ;SHIFT RIGHT
    :+:  I1*/I0*/Q4                 ;SHIFT LEFT
     +   I1* I0*/D5                 ;LOAD D5

/Q6 :=  /I1*/I0*/Q6                 ;HOLD Q6
     +  /I1* I0*/Q7                 ;SHIFT RIGHT
    :+:  I1*/I0*/Q5                 ;SHIFT LEFT
     +   I1* I0*/D6                 ;LOAD D6

/Q7 :=  /I1*/I0*/Q7                 ;HOLD Q7
     +  /I1* I0*/RILO               ;SHIFT RIGHT
    :+:  I1*/I0*/Q6                 ;SHIFT LEFT
     +   I1* I0*/D7                 ;LOAD D7

IF(/I1*I0) /LIRO = /Q0              ;LEFT IN RIGHT OUT

IF(I1*/I0) /RILO = /Q7              ;RIGHT IN LEFT OUT
```

```
FUNCTION TABLE

I1 I0 D7 D6 D5 D4 D3 D2 D1 D0 CLK /OC RILO LIRO Q7 Q6 Q5 Q4 Q3 Q2 Q1 Q0

;       DATA   IN                              Q  OUT
;INST   D7----D0   CLK /OC RILO LIRO   Q7----Q0      COMMENTS
---------------------------------------------------------------------------
  HH    LLLLLLLL    C    L    Z    Z    LLLLLLLL      LOAD ZEROS
  LL    XXXXXXXX    C    L    Z    Z    LLLLLLLL      HOLD
  HL    XXXXXXXX    C    L    L    H    LLLLLLLH      SHIFT LEFT IN A H
  HL    XXXXXXXX    C    L    L    L    LLLLLLHL      SHIFT LEFT IN A L
  HL    XXXXXXXX    C    L    L    L    LLLLLHLL      SHIFT LEFT IN A L
  HL    XXXXXXXX    C    L    L    L    LLLLHLLL      SHIFT LEFT IN A L
  HL    XXXXXXXX    C    L    L    L    LLLHLLLL      SHIFT LEFT IN A L
  HL    XXXXXXXX    C    L    L    L    LLHLLLLL      SHIFT LEFT IN A L
  HL    XXXXXXXX    C    L    L    L    LHLLLLLL      SHIFT LEFT IN A L
  HL    XXXXXXXX    C    L    H    L    HLLLLLLL      SHIFT LEFT IN A L
  HL    XXXXXXXX    C    L    L    L    LLLLLLLL      SHIFT LEFT IN A L
  LL    XXXXXXXX    X    H    Z    Z    ZZZZZZZZ      TEST HI-Z
  HH    HHHHHHHH    C    L    Z    Z    HHHHHHHH      LOAD ONES
  LL    XXXXXXXX    C    L    Z    Z    HHHHHHHH      HOLD
  LH    XXXXXXXX    C    L    L    H    LHHHHHHH      SHIFT RIGHT IN A L
  LH    XXXXXXXX    C    L    H    H    HLHHHHHH      SHIFT RIGHT IN A H
  LH    XXXXXXXX    C    L    H    H    HHLHHHHH      SHIFT RIGHT IN A H
  LH    XXXXXXXX    C    L    H    H    HHHLHHHH      SHIFT RIGHT IN A H
  LH    XXXXXXXX    C    L    H    H    HHHHLHHH      SHIFT RIGHT IN A H
  LH    XXXXXXXX    C    L    H    H    HHHHHLHH      SHIFT RIGHT IN A H
  LH    XXXXXXXX    C    L    H    H    HHHHHHLH      SHIFT RIGHT IN A H
  LH    XXXXXXXX    C    L    H    L    HHHHHHHL      SHIFT RIGHT IN A H
  LH    XXXXXXXX    C    L    H    H    HHHHHHHH      SHIFT RIGHT IN A H
  LL    XXXXXXXX    X    H    Z    Z    ZZZZZZZZ      TEST HI-Z
---------------------------------------------------------------------------
```

DESCRIPTION

THIS PAL IS AN 8-BIT SHIFT REGISTER WITH PARALLEL LOAD AND HOLD CAPABILITY. TWO FUNCTION SELECT INPUTS (I0,I1) PROVIDE ONE OF FOUR OPERATIONS WHICH OCCUR SYNCHRONOUSLY ON THE RISING EDGE OF THE CLOCK (CLK). THESE OPERATIONS ARE:

/OC	CLK	I1	I0	D7-D0	Q7-Q0	OPERATION
H	X	X	X	X	Z	HI-Z
L	C	L	L	X	L	HOLD
L	C	L	H	X	SR(Q)	SHIFT RIGHT
L	C	H	L	X	SL(Q)	SHIFT LEFT
L	C	H	H	D	D	LOAD

TWO OR MORE OCTAL SHIFT REGISTERS MAY BE CASCADED TO PROVIDE LARGER SHIFT REGISTERS. RILO AND LIRO ARE LOCATED ON PINS 14 AND 23 RESPECTIVELY, WHICH PROVIDES FOR CONVENIENT INTERCONNECTIONS WHEN TWO OR MORE OCTAL SHIFT REGISTERS ARE CASCADED TO IMPLEMENT LARGER SHIFT REGISTERS.

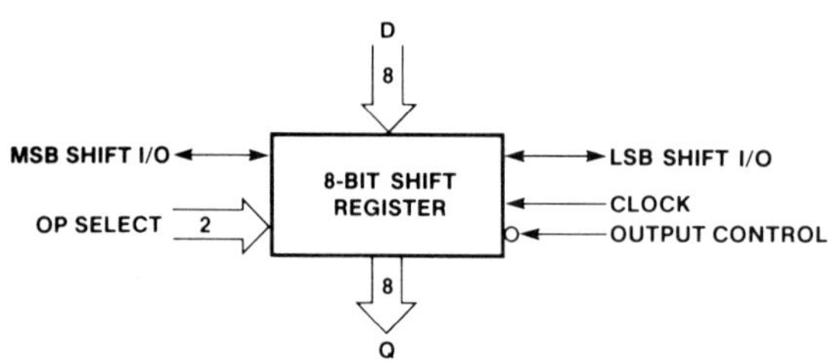

```
OCTAL SHIFT REGISTER

 1 C1000000001X0ZLLLLLLLLZ1
 2 C0XXXXXXXX0X0ZLLLLLLLLZ1
 3 C0XXXXXXXX1X0LLLLLLLLH11
 4 C0XXXXXXXX1X0LLLLLLLHL01
 5 C0XXXXXXXX1X0LLLLLLHLL01
 6 C0XXXXXXXX1X0LLLLLHLLL01
 7 C0XXXXXXXX1X0LLLLHLLLL01
 8 C0XXXXXXXX1X0LLLHLLLLL01
 9 C0XXXXXXXX1X0LLHLLLLLL01
10 C0XXXXXXXX1X0HHLLLLLLL01
11 C0XXXXXXXX1X0LLLLLLLLL01
12 X0XXXXXXXX0X1ZZZZZZZZZZ1
13 C1111111111X0ZHHHHHHHHZ1
14 C0XXXXXXXX0X0ZHHHHHHHHZ1
15 C1XXXXXXXX0X00LHHHHHHHH1
16 C1XXXXXXXX0X01HLHHHHHHH1
17 C1XXXXXXXX0X01HHLHHHHHH1
18 C1XXXXXXXX0X01HHHLHHHHH1
19 C1XXXXXXXX0X01HHHHLHHHH1
20 C1XXXXXXXX0X01HHHHHLHHH1
21 C1XXXXXXXX0X01HHHHHHLHH1
22 C1XXXXXXXX0X01HHHHHHHLL1
23 C1XXXXXXXX0X01HHHHHHHHH1
24 X0XXXXXXXX0X1ZZZZZZZZZZ1

PASS SIMULATION
```

```
OCTAL SHIFT REGISTER

              11 1111 1111 2222 2222 2233 3333 3333
  0123 4567 8901 2345 6789 0123 4567 8901 2345 6789

 0 X--- ---- ---- ---- ---- ---- ---- ---- ---- -X-- /I1*I0
 1 ---- ---X ---- ---- ---- ---- ---- ---- ---- ---- /Q0

 8 -X-- ---X ---- ---- ---- ---- ---- ---- ---- -X-- /I1*/I0*/Q0
 9 X--- ---- ---X ---- ---- ---- ---- ---- ---- -X-- /I1*I0*/Q1
10 -X-X ---- ---- ---- ---- ---- ---- ---- ---- X--- I1*/I0*/LIRO
11 X--- -X-- ---- ---- ---- ---- ---- ---- ---- X--- I1*I0*/D0

16 -X-- ---- ---X ---- ---- ---- ---- ---- ---- -X-- /I1*/I0*/Q1
17 X--- ---- ---- ---X ---- ---- ---- ---- ---- -X-- /I1*I0*/Q2
18 -X-- ---X ---- ---- ---- ---- ---- ---- ---- X--- I1*/I0*/Q0
19 X--- ---- -X-- ---- ---- ---- ---- ---- ---- X--- I1*I0*/D1

24 -X-- ---- ---- ---X ---- ---- ---- ---- ---- -X-- /I1*/I0*/Q2
25 X--- ---- ---- ---- ---X ---- ---- ---- ---- -X-- /I1*I0*/Q3
26 -X-- ---- ---X ---- ---- ---- ---- ---- ---- X--- I1*/I0*/Q1
27 X--- ---- ---- -X-- ---- ---- ---- ---- ---- X--- I1*I0*/D2

32 -X-- ---- ---- ---- ---X ---- ---- ---- ---- -X-- /I1*/I0*/Q3
33 X--- ---- ---- ---- ---- ---X ---- ---- ---- -X-- /I1*I0*/Q4
34 -X-- ---- ---- ---X ---- ---- ---- ---- ---- X--- I1*/I0*/Q2
35 X--- ---- ---- ---- -X-- ---- ---- ---- ---- X--- I1*I0*/D3

40 -X-- ---- ---- ---- ---- ---X ---- ---- ---- -X-- /I1*/I0*/Q4
41 X--- ---- ---- ---- ---- ---- ---X ---- ---- -X-- /I1*I0*/Q5
42 -X-- ---- ---- ---- ---X ---- ---- ---- ---- X--- I1*/I0*/Q3
43 X--- ---- ---- ---- ---- -X-- ---- ---- ---- X--- I1*I0*/D4

48 -X-- ---- ---- ---- ---- ---- ---X ---- ---- -X-- /I1*/I0*/Q5
49 X--- ---- ---- ---- ---- ---- ---- ---X ---- -X-- /I1*I0*/Q6
50 -X-- ---- ---- ---- ---- ---X ---- ---- ---- X--- I1*/I0*/Q4
51 X--- ---- ---- ---- ---- ---- -X-- ---- ---- X--- I1*I0*/D5

56 -X-- ---- ---- ---- ---- ---- ---- ---X ---- -X-- /I1*/I0*/Q6
57 X--- ---- ---- ---- ---- ---- ---- ---- ---X -X-- /I1*I0*/Q7
58 -X-- ---- ---- ---- ---- ---- ---X ---- ---- X--- I1*/I0*/Q5
59 X--- ---- ---- ---- ---- ---- ---- -X-- ---- X--- I1*I0*/D6

64 -X-- ---- ---- ---- ---- ---- ---- ---- ---X -X-- /I1*/I0*/Q7
65 X--- ---- ---- ---- ---- ---- ---- ---- ---- -X-X /I1*I0*/RILO
66 -X-- ---- ---- ---- ---- ---- ---- ---X ---- X--- I1*/I0*/Q6
67 X--- ---- ---- ---- ---- ---- ---- ---- -X-- X--- I1*I0*/D7

72 -X-- ---- ---- ---- ---- ---- ---- ---- ---- X--- I1*/I0
73 ---- ---- ---- ---- ---- ---- ---- ---- ---X ---- /Q7

LEGEND:  X : FUSE NOT BLOWN (L,N,0)   - : FUSE BLOWN   (H,P,1)

NUMBER OF FUSES BLOW = 1338
```

Octal Shift Register

Logic Diagram PAL20X8

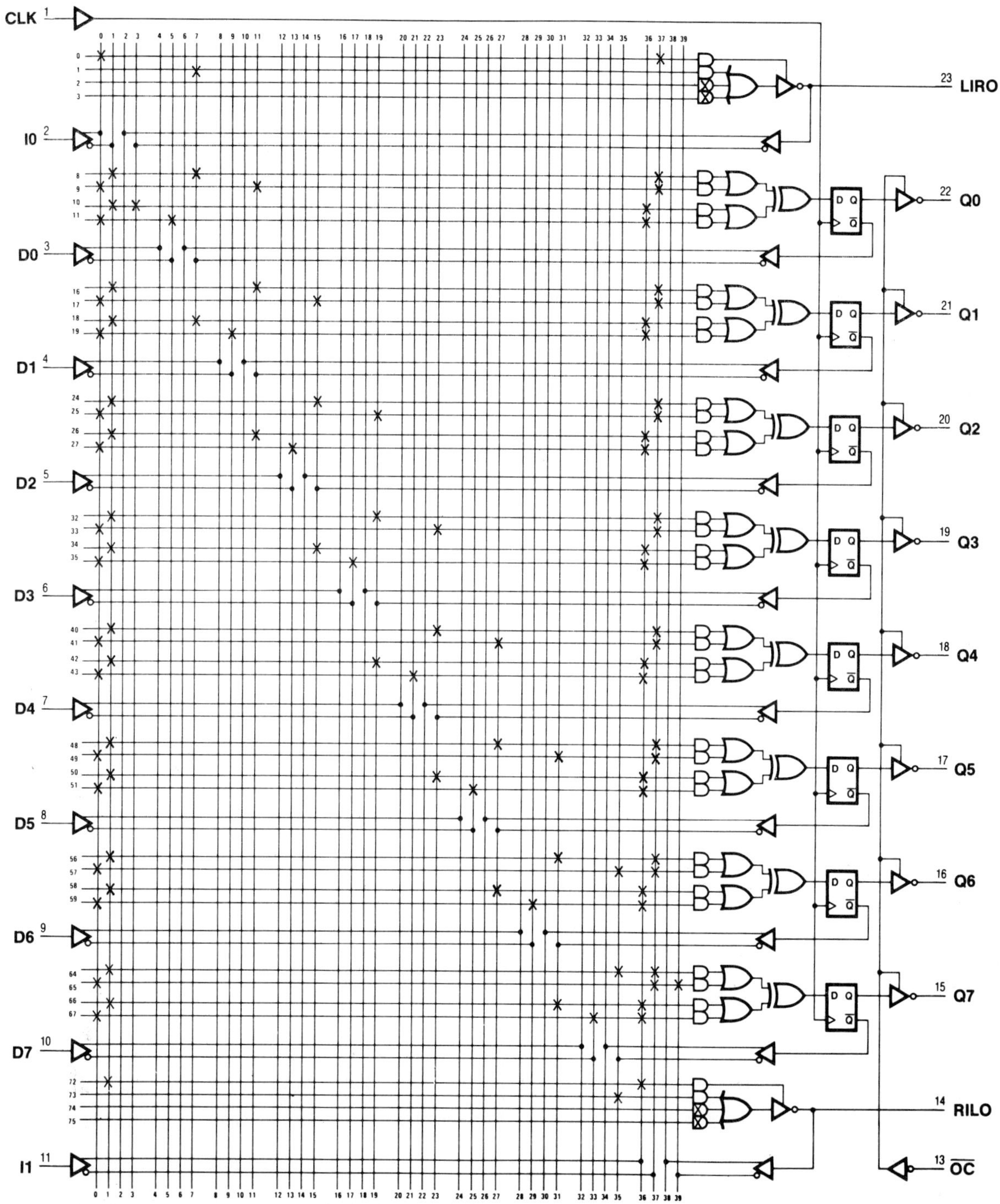

Application

16-Bit Shift Register

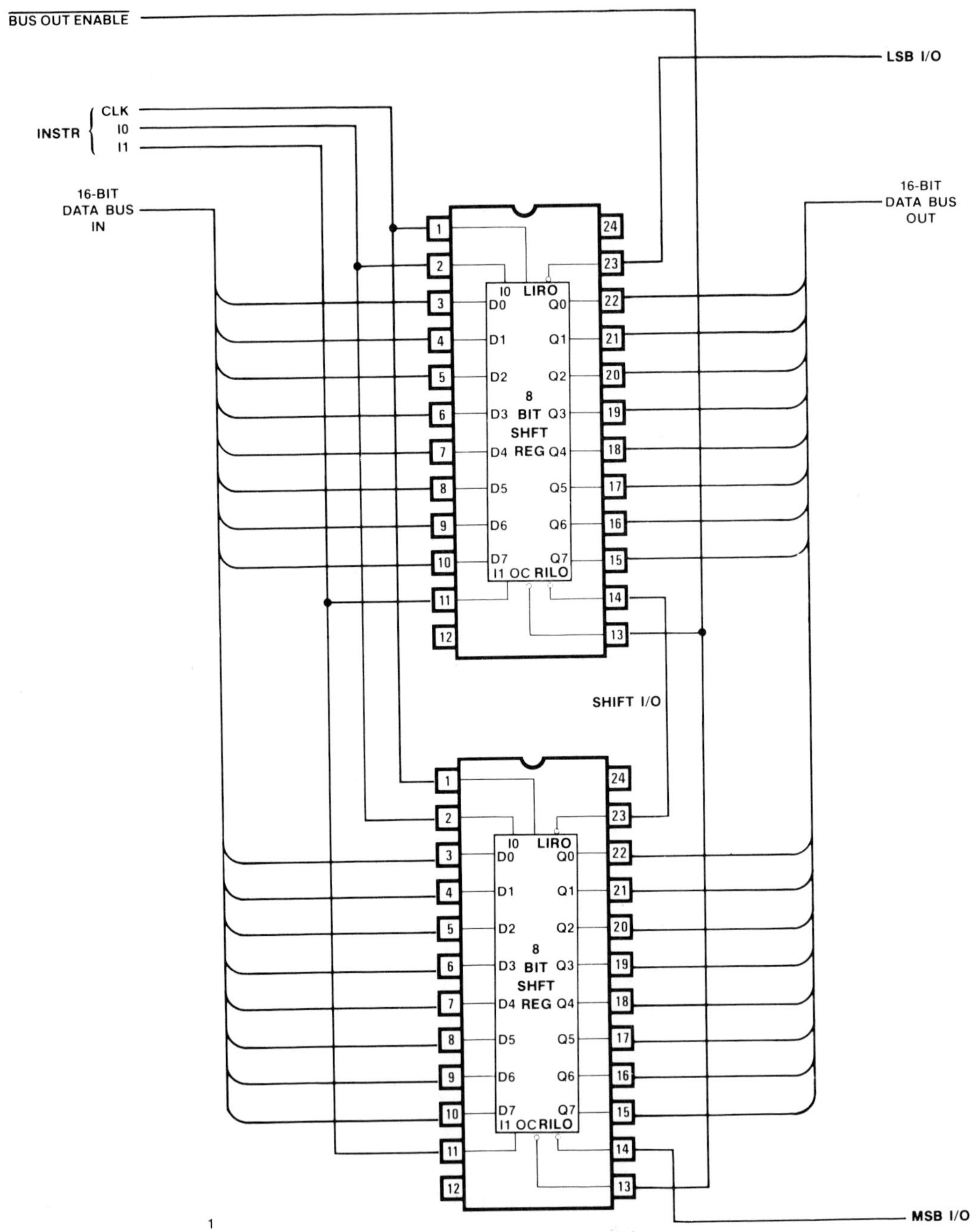

NOTE: $f_{MAX} = \frac{1}{t_{PD\ CLK\ TO\ LIRO} + t_{SU}}$

4-Bit Shift Register/Comparator

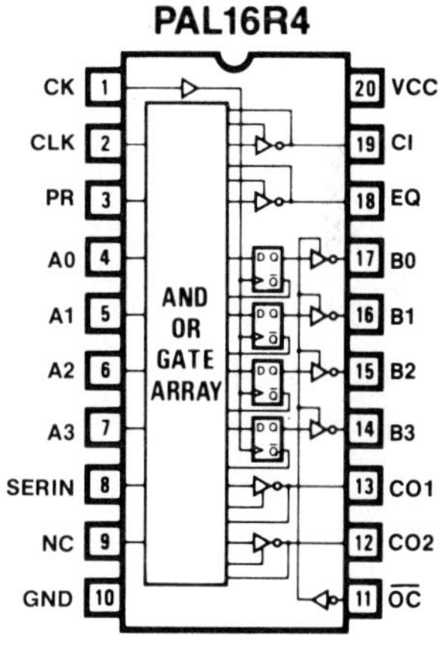

Functional Description

Frequently it is necessary to take a serial bit stream and convert it to a parallel form for storage. It is also necessary, in some cases, to monitor the same bit stream for certain patterns e.g., floppy disk file headers, RS232 ASCII characters, etc.

Using a PAL it is possible to combine these two functions.

Circuit Description

The circuit shows a 16 bit serial/parallel convertor, with three-state outputs and a compare true output (EQ). Four PAL16R4s are cascaded for this design. There is also a synchronous preset (PR) pin available. The circuit takes positive true Non-Return-To-Zero (NRZ) data with a central positive edge clock and converts it into parallel data. When the A and B inputs are equal, a negative going clock is output, with the negative (leading) edge in the center of the output data.

PAL Implementation

A PAL16R4 is used, the four flip-flops comprising the shift register and the other gates are used to compare the data and output on appropriate pulse if the compare is true. For the shift register the equations are:

B0 := /SERIN*/PR
B1 := /B0*/PR
B2 := /B1*/PR
B3 := /B2*/PR

The inputs are inverted because of the inverting output buffer on each stage. To compare two inputs A and B, the boolean equivalence operator is A ≡ B (or A :*: B).

The equations using AND-OR-INVERT logic are:

A1, A2 ≡ B1, B2 = (/A1*/B1)*(/A2*/B2) + (A1*B1)*(/A2*/B2)
+ (/A1*/B1)*(A2*B2) + (A1*B1)*(A2*B2)

So for 3 inputs we require 8 sum of products and so on. This means that we have to cascade 2 stages in the 16R4 as there are only 7 product terms available per output. Hence, compare 1 (CO1) is:

= A0*B0*A1*B1*/CI
+ A0*B0*/A1*B1*/CI
+ /A0*/B0*A1*B1*/CI
+ /A0*/B0*/A1*/B1*/CI

/CI = COMPARE IN FROM PREVIOUS STAGE

Compare Output 2 (CO2) is:
= A2*B2*A3*B3*/C*1 and so on.

On the final stage, the clock is inverted and gated with CO2. This causes a negative going pulse to be output when the A and B inputs are equal, the leading edge being at data center. This pulse is the EQ output. For a 16 bit register, the final CO2 output can have a maximum delay of 4x2x25ns = 200ns, so for a EQ pulse at data center the maximum clock frequency would be 5 MHz.

But, by using a carry-look-ahead technique, this could be increased to 7.2 MHz. In practice clock frequencies of greater than 10 MHz could be used (causing the EQ pulse leading edge to shift off center).

Conclusion

By feeding the outputs of the shift register into a bank of FIFOs (67401 or similar) a practical serial communication channel can be buffered into a microcomputer system. Using PALs the design can be tailored for use in different communication systems.

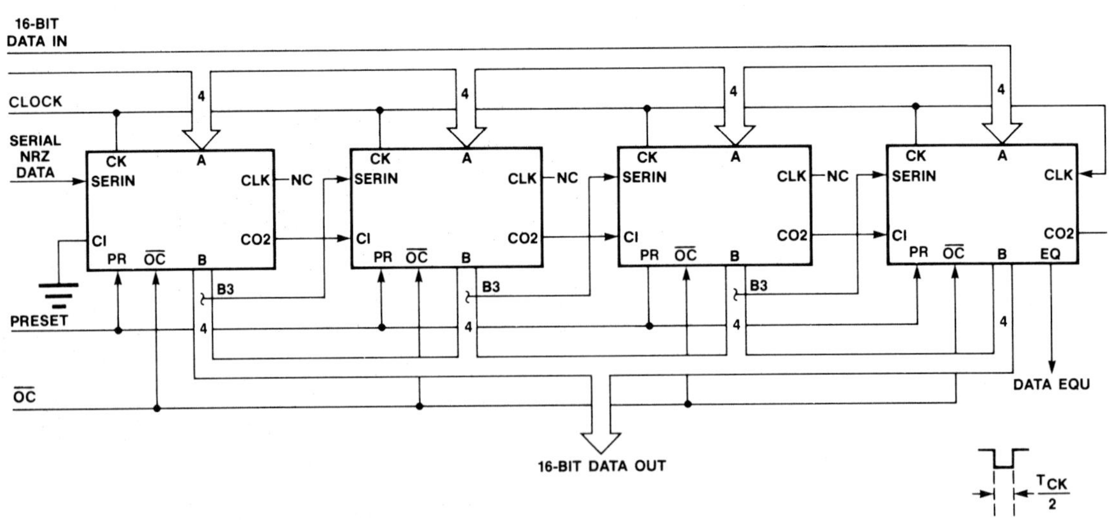

4-BIT SERIAL/PARALLEL SHIFT REGISTER/COMPARATOR WITH PRESET

```
PAL16R4                                              PAL DESIGN SPECIFICATION
SHFT4                                                   HARRY HUGHES 02/18/81
4-BIT SHIFT REGISTER/COMPARATOR
MMI ENGLAND
 CK CLK PR  A0 A1 A2 A3 SERIN NC GND
/OC CO2 CO1 B3 B2 B1 B0  EQ    CI VCC


/B0 := /SERIN*/PR                           ;SHIFT LEFT (SERIAL IN)

/B1 := /B0*/PR                              ;SHIFT LEFT

/B2 := /B1*/PR                              ;SHIFT LEFT

/B3 := /B2*/PR                              ;SHIFT LEFT

IF (VCC) /CO1 =   A0* B0* A1* B1*/CI        ;COMPARE  A0= B0 AND  A1= B1
               +  A0* B0*/A1*/B1*/CI        ;COMPARE  A0= B0 AND /A1=/B1
               + /A0*/B0* A1* B1*/CI        ;COMPARE /A0=/B0 AND  A1= B1
               + /A0*/B0*/A1*/B1*/CI        ;COMPARE /A0=/B0 AND /A1=/B1

IF (VCC) /CO2 =   A2* B2* A3* B3*/CO1       ;COMPARE  A2= B2 AND  A3= B3
               +  A2* B2*/A3*/B3*/CO1       ;COMPARE  A2= B2 AND /A3=/B3
               + /A2*/B2* A3* B3*/CO1       ;COMPARE /A2=/B2 AND  A3= B3
               + /A2*/B2*/A3*/B3*/CO1       ;COMPARE /A2=/B2 AND /A3=/B3

IF (VCC)  /EQ = /CLK*/CO2                   ;COMPARE TRUE PULSE


FUNCTION TABLE

SERIN A3 A2 A1 A0 CK /OC PR CI CO1 CO2 CLK EQ B3 B2 B1 B0

;-INPUTS-    -------CONTROL-------   OUTPUTS
;SER AAAA    C /  P  C  C  C  C  E    BBBB
;IN  3210    K OC R  I  01 02 LK Q    3210     COMMENTS
---------------------------------------------------------------------------
  X  XXXX    C L  H  X  X  X  X  X    HHHH     PRESET
  L  HHHL    C L  L  L  L  L  L  L    HHHL     SHIFT LEFT IN A L (A=B)
  L  HHLL    C L  L  L  L  L  L  L    HHLL     SHIFT LEFT IN A L (A=B)
  L  HLLL    C L  L  L  L  L  L  L    HLLL     SHIFT LEFT IN A L (A=B)
  L  LLLL    C L  L  L  L  L  L  L    LLLL     SHIFT LEFT IN A L (A=B)
  H  LLLH    C L  L  L  L  L  L  L    LLLH     SHIFT LEFT IN A H (A=B)
  H  LLHH    C L  L  L  L  L  L  L    LLHH     SHIFT LEFT IN A H (A=B)
  H  LHHH    C L  L  L  L  L  L  L    LHHH     SHIFT LEFT IN A H (A=B)
  H  HHHH    C L  L  L  L  L  L  L    HHHH     SHIFT LEFT IN A H (A=B)
  X  XXXX    L L  X  H  H  H  X  H    XXXX     PREVIOUS STAGE COMPARE NOT TRUE
  X  XXXX    L L  X  X  X  X  H  H    XXXX     COMPARE TRUE PULSE INACTIVE
  H  HHHH    L L  L  L  L  L  L  L    HHHH     COMPARE TRUE
  X  XXXX    X H  X  X  X  X  X  X    ZZZZ     TEST HI-Z
---------------------------------------------------------------------------
```

DESCRIPTION

THIS 4-BIT SHIFT REGISTER/COMPARATOR ACCEPTS POSITIVE NRZ INPUT DATA ON THE RISING EDGE OF THE CLOCK (CK) AND PRODUCES A PARALLEL OUTPUT (B) WITH A 'COMPARE TRUE PULSE' ON THE NEGATIVE EDGE OF THE CLOCK (CLK).

THE THREE-STATE OUTPUTS (B) ARE HIGH-Z WHEN THE OUTPUT CONTROL LINE (/OC) IS HIGH AND ENABLED WHEN THE OUTPUT CONTROL LINE (/OC) IS LOW.

```
4-BIT SHIFT REGISTER/COMPARATOR

 1 CX1XXXXXXX0XXHHHHXX1
 2 C0001110XX0LLHHHLL01
 3 C0000110XX0LLHHLLL01
 4 C0000010XX0LLHLLLL01
 5 C0000000XX0LLLLLLL01
 6 C0010001XX0LLLLLHL01
 7 C0011001XX0LLLLHHL01
 8 C0011101XX0LLLHHHL01
 9 C0011111XX0LLHHHHL01
10 0XXXXXXXXX0HHXXXXH11
11 01XXXXXXXX0XXXXXXHX1
12 00011111XX0LLHHHHL01
13 XXXXXXXXXX1XXZZZZXX1

PASS SIMULATION
```

```
4-BIT SHIFT REGISTER/COMPARATOR

                11 1111 1111 2222 2222 2233
   0123 4567 8901 2345 6789 0123 4567 8901


 8 ---- ---- ---- ---- ---- ---- ---- ----
 9 -X-- ---- ---- ---- ---- ---- ---- ---X /CLK*/CO2

16 ---- -X-- ---- ---- ---- ---- -X-- ---- /SERIN*/PR

24 ---- -X-- ---X ---- ---- ---- ---- ---- /B0*/PR

32 ---- -X-- ---- ---X ---- ---- ---- ---- /B1*/PR

40 ---- -X-- ---- ---- ---X ---- ---- ---- /B2*/PR

48 ---- ---- ---- ---- ---- ---- ---- ----
49 ---X ---- X-X- X-X- ---- ---- ---- ---- A0*B0*A1*B1*/CI
50 ---X ---- X-X- -X-X ---- ---- ---- ---- A0*B0*/A1*/B1*/CI
51 ---X ---- -X-X X-X- ---- ---- ---- ---- /A0*/B0*A1*B1*/CI
52 ---X ---- -X-X -X-X ---- ---- ---- ---- /A0*/B0*/A1*/B1*/CI

56 ---- ---- ---- ---- ---- ---- ---- ----
57 ---- ---- ---- ---- X-X- X-X- ---X ---- A2*B2*A3*B3*/CO1
58 ---- ---- ---- ---- X-X- -X-X ---X ---- A2*B2*/A3*/B3*/CO1
59 ---- ---- ---- ---- -X-X X-X- ---X ---- /A2*/B2*A3*B3*/CO1
60 ---- ---- ---- ---- -X-X -X-X ---X ---- /A2*/B2*/A3*/B3*/CO1


LEGEND:  X : FUSE NOT BLOWN (L,N,0)    - : FUSE BLOWN   (H,P,1)

NUMBER OF FUSES BLOWN =  462
```

4-Bit Shift Register/Comparator

Logic Diagram PAL16R4

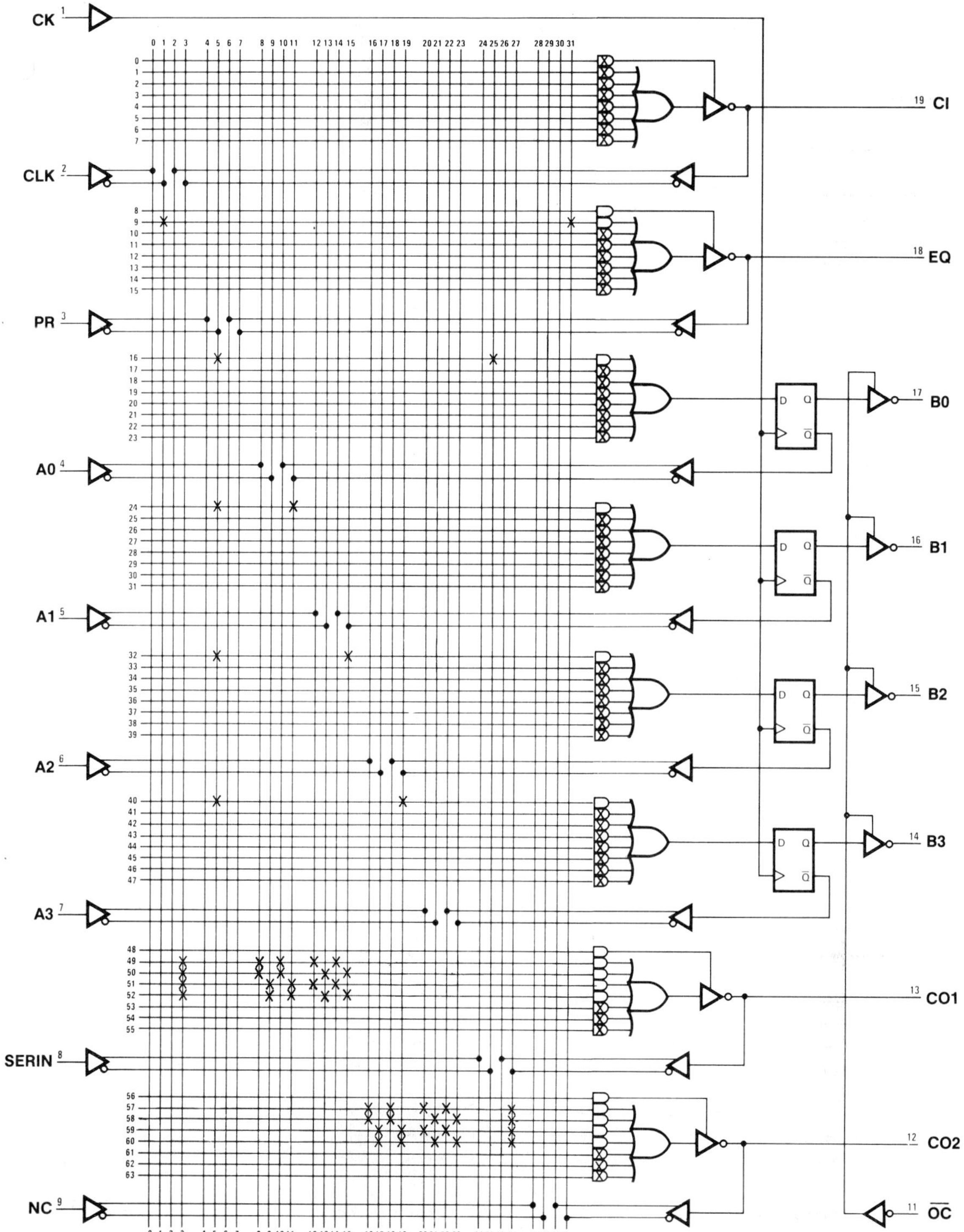

PAL
IMPORTANT, NOTES

4-Bit Counter with 2 Input Mux

PAL16R4

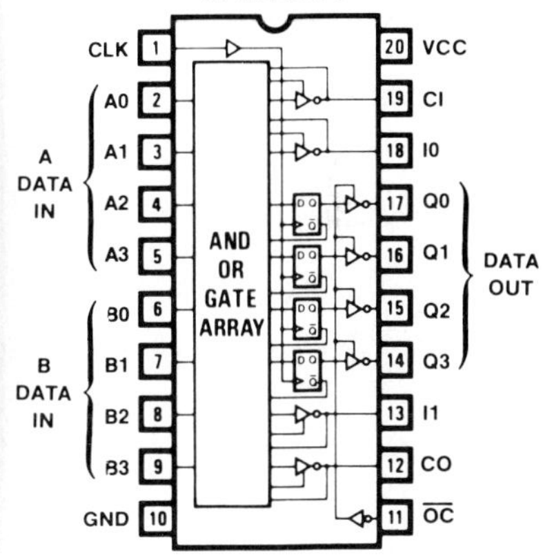

```
PAL16R4                                           PAL DESIGN SPECIFICATION
CNT4M                                               BIRKNER/COLI 07/22/81
4-BIT COUNTER WITH 2 INPUT MUX
MMI SUNNYVALE, CALIFORNIA
CLK A0 A1 A2 A3 B0 B1 B2 B3 GND
/OC CO I1 Q3 Q2 Q1 Q0 I0 CI VCC


/Q0 := /I1*/I0*/Q0                   ;HOLD Q0 (LSB)
     + /I1* I0*/A0                   ;LOAD A0
     +  I1*/I0*/B0                   ;LOAD B0
     +  I1* I0*/CI*/Q0               ;HOLD IF NO CARRY IN
     +  I1* I0* CI* Q0               ;COUNT IF CARRY IN AND Q0=H

/Q1 := /I1*/I0*/Q1                   ;HOLD Q1
     + /I1* I0*/A1                   ;LOAD A1
     +  I1*/I0*/B1                   ;LOAD B1
     +  I1* I0*/CI*/Q1               ;HOLD IF NO CARRY IN
     +  I1* I0*/Q0*/Q1               ;HOLD IF Q0,Q1=L
     +  I1* I0* CI* Q0* Q1           ;COUNT IF CARRY IN AND Q0,Q1=H

/Q2 := /I1*/I0*/Q2                   ;HOLD Q2
     + /I1* I0*/A2                   ;LOAD A2
     +  I1*/I0*/B2                   ;LOAD B2
     +  I1* I0*/CI*/Q2               ;HOLD IF NO CARRY IN
     +  I1* I0*/Q0*/Q2               ;HOLD IF Q0,Q2=L
     +  I1* I0*/Q1*/Q2               ;HOLD IF Q1,Q2=L
     +  I1* I0* CI* Q0* Q1* Q2       ;COUNT IF CARRY IN AND Q0,Q1,Q2=H

/Q3 := /I1*/I0*/Q3                   ;HOLD Q3 (MSB)
     + /I1* I0*/A3                   ;LOAD A3
     +  I1*/I0*/B3                   ;LOAD B3
     +  I1* I0*/CI*/Q3               ;HOLD IF NO CARRY IN
     +  I1* I0*/Q0*/Q3               ;HOLD IF Q0,Q3=L
     +  I1* I0*/Q1*/Q3               ;HOLD IF Q1,Q3=L
     +  I1* I0*/Q2*/Q3               ;HOLD IF Q2,Q3=L
     +  I1* I0* CI* Q0* Q1* Q2* Q3   ;COUNT IF CARRY IN AND Q0,Q1,Q2,Q3=H

IF(VCC) /CO = /CI+/Q0+/Q1+/Q2+/Q3    ;CARRY OUT IF CARRY IN AND Q0,Q1,Q2,Q3=H
```

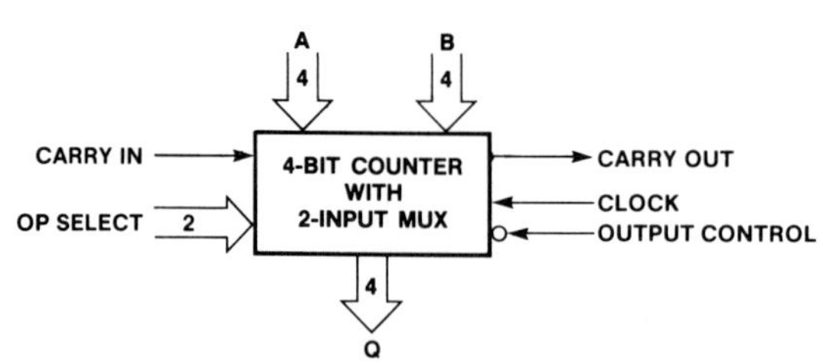

```
FUNCTION TABLE

CLK /OC I1 I0 A3 A2 A1 A0 B3 B2 B1 B0 CI CO Q3 Q2 Q1 Q0

;                  --INPUTS--          OUTPUT
;CONTROL   INSTR   AAAA  BBBB  CARRY   QQQQ      COMMENTS
;CLK /OC   I1 I0   3210  3210  CI CO   3210     (HEX VALUES)
------------------------------------------------------------------------
  C   L    L  H    LLLL  HHHH  X   X   LLLL     LOAD A (0)
  C   L    H  L    LLLL  HHHH  X   X   HHHH     LOAD B (F)
  C   L    L  H    LLLH  LHHH  X   X   LLLH     LOAD A (1)
  C   L    H  L    LLLH  LHHH  X   X   LHHH     LOAD B (7)
  C   L    L  H    LLHL  HLHH  X   X   LLHL     LOAD A (3)
  C   L    H  L    LLHL  HLHH  X   X   HLHH     LOAD B (B)
  C   L    L  H    LHLL  HHLH  X   X   LHLL     LOAD A (4)
  C   L    H  L    LHLL  HHLH  X   X   HHLH     LOAD B (D)
  C   L    L  H    HLLL  HHHL  X   X   HLLL     LOAD A (8)
  C   L    H  L    HLLL  HHHL  X   X   HHHL     LOAD B (E)
  C   L    L  H    LLLL  HHHH  X   X   LLLL     LOAD A (0)
  C   L    H  L    LLLL  HHHH  X   X   HHHH     LOAD B (F)
  C   L    H  L    XXXX  LLLH  X   X   LLLH     LOAD B (1)
  C   L    H  H    XXXX  XXXX  H   L   LLHL     INCREMENT
  C   L    H  L    XXXX  LLHH  X   X   LLHH     LOAD B (3)
  C   L    H  H    XXXX  XXXX  H   L   LHLL     INCREMENT
  C   L    L  H    LHHH  XXXX  X   X   LHHH     LOAD A (7)
  C   L    H  H    XXXX  XXXX  H   L   HLLL     INCREMENT
  C   L    L  H    HHHH  XXXX  X   X   HHHH     LOAD A (F)
  C   L    H  H    XXXX  XXXX  H   L   LLLL     INCREMENT (ROLL OVER)
  C   L    H  L    XXXX  HHLL  X   X   HHLL     LOAD B (C)
  C   L    H  H    XXXX  XXXX  H   L   HHLH     INCREMENT (D)
  C   L    L  L    XXXX  XXXX  H   L   HHLH     HOLD (D)
  C   L    H  H    XXXX  XXXX  H   L   HHHL     INCREMENT (E)
  C   L    H  H    XXXX  XXXX  H   H   HHHH     INCREMENT (F) (CARRY OUT)
  C   L    H  H    XXXX  XXXX  H   L   LLLL     INCREMENT (0) (ROLL OVER)
  C   L    H  H    XXXX  XXXX  H   L   LLLH     INCREMENT (1)
  C   L    H  H    XXXX  XXXX  L   L   LLLH     HOLD (NO CARRY IN)
  C   L    H  H    XXXX  XXXX  H   L   LLHL     INCREMENT (2)
  X   H    X  X    XXXX  XXXX  X   X   ZZZZ     TEST HI-Z
------------------------------------------------------------------------
```

DESCRIPTION

THE 4-BIT COUNTER LOADS A OR B FROM THE MUX, INCREMENTS, OR HOLDS ON THE RISING EDGE OF THE CLOCK.

/OC	CLK	I1	I0	CI	A3-A0	B3-B0	Q3-Q0	OPERATION
H	X	X	X	X	X	X	Z	HI-Z
L	C	L	L	X	X	X	Q	HOLD
L	C	L	H	X	A	X	A	LOAD A
L	C	H	L	X	X	B	B	LOAD B
L	C	H	H	L	X	X	Q	HOLD
L	C	H	H	H	X	X	Q PLUS 1	INCREMENT

```
4-BIT COUNTER WITH 2 INPUT MUX

 1 C00001111X0X0LLLL1X1
 2 C00001111X0X1HHHH0X1
 3 C10001110X0X0LLLH1X1
 4 C10001110X0X1LHHH0X1
 5 C01001101X0X0LLHL1X1
 6 C01001101X0X1HLHH0X1
 7 C00101011X0X0LHLL1X1
 8 C00101011X0X1HHLH0X1
 9 C00010111X0X0HLLL1X1
10 C00010111X0X1HHHL0X1
11 C00001111X0X0LLLL1X1
12 C00001111X0X1HHHH0X1
13 CXXXX1000X0X1LLLH0X1
14 CXXXXXXXXX0L1LLHL111
15 CXXXX1100X0X1LLHH0X1
16 CXXXXXXXXX0L1LHLL111
17 C1110XXXXX0X0LHHH1X1
18 CXXXXXXXXX0L1HLLL111
19 C1111XXXXX0X0HHHH1X1
20 CXXXXXXXXX0L1LLLL111
21 CXXXX0011X0X0HHLL1X1
22 CXXXXXXXXX0L1HHLH111
23 CXXXXXXXXX0L0HHLH011
24 CXXXXXXXXX0L1HHHL111
25 CXXXXXXXXX0H1HHHH111
26 CXXXXXXXXX0L1LLLL111
27 CXXXXXXXXX0L1LLLH111
28 CXXXXXXXXX0L1LLLH101
29 CXXXXXXXXX0L1LLHL111
30 XXXXXXXXXX1XXZZZZXX1

PASS SIMULATION
```

```
4-BIT COUNTER WITH 2 INPUT MUX

              11 1111 1111 2222 2222 2233
   0123 4567 8901 2345 6789 0123 4567 8901



16 ---- ---X ---X ---- ---- ---- ---X ---- /I1*/I0*/Q0
17 -X-- --X- ---- ---- ---- ---- ---X ---- /I1*I0*/A0
18 ---- ---X ---- ---- -X-- ---- --X- ---- I1*/I0*/B0
19 ---X --X- ---X ---- ---- ---- --X- ---- I1*I0*/CI*/Q0
20 --X- --X- --X- ---- ---- ---- --X- ---- I1*I0*CI*Q0

24 ---- ---X ---- ---X ---- ---- ---X ---- /I1*/I0*/Q1
25 ---- -XX- ---- ---- ---- ---- ---X ---- /I1*I0*/A1
26 ---- ---X ---- ---- ---- -X-- --X- ---- I1*/I0*/B1
27 ---X --X- ---- ---X ---- ---- --X- ---- I1*I0*/CI*/Q1
28 ---- --X- ---X ---X ---- ---- --X- ---- I1*I0*/Q0*/Q1
29 --X- --X- --X- --X- ---- ---- --X- ---- I1*I0*CI*Q0*Q1

32 ---- ---X ---- ---- ---X ---- ---X ---- /I1*/I0*/Q2
33 ---- --X- -X-- ---- ---- ---- ---X ---- /I1*I0*/A2
34 ---- ---X ---- ---- ---- ---- -XX- ---- I1*/I0*/B2
35 ---X --X- ---- ---- ---X ---- --X- ---- I1*I0*/CI*/Q2
36 ---- --X- ---X ---- ---X ---- --X- ---- I1*I0*/Q0*/Q2
37 ---- --X- ---- ---X ---X ---- --X- ---- I1*I0*/Q1*/Q2
38 --X- --X- --X- --X- --X- ---- --X- ---- I1*I0*CI*Q0*Q1*Q2

40 ---- ---X ---- ---- ---- ---X ---X ---- /I1*/I0*/Q3
41 ---- --X- ---- -X-- ---- ---- ---X ---- /I1*I0*/A3
42 ---- ---X ---- ---- ---- ---- --X- -X-- I1*/I0*/B3
43 ---X --X- ---- ---- ---- ---X --X- ---- I1*I0*/CI*/Q3
44 ---- --X- ---X ---- ---- ---X --X- ---- I1*I0*/Q0*/Q3
45 ---- --X- ---- ---X ---- ---X --X- ---- I1*I0*/Q1*/Q3
46 ---- --X- ---- ---- ---X ---X --X- ---- I1*I0*/Q2*/Q3
47 --X- --X- --X- --X- --X- --X- --X- ---- I1*I0*CI*Q0*Q1*Q2*Q3


56 ---- ---- ---- ---- ---- ---- ---- ----
57 ---X ---- ---- ---- ---- ---- ---- ---- /CI
58 ---- ---- ---X ---- ---- ---- ---- ---- /Q0
59 ---- ---- ---- ---X ---- ---- ---- ---- /Q1
60 ---- ---- ---- ---- ---X ---- ---- ---- /Q2
61 ---- ---- ---- ---- ---- ---X ---- ---- /Q3


LEGEND:  X : FUSE NOT BLOWN (L,N,0)   - : FUSE BLOWN   (H,P,1)

NUMBER OF FUSES BLOWN =  921
```

4-Bit Counter with 2 Input Mux

Logic Diagram PAL16R4

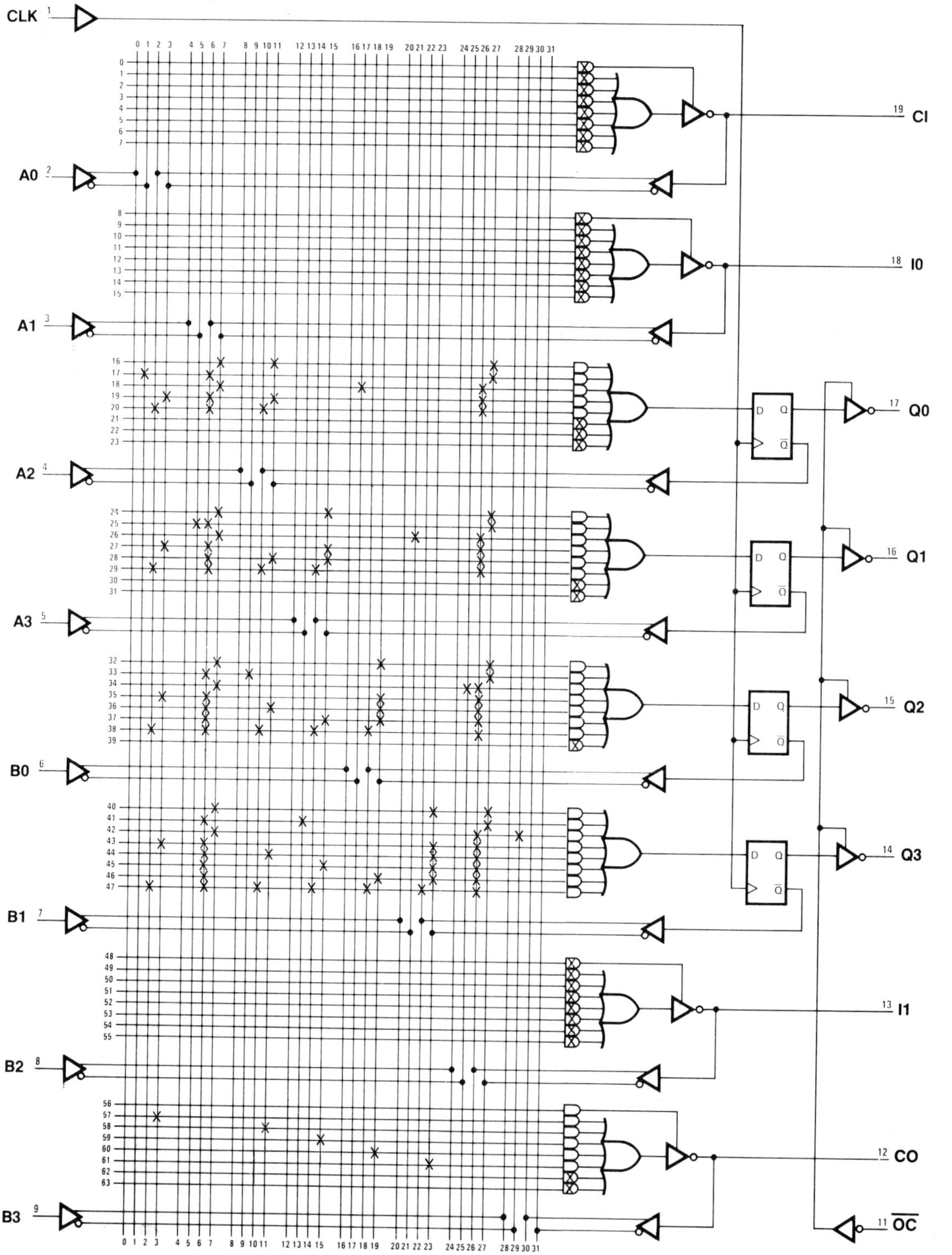

PAL
IMPORTANT,
NOTES

Octal Counter

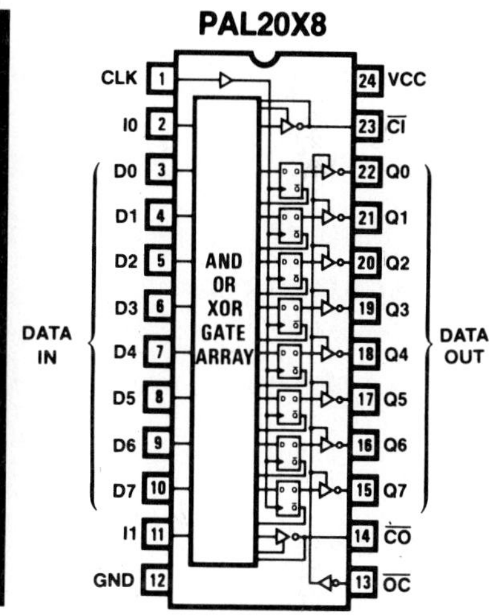

```
PAL20X8                                          PAL DESIGN SPECIFICATION
74LS461                                     BIRKNER/KAZMI/BLASCO 02/10/81
OCTAL COUNTER
MMI SUNNYVALE, CALIFORNIA
CLK  I0 D0 D1 D2 D3 D4 D5 D6 D7  I1 GND
/OC /CO Q7 Q6 Q5 Q4 Q3 Q2 Q1 Q0 /CI VCC


/Q0 :=  /I1*/I0                                ;CLEAR LSB
     +       I0*/Q0                            ;COUNT/HOLD
    :+:  I1*/I0*/D0                            ;LOAD D0 (LSB)
     +   I1* I0* CI                            ;COUNT

/Q1 :=  /I1*/I0                                ;CLEAR
     +       I0*/Q1                            ;COUNT/HOLD
    :+:  I1*/I0*/D1                            ;LOAD D1
     +   I1* I0* CI*Q0                         ;COUNT

/Q2 :=  /I1*/I0                                ;CLEAR
     +       I0*/Q2                            ;COUNT/HOLD
    :+:  I1*/I0*/D2                            ;LOAD D2
     +   I1* I0* CI*Q0*Q1                      ;COUNT

/Q3 :=  /I1*/I0                                ;CLEAR
     +       I0*/Q3                            ;COUNT/HOLD
    :+:  I1*/I0*/D3                            ;LOAD D3
     +   I1* I0* CI*Q0*Q1*Q2                   ;COUNT

/Q4 :=  /I1*/I0                                ;CLEAR
     +       I0*/Q4                            ;COUNT/HOLD
    :+:  I1*/I0*/D4                            ;LOAD D4
     +   I1* I0* CI*Q0*Q1*Q2*Q3                ;COUNT

/Q5 :=  /I1*/I0                                ;CLEAR
     +       I0*/Q5                            ;COUNT/HOLD
    :+:  I1*/I0*/D5                            ;LOAD D5
     +   I1* I0* CI*Q0*Q1*Q2*Q3*Q4             ;COUNT

/Q6 :=  /I1*/I0                                ;CLEAR
     +       I0*/Q6                            ;COUNT/HOLD
    :+:  I1*/I0*/D6                            ;LOAD D6
     +   I1* I0* CI*Q0*Q1*Q2*Q3*Q4*Q5          ;COUNT

/Q7 :=  /I1*/I0                                ;CLEAR MSB
     +       I0*/Q7                            ;COUNT/HOLD
    :+:  I1*/I0*/D7                            ;LOAD D7 (MSB)
     +   I1* I0* CI*Q0*Q1*Q2*Q3*Q4*Q5*Q6       ;COUNT

IF (VCC)  CO = CI*Q0*Q1*Q2*Q3*Q4*Q5*Q6*Q7      ;CARRY OUT
```

```
FUNCTION TABLE

CLK /OC I1 I0 D7 D6 D5 D4 D3 D2 D1 D0 /CI /CO Q7 Q6 Q5 Q4 Q3 Q2 Q1 Q0

;                    -INPUT--            -OUTPUT-
;CONTROL    INSTR    DDDDDDDD    CARRY   QQQQQQQQ    COMMENTS
;CLK /OC    I1 I0    76543210   /CI /CO  76543210   (HEX VALUES)
-------------------------------------------------------------------------------
  C   L      H  L    LLLLLLLH    X   H   LLLLLLLH   LOAD (01)
  C   L      H  H    XXXXXXXX    L   H   LLLLLLHL   INCREMENT
  C   L      H  L    LLLLLLHH    X   H   LLLLLLHH   LOAD (03)
  C   L      H  H    XXXXXXXX    L   H   LLLLLHLL   INCREMENT
  C   L      H  L    LLLLLHHH    X   H   LLLLLHHH   LOAD (07)
  C   L      H  H    XXXXXXXX    L   H   LLLLHLLL   INCREMENT
  C   L      H  L    LLLLHHHH    X   H   LLLLHHHH   LOAD (0F)
  C   L      H  H    XXXXXXXX    L   H   LLLHLLLL   INCREMENT
  C   L      H  L    LLLHHHHH    X   H   LLLHHHHH   LOAD (1F)
  C   L      H  H    XXXXXXXX    L   H   LLHLLLLL   INCREMENT
  C   L      H  L    LLHHHHHH    X   H   LLHHHHHH   LOAD (3F)
  C   L      H  H    XXXXXXXX    L   H   LHLLLLLL   INCREMENT
  C   L      H  L    LHHHHHHH    X   H   LHHHHHHH   LOAD (7F)
  C   L      H  H    XXXXXXXX    L   H   HLLLLLLL   INCREMENT
  C   L      H  L    HHHHHHHH    L   L   HHHHHHHH   LOAD (FF)
  C   L      H  H    XXXXXXXX    L   H   LLLLLLLL   INCREMENT (ROLL OVER)
  C   L      H  L    HHHHHHHH    L   L   HHHHHHHH   LOAD (FF)
  C   L      H  L    HHHHHHHL    X   H   HHHHHHHL   LOAD (FE)
  C   L      H  L    HHHHHHLH    X   H   HHHHHHLH   LOAD (FD)
  C   L      H  L    HHHHHLHH    X   H   HHHHHLHH   LOAD (FB)
  C   L      H  L    HHHHLHHH    X   H   HHHHLHHH   LOAD (F7)
  C   L      H  L    HHHLHHHH    X   H   HHHLHHHH   LOAD (EF)
  C   L      H  L    HHLHHHHH    X   H   HHLHHHHH   LOAD (DF)
  C   L      H  L    HLHHHHHH    X   H   HLHHHHHH   LOAD (BF)
  C   L      H  L    LHHHHHHH    X   H   LHHHHHHH   LOAD (7F)
  C   L      H  L    HHHHHHHH    L   L   HHHHHHHH   LOAD (FF)
  C   L      L  L    XXXXXXXX    X   H   LLLLLLLL   CLEAR
  C   L      H  H    XXXXXXXX    L   H   LLLLLLLH   INCREMENT TO (01)
  C   L      H  H    XXXXXXXX    L   H   LLLLLLHL   INCREMENT TO (02)
  C   L      H  H    XXXXXXXX    L   H   LLLLLLHH   INCREMENT TO (03)
  C   L      H  H    XXXXXXXX    L   H   LLLLLHLL   INCREMENT TO (04)
  C   L      H  H    XXXXXXXX    L   H   LLLLLHLH   INCREMENT TO (05)
  C   L      H  H    XXXXXXXX    L   H   LLLLLHHL   INCREMENT TO (06)
  C   L      H  H    XXXXXXXX    L   H   LLLLLHHH   INCREMENT TO (07)
  C   L      H  H    XXXXXXXX    L   H   LLLLHLLL   INCREMENT TO (08)
  C   L      H  H    XXXXXXXX    L   H   LLLLHLLH   INCREMENT TO (09)
  C   L      H  H    XXXXXXXX    L   H   LLLLHLHL   INCREMENT TO (0A)
  C   L      H  H    XXXXXXXX    L   H   LLLLHLHH   INCREMENT TO (0B)
  C   L      H  H    XXXXXXXX    L   H   LLLLHHLL   INCREMENT TO (0C)
  C   L      H  L    HHHHHHHL    X   H   HHHHHHHL   LOAD (FE)
  C   L      H  H    XXXXXXXX    L   L   HHHHHHHH   INCREMENT TO (FF) /CO=L
  C   L      H  H    XXXXXXXX    H   H   HHHHHHHH   CI INHIBITS COUNT AND CO
  C   L      L  H    LLLLLLLL    L   L   HHHHHHHH   HOLD SEL INHIBITS COUNT ONLY
  C   L      H  H    HHHHHHHH    L   H   LLLLLLLL   INCREMENT TO (00)
  X   H      X  X    XXXXXXXX    X   X   ZZZZZZZZ   TEST HI-Z
-------------------------------------------------------------------------------
```

DESCRIPTION

THIS IS AN 8-BIT SYNCHRONOUS COUNTER WITH PARALLEL LOAD, CLEAR, AND HOLD CAPABILITY. THE LOAD OPERATION LOADS THE INPUTS (D7-D0) INTO THE OUTPUT REGISTER (Q7-Q0). THE CLEAR OPERATION RESETS THE OUTPUT REGISTER TO ALL LOWS. THE HOLD OPERATION HOLDS THE PREVIOUS VALUE REGARDLESS OF CLOCK TRANSITIONS. THE INCREMENT OPERATION ADDS ONE TO THE OUTPUT REGISTER WHEN THE CARRY-IN IS TRUE (/CI=L), OTHERWISE THE OPERATION IS A HOLD. THE CARRY-OUT (/CO) IS TRUE (/CO=L) WHEN THE OUTPUT REGISTER (Q7-Q0) IS ALL HIGHS, OTHERWISE FALSE (/CO=H).

THESE OPERATIONS ARE EXERCISED IN THE FUNCTION TABLE AND SUMMARIZED IN THE OPERATIONS TABLE:

/OC	CLK	I1	I0	/CI	D7-D0	Q7-Q0	OPERATION
H	X	X	X	X	X	Z	HI-Z
L	C	L	L	X	X	L	CLEAR
L	C	L	H	X	X	Q	HOLD
L	C	H	L	X	D	D	LOAD
L	C	H	H	H	X	Q	HOLD
L	C	H	H	L	X	Q PLUS 1	INCREMENT

TWO OR MORE OCTAL COUNTERS MAY BE CASCADED TO PROVIDE LARGER COUNTERS. THE OPERATION CODES WERE CHOSEN SUCH THAT WHEN I1 IS HIGH, I0 MAY BE USED TO SELECT BETWEEN LOAD AND INCREMENT AS IN A PROGRAM COUNTER (JUMP/INCREMENT). ALSO, CARRY-OUT (/CO) AND CARRY-IN (/CI) ARE LOCATED ON PINS 14 AND 23 RESPECTIVELY, WHICH PROVIDES FOR CONVENIENT INTERCONNECTIONS WHEN TWO OR MORE OCTAL COUNTERS ARE CASCADED TO IMPLEMENT LARGER COUNTERS.

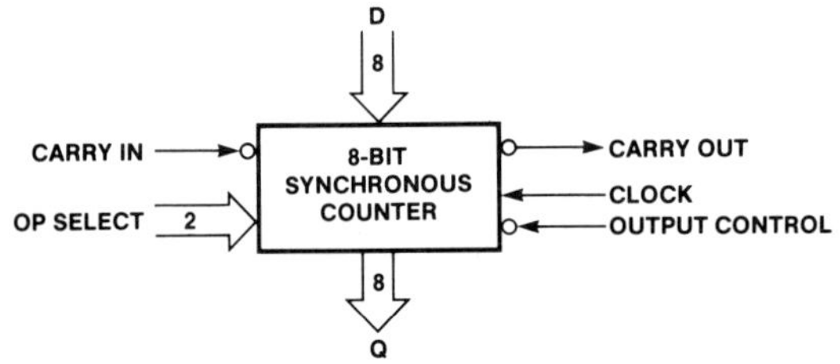

```
OCTAL COUNTER

 1 C0100000001X0HLLLLLLLHX1
 2 C1XXXXXXXX1X0HLLLLLLHL01
 3 C0110000001X0HLLLLLLHHX1
 4 C1XXXXXXXX1X0HLLLLLHLL01
 5 C0111000001X0HLLLLLHHHX1
 6 C1XXXXXXXX1X0HLLLLHLLL01
 7 C0111100001X0HLLLLHHHHX1
 8 C1XXXXXXXX1X0HLLLHLLLL01
 9 C0111110001X0HLLLHHHHHX1
10 C1XXXXXXXX1X0HLLHLLLLL01
11 C0111111001X0HLLHHHHHHX1
12 C1XXXXXXXX1X0HLHLLLLLL01
13 C0111111101X0HLHHHHHHHX1
14 C1XXXXXXXX1X0HHLLLLLLL01
15 C0111111111X0LHHHHHHHH01
16 C1XXXXXXXX1X0HLLLLLLLL01
17 C0111111111X0LHHHHHHHH01
18 C0011111111X0HHHHHHHHLX1
19 C0101111111X0HHHHHHHLHX1
20 C0110111111X0HHHHHHLHHX1
21 C0111011111X0HHHHHLHHHX1
22 C0111101111X0HHHHLHHHHX1
23 C0111110111X0HHHLHHHHHX1
24 C0111111011X0HHLHHHHHHX1
25 C0111111101X0HLHHHHHHHX1
26 C0111111111X0LHHHHHHHH01
27 C0XXXXXXXX0X0HLLLLLLLLX1
28 C1XXXXXXXX1X0HLLLLLLLH01
29 C1XXXXXXXX1X0HLLLLLLHL01
30 C1XXXXXXXX1X0HLLLLLLHH01
31 C1XXXXXXXX1X0HLLLLLHLL01
32 C1XXXXXXXX1X0HLLLLLHLH01
33 C1XXXXXXXX1X0HLLLLLHHL01
34 C1XXXXXXXX1X0HLLLLLHHH01
35 C1XXXXXXXX1X0HLLLLHLLL01
36 C1XXXXXXXX1X0HLLLLHLLH01
37 C1XXXXXXXX1X0HLLLLHLHL01
38 C1XXXXXXXX1X0HLLLLHLHH01
39 C1XXXXXXXX1X0HLLLLHHLL01
40 C0011111111X0HHHHHHHHLX1
41 C1XXXXXXXX1X0LHHHHHHHH01
42 C1XXXXXXXX1X0HHHHHHHHH11
43 C1000000000X0LHHHHHHHH01
44 C1111111111X0HLLLLLLLL01
45 XXXXXXXXXXXX1XZZZZZZZZX1

PASS SIMULATION
```

```
OCTAL COUNTER

                11 1111 1111 2222 2222 2233 3333 3333
   0123 4567 8901 2345 6789 0123 4567 8901 2345 6789


 8 -X-- ---- ---- ---- ---- ---- ---- ---- ---- -X-- /I1*/I0
 9 X--- ---X ---- ---- ---- ---- ---- ---- ---- ---- I0*/Q0
10 -X-- -X-- ---- ---- ---- ---- ---- ---- ---- X--- I1*/I0*/D0
11 X--X ---- ---- ---- ---- ---- ---- ---- ---- X--- I1*I0*CI

16 -X-- ---- ---- ---- ---- ---- ---- ---- ---- -X-- /I1*/I0
17 X--- ---- ---X ---- ---- ---- ---- ---- ---- ---- I0*/Q1
18 -X-- ---- -X-- ---- ---- ---- ---- ---- ---- X--- I1*/I0*/D1
19 X--X --X- ---- ---- ---- ---- ---- ---- ---- X--- I1*I0*CI*Q0

24 -X-- ---- ---- ---- ---- ---- ---- ---- ---- -X-- /I1*/I0
25 X--- ---- ---- ---X ---- ---- ---- ---- ---- ---- I0*/Q2
26 -X-- ---- ---- -X-- ---- ---- ---- ---- ---- X--- I1*/I0*/D2
27 X--X --X- --X- ---- ---- ---- ---- ---- ---- X--- I1*I0*CI*Q0*Q1

32 -X-- ---- ---- ---- ---- ---- ---- ---- ---- -X-- /I1*/I0
33 X--- ---- ---- ---- ---X ---- ---- ---- ---- ---- I0*/Q3
34 -X-- ---- ---- ---- -X-- ---- ---- ---- ---- X--- I1*/I0*/D3
35 X--X --X- --X- --X- ---- ---- ---- ---- ---- X--- I1*I0*CI*Q0*Q1*Q2

40 -X-- ---- ---- ---- ---- ---- ---- ---- ---- -X-- /I1*/I0
41 X--- ---- ---- ---- ---- ---X ---- ---- ---- ---- I0*/Q4
42 -X-- ---- ---- ---- ---- -X-- ---- ---- ---- X--- I1*/I0*/D4
43 X--X --X- --X- --X- --X- ---- ---- ---- ---- X--- I1*I0*CI*Q0*Q1*Q2*Q3

48 -X-- ---- ---- ---- ---- ---- ---- ---- ---- -X-- /I1*/I0
49 X--- ---- ---- ---- ---- ---- ---X ---- ---- ---- I0*/Q5
50 -X-- ---- ---- ---- ---- ---- -X-- ---- ---- X--- I1*/I0*/D5
51 X--X --X- --X- --X- --X- --X- ---- ---- ---- X--- I1*I0*CI*Q0*Q1*Q2*Q3*Q4

56 -X-- ---- ---- ---- ---- ---- ---- ---- ---- -X-- /I1*/I0
57 X--- ---- ---- ---- ---- ---- ---- ---X ---- ---- I0*/Q6
58 -X-- ---- ---- ---- ---- ---- ---- -X-- ---- X--- I1*/I0*/D6
59 X--X --X- --X- --X- --X- --X- --X- ---- ---- X--- I1*I0*CI*Q0*Q1*Q2*Q3*Q4-

64 -X-- ---- ---- ---- ---- ---- ---- ---- ---- -X-- /I1*/I0
65 X--- ---- ---- ---- ---- ---- ---- ---- ---X ---- I0*/Q7
66 -X-- ---- ---- ---- ---- ---- ---- ---- -X-- X--- I1*/I0*/D7
67 X--X --X- --X- --X- --X- --X- --X- --X- ---- X--- I1*I0*CI*Q0*Q1*Q2*Q3*Q4-

72 ---- ---- ---- ---- ---- ---- ---- ---- ---- ----
73 ---X --X- --X- --X- --X- --X- --X- --X- --X- ---- CI*Q0*Q1*Q2*Q3*Q4*Q5*Q6-

LEGEND:  X : FUSE NOT BLOWN (L,N,0)   - : FUSE BLOWN   (H,P,1)

NUMBER OF FUSES BLOW = 1243
```

Octal Counter

Logic Diagram PAL20X8

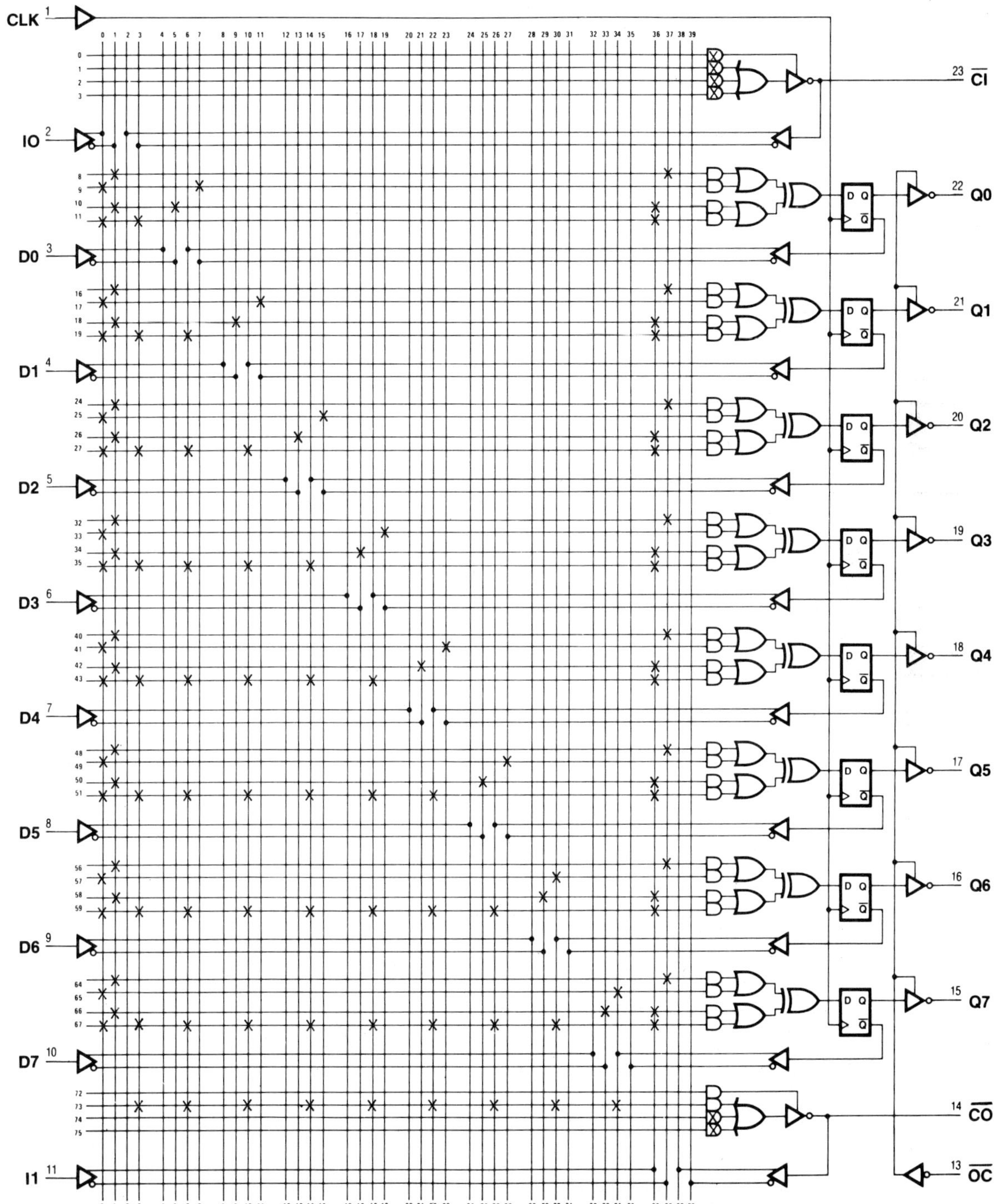

Application

16-Bit Counter

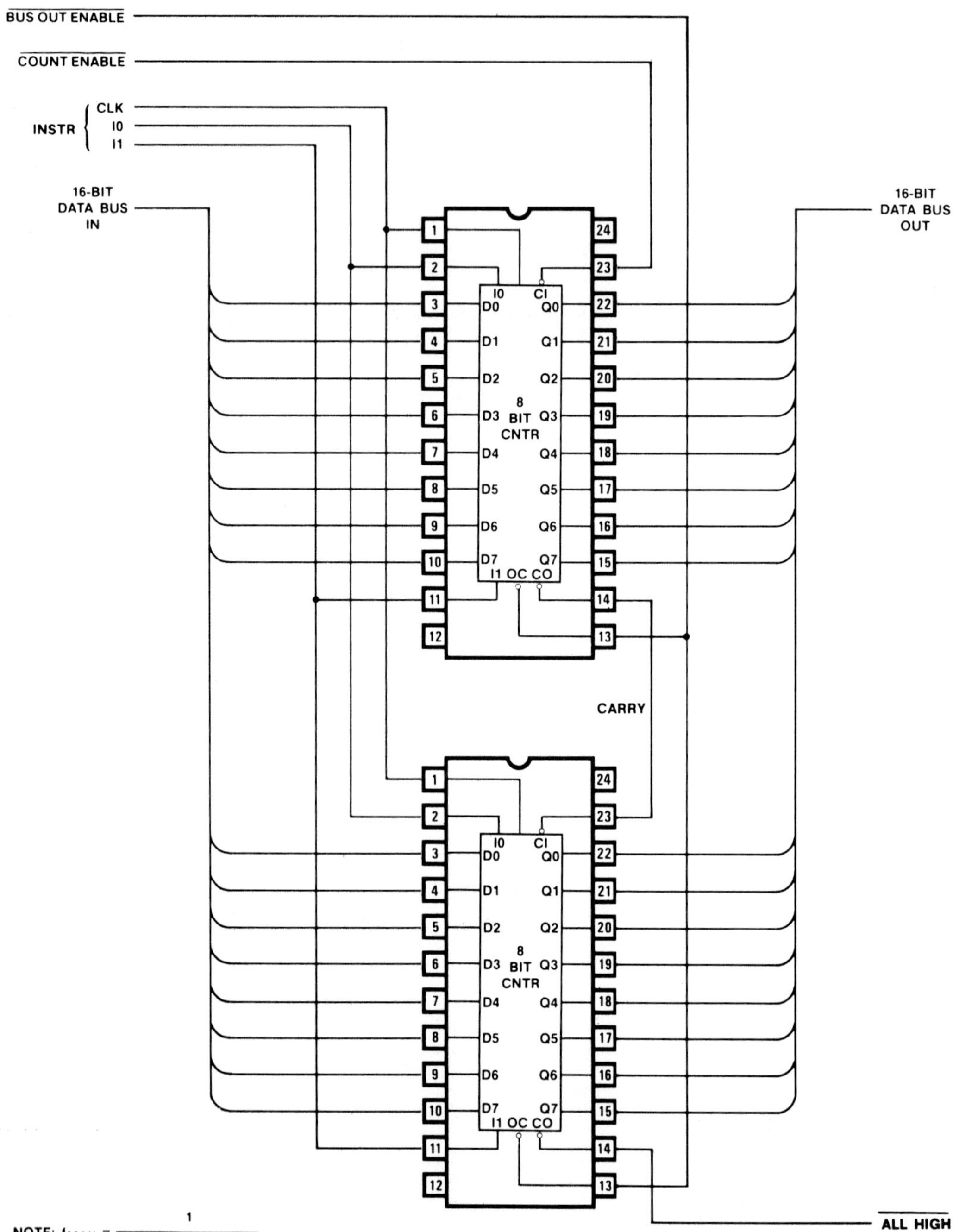

NOTE: $f_{MAX} = \frac{1}{t_{PD\ CLK\ TO\ CO} + t_{SU}}$

Octal Up/Down Counter

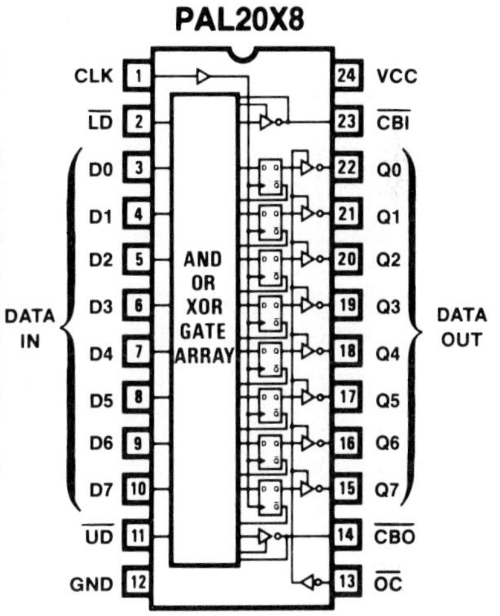

```
PAL20X8                                     PAL DESIGN SPECIFICATION
P8005                                         VINCENT COLI 07/24/81
OCTAL UP/DOWN COUNTER
MMI SUNNYVALE, CALIFORNIA
CLK /LD  D0 D1 D2 D3 D4 D5 D6 D7 /UD  GND
/OC /CBO Q7 Q6 Q5 Q4 Q3 Q2 Q1 Q0 /CBI VCC


/Q0 :=  /LD*/Q0                                          ;HOLD Q0
     +   LD*/D0                                          ;LOAD D0 (LSB)
    :+: /LD* UD* CBI                                     ;INCREMENT
     +  /LD*/UD* CBI                                     ;DECREMENT

/Q1 :=  /LD*/Q1                                          ;HOLD Q1
     +   LD*/D1                                          ;LOAD D1
    :+: /LD* UD* CBI* Q0                                 ;INCREMENT
     +  /LD*/UD* CBI*/Q0                                 ;DECREMENT

/Q2 :=  /LD*/Q2                                          ;HOLD Q2
     +   LD*/D2                                          ;LOAD D2
    :+: /LD* UD* CBI* Q0* Q1                             ;INCREMENT
     +  /LD*/UD* CBI*/Q0*/Q1                             ;DECREMENT

/Q3 :=  /LD*/Q3                                          ;HOLD Q3
     +   LD*/D3                                          ;LOAD D3
    :+: /LD* UD* CBI* Q0* Q1* Q2                         ;INCREMENT
     +  /LD*/UD* CBI*/Q0*/Q1*/Q2                         ;DECREMENT

/Q4 :=  /LD*/Q4                                          ;HOLD Q4
     +   LD*/D4                                          ;LOAD D4
    :+: /LD* UD* CBI* Q0* Q1* Q2* Q3                     ;INCREMENT
     +  /LD*/UD* CBI*/Q0*/Q1*/Q2*/Q3                     ;DECREMENT

/Q5 :=  /LD*/Q5                                          ;HOLD Q5
     +   LD*/D5                                          ;LOAD D5
    :+: /LD* UD* CBI* Q0* Q1* Q2* Q3* Q4                 ;INCREMENT
     +  /LD*/UD* CBI*/Q0*/Q1*/Q2*/Q3*/Q4                 ;DECREMENT

/Q6 :=  /LD*/Q6                                          ;HOLD Q6
     +   LD*/D6                                          ;LOAD D6
    :+: /LD* UD* CBI* Q0* Q1* Q2* Q3* Q4* Q5             ;INCREMENT
     +  /LD*/UD* CBI*/Q0*/Q1*/Q2*/Q3*/Q4*/Q5             ;DECREMENT

/Q7 :=  /LD*/Q7                                          ;HOLD Q7
     +   LD*/D7                                          ;LOAD D7 (MSB)
    :+: /LD* UD* CBI* Q0* Q1* Q2* Q3* Q4* Q5* Q6         ;INCREMENT
     +  /LD*/UD* CBI*/Q0*/Q1*/Q2*/Q3*/Q4*/Q5*/Q6         ;DECREMENT

IF(VCC) CBO =  UD* CBI* Q0* Q1* Q2* Q3* Q4* Q5* Q6* Q7 ;CARRY OUT
             + /UD* CBI*/Q0*/Q1*/Q2*/Q3*/Q4*/Q5*/Q6*/Q7 ;BORROW OUT
```

```
FUNCTION TABLE

CLK /OC /LD /UD D7 D6 D5 D4 D3 D2 D1 D0 /CBI /CBO Q7 Q6 Q5 Q4 Q3 Q2 Q1 Q0

;                    -INPUTS-             OUTPUTS
;----CONTROL----   DDDDDDDD  CARR/BORR   QQQQQQQQ     COMMENTS
;CLK /OC /LD /UD   76543210  /CBI /CBO   76543210    (HEX VALUES)
-------------------------------------------------------------------------------
  C   L   L   X    LLLLLLLH    X    X    LLLLLLLH    LOAD (01)
  C   L   H   L    XXXXXXXX    L    H    LLLLLLHL    INCREMENT
  C   L   H   H    XXXXXXXX    L    H    LLLLLLLH    DECREMENT
  C   L   L   X    LLLLLLHH    X    X    LLLLLLHH    LOAD (03)
  C   L   H   L    XXXXXXXX    L    H    LLLLLHLL    INCREMENT
  C   L   H   H    XXXXXXXX    L    H    LLLLLLHH    DECREMENT
  C   L   L   X    LLLLLHHH    X    X    LLLLLHHH    LOAD (07)
  C   L   H   L    XXXXXXXX    L    H    LLLLHLLL    INCREMENT
  C   L   H   H    XXXXXXXX    L    H    LLLLLHHH    DECREMENT
  C   L   L   X    LLLLHHHH    X    X    LLLLHHHH    LOAD (0F)
  C   L   H   L    XXXXXXXX    L    H    LLLHLLLL    INCREMENT
  C   L   H   H    XXXXXXXX    L    H    LLLLHHHH    DECREMENT
  C   L   L   X    LLLHHHHH    X    X    LLLHHHHH    LOAD (1F)
  C   L   H   L    XXXXXXXX    L    H    LLHLLLLL    INCREMENT
  C   L   H   H    XXXXXXXX    L    H    LLLHHHHH    DECREMENT
  C   L   L   X    LLHHHHHH    X    X    LLHHHHHH    LOAD (3F)
  C   L   H   L    XXXXXXXX    L    H    LHLLLLLL    INCREMENT
  C   L   H   H    XXXXXXXX    L    H    LLHHHHHH    DECREMENT
  C   L   L   X    LHHHHHHH    X    X    LHHHHHHH    LOAD (7F)
  C   L   H   L    XXXXXXXX    L    H    HLLLLLLL    INCREMENT
  C   L   H   H    XXXXXXXX    L    H    LHHHHHHH    DECREMENT
  C   L   L   X    HHHHHHHH    X    X    HHHHHHHH    LOAD (FF)
  C   L   L   X    LHHHHHHH    X    X    LHHHHHHH    LOAD (7F)
  C   L   L   X    HLHHHHHH    X    X    HLHHHHHH    LOAD (BF)
  C   L   L   X    HHLHHHHH    X    X    HHLHHHHH    LOAD (DF)
  C   L   L   X    HHHLHHHH    X    X    HHHLHHHH    LOAD (EF)
  C   L   L   X    HHHHLHHH    X    X    HHHHLHHH    LOAD (F7)
  C   L   L   X    HHHHHLHH    X    X    HHHHHLHH    LOAD (FB)
  C   L   L   X    HHHHHHLH    X    X    HHHHHHLH    LOAD (FD)
  C   L   L   X    HHHHHHHL    X    X    HHHHHHHL    LOAD (FE)
  C   L   H   L    XXXXXXXX    L    L    HHHHHHHH    INCREMENT TO (FF)  (/CBO=L)
  C   L   H   L    XXXXXXXX    L    H    LLLLLLLL    INCREMENT TO (00)  (ROLL OVER)
  C   L   H   L    XXXXXXXX    L    H    LLLLLLLH    INCREMENT TO (01)
  C   L   H   L    XXXXXXXX    L    H    LLLLLLHL    INCREMENT TO (02)
  C   L   H   L    XXXXXXXX    H    H    LLLLLLHL    HOLD
  C   L   H   L    XXXXXXXX    L    H    LLLLLLHH    INCREMENT TO (03)
  C   L   H   H    XXXXXXXX    L    H    LLLLLLHL    DECREMENT TO (02)
  C   L   H   H    XXXXXXXX    L    H    LLLLLLLH    DECREMENT TO (01)
  C   L   H   H    XXXXXXXX    L    L    LLLLLLLL    DECREMENT TO (00)  (/CBO=L)
  C   L   H   H    XXXXXXXX    L    H    HHHHHHHH    DECREMENT TO (FF) (ROLL UNDER)
  C   L   H   H    XXXXXXXX    L    H    HHHHHHHL    DECREMENT TO (FE)
  C   L   H   H    XXXXXXXX    L    H    HHHHHHLH    DECREMENT TO (FD)
  C   L   H   H    XXXXXXXX    H    H    HHHHHHLH    HOLD
  C   L   H   H    XXXXXXXX    L    H    HHHHHHLL    DECREMENT TO (FC)
  X   H   X   X    XXXXXXXX    X    X    ZZZZZZZZ    TEST HI-Z
-------------------------------------------------------------------------------
```

DESCRIPTION

THIS PAL IS AN 8-BIT SYNCHRONOUS UP/DOWN COUNTER WITH PARALLEL LOAD AND HOLD CAPABILITY. THREE FUNCTION SELECT INPUTS (/LD,/UD,/CBI) PROVIDE ONE OF FOUR OPERATIONS WHICH OCCUR SYNCHRONOUSLY ON THE RISING EDGE OF THE CLOCK (CLK). THE LOAD OPERATION LOADS THE INPUTS (D7-D0) INTO THE OUTPUT REGISTERS (Q7-Q0). THE HOLD OPERATION HOLDS THE PREVIOUS VALUE REGARDLESS OF CLOCK TRANSITIONS. THE INCREMENT OPERATION ADDS ONE TO THE OUTPUT REGISTER WHEN CARRY-IN INPUT IS TRUE (/CBI=L), OTHERWISE THE OPERATION IS A HOLD. THE CARRY-OUT (/CBO) IS TRUE (/CBO=L) WHEN THE OUTPUT REGISTER (Q7-Q0) IS ALL HIGHS, OTHERWISE FALSE (/CBO=H). THE DECREMENT OPERATION SUBTRACTS ONE FROM THE OUTPUT REGISTER WHEN THE BORROW-IN INPUT IS TRUE (/CBI=L), OTHERWISE THE OPERATION IS A HOLD. THE BORROW-OUT (/CBO) IS TRUE (/CBO=L) WHEN THE OUTPUT REGISTER (Q7-Q0) IS ALL LOWS, OTHERWISE FALSE (/CBO=H).

THESE OPERATIONS ARE EXERCISED IN THE FUNCTION TABLE AND SUMMARIZED IN THE OPERATIONS TABLE:

/OC	CLK	/LD	/UD	/CBI	D7-D0	Q7-Q0	OPERATION
H	X	X	X	X	X	Z	HI-Z
L	C	L	X	X	D	L	LOAD
L	C	H	L	H	X	Q	HOLD
L	C	H	L	L	X	Q PLUS 1	INCREMENT
L	C	H	H	H	X	Q	HOLD
L	C	H	H	L	X	Q MINUS 1	DECREMENT

THIS OCTAL COUNTER IS IMPLEMENTED WITH A SINGLE PAL20X8. CARRY/BORROW-OUT (/CBO) AND CARRY/BORROW-IN (/CBI) ARE LOCATED ON PINS 14 AND 23 RESPECTIVELY, WHICH PROVIDES FOR CONVENIENT INTERCONNECTIONS WHEN TWO OR MORE OCTAL UP/DOWN COUNTERS ARE CASCADED TO IMPLEMENT LARGER COUNTERS.

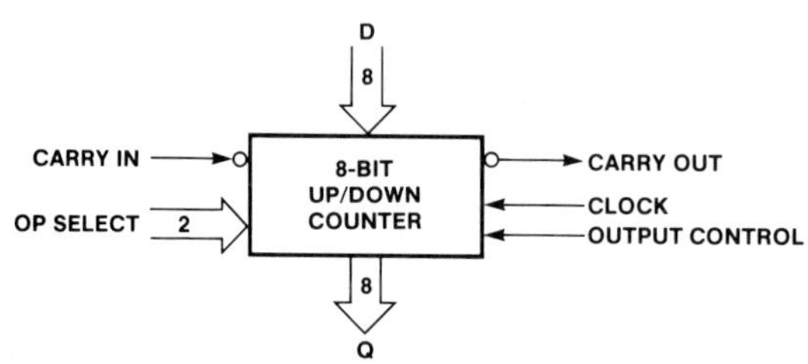

```
OCTAL UP/DOWN COUNTER

 1 C010000000XX0XLLLLLLLHX1
 2 C1XXXXXXXX0X0HLLLLLLHL01
 3 C1XXXXXXXX1X0HLLLLLLLH01
 4 C011000000XX0XLLLLLLHHX1
 5 C1XXXXXXXX0X0HLLLLLHLL01
 6 C1XXXXXXXX1X0HLLLLLLHH01
 7 C011100000XX0XLLLLLHHHX1
 8 C1XXXXXXXX0X0HLLLLHLLL01
 9 C1XXXXXXXX1X0HLLLLLHHH01
10 C011110000XX0XLLLLHHHHX1
11 C1XXXXXXXX0X0HLLLHLLLL01
12 C1XXXXXXXX1X0HLLLLHHHH01
13 C011111000XX0XLLLHHHHHX1
14 C1XXXXXXXX0X0HLLHLLLLL01
15 C1XXXXXXXX1X0HLLLHHHHH01
16 C011111100XX0XLLHHHHHHX1
17 C1XXXXXXXX0X0HLHLLLLLL01
18 C1XXXXXXXX1X0HLLHHHHHH01
19 C011111110XX0XLHHHHHHHX1
20 C1XXXXXXXX0X0HHLLLLLLL01
21 C1XXXXXXXX1X0HLHHHHHHH01
22 C011111111XX0XHHHHHHHHX1
23 C011111110XX0XLHHHHHHHX1
24 C011111101XX0XHLHHHHHHX1
25 C011111011XX0XHHLHHHHHX1
26 C011110111XX0XHHHLHHHHX1
27 C011101111XX0XHHHHLHHHX1
28 C011011111XX0XHHHHHLHHX1
29 C010111111XX0XHHHHHHLHX1
30 C001111111XX0XHHHHHHHLX1
31 C1XXXXXXXX0X0LHHHHHHHH01
32 C1XXXXXXXX0X0HLLLLLLLL01
33 C1XXXXXXXX0X0HLLLLLLLH01
34 C1XXXXXXXX0X0HLLLLLLHL01
35 C1XXXXXXXX0X0HLLLLLLHL11
36 C1XXXXXXXX0X0HLLLLLLHH01
37 C1XXXXXXXX1X0HLLLLLLHL01
38 C1XXXXXXXX1X0HLLLLLLLH01
39 C1XXXXXXXX1X0LLLLLLLLL01
40 C1XXXXXXXX1X0HHHHHHHHH01
41 C1XXXXXXXX1X0HHHHHHHHL01
42 C1XXXXXXXX1X0HHHHHHHLH01
43 C1XXXXXXXX1X0HHHHHHHLH11
44 C1XXXXXXXX1X0HHHHHHHLL01
45 XXXXXXXXXXXX1XZZZZZZZZX1

PASS SIMULATION
```

```
OCTAL UP/DOWN COUNTER

               11 1111 1111 2222 2222 2233 3333 3333
   0123 4567 8901 2345 6789 0123 4567 8901 2345 6789


 8 X--- ---X ---- ---- ---- ---- ---- ---- ---- ---- /LD*/Q0
 9 -X-- -X-- ---- ---- ---- ---- ---- ---- ---- ---- LD*/D0
10 X--X ---- ---- ---- ---- ---- ---- ---- ---- -X-- /LD*UD*CBI
11 X--X ---- ---- ---- ---- ---- ---- ---- ---- X--- /LD*/UD*CBI

16 X--- ---- ---X ---- ---- ---- ---- ---- ---- ---- /LD*/Q1
17 -X-- ---- -X-- ---- ---- ---- ---- ---- ---- ---- LD*/D1
18 X--X --X- ---- ---- ---- ---- ---- ---- ---- -X-- /LD*UD*CBI*Q0
19 X--X ---X ---- ---- ---- ---- ---- ---- ---- X--- /LD*/UD*CBI*/Q0

24 X--- ---- ---- ---X ---- ---- ---- ---- ---- ---- /LD*/Q2
25 -X-- ---- ---- -X-- ---- ---- ---- ---- ---- ---- LD*/D2
26 X--X --X- --X- ---- ---- ---- ---- ---- ---- -X-- /LD*UD*CBI*Q0*Q1
27 X--X ---X ---X ---- ---- ---- ---- ---- ---- X--- /LD*/UD*CBI*/Q0*/Q1

32 X--- ---- ---- ---- ---X ---- ---- ---- ---- ---- /LD*/Q3
33 -X-- ---- ---- ---- -X-- ---- ---- ---- ---- ---- LD*/D3
34 X--X --X- --X- --X- ---- ---- ---- ---- ---- -X-- /LD*UD*CBI*Q0*Q1*Q2
35 X--X ---X ---X ---X ---- ---- ---- ---- ---- X--- /LD*/UD*CBI*/Q0*/Q1*/Q2

40 X--- ---- ---- ---- ---- ---X ---- ---- ---- ---- /LD*/Q4
41 -X-- ---- ---- ---- ---- -X-- ---- ---- ---- ---- LD*/D4
42 X--X --X- --X- --X- --X- ---- ---- ---- ---- -X-- /LD*UD*CBI*Q0*Q1*Q2*Q3
43 X--X ---X ---X ---X ---X ---- ---- ---- ---- X--- /LD*/UD*CBI*/Q0*/Q1*/Q2-

48 X--- ---- ---- ---- ---- ---- ---X ---- ---- ---- /LD*/Q5
49 -X-- ---- ---- ---- ---- ---- -X-- ---- ---- ---- LD*/D5
50 X--X --X- --X- --X- --X- --X- ---- ---- ---- -X-- /LD*UD*CBI*Q0*Q1*Q2*Q3*-
51 X--X ---X ---X ---X ---X ---X ---- ---- ---- X--- /LD*/UD*CBI*/Q0*/Q1*/Q2-

56 X--- ---- ---- ---- ---- ---- ---- ---X ---- ---- /LD*/Q6
57 -X-- ---- ---- ---- ---- ---- ---- -X-- ---- ---- LD*/D6
58 X--X --X- --X- --X- --X- --X- --X- ---- ---- -X-- /LD*UD*CBI*Q0*Q1*Q2*Q3*-
59 X--X ---X ---X ---X ---X ---X ---X ---- ---- X--- /LD*/UD*CBI*/Q0*/Q1*/Q2-

64 X--- ---- ---- ---- ---- ---- ---- ---- ---X ---- /LD*/Q7
65 -X-- ---- ---- ---- ---- ---- ---- ---- -X-- ---- LD*/D7
66 X--X --X- --X- --X- --X- --X- --X- --X- ---- -X-- /LD*UD*CBI*Q0*Q1*Q2*Q3*-
67 X--X ---X ---X ---X ---X ---X ---X ---X ---- X--- /LD*/UD*CBI*/Q0*/Q1*/Q2-

72 ---- ---- ---- ---- ---- ---- ---- ---- ---- ----
73 ---X --X- --X- --X- --X- --X- --X- --X- --X- -X-- UD*CBI*Q0*Q1*Q2*Q3*Q4*Q-
74 ---X ---X ---X ---X ---X ---X ---X ---X ---X X--- /UD*CBI*/Q0*/Q1*/Q2*/Q3-


LEGEND:  X : FUSE NOT BLOWN (L,N,0)   - : FUSE BLOWN   (H,P,1)

NUMBER OF FUSES BLOW = 1244
```

Octal Up/Down Counter

Logic Diagram PAL20X8

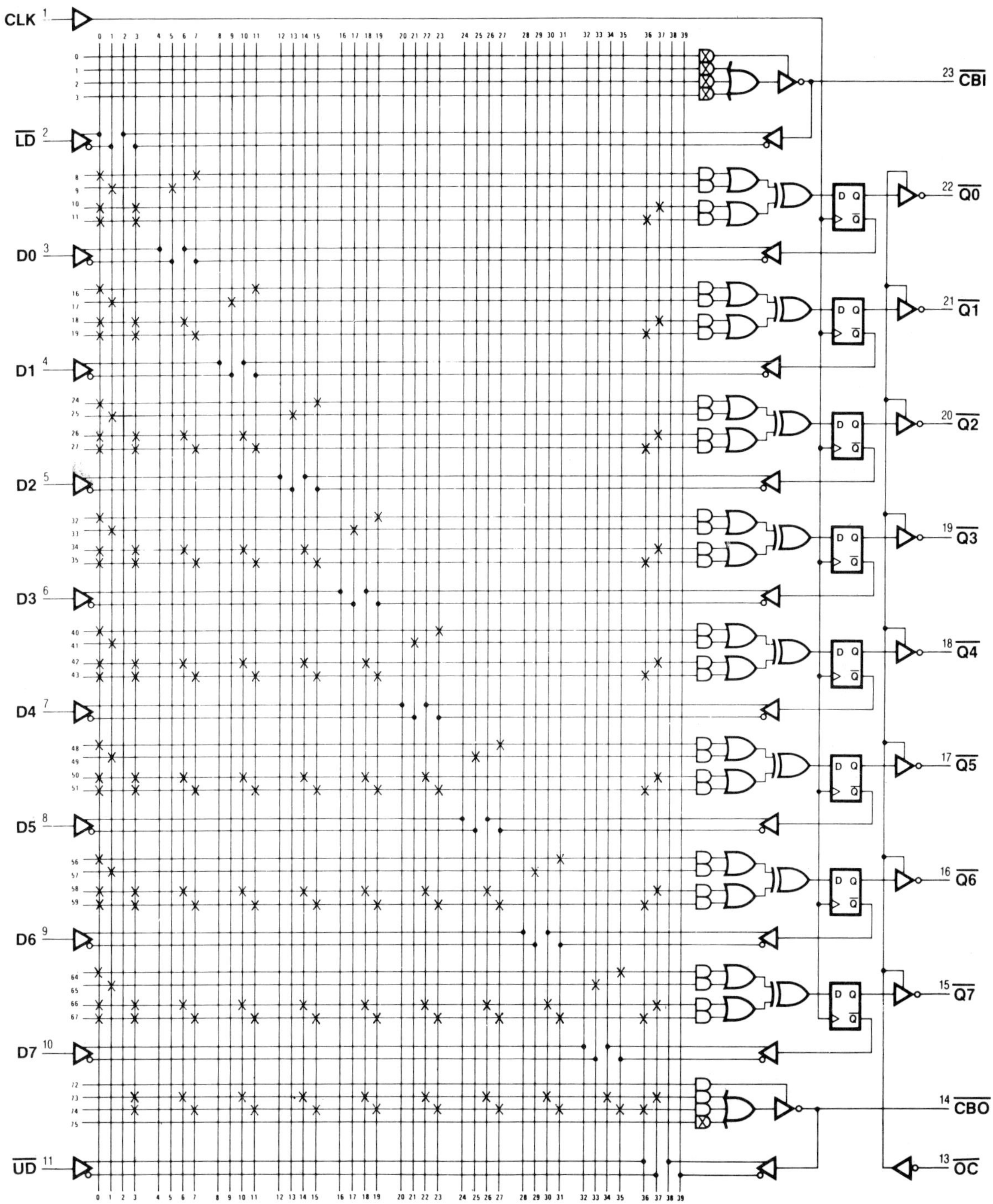

Application

16-Bit Up/Down Counter

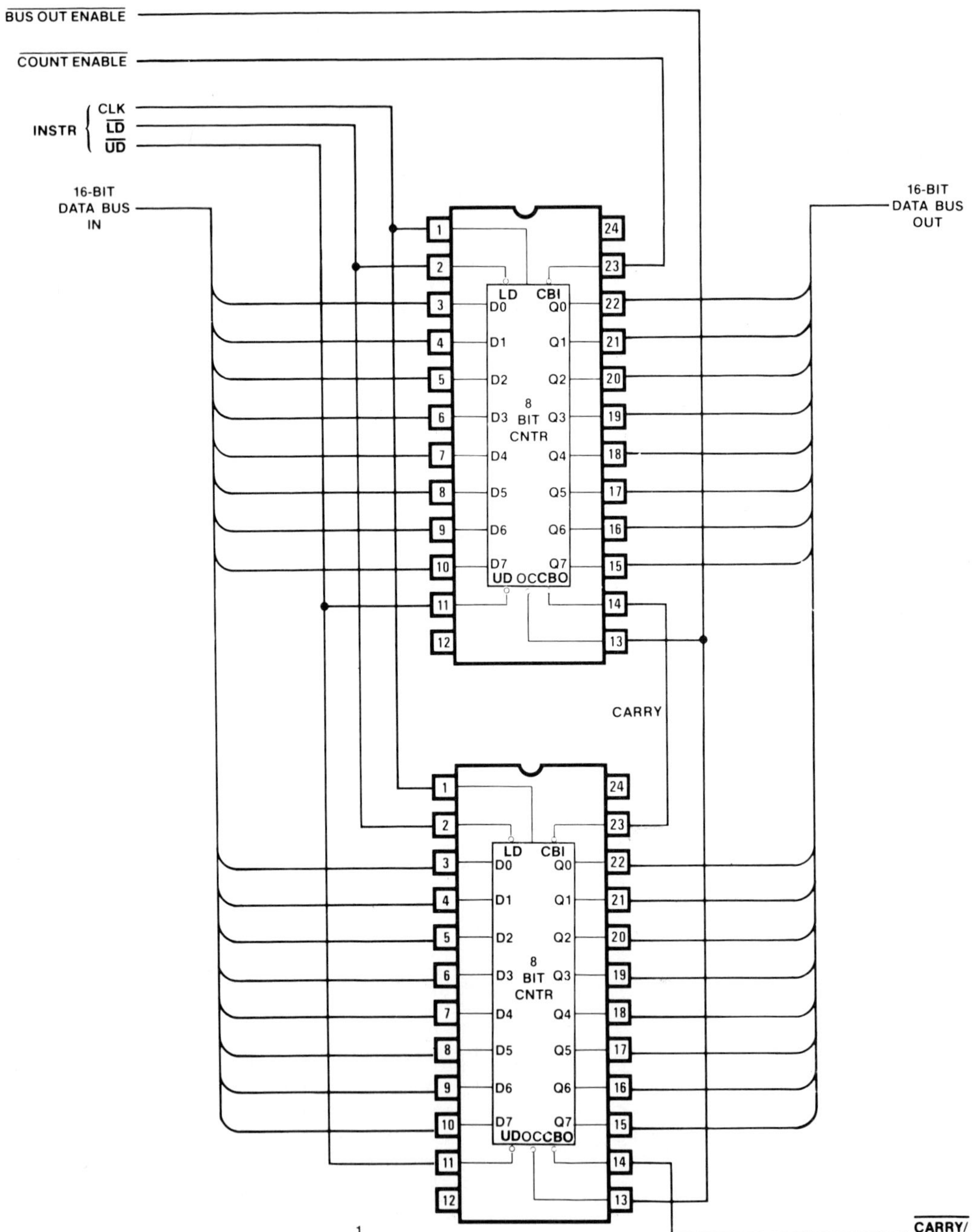

NOTE: $f_{MAX} = \frac{1}{t_{PD\,(CLK\ TO\ CBO)} + t_{SU}}$

10-Bit Counter

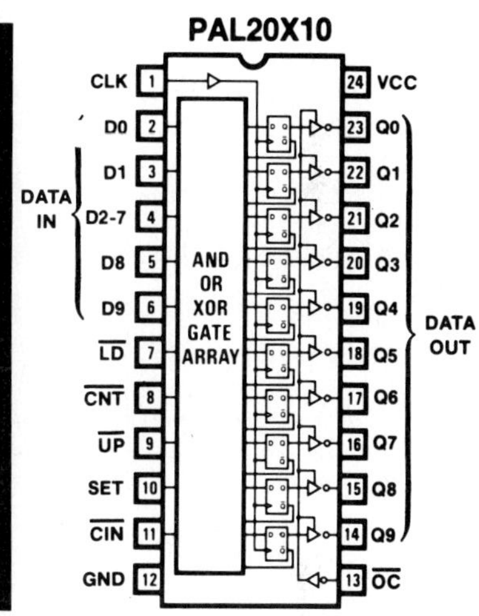

```
PAL20X10                                                    PAL DESIGN SPECIFICATION
74LS491                                                       JOHN BIRKNER 04/01/81
10-BIT COUNTER
MMI SUNNYVALE, CALIFORNIA
CLK D0 D1 D2-7 D8 D9 /LD /CNT /UP SET /CIN GND
/OC Q9 Q8 Q7 Q6 Q5 Q4 Q3 Q2 Q1 Q0 VCC

/Q0 :=  /SET* LD*/D0                                                 ;LOAD D0
     +  /SET*/LD*/Q0                                                 ;HOLD (LSB)
   :+:  /SET*/LD* CNT* CIN* UP                                       ;INCREMENT
     +  /SET*/LD* CNT* CIN*/UP                                       ;DECREMENT

/Q1 :=  /SET* LD*/D1                                                 ;LOAD D1
     +  /SET*/LD*/Q1                                                 ;HOLD
   :+:  /SET*/LD* CNT* CIN* UP* Q0                                   ;INCREMENT
     +  /SET*/LD* CNT* CIN*/UP*/Q0                                   ;DECREMENT

/Q2 :=  /SET* LD*/D2-7                                               ;LOAD D2-7
     +  /SET*/LD*/Q2                                                 ;HOLD
   :+:  /SET*/LD* CNT* CIN* UP* Q0* Q1                               ;INCREMENT
     +  /SET*/LD* CNT* CIN*/UP*/Q0*/Q1                               ;DECREMENT

/Q3 :=  /SET* LD*/D2-7                                               ;LOAD D2-7
     +  /SET*/LD*/Q3                                                 ;HOLD
   :+:  /SET*/LD* CNT* CIN* UP* Q0* Q1* Q2                           ;INCREMENT
     +  /SET*/LD* CNT* CIN*/UP*/Q0*/Q1*/Q2                           ;DECREMENT

/Q4 :=  /SET* LD*/D2-7                                               ;LOAD D2-7
     +  /SET*/LD*/Q4                                                 ;HOLD
   :+:  /SET*/LD* CNT* CIN* UP* Q0* Q1* Q2* Q3                       ;INCREMENT
     +  /SET*/LD* CNT* CIN*/UP*/Q0*/Q1*/Q2*/Q3                       ;DECREMENT

/Q5 :=  /SET* LD*/D2-7                                               ;LOAD D2-7
     +  /SET*/LD*/Q5                                                 ;HOLD
   :+:  /SET*/LD* CNT* CIN* UP* Q0* Q1* Q2* Q3* Q4                   ;INCREMENT
     +  /SET*/LD* CNT* CIN*/UP*/Q0*/Q1*/Q2*/Q3*/Q4                   ;DECREMENT

/Q6 :=  /SET* LD*/D2-7                                               ;LOAD D2-7
     +  /SET*/LD*/Q6                                                 ;HOLD
   :+:  /SET*/LD* CNT* CIN* UP* Q0* Q1* Q2* Q3* Q4* Q5               ;INCREMENT
     +  /SET*/LD* CNT* CIN*/UP*/Q0*/Q1*/Q2*/Q3*/Q4*/Q5               ;DECREMENT

/Q7 :=  /SET* LD*/D2-7                                               ;LOAD D2-7
     +  /SET*/LD*/Q7                                                 ;HOLD
   :+:  /SET*/LD* CNT* CIN* UP* Q0* Q1* Q2* Q3* Q4* Q5* Q6           ;INCREMENT
     +  /SET*/LD* CNT* CIN*/UP*/Q0*/Q1*/Q2*/Q3*/Q4*/Q5*/Q6           ;DECREMENT

/Q8 :=  /SET* LD*/D8                                                 ;LOAD D8
     +  /SET*/LD*/Q8                                                 ;HOLD
   :+:  /SET*/LD* CNT* CIN* UP* Q0* Q1* Q2* Q3* Q4* Q5* Q6* Q7       ;INCREMENT
     +  /SET*/LD* CNT* CIN*/UP*/Q0*/Q1*/Q2*/Q3*/Q4*/Q5*/Q6*/Q7       ;DECREMENT

/Q9 :=  /SET* LD*/D9                                                 ;LOAD D9
     +  /SET*/LD*/Q9                                                 ;HOLD (MSB)
   :+:  /SET*/LD* CNT* CIN* UP* Q0* Q1* Q2* Q3* Q4* Q5* Q6* Q7* Q8   ;INCREMENT
     +  /SET*/LD* CNT* CIN*/UP*/Q0*/Q1*/Q2*/Q3*/Q4*/Q5*/Q6*/Q7*/Q8   ;DECREMENT
```

```
FUNCTION TABLE

CLK /OC SET /LD /CNT /CIN /UP D9 D8 D2-7 D1 D0 Q9 Q8 Q7 Q6 Q5 Q4 Q3 Q2 Q1 Q0

;         / /
;C / S / C C /  -DATA IN-   -DATA OUT-
;L O E L N I U  DD  D  DD   QQQQQQQQQQ
;K C T D T N P  98 2-7 10   9876543210    COMMENT
--------------------------------------------------------------------------------
 C L H X X X X  XX  X  XX   HHHHHHHHHH    SET (SET=H)
 C L L L X X X  LL  L  LL   LLLLLLLLLL    CLEAR (D=L)
 C L L L X X X  HH  H  HH   HHHHHHHHHH    SET (D=H)
 C L L H H X X  LL  L  LL   HHHHHHHHHH    HOLD (/CNT=H)
 C L L L X X X  LL  L  LL   LLLLLLLLLL    CLEAR (D=L)
 C L L H H X X  XX  X  XX   LLLLLLLLLL    HOLD (/CNT=H)
 C L L H L H X  XX  X  XX   LLLLLLLLLL    HOLD (/CIN=H)
 C L L H L L L  XX  X  XX   LLLLLLLLLH    COUNT UP (NOTE 5 CNTRLS LOW NEAR GND)
 C L L H L L L  XX  X  XX   LLLLLLLLHL    COUNT UP
 C L L H L L L  XX  X  XX   LLLLLLLLHH    COUNT UP
 C L L H L L L  XX  X  XX   LLLLLLLHLL    COUNT UP
 C L L H L L H  XX  X  XX   LLLLLLLLHH    COUNT DOWN
 C L L H L L H  XX  X  XX   LLLLLLLLHL    COUNT DOWN
 C L L H L L H  XX  X  XX   LLLLLLLLLH    COUNT DOWN
 C L L H L L H  XX  X  XX   LLLLLLLLLL    COUNT DOWN
 C L L H L L H  XX  X  XX   HHHHHHHHHH    COUNT DOWN (ROLL UNDER)
 C L L H L L H  XX  X  XX   HHHHHHHHHL    COUNT DOWN
 C L L H L L H  XX  X  XX   HHHHHHHHLH    COUNT DOWN
 C L L H L L H  XX  X  XX   HHHHHHHHLL    COUNT DOWN
 C L L H L L H  XX  X  XX   HHHHHHHLHH    COUNT DOWN
 C L L H L L H  XX  X  XX   HHHHHHHLHL    COUNT DOWN
 C L L H L L H  XX  X  XX   HHHHHHHLLH    COUNT DOWN
 C L L H L L H  XX  X  XX   HHHHHHHLLL    COUNT DOWN
 C L L L X X X  LL  L  LL   LLLLLLLLLL    LOAD
 C L L H L L L  XX  X  XX   LLLLLLLLLH    COUNT UP
 C L L H H X X  XX  X  XX   LLLLLLLLLH    HOLD (/CNT=H)
 C L L H L L H  XX  X  XX   LLLLLLLLLL    COUNT DOWN
 C L L L X X X  LL  H  LL   LLHHHHHHLL    LOAD
 C L L H L L L  XX  X  XX   LLHHHHHHLH    COUNT UP
 C L L H H X X  XX  X  XX   LLHHHHHHLH    HOLD (/CNT=H)
 C L L H L L H  XX  X  XX   LLHHHHHHLL    COUNT DOWN
 C L L L X X X  HH  L  HH   HHLLLLLLHH    LOAD
 C L L H L L L  XX  X  XX   HHLLLLLHLL    COUNT UP
 C L L H H X X  XX  X  XX   HHLLLLLHLL    HOLD (/CNT=H)
 C L L H L L H  XX  X  XX   HHLLLLLLHH    COUNT DOWN
 C L L L X X X  LH  L  HL   LHLLLLLLHL    LOAD
 C L L H L L L  XX  X  XX   LHLLLLLLHH    COUNT UP
 C L L H H X X  XX  X  XX   LHLLLLLLHH    HOLD (/CNT=H)
 C L L H L L H  XX  X  XX   LHLLLLLLHL    COUNT DOWN
 C L L L X X X  HL  H  LH   HLHHHHHHLH    LOAD
 C L L H L L L  XX  X  XX   HLHHHHHHHL    COUNT UP
 C L L H H X X  XX  X  XX   HLHHHHHHHL    HOLD (/CNT=H)
 C L L H L L H  XX  X  XX   HLHHHHHHLH    COUNT DOWN
 C L L L X X X  HH  H  HH   HHHHHHHHHH    LOAD
 C L L H L L L  HH  H  HH   LLLLLLLLLL    COUNT UP (ROLL OVER)
 X H X X X X X  XX  X  XX   ZZZZZZZZZZ    TEST HI-Z
--------------------------------------------------------------------------------
```

DESCRIPTION

THE 10-BIT COUNTER CAN COUNT UP, COUNT DOWN, SET, AND LOAD 2 LSB'S (D0,D1), 2 MSB'S (D8,D9) AND 6 MIDDLE BITS (D2-7) HIGH OR LOW AS A GROUP.

SET OVERRIDES LOAD (/LD), COUNT (/CNT), AND HOLD. LOAD OVERRIDES COUNT. COUNT IS CONDITIONAL ON CARRY IN (/CIN), OTHERWISE IT HOLDS.

THESE OPERATIONS ARE EXERCISED IN THE FUNCTION TABLE AND SUMMARIZED IN THE OPERATIONS TABLE:

/OC	CLK	SET	/LD	/CNT	/CIN	/UP	D9-D0	Q9-Q0	OPERATION
H	X	X	X	X	X	X	X	Z	HI-Z
L	C	H	X	X	X	X	X	H	SET ALL HIGH
L	C	L	L	X	X	X	D	D	LOAD D
L	C	L	H	H	X	X	X	Q	HOLD (/CNT=H)
L	C	L	H	L	H	X	X	Q	HOLD (/CIN=H)
L	C	L	H	L	L	L	X	Q PLUS 1	INCREMENT
L	C	L	H	L	L	H	X	Q MINUS 1	DECREMENT

```
10-BIT COUNTER

 1 CXXXXXXXX1XX0HHHHHHHHHH1
 2 C000000XX0XX0LLLLLLLLLL1
 3 C11111 0XX0XX0HHHHHHHHHH1
 4 C000001 1X0XX0HHHHHHHHHH1
 5 C000000XX0XX0LLLLLLLLLL1
 6 CXXXXX11X0XX0LLLLLLLLLL1
 7 CXXXXX10X01X0LLLLLLLLLL1
 8 CXXXXX10000X0LLLLLLLLLH1
 9 CXXXXX10000X0LLLLLLLLHL1
10 CXXXXX10000X0LLLLLLLLHH1
11 CXXXXX10000X0LLLLLLLHLL1
12 CXXXXX10100X0LLLLLLLLHH1
13 CXXXXX10100X0LLLLLLLLHL1
14 CXXXXX10100X0LLLLLLLLLH1
15 CXXXXX10100X0LLLLLLLLLL1
16 CXXXXX10100X0HHHHHHHHHH1
17 CXXXXX10100X0HHHHHHHHHL1
18 CXXXXX10100X0HHHHHHHHLH1
19 CXXXXX10100X0HHHHHHHHLL1
20 CXXXXX10100X0HHHHHHHLHH1
21 CXXXXX10100X0HHHHHHHLHL1
22 CXXXXX10100X0HHHHHHHLLH1
23 CXXXXX10100X0HHHHHHHLLL1
24 C000000XX0XX0LLLLLLLLLL1
25 CXXXXX10000X0LLLLLLLLLH1
26 CXXXXX11X0XX0LLLLLLLLLH1
27 CXXXXX10100X0LLLLLLLLLL1
28 C001000XX0XX0LLHHHHHHLL1
29 CXXXXX10000X0LLHHHHHHLH1
30 CXXXXX11X0XX0LLHHHHHHLH1
31 CXXXXX10100X0LLHHHHHHLL1
32 C110110XX0XX0HHLLLLLLHH1
33 CXXXXX10000X0HHLLLLLHLL1
34 CXXXXX11X0XX0HHLLLLLHLL1
35 CXXXXX10100X0HHLLLLLLHH1
36 C010100XX0XX0LHLLLLLLHL1
37 CXXXXX10000X0LHLLLLLLHH1
38 CXXXXX11X0XX0LHLLLLLLHH1
39 CXXXXX10100X0LHLLLLLLHL1
40 C101010XX0XX0HLHHHHHHLH1
41 CXXXXX10000X0HLHHHHHHHL1
42 CXXXXX11X0XX0HLHHHHHHHL1
43 CXXXXX10100X0HLHHHHHHLH1
44 C111110XX0XX0HHHHHHHHHH1
45 C1111110000X0LLLLLLLLLL1
46 XXXXXXXXXXXX1ZZZZZZZZZZ1

PASS SIMULATION
```

```
10-BIT COUNTER

             11 1111 1111 2222 2222 2233 3333 3333
  0123 4567 8901 2345 6789 0123 4567 8901 2345 6789

 0 -X-- ---- ---- ---- ---- -X-- ---- ---- -X-- ---- /SET*LD*/D0
 1 ---X ---- ---- ---- ---- X--- ---- ---- -X-- ---- /SET*/LD*/Q0
 2 ---- ---- ---- ---- ---- X--- -X-- -X-- -X-- -X-- /SET*/LD*CNT*CIN*UP
 3 ---- ---- ---- ---- ---- X--- -X-- X--- -X-- -X-- /SET*/LD*CNT*CIN*/UP

 8 ---- -X-- ---- ---- ---- -X-- ---- ---- -X-- ---- /SET*LD*/D1
 9 ---- ---X ---- ---- ---- X--- ---- ---- -X-- ---- /SET*/LD*/Q1
10 --X- ---- ---- ---- ---- X--- -X-- -X-- -X-- -X-- /SET*/LD*CNT*CIN*UP*Q0
11 ---X ---- ---- ---- ---- X--- -X-- X--- -X-- -X-- /SET*/LD*CNT*CIN*/UP*/Q0

16 ---- ---- -X-- ---- ---- -X-- ---- ---- -X-- ---- /SET*LD*/D2-7
17 ---- ---- ---X ---- ---- X--- ---- ---- -X-- ---- /SET*/LD*/Q2
18 --X- --X- ---- ---- ---- X--- -X-- -X-- -X-- -X-- /SET*/LD*CNT*CIN*UP*Q0*-
19 ---X ---X ---- ---- ---- X--- -X-- X--- -X-- -X-- /SET*/LD*CNT*CIN*/UP*/Q-

24 ---- ---- -X-- ---- ---- -X-- ---- ---- -X-- ---- /SET*LD*/D2-7
25 ---- ---- ---- ---X ---- X--- ---- ---- -X-- ---- /SET*/LD*/Q3
26 --X- --X- --X- ---- ---- X--- -X-- -X-- -X-- -X-- /SET*/LD*CNT*CIN*UP*Q0*-
27 ---X ---X ---X ---- ---- X--- -X-- X--- -X-- -X-- /SET*/LD*CNT*CIN*/UP*/Q-

32 ---- ---- -X-- ---- ---- -X-- ---- ---- -X-- ---- /SET*LD*/D2-7
33 ---- ---- ---- ---- ---X X--- ---- ---- -X-- ---- /SET*/LD*/Q4
34 --X- --X- --X- --X- ---- X--- -X-- -X-- -X-- -X-- /SET*/LD*CNT*CIN*UP*Q0*-
35 ---X ---X ---X ---X ---- X--- -X-- X--- -X-- -X-- /SET*/LD*CNT*CIN*/UP*/Q-

40 ---- ---- -X-- ---- ---- -X-- ---- ---- -X-- ---- /SET*LD*/D2-7
41 ---- ---- ---- ---- ---- X--X ---- ---- -X-- ---- /SET*/LD*/Q5
42 --X- --X- --X- --X- --X- X--- -X-- -X-- -X-- -X-- /SET*/LD*CNT*CIN*UP*Q0*-
43 ---X ---X ---X ---X ---X X--- -X-- X--- -X-- -X-- /SET*/LD*CNT*CIN*/UP*/Q-

48 ---- ---- -X-- ---- ---- -X-- ---- ---- -X-- ---- /SET*LD*/D2-7
49 ---- ---- ---- ---- ---- X--- ---X ---- -X-- ---- /SET*/LD*/Q6
50 --X- --X- --X- --X- --X- X-X- -X-- -X-- -X-- -X-- /SET*/LD*CNT*CIN*UP*Q0*-
51 ---X ---X ---X ---X ---X X--X -X-- X--- -X-- -X-- /SET*/LD*CNT*CIN*/UP*/Q-

56 ---- ---- -X-- ---- ---- -X-- ---- ---- -X-- ---- /SET*LD*/D2-7
57 ---- ---- ---- ---- ---- X--- ---- ---X -X-- ---- /SET*/LD*/Q7
58 --X- --X- --X- --X- --X- X-X- -XX- -X-- -X-- -X-- /SET*/LD*CNT*CIN*UP*Q0*-
59 ---X ---X ---X ---X ---X X--X -X-X X--- -X-- -X-- /SET*/LD*CNT*CIN*/UP*/Q-

64 ---- ---- ---- -X-- ---- -X-- ---- ---- -X-- ---- /SET*LD*/D8
65 ---- ---- ---- ---- ---- X--- ---- ---- -X-X ---- /SET*/LD*/Q8
66 --X- --X- --X- --X- --X- X-X- -XX- -XX- -X-- -X-- /SET*/LD*CNT*CIN*UP*Q0*-
67 ---X ---X ---X ---X ---X X--X -X-X X--X -X-- -X-- /SET*/LD*CNT*CIN*/UP*/Q-

72 ---- ---- ---- ---- -X-- -X-- ---- ---- -X-- ---- /SET*LD*/D9
73 ---- ---- ---- ---- ---- X--- ---- ---- -X-- ---X /SET*/LD*/Q9
74 --X- --X- --X- --X- --X- X-X- -XX- -XX- -XX- -X-- /SET*/LD*CNT*CIN*UP*Q0*-
75 ---X ---X ---X ---X ---X X--X -X-X X--X -X-X -X-- /SET*/LD*CNT*CIN*/UP*/Q-
LEGEND:  X : FUSE NOT BLOWN (L,N,0)    - : FUSE BLOWN   (H,P,1)

NUMBER OF FUSES BLOW = 1350
```

10-Bit Counter

Logic Diagram PAL20X10

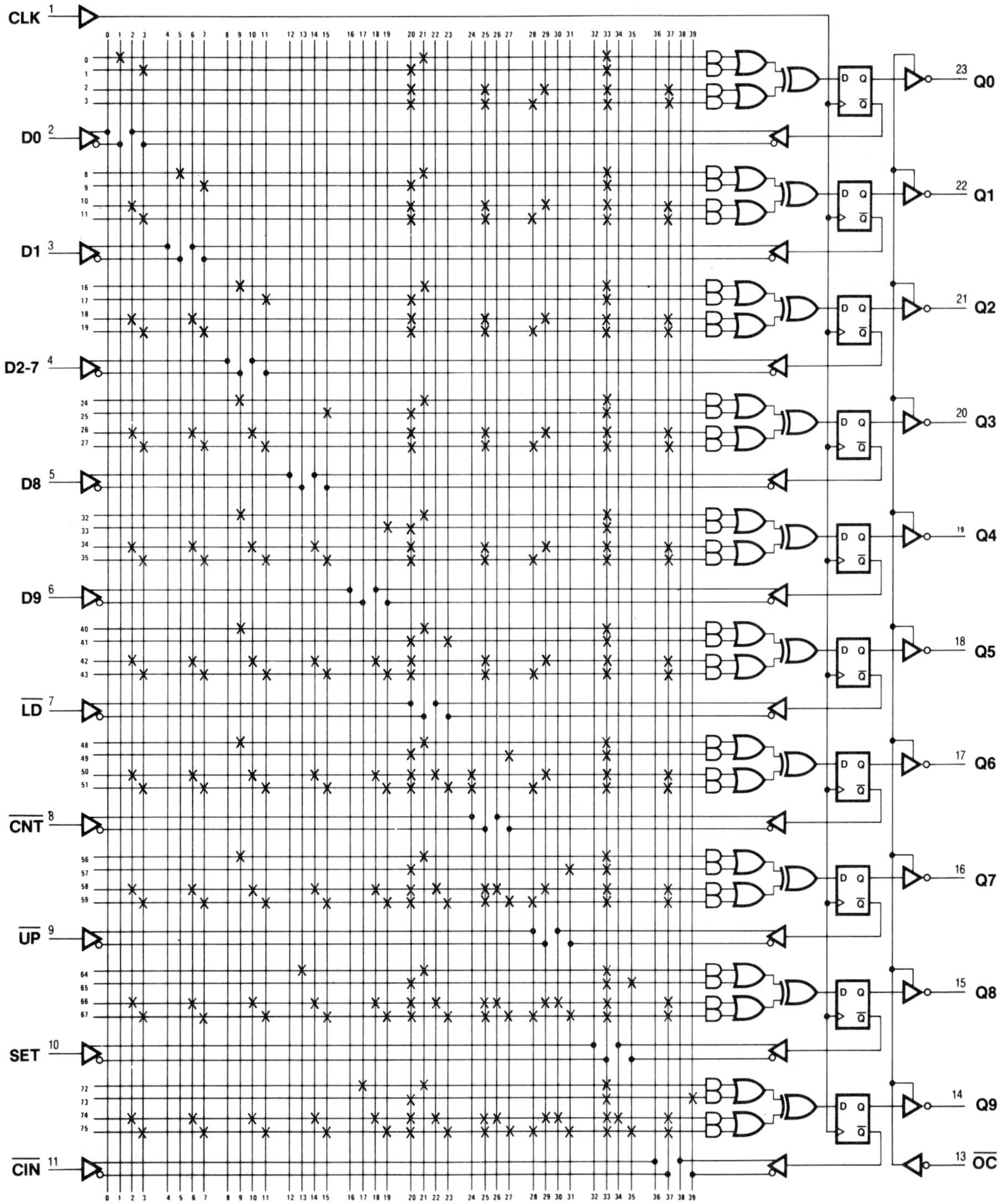

Application

CRT Horizontal Timing and Blanking

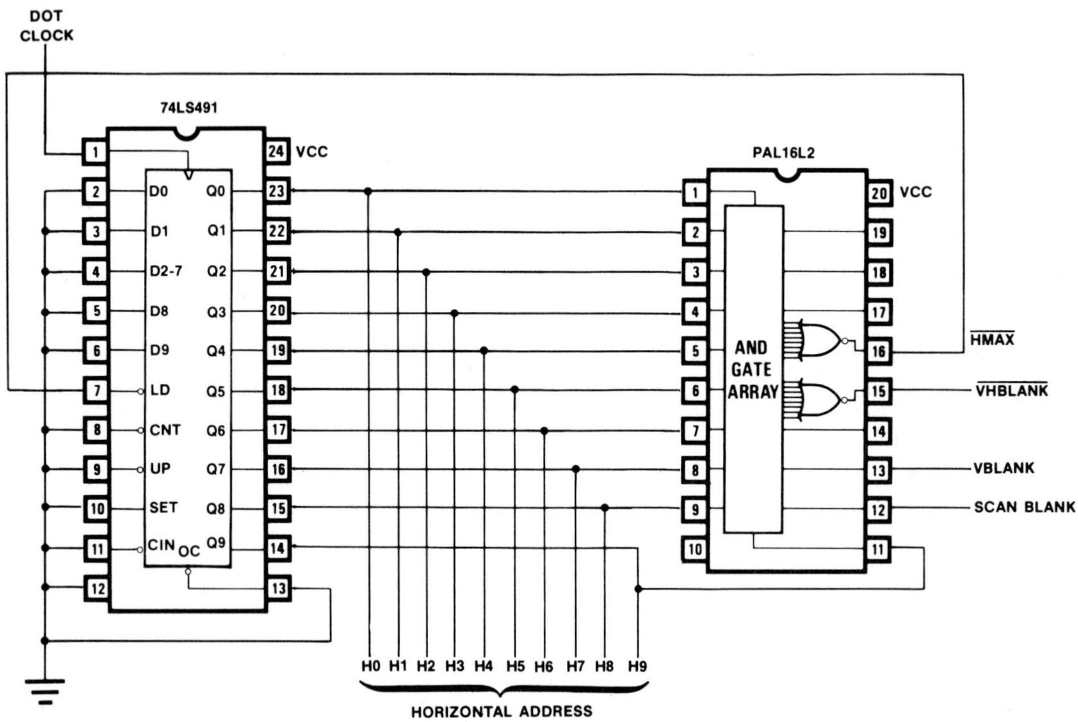

NOTE: PAL16L2 design is application dependent.

4-Bit Up/Down Counter with Shift Register and Comparator

PAL16X4

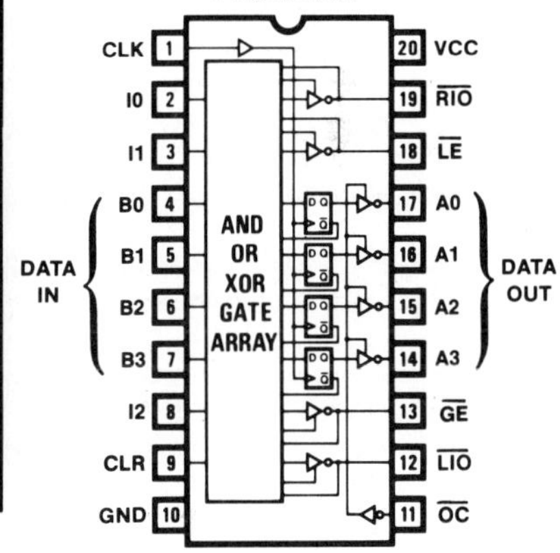

```
PAL16X4                                                   PAL DESIGN SPECIFICATION
SCNT4C                                                       BIRKNER/COLI 10/31/81
4-BIT UP/DOWN COUNTER WITH SHIFT REGISTER AND COMPARATOR
MMI SUNNYVALE, CALIFORNIA
CLK I0 I1 B0 B1 B2 B3 I2 CLR GND /OC /LIO /GE A3 A2 A1 A0 /LE /RIO VCC

IF (/I2* I1*/I0) RIO = (A0)                               ;SHIFT RIGHT OUT

/A0 :=  /I2*/I1*/I0*(/A0)*/CLR                            ;HOLD A0
     +  /I2*/I1* I0*(/B0)*/CLR                            ;LOAD B0 (LSB)
     +  /I2* I1*/I0*(/A1)*/CLR                            ;SHIFT RIGHT
     +   I2* I1*     (/A0)*/CLR                           ;HOLD (INC AND DEC)
    :+:  I2*/I1*/I0*/RIO                                  ;SHIFT LEFT
     +   I2* I1*/I0* RIO                                  ;INCREMENT IF CARRY IN
     +   I2* I1* I0* RIO                                  ;DECREMENT IF BORROW IN
     +   CLR                                              ;CLEAR LSB

/A1 :=  /I2*/I1*/I0*(/A1)*/CLR                            ;HOLD A1
     +  /I2*/I1* I0*(/B1)*/CLR                            ;LOAD B1
     +  /I2* I1*/I0*(/A2)*/CLR                            ;SHIFT RIGHT
     +   I2* I1*     (/A1)*/CLR                           ;HOLD (INC AND DEC)
    :+:  I2*/I1*/I0*(/A0)                                 ;SHIFT LEFT
     +   I2* I1*/I0*( A0)* RIO                            ;INCREMENT IF CARRY IN
     +   I2* I1* I0*(/A0)* RIO                            ;DECREMENT IF BORROW IN
     +   CLR                                              ;CLEAR

/A2 :=  /I2*/I1*/I0*(/A2)*/CLR                            ;HOLD A2
     +  /I2*/I1* I0*(/B2)*/CLR                            ;LOAD B2
     +  /I2* I1*/I0*(/A3)*/CLR                            ;SHIFT RIGHT
     +   I2* I1*     (/A2)*/CLR                           ;HOLD (INC AND DEC)
    :+:  I2*/I1*/I0*(/A1)                                 ;SHIFT LEFT
     +   I2* I1*/I0*( A1)*( A0)* RIO                      ;INCREMENT IF CARRY IN
     +   I2* I1* I0*(/A1)*(/A0)* RIO                      ;DECREMENT IF BORROW IN
     +   CLR                                              ;CLEAR

/A3 :=  /I2*/I1*/I0*(/A3)*/CLR                            ;HOLD A3
     +  /I2*/I1* I0*(/B3)*/CLR                            ;LOAD B3 (MSB)
     +  /I2* I1*/I0* /LIO*/CLR                            ;SHIFT RIGHT
     +   I2* I1*     (/A3)*/CLR                           ;HOLD (INC AND DEC)
    :+:  I2*/I1*/I0*(/A2)                                 ;SHIFT LEFT
     +   I2* I1*/I0*( A2)*( A1)*( A0)* RIO                ;INCREMENT IF CARRY IN
     +   I2* I1* I0*(/A2)*(/A1)*(/A0)* RIO                ;DECREMENT IF BORROW IN
     +   CLR                                              ;CLEAR MSB

IF ( I2) LIO = I2*/I1*/I0*( A3)                           ;SHIFT LEFT OUT
             + I2* I1*/I0*( A3)*( A2)*( A1)*( A0)* RIO    ;CARRY OUT
             + I2* I1* I0*(/A3)*(/A2)*(/A1)*(/A0)* RIO    ;BORROW OUT

IF (VCC)  LE = (A3*/B3)                                   ;B3 LT A3
             + (A3:*:B3)*(A2*/B2)                         ;B2 LT A2
             + (A3:*:B3)*(A2:*:B2)*(A1*/B1)               ;B1 LT A1
             + (A3:*:B3)*(A2:*:B2)*(A1:*:B1)*(A0*/B0)     ;B0 LT A0
             + (A3:*:B3)*(A2:*:B2)*(A1:*:B1)*(A0:*:B0)    ;B  EQ A

IF (VCC)  GE = (/A3*B3)                                   ;B3 GT A3
             + (A3:*:B3)*(/A2*B2)                         ;B2 GT A2
             + (A3:*:B3)*(A2:*:B2)*(/A1*B1)               ;B1 GT A1
             + (A3:*:B3)*(A2:*:B2)*(A1:*:B1)*(/A0*B0)     ;B0 GT A0
             + (A3:*:B3)*(A2:*:B2)*(A1:*:B1)*(A0:*:B0)    ;B  EQ A
```

```
FUNCTION TABLE

CLK /OC CLR I2 I1 I0 B3 B2 B1 B0 /GE /LE /LIO /RIO A3 A2 A1 A0

;              INST INPUT                         OUTPUT
;--CONTROL--   III  BBBB   STATUS    ---I/O---    AAAA     COMMENTS
;CLK /OC CLR   210  3210  /GE  /LE  /LIO /RIO    3210    (HEX VALUES)
-------------------------------------------------------------------------------
  C   L   H    XXX  XXXX   X    X     Z    Z     LLLL    CLEAR
  C   L   L    LHL  XXXX   X    X     L    H     HLLL    SHIFT RIGHT IN A H
  C   L   L    LHL  XXXX   X    X     H    H     LHLL    SHIFT RIGHT IN A L
  C   L   L    LLL  LHLH   L    H     Z    Z     LHLL    COMPARE B GT A
  C   L   L    LHL  XXXX   X    X     H    H     LLHL    SHIFT RIGHT IN A L
  C   L   L    LLL  LLHL   L    L     Z    Z     LLHL    COMPARE B EQ A
  C   L   L    LHL  XXXX   X    X     H    L     LLLH    SHIFT RIGHT IN A L
  C   L   L    LHL  XXXX   X    X     H    H     LLLL    SHIFT RIGHT IN A L
  C   L   L    HLH  XXXX   X    X     H    Z     HHHH    SET
  C   L   L    LLL  XXXX   X    X     Z    Z     HHHH    HOLD
  C   L   L    HLL  XXXX   X    X     L    H     HHHL    SHIFT LEFT  IN A L
  C   L   L    HLL  XXXX   X    X     L    L     HHLH    SHIFT LEFT  IN A H
  C   L   L    HLL  XXXX   X    X     L    L     HLHH    SHIFT LEFT  IN A H
  C   L   L    HLL  XXXX   X    X     H    L     LHHH    SHIFT LEFT  IN A H
  C   L   L    HLL  XXXX   X    X     L    L     HHHH    SHIFT LEFT  IN A H
  C   L   L    LLH  LLLH   X    X     Z    Z     LLLH    LOAD (1)
  C   L   L    HHL  XXXX   X    X     H    L     LLHL    INCREMENT
  C   L   L    HHH  XXXX   X    X     H    L     LLLH    DECREMENT
  C   L   L    LLH  LLHH   X    X     Z    Z     LLHH    LOAD (3)
  C   L   L    HHL  XXXX   X    X     H    L     LHLL    INCREMENT
  C   L   L    HHH  XXXX   X    X     H    L     LLHH    DECREMENT
  C   L   L    LLH  LHHH   X    X     Z    Z     LHHH    LOAD (7)
  C   L   L    HHL  XXXX   X    X     H    L     HLLL    INCREMENT
  C   L   L    HHH  XXXX   X    X     H    L     LHHH    DECREMENT
  C   L   L    LLH  HHHH   X    X     Z    Z     HHHH    LOAD (F)
  C   L   L    LLH  LHHH   X    X     Z    Z     LHHH    LOAD (7)
  C   L   L    LLH  HLHH   X    X     Z    Z     HLHH    LOAD (B)
  C   L   L    LLH  HHLH   X    X     Z    Z     HHLH    LOAD (D)
  C   L   L    LLH  HHHL   X    X     Z    Z     HHHL    LOAD (E)
  C   L   L    LLH  HLHL   X    X     Z    Z     HLHL    LOAD (A)
  C   L   L    HHL  XXXX   X    X     H    L     HLHH    INCREMENT TO (B)
  C   L   L    HHL  XXXX   X    X     H    L     HHLL    INCREMENT TO (C)
  C   L   L    LLL  HLHH   H    L     Z    Z     HHLL    COMPARE B LT A
  C   L   L    HHL  XXXX   X    X     H    L     HHLH    INCREMENT TO (D)
  C   L   L    HHL  XXXX   X    X     H    H     HHLH    HOLD NO CARRY IN (/RIO=H)
  C   L   L    HHL  XXXX   X    X     H    L     HHHL    INCREMENT TO (E)
  C   L   L    HHL  XXXX   X    X     L    L     HHHH    INCREMENT TO (F)CARRY OUT
  C   L   L    HHL  XXXX   X    X     H    L     LLLL    INCREMENT TO (0)ROLL OVER
  C   L   L    LHH  XXXX   X    X     Z    Z     HHHH    SET
  C   L   L    HHH  XXXX   X    X     H    L     HHHL    DECREMENT TO (E)
  C   L   L    LLH  LLHH   X    X     Z    Z     LLHH    LOAD (3)
  C   L   L    HHH  XXXX   X    X     H    L     LLHL    DECREMENT TO (2)
  L   L   L    HHH  LLHL   X    X     H    H     LLHL    COMPARE B EQ A
  C   L   L    HHH  XXXX   X    X     H    L     LLLH    DECREMENT TO (1)
  C   L   L    HHH  XXXX   X    X     L    L     LLLL    DECREMENT TO (0)BOROW OUT
  C   L   L    HHH  XXXX   X    X     H    L     HHHH    DECREMENT TO (F)ROLL UNDR
  X   H   X    XXX  XXXX   X    X     X    X     ZZZZ    TEST HI-Z
-------------------------------------------------------------------------------
```

DESCRIPTION

THE 4-BIT UP/DOWN COUNTER WITH SHIFT REGISTER AND COMPARATOR WILL COUNT UP, COUNT DOWN, SHIFT RIGHT, SHIFT LEFT, COMPARE GREATER THAN OR EQUAL TO, COMPARE LESS THAN OR EQUAL TO, CLEAR, SET, LOAD, OR HOLD AS SPECIFIED BY THE INSTRUCTION LINES (I2,I1,I0) AND CLEAR (CLR). ALL OPERATIONS OCCUR SYNCHRONOUSLY ON THE RISING EDGE OF THE CLOCK (CLK) EXCEPT FOR THE COMPARISION OPERATIONS WHICH ARE PERFORMED ASYNCHRONOUSLY AND WITH NO INSTRUCTION LINES REQUIRED.

THE COMPARISION OPERATIONS (/GE AND /LE) WILL COMPARE THE INPUT DATA (B) WITH THE DATA IN THE REGISTERS (A) AND SUPPLY THE FOLLOWING STATUS:

COMPARISION	/GE	/LE
B IS GREATER THAN A	L	H
B IS EQUAL TO A	L	L
B IS LESS THAN A	H	L

NOTE THAT BORROW, CARRY, AND SHIFT LEFT AND RIGHT INPUT/OUTPUTS SHARE THE SAME I/O LINES (/LIO AND /RIO) AND THESE LINES ARE INVERTED (ACTIVE LOW).

THESE OPERATIONS ARE EXERCISED IN THE FUNCTION TABLE AND SUMMARIZED IN THE OPERATIONS TABLE BELOW:

/OC	CLK	CLR	I2	I1	I0	B3-B0	/GE /LE	/LIO	/RIO	A3-A0	OPERATION
H	X	X	X	X	X	X	STATUS	X	X	Z	HI-Z
L	C	H	X	X	X	X	X X	X	X	L	CLEAR
L	C	L	L	L	L	X	STATUS	X	X	A	HOLD
L	C	L	L	L	H	B	X X	X	X	B	LOAD B
L	C	L	L	H	L	X	STATUS	RI	A0	SR(RIO)	SHIFT RIGHT
L	C	L	L	H	H	X	X X	Z	Z	H	SET
L	C	L	H	L	L	X	STATUS	A3	LI	SL(LIO)	SHIFT LEFT
L	C	L	H	L	H	X	X X	H	Z	H	SET
L	C	L	H	H	L	X	STATUS	COUT	CIN	A PLUS 1	INCREMENT IF CIN
L	C	L	H	H	H	X	STATUS	BOUT	BIN	A MINUS 1	DECREMENT IF BIN

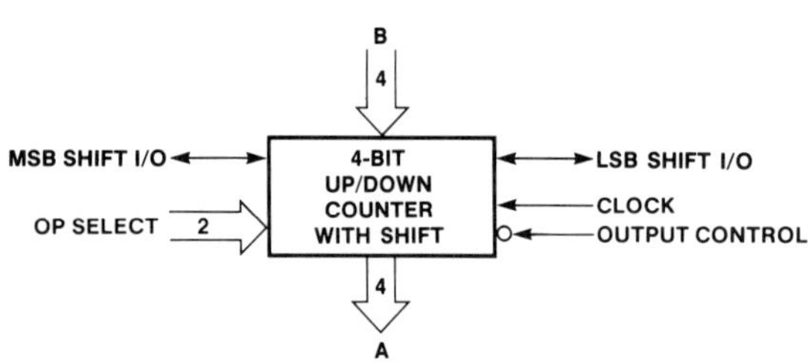

4-BIT UP/DOWN COUNTER WITH SHIFT REGISTER AND COMPARATOR

```
 1 CXXXXXXX1X0ZXLLLLXZ1
 2 C01XXXX00X00XHLLLXH1
 3 C01XXXX00X01XLHLLXH1
 4 C00101000X0ZLLHLLHZ1
 5 C01XXXX00X01XLLHLXH1
 6 C00010000X0ZLLLHLLZ1
 7 C01XXXX00X01XLLLHXL1
 8 C01XXXX00X01XLLLLXH1
 9 C10XXXX10X0HXHHHHXZ1
10 C00XXXX00X0ZXHHHHXZ1
11 C00XXXX10X0LXHHHLX11
12 C00XXXX10X0LXHHLHX01
13 C00XXXX10X0LXHLHHX01
14 C00XXXX10X0HXLHHHX01
15 C00XXXX10X0LXHHHHX01
16 C10100000X0ZXLLLHXZ1
17 C01XXXX10X0HXLLHLX01
18 C11XXXX10X0HXLLLHX01
19 C10110000X0ZXLLHHXZ1
20 C01XXXX10X0HXLHLLX01
21 C11XXXX10X0HXLLHHX01
22 C10111000X0ZXLHHHXZ1
23 C01XXXX10X0HXHLLLX01
24 C11XXXX10X0HXLHHHX01
25 C10111100X0ZXHHHHXZ1
26 C10111000X0ZXLHHHXZ1
27 C10110100X0ZXHLHHXZ1
28 C10101100X0ZXHHLHXZ1
29 C10011100X0ZXHHHLXZ1
30 C10010100X0ZXHLHLXZ1
31 C01XXXX10X0HXHLHHX01
32 C01XXXX10X0HXHHLLX01
33 C00110100X0ZHHHLLLZ1
34 C01XXXX10X0HXHHLHX01
35 C01XXXX10X0HXHHLHX11
36 C01XXXX10X0HXHHHLX01
37 C01XXXX10X0LXHHHHX01
38 C01XXXX10X0HXLLLLX01
39 C11XXXX00X0ZXHHHHXZ1
40 C11XXXX10X0HXHHHLX01
41 C10110000X0ZXLLHHXZ1
42 C11XXXX10X0HXLLHLX01
43 011010010X0HXLLHLX11
44 C11XXXX10X0HXLLLHX01
45 C11XXXX10X0LXLLLLX01
46 C11XXXX10X0HXHHHHX01
47 XXXXXXXXXX1XXZZZZXX1
```

PASS SIMULATION

```
4-BIT UP/DOWN COUNTER WITH SHIFT REGISTER AND COMPARATOR
                     11 1111 1111 2222 2222 2233
    0123 4567 8901 2345 6789 0123 4567 8901

  0 -X-- X--- ---- ---- ---- ---- -X-- ---- /I2*I1*/I0
  1 ---- ---- --XX ---- ---- ---- ---- ---- A0

  8 ---- ---- ---- ---- ---- ---- ---- ----
  9 ---- ---- ---- ---- ---- -XXX ---- ---- A3*/B3
 10 ---- ---- ---- ---- -XXX X--X ---- ---- A3:*:B3*A2*/B2
 11 ---- ---- ---- -XXX X--X X--X ---- ---- A3:*:B3*A2:*:B2*A1*/B1
 12 ---- ---- -XXX X--X X--X X--X ---- ---- A3:*:B3*A2:*:B2*A1:*:B1*A0*/B0
 13 ---- ---- X--X X--X X--X X--X ---- ---- A3:*:B3*A2:*:B2*A1:*:B1*A0:*:B0

 16 -X-- -X-- XX-- ---- ---- ---- -X-- -X-- /I2*/I1*/I0*/A0*/CLR
 17 X--- -X-- -X-X ---- ---- ---- -X-- -X-- /I2*/I1*I0*/B0*/CLR
 18 -X-- X--- ---- XX-- ---- ---- -X-- -X-- /I2*I1*/I0*/A1*/CLR
 19 ---- X--- XX-- ---- ---- ---- X--- -X-- I2*I1*/A0*/CLR
 20 -XX- -X-- ---- ---- ---- ---- X--- ---- I2*/I1*/I0*/RIO
 21 -X-X X--- ---- ---- ---- ---- X--- ---- I2*I1*/I0*RIO
 22 X--X X--- ---- ---- ---- ---- X--- ---- I2*I1*I0*RIO
 23 ---- ---- ---- ---- ---- ---- ---- X--- CLR

 24 -X-- -X-- ---- XX-- ---- ---- -X-- -X-- /I2*/I1*/I0*/A1*/CLR
 25 X--- -X-- ---- -X-X ---- ---- -X-- -X-- /I2*/I1*I0*/B1*/CLR
 26 -X-- X--- ---- ---- XX-- ---- -X-- -X-- /I2*I1*/I0*/A2*/CLR
 27 ---- X--- ---- XX-- ---- ---- X--- -X-- I2*I1*/A1*/CLR
 28 -X-- -X-- XX-- ---- ---- ---- X--- ---- I2*/I1*/I0*/A0
 29 -X-X X--- --XX ---- ---- ---- X--- ---- I2*I1*/I0*A0*RIO
 30 X--X X--- XX-- ---- ---- ---- X--- ---- I2*I1*I0*/A0*RIO
 31 ---- ---- ---- ---- ---- ---- ---- X--- CLR

 32 -X-- -X-- ---- ---- XX-- ---- -X-- -X-- /I2*/I1*/I0*/A2*/CLR
 33 X--- -X-- ---- ---- -X-X ---- -X-- -X-- /I2*/I1*I0*/B2*/CLR
 34 -X-- X--- ---- ---- ---- XX-- -X-- -X-- /I2*I1*/I0*/A3*/CLR
 35 ---- X--- ---- ---- XX-- ---- X--- -X-- I2*I1*/A2*/CLR
 36 -X-- -X-- ---- XX-- ---- ---- X--- ---- I2*/I1*/I0*/A1
 37 -X-X X--- --XX --XX ---- ---- X--- ---- I2*I1*/I0*A1*A0*RIO
 38 X--X X--- XX-- XX-- ---- ---- X--- ---- I2*I1*I0*/A1*/A0*RIO
 39 ---- ---- ---- ---- ---- ---- ---- X--- CLR

 40 -X-- -X-- ---- ---- ---- XX-- -X-- -X-- /I2*/I1*/I0*/A3*/CLR
 41 X--- -X-- ---- ---- ---- -X-X -X-- -X-- /I2*/I1*I0*/B3*/CLR
 42 -X-- X--- ---- ---- ---- ---- -X-- -XX- /I2*I1*/I0*/LIO*/CLR
 43 ---- X--- ---- ---- ---- XX-- X--- -X-- I2*I1*/A3*/CLR
 44 -X-- -X-- ---- ---- XX-- ---- X--- ---- I2*/I1*/I0*/A2
 45 -X-X X--- --XX --XX --XX ---- X--- ---- I2*I1*/I0*A2*A1*A0*RIO
 46 X--X X--- XX-- XX-- XX-- ---- X--- ---- I2*I1*I0*/A2*/A1*/A0*RIO
 47 ---- ---- ---- ---- ---- ---- ---- X--- CLR

 48 ---- ---- ---- ---- ---- ---- ---- ----
 49 ---- ---- ---- ---- ---- XXX- ---- ---- /A3*B3
 50 ---- ---- ---- ---- XXX- X--X ---- ---- A3:*:B3*/A2*B2
 51 ---- ---- ---- XXX- X--X X--X ---- ---- A3:*:B3*A2:*:B2*/A1*B1
 52 ---- ---- XXX- X--X X--X X--X ---- ---- A3:*:B3*A2:*:B2*A1:*:B1*/A0*B0
 53 ---- ---- X--X X--X X--X X--X ---- ---- A3:*:B3*A2:*:B2*A1:*:B1*A0:*:B0

 56 ---- ---- ---- ---- ---- ---- X--- ---- I2
 57 -X-- -X-- ---- ---- ---- --XX X--- ---- I2*/I1*/I0*A3
 58 -X-X X--- --XX --XX --XX --XX X--- ---- I2*I1*/I0*A3*A2*A1*A0*RIO
 59 X--X X--- XX-- XX-- XX-- XX-- X--- ---- I2*I1*I0*/A3*/A2*/A1*/A0*RIO

LEGEND:  X : FUSE NOT BLOWN (L,N,0)   - : FUSE BLOWN   (H,P,1)
NUMBER OF FUSES BLOWN = 1331
```

4-Bit Up/Down Counter with Shift Register and Comparator

Logic Diagram PAL16X4

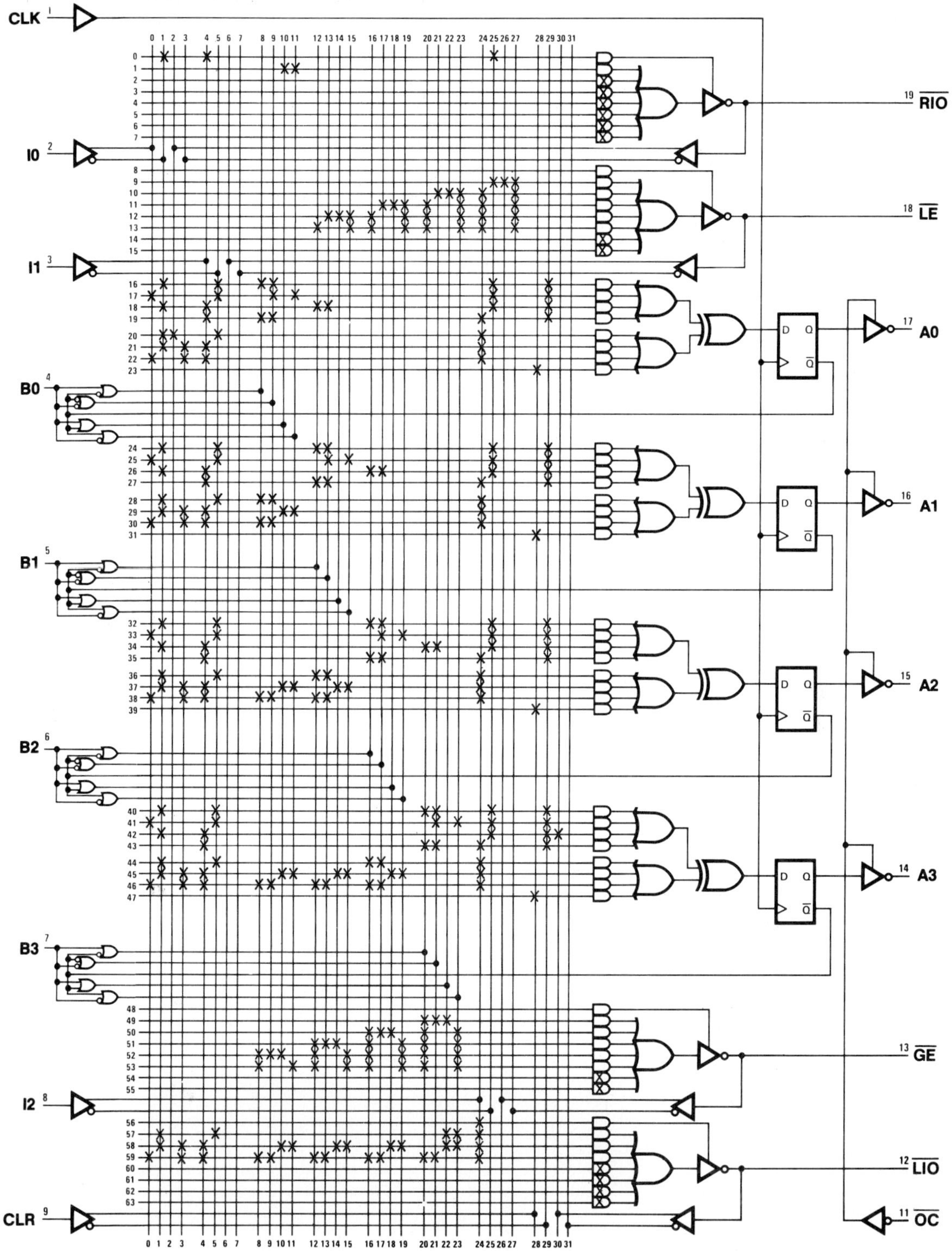

PAL
IMPORTANT.
NOTES

4-Bit Flash Gray A/D Converter

PAL20X4

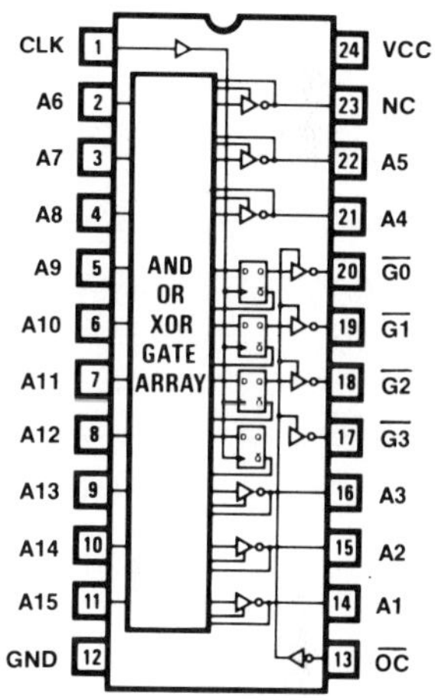

A/D and D/A Converters

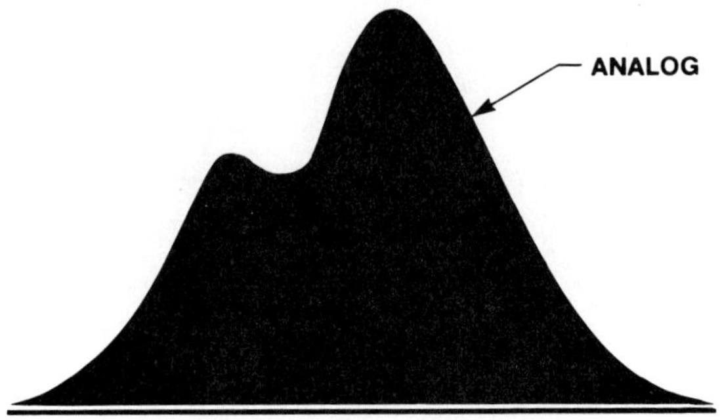

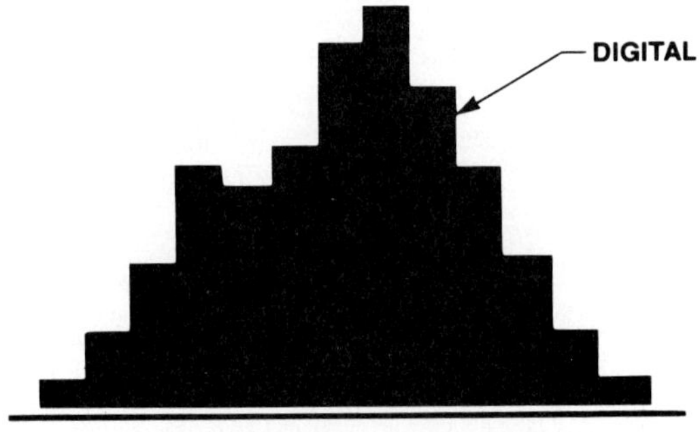

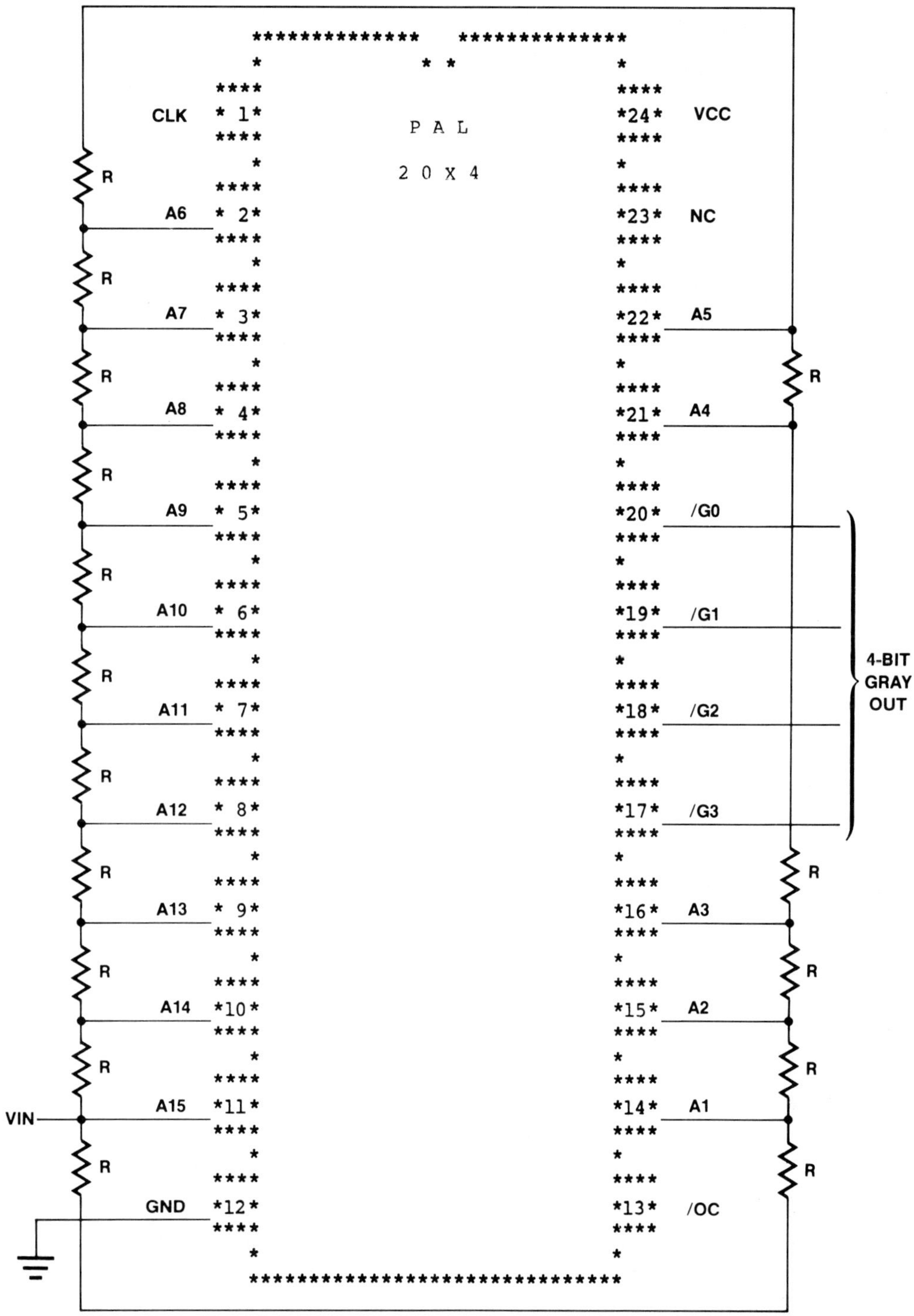
PAL
20X4
CLK
1
VCC
24
R
A6
2
NC
23
A7
3
A5
22
A8
4
A4
21
A9
5
/G0
20
A10
6
/G1
19
A11
7
/G2
18
A12
8
/G3
17
4-BIT
GRAY
OUT
A13
9
A3
16
A14
10
A2
15
VIN
A15
11
A1
14
GND
12
/OC
13

```
PAL20X4                                                PAL DESIGN SPECIFICATION
ADC4                                                     BIRKNER/COLI 07/29/81
4-BIT FLASH GRAY A/D CONVERTER
MMI SUNNYVALE, CALIFORNIA
CLK A6 A7 A8 A9 A10 A11 A12 A13 A14 A15 GND
/OC A1 A2 A3 /G3 /G2 /G1 /G0 A4 A5 NC VCC


G0 :=  /A3 * A1     ;CONVERT ANALOG TO G0 (LSB)
    +  /A7 * A5
   :+: /A11* A9
    +  /A15* A13

G1 :=  /A6 * A2     ;CONVERT ANALOG TO G1
    +  /A14* A10

G2 :=  /A12* A4     ;CONVERT ANALOG TO G2

G3 :=   A8          ;CONVERT ANALOG TO G3 (MSB)


FUNCTION TABLE

/OC CLK A15 A14 A13 A12 A11 A10 A9 A8 A7 A6 A5 A4 A3 A2 A1 G3 G2 G1 G0

;          ANALOG  INPUTS    GRAY
;CONTROL   111111           OUTPUTS    COMMENTS
;/OC CLK   543210987654321   3210      FRACTION OF Vmax
-------------------------------------------------------------
  L   C    LLLLLLLLLLLLLLL   LLLL      V=0
  L   C    LLLLLLLLLLLLLLH   LLLH      V=1/16
  L   C    LLLLLLLLLLLLLHH   LLHH      V=1/8
  L   C    LLLLLLLLLLLLHHH   LLHL      V=3/16
  L   C    LLLLLLLLLLLHHHH   LHHL      V=1/4
  L   C    LLLLLLLLLLHHHHH   LHHH      V=5/16
  L   C    LLLLLLLLLHHHHHH   LHLH      V=3/8
  L   C    LLLLLLLLHHHHHHH   LHLL      V=7/16
  L   C    LLLLLLLHHHHHHHH   HHLL      V=1/2
  L   C    LLLLLLHHHHHHHHH   HHLH      V=9/16
  L   C    LLLLLHHHHHHHHHH   HHHH      V=5/8
  L   C    LLLLHHHHHHHHHHH   HHHL      V=11/16
  L   C    LLLHHHHHHHHHHHH   HLHL      V=3/4
  L   C    LLHHHHHHHHHHHHH   HLHH      V=13/16
  L   C    LHHHHHHHHHHHHHH   HLLH      V=7/8
  L   C    HHHHHHHHHHHHHHH   HLLL      V=15/16
  H   X    XXXXXXXXXXXXXXX   ZZZZ      TEST HI-Z
-------------------------------------------------------------


DESCRIPTION

THE 4-BIT FLASH ANALOG-TO-DIGITAL CONVERTER CONVERTS AN ANALOG SIGNAL
INTO A 4-BIT GRAY CODE.  GRAY CODE IS CHOSEN TO ELIMINATE GLITCHES AT
BINARY ROLL OVER POINTS.

THE MAXIUM SAMPLE RATE IS EQUAL TO 1/tpd OF THE PAL20X4.  NOTE THAT NO
FEEDBACK PROPAGATION DELAY IS INTRODUCED.
```

```
4-BIT FLASH GRAY A/D CONVERTER

 1 C0000000000X0000HHHH00X1
 2 C0000000000X0100HHHL00X1
 3 C0000000000X0110HHLL00X1
 4 C0000000000X0111HHLH00X1
 5 C0000000000X0111HLLH10X1
 6 C0000000000X0111HLLL11X1
 7 C1000000000X0111HLHL11X1
 8 C1100000000X0111HLHH11X1
 9 C1110000000X0111LLHH11X1
10 C1111000000X0111LLHL11X1
11 C1111100000X0111LLLL11X1
12 C1111110000X0111LLLH11X1
13 C1111111000X0111LHLH11X1
14 C1111111100X0111LHLL11X1
15 C1111111110X0111LHHL11X1
16 C1111111111X0111LHHH11X1
17 XXXXXXXXXXXX1XXXZZZZXXX1

PASS SIMULATION
```

```
4-BIT FLASH GRAY A/D CONVERTER

               11 1111 1111 2222 2222 2233 3333 3333
   0123 4567 8901 2345 6789 0123 4567 8901 2345 6789



24 ---- ---- ---- ---- ---- ---- ---- ---X ---- --X- /A3*A1
25 ---- -XX- ---- ---- ---- ---- ---- ---- ---- ---- /A7*A5
26 ---- ---- ---- X--- ---- -X-- ---- ---- ---- ---- /A11*A9
27 ---- ---- ---- ---- ---- ---- ---- X--- ---- -X-- /A15*A13

32 -X-- ---- ---- ---- ---- ---- ---- ---- --X- ---- /A6*A2
33 ---- ---- ---- ---- X--- ---- ---- ---- -X-- ---- /A14*A10

40 ---- ---- --X- ---- ---- ---- -X-- ---- ---- ---- /A12*A4

48 ---- ---- X--- ---- ---- ---- ---- ---- ---- ---- A8



LEGEND:  X : FUSE NOT BLOWN (L,N,0)   - : FUSE BLOWN   (H,P,1)

NUMBER OF FUSES BLOW =  305
```

4-Bit Flash Gray A/D Converter

Logic Diagram PAL20X4

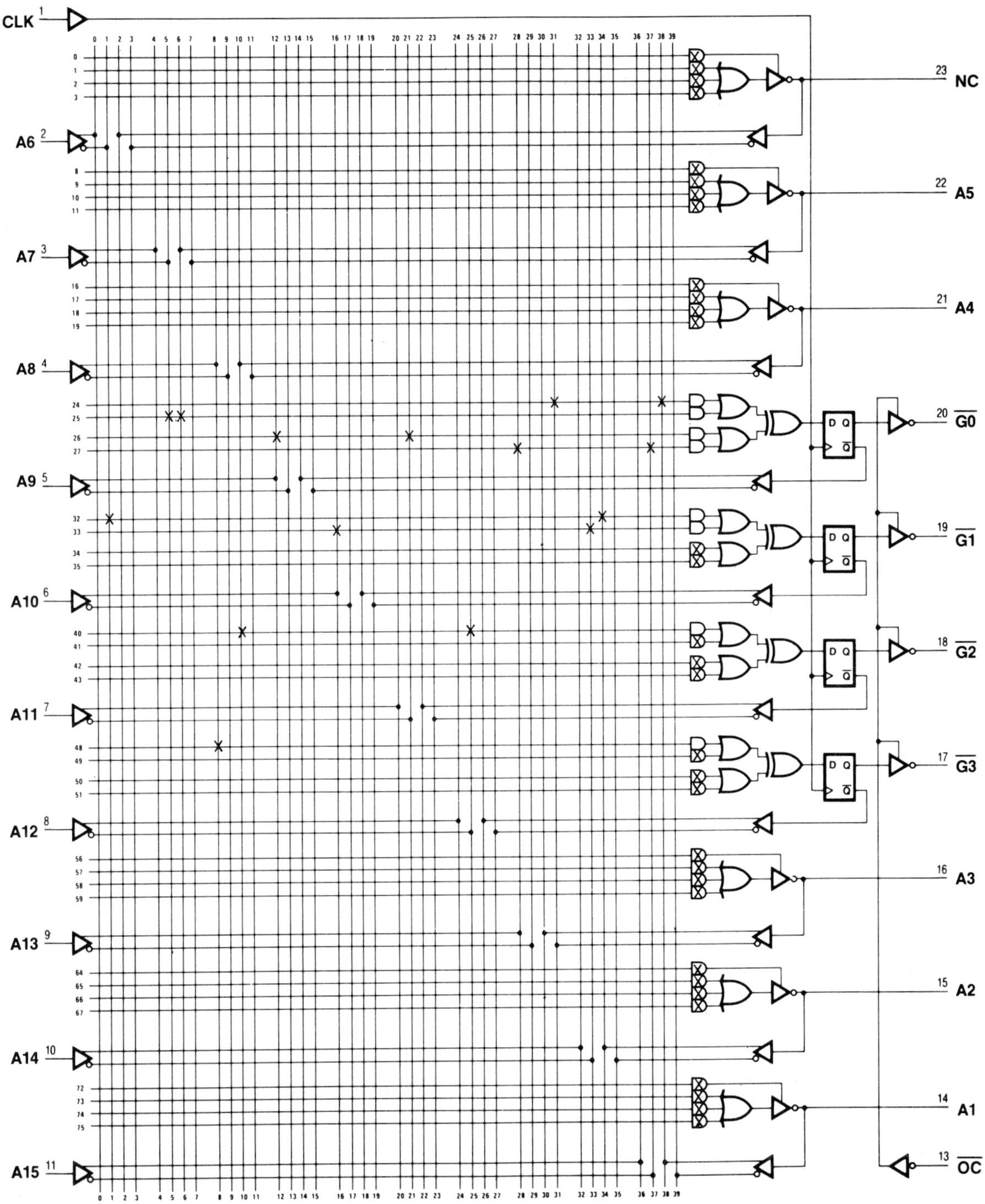

PAL
IMPORTANT,
NOTES

4-Bit Gray D/A Converter

PAL16R4

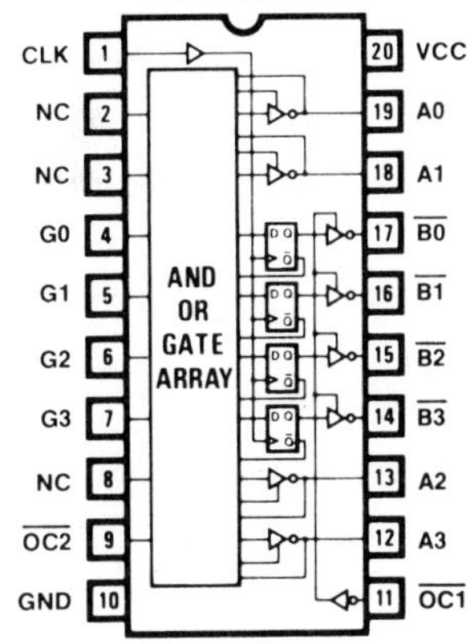

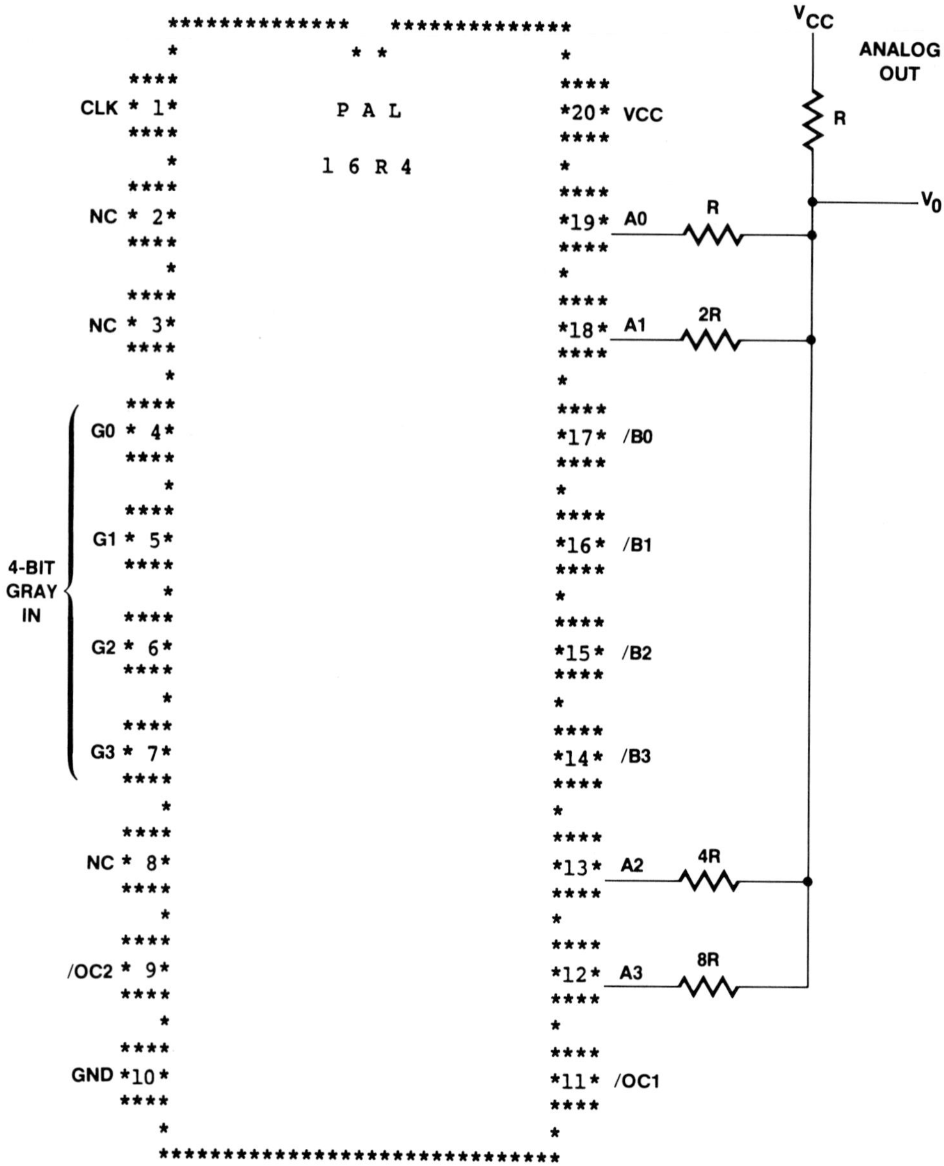

NOTE: EACH BIT CONTRIBUTES $\frac{2^N}{16}$ VOLTS

WHERE N = THE SUBSCRIPT OF B

```
PAL16R4                                                 PAL DESIGN SPECIFICATION
DAC4                                                       BIRKNER/COLI 07/30/81
4-BIT GRAY D/A CONVERTER
MMI SUNNYVALE, CALIFORNIA
 CLK NC NC  G0  G1  G2  G3 NC /OC2 GND
/OC1 A3 A2 /B3 /B2 /B1 /B0 A1  A0  VCC


B0 :=  /G0* G1* G2* G3 ;CONVERT GRAY TO B0 (LSB)
    +   G0*/G1* G2* G3
    +   G0* G1*/G2* G3
    +   G0* G1* G2*/G3
    +   G0*/G1*/G2*/G3
    +  /G0* G1*/G2*/G3
    +  /G0*/G1* G2*/G3
    +  /G0*/G1*/G2* G3

B1 :=  /G1*/G2* G3     ;CONVERT GRAY TO B1
    +  /G1* G2*/G3
    +   G1*/G2*/G3
    +   G1* G2* G3

B2 :=  /G2* G3         ;CONVERT GRAY TO B2
    +   G2*/G3

B3 :=   G3             ;CONVERT GRAY TO B3 (MSB)

IF(B0*OC2) /A0 =  B0   ;CONVERT B0 TO ANALOG

IF(B1*OC2) /A1 =  B1   ;CONVERT B1 TO ANALOG

IF(B2*OC2) /A2 =  B2   ;CONVERT B2 TO ANALOG

IF(B3*OC2) /A3 =  B3   ;CONVERT B3 TO ANALOG
```

FUNCTION TABLE

/OC1 /OC2 CLK G3 G2 G1 G0 B3 B2 B1 B0 A3 A2 A1 A0

```
;---CONTROL---   GRAY   BCD    ANALOG    COMMENTS
;/OC1 /OC2 CLK   3210   3210    3210     FRACTION OF Vmax
-----------------------------------------------------------
   L    L   C    LLLL   LLLL    ZZZZ     V=0
   L    L   C    LLLH   LLLH    ZZZL     V=1/16
   L    L   C    LLHH   LLHL    ZZLZ     V=1/8
   L    L   C    LLHL   LLHH    ZZLL     V=3/16
   L    L   C    LHHL   LHLL    ZLZZ     V=1/4
   L    L   C    LHHH   LHLH    ZLZL     V=5/16
   L    L   C    LHLH   LHHL    ZLLZ     V=3/8
   L    L   C    LHLL   LHHH    ZLLL     V=7/16
   L    L   C    HHLL   HLLL    LZZZ     V=1/2
   L    L   C    HHLH   HLLH    LZZL     V=9/16
   L    L   C    HHHH   HLHL    LZLZ     V=5/8
   L    L   C    HHHL   HLHH    LZLL     V=11/16
   L    L   C    HLHL   HHLL    LLZZ     V=3/4
   L    L   C    HLHH   HHLH    LLZL     V=13/16
   L    L   C    HLLH   HHHL    LLLZ     V=7/8
   L    L   C    HLLL   HHHH    LLLL     V=15/16
   H    X   X    XXXX   ZZZZ    XXXX     TEST HI-Z (REG)
   X    H   X    XXXX   XXXX    ZZZZ     TEST HI-Z (OC)
-----------------------------------------------------------
```

DESCRIPTION

THE 4-BIT FLASH DIGITAL-TO-ANALOG CONVERTER CONVERTS A 4-BIT GRAY CODE (G) INTO A 4-BIT BINARY CODE (B), WHICH IS THEN CONVERTED INTO ANALOG OUTPUTS (A).

ANALOG OUTPUTS (A) ARE EITHER LOW OR HI-Z WHICH ALLOWS THE CONDITIONAL THREE-STATE OUTPUTS TO PERFORM THE OPEN COLLECTOR FUNCTION THAT IS NEEDED TO DRIVE THE RESISTOR NETWORK.

```
4-BIT GRAY D/A CONVERTER

 1 CXX0000X0X0ZZHHHHZZ1
 2 CXX1000X0X0ZZHHHLZL1
 3 CXX1100X0X0ZZHHLHLZ1
 4 CXX0100X0X0ZZHHLLLL1
 5 CXX0110X0X0ZLHLHHZZ1
 6 CXX1110X0X0ZLHLHLZL1
 7 CXX1010X0X0ZLHLLHLZ1
 8 CXX0010X0X0ZLHLLLLL1
 9 CXX0011X0X0LZLHHHZZ1
10 CXX1011X0X0LZLHHLZL1
11 CXX1111X0X0LZLHLHLZ1
12 CXX0111X0X0LZLHLLLL1
13 CXX0101X0X0LLLLHHZZ1
14 CXX1101X0X0LLLLHLZL1
15 CXX1001X0X0LLLLLHLZ1
16 CXX0001X0X0LLLLLLLL1
17 XXXXXXXXXX1XXZZZZXX1
18 XXXXXXXX1XXZZXXXXZZ1

PASS SIMULATION
```

```
4-BIT GRAY D/A CONVERTER

               11 1111 1111 2222 2222 2233
   0123 4567 8901 2345 6789 0123 4567 8901

 0 ---- ---- ---X ---- ---- ---- ---- -X-- B0*OC2
 1 ---- ---- ---X ---- ---- ---- ---- ---- B0

 8 ---- ---- ---- ---X ---- ---- ---- -X-- B1*OC2
 9 ---- ---- ---- ---X ---- ---- ---- ---- B1

16 ---- ---- -X-- X--- X--- X--- ---- ---- /G0*G1*G2*G3
17 ---- ---- X--- -X-- X--- X--- ---- ---- G0*/G1*G2*G3
18 ---- ---- X--- X--- -X-- X--- ---- ---- G0*G1*/G2*G3
19 ---- ---- X--- X--- X--- -X-- ---- ---- G0*G1*G2*/G3
20 ---- ---- X--- -X-- -X-- -X-- ---- ---- G0*/G1*/G2*/G3
21 ---- ---- -X-- X--- -X-- -X-- ---- ---- /G0*G1*/G2*/G3
22 ---- ---- -X-- -X-- X--- -X-- ---- ---- /G0*/G1*G2*/G3
23 ---- ---- -X-- -X-- -X-- X--- ---- ---- /G0*/G1*/G2*G3

24 ---- ---- ---- -X-- -X-- X--- ---- ---- /G1*/G2*G3
25 ---- ---- ---- -X-- X--- -X-- ---- ---- /G1*G2*/G3
26 ---- ---- ---- X--- -X-- -X-- ---- ---- G1*/G2*/G3
27 ---- ---- ---- X--- X--- X--- ---- ---- G1*G2*G3

32 ---- ---- ---- ---- -X-- X--- ---- ---- /G2*G3
33 ---- ---- ---- ---- X--- -X-- ---- ---- G2*/G3

40 ---- ---- ---- ---- ---- X--- ---- ---- G3

48 ---- ---- ---- ---- ---X ---- ---- -X-- B2*OC2
49 ---- ---- ---- ---- ---X ---- ---- ---- B2

56 ---- ---- ---- ---- ---- ---X ---- -X-- B3*OC2
57 ---- ---- ---- ---- ---- ---X ---- ---- B3

LEGEND:  X : FUSE NOT BLOWN (L,N,0)   - : FUSE BLOWN   (H,P,1)

NUMBER OF FUSES BLOWN =  675
```

4-Bit Gray D/A Converter

Logic Diagram PAL16R4

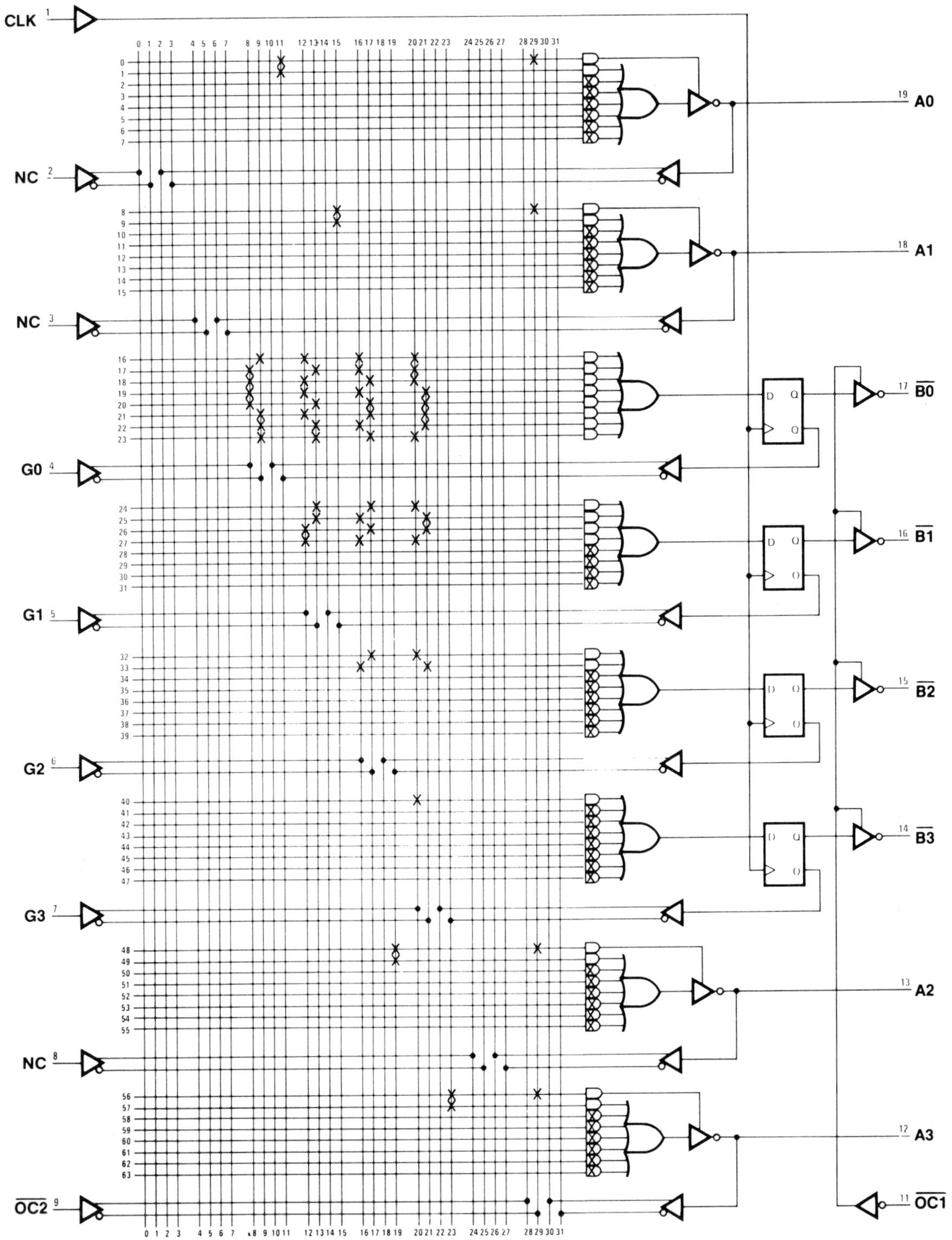

PAL
IMPORTANT, NOTES

8-Bit D/A Converter

PAL16L8

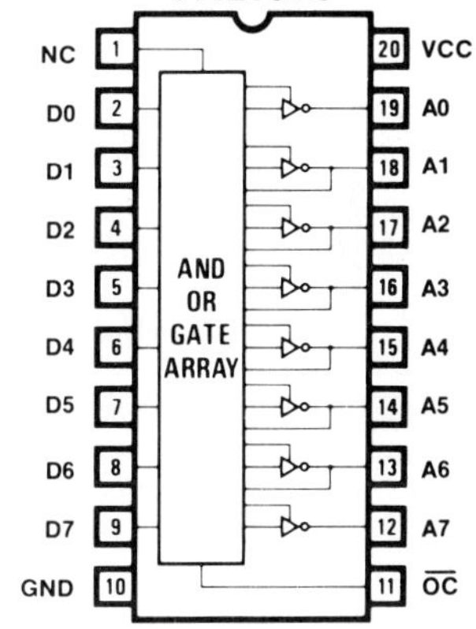

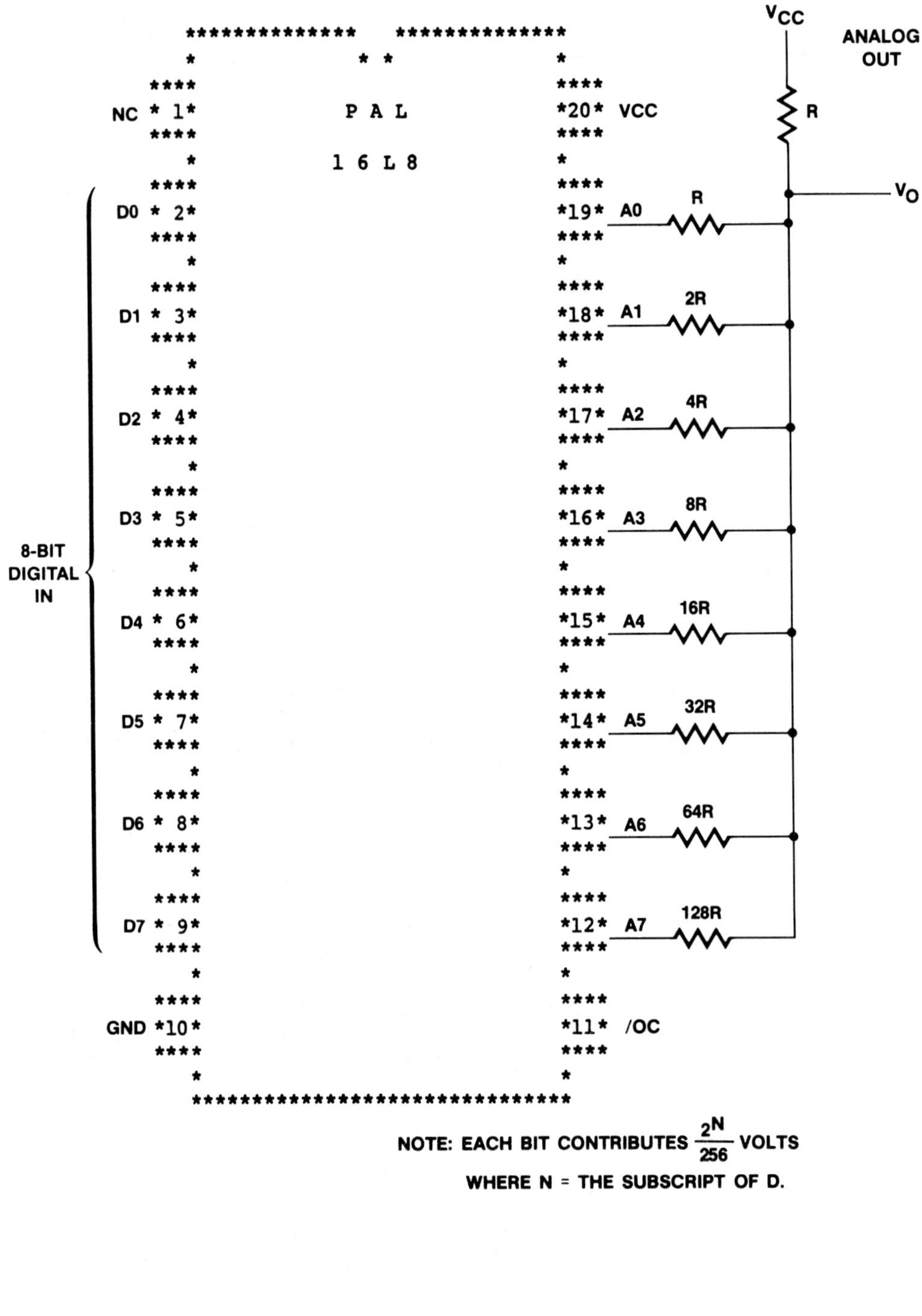

NOTE: EACH BIT CONTRIBUTES $\frac{2^N}{256}$ VOLTS
WHERE N = THE SUBSCRIPT OF D.

```
PAL16L8                                              PAL DESIGN SPECIFICATION
DAC8                                                   BIRKNER/COLI 07/29/81
8-BIT D/A CONVERTER
MMI SUNNYVALE, CALIFORNIA
 NC D0 D1 D2 D3 D4 D5 D6 D7 GND
/OC A7 A6 A5 A4 A3 A2 A1 A0 VCC


IF (D0*OC)  /A0 = D0    ;CONVERT D0 TO ANALOG (LSB)

IF (D1*OC)  /A1 = D1    ;CONVERT D1 TO ANALOG

IF (D2*OC)  /A2 = D2    ;CONVERT D2 TO ANALOG

IF (D3*OC)  /A3 = D3    ;CONVERT D3 TO ANALOG

IF (D4*OC)  /A4 = D4    ;CONVERT D4 TO ANALOG

IF (D5*OC)  /A5 = D5    ;CONVERT D5 TO ANALOG

IF (D6*OC)  /A6 = D6    ;CONVERT D6 TO ANALOG

IF (D7*OC)  /A7 = D7    ;CONVERT D7 TO ANALOG (MSB)


FUNCTION TABLE

/OC D7 D6 D5 D4 D3 D2 D1 D0 A7 A6 A5 A4 A3 A2 A1 A0

;/  DIGITAL IN   ANALOG OUT
;O   DDDDDDDD     AAAAAAAA     COMMENTS
;C   76543210     76543210     FRACTION OF Vmax
-----------------------------------------------
 L   LLLLLLLL     ZZZZZZZZ     V=0
 L   LLLLLLLH     ZZZZZZZL     V=1/256
 L   LLLLLLHL     ZZZZZZLZ     V=1/128
 L   LLLLLLHH     ZZZZZZLL     V=3/256
 L   LLLLLHLL     ZZZZZLZZ     V=1/64
 L   LLLLLHHH     ZZZZZLLL     V=7/256
 L   LLLLHLLL     ZZZZLZZZ     V=1/32
 L   LLLLHHHH     ZZZZLLLL     V=15/256
 L   LLLHLLLL     ZZZLZZZZ     V=1/16
 L   LLLHHHHH     ZZZLLLLL     V=31/256
 L   LLHLLLLL     ZZLZZZZZ     V=1/8
 L   LLHHHHHH     ZZLLLLLL     V=63/256
 L   LHLLLLLL     ZLZZZZZZ     V=1/4
 L   LHHHHHHH     ZLLLLLLL     V=127/256
 L   HLLLLLLL     LZZZZZZZ     V=1/2
 L   HLLLLLHH     LZZZZZLL     V=129/256
 L   HLLLHHHH     LZZZLLLL     V=141/256
 L   HLHHHHHH     LZLLLLLL     V=189/256
 L   HHHHHHHH     LLLLLLLL     V=255/256
 H   XXXXXXXX     ZZZZZZZZ     TEST HI-Z
-----------------------------------------------
```

DESCRIPTION

THIS PAL PERFORMS THE LOGIC NEEDED TO CONVERT AN 8-BIT DIGITAL SIGNAL INTO A 256 INCREMENT ANALOG SIGNAL.

OUTPUTS ARE EITHER LOW OR HI-Z WHICH ALLOWS THE CONDITIONAL THREE-STATE OUTPUTS TO PERFORM THE OPEN COLLECTOR FUNCTION THAT IS NEEDED TO DRIVE THE RESISTOR NETWORK.

```
8-BIT D/A CONVERTER

 1 X00000000X0ZZZZZZZZ1
 2 X10000000X0ZZZZZZZL1
 3 X01000000X0ZZZZZZLZ1
 4 X11000000X0ZZZZZZLL1
 5 X00100000X0ZZZZZLZZ1
 6 X11100000X0ZZZZZLLL1
 7 X00010000X0ZZZZLZZZ1
 8 X11110000X0ZZZZLLLL1
 9 X00001000X0ZZZLZZZZ1
10 X11111000X0ZZZLLLLL1
11 X00000100X0ZZLZZZZZ1
12 X11111100X0ZZLLLLLL1
13 X00000010X0ZLZZZZZZ1
14 X11111110X0ZLLLLLLL1
15 X00000001X0LZZZZZZZ1
16 X11000001X0LZZZZZLL1
17 X11110001X0LZZZLLLL1
18 X11111101X0LZLLLLLL1
19 X11111111X0LLLLLLLL1
20 XXXXXXXXXX1ZZZZZZZZ1

PASS SIMULATION
```

```
8-BIT D/A CONVERTER

               11 1111 1111 2222 2222 2233
   0123 4567 8901 2345 6789 0123 4567 8901

 0 X--- ---- ---- ---- ---- ---- ---- ---X D0*OC
 1 X--- ---- ---- ---- ---- ---- ---- ---- D0

 8 ---- X--- ---- ---- ---- ---- ---- ---X D1*OC
 9 ---- X--- ---- ---- ---- ---- ---- ---- D1

16 ---- ---- X--- ---- ---- ---- ---- ---X D2*OC
17 ---- ---- X--- ---- ---- ---- ---- ---- D2

24 ---- ---- ---- X--- ---- ---- ---- ---X D3*OC
25 ---- ---- ---- X--- ---- ---- ---- ---- D3

32 ---- ---- ---- ---- X--- ---- ---- ---X D4*OC
33 ---- ---- ---- ---- X--- ---- ---- ---- D4

40 ---- ---- ---- ---- ---- X--- ---- ---X D5*OC
41 ---- ---- ---- ---- ---- X--- ---- ---- D5

48 ---- ---- ---- ---- ---- ---- X--- ---X D6*OC
49 ---- ---- ---- ---- ---- ---- X--- ---- D6

56 ---- ---- ---- ---- ---- ---- ---- X--X D7*OC
57 ---- ---- ---- ---- ---- ---- ---- X--- D7

LEGEND:  X : FUSE NOT BLOWN (L,N,0)   - : FUSE BLOWN   (H,P,1)

NUMBER OF FUSES BLOWN =  488
```

8-Bit D/A Converter

Logic Diagram PAL16L8

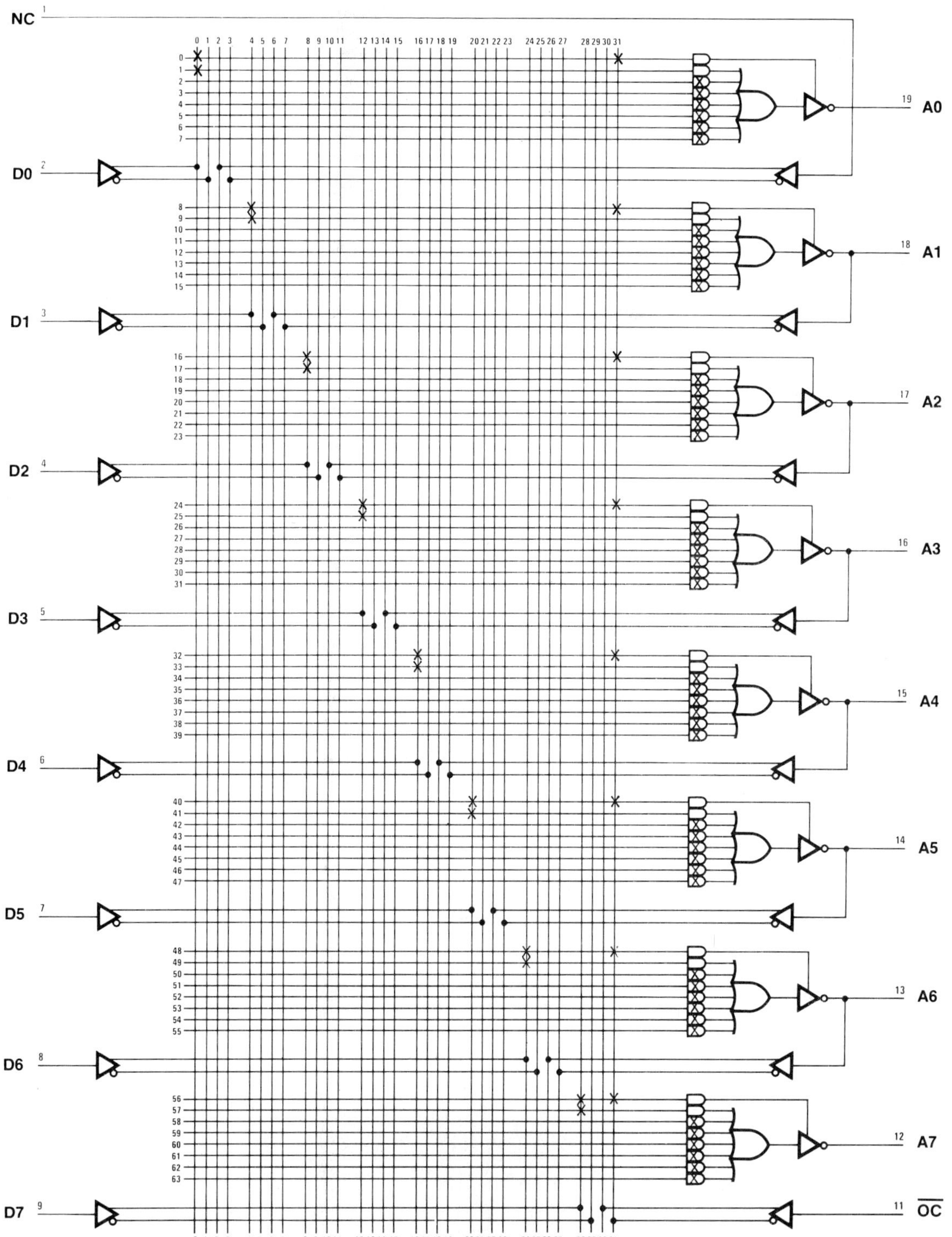

PAL
IMPORTANT,
NOTES

Octal Comparator

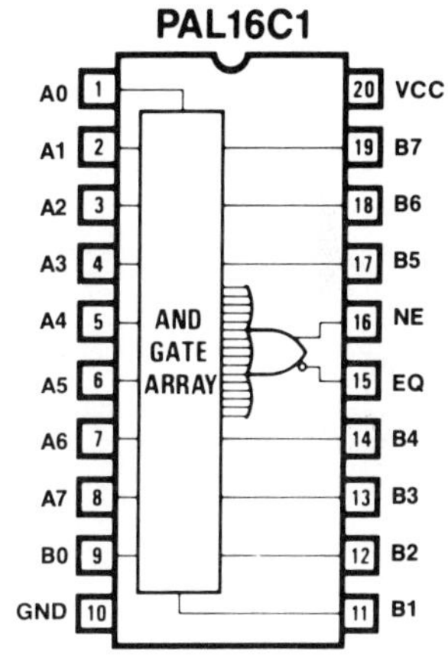

```
PAL16C1                                       PAL DESIGN SPECIFICATION
COMP8                                            BIRKNER/COLI 07/21/81
OCTAL COMPARATOR
MMI SUNNYVALE,CALIFORNIA
A0 A1 A2 A3 A4 A5 A6 A7 B0 GND
B1 B2 B3 B4 EQ NE B5 B6 B7 VCC


NE =  A0*/B0  +  /A0* B0      ;COMPARE A0 NE B0
   +  A1*/B1  +  /A1* B1      ;COMPARE A1 NE B1
   +  A2*/B2  +  /A2* B2      ;COMPARE A2 NE B2
   +  A3*/B3  +  /A3* B3      ;COMPARE A3 NE B3
   +  A4*/B4  +  /A4* B4      ;COMPARE A4 NE B4
   +  A5*/B5  +  /A5* B5      ;COMPARE A5 NE B5
   +  A6*/B6  +  /A6* B6      ;COMPARE A6 NE B6
   +  A7*/B7  +  /A7* B7      ;COMPARE A7 NE B7


FUNCTION TABLE

A7 A6 A5 A4 A3 A2 A1 A0 B7 B6 B5 B4 B3 B2 B1 B0 NE EQ

;INPUT  A   INPUT  B   OUTPUTS
;76543210   76543210    NE EQ    COMMENTS
------------------------------------------------------------
 HLLLLLLL   LLLLLLLL    H   L    A7=H, B7=L
 LHLLLLLL   LLLLLLLL    H   L    A6=H, B6=L
 LLHLLLLL   LLLLLLLL    H   L    A5=H, B5=L
 LLLHLLLL   LLLLLLLL    H   L    A4=H, A5=L
 LLLLHLLL   LLLLLLLL    H   L    A3=H, B3=L
 LLLLLHLL   LLLLLLLL    H   L    A2=H, B2=L
 LLLLLLHL   LLLLLLLL    H   L    A1=H, B1=L
 LLLLLLLH   LLLLLLLL    H   L    A0=H, B0=L
 LLLLLLLL   HLLLLLLL    H   L    A7=L, B7=H
 LLLLLLLL   LHLLLLLL    H   L    A6=L, B6=H
 LLLLLLLL   LLHLLLLL    H   L    A5=L, B5=H
 LLLLLLLL   LLLHLLLL    H   L    A4=L, B4=H
 LLLLLLLL   LLLLHLLL    H   L    A3=L, B3=H
 LLLLLLLL   LLLLLHLL    H   L    A2=L, B2=H
 LLLLLLLL   LLLLLLHL    H   L    A1=L, B1=H
 LLLLLLLL   LLLLLLLH    H   L    A0=L, B0=H
 LLLLLLLL   LLLLLLLL    L   H    TEST ALL L'S
 HHHHHHHH   HHHHHHHH    L   H    TEST ALL H'S
 HLHLHLHL   HLHLHLHL    L   H    TEST EVEN CHECKERBOARD
 LHLHLHLH   LHLHLHLH    L   H    TEST ODD  CHECKERBOARD
 HHLLHHLL   HHLLHHLL    L   H    TEST EVEN DOUBLE CHECKERBOARD
 LLHHLLHH   LLHHLLHH    L   H    TEST ODD  DOUBLE CHECKERBOARD
------------------------------------------------------------


DESCRIPTION

THE OCTAL COMPARATOR ESTABLISHES WHEN TWO 8-BIT DATA STRINGS
(A7-A0 AND B7-B0) ARE EQUIVALENT (EQ=H) OR NOT EQUIVALENT (NE=H).
```

```
OCTAL COMPARATOR

 1 000000010X0000LH0001
 2 000000100X0000LH0001
 3 000001000X0000LH0001
 4 000010000X0000LH0001
 5 000100000X0000LH0001
 6 001000000X0000LH0001
 7 010000000X0000LH0001
 8 100000000X0000LH0001
 9 000000000X0000LH0011
10 000000000X0000LH0101
11 000000000X0000LH1001
12 000000000X0001LH0001
13 000000000X0010LH0001
14 000000000X0100LH0001
15 000000000X1000LH0001
16 000000001X0000LH0001
17 000000000X0000HL0001
18 111111111X1111HL1111
19 010101010X1010HL1011
20 101010101X0101HL0101
21 001100110X0110HL0111
22 110011001X1001HL1001

PASS SIMULATION
```

OCTAL COMPARATOR

```
             11 1111 1111 2222 2222 2233
   0123 4567 8901 2345 6789 0123 4567 8901



24 --X- ---- ---- ---- ---- ---- ---- -X-- A0*/B0
25 ---X ---- ---- ---- ---- ---- ---- X--- /A0*B0
26 X--- ---- ---- ---- ---- ---- ---- ---X A1*/B1
27 -X-- ---- ---- ---- ---- ---- ---- --X- /A1*B1
28 ---- X--- ---- ---- ---- ---- ---X ---- A2*/B2
29 ---- -X-- ---- ---- ---- ---- --X- ---- /A2*B2
30 ---- ---- X--- ---- ---- ---X ---- ---- A3*/B3
31 ---- ---- -X-- ---- ---- --X- ---- ---- /A3*B3

32 ---- ---- ---- X--- ---X ---- ---- ---- A4*/B4
33 ---- ---- ---- -X-- --X- ---- ---- ---- /A4*B4
34 ---- ---- ---- ---X X--- ---- ---- ---- A5*/B5
35 ---- ---- ---- --X- -X-- ---- ---- ---- /A5*B5
36 ---- ---- ---X ---- ---- X--- ---- ---- A6*/B6
37 ---- ---- --X- ---- ---- -X-- ---- ---- /A6*B6
38 ---- ---X ---- ---- ---- ---- X--- ---- A7*/B7
39 ---- --X- ---- ---- ---- ---- -X-- ---- /A7*B7
```

LEGEND: X : FUSE NOT BLOWN (L,N,0) - : FUSE BLOWN (H,P,1)

NUMBER OF FUSES BLOWN = 480

Octal Comparator

Logic Diagram PAL16C1

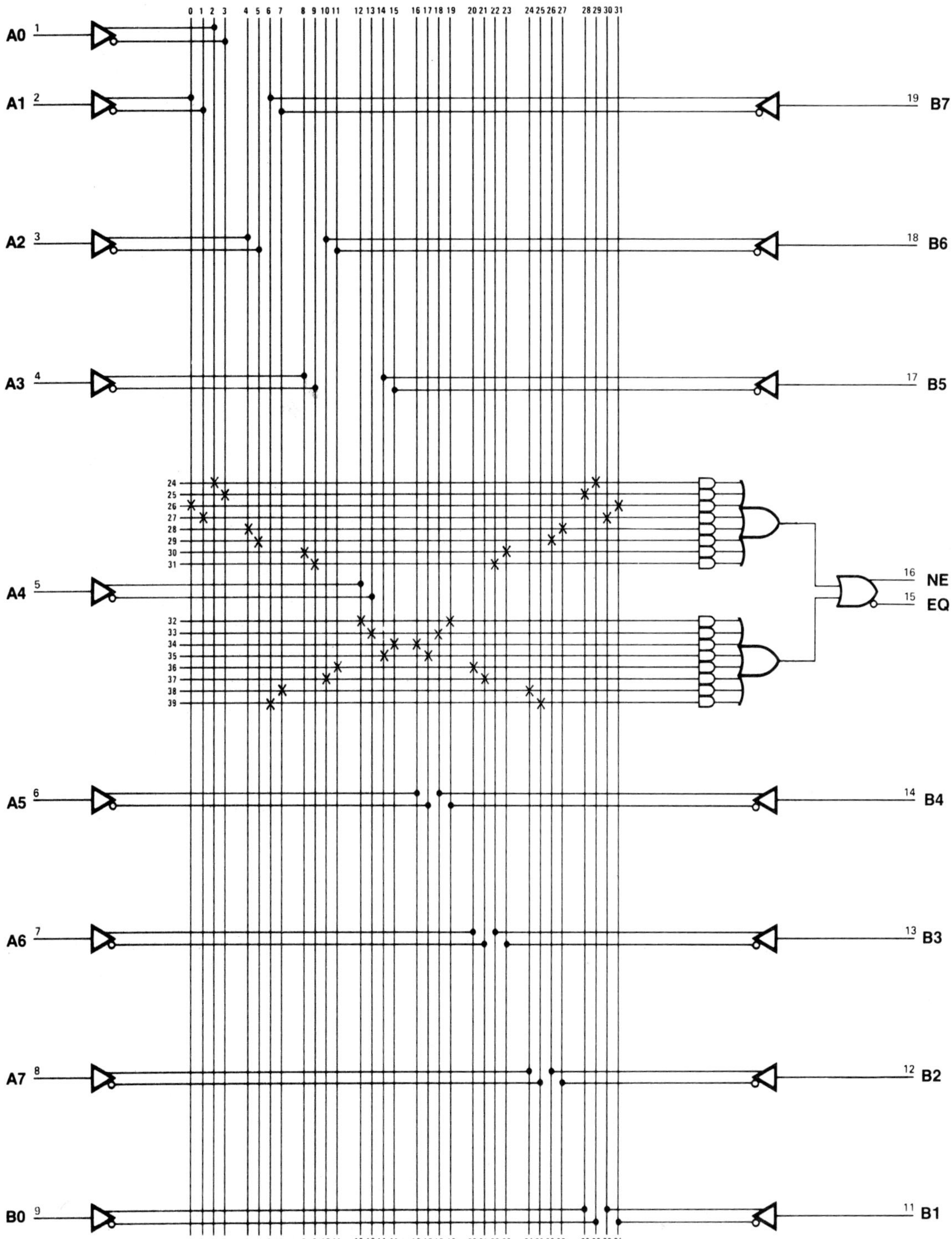

PAL
IMPORTANT
NOTES

Between Limits Comparator

PAL16X4

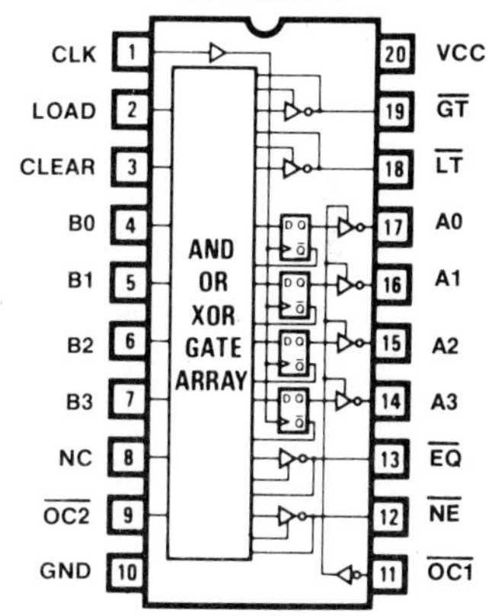

PAL16C1

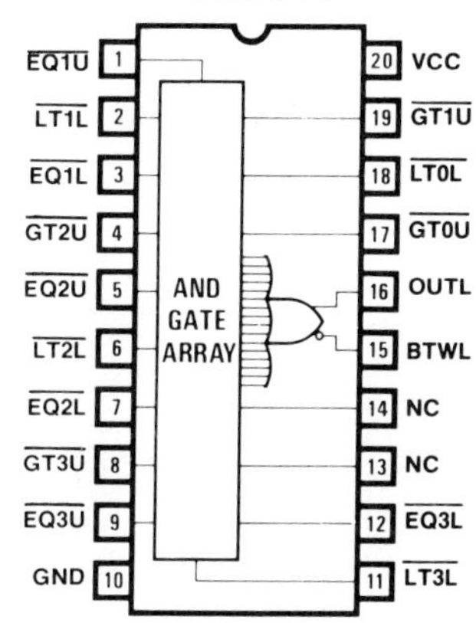

Between Limits Comparator

Logic Schematic

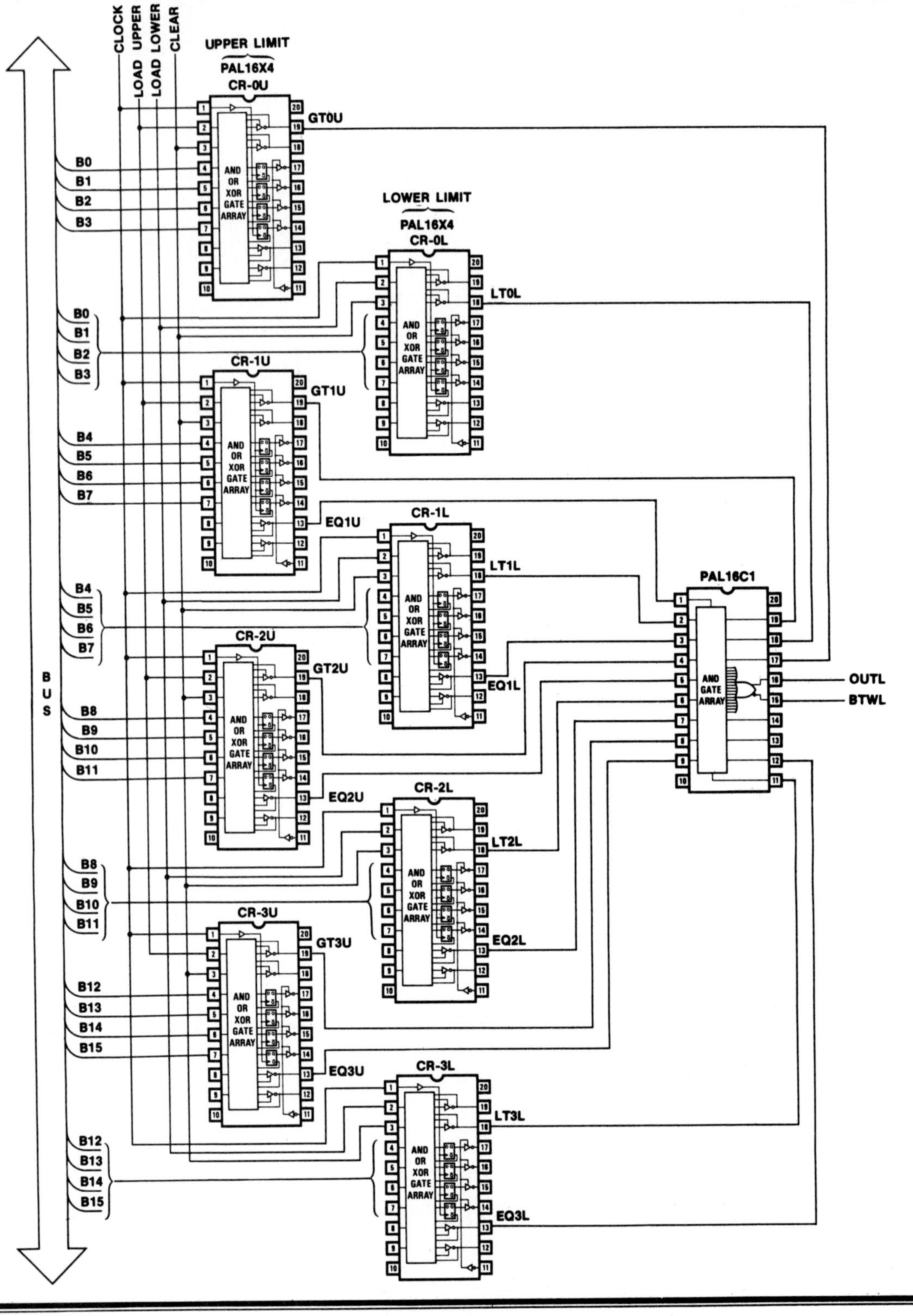

```
PAL16X4                                              PAL DESIGN SPECIFICATION
BLR                                                    BIRKNER/COLI 07/12/81
BETWEEN LIMITS COMPARATOR/REGISTER
MMI SUNNYVALE, CALIFORNIA
 CLK LOAD CLEAR B0 B1 B2 B3  NC /OC2 GND
/OC1 /NE   /EQ  A3 A2 A1 A0 /LT /GT  VCC


IF(OC2)  LT = (A3*/B3)                                                ;B3=L, A3=H
            + (A3:*:B3) * (A2*/B2)                                    ;B2=L, A2=H
            + (A3:*:B3) * (A2:*:B2) * (A1*/B1)                        ;B1=L, A1=H
            + (A3:*:B3) * (A2:*:B2) * (A1:*:B1) * (A0*/B0)            ;B0=L, A0=H

IF(OC2)  GT = (/A3*B3)                                                ;B3=H, A3=L
            + (A3:*:B3) * (/A2*B2)                                    ;B2=H, A2=L
            + (A3:*:B3) * (A2:*:B2) * (/A1*B1)                        ;B1=H, A1=L
            + (A3:*:B3) * (A2:*:B2) * (A1:*:B1) * (/A0*B0)            ;B0=H, A0=L

IF(OC2)  EQ = (A3:*:B3) * (A2:*:B2) * (A1:*:B1) * (A0:*:B0)  ;COMPARE EQUAL

IF(OC2)  NE = (A3:+:B3) + (A2:+:B2) + (A1:+:B1) + (A0:+:B0)  ;COMPARE NOT EQUAL

     /A3 := (/A3)*/LOAD       ;HOLD  REG A3
          + (/B3)* LOAD       ;LOAD  REG A3
          +  CLEAR            ;CLEAR REG A3

     /A2 := (/A2)*/LOAD       ;HOLD  REG A2
          + (/B2)* LOAD       ;LOAD  REG A2
          +  CLEAR            ;CLEAR REG A2

     /A1 := (/A1)*/LOAD       ;HOLD  REG A1
          + (/B1)* LOAD       ;LOAD  REG A1
          +  CLEAR            ;CLEAR REG A1

     /A0 := (/A0)*/LOAD       ;HOLD  REG A0
          + (/B0)* LOAD       ;LOAD  REG A0
          +  CLEAR            ;CLEAR REG A0
```

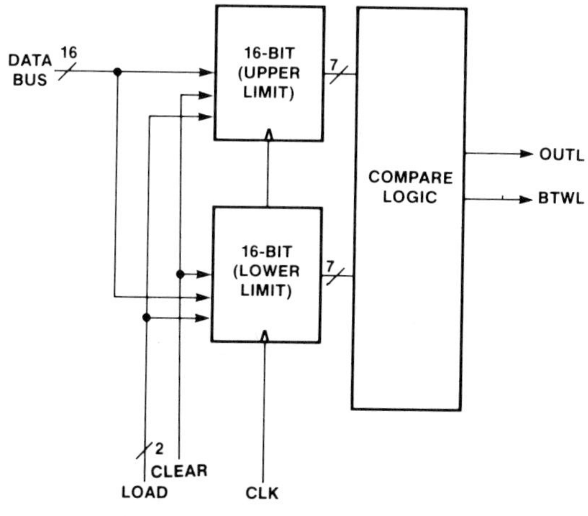

```
FUNCTION TABLE

CLK /OC1 /OC2 LOAD CLEAR B3 B2 B1 B0 A3 A2 A1 A0 LT EQ NE GT

;CONTROL                  BUS   REG
;    /OC   OPERATIONS    BBBB  AAAA   --STATUS---        COMMENTS
;CLK 1 2   LOAD CLEAR    3210  3210   LT EQ NE GT       (HEX VALUES)
--------------------------------------------------------------------------
  C  L X    X     H      XXXX  LLLL   X  X  X  X       CLEAR REG
  C  L X    H     L      LLLL  LLLL   X  X  X  X       LOAD REG (0)
  X  L L    L     L      LLLL  LLLL   L  H  L  L       COMPARE (0 EQ 0)
  X  L L    L     L      LLLH  LLLL   L  L  H  H       COMPARE (1 GT 0)
  X  L X    L     L      XXXX  LLLL   X  X  X  X       READ REG (0)
  C  L X    X     H      XXXX  LLLL   X  X  X  X       CLEAR REG
  C  L X    H     L      LHLH  LHLH   X  X  X  X       LOAD REG (5)
  X  L L    L     L      LLLL  LHLH   H  L  H  L       COMPARE (0 LT 5)
  X  L L    L     L      LHLH  LHLH   L  H  L  L       COMPARE (5 EQ 5)
  X  L L    L     L      HHHH  LHLH   L  L  H  H       COMPARE (F GT 5)
  X  L X    L     L      XXXX  LHLH   X  X  X  X       READ REG (5)
  C  L X    X     H      XXXX  LLLL   X  X  X  X       CLEAR REG
  C  L X    H     L      HLHL  HLHL   X  X  X  X       LOAD REG (A)
  X  L L    L     L      LHLL  HLHL   H  L  H  L       COMPARE (4 LT A)
  X  L L    L     L      HLHL  HLHL   L  H  L  L       COMPARE (A EQ A)
  X  L L    L     L      HLHH  HLHL   L  L  H  H       COMPARE (B GT A)
  X  L X    L     L      XXXX  HLHL   X  X  X  X       READ REG (A)
  C  L X    X     H      XXXX  LLLL   X  X  X  X       CLEAR REG
  C  L X    H     L      HHHH  HHHH   X  X  X  X       LOAD REG (F)
  X  L L    L     L      HHHL  HHHH   H  L  H  L       COMPARE (E LT F)
  X  L L    L     L      HHHH  HHHH   L  H  L  L       COMPARE (F EQ F)
  X  L X    L     L      XXXX  HHHH   X  X  X  X       READ REG (F)
  C  L X    L     L      XXXX  HHHH   X  X  X  X       HOLD (F)
  X  H X    X     X      XXXX  ZZZZ   X  X  X  X       TEST HI-Z (/OC1=H)
  X  X H    X     X      XXXX  XXXX   Z  Z  Z  Z       TEST HI-Z (/OC2=H)
--------------------------------------------------------------------------
```

DESCRIPTION

THE DEVICE CONTINUOUSLY COMPARES THE VALUE OF BUS (B3-B0) WITH THE VALUE OF THE REGISTER (A3-A0) AND REPORTS THE STATUS ON OUTPUTS LT, EQ, NE, AND GT:

```
* LT INDICATES THAT B IS  LESS   THAN A
* EQ INDICATES THAT B IS   EQUAL   TO A
* NE INDICATES THAT B IS NOT EQUAL TO A
* GT INDICATES THAT B IS GREATER THAN A
```

/OC1	/OC2	CLK	LOAD	CLEAR	STATUS LT	EQ	NE	GT	BUS B3-B0	REG A3-A0	OPERATION
H	X	X	X	X	X	X	X	X	X	Z	REG HI-Z
X	H	X	X	X	Z	Z	Z	Z	X	X	STATUS HI-Z
L	X	X	L	L	X	X	X	X	X	A	READ REG
X	X	C	H	L	X	X	X	X	B	B	LOAD REG
X	X	C	L	L	X	X	X	X	X	A	HOLD
X	X	C	X	H	X	X	X	X	X	L	CLEAR REG
X	L	X	L	L	STATUS				B	A	COMPARE

```
BETWEEN LIMITS COMPARATOR/REGISTER

  1 CX1XXXXXXX0XXLLLLXX1
  2 C100000XXX0XXLLLLXX1
  3 X000000X0X0HLLLLLHH1
  4 X001000X0X0LHLLLLHL1
  5 X00XXXXXXX0XXLLLLXX1
  6 CX1XXXXXXX0XXLLLLXX1
  7 C101010XXX0XXLHLHXX1
  8 X000000X0X0LHLHLHLH1
  9 X001010X0X0HLLHLHHH1
 10 X001111X0X0LHLHLHHL1
 11 X00XXXXXXX0XXLHLHXX1
 12 CX1XXXXXXX0XXLLLLXX1
 13 C100101XXX0XXHLHLXX1
 14 X000010X0X0LHHLHLLH1
 15 X000101X0X0HLHLHLHH1
 16 X001101X0X0LHHLHLHL1
 17 X00XXXXXXX0XXHLHLXX1
 18 CX1XXXXXXX0XXLLLLXX1
 19 C101111XXX0XXHHHHXX1
 20 X000111X0X0LHHHHHLH1
 21 X001111X0X0HLHHHHHH1
 22 X00XXXXXXX0XXHHHHXX1
 23 C00XXXXXXX0XXHHHHXX1
 24 XXXXXXXXXX1XXZZZZXX1
 25 XXXXXXXX1XXZZXXXXZZ1

PASS SIMULATION
```

```
BETWEEN LIMITS COMPARATOR/REGISTER

               11 1111 1111 2222 2222 2233
   0123 4567 8901 2345 6789 0123 4567 8901

 0 ---- ---- ---- ---- ---- ---- ---- -X-- OC2
 1 ---- ---- ---- ---- ---- XXX- ---- ---- /A3*B3
 2 ---- ---- ---- ---- XXX- X--X ---- ---- A3:*:B3*/A2*B2
 3 ---- ---- ---- XXX- X--X X--X ---- ---- A3:*:B3*A2:*:B2*/Al*Bl
 4 ---- ---- XXX- X--X X--X X--X ---- ---- A3:*:B3*A2:*:B2*Al:*:Bl*/A0*B0

 8 ---- ---- ---- ---- ---- ---- ---- -X-- OC2
 9 ---- ---- ---- ---- ---- -XXX ---- ---- A3*/B3
10 ---- ---- ---- ---- -XXX X--X ---- ---- A3:*:B3*A2*/B2
11 ---- ---- ---- -XXX X--X X--X ---- ---- A3:*:B3*A2:*:B2*Al*/Bl
12 ---- ---- -XXX X--X X--X X--X ---- ---- A3:*:B3*A2:*:B2*Al:*:Bl*A0*/B0

16 -X-- ---- XX-- ---- ---- ---- ---- ---- /A0*/LOAD
17 X--- ---- -X-X ---- ---- ---- ---- ---- /B0*LOAD
18 ---- X--- ---- ---- ---- ---- ---- ---- CLEAR

24 -X-- ---- ---- XX-- ---- ---- ---- ---- /Al*/LOAD
25 X--- ---- ---- -X-X ---- ---- ---- ---- /Bl*LOAD
26 ---- X--- ---- ---- ---- ---- ---- ---- CLEAR

32 -X-- ---- ---- ---- XX-- ---- ---- ---- /A2*/LOAD
33 X--- ---- ---- ---- -X-X ---- ---- ---- /B2*LOAD
34 ---- X--- ---- ---- ---- ---- ---- ---- CLEAR

40 -X-- ---- ---- ---- ---- XX-- ---- ---- /A3*/LOAD
41 X--- ---- ---- ---- ---- -X-X ---- ---- /B3*LOAD
42 ---- X--- ---- ---- ---- ---- ---- ---- CLEAR

48 ---- ---- ---- ---- ---- ---- ---- -X-- OC2
49 ---- ---- X--X X--X X--X X--X ---- ---- A3:*:B3*A2:*:B2*Al:*:Bl*A0:*:B0

56 ---- ---- ---- ---- ---- ---- ---- -X-- OC2
57 ---- ---- ---- ---- ---- -XX- ---- ---- A3:+:B3
58 ---- ---- ---- ---- -XX- ---- ---- ---- A2:+:B2
59 ---- ---- ---- -XX- ---- ---- ---- ---- Al:+:Bl
60 ---- ---- -XX- ---- ---- ---- ---- ---- A0:+:B0


LEGEND:  X : FUSE NOT BLOWN (L,N,0)   - : FUSE BLOWN   (H,P,1)

NUMBER OF FUSES BLOWN =  832
```

Between Limits Comparator/Register

Logic Diagram PAL16X4

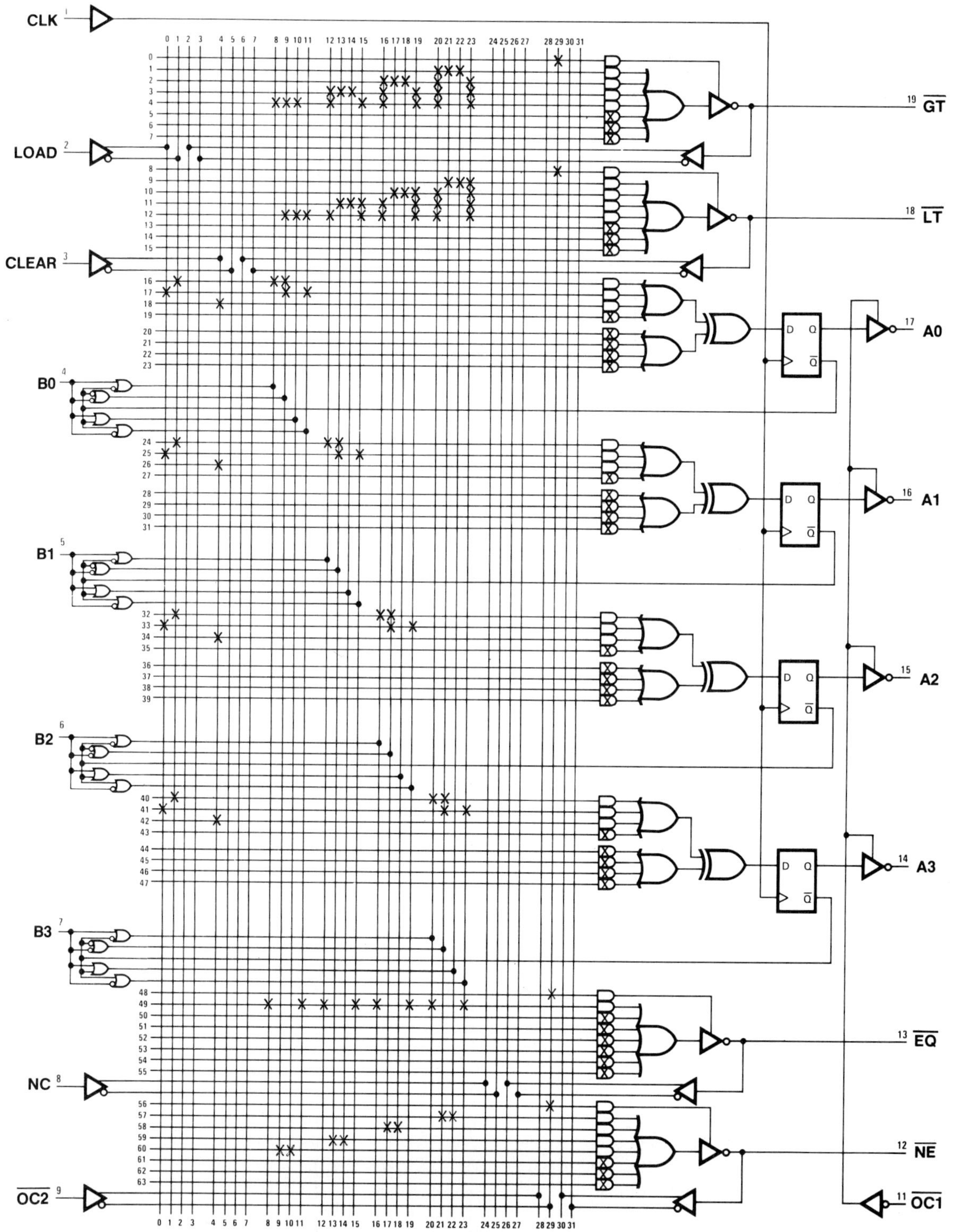

```
PAL16C1                                           PAL DESIGN SPECIFICATION
BLL                                                  BIRKNER/COLI 07/12/81
BETWEEN LIMITS COMPARATOR/LOGIC
MMI SUNNYVALE, CALIFORNIA
/EQ1U /LT1L /EQ1L /GT2U /EQ2U /LT2L /EQ2L /GT3U /EQ3U GND
/LT3L /EQ3L   NC    NC   BTWL  OUTL /GT0U /LT0L /GT1U VCC


OUTL =  GT3U                          ;GT CR-3U
     +  EQ3U * GT2U                   ;EQ CR-3U, GT CR-2U
     +  EQ3U * EQ2U * GT1U            ;EQ CR-3U, EQ CR-2U, GT CR-1U
     +  EQ3U * EQ2U * EQ1U * GT0U     ;EQ CR-3U, EQ CR-2U, EQ CR-1U, GT CR-0U
     +  LT3L                          ;LT CR-3L
     +  EQ3L * LT2L                   ;EQ CR-3L, LT CR-2L
     +  EQ3L * EQ2L * LT1L            ;EQ CR-3L, EQ CR-2L, LT CR-1L
     +  EQ3L * EQ2L * EQ1L * LT0L     ;EQ CR-3L, EQ CR-2L, EQ CR-1L, LT CR-0L


FUNCTION TABLE

GT3U EQ3U EQ3L LT3L GT2U EQ2U EQ2L LT2L GT1U EQ1U EQ1L LT1L GT0U LT0L OUTL BTWL

; COMPARATOR REGISTERS
;CR-3  CR-2  CR-1  CR-0
;GEEL  GEEL  GEEL  G  L
;TQQT  TQQT  TQQT  T  T     OUTPUTS
;UULL  UULL  UULL  U  L    OUTL  BTWL     COMMENTS
---------------------------------------------------------------
 HLLL  XXXX  XXXX  X  X     H     L       OUT OF LIMITS (GT3U=H)
 LHLL  HLLL  XXXX  X  X     H     L       OUT OF LIMITS (GT2U=H)
 LHLL  LHLL  HLLL  X  X     H     L       OUT OF LIMITS (GT1U=H)
 LHLL  LHLL  LHLL  H  L     H     L       OUT OF LIMITS (GT0U=H)
 LHLL  LHLL  LHLL  L  H     L     H       BETWEEN LIMITS
 LHLL  LHLL  LLHL  X  X     L     H       BETWEEN LIMITS
 LHLL  LHLL  LLLH  X  X     L     H       BETWEEN LIMITS
 LHLL  LLHL  XXXX  X  X     L     H       BETWEEN LIMITS
 LHLL  LLLH  XXXX  X  X     L     H       BETWEEN LIMITS
 LLHL  HLLL  XXXX  X  X     L     H       BETWEEN LIMITS
 LLHL  LHLL  XXXX  X  X     L     H       BETWEEN LIMITS
 LLHL  LLHL  HLLL  X  X     L     H       BETWEEN LIMITS
 LLHL  LLHL  LHLL  X  X     L     H       BETWEEN LIMITS
 LLHL  LLHL  LLHL  H  L     L     H       BETWEEN LIMITS
 LLHL  LLHL  LLHL  L  H     H     L       OUT OF LIMITS (LT0L=H)
 LLHL  LLHL  LLLH  X  X     H     L       OUT OF LIMITS (LT1L=H)
 LLHL  LLLH  XXXX  X  X     H     L       OUT OF LIMITS (LT2L=H)
 LLLH  XXXX  XXXX  X  X     H     L       OUT OF LIMITS (LT3L=H)
---------------------------------------------------------------


DESCRIPTION

THE BETWEEN LIMITS LOGIC CHECKS THE LT, EQ, AND GT STATUS FROM THE
COMPARATOR REGISTERS TO DETERMINE IF THE DATA IS BETWEEN THE UPPER
AND LOWER LIMITS LOADED IN THE COMPARATOR REGISTERS.  BOTH BETWEEN
LIMITS (BTWL) AND OUT OF LIMITS (OUTL) OUTPUTS ARE PROVIDED.
```

```
BETWEEN LIMITS COMPARATOR/LOGIC

 1 XXXXXXX01X11XXLHXXX1
 2 XXX011110X11XXLHXXX1
 3 111101110X11XXLHXX01
 4 011101110X11XXLH0111
 5 011101110X11XXHL1011
 6 110101110X11XXHLXX11
 7 101101110X11XXHLXX11
 8 XXX111010X11XXHLXXX1
 9 XXX110110X11XXHLXXX1
10 XXX011111X10XXHLXXX1
11 XXX101111X10XXHLXXX1
12 111111011X10XXHLXX01
13 011111011X10XXHLXX11
14 110111011X10XXHL0111
15 110111011X10XXLH1011
16 101111011X10XXLHXX11
17 XXX110111X10XXLHXXX1
18 XXXXXXX11X01XXLHXXX1

PASS SIMULATION
```

```
BETWEEN LIMITS COMPARATOR/LOGIC

                11 1111 1111 2222 2222 2233
   0123 4567 8901 2345 6789 0123 4567 8901



24 ---- ---- ---- ---- ---- ---- -X-- ---- GT3U
25 ---- ---- -X-- ---- ---- ---- ---- -X-- EQ3U*GT2U
26 ---- ---X ---- -X-- ---- ---- ---- -X-- EQ3U*EQ2U*GT1U
27 ---X ---- ---- -X-X ---- ---- ---- -X-- EQ3U*EQ2U*EQ1U*GT0U
28 ---- ---- ---- ---- ---- ---- ---- ---X LT3L
29 ---- ---- ---- ---- -X-- ---- ---X ---- EQ3L*LT2L
30 -X-- ---- ---- ---- ---- -X-- ---X ---- EQ3L*EQ2L*LT1L
31 ---- -X-- ---X ---- ---- -X-- ---X ---- EQ3L*EQ2L*EQ1L*LT0L



LEGEND:  X : FUSE NOT BLOWN (L,N,0)   - : FUSE BLOWN   (H,P,1)

NUMBER OF FUSES BLOWN =  236
```

Between Limits Comparator/Logic

Logic Diagram PAL16C1

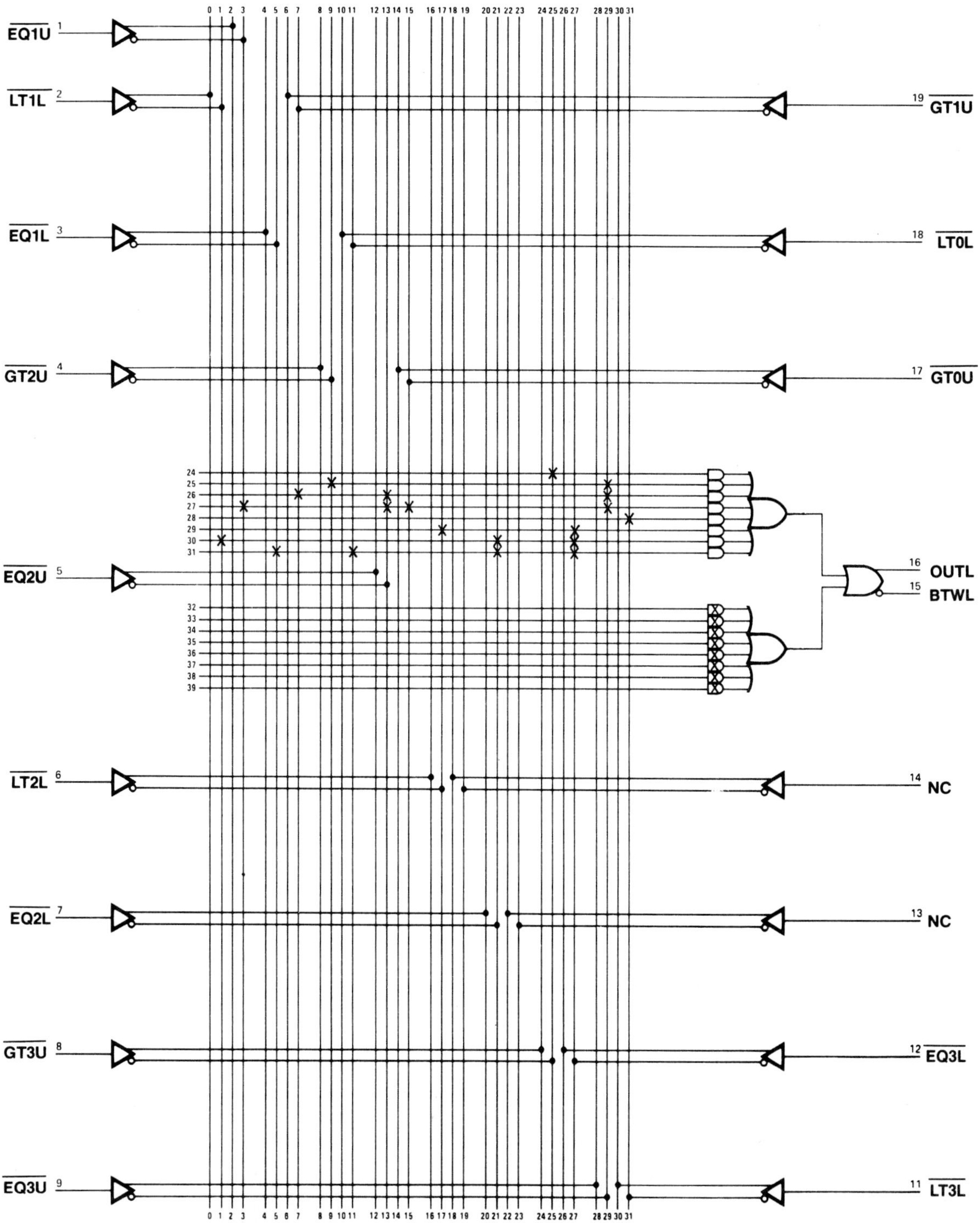

PAL
IMPORTANT,
NOTES

Memory Mapped Printer

PAL16H2

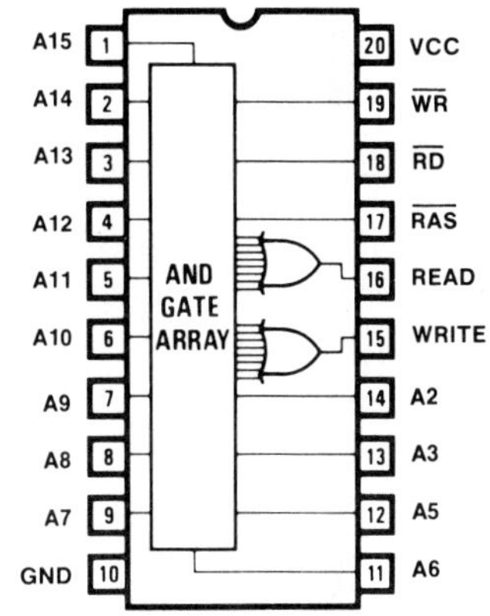

PAL20X8

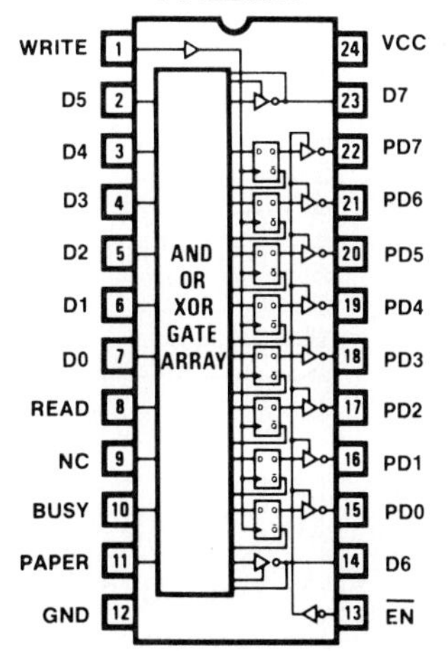

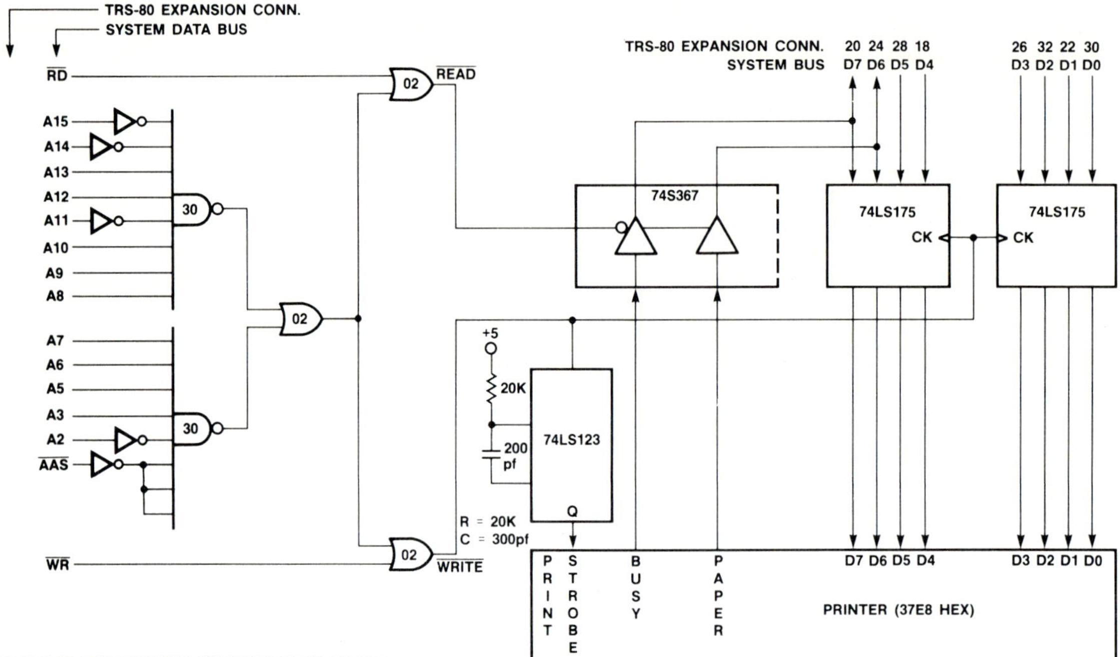

*TRS-80 IS A TRADEMARK OF TANDY RADIO SHACK

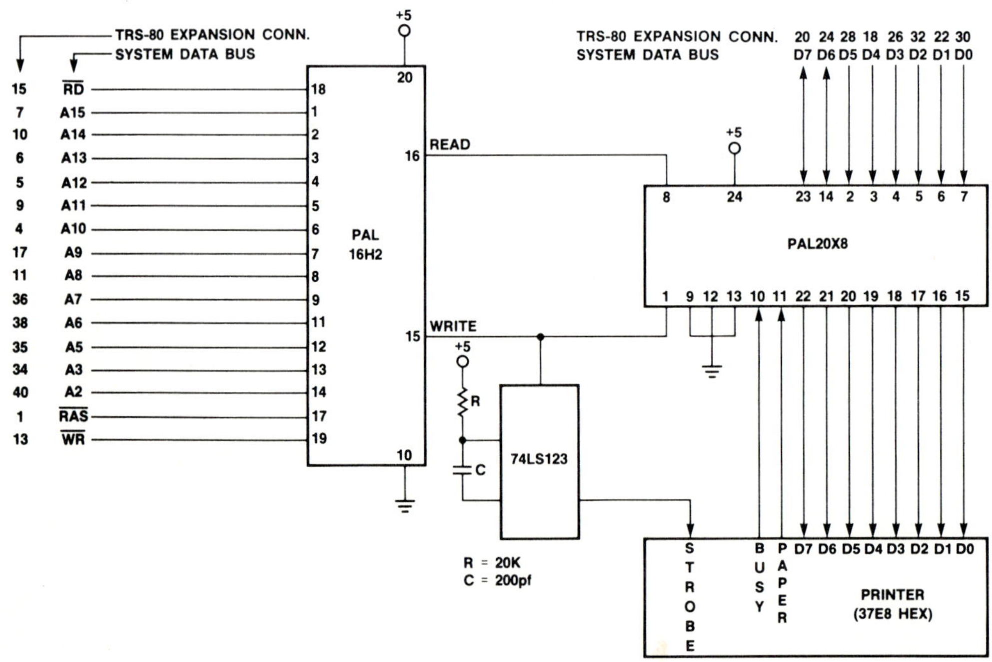

*TRS-80 IS A TRADEMARK OF TANDY RADIO SHACK

```
PAL16H2                                    PAL DESIGN SPECIFICATION
MMPD                                       DICK JONES       07/07/81
MEMORY MAPPED PRINTER DECODER
MMI FIELD APPLICATIONS ENGINEER LOMBARD, ILLINOIS
A15 A14 A13 A12 A11 A10 A9 A8 A7 GND
A6 A5 A3 A2 WRITE READ /RAS /RD /WR VCC

WRITE = /A15*/A14*A13*A12*/A11*A10*A9*A8*A7*A6*A5*A3*/A2*RAS*WR

 READ = /A15*/A14*A13*A12*/A11*A10*A9*A8*A7*A6*A5*A3*/A2*RAS*RD


FUNCTION TABLE

A15 A14 A13 A12 A11 A10 A9 A8 A7 A6 A5 A3 A2 RAS RD WR WRITE READ

;AAAA AAAA AAA AA RRW    WR
;1111 1198 765 32 ADR    RE
;5432 10          S      IA
;                        TD
;                        E       COMMENTS
-----------------------------------------------------
 LLHH LHHH HHH HL HLH    HL      WRITE WHEN 37E8 HEX
 LLHH LHHH HHH HL HHL    LH      READ WHEN 37E8 HEX
 XXXX XXXX XXX XX LXX    LL      RAS NOT PRESENT
 XXXX XXXX XXX XX HLL    LL      NOT READ OR WRITE
-----------------------------------------------------


DESCRIPTION

THIS IS A MEMORY DECODER FOR A PRINTER.  THE PRINTER
IS MAPPED TO HEX ADDRESS 37E8.  THE WRITE OR READ LINES
GO HIGH WHEN ADDRESS LINES ARE CORRECT AND A WRITE OR
READ STROBE RESPECTIVELY IS PRESENT.

THIS IS THE FIRST IC OF A 2-PAL PRINTER INTERFACE FOR
THE STANDARD CENTRONICS-TYPE PRINTER.



MEMORY MAPPED PRINTER DECODER

 1 001101111X1110HL0101
 2 001101111X1110LH0011
 3 XXXXXXXXXXXXXXLL1XX1
 4 XXXXXXXXXXXXXXLL0111

PASS SIMULATION
```

```
MEMORY MAPPED PRINTER DECODER

                11 1111 1111 2222 2222 2233
   0123 4567 8901 2345 6789 0123 4567 8901



24 -X-X X--- X--X -X-X X--X X-X- X-X- X-X- /A15*/A14*A13*A12*/A11*A10*A9*-

32 -X-X X--X X--- -X-X X--X X-X- X-X- X-X- /A15*/A14*A13*A12*/A11*A10*A9*-



LEGEND:  X : FUSE NOT BLOWN (L,N,0)   - : FUSE BLOWN   (H,P,1)

NUMBER OF FUSES BLOWN =   34
```

Memory Mapped Printer Decoder

Logic Diagram PAL16H2

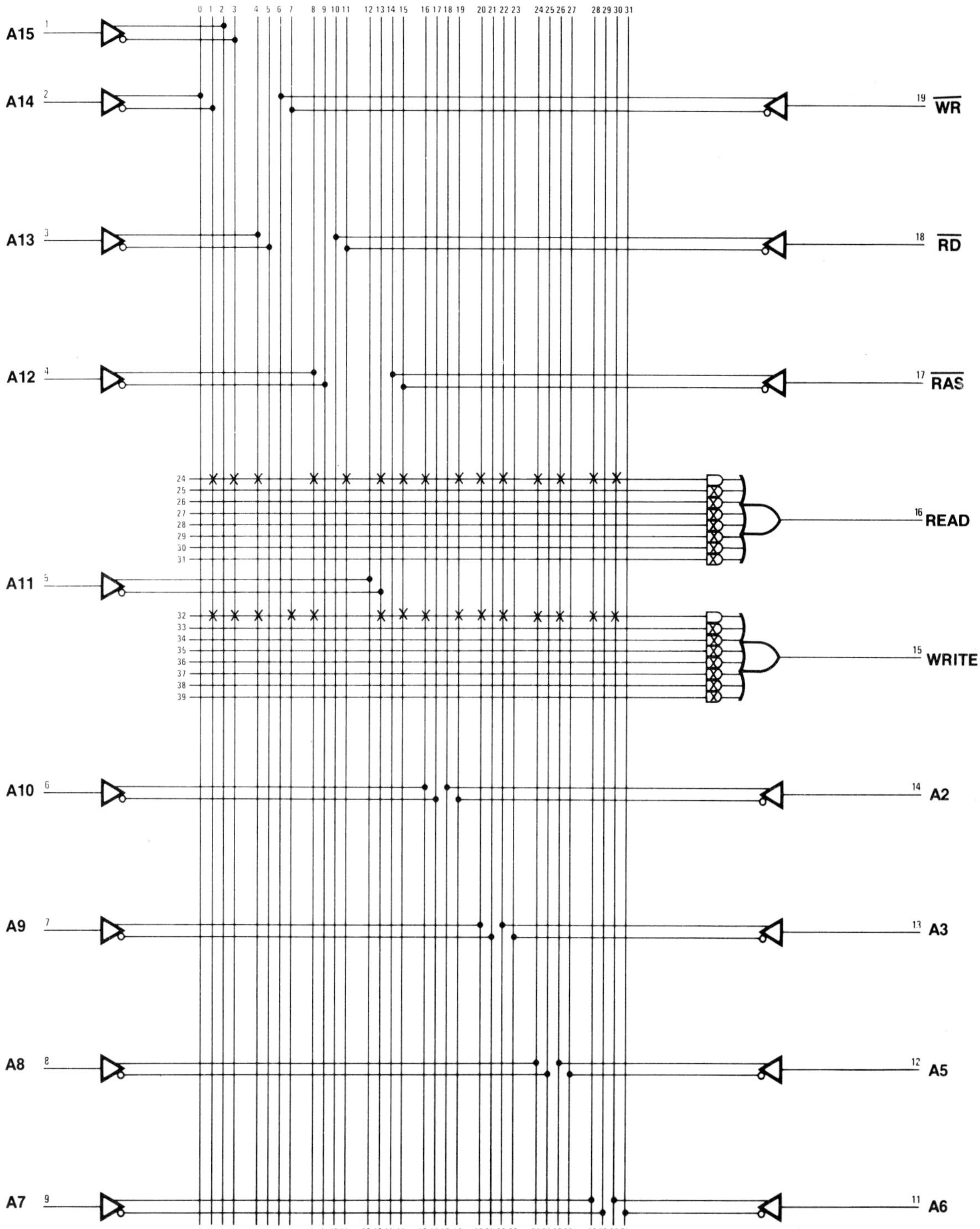

```
PAL20X8                                      PAL DESIGN SPECIFICATION
PDRM                                         DICK JONES      07/07/81
PRINTER DATA REGISTER/MUX
MMI FIELD APPLICATIONS ENGINEER LOMBARD, ILLINOIS
WRITE D5 D4 D3 D2 D1 D0 READ NC BUSY PAPER GND
/EN D6 PD0 PD1 PD2 PD3 PD4 PD5 PD6 PD7 D7 VCC


IF (READ) /D7  = /BUSY       ;READ PRINTER STATUS - BUSY

         /PD7 := /D7         ;LOAD MSB TO PRINTER

         /PD6 := /D6         ;LOAD PRINTER

         /PD5 := /D5         ;LOAD PRINTER

         /PD4 := /D4         ;LOAD PRINTER

         /PD3 := /D3         ;LOAD PRINTER

         /PD2 := /D2         ;LOAD PRINTER

         /PD1 := /D1         ;LOAD PRINTER

         /PD0 := /D0         ;LOAD LSB TO PRINTER

IF (READ) /D6  = /PAPER      ;READ PRINTER STATUS - PAPER OUT

FUNCTION TABLE

WRITE BUSY PAPER READ D7 D6 D5 D4 D3 D2 D1 D0 PD7 PD6 PD5 PD4 PD3 PD2 PD1 PD0

;WBPR DDDDDDDD PPPPPPPP
;RUAE 76543210 DDDDDDDD
;ISPA          76543210
;TYED
;E R                         COMMENTS
------------------------------------------------
 LHLH HLXXXXXX XXXXXXXX      READ PRNTR STATUS
 LLHH LHXXXXXX XXXXXXXX      READ PRNTR STATUS
 CXXL ZZXXXXXX XXXXXXXX      TEST HI-Z
 CXXL LLLLLLLL LLLLLLLL      LOAD DATA TO PRINTER
 CXXL HLHLHLHL HLHLHLHL      LOAD DATA TO PRINTER
 CXXL HHHHHHHH HHHHHHHH      LOAD DATA TO PRINTER
------------------------------------------------
```

DESCRIPTION

REGISTERED DATA FROM THE SYSTEM BUSS IS PRESENTED TO THE PRINTER WHEN A WRITE STROBE FROM THE DECODER IS PRESENT (DJPR1).

PRINTER STATUS DATA (PRINTER BUSY AND OUT OF PAPER) IS TRANSFERED TO THE SYSTEM DATA BUSS WHEN A READ STROBE FROM THE DECODER IS PRESENT.

THIS IS THE SECOND IC OF THE 2-PAL PRINTER INTERFACE FOR THE STANDARD CENTRONICS-TYPE PRINTER.

```
PRINTER DATA REGISTER/MUX

  1 0XXXXXX1X10XXLXXXXXXXXH1
  2 0XXXXXX1X01XXHXXXXXXXXL1
  3 CXXXXXX0XXXXXZXXXXXXXXZ1
  4 C0000000XXXXX0LLLLLLLL01
  5 C1010100XXXXX0LHLHLHLH11
  6 C1111110XXXXX1HHHHHHHH11

PASS SIMULATION
```

```
PRINTER DATA REGISTER/MUX

                 11 1111 1111 2222 2222 2233 3333 3333
     0123 4567 8901 2345 6789 0123 4567 8901 2345 6789

   0 ---- ---- ---- ---- ---- ---- X--- ---- ---- ---- READ
   1 ---- ---- ---- ---- ---- ---- ---- ---- -X-- ---- /BUSY

   8 ---X ---- ---- ---- ---- ---- ---- ---- ---- ---- /D7

  16 ---- ---- ---- ---- ---- ---- ---- ---- ---- ---X /D6

  24 -X-- ---- ---- ---- ---- ---- ---- ---- ---- ---- /D5

  32 ---- -X-- ---- ---- ---- ---- ---- ---- ---- ---- /D4

  40 ---- ---- -X-- ---- ---- ---- ---- ---- ---- ---- /D3

  48 ---- ---- ---- -X-- ---- ---- ---- ---- ---- ---- /D2

  56 ---- ---- ---- ---- -X-- ---- ---- ---- ---- ---- /D1

  64 ---- ---- ---- ---- ---- -X-- ---- ---- ---- ---- /D0

  72 ---- ---- ---- ---- ---- ---- X--- ---- ---- ---- READ
  73 ---- ---- ---- ---- ---- ---- ---- ---- ---- -X-- /PAPER

LEGEND:  X : FUSE NOT BLOWN (L,N,0)   - : FUSE BLOWN   (H,P,1)

NUMBER OF FUSES BLOW =  468
```

Printer Data Register/Mux

Logic Diagram PAL20X8

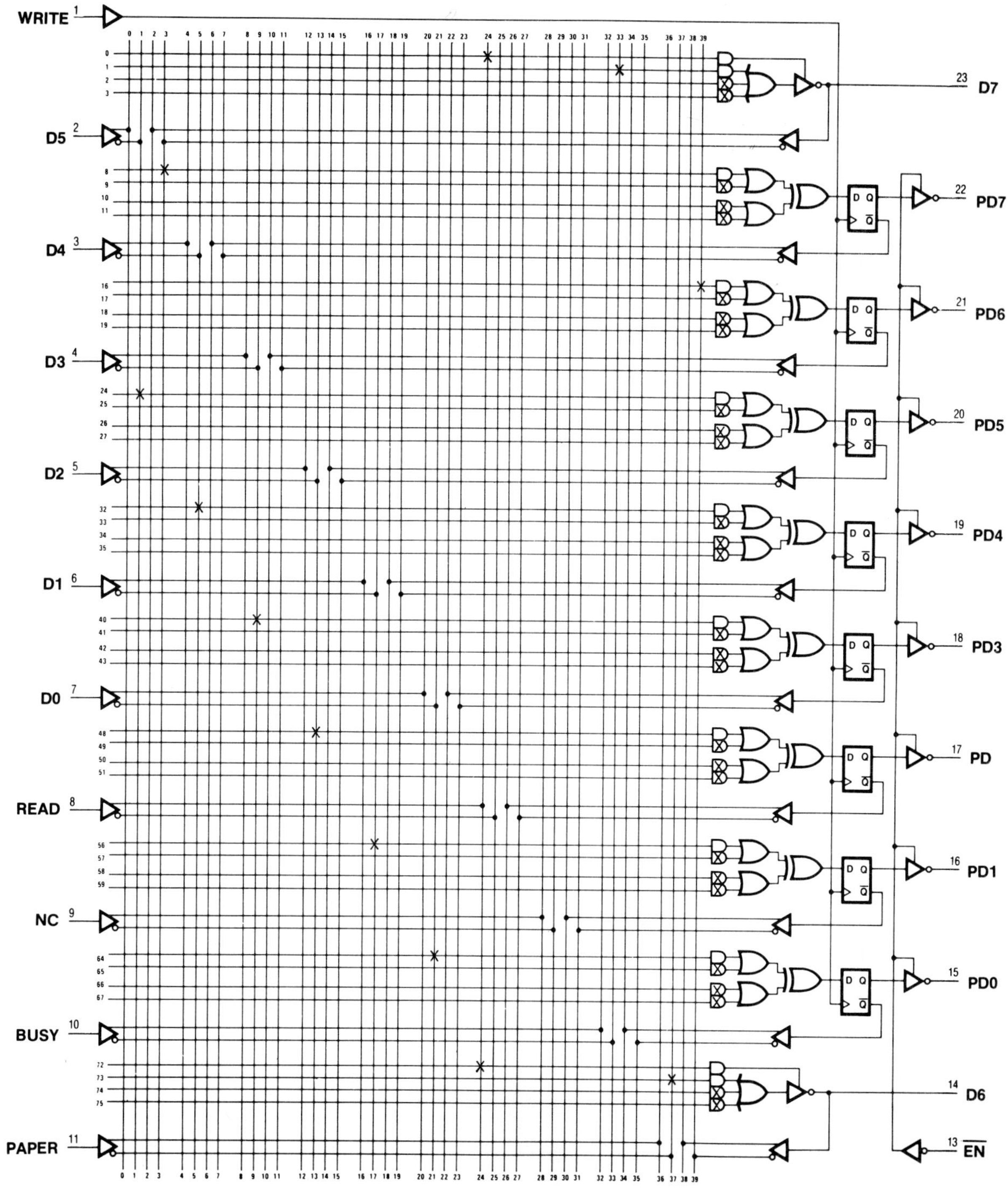

PAL
IMPORTANT,
NOTES

Craps Game

PAL16R4

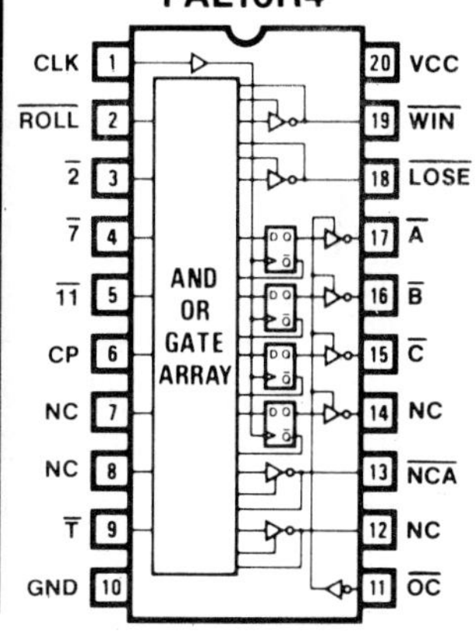

PAL16R6

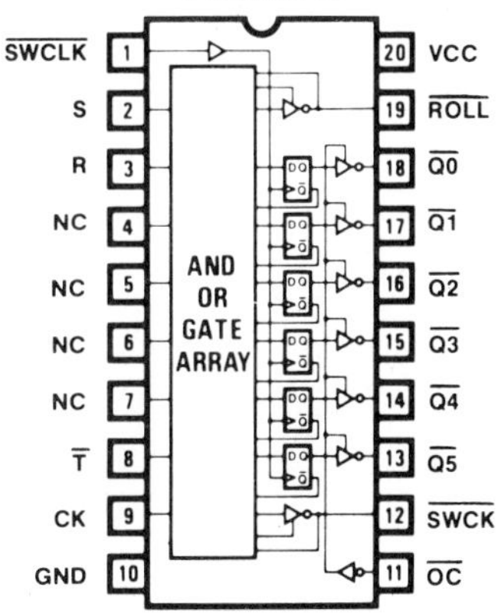

PAL16L8

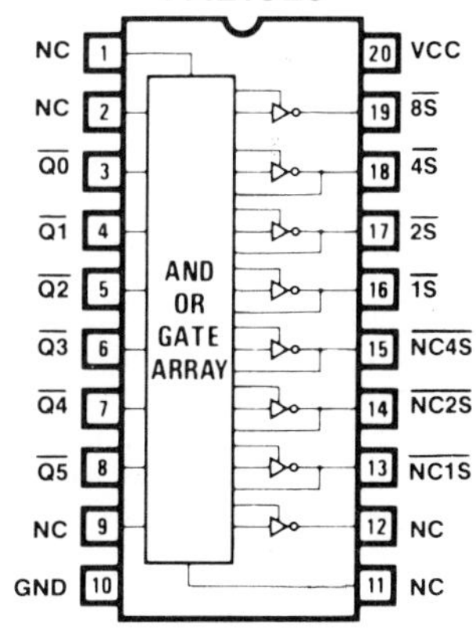

PAL16R4

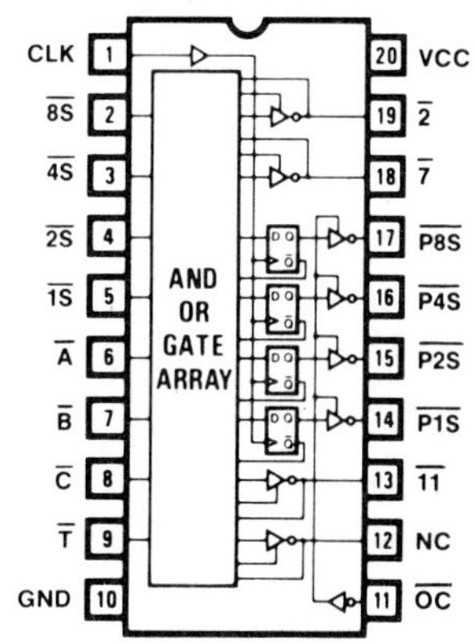

A Game of Chance

This application note describes the use of PALs to simulate the dice game "Craps". The design requirements were derived from the basic rules of the game which are listed below.

1. The player throws two dice. The number will be between 2 and 12.
2. He wins if the number is 7 or 11. He loses if the number is 2, which is called "snake eyes".
3. Any number other than 2, 7, or 11 is the player's point.
4. Player continues to roll if a point is indicated on the first roll.
5. The player loses if he throws 7 or 11 on a subsequent roll.
6. The player wins if he throws a point on a subsequent roll.
7. The player continues to roll until a win or a loss is indicated.

There are four PALs used in this design, which are:

IC1 8-State Machine and Win-Lose Decoder
IC2 36-State Machine
IC3 Dice Decoder
IC4 Store Point and /2, /7, and /11 Decode

Not included in this application note are three more ICs. These are a 74LS85 (Magnitude Comparitor), used to compare the stored point to the roll of the dice on second and subsequent rolls, and two Binary-to-Seven Segment Decoders, used to drive the LED displays.

```
PAL16R4                                                PAL DESIGN SPECIFICATION
IC1                                                      BRAD MITCHELL 04/07/81
8-STATE MACHINE AND WIN-LOSE DECODER
MMI FIELD APPLICATIONS ENGINEER DALLAS, TEXAS
CLK /ROLL /2 /7 /11 CP NC NC /T GND
/OC NC /NCA NC /C /B /A /LOSE /WIN VCC


IF(VCC) WIN  =  A* B*/C                         ;DECODE THE WIN STATE

IF(VCC) LOSE =  A*/B* C                         ;DECODE THE LOSE STATE

IF(VCC) NCA  =  A* B*/C*/ROLL                   ;STATE DECODES DERIVED
             +  A*/B* C*/ROLL                   ;FROM THE KARNAUGH MAP
             + /A* B* C*/ROLL                   ;NCA IS ADDITIONAL DECODE FOR A

          A := /A* B*/C*/ROLL* 7            * T ;STATE DECODES DERIVED
             + /A* B*/C*/ROLL   * 11        * T ;FROM THE KARNAUGH MAP
             + /A* B*/C*/ROLL        * 2    * T
             +  A*/B*/C*/ROLL*/7*/11   */CP* T
             +  A*/B*/C*/ROLL* 7            * T
             +  A*/B*/C*/ROLL   * 11        * T
             +  A*/B*/C*/ROLL          * CP* T
             +  NCA    */ROLL               * T ;PICK ADDITIONAL DECODE LOGIC
                                                ;FROM NCA

          B := /A*/B* C*/ROLL               * T ;STATE DECODES DERIVED
             + /A* B*/C*/ROLL* 7            * T ;FROM THE KARNAUGH MAP
             + /A* B*/C*/ROLL   * 11        * T
             + /A* B*/C       */7*/11*/2    * T
             +  A*/B*/C* ROLL*/7*/11   */CP* T
             +  A*/B*/C*/ROLL          * CP* T
             +  A* B   */ROLL               * T
             +     B* C* ROLL               * T

          C := /A* B*/C*/ROLL        * 2    * T
             + /A* B*/C* ROLL*/7*/11*/2     * T
             +  A*/B*/C*/ROLL* 7            * T
             +  A*/B*/C*/ROLL   * 11        * T
             + /A*/B    * ROLL              * T
             +  A    * C*/ROLL              * T
             + /A* B* C* ROLL               * T
```

```
FUNCTION TABLE

CLK ROLL 7 11 2 CP NCA T A B C LOSE WIN

;-INPUTS-              -OUTPUTS-
;CR712CNT              ABC    L W
;LO 1 PC                      O I
;KL    A                      S N
; L                           E      COMMENTS
-------------------------------------------------------------------------------
 CHXXXXXL              LLL    L L    TEST INITIATION AND GAME START
 CHXLXXLH              LLH    L L
 CHXXXXLH              LLH    L L
 CLXXXXLH              LHL    L L
 CLHLXXHH              HHL    L H    WIN BECAUSE A 7 WAS ROLLED
 CLXXXXHH              HHL    L H    HOLD WIN WHEN NOT ROLLING
 CHXXXXLH              LLL    L L    RESTART GAME
 CHXXXXLH              LLH    L L
 CLXXXXLH              LHL    L L
 CLXXHXHH              HLH    H L    LOSE BECAUSE OF 2 ON FIRST ROLL
 CLXXXXHH              HLH    H L    HOLD LOSE WHEN NOT ROLLING
 CHXXXXLH              LLL    L L    RESTART GAME
 CHXXXXLH              LLH    L L
 CLXXXXLH              LHL    L L
 CLLLLXLH              LHL    L L
 CHLLLXLH              LHH    L L
 CHXXXXLH              LHH    L L
 LLXXXXHH              XXX    L L
 CLXXXXLH              HLL    L L
 CLLLXHHH              HHL    L H    WIN BECAUSE POINT WAS MATCHED
 CHXXXXLH              LLL    L L    RESTART GAME
 CHXXXXLH              LLH    L L
 CLXXXXLH              LHL    L L
 CHLLLXLH              LHH    L L
 LLXXXXHH              XXX    L L
 CLXXXXLH              HLL    L L
 CLHHXXHH              HLH    H L    LOSE BECAUSE 7 OR 11 WAS ROLLED ON SECOND ROLL
-------------------------------------------------------------------------------------


DESCRIPTION

THIS PAL SERVES AS THE MAIN LOGIC UNIT.  IT IS THE 8 STATE MACHINE WHICH
CONTROLS WHERE WE ARE IN THE GAME.  IT ALSO DETECTS THE WIN AND LOSE STATES.
PIN /T IS USED TO INITIATE THE GAME TO STATE 000 FOR I.C. TEST EQUIPMENT.
```

```
8 STATE MACHINE & WIN-LOSE DECODER

 1 C0XXXXXX1XXXXXHHHHH1
 2 C0XX1XXX0XXXXHLHHHH1
 3 C0XXXXXX0XXXXHLHHHH1
 4 C1XXXXXX0XXXXHHLHHH1
 5 C1X01XXX0XXXXLHLLHL1
 6 C1XXXXXX0XXXXLHLLHL1
 7 C0XXXXXX0XXXXHHHHHH1
 8 C0XXXXXX0XXXXHLHHHH1
 9 C1XXXXXX0XXXXHHLHHH1
10 C10XXXXX0XXXXLLHLLH1
11 C1XXXXXX0XXXXLLHLLH1
12 C0XXXXXX0XXXXHHHHHH1
13 C0XXXXXX0XXXXHLHHHH1
14 C1XXXXXX0XXXXHHLHHH1
15 C1111XXX0XXXXHHLHHH1
16 C0111XXX0XXXXHLLHHH1
17 C0XXXXXX0XXXXHLLHHH1
18 01XXXXXX0XXXXLXXXHH1
19 C1XXXXXX0XXXXHHHLHH1
20 C1X111XX0XXXXLHLLHL1
21 C0XXXXXX0XXXXHHHHHH1
22 C0XXXXXX0XXXXHLHHHH1
23 C1XXXXXX0XXXXHHLHHH1
24 C0111XXX0XXXXHLLHHH1
25 01XXXXXX0XXXXLXXXHH1
26 C1XXXXXX0XXXXHHHLHH1
27 C1X00XXX0XXXXLLHLLH1

PASS SIMULATION
```

```
8-STATE MACHINE AND WIN-LOSE DECODER

              11 1111 1111 2222 2222 2233
   0123 4567 8901 2345 6789 0123 4567 8901

 0 ---- ---- ---- ---- ---- ---- ---- ----
 1 ---- ---- ---X ---X --X- ---- ---- ---- A*B*/C

 8 ---- ---- ---- ---- ---- ---- ---- ----
 9 ---- ---- ---X --X- ---X ---- ---- ---- A*/B*C

16 X--- ---- -XX- ---X --X- ---- ---- -X-- /A*B*/C*/ROLL*7*T
17 X--- ---- --X- -X-X --X- ---- ---- -X-- /A*B*/C*/ROLL*11*T
18 X--- -X-- --X- ---X --X- ---- ---- -X-- /A*B*/C*/ROLL*2*T
19 X--- ---- X--X X-X- -XX- ---- ---- -X-- A*/B*/C*/ROLL*/7*/11*/CP*T
20 X--- ---- -X-X --X- --X- ---- ---- -X-- A*/B*/C*/ROLL*7*T
21 X--- ---- ---X -XX- --X- ---- ---- -X-- A*/B*/C*/ROLL*11*T
22 X--- ---- ---X --X- X-X- ---- ---- -X-- A*/B*/C*/ROLL*CP*T
23 X--- ---- ---- ---- ---- ---- ---X -X-- NCA*/ROLL*T

24 X--- ---- --X- --X- ---X ---- ---- -X-- /A*/B*C*/ROLL*T
25 X--- ---- -XX- ---X --X- ---- ---- -X-- /A*B*/C*/ROLL*7*T
26 X--- ---- --X- -X-X --X- ---- ---- -X-- /A*B*/C*/ROLL*11*T
27 ---- X--- X-X- X--X --X- ---- ---- -X-- /A*B*/C*/7*/11*/2*T
28 -X-- ---- X--X X-X- -XX- ---- ---- -X-- A*/B*/C*ROLL*/7*/11*/CP*T
29 X--- ---- ---X --X- X-X- ---- ---- -X-- A*/B*/C*/ROLL*CP*T
30 X--- ---- ---X ---X ---- ---- ---- -X-- A*B*/ROLL*T
31 -X-- ---- ---- ---X ---X ---- ---- -X-- B*C*ROLL*T

32 X--- -X-- --X- ---X --X- ---- ---- -X-- /A*B*/C*/ROLL*2*T
33 -X-- X--- X-X- X--X --X- ---- ---- -X-- /A*B*/C*ROLL*/7*/11*/2*T
34 X--- ---- -X-X --X- --X- ---- ---- -X-- A*/B*/C*/ROLL*7*T
35 X--- ---- ---X -XX- --X- ---- ---- -X-- A*/B*/C*/ROLL*11*T
36 -X-- ---- --X- --X- ---- ---- ---- -X-- /A*/B*ROLL*T
37 X--- ---- ---X ---- ---X ---- ---- -X-- A*C*/ROLL*T
38 -X-- ---- --X- ---X ---X ---- ---- -X-- /A*B*C*ROLL*T


48 ---- ---- ---- ---- ---- ---- ---- ----
49 X--- ---- ---X ---X --X- ---- ---- ---- A*B*/C*/ROLL
50 X--- ---- ---X --X- ---X ---- ---- ---- A*/B*C*/ROLL
51 X--- ---- --X- ---X ---X ---- ---- ---- /A*B*C*/ROLL


LEGEND:  X : FUSE NOT BLOWN (L,N,0)   - : FUSE BLOWN   (H,P,1)

NUMBER OF FUSES BLOWN =  842
```

8-State Machine and Win-Lose Decoder

Logic Diagram PAL16R4

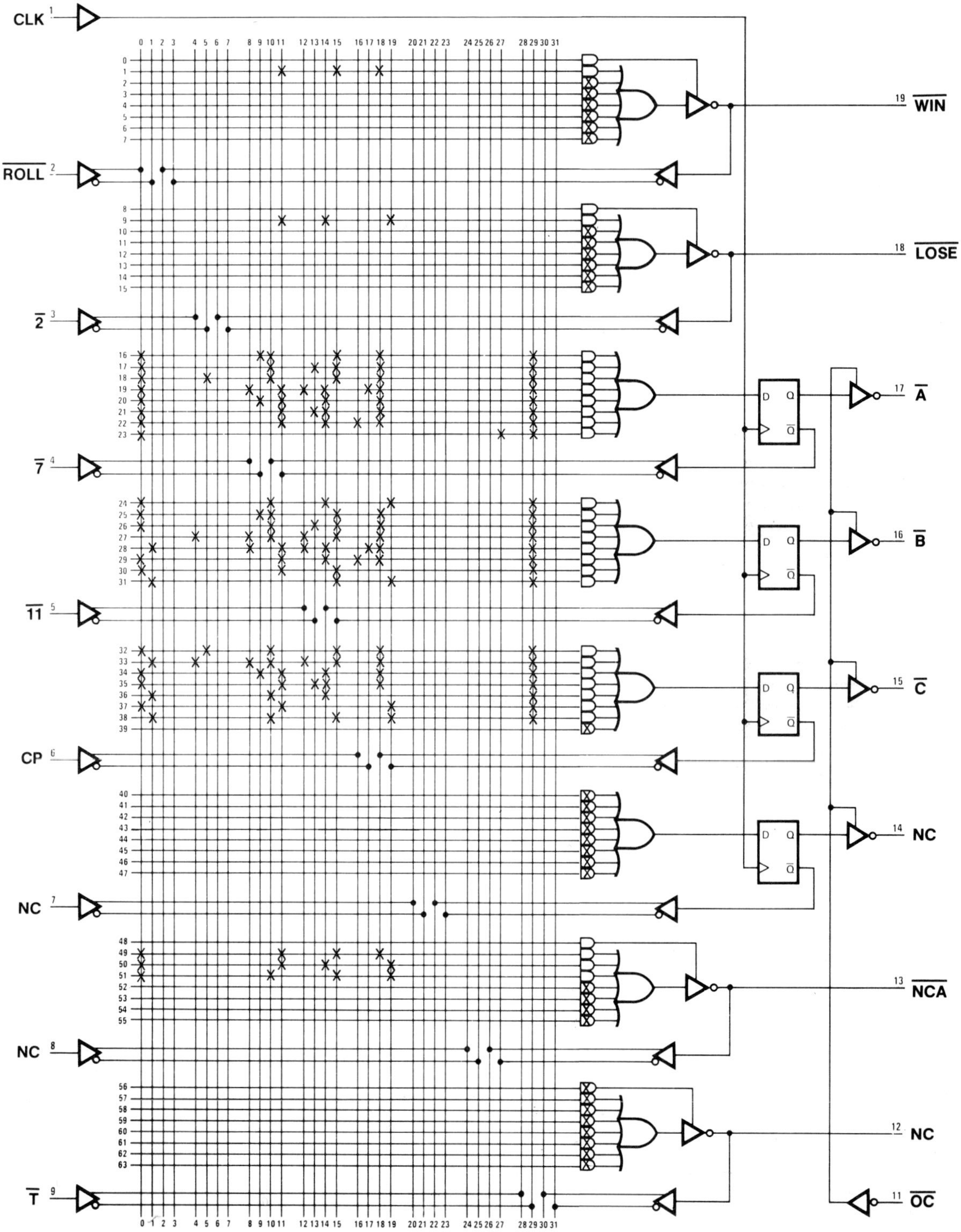

```
PAL16R6                                             PAL DESIGN SPECIFICATION
IC2                                                   BRAD MITCHELL 07/24/81
36 STATE MACHINE
MMI FIELD APLICATIONS ENGINEER DALLAS, TEXAS
/SWCLK S R NC NC NC NC /T CK GND
/OC /SWCK /Q5 /Q4 /Q3 /Q2 /Q1 /Q0 /ROLL VCC


IF(VCC) ROLL = /S                         ;R-S FLIP FLOP USED AS A
             +  R* ROLL                   ;DEBOUNCE SWITCH

IF(VCC) SWCK = /CK* ROLL                  ;SWITCH CONTROLLED CLOCK

        Q0 := /Q0    */Q2*/Q3*/Q4     *T  ;DECODE DERIVED FROM KARNAUGH MAP
            + /Q0                 */Q5*T

        Q1 := /Q0* Q1*/Q2*/Q3*/Q4     *T
            +  Q0*/Q1*/Q2*/Q3*/Q4     *T
            + /Q0* Q1             */Q5*T
            +  Q0*/Q1             */Q5*T

        Q2 :=  Q0* Q1*/Q2         */Q5*T
            +     /Q1* Q2         */Q5*T
            + /Q0    * Q2         */Q5*T

        Q3 :=  Q0* Q1* Q2*/Q3     */Q5*T
            +         /Q2* Q3     */Q5*T
            + /Q0        * Q3     */Q5*T
            +     /Q1    * Q3     */Q5*T

        Q4 :=  Q0* Q1* Q2* Q3*/Q4*/Q5*T
            +            /Q3* Q4*/Q5*T
            +     /Q1        * Q4*/Q5*T
            +         /Q2    * Q4*/Q5*T
            + /Q0            * Q4*/Q5*T

        Q5 :=  Q0* Q1* Q2* Q3* Q4*/Q5*T
            +     /Q1*/Q2*/Q3*/Q4* Q5
            + /Q0* Q1*/Q2*/Q3*/Q4* Q5
```

```
FUNCTION TABLE

SWCLK S R CK T Q5 Q4 Q3 Q2 Q1 Q0 ROLL SWCK

;  -INPUTS      --OUTPUTS--
;S S R C T      Q Q Q Q Q Q  R S
;W     K        5 4 3 2 1 0  O W
;CL                          L C
;K                           L K     COMMENTS
-----------------------------------------------------------------------------
 C X X X L      L L L L L L  X X     CYCLE THRU THE TOTAL 36 STATES (STATE 0)
 C X X X H      L L L L L H  X X     (STATE 1)
 C X X X H      L L L L H L  X X     (STATE 2)
 C X X X H      L L L L H H  X X     (STATE 3)
 C X X X H      L L L H L L  X X     (STATE 4)
 C X X X H      L L L H L H  X X     (STATE 5)
 C X X X H      L L L H H L  X X     (STATE 6)
 C X X X H      L L L H H H  X X     (STATE 7)
 C X X X H      L L H L L L  X X     (STATE 8)
 C X X X H      L L H L L H  X X     (STATE 9)
 C X X X H      L L H L H L  X X     (STATE 10)
 C X X X H      L L H L H H  X X     (STATE 11)
 C X X X H      L L H H L L  X X     (STATE 12)
 C X X X H      L L H H L H  X X     (STATE 13)
 C X X X H      L L H H H L  X X     (STATE 14)
 C X X X H      L L H H H H  X X     (STATE 15)
 C X X X H      L H L L L L  X X     (STATE 16)
 C X X X H      L H L L L H  X X     (STATE 17)
 C X X X H      L H L L H L  X X     (STATE 18)
 C X X X H      L H L L H H  X X     (STATE 19)
 C X X X H      L H L H L L  X X     (STATE 20)
 C X X X H      L H L H L H  X X     (STATE 21)
 C X X X H      L H L H H L  X X     (STATE 22)
 C X X X H      L H L H H H  X X     (STATE 23)
 C X X X H      L H H L L L  X X     (STATE 24)
 C X X X H      L H H L L H  X X     (STATE 25)
 C X X X H      L H H L H L  X X     (STATE 26)
 C X X X H      L H H L H H  X X     (STATE 27)
 C X X X H      L H H H L L  X X     (STATE 28)
 C X X X H      L H H H L H  X X     (STATE 29)
 C X X X H      L H H H H L  X X     (STATE 30)
 C X X X H      L H H H H H  X X     (STATE 31)
 C X X X H      H L L L L L  X X     (STATE 32)
 C X X X H      H L L L L H  X X     (STATE 33)
 C X X X H      H L L L H L  X X     (STATE 34)
 C X X X H      H L L L H H  X X     (STATE 35)
 C X X X H      L L L L L L  X X     (STATE 0)
 C H L L L      X X X X X X  L L     EXERCISING THE SET-RESET FLIP FLOP
 C L H H L      X X X X X X  H L     AND THE SWITCHED CLOCK
 C H H L L      X X X X X X  H H
 C H H H L      X X X X X X  H L
 C H H L L      X X X X X X  H H
 C H L H L      X X X X X X  L L
 C H H L L      X X X X X X  L L
 C H H H L      X X X X X X  L L
 C L H L L      X X X X X X  H H
 C H H H L      X X X X X X  H L
-----------------------------------------------------------------------------
```

DESCRIPTION

THIS PAL IS A 36 STATE MACHINE USED TO SIMULATE THE EXACT ROLL OF THE DICE.
THE STATE MACHINE IS SIMILAR TO THE "ELECTRONIC DICE GAME".

```
36 STATE MACHINE

 1 CXXXXXX1XXXXHHHHHHX1
 2 CXXXXXX0XXXXHHHHHLX1
 3 CXXXXXX0XXXXHHHHLHX1
 4 CXXXXXX0XXXXHHHHLLX1
 5 CXXXXXX0XXXXHHHLHHX1
 6 CXXXXXX0XXXXHHHLHLX1
 7 CXXXXXX0XXXXHHHLLHX1
 8 CXXXXXX0XXXXHHHLLLX1
 9 CXXXXXX0XXXXHHLHHHX1
10 CXXXXXX0XXXXHHLHHLX1
11 CXXXXXX0XXXXHHLHLHX1
12 CXXXXXX0XXXXHHLHLLX1
13 CXXXXXX0XXXXHHLLHHX1
14 CXXXXXX0XXXXHHLLHLX1
15 CXXXXXX0XXXXHHLLLHX1
16 CXXXXXX0XXXXHHLLLLX1
17 CXXXXXX0XXXXHLHHHHX1
18 CXXXXXX0XXXXHLHHHLX1
19 CXXXXXX0XXXXHLHHLHX1
20 CXXXXXX0XXXXHLHHLLX1
21 CXXXXXX0XXXXHLHLHHX1
22 CXXXXXX0XXXXHLHLHLX1
23 CXXXXXX0XXXXHLHLLHX1
24 CXXXXXX0XXXXHLHLLLX1
25 CXXXXXX0XXXXHLLHHHX1
26 CXXXXXX0XXXXHLLHHLX1
27 CXXXXXX0XXXXHLLHLHX1
28 CXXXXXX0XXXXHLLHLLX1
29 CXXXXXX0XXXXHLLLHHX1
30 CXXXXXX0XXXXHLLLHLX1
31 CXXXXXX0XXXXHLLLLHX1
32 CXXXXXX0XXXXHLLLLLX1
33 CXXXXXX0XXXXLHHHHHX1
34 CXXXXXX0XXXXLHHHHLX1
35 CXXXXXX0XXXXLHHHLHX1
36 CXXXXXX0XXXXLHHHLLX1
37 CXXXXXX0XXXXHHHHHHX1
38 C10XXXX10XXHXXXXXXH1
39 C01XXXX11XXHXXXXXXL1
40 C11XXXX10XXLXXXXXXL1
41 C11XXXX11XXHXXXXXXL1
42 C11XXXX10XXLXXXXXXL1
43 C10XXXX11XXHXXXXXXH1
44 C11XXXX10XXHXXXXXXH1
45 C11XXXX11XXHXXXXXXH1
46 C01XXXX10XXLXXXXXXL1
47 C11XXXX11XXHXXXXXXL1

PASS SIMULATION
```

```
36 STATE MACHINE

              11 1111 1111 2222 2222 2233
   0123 4567 8901 2345 6789 0123 4567 8901

 0 ---- ---- ---- ---- ---- ---- ---- ----
 1 -X-- ---- ---- ---- ---- ---- ---- ---- /S
 2 ---X X--- ---- ---- ---- ---- ---- ---- R*ROLL

 8 ---- --X- ---- --X- --X- --X- -X-- ---- /Q0*/Q2*/Q3*/Q4*T
 9 ---- --X- ---- ---- ---- ---- -XX- ---- /Q0*/Q5*T

16 ---- --X- ---X --X- --X- --X- -X-- ---- /Q0*Q1*/Q2*/Q3*/Q4*T
17 ---- ---X --X- --X- --X- --X- -X-- ---- Q0*/Q1*/Q2*/Q3*/Q4*T
18 ---- --X- ---X ---- ---- ---- -XX- ---- /Q0*Q1*/Q5*T
19 ---- ---X --X- ---- ---- ---- -XX- ---- Q0*/Q1*/Q5*T

24 ---- ---X ---X --X- ---- ---- -XX- ---- Q0*Q1*/Q2*/Q5*T
25 ---- ---- --X- ---X ---- ---- -XX- ---- /Q1*Q2*/Q5*T
26 ---- --X- ---- ---X ---- ---- -XX- ---- /Q0*Q2*/Q5*T

32 ---- ---X ---X ---X --X- ---- -XX- ---- Q0*Q1*Q2*/Q3*/Q5*T
33 ---- ---- ---- --X- ---X ---- -XX- ---- /Q2*Q3*/Q5*T
34 ---- --X- ---- ---- ---X ---- -XX- ---- /Q0*Q3*/Q5*T
35 ---- ---- --X- ---- ---X ---- -XX- ---- /Q1*Q3*/Q5*T

40 ---- ---X ---X ---X ---X --X- -XX- ---- Q0*Q1*Q2*Q3*/Q4*/Q5*T
41 ---- ---- ---- ---- --X- ---X -XX- ---- /Q3*Q4*/Q5*T
42 ---- ---- --X- ---- ---- ---X -XX- ---- /Q1*Q4*/Q5*T
43 ---- ---- ---- --X- ---- ---X -XX- ---- /Q2*Q4*/Q5*T
44 ---- --X- ---- ---- ---- ---X -XX- ---- /Q0*Q4*/Q5*T

48 ---- ---X ---X ---X ---X ---X -XX- ---- Q0*Q1*Q2*Q3*Q4*/Q5*T
49 ---- ---- --X- --X- --X- --X- ---X ---- /Q1*/Q2*/Q3*/Q4*Q5
50 ---- --X- ---X --X- --X- --X- ---X ---- /Q0*Q1*/Q2*/Q3*/Q4*Q5

56 ---- ---- ---- ---- ---- ---- ---- ----
57 ---X ---- ---- ---- ---- ---- ---- -X-- /CK*ROLL

LEGEND:  X : FUSE NOT BLOWN (L,N,0)   - : FUSE BLOWN   (H,P,1)

NUMBER OF FUSES BLOWN =  727
```

36-State Machine

Logic Diagram PAL16R6

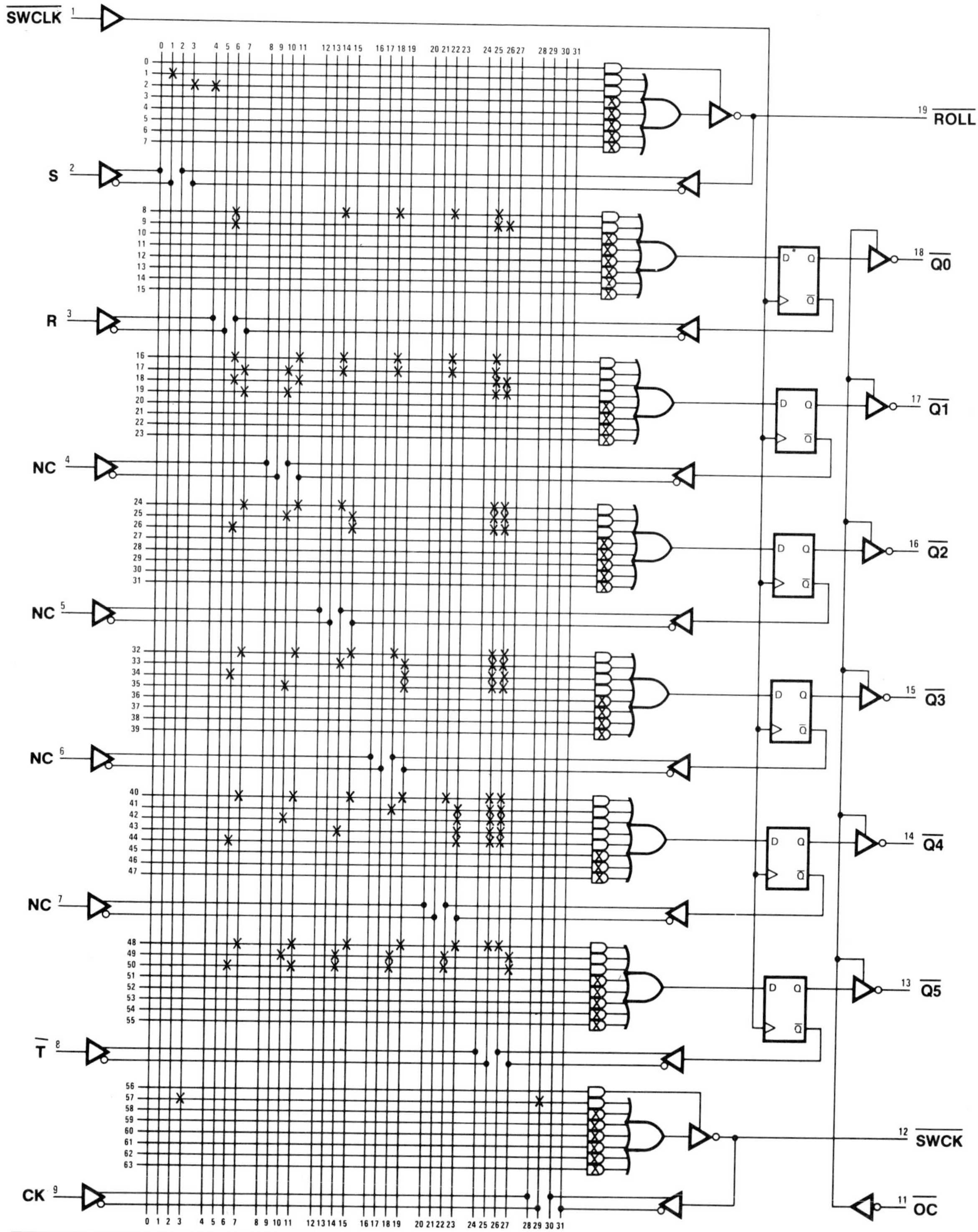

```
PAL16L8                                              PAL DESIGN SPECIFICATION
IC3                                                   BRAD MITCHELL 04/07/81
DICE DECODER
MMI FIELD APPLICATIONS ENGINEER DALLAS,TEXAS
NC NC /Q0 /Q1 /Q2 /Q3 /Q4 /Q5 NC GND
NC NC /NC1S /NC2S /NC4S /1S /2S /4S /8S VCC


IF(VCC)    1S = /Q0* Q1     */Q3* Q4*/Q5      ;THE MINIUM LOGIC REQUIRED
              + /Q0     */Q2*/Q3*/Q4* Q5      ;TO DECODE THE 1S BIT WAS DERIVED
              + /Q0* Q1* Q2*/Q3     */Q5      ;FROM THE KARNAUGH MAP
              +  Q0*/Q1* Q2* Q3     */Q5
              + /Q0     */Q2* Q3*/Q4*/Q5
              +  Q0     * Q2* Q3*/Q4*/Q5
              +  NC1S

IF(VCC) NC1S =  Q0     */Q2*/Q3*/Q4*/Q5      ;NC1S IS USED AS ADDITIONAL DECODE
              +  Q0*/Q1     */Q3*/Q4*/Q5      ;FOR 1S
              + /Q0     * Q2*/Q3* Q4*/Q5
              +  Q0*/Q1*/Q2     * Q4*/Q5
              +  Q0     */Q2* Q3* Q4*/Q5
              + /Q0* Q1* Q2     * Q4*/Q5

IF(VCC)    2S = /Q0* Q1*/Q2*/Q3*/Q4* Q5      ;FROM KARNAUGH MAP
              +  Q0*/Q1*/Q2*/Q3*/Q4
              +  Q0*/Q1*/Q2     */Q4*/Q5
              +      Q1* Q2* Q3*/Q4*/Q5
              + /Q0* Q1     * Q3*/Q4*/Q5
              + /Q0* Q1* Q2     */Q4*/Q5
              +  NC2S

IF(VCC) NC2S =  Q0* Q1     */Q3* Q4*/Q5      ;NC2S IS USED AS ADDITIONAL DECODE
              + /Q0*/Q1* Q2     * Q4*/Q5      ;FOR 2S
              + /Q0     * Q2* Q3* Q4*/Q5
              +     /Q1     */Q3*/Q4*/Q5
              +     /Q1     * Q3* Q4*/Q5

IF(VCC)    4S =  Q0* Q1*/Q2*/Q3*/Q4           ;FROM KARNAUGH MAP
              + /Q0*/Q1* Q2*/Q3     */Q5
              + /Q0* Q1* Q2* Q3     */Q5
              +     /Q1*/Q2* Q3     */Q5
              +      Q1*/Q2*/Q3     */Q5
              + /Q0         * Q3*/Q4*/Q5
              +  NC4S

IF(VCC) NC4S =             Q2* Q3*/Q4*/Q5    ;NC4S IS USED AS ADDITIONAL DECODE
              +  Q0     * Q2     */Q4*/Q5     ;FOR 4S

IF(VCC)    8S =  Q0* Q1*/Q2* Q3     */Q5      ;FROM KARNAUGH MAP
              +     /Q1*/Q2*/Q3* Q4*/Q5
              +      Q1*/Q2* Q3* Q4*/Q5
              +      Q1* Q2*/Q3* Q4*/Q5
              +     /Q1* Q2* Q3* Q4*/Q5
              +  Q0     * Q2     * Q4*/Q5
              +         /Q2*/Q3*/Q4* Q5
```

```
FUNCTION TABLE

Q5 Q4 Q3 Q2 Q1 Q0 NC4S NC2S NC1S 8S 4S 2S 1S

;   INPUTS               OUTPUTS
;Q Q Q Q Q Q   N N N     8 4 2 1
;5 4 3 2 1 0   C C C     S S S S
;              4 2 1                    COMMENTS
;              S S S                   (DICE ROLL)
-------------------------------------------------
 L L L L L L   L H L     L L H L            2
 L L L L L H   L H H     L L H H            3
 L L L L H L   L L L     L H L L            4
 L L L L H H   L L H     L H L H            5
 L L L H L L   L H L     L H H L            6
 L L L H L H   H H H     L H H H            7
 L L L H H L   L L L     L L H H            3
 L L L H H H   H L L     L H L L            4
 L L H L L L   L L L     L H L H            5
 L L H L L H   L L L     L H H L            6
 L L H L H L   L L L     L H H H            7
 L L H L H H   L L L     H L L L            8
 L L H H L L   H L L     L H L L            4
 L L H H L H   H L L     L H L H            5
 L L H H H L   H L L     L H H L            6
 L L H H H H   H L L     L H H H            7
 L H L L L L   L L L     H L L L            8
 L H L L L H   L L H     H L L H            9
 L H L L H L   L L L     L H L H            5
 L H L L H H   L H L     L H H L            6
 L H L H L L   L H H     L H H H            7
 L H L H L H   L L L     H L L L            8
 L H L H H L   L L H     H L L H            9
 L H L H H H   L H L     H L H L           10
 L H H L L L   L H L     L H H L            6
 L H H L L H   L H H     L H H H            7
 L H H L H L   L L L     H L L L            8
 L H H L H H   L L H     H L L H            9
 L H H H L L   L H L     H L H L           10
 L H H H L H   L H L     H L H H           11
 L H H H H L   L H H     L H H H            7
 L H H H H H   L L L     H L L L            8
 H L L L L L   L L L     H L L H            9
 H L L L L H   L L L     H L H L           10
 H L L L H L   L L L     H L H H           11
 H L L L H H   L L L     H H L L           12
-------------------------------------------------
```

DESCRIPTION

THIS PAL DECODES THE 36 STATE MACHINE INTO A BINARY REPRESENTATION OF THE ROLL OF THE DICE (2 THRU 12). THERE ARE 36 POSSIBLE COMBINATIONS FOR THE TWO DICE. THE NUMBERS ARE DECODED SO THAT THE PROPER ODDS ARE MAINTAINED FOR THE ROLL OF EACH NUMBER.

```
DICE DECODER

 1 XX111111XXXXHLHHLHH1
 2 XX011111XXXXLLHLLHH1
 3 XX101111XXXXHHHHHLH1
 4 XX001111XXXXLHHLHLH1
 5 XX110111XXXXHLHHLLH1
 6 XX010111XXXXLLLLLLH1
 7 XX100111XXXXHHHLLHH1
 8 XX000111XXXXHHLHHLH1
 9 XX111011XXXXHHHLHLH1
10 XX011011XXXXHHHHLLH1
11 XX101011XXXXHHHLLLH1
12 XX001011XXXXHHHHHHL1
13 XX110011XXXXHHLHHLH1
14 XX010011XXXXHHLLHLH1
15 XX100011XXXXHHLHLLH1
16 XX000011XXXXHHLLLLH1
17 XX111101XXXXHHHHHHL1
18 XX011101XXXXLHHLHHL1
19 XX101101XXXXHHHLHLH1
20 XX001101XXXXHLHHLLH1
21 XX110101XXXXLLHLLLH1
22 XX010101XXXXHHHHHHL1
23 XX100101XXXXLHHLHHL1
24 XX000101XXXXHLHHLHL1
25 XX111001XXXXHLHHLLH1
26 XX011001XXXXLLHLLLH1
27 XX101001XXXXHHHHHHL1
28 XX001001XXXXLHHLHHL1
29 XX110001XXXXHLHHLHL1
30 XX010001XXXXHLHLLHL1
31 XX100001XXXXLLHLLLH1
32 XX000001XXXXHHHHHHL1
33 XX111110XXXXHHHLHHL1
34 XX011110XXXXHHHHLHL1
35 XX101110XXXXHHHLLHL1
36 XX001110XXXXHHHHHLL1

PASS SIMULATION
```

```
DICE DECODER

                 11 1111 1111 2222 2222 2233
   0123 4567 8901 2345 6789 0123 4567 8901

 0 ---- ---- ---- ---- ---- ---- ---- ----
 1 ---- -X-- -X-- X--- -X-- ---- X--- ---- Q0*Q1*/Q2*Q3*/Q5
 2 ---- ---- X--- X--- X--- -X-- X--- ---- /Q1*/Q2*/Q3*Q4*/Q5
 3 ---- ---- -X-- X--- -X-- -X-- X--- ---- Q1*/Q2*Q3*Q4*/Q5
 4 ---- ---- -X-- -X-- X--- -X-- X--- ---- Q1*Q2*/Q3*Q4*/Q5
 5 ---- ---- X--- -X-- -X-- -X-- X--- ---- /Q1*Q2*Q3*Q4*/Q5
 6 ---- -X-- ---- -X-- ---- -X-- X--- ---- Q0*Q2*Q4*/Q5
 7 ---- ---- ---- X--- X--- X--- -X-- ---- /Q2*/Q3*/Q4*Q5

 8 ---- ---- ---- ---- ---- ---- ---- ----
 9 ---- -X-- -X-- X--- X--- X--- ---- ---- Q0*Q1*/Q2*/Q3*/Q4
10 ---- X--- X--- -X-- X--- ---- X--- ---- /Q0*/Q1*Q2*/Q3*/Q5
11 ---- X--- -X-- -X-- -X-- ---- X--- ---- /Q0*Q1*Q2*Q3*/Q5
12 ---- ---- X--- X--- -X-- ---- X--- ---- /Q1*/Q2*Q3*/Q5
13 ---- ---- -X-- X--- X--- ---- X--- ---- Q1*/Q2*/Q3*/Q5
14 ---- X--- ---- ---- -X-- X--- X--- ---- /Q0*Q3*/Q4*/Q5
15 ---- ---- ---- ---- ---X ---- ---- ---- NC4S

16 ---- ---- ---- ---- ---- ---- ---- ----
17 ---- X--- -X-- X--- X--- X--- -X-- ---- /Q0*Q1*/Q2*/Q3*/Q4*Q5
18 ---- -X-- X--- X--- X--- X--- ---- ---- Q0*/Q1*/Q2*/Q3*/Q4
19 ---- -X-- X--- X--- ---- X--- X--- ---- Q0*/Q1*/Q2*/Q4*/Q5
20 ---- ---- -X-- -X-- -X-- X--- X--- ---- Q1*Q2*Q3*/Q4*/Q5
21 ---- X--- -X-- ---- -X-- X--- X--- ---- /Q0*Q1*Q3*/Q4*/Q5
22 ---- X--- -X-- -X-- ---- X--- X--- ---- /Q0*Q1*Q2*/Q4*/Q5
23 ---- ---- ---- ---- ---- ---X ---- ---- NC2S

24 ---- ---- ---- ---- ---- ---- ---- ----
25 ---- X--- -X-- ---- X--- -X-- X--- ---- /Q0*Q1*/Q3*Q4*/Q5
26 ---- X--- ---- X--- X--- X--- -X-- ---- /Q0*/Q2*/Q3*/Q4*Q5
27 ---- X--- -X-- -X-- X--- ---- X--- ---- /Q0*Q1*Q2*/Q3*/Q5
28 ---- -X-- X--- -X-- -X-- ---- X--- ---- Q0*/Q1*Q2*Q3*/Q5
29 ---- X--- ---- X--- -X-- X--- X--- ---- /Q0*/Q2*Q3*/Q4*/Q5
30 ---- -X-- ---- -X-- -X-- X--- X--- ---- Q0*Q2*Q3*/Q4*/Q5
31 ---- ---- ---- ---- ---- ---- ---X ---- NC1S

32 ---- ---- ---- ---- ---- ---- ---- ----
33 ---- ---- ---- -X-- -X-- X--- X--- ---- Q2*Q3*/Q4*/Q5
34 ---- -X-- ---- -X-- ---- X--- X--- ---- Q0*Q2*/Q4*/Q5

40 ---- ---- ---- ---- ---- ---- ---- ----
41 ---- -X-- -X-- ---- X--- -X-- X--- ---- Q0*Q1*/Q3*Q4*/Q5
42 ---- X--- X--- -X-- ---- -X-- X--- ---- /Q0*/Q1*Q2*Q4*/Q5
43 ---- X--- ---- -X-- -X-- -X-- X--- ---- /Q0*Q2*Q3*Q4*/Q5
44 ---- ---- X--- ---- X--- X--- X--- ---- /Q1*/Q3*/Q4*/Q5
45 ---- ---- X--- ---- -X-- -X-- X--- ---- /Q1*Q3*Q4*/Q5

48 ---- ---- ---- ---- ---- ---- ---- ----
49 ---- -X-- ---- X--- X--- X--- X--- ---- Q0*/Q2*/Q3*/Q4*/Q5
50 ---- -X-- X--- ---- X--- X--- X--- ---- Q0*/Q1*/Q3*/Q4*/Q5
51 ---- X--- ---- -X-- X--- -X-- X--- ---- /Q0*Q2*/Q3*Q4*/Q5
52 ---- -X-- X--- X--- ---- -X-- X--- ---- Q0*/Q1*/Q2*Q4*/Q5
53 ---- -X-- ---- X--- -X-- -X-- X--- ---- Q0*/Q2*Q3*Q4*/Q5
54 ---- X--- -X-- -X-- ---- -X-- X--- ---- /Q0*Q1*Q2*Q4*/Q5

LEGEND:  X : FUSE NOT BLOWN (L,N,0)   - : FUSE BLOWN   (H,P,1)

NUMBER OF FUSES BLOWN = 1351
```

Dice Decoder

Logic Diagram PAL16L8

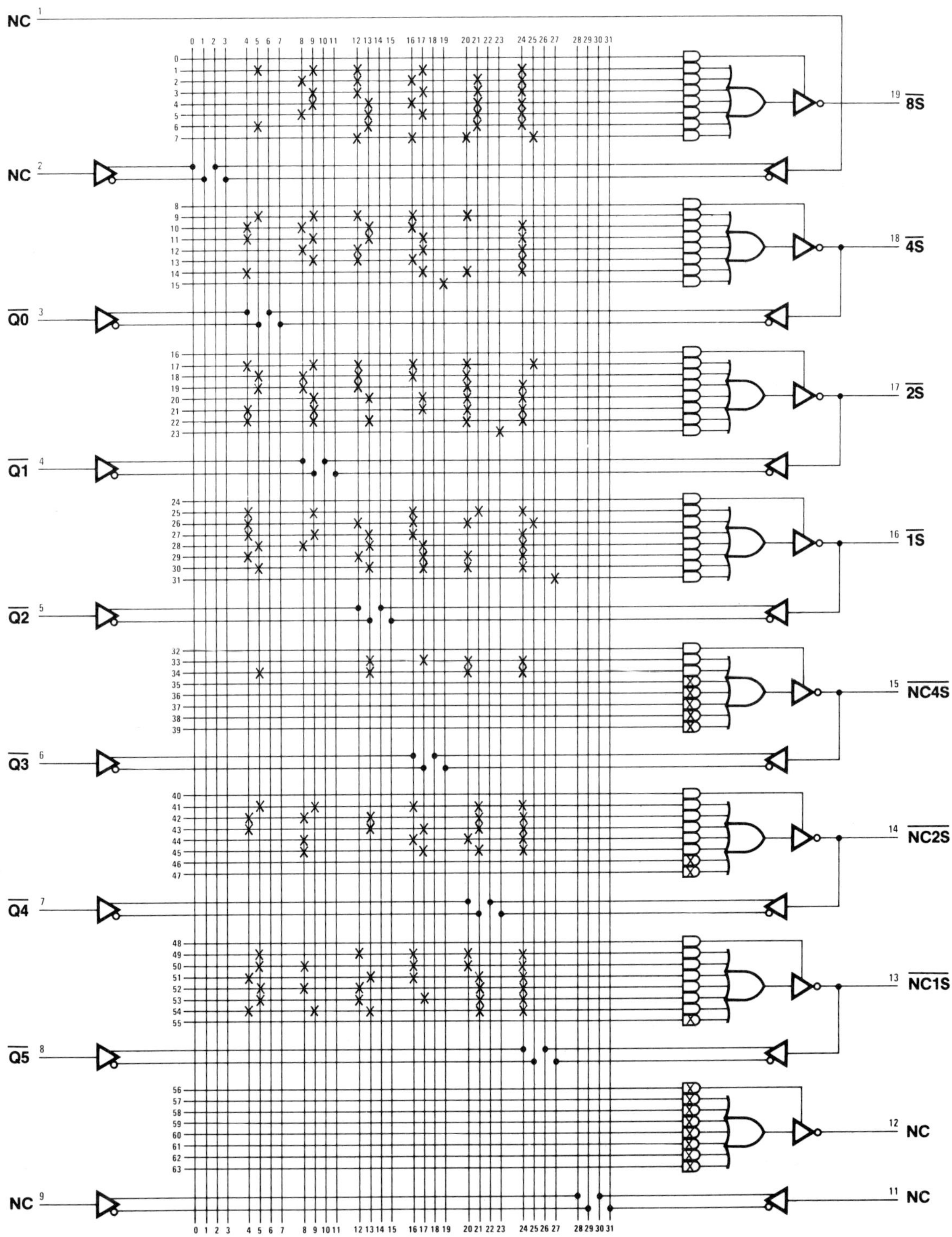

```
PAL16R4                                               PAL DESIGN SPECIFICATAION
IC4                                                     BRAD MITCHELL 07/28/81
STORE POINT /2, /7, AND /11 DECODE
MMI FIELD APPLICATIONS ENGINEER DALLAS, TEXAS
CLK /8S /4S /2S /1S /A /B /C /T GND
/OC NC /11 /P1S /P2S /P4S /P8S /7 /2 VCC


P8S :=  8S    */A* B*/C                 *T ;LOAD INTO POINT ON FIRST ROLL
     +     P8S*/A* B* C                 *T ;SAVE POINT IF NOT FIRST ROLL
     +     P8S* A*/B                    *T ;SAVE POINT
     +     P8S* A* B*/C                 *T ;SAVE POINT

P4S :=  4S    */A* B*/C                 *T ;LOAD INTO POINT IF FIRST ROLL
     +     P4S*/A* B* C                 *T ;SAVE POINT IF NOT FIRST ROLL
     +     P4S* A*/B                    *T ;SAVE POINT
     +     P4S* A* B*/C                 *T ;SAVE POINT

P2S :=  2S    */A* B*/C                 *T ;LOAD INTO POINT IF FIRST ROLL
     +     P2S*/A* B* C                 *T ;SAVE POINT IF NOT FIRST ROLL
     +     P2S* A*/B                    *T ;SAVE POINT
     +     P2S* A* B*/C                 *T ;SAVE POINT

P1S :=  1S    */A* B*/C                 *T ;LOAD INTO POINT IF FIRST ROLL
     +     P1S*/A* B* C                 *T ;SAVE POINT IF NOT FIRST ROLL
     +     P1S* A*/B                    *T ;SAVE POINT
     +     P1S* A* B*/C                 *T ;SAVE POINT

IF(VCC) 2  = /8S*/4S* 2S*/1S               ;DECODE THE NUMBER 2

IF(VCC) 7  = /8S* 4S* 2S* 1S               ;DECODE THE NUMBER 7

IF(VCC) 11 =  8S*/4S* 2S* 1S               ;DECODE THE NUMBER 11


FUNCTION TABLE

CLK 8S 4S 2S 1S  A B C T P8S P4S P2S P1S 2 7 11

;-------INPUTS-------    ----OUTPUTS----
;C 8 4 2 1  A B C  T    P P P P  2 7 1
;L S S S S              8 4 2 1      1
;K                      S S S S            COMMENTS
--------------------------------------------------------------------------
 C L L L L  L L L  L    L L L L  L L L     INITIATE ALL REGISTERS TO LOW
 C H L L H  L H L  H    H L L H  L L L     LOAD A NUMBER INTO POINT
 C L L L L  L H H  H    H L L H  L L L     SAVE THE NUMBER IN POINT
 C L L L L  H L X  H    H L L H  L L L     SAVE THE NUMBER IN POINT
 C L L L L  H H L  H    H L L H  L L L     SAVE THE NUMBER IN POINT
 C L L H L  L H L  H    L L H L  H L L     LOAD POINT & DECODE A "2"
 C L H H H  L H L  H    L H H H  L H L     LOAD POINT & DECODE A "7"
 C H L H H  L H L  H    H L H H  L L H     LOAD POINT & DECODE A "11"
--------------------------------------------------------------------------
```

DESCRIPTION

THIS PAL IS USED TO STORE THE POINT IN THE GAME. IT ALSO DECODES THE NUMBERS 2, 7, AND 11 TO BE USED IN DETERMINING WIN OR LOSE.

STORE POINT /2, /7, AND /11 DECODE

```
 1 C11111111XXXHHHHHHH1
 2 C01101010XXXHLHHLHH1
 3 C11111000XXXHLHHLHH1
 4 C111101X0XXXHLHHLHH1
 5 C11110010XXXHLHHLHH1
 6 C11011010XXXHHLHHHL1
 7 C10001010XXXHLLLHLH1
 8 C01001010XXXLLLHLHH1
```

PASS SIMULATION

```
STORE POINT AND /2, /7, AND /11 DECODE

              11 1111 1111 2222 2222 2233
   0123 4567 8901 2345 6789 0123 4567 8901

 0 ---- ---- ---- ---- ---- ---- ---- ----
 1 X--- X--- -X-- X--- ---- ---- ---- ---- /8S*/4S*2S*/1S

 8 ---- ---- ---- ---- ---- ---- ---- ----
 9 X--- -X-- -X-- -X-- ---- ---- ---- ---- /8S*4S*2S*1S

16 -X-- ---- ---- ---- X--- -X-- X--- -X-- 8S*/A*B*/C*T
17 ---- ---- ---X ---- X--- -X-- -X-- -X-- P8S*/A*B*C*T
18 ---- ---- ---X ---- -X-- X--- ---- -X-- P8S*A*/B*T
19 ---- ---- ---X ---- -X-- -X-- X--- -X-- P8S*A*B*/C*T

24 ---- -X-- ---- ---- X--- -X-- X--- -X-- 4S*/A*B*/C*T
25 ---- ---- ---- ---X X--- -X-- -X-- -X-- P4S*/A*B*C*T
26 ---- ---- ---- ---X -X-- X--- ---- -X-- P4S*A*/B*T
27 ---- ---- ---- ---X -X-- -X-- X--- -X-- P4S*A*B*/C*T

32 ---- ---- -X-- ---- X--- -X-- X--- -X-- 2S*/A*B*/C*T
33 ---- ---- ---- ---- X--X -X-- -X-- -X-- P2S*/A*B*C*T
34 ---- ---- ---- ---- -X-X X--- ---- -X-- P2S*A*/B*T
35 ---- ---- ---- ---- -X-X -X-- X--- -X-- P2S*A*B*/C*T

40 ---- ---- ---- -X-- X--- -X-- X--- -X-- 1S*/A*B*/C*T
41 ---- ---- ---- ---- X--- -X-X -X-- -X-- P1S*/A*B*C*T
42 ---- ---- ---- ---- -X-- X--X ---- -X-- P1S*A*/B*T
43 ---- ---- ---- ---- -X-- -X-X X--- -X-- P1S*A*B*/C*T

48 ---- ---- ---- ---- ---- ---- ---- ----
49 -X-- X--- -X-- -X-- ---- ---- ---- ---- 8S*/4S*2S*1S


LEGEND:  X : FUSE NOT BLOWN (L,N,0)   - : FUSE BLOWN   (H,P,1)

NUMBER OF FUSES BLOWN =  616
```

Store Point and $\overline{2}$, $\overline{7}$, and $\overline{11}$ Decode

Logic Diagram PAL16R4

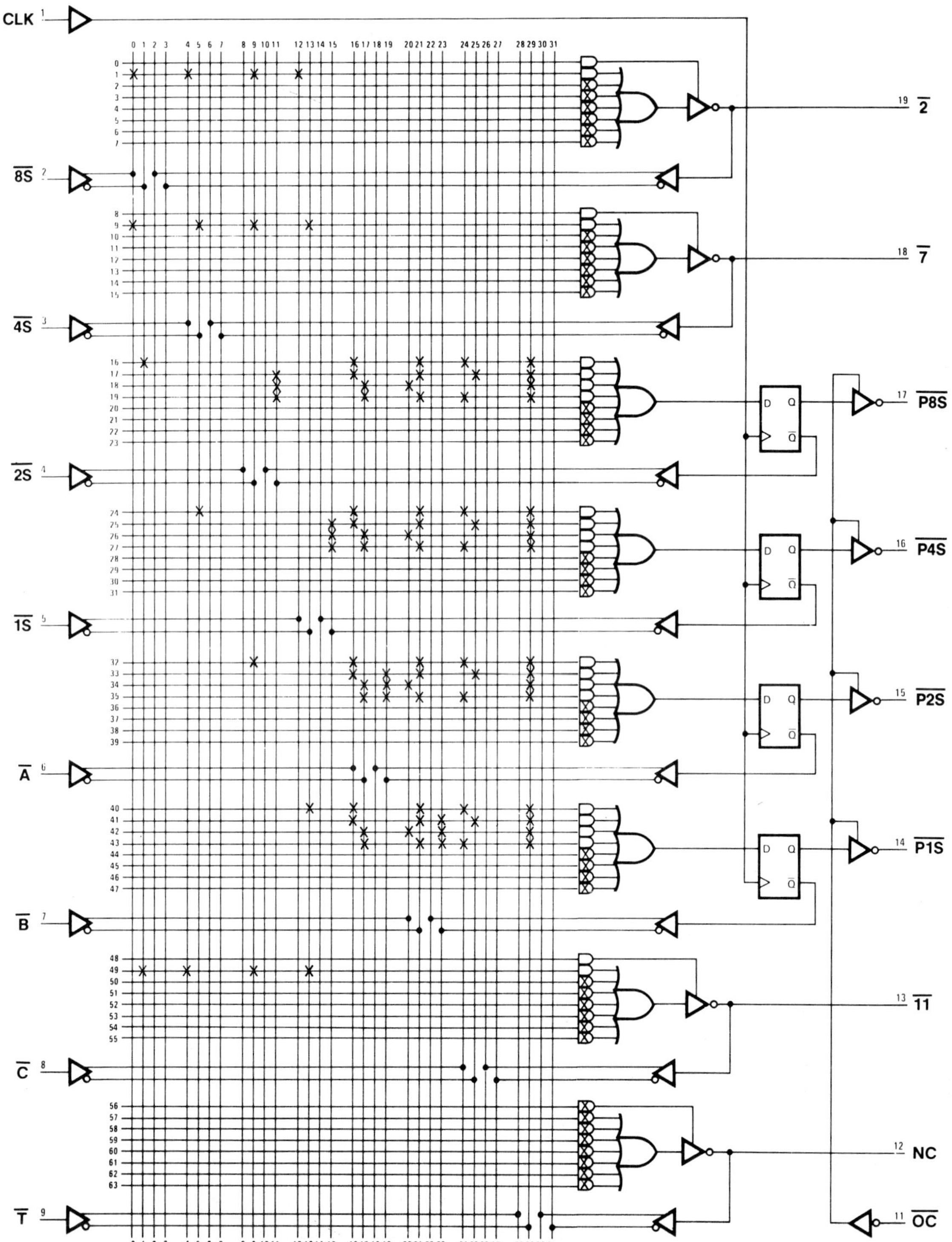

PAL
IMPORTANT,
NOTES

Traffic Signal Controller

PAL16R4

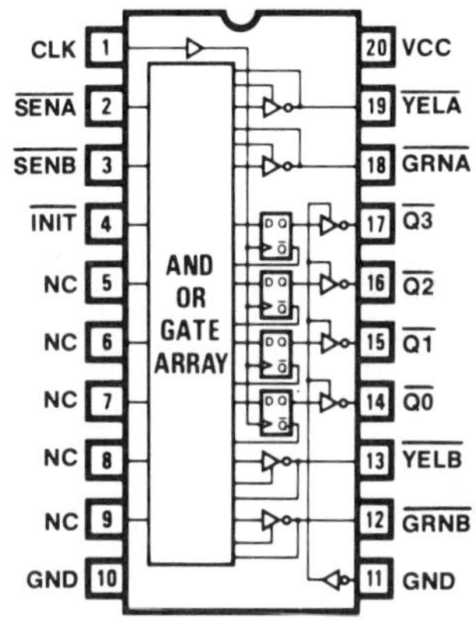

PAL16R8

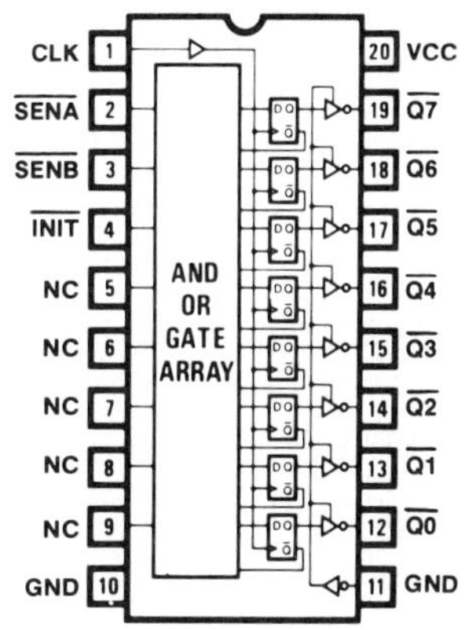

An Example of Sequential Logic Design with PALs

Figure 1 illustrates a simple traffic intersection consisting of two one-way streets, direction A and direction B. Each direction has a signal consisting of red, yellow and green lamps which are activated with appropriately named active low signals. Also, each direction has a sensor which provides an active low signal indicating the presence of an oncoming vehicle. Our controller is to manage this intersection with the sensors as inputs and the lamps as outputs, as shown in Figure 2.

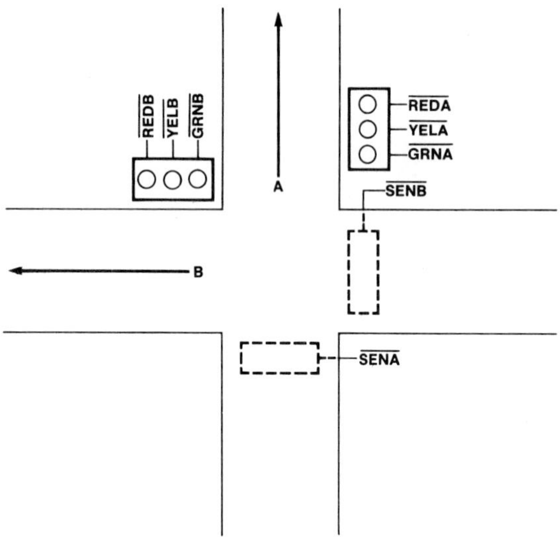

Figure 1. Traffic Intersection

Figure 2 also includes the system clock and an initialize (or reset) signal, which drives the controller to a pre-defined initial state. This raises two important issues in designing sequential logic with PALs. First, all circuit implementations of sequential logic with PALs are totally synchronous. This implies that all state variables (flip-flops) change at the same time, precisely after the rising edge of the clock. Second, PAL sequential logic designs should include a means for initialization to implement test programs and ensure reliable circuit operation.

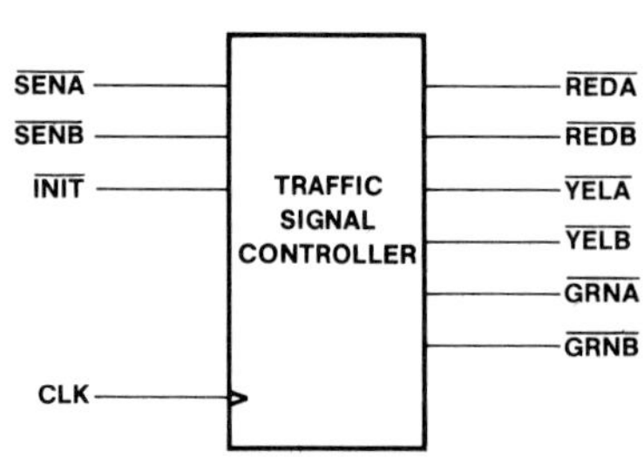

Figure 2. Traffic Signal Controller

The specifies of the controller operations are detailed with a state graph, shown in Figure 3.

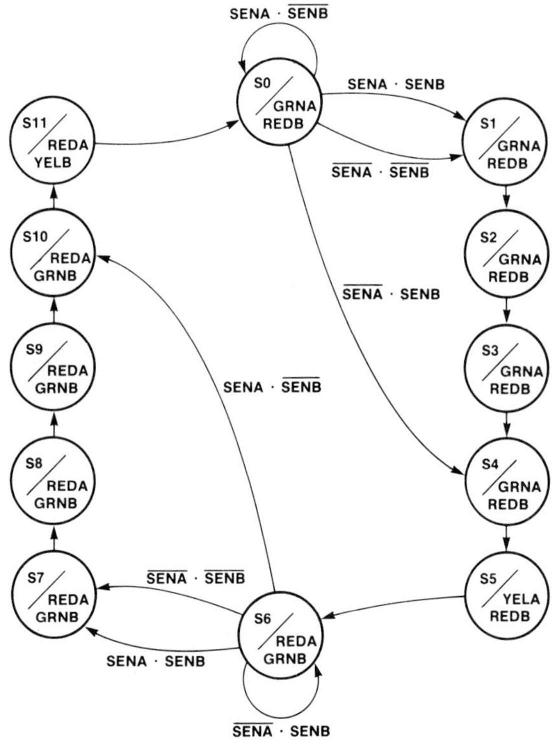

Figure 3. State Graph — Traffic Signal Controller

In this format, each bubble represents a stable state, i.e., an output configuration, lasting at least one clock cycle. Inside the bubble is the name of the state (S0–S11) and the outputs associated with that state. This particular circuit's outputs are specified to be a function of the state of the flip-flops only, and are not directly affected by the inputs. For the sake of simplicity in the state graph, the transitions involving INIT are omitted; INIT simply drives the circuit to S0 from any state, regardless of other inputs.

Another method of expressing the state graph information is with a state table, shown in Figure 4. Each row in the state table corresponds to a state (or bubble from the state graph). The first four columns give the next state for each of the possible input combinations. The output is also given for each state in the table. The state graph may be omitted but a state table is generally required to design the circuit.

The next step in the design is to assign state variables. This process also involves selecting the PAL or PALs to be used. Referring to Figures 2 and 3, the circuit requirements are seen to be 4 input, 6 output and 12 internal states. Since the intput/output pin requirements do not impose restrictions in either a 20 or 24 pin package, the states requirement will be addressed first. A PAL16R4 can implement the 12 states with its 4 flip flops. However, only 4 combinatorial outputs are available. This means that the flip-flop outputs (or state variables) will need to be utilized as circuit outputs as well. One such approach is to take advantage of the fact that REDA = $\overline{\text{REDB}}$ and implementing REDA with one flip-flop, and REDB with an external inverter.

Such a state variable assignment and resulting transition table is in Figure 5. This is generated by substituting the variable assignments into the state table.

CURRENT STATE \ NEXT STATE	INPUT SENA, SENB				OUTPUT					
	00	01	10	11	REDA	YELA	GRNA	REDB	YELB	GRNB
S0	S1	S4	S0	S1	0	0	1	1	0	0
S1	S2	S2	S2	S2	0	0	1	1	0	0
S2	S3	S3	S3	S3	0	0	1	1	0	0
S3	S4	S4	S4	S4	0	0	1	1	0	0
S4	S5	S5	S5	S5	0	0	1	1	0	0
S5	S6	S6	S6	S6	0	1	0	1	0	0
S6	S7	S6	S10	S7	1	0	0	0	0	1
S7	S8	S8	S8	S8	1	0	0	0	0	1
S8	S9	S9	S9	S9	1	0	0	0	0	1
S9	S10	S10	S10	S10	1	0	0	0	0	1
S10	S11	S11	S11	S11	1	0	0	0	0	1
S11	S0	S0	S0	S0	1	0	0	0	1	0

Figure 4. State Table — Traffic Signal Controller

CURRENT STATE	INPUT/NEXT STATE				OUTPUTS
	00	01	10	11	
0 0 0 0	0 0 0 1	0 1 0 0	0 0 0 0	0 0 0 1	0 0 1 1 0 0
0 0 0 1	0 0 1 0	0 0 1 0	0 0 1 0	0 0 1 0	0 0 1 1 0 0
0 0 1 0	0 0 1 1	0 0 1 1	0 0 1 1	0 0 1 1	0 0 1 1 0 0
0 0 1 1	0 1 0 0	0 1 0 0	0 1 0 0	0 1 0 0	0 0 1 1 0 0
0 1 0 0	0 1 0 1	0 1 0 1	0 1 0 1	0 1 0 1	0 0 1 1 0 0
0 1 0 1	1 0 0 0	1 0 0 0	1 0 0 0	1 0 0 0	0 1 0 1 0 0
1 0 0 0	1 0 0 1	1 0 0 0	1 1 0 0	1 0 0 1	1 0 0 0 0 1
1 0 0 1	1 0 1 0	1 0 1 0	1 0 1 0	1 0 1 0	1 0 0 0 0 1
1 0 1 0	1 0 1 1	1 0 1 1	1 0 1 1	1 0 1 1	1 0 0 0 0 1
1 0 1 1	1 1 0 0	1 1 0 0	1 1 0 0	1 1 0 0	1 0 0 0 0 1
1 1 0 0	1 1 0 1	1 1 0 1	1 1 0 1	1 1 0 1	1 0 0 0 0 1
1 1 0 1	0 0 0 0	0 0 0 0	0 0 0 0	0 0 0 0	1 0 0 0 1 0

STATE	Q3 Q2 Q1 Q0
S0	0 0 0 0
S1	0 0 0 1
S2	0 0 1 0
S3	0 0 1 1
S4	0 1 0 0
S5	0 1 0 1
S6	1 0 0 0
S7	1 0 0 1
S8	1 0 1 0
S9	1 0 1 1
S10	1 1 0 0
S11	1 1 0 1

Input = SENA, SENB

Current/Next State = Q3, Q2, Q1, Q0/Q3+, Q2+, Q1+, Q0+

Output = REDA, YELA, GRNA, REDB, YELB, GRNB

Figure 5. State Assignment No. 1/Transition Table

From this table, Karnaugh maps for D flip flop next state equations and output functions can be written, by transcription from the transition table, and minimized equations derived. This is shown in Figures 6 through 10. The state machine and PAL implementation follows. Note that the INIT term is simply AND'ed with all next state products to generate the initialize function.

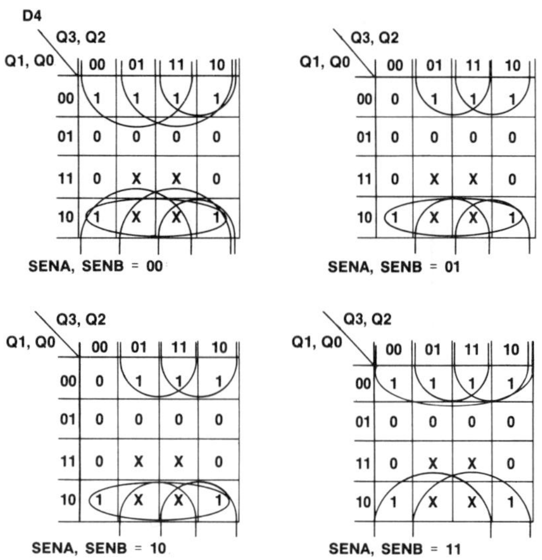

D0 = Q0 SENA SENB + Q0 SENA SENB +
Q1 Q0 + Q2 Q0 + Q3 Q0

Figure 6. K Maps for Q0+

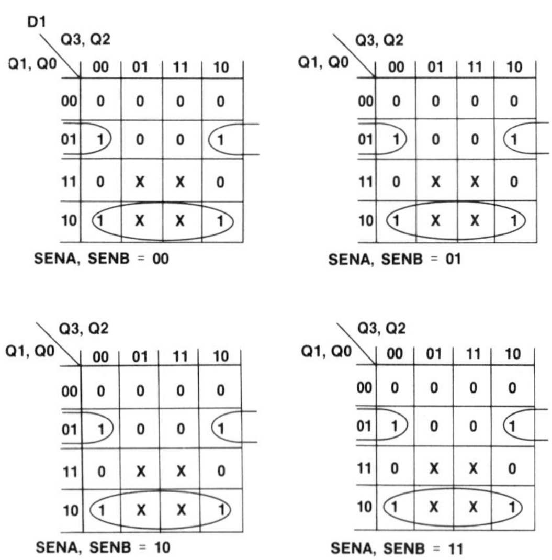

D1 = Q1 Q0 + Q2 Q1 Q0

Figure 7. K Maps for Q1+

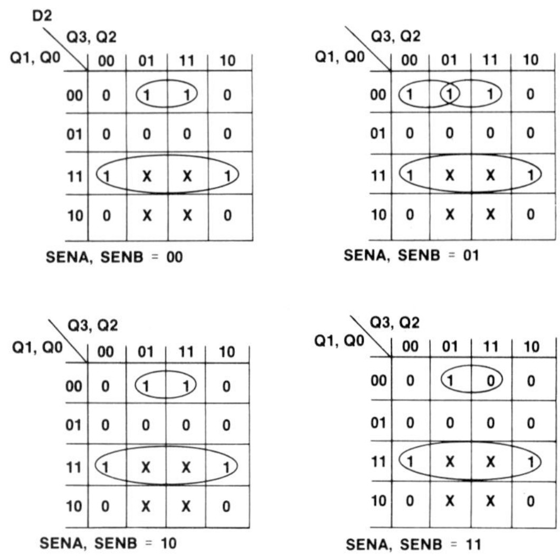

D2 = Q1 Q0 + Q2 Q1 $\overline{Q0}$ +
$\overline{SENA}$ SENB $\overline{Q3}$ $\overline{Q1}$ $\overline{Q0}$

Figure 8. K Maps for Q2+

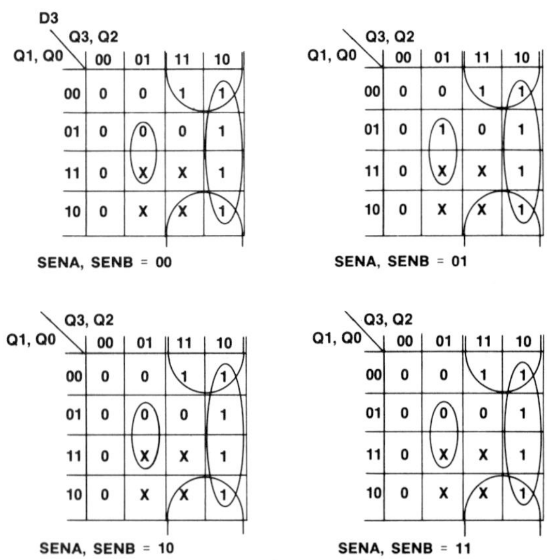

D3 = Q3 $\overline{Q0}$ + Q3, $\overline{Q2}$
Q3 Q2 Q0

Figure 9. K Maps for Q3+

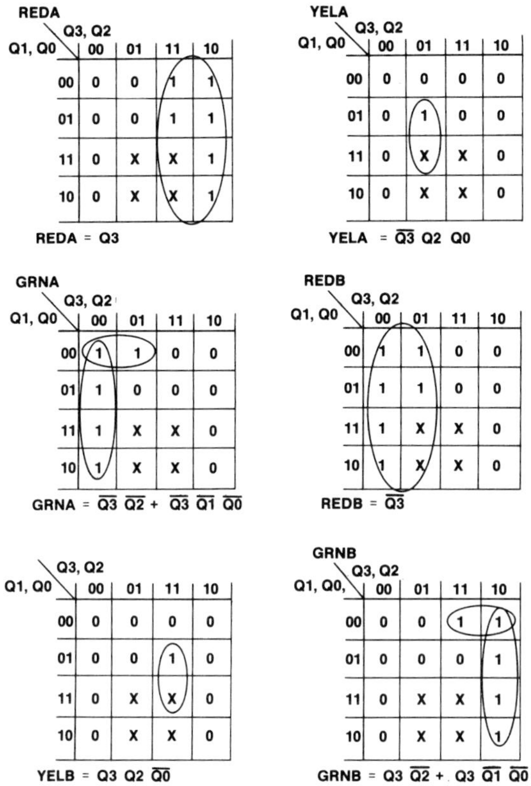

Figure 10. K Maps for Outputs

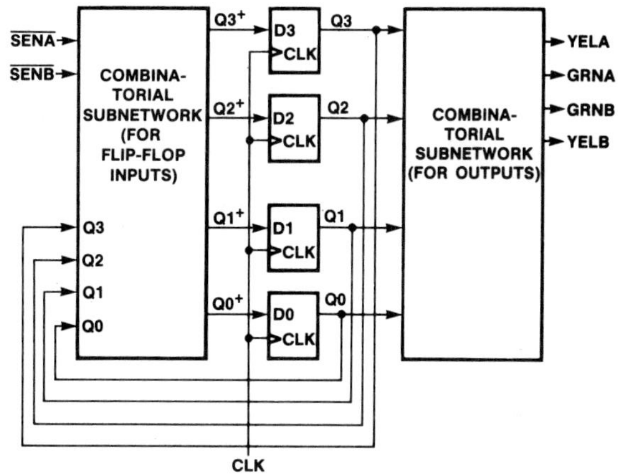

Figure 11. State Machine Traffic Signal Controller No. 1

```
PAL16R4                                                  PAL DESIGN SPECIFICATION
TRACNT1                                                  B. BRAFMAN 03/14/81
TRAFFIC SIGNAL CONTROLLER No. 1
MMI FIELD APPLICATIONS ENGINEER YORBA LINDA, CALIFORNIA
CLK /SENA /SENB /INIT NC NC NC NC NC GND
GND /GRNB /YELB /Q0 /Q1 /Q2 /Q3 /GRNA /YELA VCC


IF (VCC) YELA  =  /Q3 *   Q2 *   Q0                 ;"A" DIRECTION YELLOW LITE

IF (VCC) GRNA  =  /Q3 *  /Q2                        ;"A" DIRECTION GREEN
               +  /Q3 *  /Q1 *  /Q0

Q3  :=   Q3   *  /Q0  * /INIT
     +   Q3   *  /Q2  * /INIT
     +  /Q3   *   Q2  *   Q0   * /INIT

Q2  :=   Q1   *   Q0  * /INIT
     +   Q2   *  /Q1  *  /Q0   * /INIT
     +  /Q3   *  /Q1  *  /Q0   * /SENA *  SENB * /INIT

Q1  :=   Q1   *  /Q0  * /INIT
     +  /Q2   *  /Q1  *   Q0   * /INIT

Q0  :=  /Q0   *  /SENA *  /SENB * /INIT          ;PRODUCTS ARE FROM K-MAP
     +  /Q0   *   SENA *   SENB * /INIT
     +   Q1   *   /Q0  *  /INIT
     +   Q2   *   /Q0  *  /INIT
     +   Q3   *   /Q0  *  /INIT


IF (VCC) GRNB  =   Q3 *  /Q2                       ;"B" DIRECTION GREEN
               +   Q3 *  /Q1 *  /Q0

IF (VCC) YELB  =   Q3 *   Q2 *   Q0                ;"B" DIRECTION YELLOW
```

```
FUNCTION TABLE

/INIT  CLK  SENA  SENB     Q3 Q2 Q1 Q0   GRNA YELA GRNB YELB  ;COMMENTS
--------------------------------------------------------------------------
  L     C    X     X       L  L  L  L     X    X    X    X     S0 (INIT)
  H     C    L     L       L  L  L  H     H    L    L    L     S1
  H     C    X     X       L  L  H  L     H    L    L    L     S2
  H     C    X     X       L  L  H  H     H    L    L    L     S3
  H     C    X     X       L  H  L  L     H    L    L    L     S4
  H     C    X     X       L  H  L  H     L    H    L    L     S5
  H     C    X     X       H  L  L  L     L    L    H    L     S6
  H     C    L     L       H  L  L  H     L    L    H    L     S7
  H     C    X     X       H  L  H  L     L    L    H    L     S8
  H     C    X     X       H  L  H  H     L    L    H    L     S9
  H     C    X     X       H  H  L  L     L    L    H    L     S10
  H     C    X     X       H  H  L  H     L    L    L    H     S11
  H     C    X     X       L  L  L  L     H    L    L    L     S0
  H     C    L     H       L  H  L  L     H    L    L    L     S4
  L     C    X     X       L  L  L  L     X    X    X    X     S0 (INIT)
  H     C    H     L       L  L  L  L     H    L    L    L     S0
  H     C    H     H       L  L  L  H     H    L    L    L     S1
--------------------------------------------------------------------------
```

DESCRIPTION

THIS PAL IMPLEMENTS A SIMPLE 2 CHANNEL TRAFFIC LIGHT CONTROLLER.
IT IS INTENDED AS AN EXAMPLE IN STATE MACHINE SYNTHESIS.

```
TRAFFIC SIGNAL CONTROLLER No. 1

 1 CXX0XXXXXXXXXHHHHXX1
 2 C111XXXXXXXHHLHHHLH1
 3 CXX1XXXXXXXHHHLHHLH1
 4 CXX1XXXXXXXHHLLHHLH1
 5 CXX1XXXXXXXHHHHLHLH1
 6 CXX1XXXXXXXHHLHLHHL1
 7 CXX1XXXXXXXLHHHHLHH1
 8 C111XXXXXXXLHLHHLHH1
 9 CXX1XXXXXXXLHHLHLHH1
10 CXX1XXXXXXXLHLLHLHH1
11 CXX1XXXXXXXLHHHLLHH1
12 CXX1XXXXXXXHLLHLLHH1
13 CXX1XXXXXXXHHHHHHLH1
14 C101XXXXXXXHHHHLHLH1
15 CXX0XXXXXXXXXHHHHXX1
16 C011XXXXXXXHHHHHHLH1
17 C001XXXXXXXHHLHHHLH1

PASS SIMULATION
```

```
TRAFFIC SIGNAL CONTROLLER No. 1

              11 1111 1111 2222 2222 2233
 0123 4567 8901 2345 6789 0123 4567 8901

 0 ---- ---- ---- ---- ---- ---- ---- ----
 1 ---- ---- --X- ---X ---- ---X ---- ---- /Q3*Q2*Q0

 8 ---- ---- ---- ---- ---- ---- ---- ----
 9 ---- ---- --X- --X- ---- ---- ---- ---- /Q3*/Q2
10 ---- ---- --X- ---- --X- --X- ---- ---- /Q3*/Q1*/Q0

16 ---- ---- X--X ---- ---- --X- ---- ---- Q3*/Q0*/INIT
17 ---- ---- X--X --X- ---- ---- ---- ---- Q3*/Q2*/INIT
18 ---- ---- X-X- ---X ---- ---X ---- ---- /Q3*Q2*Q0*/INIT

24 ---- ---- X--- ---- ---X ---X ---- ---- Q1*Q0*/INIT
25 ---- ---- X--- ---X --X- --X- ---- ---- Q2*/Q1*/Q0*/INIT
26 X--- -X-- X-X- ---- --X- --X- ---- ---- /Q3*/Q1*/Q0*/SENA*SENB*/INIT

32 ---- ---- X--- ---- ---X --X- ---- ---- Q1*/Q0*/INIT
33 ---- ---- X--- --X- --X- ---X ---- ---- /Q2*/Q1*Q0*/INIT

40 X--- X--- X--- ---- ---- --X- ---- ---- /Q0*/SENA*/SENB*/INIT
41 -X-- -X-- X--- ---- ---- --X- ---- ---- /Q0*SENA*SENB*/INIT
42 ---- ---- X--- ---- ---X --X- ---- ---- Q1*/Q0*/INIT
43 ---- ---- X--- ---X ---- --X- ---- ---- Q2*/Q0*/INIT
44 ---- ---- X--X ---- ---- --X- ---- ---- Q3*/Q0*/INIT

48 ---- ---- ---- ---- ---- ---- ---- ----
49 ---- ---- ---X ---X ---- ---X ---- ---- Q3*Q2*Q0

56 ---- ---- ---- ---- ---- ---- ---- ----
57 ---- ---- ---X --X- ---- ---- ---- ---- Q3*/Q2
58 ---- ---- ---X ---- --X- --X- ---- ---- Q3*/Q1*/Q0

LEGEND:  X : FUSE NOT BLOWN (L,N,0)   - : FUSE BLOWN   (H,P,1)

NUMBER OF FUSES BLOWN =  673
```

Traffic Signal Controller No. 1

Logic Diagram PAL16R4

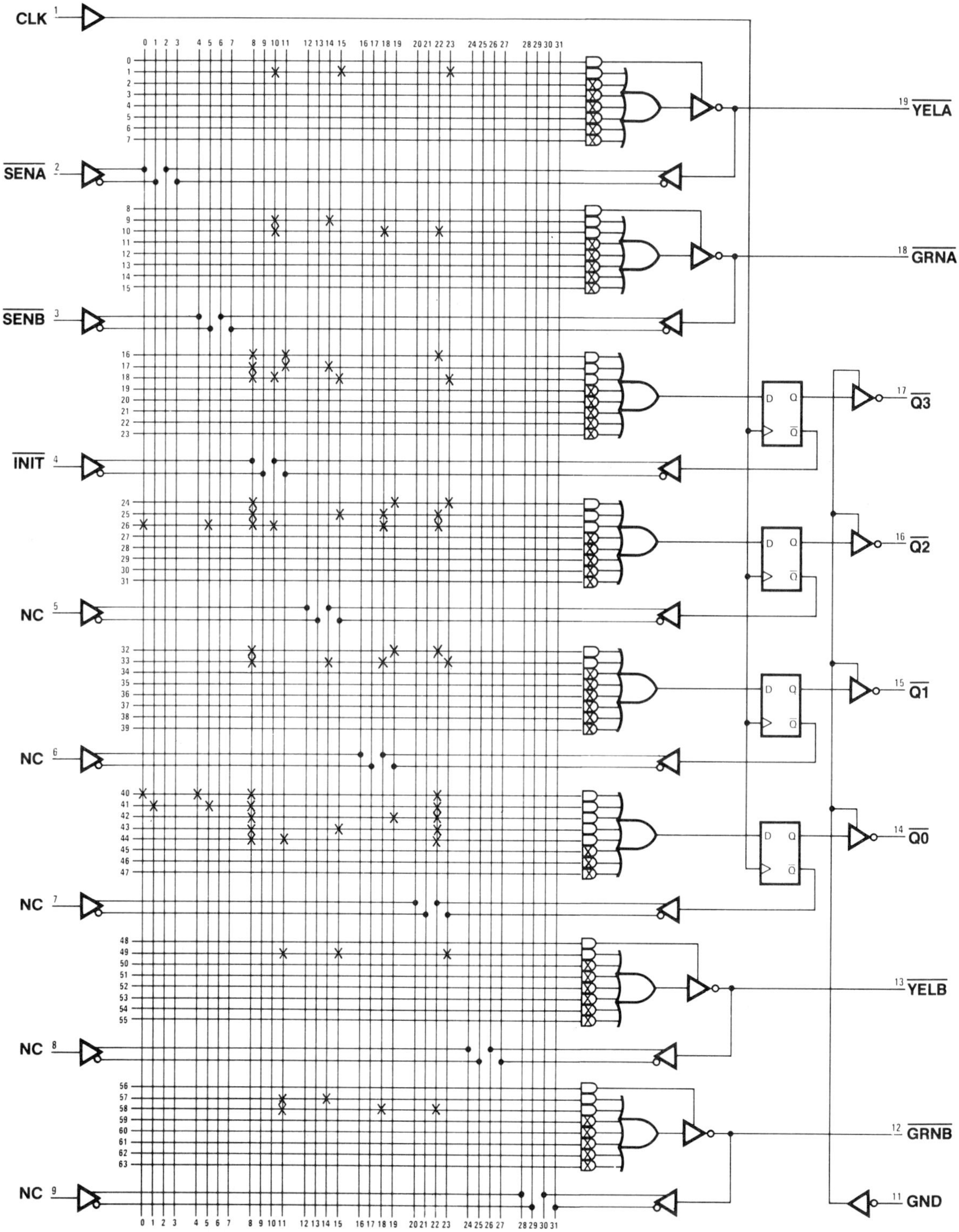

Another approach to the circuit implementation is to assign one flip-flop (state variable) per output. When this is done with PALs, no penalty in chip count need be paid. In addition, such an implementation offers higher throughput than one which uses combinatorial outputs as one layer of delay is eliminated. Once again referring to Figure 4, we see that the outputs do not change in 2 sets of 5 states. Thus, a 3-bit counter is needed to count the states in which the outputs are common. This leaves only 5 flip-flops in a PAL16R8, so we will use the REDA = REDB trick once again. Figure 13 shows a new state assignment to re-implement the circuit with this approach.

	CURRENT STATE								INPUT/NEXT STATE																															
									00								01								10								11							
	Q7	Q6	Q5	Q4	Q3	Q2	Q1	Q0	Q7	Q6	Q5	Q4	Q3	Q2	Q1	Q0	Q7	Q6	Q5	Q4	Q3	Q2	Q1	Q0	Q7	Q6	Q5	Q4	Q3	Q2	Q1	Q0	Q7	Q6	Q5	Q4	Q3	Q2	Q1	Q0
S0	0	0	1	0	0	0	0	0	0	0	1	0	0	0	0	1	0	0	1	0	0	1	0	0	0	0	1	0	0	0	0	0	0	0	1	0	0	0	0	1
S1	0	0	1	0	0	0	0	1	0	0	1	0	0	0	1	0	0	0	1	0	0	0	1	0	0	0	1	0	0	0	1	0	0	0	1	0	0	0	1	0
S2	0	0	1	0	0	0	1	0	0	0	1	0	0	0	1	1	0	0	1	0	0	0	1	1	0	0	1	0	0	0	1	1	0	0	1	0	0	0	1	1
S3	0	0	1	0	0	0	1	1	0	0	1	0	0	1	0	0	0	0	1	0	0	1	0	0	0	0	1	0	0	1	0	0	0	0	1	0	0	1	0	0
S4	0	0	1	0	0	1	0	0	0	1	0	0	0	0	0	0	0	1	0	0	0	0	0	0	0	1	0	0	0	0	0	0	0	1	0	0	0	0	0	0
S5	0	1	0	0	0	0	0	0	1	0	0	0	1	0	0	0	1	0	0	0	1	0	0	0	1	0	0	0	1	0	0	0	1	0	0	0	1	0	0	0
S6	1	0	0	0	1	0	0	0	1	0	0	0	1	0	0	1	1	0	0	0	1	0	0	0	1	0	0	0	1	1	0	0	1	0	0	0	1	0	0	1
S7	1	0	0	0	1	0	0	1	1	0	0	0	1	0	1	0	1	0	0	0	1	0	1	0	1	0	0	0	1	0	1	0	1	0	0	0	1	0	1	0
S8	1	0	0	0	1	0	1	0	1	0	0	0	1	0	1	1	1	0	0	0	1	0	1	1	1	0	0	0	1	0	1	1	1	0	0	0	1	0	1	1
S9	1	0	0	0	1	0	1	1	1	0	0	0	1	1	0	0	1	0	0	0	1	1	0	0	1	0	0	0	1	1	0	0	1	0	0	0	1	1	0	0
S10	1	0	0	0	1	1	0	0	1	0	0	1	0	0	0	0	1	0	0	1	0	0	0	0	1	0	0	1	0	0	0	0	1	0	0	1	0	0	0	0
S11	1	0	0	1	0	0	0	0	0	0	1	0	0	0	0	0	0	0	1	0	0	0	0	0	0	0	1	0	0	0	0	0	0	0	1	0	0	0	0	0

Q7 = REDA = $\overline{\text{REDB}}$ Q5 = GRNA   Q3 = GRNB   Q2, Q1, Q0 = COUNTER

Q6 = YELA   Q4 = YELB

Figure 13. State Assignment No. 2/Transition Table

This transition table would translate into 10 variable Karnaugh maps. Instead, we can simply write down the equations for each next state variable and minimize by inspection (especially if the 8 product per output restriction is exceeded). Initially we will use state names rather than state variables.

By inspection, $Q7^+$, $Q6^+$, $Q5^+$, $Q4^+$, $Q3^+$, $Q1^+$, not depend on SENA and SENB:

$Q7^+$ = S5 + S6 + S7 + S8 + S9 + S10

$Q6^+$ = S4

$Q5^+$ = S0 + S1 = S2 + S3 + S11

$Q4^+$ = S10

$Q3^+$ = S5 + S6 + S7 + S8 + S9

$Q1^+$ = S1 + S2 + S7 + S8

$Q2^+$ and $Q0^+$ do depend on SENA and SENB:

$Q2^+$ = /SENA * /SENB * (S3 + S9) [2 products]
  + /SENA * SENB * (S0 + S3 + S9) [3 products]
  + SENA * /SENB * (S3 + S6 + S9) [3 products]
  + SENA * SENB * (S3 + S9) [2 products]

Since $Q2^+$ needs 10 products as written, we minimize by Boolean manipulation:

$Q2^+$ = /SENA * /SENB * (S3 + S9) } /SENA * (S3 + S9)
  + /SENA * SENB * (S3 + S9) }
  + /SENA * SENB + (S0)   } S3 + S9
  + SENA * /SENB * (S3 + S9) } SENA * (S3 + S9)
  + SENA * SENB * (S3 + S9) }
  + SENA * SENB * (S6)

Thus,

$Q2^+$ = S3 + S9
  + /SENA * SENB * S0
  + SENA * SENB * S6

Next,

$Q0^+$ = /SENA * /SENB * (S0 + S2 + S6 + S8) [4 products]
  + /SENA * SENB * (S2 + S8) [2 products]
  + SENA * /SENB * (S2 + S8) [2 products]
  + SENA * SENB * (S0 + S2 + S6 + S8) [4 products]

$Q0^+$ = /SENA * /SENB * (S0 + S6)
  + /SENA * /SENB * (S2 + S8) } /SENA * (S2 + S8)
  + /SENA * SENB * (S2 + S8) }   } S2 + S8
  + SENA * /SENB * (S2 + S8) } SENA * (S2 + S8)
  + SENA * SENB * (S2 + S8) }
  + SENA * SENB * (S0 + S6)

$Q0^+$ + S2 + S8
  + /SENA * /SENB * (S0 + S6)
  + SENA * SENB * (S0 + S6)

The full equations (note that minimization is optional for less than 8 product sums):

```
Q7+ = /Q7 *  Q6 * /Q5 * /Q4 * /Q3 * /Q2 * /Q1 * /Q0
    +  Q7 * /Q6 * /Q5 * /Q4 *  Q3 * /Q2 * /Q1 * /Q0
    +  Q7 * /Q6 * /Q5 * /Q4 *  Q3 * /Q2 * /Q1 *  Q0
    +  Q7 * /Q6 * /Q5 * /Q4 *  Q3 * /Q2 *  Q1 * /Q0
    +  Q7 * /Q6 * /Q5 * /Q4 *  Q3 * /Q2 *  Q1 *  Q0
    +  Q7 * /Q6 * /Q5 * /Q4 *  Q3 *  Q2 * /Q1 * /Q0

Q6+ = /Q7 * /Q6 *  Q5 * /Q4 * /Q3 *  Q2 * /Q1 * /Q0

Q5+ = /Q7 * /Q6 *  Q5 * /Q4 * /Q3 * /Q2 * /Q1 * /Q0
    + /Q7 * /Q6 *  Q5 * /Q4 * /Q3 * /Q2 * /Q1 *  Q0
    + /Q7 * /Q6 *  Q5 * /Q4 * /Q3 * /Q2 *  Q1 * /Q0
    + /Q7 * /Q6 *  Q5 * /Q4 * /Q3 * /Q2 *  Q1 *  Q0
    +  Q7 * /Q6 * /Q5 *  Q4 * /Q3 * /Q2 * /Q1 * /Q0

Q4+ =  Q7 * /Q6 * /Q5 * /Q4 *  Q3 *  Q2 * /Q1 * /Q0

Q3+ = /Q7 *  Q6 * /Q5 * /Q4 * /Q3 * /Q2 * /Q1 * /Q0
    +  Q7 * /Q6 * /Q5 * /Q4 *  Q3 * /Q2 * /Q1 * /Q0
    +  Q7 * /Q6 * /Q5 * /Q4 *  Q3 * /Q2 * /Q1 *  Q0
    +  Q7 * /Q6 * /Q5 * /Q4 *  Q3 * /Q2 *  Q1 * /Q0
    +  Q7 * /Q6 * /Q5 * /Q4 *  Q3 * /Q2 *  Q1 *  Q0

Q2+ = /Q7 * /Q6 *  Q5 * /Q4 * /Q3 * /Q2 *  Q1 *  Q0
    +  Q7 * /Q6 * /Q5 * /Q4 *  Q3 * /Q2 *  Q1 *  Q0
    + /Q7 * /Q6 *  Q5 * /Q4 * /Q3 * /Q2 * /Q1 * /Q0
    * /SENA * SENB
    +  Q7 * /Q6 * /Q5 * /Q4 *  Q3 * /Q2 * /Q1 * /Q0
    *  SENA * SENB

Q1+ = /Q7 * /Q6 *  Q5 * /Q4 * /Q3 * /Q2 * /Q1 *  Q0
    + /Q7 * /Q6 *  Q5 * /Q4 * /Q3 * /Q2 *  Q1 * /Q0
    +  Q7 * /Q6 * /Q5 * /Q4 *  Q3 * /Q2 * /Q1 *  Q0
    +  Q7 * /Q6 * /Q5 * /Q4 *  Q3 * /Q2 *  Q1 * /Q0

Q0+ = /Q7 * /Q6 *  Q5 * /Q4 * /Q3 * /Q2 *  Q1 * /Q0
    +  Q7 * /Q6 * /Q5 * /Q4 *  Q3 * /Q2 *  Q1 * /Q0
    + /Q7 * /Q6 *  Q5 * /Q4 * /Q3 * /Q2 * /Q1 * /Q0
    * /SENA * /SENB
    +  Q7 * /Q6 * /Q5 * /Q4 *  Q3 * /Q2 * /Q1 * /Q0
    * /SENA * /SENB
    + /Q7 * /Q6 *  Q5 * /Q4 * /Q3 * /Q2 * /Q1 * /Q0
    *  SENA *  SENB
```

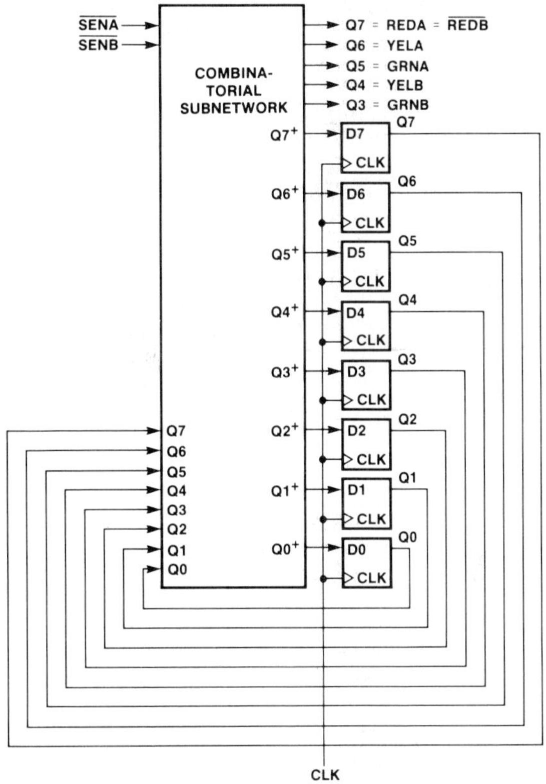

Figure 14. State Machine Traffic Signal Controller No. 2 (Note flip-flops are directly circuit outputs)

```
PAL16R8                                                    PAL DESIGN SPECIFICATION
TRACNT2                                                    B. BRAFMAN 07/16/81
TRAFFIC SIGNAL CONTROLLER No. 2
MMI FIELD APPLICATIONS ENGINEER YORBA LINDA, CALIFORNIA
CLK /SENA /SENB /INIT NC  NC NC NC NC GND
GND /Q0 /Q1 /Q2 /Q3 /Q4 /Q5 /Q6 /Q7 VCC


Q7 := /Q7 *  Q6 * /Q5 * /Q4 * /Q3 * /Q2 * /Q1 * /Q0 * /INIT
    +  Q7 * /Q6 * /Q5 * /Q4 *  Q3 * /Q2 * /Q1 * /Q0 * /INIT
    +  Q7 * /Q6 * /Q5 * /Q4 *  Q3 * /Q2 * /Q1 *  Q0 * /INIT
    +  Q7 * /Q6 * /Q5 * /Q4 *  Q3 * /Q2 *  Q1 * /Q0 * /INIT
    +  Q7 * /Q6 * /Q5 * /Q4 *  Q3 * /Q2 *  Q1 *  Q0 * /INIT
    +  Q7 * /Q6 * /Q5 * /Q4 *  Q3 *  Q2 * /Q1 * /Q0 * /INIT

Q6 := /Q7 * /Q6 *  Q5 * /Q4 * /Q3 *  Q2 * /Q1 * /Q0 * /INIT

Q5 := /Q7 * /Q6 *  Q5 * /Q4 * /Q3 * /Q2 * /Q1 * /Q0
    + /Q7 * /Q6 *  Q5 * /Q4 * /Q3 * /Q2 * /Q1 *  Q0
    + /Q7 * /Q6 *  Q5 * /Q4 * /Q3 * /Q2 *  Q1 * /Q0
    + /Q7 * /Q6 *  Q5 * /Q4 * /Q3 * /Q2 *  Q1 *  Q0
    +  Q7 * /Q6 * /Q5 *  Q4 * /Q3 * /Q2 * /Q1 * /Q0
    +  INIT                 ; PRESET THIS BIT FOR INITIALIZATION TO STATE S0

Q4 :=  Q7 * /Q6 * /Q5 * /Q4 *  Q3 *  Q2 * /Q1 * /Q0 * /INIT

Q3 := /Q7 *  Q6 * /Q5 * /Q4 * /Q3 * /Q2 * /Q1 * /Q0 * /INIT
    +  Q7 * /Q6 * /Q5 * /Q4 *  Q3 * /Q2 * /Q1 * /Q0 * /INIT
    +  Q7 * /Q6 * /Q5 * /Q4 *  Q3 * /Q2 * /Q1 *  Q0 * /INIT
    +  Q7 * /Q6 * /Q5 * /Q4 *  Q3 * /Q2 *  Q1 * /Q0 * /INIT
    +  Q7 * /Q6 * /Q5 * /Q4 *  Q3 * /Q2 *  Q1 *  Q0 * /INIT

Q2 := /Q7 * /Q6 *  Q5 * /Q4 * /Q3 * /Q2 *  Q1 *  Q0 * /INIT
    +  Q7 * /Q6 * /Q5 * /Q4 *  Q3 * /Q2 *  Q1 *  Q0 * /INIT
    + /Q7 * /Q6 *  Q5 * /Q4 * /Q3 * /Q2 * /Q1 * /Q0 * /INIT * /SENA *  SENB
    +  Q7 * /Q6 * /Q5 * /Q4 *  Q3 * /Q2 * /Q1 * /Q0 * /INIT *  SENA *  SENB

Q1 := /Q7 * /Q6 *  Q5 * /Q4 * /Q3 * /Q2 * /Q1 *  Q0 * /INIT
    + /Q7 * /Q6 *  Q5 * /Q4 * /Q3 * /Q2 *  Q1 * /Q0 * /INIT
    +  Q7 * /Q6 * /Q5 * /Q4 *  Q3 * /Q2 * /Q1 *  Q0 * /INIT
    +  Q7 * /Q6 * /Q5 * /Q4 *  Q3 * /Q2 *  Q1 * /Q0 * /INIT

Q0 := /Q7 * /Q6 *  Q5 * /Q4 * /Q3 * /Q2 *  Q1 * /Q0 * /INIT
    +  Q7 * /Q6 * /Q5 * /Q4 *  Q3 * /Q2 *  Q1 * /Q0 * /INIT
    + /Q7 * /Q6 *  Q5 * /Q4 * /Q3 * /Q2 * /Q1 * /Q0 * /INIT * /SENA * /SENB
    +  Q7 * /Q6 * /Q5 * /Q4 *  Q3 * /Q2 * /Q1 * /Q0 * /INIT * /SENA * /SENB
    + /Q7 * /Q6 *  Q5 * /Q4 * /Q3 * /Q2 * /Q1 * /Q0 * /INIT *  SENA *  SENB
    +  Q7 * /Q6 * /Q5 * /Q4 *  Q3 * /Q2 * /Q1 * /Q0 * /INIT *  SENA *  SENB
```

FUNCTION TABLE

/INIT	CLK	SENA	SENB	Q7	Q6	Q5	Q4	Q3	Q2	Q1	Q0	;COMMENTS
L	C	X	X	L	L	H	L	L	L	L	L	S0 (INIT)
H	C	L	L	L	L	H	L	L	L	L	H	S1
H	C	X	X	L	L	H	L	L	L	H	L	S2
H	C	X	X	L	L	H	L	L	L	H	H	S3
H	C	X	X	L	L	H	L	L	H	L	L	S4
H	C	X	X	L	H	L	L	L	L	L	L	S5
H	C	X	X	H	L	L	L	H	L	L	L	S6
H	C	L	L	H	L	L	L	H	L	L	H	S7
H	C	X	X	H	L	L	L	H	L	H	L	S8
H	C	X	X	H	L	L	L	H	L	H	H	S9
H	C	X	X	H	L	L	L	H	H	L	L	S10
H	C	X	X	H	L	L	H	L	L	L	L	S11
H	C	X	X	L	L	H	L	L	L	L	L	S0
H	C	L	H	L	L	H	L	L	H	L	L	S4
L	C	X	X	L	L	H	L	L	L	L	L	S0 (INIT)
H	C	H	L	L	L	H	L	L	L	L	L	S0
H	C	H	H	L	L	H	L	L	L	L	H	S1

DESCRIPTION

THIS PAL IS THE SECOND PASS AT THE TRAFFIC SIGNAL CONTROLLER IMPLEMENTATION. THE FOLLOWING SUBSTITUTIONS ARE MADE FOR STATE VARIABLES Q7-Q0:

```
Q7 = REDA = /REDB          Q5 = GRNA          Q3 = GRNB
Q6 = YELA                  Q4 = YELB          Q2,Q1,Q0 = COUNTER
```

TRAFFIC SIGNAL CONTROLLER No. 2

```
 1 CXX0XXXXXXXHHHHHLHH1
 2 C111XXXXXXXLHHHHLHH1
 3 CXX1XXXXXXXHLHHHLHH1
 4 CXX1XXXXXXXLLHHHLHH1
 5 CXX1XXXXXXXHHLHHLHH1
 6 CXX1XXXXXXXHHHHHHLH1
 7 CXX1XXXXXXXHHHLHHHL1
 8 C111XXXXXXXLHHLHHHL1
 9 CXX1XXXXXXXHLHLHHHL1
10 CXX1XXXXXXXLLHLHHHL1
11 CXX1XXXXXXXHHLLHHHL1
12 CXX1XXXXXXXHHHHLHHL1
13 CXX1XXXXXXXHHHHHLHH1
14 C101XXXXXXXHHLHHLHH1
15 CXX0XXXXXXXHHHHHLHH1
16 C011XXXXXXXHHHHHLHH1
17 C001XXXXXXXLHHHHLHH1
```

PASS SIMULATION

```
TRAFFIC SIGNAL CONTROLLER No. 2

               11 1111 1111 2222 2222 2233
   0123 4567 8901 2345 6789 0123 4567 8901

 0 --X- ---X X-X- --X- --X- --X- --X- --X- /Q7*Q6*/Q5*/Q4*/Q3*/Q2*/Q1*/Q0-
 1 ---X --X- X-X- --X- ---X --X- --X- --X- Q7*/Q6*/Q5*/Q4*Q3*/Q2*/Q1*/Q0*-
 2 ---X --X- X-X- --X- ---X --X- --X- ---X Q7*/Q6*/Q5*/Q4*Q3*/Q2*/Q1*Q0*/-
 3 ---X --X- X-X- --X- ---X --X- ---X --X- Q7*/Q6*/Q5*/Q4*Q3*/Q2*Q1*/Q0*/-
 4 ---X --X- X-X- --X- ---X --X- ---X ---X Q7*/Q6*/Q5*/Q4*Q3*/Q2*Q1*Q0*/I-
 5 ---X --X- X-X- --X- ---X ---X --X- --X- Q7*/Q6*/Q5*/Q4*Q3*Q2*/Q1*/Q0*/-

 8 --X- --X- X--X --X- --X- ---X --X- --X- /Q7*/Q6*Q5*/Q4*/Q3*Q2*/Q1*/Q0*-

16 --X- --X- ---X --X- --X- --X- --X- --X- /Q7*/Q6*Q5*/Q4*/Q3*/Q2*/Q1*/Q0
17 --X- --X- ---X --X- --X- --X- --X- ---X /Q7*/Q6*Q5*/Q4*/Q3*/Q2*/Q1*Q0
18 --X- --X- ---X --X- --X- --X- ---X --X- /Q7*/Q6*Q5*/Q4*/Q3*/Q2*Q1*/Q0
19 --X- --X- ---X --X- --X- --X- ---X ---X /Q7*/Q6*Q5*/Q4*/Q3*/Q2*Q1*Q0
20 ---X --X- --X- ---X --X- --X- --X- --X- Q7*/Q6*/Q5*Q4*/Q3*/Q2*/Q1*/Q0
21 ---- ---- -X-- ---- ---- ---- ---- ---- INIT

24 ---X --X- X-X- --X- ---X ---X --X- --X- Q7*/Q6*/Q5*/Q4*Q3*Q2*/Q1*/Q0*/-

32 --X- ---X X-X- --X- --X- --X- --X- --X- /Q7*Q6*/Q5*/Q4*/Q3*/Q2*/Q1*/Q0-
33 ---X --X- X-X- --X- ---X --X- --X- --X- Q7*/Q6*/Q5*/Q4*Q3*/Q2*/Q1*/Q0*-
34 ---X --X- X-X- --X- ---X --X- --X- ---X Q7*/Q6*/Q5*/Q4*Q3*/Q2*/Q1*Q0*/-
35 ---X --X- X-X- --X- ---X --X- ---X --X- Q7*/Q6*/Q5*/Q4*Q3*/Q2*Q1*/Q0*/-
36 ---X --X- X-X- --X- ---X --X- ---X ---X Q7*/Q6*/Q5*/Q4*Q3*/Q2*Q1*Q0*/I-

40 --X- --X- X--X --X- --X- --X- ---X ---X /Q7*/Q6*Q5*/Q4*/Q3*/Q2*Q1*Q0*/-
41 ---X --X- X-X- --X- ---X --X- ---X ---X Q7*/Q6*/Q5*/Q4*Q3*/Q2*Q1*Q0*/I-
42 X-X- -XX- X--X --X- --X- --X- --X- --X- /Q7*/Q6*Q5*/Q4*/Q3*/Q2*/Q1*/Q0-
43 -X-X -XX- X-X- --X- ---X --X- --X- --X- Q7*/Q6*/Q5*/Q4*Q3*/Q2*/Q1*/Q0*-

48 --X- --X- X--X --X- --X- --X- --X- ---X /Q7*/Q6*Q5*/Q4*/Q3*/Q2*/Q1*Q0*-
49 --X- --X- X--X --X- --X- --X- ---X --X- /Q7*/Q6*Q5*/Q4*/Q3*/Q2*Q1*/Q0*-
50 ---X --X- X-X- --X- ---X --X- --X- ---X Q7*/Q6*/Q5*/Q4*Q3*/Q2*/Q1*Q0*/-
51 ---X --X- X-X- --X- ---X --X- ---X --X- Q7*/Q6*/Q5*/Q4*Q3*/Q2*Q1*/Q0*/-

56 --X- --X- X--X --X- --X- --X- ---X --X- /Q7*/Q6*Q5*/Q4*/Q3*/Q2*Q1*/Q0*-
57 ---X --X- X-X- --X- ---X --X- ---X --X- Q7*/Q6*/Q5*/Q4*Q3*/Q2*Q1*/Q0*/-
58 X-X- X-X- X--X --X- --X- --X- --X- --X- /Q7*/Q6*Q5*/Q4*/Q3*/Q2*/Q1*/Q0-
59 X--X X-X- X-X- --X- ---X --X- --X- --X- Q7*/Q6*/Q5*/Q4*Q3*/Q2*/Q1*/Q0*-
60 -XX- -XX- X--X --X- --X- --X- --X- --X- /Q7*/Q6*Q5*/Q4*/Q3*/Q2*/Q1*/Q0-
61 -X-X -XX- X-X- --X- ---X --X- --X- --X- Q7*/Q6*/Q5*/Q4*Q3*/Q2*/Q1*/Q0*-

LEGEND:  X : FUSE NOT BLOWN (L,N,0)   - : FUSE BLOWN   (H,P,1)

NUMBER OF FUSES BLOWN =  760
```

Traffic Signal Controller No. 2

Logic Diagram PAL16R8

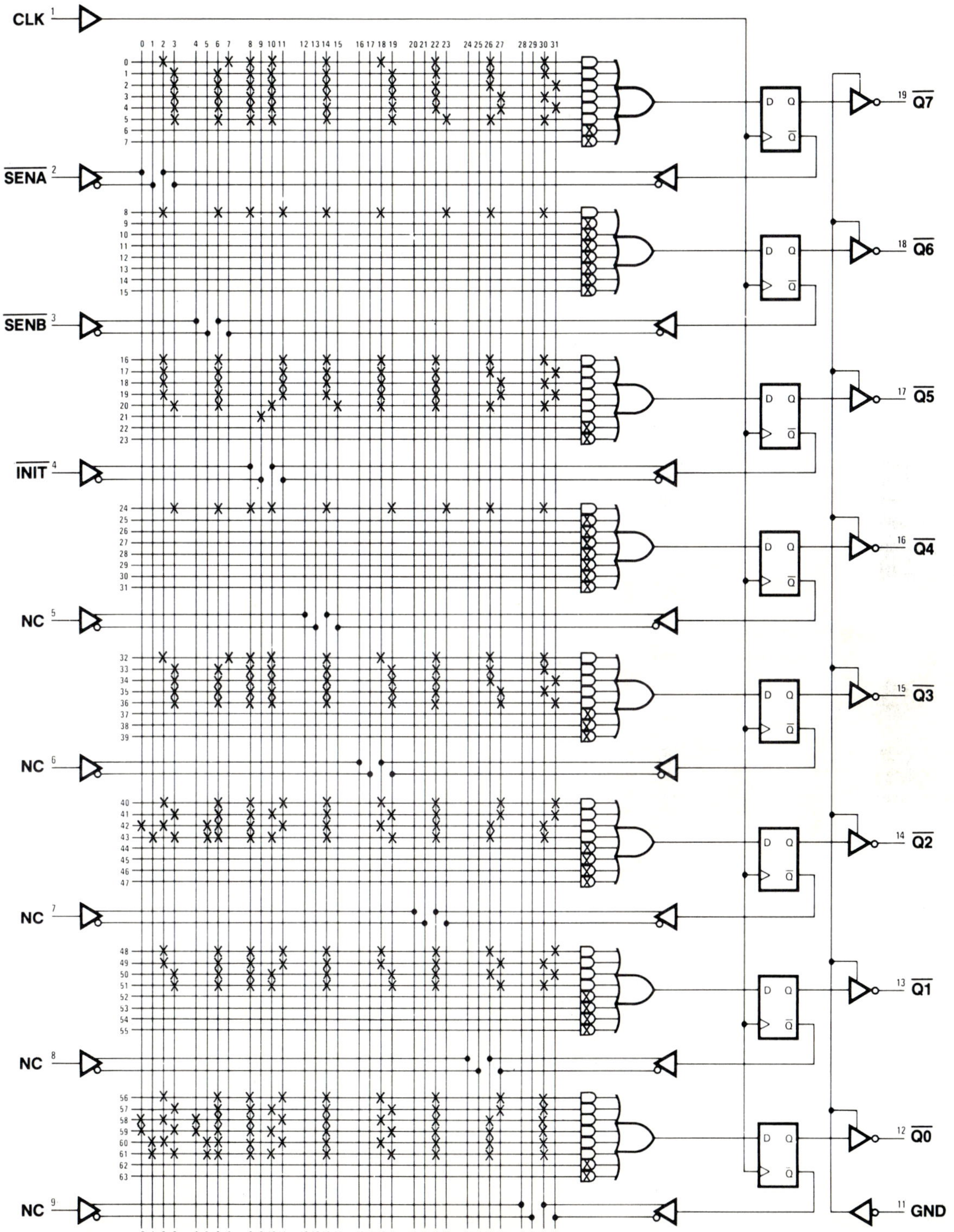

PAL
IMPORTANT,
NOTES

32-Bit CRC (Cyclical Redundancy Checking) Error Detection

PAL20X10

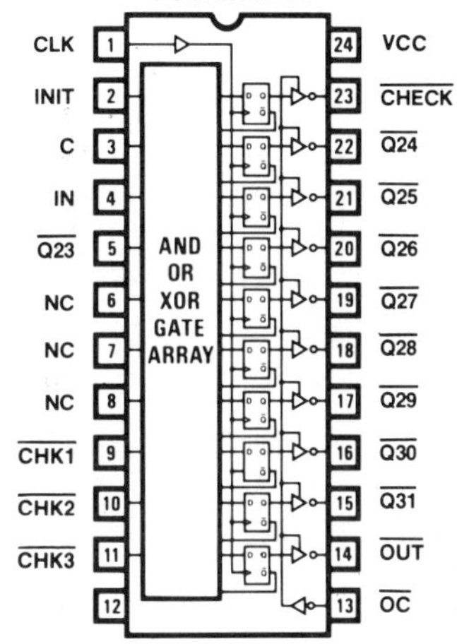

PAL20X8

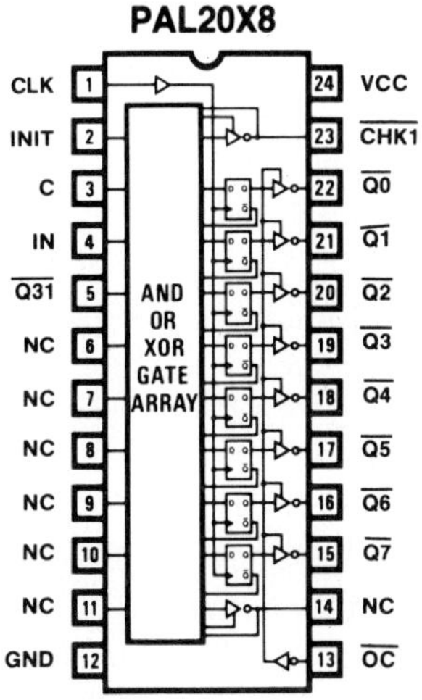

PAL20X8

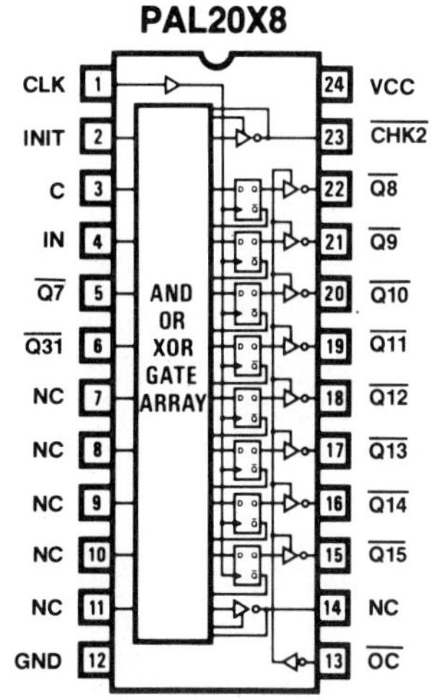

PAL20X8

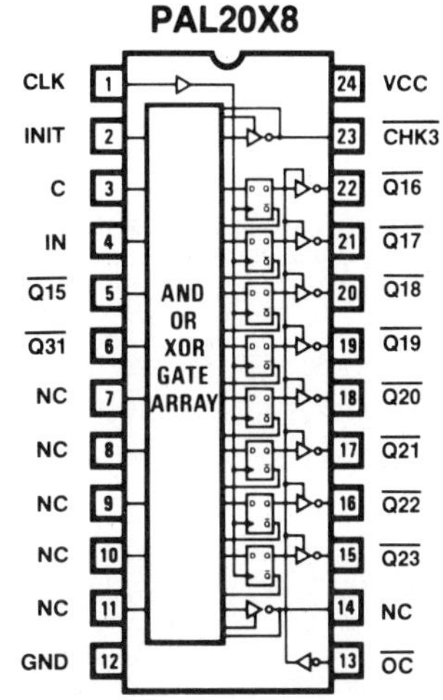

CYCLIC REDUNDANCY CHECK (CRC) USING PALS

Programmable Array Logic Devices Provide Efficient Implementation of Popular Local Network Error Checking Protocol

There is a growing interest in providing data communication links to connect several processors and peripherals into one local area network. One of the most popular networks is the Ethernet. To insure reliable communications in the network an efficient error detection scheme is required. The Ethernet protocol specifies a 32-bit cycle redundancy check (CRC).

The following application opens with a tutorial on the CRC and then shows a detailed implementation of the Ethernet CRC using PAL. The use of fuse programmable devices allows easy modification to accommodate other data communications protocols as well as other applications (CRC in disk drives, etc.), that operate at rates up to 13 Mbits/sec.

Introduction

The growing number of high speed digital links and the need for reliable communication requires implementation of efficient error detection schemes. A 32-bit CRC using PALs meets these requirements.

What is CRC ?

CRC is the acronym for Cyclic Redundancy Check, an error detection technique widely used in serial communication systems from computer to computer or from computer to peripheral devices. This technique operates on serial bits of information treated as the coefficients of a binary polynomial, P(x), and processes these bits in modulo-2 arithmetic.

The basic coding concept of the CRC is to modify the polynomial, P(x), so that it is exactly divisible by a fixed polynomial, G(x); the divisor G(x) is referred to as the generator polynomial. The modified polynomial, M(x), is transmitted. M(x) is divided by the same G(x) when received or fetched. If the remainder is zero, all bits are assumed to be correct; otherwise, a flag is set to indicate an error.

An Example Using CRC

A 6-bit message (101110) can be represented in polynomial form as:

$$P(x) = 1 + 0\,x + 1\,x^2 + 1\,x^3 + 1\,x^4 + 0\,x^5$$

or

$$P(x) = x^4 + x^3 + x^2 + 1$$

The highest power of x is attached to the least significant bit (LSB). The LSB is the first bit transmitted in communication channels. In general P(x) will not be exactly divisible by G(x); the division will generate a quotient, Q(x), and a remainder, R(x). P(x) is prescaled to insure that the order of P(x) is greater than the order of G(x) so that the remainder is always different than the message itself.

Specifically, P(x) is prescaled by x^n where n is the degree of G(x).

$$x^n\,P(x) = Q(x)\,G(x) + R(x) \qquad (1)$$

For a 3-bit CRC and $G(x) = x^3 + 1$ equation (1) becomes:

$$x^3\,(x^4 + x^3 + x^2 + 1) = (x^4 + x^3 + x^2 + x)\,(x^3 + 1) + (x^2 + x)$$

The operation is performed using modulo-2 arithmetic where the sum and difference are synonymous.
Equation 1 can equivalently be written as:

$$x^n\,P(x) - R(x) = x^n\,P(x) + R(x) = Q(x)\,G(x) = M(x)$$

M(x) is exactly divisible by G(x) and it is M(x) that is transmitted. The message M(x) is formed by adding the remaining bits, R(x), of a fixed length n to the message bits. Because the message was prescaled, addition is equivalent to appending the remainder at the end of the data bits. For the example given (remembering that LSB is sent first) the information transmitted is: 011 101110. Three redundancy bits are appended to facilitate error detection.

In conclusion when performing CRC, the transmitter will generate and append R(x) while the receiver will verify the exact division of M(x) by G(x) and signal the occurrence of an error.

Why CRC ?

Compared to other error detection schemes such as parity checking CRC is more powerful:

- all errors within n successive bits are detected
- for even G(x) all errors with an odd number of bits in error are detected (50% of all possible random errors)
- all error patterns that are not divisible by G(x) are detected

CRC is also more efficient (for large frame of information). Efficiency is defined as the number of data bits divided by the total number of bits transmitted. For example: in the Ethernet

specification the number of data bits ranges from 60 to 1500 bytes, the total number of bits transmitted will contain only an extra 32-bits (if 32-bit CRC is used) instead of an extra 60 to 1500 parity bits (if we assume one parity bit per byte of information is used.)

Implementation

A binary division that ignores the quotient but retains the remainder, R(x), is conventionally implemented with a shift register. A feedback path from the output of the last stage returns to the input of the stages corresponding to the powers of x that have non zero coefficient in the generating polynomial. At each such input, a modulo-2 adder (Exclusive OR) combines the feedback signal with the output from the previous stage.

This is equivalent to a shift subtract on each clock cycle. The example in Fig. 1 shows a 32-bit CRC where G (x), the generator polynominal, (used in ETHERNET and AUTOBAUND II) is given by:

$$G(x) = x^{32} + x^{26} + x^{23} + x^{22} + x^{16} + x^{12} + x^{11} + x^{10} + x^8 + x^7 + x^5 + x^4 + x^2 + x + 1$$

Transmitter operation:

1. Initialize shift register to all Hs. (INIT = H)
2. Data is shifted in the feedback shift register to generate R(x) and fed to the output. (Control C = H)
3. After last data bit has been processed, the complimented R(x) is shifted out for transmission. (Control C = L)

Receiver operation:

1. Initialize shift register to all Hs.
2. Data is shifted in the feedback shift register to regenerate R(x).
3. After last data bit has been processed, Control remains High and the complement of R(x) is shifted (as generated by transmitter).

If the two R(x) match, the final content of the shift register is:

X31 X0
11000111000000100110111010111011 (residue)

4) This value is tested. (Check = L indicates no error, as shown in Fig. 2)

The same hardware can perform both the transmitter and receiver function if the respective inputs are multiplexed.

PAL Configuration

Four PALs are used to implement the 32-bit CRC. The PAL interconnections are shown in Fig. 2. Eight bits of the 32-bit shift register are distributed in each PAL. The logic to check for the residue is distributed among the four PALs as shown in Fig. 3.

Summary

The lack of standardization in data communication equipment makes the use of PALs very attractive due to their flexibility and ease of design modification.

REFERENCES

The Ethernet, A Local Area Network, Data Link Layer and Physical Layer Specifications, version 1.0 (joint publication of Digital Equipment Corp., Intel Corp., and Xerox Corp., 1980).

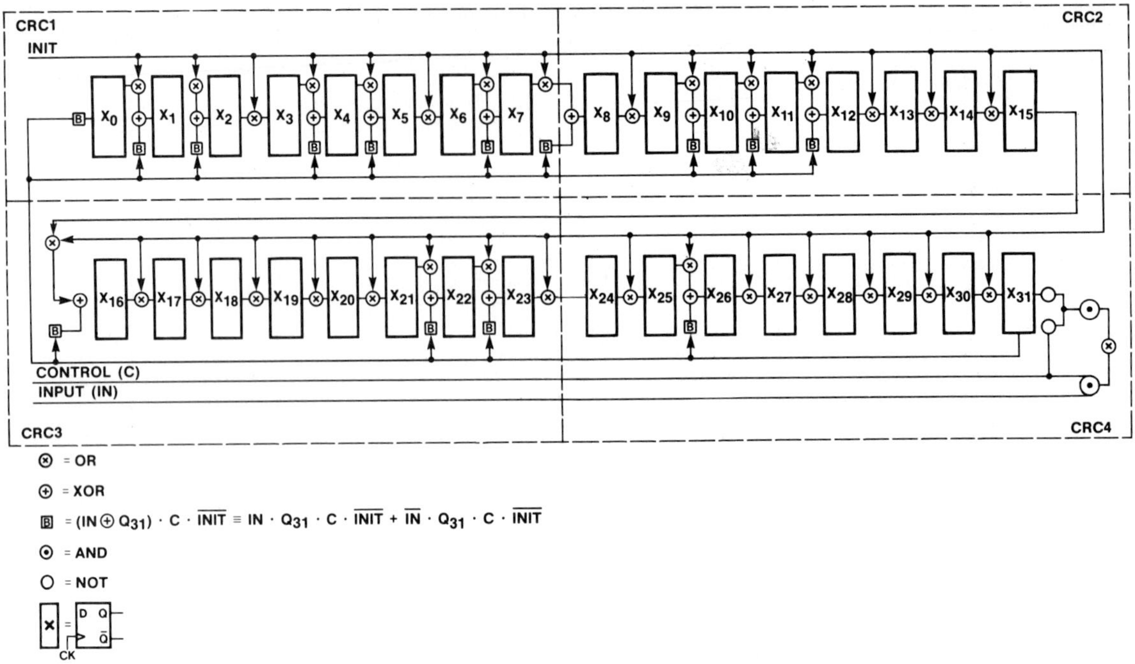
CRC1
CRC2
INIT
X_0 X_1 X_2 X_3 X_4 X_5 X_6 X_7 X_8 X_9 X_{10} X_{11} X_{12} X_{13} X_{14} X_{15}
X_{16} X_{17} X_{18} X_{19} X_{20} X_{21} X_{22} X_{23} X_{24} X_{25} X_{26} X_{27} X_{28} X_{29} X_{30} X_{31}
CONTROL (C)
INPUT (IN)
CRC3
CRC4
⊗ = OR
⊕ = XOR
B = $(IN \oplus Q_{31}) \cdot C \cdot \overline{INIT} \equiv IN \cdot \overline{Q_{31}} \cdot C \cdot \overline{INIT} + \overline{IN} \cdot Q_{31} \cdot C \cdot \overline{INIT}$
⊙ = AND
○ = NOT
X = D Q $\overline{Q}$
CK

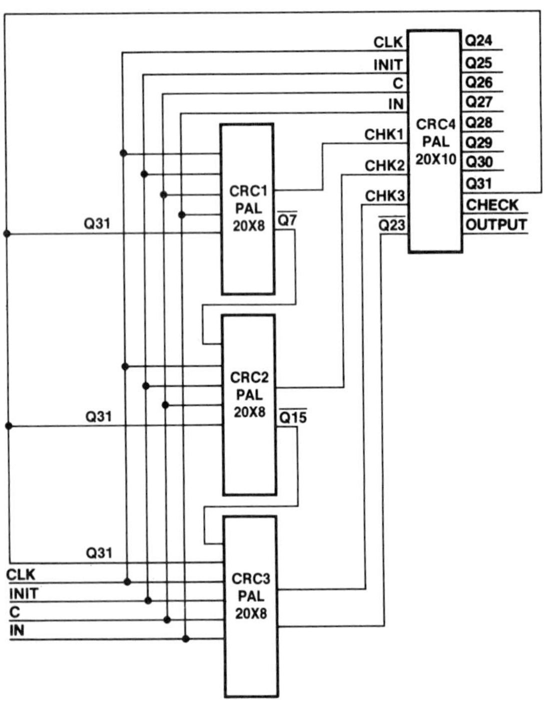
CLK
INIT
C
IN
CHK1
CHK2
CHK3
$\overline{Q23}$
CRC4 PAL 20X10
Q24 Q25 Q26 Q27 Q28 Q29 Q30 Q31
CHECK
OUTPUT
CRC1 PAL 20X8
$\overline{Q7}$
CRC2 PAL 20X8
$\overline{Q15}$
CRC3 PAL 20X8
Q31
CLK
INIT
C
IN

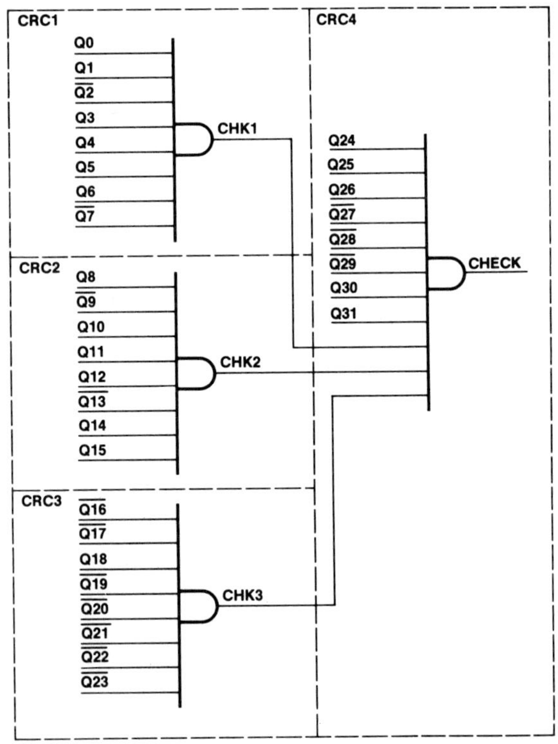
CRC1
Q0 Q1 $\overline{Q2}$ Q3 Q4 Q5 Q6 $\overline{Q7}$
CHK1
CRC2
Q8 $\overline{Q9}$ Q10 Q11 $\overline{Q12}$ $\overline{Q13}$ Q14 Q15
CHK2
CRC3
$\overline{Q16}$ $\overline{Q17}$ Q18 $\overline{Q19}$ $\overline{Q20}$ $\overline{Q21}$ $\overline{Q22}$ $\overline{Q23}$
CHK3
CRC4
Q24 Q25 Q26 $\overline{Q27}$ $\overline{Q28}$ $\overline{Q29}$ Q30 Q31
CHECK

```
PAL20X8                                               PAL DESIGN SPECIFICATION
CRC1                                                      NADIA SACHS 08/14/81
32-BIT CRC (CYCLICAL REDUNDANCY CHECKING) ERROR DETECTION, CHIP 1
MMI SUNNYVALE, CALIFORNIA
CLK INIT C IN /Q31 NC NC NC NC NC NC GND
/OC NC /Q7 /Q6 /Q5 /Q4 /Q3 /Q2 /Q1 /Q0 /CHK1 VCC


CHK1 =    Q0* Q1*/Q2* Q3* Q4* Q5* Q6*/Q7    ;CHECK BIT 1

Q0   :=  /INIT* IN* C                       ;MODULO-2
      +  /INIT* IN* C                       ;ADDITION
     :+:  Q31* C                            ;SHIFT IF C
      +   INIT                              ;INITIALIZE

Q1   :=  /INIT* C* IN*/Q31                  ;MODULO-2
      +  /INIT* C*/IN* Q31                  ;ADDITION
     :+:  Q0                                ;SHIFT
      +   INIT                              ;INITIALIZE

Q2   :=  /INIT* C* IN*/Q31                  ;MODULO-2
      +  /INIT* C*/IN* Q31                  ;ADDITION
     :+:  Q1                                ;SHIFT
      +   INIT                              ;INITIALIZE

Q3   :=   Q2                                ;SHIFT
      +   INIT                              ;INITIALIZE

Q4   :=  /INIT* C* IN*/Q31                  ;MODULO-2
      +  /INIT* C*/IN* Q31                  ;ADDITION
     :+:  Q3                                ;SHIFT
      +   INIT                              ;INITIALIZE

Q5   :=  /INIT* C* IN*/Q31                  ;MODULO-2
      +  /INIT* C*/IN* Q31                  ;ADDITION
     :+:  Q4                                ;SHIFT
      +   INIT                              ;INITIALIZE

Q6   :=   Q5                                ;SHIFT
      +   INIT                              ;INITIALIZE

Q7   :=  /INIT* C* IN*/Q31                  ;MODULO-2
      +  /INIT* C*/IN* Q31                  ;ADDITION
     :+:  Q6                                ;SHIFT
      +   INIT                              ;INITIALIZE
```

```
FUNCTION TABLE

CLK /OC INIT C IN Q31 Q7 Q6 Q5 Q4 Q3 Q2 Q1 Q0 CHK1

;                                  Q
;                                  3   QQQQQQQQ
;CLK   /OC    INIT    C    IN      1   76543210    CHK1
-------------------------------------------------------
  C     L      H      X    X       X   HHHHHHHH     X
  C     L      L      H    L       H   LHLLHLLH     X
  C     L      L      H    L       H   LLHLLHLH     X
  C     L      L      H    L       H   HHHHHHLH     X
  C     L      L      H    L       H   LHLLHHLH     X
  C     L      L      H    L       H   LLHLHHLH     X
  C     L      L      H    L       H   HHHLHHLH     X
  C     L      L      H    L       L   HHLHHLHL     X
  C     L      L      H    L       L   HLHHLHLL     X
  C     L      L      H    L       L   LHHLHLLL     X
  C     L      L      H    L       H   LHHLLHHH     X
  C     L      L      H    L       L   HHLLHHHL     X
  C     L      L      H    L       L   HLLHHHLL     X
  C     L      L      H    L       H   HLLLHHHH     X
  C     L      L      H    L       H   HLHLHLLH     X
  C     L      L      H    L       H   HHHLLHLH     X
  C     L      L      H    L       H   LHHHHHLH     X
  C     L      L      H    L       L   HHHHHLHL     X
  C     L      L      H    L       L   HHHHLHLL     X
  C     L      L      H    L       L   HHHLHLLL     X
  C     L      L      H    L       L   HHLHLLLL     X
  C     L      L      H    L       L   HLHLLLLL     X
  C     L      L      H    L       L   LHLLLLLL     X
  C     L      L      H    L       L   HLLLLLLL     X
  C     L      L      H    L       L   LLLLLLLL     X
  C     L      L      H    L       H   HLHHLHHH     X
  C     L      L      H    L       L   LHHLHHHL     X
  C     L      L      H    L       H   LHHLHLHH     X
  C     L      L      H    L       H   LHHLLLLH     X
  C     L      L      H    L       L   HHLLLLHL     X
  C     L      L      H    L       H   LLHHLLHH     X
  C     L      L      H    L       L   LHHLLHHL     X
  C     L      L      H    L       H   LHHHHLHH     X
  C     L      X      X    X       X   XXXXXXXX     H
-------------------------------------------------------
```

DESCRIPTION

FIRST 8-BIT SHIFT REGISTER AND CHECK.

32-BIT CRC (CYCLICAL REDUNDANCY CHECKING) ERROR DETECTION, CHIP 1

```
 1 C1XXXXXXXXXX0XLLLLLLLLX1
 2 C0100XXXXXXX0XHLHHLHHLX1
 3 C0100XXXXXXX0XHHLHHLHLX1
 4 C0100XXXXXXX0XLLLLLLHLX1
 5 C0100XXXXXXX0XHLHHLLHLX1
 6 C0100XXXXXXX0XHHLHLLHLX1
 7 C0100XXXXXXX0XLLLHLLHLX1
 8 C0101XXXXXXX0XLLHLLHLHX1
 9 C0101XXXXXXX0XLHLLHLHHX1
10 C0101XXXXXXX0XHLLHLHHHX1
11 C0100XXXXXXX0XHLLHHLLLX1
12 C0101XXXXXXX0XLLHHLLLHX1
13 C0101XXXXXXX0XLHHLLLHHX1
14 C0100XXXXXXX0XLHHHLLLLX1
15 C0100XXXXXXX0XLHLHLHHLX1
16 C0100XXXXXXX0XLLLHHLHLX1
17 C0100XXXXXXX0XHLLLLLHLX1
18 C0101XXXXXXX0XLLLLLHLHX1
19 C0101XXXXXXX0XLLLLHLHHX1
20 C0101XXXXXXX0XLLLHLHHHX1
21 C0101XXXXXXX0XLLHLHHHHX1
22 C0101XXXXXXX0XLHLHHHHHX1
23 C0101XXXXXXX0XHLHHHHHHX1
24 C0101XXXXXXX0XLHHHHHHHX1
25 C0101XXXXXXX0XHHHHHHHHX1
26 C0100XXXXXXX0XLHLLHLLLX1
27 C0101XXXXXXX0XHLLHLLLHX1
28 C0100XXXXXXX0XHLLHLHLLX1
29 C0100XXXXXXX0XHLLHHHHLX1
30 C0101XXXXXXX0XLLHHHHLHX1
31 C0100XXXXXXX0XHHLLHHLLX1
32 C0101XXXXXXX0XHLLHHLLHX1
33 C0100XXXXXXX0XHLLLLHLLX1
34 CXXXXXXXXXXX0XXXXXXXXXL1
```

PASS SIMULATION

```
32-BIT CRC (CYCLICAL REDUNDANCY CHECKING) ERROR DETECTION, CHIP 1

                 11 1111 1111 2222 2222 2233 3333 3333
   0123 4567 8901 2345 6789 0123 4567 8901 2345 6789

 0 ---- ---- ---- ---- ---- ---- ---- ---- ---- ----
 1 ---- ---X ---X --X- ---X ---X ---X ---X --X- ---- Q0*Q1*/Q2*Q3*Q4*Q5*Q6*/-

 8 -X-- X--- X--- ---- ---- ---- ---- ---- ---- ---- /INIT*IN*C
 9 -X-- X--- X--- ---- ---- ---- ---- ---- ---- ---- /INIT*IN*C
10 ---- X--- ---- -X-- ---- ---- ---- ---- ---- ---- Q31*C
11 X--- ---- ---- ---- ---- ---- ---- ---- ---- ---- INIT

16 -X-- X--- X--- X--- ---- ---- ---- ---- ---- ---- /INIT*C*IN*/Q31
17 -X-- X--- -X-- -X-- ---- ---- ---- ---- ---- ---- /INIT*C*/IN*Q31
18 ---- ---X ---- ---- ---- ---- ---- ---- ---- ---- Q0
19 X--- ---- ---- ---- ---- ---- ---- ---- ---- ---- INIT

24 -X-- X--- X--- X--- ---- ---- ---- ---- ---- ---- /INIT*C*IN*/Q31
25 -X-- X--- -X-- -X-- ---- ---- ---- ---- ---- ---- /INIT*C*/IN*Q31
26 ---- ---- ---X ---- ---- ---- ---- ---- ---- ---- Q1
27 X--- ---- ---- ---- ---- ---- ---- ---- ---- ---- INIT

32 ---- ---- ---- ---X ---- ---- ---- ---- ---- ---- Q2
33 X--- ---- ---- ---- ---- ---- ---- ---- ---- ---- INIT

40 -X-- X--- X--- X--- ---- ---- ---- ---- ---- ---- /INIT*C*IN*/Q31
41 -X-- X--- -X-- -X-- ---- ---- ---- ---- ---- ---- /INIT*C*/IN*Q31
42 ---- ---- ---- ---- ---X ---- ---- ---- ---- ---- Q3
43 X--- ---- ---- ---- ---- ---- ---- ---- ---- ---- INIT

48 -X-- X--- X--- X--- ---- ---- ---- ---- ---- ---- /INIT*C*IN*/Q31
49 -X-- X--- -X-- -X-- ---- ---- ---- ---- ---- ---- /INIT*C*/IN*Q31
50 ---- ---- ---- ---- ---- ---X ---- ---- ---- ---- Q4
51 X--- ---- ---- ---- ---- ---- ---- ---- ---- ---- INIT

56 ---- ---- ---- ---- ---- ---- ---X ---- ---- ---- Q5
57 X--- ---- ---- ---- ---- ---- ---- ---- ---- ---- INIT

64 -X-- X--- X--- X--- ---- ---- ---- ---- ---- ---- /INIT*C*IN*/Q31
65 -X-- X--- -X-- -X-- ---- ---- ---- ---- ---- ---- /INIT*C*/IN*Q31
66 ---- ---- ---- ---- ---- ---- ---- ---X ---- ---- Q6
67 X--- ---- ---- ---- ---- ---- ---- ---- ---- ---- INIT


LEGEND:  X : FUSE NOT BLOWN (L,N,0)   - : FUSE BLOWN   (H,P,1)

NUMBER OF FUSES BLOW = 1129
```

32-Bit CRC, Chip 1

Logic Diagram PAL20X8

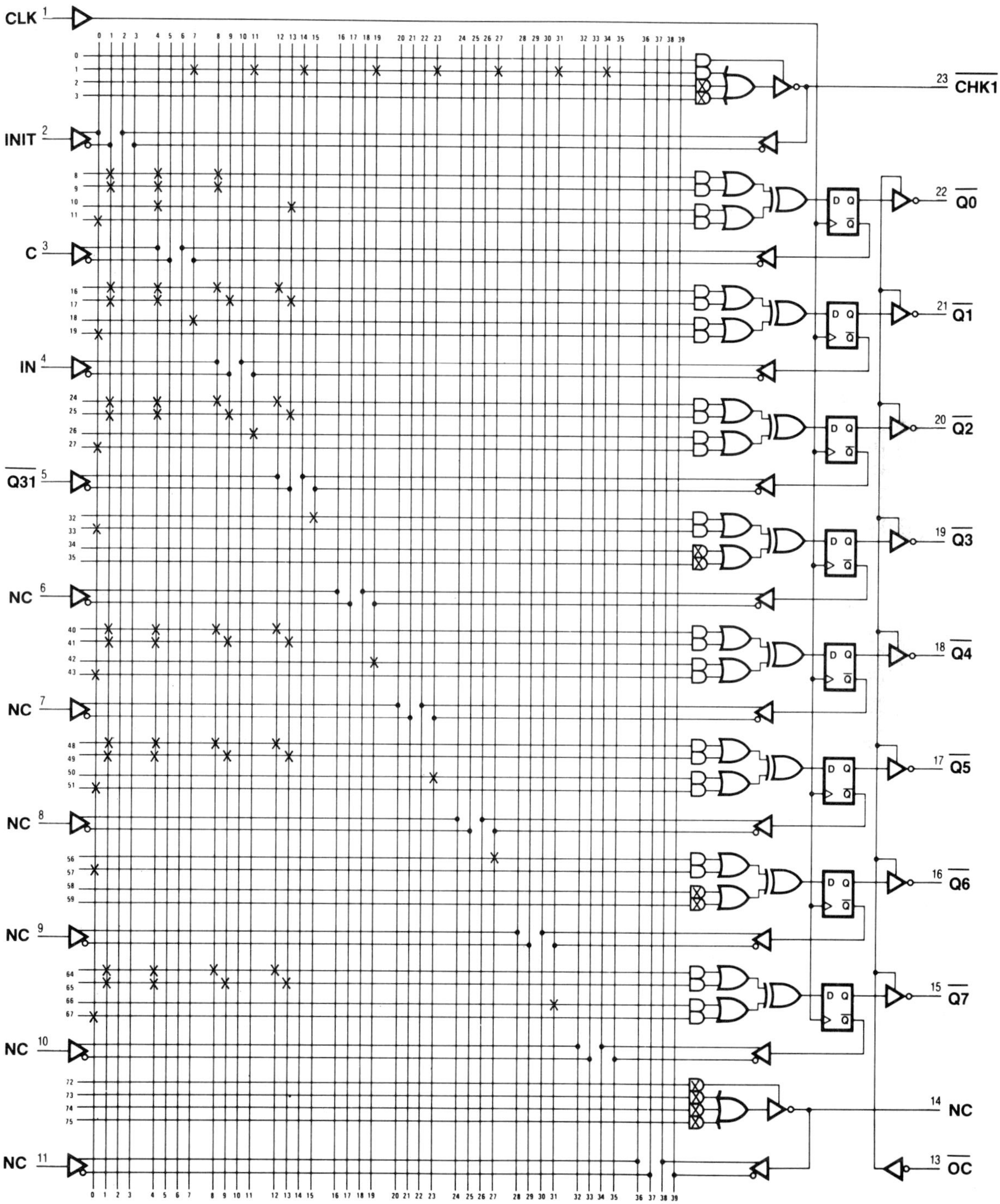

```
PAL20X8                                                    PAL DESIGN SPECIFICATION
CRC2                                                           NADIA SACHS 08/14/81
32-BIT CRC (CYCLICAL REDUNDANCY CHECKING) ERROR DETECTION, CHIP 2
MMI SUNNYVALE, CALIFORNIA
CLK INIT C IN /Q7 /Q31 NC NC NC NC NC GND
/OC NC /Q15 /Q14 /Q13 /Q12 /Q11 /Q10 /Q9 /Q8 /CHK2 VCC


CHK2 =    Q8*/Q9* Q10* Q11* Q12*/Q13* Q14* Q15    ;CHECK BIT 2

Q8   :=  /INIT* C* IN*/Q31                         ;MODULO-2
      +  /INIT* C*/IN* Q31                         ;ADDITION
    :+:   Q7                                       ;SHIFT
      +   INIT                                     ;INITIALIZE

Q9   :=   Q8                                       ;SHIFT
      +   INIT                                     ;INITIALIZE

Q10  :=  /INIT* C* IN*/Q31                         ;MODULO-2
      +  /INIT* C*/IN* Q31                         ;ADDITION
    :+:   Q9                                       ;SHIFT
      +   INIT                                     ;INITIALIZE

Q11  :=  /INIT* C* IN*/Q31                         ;MODULO-2
      +  /INIT* C*/IN* Q31                         ;ADDITION
    :+:   Q10                                      ;SHIFT
      +   INIT                                     ;INITIALIZE

Q12  :=  /INIT* C* IN*/Q31                         ;MODULO-2
      +  /INIT* C*/IN* Q31                         ;ADDITION
    :+:   Q11                                      ;SHIFT
      +   INIT                                     ;INITIALIZE

Q13  :=   Q12                                      ;SHIFT
      +   INIT                                     ;INITIALIZE

Q14  :=   Q13                                      ;SHIFT
      +   INIT                                     ;INITIALIZE

Q15  :=   Q14                                      ;SHIFT
      +   INIT                                     ;INITIALIZE
```

```
FUNCTION TABLE

CLK /OC INIT C IN Q7 Q31 Q15 Q14 Q13 Q12 Q11 Q10 Q9 Q8 CHK2

;                                   Q     QQQQQQQQ
;                              Q    3     111111
;CLK   /OC   INIT   C    IN    7    1     54321098    CHK2
------------------------------------------------------------
  C     L     H     X    X     X    X     HHHHHHHH     X
  C     L     L     H    L     H    H     HHHLLLHL     L
  C     L     L     H    L     L    H     HHLHHLLH     L
  C     L     L     H    L     L    H     HLHLHHHH     X
  C     L     L     H    L     H    H     LHLLLLHL     X
  C     L     L     H    L     L    H     HLLHHLLH     X
  C     L     L     H    L     L    H     LLHLHHHH     X
  C     L     L     H    L     H    L     LHLHHHHH     X
  C     L     L     H    L     H    L     HLHHHHHH     X
  C     L     L     H    L     H    L     LHHHHHHH     X
  C     L     L     H    L     L    H     HHHLLLHH     X
  C     L     L     H    L     L    L     HHLLLHHL     X
  C     L     L     H    L     H    L     HLLLHHLH     X
  C     L     L     H    L     H    H     LLLLLHHL     X
  C     L     L     H    L     H    H     LLLHLLLL     X
  C     L     L     H    L     H    H     LLHHHHLL     X
  C     L     L     H    L     H    H     LHHLLHLL     X
  C     L     L     H    L     L    L     HHLLHLLL     X
  C     L     L     H    L     H    L     HLLHLLLH     X
  C     L     L     H    L     H    L     LLHLLLHH     X
  C     L     L     H    L     H    L     LHLLLHHH     X
  C     L     L     H    L     H    L     HLLLHHHH     X
  C     L     L     H    L     H    L     LLLHHHHH     X
  C     L     L     H    L     L    L     LLHHHHHL     X
  C     L     L     H    L     H    L     LHHHHHLH     X
  C     L     L     H    L     L    H     HHHLLHHH     X
  C     L     L     H    L     H    L     HHLLHHHH     X
  C     L     L     H    L     L    H     HLLLLLHH     X
  C     L     L     H    L     L    H     LLLHHLHH     X
  C     L     L     H    L     L    L     LLHHLHHL     X
  C     L     L     H    L     H    H     LHHHLLLL     X
  C     L     L     H    L     L    L     HHHLLLLL     X
  C     L     L     H    L     L    H     HHLHHHLH     X
  C     L     X     X    X     X    X     XXXXXXXX     H
------------------------------------------------------------
```

DESCRIPTION

SECOND 8-BIT SHIFT REGISTER AND CHECK.

32-BIT CRC (CYCLICAL REDUNDANCY CHECKING) ERROR DETECTION, CHIP 2

```
 1 C1XXXXXXXXXX0XLLLLLLLLX1
 2 C01000XXXXXX0XLLLHHHLHH1
 3 C01010XXXXXX0XLLHLLHHLH1
 4 C01010XXXXXX0XLHLHLLLLX1
 5 C01000XXXXXX0XHLHHHHLHX1
 6 C01010XXXXXX0XLHHLLHHLX1
 7 C01010XXXXXX0XHHLHLLLLX1
 8 C01001XXXXXX0XHLHLLLLLX1
 9 C01001XXXXXX0XLHLLLLLLX1
10 C01001XXXXXX0XHLLLLLLLX1
11 C01010XXXXXX0XLLLHHHLLX1
12 C01011XXXXXX0XLLHHHLLHX1
13 C01001XXXXXX0XLHHHLLHLX1
14 C01000XXXXXX0XHHHHHLLHX1
15 C01000XXXXXX0XHHHLHHHHX1
16 C01000XXXXXX0XHHLLLLHHX1
17 C01000XXXXXX0XHLLHHLHHX1
18 C01011XXXXXX0XLLHHLHHHX1
19 C01001XXXXXX0XLHHLHHHLX1
20 C01001XXXXXX0XHHLHHHLLX1
21 C01001XXXXXX0XHLHHHLLLX1
22 C01001XXXXXX0XLHHHLLLLX1
23 C01001XXXXXX0XHHHLLLLLX1
24 C01011XXXXXX0XHHLLLLLHX1
25 C01001XXXXXX0XHLLLLLHLX1
26 C01010XXXXXX0XLLLHHLLLX1
27 C01001XXXXXX0XLLHHLLLLX1
28 C01010XXXXXX0XLHHHHHLLX1
29 C01010XXXXXX0XHHHLLHLLX1
30 C01011XXXXXX0XHHLLHLLHX1
31 C01000XXXXXX0XHLLLHHHHX1
32 C01011XXXXXX0XLLLHHHHHX1
33 C01010XXXXXX0XLLHLLLHLX1
34 CXXXXXXXXXXX0XXXXXXXXXL1
```

PASS SIMULATION

```
32-BIT CRC (CYCLICAL REDUNDANCY CHECKING) ERROR DETECTION, CHIP 2

              11 1111 1111 2222 2222 2233 3333 3333
   0123 4567 8901 2345 6789 0123 4567 8901 2345 6789

 0 ---- ---- ---- ---- ---- ---- ---- ---- ---- ----
 1 ---- ---X --X- ---X ---X ---X --X- ---X ---X ---- Q8*/Q9*Q10*Q11*Q12*/Q13-

 8 -X-- X--- X--- ---- X--- ---- ---- ---- ---- ---- /INIT*C*IN*/Q31
 9 -X-- X--- -X-- ---- -X-- ---- ---- ---- ---- ---- /INIT*C*/IN*Q31
10 ---- ---- ---- -X-- ---- ---- ---- ---- ---- ---- Q7
11 X--- ---- ---- ---- ---- ---- ---- ---- ---- ---- INIT

16 ---- ---X ---- ---- ---- ---- ---- ---- ---- ---- Q8
17 X--- ---- ---- ---- ---- ---- ---- ---- ---- ---- INIT

24 -X-- X--- X--- ---- X--- ---- ---- ---- ---- ---- /INIT*C*IN*/Q31
25 -X-- X--- -X-- ---- -X-- ---- ---- ---- ---- ---- /INIT*C*/IN*Q31
26 ---- ---- ---X ---- ---- ---- ---- ---- ---- ---- Q9
27 X--- ---- ---- ---- ---- ---- ---- ---- ---- ---- INIT

32 -X-- X--- X--- ---- X--- ---- ---- ---- ---- ---- /INIT*C*IN*/Q31
33 -X-- X--- -X-- ---- -X-- ---- ---- ---- ---- ---- /INIT*C*/IN*Q31
34 ---- ---- ---- ---X ---- ---- ---- ---- ---- ---- Q10
35 X--- ---- ---- ---- ---- ---- ---- ---- ---- ---- INIT

40 -X-- X--- X--- ---- X--- ---- ---- ---- ---- ---- /INIT*C*IN*/Q31
41 -X-- X--- -X-- ---- -X-- ---- ---- ---- ---- ---- /INIT*C*/IN*Q31
42 ---- ---- ---- ---- ---X ---- ---- ---- ---- ---- Q11
43 X--- ---- ---- ---- ---- ---- ---- ---- ---- ---- INIT

48 ---- ---- ---- ---- ---- ---X ---- ---- ---- ---- Q12
49 X--- ---- ---- ---- ---- ---- ---- ---- ---- ---- INIT

56 ---- ---- ---- ---- ---- ---- ---X ---- ---- ---- Q13
57 X--- ---- ---- ---- ---- ---- ---- ---- ---- ---- INIT

64 ---- ---- ---- ---- ---- ---- ---- ---X ---- ---- Q14
65 X--- ---- ---- ---- ---- ---- ---- ---- ---- ---- INIT


LEGEND:  X : FUSE NOT BLOWN (L,N,0)   - : FUSE BLOWN   (H,P,1)

NUMBER OF FUSES BLOW =  984
```

32-Bit CRC, Chip 2

Logic Diagram PAL20X8

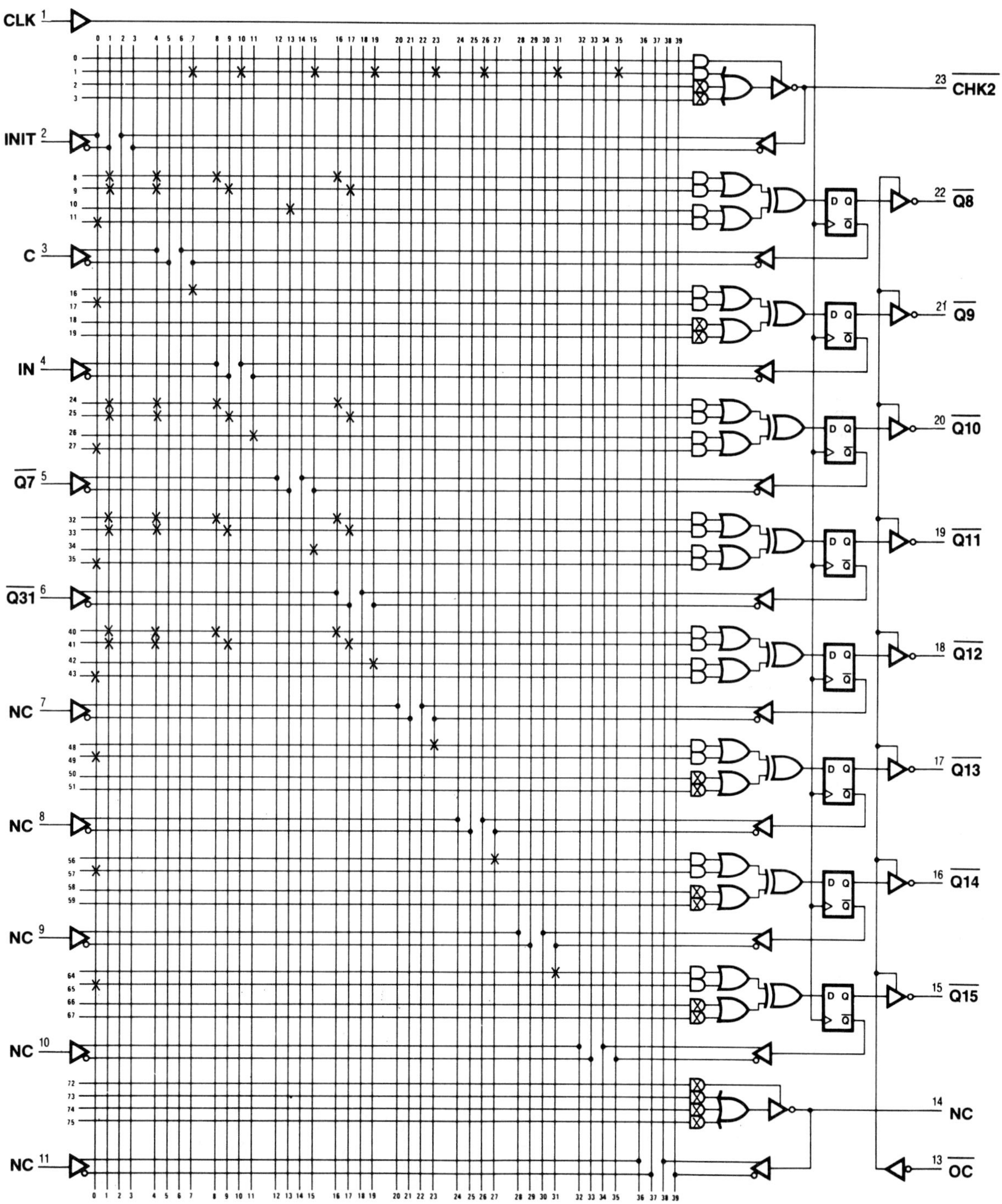

```
PAL20X8                                              PAL DESIGN SPECIFICATION
CRC3                                                    NADIA SACHS 08/14/81
32-BIT CRC (CYCLICAL REDUNDANCY CHECKING) ERROR DETECTION CHIP 3
MMI SUNNYVALE,CALIFORNIA
CLK INIT C IN /Q15 /Q31 NC NC NC NC NC GND
/OC NC /Q23 /Q22 /Q21 /Q20 /Q19 /Q18 /Q17 /Q16 /CHK3 VCC


CHK3  =  /Q16*/Q17* Q18*/Q19*/Q20*/Q21*/Q22*/Q23   ;CHECK BIT 3

Q16  :=  /INIT* C* IN*/Q31                         ;MODULO-2
      +  /INIT* C*/IN* Q31                         ;ADDITION
     :+:  Q15                                      ;SHIFT
      +   INIT                                     ;INITIALIZE

Q17  :=   Q16                                      ;SHIFT
      +   INIT                                     ;INITIALIZE

Q18  :=   Q17                                      ;SHIFT
      +   INIT                                     ;INITIALIZE

Q19  :=   Q18                                      ;SHIFT
      +   INIT                                     ;INITIALIZE

Q20  :=   Q19                                      ;SHIFT
      +   INIT                                     ;INITIALIZE

Q21  :=   Q20                                      ;SHIFT
      +   INIT                                     ;INITIALIZE

Q22  :=  /INIT* C* IN*/Q31                         ;MODULO-2
      +  /INIT* C*/IN* Q31                         ;ADDITION
     :+:  Q21                                      ;SHIFT
      +   INIT                                     ;INITIALIZE

Q23  :=  /INIT* C* IN*/Q31                         ;MODULO-2
      +  /INIT* C*/IN* Q31                         ;ADDITION
     :+:  Q22                                      ;SHIFT
      +   INIT                                     ;INITIALIZE
```

```
FUNCTION TABLE

CLK /OC INIT C IN Q15 Q31 Q23 Q22 Q21 Q20 Q19 Q18 Q17 Q16 CHK3

;                                 Q    Q    QQQQQQQQ
;                                 1    3    22221111
;CLK    /OC    INIT    C    IN    5    1    32109876    CHK3
--------------------------------------------------------------
  C      L      H      X    X     X    X    HHHHHHHH     X
  C      L      L      H    L     H    H    LLHHHHHL     L
  C      L      L      H    L     H    H    HLHHHHLL     L
  C      L      L      H    L     H    H    HLHHHLLL     X
  C      L      L      H    L     H    H    HLHHLLLL     X
  C      L      L      H    L     L    H    HLHLLLLH     X
  C      L      L      H    L     H    H    HLLLLLHL     X
  C      L      L      H    L     L    L    LLLLLHLL     X
  C      L      L      H    L     L    L    LLLLHLLL     X
  C      L      L      H    L     H    L    LLLHLLLH     X
  C      L      L      H    L     L    H    HHHLLLHH     X
  C      L      L      H    L     H    L    HHLLLHHH     X
  C      L      L      H    L     H    L    HLLLHHHH     X
  C      L      L      H    L     H    H    HHLHHHHL     X
  C      L      L      H    L     L    H    LHHHHHLH     X
  C      L      L      H    L     L    H    LLHHHLHH     X
  C      L      L      H    L     L    H    HLHHLHHH     X
  C      L      L      H    L     L    L    LHHLHHHL     X
  C      L      L      H    L     H    L    HHLHHHLH     X
  C      L      L      H    L     H    L    HLHHHLHH     X
  C      L      L      H    L     L    L    LHHHLHHL     X
  C      L      L      H    L     L    L    HHHLHHLL     X
  C      L      L      H    L     H    L    HHLHHLLH     X
  C      L      L      H    L     L    L    HLHHLLHL     X
  C      L      L      H    L     L    L    LHHLLHLL     X
  C      L      L      H    L     L    H    LLLLHLLH     X
  C      L      L      H    L     H    L    LLLHLLHH     X
  C      L      L      H    L     H    H    HHHLLHHL     X
  C      L      L      H    L     H    H    LLLLHHLL     X
  C      L      L      H    L     L    L    LLLHHLLL     X
  C      L      L      H    L     L    H    HHHHLLLH     X
  C      L      L      H    L     L    L    HHHLLLHL     X
  C      L      L      H    L     H    H    LLLLLHLL     X
  C      L      X      X    X     X    X    XXXXXXXX     H
--------------------------------------------------------------
```

DESCRIPTION

THIRD 8-BIT SHIFT REGISTER AND CHECK.

32-BIT CRC (CYCLICAL REDUNDANCY CHECKING) ERROR DETECTION CHIP 3

```
 1 C1XXXXXXXXXX0XLLLLLLLLX1
 2 C01000XXXXXX0XHHLLLLLHH1
 3 C01000XXXXXX0XLHLLLLHHH1
 4 C01000XXXXXX0XLHLLLHHHX1
 5 C01000XXXXXX0XLHLLHHHHX1
 6 C01010XXXXXX0XLHLHHHHLX1
 7 C01000XXXXXX0XLHHHHHLHX1
 8 C01011XXXXXX0XHHHHHLHHX1
 9 C01011XXXXXX0XHHHHLHHHX1
10 C01001XXXXXX0XHHHLHHHLX1
11 C01010XXXXXX0XLLLHHHLLX1
12 C01001XXXXXX0XLLHHHLLLX1
13 C01001XXXXXX0XLHHHLLLLX1
14 C01000XXXXXX0XLLHLLLLHX1
15 C01010XXXXXX0XHLLLLLHLX1
16 C01010XXXXXX0XHHLLLHLLX1
17 C01010XXXXXX0XLHLLHLLLX1
18 C01011XXXXXX0XHLLHLLLHX1
19 C01001XXXXXX0XLLHLLLHLX1
20 C01001XXXXXX0XLHLLLHLLX1
21 C01011XXXXXX0XHLLLHLLHX1
22 C01011XXXXXX0XLLLHLLHHX1
23 C01001XXXXXX0XLLHLLHHLX1
24 C01011XXXXXX0XLHLLHHLHX1
25 C01011XXXXXX0XHLLHHLHHX1
26 C01010XXXXXX0XHHHHLHHLX1
27 C01001XXXXXX0XHHHLHHLLX1
28 C01000XXXXXX0XLLLHHLLHX1
29 C01000XXXXXX0XHHHHLLHHX1
30 C01011XXXXXX0XHHHLLHHHX1
31 C01010XXXXXX0XLLLLHHHLX1
32 C01011XXXXXX0XLLLHHHLHX1
33 C01000XXXXXX0XHHHHHLHHX1
34 CXXXXXXXXXXX0XXXXXXXXXL1
```

PASS SIMULATION

```
32-BIT CRC (CYCLICAL REDUNDANCY CHECKING) ERROR DETECTION CHIP 3

                11 1111 1111 2222 2222 2233 3333 3333
   0123 4567 8901 2345 6789 0123 4567 8901 2345 6789

 0 ---- ---- ---- ---- ---- ---- ---- ---- ---- ----
 1 ---- --X- --X- ---X --X- --X- --X- --X- --X- ---- /Q16*/Q17*Q18*/Q19*/Q20-

 8 -X-- X--- X--- ---- X--- ---- ---- ---- ---- ---- /INIT*C*IN*/Q31
 9 -X-- X--- -X-- ---- -X-- ---- ---- ---- ---- ---- /INIT*C*/IN*Q31
10 ---- ---- ---- -X-- ---- ---- ---- ---- ---- ---- Q15
11 X--- ---- ---- ---- ---- ---- ---- ---- ---- ---- INIT

16 ---- ---X ---- ---- ---- ---- ---- ---- ---- ---- Q16
17 X--- ---- ---- ---- ---- ---- ---- ---- ---- ---- INIT

24 ---- ---- ---X ---- ---- ---- ---- ---- ---- ---- Q17
25 X--- ---- ---- ---- ---- ---- ---- ---- ---- ---- INIT

32 ---- ---- ---- ---X ---- ---- ---- ---- ---- ---- Q18
33 X--- ---- ---- ---- ---- ---- ---- ---- ---- ---- INIT

40 ---- ---- ---- ---- ---X ---- ---- ---- ---- ---- Q19
41 X--- ---- ---- ---- ---- ---- ---- ---- ---- ---- INIT

48 ---- ---- ---- ---- ---- ---X ---- ---- ---- ---- Q20
49 X--- ---- ---- ---- ---- ---- ---- ---- ---- ---- INIT

56 -X-- X--- X--- ---- X--- ---- ---- ---- ---- ---- /INIT*C*IN*/Q31
57 -X-- X--- -X-- ---- -X-- ---- ---- ---- ---- ---- /INIT*C*/IN*Q31
58 ---- ---- ---- ---- ---- ---- ---X ---- ---- ---- Q21
59 X--- ---- ---- ---- ---- ---- ---- ---- ---- ---- INIT

64 -X-- X--- X--- ---- X--- ---- ---- ---- ---- ---- /INIT*C*IN*/Q31
65 -X-- X--- -X-- ---- -X-- ---- ---- ---- ---- ---- /INIT*C*/IN*Q31
66 ---- ---- ---- ---- ---- ---- ---- ---X ---- ---- Q22
67 X--- ---- ---- ---- ---- ---- ---- ---- ---- ---- INIT


LEGEND:  X : FUSE NOT BLOWN (L,N,0)   - : FUSE BLOWN   (H,P,1)

NUMBER OF FUSES BLOW =  912
```

32-Bit CRC, Chip 3

Logic Diagram PAL20X8

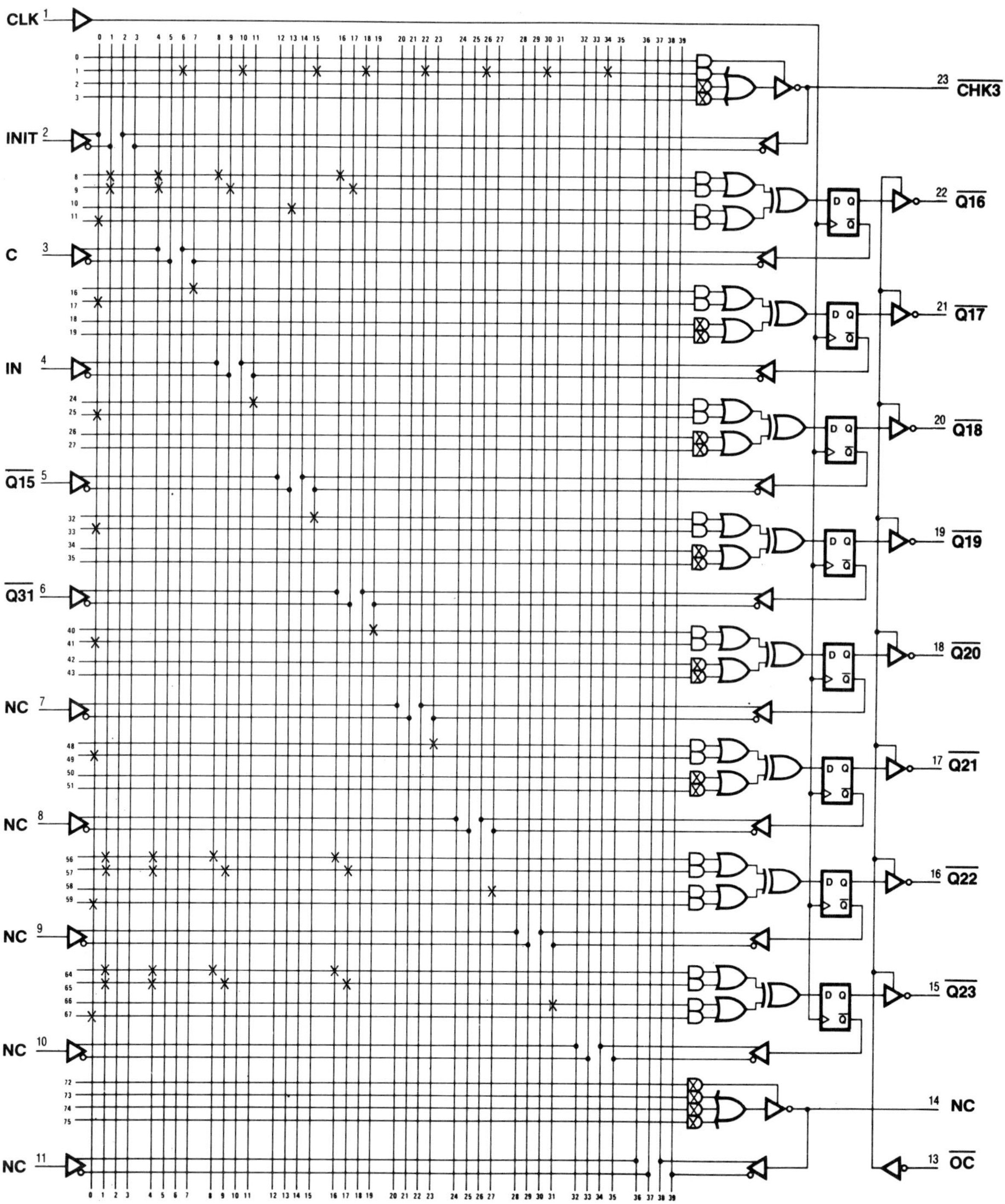

```
PAL20X10                                             PAL DESIGN SPECIFICATION
CRC4                                                    NADIA SACHS 08/14/81
32-BIT CRC (CYCLICAL REDUNDANCY CHECKING) ERROR DETECTION, CHIP 4
MMI SUNNYVALE, CALIFORNIA
CLK INIT C IN /Q23 NC NC NC /CHK1 /CHK2 /CHK3 GND
/OC /OUT /Q31 /Q30 /Q29 /Q28 /Q27 /Q26 /Q25 /Q24 /CHECK VCC


CHECK :=   CHK1* CHK2* CHK3* Q24* Q25* Q26*/Q27*/Q28*/Q29* Q30* Q31;CHECK ERROR

Q24    :=   Q23                    ;SHIFT
        +   INIT                   ;INITIALIZE

Q25    :=   Q24                    ;SHIFT
        +   INIT                   ;INITIALIZE

Q26    :=  /INIT* C* IN*/Q31       ;MODULO-2
        +  /INIT* C*/IN* Q31       ;ADDITION
      :+:   Q25                    ;SHIFT
        +   INIT                   ;INITIALIZE

Q27    :=   Q26                    ;SHIFT
        +   INIT                   ;INITIALIZE

Q28    :=   Q27                    ;SHIFT
        +   INIT                   ;INITIALIZE

Q29    :=   Q28                    ;SHIFT
        +   INIT                   ;INITIALIZE

Q30    :=   Q29                    ;SHIFT
        +   INIT                   ;INITIALIZE

Q31    :=   Q30                    ;SHIFT
        +   INIT                   ;INITIALIZE

OUT    :=   Q31*/C                 ;SERIAL
        +  /IN*  C                 ;OUT
```

```
FUNCTION TABLE

CLK /OC INIT C IN CHK1 CHK2 CHK3 Q23 Q31 Q30 Q29 Q28 Q27 Q26 Q25 Q24 OUT CHECK

;                                    Q    QQQQQQQQ
;                             CHK    2    33222222
;CLK    /OC    INIT    C    IN    123    3    10987654    OUT    CHECK
--------------------------------------------------------------------------
  C      L      H      X    L     XXX    X    HHHHHHHH     X       X
  C      L      L      H    L     XXX    H    HHHHHLHH     X       X
  C      L      L      H    L     XXX    L    HHHHLLHL     X       X
  C      L      L      H    L     XXX    H    HHHLLLLH     X       X
  C      L      L      H    L     XXX    H    HHLLLHHH     X       X
  C      L      L      H    L     XXX    H    HLLLHLHH     X       X
  C      L      L      H    L     XXX    H    LLLHLLHH     X       X
  C      L      L      H    L     XXX    H    LLHLLHHH     X       X
  C      L      L      H    L     XXX    L    LHLLHHHL     X       X
  C      L      L      H    L     XXX    L    HLLHHHLL     X       X
  C      L      L      H    L     XXX    L    LLHHHHLL     X       X
  C      L      L      H    L     XXX    H    LHHHHLLH     X       X
  C      L      L      H    L     XXX    H    HHHHLLHH     X       X
  C      L      L      H    L     XXX    H    HHHLLLHH     X       X
  C      L      L      H    L     XXX    H    HHLLLLHH     X       X
  C      L      L      H    L     XXX    L    HLLLLLHL     X       X
  C      L      L      H    L     XXX    L    LLLLLLLL     X       X
  C      L      L      H    L     XXX    H    LLLLLLLH     X       X
  C      L      L      H    L     XXX    L    LLLLLLHL     X       X
  C      L      L      H    L     XXX    H    LLLLLHLH     X       X
  C      L      L      H    L     XXX    H    LLLLHLHH     X       X
  C      L      L      H    L     XXX    L    LLLHLHHL     X       X
  C      L      L      H    L     XXX    H    LLHLHHLH     X       X
  C      L      L      H    L     XXX    H    LHLHHLHH     X       X
  C      L      L      H    L     XXX    H    HLHHLHHH     X       X
  C      L      L      H    L     XXX    L    LHHLHLHL     X       X
  C      L      L      H    L     XXX    L    HHLHLHLL     X       X
  C      L      L      H    L     XXX    L    HLHLHHLL     X       X
  C      L      L      H    L     XXX    H    LHLHHHLH     X       X
  C      L      L      H    L     XXX    L    HLHHHLHL     X       X
  C      L      L      H    L     XXX    L    LHHHLLLL     X       X
  C      L      L      H    L     XXX    H    HHHLLLLH     X       X
  C      L      L      H    L     XXX    H    HHLLLHHH     X       X
  C      L      X      X    X     HHH    X    XXXXXXXX     X       H
--------------------------------------------------------------------------
```

DESCRIPTION

FOURTH 8-BIT SHIFT REGISTER, CHECK, AND SERIAL OUT.

NOTE THAT A PAL20X8 CAN BE USED FOR THE CRC4 IF THE IMPLEMENTATION DOES NOT REQUIRE OUT AND CHECK TO BE REGISTERED OUTPUTS.

32-BIT CRC (CYCLICAL REDUNDANCY CHECKING) ERROR DETECTION, CHIP 4

```
 1 C1X0XXXXXXXX0XLLLLLLLLX1
 2 C0100XXXXXXX0XLLLLLHLLX1
 3 C0101XXXXXXX0XLLLLHHLHX1
 4 C0100XXXXXXX0XLLLHHHHLX1
 5 C0100XXXXXXX0XLLHHHLLLX1
 6 C0100XXXXXXX0XLHHHLHLLX1
 7 C0100XXXXXXX0XHHHLHHLLX1
 8 C0100XXXXXXX0XHHLHHLLLX1
 9 C0101XXXXXXX0XHLHHLLLHX1
10 C0101XXXXXXX0XLHHLLLHHX1
11 C0101XXXXXXX0XHHLLLLHHX1
12 C0100XXXXXXX0XHLLLLHHLX1
13 C0100XXXXXXX0XLLLLHHLLX1
14 C0100XXXXXXX0XLLLHHHLLX1
15 C0100XXXXXXX0XLLHHHHLLX1
16 C0101XXXXXXX0XLHHHHHLHX1
17 C0101XXXXXXX0XHHHHHHHHX1
18 C0100XXXXXXX0XHHHHHHHLX1
19 C0101XXXXXXX0XHHHHHHLHX1
20 C0100XXXXXXX0XHHHHHLHLX1
21 C0100XXXXXXX0XHHHHLHLLX1
22 C0101XXXXXXX0XHHHLHLLHX1
23 C0100XXXXXXX0XHHLHLLHLX1
24 C0100XXXXXXX0XHLHLLHLLX1
25 C0100XXXXXXX0XLHLLHLLLX1
26 C0101XXXXXXX0XHLLHLHLHX1
27 C0101XXXXXXX0XLLHLHLHHX1
28 C0101XXXXXXX0XLHLHLLHHX1
29 C0100XXXXXXX0XHLHLLLHLX1
30 C0101XXXXXXX0XLHLLLHLHX1
31 C0101XXXXXXX0XHLLLHHHHX1
32 C0100XXXXXXX0XLLLHHHHLX1
33 C0100XXXXXXX0XLLHHHLLLX1
34 CXXXXXXX000X0XXXXXXXXXL1
```

PASS SIMULATION

```
32-BIT CRC (CYCLICAL REDUNDANCY CHECKING) ERROR DETECTION, CHIP 4

               11 1111 1111 2222 2222 2233 3333 3333
   0123 4567 8901 2345 6789 0123 4567 8901 2345 6789

 0 ---- ---X ---X ---X --X- --X- --X- -X-X -X-X -X-- CHK1*CHK2*CHK3*Q24*Q25*-

 8 ---- ---- ---- -X-- ---- ---- ---- ---- ---- ---- Q23
 9 X--- ---- ---- ---- ---- ---- ---- ---- ---- ---- INIT

16 ---- ---X ---- ---- ---- ---- ---- ---- ---- ---- Q24
17 X--- ---- ---- ---- ---- ---- ---- ---- ---- ---- INIT

24 -X-- X--- X--- ---- ---- ---- ---- ---- --X- ---- /INIT*C*IN*/Q31
25 -X-- X--- -X-- ---- ---- ---- ---- ---- ---X ---- /INIT*C*/IN*Q31
26 ---- ---- ---X ---- ---- ---- ---- ---- ---- ---- Q25
27 X--- ---- ---- ---- ---- ---- ---- ---- ---- ---- INIT

32 ---- ---- ---- ---X ---- ---- ---- ---- ---- ---- Q26
33 X--- ---- ---- ---- ---- ---- ---- ---- ---- ---- INIT

40 ---- ---- ---- ---- ---X ---- ---- ---- ---- ---- Q27
41 X--- ---- ---- ---- ---- ---- ---- ---- ---- ---- INIT

48 ---- ---- ---- ---- ---- ---X ---- ---- ---- ---- Q28
49 X--- ---- ---- ---- ---- ---- ---- ---- ---- ---- INIT

56 ---- ---- ---- ---- ---- ---- ---X ---- ---- ---- Q29
57 X--- ---- ---- ---- ---- ---- ---- ---- ---- ---- INIT

64 ---- ---- ---- ---- ---- ---- ---- ---X ---- ---- Q30
65 X--- ---- ---- ---- ---- ---- ---- ---- ---- ---- INIT

72 ---- -X-- ---- ---- ---- ---- ---- ---- ---X ---- Q31*/C
73 ---- X--- -X-- ---- ---- ---- ---- ---- ---- ---- /IN*C

LEGEND:  X : FUSE NOT BLOWN (L,N,0)   - : FUSE BLOWN   (H,P,1)

NUMBER OF FUSES BLOW =  801
```

32-Bit CRC, Chip 4

Logic Diagram PAL20X10

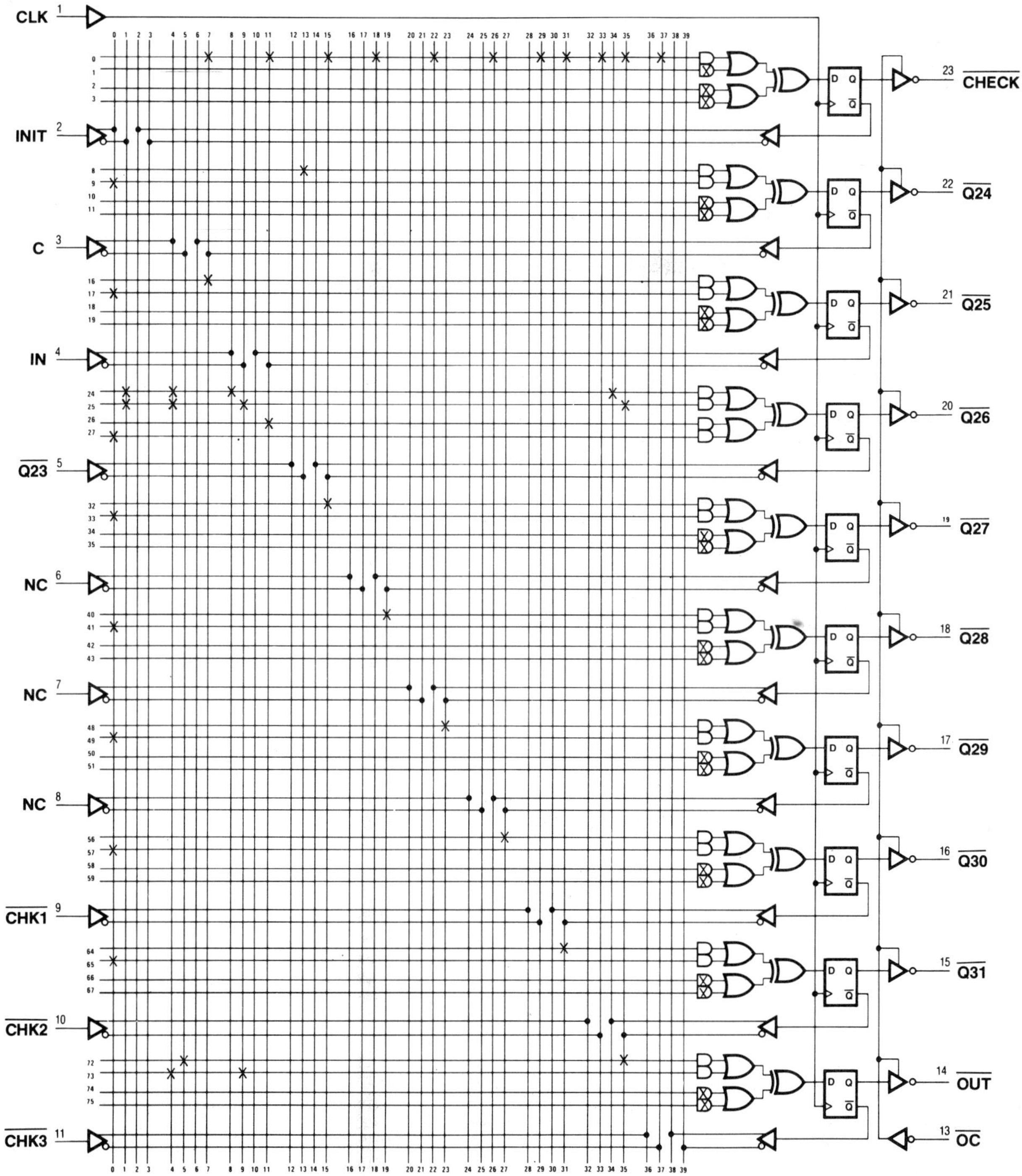

PAL
IMPORTANT,
NOTES

8-Bit Error Detection and Correction

PAL16X4

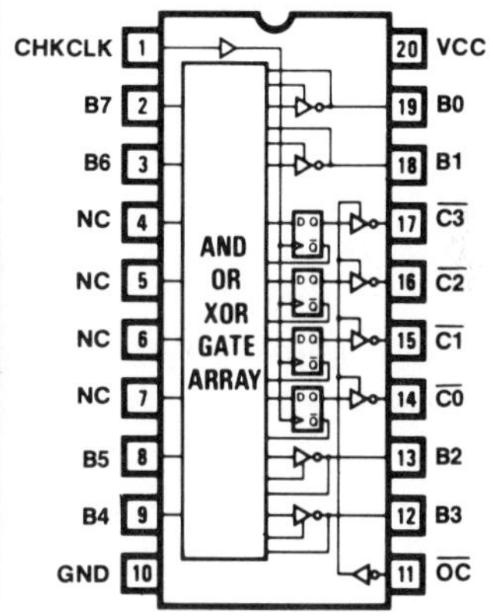

PAL16X4

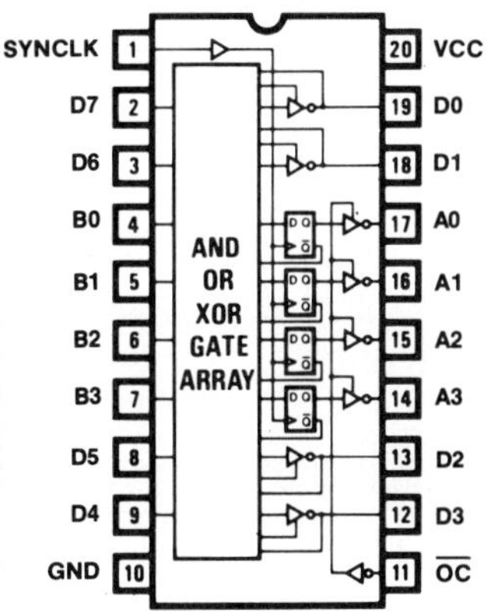

PAL16L8

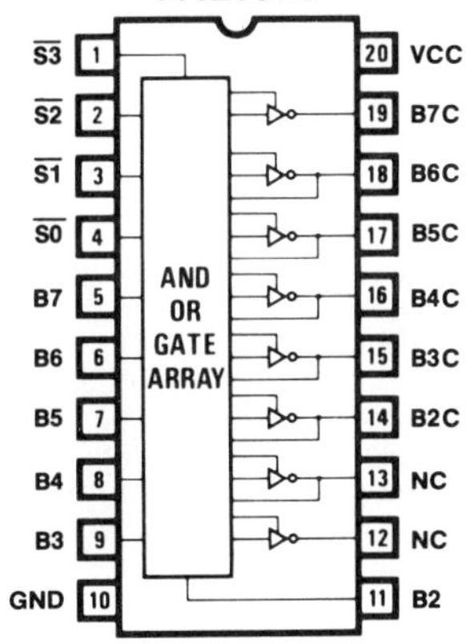

PAL16L8

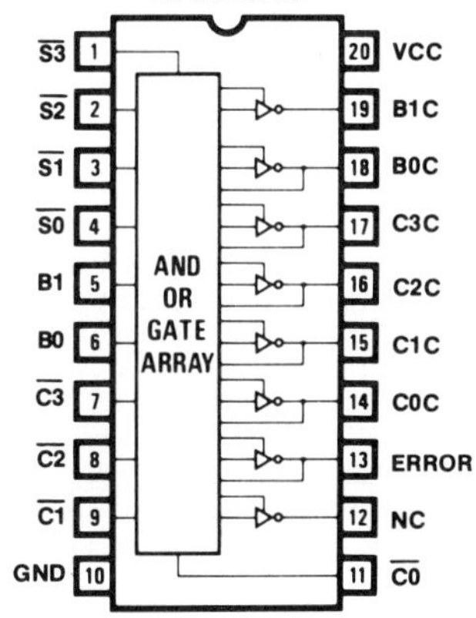

Single bit error detection and correction for an 8-bit data word requires 4 check bits, making a 12-bit code word. The simplest code to design is a 12-bit Hamming code. To arrive at the code, we set up the following matrix:

	B7	B6	B5	B4	B3	B2	B1	B0	C3	C2	C1	C0
S3	X	X	X	X					X			
S2	X				X	X	X			X		
S1		X	X		X	X		X			X	
S0		X		X	X		X	X				X

The vertical columns are in a counting pattern, excluding the single bit values of 8, 4, 2, 1. The single bit values are assigned to the check bits C3-C0. By reading horizontally across the rows of the matrix, we get the check equations by exclusive OR'ing the data bits with X's in that row and equating that to the check bit with an X in that row:

$$C3 = B7 \oplus B6 \oplus B5 \oplus B4$$
$$C2 = B7 \oplus B3 \oplus B2 \oplus B1$$
$$C1 = B6 \oplus B5 \oplus B3 \oplus B2 \oplus B0$$
$$C0 = B6 \oplus B4 \oplus B3 \oplus B1 \oplus B0$$

The check bits are stored along with the data bits in the following message format:

M12	M11	M10	M9	M8	M7	M6	M5	M4	M3	M2	M1
B7	B6	B5	B4	C3	B3	B2	B1	C2	B0	C1	C0

When a read occurs, the check bits are recalculated and compared with the stored bits to generate the 4 bit syndrome:

$$S3 = B7 \oplus B6 \oplus B5 \oplus B4 \oplus C3$$
$$S2 = B7 \oplus B3 \oplus B2 \oplus B1 \oplus C2$$
$$S1 = B6 \oplus B5 \oplus B3 \oplus B2 \oplus B0 \oplus C1$$
$$S0 = B6 \oplus B4 \oplus B3 \oplus B1 \oplus B0 \oplus C0$$

The 4 syndrome bits indicate the location of any single bit errors in the 12-bit message format which may than be corrected by inversion.

The Hamming code works by introducing enough other code words to create a difference of exactly 3 bits between legal code words. All other code words are illegal. If, in storage, one bit flips, the result is an illegal word. In addition, there is only one word in the set of legal code words from which it could have come, hence the correction.

The Hamming matrix and resultant sets of check bit and syndrome equations are selected so that when a single bit error occurs, the syndrome gives the position of that bit (either data or check) in the 12-bit message format.

Example

	B7							B0
random data word:	1	1	0	1	1	1	0	0

check bits:

$$C3 = B7 \oplus B6 \oplus B5 \oplus B4$$
$$= 1 \oplus 1 \oplus 0 \oplus 1 = 1$$
$$C2 = B7 \oplus B3 \oplus B2 \oplus B1$$
$$= 1 \oplus 1 \oplus 1 \oplus 0 = 1$$
$$C1 = B6 \oplus B5 \oplus B3 \oplus B2 \oplus B0$$
$$= 1 \oplus 0 \oplus 1 \oplus 1 \oplus 0 = 1$$
$$C0 = B6 \oplus B4 \oplus B3 \oplus B1 \oplus B0$$
$$= 1 \oplus 1 \oplus 1 \oplus 0 \oplus 0 = 1$$

message:

M12	M11	M10	M9	M8	M7	M6	M5	M4	M3	M2	M1
1	1	0	1	1	1	1	0	1	0	1	1
B7	B6	B5	B4	C3	B3	B2	B1	C2	B0	C1	C0

EDAC System Block Diagram

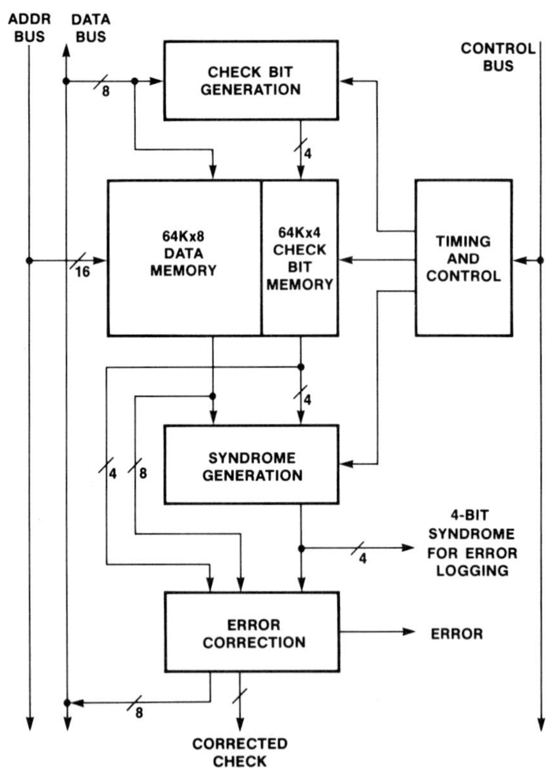

assume no error:

$$S3 = B7 \oplus B6 \oplus B5 \oplus B4 \oplus C3$$
$$= 1 \oplus 1 \oplus 0 \oplus 1 \oplus 1 = 0$$
$$S2 = B7 \oplus B3 \oplus B2 \oplus B1 \oplus C2$$
$$= 1 \oplus 1 \oplus 1 \oplus 0 \oplus 1 = 0$$
$$S1 = B6 \oplus B5 \oplus B3 \oplus B2 \oplus B0 \oplus C1$$
$$= 1 \oplus 0 \oplus 1 \oplus 1 \oplus 0 \oplus 1 = 0$$
$$S0 = B6 \oplus B4 \oplus B3 \oplus B1 \oplus B0 \oplus C0$$
$$= 1 \oplus 1 \oplus 1 \oplus 0 \oplus 0 \oplus 1 = 0$$

syndrome 0000 indicates no error

assume data bit B7 flips (1 → 0):

$$S3 = \underline{0} \oplus 1 \oplus 0 \oplus 1 \oplus 1 = 1$$
$$S2 = \underline{0} \oplus 1 \oplus 1 \oplus 0 \oplus 1 = 1$$
$$S1 = 1 \oplus 0 \oplus 1 \oplus 1 \oplus 0 \oplus 1 = 0$$
$$S0 = 1 \oplus 1 \oplus 1 \oplus 0 \oplus 0 \oplus 1 = 0$$

syndrome 1100 indicates M12 or B7 is in error

assume check bit C3 flips (1 → 0):

$$S3 = 1 \oplus 1 \oplus 0 \oplus 1 \oplus \underline{0} = 1$$
$$S2 = 1 \oplus 1 \oplus 1 \oplus 0 \oplus 1 = 0$$
$$S1 = 1 \oplus 0 \oplus 1 \oplus 1 \oplus 0 \oplus 1 = 0$$
$$S0 = 1 \oplus 1 \oplus 1 \oplus 0 \oplus 0 \oplus 1 = 0$$

syndrome 1000 indicates M8 or C3 is in error

While the check bits can be generated with a 256x4 PROM if the tolerances are loose, high performance systems will need to latch or register the check bits to meet cycle time requirements. Similarly, the syndrome bits can be generated with a 4096x4 PROM but in both cases the PAL16X4 is the high performance choice.

The worst case equations are S1 and S0 with a 6 term exclusive OR. We use 2 properties of the exclusive OR to fit the equations into the 16X4:

1. Associativity
   $A \oplus B \oplus C = (A \oplus B) \oplus C$
2. $A \oplus B \oplus C = A\overline{B}\,\overline{C} + \overline{A}B\overline{C} + \overline{A}\,\overline{B}C + ABC$

Since a 3 term exclusive OR can be realized with a 4 product sum in sum of products form, a 6 term exclusive OR can be realized by exclusive OR of 2 4 product sums. This is exactly the 16X4 configuration.

Check Bit Equations

$$C3 = B7 \oplus B6 \oplus B5 \oplus B4$$
$$= (B7 \cdot \overline{B6} + \overline{B7} \cdot B6) \oplus (B5 \cdot \overline{B4} + \overline{B5} \cdot B4)$$

$$C2 = B7 \oplus B3 \oplus B2 \oplus B1$$
$$= (B7 \cdot \overline{B3} + \overline{B7} \cdot B3) \oplus (B2 \cdot \overline{B1} + \overline{B2} \cdot B1)$$

$$C1 = B6 \oplus B5 \oplus B3 \oplus B2 \oplus B0$$
$$= (B6 \cdot B5 \cdot B3 + \overline{B6} \cdot \overline{B5} \cdot B3 + \overline{B6} \cdot B5 \cdot \overline{B3} + B6 \cdot \overline{B5} \cdot \overline{B3})$$
$$\oplus (B2 \cdot \overline{B0} + \overline{B2} \cdot \quad)$$

$$C0 = B6 \oplus B4 \oplus B3 \oplus B1 \oplus B0$$
$$= (B6 \cdot B4 \cdot B3 + \overline{B6} \cdot \overline{B4} \cdot B3 + \overline{B6} \cdot B4 \cdot \overline{B3} + B6 \cdot \overline{B4} \cdot \overline{B3})$$
$$\oplus (B1 \cdot \overline{B0} + \overline{B1} \cdot B0)$$

Syndrome Bit Equations

$$S3 = B7 \oplus B6 \oplus B5 \oplus B4 \oplus C3$$
$$= (B7 \cdot B6 \cdot B5 + \overline{B7} \cdot \overline{B6} \cdot B5 + \overline{B7} \cdot B6 \cdot \overline{B5} + B7 \cdot \overline{B6} \cdot \overline{B5})$$
$$\oplus (B4 \cdot \overline{C3} + \overline{B4} \cdot C3)$$

$$S2 = B7 \oplus B3 \oplus B2 \oplus B1 \oplus C2$$
$$= (B7 \cdot B3 \cdot B2 + \overline{B7} \cdot \overline{B3} \cdot B2 + \overline{B7} \cdot B3 \cdot \overline{B2} + B7 \cdot \overline{B3} \cdot \overline{B2})$$
$$\oplus (B1 \cdot \overline{C2} + \overline{B1} \cdot C2)$$

$$S1 = B6 \oplus B5 \oplus B3 \oplus B2 \oplus B0 \oplus C1$$
$$= (B6 \cdot B5 \cdot B3 + \overline{B6} \cdot \overline{B5} \cdot B3 + \overline{B6} \cdot B5 \cdot \overline{B3} + B6 \cdot \overline{B5} \cdot \overline{B3})$$
$$\oplus (\overline{B2} \cdot \overline{B0} \cdot C1 + \overline{B2} \cdot \overline{B0} \cdot C1 + B2 \cdot B0 \cdot \overline{C1} + B2 \cdot \overline{B0}$$

$$S0 = B6 \oplus B4 \oplus B3 \oplus B1 \oplus B0 \oplus C0$$
$$= (B6 \cdot B4 \cdot B3 + \overline{B6} \cdot \overline{B4} \cdot B3 + \overline{B6} \cdot B4 \cdot \overline{B3} + B6 \cdot \overline{B4} \cdot \overline{B3})$$
$$\oplus (B1 \cdot B0 \cdot C0 + \overline{B1} \cdot \overline{B0} \cdot C0 + \overline{B1} \cdot B0 \cdot \overline{C0} + B1 \cdot \overline{B0} \quad)$$

The error correction block decodes the 4 syndrome bits, and, if they are not 0000, inverts the indicated bit in the message format. The equations:

$$M12\ (= B7C) = S3 \cdot S2 \cdot \overline{S1} \cdot \overline{S0} \oplus B7$$
$$= S3 \cdot S2 \cdot \overline{S1} \cdot \overline{S0} \cdot \overline{B7} + \overline{(S3 \cdot S2 \cdot \overline{S1} \cdot \overline{S0})} \cdot B7$$
$$= S3 \cdot S2 \cdot \overline{S1} \cdot \overline{S0} \cdot \overline{B7} + \overline{S3} \cdot B7 + S2 \cdot B7 + S1 \cdot B7 + \overline{S0} \cdot B7$$

$$M11\ (= B6C) = S3 \cdot \overline{S2} \cdot S1 \cdot S0 \cdot \overline{B6} \cdot \overline{S3} \cdot B6 \cdot S2 \cdot B6 + \overline{S1} \cdot B6 \cdot \overline{S0} \cdot B6$$

$$M10\ (= B5C) = S3 \cdot \overline{S2} \cdot S1 \cdot \overline{S0} \cdot \overline{B5} + \overline{S3} \cdot B5 + S2 \cdot B5 + \overline{S1} \cdot B5 + S0 \cdot B5$$

$$M9\ (= B4C) = S3 \cdot \overline{S2} \cdot \overline{S1} \cdot S0 \cdot \overline{B4} + \overline{S3} \cdot B4 + S2 \cdot B4 + S1 \cdot B4 + \overline{S0} \cdot B4$$

$$M8\ (= C3C) = S3 \cdot \overline{S2} \cdot \overline{S1} \cdot \overline{S0} \cdot \overline{C3} + \overline{S3} \cdot C3 + S2 \cdot C3 + S1 \cdot C3 + S0 \cdot C3$$

$$M7\ (= B3C) = \overline{S3} \cdot S2 \cdot S1 \cdot S0 \cdot \overline{B3} + S3 \cdot B3 + \overline{S2} \cdot B3 + \overline{S1} \cdot B3 + \overline{S0} \cdot B3$$

$$M6\ (= B2C) = \overline{S3} \cdot S2 \cdot S1 \cdot \overline{S0} \cdot \overline{B2} + S3 \cdot B2 + \overline{S2} \cdot B2 + \overline{S1} \cdot B2 + S0 + B2$$

$$M5\ (= B1C) = \overline{S3} \cdot S2 \cdot \overline{S1} \cdot S0 \cdot \overline{B1} + S3 \cdot B1 + \overline{S2} \cdot B1 + S1 \cdot B1 + \overline{S0} \cdot B1$$

$$M4\ (= C2C) = \overline{S3} \cdot S2 \cdot \overline{S1} \cdot \overline{S0} \cdot \overline{C2} + S3 \cdot C2 + \overline{S2} \cdot C2 + S1 \cdot C2 + S0 \cdot C2$$

$$M3\ (= B0C) = \overline{S3} \cdot \overline{S2} \cdot S1 \cdot S0 \cdot \overline{B0} + S3 \cdot B0 + S2 \cdot B0 + \overline{S1} \cdot B0 + \overline{S0} \cdot B0$$

$$M2\ (= C1C) = \overline{S3} \cdot \overline{S2} \cdot S1 \cdot \overline{S0} \cdot \overline{C1} + S3 \cdot C1 + S2 \cdot C1 + \overline{S1} \cdot C1 + S0 \cdot C1$$

$$M1\ (= C0C) = \overline{S3} \cdot \overline{S2} \cdot \overline{S1} \cdot S0 \cdot \overline{C0} + S3 \cdot C0 + S2 \cdot C0 + S1 \cdot C0 \cdot \overline{S0} \cdot C0$$

$$ERROR = \overline{\overline{S3} \cdot \overline{S2} \cdot \overline{S1} \cdot \overline{S0}}$$

ERROR is an active high error indicator available for error logging along with the 4 syndrome bits.

To use 2 PAL16L8's for the error correction block, we need only invert the message bits to get active true outputs.

```
PAL16X4                                                PAL DESIGN SPECIFICATION
CBG                                                         B. BRAFMAN 02/16/81
CHECK BIT GENERATOR
MMI FIELD APPLICATIONS ENGINEER YORBA LINDA, CALIFORNIA
CHKCLK B7 B6 NC NC NC NC B5 B4 GND
/OC B3 B2 /C0 /C1 /C2 /C3 B1 B0 VCC


C3 :=   B7*/B6              ;B7 :+: B6
    +  /B7* B6              ;   :+:
    +   GND                 ;DO NOT BLOW THIS PRODUCT LINE
    +   GND                 ;DO NOT BLOW THIS PRODUCT LINE
   :+:  B5*/B4              ;B5 :+: B4
    +  /B5* B4

C2 :=   B7*/B3              ;B7 :+: B3
    +  /B7* B3              ;   :+:
    +   GND                 ;DO NOT BLOW THIS PRODUCT LINE
    +   GND                 ;DO NOT BLOW THIS PRODUCT LINE
   :+:  B2*/B1              ;B2 :+: B1
    +  /B2* B1

C1 :=   B6* B5* B3          ;B6 :+: B5 :+: B3
    +  /B6*/B5* B3
    +  /B6* B5*/B3          ;   :+:
    +   B6*/B5*/B3
   :+:  B2*/B0              ;B2 :+: B0
    +  /B2* B0

C0 :=   B6* B4* B3          ;B6 :+: B4 :+: B3
    +  /B6*/B4* B3
    +  /B6* B4*/B3          ;   :+:
    +   B6*/B4*/B3
   :+:  B1*/B0              ;B1 :+: B0
    +  /B1* B0
```

```
FUNCTION TABLE

CHKCLK /OC B7 B6 B5 B4 B3 B2 B1 B0 C3 C2 C1 C0

;CONTROL   8 BIT IN   CORR
;CHK  /    BBBBBBBB   CCCC
;CLK  OC   76543210   3210     COMMENTS
-------------------------------------------------
  C   L    HHHHHHHH   LLHH     ALL ONES DATA
  C   L    LHHHHHHH   HHHH     SHIFT A ZERO ACROSS
  C   L    HLHHHHHH   HLLL
  C   L    HHLHHHHH   HLLH
  C   L    HHHLHHHH   HLHL
  C   L    HHHHLHHH   LHLL
  C   L    HHHHHLHH   LHLH
  C   L    HHHHHHLH   LHHL
  C   L    HHHHHHHL   LLLL
  C   L    LLLLLLLL   LLLL     ALL ZEROS DATA
  C   L    HLLLLLLL   HHLL     SHIFT A ONE ACROSS
  C   L    LHLLLLLL   HLHH
  C   L    LLHLLLLL   HLHL
  C   L    LLLHLLLL   HLLH
  C   L    LLLLHLLL   LHHH
  C   L    LLLLLHLL   LHHL
  C   L    LLLLLLHL   LHLH
  C   L    LLLLLLLH   LLHH
-------------------------------------------------
```

```
DESCRIPTION

THIS PAL GENERATES THE 4 CHECK BITS IN A 12 BIT HAMMING CODE WORD TO
PROVIDE ERROR DETECTION AND CORRECTION ON AN 8 BIT DATA WORD.


CHECK BIT GENERATOR

 1 C11XXXX11X011LLHH111
 2 C01XXXX11X011LLLL111
 3 C10XXXX11X011HHHL111
 4 C11XXXX01X011LHHL111
 5 C11XXXX10X011HLHL111
 6 C11XXXX11X001HHLH111
 7 C11XXXX11X010LHLH111
 8 C11XXXX11X011HLLH011
 9 C11XXXX11X011HHHH101
10 C00XXXX00X000HHHH001
11 C10XXXX00X000HHLL001
12 C01XXXX00X000LLHL001
13 C00XXXX10X000HLHL001
14 C00XXXX01X000LHHL001
15 C00XXXX00X010LLLH001
16 C00XXXX00X001HLLH001
17 C00XXXX00X000LHLH101
18 C00XXXX00X000LLHH011

PASS SIMULATION
```

```
CHECK BIT GENERATOR

               11 1111 1111 2222 2222 2233
   0123 4567 8901 2345 6789 0123 4567 8901



16 X--- -X-- ---- ---- ---- ---- ---- ---- B7*/B6
17 -X-- X--- ---- ---- ---- ---- ---- ---- /B7*B6
18 XXXX XXXX XXXX XXXX XXXX XXXX XXXX XXXX
19 XXXX XXXX XXXX XXXX XXXX XXXX XXXX XXXX
20 ---- ---- ---- ---- ---- ---- X--- -X-- B5*/B4
21 ---- ---- ---- ---- ---- ---- -X-- X--- /B5*B4

24 X--- ---- ---- ---- ---- ---- ---- ---X B7*/B3
25 -X-- ---- ---- ---- ---- ---- ---- --X- /B7*B3
26 XXXX XXXX XXXX XXXX XXXX XXXX XXXX XXXX
27 XXXX XXXX XXXX XXXX XXXX XXXX XXXX XXXX
28 ---- ---X ---- ---- ---- ---- --X- ---- B2*/B1
29 ---- --X- ---- ---- ---- ---- ---X ---- /B2*B1

32 ---- X--- ---- ---- ---- ---- X--- --X- B6*B5*B3
33 ---- -X-- ---- ---- ---- ---- -X-- --X- /B6*/B5*B3
34 ---- -X-- ---- ---- ---- ---- X--- ---X /B6*B5*/B3
35 ---- X--- ---- ---- ---- ---- -X-- ---X B6*/B5*/B3
36 ---X ---- ---- ---- ---- ---- --X- ---- B2*/B0
37 --X- ---- ---- ---- ---- ---- ---X ---- /B2*B0

40 ---- X--- ---- ---- ---- ---- ---- X-X- B6*B4*B3
41 ---- -X-- ---- ---- ---- ---- ---- -XX- /B6*/B4*B3
42 ---- -X-- ---- ---- ---- ---- ---- X--X /B6*B4*/B3
43 ---- X--- ---- ---- ---- ---- ---- -X-X B6*/B4*/B3
44 ---X --X- ---- ---- ---- ---- ---- ---- B1*/B0
45 --X- ---X ---- ---- ---- ---- ---- ---- /B1*B0


LEGEND:  X : FUSE NOT BLOWN (L,N,0)   - : FUSE BLOWN   (H,P,1)

NUMBER OF FUSES BLOWN =  592
```

Check Bit Generator

Logic Diagram PAL16X4

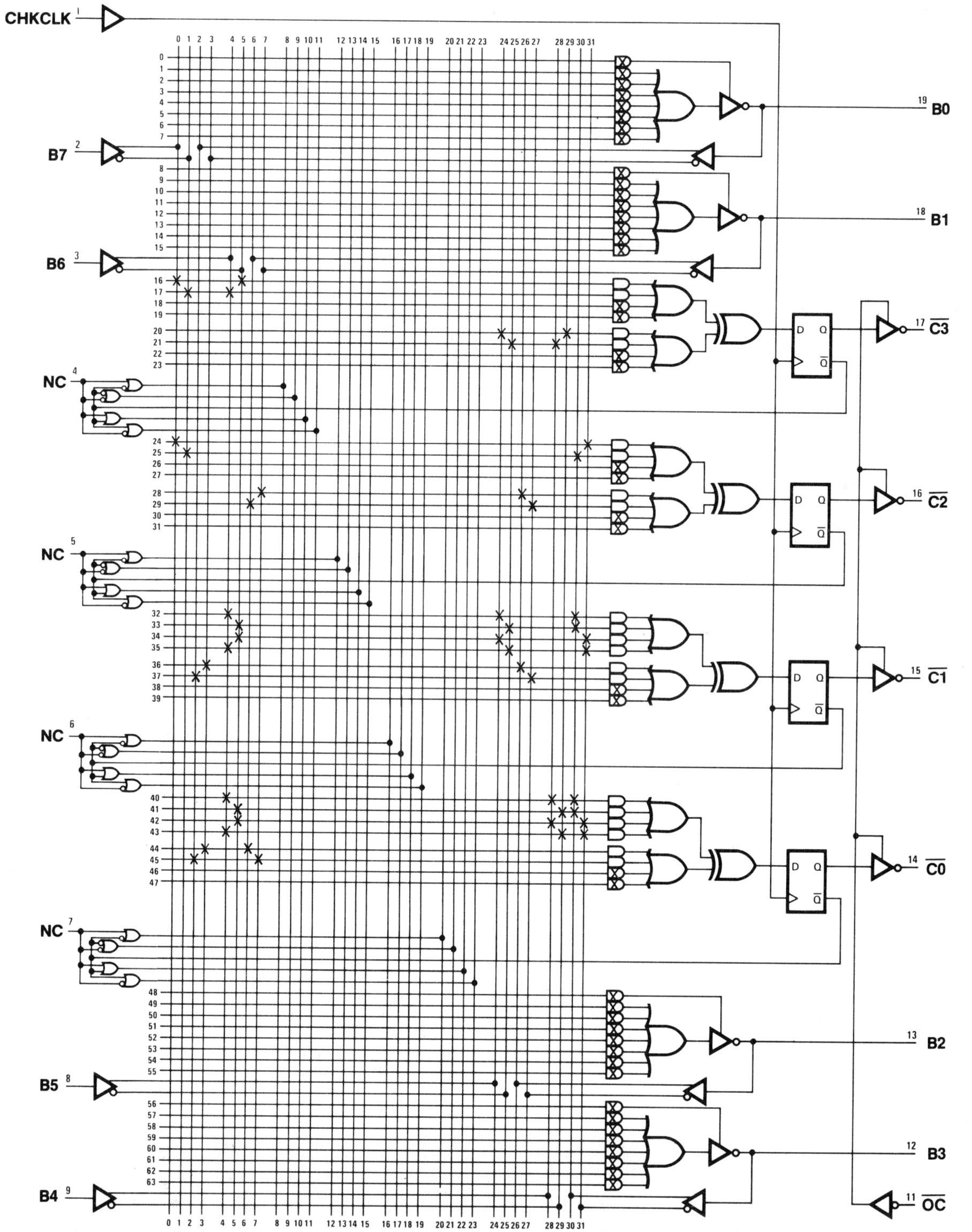

```
PAL16X4                                            PAL DESIGN SPECIFICATION
SBG                                                     B. BRAFMAN 03/13/81
SYNDROME BIT GENERATOR
MMI FIELD APPLICATIONS ENGINEER YORBA LINDA, CALIFORNIA
SYNCLK D7 D6 B0 B1 B2 B3 D5 D4 GND
/OC D3 D2 A3 A2 A1 A0 D1 D0 VCC


;    IN THE ABOVE PIN LIST, THE FOLLOWING SUBSTITUTIONS HAVE BEEN
;    MADE TO ACCOMODATE THE SPECIFIC FORMAT (FIXED SYMBOLS) FOR THE
;    ARITHMETIC PALS IN PALASM:

;         D7 MEANS B7        B0 MEANS /C3  (CHECK BIT 3)
;         D6 MEANS B6        B1 MEANS /C2  (CHECK BIT 2)
;         D5 MEANS B5        B2 MEANS /C1  (CHECK BIT 1)
;         D4 MEANS B4        B3 MEANS /C0  (CHECK BIT 0)
;         D3 MEANS B3        A0 MEANS /S3  (SYNDROME BIT 3)
;         D2 MEANS B2        A1 MEANS /S2  (SYNDROME BIT 2)
;         D1 MEANS B1        A2 MEANS /S1  (SYNDROME BIT 1)
;         D0 MEANS B0        A3 MEANS /S0  (SYNDROME BIT 0)

; B0-B7 ARE THE BITS OF THE DATA WORD.

; THE SUBSTITUTIONS APPLY BELOW WITH THE EXCEPTION OF COMMENTS.


/A0 :=    D7* D6* D5           ;B7 :+: B6 :+: B5
     +   /D7*/D6* D5
     +   /D7* D6*/D5           ;    :+:
     +    D7*/D6*/D5
    :+:   D4*(/B0)             ;B4 :+: C3
     +   /D4*( B0)

/A1 :=    D7* D3* D2           ;B7 :+: B3 :+: B2
     +   /D7*/D3* D2
     +   /D7* D3*/D2           ;    :+:
     +    D7*/D3*/D2
    :+:   D1*(/B1)             ;B1 :+: C2
     +   /D1*( B1)

/A2 :=    D6* D5* D3           ;B6 :+: B5 :+: B3
     +   /D6*/D5* D3
     +   /D6* D5*/D3           ;    :+:
     +    D6*/D5*/D3
    :+:   D2* D0*( B2)         ;B2 :+: B0 :+: C1
     +   /D2*/D0*( B2)
     +   /D2* D0*(/B2)
     +    D2*/D0*(/B2)

/A3 :=    D6* D4* D3           ;B6 :+: B4 :+: B3
     +   /D6*/D4* D3
     +   /D6* D4*/D3           ;    :+:
     +    D6*/D4*/D3
    :+:   D1* D0*( B3)         ;B1 :+: B0 :+: C0
     +   /D1*/D0*( B3)
     +   /D1* D0*(/B3)
     +    D1*/D0*(/B3)
```

FUNCTION TABLE

```
SYNCLK /OC D7 D6 D5 D4 D3 D2 D1 D0 B0 B1 B2 B3 /A0 /A1 /A2 /A3

;CONTROL   --DATA-          ////
;SYN  /    DDDDDDDD  BBBB   AAAA
;CLK  OC   76543210  0123   0123   COMMENTS
------------------------------------------
  C   L    HHHHHHHH  LLHH   LLLL   NO ERROR
  C   L    LHHHHHHH  LLHH   HHLL   D7 ERROR
  C   L    HLHHHHHH  LLHH   HLHH   D6 ERROR
  C   L    HHLHHHHH  LLHH   HLHL   D5 ERROR
  C   L    HHHLHHHH  LLHH   HLLH   D4 ERROR
  C   L    HHHHLHHH  LLHH   LHHH   D3 ERROR
  C   L    HHHHHLHH  LLHH   LHHL   D2 ERROR
  C   L    HHHHHHLH  LLHH   LHLH   D1 ERROR
  C   L    HHHHHHHL  LLHH   LLHH   D0 ERROR
  C   L    HHHHHHHH  HLHH   HLLL   B0 ERROR
  C   L    HHHHHHHH  LLHH   LLLL   NO ERROR
  C   L    HHHHHHHH  LLLH   LLHL   B2 ERROR
  C   L    HHHHHHHH  LLHL   LLLH   B1 ERROR
  C   L    LLLLLLLL  LLLL   LLLL   NO ERROR
  C   L    HLLLLLLL  LLLL   HHLL   D7 ERROR
  C   L    LHLLLLLL  LLLL   HLHH   D6 ERROR
  C   L    LLHLLLLL  LLLL   HLHL   D5 ERROR
  C   L    LLLHLLLL  LLLL   HLLH   D4 ERROR
  C   L    LLLLHLLL  LLLL   LHHH   D3 ERROR
  C   L    LLLLLHLL  LLLL   LHHL   D2 ERROR
  C   L    LLLLLLHL  LLLL   LHLH   D1 ERROR
  C   L    LLLLLLLH  LLLL   LLHH   D0 ERROR
  C   L    LLLLLLLL  HLLL   HLLL   B0 ERROR
  C   L    LLLLLLLL  LHLL   LHLL   B1 ERROR
  C   L    LLLLLLLL  LLHL   LLHL   B2 ERROR
  C   L    LLLLLLLL  LLLH   LLLH   B3 ERROR
------------------------------------------
```

DESCRIPTION

THIS PAL GENERATES THE SYNDROME BITS FOR A 12 BIT HAMMING CODE WORD AS A FUNCTION OF THE 8 DATA BITS AND THE 4 CHECK BITS TO POINT TO ANY SINGLE BIT IN ERROR.

```
SYNDROME BIT GENERATOR

 1 C11001111X011HHHH111
 2 C01001111X011HHLL111
 3 C10001111X011LLHL111
 4 C11001101X011HLHL111
 5 C11001110X011LHHL111
 6 C11001111X001LLLH111
 7 C11001111X010HLLH111
 8 C11001111X011LHLH011
 9 C11001111X011LLHH101
10 C11101111X011HHHL111
11 C11001111X011HHHH111
12 C11000111X011HLHH111
13 C11001011X011LHHH111
14 C00000000X000HHHH001
15 C10000000X000HHLL001
16 C01000000X000LLHL001
17 C00000010X000HLHL001
18 C00000001X000LHHL001
19 C00000000X010LLLH001
20 C00000000X001HLLH001
21 C00000000X000LHLH101
22 C00000000X000LLHH011
23 C00100000X000HHHL001
24 C00010000X000HHLH001
25 C00001000X000HLHH001
26 C00000100X000LHHH001

PASS SIMULATION
```

```
SYNDROME BIT GENERATOR

              11 1111 1111 2222 2222 2233
   0123 4567 8901 2345 6789 0123 4567 8901



16 X--- X--- ---- ---- ---- ---- X--- ---- D7*D6*D5
17 -X-- -X-- ---- ---- ---- ---- X--- ---- /D7*/D6*D5
18 -X-- X--- ---- ---- ---- ---- -X-- ---- /D7*D6*/D5
19 X--- -X-- ---- ---- ---- ---- -X-- ---- D7*/D6*/D5
20 ---- ---- -X-X ---- ---- ---- ---- X--- D4*/B0
21 ---- ---- X-X- ---- ---- ---- ---- -X-- /D4*B0

24 X--- ---- ---- ---- ---- ---- --X- --X- D7*D3*D2
25 -X-- ---- ---- ---- ---- ---- --X- ---X /D7*/D3*D2
26 -X-- ---- ---- ---- ---- ---- ---X --X- /D7*D3*/D2
27 X--- ---- ---- ---- ---- ---- ---X ---X D7*/D3*/D2
28 ---- --X- ---- -X-X ---- ---- ---- ---- D1*/B1
29 ---- ---X ---- X-X- ---- ---- ---- ---- /D1*B1

32 ---- X--- ---- ---- ---- ---- X--- --X- D6*D5*D3
33 ---- -X-- ---- ---- ---- ---- -X-- --X- /D6*/D5*D3
34 ---- -X-- ---- ---- ---- ---- X--- ---X /D6*D5*/D3
35 ---- X--- ---- ---- ---- ---- -X-- ---X D6*/D5*/D3
36 --X- ---- ---- ---- X-X- ---- --X- ---- D2*D0*B2
37 ---X ---- ---- ---- X-X- ---- ---X ---- /D2*/D0*B2
38 --X- ---- ---- ---- -X-X ---- ---X ---- /D2*D0*/B2
39 ---X ---- ---- ---- -X-X ---- --X- ---- D2*/D0*/B2

40 ---- X--- ---- ---- ---- ---- ---- X-X- D6*D4*D3
41 ---- -X-- ---- ---- ---- ---- ---- -XX- /D6*/D4*D3
42 ---- -X-- ---- ---- ---- ---- ---- X--X /D6*D4*/D3
43 ---- X--- ---- ---- ---- ---- ---- -X-X D6*/D4*/D3
44 --X- --X- ---- ---- ---- X-X- ---- ---- D1*D0*B3
45 ---X ---X ---- ---- ---- X-X- ---- ---- /D1*/D0*B3
46 --X- ---X ---- ---- ---- -X-X ---- ---- /D1*D0*/B3
47 ---X --X- ---- ---- ---- -X-X ---- ---- D1*/D0*/B3


LEGEND:  X : FUSE NOT BLOWN (L,N,0)   - : FUSE BLOWN   (H,P,1)

NUMBER OF FUSES BLOWN =  828
```

Syndrome Bit Generator

Logic Diagram PAL16X4

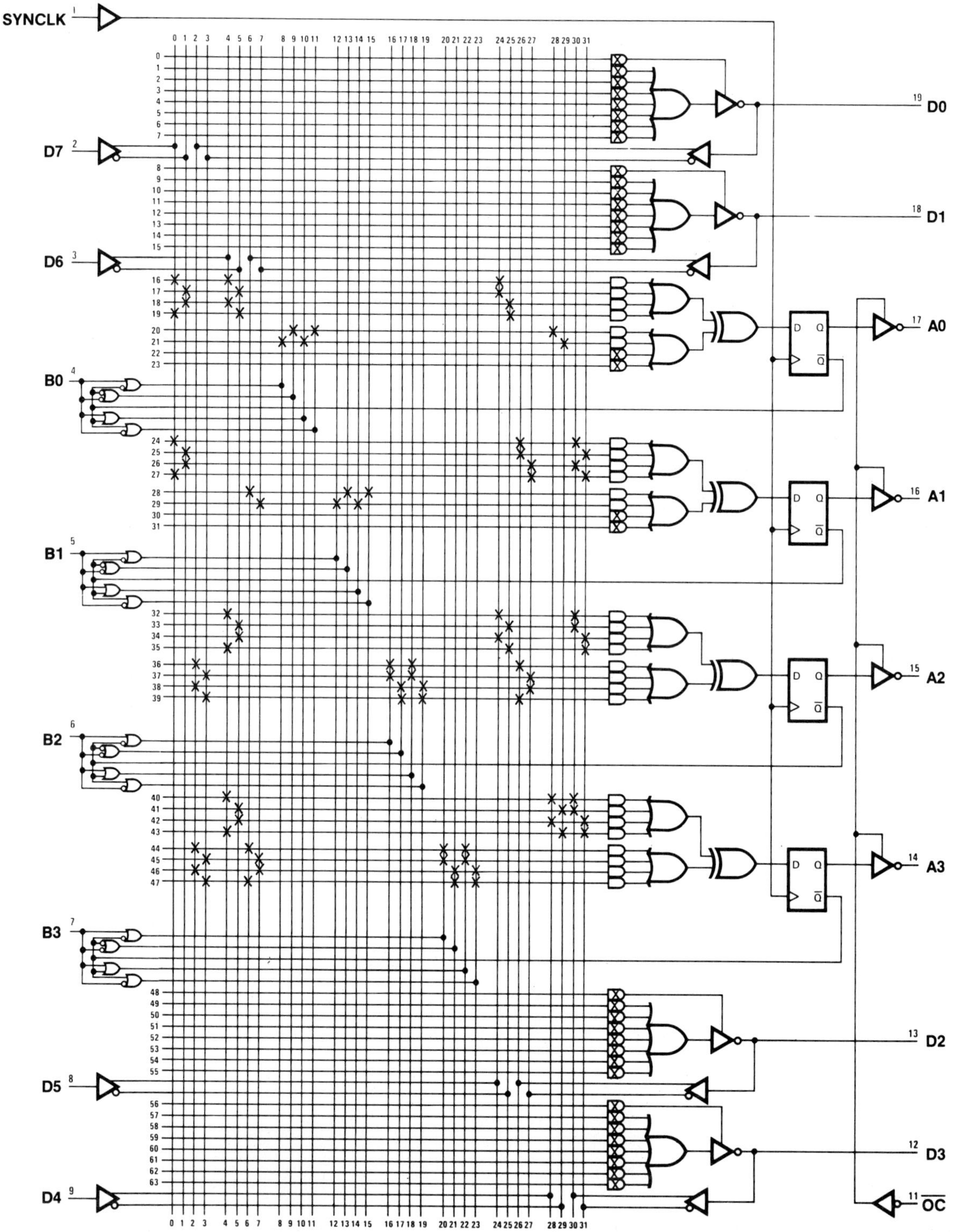

```
PAL16L8                                                 PAL DESIGN SPECIFICATION
ECU1                                                         B. BRAFMAN 03/13/81
ERROR CORRECTION UNIT No. 1
MMI FIELD APPLICATIONS ENGINEER YORBA LINDA, CALIFORNIA
/S3 /S2 /S1 /S0 B7  B6  B5  B4  B3  GND
 B2  NC  NC B2C B3C B4C B5C B6C B7C VCC


IF (VCC) /B7C =  S3* S2*/S1*/S0* B7      ;CORRECTION OF B7
              + /S3*/B7                  ;NO CORRECTION
              + /S2*/B7                  ;NO CORRECTION
              +  S1*/B7                  ;NO CORRECTION
              +  S0*/B7                  ;NO CORRECTION

IF (VCC) /B6C =  S3*/S2* S1* S0* B6      ;CORRECTION OF B6
              + /S3*/B6                  ;NO CORRECTION
              +  S2*/B6                  ;NO CORRECTION
              + /S1*/B6                  ;NO CORRECTION
              + /S0*/B6                  ;NO CORRECTION

IF (VCC) /B5C =  S3*/S2* S1*/S0* B5      ;CORRECTION OF B5
              + /S3*/B5                  ;NO CORRECTION
              +  S2*/B5                  ;NO CORRECTION
              + /S1*/B5                  ;NO CORRECTION
              +  S0*/B5                  ;NO CORRECTION

IF (VCC) /B4C =  S3*/S2*/S1* S0* B4      ;CORRECTION OF B4
              + /S3*/B4                  ;NO CORRECTION
              +  S2*/B4                  ;NO CORRECTION
              +  S1*/B4                  ;NO CORRECTION
              + /S0*/B4                  ;NO CORRECTION

IF (VCC) /B3C = /S3* S2* S1* S0* B3      ;CORRECTION OF B3
              +  S3*/B3                  ;NO CORRECTION
              + /S2*/B3                  ;NO CORRECTION
              + /S1*/B3                  ;NO CORRECTION
              + /S0*/B3                  ;NO CORRECTION

IF (VCC) /B2C = /S3* S2* S1*/S0* B2      ;CORRECTION OF B2
              +  S3*/B2                  ;NO CORRECTION
              + /S2*/B2                  ;NO CORRECTION
              + /S1*/B2                  ;NO CORRECTION
              +  S0*/B2                  ;NO CORRECTION
```

```
FUNCTION TABLE

S3 S2 S1 S0 B7 B6 B5 B4 B3 B2 B7C B6C B5C B4C B3C B2C

;SYNDROME    INPUT     CORRECTED
;  SSSS      BBBBBB     BBBBBB
;  3210      765432     765432          COMMENTS
-------------------------------------------------
   LLLL      HHHHHH     HHHHHH          NO ERROR
   LLLL      LLLLLL     LLLLLL          NO ERROR
   HHLL      HHHHHH     LHHHHH          CORRECT B7
   HHLL      LLLLLL     HLLLLL          CORRECT B7
   HLHH      HHHHHH     HLHHHH          CORRECT B6
   HLHH      LLLLLL     LHLLLL          CORRECT B6
   HLHL      HHHHHH     HHLHHH          CORRECT B5
   HLHL      LLLLLL     LLHLLL          CORRECT B5
   HLLH      HHHHHH     HHHLHH          CORRECT B4
   HLLH      LLLLLL     LLLHLL          CORRECT B4
   LHHH      HHHHHH     HHHHLH          CORRECT B3
   LHHH      LLLLLL     LLLLHL          CORRECT B3
   LHHL      HHHHHH     HHHHHL          CORRECT B2
   LHHL      LLLLLL     LLLLLH          CORRECT B2
-------------------------------------------------


DESCRIPTION

THIS PAL PERFORMS ERROR CORRECTION ON BITS B2-B7 BASED ON THE 4-BIT
ERROR SYNDROME S0-S3.


ERROR CORRECTION UNIT #1

 1 111111111X1XXHHHHHH1
 2 111100000X0XXLLLLLL1
 3 001111111X1XXHHHHHL1
 4 001100000X0XXLLLLLH1
 5 010011111X1XXHHHHLH1
 6 010000000X0XXLLLLHL1
 7 010111111X1XXHHHLHH1
 8 010100000X0XXLLLHLL1
 9 011011111X1XXHHLHHH1
10 011000000X0XXLLHLLL1
11 100011111X1XXHLHHHH1
12 100000000X0XXLHLLLL1
13 100111111X1XXLHHHHH1
14 100100000X0XXHLLLLL1

PASS SIMULATION
```

```
ERROR CORRECTION UNIT No. 1

               11 1111 1111 2222 2222 2233
   0123 4567 8901 2345 6789 0123 4567 8901

 0 ---- ---- ---- ---- ---- ---- ---- ----
 1 -X-X X--- X--- X--- ---- ---- ---- ---- S3*S2*/S1*/S0*B7
 2 --X- ---- ---- -X-- ---- ---- ---- ---- /S3*/B7
 3 X--- ---- ---- -X-- ---- ---- ---- ---- /S2*/B7
 4 ---- -X-- ---- -X-- ---- ---- ---- ---- S1*/B7
 5 ---- ---- -X-- -X-- ---- ---- ---- ---- S0*/B7

 8 ---- ---- ---- ---- ---- ---- ---- ----
 9 X--X -X-- -X-- ---- X--- ---- ---- ---- S3*/S2*S1*S0*B6
10 --X- ---- ---- ---- -X-- ---- ---- ---- /S3*/B6
11 -X-- ---- ---- ---- -X-- ---- ---- ---- S2*/B6
12 ---- X--- ---- ---- -X-- ---- ---- ---- /S1*/B6
13 ---- ---- X--- ---- -X-- ---- ---- ---- /S0*/B6

16 ---- ---- ---- ---- ---- ---- ---- ----
17 X--X -X-- X--- ---- ---- X--- ---- ---- S3*/S2*S1*/S0*B5
18 --X- ---- ---- ---- ---- -X-- ---- ---- /S3*/B5
19 -X-- ---- ---- ---- ---- -X-- ---- ---- S2*/B5
20 ---- X--- ---- ---- ---- -X-- ---- ---- /S1*/B5
21 ---- ---- -X-- ---- ---- -X-- ---- ---- S0*/B5

24 ---- ---- ---- ---- ---- ---- ---- ----
25 X--X X--- -X-- ---- ---- ---- X--- ---- S3*/S2*/S1*S0*B4
26 --X- ---- ---- ---- ---- ---- -X-- ---- /S3*/B4
27 -X-- ---- ---- ---- ---- ---- -X-- ---- S2*/B4
28 ---- -X-- ---- ---- ---- ---- -X-- ---- S1*/B4
29 ---- ---- X--- ---- ---- ---- -X-- ---- /S0*/B4

32 ---- ---- ---- ---- ---- ---- ---- ----
33 -XX- -X-- -X-- ---- ---- ---- ---- X--- /S3*S2*S1*S0*B3
34 ---X ---- ---- ---- ---- ---- ---- -X-- S3*/B3
35 X--- ---- ---- ---- ---- ---- ---- -X-- /S2*/B3
36 ---- X--- ---- ---- ---- ---- ---- -X-- /S1*/B3
37 ---- ---- X--- ---- ---- ---- ---- -X-- /S0*/B3

40 ---- ---- ---- ---- ---- ---- ---- ----
41 -XX- -X-- X--- ---- ---- ---- ---- --X- /S3*S2*S1*/S0*B2
42 ---X ---- ---- ---- ---- ---- ---- ---X S3*/B2
43 X--- ---- ---- ---- ---- ---- ---- ---X /S2*/B2
44 ---- X--- ---- ---- ---- ---- ---- ---X /S1*/B2
45 ---- ---- -X-- ---- ---- ---- ---- ---X S0*/B2


LEGEND:  X : FUSE NOT BLOWN (L,N,0)    - : FUSE BLOWN   (H,P,1)

NUMBER OF FUSES BLOWN = 1074
```

Error Correction Unit No. 1

Logic Diagram PAL16L8

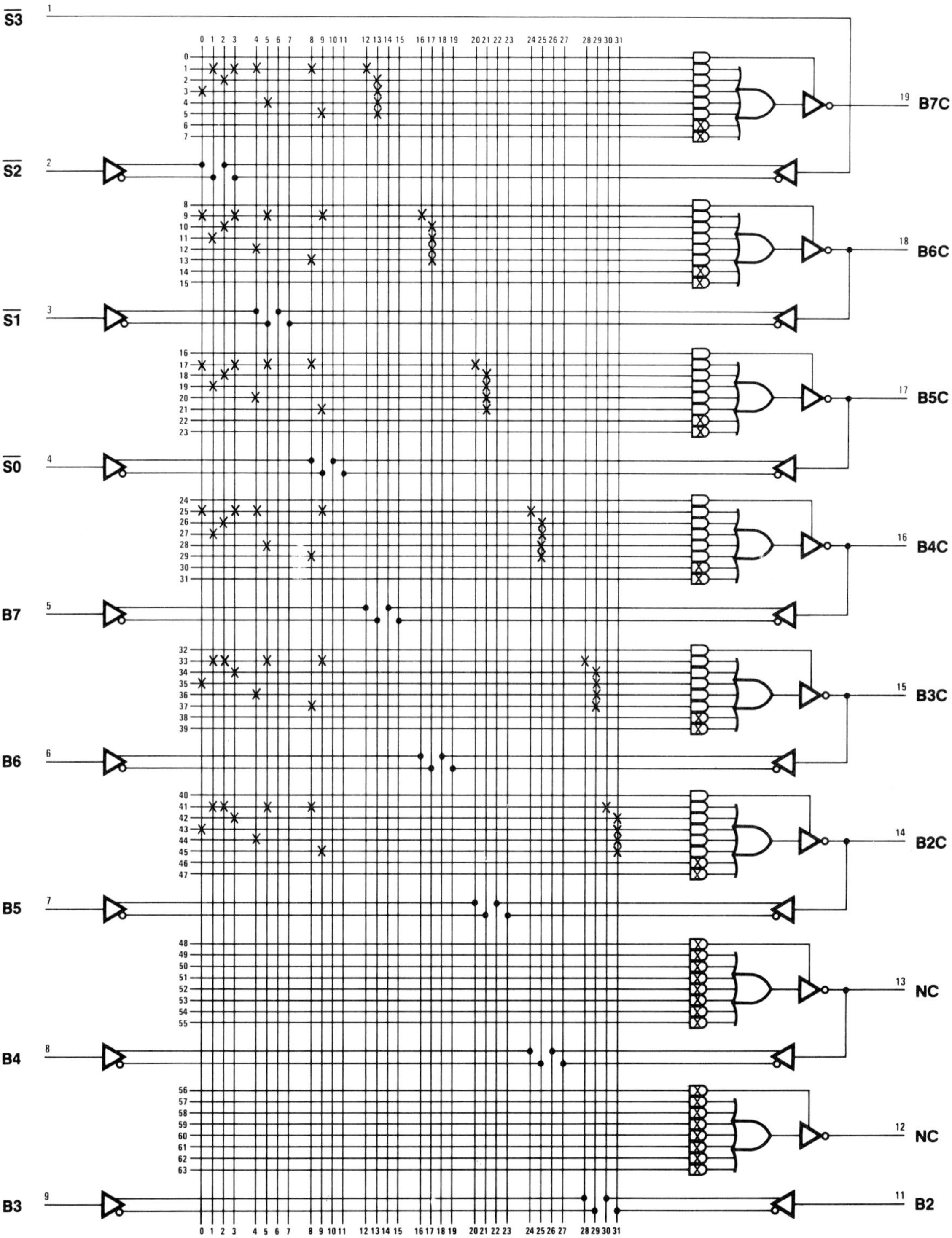

```
PAL16L8                                                 PAL DESIGN SPECIFICATION
ECU2                                                        B. BRAFMAN 03/13/81
ERROR CORRECTION UNIT No. 2
MMI FIELD APPLICATIONS ENGINEER  YORBA LINDA, CALIFORNIA
/S3 /S2 /S1 /S0 B1 B0 /C3 /C2 /C1 GND
/C0 NC ERROR C0C C1C C2C C3C B0C B1C VCC


IF (VCC) /B1C = /S3* S2*/S1* S0* B1     ;CORRECTION OF B1
              +  S3*/B1                 ;NO CORRECTION
              + /S2*/B1                 ;NO CORRECTION
              +  S1*/B1                 ;NO CORRECTION

IF (VCC) /B0C = /S3*/S2* S1* S0* B0     ;CORRECTION OF B0
              +  S3*/B0                 ;NO CORRECTION
              +  S2*/B0                 ;NO CORRECTION
              + /S1*/B0                 ;NO CORRECTION
              + /S0*/B0                 ;NO CORRECTION

IF (VCC) /C3C =  S3*/S2*/S1*/S0* C3     ;CORRECTION OF C3
              + /S3*/C3                 ;NO CORRECTION
              +  S2*/C3                 ;NO CORRECTION
              +  S1*/C3                 ;NO CORRECTION
              +  S0*/C3                 ;NO CORRECTION

IF (VCC) /C2C = /S3* S2*/S1*/S0* C2     ;CORRECTION OF C2
              +  S3*/C2                 ;NO CORRECTION
              + /S2*/C2                 ;NO CORRECTION
              +  S1*/C2                 ;NO CORRECTION
              +  S0*/C2                 ;NO CORRECTION

IF (VCC) /C1C = /S3*/S2* S1*/S0* C1     ;CORRECTION OF C1
              +  S3*/C1                 ;NO CORRECTION
              +  S2*/C1                 ;NO CORRECTION
              + /S1*/C1                 ;NO CORRECTION
              +  S0*/C1                 ;NO CORRECTION

IF (VCC) /C0C = /S3*/S2*/S1* S0* C0     ;CORRECTION OF C0
              +  S3*/C0                 ;NO CORRECTION
              +  S2*/C0                 ;NO CORRECTION
              +  S1*/C0                 ;NO CORRECTION
              + /S0*/C0                 ;NO CORRECTION

IF (VCC) /ERROR = /S3*/S2*/S1*/S0       ;NO ERROR!
```

FUNCTION TABLE

```
S3 S2 S1 S0 B1 B0 C3 C2 C1 C0 B1C B0C C3C C2C C1C C0C ERROR

;                    BB   CCCC
;SSSS  BB   CCCC    10   3210
;3210  10   3210    CC   CCCC  ERROR     COMMENTS
-----------------------------------------------------
 LLLL  HH   XXXX    HH   XXXX    L       NO ERROR
 LLLL  XX   HHHH    XX   HHHH    L       NO ERROR
 LLLL  LL   XXXX    LL   XXXX    L       NO ERROR
 LLLL  XX   LLLL    XX   LLLL    L       NO ERROR
 LHLH  HH   XXXX    LH   XXXX    H       CORRECT B1
 LHLH  LL   XXXX    HL   XXXX    H       CORRECT B1
 LLHH  HH   XXXX    HL   XXXX    H       CORRECT B0
 LLHH  LL   XXXX    LH   XXXX    H       CORRECT B0
 HLLL  XX   HHHH    XX   LHHH    H       CORRECT C3
 HLLL  XX   LLLL    XX   HLLL    H       CORRECT C3
 LHLL  XX   HHHH    XX   HLHH    H       CORRECT C2
 LHLL  XX   LLLL    XX   LHLL    H       CORRECT C2
 LLHL  XX   HHHH    XX   HHLH    H       CORRECT C1
 LLHL  XX   LLLL    XX   LLHL    H       CORRECT C1
 LLLH  XX   HHHH    XX   HHHL    H       CORRECT C0
 LLLH  XX   LLLL    XX   LLLH    H       CORRECT C0
-----------------------------------------------------
```

DESCRIPTION

THIS PAL PERFORMS ERROR CORRECTION ON BITS B0-B1 AND CHECKS BITS C0-C3 BASED ON THE 4 BIT ERROR SYNDROME S0-S3.

ERROR CORRECTION UNIT #2

```
 1 111111XXXXXXLXXXXHH1
 2 1111XX000X0XLHHHHXX1
 3 111100XXXXXXLXXXXLL1
 4 1111XX111X1XLLLLLXX1
 5 101011XXXXXXHXXXXHL1
 6 101000XXXXXXHXXXXLH1
 7 110011XXXXXXHXXXXLH1
 8 110000XXXXXXHXXXXHL1
 9 0111XX000X0XHHHHLXX1
10 0111XX111X1XHLLLHXX1
11 1011XX000X0XHHHLHXX1
12 1011XX111X1XHLLHLXX1
13 1101XX000X0XHHLHHXX1
14 1101XX111X1XHLHLLXX1
15 1110XX000X0XHLHHHXX1
16 1110XX111X1XHHLLLXX1
```

PASS SIMULATION

ERROR CORRECTION UNIT No. 2

```
                 11 1111 1111 2222 2222 2233
   0123 4567 8901 2345 6789 0123 4567 8901

 0 ---- ---- ---- ---- ---- ---- ---- ----
 1 -XX- X--- -X-- X--- ---- ---- ---- ---- /S3*S2*/S1*S0*B1
 2 ---X ---- ---- -X-- ---- ---- ---- ---- S3*/B1
 3 X--- ---- ---- -X-- ---- ---- ---- ---- /S2*/B1
 4 ---- -X-- ---- -X-- ---- ---- ---- ---- S1*/B1

 8 ---- ---- ---- ---- ---- ---- ---- ----
 9 X-X- -X-- -X-- ---- X--- ---- ---- ---- /S3*/S2*S1*S0*B0
10 ---X ---- ---- ---- -X-- ---- ---- ---- S3*/B0
11 -X-- ---- ---- ---- -X-- ---- ---- ---- S2*/B0
12 ---- X--- ---- ---- -X-- ---- ---- ---- /S1*/B0
13 ---- ---- X--- ---- -X-- ---- ---- ---- /S0*/B0

16 ---- ---- ---- ---- ---- ---- ---- ----
17 X--X X--- X--- ---- ---- -X-- ---- ---- S3*/S2*/S1*/S0*C3
18 --X- ---- ---- ---- ---- X--- ---- ---- /S3*/C3
19 -X-- ---- ---- ---- ---- X--- ---- ---- S2*/C3
20 ---- -X-- ---- ---- ---- X--- ---- ---- S1*/C3
21 ---- ---- -X-- ---- ---- X--- ---- ---- S0*/C3

24 ---- ---- ---- ---- ---- ---- ---- ----
25 -XX- X--- X--- ---- ---- ---- -X-- ---- /S3*S2*/S1*/S0*C2
26 ---X ---- ---- ---- ---- ---- X--- ---- S3*/C2
27 X--- ---- ---- ---- ---- ---- X--- ---- /S2*/C2
28 ---- -X-- ---- ---- ---- ---- X--- ---- S1*/C2
29 ---- ---- -X-- ---- ---- ---- X--- ---- S0*/C2

32 ---- ---- ---- ---- ---- ---- ---- ----
33 X-X- -X-- X--- ---- ---- ---- ---- -X-- /S3*/S2*S1*/S0*C1
34 ---X ---- ---- ---- ---- ---- ---- X--- S3*/C1
35 -X-- ---- ---- ---- ---- ---- ---- X--- S2*/C1
36 ---- X--- ---- ---- ---- ---- ---- X--- /S1*/C1
37 ---- ---- -X-- ---- ---- ---- ---- X--- S0*/C1

40 ---- ---- ---- ---- ---- ---- ---- ----
41 X-X- X--- -X-- ---- ---- ---- ---- ---X /S3*/S2*/S1*S0*C0
42 ---X ---- ---- ---- ---- ---- ---- --X- S3*/C0
43 -X-- ---- ---- ---- ---- ---- ---- --X- S2*/C0
44 ---- -X-- ---- ---- ---- ---- ---- --X- S1*/C0
45 ---- ---- X--- ---- ---- ---- ---- --X- /S0*/C0

48 ---- ---- ---- ---- ---- ---- ---- ----
49 X-X- X--- X--- ---- ---- ---- ---- ---- /S3*/S2*/S1*/S0
```

LEGEND: X : **FUSE** NOT BLOWN (L,N,0)   - : FUSE BLOWN   (H,P,1)

NUMBER OF FUSES BLOWN = 1104

Error Correction Unit No. 2

Logic Diagram PAL16L8

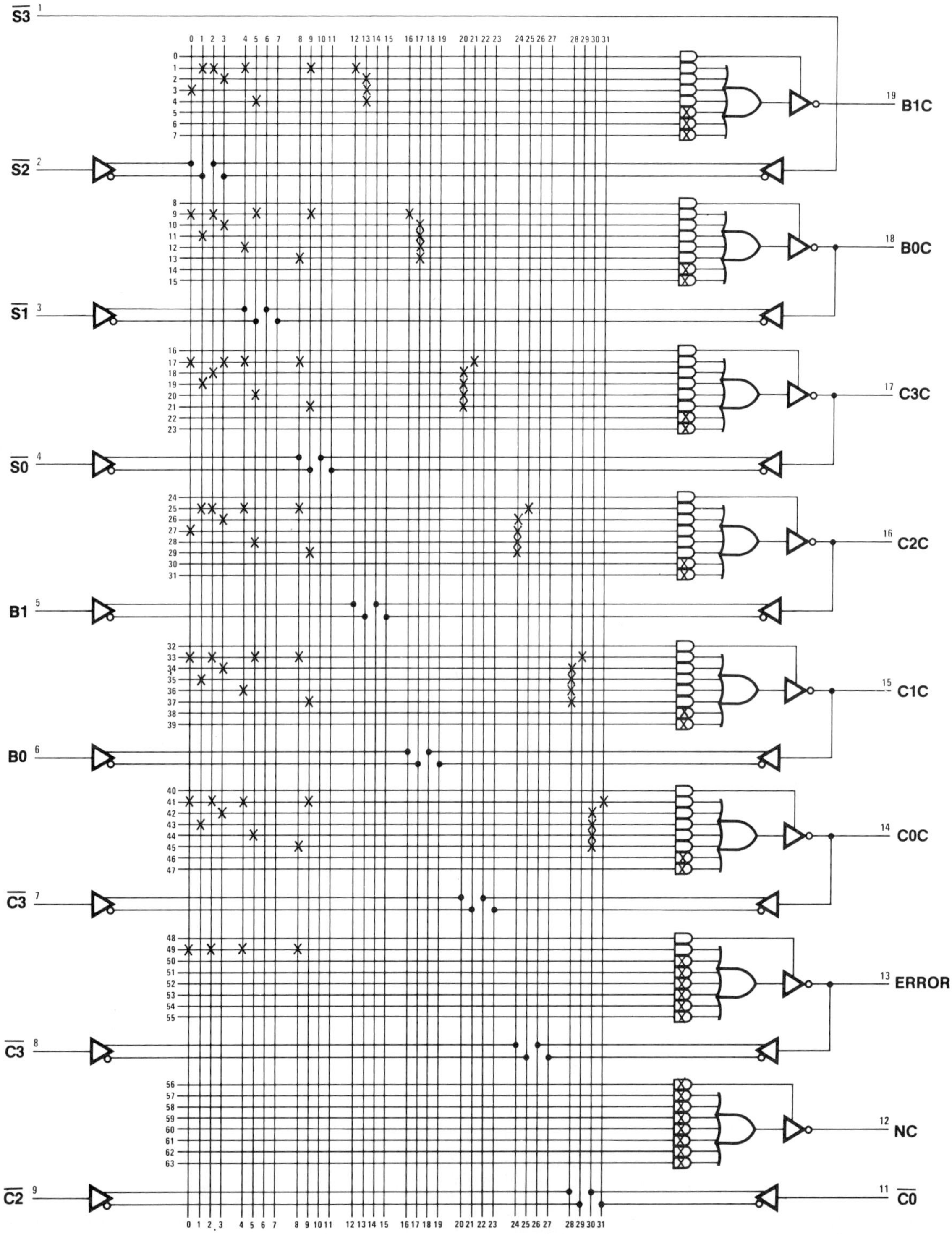

PAL
IMPORTANT
NOTES

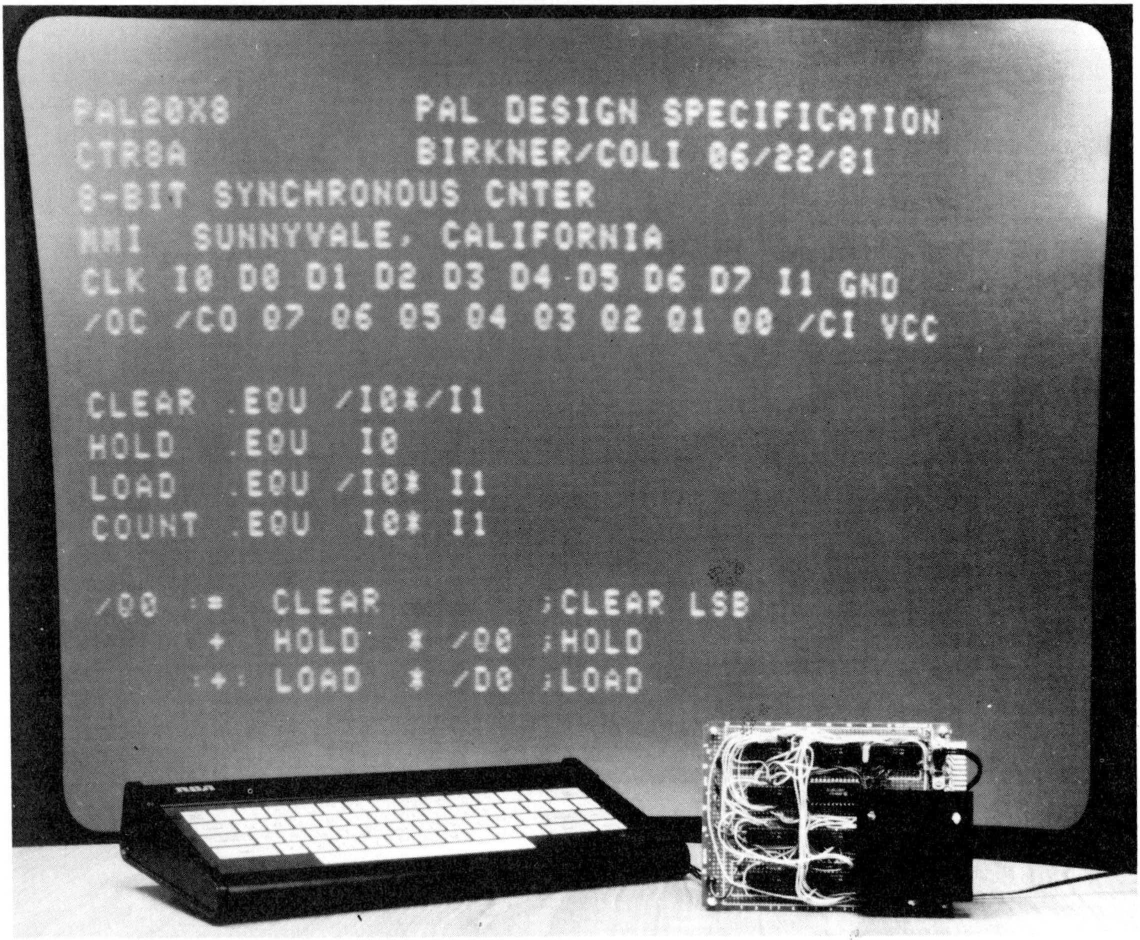

Introduction to Video Section

Computer graphics is a rapidly growing field in the computer industry. It enables communication between the human being and the computer. The human eye can absorb information displayed in diagrams, numbers, letters and images much faster than it can absorb tables with numbers only. Computer graphics is penetrating into almost every professional field and the "video games" syndrome is spreading into more and more living rooms.

The PAL family teams up to help the wide-spread use of computer graphics. By using high speed PALs, the designer can implement simulations and real time systems in an efficient way.

The following designs are examples of the use of PALs in the video world.

1. **10 BIT COUNTER [SN54/74LS491]** This is ideal for video synch generation for CRT graphics including video games. This counter provides the vertical and horizontal coordinates required to address the graphic data. Video resolution is usually 9 or 10 bits in the vertical and horizontal which in the past was supplied by three LS161's. These, of course, can be replaced by one LS491. This counter can also count down which allows screen coordinate reversal.
2. Analog to digital and digital to analog converters, change analog signal into an equivalent digital code and vice versa. This function is commonly required in a digital system when the analog information has to be stored and then shown as a displacement on a CRT.
3. The video logic design shows the reduction in the number of parts on a video-interface board using PALs.
4. The video-controller board is an example of how to implement a video system using PALs.

Implementing a Video Controller Using Programmable Array Logic

by Ehud "Udi" Gordon

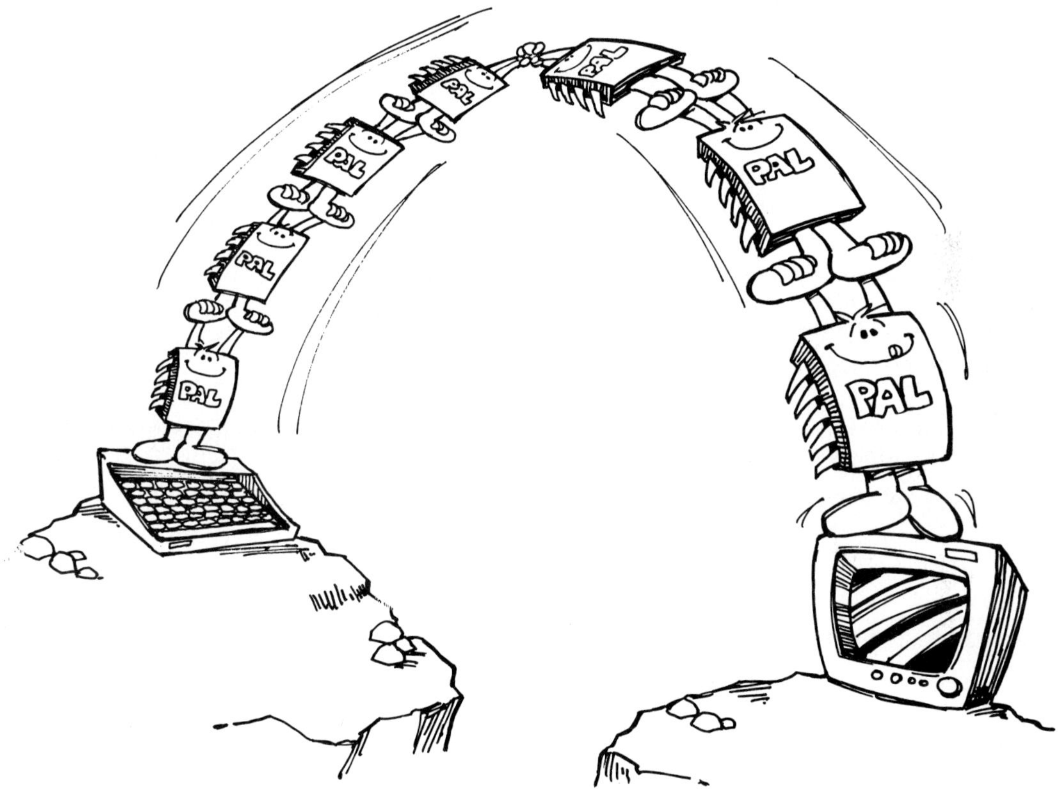

The use of video is definitely a sign of the times and will be with us into the future. The video-controller board is the bridge between the outside world and the screen. There are many possibilities to implement the video-controller board, but an efficient one uses PALs. The following will simplify the construction of a video-controller board and will assist the designer in eliminating board space problems. PALs are the backbone of this application.

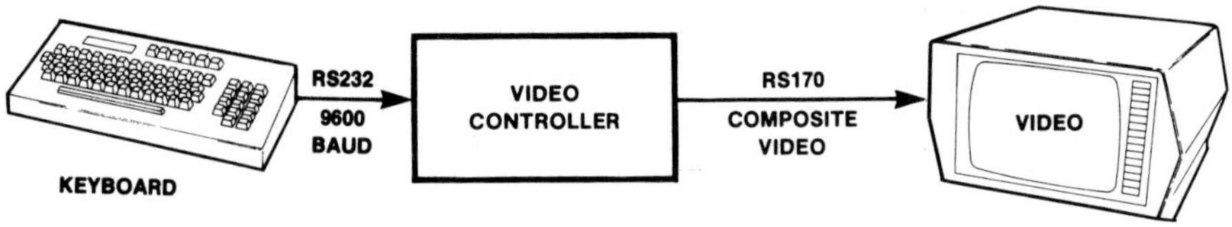

Overview

There are words that belong to specific concepts within the video industry. For a clear understanding of how the video-controller board works we need to define some of them:

FRAME — A single complete picture

SCANNING — The process of analyzing successively, according to a predetermined method, the light values of picture elements which constitute the total picture area

FRAME FREQUENCY — The number of times per second the picture area is completely scanned

The frame frequency has been standardized at 30 frames per second, which gives a satisfactory illusion of motion continuity, although the individual picture elements are transmitted one after the other. A frequency of 30 frames per second is equal to half the power-line frequency in most locations. Using this standardized rate, the entire screen is illuminated 30 times per second. This is too slow to give the impression of a truly steady light, so a flickering occurs.

To overcome the flickering problem it is common to use the **INTERLACED SCANNING METHOD**. In this method the screen is divided into 525 lines and into two fields. There is an odd numbered field and an even numbered field. Each of these fields is made up of one-half of the screen by dividing the frame into odd and even numbered lines. First, all the odd numbered lines 1, 3, 5, ... are scanned from top to bottom. After scanning a total of 262.5 odd numbered lines, the even numbered lines are scanned from top to bottom, for the total of 525 lines. Each scanning period from top to bottom is 1/60 of a second and is called a **FIELD**. Two fields constitute a frame.

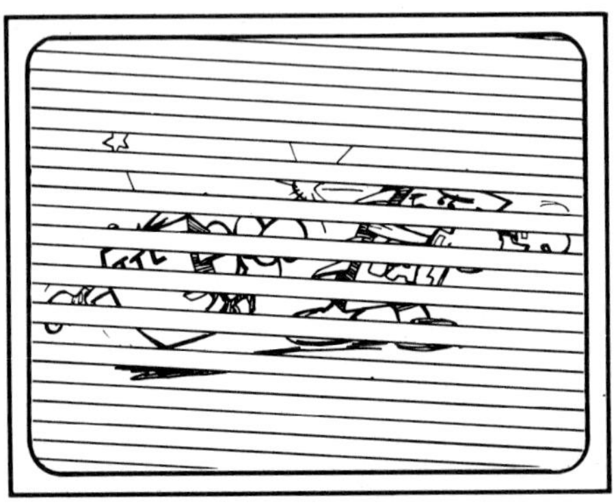

Figure 1a. Odd Numbered Lines Scanned Generate the Odd Field

Figure 1b. Even Numbered Lines Scanned Generate the Even Field

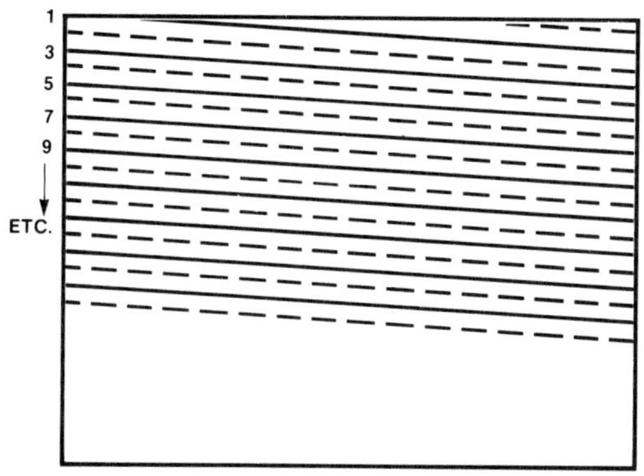

Figure 1c. The Solid Lines 1, 3, 5, . . . Represent the Odd Field. The Dashed Lines 2, 4, 6 . . . Represent the Even Field

Figure 1d. The Odd and Even Fields Combined Generate One Frame

FIELD FREQUENCY — The number of times per second the field is completely scanned

The field frequency has been standardized at 60 fields per second. At this rate, the screen gets illuminated 60 times per second which results in the disappearance of the flickering. (Notice that the frame frequency is still 1/30 of a second.)

At the end of each scan line the electron beam moves rapidly from right to left on the screen which gives the horizontal retrace. Then it moves across the next odd/even numbered scan line and returns retracing right to left. While the beam retraces, blanking pulses are transmitted which blank out the total screen for this time period.

A HORIZONTAL SYNCHRONIZED PULSE is used to time the start of each horizontal scan line. The rate of the horizontal synchronizing pulse is equal to the total number of lines per frame multiplied by the number of frames transmitted per second:

$$525 \text{ lines} * 30 \text{ frames} = 15750 \text{ pulses/second}$$

A VERTICAL SYNCHRONIZED PULSE is used to time the start of each field. It occurs at the end of each field and causes the beam to go from bottom to top of the screen. During the vertical retrace, blanking pulses are transmitted which blank out the total screen for this time period. The rate of the vertical synchronizing pulse is equal to the number of fields transmitted per second: 60 pulses/second.

Figure 2. Horizontal Scanned Lines With the Retraces

Figure 3. Composite Video Signal

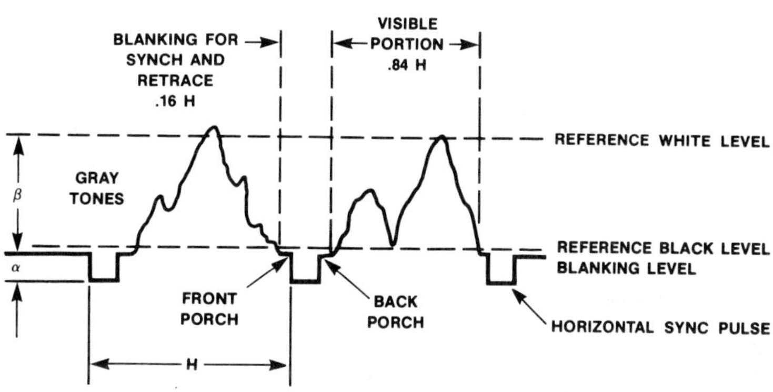

β = 1.0 ± 0.05 Volts
α = 0.4 ± 0.05β Volts
H = Time From Start of One Line to Start of Next Line

A picture signal is defined as voltage levels which when combined with the synchronizing pulses generate **A COMPOSITE VIDEO SIGNAL**. There are two reference voltage levels; i.e., a high voltage level = white and a low voltage level = black (see Figure 3). In between these reference levels are the gray tones. The synchronizing pulses are below the black level so they do not produce light.

The horizontal and vertical pulses along with the picture signals constitute a frame where 15,750 horizontal lines are scanned every second making one complete horizontal cycle of approximately 63.5 microsceonds (commonly called 1H). Because of the front and the back porches (see Figure 3) that are used for retrace time and synchronization, the visible portion lasts approximately 54 microseconds. The time from the start of one field to the start of the next field is 262.5H or 1V.

Figure 6 illustrates the relationship between (a) the horizontal and vertical sweeps and (b) the line and the field blanking. A field blanking signal starts at Point A which is the initiation of the vertical retrace where the electron beam is at the bottom of the screen. During the vertical retrace period, the beam moves back and forth across the screen until it reaches the top of the screen (see Figure 5). The field remains blank until the beam reaches Point B. From Point B the beam is visible until it nears the right edge of the screen. At this time, horizontal blanking occurs and the beam moves from the right edge to the left edge of the screen. Horizontal blanking occurs 263 times for each field. At Point C, a new vertical retrace for the next field is initiated. At Point D, the beam finishes the scan of the entire screen for one frame. This point corresponds to Point A in the first field, so a field blanking occurs again.

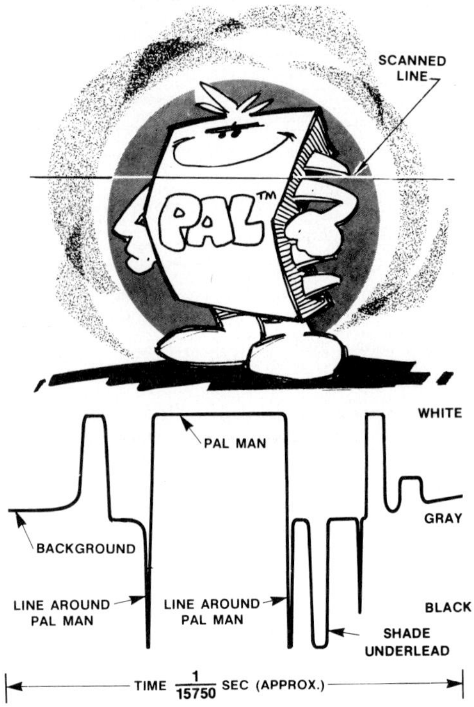

Figure 4. A Waveform of Video Voltage Produced by Scanning One Line on a Televised Screen

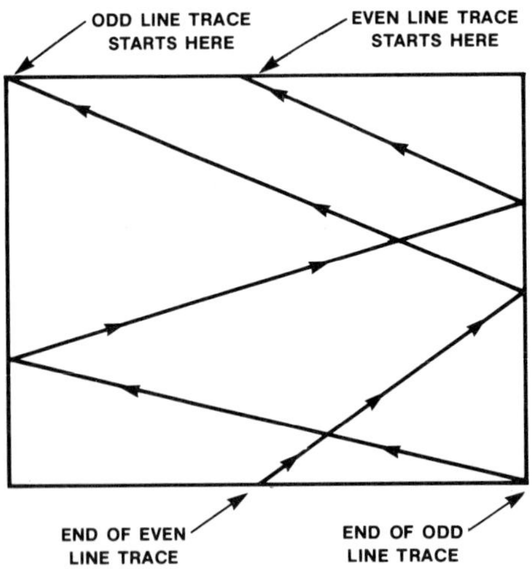

Figure 5. Vertical Retraces for the Odd and Even Fields

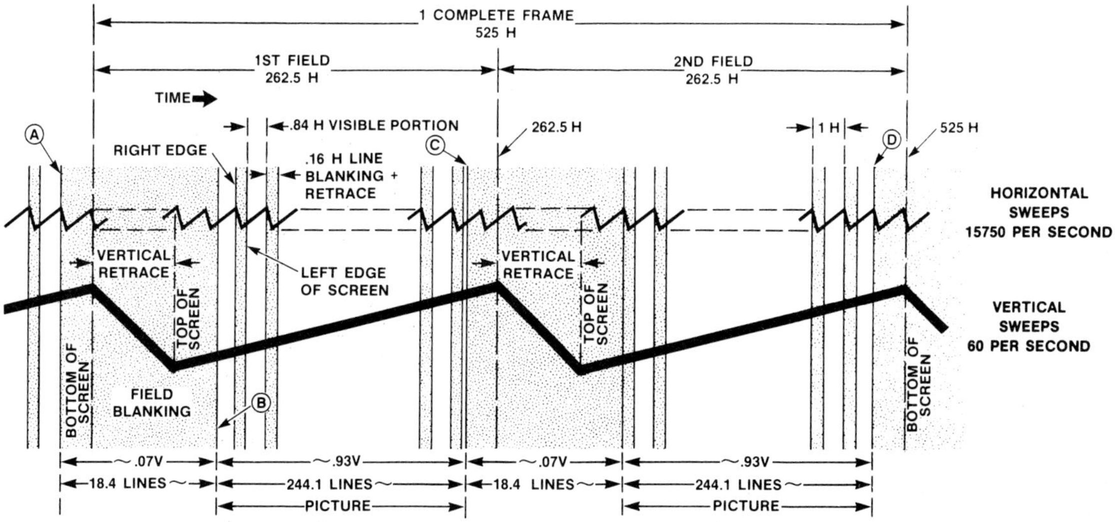

Figure 6. Vertical and Horizontal Sweeps, and Blanking Within a Frame

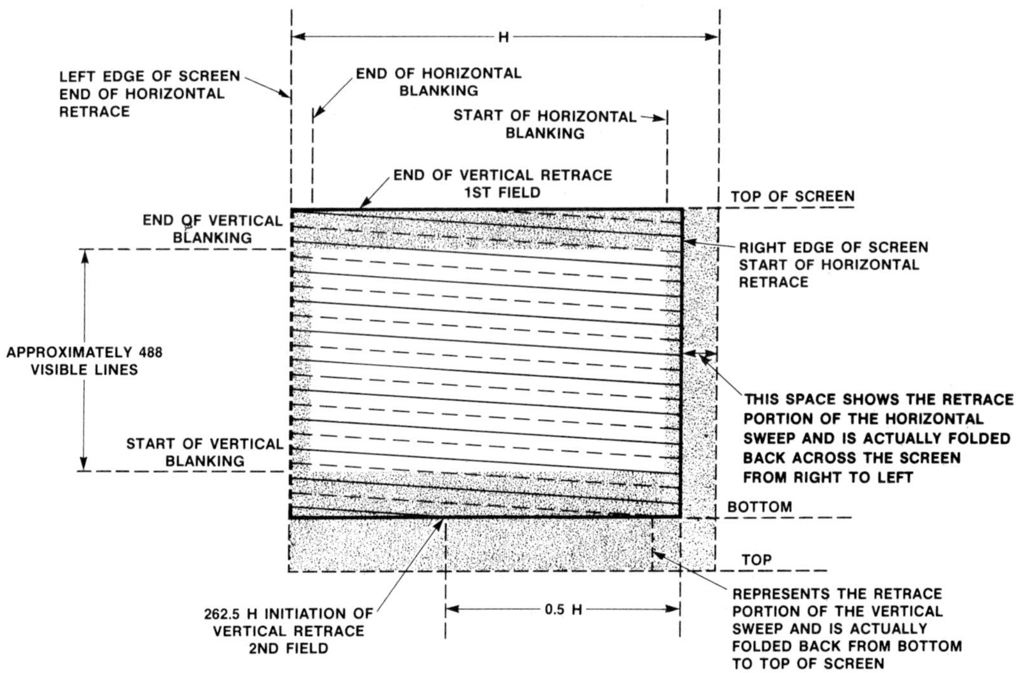

Figure 7. Effect of Vertical and Horizontal Blanking on the Screen

Figure 7 shows the actual movement of the beam and the effect of the line and the field blanking on the screen. The shaded portions at the top and bottom of the screen represent field blanking, while the shaded portion at the left and right edges of the screen represent line blanking. The combination of the shaded portions with the unshaded portions represent the available screen size, if no retracing were necessary.

From a single scan line to a complete picture which defines a frame, we have presented the concept and the process for sending information (a composite video signal) to a video receiver.

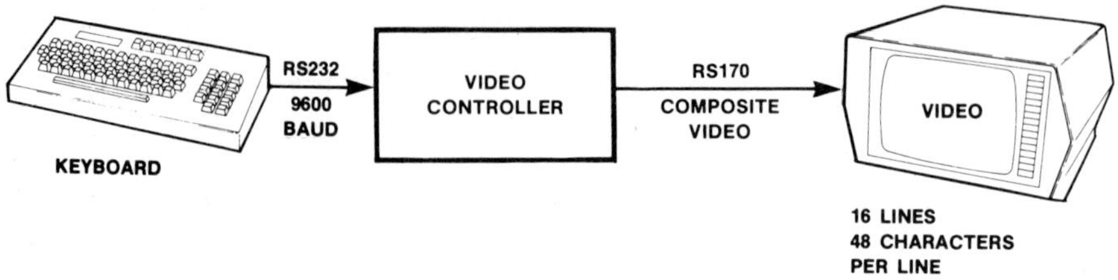

Figure 8. A Very Simplified Diagram

From the Keyboard to the Video Controller

The input to our video controller comes from a keyboard terminal or a computer. The information is transferred via an RS232 port to the video controller, one bit at a time. Each character is represented in ASCII code and is detected by the video controller only if a start signal was first issued.

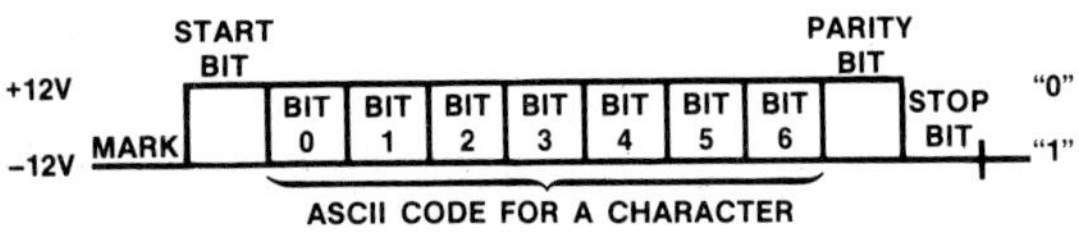

Figure 9. Each Character Consists of 10 Bits
1 Start Bit
7 ASCII Bits
1 Parity Bit
1 Stop Bit

The design is based on using 260 scan lines and an 8 MHz crystal. In order to obtain the standard horizontal period of 63.5 microseconds, each horizontal line is divided into 512 cycles giving a line period of 512/8 = 64.0 microseconds. The frequency of the electron beam is equal to the power line frequency (60 Hz) so in a clear environment (without noise) the picture is clear and steady.

$$\text{FRAME RATE} = \frac{8\ \text{MHz}}{260\ \text{scan lines} * 512\ \text{cycles per line}} = 60.09\ \text{Hz}$$

These figures and calculations are explained and diagrammed in detail in the section on implementation.

From the Video Controller to the Video Screen

Our video controller uses a **NON-INTERLACED METHOD** for scanning (see Figrue 10). In this method, the traced lines are adjacent and each frame consists of 260 scanned lines. Each field is equal to a frame which changes the definition of a field so that a complete frame is now transmitted in 1/60 of a second.

Figure 11 shows the horizontal and the vertical sweeps which cut in half the common frame frequency and now generate two frames for the same amount of time. At the end of each horizontal line, the electron beam moves rapidly from the right edge to the left edge of the screen while blanking pulses are transmitted (Points C–D in Figure 11).

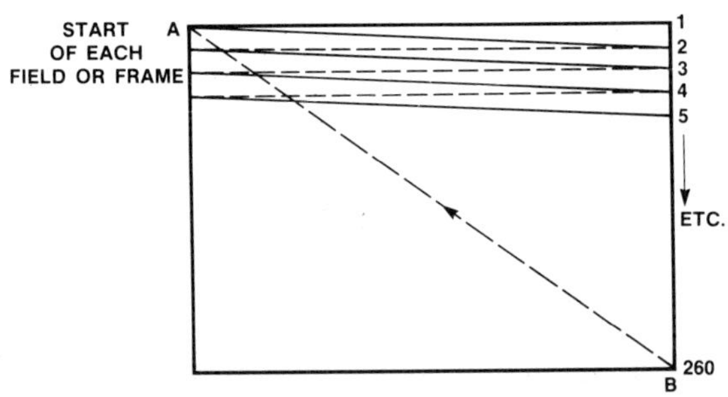

Figure 10. Non-interlaced Scanning. 260 Solid Lines Represent a Frame. The Dashed Lines are the Retrace Lines.

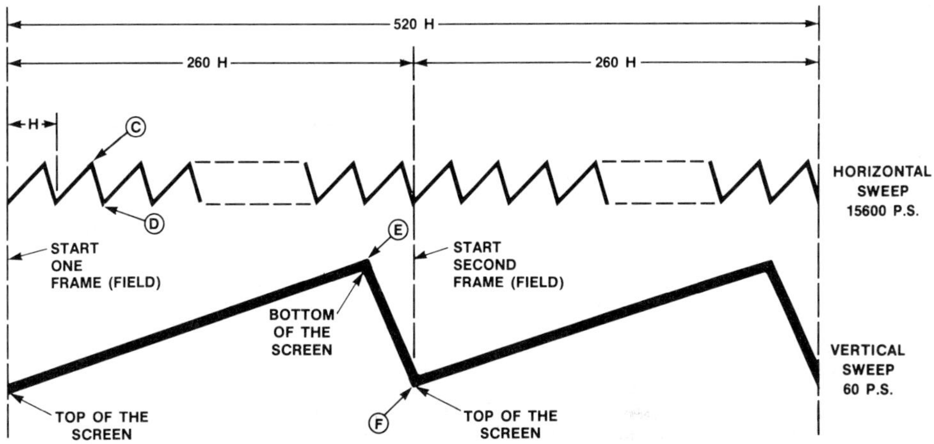

Figure 11. 520 Horizontal Lines Generate Two Fields Which Constitute Two Frames in A Non-interlaced Scanning

At the end of 260 horizontal lines, the electron beam is blanked out while it goes back from the bottom to the top of the screen (Points E-F in Figure 11).

The video controller can display a maximum of 16 visible character-lines with 48 visible characters per character-line. Each character is produced by a 5×7 character generator. A character-line on the screen consists of twelve dot-lines: seven dot-lines for the character and five blank dot-lines for space between the character-lines. Each dot in a dot-line is called a **PIXEL**.

Figure 12 shows one character-line with the characters "U, D, I" and all the pixels that built these three characters on the screen. These pixels or character elements are sent one after the other in an orderly sequence across the dot-line. Twelve dot-lines are rapidly transmitted to create one character-line. This is called **SUCCESSIVE METHOD OF TRANSMISSION** (see Figure 13).

Figure 12. One Character-line With Three Characters

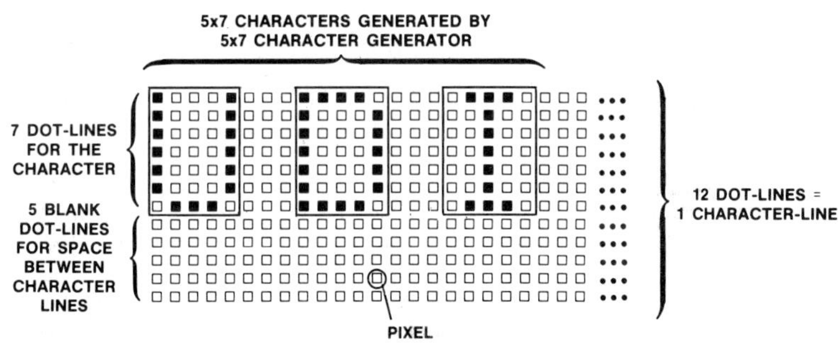

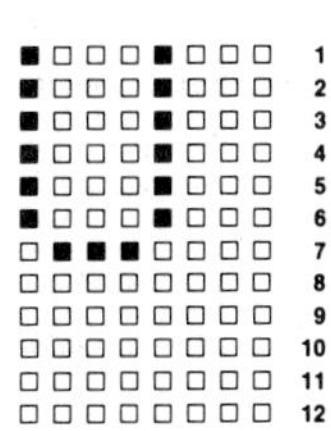

Figure 13. Successive Method of Transmission. For Simplicity Assume Only One Character 'U'. Each Dot-line is Sent in Orderly Sequence.

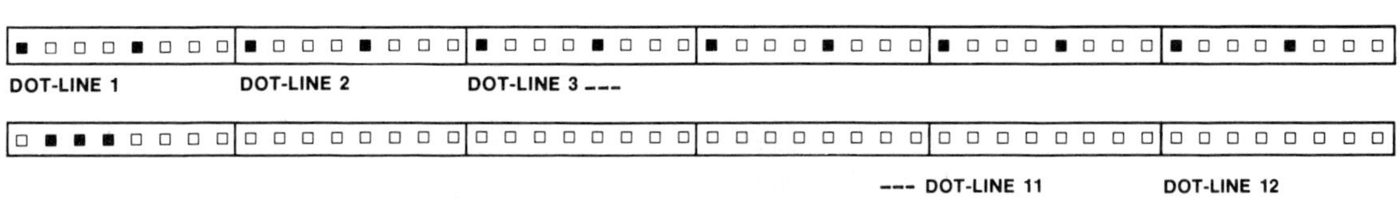

Implementation

Our video-controller board is divided into two subsystems which are connected by a RAM. The RAM is time shared by the two subsystems and provides the effect of a multi-port RAM. An 8-bit ASCII code is entered into the system through a "write only" port which is connected by the RS232 interface. The code is written into the RAM in locations indicated by pointers "SCROL" and "CURS". We don't write every cycle, but we read every cycle. The code is read from the RAM from locations indicated by pointers "LINES" and "CHAR" and transferred through a "read only" port to a character generator that generates the pixels for the screen. The "read" is done continuously so the picture looks steady. "Write" is done upon receipt of a special signal.

To build the video-controller board we used a RAM, a character generator and counters that are used as pointers/special module counters. Monolithic Memories' PALs provide an excellent replacement for TTL counters. They can be programmed to count in any desired mode. The PAL meets the requirements of the standard TTL SSI/MSI of 25 nsec propagation delay while reducing the chip count on the board. The PAL can generate non-standard functions which are not available on standard chips. By customizing the PAL to give only the functions that are needed, the user can save board space. The following is a detailed design of a video controller using Monolithic Memories PALs.

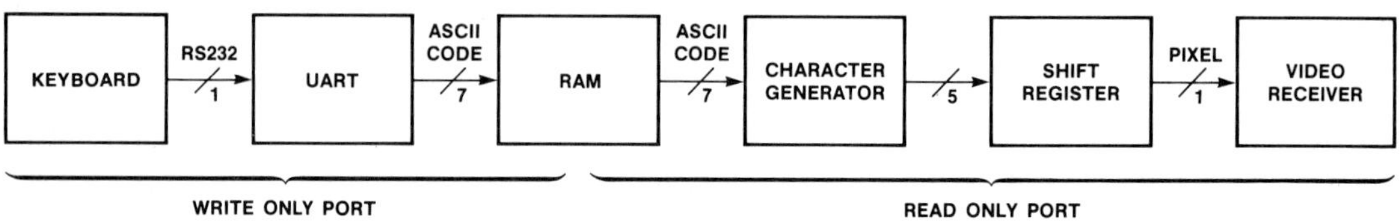

Figure 14. The RAM Divides the Board into Two Subsystems:
a) Write Only Subsystem; From the Keyboard to the RAM.
b) Read Only Subsystem; From the RAM to the Video Receiver.

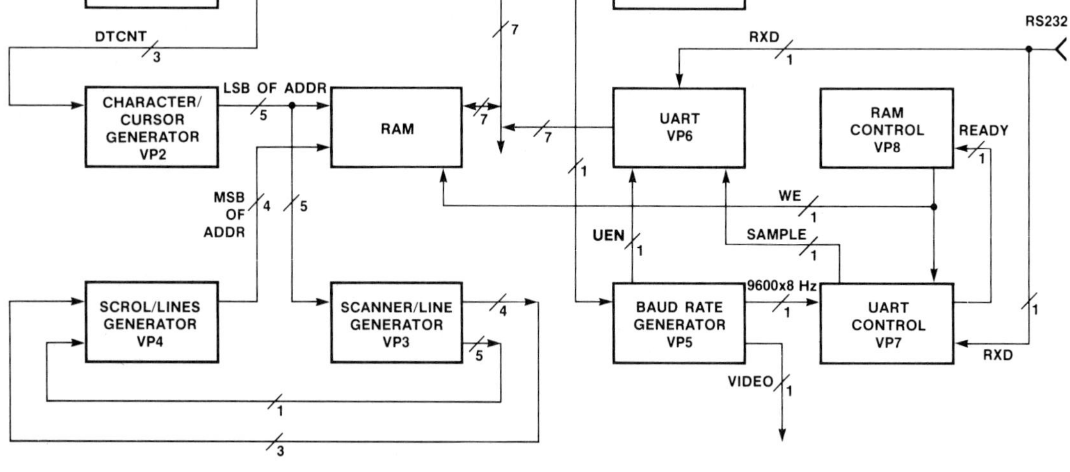

Figure 15. Block Diagram of the Video Controller

NOTES:

1. VP1 is a shift register for the dots in a dot-line of each character. "DTCNT" counts 8 dots for each character (PAL20X8).
2. VP2 generates the 5 least significant bits of the address to the RAM (PAL20X10): "CHAR", when reading from the RAM; "CURS", when writing into the RAM.
3. VP3 counts 12 dot-lines per 1 character-line and the number of lines in the whole screen (PAL20X10).
4. VP4 generates the 4 most significant bits of the address to the RAM (PAL20X10): "LINES", when reading from the RAM, "SCROL", when writing into the RAM.
5. VP5 generates the baud rate and the composite video signal (PAL20X8).
6. VP6 is a shift register. It loads the ASCII bits in serial form from the RXD line (PAL20X8).
7. VP7 generates the "SAMPLE" pulses, the "READY" signal when a code for a character is in the UART, and detects a false "START" signal (PAL20X10).
8. VP8 controls the RAM (PAL20X10).
9. Monolithic Memories' 6055 is used as a character generator.
10. Hitachi HM6116P: 2048 words x 8 bits high speed static CMOS RAM is used in our design.

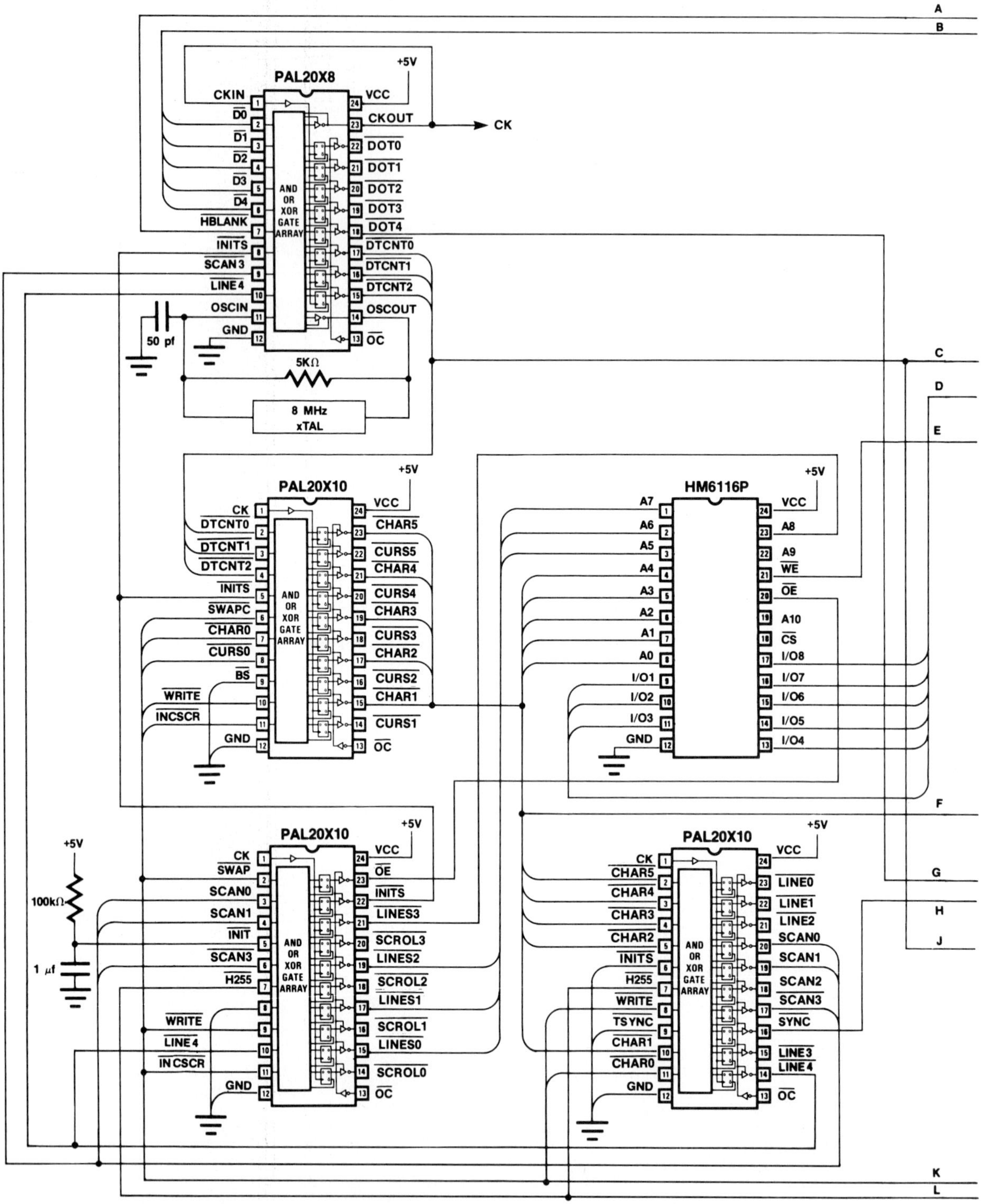
A
B
PAL20X8
+5V
CKIN
D0
D1
D2
D3
D4
HBLANK
INITS
SCAN3
LINE4
OSCIN
GND
VCC
CKOUT
CK
DOT0
DOT1
DOT2
DOT3
DOT4
DTCNT0
DTCNT1
DTCNT2
OSCOUT
OC
AND OR XOR GATE ARRAY
50 pf
5KΩ
8 MHz xTAL
C
D
E
PAL20X10
CK
DTCNT0
DTCNT1
DTCNT2
INITS
SWAPC
CHAR0
CURS0
BS
WRITE
INCSCR
GND
VCC
CHAR5
CURS5
CHAR4
CURS4
CHAR3
CURS3
CHAR2
CURS2
CHAR1
CURS1
OC
HM6116P
A7
A6
A5
A4
A3
A2
A1
A0
I/O1
I/O2
I/O3
GND
VCC
A8
A9
WE
OE
A10
CS
I/O8
I/O7
I/O6
I/O5
I/O4
F
PAL20X10
CK
SWAP
SCAN0
SCAN1
INIT
SCAN3
H255
WRITE
LINE4
INCSCR
GND
VCC
OE
INITS
LINES3
SCROL3
LINES2
SCROL2
LINES1
SCROL1
LINES0
SCROL0
OC
100kΩ
1 μf
PAL20X10
CK
CHAR5
CHAR4
CHAR3
CHAR2
INITS
H255
WRITE
TSYNC
CHAR1
CHAR0
GND
VCC
LINE0
LINE1
LINE2
SCAN0
SCAN1
SCAN2
SCAN3
SYNC
LINE3
LINE4
OC
G
H
J
K
L

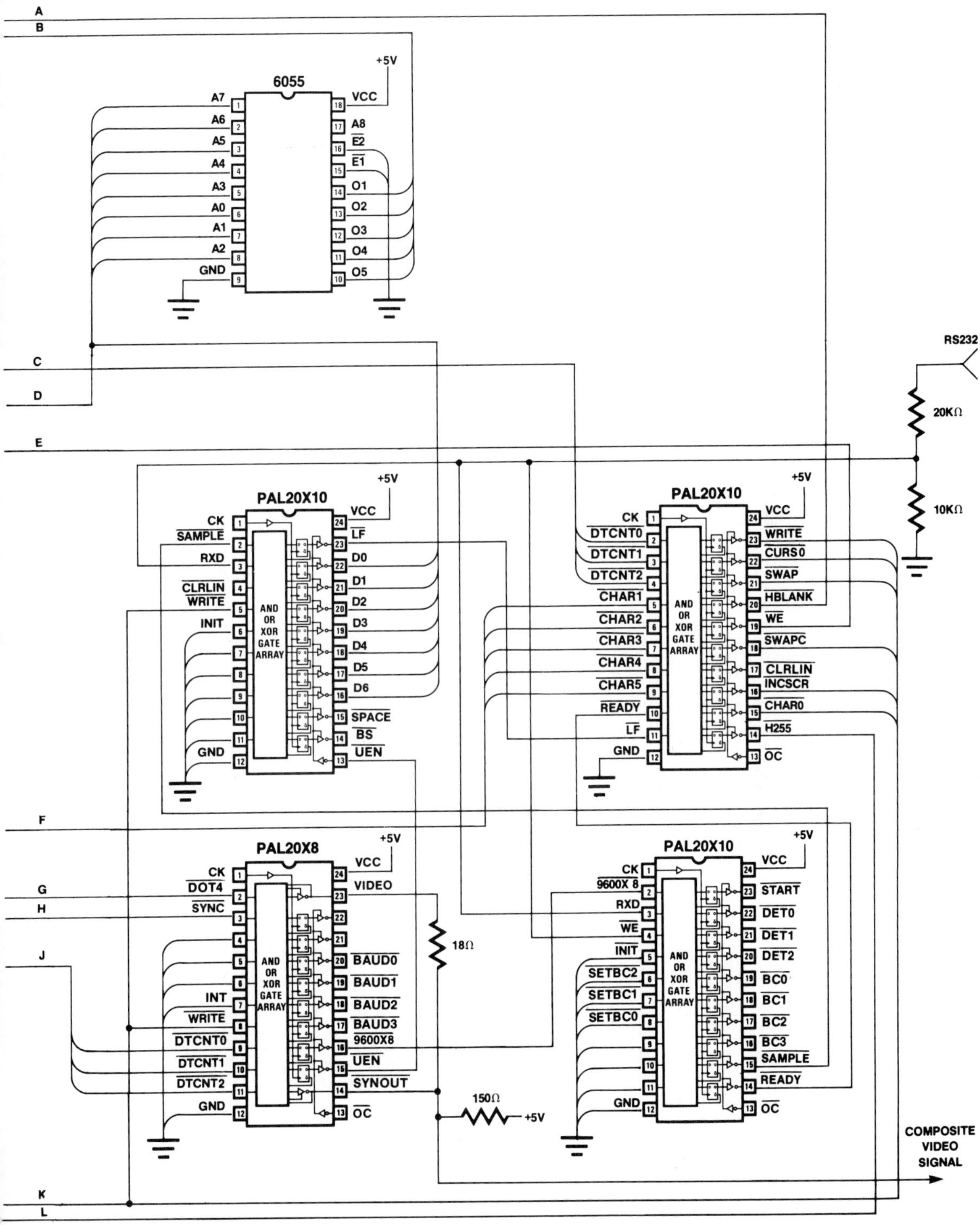
A
B
C
D
E
F
G
H
J
K
L
6055
+5V
A7
A6
A5
A4
A3
A0
A1
A2
GND
VCC
A8
E2
E1
O1
O2
O3
O4
O5
RS232
20KΩ
10KΩ
PAL20X10
CK
SAMPLE
RXD
CLRLIN
WRITE
INIT
GND
AND OR XOR GATE ARRAY
VCC
LF
D0
D1
D2
D3
D4
D5
D6
SPACE
BS
UEN
PAL20X10
CK
DTCNT0
DTCNT1
DTCNT2
CHAR1
CHAR2
CHAR3
CHAR4
CHAR5
READY
LF
GND
AND OR XOR GATE ARRAY
VCC
WRITE
CURS0
SWAP
HBLANK
WE
SWAPC
CLRLIN
INCSCR
CHAR0
H255
OC
PAL20X8
CK
DOT4
SYNC
INT
WRITE
DTCNT0
DTCNT1
DTCNT2
GND
AND OR XOR GATE ARRAY
VCC
VIDEO
BAUD0
BAUD1
BAUD2
BAUD3
9600X8
UEN
SYNOUT
OC
18Ω
150Ω
+5V
PAL20X10
CK
9600X 8
RXD
WE
INIT
SETBC2
SETBC1
SETBC0
GND
AND OR XOR GATE ARRAY
VCC
START
DET0
DET1
DET2
BC0
BC1
BC2
BC3
SAMPLE
READY
OC
COMPOSITE VIDEO SIGNAL

Solder Side

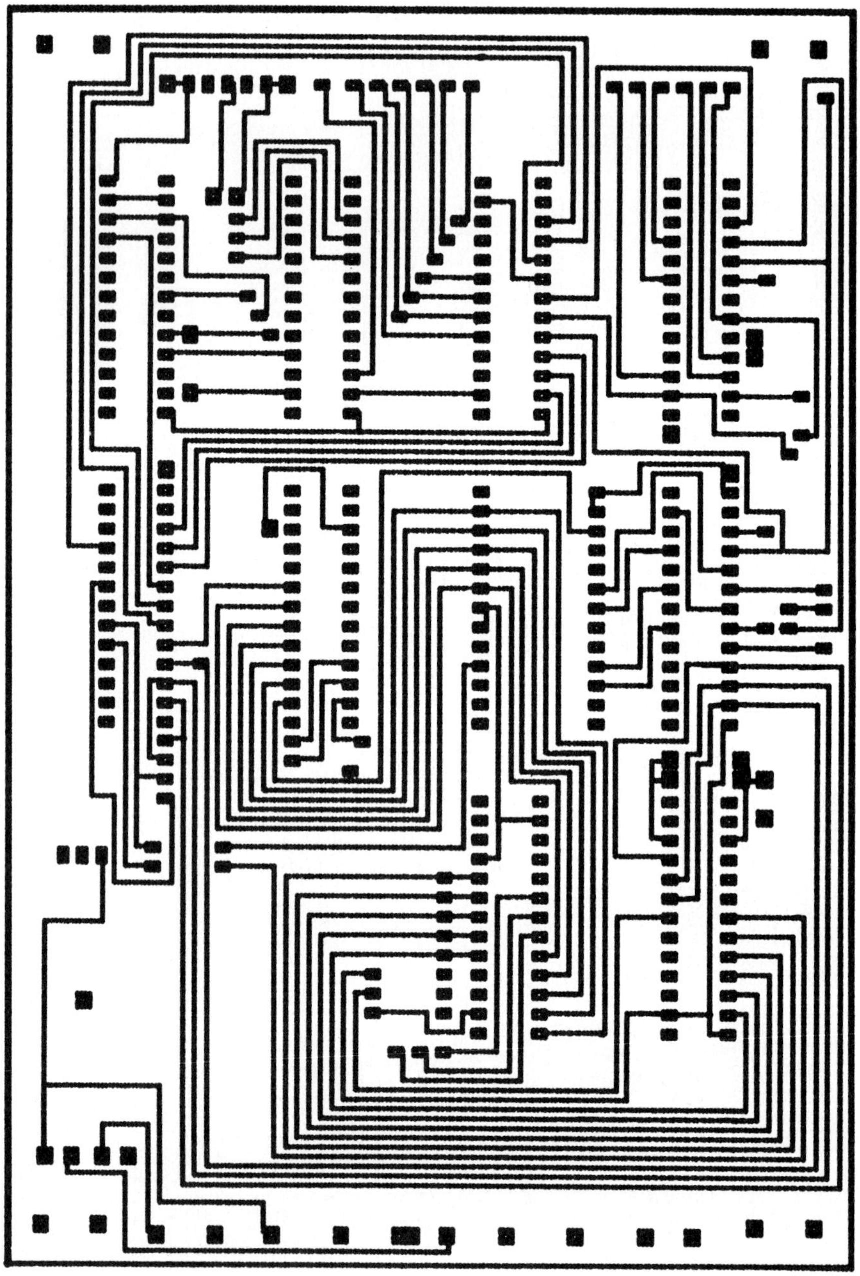

Component Side

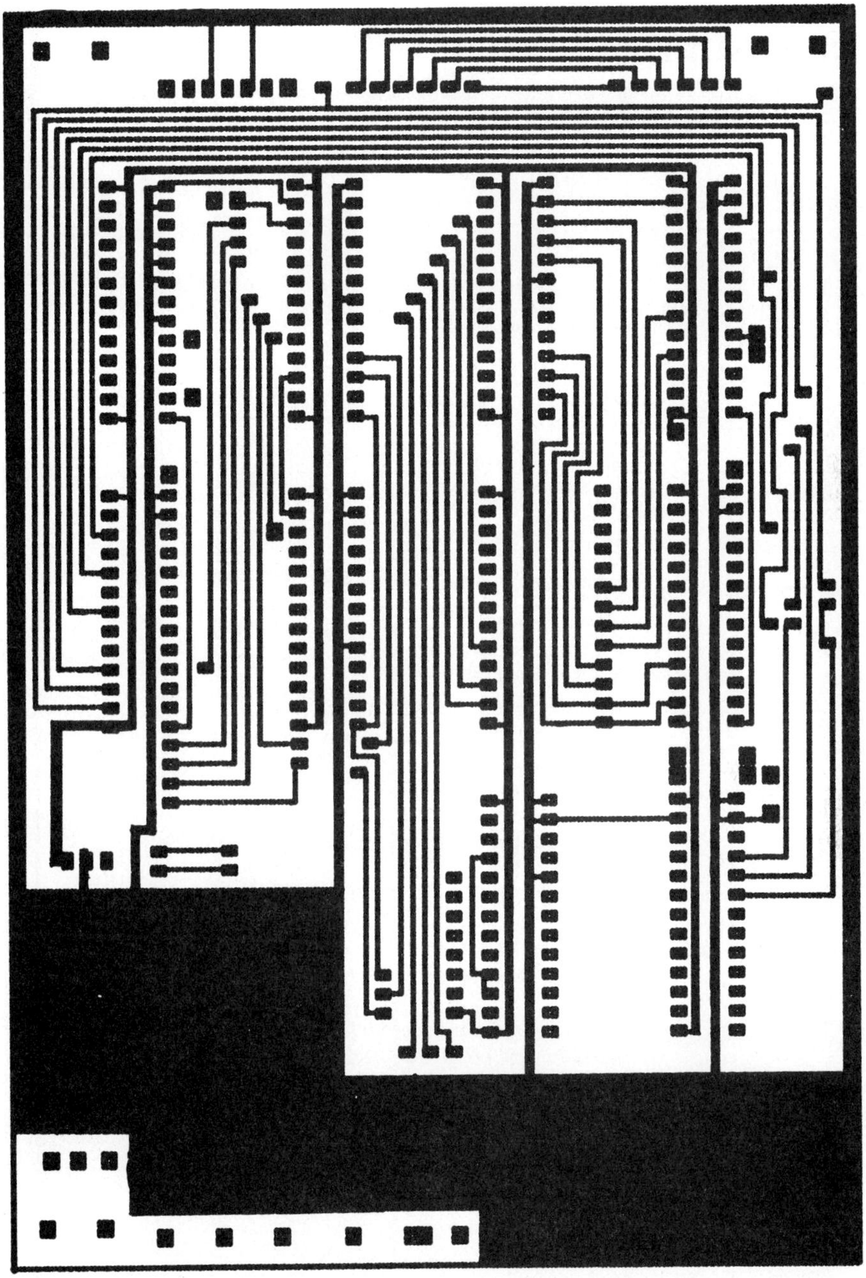

Video Controller Specifications

The Video controller provides a 16 line by 48 character display for use with standard CRT monitors and televisions. The controller "listens" to standard RS232C serial data via a 25 pin DB-25 plug/socket pair inserted into any Computer/Terminal RS232C interface. The controller stores the serial data in a 2Kx8 RAM and continuously displays it on the RS170 composite video output. Eight PALs and one character generator provide the control circuitry, mounted on a 5x7 inch PCB.

lines per frame	16
characters per line	48
character format	5x7
ASCII character set	64 (upper case)
scanning method	non-interlace
scans per frame	260 (312 optional)
scans per line	12
frame period	16.64 milli seconds (19.968 optional)
scan period	64 micro seconds
character period	1 micro second
dot period	125 nano seconds
input specification	RS232C
speed	9600 Baud (4800,2400,1200 optional)
format	7 bits, mark parity, one stop bit
low level	-3 to -12 Volts
high level	+6 to +12 Volts
input impedance	30K Ohm
input connector	25 pin DB-25P/DB-25S
output specification	RS170 (composite video)
sync pulse	4 micro seconds
horizontal blanking	16 micro seconds
sync level	0.4 Volts
black level	0.8 Volts
white level	1.8 Volts
output drive	75 Ohm termination
output connector	RCA Audio Jack
power	12 Watts
input voltage	100-120 Volts AC (200-240 optional)
line frequency	50/60 Hz
card size	5x7x1 inches

Dot Generator

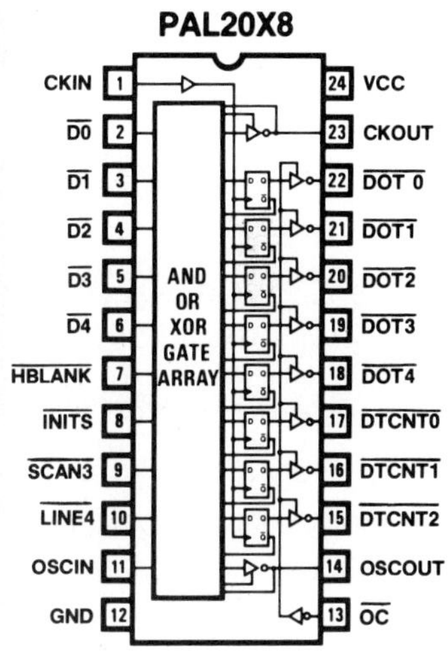

```
PAL20X8                                    PAL DESIGN SPECIFICATION
VP1                                        BIRKNER/KAZMI/UDI 7/7/81
DOT GENERATOR
MMI SUNNYVALE, CALIFORNIA
CKIN /D0 /D1 /D2 /D3 /D4 /HBLANK /INITS /SCAN3 /LINE4 OSCIN GND
/OC OSCOUT /DTCNT2 /DTCNT1 /DTCNT0 /DOT4 /DOT3 /DOT2 /DOT1 /DOT0
CKOUT VCC


IF(VCC) /CKOUT = /OSCOUT

 DOT0    :=  /HBLANK*/LINE4*/SCAN3*DTCNT2*DTCNT1*DTCNT0*D0    ;LOAD

 DOT1    :=  /HBLANK*/LINE4*/SCAN3*DTCNT2*DTCNT1*DTCNT0*D1    ;LOAD
          +  /HBLANK*/LINE4*/SCAN3*/DTCNT2*DOT0               ;SHIFT

 DOT2    :=  /HBLANK*/LINE4*/SCAN3*DTCNT2*DTCNT1*DTCNT0*D2    ;LOAD
          +  /HBLANK*/LINE4*/SCAN3*/DTCNT2*DOT1               ;SHIFT

 DOT3    :=  /HBLANK*/LINE4*/SCAN3*DTCNT2*DTCNT1*DTCNT0*D3    ;LOAD
          +  /HBLANK*/LINE4*/SCAN3*/DTCNT2*DOT2               ;SHIFT

 DOT4    :=  /HBLANK*/LINE4*/SCAN3*DTCNT2*DTCNT1*DTCNT0*D4    ;LOAD
          +  /HBLANK*/LINE4*/SCAN3*/DTCNT2*DOT3               ;SHIFT

 DTCNT0  :=  /INITS*DTCNT0                                    ;HOLD
          +  /INITS*DTCNT0                                    ;EXTEND
        :+:  /INITS                                           ;INC

 DTCNT1  :=  /INITS*DTCNT1                                    ;HOLD
          +  /INITS*DTCNT1                                    ;EXTEND
        :+:  /INITS*DTCNT0                                    ;INC

 DTCNT2  :=  /INITS*DTCNT2                                    ;HOLD
          +  /INITS*DTCNT2                                    ;EXTEND
        :+:  /INITS*DTCNT0*DTCNT1                             ;INC

IF(VCC) /OSCOUT = OSCIN
```

FUNCTION TABLE

```
CKIN D4 D3 D2 D1 D0 HBLANK INITS SCAN3 LINE4 OSCIN /OC OSCOUT DTCNT2
DTCNT1 DTCNT0 DOT4 DOT3 DOT2 DOT1 DOT0 CKOUT

;            H                 O
;            B  I  S  L  O     S                C
; C          L  N  C  I  S     C                K
; K          A  I  A  N  C  /  O                O
; I DATA IN  N  T  N  E  I  O  U  DTCNT   DOT   U
; N D4---D0  K  S  3  4  N  C  T   210   43210  T  COMMENTS
---------------------------------------------------------------------------
  C  XXXXX   X  H  X  X  X  L  X   LLL   XXXXX  X  INITIALIZE DTCNT
  C  XXXXX   X  L  X  X  X  L  X   LLH   XXXXX  X  INC DTCNT
  C  XXXXX   X  L  X  X  X  L  X   LHL   XXXXX  X  INC DTCNT
  C  XXXXX   X  L  X  X  L  L  H   LHH   XXXXX  H  INC DTCNT, OSCILIN = L
  C  XXXXX   X  L  X  X  H  L  L   HLL   XXXXX  L  INC DTCNT, OSCILIN = H
  C  XXXXX   X  L  X  X  X  L  X   HLH   XXXXX  X  INC DTCNT
  C  XXXXX   X  L  X  X  X  L  X   HHL   XXXXX  X  INC DTCNT
  C  XXXXX   X  L  X  X  X  L  X   HHH   XXXXX  X  INC DTCNT
  C  LHLHL   L  L  L  L  X  L  X   LLL   LHLHL  X  DATA IS LOADED
  C  XXXXX   L  L  L  L  X  L  X   LLH   HLHLL  X  OUTPUT TO SCREEN = H
  C  XXXXX   L  L  L  L  X  L  X   LHL   LHLLL  X  OUTPUT TO SCREEN = L
  C  XXXXX   L  L  L  L  X  L  X   LHH   HLLLL  X  OUTPUT TO SCREEN = H
  C  XXXXX   L  L  L  L  X  L  X   HLL   LLLLL  X  OUTPUT TO SCREEN = L
  C  XXXXX   L  L  L  L  X  L  X   HLH   LLLLL  X  SEND BLANK TO SCREEN
  C  XXXXX   L  L  L  L  X  L  X   HHL   LLLLL  X  SEND BLANK TO SCREEN
  C  XXXXX   L  L  L  L  X  L  X   HHH   LLLLL  X  SEND BLANK TO SCREEN
  C  HLHLH   L  L  L  L  X  L  X   LLL   HLHLH  X  NEW DATA IS LOADED
  C  XXXXX   L  L  L  L  X  L  X   LLH   LHLHL  X  OUTPUT TO SCREEN = L
---------------------------------------------------------------------------
```

DESCRIPTION

THE DOT GENERATOR PROVIDES THE OSCILLATOR/CLOCK DRIVER, THE DOT SHIFT REGISTER AND THE 3-BIT DOT COUNTER. IT IS LOADED WITH THE 5 DOTS GENERATED BY THE CHARACTER GENERATOR. THESE DOTS ARE SHIFTED OUT THROUGH A SHIFT REGISTER, ONE DOT AT A TIME AND DISPLAYED ON THE SCREEN. "DTCNT" COUNTS UNTIL 8: 5 COUNTS FOR THE CHARACTER AND 3 COUNTS FOR SPACE BETWEEN CHARACTERS.

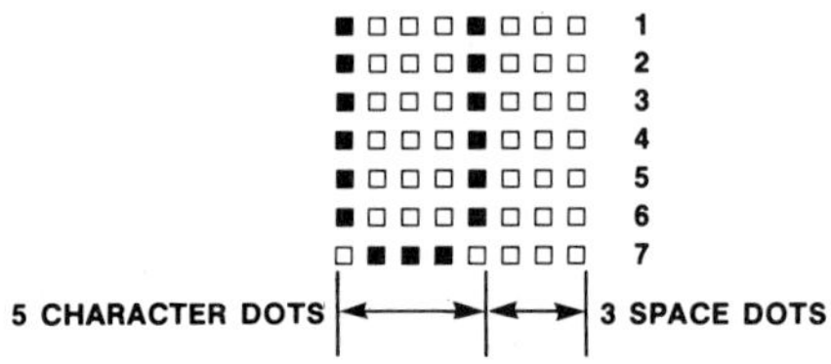

THE 20X8 IS A REGISTERED PAL. DATA SHOULD BE VALID AND STABLE ON THE INPUT PINS ONE CYCLE BEFORE IT APPEARS ON THE OUTPUT PINS. THE REGISTER IS TRIGGERED ON THE RISING EDGE OF THE CLOCK AND THE DATA IS AVAILABLE ON THE OUTPUT PINS DURING THE NEXT CLOCK CYCLE.

"DTCNT" CAN BE INITIALIZED, CAN COUNT AND CAN HOLD.

"HBLANK" IS A SIGNAL FOR THE END OF ONE DOT LINE (48 CHARACTERS).

"LINE4" IS SET WHEN 16 LINES ARE DISPLAYED ON THE SCREEN.

"SCAN3" IS SET WHEN 7 DOT LINES ARE DISPLAYED.

"DOT" IS A SHIFT REGISTER. IT CAN BE LOADED OR CAN SHIFT LEFT.

WHEN "LINE4" AND/OR "SCAN3" ARE SET, "DOT" SENDS BLANK DOTS TO THE SCREEN FOR GENERATING SPACES BETWEEN CHARACTER LINES AND FOR THE MARGINS OF THE SCREEN. THE OUTPUT FROM THE REGISTER TO THE SCREEN IS THROUGH "DOT4".

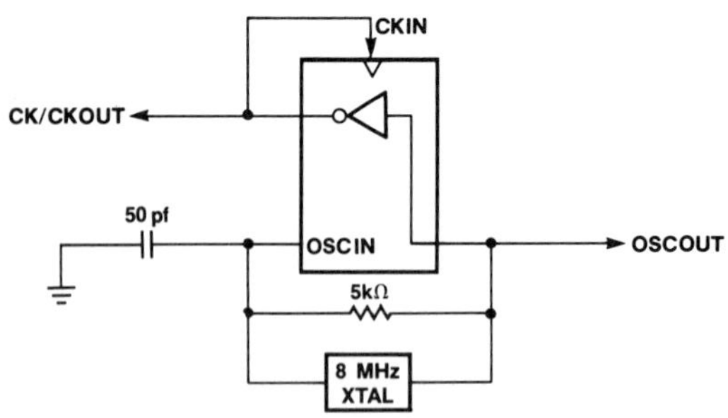

CLOCK GENERATOR

```
DOT GENERATOR

 1 CXXXXXX0XXXX0XHHHXXXXXX1
 2 CXXXXXX1XXXX0XHHLXXXXXX1
 3 CXXXXXX1XXXX0XHLHXXXXXX1
 4 CXXXXXX1XX0X0HHLLXXXXXH1
 5 CXXXXXX1XX1X0LLHHXXXXXL1
 6 CXXXXXX1XXXX0XLHLXXXXXX1
 7 CXXXXXX1XXXX0XLLHXXXXXX1
 8 CXXXXXX1XXXX0XLLLXXXXXX1
 9 C101011111XX0XHHHHLHLHX1
10 CXXXXX1111XX0XHHLLHLHHX1
11 CXXXXX1111XX0XHLHHLHHHX1
12 CXXXXX1111XX0XHLLLHHHHX1
13 CXXXXX1111XX0XLHHHHHHHX1
14 CXXXXX1111XX0XLHLHHHHHX1
15 CXXXXX1111XX0XLLHHHHHHX1
16 CXXXXX1111XX0XLLLHHHHHX1
17 C010101111XX0XHHHLHLHLX1
18 CXXXXX1111XX0XHHLHLHLHX1

PASS SIMULATION
```

DOT GENERATOR

```
                11 1111 1111 2222 2222 2233 3333 3333
   0123 4567 8901 2345 6789 0123 4567 8901 2345 6789

 0 ---- ---- ---- ---- ---- ---- ---- ---- ---- ----
 1 ---- ---- ---- ---- ---- ---- ---- ---- ---- ---X /OSCOUT

 8 -X-- ---- ---- ---- ---- X--- ---X X--X X--X ---- /HBLANK*/LINE4*/SCAN3*D-

16 ---- -X-- ---- ---- ---- X--- ---X X--X X--X ---- /HBLANK*/LINE4*/SCAN3*D-
17 ---- ---X ---- ---- ---- X--- ---- X--- X-X- ---- /HBLANK*/LINE4*/SCAN3*/-

24 ---- ---- -X-- ---- ---- X--- ---X X--X X--X ---- /HBLANK*/LINE4*/SCAN3*D-
25 ---- ---- ---X ---- ---- X--- ---- X--- X-X- ---- /HBLANK*/LINE4*/SCAN3*/-

32 ---- ---- ---- -X-- ---- X--- ---X X--X X--X ---- /HBLANK*/LINE4*/SCAN3*D-
33 ---- ---- ---- ---X ---- X--- ---- X--- X-X- ---- /HBLANK*/LINE4*/SCAN3*/-

40 ---- ---- ---- ---- -X-- X--- ---X X--X X--X ---- /HBLANK*/LINE4*/SCAN3*D-
41 ---- ---- ---- ---- ---X X--- ---- X--- X-X- ---- /HBLANK*/LINE4*/SCAN3*/-

48 ---- ---- ---- ---- ---- ---- X--X ---- ---- ---- /INITS*DTCNT0
49 ---- ---- ---- ---- ---- ---- X--X ---- ---- ---- /INITS*DTCNT0
50 ---- ---- ---- ---- ---- ---- X--- ---- ---- ---- /INITS

56 ---- ---- ---- ---- ---- ---- X--- ---X ---- ---- /INITS*DTCNT1
57 ---- ---- ---- ---- ---- ---- X--- ---X ---- ---- /INITS*DTCNT1
58 ---- ---- ---- ---- ---- ---- X--X ---- ---- ---- /INITS*DTCNT0

64 ---- ---- ---- ---- ---- ---- X--- ---- ---X ---- /INITS*DTCNT2
65 ---- ---- ---- ---- ---- ---- X--- ---- ---X ---- /INITS*DTCNT2
66 ---- ---- ---- ---- ---- ---- X--X ---X ---- ---- /INITS*DTCNT0*DTCNT1

72 ---- ---- ---- ---- ---- ---- ---- ---- ---- ----
73 ---- ---- ---- ---- ---- ---- ---- ---- ---- X--- OSCIN

LEGEND:  X : FUSE NOT BLOWN (L,N,0)   - : FUSE BLOWN   (H,P,1)

NUMBER OF FUSES BLOW =  805
```

Dot Generator

Logic Diagram PAL20X 8

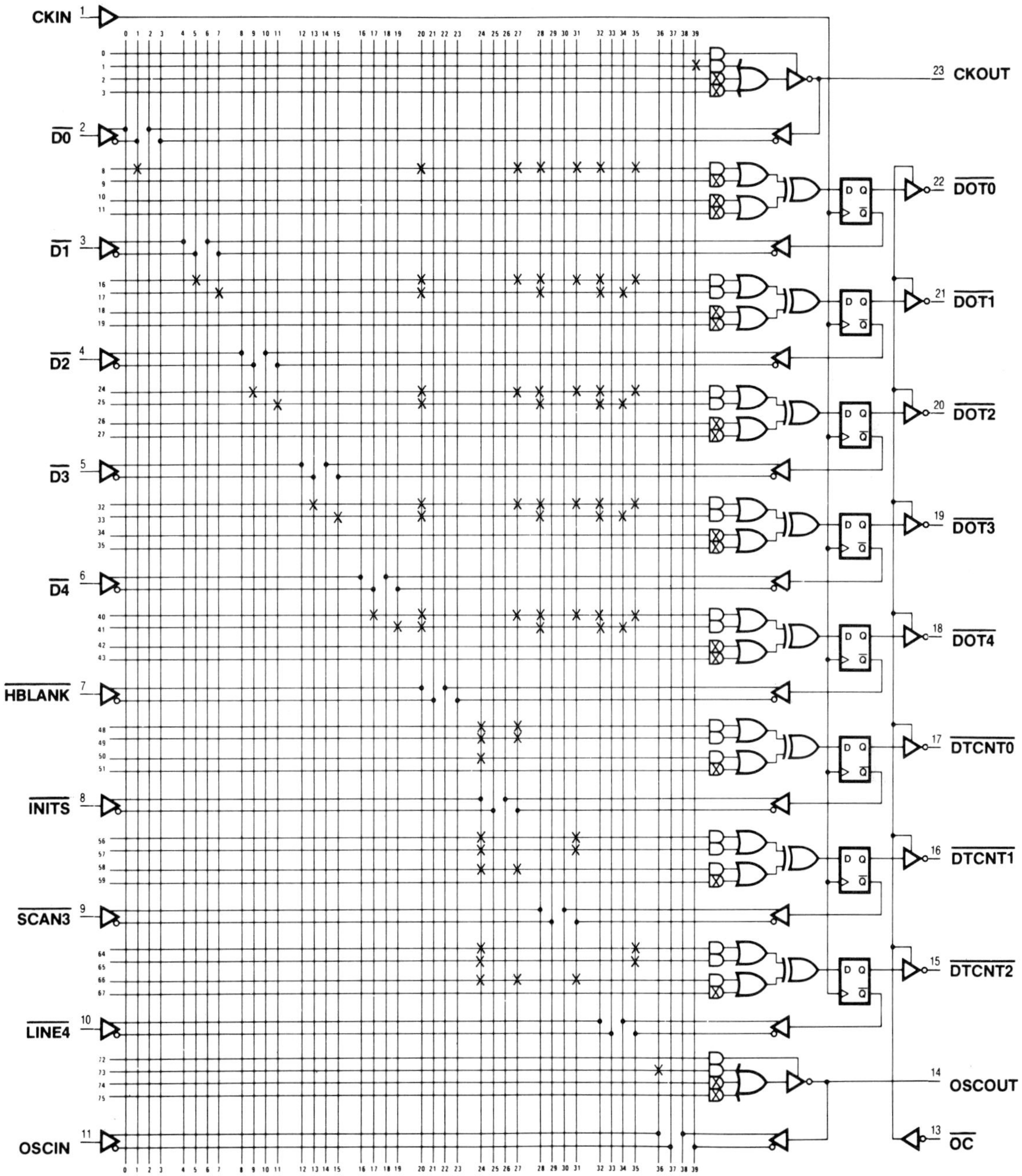

PAL
IMPORTANT,
NOTES

CHAR/CURS Generator

PAL20X10

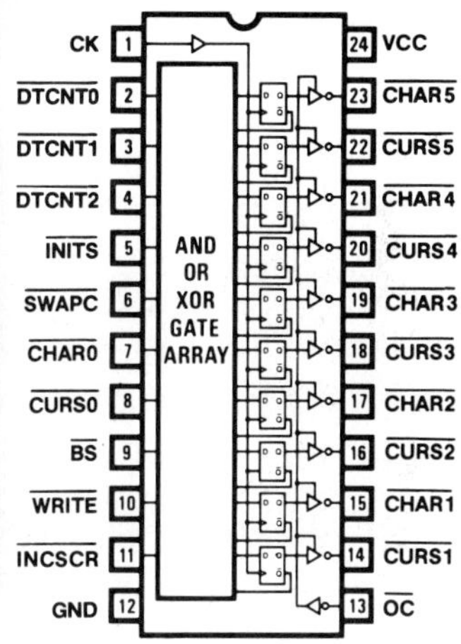

```
PAL20X10                                     PAL DESIGN SPECIFICATION
VP2                                          BIRKNER/KAZMI/UDI 7/9/81
CHAR/CURS GENERATOR
MMI SUNNYVALE, CALIFORNIA
CK /DTCNT0 /DTCNT1 /DTCNT2 /INITS /SWAPC /CHAR0 /CURS0 /BS /WRITE /INCSCR GND
/OC /CURS1 /CHAR1 /CURS2 /CHAR2 /CURS3 /CHAR3 /CURS4 /CHAR4 /CURS5 /CHAR5 VCC

 CHAR1 :=  SWAPC*/INITS*CURS1                            ;SWAP WITH CURS
       + /SWAPC*/INITS*DTCNT0*DTCNT1*DTCNT2*CHAR0        ;INC
      :+:/SWAPC*/INITS*CHAR1                             ;HOLD

 CHAR2 :=  SWAPC*/INITS*CURS2                            ;SWAP WITH CURS
       + /SWAPC*/INITS*DTCNT0*DTCNT1*DTCNT2              ;INC
               * CHAR0*CHAR1
      :+:/SWAPC*/INITS*CHAR2                             ;HOLD

 CHAR3 :=  SWAPC*/INITS*CURS3                            ;SWAP WITH CURS
       + /SWAPC*/INITS*DTCNT0*DTCNT1*DTCNT2              ;INC
               * CHAR0*CHAR1*CHAR2
      :+:/SWAPC*/INITS*CHAR3                             ;HOLD

 CHAR4 :=  SWAPC*/INITS*CURS4                            ;SWAP WITH CURS
       + /SWAPC*/INITS*DTCNT0*DTCNT1*DTCNT2              ;INC
               * CHAR0*CHAR1*CHAR2*CHAR3
      :+:/SWAPC*/INITS*CHAR4                             ;HOLD

 CHAR5 :=  SWAPC*/INITS*CURS5                            ;SWAP WITH CURS
       + /SWAPC*/INITS*DTCNT0*DTCNT1*DTCNT2              ;INC
               * CHAR0*CHAR1*CHAR2*CHAR3*CHAR4
      :+:/SWAPC*/INITS*CHAR5                             ;HOLD

 CURS1 :=  SWAPC*/INITS*/INCSCR*CHAR1                    ;SWAP WITH CHAR
       + /SWAPC*/INITS*/INCSCR*CURS1                     ;HOLD
      :+:/SWAPC*/INITS*/INCSCR                           ;INC
               * WRITE* DTCNT2*DTCNT1*/DTCNT0*CURS0

 CURS2 :=  SWAPC*/INITS*/INCSCR*CHAR2                    ;SWAP WITH CHAR
       + /SWAPC*/INITS*/INCSCR*CURS2                     ;HOLD
      :+:/SWAPC*/INITS*/INCSCR                           ;INC
               * WRITE* DTCNT2*DTCNT1*/DTCNT0
               * CURS0* CURS1

 CURS3 :=  SWAPC*/INITS*/INCSCR*CHAR3                    ;SWAP WITH CHAR
       + /SWAPC*/INITS*/INCSCR*CURS3                     ;HOLD
      :+:/SWAPC*/INITS*/INCSCR                           ;INC
               * WRITE* DTCNT2*DTCNT1*/DTCNT0
               * CURS0* CURS1*CURS2

 CURS4 :=  SWAPC*/INITS*/INCSCR*CHAR4                    ;SWAP WITH CHAR
       + /SWAPC*/INITS*/INCSCR*CURS4                     ;HOLD
      :+:/SWAPC*/INITS*/INCSCR                           ;INC
               * WRITE* DTCNT2*DTCNT1*/DTCNT0
               * CURS0* CURS1*CURS2*CURS3

 CURS5 :=  SWAPC*/INITS*/INCSCR*CHAR5                    ;SWAP WITH CHAR
       + /SWAPC*/INITS*/INCSCR*CURS5                     ;HOLD
      :+:/SWAPC*/INITS*/INCSCR                           ;INC
               * WRITE* DTCNT2*DTCNT1*/DTCNT0
               * CURS0* CURS1*CURS2*CURS3*CURS4
```

```
FUNCTION TABLE

CK     DTCNT2 DTCNT1 DTCNT0 INITS SWAPC BS    WRITE INCSCR /OC    CURS5 CURS4
CURS3 CURS2   CURS1   CURS0   CHAR5 CHAR4 CHAR3 CHAR2 CHAR1   CHAR0

;                              I
;           I  S        W  N
;           N  W        R  C
;           I  A        I  S  /
; C  DTCNT  T  P  B  T  C  O    CURS       CHAR
; K   210   S  C  S  E  R  C   54321 0   54321 0    COMMENTS
------------------------------------------------------------------------------
  C   XXX   H  X  X  X  X  L   LLLLL L   LLLLL L    INITIALIZE CHAR AND CURS
  C   LLL   L  L  X  X  L  L   LLLLL L   LLLLL H    INCREMENT CHAR, HOLD CURS
  C   LLH   L  L  X  X  L  L   LLLLL L   LLLLL H    HOLD CHAR AND CURS
  C   LHL   L  L  X  X  L  L   LLLLL L   LLLLL H    HOLD CHAR AND CURS
  C   LHH   L  L  X  X  L  L   LLLLL L   LLLLL H    HOLD CHAR AND CURS
  C   HLL   L  L  X  X  L  L   LLLLL L   LLLLL H    HOLD CHAR AND CURS
  C   HLH   L  L  X  X  L  L   LLLLL L   LLLLL H    HOLD CHAR AND CURS
  C   HHL   L  L  X  X  L  L   LLLLL L   LLLLL H    HOLD CHAR AND CURS
  C   HHH   L  L  X  X  L  L   LLLLL L   LLLLH H    INCREMENT CHAR
  C   LLL   L  L  X  X  L  L   LLLLL L   LLLLH L    HOLD CHAR AND CURS
  C   LLH   L  L  X  X  L  L   LLLLL L   LLLLH L    HOLD CHAR AND CURS
  C   HHH   L  L  X  X  L  L   LLLLL L   LLLLH L    INCREMENT CHAR
  C   LLL   L  L  X  X  L  L   LLLLL L   LLLLH H    CHAR = 3
  C   LLH   L  L  X  X  L  L   LLLLL L   LLLLH H    HOLD CHAR AND CURS
  C   LHL   L  L  X  X  L  L   LLLLL L   LLLLH H    HOLD CHAR AND CURS
  C   LHH   L  H  X  X  L  L   LLLLH H   LLLLL L    SWAP CHAR AND CURS
  C   HLL   L  L  X  X  L  L   LLLLH H   LLLLL H    SET CHAR0
  C   HHH   L  L  X  X  L  L   LLLLH H   LLLLH H    INCREMENT CHAR TO 3
  C   HHH   L  L  X  X  L  L   LLLLH H   LLLHL H    INCREMENT CHAR, HOLD CURS
  C   LLL   L  L  X  X  L  L   LLLLH H   LLLHL L    CHAR = 4
  C   HHL   L  L  X  L  L  L   LLLLH H   LLLHL L    HOLD CHAR AND CURS
  C   HHH   L  L  X  X  L  L   LLLLH H   LLLHL L    INCREMENT CHAR
  C   LLL   L  L  X  X  L  L   LLLLH H   LLLHL H    CHAR = 5
  C   HHH   L  L  X  X  L  L   LLLLH H   LLLHH H    INCREMENT CHAR
  C   LLL   L  L  X  X  L  L   LLLLH H   LLLHH L    CHAR = 6
  C   LLL   L  L  X  X  L  L   LLLLH H   LLLHH H    CHAR = 7
  C   HHH   L  L  X  X  L  L   LLLLH H   LLHLL H    INCREMENT CHAR
  C   HHH   L  L  X  X  L  L   LLLLH H   LLHLL L    CHAR = 8
  C   HHH   L  L  X  X  L  L   LLLLH H   LLHLH H    INCREMENT CHAR TO 11
  C   LLL   L  L  X  X  L  L   LLLLH H   LLHLH H    CHAR = 11
  C   HHH   L  L  X  X  L  L   LLLLH H   LLHHL H    SET CHAR0, INC CHAR BY 2
  C   HHH   L  L  X  X  L  L   LLLLH H   LLHHH H    CHAR = 15
  C   HHH   L  L  X  X  L  L   LLLLH H   LHLLL H    CHAR = 17
  C   HHL   L  L  X  H  L  L   LLLHL H   LHLLL H    INCREMENT CURS
  C   HHH   L  L  X  X  L  L   LLLHL L   LHLLH H    CHAR = 19, CURS = 4
  C   HHL   L  L  X  H  L  L   LLLHH H   LHLLH H    CURS = 7
  C   HHH   L  L  X  X  L  L   LLLHH H   LHLHL H    CHAR = 21
  C   HHL   L  L  X  H  L  L   LLHLL H   LHLHL H    CURS = 9
  C   HHH   L  L  X  X  L  L   LLHLL H   LHLHH H    CHAR = 23
  C   HHL   L  L  X  H  L  L   LLHLH H   LHLHH H    CURS = 11
  C   HHH   L  L  X  X  L  L   LLHLH H   LHHLL H    CHAR = 25
  C   HHL   L  L  X  H  L  L   LLHHL H   LHHLL H    CURS = 13
```

```
  C   HHH   L  L  X  X  L  L  LLHHL H  LHHLH H   CHAR = 27
  C   HHL   L  L  X  H  L  L  LLHHH H  LHHLH H   CURS = 15
  C   HHH   L  L  X  X  L  L  LLHHH H  LHHHL H   CHAR = 29
  C   HHH   L  L  X  X  L  L  LLHHH H  LHHHH H   CHAR = 31
  C   HHH   L  L  X  X  L  L  LLHHH H  HLLLL H   CHAR = 33
  C   HHH   L  L  X  X  L  L  LLHHH H  HLLLH H   CHAR = 35
  C   HHH   L  L  X  X  L  L  LLHHH H  HLLHL H   CHAR = 37
  C   HHH   L  L  X  X  L  L  LLHHH H  HLLHH H   CHAR = 39
  C   HHH   L  L  X  X  L  L  LLHHH H  HLHLL H   CHAR = 41
  C   HHH   L  L  X  X  L  L  LLHHH H  HLHLH H   CHAR = 43
  C   HHH   L  L  X  X  L  L  LLHHH H  HLHHL H   CHAR = 45
  C   HHH   L  L  X  X  L  L  LLHHH H  HLHHH H   CHAR = 47
  C   HHH   L  L  X  X  L  L  LLHHH H  HHLLL H   CHAR = 49
  C   HHH   L  L  X  X  L  L  LLHHH H  HHLLH H   CHAR = 51
  C   HHH   L  L  X  X  L  L  LLHHH H  HHLHL H   CHAR = 53
  C   HHH   L  L  X  X  L  L  LLHHH H  HHLHH H   CHAR = 55
  C   HHH   L  L  X  X  L  L  LLHHH H  HHHLL H   CHAR = 57
  C   HHH   L  L  X  X  L  L  LLHHH H  HHHLH H   CHAR = 59
  C   HHH   L  L  X  X  L  L  LLHHH H  HHHHL H   CHAR = 61
  C   HHH   L  L  X  X  L  L  LLHHH H  HHHHH H   CHAR = 63
  C   LLL   L  L  X  X  L  L  LLHHH H  HHHHH H   CHAR = 63, DTCNT = 0
  C   LLH   L  L  X  X  L  L  LLHHH H  HHHHH H   CHAR = 63, DTCNT = 1
  C   LHL   L  L  X  X  L  L  LLHHH H  HHHHH H   CHAR = 63, DTCNT = 2
  C   LHH   L  L  X  X  L  L  LLHHH H  HHHHH H   CHAR = 63, DTCNT = 3
  C   HLL   L  L  X  X  L  L  LLHHH H  HHHHH H   CHAR = 63, DTCNT = 4
  C   HLH   L  L  X  X  L  L  LLHHH H  HHHHH H   CHAR = 63, DTCNT = 5
  C   HHL   L  L  X  H  L  L  LHLLL H  HHHHH H   INCREMENT CURS
  C   HHH   L  L  X  X  L  L  LHLLL L  LLLLL H   CURS = 14, INCREMENT CHAR
  C   HHH   L  L  X  X  L  L  LHLLL L  LLLLL L   CURS = 14, CHAR = 0
-------------------------------------------------------------------------
```

DESCRIPTION

"CHAR" AND "CURS" COUNT THE NUMBER OF CHARACTERS PER LINE. THEY ARE ALSO USED AS POINTERS TO THE RAM. "CURS" IS USED WHEN A CHARACTER IS WRITTEN INTO THE RAM AND "CHAR" WHEN A CHARACTER IS READ FROM THE RAM. "CURS" IS ALWAYS POINTED TO THE NEXT AVAILABLE LOCATION IN THE RAM WHERE A NEW CHARACTER CAN BE STORED.

"CHAR" IS INCREMENTED AT THE END OF 8 PIXELS MEANING IT COUNTS AFTER EACH CHARACTER. IT COUNTS FROM 0 TO 63 ALTHOUGH ONLY 48 CHARACTERS ARE VISIBLE. THE HORIZONTAL SYNC PULSE IS GIVEN BETWEEN CHARACTERS 56 AND 59. DURING THE COUNTS OF CHAR FROM 48 TO 63, BLACK SIGNALS ARE TRANSMITTED TO THE SCREEN. "CURS" IS INCREMENTED FOR ANY OPERATION ON THE KEY BOARD. THE TWO POINTERS USE THE RAM IN INTERLIVED FASHION. READ IS DONE EVERY CYCLE, BUT WRITE IS DONE ONLY WHEN A WRITE SIGNAL IS GIVEN. THE WRITE SIGNAL IS SET WHEN A NEW CHARACTER ENTERS THE SYSTEM THROUGH THE RS232 PORT.

THE FUNCTION TABLE ABOVE DESCRIBES OPERATIONS OF READ AND WRITE FOR A CERTAIN LINE. WHEN THIS LINE WAS PRINTED, 64 CHARACTERS WERE READ AND 15 CHARACTERS WERE WRITTEN.

SIGNALS CHAR0, CURS0, SWAPC, WRITE AND INCSCR ARE DERIVED IN PAL VP8.

CHAR/CURS GENERATOR

```
 1 CXXX0X11XXXX0HHHHHHHHHH1
 2 C1111101XX1X0HHHHHHHHHH1
 3 C0111101XX1X0HHHHHHHHHH1
 4 C1011101XX1X0HHHHHHHHHH1
 5 C0011101XX1X0HHHHHHHHHH1
 6 C1101101XX1X0HHHHHHHHHH1
 7 C0101101XX1X0HHHHHHHHHH1
 8 C1001101XX1X0HHHHHHHHHH1
 9 C0001101XX1X0HLHHHHHHHH1
10 C1111111XX1X0HLHHHHHHHH1
11 C0111111XX1X0HLHHHHHHHH1
12 C0001111XX1X0HLHHHHHHHH1
13 C1111101XX1X0HLHHHHHHHH1
14 C0111101XX1X0HLHHHHHHHH1
15 C1011101XX1X0HLHHHHHHHH1
16 C0011010XX1X0LHHHHHHHHH1
17 C1101100XX1X0LHHHHHHHHH1
18 C0001100XX1X0LLHHHHHHHH1
19 C0001100XX1X0LHHLHHHHHH1
20 C1111110XX1X0LHHLHHHHHH1
21 C1001110X11X0LHHLHHHHHH1
22 C0001110XX1X0LHHLHHHHHH1
23 C1111100XX1X0LHHLHHHHHH1
24 C0001100XX1X0LLHLHHHHHH1
25 C1111110XX1X0LLHLHHHHHH1
26 C1111100XX1X0LLHLHHHHHH1
27 C0001100XX1X0LHHHHLHHHH1
28 C0001110XX1X0LHHHHLHHHH1
29 C0001100XX1X0LLHHHLHHHH1
30 C1111100XX1X0LLHHHLHHHH1
31 C0001100XX1X0LHHLHLHHHH1
32 C0001100XX1X0LLHLHLHHHH1
33 C0001100XX1X0LHHHHHHLHH1
34 C1001100X01X0HHLHHHHLHH1
35 C0001101XX1X0HLLHHHHLHH1
36 C1001100X01X0LLLHHHHLHH1
37 C0001100XX1X0LHLLHHHLHH1
38 C1001100X01X0HHHLLHHLHH1
39 C0001100XX1X0HLHLLHHLHH1
40 C1001100X01X0LLHLLHHLHH1
41 C0001100XX1X0LHHHLLHLHH1
42 C1001100X01X0HHLHLLHLHH1
43 C0001100XX1X0HLLHLLHLHH1
44 C1001100X01X0LLLHLLHLHH1
45 C0001100XX1X0LHLLLLHLHH1
46 C0001100XX1X0LLLLLLHLHH1
47 C0001100XX1X0LHLHLHHHHL1
48 C0001100XX1X0LLLHLHHHHL1
49 C0001100XX1X0LHLLLHHHHL1
50 C0001100XX1X0LLLLLHHHHL1
51 C0001100XX1X0LHLHLLHHHL1
52 C0001100XX1X0LLLHLLHHHL1
53 C0001100XX1X0LHLLLLHHHL1
54 C0001100XX1X0LLLLLLHHHL1
55 C0001100XX1X0LHLHLHHLHL1
56 C0001100XX1X0LLLHLHHLHL1
57 C0001100XX1X0LHLLLHHLHL1
58 C0001100XX1X0LLLLLHHLHL1
59 C0001100XX1X0LHLHLLHLHL1
60 C0001100XX1X0LLLHLLHLHL1
61 C0001100XX1X0LHLLLLHLHL1
62 C0001100XX1X0LLLLLLHLHL1
63 C1111100XX1X0LLLLLLHLHL1
64 C0111100XX1X0LLLLLLHLHL1
65 C1011100XX1X0LLLLLLHLHL1
66 C0011100XX1X0LLLLLLHLHL1
67 C1101100XX1X0LLLLLLHLHL1
68 C0101100XX1X0LLLLLLHLHL1
69 C1001100X01X0HLHLHLLLHL1
70 C0001101XX1X0HHHHHHLHHH1
71 C0001111XX1X0HHHHHHLHHH1
```

PASS SIMULATION

CHAR/CURS GENERATOR

```
                11 1111 1111 2222 2222 2233 3333 3333
   0123 4567 8901 2345 6789 0123 4567 8901 2345 6789

 0 ---- ---X ---- X--- -X-- ---- ---- ---- ---- ---- SWAPC*/INITS*CURS5
 1 -X-- -X-- -X-X X--- X--X -X-- ---X ---- ---X ---- /SWAPC*/INITS*DTCNT0*DT-
 2 ---X ---- ---- X--- X--- ---- ---- ---- ---- ---- /SWAPC*/INITS*CHAR5

 8 ---X ---- ---- X--- -X-- ---- ---- ---- ---- X--- SWAPC*/INITS*/INCSCR*CH-
 9 ---- ---X ---- X--- X--- ---- ---- ---- ---- X--- /SWAPC*/INITS*/INCSCR*C-
10 X--- -X-- -X-- X--X X--- ---X -X-- ---X -X-- X--X /SWAPC*/INITS*/INCSCR*W-

16 ---- ---- ---- X--X -X-- ---- ---- ---- ---- ---- SWAPC*/INITS*CURS4
17 -X-- -X-- -X-- X--- X--X -X-- ---X ---- ---X ---- /SWAPC*/INITS*DTCNT0*DT-
18 ---- ---- ---X X--- X--- ---- ---- ---- ---- ---- /SWAPC*/INITS*CHAR4

24 ---- ---- ---X X--- -X-- ---- ---- ---- ---- X--- SWAPC*/INITS*/INCSCR*CH-
25 ---- ---- ---- X--X X--- ---- ---- ---- ---- X--- /SWAPC*/INITS*/INCSCR*C-
26 X--- -X-- -X-- X--- X--- ---X -X-- ---X -X-- X--X /SWAPC*/INITS*/INCSCR*W-

32 ---- ---- ---- X--- -X-- ---X ---- ---- ---- ---- SWAPC*/INITS*CURS3
33 -X-- -X-- -X-- X--- X--- -X-- ---X ---- ---X ---- /SWAPC*/INITS*DTCNT0*DT-
34 ---- ---- ---- X--- X--X ---- ---- ---- ---- ---- /SWAPC*/INITS*CHAR3

40 ---- ---- ---- X--- -X-X ---- ---- ---- ---- X--- SWAPC*/INITS*/INCSCR*CH-
41 ---- ---- ---- X--- X--- ---X ---- ---- ---- X--- /SWAPC*/INITS*/INCSCR*C-
42 X--- -X-- -X-- X--- X--- ---- -X-- ---X -X-- X--X /SWAPC*/INITS*/INCSCR*W-

48 ---- ---- ---- X--- -X-- ---- ---- ---X ---- ---- SWAPC*/INITS*CURS2
49 -X-- -X-- -X-- X--- X--- -X-- ---- ---- ---X ---- /SWAPC*/INITS*DTCNT0*DT-
50 ---- ---- ---- X--- X--- ---- ---X ---- ---- ---- /SWAPC*/INITS*CHAR2

56 ---- ---- ---- X--- -X-- ---- ---X ---- ---- X--- SWAPC*/INITS*/INCSCR*CH-
57 ---- ---- ---- X--- X--- ---- ---- ---X ---- X--- /SWAPC*/INITS*/INCSCR*C-
58 X--- -X-- -X-- X--- X--- ---- -X-- ---- -X-- X--X /SWAPC*/INITS*/INCSCR*W-

64 ---- ---- ---- X--- -X-- ---- ---- ---- ---- ---X SWAPC*/INITS*CURS1
65 -X-- -X-- -X-- X--- X--- -X-- ---- ---- ---- ---- /SWAPC*/INITS*DTCNT0*DT-
66 ---- ---- ---- X--- X--- ---- ---- ---- ---X ---- /SWAPC*/INITS*CHAR1

72 ---- ---- ---- X--- -X-- ---- ---- ---- ---X X--- SWAPC*/INITS*/INCSCR*CH-
73 ---- ---- ---- X--- X--- ---- ---- ---- ---- X--X /SWAPC*/INITS*/INCSCR*C-
74 X--- -X-- -X-- X--- X--- ---- -X-- ---- -X-- X--- /SWAPC*/INITS*/INCSCR*W-

LEGEND:  X : FUSE NOT BLOWN (L,N,0)   - : FUSE BLOWN   (H,P,1)

NUMBER OF FUSES BLOW = 1040
```

CHAR/CURS Generator

Logic Diagram PAL20X10

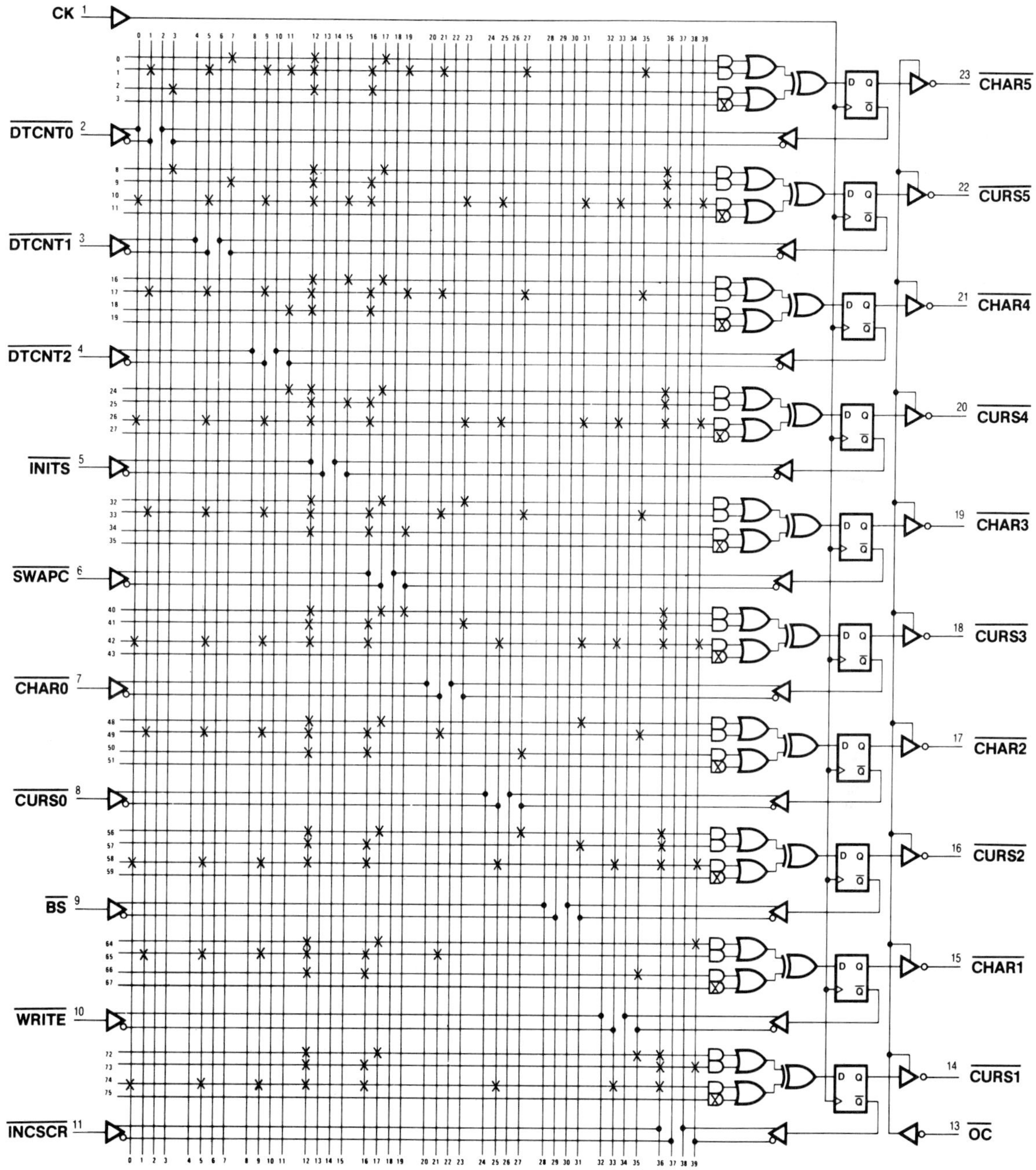

PAL
IMPORTANT, NOTES

SCAN/LINE Generator

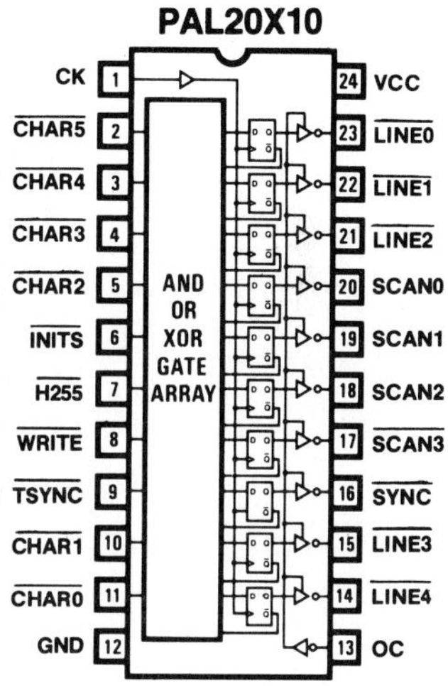

```
PAL20X10                                          PAL DESIGN SPECIFICATION
VP3                                               BIRKNER/UDI      7/13/81
SCAN/LINE GENERATOR
MMI SUNNYVALE, CALIFORNIA
 CK /CHAR5 /CHAR4 /CHAR3 /CHAR2 /INITS /H255 /WRITE /TSYNC /CHAR1 /CHAR0 GND
/OC /LINE4 /LINE3 /SYNC /SCAN3  SCAN2  SCAN1  SCAN0 /LINE2 /LINE1 /LINE0 VCC


/SCAN0   :=  INITS                                    ;INITIALIZE
          + /INITS*/SCAN0                             ;HOLD
         :+:/INITS*H255                               ;INCREMENT

/SCAN1   :=  INITS                                    ;INITIALIZE
          + /INITS*/SCAN1                             ;HOLD
         :+:/INITS*H255*SCAN0                         ;INCREMENT

/SCAN2   :=  INITS                                    ;INITIALIZE
          + /INITS*/SCAN2                             ;HOLD
         :+:/INITS*H255*SCAN0*SCAN1*/SCAN3            ;INC IN MODULUS 12

 SCAN3   := /INITS*SCAN3                              ;HOLD
          + /INITS*H255*LINE4*LINE2*LINE0             ;DETECT SCAN LINE 260
                 *SCAN2*SCAN1*SCAN0                   ;FOR VERTICAL RETRACE
         :+:/INITS*H255*SCAN0*SCAN1*SCAN2             ;INCREMENT
          + /INITS*H255*SCAN3*SCAN1*SCAN0             ;MODULE 12 CORRECTION
                                                      ;INITIAL WHEN INITS=H
LINE0    := /INITS*LINE0                              ;HOLD
          + /TSYNC                                    ;TEST SYNC
         :+:/INITS*H255*SCAN3*SCAN1*SCAN0             ;INCREMENT
          + /INITS*H255*LINE4*LINE2*LINE0             ;DETECT LINE 21 7/12
                 *SCAN2*SCAN1*SCAN0                   ;FOR VERTICAL RETRACE

LINE1    := /INITS*LINE1                              ;HOLD
          + /TSYNC                                    ;TEST SYNC
         :+:/INITS*H255*SCAN3*SCAN1*SCAN0*LINE0       ;INCREMENT

LINE2    := /INITS*LINE2                              ;HOLD
          + /INITS*LINE2                              ;EXTEND
         :+:/INITS*H255*SCAN3*SCAN1*SCAN0*LINE0*LINE1 ;INCREMENT
          + /INITS*H255*LINE4*LINE2*LINE0             ;DETECT LINE 21 7/12
                 *SCAN2*SCAN1*SCAN0                   ;FOR VERTICAL RETRACE

LINE3    := /INITS*LINE3                              ;HOLD
          + /INITS*LINE3                              ;EXTEND
         :+:/INITS*H255*SCAN3*SCAN1*SCAN0             ;INCREMENT
                 *LINE2*LINE1*LINE0

LINE4    := /INITS*LINE4                              ;HOLD
          + /TSYNC                                    ;TEST SYNC
         :+:/INITS*H255*SCAN3*SCAN1*SCAN0             ;INCREMENT
                 *LINE3*LINE2*LINE1*LINE0
          + /INITS*H255*LINE4*LINE2*LINE0             ;DETECT LINE 21 7/12
                 *SCAN2*SCAN1*SCAN0                   ;FOR VERTICAL RETRACE

 SYNC    :=   CHAR5*CHAR4*/CHAR3*CHAR2*/WRITE           ;CHAR 52-55 HORIZ SYNC
          +   LINE0*LINE1*/LINE2*LINE4*/SCAN2*/SCAN3*SYNC;VERTICAL SYNC
         :+:  LINE0*LINE1*/LINE2*LINE4*/SCAN2*/SCAN3*SYNC;WHEN LINE=19 SCAN 0-3
              *CHAR5*CHAR4*/CHAR3*/CHAR2                ;AND CHAR 48-51
```

Vertical Sync

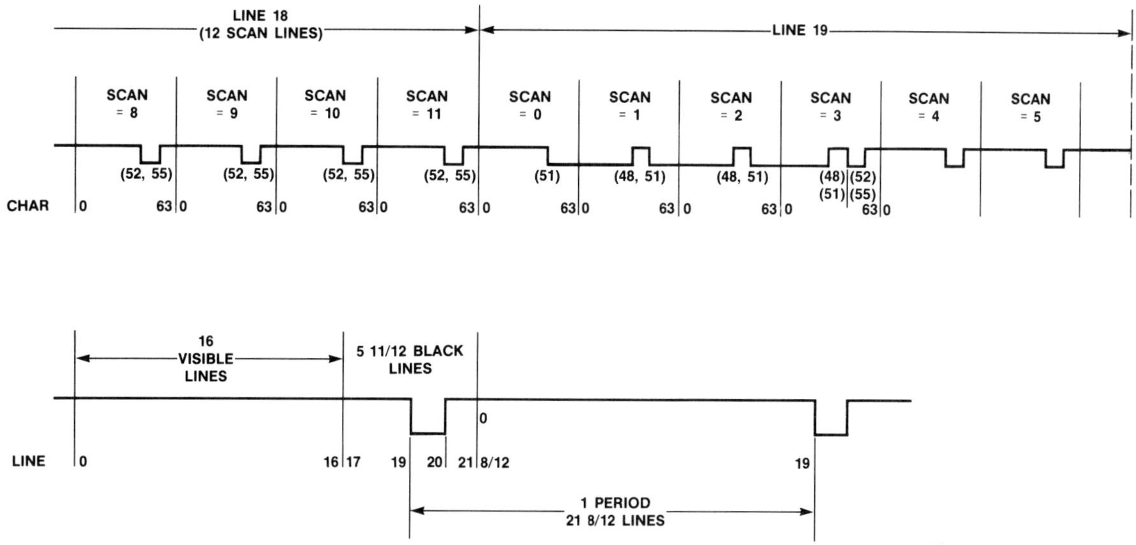

12 dot-lines generate one-character line. The total number of scanned lines is 260 or 21 8/12 character-lines. Out of the 21 8/12 character lines only 16 lines are visible. The vertical sync pulse is asserted during Line 19.

Horizontal Sync

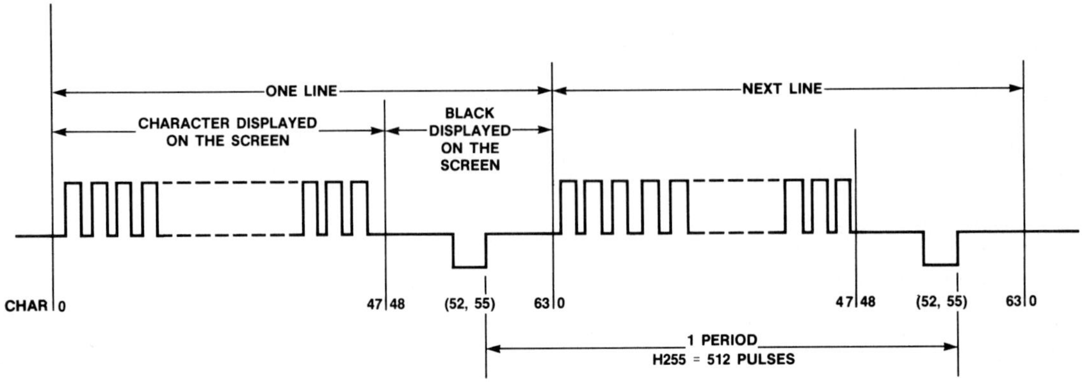

One character is represented in 8 pulses. Then the 512 pulses cause "CHAR" to count from 0 to 63. Out of the 64 characters only 48 characters are visible on the screen. The horizontal sync pulse is asserted during "CHAR" position 52 through and including "CHAR" 55.

```
SCAN/LINE GENERATOR

 1 CXXXX0XX0XXX0HHXHLLLHHH1
 2 CXXXX10X0XXX0HHXHLLHHHH1
 3 CXXXX10X0XXX0HHXHLHLHHH1
 4 CXXXX10X0XXX0HHXHLHHHHH1
 5 CXXXX10X0XXX0HHXHHLLHHH1
 6 CXXXX10X0XXX0HHXHHLHHHH1
 7 CXXXX10X0XXX0HHXHHHLHHH1
 8 CXXXX10X0XXX0HHXHHHHHHH1
 9 CXXXX10X0XXX0HHXLLLLHHH1
10 CXXXX10X0XXX0HHXLLLHHHH1
11 CXXXX10X0XXX0HHXLLHLHHH1
12 CXXXX10X0XXX0HHXLLHHHHH1
13 CXXXX10X0XXX0HHXHLLLHHL1
14 CXXXX10X0XXX0HHXHLLHHHL1
15 CXXXX10X0XXX0HHXHLHLHHL1
16 CXXXX10X0XXX0HHXHLHHHHL1
17 CXXXX0XX0XXX0HHXHLLLHHH1
18 C001111X1XXX0LHHHLLLHLL1
19 C001110X0XXX0LHHHLLHHLL1
20 C001110X0XXX0LHHHLHLHLL1
21 C001110X0XXX0LHHHLHHHLL1
22 C001110X0XXX0LHHHHLLHLL1
23 C001110X0XXX0LHHHHLHHLL1
24 C00101110XXX0XXLXXXXXXX1

PASS SIMULATION
```

SCAN/LINE GENERATOR

```
                 11 1111 1111 2222 2222 2233 3333 3333
   0123 4567 8901 2345 6789 0123 4567 8901 2345 6789

 0 ---X ---- ---- ---- X--- ---- ---- ---- ---- ---- /INITS*LINE0
 1 ---- ---- ---- ---- ---- ---- ---- X--- ---- ---- /TSYNC
 2 ---- ---- ---- --X- X-X- -X-- ---X ---- ---- ---- /INITS*H255*SCAN3*SCAN1-
 3 ---X ---- ---X --X- X-X- -XX- ---- ---- ---- ---X /INITS*H255*LINE4*LINE2-

 8 ---- ---X ---- ---- X--- ---- ---- ---- ---- ---- /INITS*LINE1
 9 ---- ---- ---- ---- ---- ---- ---- X--- ---- ---- /TSYNC
10 ---X ---- ---- --X- X-X- -X-- ---X ---- ---- ---- /INITS*H255*SCAN3*SCAN1-

16 ---- ---- ---X ---- X--- ---- ---- ---- ---- ---- /INITS*LINE2
17 ---- ---- ---X ---- X--- ---- ---- ---- ---- ---- /INITS*LINE2
18 ---X ---X ---- --X- X-X- -X-- ---X ---- ---- ---- /INITS*H255*SCAN3*SCAN1-
19 ---X ---- ---X --X- X-X- -XX- ---- ---- ---- ---X /INITS*H255*LINE4*LINE2-

24 ---- ---- ---- ---- -X-- ---- ---- ---- ---- ---- INITS
25 ---- ---- ---- ---X X--- ---- ---- ---- ---- ---- /INITS*/SCAN0
26 ---- ---- ---- ---- X--- -X-- ---- ---- ---- ---- /INITS*H255

32 ---- ---- ---- ---- -X-- ---- ---- ---- ---- ---- INITS
33 ---- ---- ---- ---- X--X ---- ---- ---- ---- ---- /INITS*/SCAN1
34 ---- ---- ---- --X- X--- -X-- ---- ---- ---- ---- /INITS*H255*SCAN0

40 ---- ---- ---- ---- -X-- ---- ---- ---- ---- ---- INITS
41 ---- ---- ---- ---- X--- ---X ---- ---- ---- ---- /INITS*/SCAN2
42 ---- ---- ---- --X- X-X- -X-- --X- ---- ---- ---- /INITS*H255*SCAN0*SCAN1-

48 ---- ---- ---- ---- X--- ---- ---X ---- ---- ---- /INITS*SCAN3
49 ---X ---- ---X --X- X-X- -XX- ---- ---- ---- ---X /INITS*H255*LINE4*LINE2-
50 ---- ---- ---- --X- X-X- -XX- ---- ---- ---- ---- /INITS*H255*SCAN0*SCAN1-
51 ---- ---- ---- --X- X-X- -X-- ---X ---- ---- ---- /INITS*H255*SCAN3*SCAN1-

56 -X-- -X-- X--- -X-- ---- ---- X--- ---- ---- ---- CHAR5*CHAR4*/CHAR3*CHAR-
57 ---X ---X --X- ---- ---- ---X --X- ---X ---- ---X LINE0*LINE1*/LINE2*LINE-
58 -X-X -X-X X-X- X--- ---- ---X --X- ---X ---- ---X LINE0*LINE1*/LINE2*LINE-

64 ---- ---- ---- ---- X--- ---- ---- ---- ---X ---- /INITS*LINE3
65 ---- ---- ---- ---- X--- ---- ---- ---- ---X ---- /INITS*LINE3
66 ---X ---X ---X --X- X-X- -X-- ---X ---- ---- ---- /INITS*H255*SCAN3*SCAN1-

72 ---- ---- ---- ---- X--- ---- ---- ---- ---- ---X /INITS*LINE4
73 ---- ---- ---- ---- ---- ---- ---- X--- ---- ---- /TSYNC
74 ---X ---X ---X --X- X-X- -X-- ---X ---- ---X ---- /INITS*H255*SCAN3*SCAN1-
75 ---X ---- ---X --X- X-X- -XX- ---- ---- ---- ---X /INITS*H255*LINE4*LINE2-
```

LEGEND: X : FUSE NOT BLOWN (L,N,0) - : FUSE BLOWN (H,P,1)

NUMBER OF FUSES BLOW = 1222

SCAN/LINE Generator

Logic Diagram PAL20X10

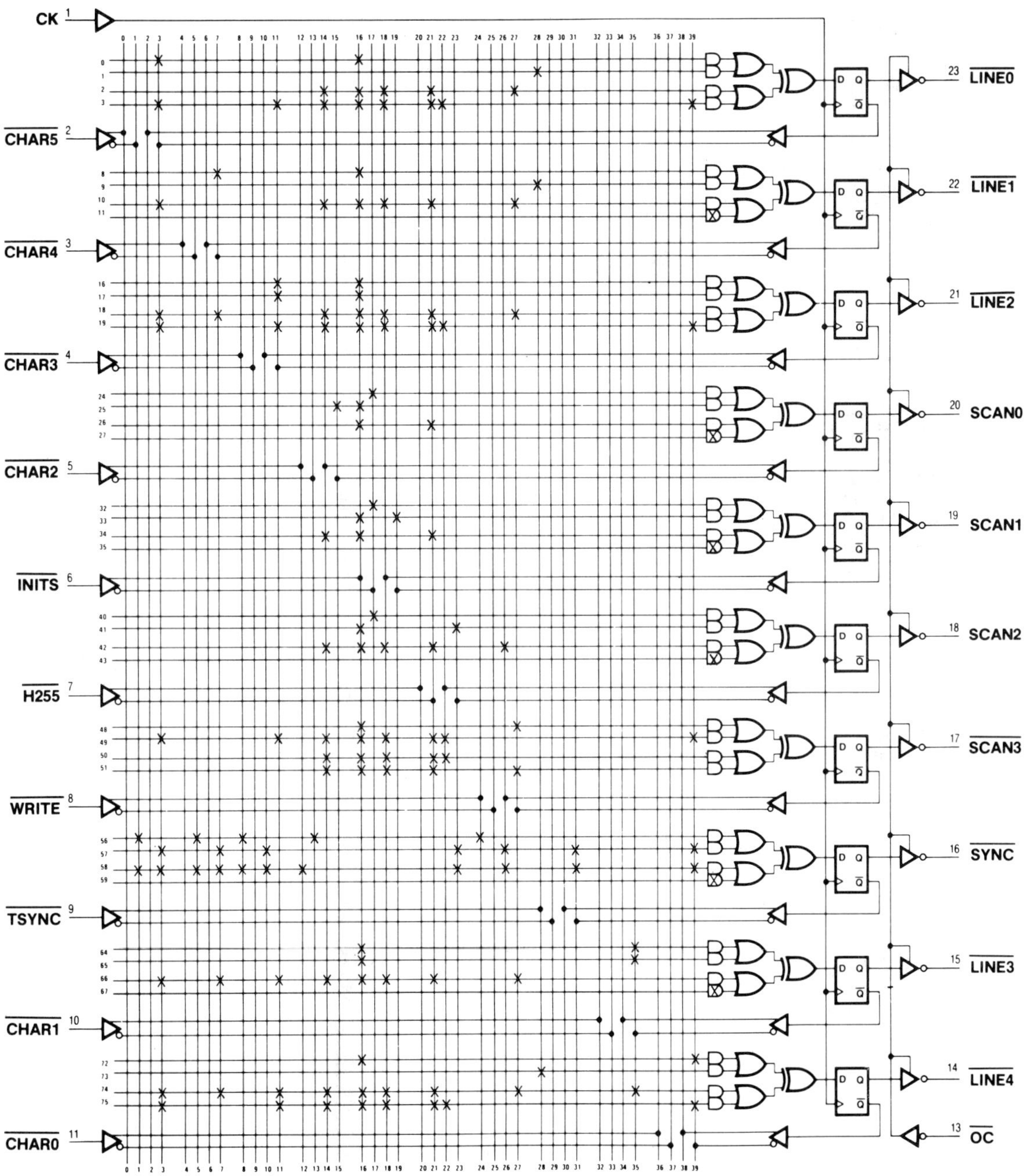

PAL
IMPORTANT
NOTES

LINES/SCROL Generator

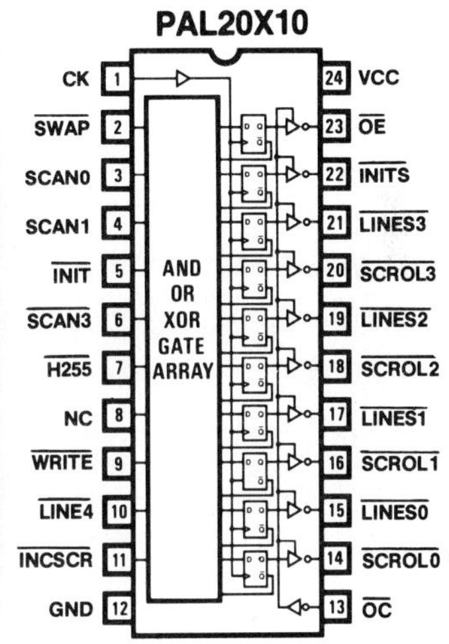

```
PAL20X10                                      PAL DESIGN SPECIFICATION
VP4                                           BIRKNER/UDI      7/14/81
LINES/SCROL GENERATOR
MMI SUNNYVALE, CALIFORNIA
 CK /SWAP    SCAN0   SCAN1  /INIT   /SCAN3   /H255   NC     /WRITE  /LINE4
/INCSCR GND /OC     /SCROL0 /LINES0 /SCROL1 /LINES1 /SCROL2 /LINES2 /SCROL3
/LINES3 /INITS /OE  VCC

LINES0  :=  /SWAP*/INITS*LINES0                  ;HOLD
         +   SWAP*/INITS*SCROL0                  ;SWAP WITH SCROL
        :+: /SWAP*/INITS*H255*/LINE4             ;INC (12 DOT LINES)
                 * SCAN3*SCAN1*SCAN0
         +  /SWAP*/INITS*INCSCR                  ;INC (LF)

SCROL0  :=  /SWAP*/INITS*SCROL0                  ;HOLD
         +   SWAP*/INITS*LINES0                  ;SWAP WITH LINES
        :+: /SWAP*/INITS*INCSCR                  ;INC (LF OR CHAR = 47)
         +         INITS                         ;INITIALIZE

LINES1  :=  /SWAP*/INITS*LINES1                  ;HOLD
         +   SWAP*/INITS*SCROL1                  ;SWAP WITH SCROL
        :+: /SWAP*/INITS*H255*/LINE4             ;INC (12 DOT LINES)
                 * SCAN3*SCAN1*SCAN0*LINES0
         +  /SWAP*/INITS*INCSCR*LINES0           ;INC (LF)

SCROL1  :=  /SWAP*/INITS*SCROL1                  ;HOLD
         +   SWAP*/INITS*LINES1                  ;SWAP WITH LINES
        :+: /SWAP*/INITS*INCSCR*SCROL0           ;INC (LF OR CHAR = 47)
         +         INITS                         ;INITIALIZE

LINES2  :=  /SWAP*/INITS*LINES2                  ;HOLD
         +   SWAP*/INITS*SCROL2                  ;SWAP WITH SCROL
        :+: /SWAP*/INITS*H255*/LINE4             ;INC (12 DOT LINES)
                 * SCAN3*SCAN1*SCAN0
                 *LINES1*LINES0
         +  /SWAP*/INITS*INCSCR                  ;INC (LF)
                 *LINES1*LINES0

SCROL2  :=  /SWAP*/INITS*SCROL2                  ;HOLD
         +   SWAP*/INITS*LINES2                  ;SWAP WITH LINES
        :+: /SWAP*/INITS*INCSCR*SCROL0*SCROL1    ;INC (LF OR CHAR = 47)
         +         INITS                         ;INITIALIZE

LINES3  :=  /SWAP*/INITS*LINES3                  ;HOLD
         +   SWAP*/INITS*SCROL3                  ;SWAP WITH SCROL
        :+: /SWAP*/INITS*H255*/LINE4             ;INC (12 DOT LINES)
                 * SCAN3*SCAN1*SCAN0
                 *LINES2*LINES1*LINES0
         +  /SWAP*/INITS*INCSCR                  ;INC (LF)
                 *LINES2*LINES1*LINES0

SCROL3  :=  /SWAP*/INITS*SCROL3                  ;HOLD
         +   SWAP*/INITS*LINES3                  ;SWAP WITH LINES
        :+: /SWAP*/INITS*INCSCR                  ;INC (LF OR CHAR = 47)
                 *SCROL2*SCROL1*SCROL0
         +         INITS                         ;INITIALIZE

INITS   :=  INIT*H255                            ;INITIALIZATION SIGNAL

OE      := /WRITE                                ;ENABLE THREE STATE OF RAM
```

```
FUNCTION TABLE

CK     SWAP   SCAN3  SCAN1  SCAN0  INIT   H255   WRITE LINE4  INCSCR /OC
SCROL3 SCROL2 SCROL1 SCROL0 LINES3 LINES2 LINES1 LINES0  INITS   OE

;                             I
;                    W   L    N                   I
;   S          I  H  R   I    C                   N
;   W          N  2  I   N    S  /                I
; C A  SCAN    I  5  T   E    C  O  SCROL  LINES  T  O
; K P   310    T  5  E   4    R  C  3210   3210   S  E   COMMENTS
--------------------------------------------------------------------------
  C X   XXX    H  H  X   X    X  L  XXXX   XXXX   H  X   SET INITIALIZE BIT
  C X   XXX    L  X  X   X    X  L  HHHH   LLLL   L  X   INITIALIZE COUNTERS
  C L   XXX    L  L  X   X    L  L  HHHH   LLLL   L  X   INITS = L
  C L   HHH    L  H  X   L    L  L  HHHH   LLLH   L  X   INC LINES, HOLD SCROL
  C L   HHH    L  H  X   L    L  L  HHHH   LLHL   L  X   INC LINES, HOLD SCROL
  C L   HHH    L  H  X   L    L  L  HHHH   LLHH   L  X   INC LINES, SCAN = 11
  C L   HHH    L  H  X   L    L  L  HHHH   LHLL   L  X   INC LINES, SCAN = 11
  C L   XXX    L  H  X   X    H  L  LLLL   LHLH   L  X   INC LINES & SCROL: LF
  C L   XXX    L  X  X   X    H  L  LLLH   LHHL   L  X   INC LINES & SCROL: LF
  C L   XXX    L  L  X   X    L  L  LLLH   LHHL   L  X   HOLD LINES & SCROL
  C H   XXX    L  L  X   X    L  L  LHHL   LLLH   L  X   SWAP LINES & SCROL
  C L   XXX    L  X  X   X    H  L  LHHH   LLHL   L  X   INC LINES & SCROL
  C X   XXX    X  X  L   X    X  L  XXXX   XXXX   X  H   SET OE
  C X   XXX    X  X  H   X    X  L  XXXX   XXXX   X  L   CLEAR OE
--------------------------------------------------------------------------


DESCRIPTION

"SCROL" AND "LINES" ARE COUNTERS AND POINTERS TO THE RAM. "LINES" IS A
POINTER TO THE LINE THAT IS READ FROM THE RAM. "SCROL" IS A POINTER
TO THE LOCATION IN THE RAM WHERE A NEW LINE CAN BE STORED.  BOTH OF THEM
COUNT UP TO A MAXIMUM OF 16 LINES.

THE BIT "SWAP" ENABLES THE TWO COUNTERS TO TALK TO THE SAME ADDRESS LINES
OF THE RAM.

THE NEXT FIGURE SHOWS ALL THE POINTERS THAT HAVE BEEN DESCRIBED.

"W" MEANS WRITING INTO THE RAM, "R" MEANS READING FROM THE RAM AND "C"
IS A TEMPORARY POINTER.
$
```

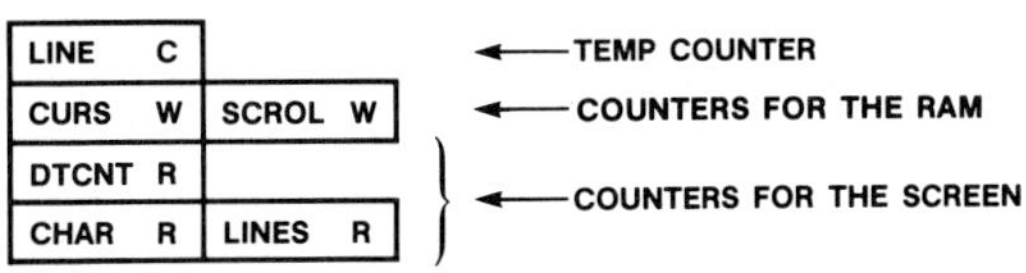

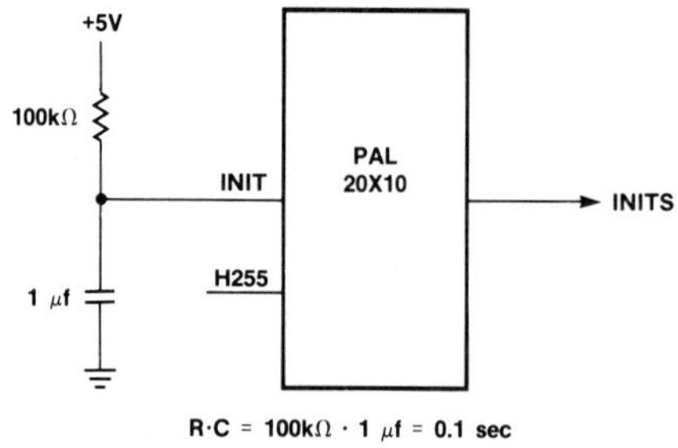

Initialization of the system when power (+5V) is turned on.

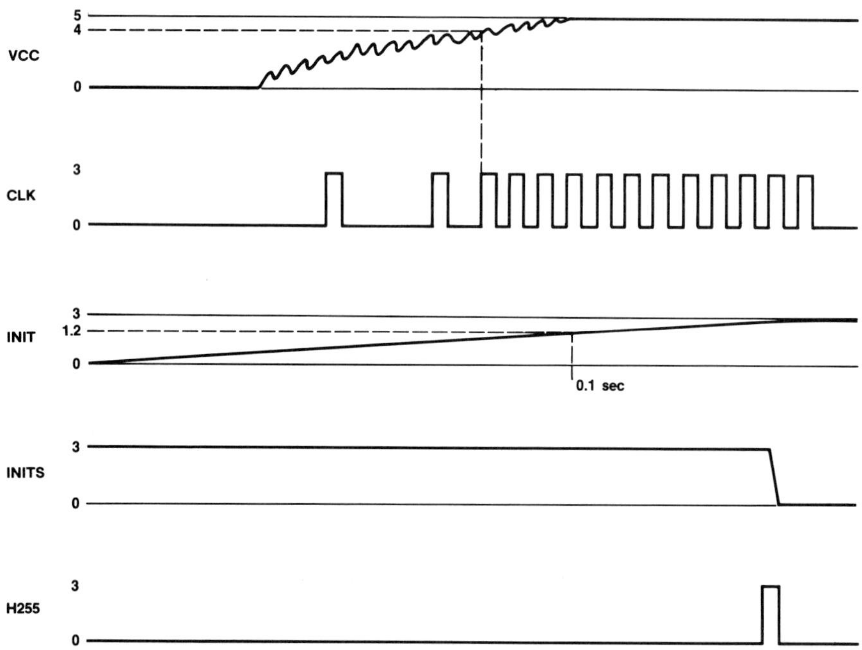

```
LINES/SCROL GENERATOR

 1 CXXX0X0XXXXX0XXXXXXXXXLX1
 2 CXXX1XXXXXXX0LHLHLHLHHX1
 3 C1XX1X1XXX1X0LHLHLHLHHX1
 4 C11100XX11X0LLLHLHLHHX1
 5 C11100XX11X0LHLLLHLHHX1
 6 C11100XX11X0LLLLLHLHHX1
 7 C11100XX11X0LHLHLLLHHX1
 8 C1XX1X0XXX0X0HLHHHLHHHX1
 9 C1XX1XXXXX0X0LHHLHLHHHX1
10 C1XX1X1XXX1X0LHHLHLHHHX1
11 C0XX1X1XXX1X0HLLHLHHHHX1
12 C1XX1XXXXX0X0LHLLLHHHHX1
13 CXXXXXXX1XXX0XXXXXXXXXXL1
14 CXXXXXXX0XXX0XXXXXXXXXXH1

PASS SIMULATION
```

LINES/SCROL GENERATOR

```
                 11 1111 1111 2222 2222 2233 3333 3333
   0123 4567 8901 2345 6789 0123 4567 8901 2345 6789

 0 ---- ---- ---- ---- ---- ---- ---- X--- ---- ---- /WRITE

 8 ---- ---- ---- -X-- ---- -X-- ---- ---- ---- ---- INIT*H255

16 X--- --X- ---X ---- ---- ---- ---- ---- ---- ---- /SWAP*/INITS*LINES3
17 -X-- --X- ---- ---X ---- ---- ---- ---- ---- ---- SWAP*/INITS*SCROL3
18 X--- X-X- X--- ---- -X-X -X-- ---X ---- X--X ---- /SWAP*/INITS*H255*/LINE-
19 X--- --X- ---- ---- ---X ---- ---X ---- ---X -X-- /SWAP*/INITS*INCSCR*LIN-

24 X--- --X- ---- ---X ---- ---- ---- ---- ---- ---- /SWAP*/INITS*SCROL3
25 -X-- --X- ---X ---- ---- ---- ---- ---- ---- ---- SWAP*/INITS*LINES3
26 X--- --X- ---- ---- ---- ---X ---- ---X ---- -X-X /SWAP*/INITS*INCSCR*SCR-
27 ---- ---X ---- ---- ---- ---- ---- ---- ---- ---- INITS

32 X--- --X- ---- ---- ---X ---- ---- ---- ---- ---- /SWAP*/INITS*LINES2
33 -X-- --X- ---- ---- ---- ---X ---- ---- ---- ---- SWAP*/INITS*SCROL2
34 X--- X-X- X--- ---- -X-- -X-- ---X ---- X--X ---- /SWAP*/INITS*H255*/LINE-
35 X--- --X- ---- ---- ---- ---- ---X ---- ---X -X-- /SWAP*/INITS*INCSCR*LIN-

40 X--- --X- ---- ---- ---- ---X ---- ---- ---- ---- /SWAP*/INITS*SCROL2
41 -X-- --X- ---- ---- ---X ---- ---- ---- ---- ---- SWAP*/INITS*LINES2
42 X--- --X- ---- ---- ---- ---- ---- ---X ---- -X-X /SWAP*/INITS*INCSCR*SCR-
43 ---- ---X ---- ---- ---- ---- ---- ---- ---- ---- INITS

48 X--- --X- ---- ---- ---- ---- ---X ---- ---- ---- /SWAP*/INITS*LINES1
49 -X-- --X- ---- ---- ---- ---- ---- ---X ---- ---- SWAP*/INITS*SCROL1
50 X--- X-X- X--- ---- -X-- -X-- ---- ---- X--X ---- /SWAP*/INITS*H255*/LINE-
51 X--- --X- ---- ---- ---- ---- ---- ---- ---X -X-- /SWAP*/INITS*INCSCR*LIN-

56 X--- --X- ---- ---- ---- ---- ---- ---X ---- ---- /SWAP*/INITS*SCROL1
57 -X-- --X- ---- ---- ---- ---- ---X ---- ---- ---- SWAP*/INITS*LINES1
58 X--- --X- ---- ---- ---- ---- ---- ---- ---- -X-X /SWAP*/INITS*INCSCR*SCR-
59 ---- ---X ---- ---- ---- ---- ---- ---- ---- ---- INITS

64 X--- --X- ---- ---- ---- ---- ---- ---- ---X ---- /SWAP*/INITS*LINES0
65 -X-- --X- ---- ---- ---- ---- ---- ---- ---- ---X SWAP*/INITS*SCROL0
66 X--- X-X- X--- ---- -X-- -X-- ---- ---- X--- ---- /SWAP*/INITS*H255*/LINE-
67 X--- --X- ---- ---- ---- ---- ---- ---- ---- -X-- /SWAP*/INITS*INCSCR

72 X--- --X- ---- ---- ---- ---- ---- ---- ---- ---X /SWAP*/INITS*SCROL0
73 -X-- --X- ---- ---- ---- ---- ---- ---- ---X ---- SWAP*/INITS*LINES0
74 X--- --X- ---- ---- ---- ---- ---- ---- ---- -X-- /SWAP*/INITS*INCSCR
75 ---- ---X ---- ---- ---- ---- ---- ---- ---- ---- INITS
```

LEGEND: X : FUSE NOT BLOWN (L,N,0) - : FUSE BLOWN (H,P,1)

NUMBER OF FUSES BLOW = 1235

LINES/SCROL Generator

Logic Diagram PAL20X10

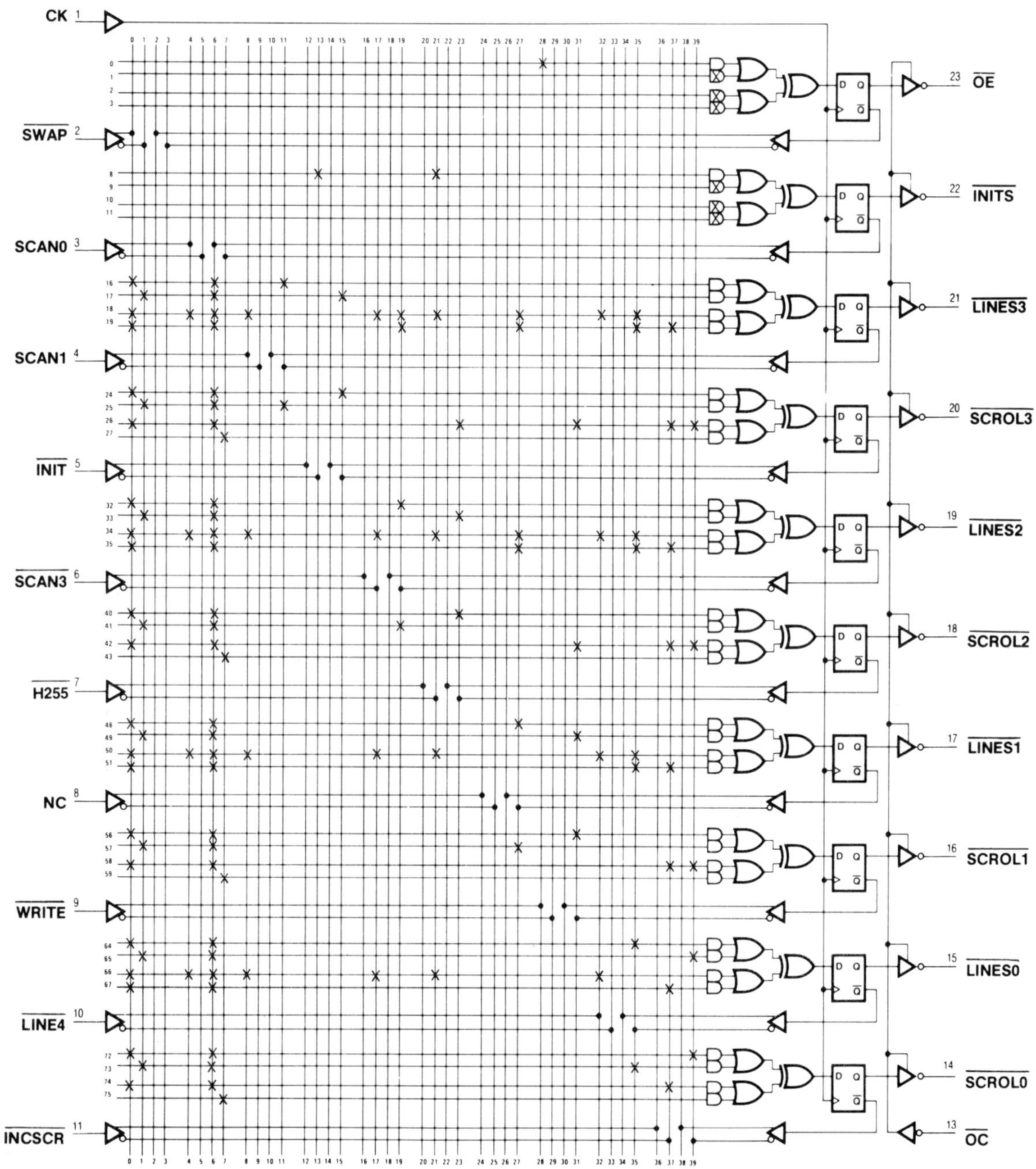

PAL
IMPORTANT
NOTES

Composite Video/Baud Rate Generator

PAL20X10

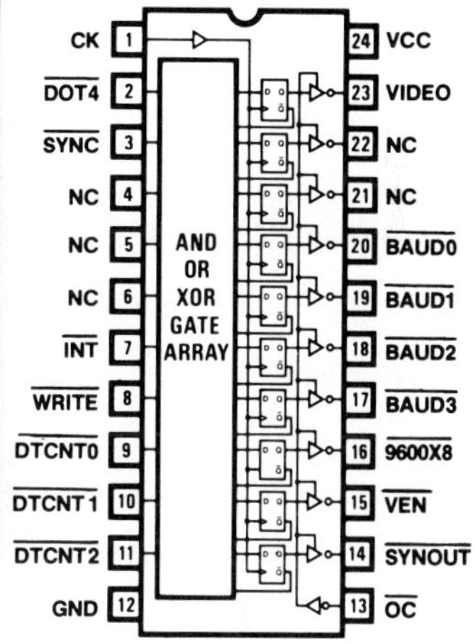

```
PAL20X8                                             PAL DESIGN  SPECIFICATION
VP5                                                 BIRKNER/KAZMI/UDI 7/14/81
COMPOSITE VIDEO/BAUD RATE GENERATOR
MMI SUNNYVALE, CALIFORNIA
CK /DOT4 /SYNC   NC  NC  NC   INT  /WRITE /DTCNT0 /DTCNT1 /DTCNT2 GND
/OC /SYNOUT  /UEN /9600X8 /BAUD3 /BAUD2 /BAUD1 /BAUD0 NC NC VIDEO VCC


IF( SYNC )  SYNOUT =  SYNC                          ;SYNC PULSE

IF( /DOT4 ) /VIDEO = /DOT4                          ;PIXEL TO THE SCREEN

9600X8 := INT                                       ;TO INITIALIZE COUNTER BAUD
       + BAUD3*BAUD2*DTCNT2*DTCNT1*/DTCNT0          ;104/8 = 13, MODULE 102
                                                    ;COUNTS 103 = 12 6/8
BAUD0 := /9600X8*BAUD0                              ;HOLD
      + /9600X8*BAUD0                               ;EXTEND
      :+:/9600X8*DTCNT2*DTCNT1*DTCNT0               ;INC

BAUD1 := /9600X8*BAUD1                              ;HOLD
      + /9600X8*BAUD1                               ;EXTEND
      :+:/9600X8*DTCNT2*DTCNT1*DTCNT0*BAUD0         ;INC

BAUD2 := /9600X8*BAUD2                              ;HOLD
      + /9600X8*BAUD2                               ;EXTEND
      :+:/9600X8*DTCNT2*DTCNT1*DTCNT0               ;INC
                *BAUD1*BAUD0

BAUD3 := /9600X8*BAUD3                              ;HOLD
      + /9600X8*BAUD3                               ;EXTEND
      :+:/9600X8*DTCNT2*DTCNT1*DTCNT0               ;INC
                *BAUD2*BAUD1*BAUD0

UEN   := WRITE*/DTCNT2*DTCNT1                       ;DTCNT = 2,3
      + WRITE* DTCNT2*/DTCNT1*/DTCNT0               ;DTCNT = 4
```

```
FUNCTION TABLE

CK DOT4 SYNC INT WRITE DTCNT2 DTCNT1 DTCNT0 /OC SYNOUT UEN
9600X8 BAUD3 BAUD2 BAUD1 BAUD0 VIDEO

;                          S     9
;             W            Y     6        V
;    D  S     R            N     0        I
;    O  Y  I  I         /  O  U  0        D
; C  T  N  N  T  DTCNT  E  U  E  X  BAUD  E
; K  4  C  T  E   210   N  T  N  8  3210  O   COMMENTS
-----------------------------------------------------------------------------
  L  X  H  X  X   XXX   L  H  X  X  XXXX  X   CHECK SYNOUT FOR H
  L  X  L  X  X   XXX   L  L  X  X  XXXX  X   CHECK SYNOUT FOR L
  L  L  X  X  X   XXX   L  X  X  X  XXXX  L   VIDEO = L
  L  H  X  X  X   XXX   L  X  X  X  XXXX  H   VIDEO = H
  C  X  X  H  X   LLL   L  X  X  H  XXXX  X   SET 9600X8
  C  X  X  L  X   LLL   L  X  X  L  LLLL  X   INITIALIZE BAUD COUNTER
  C  X  X  L  X   HHH   L  X  X  L  LLLH  X   INC BAUD
  C  X  X  L  X   HHH   L  X  X  L  LLHL  X   INC BAUD
  C  X  X  L  X   HHH   L  X  X  L  LLHH  X   INC BAUD
  C  X  X  L  X   HHH   L  X  X  L  LHLL  X   INC BAUD
  C  X  X  L  X   HLH   L  X  X  L  LHLL  X   HOLD BAUD: DTCNT NEQ HHH
  C  X  X  L  X   HHH   L  X  X  L  LHLH  X   INC BAUD
  C  X  X  L  X   HHH   L  X  X  L  LHHL  X   INC BAUD
  C  X  X  L  X   HHH   L  X  X  L  LHHH  X   INC BAUD
  C  X  X  L  X   HHH   L  X  X  L  HLLL  X   INC BAUD
  C  X  X  L  X   HHH   L  X  X  L  HLLH  X   INC BAUD
  C  X  X  L  X   HHH   L  X  X  L  HLHL  X   INC BAUD
  C  X  X  L  X   HHH   L  X  X  L  HLHH  X   INC BAUD
  C  X  X  L  X   HHH   L  X  X  L  HHLL  X   INC BAUD
  C  X  X  L  H   LLL   L  X  L  L  HHLL  X   HOLD BAUD
  C  X  X  L  H   LLH   L  X  L  L  HHLL  X   HOLD BAUD
  C  X  X  L  H   LHL   L  X  H  L  HHLL  X   HOLD BAUD, SET UEN
  C  X  X  L  H   LHH   L  X  H  L  HHLL  X   HOLD BAUD, SET UEN
  C  X  X  L  H   HLL   L  X  H  L  HHLL  X   HOLD BAUD, SET UEN
  C  X  X  L  H   HLH   L  X  L  L  HHLL  X   HOLD BAUD
  C  X  X  L  H   HHL   L  X  L  H  HHLL  X   SET 9600X8, HOLD BAUD
  C  X  X  L  H   HHH   L  X  L  L  LLLL  X   INITIALIZE BAUD
--------------------------------------------------------------------------------
```

DESCRIPTION

THIS PAL GENERATES THE BAUD RATE, THE VIDEO AND THE SYNC SIGNALS WHICH ARE COMBINED AT THE OUTPUTS TO FORM THE COMPOSITE VIDEO SIGNAL, AND THE "UEN" SIGNAL WHICH ENABLE THE "UART".

EVERY CHARACTER CONSISTS OF 10 BITS: 1 START BIT, 7 ASCII CODE BITS, 1 PARITY BIT, AND 1 STOP BIT. THE CHARACTER RATE IS 9600 Hz. EACH BIT IS DIVIDED INTO 8 SMALL BITS SO THE NUMBER OF BITS PER SECOND REQUIRED FOR OUR SYSTEM IS 9600*8 = 76800 OR 76800 Hz.

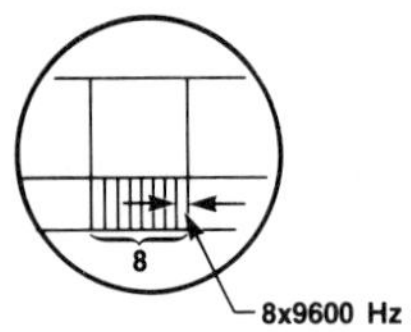

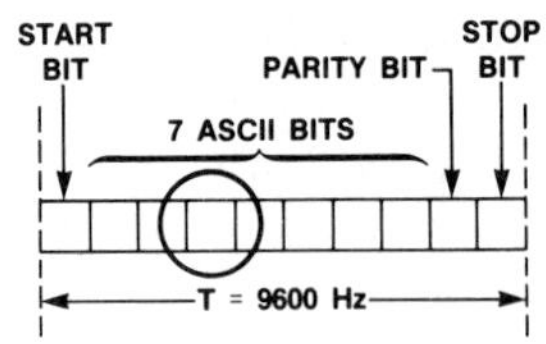

T = 1/76800 = 13 MICROSECOND
THE CLOCK FREQUENCY IS 8000000 Hz.
WE NEED TO DIVIDE THE CLOCK FREQUENCY BY 104 TO GENERATE A FREQUENCY OF 76800 Hz.

8000000/76800 = 104 = 13*8

"DTCNT" COUNTS 8, AND "BAUD" COUNTS 13. TO GET 104 COUNTS WE NEED TO COUNT FROM 0 TO 103. BECAUSE THERE IS ONE CLOCK CYCLE DELAY UNTIL THE DATA IS AVAILABLE ON THE OUTPUT PINS (REGISTERED PAL), MODULE 104 IS DETECTED BY COUNT 102 WHICH IS EQUAL TO 102/8 = 12 6/8.

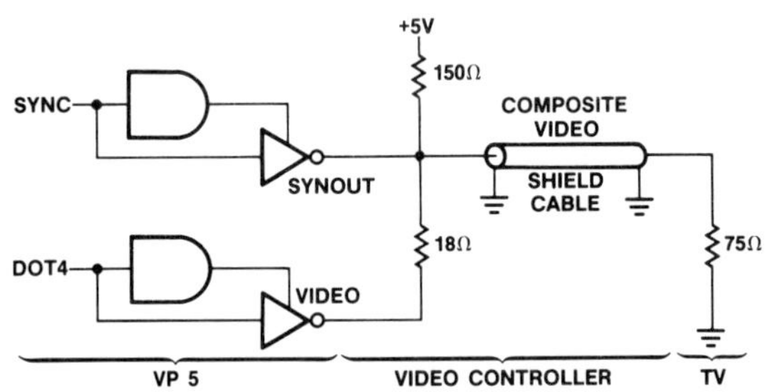

$$\frac{18}{150 + 18} * 4.6 = 0.49V$$

$$\frac{75}{150 + 75} * 5 = 1.66V$$

When SYNC = H the output is at 0.4V.

DIGITAL TO ANALOG CONVERTER

SYNOUT	VIDEO	COMPOSITE VIDEO
L	L	1.7V
L	H	0.9V
H	L	0.4V
H	H	0.4V

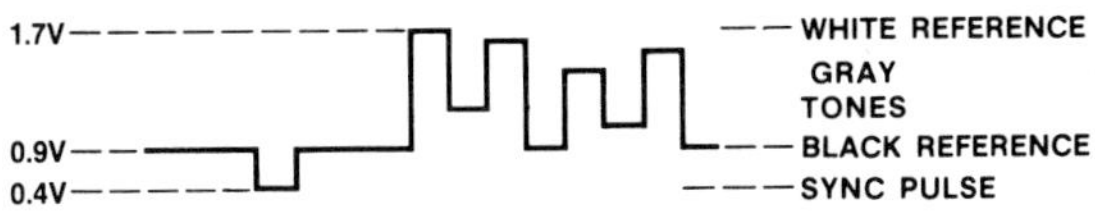

COMPOSITE VIDEO SIGNAL

COMPOSITE VIDEO/BAUD RATE GENERATOR

```
 1 0X0XXXXXXXXX0LXXXXXXXXX1
 2 0X1XXXXXXXXX01XXXXXXXXX1
 3 01XXXXXXXXXX0XXXXXXXXXL1
 4 00XXXXXXXXXX0XXXXXXXXX11
 5 CXXXXX1X111X0XXLXXXXXXX1
 6 CXXXXX0X111X0XXHHHHHXXX1
 7 CXXXXX0X000X0XXHHHHLXXX1
 8 CXXXXX0X000X0XXHHHLHXXX1
 9 CXXXXX0X000X0XXHHHLLXXX1
10 CXXXXX0X000X0XXHHLHHXXX1
11 CXXXXX0X010X0XXHHLHHXXX1
12 CXXXXX0X000X0XXHHLHLXXX1
13 CXXXXX0X000X0XXHHLLHXXX1
14 CXXXXX0X000X0XXHHLLLXXX1
15 CXXXXX0X000X0XXHLHHHXXX1
16 CXXXXX0X000X0XXHLHHLXXX1
17 CXXXXX0X000X0XXHLHLHXXX1
18 CXXXXX0X000X0XXHLHLLXXX1
19 CXXXXX0X000X0XXHLLHHXXX1
20 CXXXXX00111X0XHHLLHHXXX1
21 CXXXXX00011X0XHHLLHHXXX1
22 CXXXXX00101X0XLHLLHHXXX1
23 CXXXXX00001X0XLHLLHHXXX1
24 CXXXXX00110X0XLHLLHHXXX1
25 CXXXXX00010X0XHHLLHHXXX1
26 CXXXXX00100X0XHLLLHHXXX1
27 CXXXXX00000X0XHHHHHHXXX1
```

PASS SIMULATION

COMPOSITE VIDEO/BAUD RATE GENERATOR

```
             11 1111 1111 2222 2222 2233 3333 3333
 0123 4567 8901 2345 6789 0123 4567 8901 2345 6789

 0 X--- ---- ---- ---- ---- ---- ---- ---- ---- ---- /DOT4
 1 X--- ---- ---- ---- ---- ---- ---- ---- ---- ---- /DOT4



24 ---- ---- ---- ---X ---- ---- ---- --X- ---- ---- /9600X8*BAUD0
25 ---- ---- ---- ---X ---- ---- ---- --X- ---- ---- /9600X8*BAUD0
26 ---- ---- ---- ---- ---- ---- ---- -XX- -X-- -X-- /9600X8*DTCNT2*DTCNT1*D-

32 ---- ---- ---- ---- ---X ---- ---- --X- ---- ---- /9600X8*BAUD1
33 ---- ---- ---- ---- ---X ---- ---- --X- ---- ---- /9600X8*BAUD1
34 ---- ---- ---- ---X ---- ---- ---- -XX- -X-- -X-- /9600X8*DTCNT2*DTCNT1*D-

40 ---- ---- ---- ---- ---- ---X ---- --X- ---- ---- /9600X8*BAUD2
41 ---- ---- ---- ---- ---- ---X ---- --X- ---- ---- /9600X8*BAUD2
42 ---- ---- ---- ---X ---X ---- ---- -XX- -X-- -X-- /9600X8*DTCNT2*DTCNT1*D-

48 ---- ---- ---- ---- ---- ---- ---X --X- ---- ---- /9600X8*BAUD3
49 ---- ---- ---- ---- ---- ---- ---X --X- ---- ---- /9600X8*BAUD3
50 ---- ---- ---- ---X ---X ---X ---- -XX- -X-- -X-- /9600X8*DTCNT2*DTCNT1*D-

56 ---- ---- ---- ---- ---- X--- ---- ---- ---- ---- INT
57 ---- ---- ---- ---- ---- ---X ---X X--- -X-- -X-- BAUD3*BAUD2*DTCNT2*DTCN-

64 ---- ---- ---- ---- ---- ---- -X-- ---- -X-- X--- WRITE*/DTCNT2*DTCNT1
65 ---- ---- ---- ---- ---- ---- -X-- X--- X--- -X-- WRITE*DTCNT2*/DTCNT1*/D-

72 ---- -X-- ---- ---- ---- ---- ---- ---- ---- ---- SYNC
73 ---- -X-- ---- ---- ---- ---- ---- ---- ---- ---- SYNC


LEGEND:  X : FUSE NOT BLOWN (L,N,0)   - : FUSE BLOWN   (H,P,1)

NUMBER OF FUSES BLOW =  745
```

Composite Video/Baud Rate Generator

Logic Diagram PAL20X 8

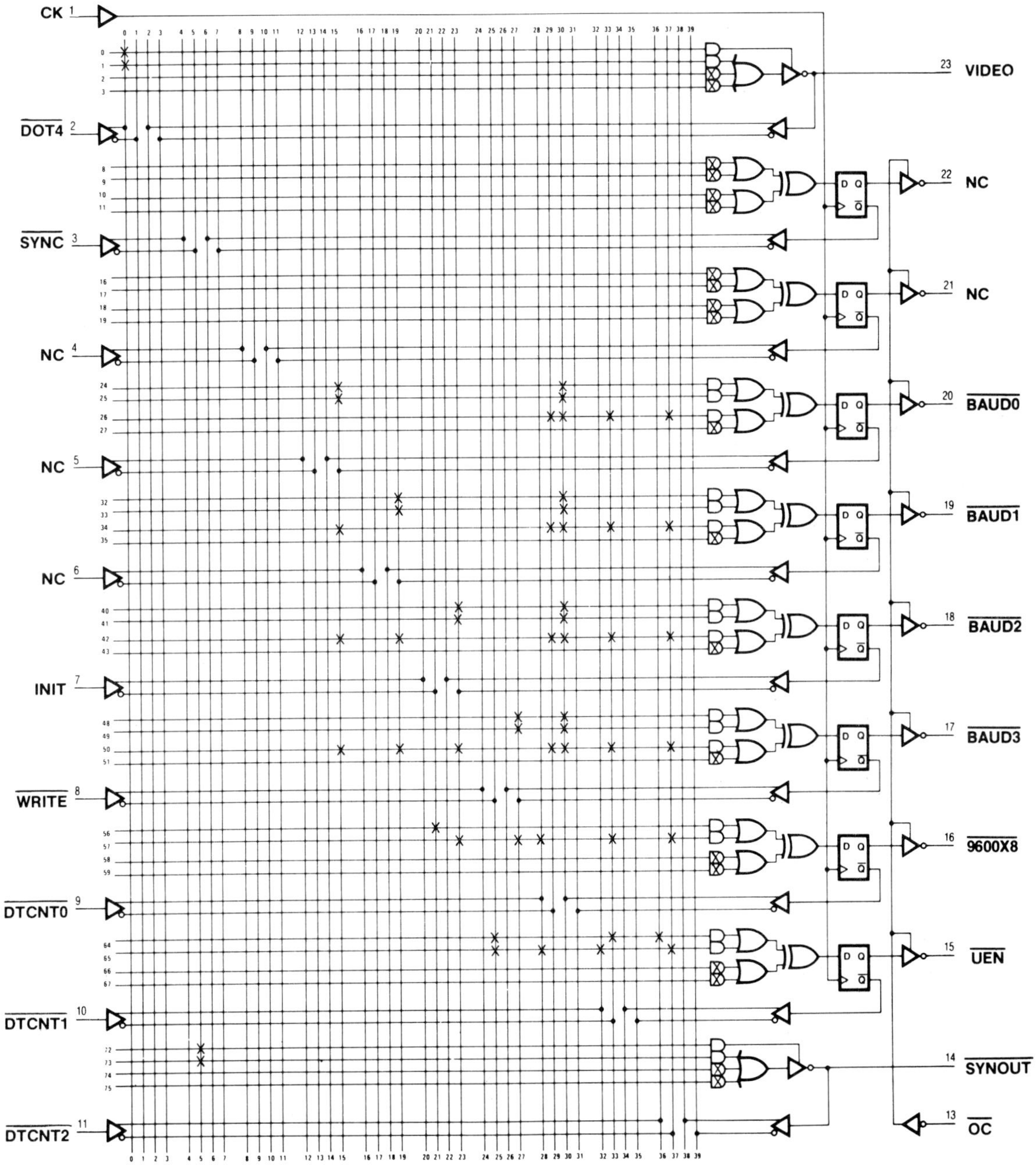

PAL
IMPORTANT, NOTES

UART Shift Register and Control Key Detect

PAL20X10

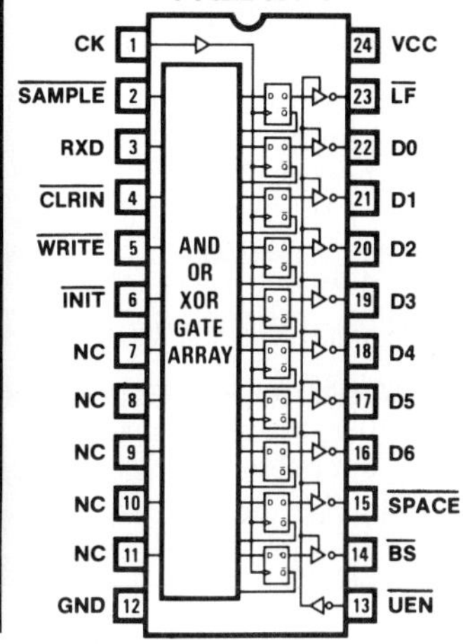

```
PAL20X10                                        PAL DESIGN SPECIFICATION
VP6                                             BIRKNER/UDI      21/7/81
UART SHIFT REGISTER AND CONTROL KEY DETECT
MMI SUNNYVALE, CALIFORNIA
CK /SAMPLE RXD /CLRLIN /WRITE  INIT NC NC NC NC NC GND
/UEN /BS  /SPACE  D6  D5  D4  D3  D2  D1  D0  /LF  VCC


/D0  := /D0*/SAMPLE                             ;HOLD
     +  SPACE                                   ;SET SPACE CODE
    :+:/D1* SAMPLE                              ;SHIFT

/D1  := /D1*/SAMPLE                             ;HOLD
     +  SPACE                                   ;SET SPACE CODE
    :+:/D2* SAMPLE                              ;SHIFT

/D2  := /D2*/SAMPLE                             ;HOLD
     +  SPACE                                   ;SET SPACE CODE
    :+:/D3* SAMPLE                              ;SHIFT

/D3  := /D3*/SAMPLE                             ;HOLD
     +  SPACE                                   ;SET SPACE CODE
    :+:/D4* SAMPLE                              ;SHIFT

/D4  := /D4*/SAMPLE                             ;HOLD
     +  SPACE                                   ;SET SPACE CODE
    :+:/D5* SAMPLE                              ;SHIFT

/D5  := /INIT*/D5*/SAMPLE*/SPACE                ;SET SPACE CODE INSTEAD
     + /D5*/SAMPLE*/SPACE                       ;OF ANY CONTROL CODE
    :+:/INIT*/D6*SAMPLE*/SPACE                  ;SHIFT

/D6  := /INIT*/D6*/SAMPLE                       ;HOLD
     +  SPACE                                   ;SET SPACE CODE
    :+:/INIT* RXD*SAMPLE                        ;DATA IS SHIFTED IN


SPACE := WRITE*/D6*/D5                          ;DETECT CTRL CHAR
       + CLRLIN                                 ;AND CLEAR LINE

 LF := /D6*/D5*/D4*D3*/D2*D1*/D0                ;LINE FEED = HEX 0A
          *WRITE                                ;LATCH ON WRITE
       + LF*WRITE                               ;HOLD DURING WRITE
```

FUNCTION TABLE

```
CK SAMPLE RXD CLRLIN WRITE INIT /UEN /BS SPACE D6 D5 D4 D3 D2 D1 D0 LF

;     S     C
;     A     L  W           S
;     M     R  R  I  /     P
;     P  R  L  I  N  U  /  A
; C   L  X  I  T  I  E  B  C  DATA  OUT  L
; K   E  D  N  E  T  N  S  E  D6-----D0  F   COMMENTS
------------------------------------------------------------------------------
  C   X  X  L  L  L  L  X  L   XXXXXXX   X   INITIALIZE "SPACE"
  C   H  X  L  L  H  L  X  L   HHXXXXX   X   INITIALIZE D6 AND D5
  C   X  X  L  L  L  L  X  L   XXXXXXX   X   HOLD "SPACE" LO
  C   H  L  L  X  L  L  X  L   HXXXXXX   X   SHIFT IN 1'ST BIT OF "U" CODE
  C   H  H  L  X  L  L  X  L   LHXXXXX   X   SHIFT IN 2'ND BIT OF "U" CODE
  C   H  L  L  X  L  L  X  L   HLHXXXX   X   SHIFT IN 3'RD BIT OF "U" CODE
  C   H  H  L  X  L  L  X  L   LHLHXXX   X   SHIFT IN 4'TH BIT OF "U" CODE
  C   H  L  L  X  L  L  X  L   HLHLHXX   X   SHIFT IN 5'TH BIT OF "U" CODE
  C   H  H  L  X  L  L  X  L   LHLHLHX   X   SHIFT IN 6'TH BIT OF "U" CODE
  C   H  L  L  X  L  L  X  L   HLHLHLH   X   OUTPUT "U" CODE, STORE IN RAM
  C   H  H  L  X  L  L  X  L   LHLHLHL   X   SHIFT IN 1'ST BIT OF "LF" CODE
  C   H  L  L  X  L  L  X  L   HLHLHLH   X   SHIFT IN 2'ND BIT OF "LF" CODE
  C   H  H  L  X  L  L  X  L   LHLHLHL   X   SHIFT IN 3'RD BIT OF "LF" CODE
  C   H  L  L  X  L  L  X  L   HLHLHLH   X   SHIFT IN 4'TH BIT OF "LF" CODE
  C   H  H  L  X  L  L  X  L   LHLHLHL   X   SHIFT IN 5'TH BIT OF "LF" CODE
  C   H  H  L  X  L  L  X  L   LLHLHLH   X   SHIFT IN 6'TH BIT OF "LF" CODE
  C   H  H  L  L  L  L  X  L   LLLHLHL   X   DETECT "LF" CODE
  C   L  X  L  H  L  L  X  H   LLLHLHL   H   HOLD DURING WRITE
  C   L  X  L  L  L  L  X  L   LHLLLLL   X   WRITE "SPACE" CODE INTO RAM
------------------------------------------------------------------------------
```

DESCRIPTION

THE "UART" SHIFT REGISTER IS A SEVEN BIT REGISTER FOR THE SEVEN BIT ASCII CODE. THE INFORMATION ENTERS THE SHIFT REGISTER IN D6, ONE BIT AT A TIME. IT COMES THROUGH RXD PIN WHICH IS THE TRANSMIT OR THE RECEIVE LINE OF THE RS232. THE OUTPUTS ARE TRANSFERED IN PARALLEL TO THE RAM. "UEN" ENABLES THE THREE STATE FOR THESE OUTPUTS. WHEN BITS D6 AND D5 TOGETHER IN THE ASCII CODE ARE ZEROES OR WHEN THE "CLRLIN" BIT IS SET, A "SPACE" CODE IS SHIFTED INTO THE "UART" REGISTER. THE SPACE CODE PRINTS A BLANK SPACE ON THE SCREEN. "SPACE" IN ASCII CODE IS 0100000 = 20 HEX.

ASCII Code System and Character Set

D6, D5 — **CONTROL CHARACTERS ARE DETECTED WHEN D6, D5 = 0,0**

8 7 6 5 / 4 3 2 1	0 0 0 0	0 0 0 1	0 0 1 0	0 0 1 1	0 1 0 0	0 1 0 1	0 1 1 0	0 1 1 1
0 0 0 0	NUL	DLE	SP	0	@	P	`	p
0 0 0 1	SOH	DC1	!	1	A	Q	a	q
0 0 1 0	STX	DC2	"	2	B	R	b	r
0 0 1 1	ETX	DC3	#	3	C	S	c	s
0 1 0 0	EOT	DC4	$	4	D	T	d	t
0 1 0 1	ENQ	NAK	%	5	E	U	e	u
0 1 1 0	ACK	SYN	&	6	F	V	f	v
0 1 1 1	BEL	ETB	'	7	G	W	g	w
1 0 0 0	BS	CAN	(	8	H	X	h	x
1 0 0 1	HT	EM	)	9	I	Y	i	y
1 0 1 0	LF	SUB	*	:	J	Z	j	z
1 0 1 1	VT	ESC	+	;	K	[	k	{
1 1 0 0	FF	FS	,	<	L	\	l	¦
1 1 0 1	CR	GS	-	=	M	]	m	}
1 1 1 0	SO	RS	.	>	N	∧	n	~
1 1 1 1	SI	US	/	?	O	—	o	DEL

- Printable Characters
- Printer Control Characters
- Codes Generated and Transmitted by the Terminal
- ASR Control Codes
- Extended Line Control

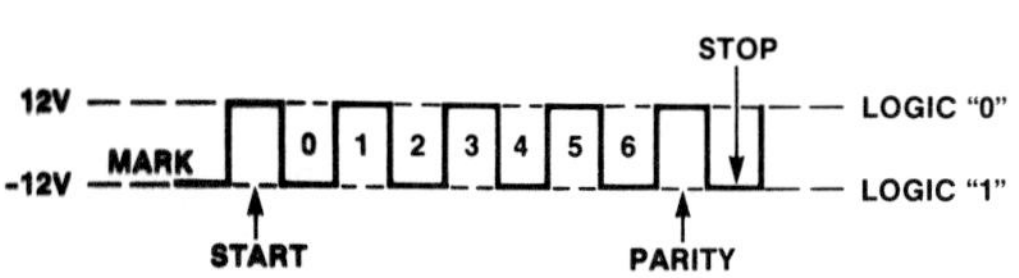

POLARITY CONVENTION FOR RS232

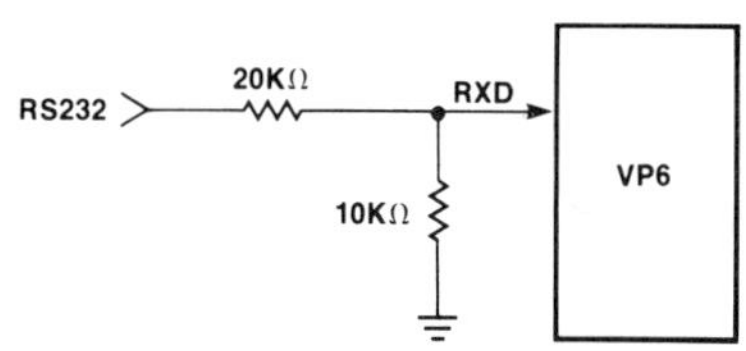

The voltages of the RS232 signals are between +12V and -12V. In order to get a logic one at 4V we built the above circuit.

UART SHIFT REGISTER AND CONTROL KEY DETECT

```
 1 CXX110XXXXXX0XHXXXXXXXX1
 2 C0X111XXXXXX0XHHHXXXXXX1
 3 CXX110XXXXXX0XHXXXXXXXX1
 4 C001X0XXXXXX0XHHXXXXXXX1
 5 C011X0XXXXXX0XHLHXXXXXX1
 6 C001X0XXXXXX0XHHLHXXXXX1
 7 C011X0XXXXXX0XHLHLHXXXX1
 8 C001X0XXXXXX0XHHLHLHXXX1
 9 C011X0XXXXXX0XHLHLHLHXX1
10 C001X0XXXXXX0XHHLHLHLHX1
11 C011X0XXXXXX0XHLHLHLHLX1
12 C001X0XXXXXX0XHHLHLHLHX1
13 C011X0XXXXXX0XHLHLHLHLX1
14 C001X0XXXXXX0XHHLHLHLHX1
15 C011X0XXXXXX0XHLHLHLHLX1
16 C011X0XXXXXX0XHLLHLHLHX1
17 C01110XXXXXX0XHLLLHLHLX1
18 C1X100XXXXXX0XLLLLHLHLL1
19 C1X110XXXXXX0XHLHLLLLLX1
```

PASS SIMULATION

```
UART SHIFT REGISTER AND CONTROL KEY DETECT

               11 1111 1111 2222 2222 2233 3333 3333
   0123 4567 8901 2345 6789 0123 4567 8901 2345 6789

 0 ---- ---X --X- -X-X --X- ---X ---X ---X ---- ---- /D6*/D5*/D4*D3*/D2*D1*/-
 1 ---X ---- ---- -X-- ---- ---- ---- ---- ---- ---- LF*WRITE

 8 X--- ---X ---- ---- ---- ---- ---- ---- ---- ---- /D0*/SAMPLE
 9 ---- ---- ---- ---- ---- ---- ---- ---- ---X ---- SPACE
10 -X-- ---- ---X ---- ---- ---- ---- ---- ---- ---- /D1*SAMPLE

16 X--- ---- ---X ---- ---- ---- ---- ---- ---- ---- /D1*/SAMPLE
17 ---- ---- ---- ---- ---- ---- ---- ---- ---X ---- SPACE
18 -X-- ---- ---- ---X ---- ---- ---- ---- ---- ---- /D2*SAMPLE

24 X--- ---- ---- ---X ---- ---- ---- ---- ---- ---- /D2*/SAMPLE
25 ---- ---- ---- ---- ---- ---- ---- ---- ---X ---- SPACE
26 -X-- ---- ---- ---- ---X ---- ---- ---- ---- ---- /D3*SAMPLE

32 X--- ---- ---- ---- ---X ---- ---- ---- ---- ---- /D3*/SAMPLE
33 ---- ---- ---- ---- ---- ---- ---- ---- ---X ---- SPACE
34 -X-- ---- ---- ---- ---- ---X ---- ---- ---- ---- /D4*SAMPLE

40 X--- ---- ---- ---- ---- ---X ---- ---- ---- ---- /D4*/SAMPLE
41 ---- ---- ---- ---- ---- ---- ---- ---- ---X ---- SPACE
42 -X-- ---- ---- ---- ---- ---- ---X ---- ---- ---- /D5*SAMPLE

48 X--- ---- ---- ---- -X-- ---- ---X ---- --X- ---- /INIT*/D5*/SAMPLE*/SPACE
49 X--- ---- ---- ---- ---- ---- ---X ---- --X- ---- /D5*/SAMPLE*/SPACE
50 -X-- ---- ---- ---- -X-- ---- ---- ---X --X- ---- /INIT*/D6*SAMPLE*/SPACE

56 X--- ---- ---- ---- -X-- ---- ---- ---X ---- ---- /INIT*/D6*/SAMPLE
57 ---- ---- ---- ---- ---- ---- ---- ---- ---X ---- SPACE
58 -X-- X--- ---- ---- -X-- ---- ---- ---- ---- ---- /INIT*RXD*SAMPLE

64 ---- ---- ---- -X-- ---- ---- ---X ---X ---- ---- WRITE*/D6*/D5
65 ---- ---- -X-- ---- ---- ---- ---- ---- ---- ---- CLRLIN


LEGEND:  X : FUSE NOT BLOWN (L,N,0)   - : FUSE BLOWN   (H,P,1)

NUMBER OF FUSES BLOW =  943
```

UART Shift Register and Control Detect

Logic Diagram PAL20X10

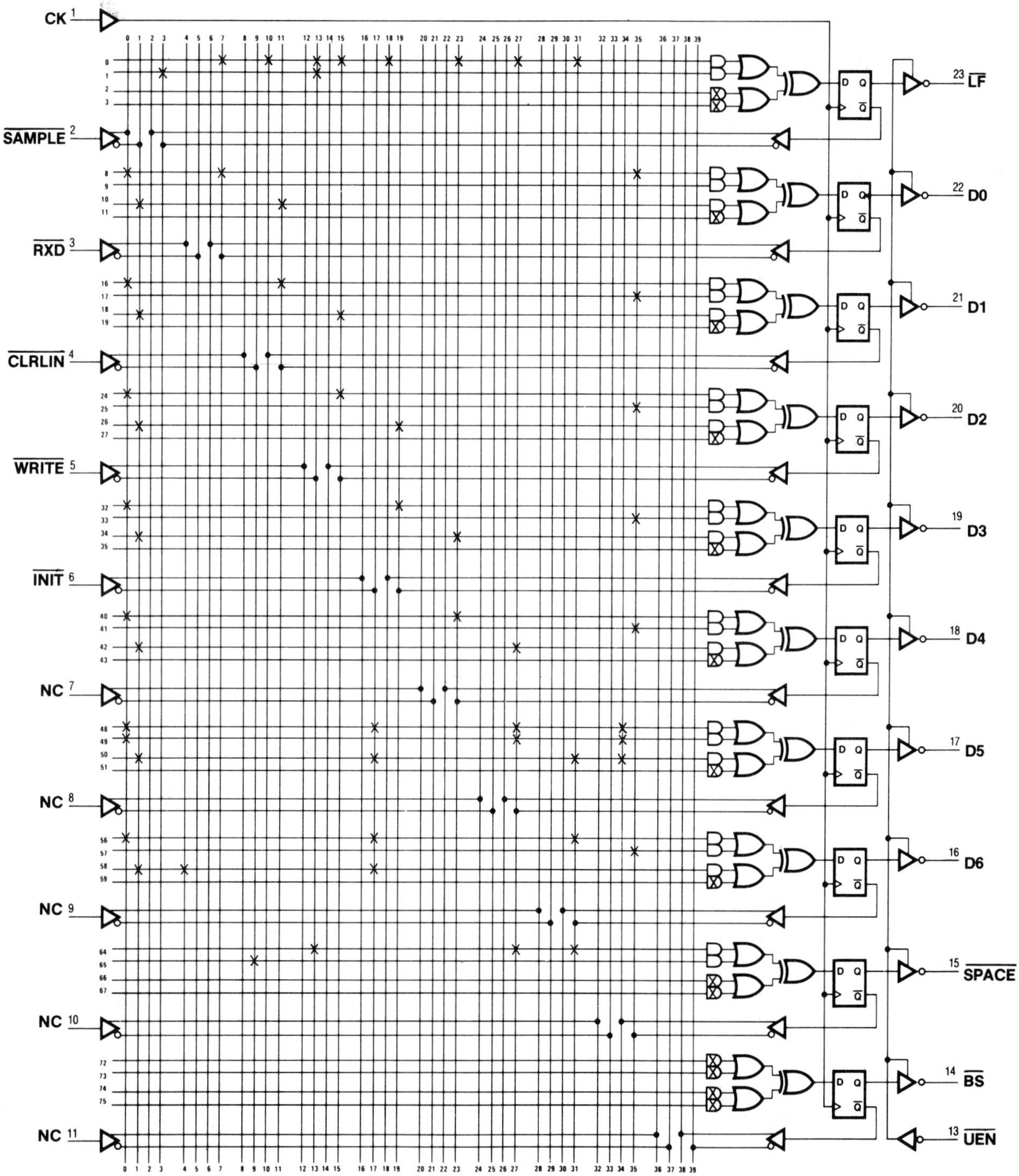

PAL
IMPORTANT,
NOTES

UART Control

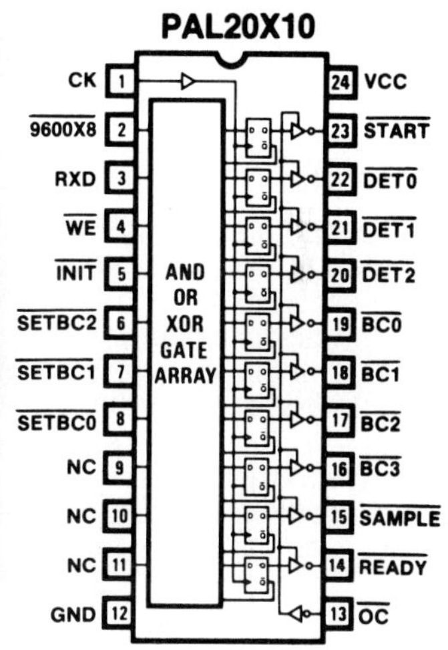

```
PAL20X10                                        PAL DESIGN SPECIFICATION
VP7                                             BIRKNER/UDI      7/28/81
UART CONTROL
MMI SUNNYVALE, CALIFORNIA
CK /9600X8  RXD /WE  /INIT /SETBC2 /SETBC1 /SETBC0  NC  NC  NC  GND
/OC /READY /SAMPLE /BC3 /BC2 /BC1 /BC0 /DET2 /DET1 /DET0 /START VCC


START := /READY*START                           ;HOLD
       + /READY*RXD                             ;DETECT START BIT
      :+:/READY*START*BC3*BC2*BC1*BC0           ;FILTER FALSE START
                    */DET2*/DET1*DET0*/RXD      ;CANCEL START IF NO RXD

DET0  := START*DET0                             ;HOLD
       + START*DET0                             ;EXTEND
      :+:START*9600X8                           ;CARRY

DET1  := START*DET1                             ;HOLD
       + START*DET1                             ;EXTEND
      :+:START*9600X8*DET0                      ;CARRY

DET2  := START*DET2                             ;HOLD
       + START*DET2                             ;EXTEND
      :+:START*9600X8*DET0*DET1                 ;CARRY

BC0   := /SETBC0*BC0                            ;HOLD
       + /SETBC0*READY                          ;SET BC TO -1 ON READY
      :+:/SETBC0*START*9600X8*DET0*DET1*DET2    ;CARRY
       +  SETBC0                                ;SET BC TO 7 FOR TESTING

BC1   := /SETBC1*BC1                            ;HOLD
       + /SETBC1*READY                          ;SET BC TO -1 ON READY
      :+:/SETBC1*START*9600X8*DET0*DET1*DET2    ;CARRY
                              *BC0
       +  SETBC1                                ;SET BC TO 7 FOR TESTING

BC2   := /SETBC2*BC2                            ;HOLD
       + /SETBC2*READY                          ;SET BC TO -1 ON READY
      :+:/SETBC2*START*9600X8*DET0*DET1*DET2    ;CARRY
                              *BC0*BC1
       +  SETBC2                                ;SET BC TO 7 FOR TESTING

BC3   := BC3                                    ;HOLD
       + READY                                  ;SET BC TO -1 ON READY
      :+:START*9600X8*DET0*DET1*DET2            ;CARRY
                              *BC0*BC1*BC2

SAMPLE := START*9600X8*/DET2*DET1*/DET0*/BC3    ;DET=2 & BC=0..7
        + START*9600X8*/DET2*DET1*/DET0*/BC3    ;EXTEND
       :+:START*9600X8*/DET2*DET1*/DET0         ;CANCEL BC = 7
                         */BC3*BC2*BC1*BC0

READY := /INIT*/WE*READY                        ;HOLD
       + /INIT*/WE*START*BC3*/BC2*/BC1*/BC0     ;SET ON BC=8
      :+: INIT                                  ;INITIAL READY, START & BC
```

FUNCTION TABLE

CK 9600X8 RXD /WE INIT SETBC2 SETBC1 SETBC0 /OC READY
SAMPLE BC3 BC2 BC1 BC0 DET2 DET1 DET0 START

CK	9600X8	RXD	/WE	INIT	SETBC 210	/OC	READY	SAMPLE	BC 3210	DET 210	START	COMMENTS
C	X	X	X	H	XXX	L	H	X	XXXX	XXX	X	INITIAL READY
C	X	L	H	L	XXX	L	H	X	HHHH	XXX	L	CLEAR START & INITIAL BC
C	X	L	L	L	XXX	L	L	X	HHHH	LLL	L	INITIAL DET & CLEAR READY
C	X	H	L	L	XXX	L	L	X	HHHH	LLL	H	SET START
C	H	L	L	L	LLL	L	L	L	HHHH	LLH	H	NO RXD, DETECT FALSE START
C	H	L	L	L	LLL	L	L	L	HHHH	LHL	L	CLEAR START (NOISE ON RXD)
C	H	H	L	L	LLL	L	L	L	HHHH	LLL	H	INITIALIZE DET
C	H	H	L	L	LLL	L	L	L	HHHH	LLH	H	NOW IT IS A REAL SIGNAL
C	H	H	L	L	LLL	L	L	L	HHHH	LHL	H	INC DET, NO SAMPLING
C	H	H	L	L	LLL	L	L	L	HHHH	LHH	H	NO SAMPLE, START BIT OF INFO
C	H	H	L	L	LLL	L	L	L	HHHH	HLL	H	INC DET, NO SAMPLING
C	H	H	L	L	LLL	L	L	L	HHHH	HLH	H	INC DET, NO SAMPLING
C	H	H	L	L	LLL	L	L	L	HHHH	HHL	H	INC DET, NO SAMPLING
C	H	H	L	L	LLL	L	L	L	HHHH	HHH	H	INC DET, NO SAMPLING
C	H	H	L	L	LLL	L	L	L	LLLL	LLL	H	INC DET AND BIT COUNTER
C	H	H	L	L	LLL	L	L	L	LLLL	LLH	H	1'ST BIT OF ASCII CODE
C	H	H	L	L	LLL	L	L	L	LLLL	LHL	H	INC DET
C	H	H	L	L	LLL	L	L	H	LLLL	LHH	H	SAMPLE THE 1'ST INFO BIT
C	H	H	L	L	LLL	L	L	L	LLLL	HLL	H	INC DET
C	H	H	L	L	LLL	L	L	L	LLLL	HLH	H	INC DET
C	H	H	L	L	LLL	L	L	L	LLLL	HHL	H	INC DET
C	H	H	L	L	LLL	L	L	L	LLLL	HHH	H	INC DET
C	H	H	L	L	LLL	L	L	L	LLLH	LLL	H	INC DET AND BIT COUNTER
C	H	H	L	L	LLL	L	L	L	LLLH	LLH	H	2'ND BIT OF ASCII CODE
C	H	H	L	L	LLL	L	L	L	LLLH	LHL	H	INC DET
C	H	H	L	L	LLL	L	L	H	LLLH	LHH	H	SAMPLE 2'ND BIT OF INFO
C	H	H	L	L	LLL	L	L	L	LLLH	HLL	H	INC DET
C	H	H	L	L	LLL	L	L	L	LLLH	HLH	H	INC DET
C	H	H	L	L	LLL	L	L	L	LLLH	HHL	H	INC DET
C	H	H	L	L	LLL	L	L	L	LLLH	HHH	H	INC DET
C	H	H	L	L	HLH	L	L	L	LHHH	LLL	H	SET BIT COUNTER TO 7
C	H	H	L	L	LLL	L	L	L	LHHH	LLH	H	7'TH BIT OF ASCII CODE
C	H	H	L	L	LLL	L	L	L	LHHH	LHL	H	INC DET
C	H	H	L	L	LLL	L	L	L	LHHH	LHH	H	NO SAMPLE 7'TH BIT ALWAYS 0
C	H	H	L	L	LLL	L	L	L	LHHH	HLL	H	INC DET
C	H	H	L	L	LLL	L	L	L	LHHH	HLH	H	INC DET
C	H	H	L	L	LLL	L	L	L	LHHH	HHL	H	INC DET
C	H	H	L	L	LLL	L	L	L	LHHH	HHH	H	INC DET
C	H	H	L	L	LLL	L	L	L	HLLL	LLL	H	INC DET AND BIT COUNTER
C	H	H	H	L	LLL	L	H	L	HLLL	LLH	H	SET THE READY SIGNAL
C	H	H	L	L	LLL	L	L	L	HHHH	LHL	L	SET START BIT & INITIAL BC
C	H	H	L	L	LLL	L	L	L	HHHH	LLL	H	REPEATE FOR NEXT CHARACTER

DESCRIPTION

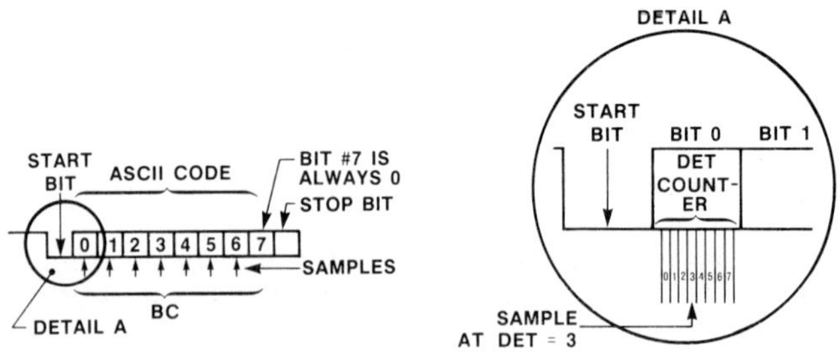

"BC" IS A COUNTER FOR THE ASCII CODE BITS. A SAMPLE FROM EACH ASCII BIT IS TAKEN WHEN "DET" = 3.

THE "START" SIGNAL IS SET WHEN A START BIT IS DETECTED ON THE RXD LINE AND REMAINS SET UNTIL THE LAST ASCII BIT OF THE CHARACTER THAT IS SAMPLED. AFTER ALL THE 7 BITS OF THE ASCII CODE WERE SAMPLED, A WRITE SIGNAL IS SENT TO THE RAM AND THE 7 BITS (A CODE FOR A CHARACTER) ARE WRITTEN IN PARALLEL INTO THE RAM.

WHEN "BC" COUNTS 8 THE "READY" SIGNAL GOES HIGH, "START" GOES LOW AND READY TO BE SET AGAIN IF A NEW START BIT IS DETECTED. A NEW CODE FOR A NEW CHARACTER WILL START TO BE SAMPLED.

BUT

ASSUME THAT A NOISE OCCURS ON THE RXD LINE WHICH SET THE "START" SIGNAL.

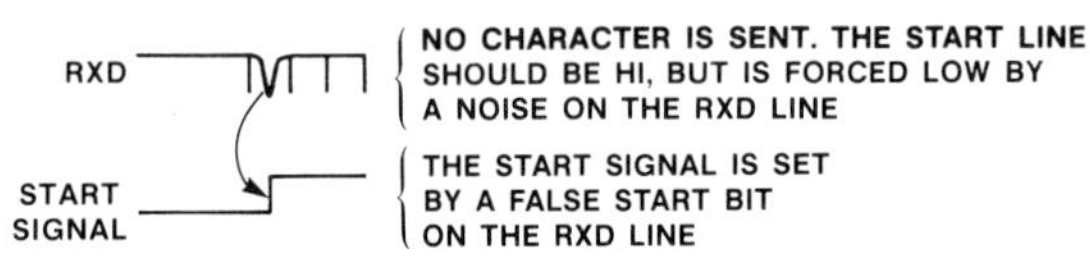

TO DETERMINE IF THIS IS A TRUE OR FALSE START, WE CHECK THE RXD LINE. IF THE RXD LINE IS NOT SET, WE KNOW THAT NO CHARACTER WAS SENT ON THE RS232 LINE; THEREFORE, A NOISE/FALSE SIGNAL WAS DETECTED.

ERROR ANALYSIS FOR SAMPLING

SINCE BOTH A TRANSMITTER AND A RECEIVER ARE USED IN OBTAINING INFORMATION, AN ERROR CAN OCCUR THAT INVOLVES BOTH OF THESE COMPONENTS.

ASSUME: ERROR IN TRANSMITTING FREQUENCY = EX
ERROR IN RECEIVING FREQUENCY = ER
THEN THE TOTAL ERROR FOR ONE BIT OF INFORMATION IS (EX + ER).
AND THE TOTAL ERROR FOR THE N'TH BIT OF INFORMATION IS N*(EX + ER).

WHEN COUNTER "DET" IS EQUAL 3, WE HAVE THE IDEAL BIT FOR SAMPLING.
THE MAXIMUM ERROR THAT IS ALLOWED DUE TO THE TOLERANCES IN THE FREQUENCIES IN BOTH TRANSMITTER AND RECEIVER, WILL BE WHEN THE SAMPLE IS TAKEN AT "DET" = 0 OR AT "DET" = 6, AS SHOWN HERE:

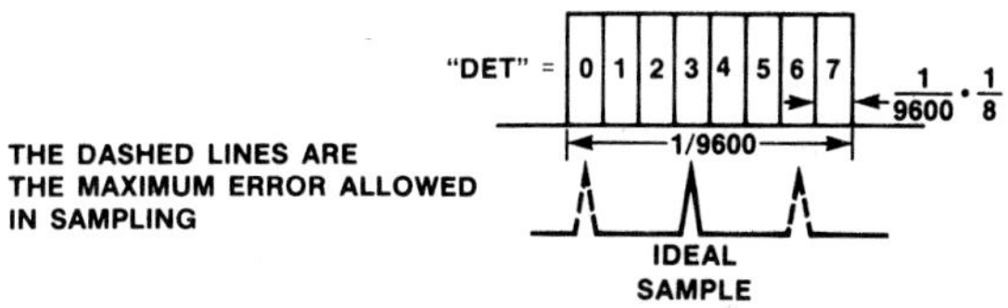

THE FREQUENCY FOR EACH BIT OF INFORMATION IS 1/9600 Hz (104 MICROSECOND).
EACH BIT OF INFORMATION IS DIVIDED INTO EIGHT TIME SLOTS.

THE TOTAL ERROR ALLOWED FOR THE 7'TH BIT OF INFORMATION IS:

7 * (EX + ER) = (1/9600) * (3/8)

THE TOTAL ERROR ALLOWED FOR ONE BIT OF INFORMATION IS:

(EX + ER) = 104 * (3/8) * (1/7) = 5.5 MICROSECOND

THE FREQUENCY RATE BETWEEN RS232 AND THE RXD LINE FOR EVERY BIT OF INFORMATION SHOULD BE BETWEEN 10150 Hz AND 9130 Hz.

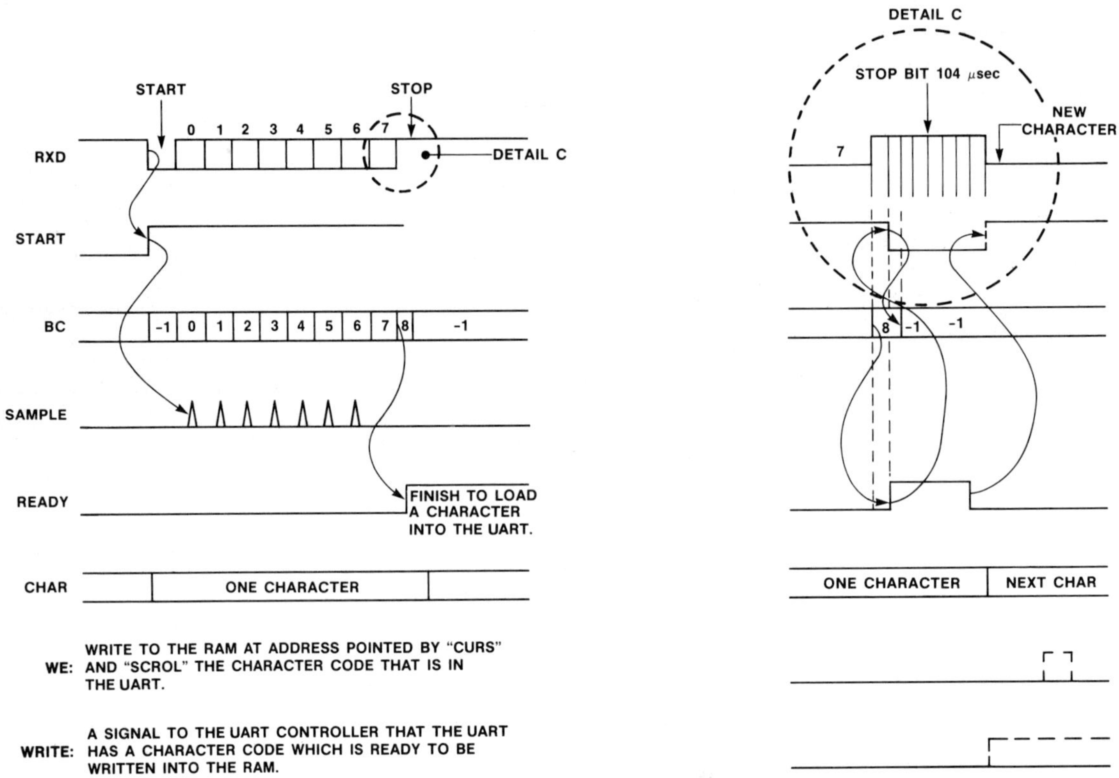

Timing diagram for detecting a character and writing it into the RAM. Signals "WRITE" and "WE" are explained and derived in the next PAL specification VP8.

```
UART CONTROL

 1 CXXX0XXXXXXX0LXXXXXXXXX1
 2 CX011XXXXXXX0LXLLLLXXXH1
 3 CX001XXXXXXX0HXLLLLHHHH1
 4 CX101XXXXXXX0HXLLLLHHHL1
 5 C0001111XXXX0HHLLLLHHLL1
 6 C0001111XXXX0HHLLLLHLHH1
 7 C0101111XXXX0HHLLLLHHHL1
 8 C0101111XXXX0HHLLLLHHLL1
 9 C0101111XXXX0HHLLLLHLHL1
10 C0101111XXXX0HHLLLLHLLL1
11 C0101111XXXX0HHLLLLLHHL1
12 C0101111XXXX0HHLLLLLHLL1
13 C0101111XXXX0HHLLLLLLHL1
14 C0101111XXXX0HHLLLLLLLL1
15 C0101111XXXX0HHHHHHHHHL1
16 C0101111XXXX0HHHHHHHHLL1
17 C0101111XXXX0HHHHHHHLHL1
18 C0101111XXXX0HLHHHHHLLL1
19 C0101111XXXX0HHHHHHLHHL1
20 C0101111XXXX0HHHHHHLHLL1
21 C0101111XXXX0HHHHHHLLHL1
22 C0101111XXXX0HHHHHHLLLL1
23 C0101111XXXX0HHHHHLHHHL1
24 C0101111XXXX0HHHHHLHHLL1
25 C0101111XXXX0HHHHHLHLHL1
26 C0101111XXXX0HLHHHLHLLL1
27 C0101111XXXX0HHHHHLLHHL1
28 C0101111XXXX0HHHHHLLHLL1
29 C0101111XXXX0HHHHHLLLHL1
30 C0101111XXXX0HHHHHLLLLL1
31 C0101010XXXX0HHHLLLHHHL1
32 C0101111XXXX0HHHLLLHHLL1
33 C0101111XXXX0HHHLLLHLHL1
34 C0101111XXXX0HHHLLLHLLL1
35 C0101111XXXX0HHHLLLLHHL1
36 C0101111XXXX0HHHLLLLHLL1
37 C0101111XXXX0HHHLLLLLHL1
38 C0101111XXXX0HHHLLLLLLL1
39 C0101111XXXX0HHLHHHHHHL1
40 C0111111XXXX0LHLHHHHHLL1
41 C0101111XXXX0HHLLLLHLHH1
42 C0101111XXXX0HHLLLLHHHL1

PASS SIMULATION
```

```
UART CONTROL

                11 1111 1111 2222 2222 2233 3333 3333
   0123 4567 8901 2345 6789 0123 4567 8901 2345 6789

 0 ---X ---- ---- ---- ---- ---- ---- ---- ---- --X- /READY*START
 1 ---- X--- ---- ---- ---- ---- ---- ---- ---- --X- /READY*RXD
 2 ---X -X-X --X- --X- ---X ---X ---X ---X ---- --X- /READY*START*BC3*BC2*BC-

 8 ---X ---X ---- ---- ---- ---- ---- ---- ---- ---- START*DET0
 9 ---X ---X ---- ---- ---- ---- ---- ---- ---- ---- START*DET0
10 -X-X ---- ---- ---- ---- ---- ---- ---- ---- ---- START*9600X8

16 ---X ---- ---X ---- ---- ---- ---- ---- ---- ---- START*DET1
17 ---X ---- ---X ---- ---- ---- ---- ---- ---- ---- START*DET1
18 -X-X ---X ---- ---- ---- ---- ---- ---- ---- ---- START*9600X8*DET0

24 ---X ---- ---- ---X ---- ---- ---- ---- ---- ---- START*DET2
25 ---X ---- ---- ---X ---- ---- ---- ---- ---- ---- START*DET2
26 -X-X ---X ---X ---- ---- ---- ---- ---- ---- ---- START*9600X8*DET0*DET1

32 ---- ---- ---- ---- ---X ---- X--- ---- ---- ---- /SETBC0*BC0
33 ---- ---- ---- ---- ---- ---- X--- ---- ---- ---X /SETBC0*READY
34 -X-X ---X ---X ---X ---- ---- X--- ---- ---- ---- /SETBC0*START*9600X8*DE-
35 ---- ---- ---- ---- ---- ---- -X-- ---- ---- ---- SETBC0

40 ---- ---- ---- ---- ---- X--X ---- ---- ---- ---- /SETBC1*BC1
41 ---- ---- ---- ---- ---- X--- ---- ---- ---- ---X /SETBC1*READY
42 -X-X ---X ---X ---X ---X X--- ---- ---- ---- ---- /SETBC1*START*9600X8*DE-
43 ---- ---- ---- ---- ---- -X-- ---- ---- ---- ---- SETBC1

48 ---- ---- ---- ---- X--- ---- ---X ---- ---- ---- /SETBC2*BC2
49 ---- ---- ---- ---- X--- ---- ---- ---- ---- ---X /SETBC2*READY
50 -X-X ---X ---X ---X X--X ---X ---- ---- ---- ---- /SETBC2*START*9600X8*DE-
51 ---- ---- ---- ---- -X-- ---- ---- ---- ---- ---- SETBC2

56 ---- ---- ---- ---- ---- ---- ---- ---X ---- ---- BC3
57 ---- ---- ---- ---- ---- ---- ---- ---- ---- ---X READY
58 -X-X ---X ---X ---X ---X ---X ---X ---- ---- ---- START*9600X8*DET0*DET1*-

64 -X-X --X- ---X --X- ---- ---- ---- --X- ---- ---- START*9600X8*/DET2*DET1-
65 -X-X --X- ---X --X- ---- ---- ---- --X- ---- ---- START*9600X8*/DET2*DET1-
66 -X-X --X- ---X --X- ---X ---X ---X --X- ---- ---- START*9600X8*/DET2*DET1-

72 ---- ---- X--- X--- ---- ---- ---- ---- ---- ---X /INIT*/WE*READY
73 ---X ---- X--- X--- --X- --X- --X- ---X ---- ---- /INIT*/WE*START*BC3*/BC-
74 ---- ---- ---- -X-- ---- ---- ---- ---- ---- ---- INIT

LEGEND:  X : FUSE NOT BLOWN (L,N,0)   - : FUSE BLOWN   (H,P,1)

NUMBER OF FUSES BLOW = 1207
```

UART Control

Logic Diagram PAL20X10

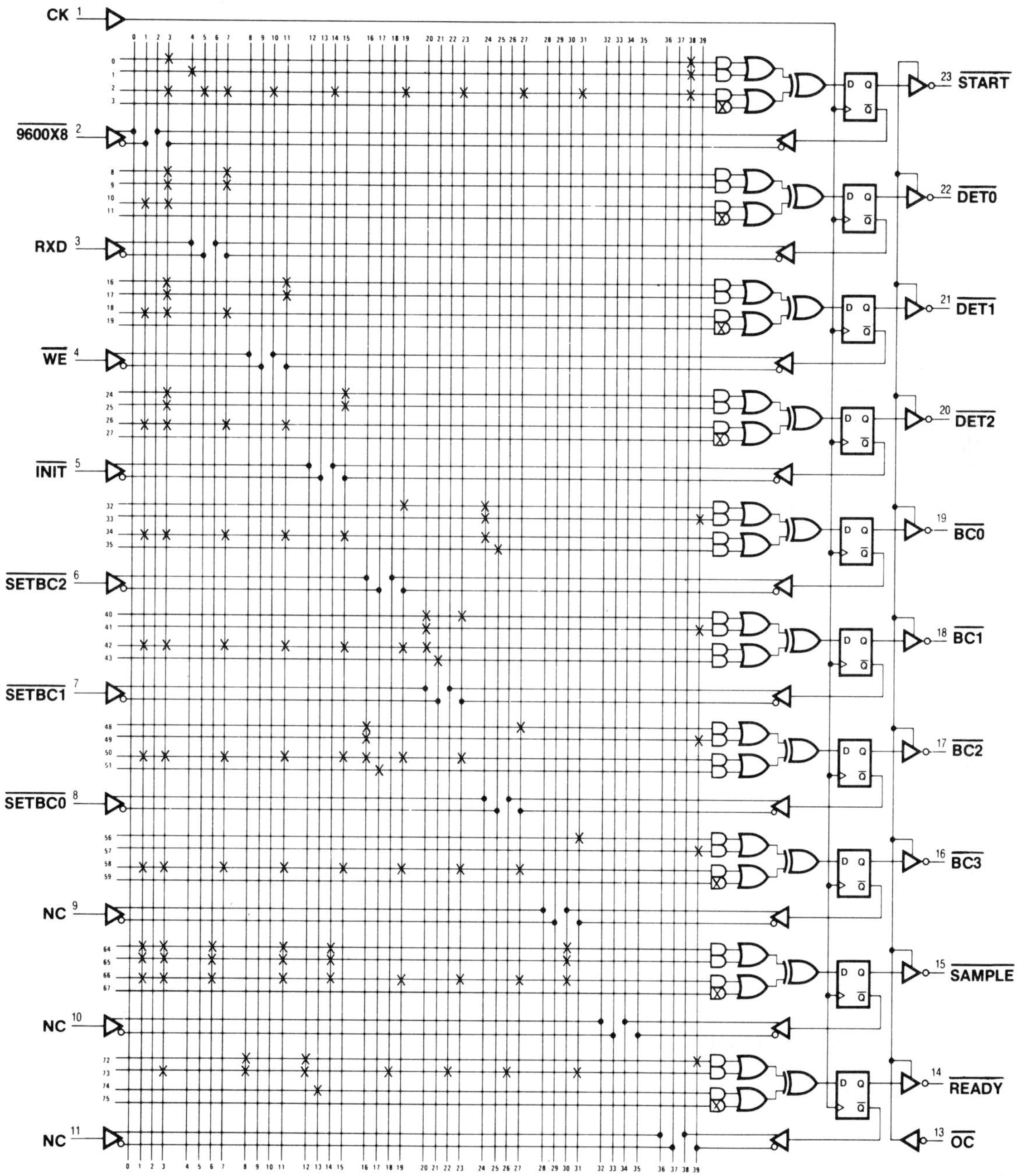

PAL
IMPORTANT, NOTES

RAM Control

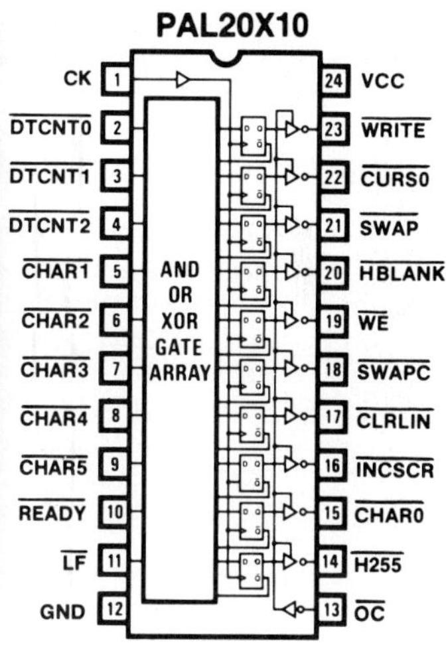
PAL20X10
CK
DTCNT0
DTCNT1
DTCNT2
CHAR1
CHAR2
CHAR3
CHAR4
CHAR5
READY
LF
GND
AND
OR
XOR
GATE
ARRAY
VCC
WRITE
CURS0
SWAP
HBLANK
WE
SWAPC
CLRLIN
INCSCR
CHAR0
H255
OC

```
PAL20X10                                          PAL DESIGN SPECIFICATION
VP8                                               BIRKNER/UDI      7/29/81
RAM CONTROL
MMI SUNNYVALE, CALIFORNIA
CK /DTCNT0 /DTCNT1 /DTCNT2 /CHAR1 /CHAR2 /CHAR3 /CHAR4 /CHAR5 /READY /LF GND
/OC /H255 /CHAR0 /INCSCR /CLRLIN /SWAPC /WE /HBLANK /SWAP /CURS0 /WRITE  VCC


WRITE:=READY*/DTCNT2*/DTCNT1*/DTCNT0*/H255                      ;SET WHEN DTCNT=0
            *CHAR5*CHAR4*CHAR3*CHAR2*CHAR1*CHAR0                ;& CHAR=63
      + WRITE*/DTCNT2*/H255                                     ;HOLD AT 0,1,2,3
     :+:WRITE* DTCNT2*/DTCNT1*/H255                             ;HOLD AT 4,5
      + CLRLIN*/DTCNT2*/DTCNT1*/DTCNT0                          ;SET AT DTCNT=0

SWAP := WRITE*/DTCNT2*/DTCNT1*DTCNT0                            ;SWAP AT DTCNT=1
      + WRITE* DTCNT2*/DTCNT1*/DTCNT0                           ;SWAP BACK AT 4

SWAPC:= WRITE*/DTCNT2*/DTCNT1*DTCNT0*/CLRLIN                    ;SWAP AT DTCNT=1
      + WRITE* DTCNT2*/DTCNT1*/DTCNT0*/CLRLIN                   ;SWAP BACK AT 4
     :+:CHAR5*CHAR4*/CHAR3*LF                                   ;TEST CONDITION

WE   := WRITE*/DTCNT2*DTCNT1*DTCNT0                             ;ENABLE WRITE

INCSCR  := WRITE*DTCNT2*/DTCNT1*DTCNT0*/CLRLIN*/H255*LF         ;DETECT LINEFEED
         + WRITE* CHAR5*/CHAR4*CHAR3*CHAR2*CHAR1*CHAR0          ;CURS=47, LAST
                */CLRLIN*/H255                                  ;VISIBLE CHAR ON
                * DTCNT2*/DTCNT1*DTCNT0                         ;LINE. DTCNT=5
        :+:CHAR5*CHAR4*/CHAR3*LF                                ;TEST CONDITION

H255    := CHAR5*CHAR4*CHAR3*CHAR2*CHAR1*CHAR0                  ;END OF LINE
           *DTCNT2*DTCNT1*/DTCNT0                               ;DTCNT=6

CLRLIN := INCSCR                                                ;SET ON LINE END
        + CLRLIN*CHAR5*CHAR4*CHAR3*CHAR2*CHAR1*CHAR0            ;HOLD THIS WRITE
       :+:CLRLIN*/CHAR5                                         ;HOLD, CHAR=0-31
        + CLRLIN*/CHAR4                                         ;HOLD, CHAR=32-47

HBLANK := CHAR5*CHAR4                                           ;CHAR=48-63
        + CHAR5*CHAR4                                           ;EXTEND
       :+:CHAR5*CHAR4*/CHAR3*/CHAR2*/CHAR1*/CHAR0*/DTCNT2 ;CANCEL 48-48.5
        + CHAR5*CHAR4*/CHAR3*/CHAR2*/CHAR1*/CHAR0*/DTCNT1 ;CANCEL 48.5-48.75

CHAR0 :=  SWAPC*CURS0                                           ;SWAP WITH CURS
       + /SWAPC*CHAR0                                           ;HOLD
      :+:/SWAPC*DTCNT0*DTCNT1*DTCNT2                            ;INC

CURS0 :=  SWAPC*/INCSCR*CHAR0                                   ;SWAP WITH CHAR
       + /SWAPC*/INCSCR*CURS0                                   ;HOLD
      :+:/SWAPC*/INCSCR*WRITE*/CLRLIN*DTCNT2*DTCNT1*/DTCNT0 ;INC
```

```
FUNCTION TABLE

CK DTCNT2 DTCNT1 DTCNT0 CHAR5 CHAR4 CHAR3 CHAR2 CHAR1 CHAR0 READY
LF /OC  H255   INCSCR CLRLIN  SWAPC  /WE HBLANK  SWAP CURS0  WRITE


;                                     I   C           H
;                       R             N   L   S       B       C   W
;                       E         H   C   R   W       L   S   U   R
;                       A     /   2   S   L   A   /   A   W   R   I
; C  DTCNT    CHAR      D   L   O   5   C   I   P   W   N   A   S   T
; K   210    54321 0    Y   F   C   5   R   N   C   E   K   P   0   E    COMMENTS
-------------------------------------------------------------------------------
  C   LLL    HHLXX X   X   H   L   X   H   X   H   X   X   X   X   X    SET INCSCR,SWAPC
  C   HHL    HHLXX X   X   H   L   X   H   H   H   X   X   X   L   X    CLRLIN=H,CURS=L
  C   LLL    HHLXX X   X   H   L   L   H   H   H   X   X   X   L   H    SET WRITE
  C   LLH    LLLXX X   X   X   L   L   L   L   L   X   X   X   L   H    INCSCS,CLRLIN=L
  C   HHL    LLXXX X   L   X   L   L   L   L   L   X   X   X   X   L    SWAP CURS0,CHAR0
  C   HHL    HHLXX X   X   H   L   X   H   X   H   X   X   X   X   X    SET INCSCR,CWAPC
  C   HHL    HHLXX X   X   H   L   X   H   H   H   X   X   X   L   X    CLRLIN=H
  C   LLL    HHLXX X   X   H   L   L   H   H   H   X   X   X   X   H    SET WRITE SIGNAL
  C   LLH    XXXXX X   L   X   L   L   X   X   X   X   X   X   X   H    HOLD WRITE
  C   LHL    XXXXX X   L   X   L   L   X   X   X   H   X   X   X   H    HOLD WRITE
  C   LHH    XXXXX X   L   X   L   L   X   X   X   L   X   X   X   H    ENABLE WRITE
  C   HLL    XXXXX X   L   X   L   L   X   X   X   H   X   X   X   H    HOLD WRITE
  C   HLH    XXXXX X   L   X   L   L   X   X   X   X   X   X   X   H    HOLD WRITE
  C   HHL    XXXXX X   L   X   L   L   X   X   L   X   X   X   X   L    CLEAR WRITE SIGNAL
  C   HHH    XXXXX H   L   X   L   L   L   X   L   X   X   X   X   L    CHAR0=H, INCSCR=L
  C   LLL    XXXXX H   L   X   L   L   L   X   L   X   X   X   X   L    HOLD
  C   LLH    XXXXX H   L   X   L   L   L   X   L   X   X   X   X   L    HOLD
  C   LHL    XXXXX H   L   X   L   L   L   X   L   X   X   X   X   L    HOLD
  C   LHH    XXXXX H   L   X   L   L   L   X   L   X   X   X   X   L    HOLD
  C   HLL    XXXXX H   L   X   L   L   L   X   L   X   X   X   X   L    HOLD
  C   HLH    XXXXX H   L   X   L   L   L   X   L   X   X   X   X   L    HOLD
  C   HHL    HHHHH H   L   X   L   H   L   X   L   X   X   X   X   X    END OF LINE
  C   HHH    HHLXX L   L   L   L   L   L   L   L   X   X   X   X   X    CLEAR CLRLIN & H255
  C   LLL    HHHXX L   H   L   L   L   L   L   L   X   H   X   X   L    SET HBLANK
  C   HHH    HHLXX H   L   L   L   L   L   L   L   X   H   X   L   L    SET CURS0 LO
  C   LLL    HHLLL H   H   L   L   L   L   L   L   X   H   X   L   X    HBLANK=L
  C   LHH    HHLXX H   L   L   L   L   L   L   L   X   X   L   L   L    HOLD
  C   HHL    HHLXX H   L   H   L   L   H   L   H   X   X   L   L   L    SET INCSCR
  C   XXX    HHLXX L   L   L   L   L   L   H   X   X   X   X   L   L    SET CLRLIN
  C   LLL    LLXXX L   L   L   L   L   L   H   X   X   X   X   L   H    HOLD CLRLIN,SET WRITE
  C   LLL    LLXXX L   L   L   L   L   L   H   X   X   X   X   L   L    CLR WRITE,HOLD CLRLIN
  C   LLL    HHLXX L   L   L   L   L   L   L   X   X   X   X   L   H    CLEAR CLRLIN
  C   LLH    XXXXX L   L   L   L   L   L   L   H   X   X   H   L   H    SET SWAP & SWAPC
-------------------------------------------------------------------------------
```

DESCRIPTION

THIS PAL CONTROLS BOTH THE TIMING FOR WRITING A CHARACTER INTO THE RAM AND THE TIMING FOR READING A CHARACTER FROM THE RAM.

"WRITE" IS A SIGNAL THAT DATA IS AVAILABLE AND CAN BE WRITTEN INTO THE RAM WHEN "DTCNT" IS BETWEEN 0 AND 5.

"SWAP" AND "SWAPC" SWAP POINTERS TO ENABLE WRITING AND READING BY ADDRESSING THE RAM THROUGH THE SAME ADDRESS LINES.

"UEN" ENABLES THE UART.

"WE" WRITES TO THE RAM THE DATA THAT IS IN THE UART REGISTER.

"INCSCR" IS A SIGNAL THAT DETECT LINEFEED AND 48 CHARACTERS PER LINE.

"CLRLIN" ERASES EARLIER INFORMATION AND ALLOWS TO WRITE TO THAT LOCATION. WHEN THE "LF" KEY IS PUSHED, THE CLRLIN SIGNAL IS SET. IT REMAINS SET AS LONG AS A WRITE IS DONE TO THIS LOCATION.

"H255" DETECTS END OF LINE.

"HBLANK" BLANK OUT THE SCREEN WHEN "CHAR" IS BETWEEN 48 AND 63.

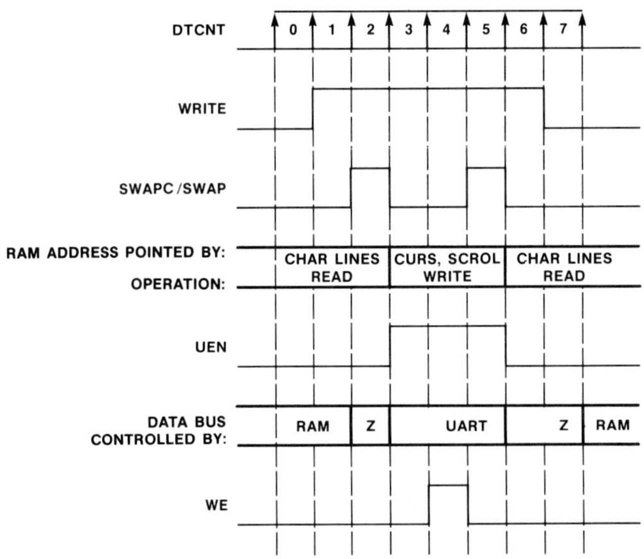

WRITE and READ signals to the RAM for one character code (when CHAR = 63). (Z = THREE STATE)

```
RAM CONTROL

 1 C111XX100X0X0XXLXLXXXXX1
 2 C100XX100X0X0XXLLLXXXHX1
 3 C111XX100X0X0HXLLLXXXHL1
 4 C011XX111XXX0HXHHHXXXHL1
 5 C100XXX111XX0HXHHHXXXXH1
 6 C100XX100X0X0XXLXLXXXXX1
 7 C100XX100X0X0XXLLLXXXHX1
 8 C111XX100X0X0HXLLLXXXXL1
 9 C011XXXXX1XX0HXXXXXXXXL1
10 C101XXXXX1XX0HXXXXHXXXL1
11 C001XXXXX1XX0HXXXXLXXXL1
12 C110XXXXX1XX0HXXXXHXXXL1
13 C010XXXXX1XX0HXXXXXXXXL1
14 C100XXXXX1XX0HXXXHXXXXH1
15 C000XXXXX1XX0HLHXHXXXXH1
16 C111XXXXX1XX0HLHXHXXXXH1
17 C011XXXXX1XX0HLHXHXXXXH1
18 C101XXXXX1XX0HLHXHXXXXH1
19 C001XXXXX1XX0HLHXHXXXXH1
20 C110XXXXX1XX0HLHXHXXXXH1
21 C010XXXXX1XX0HLHXHXXXXH1
22 C100000001XX0LLHXHXXXXX1
23 C000XX10011X0HHHHHXXXXX1
24 C111XX00001X0HHHHHXLXXH1
25 C000XX10011X0HLHHHXLXHH1
26 C1111110001X0HLHHHXLXHX1
27 C001XX10011X0HLHHHXXHHH1
28 C100XX10010X0HLLHLXXHHH1
29 CXXXXX10011X0HHHLXXXXHH1
30 C111XXX1111X0HHHLXXXXHL1
31 C111XXX1111X0HHHLXXXXHH1
32 C111XX10011X0HHHHXXXXHL1
33 C011XXXXX11X0HHHHLXXLHL1

PASS SIMULATION
```

```
RAM CONTROL

                 11 1111 1111 2222 2222 2233 3333 3333
   0123 4567 8901 2345 6789 0123 4567 8901 2345 6789

 0 X--- X--- X--- -X-- -X-- -X-- -X-- -X-- -X-X --X- READY*/DTCNT2*/DTCNT1*/-
 1 ---X ---- X--- ---- ---- ---- ---- ---- ---- --X- WRITE*/DTCNT2*/H255
 2 ---X X--- -X-- ---- ---- ---- ---- ---- ---- --X- WRITE*DTCNT2*/DTCNT1*/H-
 3 X--- X--- X--- ---- ---- ---- ---X ---- ---- ---- CLRLIN*/DTCNT2*/DTCNT1*-

 8 ---- ---- ---- ---- ---- ---X ---- --X- ---X ---- SWAPC*/INCSCR*CHAR0
 9 ---- ---X ---- ---- ---- --X- ---- --X- ---- ---- /SWAPC*/INCSCR*CURS0
10 X--X -X-- -X-- ---- ---- --X- --X- --X- ---- ---- /SWAPC*/INCSCR*WRITE*/C-

16 -X-X X--- X--- ---- ---- ---- ---- ---- ---- ---- WRITE*/DTCNT2*/DTCNT1*D-
17 X--X X--- -X-- ---- ---- ---- ---- ---- ---- ---- WRITE*DTCNT2*/DTCNT1*/D-

24 ---- ---- ---- ---- ---- ---- -X-- -X-- ---- ---- CHAR5*CHAR4
25 ---- ---- ---- ---- ---- ---- -X-- -X-- ---- ---- CHAR5*CHAR4
26 ---- ---- X--- X--- X--- X--- -X-- -X-- --X- ---- CHAR5*CHAR4*/CHAR3*/CHA-
27 ---- X--- ---- X--- X--- X--- -X-- -X-- --X- ---- CHAR5*CHAR4*/CHAR3*/CHA-

32 -X-X -X-- X--- ---- ---- ---- ---- ---- ---- ---- WRITE*/DTCNT2*DTCNT1*DT-

40 -X-X X--- X--- ---- ---- ---- --X- ---- ---- ---- WRITE*/DTCNT2*/DTCNT1*D-
41 X--X X--- -X-- ---- ---- ---- --X- ---- ---- ---- WRITE*DTCNT2*/DTCNT1*/D-
42 ---- ---- ---- ---- ---- X--- -X-- -X-- ---- -X-- CHAR5*CHAR4*/CHAR3*LF

48 ---- ---- ---- ---- ---- ---- ---- ---X ---- ---- INCSCR
49 ---- ---- ---- -X-- -X-- -X-- -X-X -X-- ---X ---- CLRLIN*CHAR5*CHAR4*CHAR-
50 ---- ---- ---- ---- ---- ---- ---X X--- ---- ---- CLRLIN*/CHAR5
51 ---- ---- ---- ---- ---- ---- X--X ---- ---- ---- CLRLIN*/CHAR4

56 -X-X X--- -X-- ---- ---- ---- --X- ---- ---- -XX- WRITE*DTCNT2*/DTCNT1*DT-
57 -X-X X--- -X-- -X-- -X-- -X-- X-X- -X-- ---X --X- WRITE*CHAR5*/CHAR4*CHAR-
58 ---- ---- ---- ---- ---- X--- -X-- -X-- ---- -X-- CHAR5*CHAR4*/CHAR3*LF

64 ---- ---X ---- ---- ---- ---X ---- ---- ---- ---- SWAPC*CURS0
65 ---- ---- ---- ---- ---- --X- ---- ---- ---X ---- /SWAPC*CHAR0
66 -X-- -X-- -X-- ---- ---- --X- ---- ---- ---- ---- /SWAPC*DTCNT0*DTCNT1*DT-

72 X--- -X-- -X-- -X-- -X-- -X-- -X-- -X-- ---X ---- CHAR5*CHAR4*CHAR3*CHAR2-

LEGEND:  X : FUSE NOT BLOWN (L,N,0)   - : FUSE BLOWN   (H,P,1)

NUMBER OF FUSES BLOW =  989
```

RAM Control

Logic Diagram PAL20X10

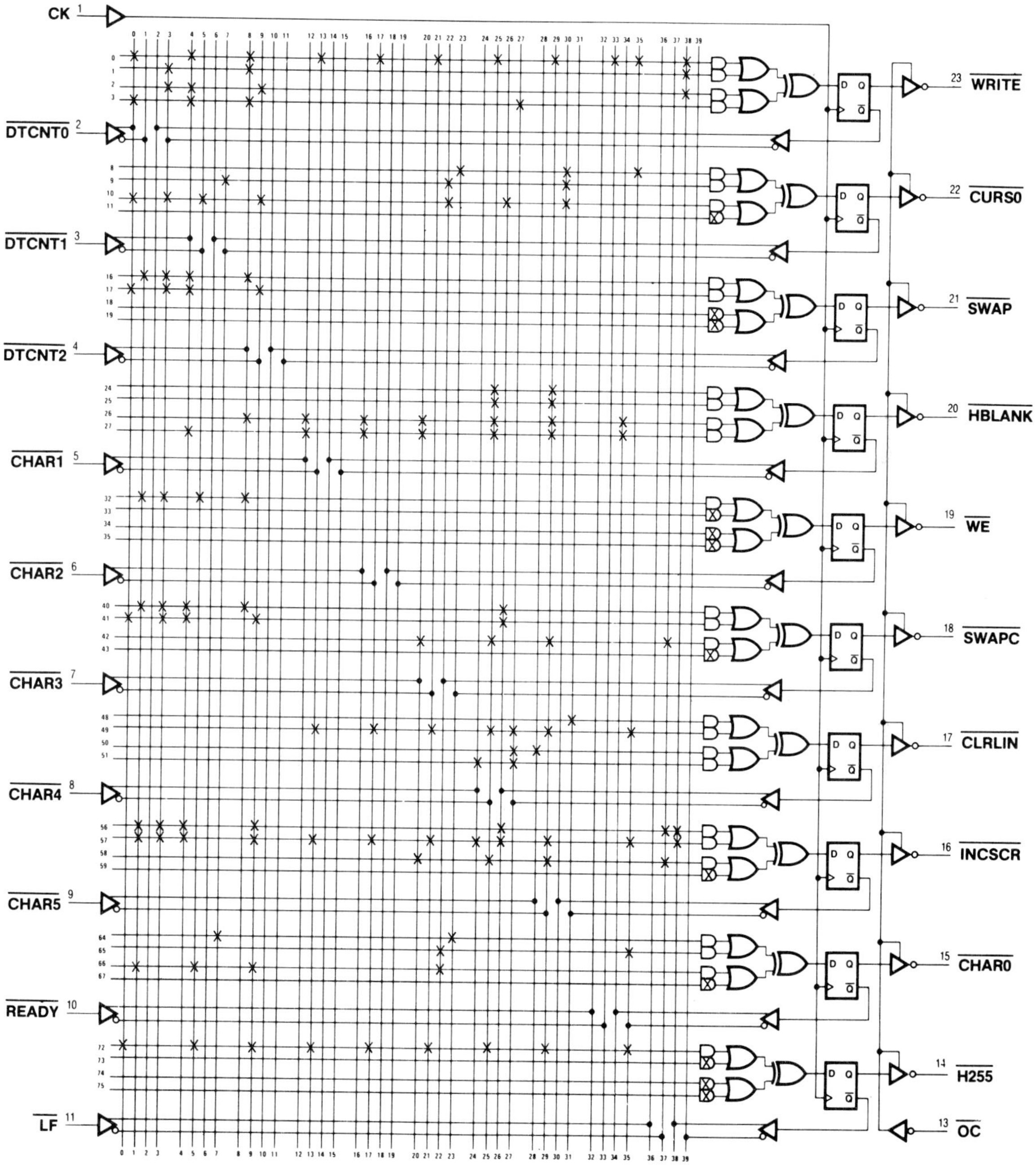

Summary

This paper conveys the message that a video-controller board can be designed in an efficient way by using PALs. The above video controller was developed and is used by Monolithic Memories, Inc.

We have presented the basic vocabulary and processes that are presently common to the industry with an explanation of how we developed our video-controller board.

Boolean transfer function equations, function tables, descriptions, simulations and fuse-plots are all offered within our PAL specifications. These were developed on the company in-house computer and are available from Monolithic Memories.

Video Controller Computer Interface

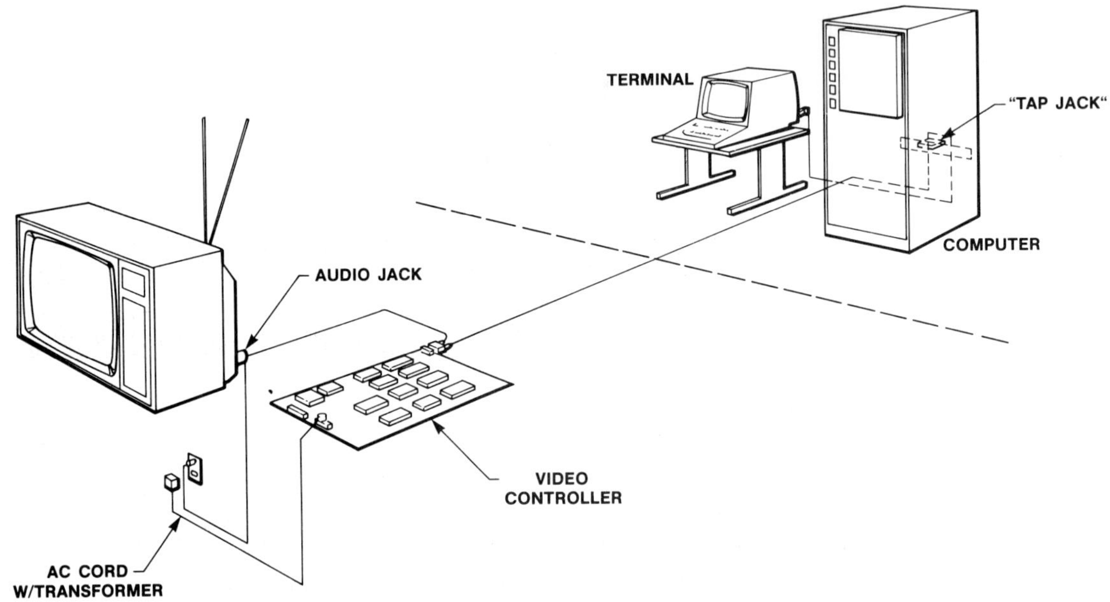

References

1. *Color TV Training Manual*
   by Howard W. Sams
   Howard W. Sams & Co., Inc.
   The Bobb-Merrill Co., Inc.

2. *Television Fundamentals Theory, Circuit and Servicing*
   Fowler and Lippert
   McGraw Hill

3. *Principles of Interactive Computer Graphics*
   by William M. Newman and Robert F. Sproull
   McGraw Hill

4. *John Birkner, personal Communication, 1981*

SINGLE-CHIP CONTROLLER INCREASES MICROPROCESSOR THROUGHPUT

Design technique uses semicustom logic to minimize hardware in a DMA controller that combines fast response with the potential to service multiple input or output devices and the flexibility to handle many different applications

Alan W. Bentley

Cubic Corporation
9333 Balboa Ave, San Diego, CA 92123

Microprocessors have a broad range of capabilities; yet they are unable to perform specific functions efficiently without hardware augmentation. One such function is transfer of blocks of data to or from processor controlled memory. Under specific conditions, such blocks may be moved efficiently by direct memory access. Data must be sequentially ordered, a starting address must be specified for both the processor associated memory and the external source or destination, and the data block length must be specified. When these three conditions are met, data transfer responsibility passes to a hardware controller, and data moves rapidly because instruction processing is eliminated during the transfer.

Although direct memory access (DMA) efficiently transfers blocks of data between a source and a destination, it normally interfaces memory with only a single external device and is unable to move data between memory and a distributed network. The need to interface a microprocessor with a network of distributed devices led to a generalized concept that can be structured to transfer data rapidly in either direction.

This concept is analogous to the DMA function in that blocks of sequential data are transferred to or from memory. It differs in that, externally, each data word has an associated device location. Implementing the transfer function in terms of this concept increases the data transfer rate while imposing four constraints on the system: the data block length must be constant; data must occupy sequential memory locations; the distributed devices are always serviced in the same sequence; and each implementation is committed to either input or output.

Controller Design Objectives

Conceptually, the controller accepts data transfer responsibility from the microprocessor upon command; steps through the data block, sequentially creating data paths between memory and various external devices; then returns control to the microprocessor. Functionally, upon receipt of the transfer mode command, the controller places the central processing unit (CPU) in the 3-state mode, generates all

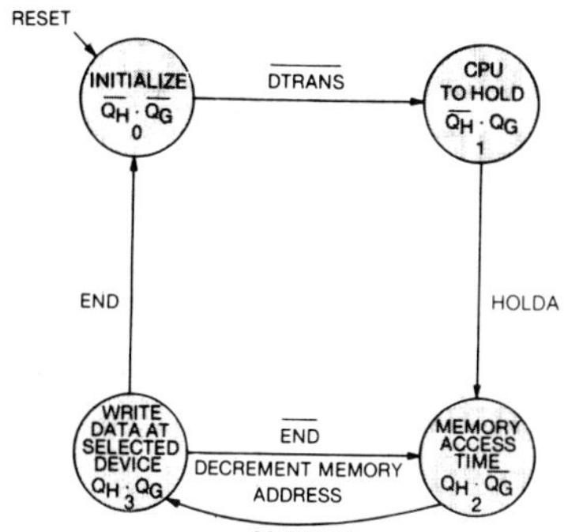

COMPLETE STATE DIAGRAM

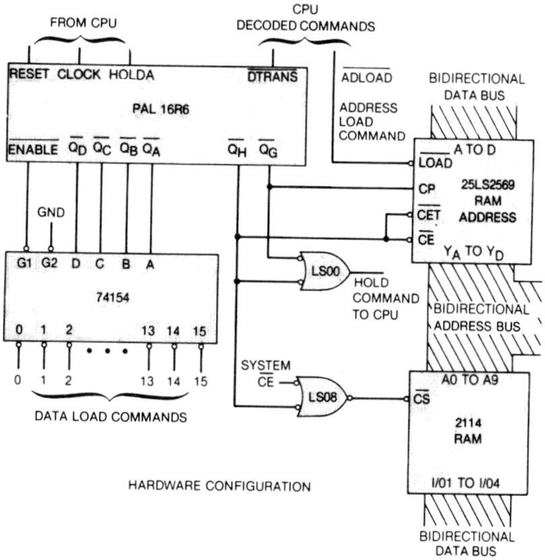

HARDWARE CONFIGURATION

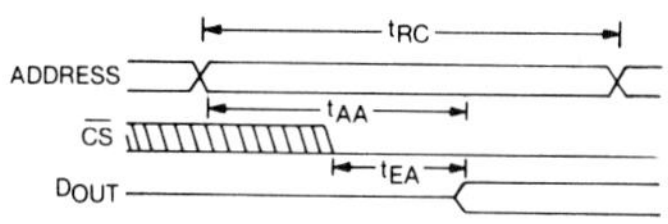

t_{RC} = READ CYCLE TIME
t_{AA} = ACCESS TIME - ADDRESS TO D_{OUT}
t_{EA} = ACCESS TIME - CHIP SELECT TO D_{OUT}

RAM TIMING REQUIREMENTS

GENERAL

1. CPU HOLD COMMAND IS $Q_G + Q_H$ (STATE 1, 2, OR 3)
2. STATE 2 IS ENTERED UPON RECEIPT OF HOLDA (CPU IN HOLD, CPU ADDRESS AND DATA BUSES 3-STATE)
3. IN STATES 2 AND 3 RAM ADDRESS COUNTER OUTPUT IS REMOVED FROM 3-STATE MODE AND ITS COUNT CAPABILITY ENABLED THROUGH $\overline{CET}$
4. AT TRANSITION FROM STATE 3 TO STATE 2, BOTH DATA COUNTER AND RAM COUNTER ADDRESS ARE DECREMENTED BY RISING EDGE OF $\overline{Q_G}$
5. UPON COMPLETION OF DATA TRANSFER (END), STATE 0 IS ENTERED FROM STATE 3, DATA COUNTER IS SET AT ITS INITIAL COUNT, ADDRESS COUNTER IS PLACED IN 3-STATE MODE, AND HOLD COMMAND TO CPU IS RELEASED

SPECIFIC (TRANSFER CPU MEMORY TO EXTERNAL DEVICES)

1. RAM IS SELECTED IN STATES 2 AND 3, $\overline{Q_H}$
2. IN STATE 3, ENABLE SELECTS DEMULTIPLEXER, AND CONTENTS OF DATA COUNTER ($\overline{Q_A}$ THROUGH Q_D) ARE DECODED TO GENERATE DATA LOAD (WRITE ENABLE) PULSE

SEQUENCE OF EVENTS

Fig 1 Transfer from CPU memory to device. PAL implements two categories of Boolean expressions, data counters that control destination selection and state equations that control sequence of events shown in state diagram

required timing and control signals, sequentially creates the data paths, and transfers data through each path. Upon completion of the data transfer, it relinquishes control to the microprocessor, which then resumes instruction processing.

Increased throughput is the implementation rationale; therefore, the two primary design objectives are to enter and leave the data transfer mode in a minimum number of clock periods and to transfer one data word every two clock periods. This transfer rate allows one clock period to establish each data path, with the write pulse created in the second period to complete the transfer. Secondary design objectives relate to implementation and allow modification to meet varying applications using a minimal amount of additional circuitry.

Design approaches that meet these objectives include use of a state sequencer to meet the control transfer and data transmission timing requirements, and use of fusible link, semicustom logic to meet the circuit flexibility and minimization requirements. A simplified microprocessor interface is achieved by incorporating the microprocessor clock and hold capabilities into the sequencer design.

State Sequencer

The state sequencer organizes and concentrates logical functions to realize the high density capabilities of semicustom logic. What determines the number of control flipflops is the number of required states; therefore,

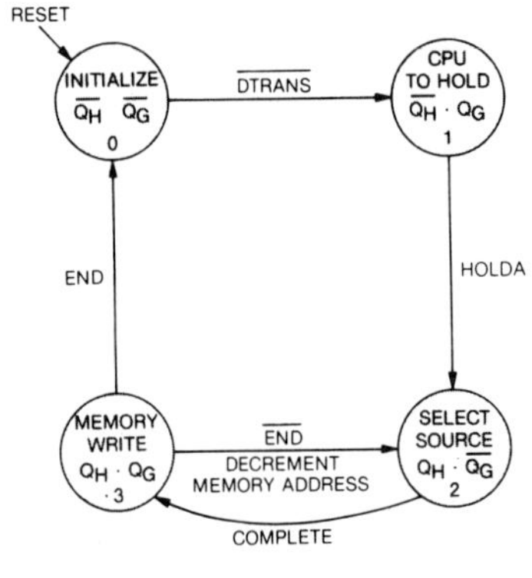

STATE DIAGRAM

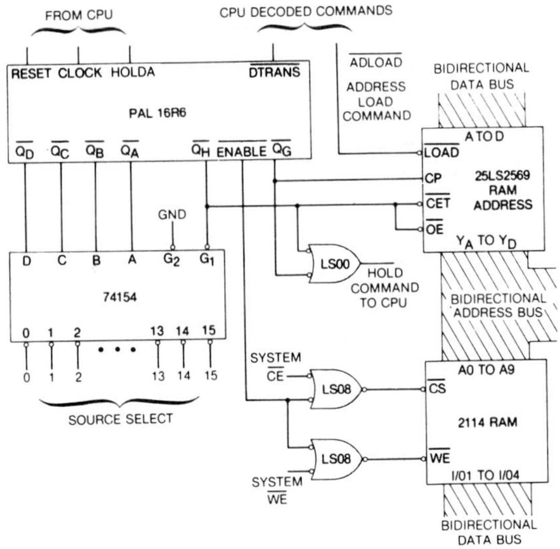

HARDWARE CONFIGURATION

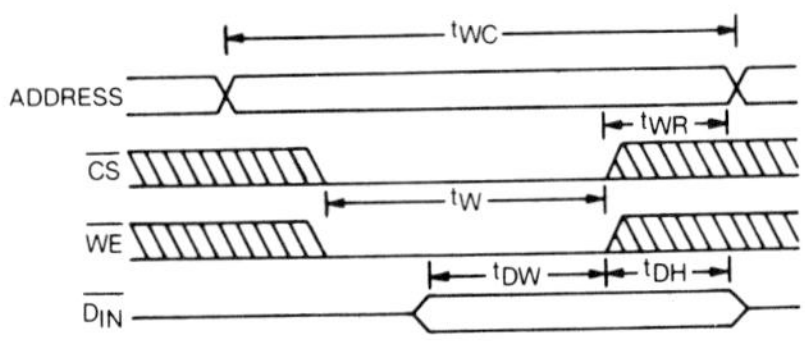

t_{WC} = WRITE CYCLE TIME

t_W = WRITE TIME

t_{DW} = DATA TO WRITE TIME OVERLAP

t_{DH} = DATA HOLD TIME FROM WRITE TIME

t_{WR} = WRITE RELEASE TIME

RAM TIMING REQUIREMENTS

GENERAL

1. CPU HOLD COMMAND IS $Q_G + Q_H$ (STATE 1, 2, OR 3)
2. STATE 2 IS ENTERED UPON RECEIPT OF HOLDA (CPU IN HOLD, CPU ADDRESS AND DATA BUSES 3-STATE)
3. IN STATES 2 AND 3 RAM ADDRESS COUNTER OUTPUT IS REMOVED FROM 3-STATE MODE AND ITS COUNT CAPABILITY ENABLED THROUGH $\overline{CET}$
4. AT TRANSITION FROM STATE 3 TO STATE 2, BOTH DATA COUNTER AND RAM COUNTER ADDRESS ARE DECREMENTED BY RISING EDGE OF $\overline{Q_G}$
5. UPON COMPLETION OF DATA TRANSFER (END), STATE 0 IS ENTERED FROM STATE 3. DATA COUNTER IS SET AT ITS INITIAL COUNT, ADDRESS COUNTER IS PLACED IN 3-STATE MODE, AND HOLD COMMAND TO CPU IS RELEASED

SPECIFIC (TRANSFER EXTERNAL SOURCE TO CPU MEMORY)

1. IN STATES 2 AND 3 ($\overline{Q_H}$) DEMULTIPLEXER IS ENABLED, DECODES DATA COUNTER CONTENTS, AND SELECTS EXTERNAL SOURCE
2. DURING STATE 3 $\overline{ENABLE}$ IS RAM CHIP SELECT AND WRITE ENABLE, WRITING SOURCE DATA WORD IN SELECTED ADDRESS LOCATION

SEQUENCE OF EVENTS

Fig 2 Transfer from device to CPU memory. Similar to Fig 1, with hardware configuration and state diagram modified to transfer data in opposite direction

performing all logic functions in four states reduces the sequencer design requirement to two flipflops and helps meet the secondary design objective. These four states are idle, when the CPU has system control; transitional, while the CPU is entering the hold mode and relinquishing control; and two data transfer, one permitting address and data stabilization, and the other creating the write command (Figs 1 and 2).

In this application, both flipflops are reset in the idle state ($\overline{Q}_H$,$\overline{Q}_G$, state 0) awaiting a software generated command ($\overline{DTRANS}$), which sets the G flipflop, advances the sequencer to state 1 ($\overline{Q}_H$,Q_G), and initiates a CPU hold command, sustained until the sequencer returns to state 0. The CPU tests its hold command input each machine cycle and, upon sensing a command, enters the hold state, placing its data bus, address bus, and some control lines in the 3-state mode. It remains in this state until the hold command is released by the sequencer.

When it enters the hold state, the CPU issues a hold acknowledge (HOLD). Upon receipt of HOLDA, the sequencer advances to state 2 ($Q_H,\overline{Q}_G$), which completes transfer of the data handling function from the CPU to the controller. It then toggles between state 2 and state 3 (Q_H,Q_G), processing one data word each cycle until the preestablished number of data words have been transferred (END). Then, the sequencer returns to state 0 and releases the hold command, allowing resumption of instruction processing by the CPU.

While the sequence of states is the same for data transfer in either direction, the events that occur within states 2 and 3 differ. During transfer of data from memory to external devices, state 2 is memory access time and state 3 generates the load command for the specific device. When leaving state 3, the edge of the G flipflop ($\overline{Q}_G$) advances the memory address counter. When data from external devices are read into memory, state 2 time is used to select the external source and stabilize the data. The memory write enable pulse is generated by state 3, and leaving state 3 changes the memory address counter. Transfer states ST2 and ST3 are identified by the output of the H flipflop, which activates the random access memory (RAM) address counter outputs, enables address counting, and, additionally, selects either the RAM or the multiplexer when transferring to or from the external devices, respectively.

Programmed Array Logic

Utilizing semicustom integrated circuitry satisfies the requirement for logic minimization and design flexibility. This approach increases logic density by mitigating two factors that increase random logic package count: function partitioning and pin limitation. To maximize these benefits, the programmable logic chip must contain AND, OR, and flipflop functions, as well as internal feedback. Flipflop functions are required to implement the sequencer and, additionally, a counter that is decremented at the completion of each data transfer (state 3 to state 2 transition). The counter serves a dual purpose: the demultiplexed count selects external devices and, by monitoring the count, the controller determines completion of the data block transfer (END).

Data block length determines the number of counters and demultiplexers required. With three counters and a 3 to 8 demultiplexer (74138), block lengths up to eight may be accommodated. With four counters and a 4 to 16 demultiplexer (74157), the block length may be extended to 16. An increase to six counters will allow block length expansion to 64, with additional demultiplexers. This approach focuses on design for a block length of 16 words so that the flipflops and associated input decoding can be contained on one fusible link, programmable array logic (PAL) integrated circuit.

PAL 16R6 contains six D flipflops (registers) connected to a common clock input. Output Q of each register is available externally through an inverting, 3-state buffer ($\overline{Q}$). Input D of each register is an 8-input OR gate, each input a programmable AND combination of the available terms. Each gate array must be true to set the register on the following clock pulse or false to allow the register to reset. Thus, Boolean expressions state the conditions that cause the registers to become or remain set.

Two additional, non-register, AND-OR gate outputs and the six register outputs have internal feedback paths. With the eight available inputs, they become the 16 terms available when implementing Boolean expressions.

Boolean Expressions

Six counter equations are shown in Fig 3. For a maximum block length of 16, the four least significant counts (A through D) are required; expansion up to length 32 requires equation E; equation F must be implemented for block lengths between 33 and 64. The counter flipflops are held set during states 0 and 1. States 2 and 3 require only one clock period each; hence, from leaving state 1 until completion of data transmission and return to state 0, there is a state transition in every clock cycle.

During this interval, each equation must establish the condition of its counter flipflop for the following state. When entering state 2 from state 1, the counter flipflops are set as established by state 1. Since it is necessary to change the counter on the transition from state 3 to state 2, the counting decision must be made during state 3, and the new count must be established when entering state 2. The counter register content must be maintained during state 2 to prevent change at the transition from state 2 to 3.

Fig 3 also shows the 2-state sequencer equations. Equation G is independent of block length, and equation H

$$Q_F = \overline{Q_H} + Q_H \cdot \overline{Q_G} \cdot Q_F + Q_H \cdot Q_G (Q_F \cdot Q_E + Q_F \cdot Q_D + Q_F \cdot Q_C + Q_F \cdot Q_B + Q_F \cdot Q_A)$$

$$Q_E = \overline{Q_H} + Q_H \cdot \overline{Q_G} \cdot Q_E + Q_H \cdot Q_G (Q_E \cdot Q_D + Q_E \cdot Q_C + Q_E \cdot Q_B + Q_E \cdot Q_A + \overline{Q_E} \cdot \overline{Q_D} \cdot \overline{Q_C} \cdot \overline{Q_B} \cdot \overline{Q_A})$$

$$Q_D = \overline{Q_H} + Q_H \cdot \overline{Q_G} \cdot Q_D + Q_H \cdot Q_G (Q_D \cdot Q_C + Q_D \cdot Q_B + Q_D \cdot Q_A + \overline{Q_D} \cdot \overline{Q_C} \cdot \overline{Q_B} \cdot \overline{Q_A})$$

$$Q_C = \overline{Q_H} + Q_H \cdot \overline{Q_G} \cdot Q_C + Q_H \cdot Q_G (Q_C \cdot Q_B + Q_C \cdot Q_A + \overline{Q_C} \cdot \overline{Q_B} \cdot \overline{Q_A})$$

$$Q_B = \overline{Q_H} + Q_H \cdot \overline{Q_G} \cdot Q_B + Q_H \cdot Q_G (Q_B \cdot Q_A + \overline{Q_B} \cdot \overline{Q_A})$$

$$Q_A = \overline{Q_H} + Q_H \cdot \overline{Q_G} \cdot Q_A + Q_H \cdot Q_G \cdot \overline{Q_A}$$

$$Q_G = \overline{\text{RESET}} (\overline{Q_H} \cdot \overline{Q_G} \cdot \overline{\text{DTRANS}} + \overline{Q_H} \cdot Q_G \cdot \overline{\text{HOLDA}} + Q_H \cdot \overline{Q_G})$$

$$Q_H = \overline{\text{RESET}} [\overline{Q_H} \cdot Q_G \cdot \text{HOLDA} + Q_H \cdot \overline{Q_G} + Q_H \cdot Q_G (\overline{\text{END}})]$$

Fig 3 Boolean statements. PAL registers implement data counter and state controller equations. Control equation G is independent of block length. Control equation H must be expanded by expression for $\overline{\text{END}}$ to establish block length incorporates the block length ($\overline{END}$) decoding. The table, Block Length Control, shows the expressions for $\overline{END}$, when six counters are used, organized by remainder of a modulo 16 number. For shorter block lengths, references to unimplemented counters are ignored. Both control flipflops are reset (expressions false) when the computer issues a RESET command, establishing state 0. This state is maintained until the CPU issues $\overline{DTRANS}$, advancing the sequencer to state 1 by setting G.

A hold command is generated by the sequencer, which waits in state 1 until the CPU responds with HOLDA, verifying that it has stopped instruction processing and that its buses are 3-stated. HOLDA resets G and sets H, advancing the sequencer to state 2. The G flipflop then toggles, causing the sequencer to cycle between states 2 and 3. H remains set during both states but tests the content of the data counter during state 3 to determine if data transmission is complete ($\overline{END}$ expression false). $\overline{END}$ false also causes the H flipflop to reset at the completion of state 3, returning the sequencer to state 0 and releasing the hold command to the CPU.

Block Length Control*

Remainder	$\overline{END}$ Expression
1	$Q_F + Q_E$
2	$Q_F + Q_E + Q_A$
3	$Q_F + Q_E + Q_B$
4	$Q_F + Q_E + Q_B + Q_A$
5	$Q_F + Q_E + Q_C$
6	$Q_F + Q_E + Q_C + Q_A$
7	$Q_F + Q_E + Q_C + Q_B$
8	$Q_F + Q_E + Q_C + Q_B + Q_A$
9	$Q_F + Q_E + Q_D$
10	$Q_F + Q_E + Q_D + Q_A$
11	$Q_F + Q_E + Q_D + Q_B$
12	$Q_F + Q_E + Q_D + Q_B + Q_A$
13	$Q_F + Q_E + Q_D + Q_C$
14	$Q_F + Q_E + Q_D + Q_C + Q_A$
15	$Q_F + Q_E + Q_D + Q_C + Q_B$
0	$Q_F + Q_E + Q_D + Q_C + Q_B + Q_A$

*Required to complete equation H in Fig 3, $\overline{END}$ expressions are listed by modulo 16 remainder of data word count. Counter F is not required for block sizes less than 33. Counter E is not required for block sizes less than 17. Single word transmission is a trivial solution

Implementation

System parameters were developed for use with the model 8085 microprocessor, the 2114 bidirectional RAM, and the 25LS2569 binary up/down counter. Attributes of these components that help meet the design goals are (a) availability of the CPU interface signals reset, clock out, hold, and hold

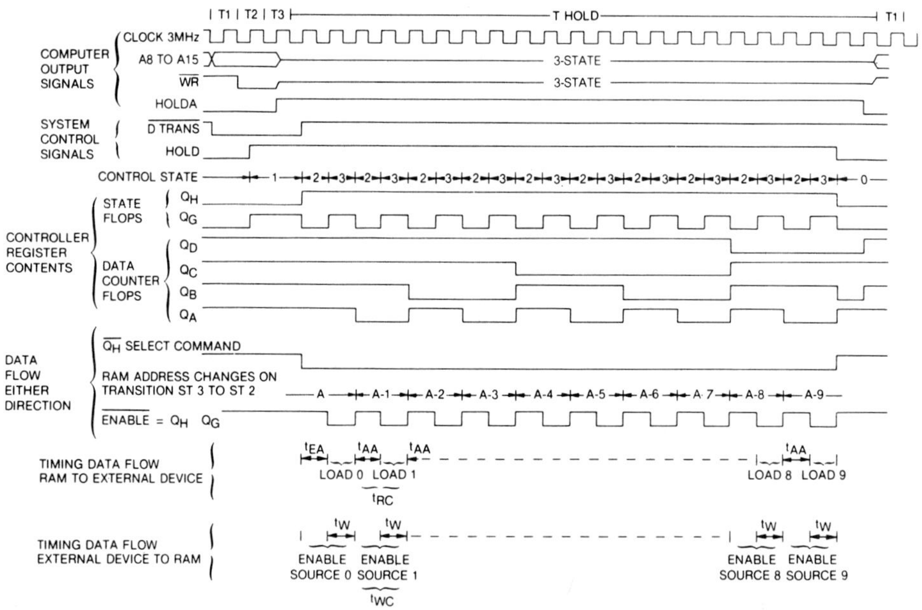

Fig 4 8085 timing and interface signals. Register contents reflect state controller interaction with computer commands. Control states reflect state flipflop outputs. Signals common to transfer in either direction are grouped. Current RAM address starts at A and decreases during successive cycles. Memory timing, shown for data flow both from and to RAM, relates to RAM timing requirements for Fig 1 and Fig 2, respectively acknowledge; (b) the RAM's high density, 4-bit data word, bidirectional data bus, and simplified dual control line interface; and (c) the counter synchronized load, increment, and decrement controls, and also its 3-state output and cascading capabilities. Additionally, the response and operating speeds of the RAM and counter are compatible with the microprocessor clock.

Figs 1, 2, and 4 show the configuration and timing relationships achieved by using these components. Microprocessor choice establishes the system clock rate and the method of passing control between the microprocessor and the data controller. The method of implementing the data controller, which meets the dual requirements of simplicity and high throughput, restricts RAM selection. In Figs 1 and 2, t_{RC} and t_{WC} cannot exceed two clock periods. When moving data to external devices, the devices must be able to function within the constraints of t_{AA} and t_{EA}. When moving data to the CPU memory, its write requirements, t_W and t_{DW}, must be less than one clock period. Because of the controller structure, t_{DH} and t_{WR} must both be zero, a restriction satisfied by many RAMs currently available.

Adaptation

Distributed data port servicing is the primary functional requirement of the data controller, and the specific number of ports is a parameter written into the Boolean expressions implemented by a member of the PAL family. The inherent flexibility arising from implementation of many of the logic functions by easily modified Boolean expressions can be demonstrated by extending the application requirements to include program control of the data block length. Now, the design objectives are to incorporate this feature with minimal hardware reconfiguration and to retain all the operational attributes of the original DMA controller.

Although the state sequencer remains conceptually unchanged, its interaction with the data counter must be modified to implement a variable block length. The original concept has a fixed data block length, with the data counter starting at all 1s and decrementing to a predetermined end count. Its advantages are that the CPU interface is minimized and that all data ports are serviced during each DMA cycle. To implement the variable block length feature, the CPU loads the data counter with the actual count; then during data transfer, the state sequencer decrements the count to 0, the end count that terminates the operation.

It is desirable to implement the state sequencer and data counter on a single programmable chip while maximizing the data counter length. To achieve this, a 16R8 programmable logic chip replaces the 16R6 used previously. This change increases the number of registers by two at the expense of the two gated outputs. The chip configuration now offers eight data inputs; eight D registers, each with an inverting output; a register clock input; and a 3-state control input.

Of the eight registers, two are required for the state sequencer, allowing a maximum block length of 64 in a single-chip implementation. However, three control lines are required: $\overline{\text{HOLDA}}$ and $\overline{\text{DTRANS}}$, as in the original concept, plus a software generated $\overline{\text{LOADA}}$, which transfers the content of the data bus to the data registers. Additionally, the $\overline{\text{LOADA}}$ command must be used to initialize the state counter (Fig 5). With this approach, five inputs remain for the data bus, limiting the block size to 32 words.

An alternative configuration using only three data bits allows loading of the six flipflops in two instruction cycles

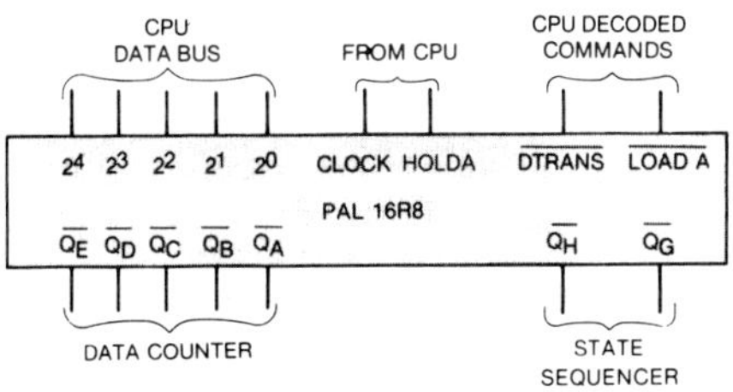

DATA COUNTERS

$$Q_E = \overline{\text{LOAD A}} \cdot 2^4 + Q_E(\overline{Q_H} + Q_H \cdot \overline{Q_G}) + Q_H \cdot Q_G \cdot Q_E(Q_D + Q_C + Q_B + Q_A)$$

$$Q_D = \overline{\text{LOAD A}} \cdot 2^3 + Q_D(\overline{Q_H} + Q_H \cdot \overline{Q_G}) + Q_H \cdot Q_G[Q_D(Q_C + Q_B + Q_A) + \overline{Q_D} \cdot \overline{Q_C} \cdot \overline{Q_B} \cdot \overline{Q_A}]$$

$$Q_C = \overline{\text{LOAD A}} \cdot 2^2 + Q_C(\overline{Q_H} + Q_H \cdot \overline{Q_G}) + Q_H \cdot Q_G[Q_C(Q_B + Q_A) + \overline{Q_C} \cdot \overline{Q_B} \cdot \overline{Q_A}]$$

$$Q_B = \overline{\text{LOAD A}} \cdot 2^1 + Q_B(\overline{Q_H} + Q_H \cdot \overline{Q_G}) + Q_H \cdot Q_G(Q_B \cdot Q_A + \overline{Q_B} \cdot \overline{Q_A})$$

$$Q_A = \overline{\text{LOAD A}} \cdot 2^0 + Q_A(\overline{Q_H} + Q_H \cdot \overline{Q_G}) + Q_H \cdot Q_G \cdot \overline{Q_A}$$

STATE CONTROLLER

$$Q_G = \text{LOAD A}(\overline{Q_H} \cdot \overline{Q_G} \cdot \overline{\text{DTRANS}} + \overline{Q_H} \cdot Q_G \cdot \overline{\text{HOLDA}} + Q_H \cdot \overline{Q_G})$$

$$Q_H = \text{LOAD A}[\overline{Q_H} \cdot Q_G \cdot \text{HOLDA} + Q_H \cdot \overline{Q_G} + Q_H \cdot Q_G(Q_E + Q_D + Q_C + Q_B + Q_A)]$$

Fig 5 Adding program control over block length. Hardware configuration and Boolean expressions are modified to implement program control of data block length. Data input limitation prevents use of one register, restricting block length to 32 words

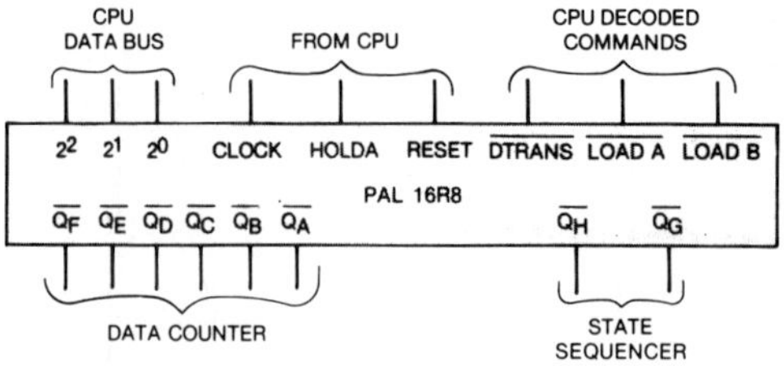

DATA COUNTERS

$$Q_F = \overline{\text{LOAD B}} \cdot 2^2 + Q_F(\overline{Q_H} + Q_H \cdot \overline{Q_G}) + Q_H \cdot Q_G \cdot Q_F(Q_E + Q_D + Q_C + Q_B + Q_A)$$

$$Q_E = \overline{\text{LOAD B}} \cdot 2^1 + Q_E(\overline{Q_H} + Q_H \cdot \overline{Q_G}) + Q_H \cdot Q_G[Q_E(Q_D + Q_C + Q_B + Q_A) + \overline{Q_E} \cdot \overline{Q_D} \cdot \overline{Q_C} \cdot \overline{Q_B} \cdot \overline{Q_A}]$$

$$Q_D = \overline{\text{LOAD B}} \cdot 2^0 + Q_D(\overline{Q_H} + Q_H \cdot \overline{Q_G}) + Q_H \cdot Q_G[Q_D(Q_C + Q_B + Q_A) + \overline{Q_D} \cdot \overline{Q_C} \cdot \overline{Q_B} \cdot \overline{Q_A}]$$

$$Q_C = \overline{\text{LOAD A}} \cdot 2^2 + Q_C(\overline{Q_H} + Q_H \cdot \overline{Q_G}) + Q_H \cdot Q_G[Q_C(Q_B + Q_A) + \overline{Q_C} \cdot \overline{Q_B} \cdot \overline{Q_A}]$$

$$Q_B = \overline{\text{LOAD A}} \cdot 2^1 + Q_B(\overline{Q_H} + Q_H \cdot \overline{Q_G}) + Q_H \cdot Q_G(Q_B \cdot Q_A + \overline{Q_B} \cdot \overline{Q_A})$$

$$Q_A = \overline{\text{LOAD A}} \cdot 2^0 + Q_A(\overline{Q_H} + Q_H \cdot \overline{Q_G}) + Q_H \cdot Q_G \cdot \overline{Q_A}$$

STATE CONTROLLER

$$Q_G = \overline{\text{RESET}}(\overline{Q_H} \cdot \overline{Q_G} \cdot \overline{\text{DTRANS}} + \overline{Q_H} \cdot Q_G \cdot \overline{\text{HOLDA}} + Q_H \cdot \overline{Q_G})$$

$$Q_H = \overline{\text{RESET}}[\overline{Q_H} \cdot Q_G \cdot \text{HOLDA} + Q_H \cdot \overline{Q_G} + Q_H \cdot Q_G(Q_F + Q_E + Q_D + Q_C + Q_B + Q_A)]$$

Fig 6 Extending block length. Additional modification increases block length to 64 words by using all internal registers. All capabilities of previous configuration have been maintained across both modifications

by implementing a second load command, $\overline{\text{LOADB}}$. The DMA controller now handles block lengths as long as 64 data words, and the RESET command can be used to initialize the state counter as in the original concept (Fig 6).

Summary

Generally, a design approach and its means of implementation should be complementary. Specifically, the controller design objectives are met by utilizing a state sequencer, and implementation compatibility is assured by such features of semicustom logic as multiple storage elements with internal feedback paths, dense gating arrays, and interconnection flexibility.

The process of creating a state sequencer to solve a design problem results in a series of Boolean expressions that define the controller capability and the gate array that must be effected. Several partially dedicated gating and register arrays constitute the semicustom logic family. After the most suitable array configuration is selected, the interconnections, as expressed by Boolean statements, are completed to implement the design. This creates a unique logic pattern whose dense gating contributes to chip count minimization. Design variations can be accommodated by restructuring the gating arrays with minimal hardware reconfiguration. Thus, the system can be tailored to the original operating requirements and yet be easily adapted if modifications are desired.

Bibliography

"MCS-85 Users Manual," Intel Corp, Santa Clara, Calif, 1978

J. Nissim, "DMA Controller Capitalizes on Clock Cycles to Bypass CPU," *Computer Design*, Jan 1978, pp 117-124

"Programmable Array Logic Handbook," Monolithic Memories Inc, Sunnyvale, Calif, 1978

Alan W. Bentley is a design specialist, technically responsible for the development of a high speed data processing and display system at Cubic Corp. He is also an instructor in the Engineering Department of San Diego Community College. He has a BS degree in electrical engineering from Tufts University, an MBA from United States International University, and an MA from San Diego State University.

FPLA ARBITER CONCEPT ADAPTS TO APPLICATION NEEDS

Field programmable logic implements efficient, easily customized arbiter whose versatile Boolean statement format meets numerous system requirements

Alan W. Bentley Cubic Corporation
9333 Balboa Ave, San Diego, CA 92123

Today's trends toward shared resources, multiprocessing, and decentralized, bus oriented system organization underscore the demand for arbiters that work independently and issue grants according to predetermined algorithms. Functionally, a requirement for stable processing of system requests is created when several processors use a common device and each requests service asynchronously. It is the arbiter's task to issue grants for sequential access in accordance with a preestablished algorithm. By using a versatile Boolean statement format to express its algorithms, an arbiter can be customized to interface with single-array, multiple-array, and hybrid logic configurations. Designing arbiters to be flexible in implementing algorithms can help to meet the demand for cost-effective data processing systems and bring heretofore expensive, hence scarce, devices into wider use.

Arbiter Interface

From the system's perspective of the interface, when a system is ready for service from the device, it raises a request line. The arbiter responds by issuing a grant to the system that clears it to conduct transactions with the device. Upon completion of service, the system drops its request line. The arbiter, in turn, cancels the grant and is then free to issue a grant to the next pending request.

Stable system requests are necessary because all requests and grants are evaluated each clock period. These requests are generated asynchronously and are synchronized through a set of input latches. If a 2-phase balanced clock is used, with requests synchronized on phase 0 and grants issued or released on phase 1, the maximum time from a system request for service until synchronization of that request is one clock period. Minimum time from completion of the transaction to release of the synchronized request is the system's internal delay, as it drops the request line, plus the setup time of the synchronizing latches. At the completion of a transaction, there is a half-clock period, the time from phase 0 to phase 1, when a unique signal combination exists—a grant issued to a system that does not have a synchronized request. During this half-period, all other synchronized requests are examined and, according to the servicing algorithm, the recipient of the next sequential grant is determined. Then, on phase 1, the existing (unsolicited) grant is canceled and the next grant issued.

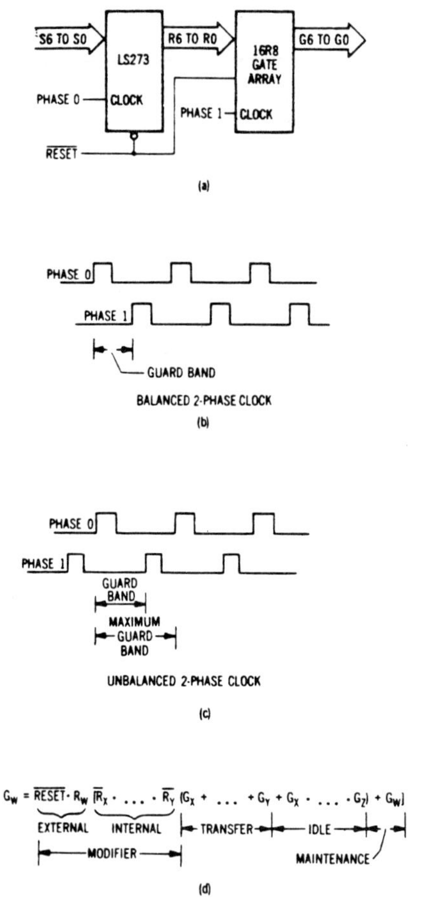

Fig 1 Arbiter circuitry, timing, and grant expression format. In (a), S6 to S0 are system requests. Latch outputs R6 to R0 are synchronized requests that arbiter algorithm converts to system grants, G6 to G0. Unbalanced clock phases increase guard band (b and c), with maximum guard band needing only one phase. Logic equation for algorithm (d) combines four subexpressions

The sum of the requesting system's internal delay in dropping its request line, the synchronizing latch setup time, and one-half the clock period, act as a guard band to ensure separation of systems interacting with the device. Arbiter clock frequency, therefore, is a major factor in determining guard band time. For a given arbiter clock frequency, the guard band can be increased by unbalancing the clock, increasing the time between phase 0 and phase 1 to more than half the clock period. The limiting case occurs when the time between phase 0 and phase 1 is increased until it equals the clock period. This makes phase 0 and phase 1 coincident, requires only a single-phase clock, and maximizes the guard band for a given clock frequency. The limiting case relies on the propagation delay of the latch flipflops and the setup time of the array logic grant flipflops to ensure a delay of one clock period between release of the synchronized request and the associated grant. Start of the guard band signifies completion of the current transaction, and guard band time is used to determine the next grant recipient; then, at the start of the next clock period, the current grant will be canceled, and, if one or more requests are pending, the next grant issued.

Octal D flipflops (LS273) are used to synchronize the input requests, and a programmable gate array (16R8) is used to evaluate the requests and issue grants. In the 2-phase clock, phase 0 synchronizes requests and phase 1 issues grants (Fig 1). Both the octal flipflops and the logic array are 20-pin packages. In addition to the clock and 3-state control inputs, the logic array has 8 data inputs and 8 D flipflop outputs. The Q output of each flipflop is inverted and buffered, and is a 3-state output; the $\overline{Q}$ output is returned to the array internally, where the 8 flipflop settings and the 8 data inputs are complemented and are available in both original and complement form at 8-input OR gates. There are eight OR gates, each forming the D input for one of the eight flipflops.

By programming through fusable links, the set condition of each flipflop is established from the eight data inputs, the current state of the eight flipflops, and the complements of both. Each flipflop's set condition can be represented as a Boolean expression of up to eight ORed statements. Each statement is created by ANDing terms drawn from the data inputs, the flipflop status, and their complements. Limiting parameters of this configuration are the 8 data inputs and the fixed 8-term OR gate at the D input of each flipflop. Boolean expressions implemented through the programmable fuses must be true when the flipflop is to be set or maintained in the set state, and false when the flipflop is to be reset or to remain reset.

Single-Array Configuration

Any of several servicing algorithms, expressed as Boolean statements, can be implemented with a single logic array that will process service requests for up to seven systems. The first two algorithms represent the organizational extremes. "Priority service" algorithm has a strict priority ranking from R6 to R0: a grant will be issued only if no higher priority system has a pending request. The other extreme is the "polled service" algorithm; here, all systems place equal demand on the device and are serviced through a rotating, or "round-robin," method. In this case, when one transaction has been completed, the following grant is issued in response to the next ranking request (eg, next lower number). Circular continuity is maintained by having R6 follow R0 in the granting sequence. Between the extremes, algorithms 3 and 4 represent hybrid organizations. The "executive and polled service" algorithm allows a single, high priority executive system (R6), with the remaining systems (R5 to R0) equal and polled in a

ALGORITHM 1: PRIORITY SERVICE

$$G6 = \overline{RESET} \cdot R6\,[G5 \cdot \overline{R5} + G4 \cdot \overline{R4} + G3 \cdot \overline{R3} + G2 \cdot \overline{R2} + G1 \cdot \overline{R1} + G0 \cdot \overline{R0} + \overline{G5} \cdot \overline{G4} \cdot \overline{G3} \cdot \overline{G2} \cdot \overline{G1} \cdot \overline{G0} + G6]$$

$$G5 = \overline{RESET} \cdot R5\,[\overline{R6}\,(G6 + G4 \cdot \overline{R4} + G3 \cdot \overline{R3} + G2 \cdot \overline{R2} + G1 \cdot \overline{R1} + G0 \cdot \overline{R0} + \overline{G6} \cdot \overline{G4} \cdot \overline{G3} \cdot \overline{G2} \cdot \overline{G1} \cdot \overline{G0}) + G5]$$

$$G4 = \overline{RESET} \cdot R4\,[\overline{R6} \cdot \overline{R5}\,(G6 + G5 + G3 \cdot \overline{R3} + G2 \cdot \overline{R2} + G1 \cdot \overline{R1} + G0 \cdot \overline{R0} + \overline{G6} \cdot \overline{G5} \cdot \overline{G3} \cdot \overline{G2} \cdot \overline{G1} \cdot \overline{G0}) + G4]$$

$$G3 = \overline{RESET} \cdot R3\,[\overline{R6} \cdot \overline{R5} \cdot \overline{R4}\,(G6 + G5 + G4 + G2 \cdot \overline{R2} + G1 \cdot \overline{R1} + G0 \cdot \overline{R0} + \overline{G6} \cdot \overline{G5} \cdot \overline{G4} \cdot \overline{G2} \cdot \overline{G1} \cdot \overline{G0}) + G3]$$

$$G2 = \overline{RESET} \cdot R2\,[\overline{R6} \cdot \overline{R5} \cdot \overline{R4} \cdot \overline{R3}\,(G6 + G5 + G4 + G3 + G1 \cdot \overline{R1} + G0 \cdot \overline{R0} + \overline{G6} \cdot \overline{G5} \cdot \overline{G4} \cdot \overline{G3} \cdot \overline{G1} \cdot \overline{G0}) + G2]$$

$$G1 = \overline{RESET} \cdot R1\,[\overline{R6} \cdot \overline{R5} \cdot \overline{R4} \cdot \overline{R3} \cdot \overline{R2}\,(G6 + G5 + G4 + G3 + G2 + G0 \cdot \overline{R0} + \overline{G6} \cdot \overline{G5} \cdot \overline{G4} \cdot \overline{G3} \cdot \overline{G2} \cdot \overline{G0}) + G1]$$

$$G0 = \overline{RESET} \cdot R0\,[\overline{R6} \cdot \overline{R5} \cdot \overline{R4} \cdot \overline{R3} \cdot \overline{R2} \cdot \overline{R1}\,(G6 + G5 + G4 + G3 + G2 + G1 + \overline{G6} \cdot \overline{G5} \cdot \overline{G4} \cdot \overline{G3} \cdot \overline{G2} \cdot \overline{G1}) + G0]$$

ALGORITHM 2: POLLED SERVICE

$$G6 = \overline{RESET} \cdot R6\,[\overline{R0}\,(G0 + G1 \cdot \overline{R1} + G2 \cdot \overline{R2} \cdot \overline{R1} + G3 \cdot \overline{R3} \cdot \overline{R2} \cdot \overline{R1} + G4 \cdot \overline{R4} \cdot \overline{R3} \cdot \overline{R2} \cdot \overline{R1} + G5 \cdot \overline{R5} \cdot \overline{R4} \cdot \overline{R3} \cdot \overline{R2} \cdot \overline{R1}) \\ + \overline{G5} \cdot \overline{G4} \cdot \overline{G3} \cdot \overline{G2} \cdot \overline{G1} \cdot \overline{G0} + G6]$$

$$G5 = \overline{RESET} \cdot R5\,[\overline{R6}\,(G6 + G0 \cdot \overline{R0} + G1 \cdot \overline{R1} \cdot \overline{R0} + G2 \cdot \overline{R2} \cdot \overline{R1} \cdot \overline{R0} + G3 \cdot \overline{R3} \cdot \overline{R2} \cdot \overline{R1} \cdot \overline{R0} + G4 \cdot \overline{R4} \cdot \overline{R3} \cdot \overline{R2} \cdot \overline{R1} \cdot \overline{R0} \\ + \overline{G6} \cdot \overline{G4} \cdot \overline{G3} \cdot \overline{G2} \cdot \overline{G1} \cdot \overline{G0}) + G5]$$

$$G4 = \overline{RESET} \cdot R4\,[\overline{R5}\,(G5 + G6 \cdot \overline{R6} + G0 \cdot \overline{R0} \cdot \overline{R6} + G1 \cdot \overline{R1} \cdot \overline{R0} \cdot \overline{R6} + G2 \cdot \overline{R2} \cdot \overline{R1} \cdot \overline{R0} \cdot \overline{R6} + G3 \cdot \overline{R3} \cdot \overline{R2} \cdot \overline{R1} \cdot \overline{R0} \cdot \overline{R6} \\ + \overline{R6} \cdot \overline{G6} \cdot \overline{G5} \cdot \overline{G3} \cdot \overline{G2} \cdot \overline{G1} \cdot \overline{G0}) + G4]$$

$$G3 = \overline{RESET} \cdot R3\,[\overline{R4}\,(G4 + G5 \cdot \overline{R5} + G6 \cdot \overline{R6} \cdot \overline{R5} + G0 \cdot \overline{R0} \cdot \overline{R6} \cdot \overline{R5} + G1 \cdot \overline{R1} \cdot \overline{R0} \cdot \overline{R6} \cdot \overline{R5} + G2 \cdot \overline{R2} \cdot \overline{R1} \cdot \overline{R0} \cdot \overline{R6} \cdot \overline{R5} \\ + \overline{R6} \cdot \overline{R5} \cdot \overline{G6} \cdot \overline{G5} \cdot \overline{G4} \cdot \overline{G2} \cdot \overline{G1} \cdot \overline{G0}) + G3]$$

$$G2 = \overline{RESET} \cdot R2\,[\overline{R3}\,(G3 + G4 \cdot \overline{R4} + G5 \cdot \overline{R5} \cdot \overline{R4} + G6 \cdot \overline{R6} \cdot \overline{R5} \cdot \overline{R4} + G0 \cdot \overline{R0} \cdot \overline{R6} \cdot \overline{R5} \cdot \overline{R4} + G1 \cdot \overline{R1} \cdot \overline{R0} \cdot \overline{R6} \cdot \overline{R5} \cdot \overline{R4} \\ + \overline{R6} \cdot \overline{R5} \cdot \overline{R4} \cdot \overline{G6} \cdot \overline{G5} \cdot \overline{G4} \cdot \overline{G3} \cdot \overline{G1} \cdot \overline{G0}) + G2]$$

$$G1 = \overline{RESET} \cdot R1\,[\overline{R2}\,(G2 + G3 \cdot \overline{R3} + G4 \cdot \overline{R4} \cdot \overline{R3} + G5 \cdot \overline{R5} \cdot \overline{R4} \cdot \overline{R3} + G6 \cdot \overline{R6} \cdot \overline{R5} \cdot \overline{R4} \cdot \overline{R3} + G0 \cdot \overline{R0} \cdot \overline{R6} \cdot \overline{R5} \cdot \overline{R4} \cdot \overline{R3} \\ + \overline{R6} \cdot \overline{R5} \cdot \overline{R4} \cdot \overline{R3} \cdot \overline{G6} \cdot \overline{G5} \cdot \overline{G4} \cdot \overline{G3} \cdot \overline{G2} \cdot \overline{G0}) + G1]$$

$$G0 = \overline{RESET} \cdot R0\,[\overline{R1}\,(G1 + G2 \cdot \overline{R2} + G3 \cdot \overline{R3} \cdot \overline{R2} + G4 \cdot \overline{R4} \cdot \overline{R3} \cdot \overline{R2} + G5 \cdot \overline{R5} \cdot \overline{R4} \cdot \overline{R3} \cdot \overline{R2} + G6 \cdot \overline{R6} \cdot \overline{R5} \cdot \overline{R4} \cdot \overline{R3} \cdot \overline{R2} \\ + \overline{R6} \cdot \overline{R5} \cdot \overline{R4} \cdot \overline{R3} \cdot \overline{R2} \cdot \overline{G6} \cdot \overline{G5} \cdot \overline{G4} \cdot \overline{G3} \cdot \overline{G2} \cdot \overline{G1}) + G0]$$

ALGORITHM 3: EXECUTIVE AND POLLED SERVICE

G6 = SAME AS G6 EQUATION, ALGORITHM 1

$$G5 = \overline{RESET} \cdot R5\,[\overline{R6}\,(G6 + G0 \cdot \overline{R0} + G1 \cdot \overline{R1} \cdot \overline{R0} + G2 \cdot \overline{R2} \cdot \overline{R1} \cdot \overline{R0} + G3 \cdot \overline{R3} \cdot \overline{R2} \cdot \overline{R1} \cdot \overline{R0} + G4 \cdot \overline{R4} \cdot \overline{R3} \cdot \overline{R2} \cdot \overline{R1} \cdot \overline{R0} \\ + \overline{G6} \cdot \overline{G4} \cdot \overline{G3} \cdot \overline{G2} \cdot \overline{G1} \cdot \overline{G0}) + G5]$$

$$G4 = \overline{RESET} \cdot R4\,[\overline{R6} \cdot \overline{R5}\,(G6 + G5 + G0 \cdot \overline{R0} + G1 \cdot \overline{R1} \cdot \overline{R0} + G2 \cdot \overline{R2} \cdot \overline{R1} \cdot \overline{R0} + G3 \cdot \overline{R3} \cdot \overline{R2} \cdot \overline{R1} \cdot \overline{R0} \\ + \overline{G6} \cdot \overline{G5} \cdot \overline{G3} \cdot \overline{G2} \cdot \overline{G1} \cdot \overline{G0}) + G4]$$

$$G3 = \overline{RESET} \cdot R3\,[\overline{R6} \cdot \overline{R4}\,(G6 \cdot \overline{R5} + G4 + G5 \cdot \overline{R5} + G0 \cdot \overline{R0} \cdot \overline{R5} + G1 \cdot \overline{R1} \cdot \overline{R0} \cdot \overline{R5} + G2 \cdot \overline{R2} \cdot \overline{R1} \cdot \overline{R0} \cdot \overline{R5} \\ + \overline{R5} \cdot \overline{G6} \cdot \overline{G5} \cdot \overline{G4} \cdot \overline{G2} \cdot \overline{G1} \cdot \overline{G0}) + G3]$$

$$G2 = \overline{RESET} \cdot R2\,[\overline{R6} \cdot \overline{R3}\,(G6 \cdot \overline{R5} \cdot \overline{R4} + G3 + G4 \cdot \overline{R4} + G5 \cdot \overline{R5} \cdot \overline{R4} + G0 \cdot \overline{R0} \cdot \overline{R5} \cdot \overline{R4} + G1 \cdot \overline{R1} \cdot \overline{R0} \cdot \overline{R5} \cdot \overline{R4} \\ + \overline{R5} \cdot \overline{R4} \cdot \overline{G6} \cdot \overline{G5} \cdot \overline{G4} \cdot \overline{G3} \cdot \overline{G1} \cdot \overline{G0}) + G2]$$

$$G1 = \overline{RESET} \cdot R1\,[\overline{R6} \cdot \overline{R2}\,(G6 \cdot \overline{R5} \cdot \overline{R4} \cdot \overline{R3} + G2 + G3 \cdot \overline{R3} + G4 \cdot \overline{R4} \cdot \overline{R3} + G5 \cdot \overline{R5} \cdot \overline{R4} \cdot \overline{R3} + G0 \cdot \overline{R0} \cdot \overline{R5} \cdot \overline{R4} \cdot \overline{R3} \\ + \overline{R5} \cdot \overline{R4} \cdot \overline{R3} \cdot \overline{G6} \cdot \overline{G5} \cdot \overline{G4} \cdot \overline{G3} \cdot \overline{G2} \cdot \overline{G0}) + G1]$$

$$G0 = \overline{RESET} \cdot R0\,[\overline{R6} \cdot \overline{R1}\,(G6 \cdot \overline{R5} \cdot \overline{R4} \cdot \overline{R3} \cdot \overline{R2} + G1 + G2 \cdot \overline{R2} + G3 \cdot \overline{R3} \cdot \overline{R2} + G4 \cdot \overline{R4} \cdot \overline{R3} \cdot \overline{R2} + G5 \cdot \overline{R5} \cdot \overline{R4} \cdot \overline{R3} \cdot \overline{R2} \\ + \overline{R5} \cdot \overline{R4} \cdot \overline{R3} \cdot \overline{R2} \cdot \overline{G6} \cdot \overline{G5} \cdot \overline{G4} \cdot \overline{G3} \cdot \overline{G2} \cdot \overline{G1}) + G0]$$

ALGORITHM 4: DECLINING PRIORITY AND POLLED SERVICE

G6 = SAME AS G6 EQUATION, ALGORITHM 1

G5 = SAME AS G5 EQUATION, ALGORITHM 1

G4 = SAME AS G4 EQUATION, ALGORITHM 1

$$G3 = \overline{RESET} \cdot R3\,[\overline{R6} \cdot \overline{R5} \cdot \overline{R4}\,(G6 + G5 + G4 + G0 \cdot \overline{R0} + G1 \cdot \overline{R1} \cdot \overline{R0} \\ + G2 \cdot \overline{R2} \cdot \overline{R1} \cdot \overline{R0} + \overline{G6} \cdot \overline{G5} \cdot \overline{G4} \cdot \overline{G2} \cdot \overline{G1} \cdot \overline{G0}) + G3]$$

$$G2 = \overline{RESET} \cdot R2\,[\overline{R6} \cdot \overline{R5} \cdot \overline{R4} \cdot \overline{R3}\,(G6 + G5 + G4 + G3 + G0 \cdot \overline{R0} \\ + G1 \cdot \overline{R1} \cdot \overline{R0} + \overline{G6} \cdot \overline{G5} \cdot \overline{G4} \cdot \overline{G3} \cdot \overline{G1} \cdot \overline{G0}) + G2]$$

$$G1 = \overline{RESET} \cdot R1\,[\overline{R6} \cdot \overline{R5} \cdot \overline{R4} \cdot \overline{R2}\,(G6 \cdot \overline{R3} + G5 \cdot \overline{R3} + G4 \cdot \overline{R3} + G3 \cdot \overline{R3} + G2 \\ + G0 \cdot \overline{R0} \cdot \overline{R3} + \overline{R3} \cdot \overline{G6} \cdot \overline{G5} \cdot \overline{G4} \cdot \overline{G3} \cdot \overline{G2} \cdot \overline{G0}) + G1]$$

$$G0 = \overline{RESET} \cdot R0\,[\overline{R6} \cdot \overline{R5} \cdot \overline{R4} \cdot \overline{R1}\,(G6 \cdot \overline{R3} \cdot \overline{R2} + G5 \cdot \overline{R3} \cdot \overline{R2} + G4 \cdot \overline{R3} \cdot \overline{R2} \\ + G3 \cdot \overline{R3} \cdot \overline{R2} + G2 \cdot \overline{R2} + G1 + \overline{R3} \cdot \overline{R2} \cdot \overline{G6} \cdot \overline{G5} \cdot \overline{G4} \cdot \overline{G3} \cdot \overline{G2} \cdot \overline{G1}) + G0]$$

circular pattern by decreasing number (R5 follows R0). The other hybrid algorithm, "declining priority and polled service," services three systems in declining priority (R6 to R4), and allocates four systems the lowest priority; R3 to R0 have equal priority and are polled in a circular pattern by decreasing number (R3 follows R0).

In each configuration, the eight inputs consist of a RESET command and seven synchronized requests. Outputs are the seven corresponding grants, each the set output of a flipflop, buffered and inverted. When activated, the RESET command negates all expressions, resetting all grant flipflops. After a synchronized request is received, the appropriate expression becomes true, and the grant flipflop is set at the following clock edge. Upon completion of the transaction, the grant is released one clock period following the clock edge that terminates its synchronized request. This interval, when the grant is true and its synchronized request is false, denotes the completion of the service cycle. If one or more synchronized requests are pending, all expressions are evaluated, and, based on the servicing sequence expressed by the Boolean statements, the next grant is issued. If at the completion of a grant there are no pending requests, then all grant flipflops are reset and the device reverts to the idle state.

When the device is idle, all synchronized requests are scanned each clock period. Detection of a single synchronized request causes a grant to be issued at the following clock edge. If two or more requests are synchronized simultaneously, the expressions must provide a hierarchical method for issuing the initial grant. If the systems are organized from highest to lowest priority, the issuing of an initial grant follows the same seniority pattern. However, if all systems polled are of equal priority, the initial grant hierarchy must be established arbitrarily; in these examples, the grant hierarchy is based on highest to lowest sequence, systems R6 to R0. All these factors are apparent in the Boolean statements that implement the various grant algorithms. Each statement is the D input of a flipflop, and when a statement is true, the corresponding flipflop becomes (or remains) set at the following clock edge, issuing (or maintaining) a grant. As grants must be issued sequentially, the statements must be interlocked to prevent multiple flipflop settings.

The format set forth in the Boolean expressions of algorithms 1 through 4 [compare Fig 1(d)] is used when writing all statements. It consists of four sections: a modifier divided into an external and an internal portion, a transfer expression, an idle expression, and a maintenance expression. The external modifier, which operates on the entire contents of each statement, is the $\overline{\text{RESET}}$ term ANDed with the appropriate synchronized request. This establishes the basic requirement that RESET not be issued—and that the synchronized request be present—to consider whether to issue or to maintain a grant. The internal modifier operates on the transfer and idle expressions, and is the AND of synchronized requests that must be false for a specific grant to be issued. Since in a complete or partial priority structure, the highest numbered system (R6) always takes precedence, the internal modifier for the G6 expression is nonexistent.

The transfer expression identifies the completion of a transaction through the combination of a grant with its corresponding request. In conjunction with the modifiers, the transfer expression evaluates the pending requests to determine the next sequential grant. If one or several simultaneous requests are synchronized when grants are not active, the idle expression, in conjunction with the modifiers, determines which grant will be issued according to the established priority. The maintenance expression, the set output of the grant flipflop, maintains an established grant until its external modifier becomes false.

There are at least two other practical hybrid combinations: two prioritized systems with the remaining five polled, and four prioritized systems with the remaining three polled. Expressions for these two configurations can be derived from the four examples just discussed.

Multiple-Array Configuration

The single-array configuration handles up to seven systems with a broad selection of operation modes and is suitable for a configuration that has a limited number of systems with high rates of interaction with the device. When there is a large number of systems that have low rates of interaction individually, it is necessary to scan blocks of synchronized requests rapidly in order to minimize response time, thereby maximizing device

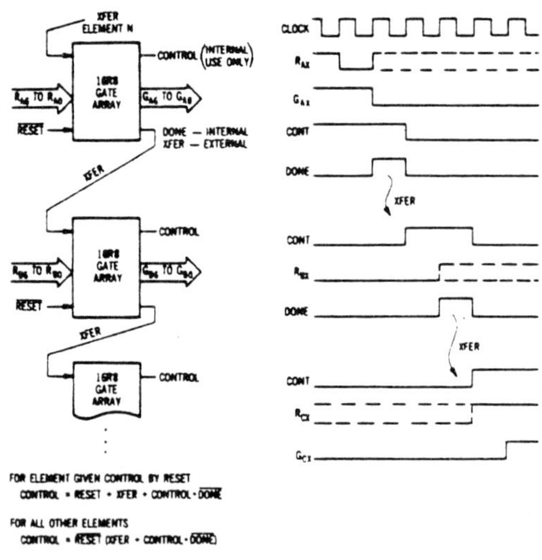

Fig 2 Multiple-array configuration. Each of n elements can service six systems arranged in circular (ie, polled or "round-robin") configuration. RESET issues control to one element. Then, as systems are serviced, DONE and CONTROL commands pass control function among elements as shown

utilization. This is accomplished by using the same 8-register programmable array device, with 6 of the registers issuing grants and the remaining 2 used to transfer the control and done commands. Devices thus organized become elements in a daisy chain configuration that is, in theory, infinitely expandable. Within the daisy chain, the element whose control flipflop is set is empowered to issue grants. Each element, while completing its last transaction, clears the grant flipflop, and, on the same clock edge, sets the done flipflop for one clock cycle. (See Fig 2.) Output of the done flipflop serves as an inhibit command within the element, and externally as a transfer (XFER) command to set the control flipflop of the next element.

Upon receipt of control, if one or more requests are pending, they are evaluated and a grant is issued at the next clock edge; if there are no requests, the clock edge instead sets the done flipflop to again transfer the control capability. Within an element, the same clock edge releases a completed grant and initiates a new grant, as was the case in the single-array configuration; among elements, there is a 2-period delay between succesive grants for sequencing of the done and control flipflops. Therefore, if the device is idle, an element that monitors six system requests is scanned each two clock cycles as the control function is sequenced through the elements.

Since this configuration can be expanded to accommodate servicing of numerous inputs, the elements are polled and equally weighted. However, within each element a protocol for responding to requests must be established; in these examples, priority is from the highest to the lowest number (R5 to R0). Algorithms 5 and 6 are variations of this configuration. In the "multiple-array polling" algorithm, the element retains control and services all requests in a declining polling sequence; control is relinquished only when there are no remaining requests. In the "multiple-array priority" algorithm, requests are serviced in a strict order of declining priority (ie, decreasing request numbers), and control is released in the absence of requests or upon completion of a device service period when no lower numbered systems have pending requests. In an application, these two configurations can be intermixed because the element interfaces are identical. The

ALGORITHM 5: MULTIPLE-ARRAY POLLING

$$\begin{aligned}G5 = {} & \overline{\text{RESET}} \cdot \overline{\text{DONE}} \cdot \text{CONT} \cdot R5\,[\overline{R0}\,(G0 + G1 \cdot \overline{R1} + G2 \cdot \overline{R2} \cdot \overline{R1} + G3 \cdot \overline{R3} \cdot \overline{R2} \cdot \overline{R1} \\ & + G4 \cdot \overline{R4} \cdot \overline{R3} \cdot \overline{R2} \cdot \overline{R1}) + \overline{G4} \cdot \overline{G3} \cdot \overline{G2} \cdot \overline{G1} \cdot \overline{G0} + G5]\end{aligned}$$

$$\begin{aligned}G4 = {} & \overline{\text{RESET}} \cdot \overline{\text{DONE}} \cdot \text{CONT} \cdot R4\,[\overline{R5}\,(G5 + G0 \cdot \overline{R0} + G1 \cdot \overline{R1} \cdot \overline{R0} + G2 \cdot \overline{R2} \cdot \overline{R1} \cdot \overline{R0} \\ & + G3 \cdot \overline{R3} \cdot \overline{R2} \cdot \overline{R1} \cdot \overline{R0} + \overline{G5} \cdot \overline{G3} \cdot \overline{G2} \cdot \overline{G1} \cdot \overline{G0}) + G4]\end{aligned}$$

$$\begin{aligned}G3 = {} & \overline{\text{RESET}} \cdot \overline{\text{DONE}} \cdot \text{CONT} \cdot R3\,[\overline{R4}\,(G4 + G5 \cdot \overline{R5} + G0 \cdot \overline{R0} \cdot \overline{R5} + G1 \cdot \overline{R1} \cdot \overline{R0} \cdot \overline{R5} \\ & + G2 \cdot \overline{R2} \cdot \overline{R1} \cdot \overline{R0} \cdot \overline{R5} + \overline{R5} \cdot \overline{G5} \cdot \overline{G4} \cdot \overline{G2} \cdot \overline{G1} \cdot \overline{G0}) + G3]\end{aligned}$$

$$\begin{aligned}G2 = {} & \overline{\text{RESET}} \cdot \overline{\text{DONE}} \cdot \text{CONT} \cdot R2\,[\overline{R3}\,(G3 + G4 \cdot \overline{R4} + G5 \cdot \overline{R5} \cdot \overline{R4} + G0 \cdot \overline{R0} \cdot \overline{R5} \cdot \overline{R4} \\ & + G1 \cdot \overline{R1} \cdot \overline{R0} \cdot \overline{R5} \cdot \overline{R4} + \overline{R5} \cdot \overline{R4} \cdot \overline{G5} \cdot \overline{G4} \cdot \overline{G3} \cdot \overline{G1} \cdot \overline{G0}) + G2]\end{aligned}$$

$$\begin{aligned}G1 = {} & \overline{\text{RESET}} \cdot \overline{\text{DONE}} \cdot \text{CONT} \cdot R1\,[\overline{R2}\,(G2 + G3 \cdot \overline{R3} + G4 \cdot \overline{R4} \cdot \overline{R3} + G5 \cdot \overline{R5} \cdot \overline{R4} \cdot \overline{R3} \\ & + G0 \cdot \overline{R0} \cdot \overline{R5} \cdot \overline{R4} \cdot \overline{R3} + \overline{R5} \cdot \overline{R4} \cdot \overline{R3} \cdot \overline{G5} \cdot \overline{G4} \cdot \overline{G3} \cdot \overline{G2} \cdot \overline{G0}) + G1]\end{aligned}$$

$$\begin{aligned}G0 = {} & \overline{\text{RESET}} \cdot \overline{\text{DONE}} \cdot \text{CONT} \cdot R0\,[\overline{R1}\,(G1 + G2 \cdot \overline{R2} + G3 \cdot \overline{R3} \cdot \overline{R2} + G4 \cdot \overline{R4} \cdot \overline{R3} \cdot \overline{R2} \\ & + G5 \cdot \overline{R5} \cdot \overline{R4} \cdot \overline{R3} \cdot \overline{R2} + \overline{R5} \cdot \overline{R4} \cdot \overline{R3} \cdot \overline{R2} \cdot \overline{G5} \cdot \overline{G4} \cdot \overline{G3} \cdot \overline{G2} \cdot \overline{G1}) + G0]\end{aligned}$$

$$\text{DONE} = \overline{\text{RESET}} \cdot \text{CONT} \cdot \overline{\text{DONE}} \cdot \overline{R5} \cdot \overline{R4} \cdot \overline{R3} \cdot \overline{R2} \cdot \overline{R1} \cdot \overline{R0}$$

CONT = CONTROL (SEE FIG 2)

ALGORITHM 6: MULTIPLE-ARRAY PRIORITY

$$G5 = \overline{\text{RESET}} \cdot \overline{\text{DONE}} \cdot \text{CONT} \cdot \overline{G4} \cdot \overline{G3} \cdot \overline{G2} \cdot \overline{G1} \cdot \overline{G0} \cdot R5$$

$$G4 = \overline{\text{RESET}} \cdot \overline{\text{DONE}} \cdot \text{CONT} \cdot \overline{G3} \cdot \overline{G2} \cdot \overline{G1} \cdot \overline{G0} \cdot R4\,[\overline{R5} + G4]$$

$$G3 = \overline{\text{RESET}} \cdot \overline{\text{DONE}} \cdot \text{CONT} \cdot \overline{G2} \cdot \overline{G1} \cdot \overline{G0} \cdot R3\,[\overline{R4}\,(\overline{R5} + G4) + G3]$$

$$G2 = \overline{\text{RESET}} \cdot \overline{\text{DONE}} \cdot \text{CONT} \cdot \overline{G1} \cdot \overline{G0} \cdot R2\,[\overline{R3}\,(\overline{R5} \cdot \overline{R4} + G4 \cdot \overline{R4} + G3) + G2]$$

$$\begin{aligned}G1 = {} & \overline{\text{RESET}} \cdot \overline{\text{DONE}} \cdot \text{CONT} \cdot \overline{G0} \cdot R1\,[\overline{R2}\,(\overline{R5} \cdot \overline{R4} \cdot \overline{R3} + G4 \cdot \overline{R4} \cdot \overline{R3} \\ & + G3 \cdot \overline{R3} + G2) + G1]\end{aligned}$$

$$\begin{aligned}G0 = {} & \overline{\text{RESET}} \cdot \overline{\text{DONE}} \cdot \text{CONT} \cdot R0\,[\overline{R1}\,(\overline{R5} \cdot \overline{R4} \cdot \overline{R3} \cdot \overline{R2} + G4 \cdot \overline{R4} \cdot \overline{R3} \cdot \overline{R2} \\ & + G3 \cdot \overline{R3} \cdot \overline{R2} + G2 \cdot \overline{R2} + G1) + G0]\end{aligned}$$

$$\begin{aligned}\text{DONE} = {} & \overline{\text{RESET}} \cdot \overline{\text{DONE}} \cdot \text{CONT} \cdot \overline{R0}\,[\overline{R1}\,(\overline{R5} \cdot \overline{R4} \cdot \overline{R3} \cdot \overline{R2} + G4 \cdot \overline{R4} \cdot \overline{R3} \cdot \overline{R2} \\ & + G3 \cdot \overline{R3} \cdot \overline{R2} + G2 \cdot \overline{R2} + G1) + G0]\end{aligned}$$

CONT = CONTROL (SEE FIG 2)

differences are within the elements—ie, the methods used when evaluating requests to issue grants and when generating the transfer command. Since only one element can have a set control flipflop and the associated authority to issue grants, one control flipflop must be set, and all others reset, during initialization. During implementation, the system start of poll (established by RESET) must be selected, and each element's control equation implemented accordingly. (See Fig 2.)

The Boolean statements in algorithms 5 and 6 are configured in the format shown in Fig 1(d). In algorithm 5, the external modifier has two additional terms, CONT and DONE, both establishing that the element has control. The remainder of the terms is similar in content to the terms in algorithm 2, and, with the exception of the idle expression, also similar in concept. Since an element does not retain control in the idle state, this term instead establishes the initial grant upon receipt of the control function. Subsequent grants are issued through the transfer expression, and when all requests are satisfied, the done flipflop is set for one period, initiating a transfer of control to the next element.

Hybrid Configuration

Single- and multiple-array configurations have limitations. The single-array concept services only seven systems, but offers flexibility in configuring the response patterns. Conversely, the multiple-array configuration can handle a large (theoretically unlimited) number of systems, but is not flexible in configuring response patterns because the control function must cycle through elements in a prescribed sequence. By restructuring the control lines, designers can interconnect elements in a hierarchical fashion, both increasing the number of systems serviced and providing service flexibility. An example that consists of two elements, each servicing six systems, is shown in Fig 3. The two elements are labeled "upper" and "lower" to denote their relative priorities. Each element has a control flipflop whose output is an input to the other element.

The control flipflop of the upper element is set whenever it has a synchronized request, and is a DEMAND for control. The control flipflop of the lower element is set when it receives a demand and does not have an active grant; it is a RELEASE of control. Thus, the upper element DEMANDs and receives control when it has a request. When all upper element requests are satisfied, the demand flipflop is reset and control shifts to the lower element by default. The control equations for the upper and lower elements are shown in Fig 3, along with the format for the grant equations and one sample grant equation for each element. Because the equations for the hybrid configuration are similar to those for the single-array configuration, the grant equations are modifications of those shown in algorithms 1 through 4. When in the idle state, the default location for control is in the lower element; therefore, the equation for the upper element does not require an idle section.

Efficient transfer of control and prevention of inadvertent simultaneous grant issuance during the transition sequence are primary considerations in arbiter

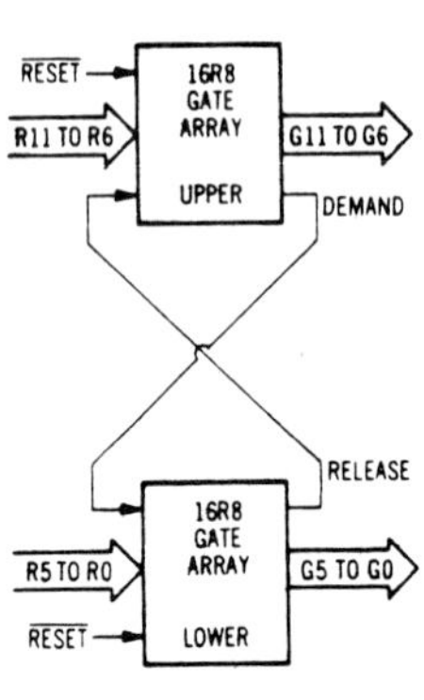

UPPER ELEMENT

$$DEMAND = \overline{RESET}\,(R11 + R10 + R9 + R8 + R7 + R6)$$

$$G_X = \underbrace{\overline{RESET} \cdot DEM \cdot REL \cdot R_X}_{EXTERNAL}\,[\underbrace{\quad}_{INTERNAL}(\qquad) + G_X]$$

MODIFIER — TRANSFER — / MAINTENANCE

EXAMPLE FROM ALGORITHM 1

$$G9 = \overline{RESET} \cdot DEM \cdot REL \cdot R9\,[\overline{R11} \cdot \overline{R10}\,(G11 + G10 + G8 \cdot \overline{R8} + G7 \cdot \overline{R7} + G6 \cdot \overline{R6}) + G9]$$

LOWER ELEMENT

$$RELEASE = \overline{RESET} \cdot DEM\,[G5 \cdot \overline{R5} + G4 \cdot \overline{R4} + G3 \cdot \overline{R3} + G2 \cdot \overline{R2} + G1 \cdot \overline{R1} + G0 \cdot \overline{R0} + \overline{G5} \cdot \overline{G4} \cdot \overline{G3} \cdot \overline{G2} \cdot \overline{G1} \cdot \overline{G0}]$$

$$G_Y = \underbrace{\overline{RESET} \cdot R_Y}_{EXTERNAL}\,[\underbrace{\overline{DEM} \cdot \overline{REL}}_{INTERNAL}\,(\qquad + \qquad) + G_Y]$$

MODIFIER — TRANSFER — IDLE — / MAINTENANCE

EXAMPLE FROM ALGORITHM 2

$$G2 = \overline{RESET} \cdot R2\,[\overline{DEM} \cdot \overline{REL} \cdot \overline{R3}\,(G3 + G4 \cdot \overline{R4} + G5 \cdot \overline{R5} \cdot \overline{R4} + G0 \cdot \overline{R0} \cdot \overline{R5} \cdot \overline{R4} + G1 \cdot \overline{R1} \cdot \overline{R0} \cdot \overline{R5} \cdot \overline{R4} + \overline{R5} \cdot \overline{R4} \cdot \overline{G5} \cdot \overline{G4} \cdot \overline{G3} \cdot \overline{G1} \cdot \overline{G0}) + G2]$$

Fig 3 Hybrid configuration. Two elements have hierarchical structure. Upper element demands control when request is pending, thereby preventing lower element from issuing grants and gaining control when lower element becomes idle. Modified grant expression format and typical grant expression appear for each element. Release expression is also shown. Each element offers full flexibility shown in algorithms 1 to 4

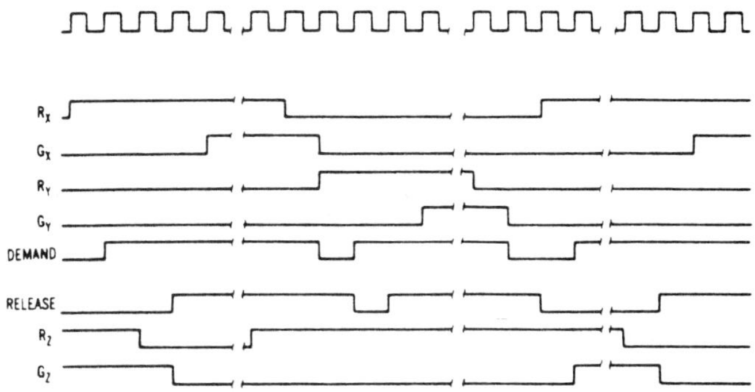

Fig 4 Hybrid configuration timing. Diagram shows timing relationship as control function passes between upper and lower elements. At left, control passes from lower element to upper element upon completion of G_Z. In second sector, upper element releases control and reestablishes demand during same clock period (adverse situation). Lower element with pending request must reinitiate release, causing 3-period delay between grants. In two right sectors, upper element releases control and reestablishes demand one clock period later. Lower element issues grant for its pending request and releases control upon completion of service

design. Control equations and modifier sections of the grant equations, respectively, fulfill these design requirements. Three transitional sequences for hybrid configuration are shown in the timing diagram. (See Fig 4.)

Summary

The increased desirability of sharing resources among several systems has increased the requirements for arbiters that can function independently. Such arbiters enhance the profitability of shared resource data processing systems. A versatile Boolean statement format can implement efficient control protocol and grant algorithms in field programmable logic. The flexibility and logic density of register arrays can facilitate efficient custom arbiter implementation.

Bibliography

K. Søe Højberg, "Queue Handling Arbiter Solves Shared Resource Conflicts," *Computer Design,* Nov 1979, pp 129-135

James Nadir and Bruce McCormick, "Bus Arbiter Streamlines Multiprocessor Design," *Computer Design,* June 1980, pp 103-109

Emil Petriu, "N-Channel Asynchronous Arbiter Resolves Resource Allocation Conflicts," *Computer Design,* Aug 1980, pp 126-132

About the Author:

Alan W. Bentley is a design specialist, responsible for the technical development of a high speed data processing and display system at Cubic Corporation. He is also an instructor in the Engineering Department of San Diego Community College. He has a BS degree in electrical engineering from Tufts University, an MBA from United States International University, and an MA from San Diego State University.

Programmable Array Logic Leads to Flexible Application of 8-Bit Wide Memories

Bernard Brafman

Introduction

The flexible application of memory devices in small microprocessor based systems have been enhanced by the introduction of 8-bit wide static random access memories. These devices have pinouts and operating characteristics that are similar to those of read only and programmable read only memories. Thus, the configuration of both read/write and read only memories can be simplified to meet changing system requirements. For example, this flexibility allows a single printed circuit board to be used in several different product configurations, from fixed program intensive (large read only memory requirements) to data intensive (large read/write memory requirements). Using programmable logic technology in conjunction with 8-bit wide memory devices adds even more flexibility and helps to reduce parts count.

To provide for the simple substitution of parts, a printed circuit (PC) board must be developed that allows interchangeability among the memory sockets of 8k-, 16k-, and 64k-memory devices, both random access memory (RAM) and programmable read only memory (P/ROM), or read only memory (ROM). A method must be created also to define flexibly the addressing of these parts to accommodate varying address space requirements. The first task is physical — e.g., some 64k devices have 28 pins while others have 24 pins. To be most flexible, the PC board will have a 28-pin socket with jumpers to allow the use of either 24- or 28-pin devices. Socket interchangeability also necessitates an examination of the timing requirements of the target memory devices and microprocessor, since differences exist in setup or prechange or hold times for address and data, and control signal interactions. Some systems will need additional gating or delays to ensure flexibility. Such timing information is easily found in application notes published by both microprocessor and memory manufacturers.

The second task is to implement decoding schemes for the selection of the appropriate devices in the memory array. One method uses hardwired discrete logic. This alternative is not viable because high configurability requires an excessive use of space consuming jumpers and also results in unused logic on the PC board. Programmable logic, on the other hand, implements the requisite configurably in fuses on silicon, not on the PC board, and consolidates several integrated circuit (IC) packages into one.

Design Tradeoffs

The choices in programmable logic are programmable logic arrays (PLAs), P/PROMs, and programmable array logic (PAL®). PLAs must be ruled out since their 2-fuse array structure, while awarding some versatility, uses up too much board space. PLAs are implemented in 0.6 in. (1.5 cm), 28-pin packages; the job can be done with smaller 0.3 in. (0.8 cm), 16- or 20-pin packages when P/ROMs or PALs are used.

While P/ROMs are frequently employed in such applications, there are compelling reasons to consider the use of PAL. First, any P/ROM with an adequate number of input and output pins to replace the required external logic consumes more power than a comparable PAL. For example, providing control signals for four memory devices requires four chip enables and at least one output enable signal. These signals must be derived from at least six address lines and generally three and often four control signals. In such a case, the programmable logic device must have ten inputs and five outputs. For a PROM, this would be an 8K, 20 or 24-pin device, organized as 1Kx8. Typically, a commercial 8K bipolar PROM has an I_{CC} of 190 mA over temperature, as compared with 90 mA for a 10-input, 8-output PAL. Even if external logic were employed, so that a 1K PROM, organized as 256x4 were used, the I_{CC} would by typically 130 mA over temperature.

PALs are not susceptible to the "glitching" characteristics of PROMs during the access time from address. To combat glitching, the PROM must be used with registers or, if the control signals are active low only, open collector with pullup resistors for the outputs. Generally, a processor control signal or its derivative serves as the clock for the register or output enable to the PROM, an example of increasing parts count and costs in an attempt to overcome an implementation detail. While the technique usually employed to generate the fuse pattern, or programming, for PROMs is manual, a useful and uniform design tool exists for configuring PALs. A FORTRAN IV program called PALASM (for PAL assembler) is available on the National CSS timeshare network or as source code at no charge for any machine that supports a FORTRAN environment. PALASM converts logic equations describing the function of the target device directly into a fuse pattern format that is compatible with the several PROM programmers which support PAL programming. This assembler allows simple, rapid, and complete design and documentation of PAL configurations in a format useful for communication between engineers. Finally, like PROMs, PALs have a masked counterpart, hard array logic (HAL). HALs are plug compatible with the corresponding PAL, and offer significant cost reductions for high volume applications.

Implementation Example

A typical design with memory device interchangeability, is the 6802 microprocessor based instrument required to have four sockets capable of accepting 2kx8 static RAMs, 2kx8 erasable programmable read only memories (EPROMs), or 4kx8 EPROMs. The four chip enable signals ($\overline{CE}_1$, $\overline{CE}_2$, $\overline{CE}_3$, and $\overline{CE}_4$), the common output enable (OE), and the common read/write control (R/$\overline{W}$) are compatible with the devices selected so that no special gating is needed. The programmable logic device will have as inputs the five high order address bits A_{11} through A_{15} and the control signals VMA (valid memory address) and E (enable). While R/$\overline{W}$ may be used directly for write enable ($\overline{WE}$), it is needed to generate $\overline{OE}$. (See Fig. 1.).

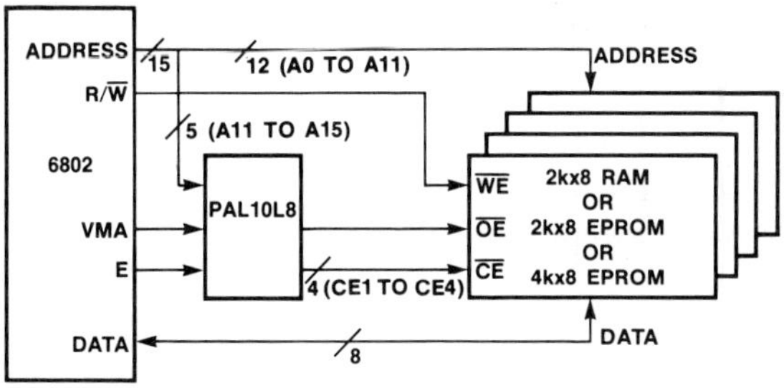

Fig. 1. 6802 based system. Block diagram outlines system's capability to accept 2kx8 static RAMs, 2kx8 EPROMs, or 4kx8 EPROMs.

The programmable logic device requires eight inputs and five outputs. PAL10L8 and PAL12L6 meet both the input and output pin requirements. The PAL10L8 has been selected for this discussion because the three outputs are left unused and are available for logic replacement. (See Fig. 2.). Internally, the PAL10L8 generates eight 2-term OR sums, each sum composed of two 10-term AND products. Each of the products may be connected to any of the input signals or its complement.

PAL10L8

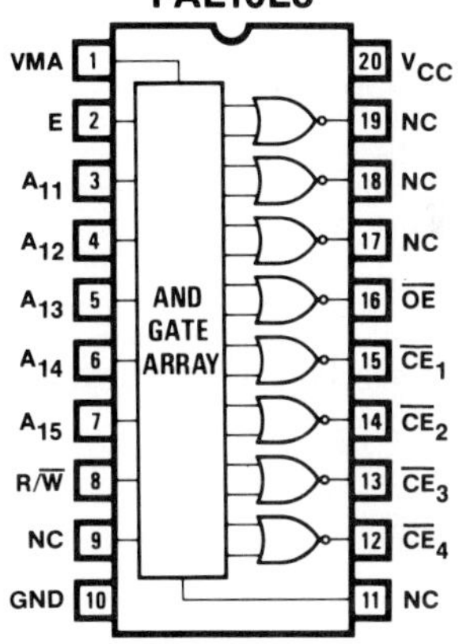

GND = GROUND
NC = NOT CONNECTED

Fig. 2. PAL10L8 pinout. Device generates eight 2-term OR sums, each composed of two 10-term AND products.

While there are 81 unique combinations of the three memory devices in the four sockets, there are only 16 distinct decoding schemes implementing either a 2k- or 4k-deep device in any of the four sockets; these 16 schemes are set forth in "Address Ranges of 16 Device Combinations." See "PAL Design Specifications," which can also include a function or truth table, for a description of the arbitrary pinout shown in Fig. 2; this pinout may be altered simply by switching the elements of the pin list on line 5 on both design specifications. Notice that the chip enables and output enable are inverted in the pin list and true in the equations. This is to keep expressions in the sum-of-products form for PALASM, which expects equations summed at the node before the inversion for active low PALs. Also, there are two unused inputs and three unused outputs that may be applied to reduce logic elsewhere in the system.

ADDRESS RANGES FOR 16 COMBINATIONS OF DEVICES

CE_1	CE_2	CE_3	CE_4	CONFIGURATION
0000-07FF	0800-0FFF	1000-17FF	1800-1FFF	2k, 2k, 2k, 2k
0000-07FF	0800-0FFF	1000-17FF	1800-27FF	2k, 2k, 2k, 4k
0000-07FF	0800-0FFF	1000-1FFF	2000-27FF	2k, 2k, 4k, 2k
0000-07FF	0800-0FFF	1000-1FFF	2000-2FFF	2k, 2k, 4k, 4k
0000-07FF	0800-17FF	1800-1FFF	2000-27FF	2k, 4k, 2k, 2k
0000-07FF	0800-17FF	1800-1FFF	2000-2FFF	2k, 4k, 2k, 4k
0000-07FF	0800-17FF	1800-27FF	2800-2FFF	2k, 4k, 4k, 2k
0000-C7FF	0800-17FF	1800-27FF	2800-37FF	2k, 4k, 4k, 4k
0000-0FFF	1000-17FF	1800-1FFF	2000-27FF	4k, 2k, 2k, 2k
0000-0FFF	1000-17FF	1800-1FFF	2000-2FFF	4k, 2k, 2k, 4k
0000-0FFF	1000-17FF	1800-27FF	2800-2FFF	4k, 2k, 4k, 2k
0000-0FFF	1000-17FF	1800-27FF	2800-37FF	4k, 2k, 4k, 4k
0000-0FFF	1000-1FFF	2000-27FF	2800-2FFF	4k, 4k, 2k, 2k
0000-0FFF	1000-1FFF	2000-27FF	2800-37FF	4k, 4k, 2k, 4k
0000-0FFF	1000-1FFF	2000-2FFF	3000-37FF	4k, 4k, 4k, 2k
0000-0FFF	1000-1FFF	2000-2FFF	3000-3FFF	4k, 4k, 4k, 4k

```
PAL10L8
PN1001                                                  B. BRAFMAN 12/10/80
ADDRESS DECODER  (EXAMPLE 1)
MMI SUNNYVALE, CALIFORNIA
VMA E A11 A12 A13 A14 A15 RW NC GND        } PIN LIST OF SYMBOLIC NAMES
NC /CE4 /CE3 /CE2 /CE1 /OE NC NC NC VCC

CE1 = /A15 * /A14 * /A13 * /A12 * VMA * E
CE2 = /A15 * /A14 * /A13 *  A12 * VMA * E    } LOGIC EQUATIONS
CE3 = /A15 * /A14 *  A13 * /A12 * VMA * E
CE4 = /A15 * /A14 *  A13 *  A12 * VMA * E
OE  = E * RW

DESCRIPTION
 THIS PART GENERATES CHIP ENABLES AND OUTPUT ENABLE FOR
 TWO 4k X 8 PROMS AND TWO 2k X 8 STATIC RAMS AS FOLLOWS:
          CE1--0000-0FFF                                 } OPERATION
          CE2--1000-1FFF
          CE3--2000-27FF
          CE4--2800-2FFF
```

```
PAL10L8
PN1002                                                  B. BRAFMAN 12/10/80
ADDRESS DECODER  (EXAMPLE 2)
MMI SUNNYVALE, CALIFORNIA
VMA E A11 A12 A13 A14 A15 RW NC GND        } PIN LIST OF SYMBOLIC NAMES
NC /CE4 /CE3 /CE2 /CE1 /OE NC NC NC VCC

CE1 = /A15 * /A14 * /A13 * /A12 * /A11 * VMA * E
CE2 = /A15 * /A14 * /A13 * /A12 *  A11 * VMA * E
CE3 = /A15 * /A14 * /A13 *  A12 * /A11 * VMA * E   } LOGIC EQUATIONS
CE4 = /A15 * /A14 * /A13 *  A12 *  A11 * VMA * E
    + /A15 * /A14 *  A13 * /A12 *  A11 * VMA * E
OE  = E * RW

DESCRIPTION
 THIS PART GENERATES CHIP ENABLES AND OUTPUT ENABLE FOR
 THREE 2k X 8 STATIC RAMS AND ONE 4k X 8 PROM AS FOLLOWS:
          CE1--0000-07FF                                 } OPERATION
          CE2--8000-0FFF
          CE3--1000-17FF
          CE4--1800-27FF
```

Summary

The combination of 8-bit wide memory devices and programmable array logic allows designers to implement highly flexible microprocessor based designs with minimal chip count and reduced overall costs. PALASM serves as a useful tool for expediting prototype cycles and documenting PAL designs; this can reduce future problems when changes must be made by designers unfamiliar with the original design. Finally, products with high volume in a specific configuration may switch over to mask programmable array logic, HAL, to reduce costs further.

PAL: Quick Turnaround Alternative to Gate Arrays

Shlomo Waser

Abstract

The first part of the paper will describe the PAL family including the second generation to be introduced shortly, and the HAL, which is a gate array with fusible prototype.

The second part will address the PAL software support tools with emphasis on HDL (Hardware Description Language), design verification via function tables, simulation and automatic test vector generation.

Introduction

The Part Number Problem

As the capability of the semiconductor industry to integrate more and more logic into a single chip, a unique problem has arisen; how to define a common chip that will have enough volume to justify the tremendous design costs associated with high degree of integration. Let us illustrate this with an example: Back in the '60s when the integration capability was below 10 gates per chip, we made quad NAND gates and similar SSI. Everybody that made digital systems could use a quad NAND so there was no volume problem. But in the '80s, we can put thousands of gates per chip and the design cost is measured in millions of dollars. As long as we provide memories and microprocessors, there are always enough customers that have common requirements to request large volume. So in the '80s, we don't have a problem with memories and microprocessors, but we do have a problem with what to do with the rest of the required components. Especially the components that are unique to special systems and there is no chance that there will be enough volume generated to justify the large design cost.

The SSI/MSI Solution

One solution to the above problem is to use SSI gates and construct the desired function. This is an undesirable solution since it does not take advantage of the increased integration available nowadays.

The Custom Solution

If the special function has enough volume, a custom design is justified economically, provided the long design cycle associated with custom is acceptable.

The Programmable Solution

There is a big void between the undesirable SSI solutions and the uneconomical custom. This void is now being addressed by semi-custom approaches. Three semi-custom approaches are generally available (in increasing order with gate densities):

1. Fuse programmable logic (PAL, FPLA, and PROM)
2. Gate Arrays
3. Standard Cells

It is estimated that by 1990, half of the semiconductor market will be made of programmable system components. This paper will focus on only the PAL approach to semi-custom, but will compare the PAL to other alternatives.

The PAL Family

The First Generation: PAL20

The PAL is an abbreviation for Programmable Array Logic. The PAL was invented and patented by John Birkner of Monolithic Memories, Inc. The family is made of 15 different parts. All are housed in 20-pin DIP, and are fuse programmable by the user. Of the 15 different parts, 9 are combinatorial and 6 are registered for sequential operations. Figure 1 illustrates the use of a combinatorial PAL to perform address decoding in a typical microprocessor system.

Each PAL is made of one or more of the following cells:

- AND-OR/NOR cell used for combinatorial logic (Figure 2)
- Registered cell with internal feedback. Used to implement sequential logic (Figure 3).
- Programmable I/O cells enable the user to dynamically change the pin function from input to output and vice versa. This feature is very useful for bidirectional communication (Figure 4).

Figure 5 is a general block diagram of a state machine. The state of the machine is determined by the contents of the output register while the next state is a function of the present state and some input variables. Figure 6 depicts the implementation of this classic structure by a registered PAL. Note that the present state information is fed back to the combinatorial network via the internal feedback, thus conserving the use of precious pins.

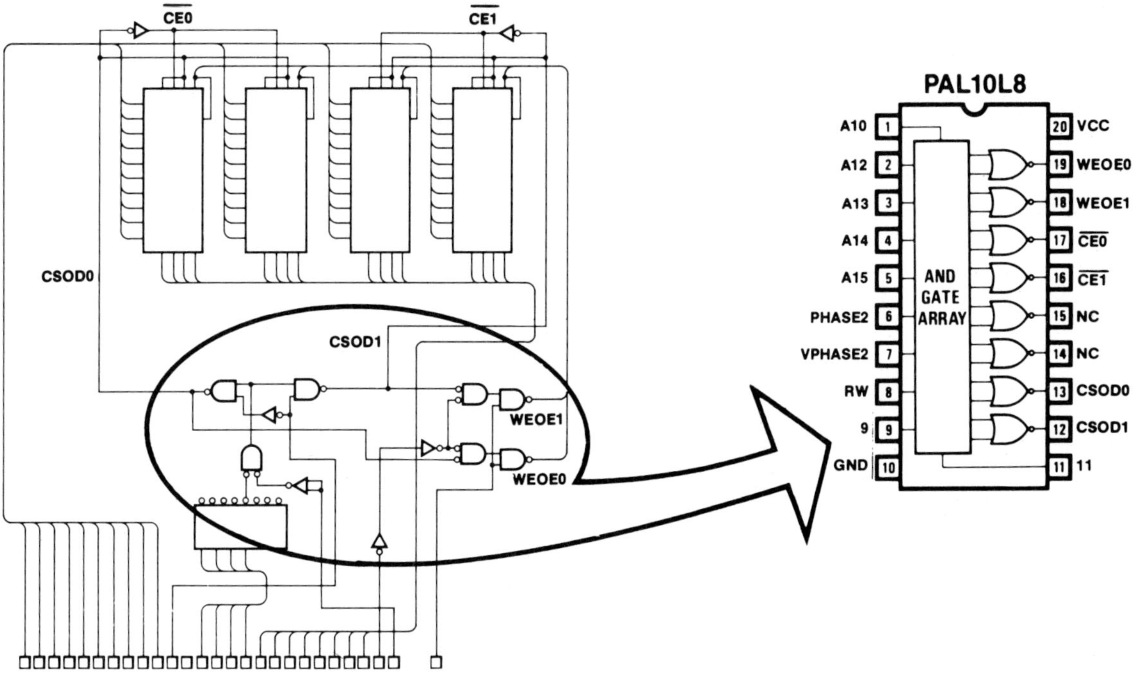

Figure 1. Using PAL to Replace Random Logic in 6800 Microprocessor Bus

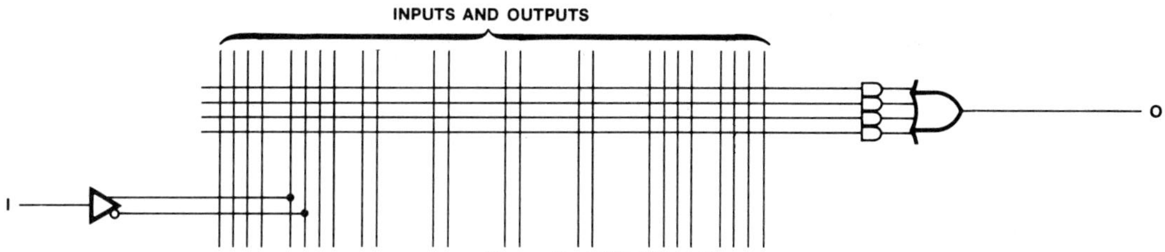

Figure 2. AND-OR Cell

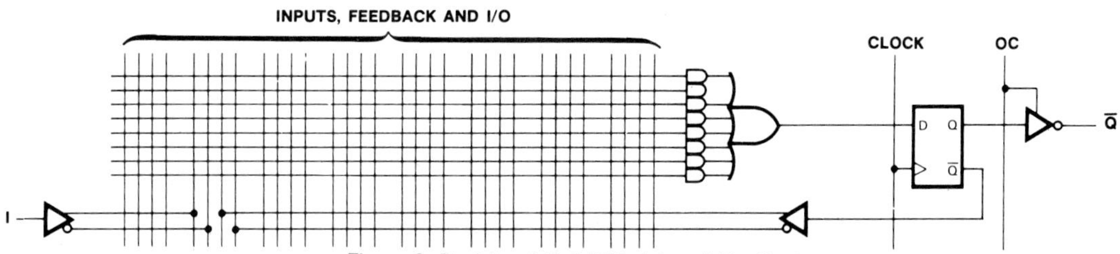

Figure 3. Registered Cell With Internal Feedback

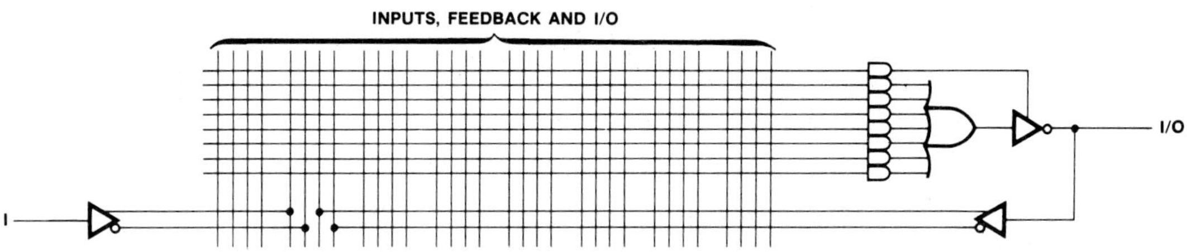

Figure 4. Programmable I/O Cell

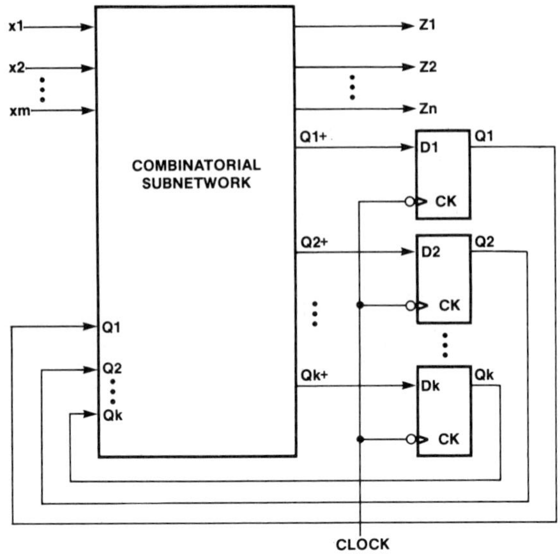

Figure 5. State Machine Block Diagram

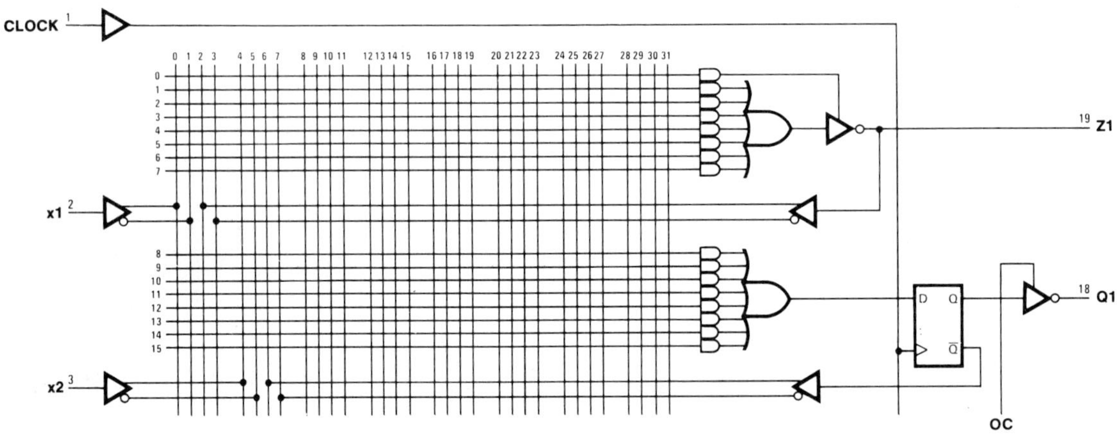

Figure 6. Section of a PAL16R6 Logic Diagram

The Second Generation: PAL24

The PAL24 is an evolution of the PAL20 and similarly has combinatorial and registered parts. However, in the combinatorial circuits, it is now possible to decode simultaneously up to 20 inputs. The registered parts now have as many as 10 outputs, but the important thing to note about the architecture of the registered part is the addition of a new cell: "AND-OR-EXOR" as illustrated in Figure 7. The significance of the cell is for implementing various types of counters. Figure 8 shows the logic diagram for the PAL20X8 that can be easily programmed to implement an octal counter.

PAL20X8

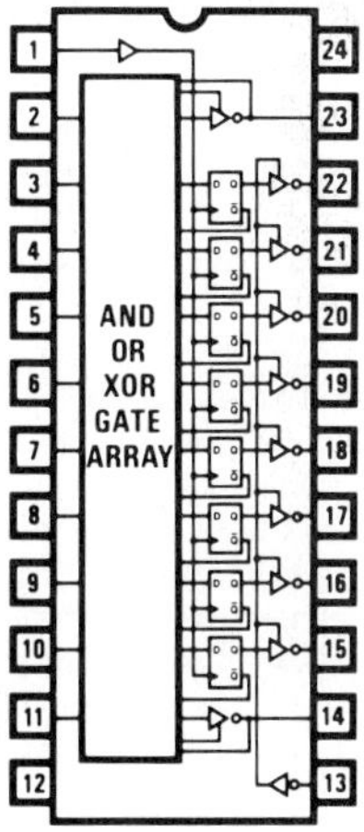

Figure 8. PAL20X8

PAL Performance: Present and Future

The most critical parameter for the PAL performance is the propagation delay for the combinatorial cells and the set-up time for the registered cells. These two parameters are equal in the PAL family and are listed below as function of time:

	1979	1981	1982	1983
$t_{PD} = t_{SU}$	40 ns	35 ns	25 ns	15 ns

These numbers are worst case for commercial temperature and supply ranges. Add 5 ns to get the worst case numbers for military temperature and supply.

PAL — Industry Standard

The PAL has been accepted as an industry standard and is being manufactured under license by National Semiconductor (NSC). In addition, it was announced by Texas Instruments (TI). It is very significant to note that TI and NSC, who are the leaders in the TTL market have recognized that PAL will eventually replace the present TTL. The PAL20 was adopted by the JEDEC 42.1 Committee as a de facto standard and it further proposed that the PAL24 be also adopted.

HAL — Hard Array Logic

The HAL to a PAL is the same as a ROM to a PROM. Instead of having a fuse mask, a metal mask is used. This technique reduces the PAL price almost by a factor of two. The HAL is similar to a gate array. Both are customized in the last fabrication stage by applying a unique metal mask to otherwise standard wafer. However, the HAL is the only gate array in the market with a fusible prototype.

PAL vs Other Alternatives

PAL Advantages Over SSI/MSI

The PAL can replace from 4-10 SSI/MSI and consequently it reduces the board space required for a function. It also increases reliability by moving the interconnections from the less reliable PC solder connections to the silicon chip. Since the PAL is programmable, it expedites the prototyping and debugging process as compared to conventional SSI/MSI. Last but not least, is the PAL security fuse which makes it impossible to copy the contents of a PAL.

PAL vs Gate Arrays

Gate arrays typically have higher gate density than a PAL. However, they have several drawbacks. The turn-around time for gate array is 2–4 months for the first silicon and typically two iterations are required to get a completely functional unit. Thus, the actual turn-around time is 4–8 months. By contrast, a PAL can be programmed in a few minutes and if several iterations are required, the total turn-around time is still measured in hours, not in months. Even if a customer selects to go with HAL (which has a turn-around time similar to gate arrays), he still does not lose time since he can use the PAL as his fusible prototype to build the first systems.

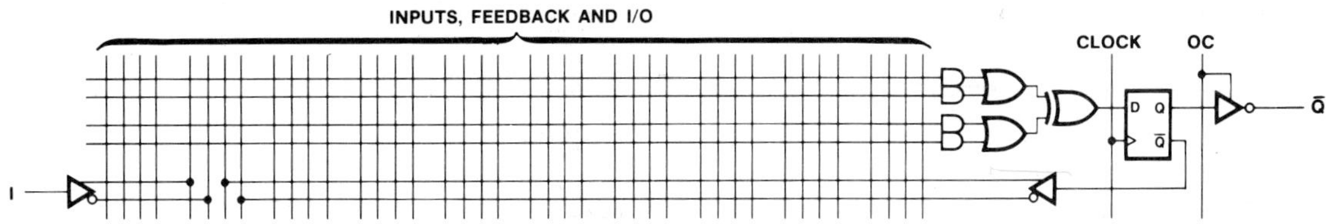

Figure 7. Registered Cell Using XOR Gate

Gate array development cost is estimated to be $20-$50K per circuit, this compared with less than $1K for HAL mask charges or nothing if only PAL is used.

Finally, at the time of writing this paper, the PAL is multi-sourced while gate arrays are single sourced.

PAL vs FPLA

Both approaches use AND array followed by OR array. In the FPLA, both arrays are programmable while in the PAL, only the AND array is programmable. The FPLA approach is academically more flexible but in practicality this flexibility costs time delay and power dissipation. The PAL with its programmable AND array is an engineering trade-off, since the majority of the TTL applications can be implemented by the single programmable array while increasing speed and saving power dissipation.

PROMs Complements the PAL

In few applications, we find that the PAL does not have sufficient product-terms to implement a certain function (especially arithmetic functions). In cases like this, the PROM has a clear advantage since it has all possible product-terms for a given number of inputs. For example: to build a 4x4 multiplier, only 8 inputs and 8 outputs are required; but the number of product terms is more than the 8 available in PAL. Thus, a 256x8 PROM can be used to implement this multiplier (since a 256 words PROM has 8 address lines).

PAL Design Specifications

Motivation

The PAL design specifications serve two functions which are very critical to any user who customizes his own chip:

(a) Documenting the customized function on a computerized data sheet form so that retrieving and updating are easily accomplished.

(b) Automating the design process, i.e., only logic equations are necessary in specifying a new function. The translation of these logic-equations to physcial fuse pattern should be transparent to the user.

The Specifications

The following items constitute the total specs:

- PAL part number
- Heading on user and function
- Pin list
- Logic equations
- Function table (optional)
- Description (optional)

Let us illustrate these specs by going though an example of a 24-pin PAL which is customized as an octal counter. This octal synchronous counter can perform 4 operations. Each operation is selected by a two bit code:

I1	I0	
0	0	Clear
0	1	Hold
1	0	Load
1	1	Increment

The counter has 8 data outputs which are called, “Q0” through “Q7” and 8 data inputs which are called “D0” through “D7”, where “D0” is the LSB.

So now we are ready to go through the detailed specifications. The first 4 lines are specified in the following way:

- Line 1 specifies that the device is PAL20X8
- Line 2 specifies user part number
- Line 3 is the device application name
- Line 4 is the user's company name, city and state

```
PAL20X8                                PAL DESIGN SPECIFICATION
74LS461                         BIRKNER/KAZMI/BLASCO 02/10/81
OCTAL COUNTER
MMI SUNNYVALE, CALIFORNIA
```

- Line 5 is the beginning of the pin list. In our case there are 24-pins:

  Pin 1 is the clock pin called "CLK"

  Pin 2 is a select line called "I0"

  Pin 3 is the LSB of the input called "D0," and so forth.

```
CLK  I0 D0 Dl D2 D3 D4 D5 D6 D7  Il GND
/OC /CO Q7 Q6 Q5 Q4 Q3 Q2 Q1 Q0 /CI VCC
```

Logic-equations follow the pin list:

```
/Q0 :=  /Il*/I0                              ;CLEAR LSB
     +       I0 * /Q0                        ;COUNT/HOLD
    :+:  Il*/I0 * /D0                        ;LOAD D0 (LSB)
     +   Il* I0 * CI                         ;COUNT

/Q1 :=  /Il*/I0                              ;CLEAR
     +       I0 * /Q1                        ;COUNT/HOLD
    :+:  Il*/I0 * /Dl                        ;LOAD Dl
     +   Il* I0 * CI*Q0                      ;COUNT

/Q2 :=  /Il*/I0                              ;CLEAR
     +       I0 * /Q2                        ;COUNT/HOLD
    :+:  Il*/I0 * /D2                        ;LOAD D2
     +   Il* I0 * CI*Q0*Ql                   ;COUNT

/Q3 :=  /Il*/I0                              ;CLEAR
     +       I0 * /Q3                        ;COUNT/HOLD
    :+:  Il*/I0 * /D3                        ;LOAD D3
     +   Il* I0 * CI*Q0*Ql*Q2                ;COUNT

/Q4 :=  /Il*/I0                              ;CLEAR
     +       I0 * /Q4                        ;COUNT/HOLD
    :+:  Il*/I0 * /D4                        ;LOAD D4
     +   Il* I0 * CI*Q0*Ql*Q2*Q3             ;COUNT

/Q5 :=  /Il*/I0                              ;CLEAR
     +       I0 * /Q5                        ;COUNT/HOLD
    :+:  Il*/I0 * /D5                        ;LOAD D5
     +   Il* I0 * CI*Q0*Ql*Q2*Q3*Q4          ;COUNT

/Q6 :=  /Il*/I0                              ;CLEAR
     +       I0 * /Q6                        ;COUNT/HOLD
    :+:  Il*/I0 * /D6                        ;LOAD D6
     +   Il* I0 * CI*Q0*Ql*Q2*Q3*Q4*Q5       ;COUNT

/Q7 :=  /Il*/I0                              ;CLEAR MSB
     +       I0 * /Q7                        ;COUNT/HOLD
    :+:  Il*/I0 * /D7                        ;LOAD D7 (MSB)
     +   Il* I0 * CI*Q0*Ql*Q2*Q3*Q4*Q5*Q6    ;COUNT

IF (VCC)  CO = CI*Q0*Ql*Q2*Q3*Q4*Q5*Q6*Q7    ;CARRY OUT
```

Following the logic equations, a FUNCTION TABLE is given. Note that the FUNCTION TABLE includes some basic test information:

```
FUNCTION TABLE

CLK /OC I1 I0 D7 D6 D5 D4 D3 D2 D1 D0 /CI /CO Q7 Q6 Q5 Q4 Q3 Q2 Q1 Q0

;                      -INPUT--               -OUTPUT-
;CONTROL      INSTR   DDDDDDDD    CARRY      QQQQQQQQ     COMMENTS
;CLK /OC      I1 I0   76543210   /CI /CO     76543210    (HEX VALUES)
-----------------------------------------------------------------------------
;BASIC LOAD TEST AND INCREMENT-WITH-CARRY TESTS
  C   L       H  L    LLLLLLLH    X    H     LLLLLLLH    LOAD (01)
  C   L       H  H    XXXXXXXX    L    H     LLLLLLHL    INCREMENT
  C   L       H  L    LLLLLLHH    X    H     LLLLLLHH    LOAD (03)
  C   L       H  H    XXXXXXXX    L    H     LLLLLHLL    INCREMENT
  C   L       H  L    LLLLLHHH    X    H     LLLLLHHH    LOAD (07)
  C   L       H  H    XXXXXXXX    L    H     LLLLHLLL    INCREMENT
  C   L       H  L    LLLLHHHH    X    H     LLLLHHHH    LOAD (0F)
  C   L       H  H    XXXXXXXX    L    H     LLLHLLLL    INCREMENT
  C   L       H  L    LLLHHHHH    X    H     LLLHHHHH    LOAD (1F)
  C   L       H  H    XXXXXXXX    L    H     LLHLLLLL    INCREMENT
  C   L       H  L    LLHHHHHH    X    H     LLHHHHHH    LOAD (3F)
  C   L       H  H    XXXXXXXX    L    H     LHLLLLLL    INCREMENT
  C   L       H  L    LHHHHHHH    X    H     LHHHHHHH    LOAD (7F)
  C   L       H  H    XXXXXXXX    L    H     HLLLLLLL    INCREMENT
  C   L       H  L    HHHHHHHH    L    L     HHHHHHHH    LOAD (FF)
  C   L       H  H    XXXXXXXX    L    H     LLLLLLLL    INCREMENT (ROLL OVER)
;COMPLEMENT LOAD TESTS
  C   L       H  L    HHHHHHHH    L    L     HHHHHHHH    LOAD (FF)
  C   L       H  L    HHHHHHHL    X    H     HHHHHHHL    LOAD (FE)
  C   L       H  L    HHHHHHLH    X    H     HHHHHHLH    LOAD (FD)
  C   L       H  L    HHHHHLHH    X    H     HHHHHLHH    LOAD (FB)
  C   L       H  L    HHHHLHHH    X    H     HHHHLHHH    LOAD (F7)
  C   L       H  L    HHHLHHHH    X    H     HHHLHHHH    LOAD (EF)
  C   L       H  L    HHLHHHHH    X    H     HHLHHHHH    LOAD (DF)
  C   L       H  L    HLHHHHHH    X    H     HLHHHHHH    LOAD (BF)
  C   L       H  L    LHHHHHHH    X    H     LHHHHHHH    LOAD (7F)
  C   L       H  L    HHHHHHHH    L    L     HHHHHHHH    LOAD (FF)
;SHORT COUNT SEQUENCE - CONSECUTIVE COUNTS
  C   L       L  L    XXXXXXXX    X    H     LLLLLLLL    CLEAR
  C   L       H  H    XXXXXXXX    L    H     LLLLLLLH    INCREMENT TO (01)
  C   L       H  H    XXXXXXXX    L    H     LLLLLLHL    INCREMENT TO (02)
  C   L       H  H    XXXXXXXX    L    H     LLLLLLHH    INCREMENT TO (03)
  C   L       H  H    XXXXXXXX    L    H     LLLLLHLL    INCREMENT TO (04)
;COUNT HOLD CHECK - CO GATING CHECK
  C   L       H  L    HHHHHHHL    X    H     HHHHHHHL    LOAD (FE)
  C   L       H  H    XXXXXXXX    L    L     HHHHHHHH    INCREMENT TO (FF) /CO=L
  C   L       H  H    XXXXXXXX    H    H     HHHHHHHH    CI INHIBITS COUNT AND CO
  C   L       L  H    LLLLLLLL    L    L     HHHHHHHH    HOLD SEL INHIBITS COUNT ONLY
  C   L       H  H    HHHHHHHH    L    H     LLLLLLLL    INCREMENT TO (00)
;TEST OUTPUT CONTROL (/OC) FOR THREE-STATE OUTPUTS
  X   H       X  X    XXXXXXXX    X    X     ZZZZZZZZ    TEST HI-Z
-----------------------------------------------------------------------------
```

Finally, it is highly recommended that a description be a part of this computerized data sheet.

```
THIS IS AN 8-BIT SYNCHRONOUS COUNTER WITH PARALLEL LOAD, CLEAR, AND HOLD
CAPABILITY.  THE LOAD OPERATION LOADS THE INPUTS (D7-D0) INTO THE OUTPUT
REGISTER (Q7-Q0).  THE CLEAR OPERATION RESETS THE OUTPUT REGISTER TO ALL LOWS.
THE HOLD OPERATION HOLDS THE PREVIOUS VALUE REGARDLESS OF CLOCK TRANSITIONS.
THE INCREMENT OPERATION ADDS ONE TO THE OUTPUT REGISTER WHEN THE CARRY-IN IS
TRUE (/CI=L), OTHERWISE THE OPERATION IS A HOLD.  THE CARRY-OUT (/CO) IS TRUE
(/CO=L) WHEN THE OUTPUT REGISTER (Q7-Q0) IS ALL HIGHS, OTHERWISE FALSE (/CO=H).

THESE OPERATIONS ARE EXERCISED IN THE FUNCTION TABLE AND SUMMARIZED IN THE
OPERATIONS TABLE:

     /OC  CLK  I1  I0  /CI  D7-D0  Q7-Q0     OPERATION
     ------------------------------------------------
      H    X   X   X    X     X      Z       HI-Z
      L    C   L   L    X     X      L       CLEAR
      L    C   L   H    X     X      Q       HOLD
      L    C   H   L    X     D      D       LOAD
      L    C   H   H    H     X      Q       HOLD
      L    C   H   H    L     X   Q PLUS 1   INCREMENT
     ------------------------------------------------
```

CAD Software for PAL

PALASM

PALASM is a software which translates the LOGIC EQUATIONS to a fuse pattern. The output of the PALASM is in a format compatible with either a PAL or a PROM programmer. The user needs to specify only his "block-box" description and the programmer will blow the corresponding fuse pattern.

PALASM also uses the FUNCTION TABLE to perform two critical operations for the semi-custom user:

- Design Verification — Each entry of the FUNCTION TABLE is checked against the logic equations and any inconsistency is flagged as an error.
- Test Vectors — Each entry of the FUNCTION TABLE is translated to a universal test vector, so there is a way of testing the customized PAL once it is fabricated

PALASM is written in FORTRAN IV and it resides on an IBM 370/168. Users can access the program by calling the NCSS time-share network. Additionally, Monolithic Memories makes the source code of PALASM available to users at no cost. PALASM is presently running on quite a few computers at customer sites. Several examples of such computers are the DEC PDP/11, DG NOVA, HP2100, MDS800, and many others.

An example of the test-vectors generated from the FUNCTION TABLE of the octal counter is given at right:

```
 1 C0100000001X0HLLLLLLLHX1
 2 C1XXXXXXXX1X0HLLLLLLHL01
 3 C0110000001X0HLLLLLLHHX1
 4 C1XXXXXXXX1X0HLLLLLHLL01
 5 C0111000001X0HLLLLLHHHX1
 6 C1XXXXXXXX1X0HLLLLHLLL01
 7 C0111100001X0HLLLLHHHHX1
 8 C1XXXXXXXX1X0HLLLHLLLL01
 9 C0111110001X0HLLLHHHHHX1
10 C1XXXXXXXX1X0HLLHLLLLL01
11 C0111111001X0HLLHHHHHHX1
12 C1XXXXXXXX1X0HLHLLLLLL01
13 C0111111101X0HLHHHHHHHX1
14 C1XXXXXXXX1X0HHLLLLLLL01
15 C0111111111X0LHHHHHHHH01
16 C1XXXXXXXX1X0HLLLLLLLL01
17 C0111111111X0LHHHHHHHH01
18 C0011111111X0HHHHHHHHLX1
19 C0101111111X0HHHHHHHLHX1
20 C0110111111X0HHHHHHLHHX1
21 C0111011111X0HHHHHLHHHX1
22 C0111101111X0HHHHLHHHHX1
23 C0111110111X0HHHLHHHHHX1
24 C0111111011X0HHLHHHHHHX1
25 C0111111101X0HLHHHHHHHX1
26 C0111111111X0LHHHHHHHH01
27 C0XXXXXXXX0X0HLLLLLLLLX1
28 C1XXXXXXXX1X0HLLLLLLLH01
29 C1XXXXXXXX1X0HLLLLLLHL01
30 C1XXXXXXXX1X0HLLLLLLHH01
31 C1XXXXXXXX1X0HLLLLLHLL01
32 C0011111111X0HHHHHHHHLX1
33 C1XXXXXXXX1X0LHHHHHHHH01
34 C1XXXXXXXX1X0HHHHHHHHH11
35 C1000000000X0LHHHHHHHH01
36 C1111111111X0HLLLLLLLL01
37 XXXXXXXXXXXX1XZZZZZZZZX1
```

Testability

The test vectors which resulted from the FUNCTION TABLE are referred to as basic test vector and they indeed guarantee that the part is functioning according to each entry in the FUNCTION TABLE. However, to increase the confidence level that the device will not "misbehave" (when unspecified inputs are applied) it is necessary to insure that all nodes are toggled during the testing. Monolithic Memories has an automatic test-vector generation program which is used to test HAL, the software uses the basic test-vectors as seed vector and from there it iteratively adds more test vectors until all nodes have been toggled.

It is important to note that for testability it is always necessary to have an initiallization mechanism, e.g., in the octal counter when I0 = I1 = 0, the counter is cleared to all zeros.

HMSI: Dedicated HAL Functions

In general, the PAL and HAL are programmed according to user specifications. However, as an aid to customers, we make certain dedicated 24-pin HAL. For example:

- Octal Counter
- 10-Bit Counter
- 16:1 MUX and several other "new" TTL functions

PAL and the Military

Bipolar Technology

The PALs are fabricated using bipolar Schottky technology which has been proven to be much more reliable at extreme temperatures than the MOS technology. The PAL is being programmed by blowing TiW fusible links which has proven reliability on PROMs. The fusible link technique is much more reliable than the EPROM or EEPROM which use a stored charge that leaks with time and has a questionable operation at the military temperature range.

Low-Volume

Low-volume requirement has been a continuous problem to the military market place, but with PALs obviously the low-volume requirement can be satisfied by customizing as little as one chip at a time.

Obsolete SSI/MSI

Anytime the demand for ICs exceeds the available supply, the semiconductor manufacturer stops producing the least profitable ICs. As the labor cost increases and the silicon cost decreases, SSI/MSI devices (which are labor intensive) are the first to become obsolete. With the fast turn-around time of the PAL. These TTL devices can be quickly reduced by PAL.

Leadless Packages

The PAL is also available in the space saving leadless chip carriers (LLC). These carriers are made according to JEDEC outline (Type B) with 50 mil centers and 75 mil package thickness. The 20-pin LCC is 350x350 mils and occupies only 40% of the space required by the equivalent of 20-pin DIP.

Military Processing

PALs, like all other Monolithic Memories' products, can be processed to meet the HI-REL requirements of MIL-STD-883B. This processing is available for both LCC and DIP packages and also for dice where they are visually inspected by method 2010B and are shipped in a standard waffle pack.

Summary

The PAL family is already a valuable semi-custom approach in the commercial market place. It will even be more valuable to the military market that has been looking for a solution to the problem of low-volume requirement.

The PAL, which is implemented in bipolar technology, presents a high reliability programmable solution to the demanding needs of the military market.

High Speed/Low Cost Fuse Link Arrays Compete with TTL 74S/LS

John Birkner/Wescon 78

Random Logic has remained virtually impenetrable by today's state of the art LSI technology. This fact is dramatically evidenced by the high percentage of TTL 74S/LS logic found in currently introduced small board computers based on MOS microprocessors, and also high performance minicomputers based on bipolar bit slice chip sets.

LSI has vastly reduced the well defined, regular logic functions found in these systems because of the wide appeal, thus, high volume and low cost. When the regular functions are applied to the specific needs of a particular systems manufacturer, however, individual interfacing requirements demand additional logic not available in LSI functions. The present solution is to use standard SSI/MSI logic functions at a high cost in chip count, assembly/test labor and reliability.

To answer the need for LSI Random Logic, a family of fuse Programmable Array Logic devices (PAL) has recently been introduced. This family meets the speed requirements of competing TTL SSI/MSI with typical 25ns propogation and set up delays while reducing chip count 4 to 1.

Total system cost using PALs is comparable with SSI/MSI, yet design time and inventory costs are reduced. The 15 part family utilizes the latest improvements in bipolar Schottky fusible link technology with the proven reliability track record of bipolar PROMs. Titanium-tungsten fuses and emitter follower arrays are used to achieve the 25ns delays through three levels of logic.

DEFINING THE PROBLEM

Increasing the logic function density per chip is the name of the game in the integrated circuit industry. The standard procedure is to identify a logical block which is common to many applications and users, and then to integrate that function onto a single chip. The problem with integrating the random and irregular functions which are so prevalent in today's digital systems is to identify a common denominator which can provide a generalized solution that meets cost and performance goals.

A Decade of TTL

The growth of TTL SSI/MSI during the last decade provides a wealth of knowledge about the elements that designers need to build digital systems. This family of devices was defined by many users and manufacturers over many years and is, therefore, an evolutionary, emperical data base from which we can extrapolate generalized logical primatives for LSI implementation.

The Primitives

SSI/MSI functions can be classified as either combinatorial or sequential. Combinatorial includes the basic gates, AND-OR-INVRT gates, Multiplexors, de-multiplexors and priority encoders. More complex combinatorial includes arithmetic functions such as comparitors, adders, and ALUs. The common denominator among the simple combinatorial elements is the sum of products. An additional primative in the arithmetic elements is a high density of Exclusive-ORs.

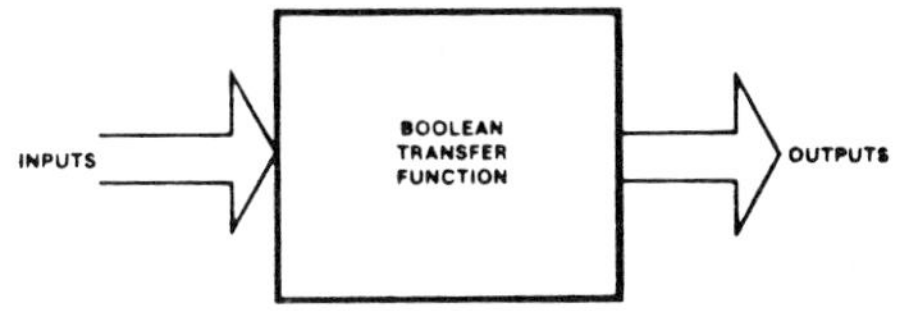

Figure 1: Combinatorial Function

Sequential includes all the registered functions such as counters, shift registers, registered multi-pliexors, accumulators, and registered encoders. The common denominator of these sequential elements is a register driven by a combinatorial element whose inputs are both external and internal from the register. All of the sequential devices may be described as simple state machines.

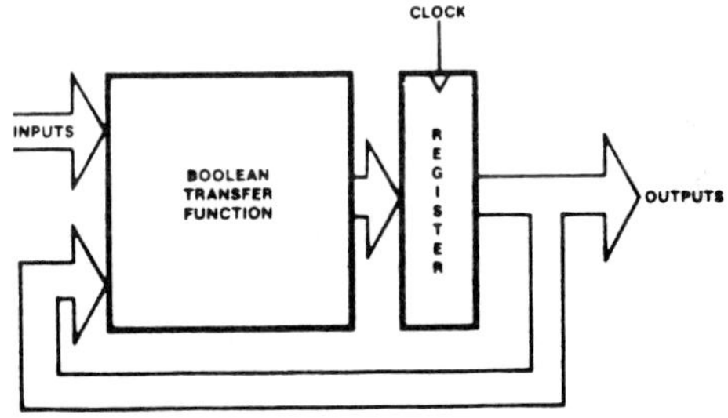

Figure 2: Sequential Function

Both the combinatorial and the sequential functions may have the optional characteristic of three-state outputs. That is, the output function may be disconnected as a driving source by placing the outputs in a high impedance state (High-Z)

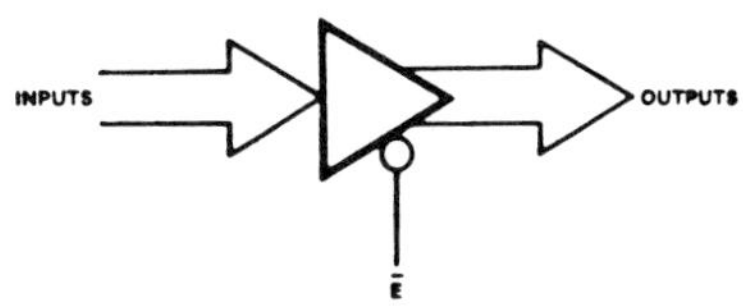

Figure 3: Three-State Output Gate

Definition of Terms

Before we can rigorously define the basic logical primitives, we first need a precise language which unambiguously describes the transfer functions.

Definitions:

- = Equality, after the propogation time, t_{PD}, from any input change.
- := Replaced by, after the propogation delay, t_{PD}, from the low to high transition of the clock.
- IF Conditional Equality, after the propogation delay, t_{PD}, from the enabling condition. Otherwide, high impedance (High-Z).
- / Complement, Boolean operator, placed to the left of a Boolean variable.
- * AND, Boolean operator.
- + OR, Boolean operator.
- :+: XOR, Boolean operator.
- ( ) Parenthetical separators.

hierarchical order / * + :+:
where / is evaluated first.

Given these definitions, we can formulate rigorous logical descriptions of standard SSI/MSI functions.

Rigorous Statement of Primitives

We can now state, in equation form, a generalized set of equations suitable for LSI implementation.

For an input vector X and an output vector Y, a combinatorial function is described as,

$$Y = f(X)$$

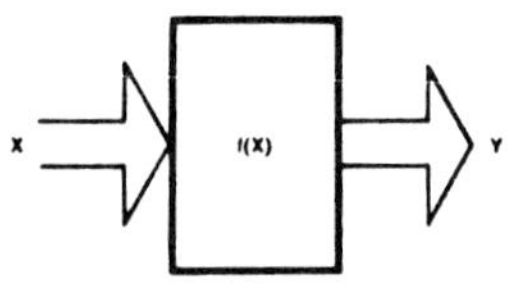

where f is Boolean sum of products transfer function.

A three state combinatorial function is described as,

$$IF\ (\ f_1(X)\ )\quad Z = f_2(X)$$

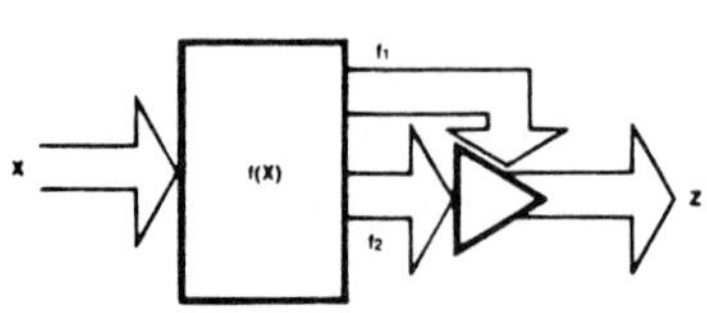

A sequential function is described as,

$$Y := f(X,\ Y)$$
$$IF(E)\ Y^{1} = Y$$

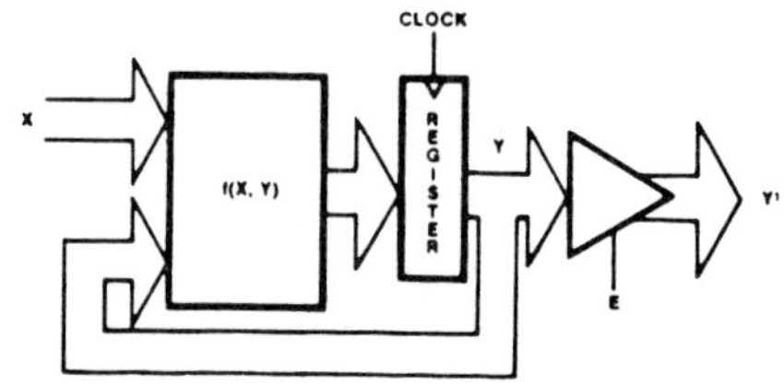

Combining sequential, combinatorial and three-state we now have,

$$IF\ (\ f_1(X,\ Y)\ )\ Z = f_2(X,\ Y)$$
$$Y: = f_3(X,\ Y)$$
$$IF\ (E)\quad Y^{1} = Y$$

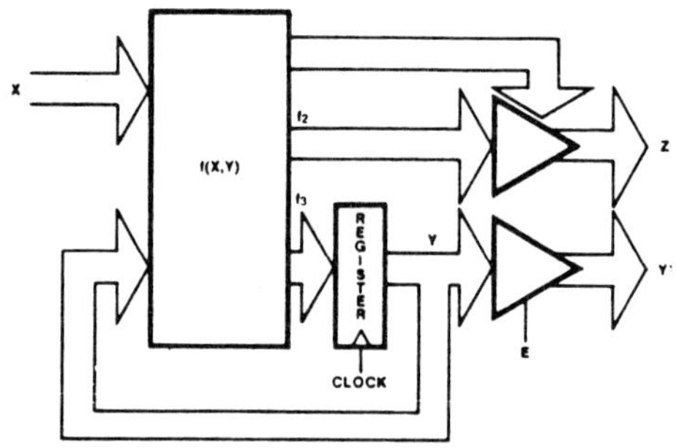

The above generalized Boolean functions are a super set of virtually all of the standard SSI/MSI functions.

For an LSI implementation to provide a better solution than existing SSI/MSI it must meet the following requirements:

1. Reduce package count
2. Match or improve performance.
3. Reduce System Cost.

The Programmable Array Logic (PAL) family was designed to meet these requirements.

COMBINATORIAL EXAMPLE:

4 to 1 Mux with three-state Outputs (74LS253)

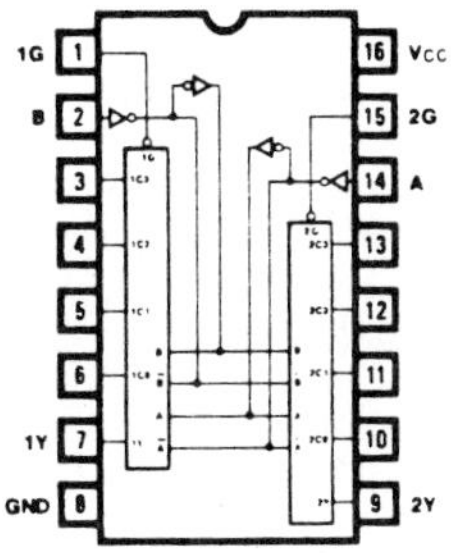

4 to 1 Mux Logic Symbol

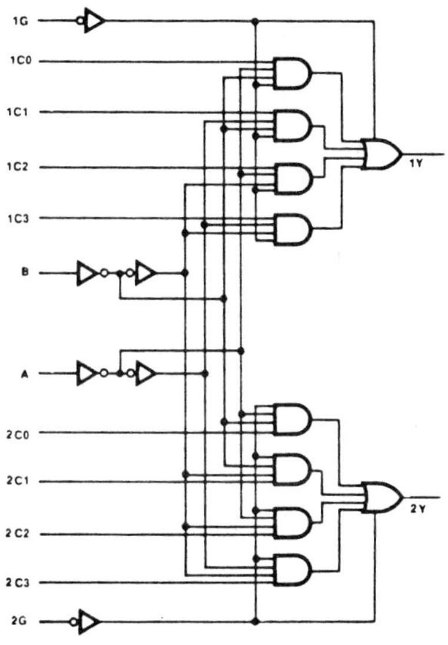

4 to 1 Mux Logic Diagram

EQUATIONS:

IF(/1G) 1Y = /A* /B* 1C0 +
A*/B*1C1 +
/A* B*1C2 +
A* B*1C3

IF(/2G) 2Y = /A*/B*2C0 +
A*/B*2C1 +
/A*B*2C2 +
A*B*2C3

SEQUENTIAL EXAMPLE:

4 BIT UP/DOWN COUNTER (74LS169)

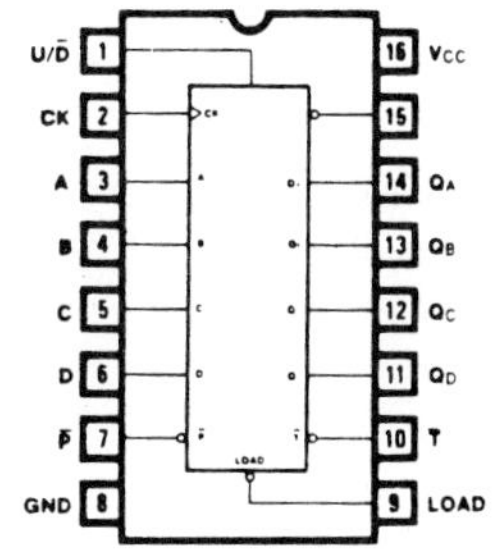

Up/Down Counter Logic Symbol

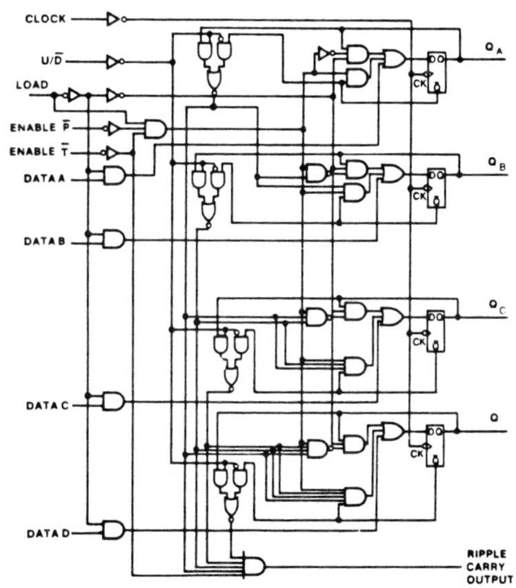

Up/Down Counter Logic Diagram

EQUATIONS:

QA : = LOAD*A + /LOAD*QA :+:
/LOAD*P*T

QB : = LOAD*B + /LOAD*QB :+:
/LOAD*P*T*UD*QA +
/LOAD*P*T/UD*/QA

QC : = LOAD*C + /LOAD*QC :+:
/LOAD*P*T*UD*QA*QB +
/LOAD*P*T*/UD*/QA*/QB

QD : = LOAD*D + /LOAD*QD :+:
/LOAD*P*T*UD*QA*QB*QC +
/LOAD*P*T*/UD*/QA*/QB*/QC

/CARRY = T*UD*QA*QB*QC*QD + T*/UD*
/QA*/QB*/QC*/QD

THE PROGRAMMABLE LSI SOLUTION

A family of 15 PAL devices are manufactured by Monolithic Memories, Inc. which provide a range of logic functions including combinatorial, three-state, sequential, and arithmetic sequential. The TTL devices utilize a platinum Silicide Schottky process and Titanium Tungsten fuse links to form a single programmable emitter follower AND array which drives a fixed OR array as shown in Figure 4.

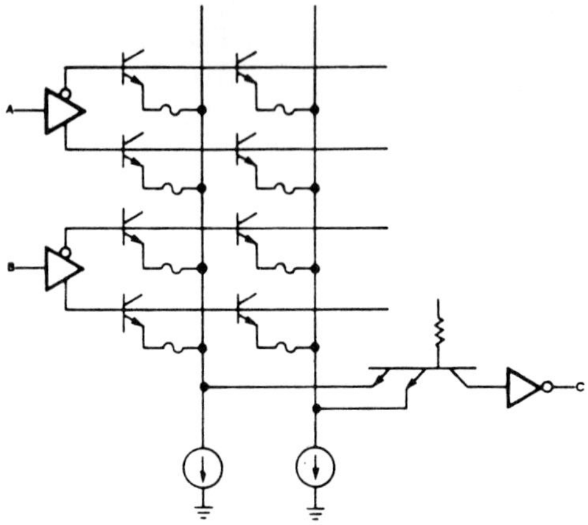

Figure 4: AND-OR Circuit Diagram

The AND-OR array is described logically by a distributed AND gate symbol to facilitate ease of drawing. (Conventional AND symbol with single input rail where X indicates a diode and a fuse.)

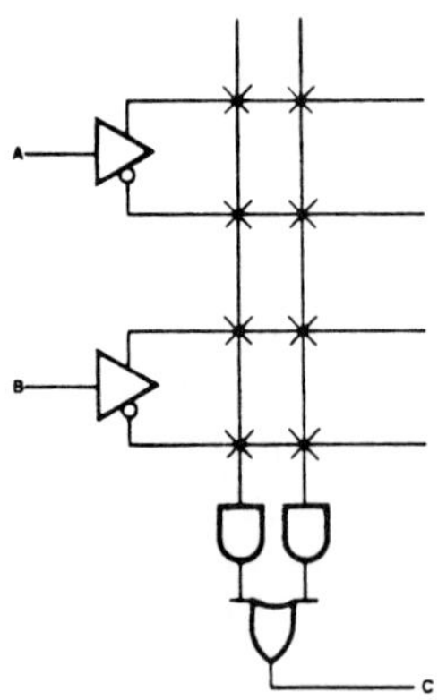

Figure 5: AND-OR Logic Diagram

Basic Combinatorial Cell

The basic combinatorial cell implements the sum of products over a range of input-output pin ratios. All combinatorial output drivers conform to the Low Power Schottky TTL electrical characteristics for totempole drivers. e.g., I_{OL} = 8mA.

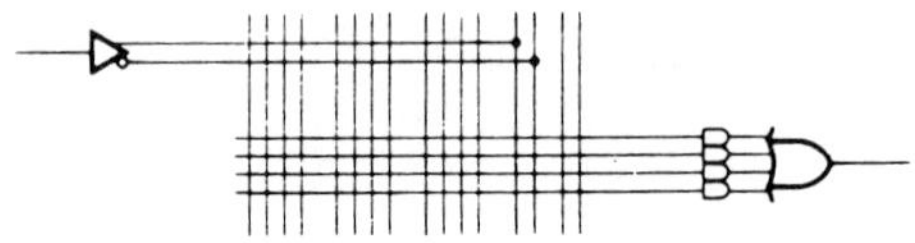

Figure 6: Combinatorial Cell

Programmable I/O

A more complex combinatorial cell incorporates three-state drivers where the enable function is programmable. This allows a pin to be allocated as an input, an output, or dynamically I/O. All three-state outputs are designed to meet the Low Power Schottky TTL three-state bus standard of 24mA I_{OL}.

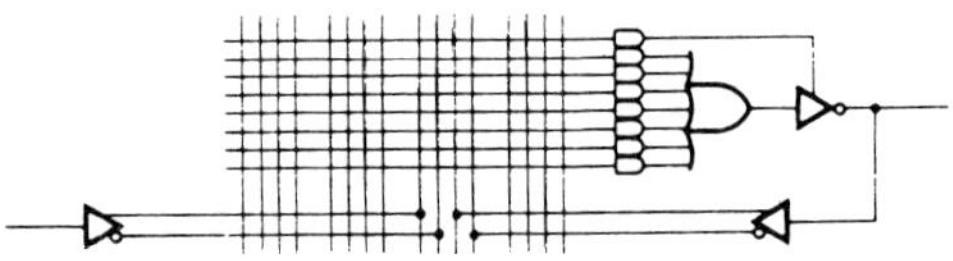

Figure 7: Programmable I/O Cell

Registered Feedback Cell

A D-type Register at the output of a combinatorial cell forms the state machine primative. This cell can be used to implement regular state sequences such as count and shift, but more importantly, it can be used to implement random state sequences not available as standard functions.

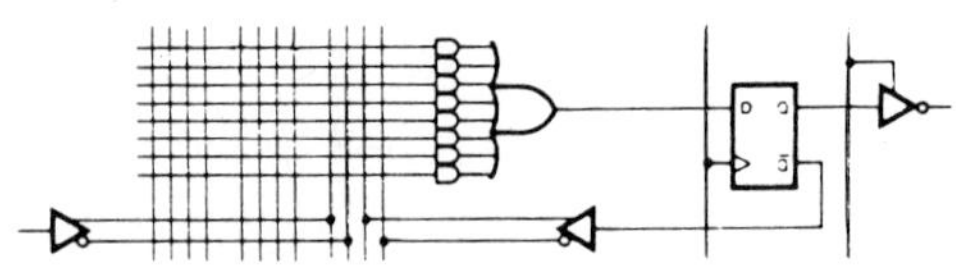

Figure 8: Registered Feedback Cell

Arithmetic Cell

The most complex of the PAL cells includes an exclusive OR and a gated feedback to implement basic arithmetic operations such as greater than, less than, add and subtract.

The register forms an accumulator while the combinatorial network forms an ALU.

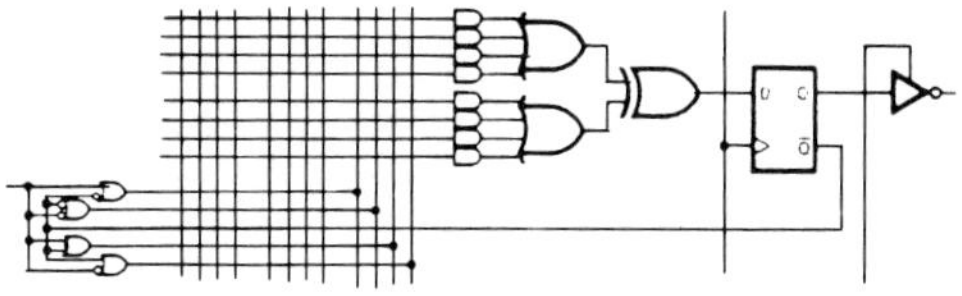

Figure 9: Arithmetic Cell

Structured Pinouts

The 15 PALs are packaged in the popular 20 pin 300 mil wide Skinny DIP™. Input pins are generally to the left while output pins and I/O pins are to the right. This feature conveniences PC board layout and allows the Pinout/Logic Symbol to be a Block diagram.

PALs: Programmable Logic Functions Help Minimize Hardware

John Birkner/Wescon 79

Taking advantage of PROM on-the-spot programmability, the PALs offer a range of logic replacement capabilities — from random gates to complex arithmetic circuits. Using a programmable AND array to feed a fixed OR array, PALs permit compact realizations of sum-of-products expressions. This paper will provide an overview of the PAL family, a basic understanding of the PAL structure, some guidelines as to how systems can be partitioned to take advantage of the PALs and a design example.

The Problem

A look at the three[1] billion dollar digital integrated circuit marketplace provides insight into the needs of systems designers. First, Figure 1 breaks out the dollar marketplace into four major areas.

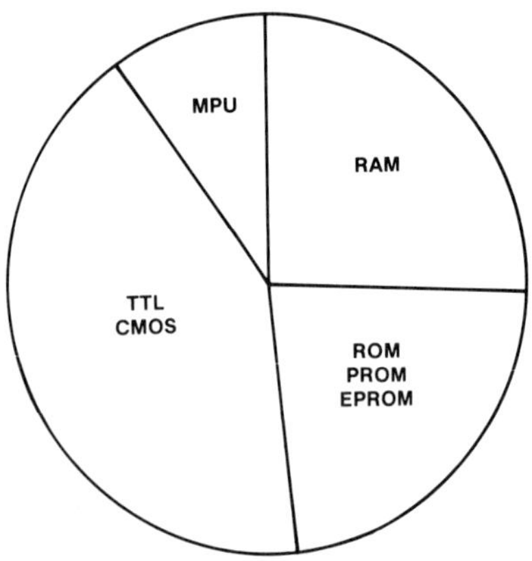

Figure 1. $ Digital IC Marketplace

As the average system should contain a similar percentage cost of silicon for MPU, RAM, ROM/PROM/EPROM, TTL/CMOS, it is of particular interest to note the high percentage of Random Logic; e.g., TTL/CMOS. In spite of the great microprocessor revolution, the systems marketplace spends 35% of its dollars on random logic. To make this point shockingly clear, Figure 2 shows the three billion *unit* marketplace for MPU, RAM, ROM/PROM/EPROM, TTL/CMOS.

The systems marketplace devotes 87% of its IC chip count to TTL/CMOS. Dramatic evidence of this fact is demonstrated by observing the high percentage of 16 and 20 pin DIPs on today's small board computers and microprocessor systems.

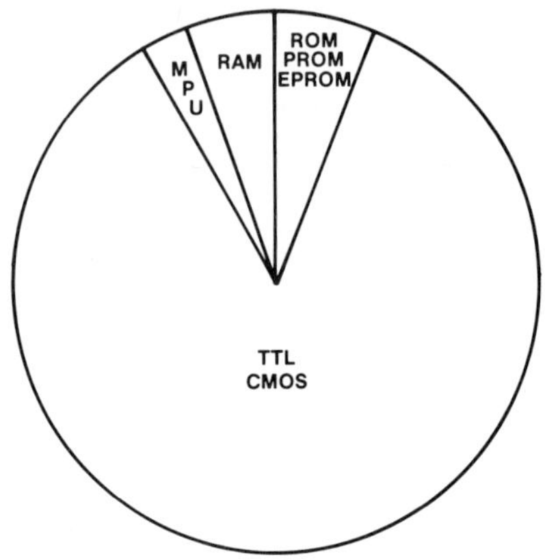

Figure 2. Unit Digital IC Marketplace

Comparison of Figure 1 and Figure 2 along with some quick arithmetic shows the ASP (Average Selling Price) of the MPU, RAM, ROM/PROM/EPROM is around $4.00, whereas, the ASP of TTL/CMOS is around $.50. As a ball-park cost of placing an IC on a board is around $1.00 (board cost, assembly and test), the major cost of using the TTL/CMOS is the overhead, not the silicon.

Programmable Logic

Semiconductor manufacturers have been busy designing a host of programmable logic devices to meet the challenge of integrating this last holdout to LSI, namely random logic gates/muxes/decoders/flip-flops. For the system designer, programmable logic holds the promise of balancing the level of integration of his digital ICs while still further reducing the printed circuit board real estate required per system. Further, programmable logic gives the user a custom IC which he can buy as an inexpensive high volume/multiple sourced virgin device, then customize on commonly available programmers.

The first and most common programmable logic device suitable for logic replacement is the bipolar PROM. Available in a wide variety of input/output pin ratios, the PROM transforms an input variable (address lines) to a desired output condition (data out) with a propagation delay in the range of 50 to 80 nanoseconds. Normally thought of as a memory, the PROM is a sum of products, boolean transfer function which will transform all possible input vectors to any desired output vector. Caution! PROM outputs glitch during the propagation delay of any input change. This is true as any input change causes the source of data to move from one product to another where there may be a gap, overlap, or a third product causing unpredictable outputs. Figure 3 shows a PROM architecture in sum of products form.

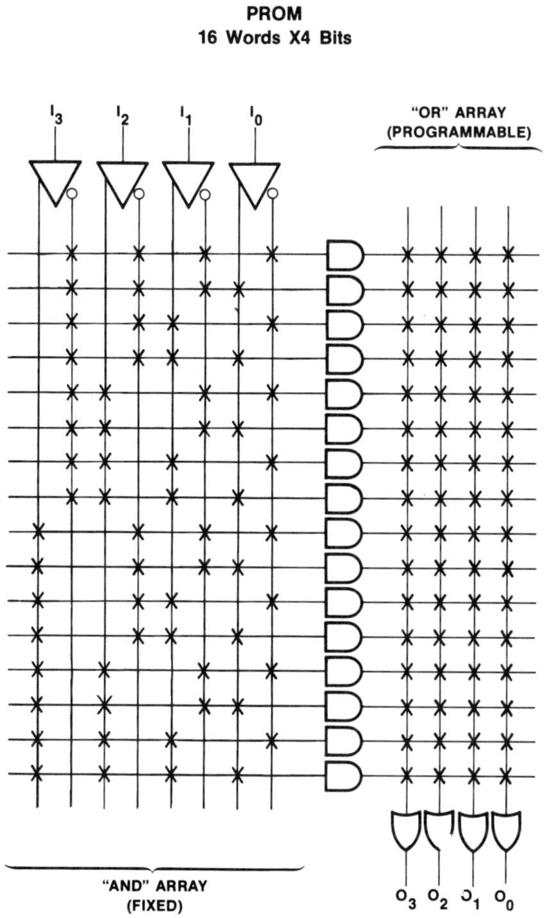

Figure 3. PROM Architecture

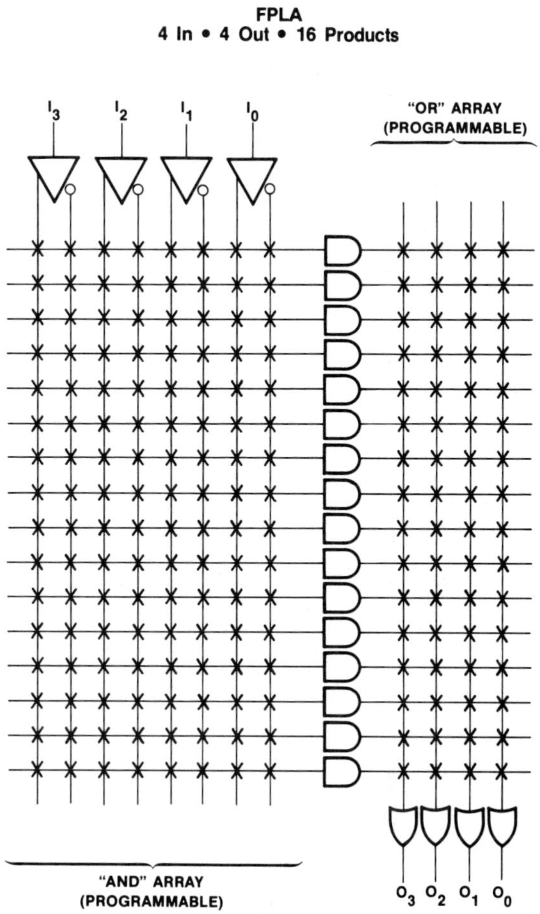

Figure 4. FPLA Architecture

The first programmable logic device designed specifically for logic replacement was the FPLA. The programmable AND array overcomes the previous glitch problem in the PROM and allows more input variables. Figure 4 shows an FPLA architecture with programmable AND and programmable OR arrays.

A recent entry into the programmable logic marketplace is the PAL[2] (Programmable Array Logic). The PAL architecture is a complement of the PROM architecture as the AND array is programmable and the OR array is fixed. The architecture affords simple programming in existing PROM programmers plus a fast propagation time of 40 nanoseconds maximum over the commercial V_{CC} and temperature ranges. In addition, PALs have additional output options of Registers and I/O as summarized in Figure 6. Figure 5 shows the PAL architecture with programmable AND array and fixed OR array.

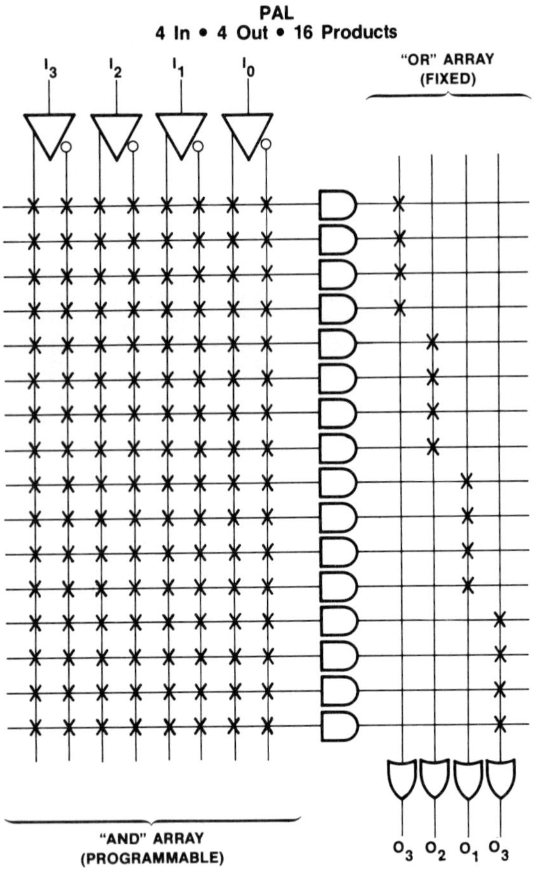

Figure 5. PAL Architecture

	AND	OR	OUTPUT OPTIONS
PROM	Fixed	Prog	TS, OC
FPLA	Prog	Prog	TS, OC, Fusible Polarity
FPGA	Prog	None	TS, OC, Fusible Polarity
PMUX	Fix/Prog	Fixed	TS
PAL	Prog	Fixed	TS, Registered, Feedback, I/O

Figure 6. Programmable Logic Summary

PALs — A Family of 15

Fifteen PALs provide a family approach to the replacement of random logic gates, muxs, decoders and flip-flops at a greater than 4 to 1 chip count reduction. The die sizes range from 13K square mils to 19K square mils which compare to 2K PROM and 4K PROM die sizes which sell in the $2.00 to $4.00 range. Two major semiconductor manufacturers are now supplying PALs with a third to appear shortly.

A description of the family is shown in Table 1 below.

PART NUMBER	DESCRIPTION
PAL10H8	Octal 10 Input And-Or Gate Array
PAL12H6	Hex 12 Input And-Or Gate Array
PAL14H4	Quad 14 Input And-Or Gate Array
PAL16H2	Dual 16 Input And-Or Gate Array
PAL16C1	16 Input And-Or/And-Or-Invert Gate Array
PAL10L8	Octal 10 Input And-Or-Invert Gate Array
PAL12L6	Hex 12 Input And-Or-Invert Gate Array
PAL14L4	Quad 14 Input And-Or-Invert Gate Array
PAL16L2	Dual 16 Input And-Or-Invert Gate Array
PAL16L8	Octal 16 Input And-Or-Invert Gate Array
PAL16R8	Octal 16 Input Registered And-Or Gate Array
PAL16R6	Hex 16 Input Registered And-Or Gate Array
PAL16R4	Quad 16 Input Registered And-Or Gate Array
PAL16X4	Quad 16 Input Registered And-Or-Xor Gate Array
PAL16A4	Quad 16 Input Registered And-Carry-Or-Xor Gate

Table 1. PAL Family

Ranging in complexity from simple gates to complex arithmetic functions the PAL Family can functionally replace up to 90% of the 7400 Series TTL.

A Simple Example

To demonstrate a PAL implementation, consider the following Boolean functions:

```
B = A
D = /C
G = E * F
J = H + I
M = /K + /L
P = /N * /O
```

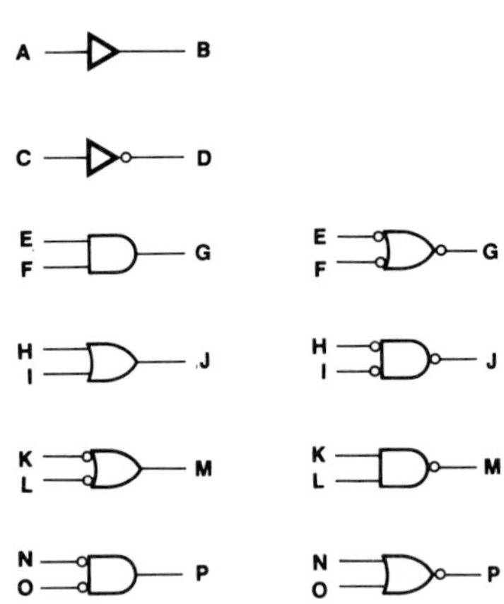

Choosing the PAL10H8, these functions are now implemented as shown in the logic symbol of Figure 7.

PAL10H8

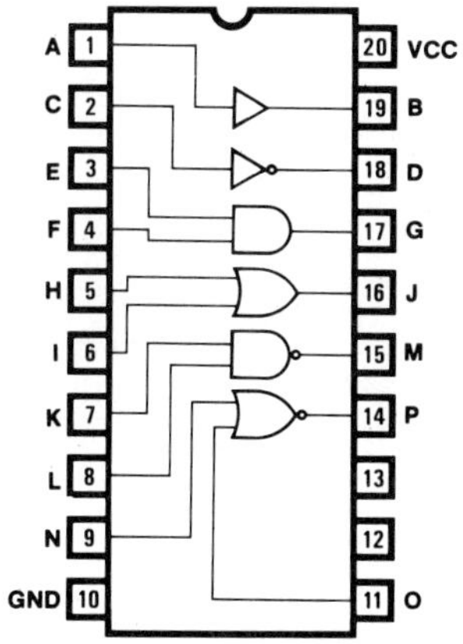

Logic Symbol

Figure 7. Example Gates Logic Symbol

Example Gates No. 1

Logic Diagram PAL10H8

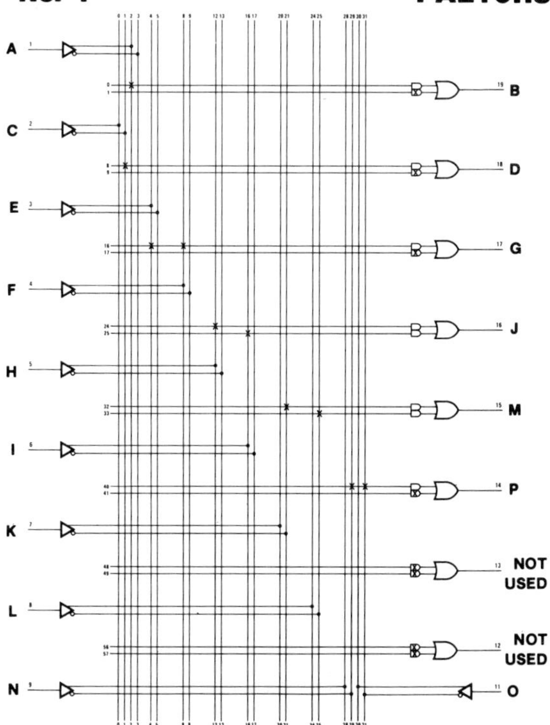

Figure 8. Example Gates Logic Diagram

The functions are described by the logic diagram of Figure 8. The buffer which connects Pin 1 (A) to Pin 19 (B) is formed by the single "X" placed at the intersection of product term 0 (top horizontal line) and input line 2 (far left vertical line). The "X" is a shorthand expression for an intact fuse connecting the product line (AND gate) to the input line thru an NPN transistor. The absence of an "X" indicates a blown fuse. The AND gate is formed by two "Xs" on the same line which signifies ANDing as all "Xed" inputs on the single rail AND symbol are ANDed together. The OR function is formed by two "Xs" on different product lines.

This example has shown the implementation of common gate structures. The versatility of the PAL is demonstrated by some not so common gate structures shown below. Figure 9 shows a PAL implementation of those gates.

C = A * /B

F = D + /E

I = G*/H + /G*H

L = J*K + /J*/K

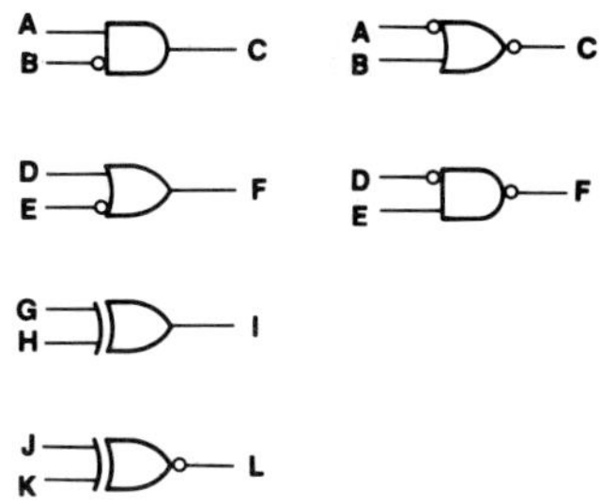

PAL10H8

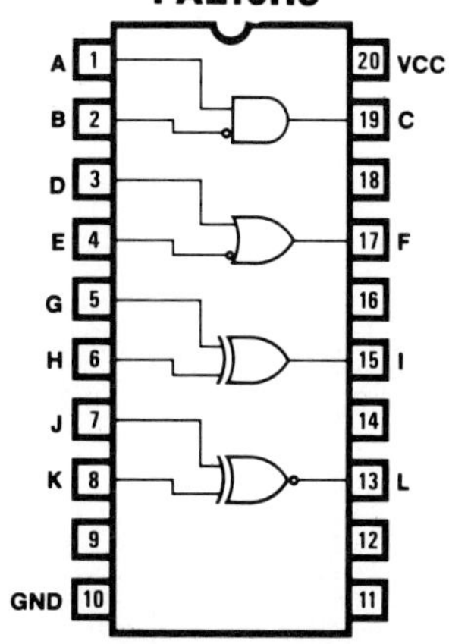

Logic Symbol

Figure 9. Example Gates Logic Symbol

Partitioning System Logic for PALs

The sum of products Boolean transfer function is the common denominator and basic primitive of all digital logic systems. From the sum of products, not only can all the gate functions be derived, but so also can latches, edge triggered registers, MUXs, encoders and decoders. The first nine PALs (PAL10H8 thru PAL16L2) implement a variety of input/output pin ratios and product terms per output. Input pin loading is less than 0.25 mA while output drive is 8 mA sink and 3.2 mA source. A typical gate configuration is shown in Figure 10.

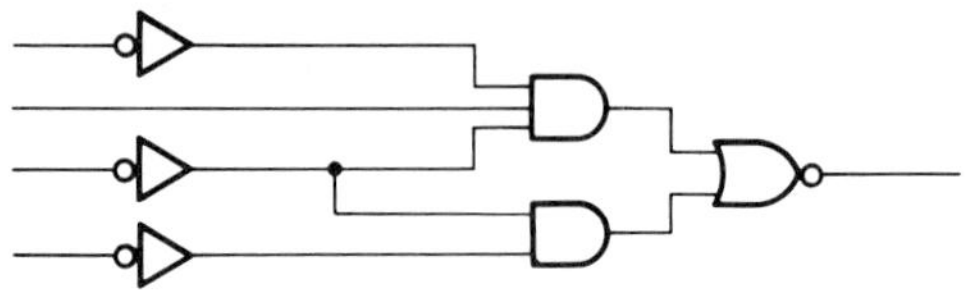

Figure 10. Typical Sum of Products

Three-state buses are commonly used in TTL systems to reduce interconnect densities by sharing signal lines. The PAL16L8 thru PAL16A4 output drivers are all three-state outputs which sink 24 mA, compatible with the low power Schottky three state standard. This 24 mA sink is sufficient to drive many standard buses including the Intel Multibus.

The PAL three-state outputs are of two types. First, the register outputs are controlled by a common enable pin for parallel bus enabling. Second, the combinatorial outputs are individually controlled by a product term. This feature allows an open collector configuration to be logically derived as required in bus-shared control signals such as memory transfer acknowledge. The latter type is shown in Figure 11.

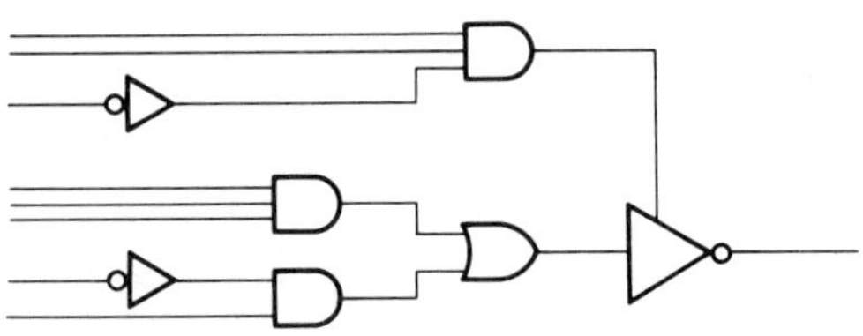

Figure 11. Three-State Driver with Individual Enable

Latch circuits can be implemented as shown in Figure 12. The PAL16L8 is commonly used for this function as six of the eight outputs are internally connected to an array input line. Edge triggered flip flops can be constructed from two latches where individual clocking is required.

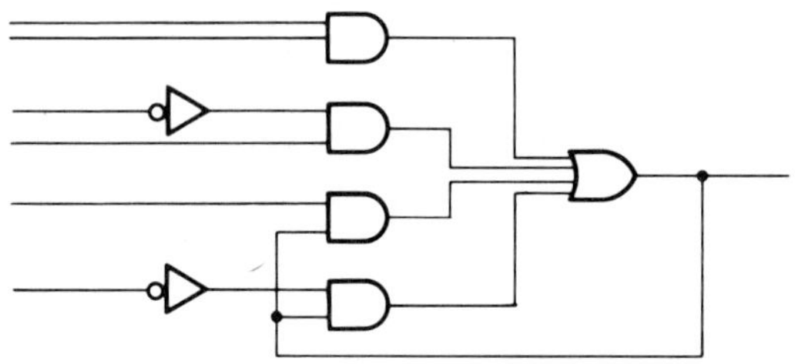

Figure 12. Latch Circuit

Control logic containing D-type or J-K flip-flops is common among memory, processor and controller interfaces. This logic can generally be classified as state-sequence logic or small-state machines. The PAL types PAL16R8, PAL16R6 and PAL16R4 contain output registers with feedback which can implement simple state-sequences. Figure 13 shows a typical control logic configuration.

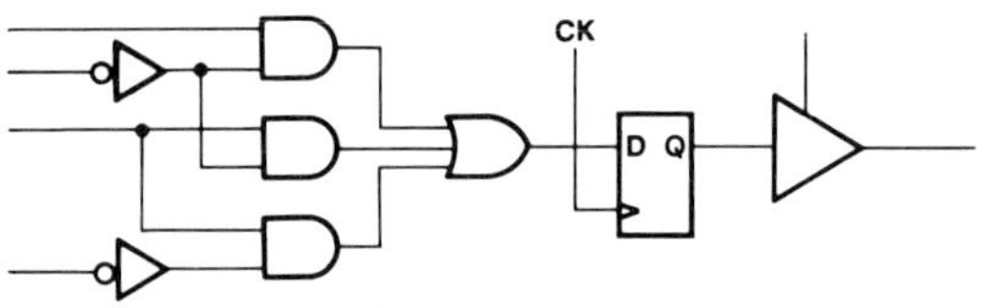

Figure 13. Registered Sum of Products

Design Example

A typical control logic problem is the memory to processor handshake on memory transfer used in many computer architectures. The processor makes a transfer request by activating a request line (REQ) and specifies a read or write operation on a Read/Write line (R/W).

During a read operation the processor waits for a Data Available signal at which time the data bus is sampled and the request line lowered, completing the cycle. During a write operation, the processor places data on the bus and waits for a write complete signal after the write cycle is finished. Upon write complete, the request line is lowered, completing the cycle. This handshaking operation is described in the timing diagram of Figure 14.

The memory-board logic to implement this function may be designed with gates and edge triggered flip flops as shown in Figure 15. This particular design would require about five SSI/MSI packages. The same design is implemented in Figure 16 by a single PAL16R8.

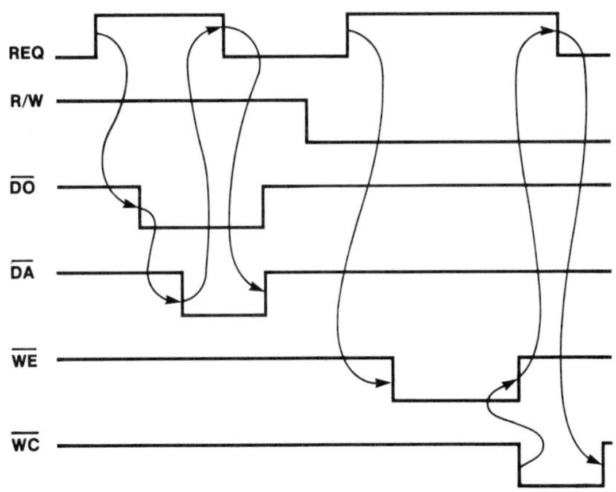

Figure 14. Memory Handshake Timing

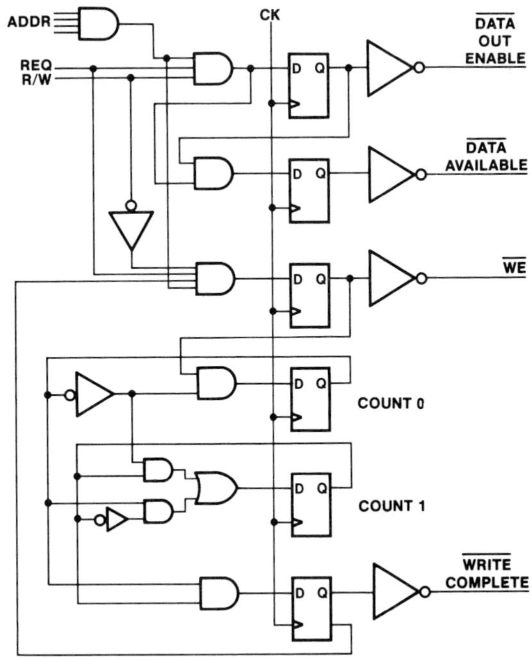

Figure 15. Memory Handshake Logic

Logic Diagram PAL16R8

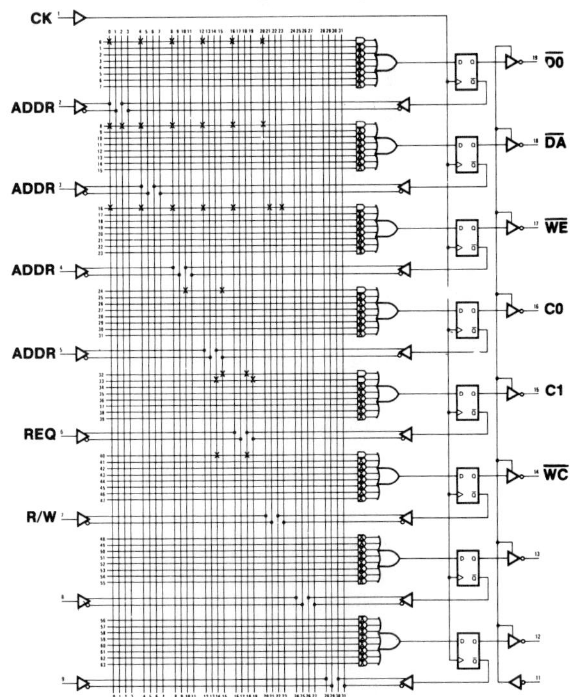

Figure 16. PAL Memory Handshake Logic

Bibliography

1. Semiconductor Industry Association, 1979, first four months report.
2. John Birkner, High Speed/Low Cost Fuse Link Arrays Compete with TTL 74S/LS, WESCON '78.

Gate Arrays Logjam Test Engineering

John Birkner/Wescon 80

Gate arrays give logic designers the ability to create numerous semi-custom ICs in a relatively short amount of time. The number of unique patterns may vary from 10 to 200 for a typical new systems design. When the new system is transferred to production, the Test Engineering department is faced with one to two work weeks per pattern. Systems manufacturers, using gate arrays for the first time, are cautioned to plan for the increased demands on Test Engineering, or they will find a logjam in testing. This paper examines the problems and solutions in testing gate arrays and semicustom logic.

Definitions

Many terms have recently appeared to describe the host of integrated circuits which are configured late in the manufacturing process. These ICs are most generally described as uncommitted logic. More specifically, there are classifications such as semicustom logic, gate arrays, programmable logic arrays, field programmable logic arrays, programmable array logic and hard array logic.

All of these devices provide the systems designer with common advantages; higher board density, lower power, higher speed, etc. For the purposes of this discussion, they will all be classified as gate arrays. The specific example chosen for this discussion will be hard array logic, HAL, and its programmable counterpart, PAL.

Replacing PCBs With Silicon

The problem of testing digital logic is steadily moving from the printed circuit board (PCB) to the LSI chip. In the case of gate arrays, the etched lines which connected the random assortment of SSI/MSI gates and flip flops is being lifted from the PCB and placed on silicon. Test engineers, who complain that the new gate arrays create a testing problem, forget that they once tested that same logic on the PCB.

Gate arrays don't create new testing problems; they just move the old testing problem from the PCB onto the silicon chip. This may be viewed as an opportunity to structure the testing problem in the more regular environment of a fixed package, structured array. We must be more clever, however, in generating our test programs without the aid of internal test points which were available on the PCB.

The Logjam

Testing LSI logic is certainly not a new problem. Standard LSI chips, like the microprocessor and the variety of special purpose controllers, are regularly tested. The new problem lies in large numbers of gate array patterns which can be quickly designed and fabricated.

For a single systems design, a few design engineers can create as many as 200 new and unique gate array patterns. At one week per pattern, this translates to four work years of test engineering time.

Test Vectors

Test programs for LSI devices consist of electrical, switching and functional tests. The electrical and switching characteristics are tested by the semiconductor manufacturer, and may be optionally tested by the user. The function test is supplied to the manufacturer by the user. It consists of a list of test vectors, which specify for each pin, instructions for driving high or low, or testing high or low, or not driving and not testing.

The time consuming job for the user is the generation of test vectors. At this time, work is under way toward automating the generation of test vectors, thus far with some success. Even with automated programs, manual intervention and human interaction make the task time consuming. In addition, the automated programs are not self starting. They need manually generated seed vectors.

Responsibility of the Designer

When a new system is transferred to production, the systems designer hands over the responsibility for the system to the test engineering department who now determines how and what tests should be performed to ensure proper operation of the system. At this pont the systems designer transmits the necessary information for understanding the system operation. Unfortunately, much information is lost at this point. All too often continuity is broken and while the systems designer is off designing the next great project, the test engineer is left to struggle with understanding how the system works. This struggle is exaggerated when system complexity is increased by the use of gate arrays.

It is the design engineer who best knows the operation of his gate array design, and it is the design engineer who can quickly specify a few seed vectors to give the test engineer a starting point or to give the automatic vector generator a starting point. The problem at hand is to entice designers into this task.

Tools for the Designer

The first step toward luring the designer into providing test vector information is to give him a standard format for specifying the vectors. The format should be easy to understand and convenient to write down either on paper or, preferably, into a computer terminal. Fortunately, there is a format that already exists, which with slight modification, will suit our purpose. The format is the well known "Function Table" format found in the Texas Instruments TTL *Databook* and accepted by JEDEC. Let us now redefine that format as follows:

Function Table

The function table begins with the keyword, "FUNCTION TABLE." It is followed by a pin list which symbolically defines each pin. The pin list is followed by a dashed line, e.g.-------(length optional), which in turn is followed by a list of vectors, one vector per line. A vector is a sequence of states in order of the pin list followed by an optional comment. The vector list is followed by another dashed line.

Definition of States

```
H    HIGH LEVEL

L    LOW LEVEL

C    TRANSITION FROM LOW TO HIGH

X    IRRELEVANT

Z    OFF (HIGH IMPEDANCE)
```

With this definition, let us now write a function Table for a simple two input AND Gate having inputs A and B with output C.

```
FUNCTION TABLE

A  B  C
--------------
L  L  L
H  L  L
L  H  L
H  H  H
--------------
```

The second step in persuading the designer into providing test vectors is to combine the Function Table with the gate array design specification so as to provide one document with design and functional information.

The real objective here is to give the designer a format to mimic the data sheet format which he is accustomed to seeing for standard TTL components.

This is the approach taken to specify designs for Hard Array Logic, HAL, the mask version of Programmable Array Logic, PAL. The design specification is a computer file which contains part number, name of device, symbolic pin list, design equations and a Function Table.

Outsmarting the Designer

Providing just the format for specifying test vector information is not likely to seduce the busy systems designer into such a boring task. We have to be a bit more clever to snare him. Fortunately, we can charm him with a decoy, gate array simulation.

Gate Array Simulation

The systems designer is impressed with computer-aided tools that help him in his design task. What if he had a computer program which would simulate his gate array design and tell him if it works as he wants it to? Would he use it? This author is betting that he will.

A simulator has been added to the PAL Assembler, PALASM, which reads the Function Table and simulates the device as specified in the state equations which specify the transfer function. Inconsistencies between the Function Table and the transfer function are reported as errors. The simulator checks the operation of the gate array against the equations, thus verifying the designer's intention for the device. What the designer perhaps will never realize is that he has also provided seed vectors for test engineering.

Future Considerations

The test vector generation problem is generally considered to be one of starting with the transfer function and synthesizing the state table. The engineering problem is just the reverse. That is, the designer starts off with the state table and he synthesizes the transfer function. A challenge for gate array manufacturers is to provide their customers with computer-aided tools to automatically generate gate arrays from state tables.

High Level Language for Programmable Array Logic

John Birkner/Wescon 81

Introduction

Standards for silicon definition languages are under consideration by semiconductor manufacturers in order to provide a means of communication between vendor and customer for specifying semicustom ICs. The objective of an industry standard language is to provide a hardware-independent, manufacturer-independent, user-independent, unambiguous definition of an IC. So far, the debates in subcommittees, ranging from what symbol to use for an AND gate to whether there should be a standard at all, would indicate that many standards will evolve.

Digital machines are most efficiently defined by explicit Boolean state equations. These equations are unambiguous, they are easily simulated, and they can be readily expanded to systems of machines. This paper discusses such an equation-implemented language as applied to Programmable Array Logic.

Logic Schematics Fall Short

The predominant hardware description language of today is the logic schematic. The predominant hardware verification technique of today is the hardware prototype. These tools are inadequate for the development of silicon hardware.

The logic schematic may be a fine tool for human understanding of a digital system, but is is quite awkward to input it into a computer for generation of photolithographic plates used in making semicustom or custom ICs. Likewise, the hardware prototype is an awkward means of design verification of an IC. Differences in propagation delay, circuit implementation, and logic implementation degrade the effectiveness of the hardware emulation. Also, the manual interaction increases the probability of error, especially in high complexity logic systems. The cost of an error in making an IC is tens and thousands of dollars and months of delay. The cost of multiple errors is years of delay, which often kills the project.

TTL 7400-series logic schematics are commonly submitted to semiconductor vendors for implementation in semicustom or custom ICs. The semiconductor manufacturer then makes a choice as to whether to implement the function exactly as shown on the schematic, or to optimize the design to the particular circuit technique.

If the vendor implements the TTL function exactly as shown, the user will pay the price of extra die size. If the vendor optimizes the design, he must understand it, at a high cost of engineering development time. In either case, the vendor is subject to the risk that the IC version will not operate identically to the TTL version. Figure 1 demonstrates the risk of copying TTL logic directly. The 74LS161 four-bit counter is asynchronously set to zero when the count reaches 12. Will this circuit hazard operate the same when it is forged into one piece of silicon? Or, will it oscillate?

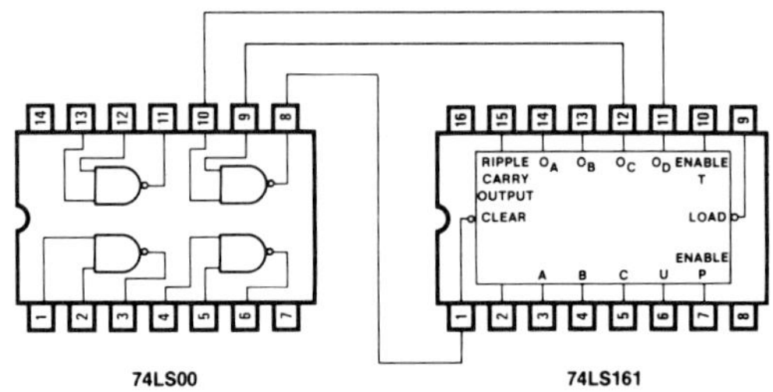

Figure 1. Common Circuit Hazard

Testability is another common trap for the semiconductor vendor. The user's TTL prototype may work fine in his system and also be virtually untestable. A frequent example is the clock phase generator which has no initialize control pin. Without a known initial state, the tester must sequence the device until a recognizable pattern is observed. Most IC testers do not have this capability.

Discipline for Semicustom Users

Successful use of semicustom logic is best achieved when the user understands the vendors manufacturing cycle and when the user participates in that cycle. The production of a semicustom IC is basically the same as that required for a standard IC, with the exception that the user takes part in some of the steps. The major steps are outlined below.

1. Define
2. Simulate
3. Build
4. Test

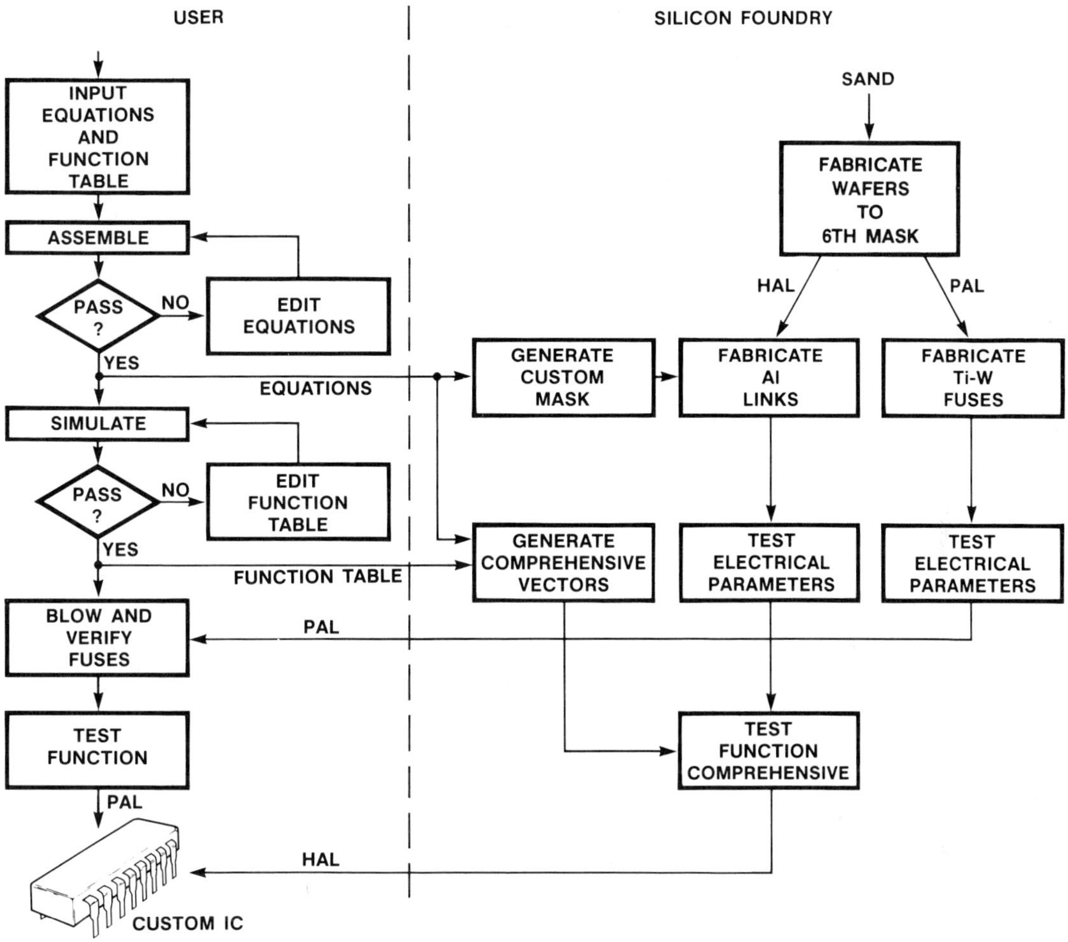

Figure 2. PAL/HAL Development Cycle

These four steps are demonstrated in the diagram above for the development of PAL, Programmable Array Logic, and HAL, Hard Array Logic. The user begins by defining his logic functions using Boolean logic equations. These equations are automatically assembled into hardware routing instructions by the PAL assembler, PALASM. Syntax errors are reported. The user edits and reassembles, repeating the process until no syntax errors are reported.

The user then inputs a Function Table to verify his design. PALASM simulates the PAL/HAL, using the equations, and executes the Function Table on the simulated device. Simulation errors are reported. The user corrects the Function Table and/or equations until no simulation errors occur. This completes the design verification process.

The automatic routing instructions from PALASM may now be used to generate a custom mask for fabrication of a HAL. Aluminum links implement the logic equations, providing a semicustom device. Comprehensive Test vectors are generated using the Function Table as seed vectors. One hundred percent coverage for stuck-high/low test conditions is usually achieved with fewer than 200 vectors.

HALs are cost-effective in volumes of 1000 or above. For lower volumes, the programmable version, PAL, may be programmed by the user on low-cost programmers. The HAL is unique in that it is a semicustom device that has a programmable prototype, the PAL.

Equations Simplify

"Our life is frittered away by detail . . . Simplify, simplify."

Thoreau

Hardware Description Languages most often use network topology to specify the interconnection of gates and flipflops. Propagation delays are individually specified; wire lists are generated; long lists of generally unreadable network interconnection are printed out.

Explicit Boolean equations are a much simpler method of writing logic functions. They are easily interpreted and can be readily commented. An example of an AND gate feeding an OR gate with a comment is shown below.

F = A*B + C ; This is a comment

The AND gate is symbolized by "*" and the OR gate is symbolized by "+".

Function Table Simulates

Equations are easily simulated and can be exercised by HIGHs and LOWs specified in a Function Table. A simulation of the above equations is implemented in the Function Table below.

```
FUNCTION TABLE

A B C  F
-------------------------
L L L  L TEST OUTPUT LOW
H H L  H TEST OUTPUT HIGH
L L H  H TEST OUTPUT HIGH
-------------------------
```

The simulation is now used to generate test vectors and may also be used as seed vectors for automatic generation of comprehensive test vectors until a 100% coverage of stuck-high/low conditions is achieved.

Design Verification

The design verification performed by a user in the PAL/HAL development cycle of Figure 2 is now demonstrated in a real example. What follows is a computer printout from the terminal of a PAL Development System during a development session. Two errors are intentionally made during the session. First, a syntax error, then a simulation error is made to demonstrate the corrective feedback in the development cycle.

EXAMPLE SESSION #1

```
+INPUT
PAL10L8                    PAL DESIGN SPECIFICATION
PN12345                    J. BIRKNER          6/9/81
EXAMPLE
MMI SUNNYVALE, CA
A B C X X X X X X GND X X X X X X X X /F VCC
F = A*B + E ;THIS IS A COMMENT
FUNCTION TABLE
A B C  F
--------------------------
L L L  L  TEST OUTPUT LOW
H H L  L  TEST OUTPUT HIGH
L L H  H  TEST OUTPUT HIGH
--------------------------

+ASSEMBLE
ASSEMBLY ERROR = E

FAIL
+EDIT
   PAL10L8                    PAL DESIGN SPECIFICATION
#  PN12345                    J. BIRKNER          6/9/81
#  EXAMPLE
#  MMI SUNNYVALE, CA
#  A B C X X X X X X GND X X X X X X X X /F VCC
#  F = A*B + E ;THIS IS A COMMENT
#CEF = A*B + C
   F = A*B + C ;THIS IS A COMMENT
#
#Q

+SIMULATE
01 000XXXXXXXXXXXXXXXH1
VECTOR ERROR 02 F

FAIL
+EDIT
   PAL10L8                    PAL DESIGN SPECIFICATION
#  PN12345                    J. BIRKNER          6/9/81
#  EXAMPLE
#  MMI SUNNYVALE, CA
#  A B C X X X X X X GND X X X X X X X X /F VCC
#  F = A*B + C ;THIS IS A COMMENT
#  FUNCTION TABLE
#  A B C  F
#  --------------------------
#  L L L  L  TEST OUTPUT LOW
#  H H L  L  TEST OUTPUT HIGH
#CLH H L  H
   H H L  H  TEST OUTPUT HIGH
#
#Q

+SIMULATE
01 000XXXXXXXXXXXXXXXH1
02 110XXXXXXXXXXXXXXXL1
03 001XXXXXXXXXXXXXXXL1


PASS
+
```

A more complex example is an 8-bit synchronous counter as shown in Figure 3. Example Session #2 reads, assembles and simulates the PAL Design Specification.

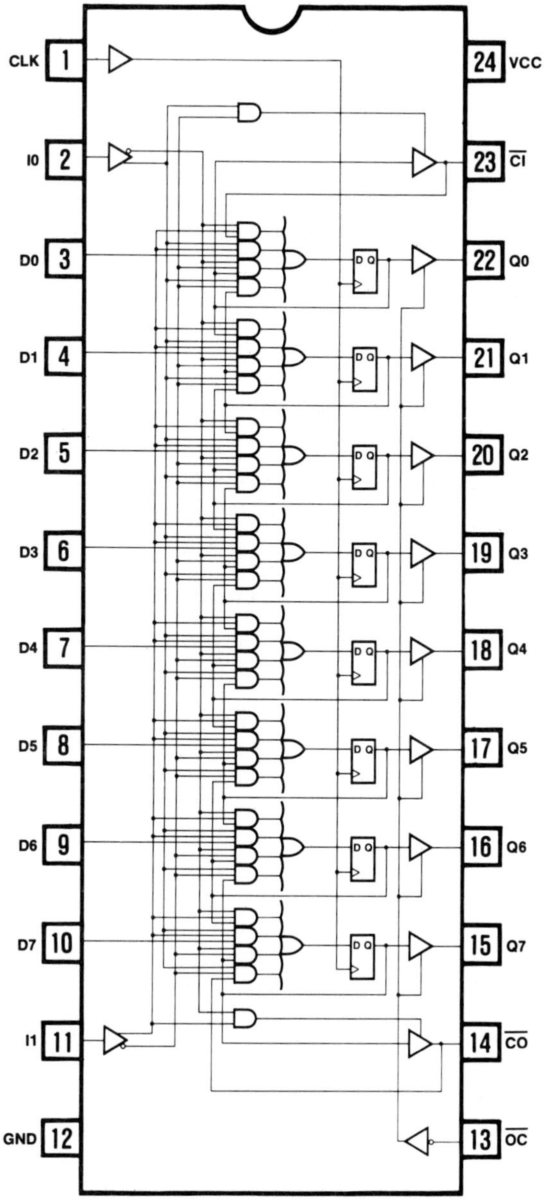

Figure 3. 8-Bit Synchronous Counter

EXAMPLE SESSION #2

```
+READ
PAL20X8                    PAL DESIGN SPECIFICATION
CTR8A              BIRKNER/KAZMI/BLASCO     2/10/81
8-BIT SYNCHRONOUS COUNTER
MMI  SUNNYVALE, CALIFORNIA
CLK I0 D0 D1 D2 D3 D4 D5 D6 D7 I1 GND
/EN /CO Q7 Q6 Q5 Q4 Q3 Q2 Q1 Q0 /CI VCC

/Q0  :=  /I1*/I0                     ;CLEAR LSB
      +       I0 * /Q0               ;COUNT/HOLD
    :+:  I1*/I0 * /D0                ;LOAD D0 (LSB)
      +  I1* I0 * CI                 ;COUNT

/Q1  :=  /I1*/I0
      +       I0 * /Q1
    :+:  I1*/I0 * /D1
      +  I1* I0 * CI*Q0

/Q2  :=  /I1*/I0
      +       I0 * /Q2
    :+:  I1*/I0 * /D2
      +  I1* I0 * CI*Q0*Q1

/Q3  :=  /I1*/I0
      +       I0 * /Q3
    :+:  I1*/I0 * /D3
      +  I1* I0 * CI*Q0*Q1*Q2

/Q4  :=  /I1*/I0
      +       I0 * /Q4
    :+:  I1*/I0 * /D4
      +  I1* I0 * CI*Q0*Q1*Q2*Q3

/Q5  :=  /I1*/I0
      +       I0 * /Q5
    :+:  I1*/I0 * /D5
      +  I1* I0 * CI*Q0*Q1*Q2*Q3*Q4

/Q6  :=  /I1*/I0
      +       I0 * /Q6
    :+:  I1*/I0 * /D6
      +  I1* I0 * CI*Q0*Q1*Q2*Q3*Q4*Q5

/Q7  :=  /I1*/I0
      +       I0 * /Q7
    :+:  I1*/I0 * /D7
      +  I1* I0 * CI*Q0*Q1*Q2*Q3*Q4*Q5*Q6

IF (VCC)  CO = CI*Q0*Q1*Q2*Q3*Q4*Q5*Q6*Q7
```

```
FUNCTION TABLE

I1 I0 D7 D6 D5 D4 D3 D2 D1 D0 /CI CLK /EN
Q7 Q6 Q5 Q4 Q3 Q2 Q1 Q0 /CO

; SEL     INPUTS     CONTROL     OUTPUTS
;I1 I0  7------0 /CI CLK /EN 7------0 /CO
----------------------------------------------
  L L   HHHHHHHH  L    C    L  LLLLLLLL  H
  H L   LLLLLLLH  X    C    L  LLLLLLLH  H
  H H   XXXXXXXX  L    C    L  LLLLLLHL  H
  H L   LLLLLLHH  X    C    L  LLLLLLHH  H
  H H   XXXXXXXX  L    C    L  LLLLLHLL  H
  H L   LLLLLHHH  X    C    L  LLLLLHHH  H
  H H   XXXXXXXX  L    C    L  LLLLHLLL  H
  H L   LLLLHHHH  X    C    L  LLLLHHHH  H
  H H   XXXXXXXX  L    C    L  LLLHLLLL  H
  H L   LLLHHHHH  X    C    L  LLLHHHHH  H
  H H   XXXXXXXX  L    C    L  LLHLLLLL  H
  H L   LLHHHHHH  X    C    L  LLHHHHHH  H
  H H   XXXXXXXX  L    C    L  LHLLLLLL  H
  H L   LHHHHHHH  X    C    L  LHHHHHHH  H
  H H   XXXXXXXX  L    C    L  HLLLLLLL  H
  H L   HHHHHHHH  L    C    L  HHHHHHHH  L
  H H   XXXXXXXX  L    C    L  LLLLLLLL  H
  H L   HHHHHHHH  L    C    L  HHHHHHHH  L
  H L   HHHHHHHL  X    C    L  HHHHHHHL  H
  H L   HHHHHHLH  X    C    L  HHHHHHLH  H
  H L   HHHHHLHH  X    C    L  HHHHHLHH  H
  H L   HHHHLHHH  X    C    L  HHHHLHHH  H
  H L   HHHLHHHH  X    C    L  HHHLHHHH  H
  H L   HHLHHHHH  X    C    L  HHLHHHHH  H
  H L   HLHHHHHH  X    C    L  HLHHHHHH  H
  H L   LHHHHHHH  X    C    L  LHHHHHHH  H
  H L   HHHHHHHH  L    C    L  HHHHHHHH  L
  L L   XXXXXXXX  X    C    L  LLLLLLLL  H
  H H   XXXXXXXX  L    C    L  LLLLLLLH  H
  H H   XXXXXXXX  L    C    L  LLLLLLHL  H
  H H   XXXXXXXX  L    C    L  LLLLLLHH  H
  H H   XXXXXXXX  L    C    L  LLLLLHLL  H
  H L   HHHHHHHL  X    C    L  HHHHHHHL  H
  H H   XXXXXXXX  L    C    L  HHHHHHHH  L
  H H   XXXXXXXX  H    C    L  HHHHHHHH  H
  L H   LLLLLLLL  L    C    L  HHHHHHHH  L
  H H   HHHHHHHH  L    C    L  LLLLLLLL  H
----------------------------------------------
```

```
+ASSEMBLE


PASS
+SIMULATE
01 C0111111110X0HLLLLLLLL01
02 C0100000001X0HLLLLLLLHX1
03 C1XXXXXXXX1X0HLLLLLLHL01
04 C0110000001X0HLLLLLLHHX1
05 C1XXXXXXXX1X0HLLLLLHLL01
06 C0111000001X0HLLLLLHHHX1
07 C1XXXXXXXX1X0HLLLLHLLL01
08 C0111100001X0HLLLLHHHHX1
09 C1XXXXXXXX1X0HLLLHLLLL01
10 C0111110001X0HLLLHHHHHX1
11 C1XXXXXXXX1X0HLLHLLLLL01
12 C0111111001X0HLLHHHHHHX1
13 C1XXXXXXXX1X0HLHLLLLLL01
14 C0111111101X0HLHHHHHHHX1
15 C1XXXXXXXX1X0HHLLLLLLL01
16 C0111111111X0LHHHHHHHH01
17 C1XXXXXXXX1X0HLLLLLLLL01
18 C0111111111X0LHHHHHHHH01
19 C0011111111X0HHHHHHHHLX1
20 C0101111111X0HHHHHHHLHX1
21 C0110111111X0HHHHHHLHHX1
22 C0111011111X0HHHHHLHHHX1
23 C0111101111X0HHHHLHHHHX1
24 C0111110111X0HHHLHHHHHX1
25 C0111111011X0HHLHHHHHHX1
26 C0111111101X0HLHHHHHHHX1
27 C0111111111X0LHHHHHHHH01
28 C0XXXXXXXX0X0HLLLLLLLLX1
29 C1XXXXXXXX1X0HLLLLLLLH01
30 C1XXXXXXXX1X0HLLLLLLHL01
31 C1XXXXXXXX1X0HLLLLLLHH01
32 C1XXXXXXXX1X0HLLLLLHLL01
33 C0011111111X0HHHHHHHHLX1
34 C1XXXXXXXX1X0LHHHHHHHH01
35 C1XXXXXXXX1X0HHHHHHHHH11
36 C1000000000X0LHHHHHHHH01
37 C1111111111X0HLLLLLLLL01


PASS
+
```

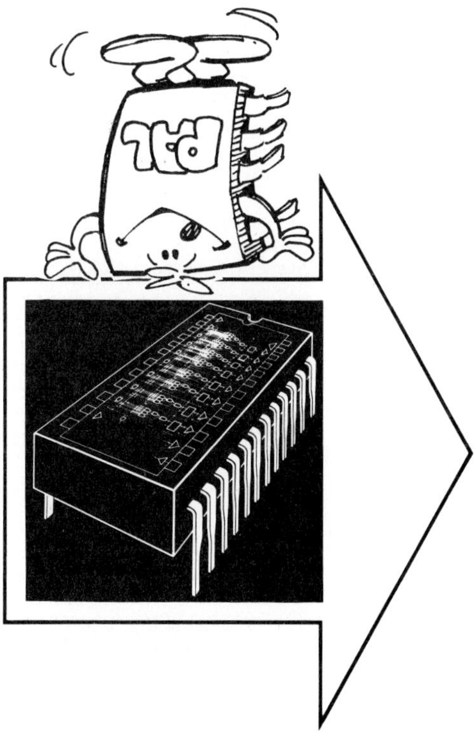

Programmable Array Logic Family

PAL® Series 20

U.S. Patent 4124899

Features/Benefits

- **Programmable replacement for conventional TTL logic.**
- **Reduces IC inventories substantially and simplifies their control.**
- **Reduces chip count by 4 to 1.**
- **Expedites and simplifies prototyping and board layout.**
- **Saves space with 20-pin SKINNY DIP® packages.**
- **High speed: 25ns typical propagation delay.**
- **Programmed on standard PROM programmers.**
- **Programmable three-state outputs.**
- **Special feature reduces possibility of copying by competitors.**

PART NUMBER	PKG	DESCRIPTION
PAL10H8	N,J,F	Octal 10 Input And-Or Gate Array
PAL12H6	N,J,F	Hex 12 Input And-Or Gate Array
PAL14H4	N,J,F	Quad 14 Input And-Or Gate Array
PAL16H2	N,J,F	Dual 16 Input And-Or Gate Array
PAL16C1	N,J,F	16 Input And-Or/And-Or-Invert Gate Array
PAL10L8	N,J,F	Octal 10 Input And-Or-Invert Gate Array
PAL12L6	N,J,F	Hex 12 Input And-Or-Invert Gate Array
PAL14L4	N,J,F	Quad 14 Input And-Or-Invert Gate Array
PAL16L2	N,J,F	Dual 16 Input And-Or-Invert Gate Array
PAL16L8	N,J,F	Octal 16 Input And-Or-Invert Gate Array
PAL16R8	N,J,F	Octal 16 Input Registered And-Or Gate Array
PAL16R6	N,J,F	Hex 16 Input Registered And-Or Gate Array
PAL16R4	N,J,F	Quad 16 Input Registered And-Or Gate Array
PAL16X4	N,J	Quad 16 Input Registered And-Or-Xor Gate Array
PAL16A4	N,J	Quad 16 Input Registered And-Carry-Or-Xor Gate

Description

The PAL family utilizes an advanced Schottky TTL process and the Bipolar PROM fusible link technology to provide user programmable logic for replacing conventional SSI/MSI gates and flip-flops at reduced chip count.

The family lets the systems engineer "design his own chip" by blowing fusible links to configure AND and OR gates to perform his desired logic function. Complex interconnections which previously required time-consuming layout are thus "lifted" from PC board etch and placed on silicon where they can be easily modified during prototype check-out or production.

The PAL transfer function is the familiar sum of products. Like the PROM, the PAL has a single array of fusible links. Unlike the PROM, the PAL is a programmable AND array driving a fixed OR array (the PROM is a fixed AND array driving a programmable OR array). In addition the PAL provides these options:

- Variable input/output pin ratio
- Programmable three-state outputs
- Registers with feedback
- Arithmetic capability

Unused inputs are tied directly to V_{CC} or GND. Product terms with all fuses blown assume the logical high state, and product terms connected to both true and complement of any single input assume the logical low state. Registers consist of D type flip-flops which are loaded on the low to high transition of the clock. PAL Logic Diagrams are shown with all fuses blown, enabling the designer use of the diagrams as coding sheets.

The entire PAL family is programmed on inexpensive conventional PROM programmers with appropriate personality and socket adapter cards. Once the PAL is programmed and verified, two additional fuses may be blown to defeat verification. This feature gives the user a proprietary circuit which is very difficult to copy.

Ordering Information

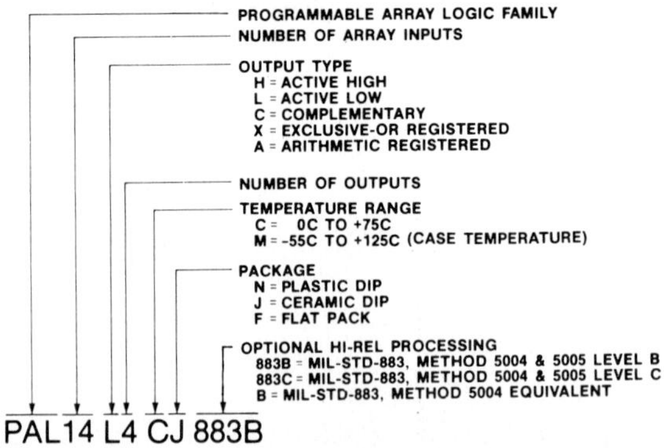

PAL® is a registered trademark of Monolithic Memories

PAL10H8

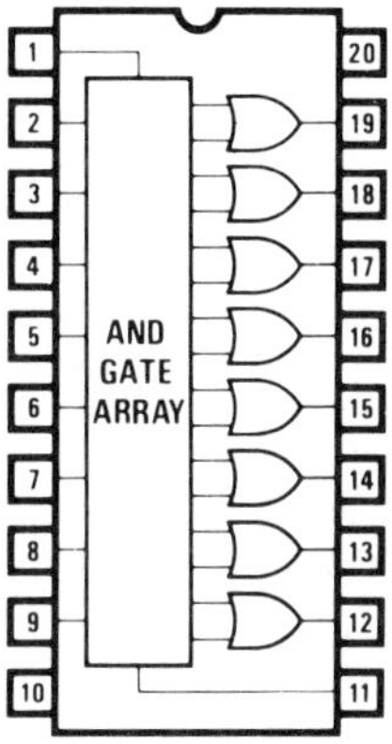

PAL12H6

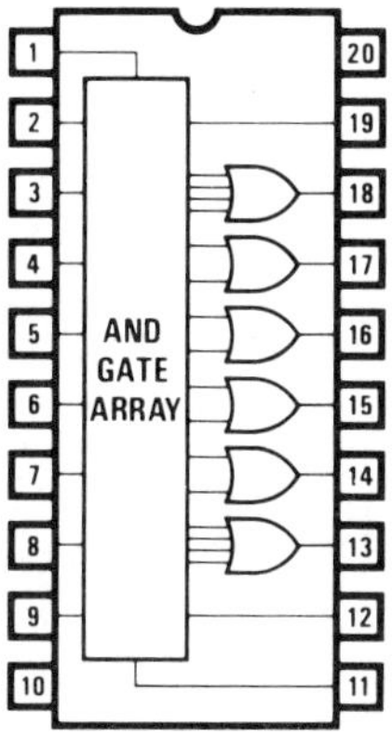

PAL14H4

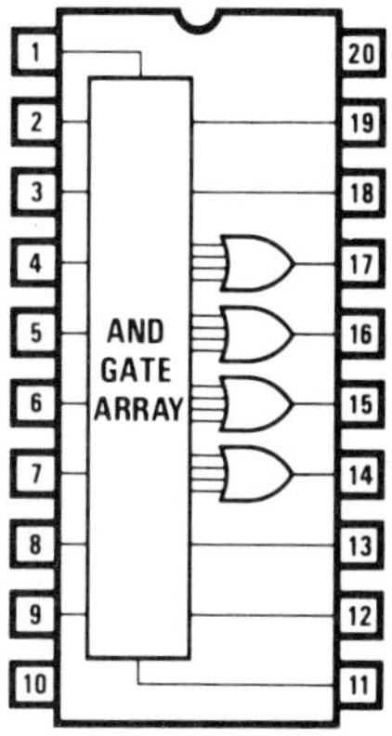

PAL16H2

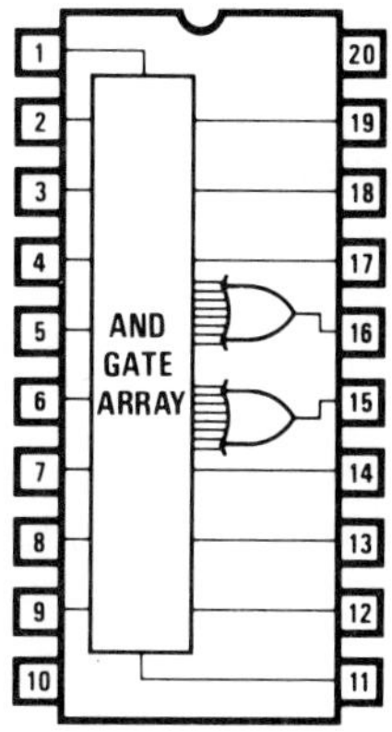

PAL16C1

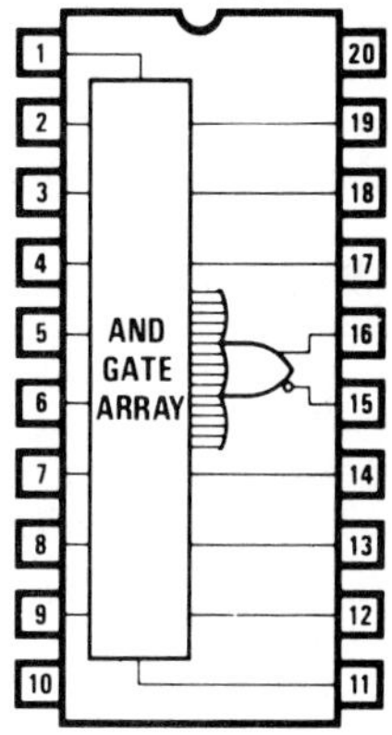

PAL10L8

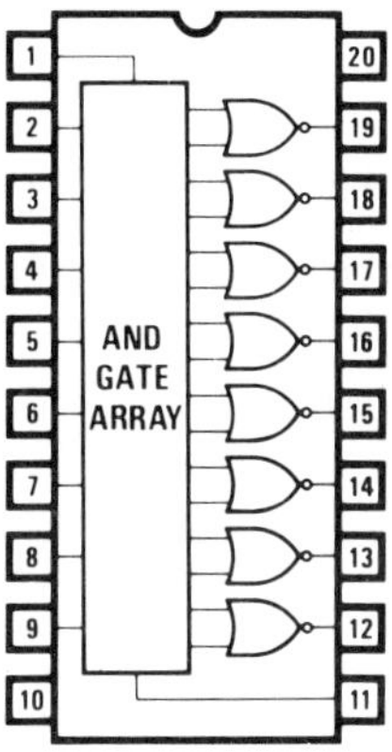

PAL12L6

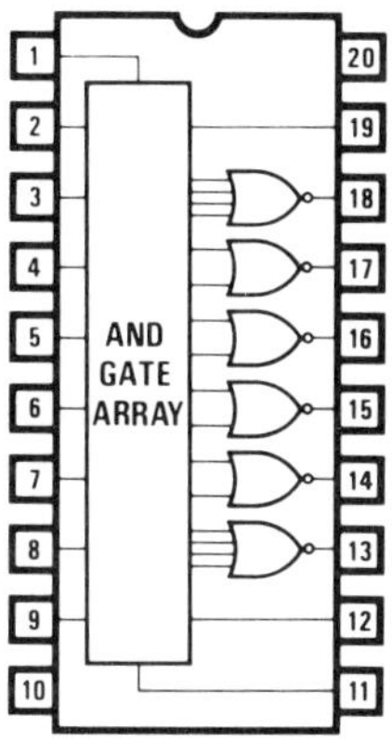

PAL14L4

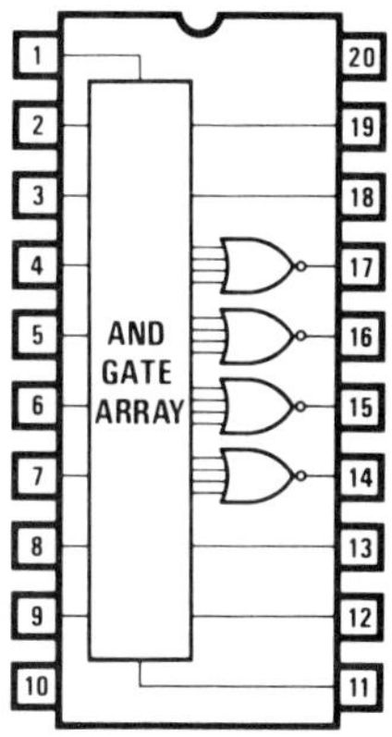

PAL16L2

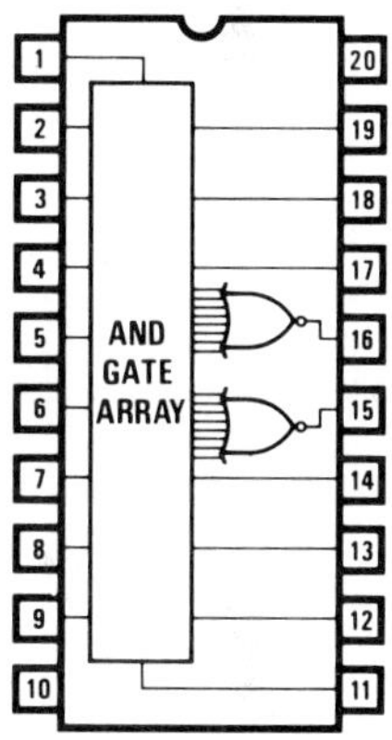

PAL16L8

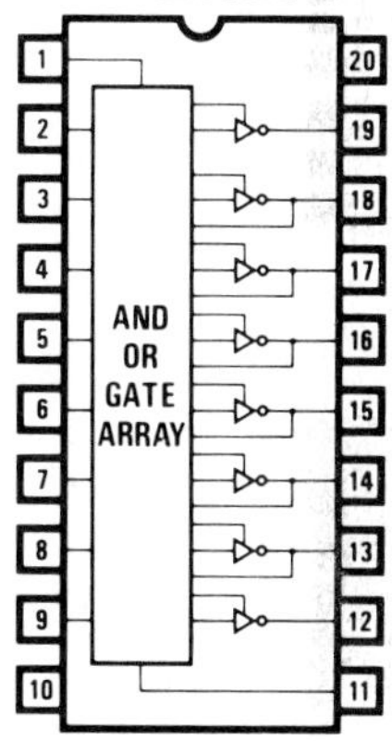

PAL16R8

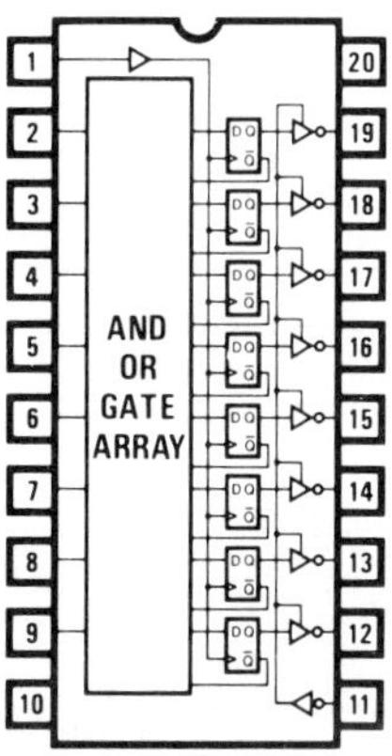

PAL16R6

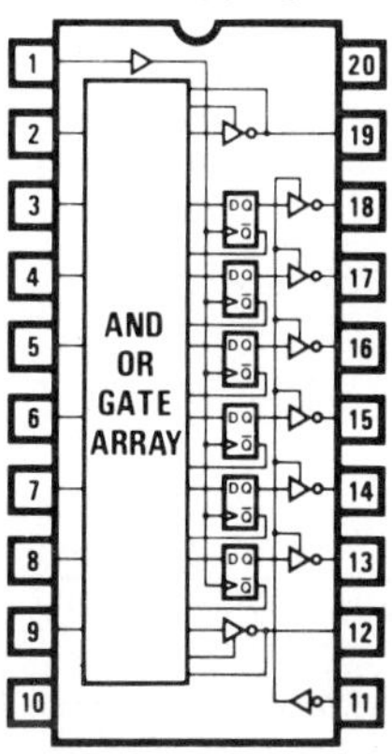

PAL16R4

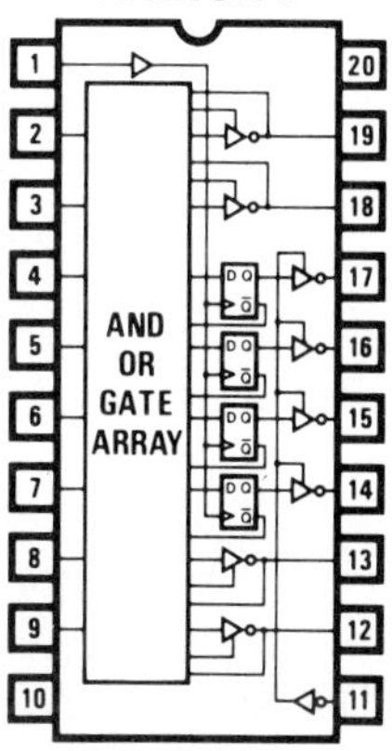

PAL16X4

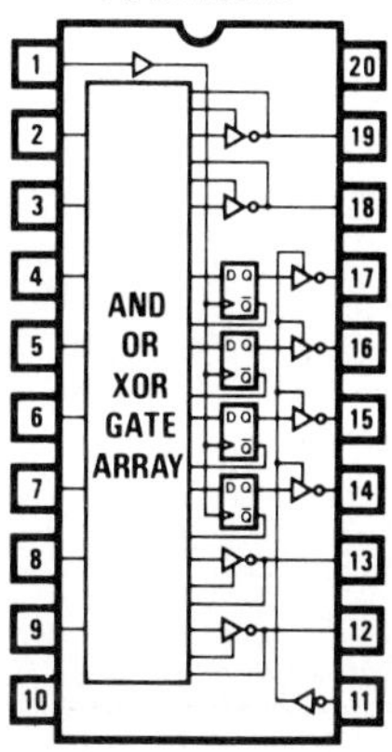

PAL16A4

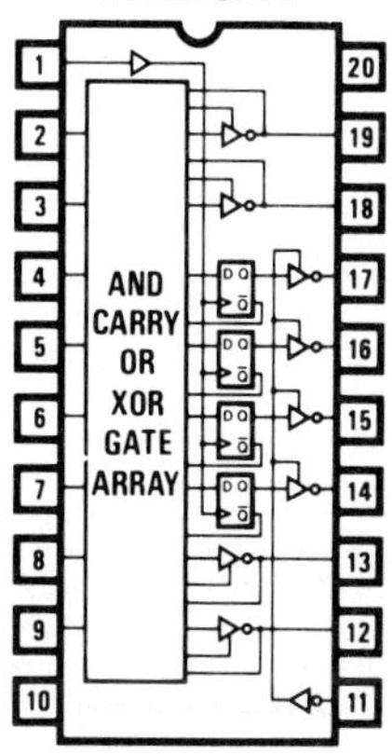

Absolute Maximum Ratings

	Operating
Supply Voltage, V_{CC}	7
Input Voltage	5.5V
Off-state output Voltage	5.5V
Storage temperature	−65° to +150°C

Operating Conditions

SYMBOL	PARAMETER		MILITARY MIN	MILITARY TYP	MILITARY MAX	COMMERCIAL MIN	COMMERCIAL TYP	COMMERCIAL MAX	UNIT
V_{CC}	Supply voltage		4.5	5	5.5	4.75	5	5.25	V
t_w	Width of clock	Low	25	10		25	10		ns
		High	25	10		25	10		
t_{su}	Set up time from input or feedback	16R8 16R6 16R4	45	25		35	25		ns
		16X4 16A4	55	30		45	30		
t_h	Hold time		0	−15		0	−15		ns
T_A	Operating free-air temperature		−55			0	5	75	°C
T_C	Operating case temperature				125				°C

Electrical Characteristics Over Operating Conditions

SYMBOL	PARAMETER	TEST CONDITIONS			MIN	TYP	MAX	UNIT
V_{IL}*	Low-level input voltage						0.8	V
V_{IH}*	High-level input voltage				2			V
V_{IC}	Input clamp voltage	V_{CC} = MIN		I_I = −18mA		−0.8	−1.5	V
I_{IL}	Low-level input current †	V_{CC} = MAX		V_I = 0.4V		−0.02	−0.25	mA
I_{IH}	High-level input current †	V_{CC} = MAX		V_I = 2.4V			25	μA
I_I	Maximum input current	V_{CC} = MAX		V_I = 5.5V			1	mA
V_{OL}	Low-level output voltage	V_{CC} = MIN, V_{IL} = 0.8V, V_{IH} = 2V	10H8, 12H6, 14H4, 16H2, 16C1, 10L8, 12L6, 14L4, 16L2	MIL COM I_{OL} = 8mA		0.3	0.5	V
			16L8 16R8 16R6 16R4 16X4 16A4	MIL I_{OL} = 12mA				
				COM I_{OL} = 24mA				
V_{OH}	High-level output voltage	V_{CC} = MIN, V_{IL} = 0.8V, V_{IH} = 2V	MIL	I_{OH} = −2mA	2.4	2.8		V
			COM	I_{OH} = −3.2mA				
I_{OZL}	Off-state output current †	V_{CC} = MAX, V_{IL} = 0.8V, V_{IH} = 2V	16L8 16R8 16R6 16R4 16X4 16A4	V_O = 0.4V			−100	μA
I_{OZH}				V_O = 2.4V			100	μA
I_{OS}	Output short-circuit current **	V_{CC} = 5V		V_O = 0V	−30	−70	−130	mA
I_{CC}	Supply current	V_{CC} = MAX	10H8, 12H6, 14H4, 16H2, 16C1, 10L8, 12L6, 14L4, 16L2			55	90	mA
			16R4, 16R6, 16R8, 16L8			120	180	
			16X4			160	225	
			16A4			170	240	

† I/O pin leakage is the worst case of I_{OZX} or I_{IX} e.g., I_{IL} and I_{OZH}.

†† All typical values are at V_{CC} = 5V, T_A = 25°C.

* These are absolute voltages with respect to pin 10 on the device and includes all overshoots due to system and/or tester noise. Do not attempt to test these values without suitable equipment.

** Only one output shorted at a time.

Switching Characteristics

Over Operating Conditions

SYMBOL	PARAMETER		TEST CONDITIONS	MILITARY MIN	MILITARY TYP	MILITARY MAX	COMMERCIAL MIN	COMMERCIAL TYP	COMMERCIAL MAX	UNIT
t_{PD}	Input to output	10H8 12H6 14H4 16H2 10L8 12L6 14L4 16L2	$R_1 = 560\Omega$ $R_2 = 1.1k\Omega$		25	45		25	35	ns
		16C1			25	45		25	40	
t_{PD}	Input or feed-back to output	16R6 16R4 16L8	$R_1 = 200\Omega$ $R_2 = 390\Omega$		25	45		25	35	ns
		16X4 16A4			30	45		30	40	
t_{CLK}	Clock to output or feedback				15	25		15	25	ns
t_{PZY}	Pin 11 to output enable				15	25		15	25	ns
t_{PXZ}	Pin 11 to output disable				15	25		15	25	ns
t_{PZX}	Input to output enable	16R6 16R4 16L8			25	45		25	35	ns
		16X4 16A4			30	45		30	40	
t_{PXZ}	Input to output disable	16R6 16R4 16L8			25	45		25	35	ns
		16X4 16A4			30	45		30	40	
f_{MAX}	Maximum frequency	16R8 16R6 16R4		14	25		16	25		MHz
		16X4 16A4		12	22		14	22		

Test Load

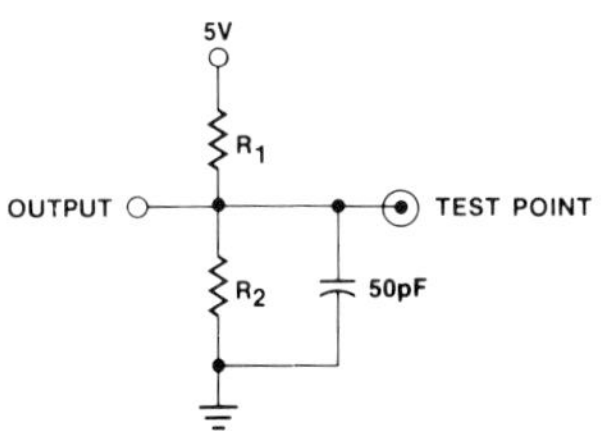

Schematic of Inputs and Outputs

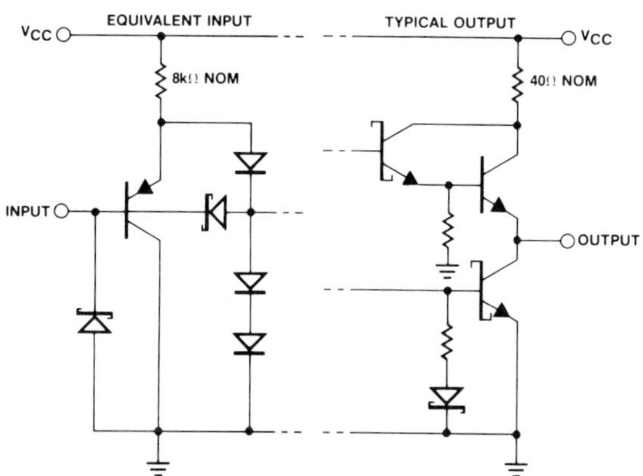

Available Programmers

MANUFACTURER	PERSONALITY CARD SET	SOCKET ADAPTER CONFIGURATION
Data I/O Corporation	909-1427	715 1428-1 715 1428-2 715 1428-3
Pro-Log Corporation	PM9068	
Stag Systems	PM202	AM10H8 AM10L8 AM12H6 AM12L6 AM14H4 AM14L4 AM16H2 AM16L2 AM16C1
Structured Design	SD20/24	

Programming

PAL fuses are programmed using a low-voltage linear-select procedure which is common to all 15 PAL types. The array is divided into two groups, products 0 thru 31 and products 32 thru 63, for which pin identifications are shown in Pin Configurations below. To program a particular fuse, both an input line and a product line are selected according to the following procedure:

Step 1 Raise Output Disable, OD, to V_{IHH}

Step 2 Select an input line by specifying $I_0, I_1, I_2, I_3, I_4, I_5, I_6, I_7$ and L/R as shown in Table 1.

Step 3 Select a product line by specifying A_0, A_1 and A_2 one-of-eight select as shown in Table 2.

Step 4 Raise V_{CC} (pin 20) to V_{IHH}

Step 5 Program the fuse by pulsing the output pins, O, of the selected product group to V_{IHH} as shown in Programming Waveform.

Step 6 Lower V_{CC} (pin 20) to 6.0 V

Step 7 Pulse the CLOCK pin and verify the output pin, O, to be Low for active Low PAL types or High for active High PAL types.

Step 8 Lower V_{CC} (pin 20) to 4.5 V and repeat step 7.

Step 9 Should the output not verify, repeat steps 1 thru 8 up to five (5) times.

This procedure is repeated for all fuses to be blown (see Programming Waveforms).

To prevent further verification, two last fuses may be blown by raising pin 1 and pin 11 to V_P. V_{CC} is not required during this operation.

Voltage Legend

L = Low-level input voltage, V_{IL}
H = High-level input voltage, V_{IH}
HH = High-level program voltage, V_{IHH}
Z = High impedance (e.g., 10kΩ to 5.0V)

INPUT LINE NUMBER	PIN IDENTIFICATION								
	I_7	I_6	I_5	I_4	I_3	I_2	I_1	I_0	L/R
0	HH	HH	HH	HH	HH	HH	HH	L	Z
1	HH	HH	HH	HH	HH	HH	HH	H	Z
2	HH	HH	HH	HH	HH	HH	HH	L	HH
3	HH	HH	HH	HH	HH	HH	HH	H	HH
4	HH	HH	HH	HH	HH	HH	L	HH	Z
5	HH	HH	HH	HH	HH	HH	H	HH	Z
6	HH	HH	HH	HH	HH	HH	L	HH	HH
7	HH	HH	HH	HH	HH	HH	H	HH	HH
8	HH	HH	HH	HH	HH	L	HH	HH	Z
9	HH	HH	HH	HH	HH	H	HH	HH	Z
10	HH	HH	HH	HH	HH	L	HH	HH	HH
11	HH	HH	HH	HH	HH	H	HH	HH	HH
12	HH	HH	HH	HH	L	HH	HH	HH	Z
13	HH	HH	HH	HH	H	HH	HH	HH	Z
14	HH	HH	HH	HH	L	HH	HH	HH	HH
15	HH	HH	HH	HH	H	HH	HH	HH	HH
16	HH	HH	HH	L	HH	HH	HH	HH	Z
17	HH	HH	HH	H	HH	HH	HH	HH	Z
18	HH	HH	HH	L	HH	HH	HH	HH	HH
19	HH	HH	HH	H	HH	HH	HH	HH	HH
20	HH	HH	L	HH	HH	HH	HH	HH	Z
21	HH	HH	H	HH	HH	HH	HH	HH	Z
22	HH	HH	L	HH	HH	HH	HH	HH	HH
23	HH	HH	H	HH	HH	HH	HH	HH	HH
24	HH	L	HH	HH	HH	HH	HH	HH	Z
25	HH	H	HH	HH	HH	HH	HH	HH	Z
26	HH	L	HH	HH	HH	HH	HH	HH	HH
27	HH	H	HH	HH	HH	HH	HH	HH	HH
28	L	HH	HH	HH	HH	HH	HH	HH	Z
29	H	HH	HH	HH	HH	HH	HH	HH	Z
30	L	HH	HH	HH	HH	HH	HH	HH	HH
31	H	HH	HH	HH	HH	HH	HH	HH	HH

Table 1 Input Line Select

PRODUCT LINE NUMBER	PIN IDENTIFICATION						
	O_3	O_2	O_1	O_0	A_2	A_1	A_0
0, 32	Z	Z	Z	HH	Z	Z	Z
1, 33	Z	Z	Z	HH	Z	Z	HH
2, 34	Z	Z	Z	HH	Z	HH	Z
3, 35	Z	Z	Z	HH	Z	HH	HH
4, 36	Z	Z	Z	HH	HH	Z	Z
5, 37	Z	Z	Z	HH	HH	Z	HH
6, 38	Z	Z	Z	HH	HH	HH	Z
7, 39	Z	Z	Z	HH	HH	HH	HH
8, 40	Z	Z	HH	Z	Z	Z	Z
9, 41	Z	Z	HH	Z	Z	Z	HH
10, 42	Z	Z	HH	Z	Z	HH	Z
11, 43	Z	Z	HH	Z	Z	HH	HH
12, 44	Z	Z	HH	Z	HH	Z	Z
13, 45	Z	Z	HH	Z	HH	Z	HH
14, 46	Z	Z	HH	Z	HH	HH	Z
15, 47	Z	Z	HH	Z	HH	HH	HH
16, 48	Z	HH	Z	Z	Z	Z	Z
17, 49	Z	HH	Z	Z	Z	Z	HH
18, 50	Z	HH	Z	Z	Z	HH	Z
19, 51	Z	HH	Z	Z	Z	HH	HH
20, 52	Z	HH	Z	Z	HH	Z	Z
21, 53	Z	HH	Z	Z	HH	Z	HH
22, 54	Z	HH	Z	Z	HH	HH	Z
23, 55	Z	HH	Z	Z	HH	HH	HH
24, 56	HH	Z	Z	Z	Z	Z	Z
25, 57	HH	Z	Z	Z	Z	Z	HH
26, 58	HH	Z	Z	Z	Z	HH	Z
27, 59	HH	Z	Z	Z	Z	HH	HH
28, 60	HH	Z	Z	Z	HH	Z	Z
29, 61	HH	Z	Z	Z	HH	Z	HH
30, 62	HH	Z	Z	Z	HH	HH	Z
31, 63	HH	Z	Z	Z	HH	HH	HH

Table 2 Product Line Select

Pin Configurations for Programming

PRODUCTS 0 THRU 31

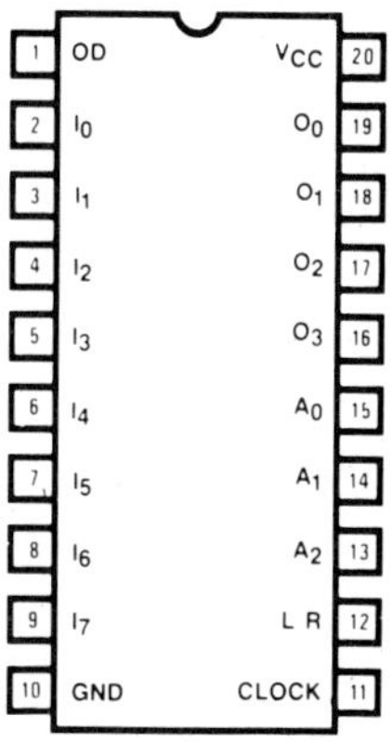

PRODUCTS 32 THRU 63

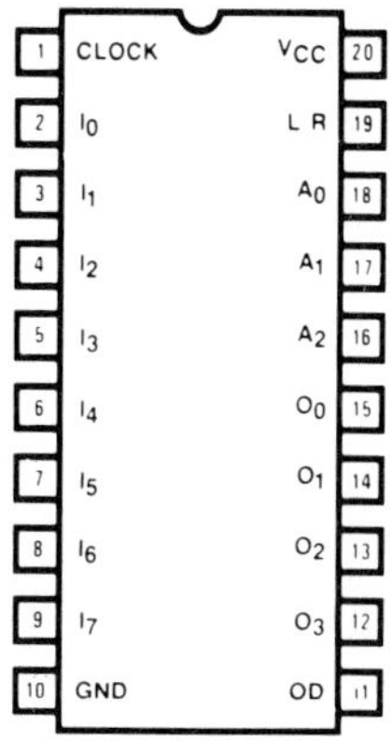

Programming Parameters $T_A = 25°C$

SYMBOL	PARAMETER		LIMITS MIN	TYP	MAX	UNIT
V_{IHH}	Program-level input voltage		11	11.5	12	V
I_{IHH}	Program-level input current	Output Program Pulse			50	mA
		OD, L/R			25	mA
		All Other Inputs			5	mA
I_{CCH}	Program Supply Current				400	mA
T_P	Program Pulse Width		10		50	μs
t_D	Delay time		100			ns
t_{DV}	Delay Time to Verify		100			μs
	Program Pulse duty cycle				25	%
V_P	Verify-Protect-input voltage		20	21	22	V
I_P	Verify-Protect-input current				400	mA
T_{PP}	Verify-Protect Pulse Width		20		50	msec

Programming Waveforms

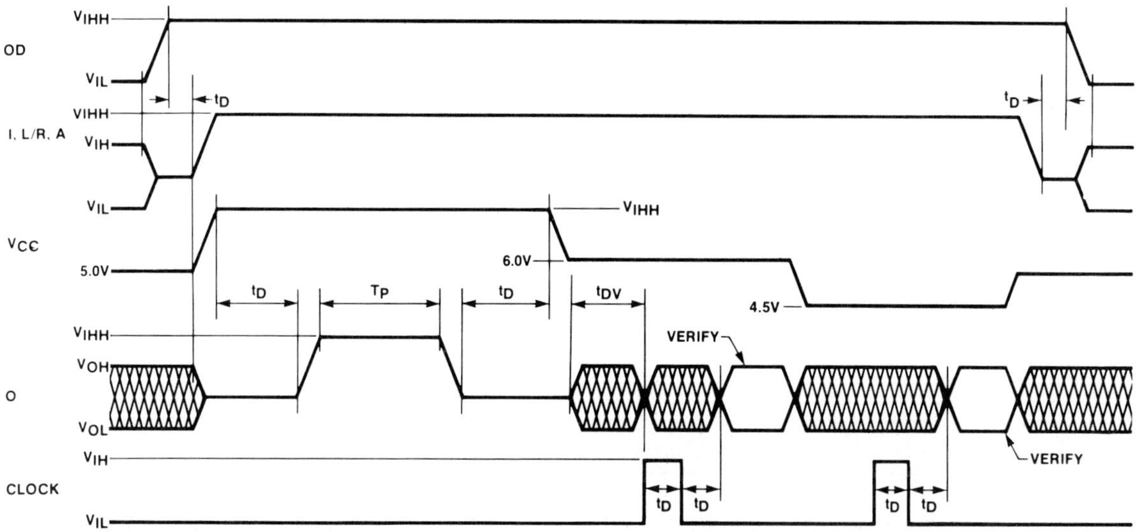

PAL
PART NUMBER

PAL DESIGN SPECIFICATION

USER'S PART NUMBER — REV — NAME — DATE / /

TITLE

COMPANY, CITY, STATE

PIN 1	PIN 2	PIN 3	PIN 4	PIN 5
PIN 6	PIN 7	PIN 8	PIN 9	GND PIN 10
PIN 11	PIN 12	PIN 13	PIN 14	PIN 15
PIN 16	PIN 17	PIN 18	PIN 19	VCC PIN 20

EQUATIONS

Description

LEGEND:	= EQUAL	+ OR	:+: XOR	/ COMPLEMENT
	:= REPLACED BY	* AND	:*: XNOR	( ) THREE-STATE

F 110

FUNCTION TABLE

PIN A	PIN B	PIN C	PIN D	PIN E
PIN F	PIN G	PIN H	PIN I	PIN J
PIN K	PIN L	PIN M	PIN N	PIN O
PIN P	PIN Q	PIN R		

; ____ COMMENT

; A B C D E F G H I J K L M N O P Q R COMMENT

LEGEND: H HIGH, L LOW, C CLOCK, X IRRELEVANT, Z OFF

F 109

Programmable Array Logic Family

PAL® Series 24

U.S. Patent 4124899

Features/Benefits

- **Programmable replacement for conventional TTL logic.**
- **Reduces IC inventories substantially and simplifies their control.**
- **Reduces chip count by 5 to 1.**
- **Expedites and simplifies prototyping and board layout.**
- **Saves space with 24-pin SKINNYDIP™ packages.**
- **Programmed on standard PROM programmers.**
- **Programmable three-state outputs.**
- **Special feature reduces possibility of copying by competitors.**

PART NUMBER	PKG	DESCRIPTION
PAL12L10	J,N	Deca 12 Input And-Or-Invert Gate Array
PAL14L8	J,N	Octal 14 Input And-Or-Invert Gate Array
PAL16L6	J,N	Hex 16 Input And-Or-Invert Gate Array
PAL18L4	J,N	Quad 18 Input And-Or-Invert Gate Array
PAL20L2	J,N	Dual 20 Input And-Or-Invert Gate Array
PAL20C1	J,N	20 Input And-Or/And-Or Invert Gate Array
PAL20L10	J,N	Deca 20 Input And-Or-Invert Gate Array
PAL20X10	J,N	Deca 20 Input Registered And-Or-Xor Gate Array
PAL20X8	J,N	Octal 20 Input Registered And-Or-Xor Gate Array
PAL20X4	J,N	Quad 20 Input Registered And-Or-Xor Gate Array

Description

The PAL Series 24 family complements the PAL Series 20 family by providing two additional inputs and two additional outputs, allowing more complex functions in a single package. This new family is made feasible by the Monolithic Memories new and revolutionary 24-pin SKINNYDIP™.

In addition to providing more logic function per chip, 24 pins allows for many natural functions which were previously unavailable in skinny 300 mil-wide packages. Examples include:

- 8-bit parallel-in parallel-out counters
- 8-bit parallel-in parallel-out shift registers
- 16-Line-to-1-Line Multiplexors
- Dual 8-Line-to-1-Line Multiplexors
- Quad 4-Line-to-1-Line Multiplexors

These natural functions provide twice the density of traditional 16-pin packages.

The PAL family utilizes an advanced Schottky TTL process and the Bipolar PROM fusible link technology to provide user programmable logic for replacing conventional SSI/MSI gates and flip-flops at reduced chip count.

The family lets the systems engineer "design his own chip" by blowing fusible links to configure AND and OR gates to perform his desired logic function. Complex interconnections which previously required time-consuming layout are thus "lifted" from PC board etch and placed on silicon where they can be easily modified during prototype check-out or production.

The PAL transfer function is the familiar sum of products. Like the PROM, the PAL has a single array of fusible links. Unlike the PROM, the PAL is a programmable AND array driving a fixed OR array (the PROM is a fixed AND array driving a programmable OR array). In addition the PAL provides these options:

- Variable input/output pin ratio
- Programmable three-state outputs
- Registers with feedback

Unused inputs are tied directly to V_{CC} or GND. Product terms with all fuses blown assume the logical high state, and product terms connected to both true and complement of any single input assume the logical low state. Registers consist of D type flip-flops which are loaded on the low to high transition of the clock. PAL Logic Diagrams are shown with all fuses blown, enabling the designer use of the diagrams as coding sheets.

To design a PAL, the user writes the logic equations using PAL DESIGN SPECIFICATION standard format (F108). This specification may be submitted to Monolithic Memories where it is computer processed and assigned a bit pattern number, eg P0123. Monolithic Memories accepts the PAL DESIGN SPECIFICATION in one of the three forms:

1. Computer generated listings.
2. Typed or hand-written forms F107 and F108.
3. Direct on line data transmission to Monolithic Memories Timeshare computer system via telephone (local telephone network to major U.S. cities, London and Paris) or TWX online Boston TWX No.).

The entire PAL family is programmed on inexpensive conventional PROM programmers with appropriate personality and socket adapter cards. Once the PAL is programmed and verified, two additional fuses may be blown to defeat verification. This feature gives the user a proprietary circuit which is very difficult to copy.

Ordering Information

PROGRAMMABLE ARRAY LOGIC FAMILY

NUMBER OF ARRAY INPUTS

OUTPUT TYPE
L = ACTIVE LOW
C = COMPLEMENTARY
X = EXCLUSIVE OR REGISTERED
R = REGISTERED

NUMBER OF OUTPUTS

TEMPERATURE RANGE
C = 0C TO +75C
M = -55C TO +125C (CASE TEMPERATURE)

PACKAGE
N = PLASTIC DIP
J = CERAMIC DIP

HI-REL SCREENING LEVEL SEE "SCREENING OPTIONS

PAL20X8CJ 883B

SKINNYDIP is a registered trademark of Monolithic Memories

PAL12L10

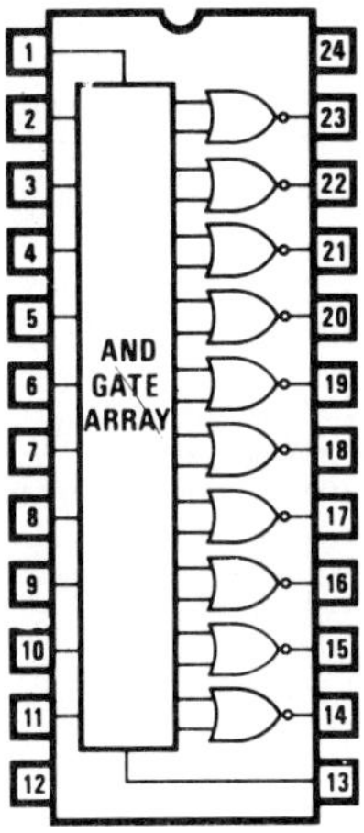

PAL14L8

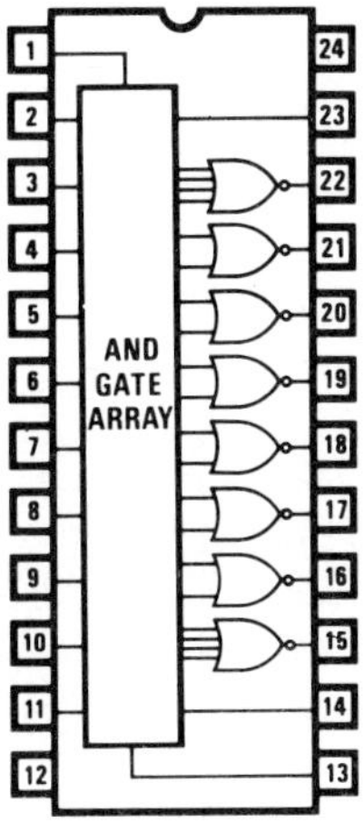

PAL16L6

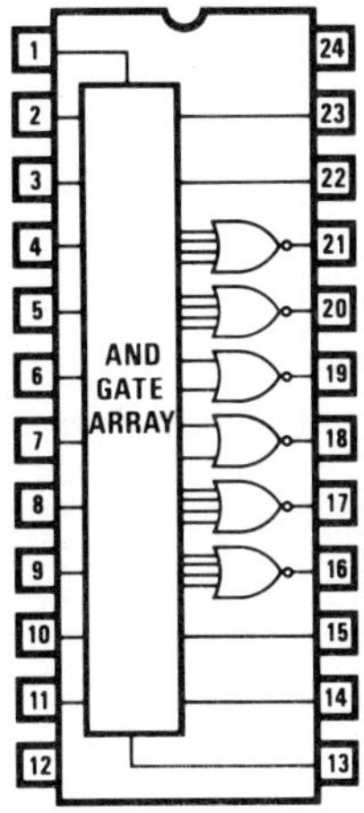

PAL18L4

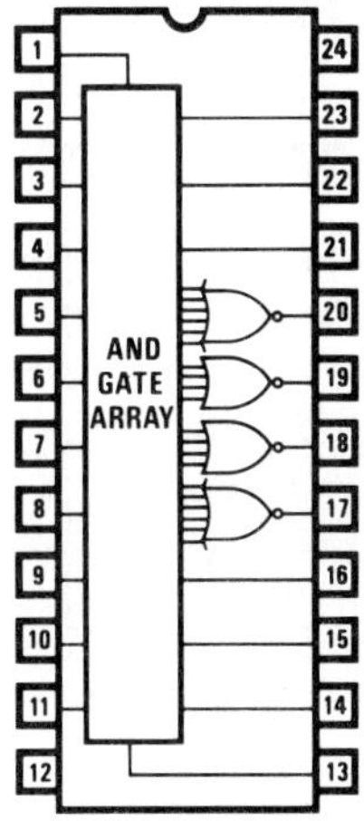

PAL20L2

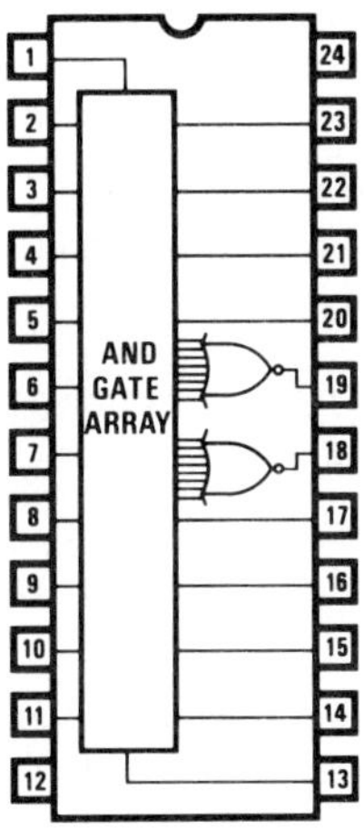

PAL20C1

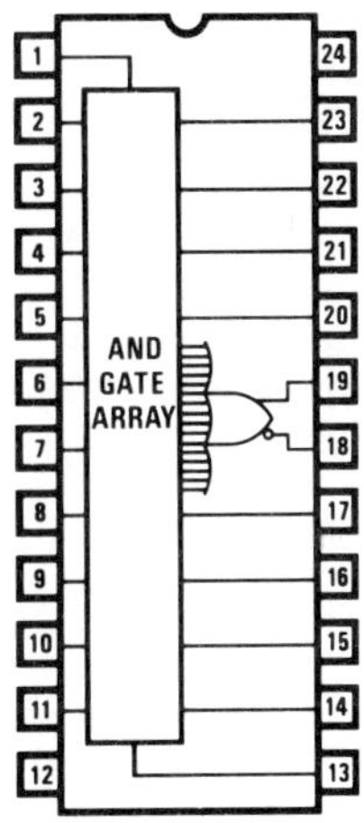

PAL20L10

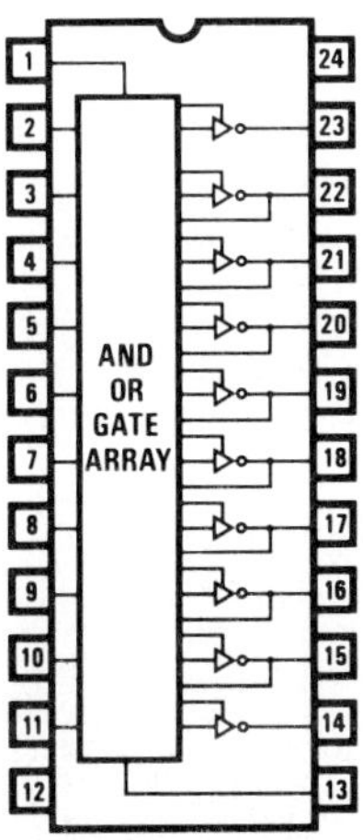

PAL20X10

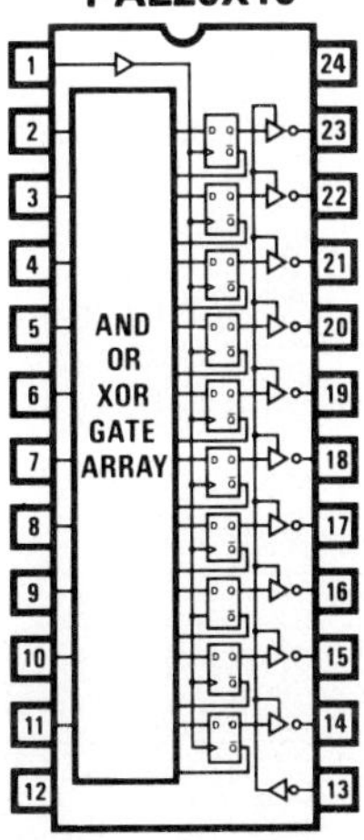

PAL20X8

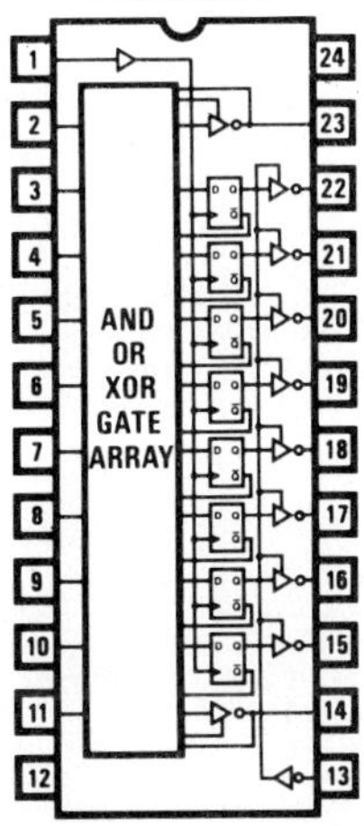

PAL20X4

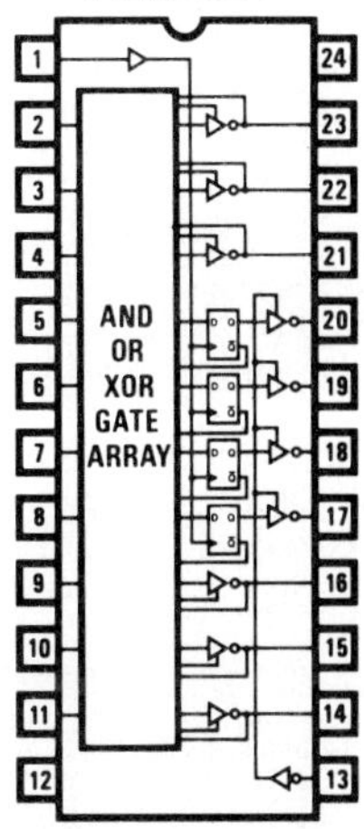

Absolute Maximum Ratings

	Operating	Programming
Supply Voltage, V_{CC}	7	12V
Input Voltage	5.5V	12V*
Off-state output Voltage	5.5V	12V
Storage temperature	−65° to +150°C	

Operating Conditions

SYMBOL	PARAMETER		MILITARY MIN	MILITARY TYP	MILITARY MAX	COMMERCIAL MIN	COMMERCIAL TYP	COMMERCIAL MAX	UNIT
V_{CC}	Supply voltage		4.5	5	5.5	4.75	5	5.25	V
t_w	Width of clock	Low	40	20		35	20		ns
		High	30	10		25	10		ns
t_{su}	Set up time		60	38		50	38		ns
t_h	Hold time		0	−15		0	−15		ns
T_A	Operating free air temperature		−55			0		75	°C
T_C	Operating case temperature				125				°C

Electrical Characteristics Over Operating Conditions

SYMBOL	PARAMETER	TEST CONDITIONS			MIN	TYP††	MAX	UNIT
V_{IL}	Low-level input voltage						0.8	V
V_{IH}	High-level input voltage				2			V
V_{IC}	Input clamp voltage	V_{CC} = MIN	I_I = −18mA			−0.8	−1.5	V
I_{IL}	Low-level input current †	V_{CC} = MAX	V_I = 0.4V			−0.02	−0.25	mA
I_{IH}	High-level input current †	V_{CC} = MAX	V_I = 2.4V				25	μA
I_I	Maximum input current	V_{CC} = MAX	V_I = 5.5V				1	mA
V_{OL}	Low-level output voltage	V_{CC} = MIN, V_{IL} = 0.8V, V_{IH} = 2V	12L10, 14L8, 16L6 18L4, 20L2, 20C1	I_{OL} = 8mA		0.3	0.5	V
			20L10, 20X10 20X8, 20X4	MIL I_{OL} = 12mA				
				COM I_{OL} = 24mA				
V_{OH}	High-level output voltage	V_{CC} = MIN, V_{IL} = 0.8V, V_{IH} = 2V	I_{OH} = −2mA	MIL	2.4	2.8		V
			I_{OH} = −3.2mA	COM				
I_{OZL}	Off-state output current †	V_{CC} = MAX, V_{IL} = 0.8V, V_{IH} = 2V	V_O = 0.4V				−100	μA
I_{OZH}			V_O = 2.4V				100	μA
I_{OS}	Output short-circuit current **	V_{CC} = 5V	V_O = 0V		−30	−70	−130	mA
I_{CC}	Supply current	V_{CC} = MAX	12L10, 14L8, 16L6, 18L4, 20L2, 20C1			60	100	mA
			20X4, 20X8, 20X10			120	180	
			20L10			90	165	

† I/O pin leakage is the worst case of I_{OZX} or I_{IX} e.g. I_{IX} and I_{OZH}

†† All typical values are at V_{CC} = 5V, T_A = 25°C.

* Pins 1 and 13 may be raised to 22V max.

** Only one output shorted at a time.

Switching Characteristics

Over Operating Conditions

SYMBOL	PARAMETER		TEST CONDITIONS	MILITARY MIN	MILITARY TYP	MILITARY MAX	COMMERCIAL MIN	COMMERCIAL TYP	COMMERCIAL MAX	UNIT
t_{PD}	Input to output	12L10, 14L8, 16L6, 18L4, 20L2, 20C1	$R_1 = 560\Omega$ $R_2 = 1.1k\Omega$		25	45		25	40	ns
t_{PD}	Input or feedback to output		20L10, 20X10 20X8, 20X4 $R_1 = 200\Omega$ $R_2 = 390\Omega$		35	60		35	50	ns
t_{CLK}	Clock to output or feedback				20	35		20	30	ns
t_{PZX}	Pin 13 to output enable				20	45		20	35	ns
t_{PXZ}	Pin 13 to output disable				20	45		20	35	ns
t_{PZX}	Input to output enable				35	55		35	45	ns
t_{PXZ}	Input to output disable				35	55		35	45	ns
f_{MAX}	Maximum frequency			10.5	16		12.5	16		MHz

Test Load

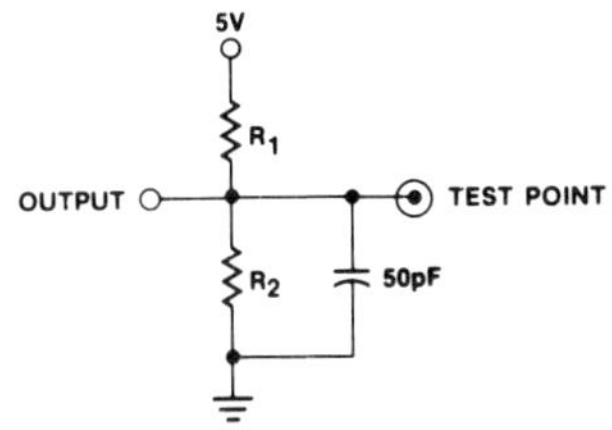

Schematic of Inputs and Outputs

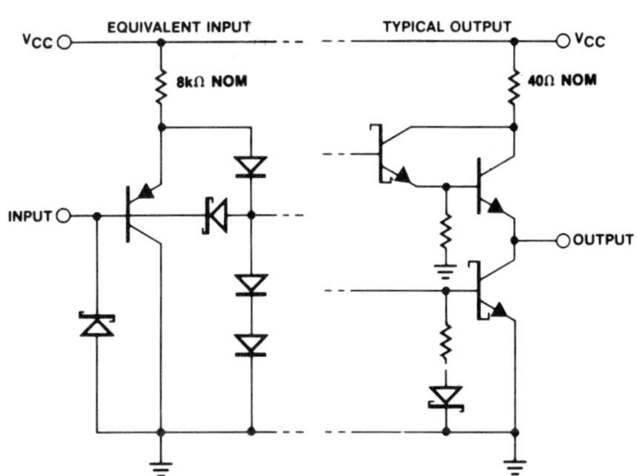

Programming

PAL fuses are programmed using a low-voltage linear-select procedure which is common to all PAL types. The array is divided into two groups, products 0 thru 39 and products 40 thru 79, for which pin identifications are shown in Pin Configurations below. To program a particular fuse, both an input line and a product line are selected according to the following procedure:

Step 1 Raise Output Disable, OD, to V_{IHH}.

Step 2 Select an input line by specifying I_0, I_1, I_2, I_3, I_4, I_5, I_6, I_7, I_8, I_9 and L/R as shown in Table 1.

Step 3 Select a product line by specifying A_0, A_1 and A_2 one-of-eight select as shown in Table 2.

Step 4 Raise V_{CC} (pin 24) to V_{IHH}.

Step 5 Program the fuse by pulsing the output pins, O, of the selected product group to V_{IHH} as shown in Programming Waveform.

Step 6 Lower V_{CC} (pin 24) to 6.0 V.

Step 7 Pulse the CLOCK pin and verify the output pin, O, to be Low for active Low PAL types or High for active High PAL types.

Step 8 Lower V_{CC} (pin 24) to 4.5 V and repeat step 7.

Step 9 Should the output not verify, repeat steps 1 thru 8 up to five (5) times.

This procedure is repeated for all fuses to be blown (see Programming Waveforms).

To prevent further verification, two last fuses may be blown by raising pin 1 and pin 13 to V_P. V_{CC} is not required during this operation.

Voltage Legend

L = Low-level input voltage, V_{IL}
H = High-level input voltage, V_{IH}
HH = High-level program voltage, V_{IHH}
Z = High impedance (e.g. 10K Ω to 5.0V)

INPUT LINE NUMBER	PIN IDENTIFICATION										
	I_9	I_8	I_7	I_6	I_5	I_4	I_3	I_2	I_1	I_0	L/R
0	HH	HH	HH	HH	HH	HH	HH	HH	HH	L	Z
1	HH	HH	HH	HH	HH	HH	HH	HH	HH	H	Z
2	HH	HH	HH	HH	HH	HH	HH	HH	HH	L	HH
3	HH	HH	HH	HH	HH	HH	HH	HH	HH	H	HH
4	HH	HH	HH	HH	HH	HH	HH	HH	L	HH	Z
5	HH	HH	HH	HH	HH	HH	HH	HH	H	HH	Z
6	HH	HH	HH	HH	HH	HH	HH	HH	L	HH	HH
7	HH	HH	HH	HH	HH	HH	HH	HH	H	HH	HH
8	HH	HH	HH	HH	HH	HH	HH	L	HH	HH	Z
9	HH	HH	HH	HH	HH	HH	HH	H	HH	HH	Z
10	HH	HH	HH	HH	HH	HH	HH	L	HH	HH	HH
11	HH	HH	HH	HH	HH	HH	HH	H	HH	HH	HH
12	HH	HH	HH	HH	HH	HH	L	HH	HH	HH	Z
13	HH	HH	HH	HH	HH	HH	H	HH	HH	HH	Z
14	HH	HH	HH	HH	HH	HH	L	HH	HH	HH	HH
15	HH	HH	HH	HH	HH	HH	H	HH	HH	HH	HH
16	HH	HH	HH	HH	HH	L	HH	HH	HH	HH	Z
17	HH	HH	HH	HH	HH	H	HH	HH	HH	HH	Z
18	HH	HH	HH	HH	HH	L	HH	HH	HH	HH	HH
19	HH	HH	HH	HH	HH	H	HH	HH	HH	HH	HH
20	HH	HH	HH	HH	L	HH	HH	HH	HH	HH	Z
21	HH	HH	HH	HH	H	HH	HH	HH	HH	HH	Z
22	HH	HH	HH	HH	L	HH	HH	HH	HH	HH	HH
23	HH	HH	HH	HH	H	HH	HH	HH	HH	HH	HH
24	HH	HH	HH	L	HH	HH	HH	HH	HH	HH	Z
25	HH	HH	HH	H	HH	HH	HH	HH	HH	HH	Z
26	HH	HH	HH	L	HH	HH	HH	HH	HH	HH	HH
27	HH	HH	HH	H	HH	HH	HH	HH	HH	HH	HH
28	HH	HH	L	HH	HH	HH	HH	HH	HH	HH	Z
29	HH	HH	H	HH	HH	HH	HH	HH	HH	HH	Z
30	HH	HH	L	HH	HH	HH	HH	HH	HH	HH	HH
31	HH	HH	H	HH	HH	HH	HH	HH	HH	HH	HH
32	HH	L	HH	HH	HH	HH	HH	HH	HH	HH	Z
33	HH	H	HH	HH	HH	HH	HH	HH	HH	HH	Z
34	HH	L	HH	HH	HH	HH	HH	HH	HH	HH	HH
35	HH	H	HH	HH	HH	HH	HH	HH	HH	HH	HH
36	L	HH	HH	HH	HH	HH	HH	HH	HH	HH	Z
37	H	HH	HH	HH	HH	HH	HH	HH	HH	HH	Z
38	L	HH	HH	HH	HH	HH	HH	HH	HH	HH	HH
39	H	HH	HH	HH	HH	HH	HH	HH	HH	HH	HH

Table 1 Input Line Select

PRODUCT LINE NUMBER	PIN IDENTIFICATION							
	O_4	O_3	O_2	O_1	O_0	A_2	A_1	A_0
0, 40	Z	Z	Z	Z	HH	Z	Z	Z
1, 41	Z	Z	Z	Z	HH	Z	Z	HH
2, 42	Z	Z	Z	Z	HH	Z	HH	Z
3, 43	Z	Z	Z	Z	HH	Z	HH	HH
4, 44	Z	Z	Z	Z	HH	HH	Z	Z
5, 45	Z	Z	Z	Z	HH	HH	Z	HH
6, 46	Z	Z	Z	Z	HH	HH	HH	Z
7, 47	Z	Z	Z	Z	HH	HH	HH	HH
8, 48	Z	Z	Z	HH	Z	Z	Z	Z
9, 49	Z	Z	Z	HH	Z	Z	Z	HH
10, 50	Z	Z	Z	HH	Z	Z	HH	Z
11, 51	Z	Z	Z	HH	Z	Z	HH	HH
12, 52	Z	Z	Z	HH	Z	HH	Z	Z
13, 53	Z	Z	Z	HH	Z	HH	Z	HH
14, 54	Z	Z	Z	HH	Z	HH	HH	Z
15, 55	Z	Z	Z	HH	Z	HH	HH	HH
16, 56	Z	Z	HH	Z	Z	Z	Z	Z
17, 57	Z	Z	HH	Z	Z	Z	Z	HH
18, 58	Z	Z	HH	Z	Z	Z	HH	Z
19, 59	Z	Z	HH	Z	Z	Z	HH	HH
20, 60	Z	Z	HH	Z	Z	HH	Z	Z
21, 61	Z	Z	HH	Z	Z	HH	Z	HH
22, 62	Z	Z	HH	Z	Z	HH	HH	Z
23, 63	Z	Z	HH	Z	Z	HH	HH	HH
24, 64	Z	HH	Z	Z	Z	Z	Z	Z
25, 65	Z	HH	Z	Z	Z	Z	Z	HH
26, 66	Z	HH	Z	Z	Z	Z	HH	Z
27, 67	Z	HH	Z	Z	Z	Z	HH	HH
28, 68	Z	HH	Z	Z	Z	HH	Z	Z
29, 69	Z	HH	Z	Z	Z	HH	Z	HH
30, 70	Z	HH	Z	Z	Z	HH	HH	Z
31, 71	Z	HH	Z	Z	Z	HH	HH	HH
32, 72	HH	Z	Z	Z	Z	Z	Z	Z
33, 73	HH	Z	Z	Z	Z	Z	Z	HH
34, 74	HH	Z	Z	Z	Z	Z	HH	Z
35, 75	HH	Z	Z	Z	Z	Z	HH	HH
36, 76	HH	Z	Z	Z	Z	HH	Z	Z
37, 77	HH	Z	Z	Z	Z	HH	Z	HH
38, 78	HH	Z	Z	Z	Z	HH	HH	Z
39, 79	HH	Z	Z	Z	Z	HH	HH	HH

Table 2 Product Line Select

Pin Configurations for Programming

PRODUCTS 0 THRU 39

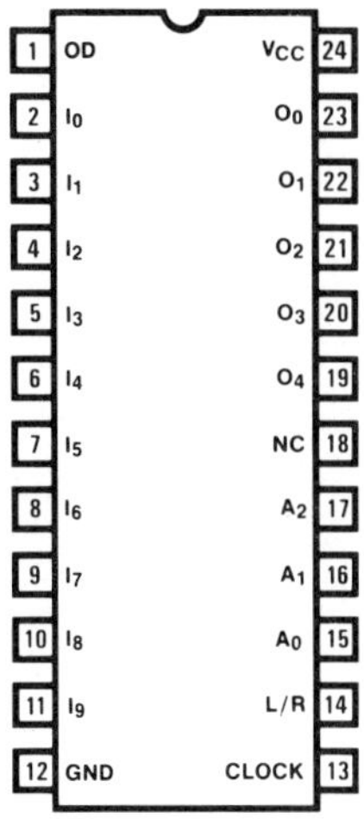

PRODUCTS 40 THRU 79

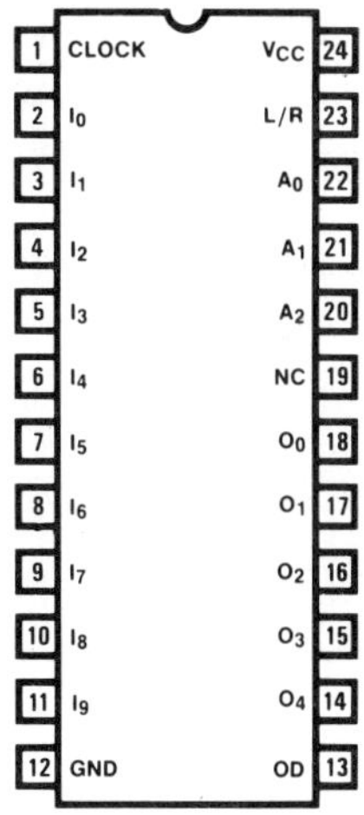

Programming Parameters $T_A = 25°C$

SYMBOL	PARAMETER		LIMITS MIN	TYP	MAX	UNIT
V_{IHH}	Program-level input voltage		11.5	11.75	12	V
I_{IHH}	Program-level input current	Output Program Pulse			50	mA
		OD, L/R			50	
		All Other Inputs			5	
I_{CCH}	Program Supply Current				400	mA
T_P	Program Pulse Width		10		50	μs
t_D	Delay time		100			ns
t_{DV}	Delay Time to Verify		100			μs
	Program Pulse duty cycle				25	%
V_P	Verify-Protect-input voltage		20	21	22	V
I_P	Verify-Protect-input current				400	mA
T_{PP}	Verify-Protect Pulse Width		20		50	msec

Programming Waveforms

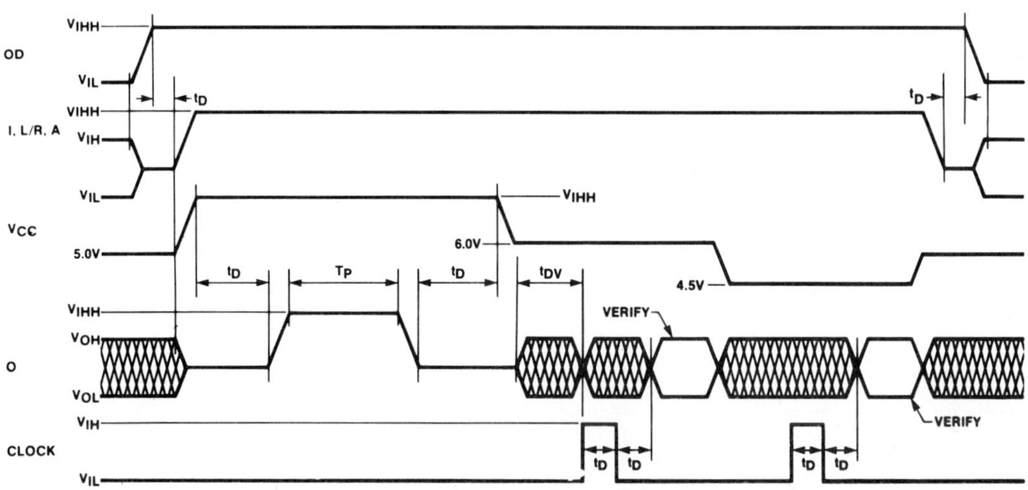

PAL
PART NUMBER

PAL DESIGN SPECIFICATION

USER'S PART NUMBER	REV	NAME	/ / DATE

TITLE

COMPANY, CITY, STATE

PIN 1	PIN 2	PIN 3	PIN 4	PIN 5	PIN 6
					GND
PIN 7	PIN 8	PIN 9	PIN 10	PIN 11	PIN 12
PIN 13	PIN 14	PIN 15	PIN 16	PIN 17	PIN 18
					VCC
PIN 19	PIN 20	PIN 21	PIN 22	PIN 23	PIN 24

EQUATIONS

DESCRIPTION:

LEGEND:	=	EQUAL	+	OR	:+:	XOR	/	COMPLEMENT
	:=	REPLACED BY	*	AND	:*:	XNOR	( )	THREE-STATE

F 108

FUNCTION TABLE

PIN A	PIN B	PIN C	PIN D	PIN E	PIN F
PIN G	PIN H	PIN I	PIN J	PIN K	PIN L
PIN M	PIN N	PIN O	PIN P	PIN Q	PIN R
PIN S	PIN T	PIN U	PIN V		

;
COMMENT

;

A	B	C	D	E	F	G	H	I	J	K	L	M	N	O	P	Q	R	S	T	U	V	COMMENT

LEGEND: H HIGH C CLOCK Z OFF
L LOW X IRRELEVANT

F 107

Hard Array Logic Family

HAL Series 20 Data Sheet

Features/Benefits

- **Gate array equivalent of up to 200 gates.**
- **Semi-custom solution**
- **Reduces SSI/MSI chip count greater than 4 to 1.**
- **Prototype using field-programmable version — PAL.**
- **Cost savings up to 40% compared to PAL.**
- **Security link disabled for design secrecy.**
- **Test and simulation made simple with PALASM Function Table.**
- **Saves space with 20-pin SKINNYDIP™ packages.**
- **Power consumption is directly proportional to logic complexity.**

Description

The HAL family utilizes standard Low-Power Schottky TTL process and automated mask pattern generation directly from logic equations to provide a semi-custom gate array for replacing conventional SSI/MSI gates and flip-flops at reduced chip count.

The family lets the systems engineer "design his own chip" by AND and OR gates to perform his desired logic function. Complex interconnections which previously required time-consuming layout are thus "lifted" from PC board etch and placed on silicon where they can be easily modified during prototype check-out or production.

The HAL transfer function is the familiar sum of products. Like the ROM, the HAL has a single array of selectable gates. Unlike the ROM, the HAL is a selectable AND array driving a fixed OR array (the ROM is a fixed AND array driving a selectable OR array). In addition the HAL provides these options:

- Variable input/output pin ratio
- Programmable three-state outputs
- Registers with feedback
- Arithmetic capability

Unused inputs are tied directly to V_{CC} or GND. Product terms with all fuses blown assume the logical high state, and product terms connected to both true and complement of any single input assume the logical low state. Registers consist of D type flip-flops which are loaded on the low-to-high transition of the clock. HAL Logic Diagrams are shown with all fuses blown, enabling the designer to use the diagrams as coding sheets.

To design a HAL, the user first programs and debugs a PAL using PALASM and the "PAL DESIGN SPECIFICATION" standard format. This specification is submitted to Monolithic Memories where it is computer processed and assigned a bit pattern number, e.g. P01234.

PART NUMBER	PKG	DESCRIPTION
HAL10H8	J,N,F	Octal 10 Input And-Or Gate Array
HAL12H6	J,N,F	Hex 12 Input And-Or Gate Array
HAL14H4	J,N,F	Quad 14 Input And-Or Gate Array
HAL16H2	J,N,F	Dual 16 Input And-Or Gate Array
HAL16C1	J,N,F	16 Input And-Or/And-Or-Invert Gate Array
HAL10L8	J,N,F	Octal 10 Input And-Or-Invert Gate Array
HAL12L6	J,N,F	Hex 12 Input And-Or-Invert Gate Array
HAL14L4	J,N,F	Quad 14 Input And-Or-Invert Gate Array
HAL16L2	J,N,F	Dual 16 Input And-Or-Invert Gate Array
HAL16L8	J,N,F	Octal 16 Input And-Or-Invert Gate Array
HAL16R8	J,N,F	Octal 16 Input Registered And-Or Gate Array
HAL16R6	J,N,F	Hex 16 Input Registered And-Or Gate Array
HAL16R4	J,N,F	Quad 16 Input Registered And-Or Gate Array
HAL16X4	J,N,F	Quad 16 Input Registered And-Or-Xor Gate Array
HAL16A4	J,N,F	Quad 16 Input Registered And-Carry-Or-Xor Gate

Monolithic Memories accepts the PAL DESIGN SPECIFICATION in one of three forms:

1. Computer generated listing.
2. Typed or hand-written forms F109 and F110. See example on pages 6-7 and forms on pages 23-24.
3. Direct online data transmission to Monolithic Memories Timeshare computer system via telephone (local telephone network to major US cities, London and Paris) or TWX (online Boston TWX no.).

Monolithic Memories will provide a PAL sample for customer qualification. The user then submits a purchase order for a HAL of the specified bit pattern number, e.g. HAL14L4 P01234. See Ordering Information below.

Ordering Information

HARD ARRAY LOGIC FAMILY
NUMBER OF ARRAY INPUTS
OUTPUT YPE
H = ACTIVE HIGH
L = ACTIVE LOW
C = COMPLEMENTARY
R = REGISTERED
X = EXCLUSIVE-OR REGISTERED
A = ARITHMETIC REGISTERED
NUMBER OF OUTPUTS
TEMPERATURE RANGE
C = 0C TO +75C
M = -55C TO +125C (CASE TEMPERATURE)
PACKAGE
N = PLASTIC DIP
J = CERAMIC DIP
F = FLAT PACK
OPTIONAL HI-REL PROCESSING
883 = MIL-STD-883, METHOD 5004 & 5005 LEVEL B
883C = MIL-STD-883, METHOD 5004 & 5005 LEVEL C
B = MIL-STD-883, METHOD 5004 EQUIVALENT
C = MIL-STD-883, METHOD 5004 EQUIVALENT
BIT PATTERN NUMBER

HAL14 L4 CJ 883B P01234

HAL10H8

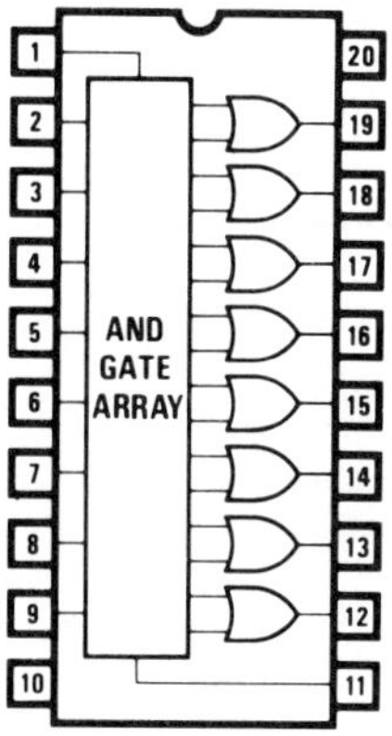

HAL12H6

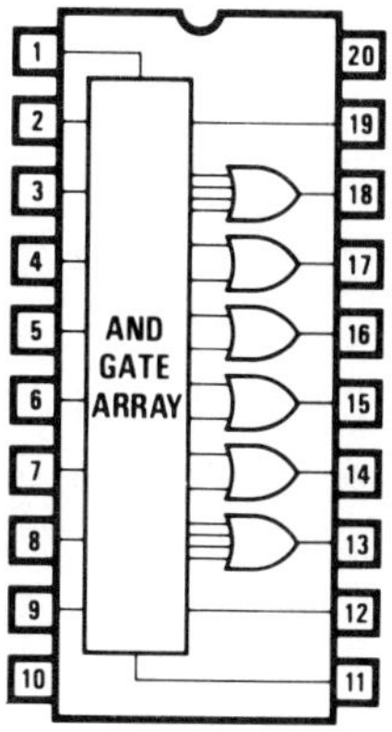

HAL14H4

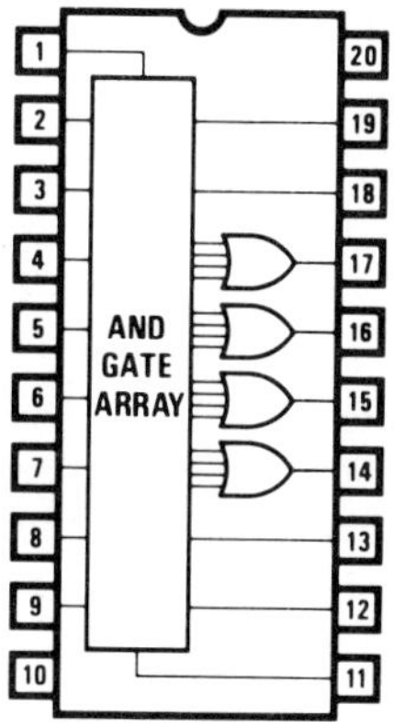

HAL16H2

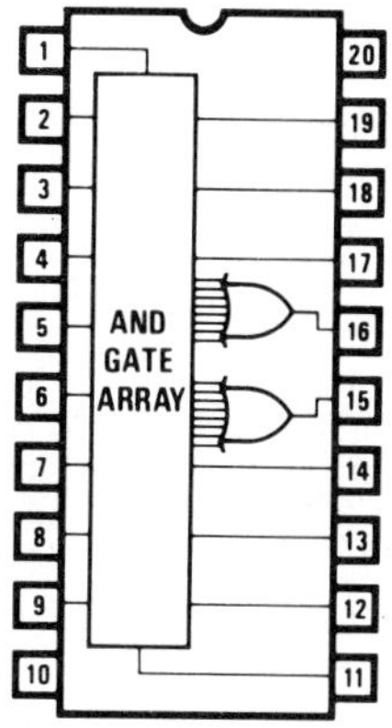

HAL16C1

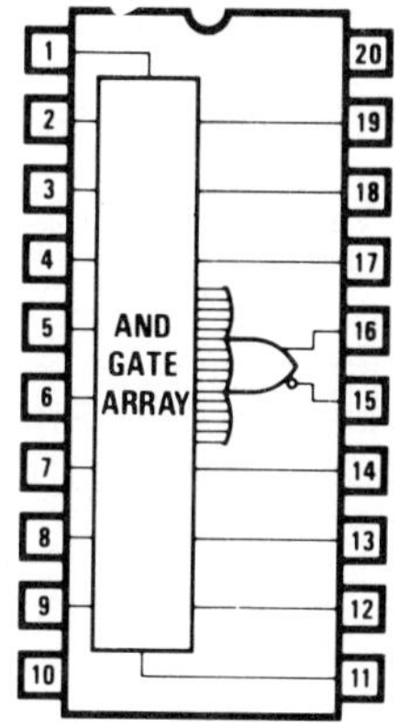

HAL10L8

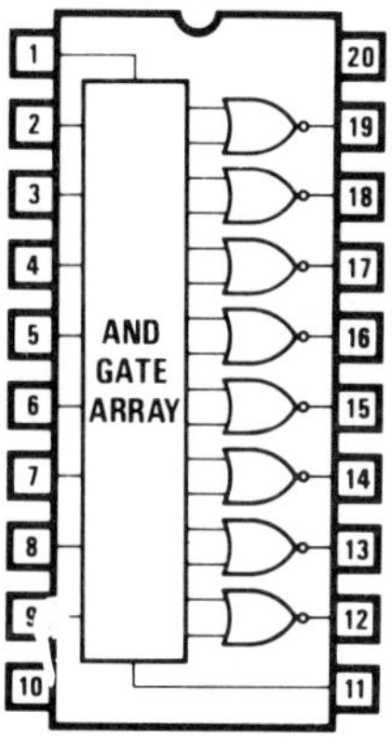

HAL12L6

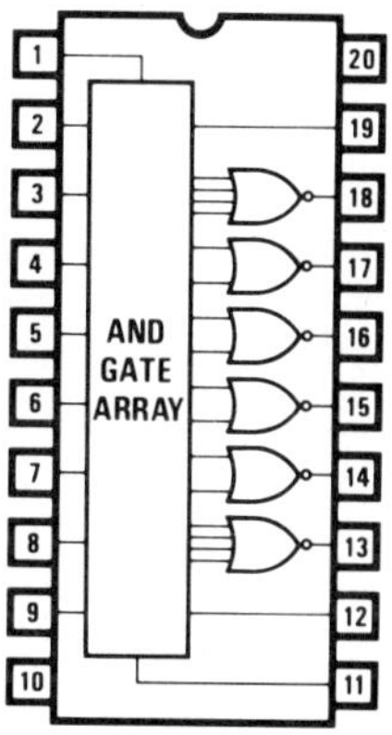

HAL14L4

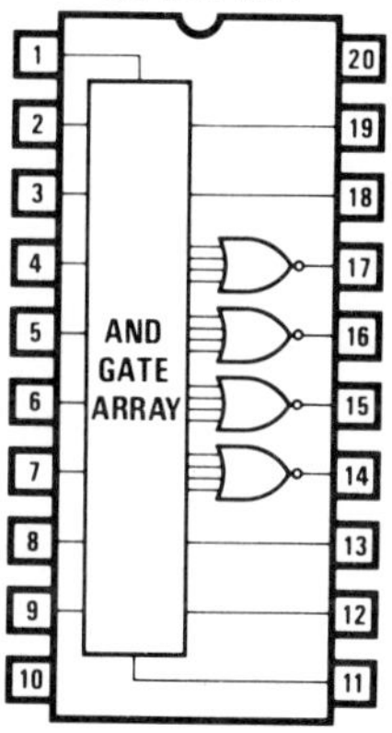

HAL16L2

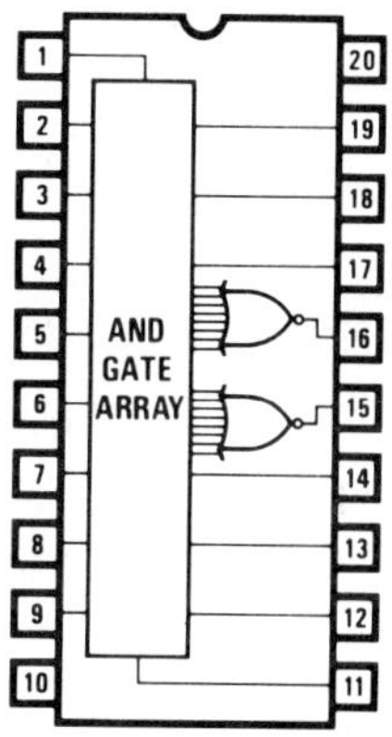

HAL16L8

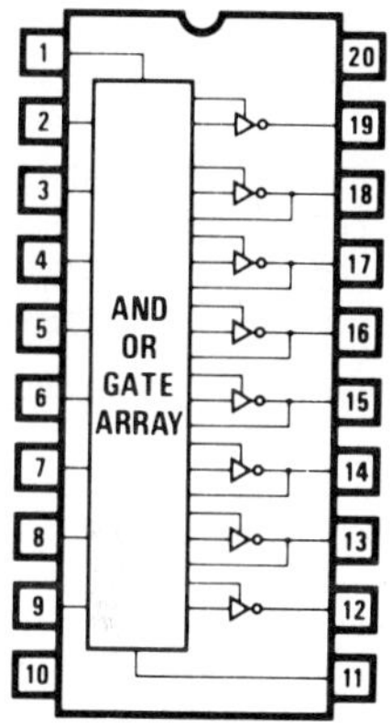

HAL16R8

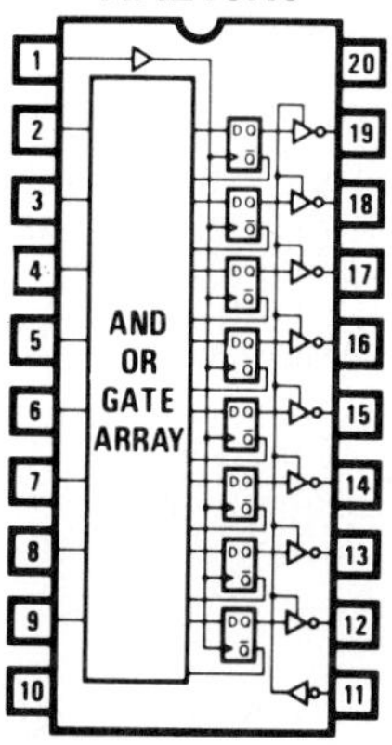

HAL16R6

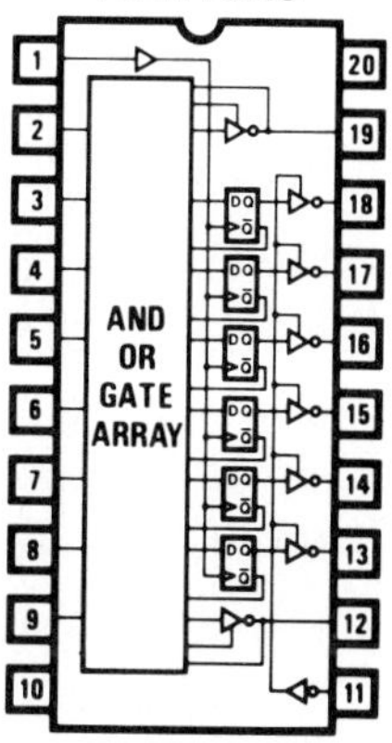

HAL16R4

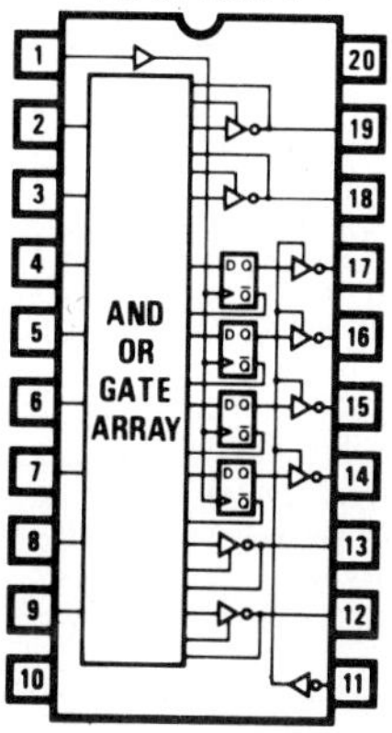

HAL16X4

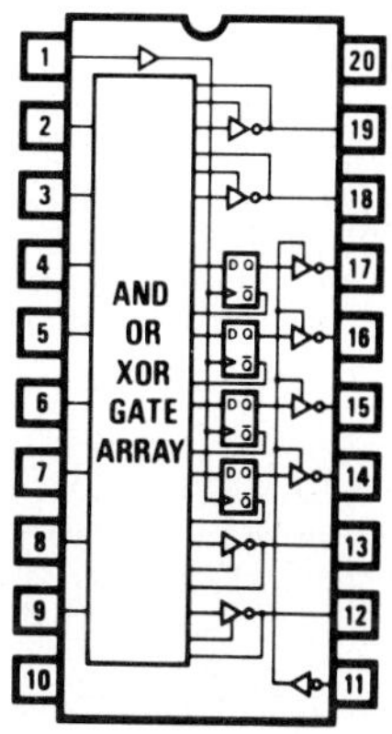

HAL16A4

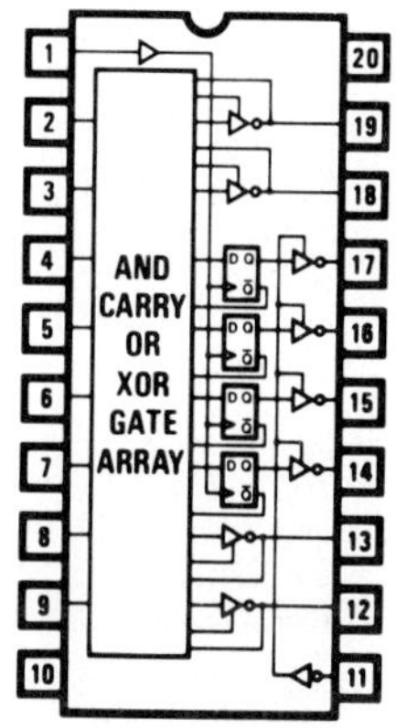

Absolute Maximum Ratings

	Operating
Supply Voltage, V_{CC}	7
Input Voltage	5.5V
Off-state output Voltage	5.5V
Storage temperature	−65° to +150°C

Operating Conditions

SYMBOL	PARAMETER		MILITARY MIN	MILITARY TYP	MILITARY MAX	COMMERCIAL MIN	COMMERCIAL TYP	COMMERCIAL MAX	UNIT
V_{CC}	Supply voltage		4.5	5	5.5	4.75	5	5.25	V
t_w	Width of clock	Low	25	10		25	10		ns
		High	25	10		25	10		ns
t_{su}	Set up time from input or feedback	16R8 16R6 16R4	45	25		35	25		ns
		16X4 16A4	55	30		45	30		ns
t_h	Hold time		0	−15		0	−15		ns
T_A	Operating free-air temperature		−55			0	5	75	°C
T_C	Operating case temperature				125				°C

Electrical Characteristics Over Operating Conditions

SYMBOL	PARAMETER	TEST CONDITIONS			MIN	TYP ††	MAX	UNIT
V_{IL}*	Low-level input voltage						0.8	V
V_{IH}*	High-level input voltage				2			V
V_{IC}	Input clamp voltage	V_{CC} = MIN		I_I = −18mA		−0.8	−1.5	V
I_{IL}	Low-level input current †	V_{CC} = MAX		V_I = 0.4V		−0.02	−0.25	mA
I_{IH}	High-level input current †	V_{CC} = MAX		V_I = 2.4V			25	μA
I_I	Maximum input current	V_{CC} = MAX		V_I = 5.5V			1	mA
V_{OL}	Low-level output voltage	V_{CC} = MIN, V_{IL} = 0.8V, V_{IH} = 2V	10H8, 12H6, 14H4, 16H2, 16C1, 10L8, 12L6, 14L4, 16L2	MIL, COM I_{OL} = 8mA		0.3	0.5	V
			16L8 16R8 16R6 16R4 16X4 16A4	MIL I_{OL} = 12mA				
				COM I_{OL} = 24mA				
V_{OH}	High-level output voltage	V_{CC} = MIN, V_{IL} = 0.8V, V_{IH} = 2V	MIL	I_{OH} = −2mA	2.4	2.8		V
			COM	I_{OH} = −3.2mA				
I_{OZL}	Off-state output current †	V_{CC} = MAX, V_{IL} = 0.8V, V_{IH} = 2V	16L8 16R8 16R6 16R4 16X4 16A4	V_O = 0.4V			−100	μA
I_{OZH}				V_O = 2.4V			100	μA
I_{OS}	Output short-circuit current **	V_{CC} = 5V		V_O = 0V	−30	−70	−130	mA
I_{CC}	Supply current	V_{CC} = MAX	10H8, 12H6, 14H4, 16H2, 16C1, 10L8, 12L6, 14L4, 16L2			55	90	mA
			16R4, 16R6, 16R8, 16L8			See Table 1	180	mA
			16X4			160	225	mA
			16A4			170	240	mA

† I/O pin leakage is the worst case of I_{OZX} or I_{IX} e.g. I_{IL} and I_{OZH}

†† All typical values are at V_{CC} = 5V, T_A = 25°C.

* These are absolute voltages with respect to pin 10 on the device and includes all overshoots due to system and/or tester noise. Do not attempt to test these values without suitable equipment.

** Only one output shorted at a time.

Switching Characteristics

Over Operating Conditions

SYMBOL	PARAMETER		TEST CONDITIONS	MILITARY MIN	MILITARY TYP	MILITARY MAX	COMMERCIAL MIN	COMMERCIAL TYP	COMMERCIAL MAX	UNIT
t_{PD}	Input to output	10H8 12H6 14H4 16H2 10L8 12L6 14L4 16L2	$R_1 = 560\Omega$ $R_2 = 1.1k\Omega$		25	45		25	35	ns
		16C1			25	45		25	40	
t_{PD}	Input or feed-back to output	16R6 16R4 16L8	$R_1 = 200\Omega$ $R_2 = 390\Omega$		25	45		25	35	ns
		16X4 16A4			30	45		30	40	
t_{CLK}	Clock to output or feedback				15	25		15	25	ns
t_{PZY}	Pin 11 to output enable				15	25		15	25	ns
t_{PXZ}	Pin 11 to output disable				15	25		15	25	ns
t_{PZX}	Input to output enable	16R6 16R4 16L8			25	45		25	35	ns
		16X4 16A4			30	45		30	40	
t_{PXZ}	Input to output disable	16R6 16R4 16L8			25	45		25	35	ns
		16X4 16A4			30	45		30	40	
f_{MAX}	Maximum frequency	16R8 16R6 16R4		14	25		16	25		MHz
		16X4 16A4		12	22		14	22		

Test Load

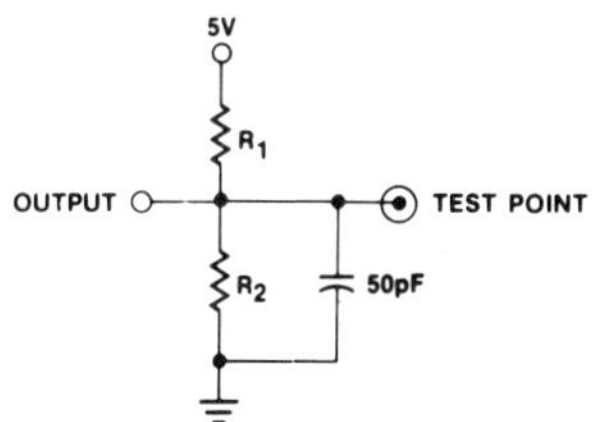

NUMBER OF PRODUCT TERMS	HAL16L8, 16R4 16R6, 16R8	HAL16X4	HAL16A4
0	99	97	108
1-4	101	101	113
5-8	104	106	117
9-12	106	110	122
13-16	108	115	126
17-20	110	119	131
21-24	113	124	135
25-28	115	128	140
29-32	117	133	144
33-36	119	137	149
37-40	122	142	153
41-44	124	146	158
45-48	126	151	162
49-52	128	155	167
53-56	131	160	171
57-60	133	164	176
61-64	135	169	180

Table 1. Typical I_{CC} vs. Number of Products Used

Schematic of Inputs and Outputs

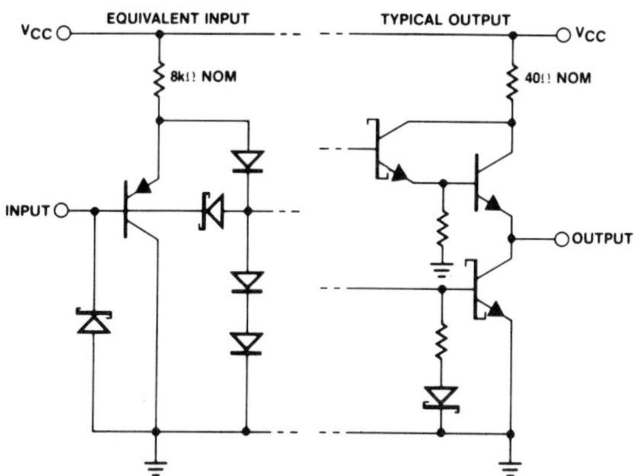

HAL 1246
PART NUMBER

HAL DESIGN SPECIFICATION

PN 1234	A	KAZMI	2/6/81
USER'S PART NUMBER	REV	NAME	DATE

BASIC GATES EXAMPLE
TITLE

MONOLITHIC MEMORIES, CALIFORNIA
COMPANY, CITY, STATE

C	D	F	G	M
PIN 1	PIN 2	PIN 3	PIN 4	PIN 5
N	P	Q	I	GND
PIN 6	PIN 7	PIN 8	PIN 9	PIN 10
J	K	L	R	O
PIN 11	PIN 12	PIN 13	PIN 14	PIN 15
H	E	B	A	VCC
PIN 16	PIN 17	PIN 18	PIN 19	PIN 20

EQUATIONS

```
B = /A                  ; INVERTER
E = C * D               ; AND GATE
H = F + G               ; OR GATE
L = /I + /J + /K        ; NAND GATE
O = /M * /N             ; NOR GATE
R = P * /Q + /P * Q     ; XOR GATE
```

DESCRIPTION

THIS EXAMPLE ILLUSTRATES ARRAY LOGIC TO IMPLEMENT BASIC GATES.

LEGEND:	= EQUAL	+ OR	:+: XOR	/ COMPLEMENT
	:= REPLACED BY	* AND	:*: XNOR	( ) THREE-STATE

F 110

FUNCTION TABLE

A	B	C	D	E
PIN A	PIN B	PIN C	PIN D	PIN E
F	G	H	I	J
PIN F	PIN G	PIN H	PIN I	PIN J
K	L	M	N	O
PIN K	PIN L	PIN M	PIN N	PIN O
P	Q	R		
PIN P	PIN Q	PIN R		

; INV AND OR NAND NOR XOR
COMMENT

;A	B	C	D	E	F	G	H	I	J	K	L	M	N	O	P	Q	R	COMMENT
A	B	C	D	E	F	G	H	I	J	K	L	M	N	O	P	Q	R	
L	H	X	X	X	X	X	X	X	X	X	X	X	X	X	X	X	X	INVERTER
H	L	X	X	X	X	X	X	X	X	X	X	X	X	X	X	X	X	INVERTER
X	X	L	L	L	X	X	X	X	X	X	X	X	X	X	X	X	X	AND
X	X	L	H	L	X	X	X	X	X	X	X	X	X	X	X	X	X	AND
X	X	H	L	L	X	X	X	X	X	X	X	X	X	X	X	X	X	AND
X	X	H	H	H	X	X	X	X	X	X	X	X	X	X	X	X	X	AND
X	X	X	X	X	L	L	L	X	X	X	X	X	X	X	X	X	X	OR
X	X	X	X	X	L	H	H	X	X	X	X	X	X	X	X	X	X	OR
X	X	X	X	X	H	L	H	X	X	X	X	X	X	X	X	X	X	OR
X	X	X	X	X	H	H	H	X	X	X	X	X	X	X	X	X	X	OR
X	X	X	X	X	X	X	X	L	L	L	H	X	X	X	X	X	X	NAND
X	X	X	X	X	X	X	X	L	L	H	H	X	X	X	X	X	X	NAND
X	X	X	X	X	X	X	X	L	H	L	H	X	X	X	X	X	X	NAND
X	X	X	X	X	X	X	X	H	L	L	H	X	X	X	X	X	X	NAND
X	X	X	X	X	X	X	X	H	H	H	L	X	X	X	X	X	X	NAND
X	X	X	X	X	X	X	X	X	X	X	X	L	L	H	X	X	X	NOR
X	X	X	X	X	X	X	X	X	X	X	X	L	H	L	X	X	X	NOR
X	X	X	X	X	X	X	X	X	X	X	X	H	L	L	X	X	X	NOR
X	X	X	X	X	X	X	X	X	X	X	X	H	H	L	X	X	X	NOR
X	X	X	X	X	X	X	X	X	X	X	X	X	X	X	L	L	L	XOR

LEGEND: H HIGH, L LOW, C CLOCK, X IRRELEVANT, Z OFF

F 109

PAL
IMPORTANT,
NOTES

Logic Diagram HAL10H8

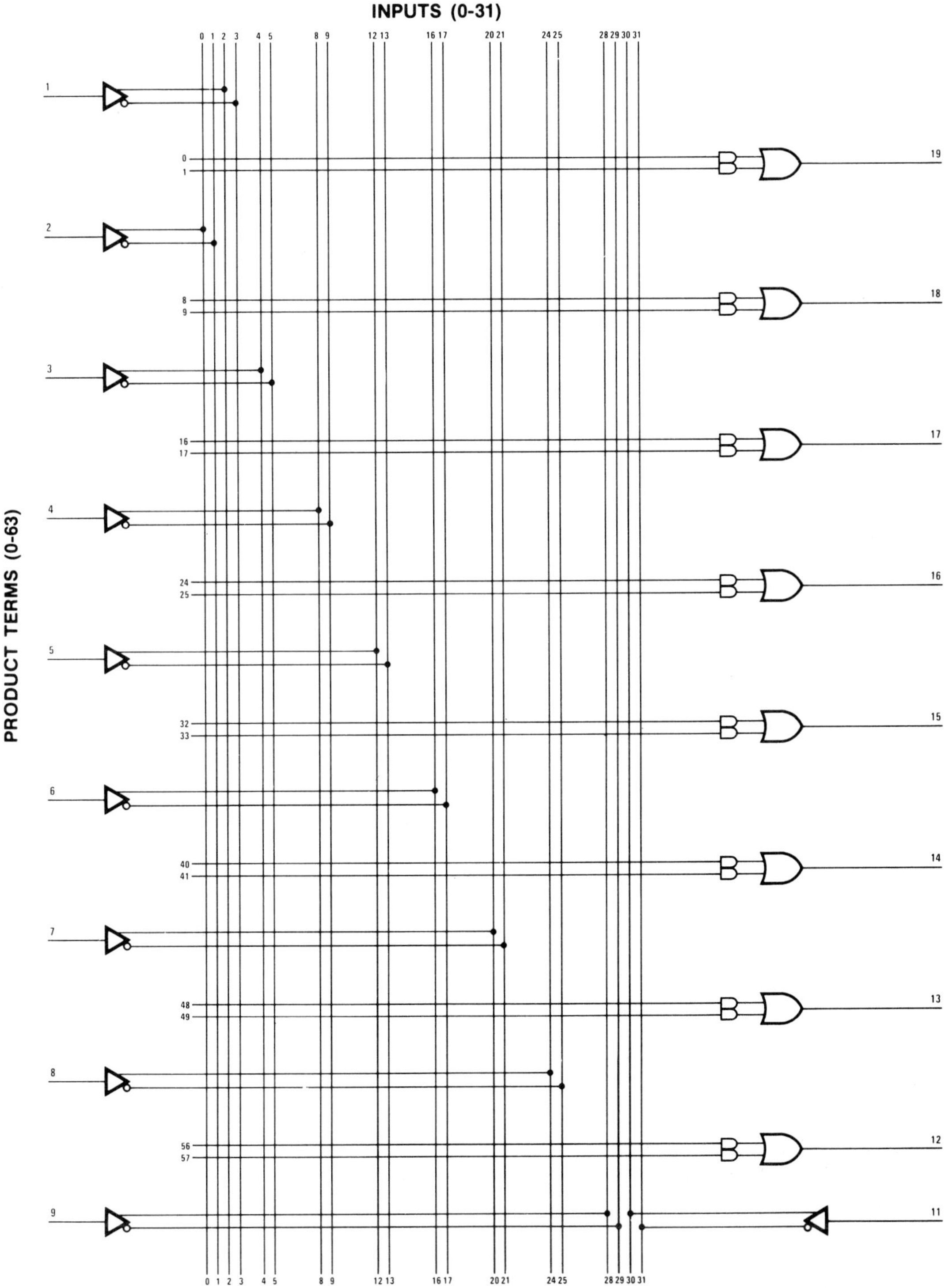

Logic Diagram HAL12H6

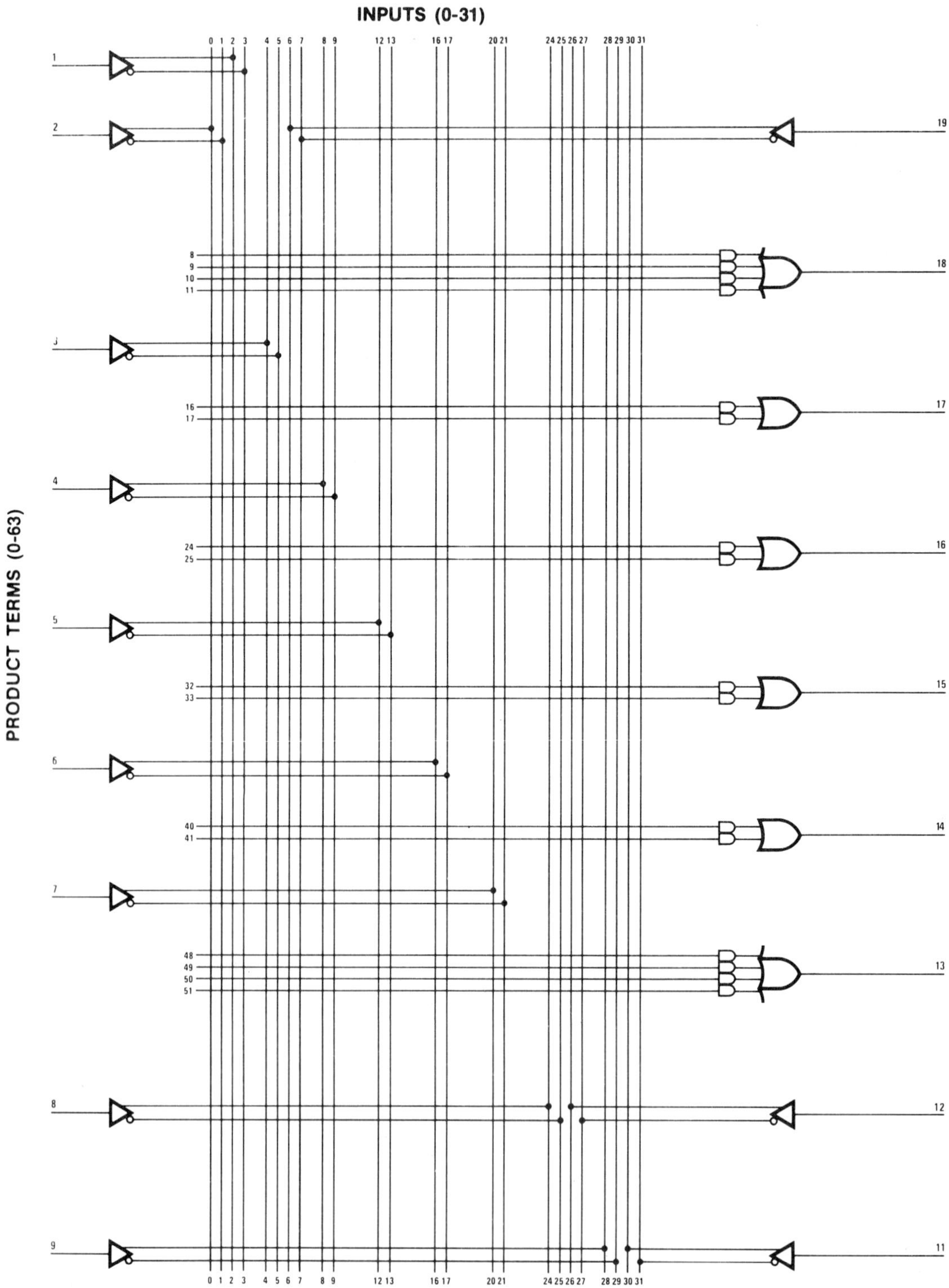

Logic Diagram HAL14H4

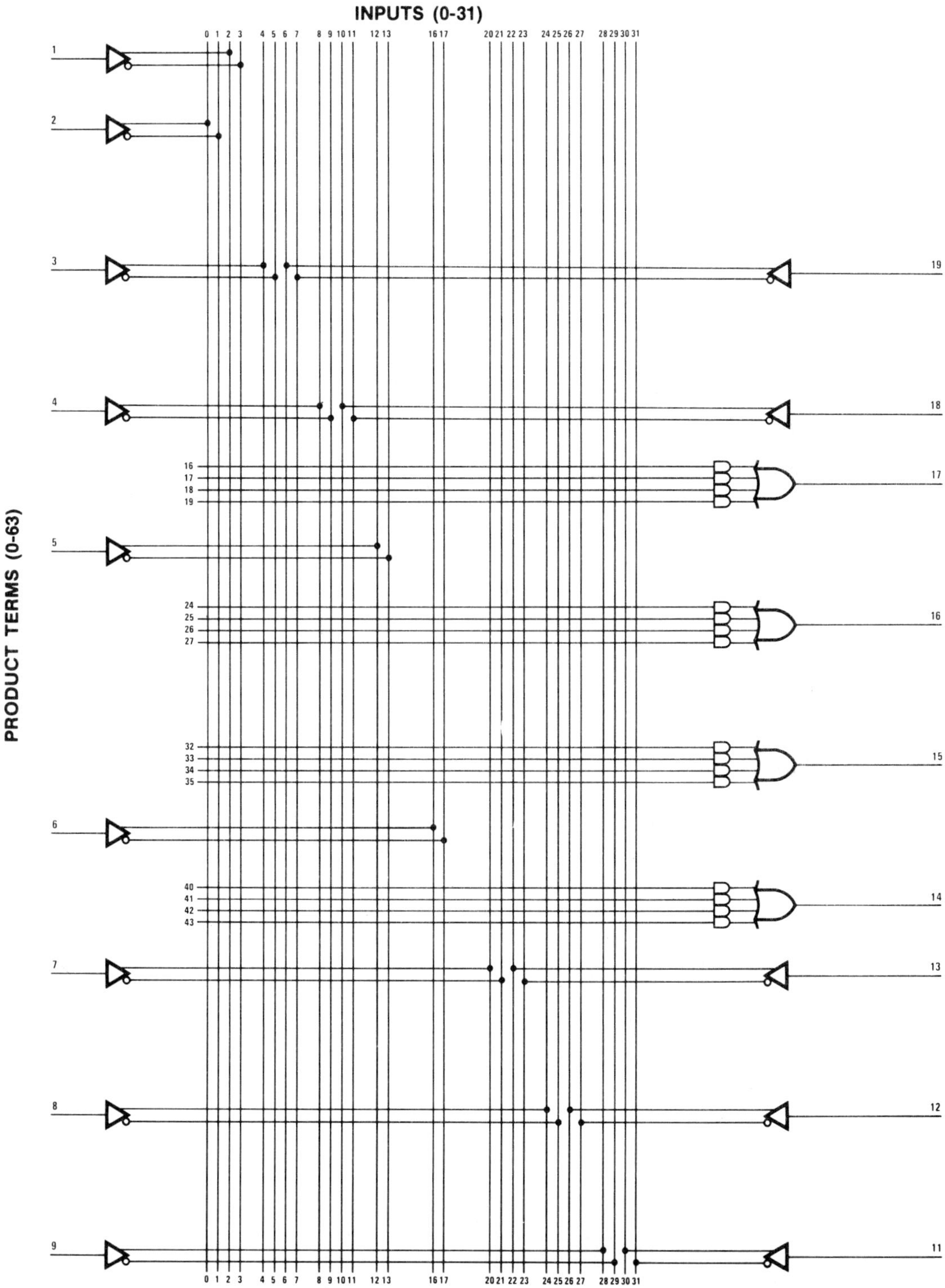

Logic Diagram HAL16H2

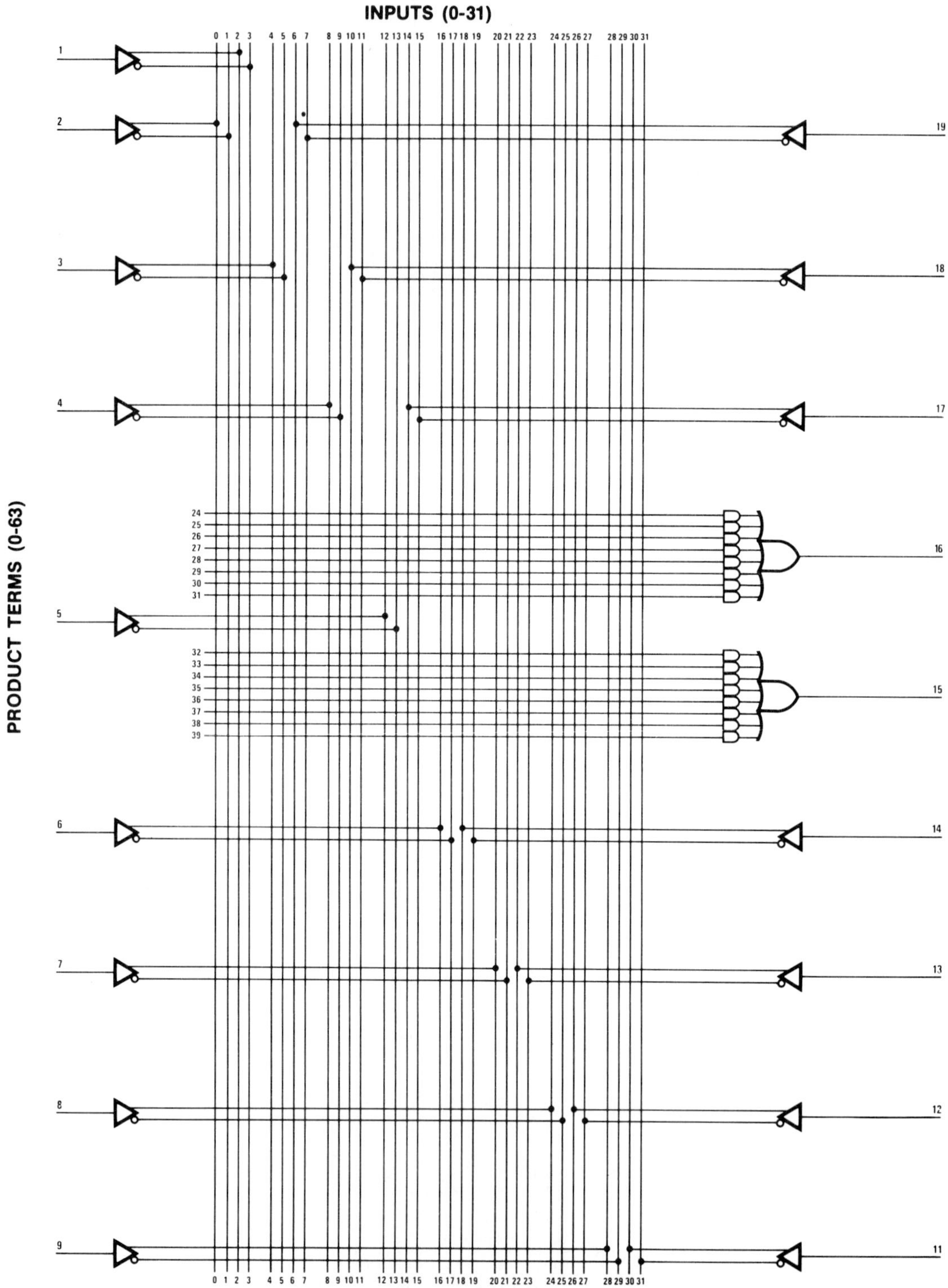

Logic Diagram HAL16C1

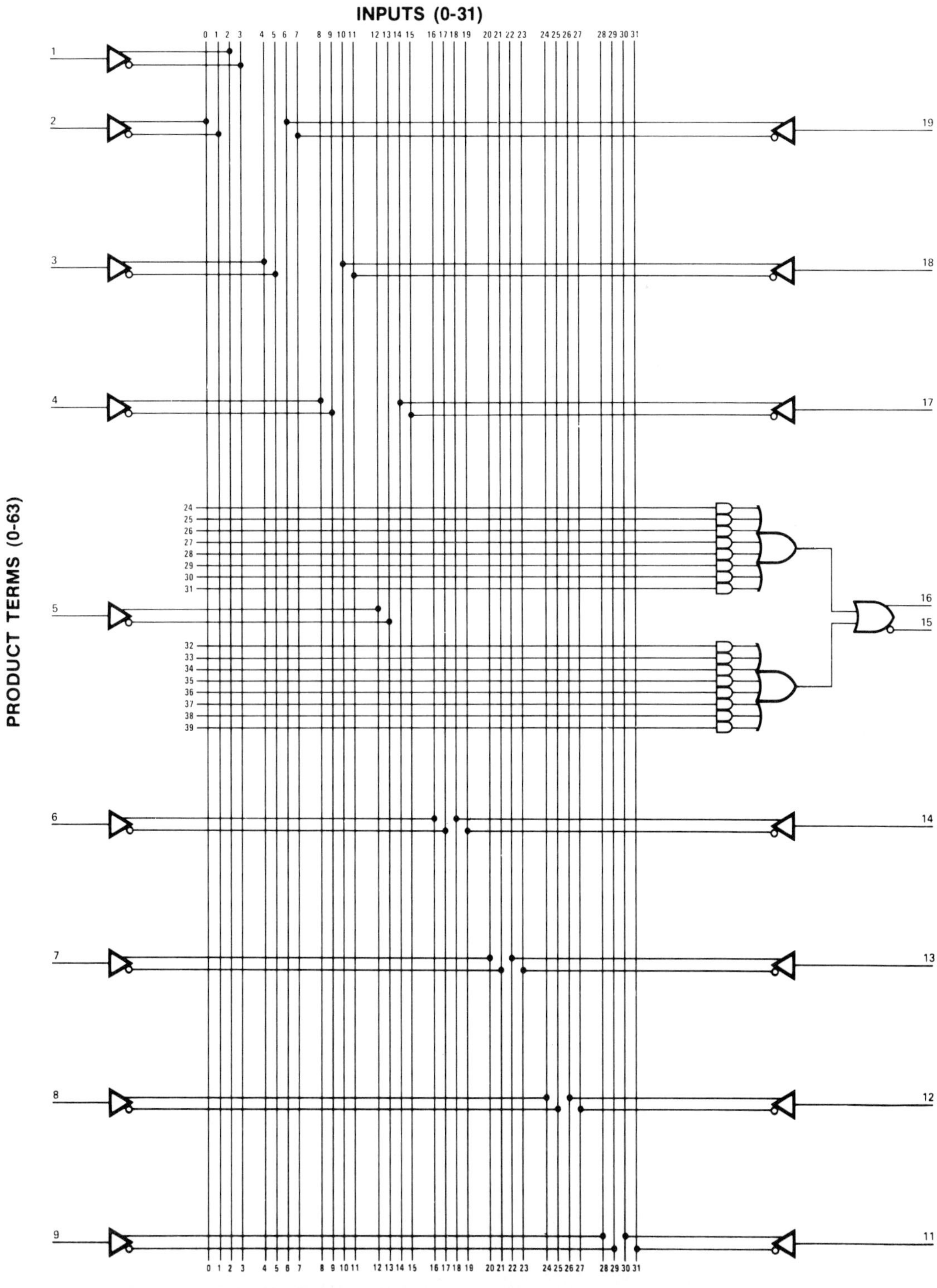

Logic Diagram HAL10L8

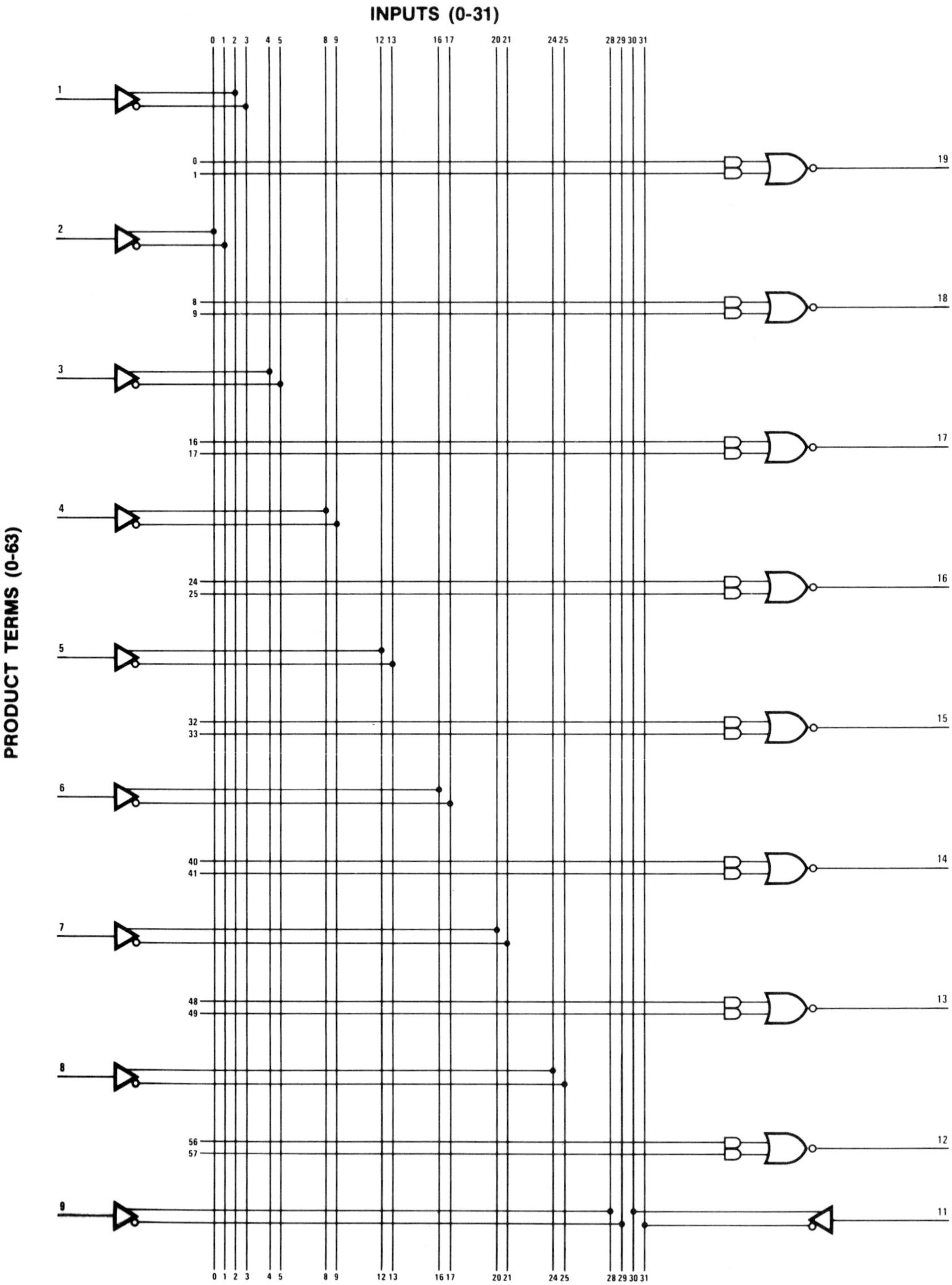

Logic Diagram HAL12L6

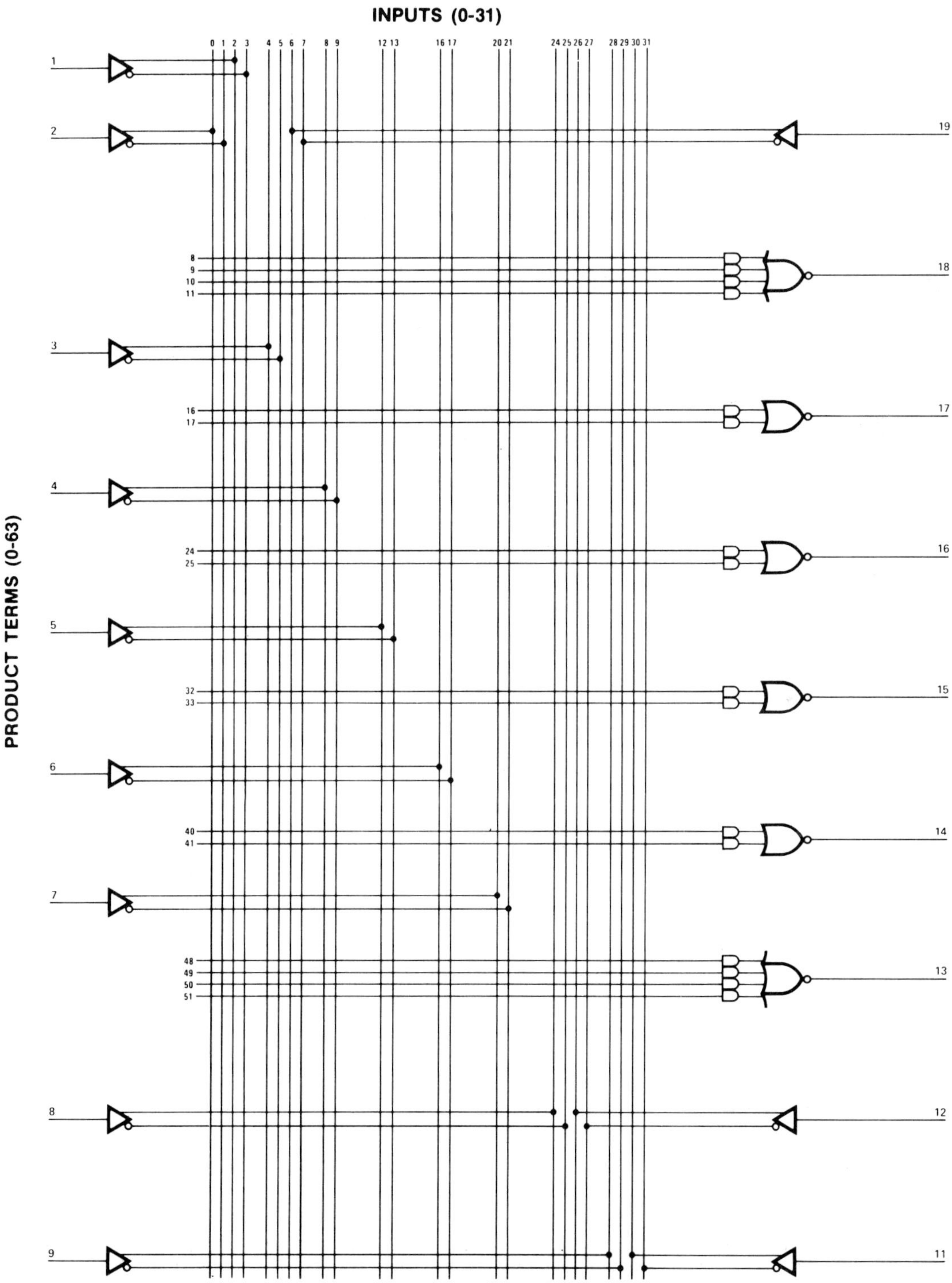

Logic Diagram HAL14L4

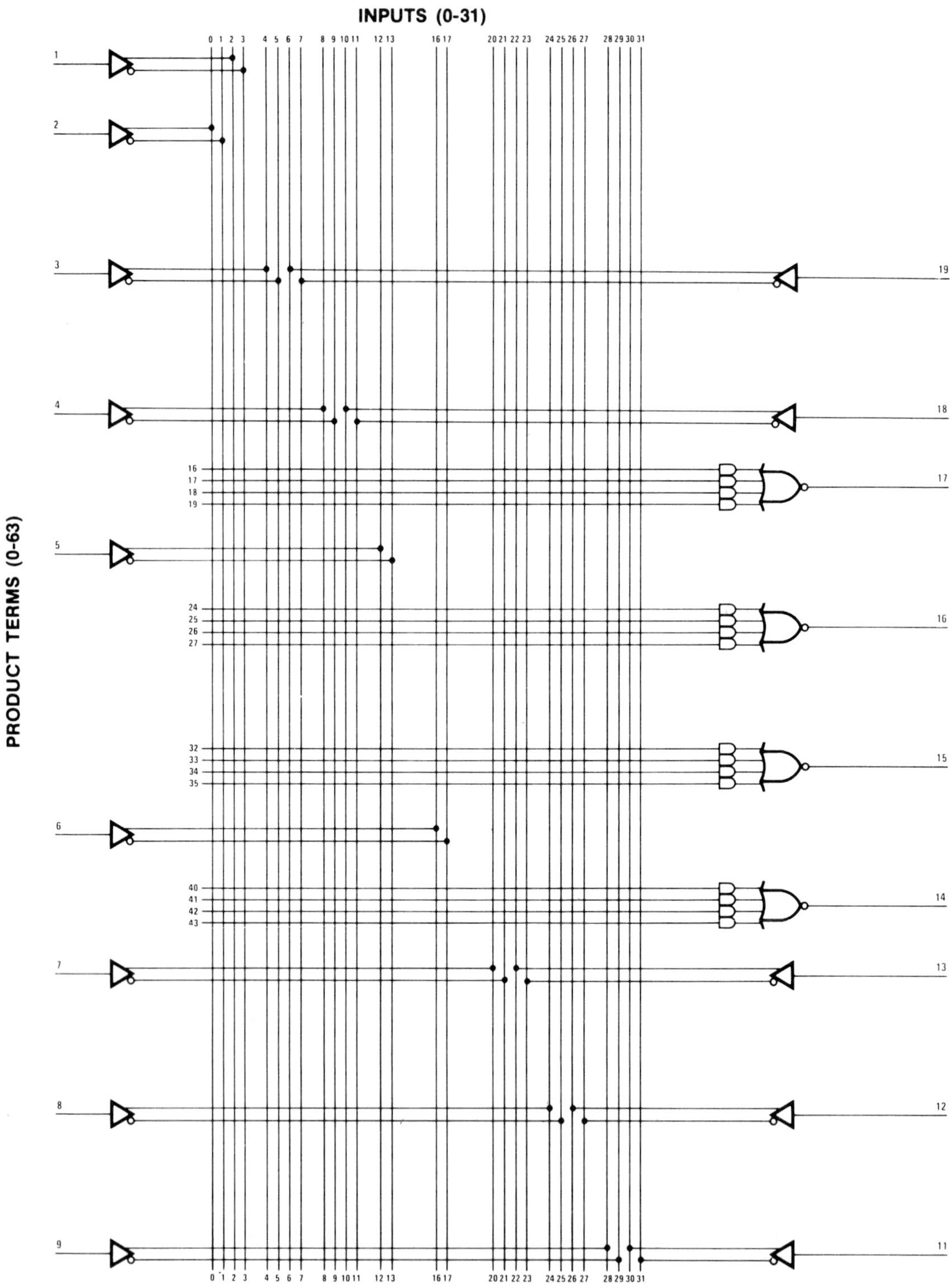

Logic Diagram HAL16L2

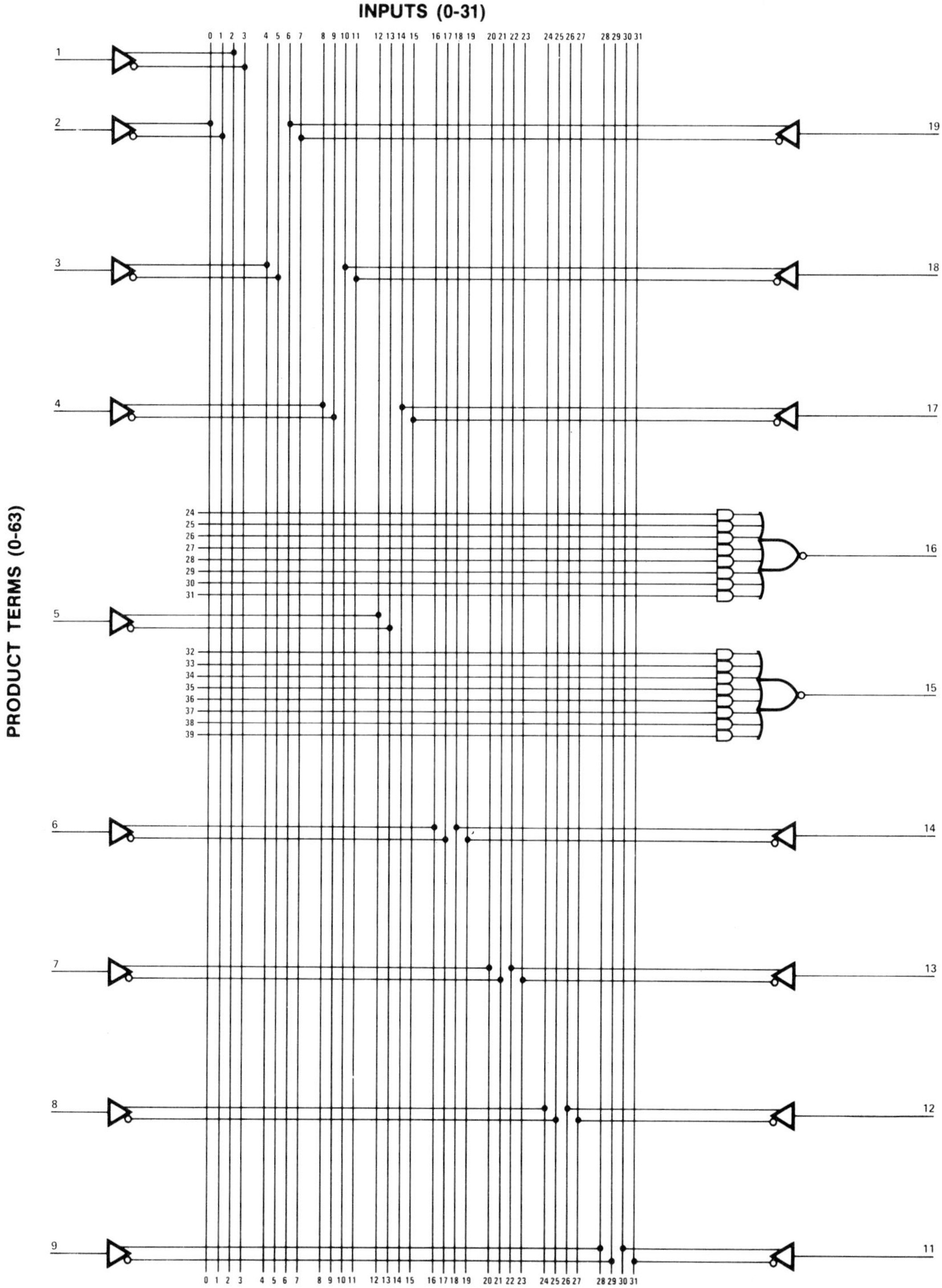

Logic Diagram HAL16L8

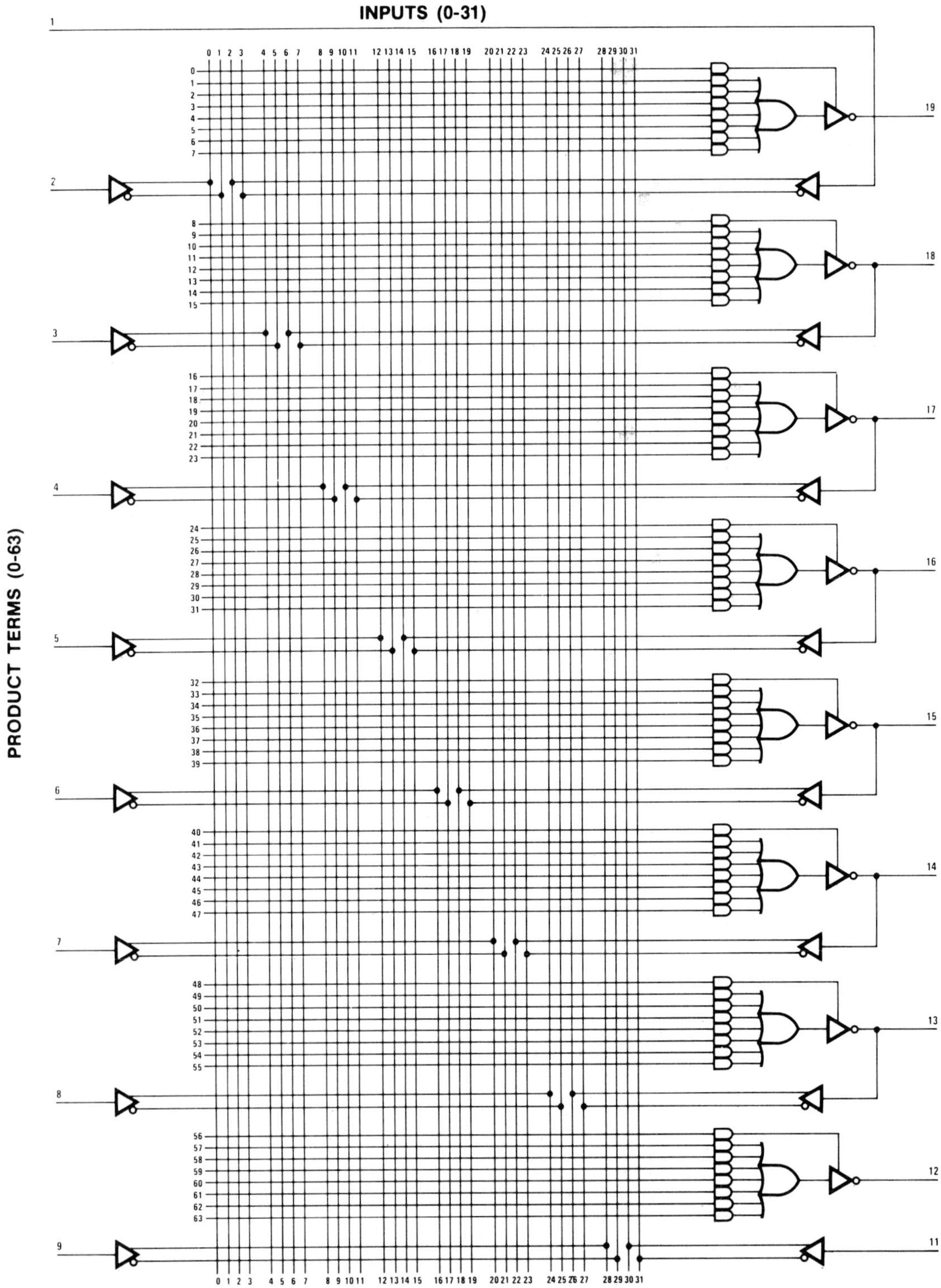

Logic Diagram HAL16R8

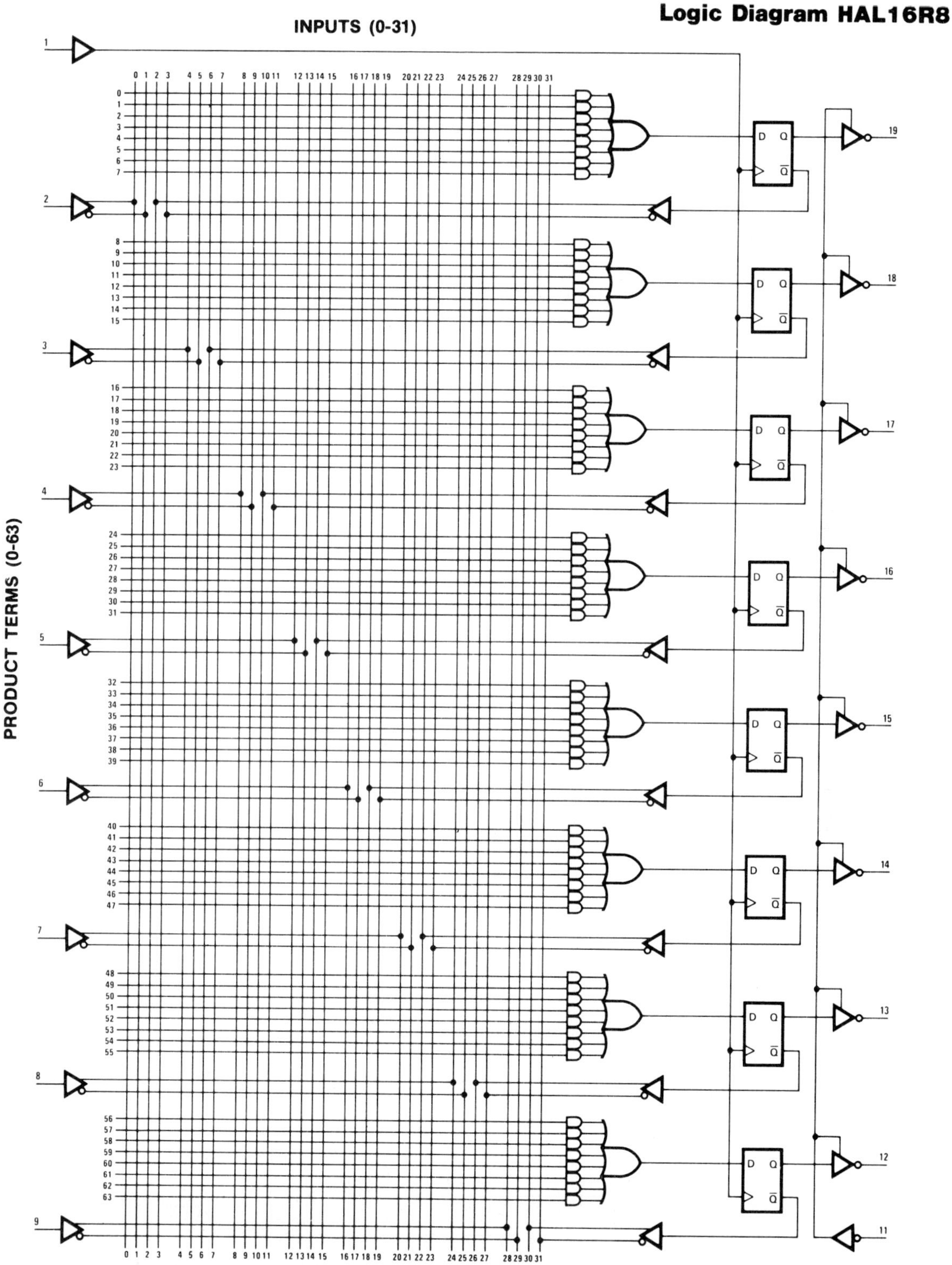

Logic Diagram HAL16R6

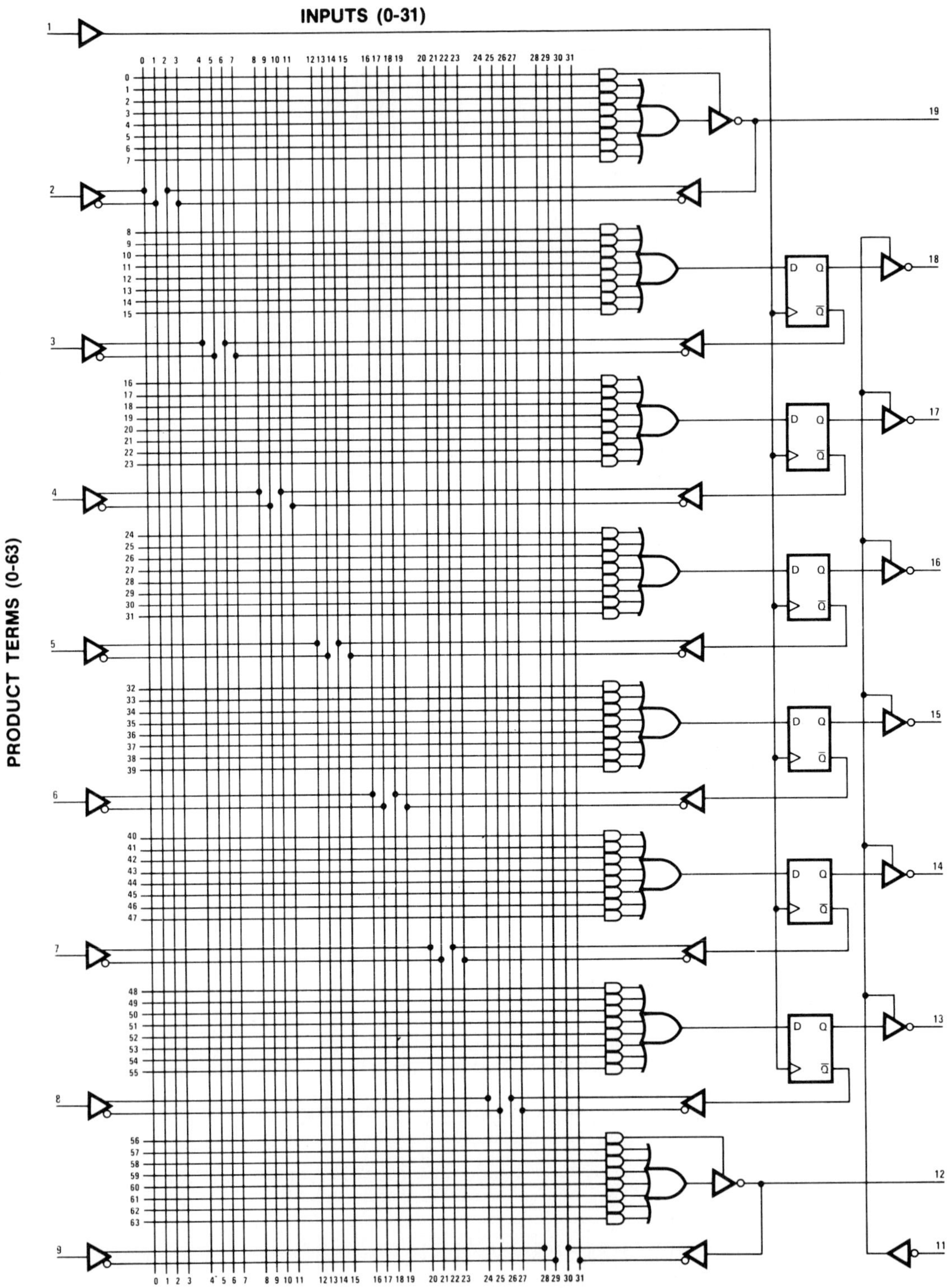

Logic Diagram HAL16R4

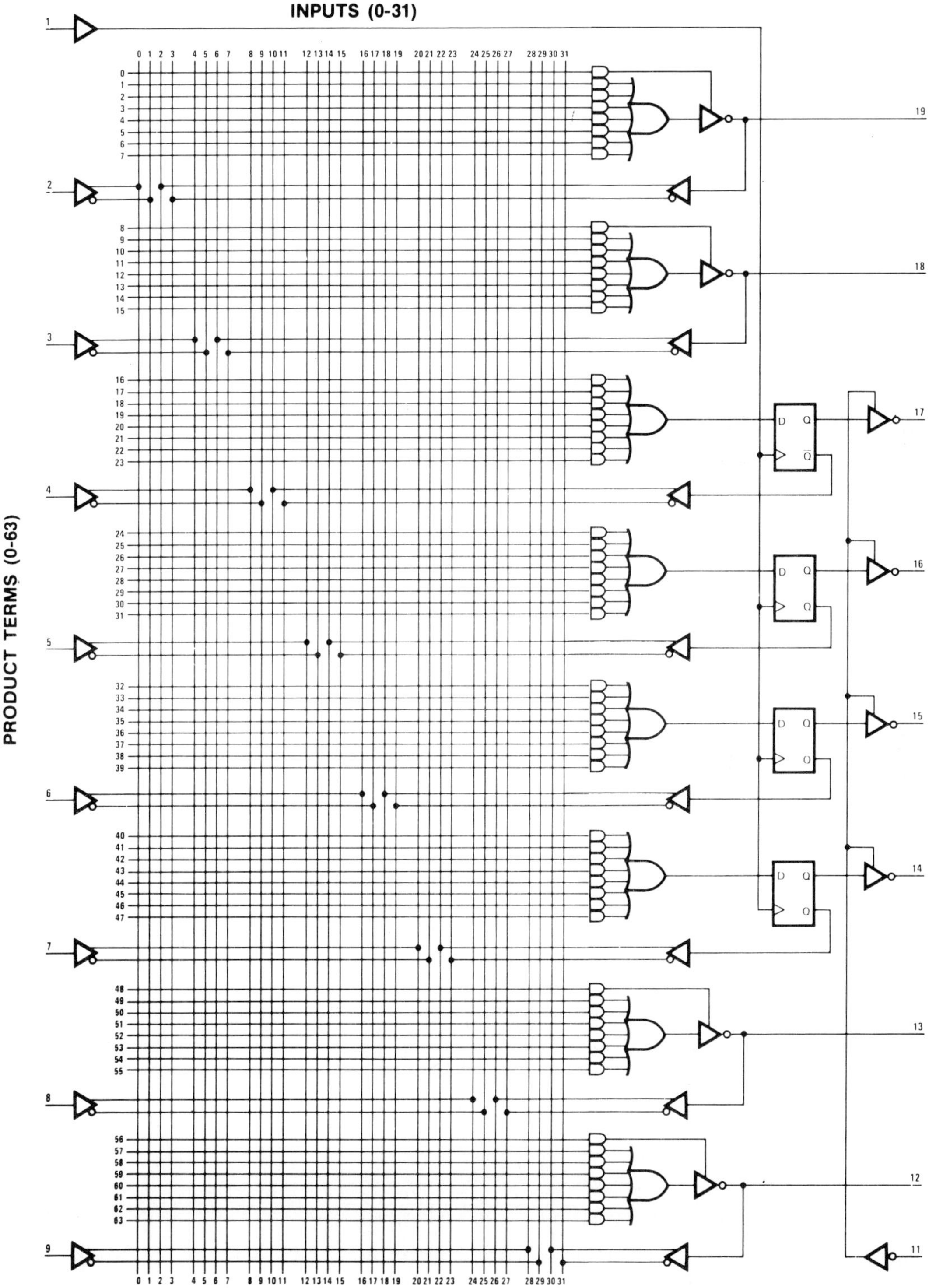

Logic Diagram HAL16X4

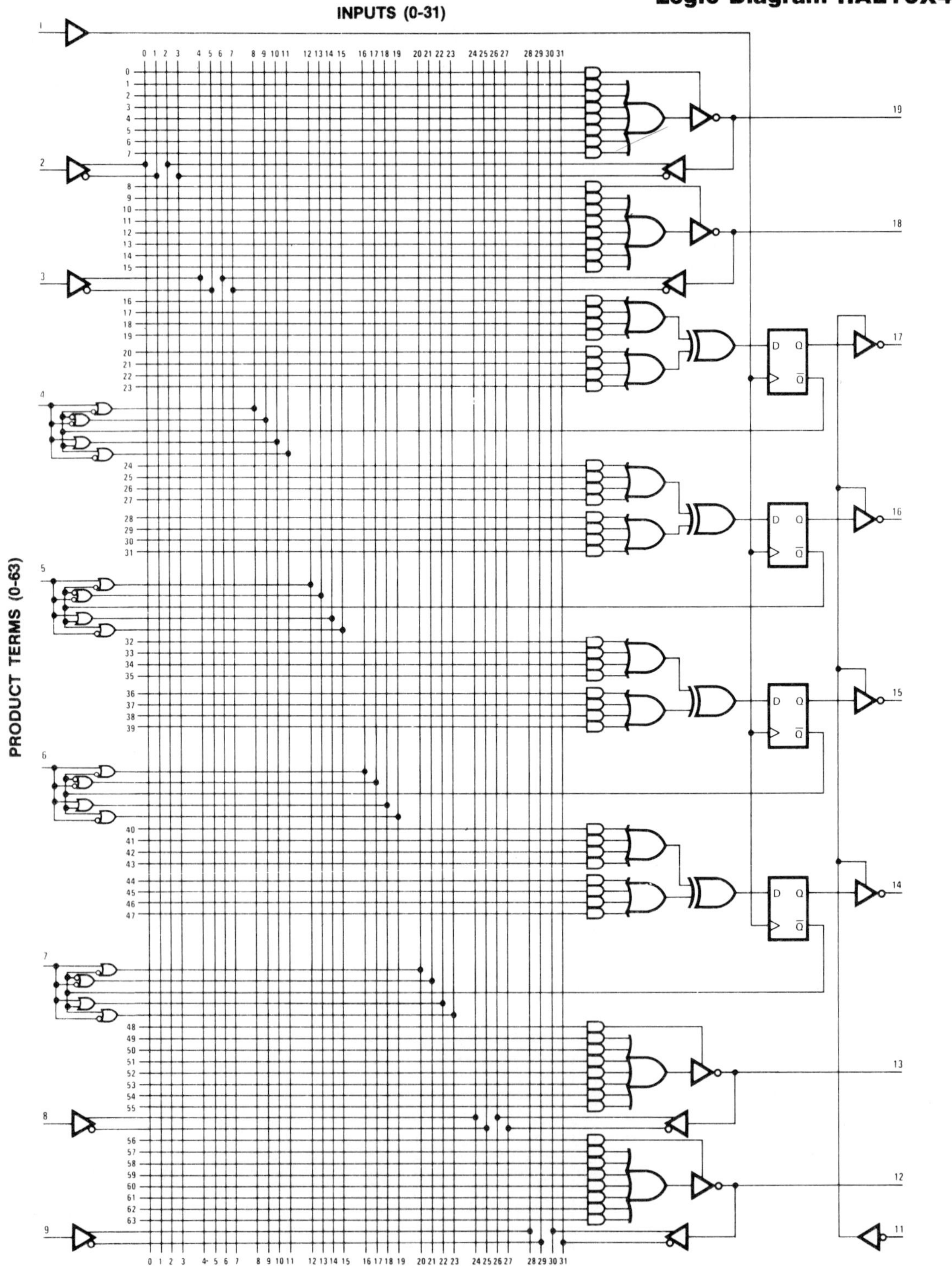

Logic Diagram HAL16A4

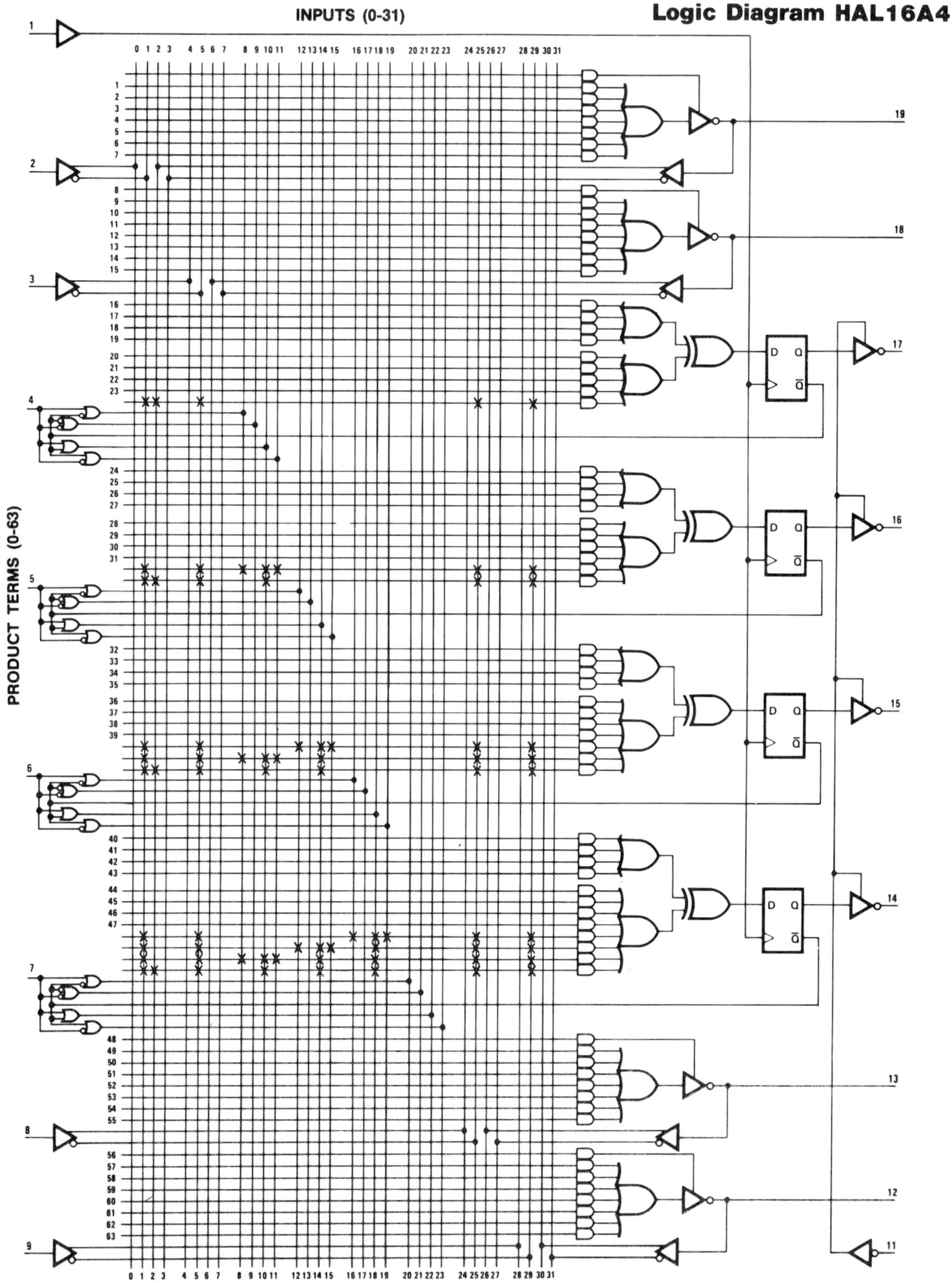

HAL
PART NUMBER

HAL DESIGN SPECIFICATION

USER'S PART NUMBER | REV | NAME | DATE / /

TITLE

COMPANY, CITY, STATE

PIN 1	PIN 2	PIN 3	PIN 4	PIN 5
PIN 6	PIN 7	PIN 8	PIN 9	GND PIN 10
PIN 11	PIN 12	PIN 13	PIN 14	PIN 15
PIN 16	PIN 17	PIN 18	PIN 19	VCC PIN 20

EQUATIONS

DESCRIPTION

LEGEND:

= EQUAL	+ OR	:+: XOR	/ COMPLEMENT
:= REPLACED BY	* AND	:*: XNOR	( ) THREE-STATE

F 110

FUNCTION TABLE

______ PIN A	______ PIN B	______ PIN C	______ PIN D	______ PIN E
______ PIN F	______ PIN G	______ PIN H	______ PIN I	______ PIN J
______ PIN K	______ PIN L	______ PIN M	______ PIN N	______ PIN O
______ PIN P	______ PIN Q	______ PIN R		

; ____
COMMENT

A	B	C	D	E	F	G	H	I	J	K	L	M	N	O	P	Q	R	COMMENT

LEGEND: H HIGH, L LOW, C CLOCK, X IRRELEVANT, Z OFF

F 109

Hard Array Logic Family

HAL Series 24 Data Sheet

Features/Benefits

- **Gate array equivalent of up to 300 gates.**
- **Semi-custom solution**
- **Reduces SSI/MSI chip count greater than 5 to 1**
- **Prototype using field-programmable version — PAL.**
- **Cost savings up to 40% compared to PAL**
- **Security link disabled for design secrecy.**
- **Test and simulation made simple with PALASM Function Table**
- **Saves space with 24-pin SKINNYDIP™ packages**

Description

The HAL family utilizes standard Low-Power Schottky TTL process and automated mask pattern generation directly from logic equations to provide a semi-custom gate array for replacing conventional SSI/MSI gates and flip-flops at reduced chip count.

The family lets the systems engineer "design his own chip" by AND and OR gates to perform his desired logic function. Complex interconnections which previously required time-consuming layout are thus "lifted" from PC board etch and placed on silicon where they can be easily modified during prototype check-out or production.

The HAL transfer function is the familiar sum of products. Like the ROM, the HAL has a single array of selectable gates. Unlike the ROM, the HAL is a selectable AND array driving a fixed OR array (the ROM is a fixed AND array driving a selectable OR array). In addition the HAL provides thee options:

- Variable input/output pin ratio
- Programmable three-state outputs
- Registers with feedback
- Exclusive-OR gates

Unused inputs are tied directly to V_{CC} or GND. Product terms with all fuses blown assume the logical high state, and product terms connected to both true and complement of any single input assume the logical low state. Registers consist of D type flip-flops which are loaded on the low-to-high transition of the clock. HAL Logic Diagrams are shown with all fuses blown, enabling the designer to use the diagrams as coding sheets.

SKINNYDIP is a registered trademark of Monolithic Memories

PART NUMBER	PKG	DESCRIPTION
HAL12L10	J,N,F	Deca 12 Input And-Or-Invert Gate Array
HAL14L8	J,N,F	Octal 14 Input And-Or-Invert Gate Array
HAL16L6	J,N,F	Hex 16 Input And-Or-Invert Gate Array
HAL18L4	J,N,F	Quad 18 Input And-Or-Invert Gate Array
HAL20L2	J,N,F	Dual 20 Input And-Or-Invert Gate Array
HAL20C1	J,N,F	20 Input And-Or/And-Or Invert Gate Array
HAL20L10	J,N,F	Deca 20 Input And-Or-Invert Gate Array
HAL20X10	J,N,F	Deca 20 Input Registered And-Or-Xor Gate Array
HAL20X8	J,N,F	Octal 20 Input Registered And-Or-Xor Gate Array
HAL20X4	J,N,F	Quad 20 Input Registered And-Or-Xor Gate Array

To design a HAL, the user first programs and debugs a PAL using PALASM and the "PAL DESIGN SPECIFICATION" standard format. This specification is submitted to Monolithic Memories where it is computer processed and assigned a bit pattern number, e.g., P01234. Monolithic Memories accepts the PAL DESIGN SPECIFICATION in one of three forms:

1. Computer generated listing.
2. Typed or hand-written forms F107 and F108. See example on pages 7-30, 7-31 and forms on pages 7-42 and 7-43.
3. Direct online data transmission to Monolithic Memories Timeshare computer system via telephone (local telephone network to major US cities, London and Paris) or TWX (online Boston TWX no.).

Monolithic Memories will provide a PAL sample for customer qualification. The user then submits a purchase order for a HAL of the specified bit pattern number, e.g., HAL18L4 P01234. See Ordering Information below.

Ordering Information

HAL 18 L4 CJ 883B P01234

- HAL — HARD ARRAY LOGIC FAMILY
- 18 — NUMBER OF ARRAY INPUTS
- L — OUTPUT TYPE
  - L = ACTIVE LOW
  - C = COMPLEMENTARY
  - X = EXCLUSIVE-OR REGISTERED
- 4 — NUMBER OF OUTPUTS
- C — TEMPERATURE RANGE
  - C = 0C TO +75C
  - M = -55C TO +125C (CASE TEMPERATURE)
- J — PACKAGE
  - N = PLASTIC DIP
  - J = CERAMIC DIP
  - F = FLAT PACK
- 883B — OPTIONAL HI-REL PROCESSING
  - 883B = MIL-STD-883, METHOD 5004 & 5005 LEVEL B
  - 883C = MIL-STD-883, METHOD 5004 & 5005 LEVEL C
  - B = MIL-STD-883, METHOD 5004 EQUIVALENT
  - C = MIL-STD-883, METHOD 5004 EQUIVALENT
- P01234 — BIT PATTERN NUMBER

HAL12L10

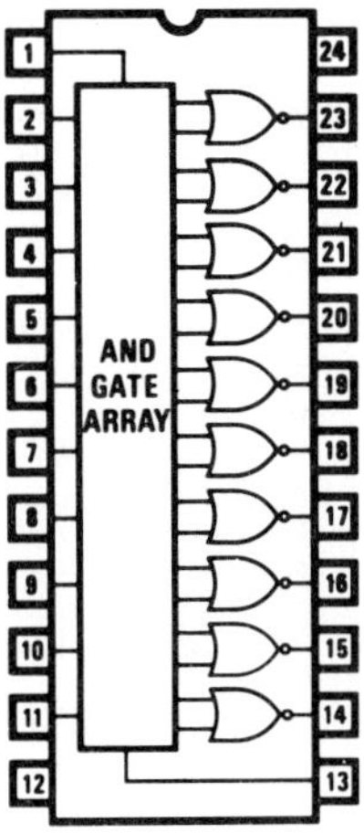

HAL14L8

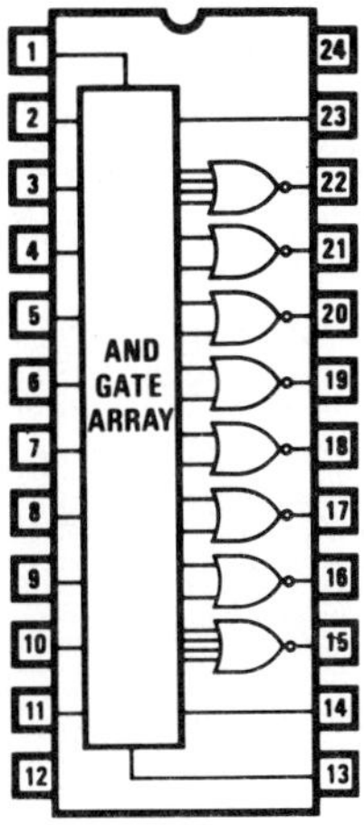

HAL16L6

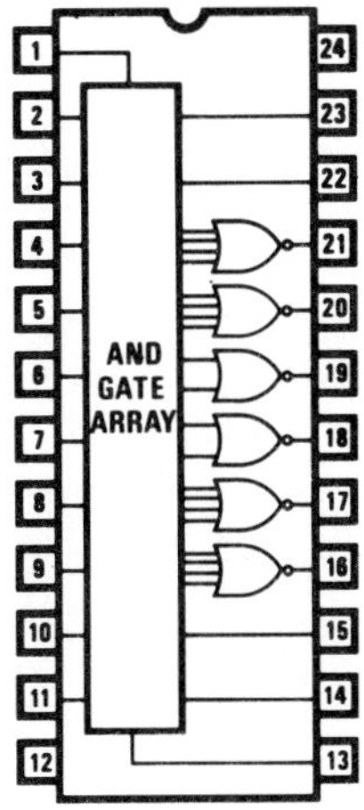

HAL18L4

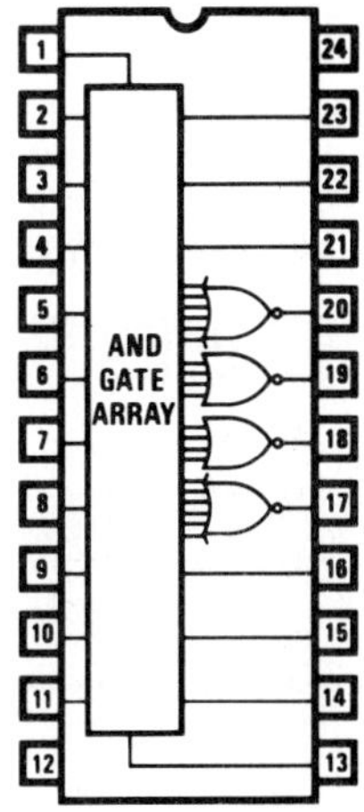

HAL20L2

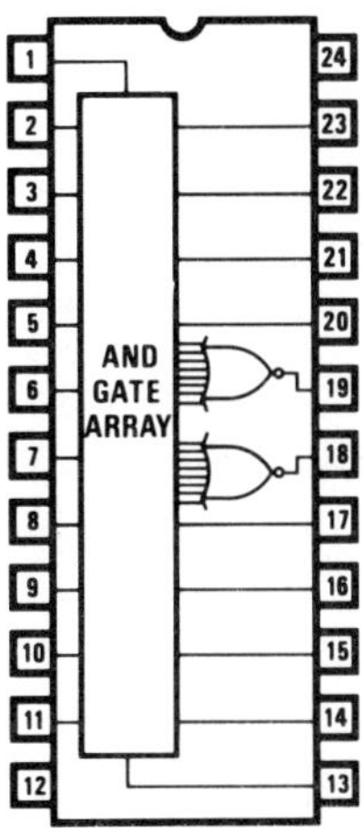

HAL20C1

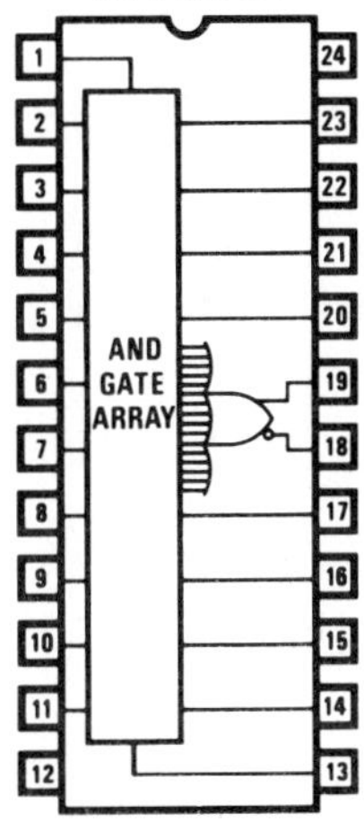

HAL20L10

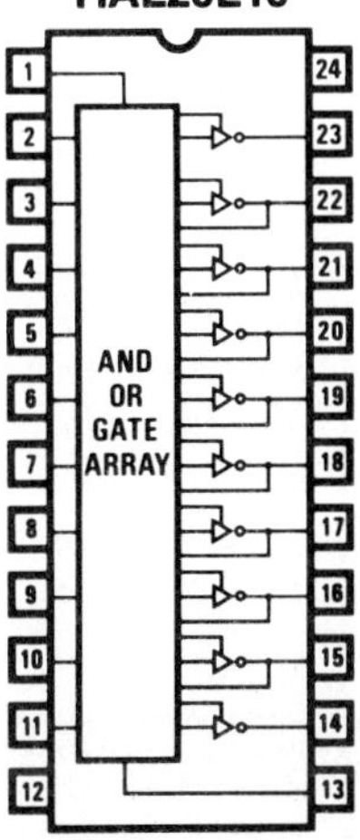

HAL20X10

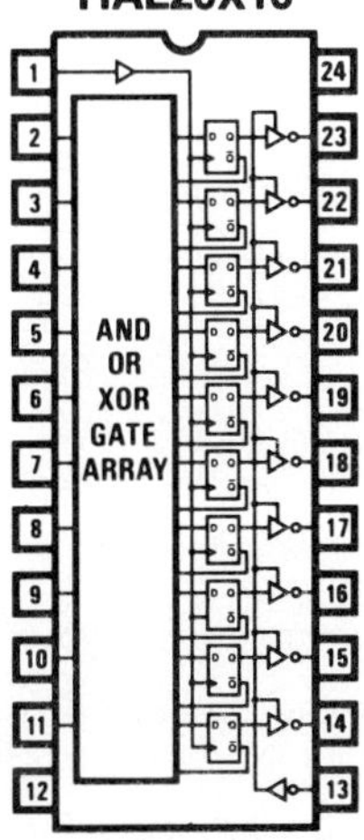

HAL20X8

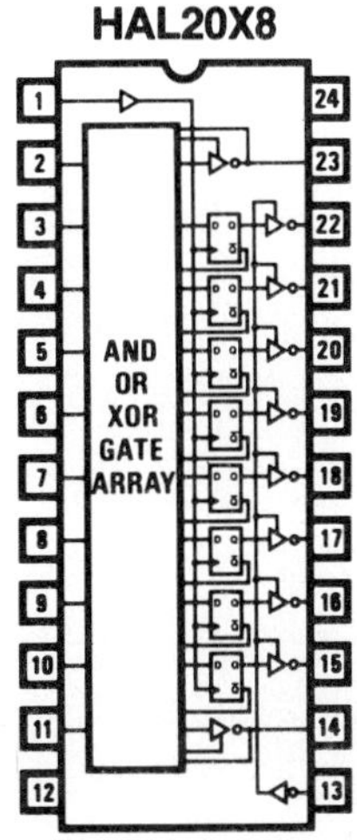

HAL20X4

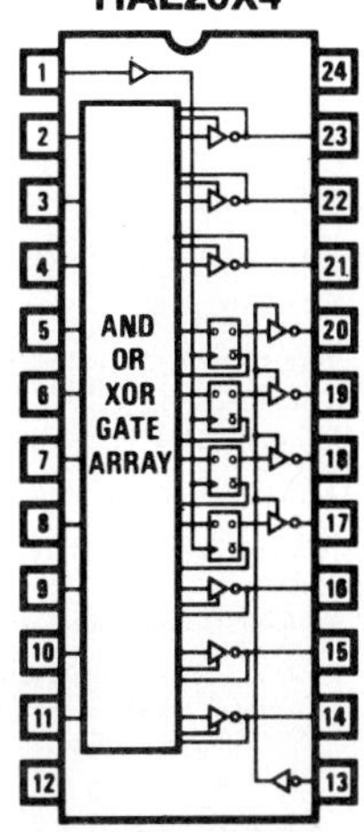

Absolute Maximum Ratings

	Operating	Programming
Supply Voltage, VCC	7	12V
Input Voltage	5.5V	12V*
Off-state output Voltage	5.5V	12V
Storage temperature	−65° to +150°C	

Operating Conditions

SYMBOL	PARAMETER		MILITARY MIN	MILITARY TYP	MILITARY MAX	COMMERCIAL MIN	COMMERCIAL TYP	COMMERCIAL MAX	UNIT
V_{CC}	Supply voltage		4.5	5	5.5	4.75	5	5.25	V
t_w	Width of clock	Low	40	20		35	20		ns
		High	30	10		25	10		
t_{su}	Set up time		60	38		50	38		ns
t_h	Hold time		0	−15		0	−15		
T_A	Operating free air temperature		−55			0		75	°C
T_C	Operating case temperature				125				°C

Electrical Characteristics Over Operating Conditions

SYMBOL	PARAMETER	TEST CONDITIONS			MIN	TYP††	MAX	UNIT
V_{IL}	Low-level input voltage						0.8	V
V_{IH}	High-level input voltage				2			V
V_{IC}	Input clamp voltage	V_{CC} = MIN	I_I = −18mA			−0.8	−1.5	V
I_{IL}	Low-level input current †	V_{CC} = MAX	V_I = 0.4V			−0.02	−0.25	mA
I_{IH}	High-level input current †	V_{CC} = MAX	V_I = 2.4V				25	μA
I_I	Maximum input current	V_{CC} = MAX	V_I = 5.5V				1	mA
V_{OL}	Low-level output voltage	V_{CC} = MIN, V_{IL} = 0.8V, V_{IH} = 2V	12L10, 14L8, 16L6, 18L4, 20L2, 20C1	I_{OL} = 8mA		0.3	0.5	V
			20L10, 20X10, 20X8, 20X4	MIL I_{OL} = 12mA				
				COM I_{OL} = 24mA				
V_{OH}	High-level output voltage	V_{CC} = MIN, V_{IL} = 0.8V, V_{IH} = 2V	I_{OH} = −2mA	MIL	2.4	2.8		V
			I_{OH} = −3.2mA	COM				
I_{OZL}	Off-state output current †	V_{CC} = MAX, V_{IL} = 0.8V, V_{IH} = 2V	V_O = 0.4V				−100	μA
I_{OZH}			V_O = 2.4V				100	μA
I_{OS}	Output short-circuit current**	V_{CC} = 5V	V_O = 0V		−30	−70	−130	mA
I_{CC}	Supply current	V_{CC} = MAX	12L10, 14L8, 16L6, 18L4, 20L2, 20C1			60	100	mA
			20X4, 20X8, 20X10			120	180	
			20L10			90	165	

† I/O pin leakage is the worst case of I_{OZX} or I_{IX} e.g. I_{IX} and I_{OZH}

†† All typical values are at V_{CC} = 5V, T_A = 25°C.

* Pins 1 and 13 may be raised to 22V max.

** Only one output shorted at a time.

Switching Characteristics

Over Operating Conditions

SYMBOL	PARAMETER	TEST CONDITIONS	MILITARY MIN	MILITARY TYP	MILITARY MAX	COMMERCIAL MIN	COMMERCIAL TYP	COMMERCIAL MAX	UNIT
t_{PD}	Input to output — 12L10, 14L8, 16L6, 18L4, 20L2, 20C1	R_1 = 560Ω, R_2 = 1.1kΩ		25	45		25	40	ns
t_{PD}	Input or feedback to output	20L10, 20X10, 20X8, 20X4, R_1 = 200Ω, R_2 = 390Ω		35	60		35	50	ns
t_{CLK}	Clock to output or feedback			20	35		20	30	ns
t_{PZX}	Pin 13 to output enable			20	45		20	35	ns
t_{PXZ}	Pin 13 to output disable			20	45		20	35	ns
t_{PZX}	Input to output enable			35	55		35	45	ns
t_{PXZ}	Input to output disable			35	55		35	45	ns
f_{MAX}	Maximum frequency		10.5	16		12.5	16		MHz

Test Load

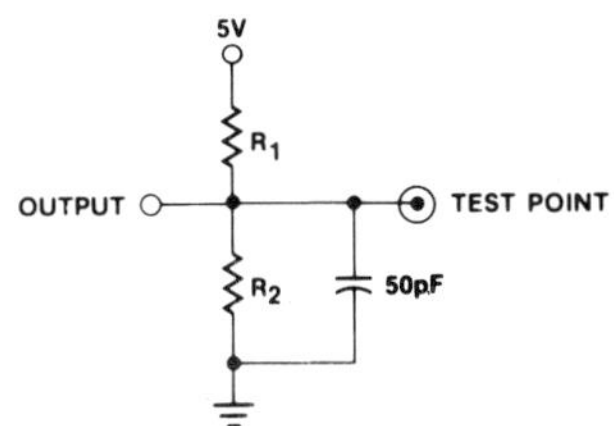

Schematic of Inputs and Outputs

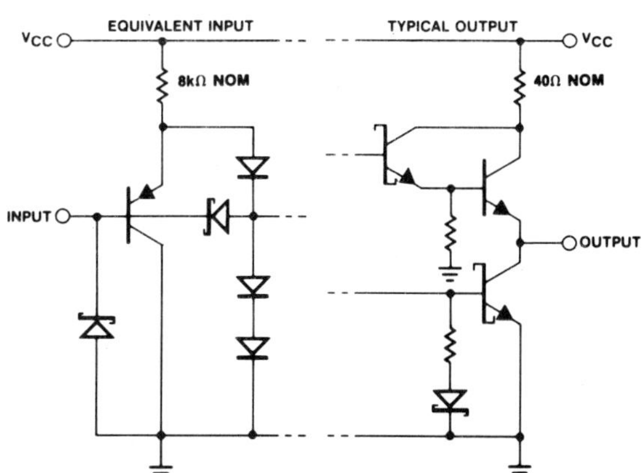

HAL 20X10 **HAL DESIGN SPECIFICATION**

PART NUMBER	REV	NAME	DATE
INT 8C2	0	BIRKNER	2/28/81

USER'S PART NUMBER

NONAL REGISTER

TITLE

MMI SUNNYVALE, CA

COMPANY, CITY, STATE

CK	D0	D1	D2	D3	D4
PIN 1	PIN 2	PIN 3	PIN 4	PIN 5	PIN 6
D5	D6	D7	D8	/LD	GND
PIN 7	PIN 8	PIN 9	PIN 10	PIN 11	PIN 12
IOE	NC	Q8	Q7	Q7	Q5
PIN 13	PIN 14	PIN 15	PIN 16	PIN 17	PIN 18
Q4	Q3	Q2	Q1	Q0	VCC
PIN 19	PIN 20	PIN 21	PIN 22	PIN 23	PIN 24

EQUATIONS

```
/Q0 := /Q0 * /LD        ; HOLD Q0
     + /D0 * LD         ; LOAD D0
/Q1 := /Q1 * /LD        ; HOLD Q1
     + /D1 * LD         ; LOAD D1
/Q2 := /Q2 * /LD        ; HOLD Q2
     + /D2 * LD         ; LOAD D2
/Q3 := /Q3 * /LD        ; HOLD Q3
     + /D3 * LD         ; LOAD D3
/Q4 := /Q4 * /LD        ; HOLD Q4
     + /D4 * LD         ; LOAD D4
/Q5 := /Q5 * /LD        ; HOLD Q5
     + /D5 * LD         ; LOAD D5
/Q6 := /Q6 * /LD        ; HOLD Q6
     + /D6 * LD         ; LOAD D6
/Q7 := /Q7 * /LD        ; HOLD Q7
     + /D7 * LD         ; LOAD D7
/Q8 := /Q8 * /LD        ; HOLD Q8
     + /D8 * LD         ; LOAD D8
```

DESCRIPTION:

THE NONAL REGISTER IS A 9-BIT REGISTER THAT LOADS THE DATA INPUTS IF LOAD LINE IS SELECTED OTHERWISE HOLDS THE ORIGINAL DATA.

LEGEND:	= EQUAL	+ OR	:+: XOR	/ COMPLEMENT
	:= REPLACED BY	* AND	:*: XNOR	( ) THREE-STATE

F 108

FUNCTION TABLE

CK	OE	LD	D8	D7	D6
PIN A	PIN B	PIN C	PIN D	PIN E	PIN F
D5	D4	D3	D2	D1	D0
PIN G	PIN H	PIN I	PIN J	PIN K	PIN L
Q8	Q7	Q6	Q5	Q4	Q3
PIN M	PIN N	PIN O	PIN P	PIN Q	PIN R
Q2	Q1	Q0			
PIN S	PIN T	PIN U	PIN V		

; DATA IN DATA OUT

COMMENT

CK	OE	LD	D8	D7	D6	D5	D4	D3	D2	D1	D0	Q8	Q7	Q6	Q5	Q4	Q3	Q2	Q1	Q0		COMMENT
A	B	C	D	E	F	G	H	I	J	K	L	M	N	O	P	Q	R	S	T	U	V	
C	L	X	X	X	X	X	X	X	X	X	X	Z	Z	Z	Z	Z	Z	Z	Z	Z		TEST HI-Z
C	H	H	L	L	L	L	L	L	L	L	L	L	L	L	L	L	L	L	L	L		LOAD ALL ZEROS
C	H	L	X	X	X	X	X	X	X	X	X	L	L	L	L	L	L	L	L	L		HOLD ALL ZEROS
C	H	H	H	H	H	H	H	H	H	H	H	H	H	H	H	H	H	H	H	H		LOAD ALL ONES
C	H	L	X	X	X	X	X	X	X	X	X	H	H	H	H	H	H	H	H	H		HOLD ALL ONES
C	H	H	L	H	L	H	L	H	L	H	L	L	H	L	H	L	H	L	H	L		TEST EVEN CHECKERBOARD
C	H	H	H	L	H	L	H	L	H	L	H	H	L	H	L	H	L	H	L	H		TEST ODD CHECKERBOARD

LEGEND: H HIGH C CLOCK Z OFF
L LOW X IRRELEVANT

Logic Diagram HAL12L10

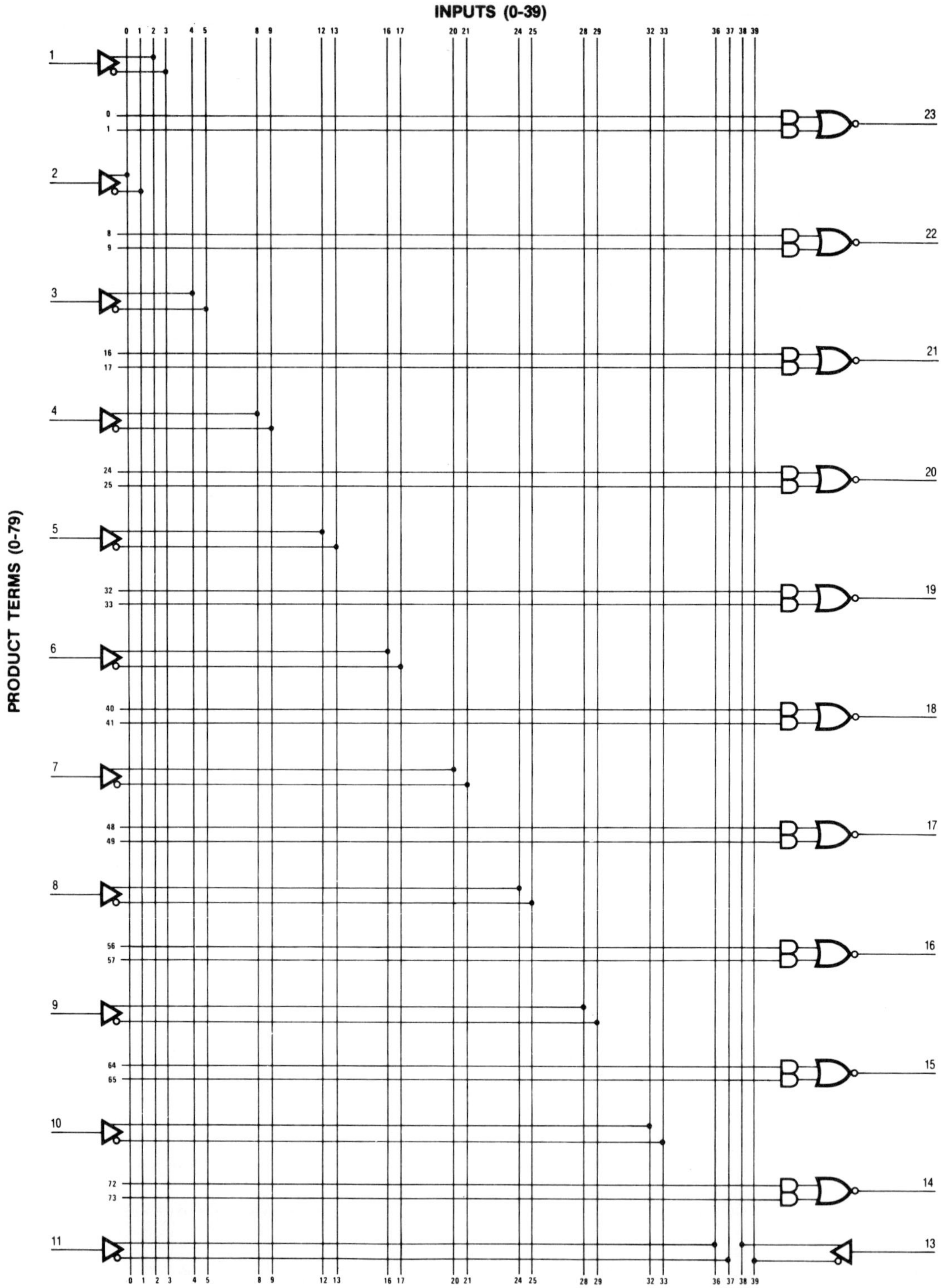

Logic Diagram HAL14L8

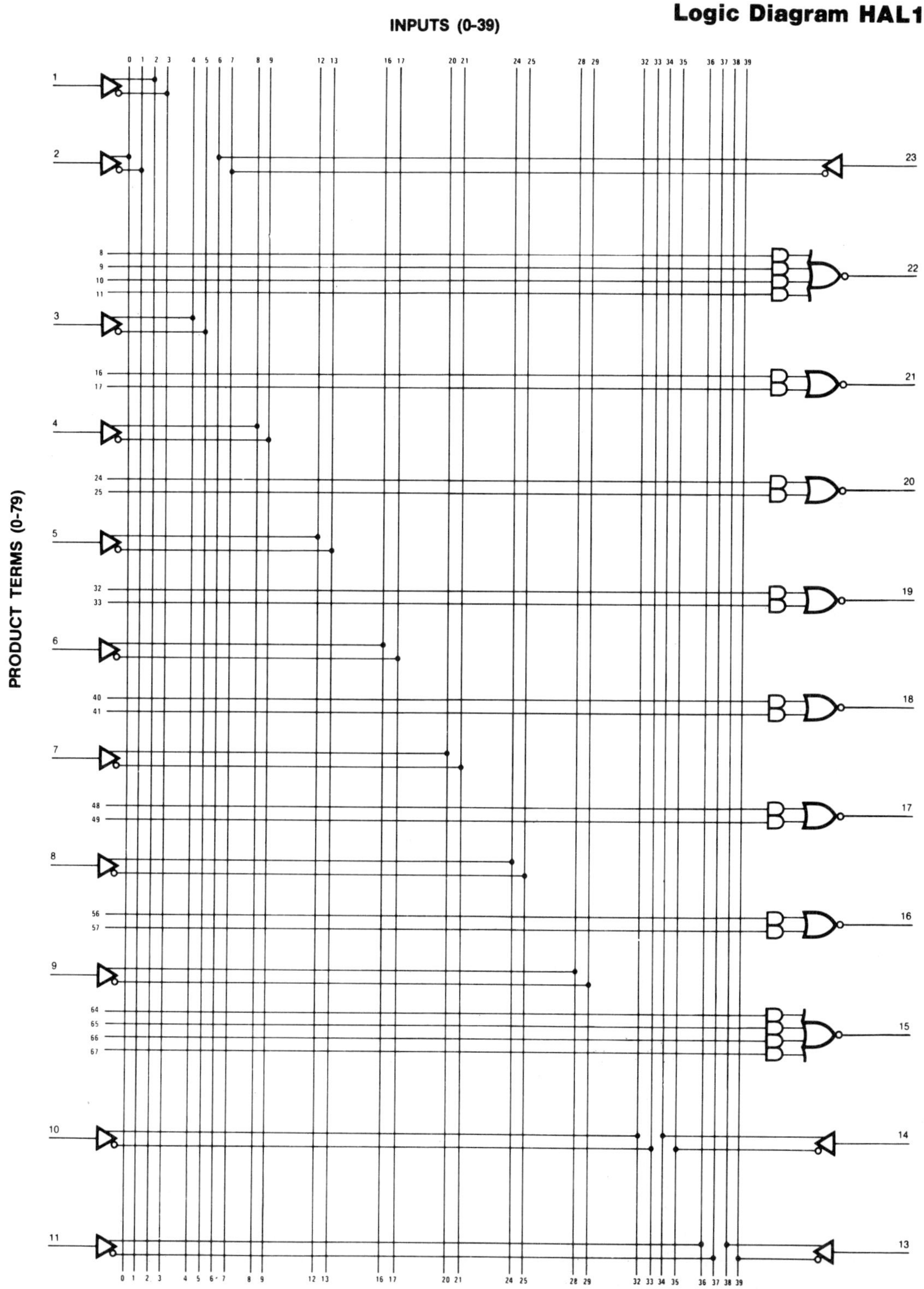

Logic Diagram HAL16L6

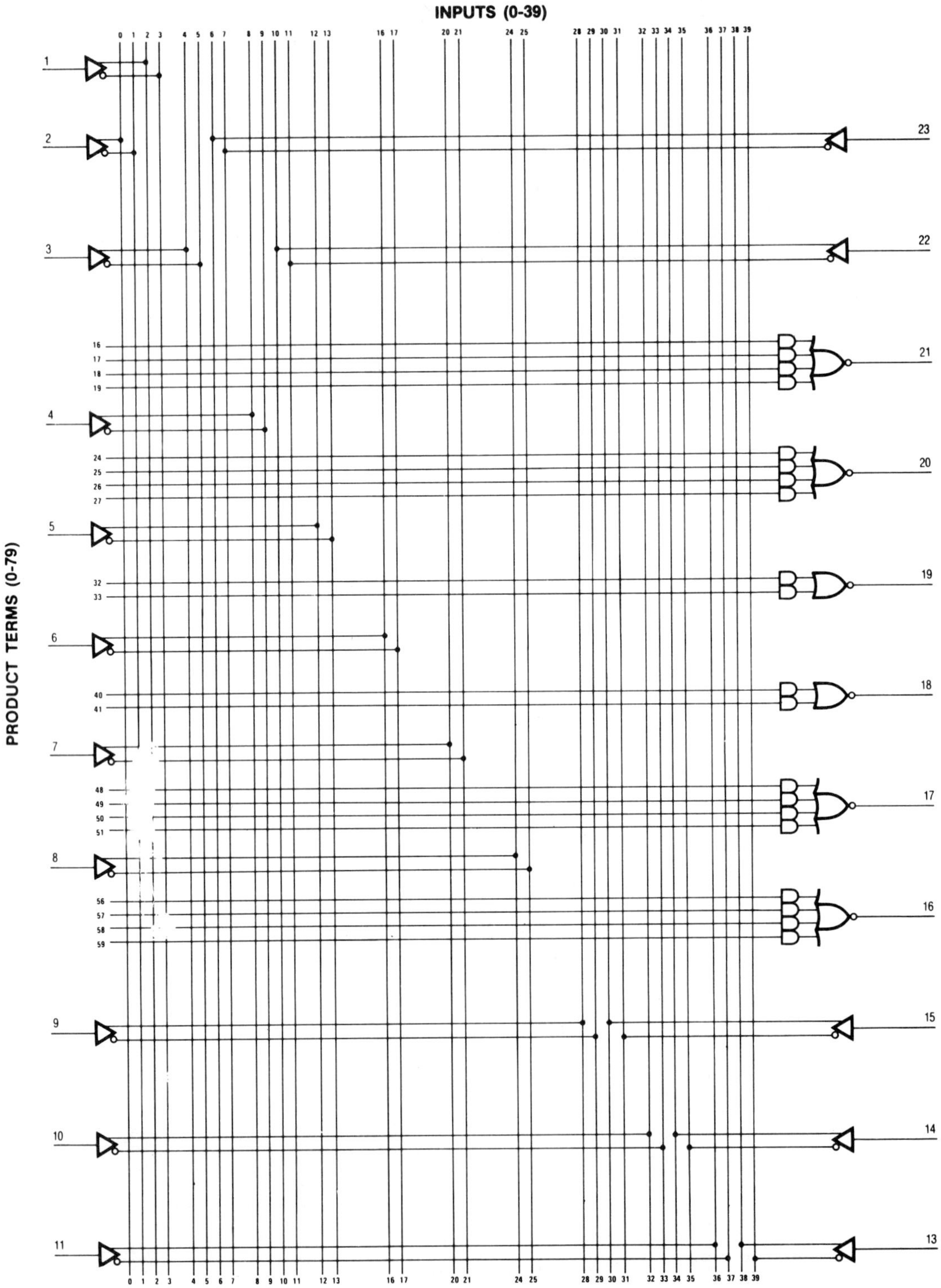

Logic Diagram HAL18L4

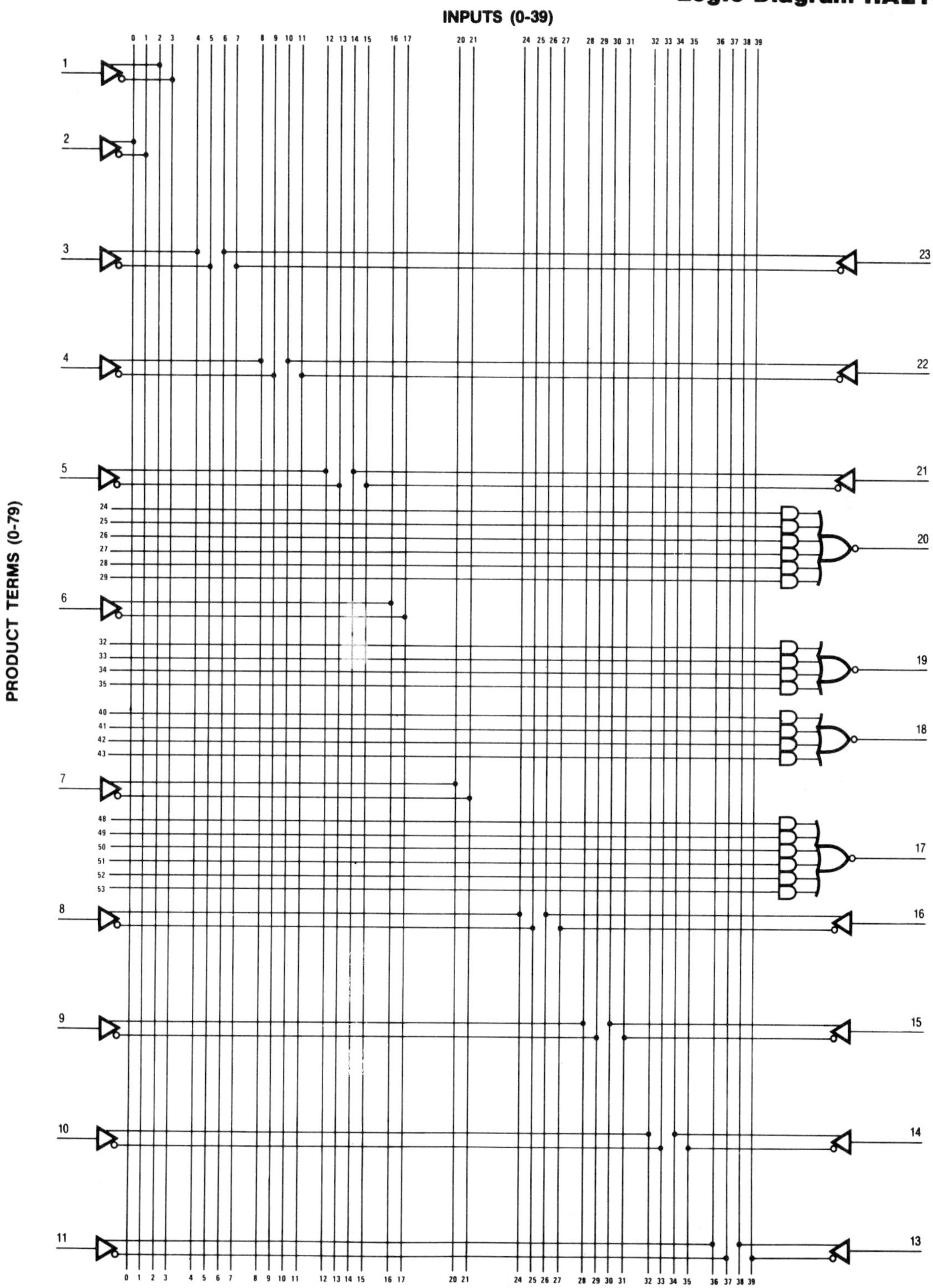

Logic Diagram HAL20L2

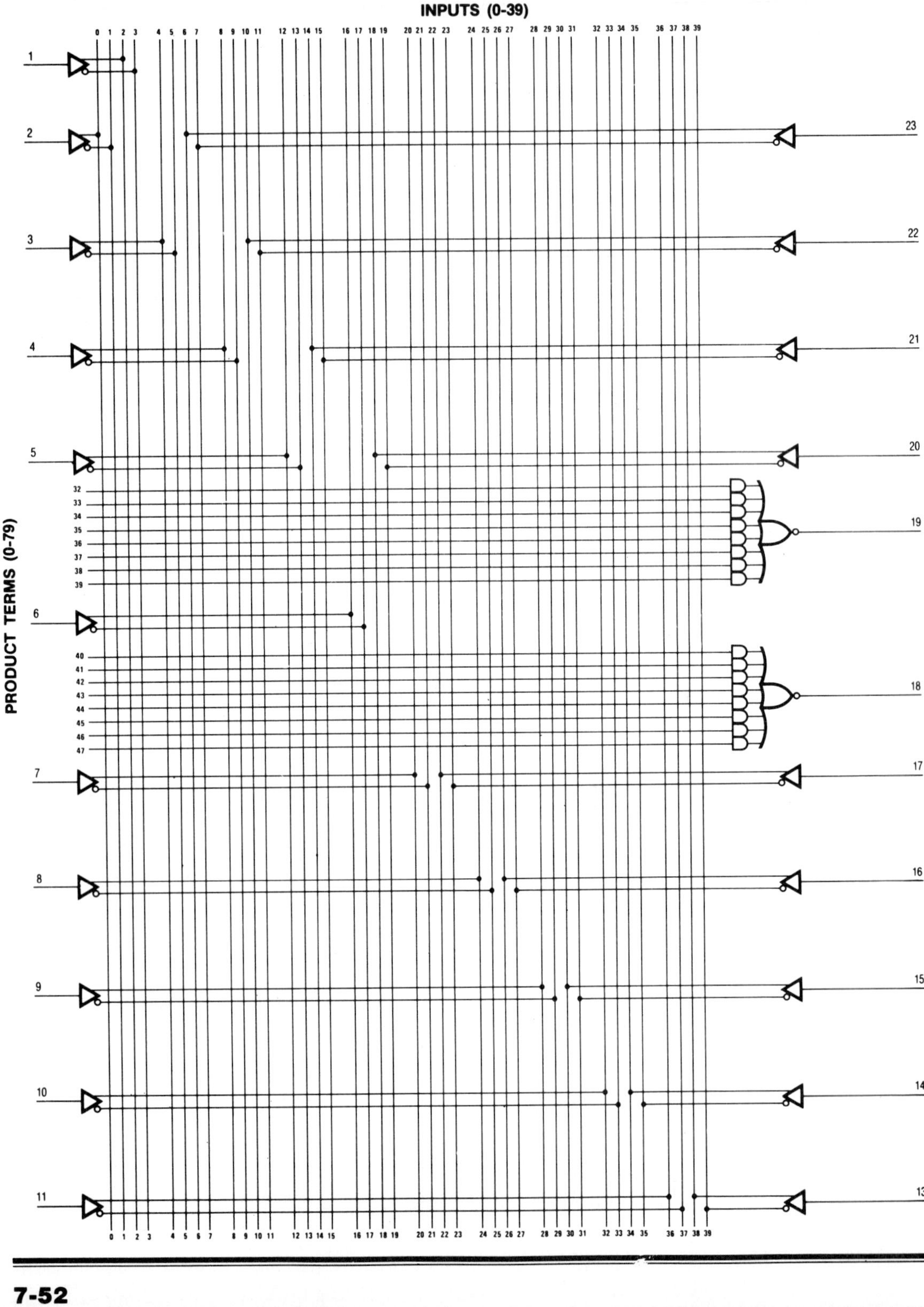

Logic Diagram HAL20C1

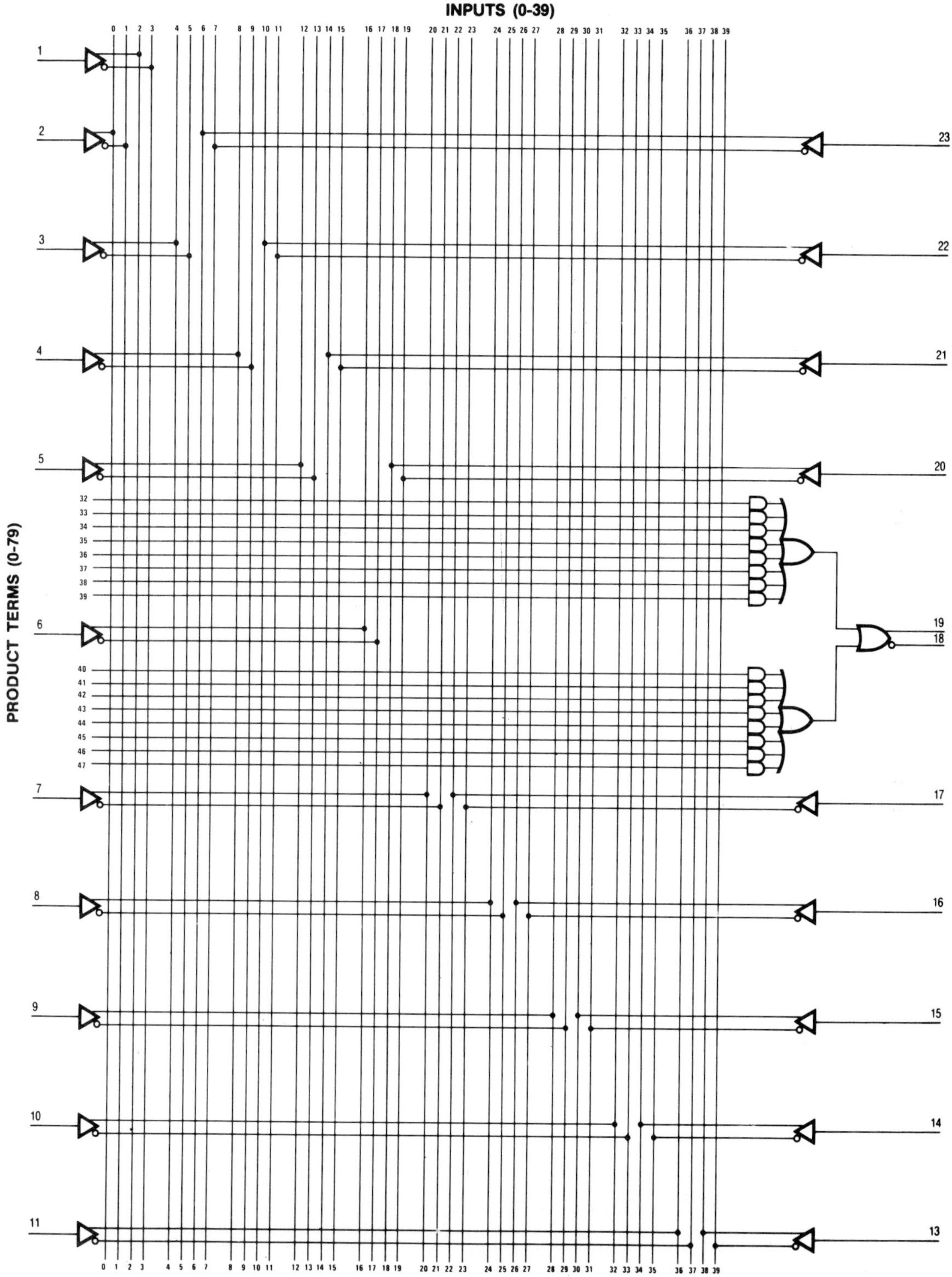

Logic Diagram HAL20L10

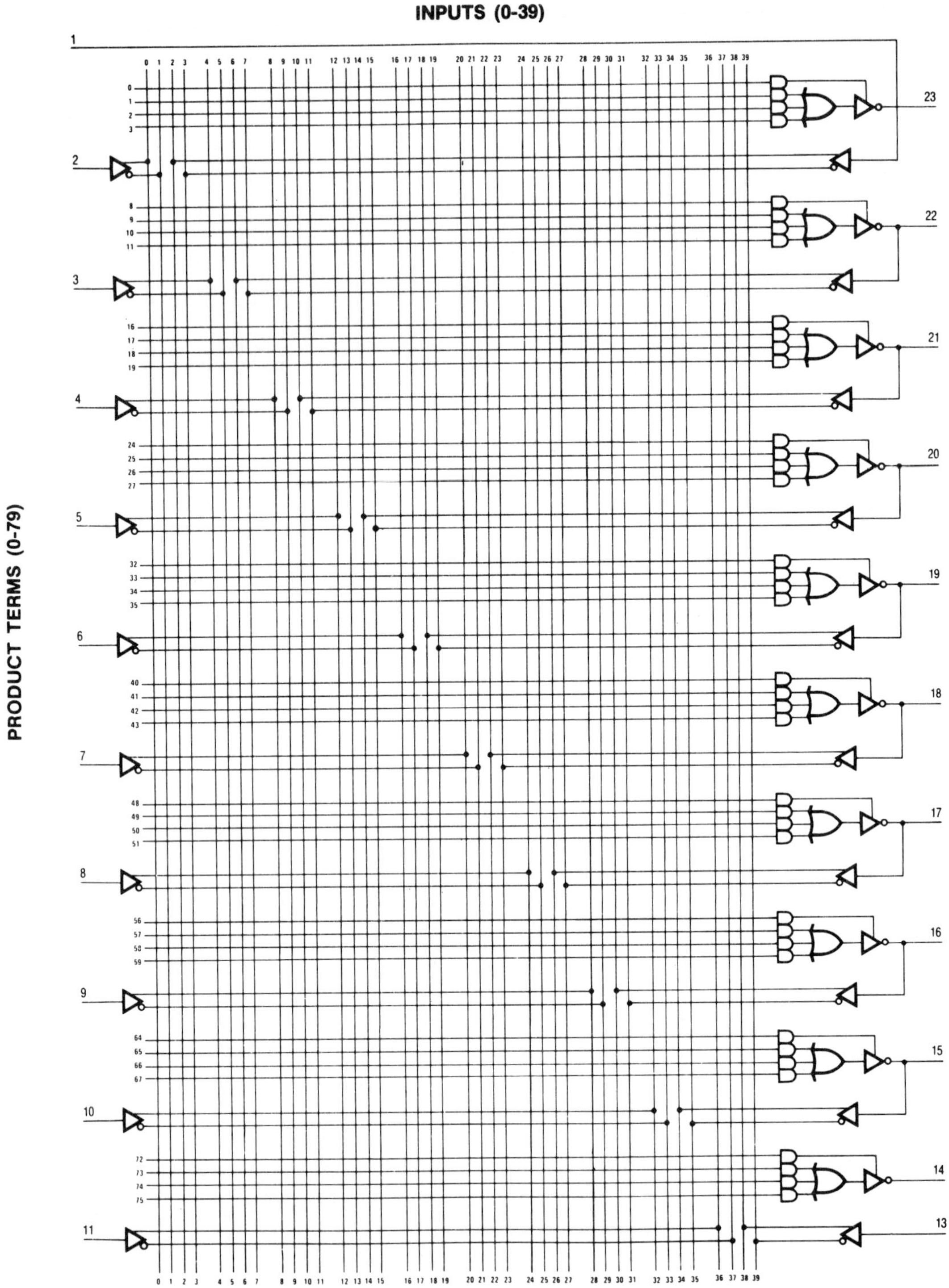

Logic Diagram HAL20X10

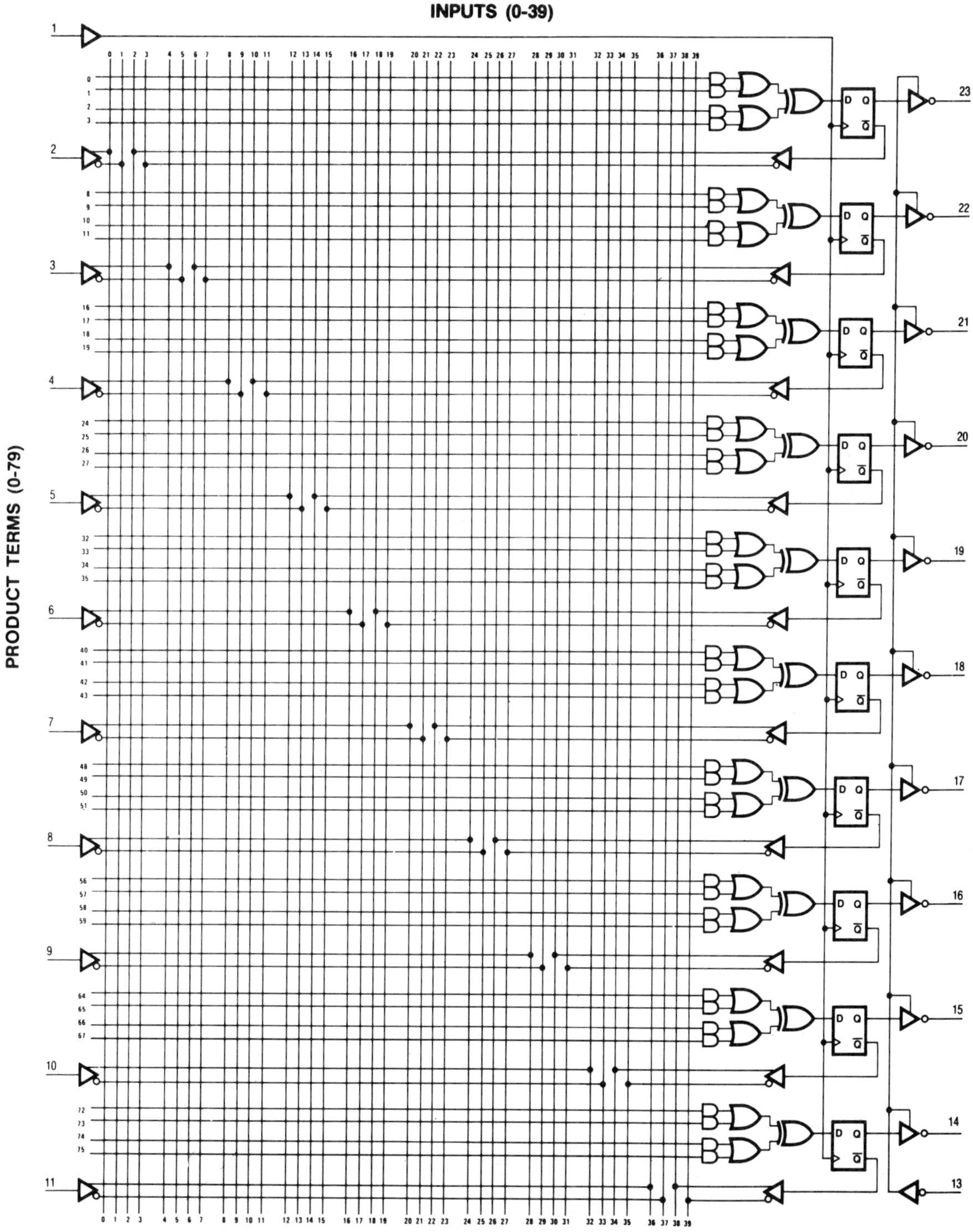

Logic Diagram HAL20X8

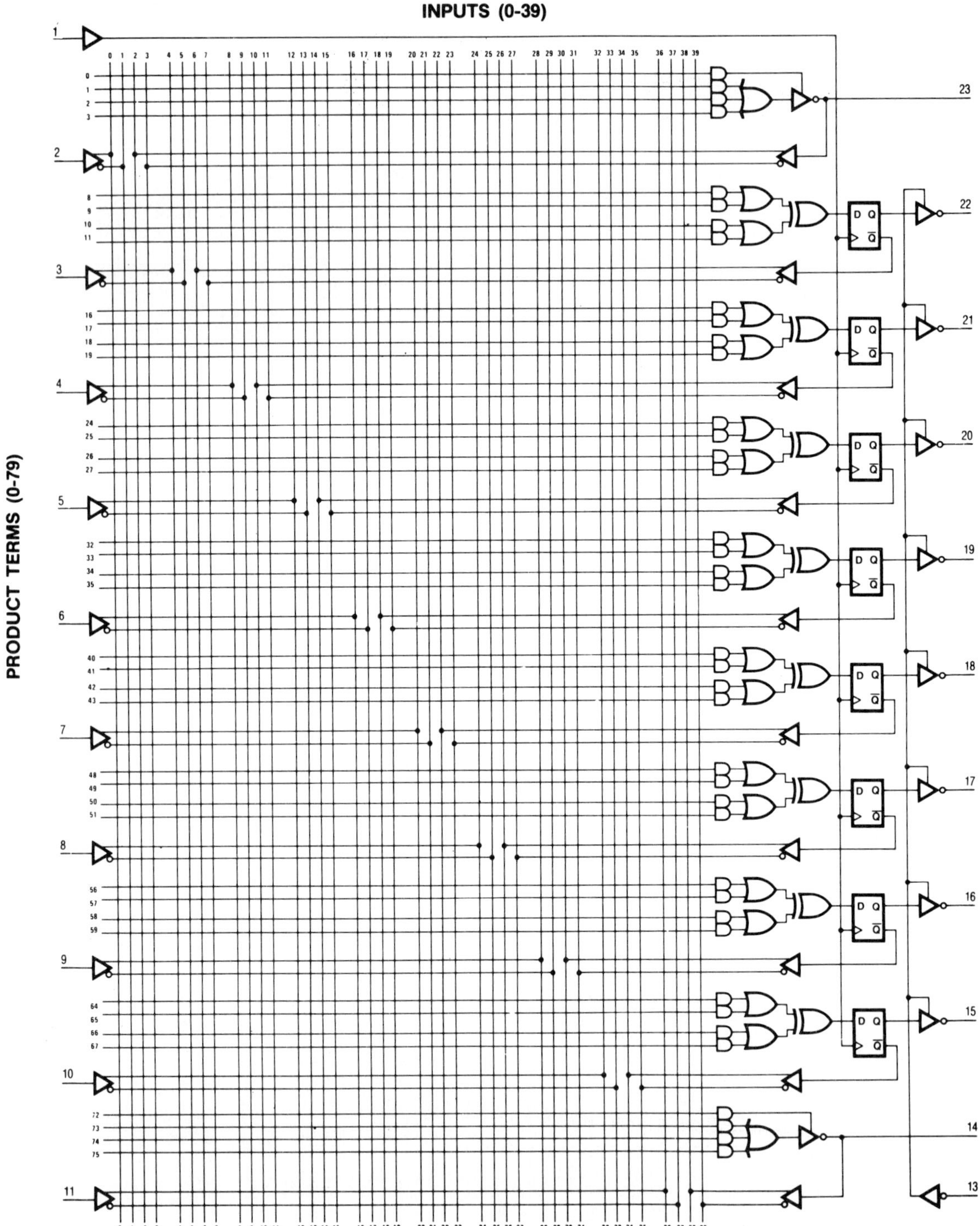

Logic Diagram HAL20X4

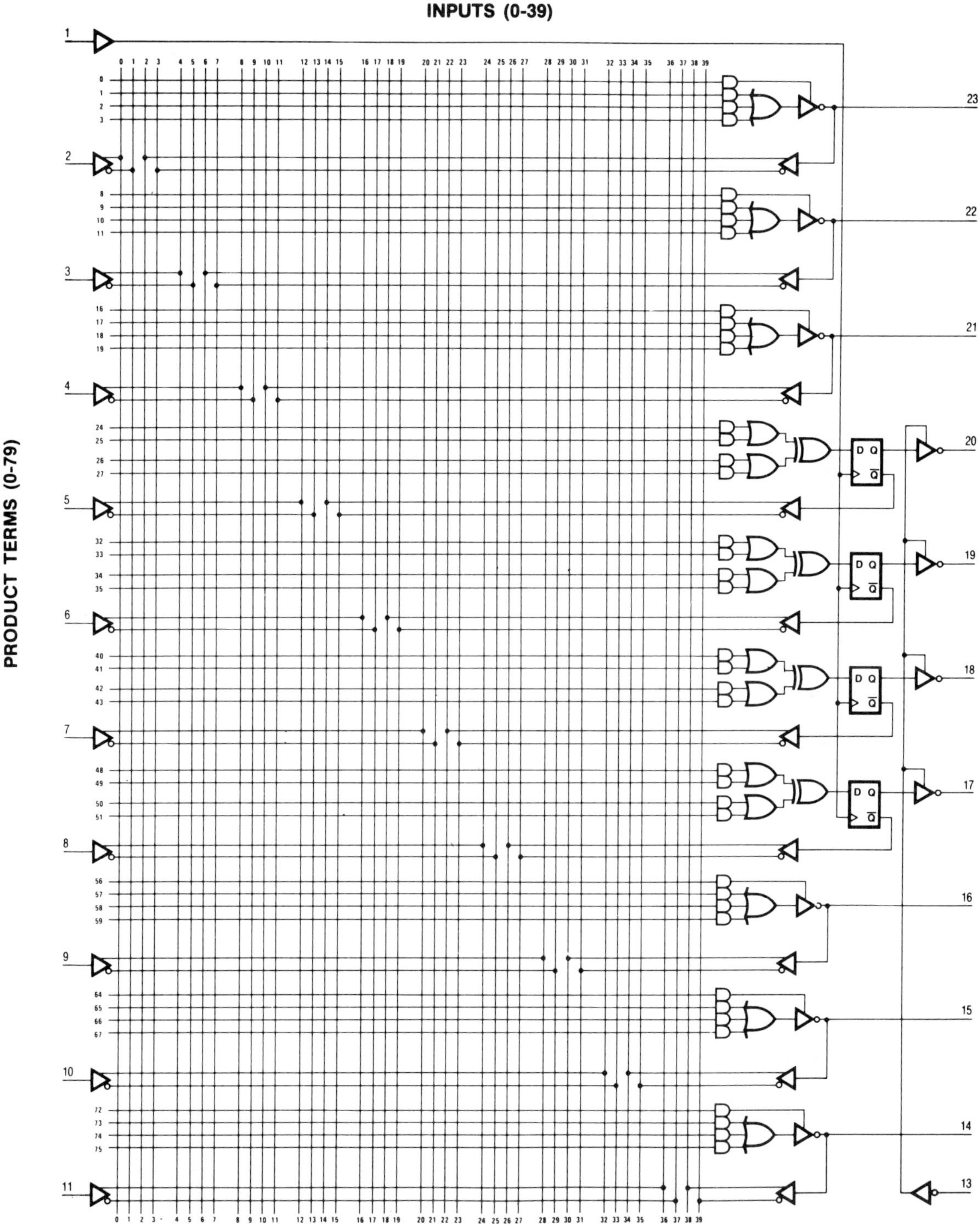

HAL
PART NUMBER

HAL DESIGN SPECIFICATION

USER'S PART NUMBER | REV | NAME | DATE / /

TITLE

COMPANY, CITY, STATE

PIN 1	PIN 2	PIN 3	PIN 4	PIN 5	PIN 6
					GND
PIN 7	PIN 8	PIN 9	PIN 10	PIN 11	PIN 12
PIN 13	PIN 14	PIN 15	PIN 16	PIN 17	PIN 18
					VCC
PIN 19	PIN 20	PIN 21	PIN 22	PIN 23	PIN 24

EQUATIONS

DESCRIPTION:

LEGEND:

= EQUAL	+ OR	:+: XOR	/ COMPLEMENT
:= REPLACED BY	* AND	:*: XNOR	( ) THREE-STATE

F 108

FUNCTION TABLE

PIN A	PIN B	PIN C	PIN D	PIN E	PIN F
PIN G	PIN H	PIN I	PIN J	PIN K	PIN L
PIN M	PIN N	PIN O	PIN P	PIN Q	PIN R
PIN S	PIN T	PIN U	PIN V		

;
COMMENT

A	B	C	D	E	F	G	H	I	J	K	L	M	N	O	P	Q	R	S	T	U	V	COMMENT

LEGEND: H HIGH, L LOW, C CLOCK, X IRRELEVANT, Z OFF

F 107

PAL
IMPORTANT NOTES

Low Power Programmable Array Logic Family

PAL® Series 20-2/-4

U.S. Patent 4124899

July 1982

Features/Benefits

- **Low power: 1/2 and 1/4 power options off standard PAL**
- **Programmable replacement for TTL logic**
- **Reduces IC inventories**
- **Reduces chip count by more than 4 to 1**
- **Expedites prototyping and board layout**
- **Save space with 20-pin SKINNYDIP® packages**
- **Programmed on standard PROM programmers**
- **Programmable three-state outputs**
- **Last fuse reduces possibility of copying**

Description

The PAL family utilizes an advanced Schottky Low Power TTL process and the Bipolar PROM fusible link technology to provide user programmable logic for replacing conventional Low Power SSI/MSI gates and flip-flops at reduced chip count.

The family lets the systems engineer "design his own chip" by blowing fusible links to configure AND and OR gates to perform his desired logic function. Complex interconnections which previously required time-consuming layout are thus "lifted" from PC board etch and placed on silicon where they can be easily modified during prototype check-out or production.

The PAL transfer function is the familiar sum of products. Like the PROM, the PAL has a single array of fusible links. Unlike the PROM, the PAL is a programmable AND array driving a fixed OR array (the PROM is a fixed AND array driving a programmable OR array). In addition the PAL provides these options:

- Variable input/output pin ratio
- Programmable three-state outputs
- Registers with feedback

Unused inputs are tied directly to V_{CC} or GND. Product terms with all fuses blown assume the logical high state, and product terms connected to both true and complement of any single input assume the logical low state. Registers consist of D type flip-flops which are loaded on the low to high transition of the clock. PAL Logic Diagrams are shown with all fuses blown, enabling the designer use of the diagrams as coding sheets.

The entire PAL family is programmed on inexpensive conventional PROM programmers with appropriate personality and socket adapter cards. Once the PAL is programmed and verified, two additional fuses may be blown to defeat verification. This feature gives the user a proprietary circuit which is very difficult to copy.

PART NUMBER	PKG	GATE ARRAY DESCRIPTION
PAL10H8-2	N,J,F,L	Octal 10 Input And-Or
PAL12H6-2	N,J,F,L	Hex 12 Input And-Or
PAL14H4-2	N,J,F,L	Quad 14 Input And-Or
PAL16H2-2	N,J,F,L	Dual 16 Input And-Or
PAL16C1-2	N,J,F,L	16 Input And-Or/And-Or-Invert
PAL10L8-2	N,J,F,L	Octal 10 Input And-Or-Invert
PAL12L6-2	N,J,F,L	Hex 12 Input And-Or-Invert
PAL14L4-2	N,J,F,L	Quad 14 Input And-Or Invert
PAL16L2-2	N,J,F,L	Dual 16 Input And-Or-Invert
PAL16L8-2	N,J,F,L	Octal 16 Input And-Or-Invert
PAL16R8-2	N,J,F,L	Octal 16 Input Registered And-Or
PAL16R6-2	N,J,F,L	Hex 16 Input Registered And-Or
PAL16R4-2	N,J,F,L	Quad 16 Input Registered And-Or
PAL16L8-4	N,J,F,L	Octal 16 Input And-Or-Invert
PAL16R8-4	N,J,F,L	Octal 16 Input Registered And-Or
PAL16R6-4	N,J,F,L	Hex 16 Input Registered And-Or
PAL16R4-4	N,J,F,L	Quad 16 Input Registered And-Or

Ordering Information

HARD ARRAY LOGIC FAMILY
NUMBER OF ARRAY INPUTS
OUTPUT TYPE
L = ACTIVE LOW
C = COMPLEMENTARY
X = EXCLUSIVE-OR REGISTERED
A = ARITHMETIC REGISTERED
NUMBER OF OUTPUTS
SPEED/POWER
A = HIGH SPEED
-2 = 1/2 POWER
-4 = 1/4 POWER
TEMPERATURE RANGE
C = 0C TO +75C
M = -55C TO +125C
(CASE TEMPERATURE)
PACKAGE
N = PLASTIC DIP
J = CERAMIC DIP
F = FLAT PACK
L = LEADLESS CHIP CARRIER
OPTIONAL HI-REL PROCESSING
883B = MIL-STD-883, METHOD 5004 & 5005 LEVEL B
883C = MIL-STD-883, METHOD 5004 & 5005 LEVEL C
B = MIL-STD-883, METHOD 5004 EQUIVALENT
C = MIL-STD-883, METHOD 5004 EQUIVALENT
BIT PATTERN NUMBER

PAL 14 L4 -2 C J 883B P01234

PAL® is a registered trademark of Monolithic Memories

1165 East Arques Avenue, Sunnyvale, CA 94086 Tel: (408) 739-3535 TWX: 910-339-9229 **Monolithic Memories** MMI

PAL10H8-2

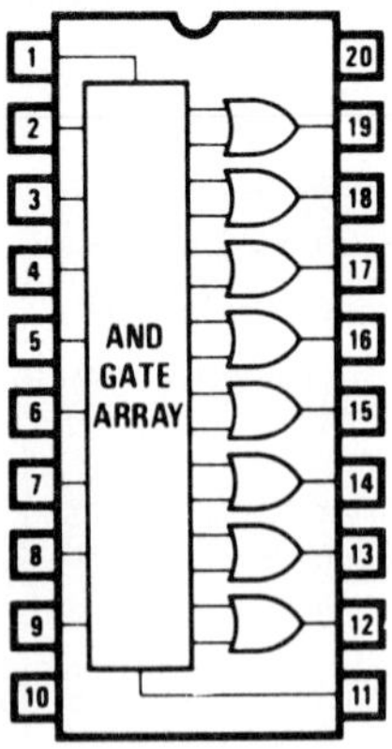

PAL12H6-2

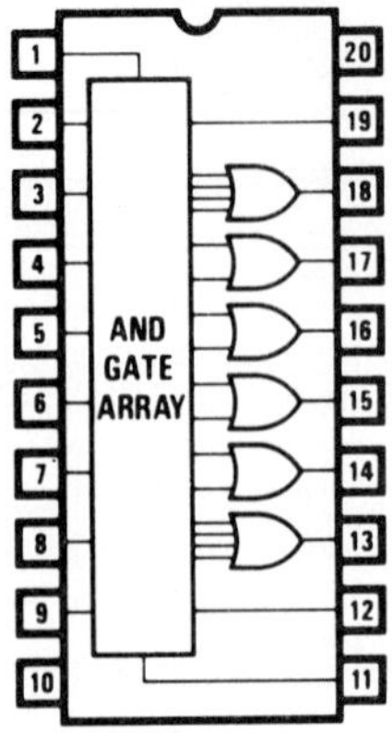

PAL14H4-2

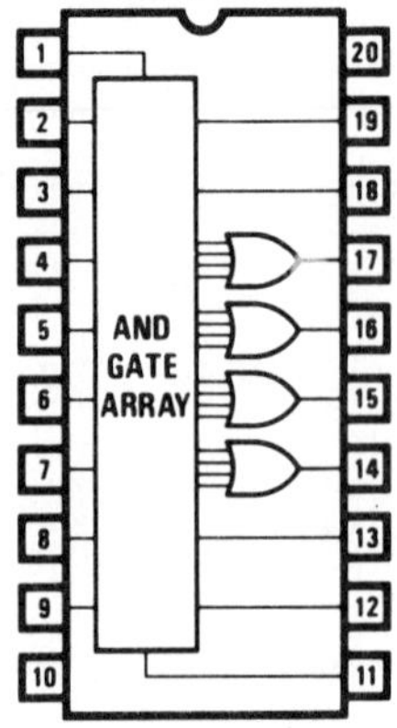

PAL16H2-2

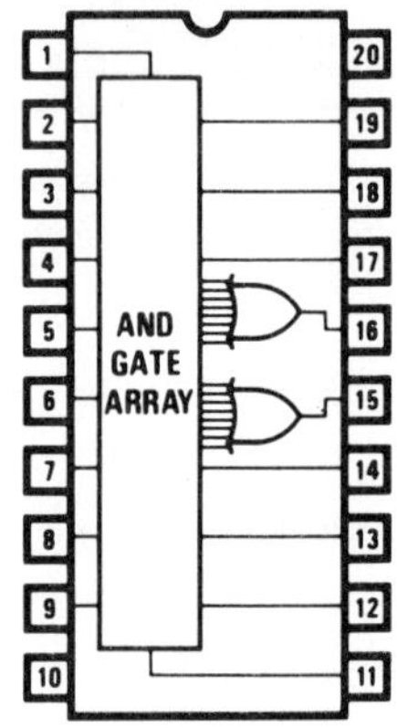

PAL16C1-2

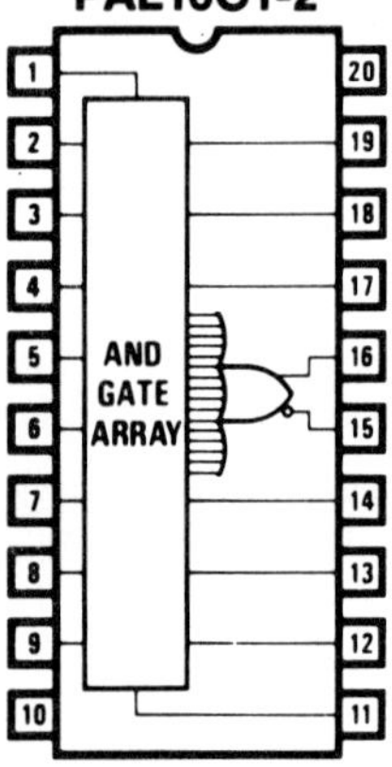

PAL10L8-2

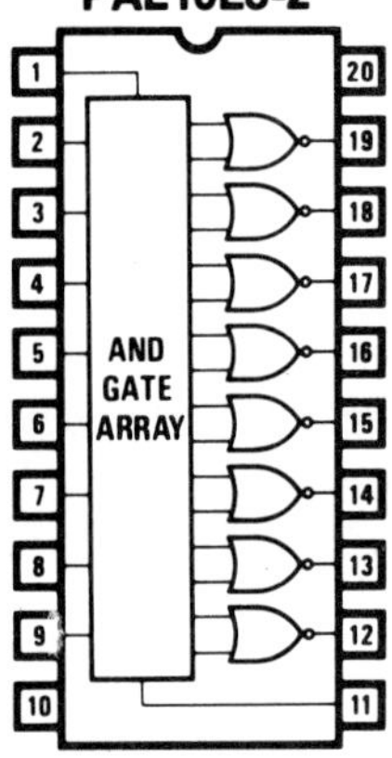

PAL12L6-2

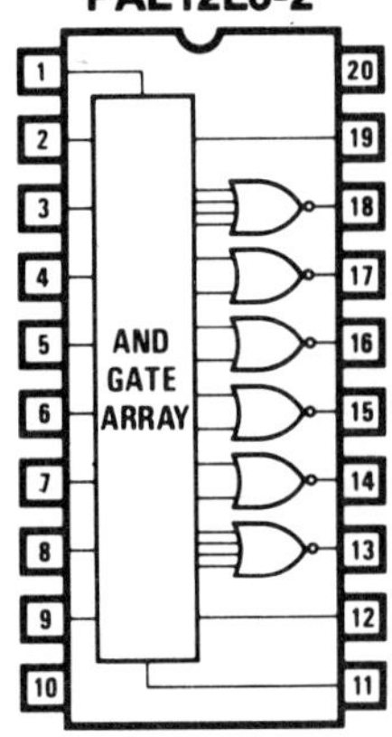

PAL14L4-2

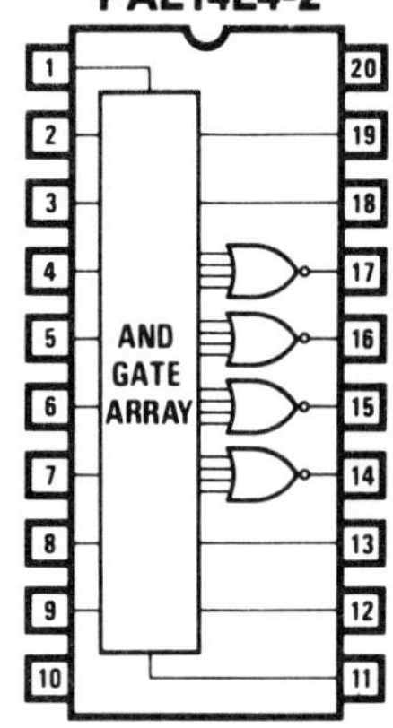

PAL16L2-2

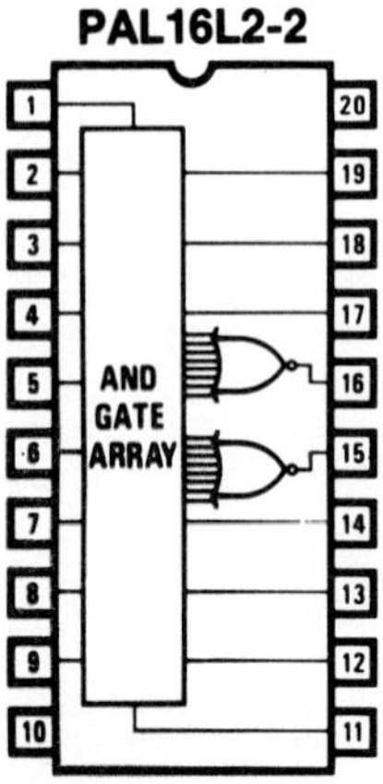

PAL16L8-2

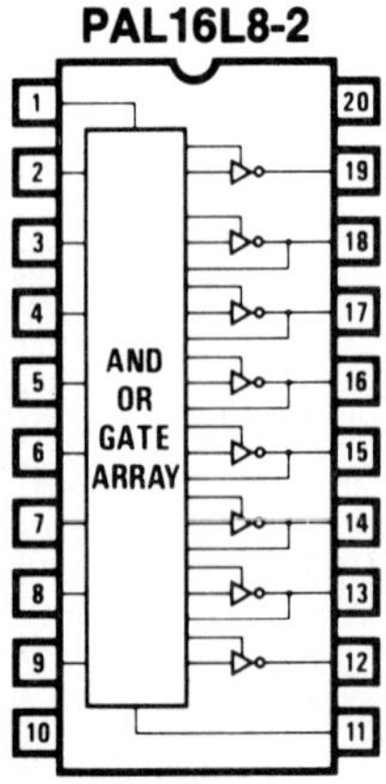

PAL16R8-2

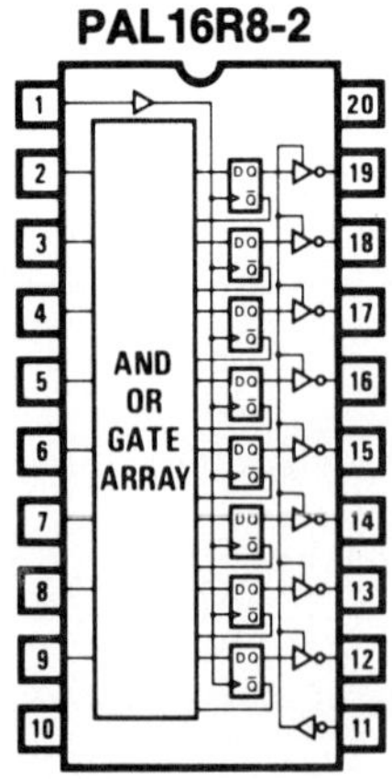

PAL16R6-2

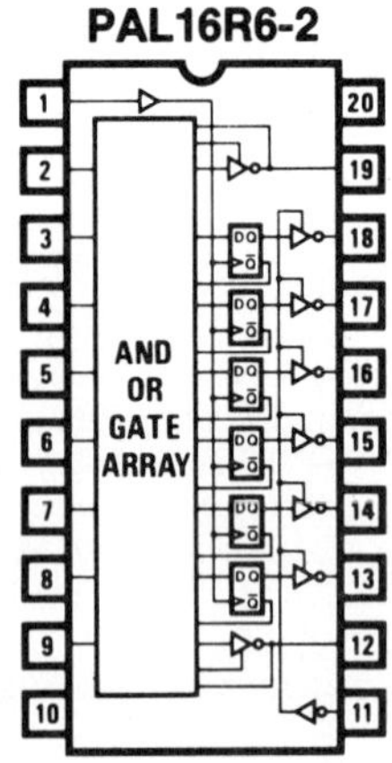

PAL16R4-2

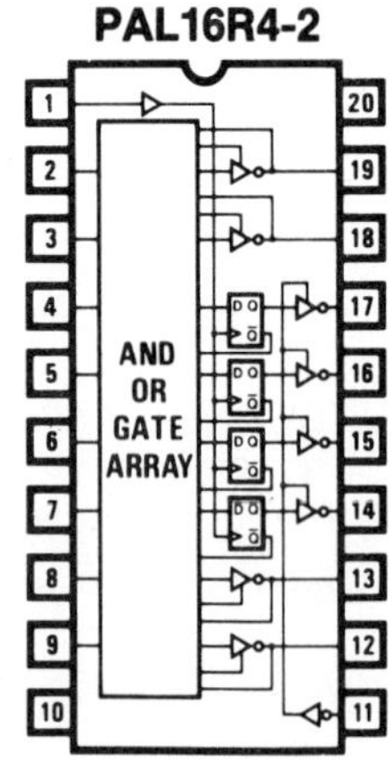

PAL16L8-4

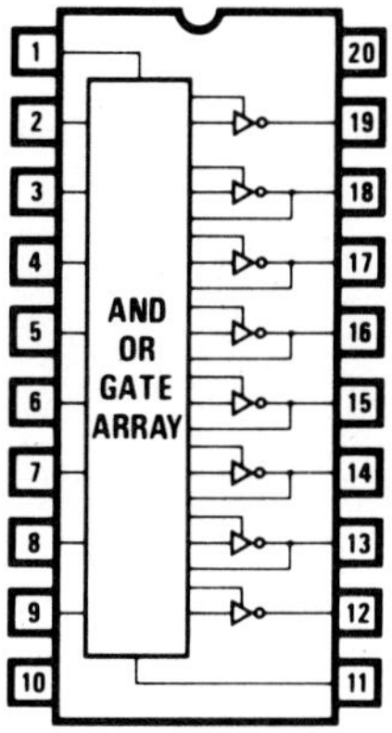

PAL16R8-4

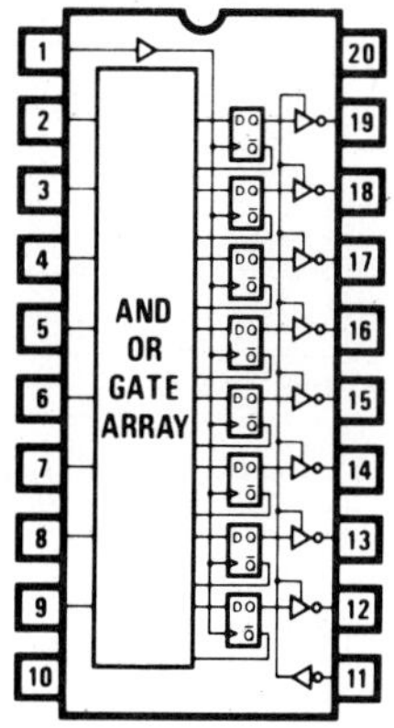

PAL16R6-4

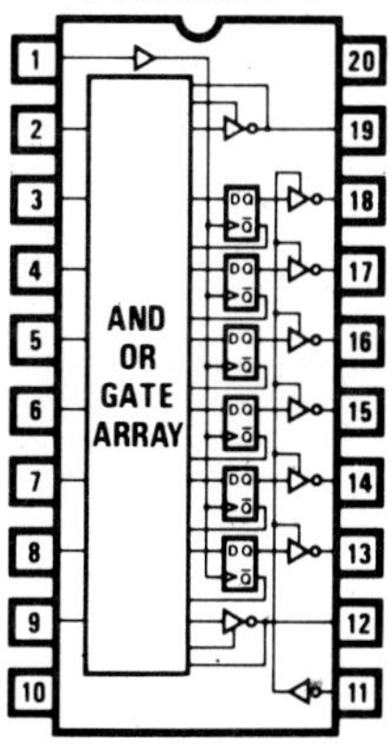

PAL16R4-4

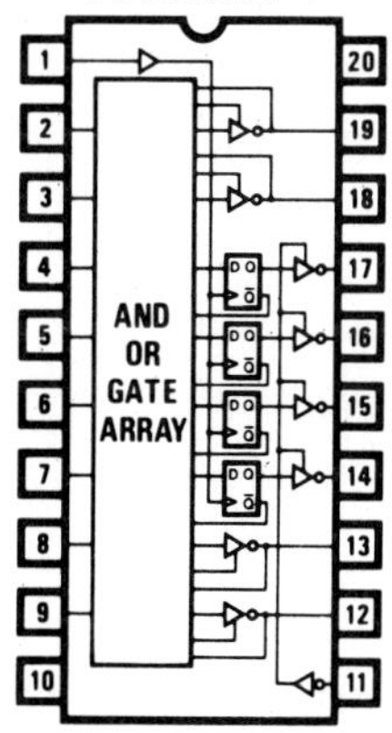

Absolute Maximum Ratings

	Operating	Programming
Supply Voltage, V_{CC}	−0.5 to 7.0V	−0.5 to 12.0V
Input Voltage	−1.5 to 5.5V	−1.0 to 12.0V⊕
Off-state output Voltage	5.5V	12.0V
Storage temperature		−65° to +150°C

Operating Conditions

SYMBOL	PARAMETER			MILITARY MIN	MILITARY TYP	MILITARY MAX	COMMERCIAL MIN	COMMERCIAL TYP	COMMERCIAL MAX	UNIT
V_{CC}	Supply voltage			4.5	5	5.	4.75	5	5.25	V
t_w	Width of clock	16R8-2 16R6-2 16R4-2	Low	50	25		40	25		ns
			High	50	25		40	25		ns
t_{su}	Set up time from input or feedback	16R8-2 16R6-2 16R4-2		70	40		55	40		ns
t_h	Hold time			0	−15		0	−15		ns
T_A	Operating free-air temperature			−55			0	5	75	°C
T_C	Operating case temperature					125				°C

Electrical Characteristics Over Operating Conditions

SYMBOL	PARAMETER	TEST CONDITIONS			MIN	TYP	MAX	UNIT
V_{IL}*	Low-level input voltage						0.8	V
V_{IH}*	High-level input voltage				2			V
V_{IC}	Input clamp voltage	V_{CC} = MIN		II = −18mA		−0.8	−1.5	V
I_{IL}	Low-level input current†	V_{CC} = MAX		VI = 0.4V		−0.02	−0.25	mA
I_{IH}	High-level input current†	V_{CC} = MAX		VI = 2.4V			25	μA
I_I	Maximum input current	V_{CC} = MAX		VI = 5.5V			1	mA
V_{OL}	Low-level output voltage	V_{CC} = MIN, V_{IL} = 0.8V, V_{IH} = 2V	10L8-2 10H8-2 12L6-2 12H6-2 14L4-2 14H4-2 16L2-2 16H2-2 16C1-2	MIL I_{OL} = 4mA		0.3	0.5	V
				COM I_{OL} = 4mA				
			16L8-2 16R8-2	MIL I_{OL} = 4mA				
			16R6-2 16R4-2	COM I_{OL} = 8mA				
V_{OH}	High-level output voltage	V_{CC} = MIN, V_{IL} = 0.8V, V_{IH} = 2V	10L8-2 10H8-2 12L6-2 12H6-2 14L4-2 14H4-2 16L2-2 16H2-2 16C1-2	MIL I_{OH} = −1mA	2.4	2.8		V
				COM I_{OH} = −1mA				
			16L8-2 16R8-2	MIL I_{OH} = −1mA				
			16R6-2 16R4-2	COM I_{OH} = −1mA				
I_{OZL}	Off-state output current†	V_{CC} = MAX, V_{IL} = 0.8V, V_{IH} = 2V	16L8-2 16R8-2 16R6-2 16R4-2	V_O = 0.4V			−100	μA
I_{OZH}				V_O = 2.4V			100	μA
I_{OS}	Output short-circuit current**	V_{CC} = 5V		V_O = 0V	−30	−70	−130	mA
I_{CC}	Supply current	V_{CC} = MAX	10H8-2 12H6-2 14H4-2 16H2-2 16C1-2 10L8-2 12L6-2 14L4-2 16L2-2			30	45	mA
			16R4-2 16R6-2 16R8-2 16L8-2			60	90	mA

* These are absolute voltages with respect to pin 10 on the device and includes all overshoots due to system and/or tester noise. Do not attempt to test these values without suitable equipment.

⊕ Pins 1 and 11 may be raised to 22V MAX.

** Only one output shorted at a time.

† I/O pin leakage is the worst case of I_{OZX} or I_{IX} e.g., I_{IL} and I_{OZH}.

†† All typical values are at V_{CC} = 5V, T_A = 25°C.

Switching Characteristics

Over Operating Conditions

SYMBOL	PARAMETER		TEST CONDITIONS	MILITARY MIN	MILITARY TYP	MILITARY MAX	COMMERCIAL MIN	COMMERCIAL TYP	COMMERCIAL MAX	UNIT
t_{PD}	Input to output	10H8-2 12H6-2 14H4-2 16H2-2 10L8-2 12L6-2 14L4-2 16L2-2 16C1-2	R_1 = 1.12kΩ R_2 = 2.2kΩ		45	80		45	60	ns
t_{PD}	Input or feed-back to output	16R6-2 16R4-2 16L8-2	R_1 = 400Ω R_2 = 780Ω		30	65		30	50	ns
t_{CLK}	Clock to output or feedback — 2				20	50		20	40	ns
$t_{PXZ/ZY}$	Pin 11 to output disable/enable — 2				15	40		15	30	ns
t_{PZX}	Input to output enable	16R6-2 16R4-2 16L8-2			30	65		30	50	ns
t_{PXZ}	Input to output disable	16R6-2 16R4-2 16L8-2			30	65		30	50	ns
f_{MAX}	Maximum frequency	16R8-2 16R6-2 16R4-2		8	20		11	20		MHz

Test Load

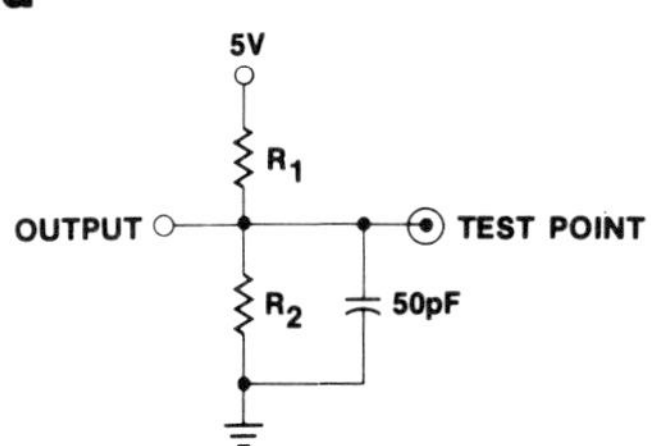

Available Programmers

MANUFACTURER	PERSONALITY CARD SET	SOCKET ADAPTER CONFIGURATION
Data I/O Corporation	909-1427	715 1428-1 715 1428-2 715 1428-3
Pro-Log Corporation	PM9068	
Stag Systems	PM202	AM10H8 AM10L8 AM12H6 AM12L6 AM14H4 AM14L4 AM16H2 AM16L2 AM16C1
Structured Design	SD20/24	

Schematic of Inputs and Outputs

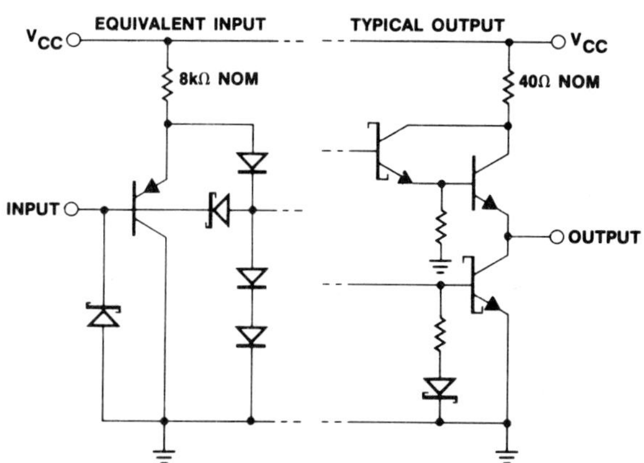

Absolute Maximum Ratings

	Operating	Programming
Supply Voltage, V_{CC}	-0.5 to 7.0V	-0.5 to 12.0V
Input Voltage	-1.5 to 5.5V	-1.0 to 12.0V⊕
Off-state output Voltage	5.5V	12.0V
Storage temperature		-65° to +150°C

Operating Conditions

SYMBOL	PARAMETER			MILITARY MIN	MILITARY TYP	MILITARY MAX	COMMERCIAL MIN	COMMERCIAL TYP	COMMERCIAL MAX	UNIT
V_{CC}	Supply voltage			4.5	5	5.5	4.75	5	5.25	V
t_w	Width of clock	16R8-4 16R6-4 16R4-4	Low	70	25		50	25		ns
			High	70	25		50	25		ns
t_{su}	Set up time from input or feedback	16R8-4 16R6-4 16R4-4		120	45		100	45		ns
t_h	Hold time			0	-15		0	-15		ns
T_A	Operating free-air temperature			-55			0	5	75	°C
T_C	Operating case temperature					125				°C

Electrical Characteristics Over Operating Conditions

SYMBOL	PARAMETER	TEST CONDITIONS			MIN	TYP	MAX	UNIT
V_{IL}*	Low-level input voltage						0.8	V
V_{IH}*	High-level input voltage				2			V
V_{IC}	Input clamp voltage	V_{CC} = MIN		II = -18mA		-0.8	-1.5	V
I_{IL}	Low-level input current†	V_{CC} = MAX		VI = 0.4V		-0.02	-0.25	mA
I_{IH}	High-level input current†	V_{CC} = MAX		VI = 2.4V			25	μA
I_I	Maximum input current	V_{CC} = MAX		VI = 5.5V			1	mA
V_{OL}	Low-level output voltage	V_{CC} = MIN, V_{IL} = 0.8V, V_{IH} = 2V	16L8-4 16R8-4 16R6-4 16R4-4	MIL I_{OL} = 4mA COM I_{OL} = 4mA		0.3	0.5	V
V_{OH}	High-level output voltage	V_{CC} = MIN, V_{IL} = 0.8V, V_{IH} = 2V	16L8-4 16R8-4 16R6-4 16R4-4	MIL I_{OH} = -1mA COM I_{OH} = -1mA	2.4	2.8		V
I_{OZL}	Off-state output current†	V_{CC} = MAX, V_{IL} = 0.8V, V_{IH} = 2V	16L8-4 16R8-4 16R6-4 16R4-4	V_O = 0.4V			-100	μA
I_{OZH}				V_O = 2.4V			100	μA
I_{OS}	Output short-circuit current**	V_{CC} = 5V		VO = 0V	-30	-70	-130	mA
I_{CC}	Supply current	V_{CC} = MAX	16R4-4 16R6-4 16R8-4 16L8-4			30	50	mA

* These are absolute voltages with respect to pin 10 on the device and includes all overshoots due to system and/or tester noise. Do not attempt to test these values without suitable equipment.

⊕ Pins 1 and 11 may be raised to 22V MAX.

** Only one output shorted at a time.

† I/O pin leakage is the worst case of I_{OZX} or I_{IX} e.g., I_{IL} and I_{OZH}.

†† All typical values are at V_{CC} = 5V, T_A = 25°C.

Switching Characteristics

Over Operating Conditions

SYMBOL	PARAMETER		TEST	MILITARY MIN	MILITARY TYP	MILITARY MAX	COMMERCIAL MIN	COMMERCIAL TYP	COMMERCIAL MAX	UNIT
t_{PD}	Input or feed-back to output	16R6-4 16R4-4 16L8-4	$R_1 = 800\ \Omega$ $R_2 = 1.56K\ \Omega$		55	100		55	80	ns
t_{CLK}	Clock to output or feedback — 4				40	80		40	60	ns
$t_{PXZ/ZY}$	Pin 11 to output disable/enable — 4				25	50		25	40	ns
t_{PZX}	Input to output enable	16R6-4 16R4-4 16L8-4			50	100		50	75	ns
t_{PXZ}	Input to output disable	16R6-4 16R4-4 16L8-4			50	100		50	75	ns
f_{MAX}	Maximum frequency	16R8-4 16R6-4 16R4-4		5	10		7	10		MHz

Test Load

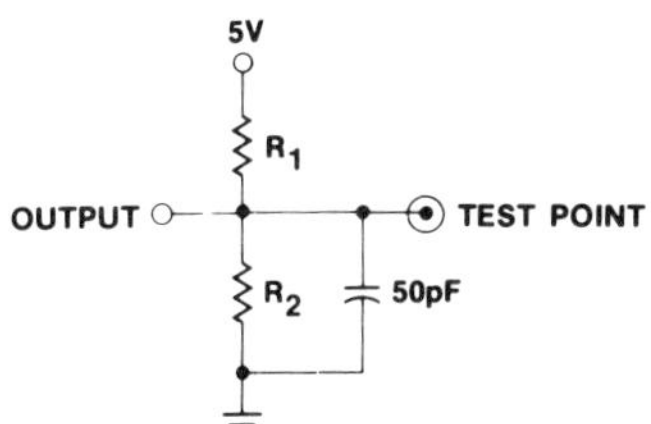

Schematic of Inputs and Outputs

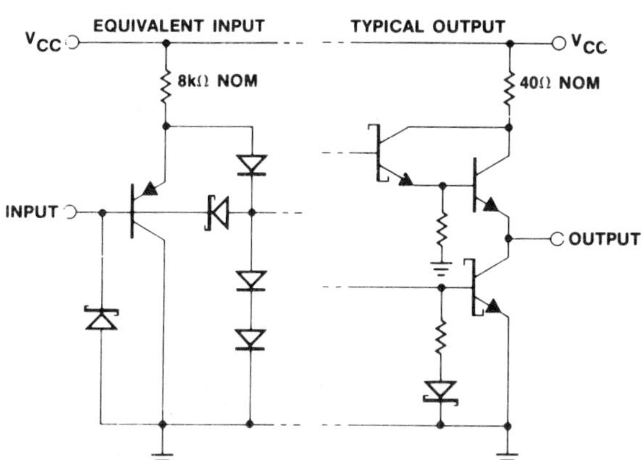

Available Programmers

MANUFACTURER	PERSONALITY CARD SET	SOCKET ADAPTER CONFIGURATION
Data I/O Corporation	909-1427	715 1428-1 715 1428-2 715 1428-3
Pro-Log Corporation	PM9068	
Stag Systems	PM202	AM10H8 AM10L8 AM12H6 AM12L6 AM14H4 AM14L4 AM16H2 AM16L2 AM16C1
Structured Design	SD20/24	

Programming

PAL fuses are programmed using a low-voltage linear-select procedure which is common to all 19 PAL types. The array is divided into two groups, products 0 thru 31 and products 32 thru 63, for which pin identifications are shown in Pin Configurations below. To program a particular fuse, both an input line and a product line are selected according to the following procedure:

Step 1 Raise Output Disable, OD, to V_{IHH}

Step 2 Select an input line by specifying $I_0, I_1, I_2, I_3, I_4, I_5, I_6, I_7$ and L/R as shown in Table 1.

Step 3 Select a product line by specifying A_0, A_1 and A_2 one-of-eight select as shown in Table 2.

Step 4 Raise V_{CC} (pin 20) to V_{IHH}

Step 5 Program the fuse by pulsing the output pins, O, of the selected product group to V_{IHH} as shown in Programming Waveform.

Step 6 Lower V_{CC} (pin 20) to 6.0 V

Step 7 Pulse the CLOCK pin and verify the output pin, O, to be Low for active Low PAL types or High for active High PAL types.

Step 8 Lower V_{CC} (pin 20) to 4.5 V and repeat step 7.

Step 9 Should the output not verify, repeat steps 1 thru 8 up to five (5) times.

This procedure is repeated for all fuses to be blown (see Programming Waveforms).

To prevent further verification, two last fuses may be blown by raising pin 1 and pin 11 to V_P. V_{CC} is not required during this operation.

Voltage Legend

L = Low-level input voltage, V_{IL}
H = High-level input voltage, V_{IH}
HH = High-level program voltage, V_{IHH}
Z = High impedance (e.g., 10kΩ to 5.0V)

INPUT LINE NUMBER	PIN IDENTIFICATION								
	I_7	I_6	I_5	I_4	I_3	I_2	I_1	I_0	L/R
0	HH	HH	HH	HH	HH	HH	HH	L	Z
1	HH	HH	HH	HH	HH	HH	HH	H	Z
2	HH	HH	HH	HH	HH	HH	HH	L	HH
3	HH	HH	HH	HH	HH	HH	HH	H	HH
4	HH	HH	HH	HH	HH	HH	L	HH	Z
5	HH	HH	HH	HH	HH	HH	H	HH	Z
6	HH	HH	HH	HH	HH	HH	L	HH	HH
7	HH	HH	HH	HH	HH	HH	H	HH	HH
8	HH	HH	HH	HH	HH	L	HH	HH	Z
9	HH	HH	HH	HH	HH	H	HH	HH	Z
10	HH	HH	HH	HH	HH	L	HH	HH	HH
11	HH	HH	HH	HH	HH	H	HH	HH	HH
12	HH	HH	HH	HH	L	HH	HH	HH	Z
13	HH	HH	HH	HH	H	HH	HH	HH	Z
14	HH	HH	HH	HH	L	HH	HH	HH	HH
15	HH	HH	HH	HH	H	HH	HH	HH	HH
16	HH	HH	HH	L	HH	HH	HH	HH	Z
17	HH	HH	HH	H	HH	HH	HH	HH	Z
18	HH	HH	HH	L	HH	HH	HH	HH	HH
19	HH	HH	HH	H	HH	HH	HH	HH	HH
20	HH	HH	L	HH	HH	HH	HH	HH	Z
21	HH	HH	H	HH	HH	HH	HH	HH	Z
22	HH	HH	L	HH	HH	HH	HH	HH	HH
23	HH	HH	H	HH	HH	HH	HH	HH	HH
24	HH	L	HH	HH	HH	HH	HH	HH	Z
25	HH	H	HH	HH	HH	HH	HH	HH	Z
26	HH	L	HH	HH	HH	HH	HH	HH	HH
27	HH	H	HH	HH	HH	HH	HH	HH	HH
28	L	HH	HH	HH	HH	HH	HH	HH	Z
29	H	HH	HH	HH	HH	HH	HH	HH	Z
30	L	HH	HH	HH	HH	HH	HH	HH	HH
31	H	HH	HH	HH	HH	HH	HH	HH	HH

Table 1 Input Line Select

PRODUCT LINE NUMBER	PIN IDENTIFICATION						
	O_3	O_2	O_1	O_0	A_2	A_1	A_0
0, 32	Z	Z	Z	HH	Z	Z	Z
1, 33	Z	Z	Z	HH	Z	Z	HH
2, 34	Z	Z	Z	HH	Z	HH	Z
3, 35	Z	Z	Z	HH	Z	HH	HH
4, 36	Z	Z	Z	HH	HH	Z	Z
5, 37	Z	Z	Z	HH	HH	Z	HH
6, 38	Z	Z	Z	HH	HH	HH	Z
7, 39	Z	Z	Z	HH	HH	HH	HH
8, 40	Z	Z	HH	Z	Z	Z	Z
9, 41	Z	Z	HH	Z	Z	Z	HH
10, 42	Z	Z	HH	Z	Z	HH	Z
11, 43	Z	Z	HH	Z	Z	HH	HH
12, 44	Z	Z	HH	Z	HH	Z	Z
13, 45	Z	Z	HH	Z	HH	Z	HH
14, 46	Z	Z	HH	Z	HH	HH	Z
15, 47	Z	Z	HH	Z	HH	HH	HH
16, 48	Z	HH	Z	Z	Z	Z	Z
17, 49	Z	HH	Z	Z	Z	Z	HH
18, 50	Z	HH	Z	Z	Z	HH	Z
19, 51	Z	HH	Z	Z	Z	HH	HH
20, 52	Z	HH	Z	Z	HH	Z	Z
21, 53	Z	HH	Z	Z	HH	Z	HH
22, 54	Z	HH	Z	Z	HH	HH	Z
23, 55	Z	HH	Z	Z	HH	HH	HH
24, 56	HH	Z	Z	Z	Z	Z	Z
25, 57	HH	Z	Z	Z	Z	Z	HH
26, 58	HH	Z	Z	Z	Z	HH	Z
27, 59	HH	Z	Z	Z	Z	HH	HH
28, 60	HH	Z	Z	Z	HH	Z	Z
29, 61	HH	Z	Z	Z	HH	Z	HH
30, 62	HH	Z	Z	Z	HH	HH	Z
31, 63	HH	Z	Z	Z	HH	HH	HH

Table 2 Product Line Select

Pin Configurations for Programming

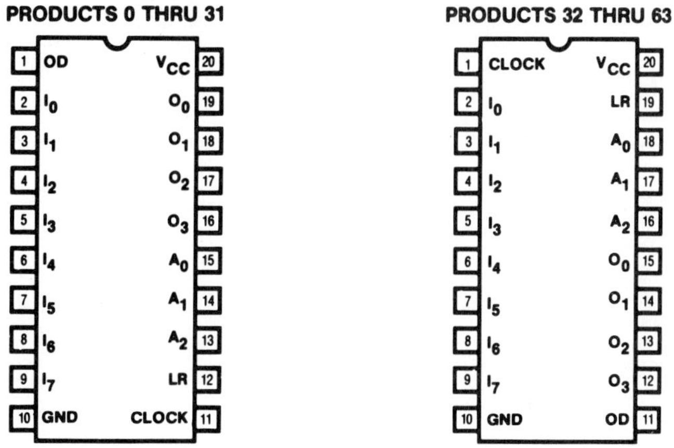

Programming Parameters $T_A = 25°C$

SYMBOL	PARAMETER		LIMITS MIN	TYP	MAX	UNIT
V_{IHH}	Program-level input voltage		11	11.5	12	V
I_{IHH}	Program-level input current	Output Program Pulse			50	mA
		OD, L/R			25	
		All Other Inputs			5	
I_{CCH}	Program Supply Current				400	mA
T_P	Program Pulse Width		10		50	μs
t_D	Delay time		100			ns
t_{DV}	Delay Time to Verify		100			μs
	Program Pulse duty cycle				25	%
V_P	Verify-Protect-input voltage		20	21	22	V
I_P	Verify-Protect-input current				400	mA
T_{PP}	Verify-Protect Pulse Width		20		50	msec

Programming Waveforms

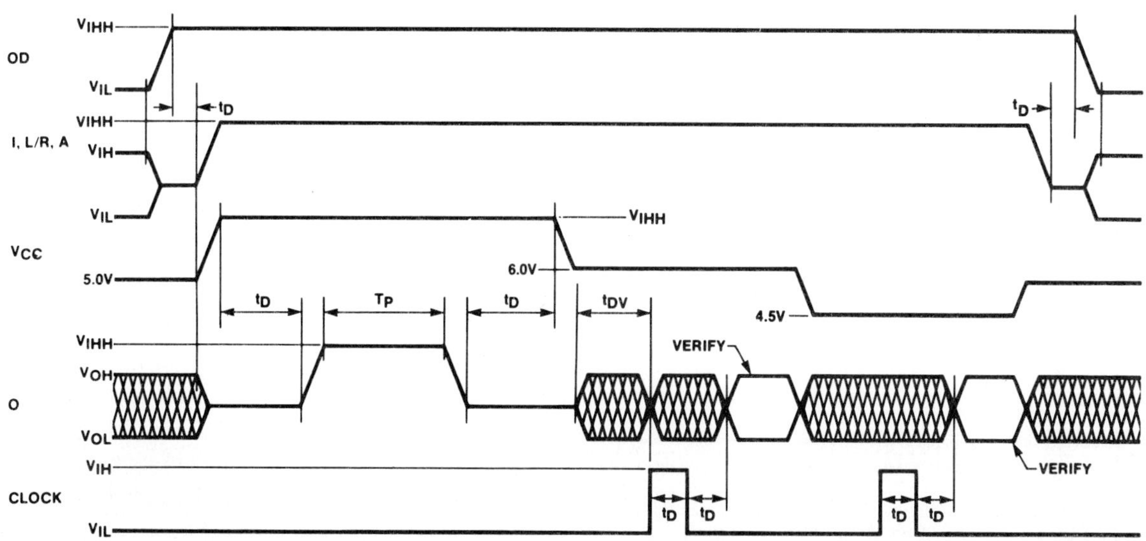

High Speed Programmable Array Logic Family

PAL® Series 20A

U.S. Patent 4124899

March 1982

Features/Benefits

- **15ns typical propagation delay**
- **Programmable replacement for TTL logic**
- **Reduces IC inventories**
- **Reduces chip count by greater than 4 to 1**
- **Expedites prototyping and board layout**
- **Saves space with 20-pin SKINNYDIP™ packages**
- **Programmed on standard PROM programmers**
- **Programmable three-state outputs**
- **Last fuse prevents duplication on a PROM/PAL programmer**

PART NUMBER	PKG	GATE ARRAY DESCRIPTION
PAL16L8A	N,J,F,L	Octal 16 Input And-Or-Invert
PAL16R8A	N,J,F,L	Octal 16 Input Registered And-Or
PAL16R6A	N,J,F,L	Hex 16 Input Registered And-Or
PAL16R4A	N,J,F,L	Quad 16 Input Registered And-Or

Description

The PAL Series 20A family utilizes Monolithic Memories advanced self-aligned washed emitter high speed bipolar process and the bipolar PROM fusible link technology to provide user programmable logic for replacing conventional SSI/MSI gates and flip-flops at reduced chip count.

The family lets the systems engineer "design his own chip" by blowing fusible links to configure AND and OR gates to perform his desired logic function. Complex interconnections which previously required time-consuming layout are thus "lifted" from the PC board and are placed on silicon where they can be easily modified during prototype check-out or production.

The PAL transfer function is the familiar sum of products. Like the PROM, the PAL has a single array of fusible links. Unlike the PROM, the PAL is a programmable AND array driving a fixed OR array (the PROM is a fixed AND array driving a programmable OR array). In addition the PAL provides these options:

- Variable input/output pin ratio
- Programmable three-state outputs
- Registers with feedback

Unused inputs are tied directly to V_{CC} or GND. Product terms with all fuses blown assume the logical high state, and product terms connected to both true and complement of any single input assume the logical low state. Registers consist of D type flip-flops which are loaded on the low to high transition of the clock. PAL Logic Diagrams are shown with all fuses blown, enabling the designer use of the diagrams as coding sheets.

The entire PAL family is programmed on inexpensive conventional PROM programmers with appropriate personality and socket adapter cards. Once the PAL is programmed and verified, two additional fuses may be blown to defeat verification. This feature gives the user a proprietary circuit which is very difficult to copy.

Ordering Information

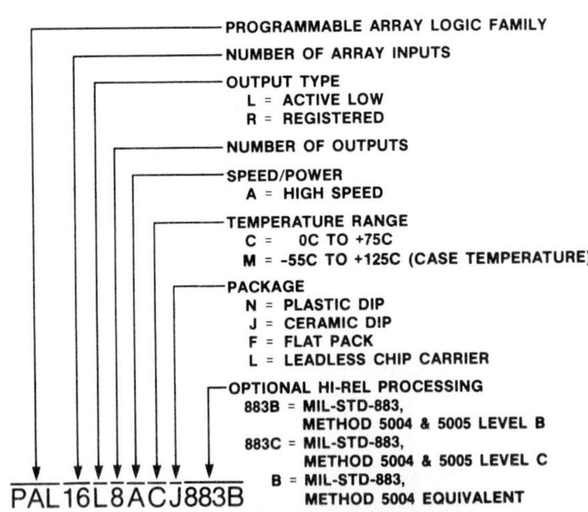

PAL® is a registered trademark of Monolithic Memories.

PAL16L8A

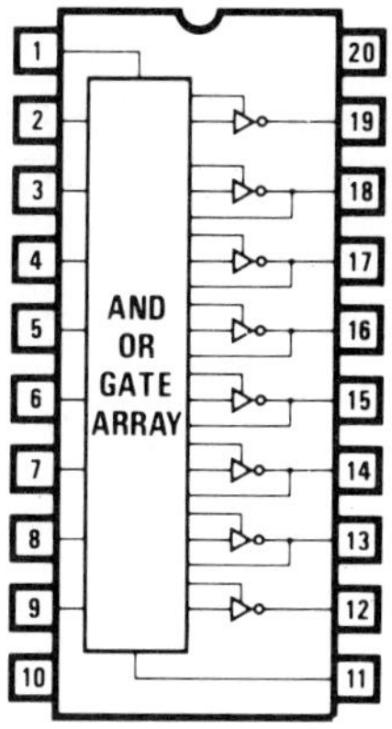

PAL16R8A

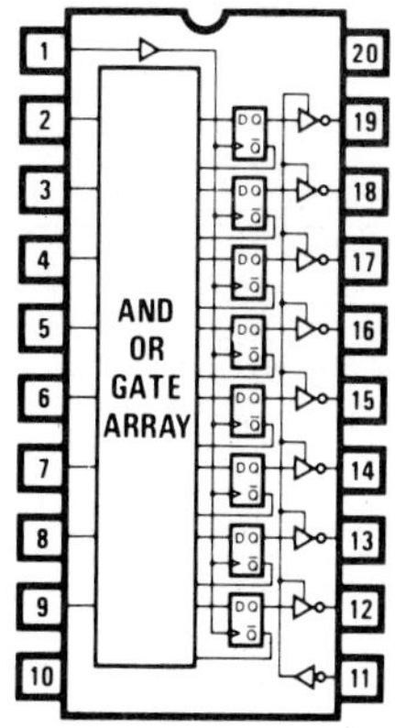

PAL16R6A

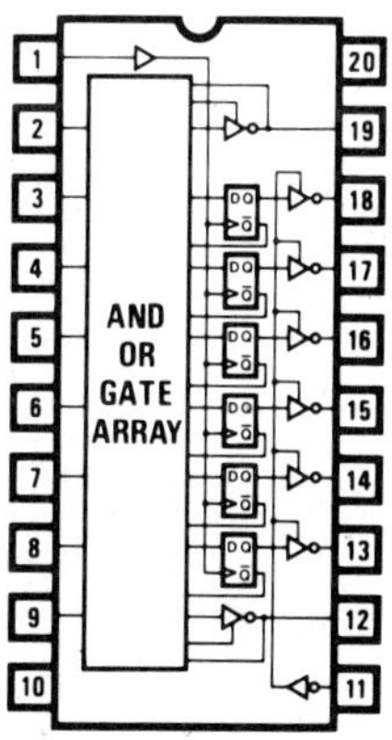

PAL16R4A

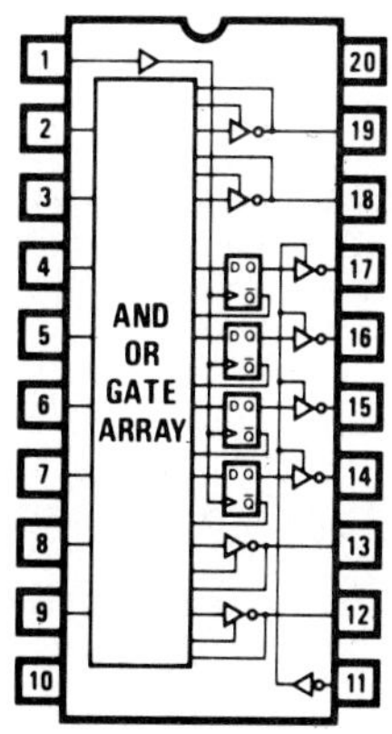

Absolute Maximum Ratings

	Operating	Programming
Supply Voltage, V_{CC}	-0.5 to 7.0V	-0.5 to 12.0V
Input Voltage	-1.5 to 5.5V	-1.0 to 12.0V⊕
Off-state output Voltage	5.5V	12.0V
Storage temperature		-65° to +150°C

Operating Conditions

SYMBOL	PARAMETER		MILITARY MIN	MILITARY TYP	MILITARY MAX	COMMERCIAL MIN	COMMERCIAL TYP	COMMERCIAL MAX	UNIT
V_{CC}	Supply voltage		4.5	5	5.5	4.75	5	5.25	V
t_w	Width of clock	Low	20	10		15	10		ns
		High	20	10		15	10		
t_{su}	Set up time from input or feedback to clock	16R8A 16R6A 16R4A	30	16		25	16		ns
t_h	Hold time		0	-10		0	-10		ns
T_A	Operating free-air temperature		-55			0	25	75	°C
T_C	Operating case temperature				125				°C

Electrical Characteristics Over Operating Conditions

SYMBOL	PARAMETER	TEST CONDITIONS			MIN	TYP	MAX	UNIT
V_{IL}*	Low-level input voltage						0.8	V
V_{IH}*	High-level input voltage				2			V
V_{IC}	Input clamp voltage	V_{CC} = MIN		I_I = −18mA		-0.8	−1.5	V
I_{IL}	Low-level input current †	V_{CC} = MAX		V_I = 0.4V		-0.02	−0.25	mA
I_{IH}	High-level input current †	V_{CC} = MAX		V_I = 2.4V			25	μA
I_I	Maximum input current	V_{CC} = MAX		V_I = 5.5V			1	mA
V_{OL}	Low-level output voltage	V_{CC} = MIN, V_{IL} = 0.8V, V_{IH} = 2V	MIL	I_{OL} = 12mA		0.3	0.5	V
			COM	I_{OL} = 24mA				
V_{OH}	High-level output voltage	V_{CC} = MIN, V_{IL} = 0.8V, V_{IH} = 2V	MIL	I_{OH} = −2mA	2.4	2.8		V
			COM	I_{OH} = −3.2mA				
I_{OZL}	Off-state output current †	V_{CC} = MAX, V_{IL} = 0.8V, V_{IH} = 2V		V_O = 0.4V			−100	μA
I_{OZH}				V_O = 2.4V			100	μA
I_{OS}	Output short-circuit current **	V_{CC} = 5V		V_O = 0V	−30	−70	−130	mA
I_{CC}	Supply current	V_{CC} = MAX				120	180	mA

† I/O pin leakage is the worst case of I_{OZX} or I_{IX} e.g., I_{IL} and I_{OZH}.

†† All typical values are at V_{CC} = 5V, T_A = 25°C.

* These are absolute voltages with respect to pin 10 on the device and includes all overshoots due to system and/or tester noise. Do not attempt to test these values without suitable equipment.

** Only one output shorted at a time.

⊕Pins 1 and 11 may be raised to 22V max.

Switching Characteristics

Over Operating Conditions

SYMBOL	PARAMETER		TEST CONDITIONS	MILITARY MIN	MILITARY TYP	MILITARY MAX	COMMERCIAL MIN	COMMERCIAL TYP	COMMERCIAL MAX	UNIT
t_{PD}	Input or feed-back to output	16R6A 16R4A 16L8A	$R_1 = 200\Omega$ $R_2 = 390\Omega$		15	30		15	25	ns
t_{CLK}	Clock to output or feedback				10	20		10	15	ns
t_{PZX}	Pin 11 to output enable				10	25		10	20	ns
t_{PXZ}	Pin 11 to output disable				11	25		11	20	ns
t_{PZX}	Input to output enable	16R6A 16R4A 16L8A			10	30		10	25	ns
t_{PXZ}	Input to output disable	16R6A 16R4A 16L8A			13	30		13	25	ns
f_{MAX}	Maximum frequency	16R8A 16R6A 16R4A		20	30		25	30		MHz

Test Load

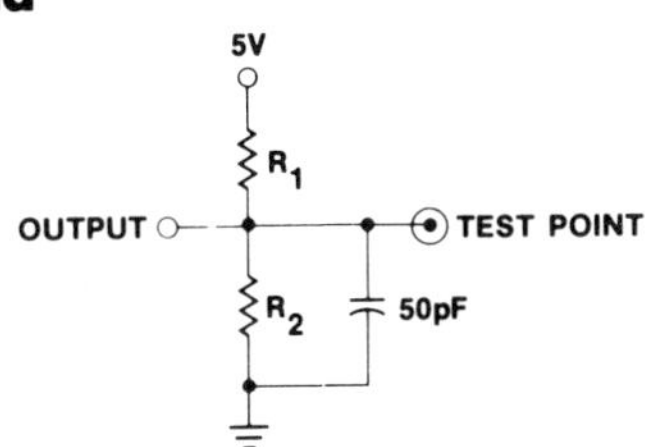

Available Programmers

MANUFACTURER	PERSONALITY CARD SET	SOCKET ADAPTER CONFIGURATION
Data I/O Corporation	909-1427	715 1428-1 715 1428-2 715 1428-3
Pro-Log Corporation	PM9068	
Stag Systems	PM202	AM10H8 AM10L8 AM12H6 AM12L6 AM14H4 AM14L4 AM16H2 AM16L2 AM16C1
Structured Design	SD20/24	
Kontron	MPP-80S	

Schematic of Inputs and Outputs

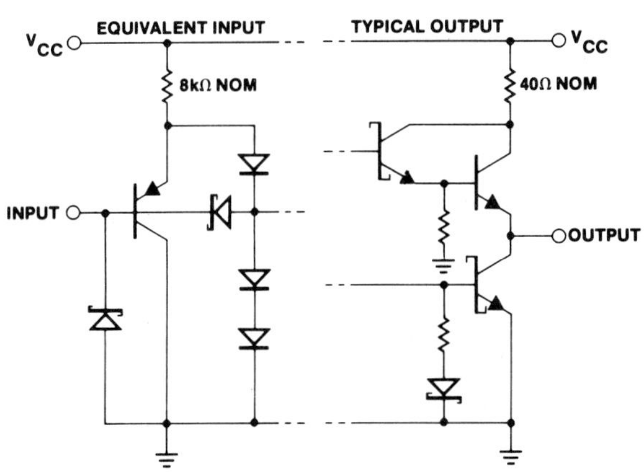

Programming

PAL fuses are programmed using a low-voltage linear-select procedure which is common to all 4 PAL types. The array is divided into two groups, products 0 thru 31 and products 32 thru 63, for which pin identifications are shown in Pin Configurations below. To program a particular fuse, both an input line and a product line are selected according to the following procedure:

Step 1 Raise Output Disable, OD, to V_{IHH}

Step 2 Select an input line by specifying $I_0, I_1, I_2, I_3, I_4, I_5, I_6, I_7$ and L/R as shown in Table 1.

Step 3 Select a product line by specifying A_0, A_1 and A_2 one-of-eight select as shown in Table 2.

Step 4 Raise V_{CC} (pin 20) to V_{IHH}

Step 5 Program the fuse by pulsing the output pins, O, of the selected product group to V_{IHH} as shown in Programming Waveform.

Step 6 Lower V_{CC} (pin 20) to 6.0 V

Step 7 Pulse the CLOCK pin and verify the output pin, O, to be Low for active Low PAL types or High for active High PAL types.

Step 8 Lower V_{CC} (pin 20) to 4.5 V and repeat step 7.

Step 9 Should the output not verify, repeat steps 1 thru 8 up to five (5) times.

This procedure is repeated for all fuses to be blown (see Programming Waveforms).

To prevent further verification, two last fuses may be blown by raising pin 1 and pin 11 to V_P. V_{CC} is not required during this operation.

Voltage Legend

L = Low-level input voltage, V_{IL}
H = High-level input voltage, V_{IH}
HH = High-level program voltage, V_{IHH}
Z = High impedance (e.g., 10kΩ to 5.0V)

INPUT LINE NUMBER	PIN IDENTIFICATION								
	I_7	I_6	I_5	I_4	I_3	I_2	I_1	I_0	L/R
0	HH	HH	HH	HH	HH	HH	HH	L	Z
1	HH	HH	HH	HH	HH	HH	HH	H	Z
2	HH	HH	HH	HH	HH	HH	HH	L	HH
3	HH	HH	HH	HH	HH	HH	HH	H	HH
4	HH	HH	HH	HH	HH	HH	L	HH	Z
5	HH	HH	HH	HH	HH	HH	H	HH	Z
6	HH	HH	HH	HH	HH	HH	L	HH	HH
7	HH	HH	HH	HH	HH	HH	H	HH	HH
8	HH	HH	HH	HH	HH	L	HH	HH	Z
9	HH	HH	HH	HH	HH	H	HH	HH	Z
10	HH	HH	HH	HH	HH	L	HH	HH	HH
11	HH	HH	HH	HH	HH	H	HH	HH	HH
12	HH	HH	HH	HH	L	HH	HH	HH	Z
13	HH	HH	HH	HH	H	HH	HH	HH	Z
14	HH	HH	HH	HH	L	HH	HH	HH	HH
15	HH	HH	HH	HH	H	HH	HH	HH	HH
16	HH	HH	HH	L	HH	HH	HH	HH	Z
17	HH	HH	HH	H	HH	HH	HH	HH	Z
18	HH	HH	HH	L	HH	HH	HH	HH	HH
19	HH	HH	HH	H	HH	HH	HH	HH	HH
20	HH	HH	L	HH	HH	HH	HH	HH	Z
21	HH	HH	H	HH	HH	HH	HH	HH	Z
22	HH	HH	L	HH	HH	HH	HH	HH	HH
23	HH	HH	H	HH	HH	HH	HH	HH	HH
24	HH	L	HH	HH	HH	HH	HH	HH	Z
25	HH	H	HH	HH	HH	HH	HH	HH	Z
26	HH	L	HH	HH	HH	HH	HH	HH	HH
27	HH	H	HH	HH	HH	HH	HH	HH	HH
28	L	HH	HH	HH	HH	HH	HH	HH	Z
29	H	HH	HH	HH	HH	HH	HH	HH	Z
30	L	HH	HH	HH	HH	HH	HH	HH	HH
31	H	HH	HH	HH	HH	HH	HH	HH	HH

Table 1 Input Line Select

PRODUCT LINE NUMBER	PIN IDENTIFICATION						
	O_3	O_2	O_1	O_0	A_2	A_1	A_0
0, 32	Z	Z	Z	HH	Z	Z	Z
1, 33	Z	Z	Z	HH	Z	Z	HH
2, 34	Z	Z	Z	HH	Z	HH	Z
3, 35	Z	Z	Z	HH	Z	HH	HH
4, 36	Z	Z	Z	HH	HH	Z	Z
5, 37	Z	Z	Z	HH	HH	Z	HH
6, 38	Z	Z	Z	HH	HH	HH	Z
7, 39	Z	Z	Z	HH	HH	HH	HH
8, 40	Z	Z	HH	Z	Z	Z	Z
9, 41	Z	Z	HH	Z	Z	Z	HH
10, 42	Z	Z	HH	Z	Z	HH	Z
11, 43	Z	Z	HH	Z	Z	HH	HH
12, 44	Z	Z	HH	Z	HH	Z	Z
13, 45	Z	Z	HH	Z	HH	Z	HH
14, 46	Z	Z	HH	Z	HH	HH	Z
15, 47	Z	Z	HH	Z	HH	HH	HH
16, 48	Z	HH	Z	Z	Z	Z	Z
17, 49	Z	HH	Z	Z	Z	Z	HH
18, 50	Z	HH	Z	Z	Z	HH	Z
19, 51	Z	HH	Z	Z	Z	HH	HH
20, 52	Z	HH	Z	Z	HH	Z	Z
21, 53	Z	HH	Z	Z	HH	Z	HH
22, 54	Z	HH	Z	Z	HH	HH	Z
23, 55	Z	HH	Z	Z	HH	HH	HH
24, 56	HH	Z	Z	Z	Z	Z	Z
25, 57	HH	Z	Z	Z	Z	Z	HH
26, 58	HH	Z	Z	Z	Z	HH	Z
27, 59	HH	Z	Z	Z	Z	HH	HH
28, 60	HH	Z	Z	Z	HH	Z	Z
29, 61	HH	Z	Z	Z	HH	Z	HH
30, 62	HH	Z	Z	Z	HH	HH	Z
31, 63	HH	Z	Z	Z	HH	HH	HH

Table 2 Product Line Select

Pin Configurations for Programming

PRODUCTS 0 THRU 31

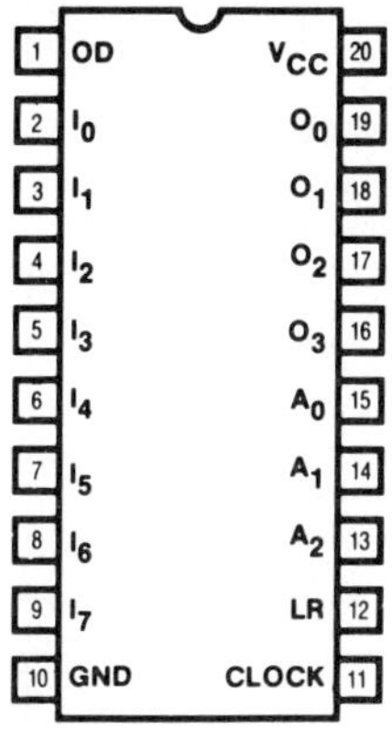

PRODUCTS 32 THRU 63

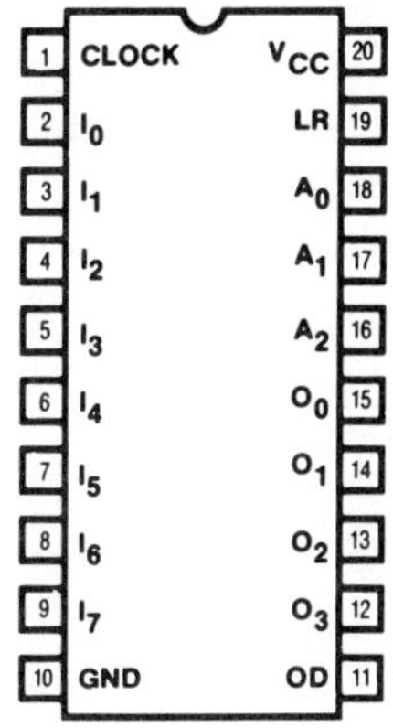

Programmer Requirement $T_A = 25°C$

SYMBOL	DEFINITION		LIMITS MIN	TYP	MAX	UNIT
V_{IHH}	Program-level input voltage		11	11.5	12	V
I_{IHH}	Program-level input current	Output Program Pulse			50	mA
		OD, L/R			25	mA
		All Other Inputs			5	mA
I_{CCH}	Program Supply Current				400	mA
T_P	Program Pulse Width		10		50	μs
t_D	Delay time		100			ns
t_{DV}	Delay Time to Verify		100			μs
	Program Pulse duty cycle				25	%
V_P	Verify-Protect-input voltage		20	21	22	V
I_P	Verify-Protect-input current				400	mA
T_{PP}	Verify-Protect Pulse Width		20		50	msec

Programming Waveforms

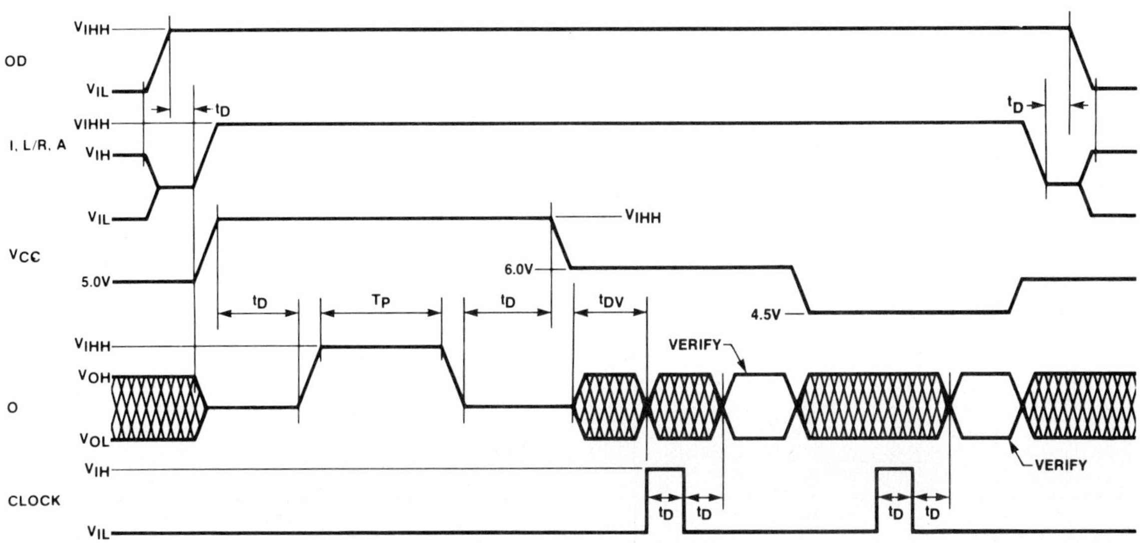

Package Drawings

UNLESS OTHERWISE SPECIFIED:
ALL DIMENSIONS MIN.-MAX. IN INCHES
ALL DIMENSIONS MIN.-MAX. IN MILLIMETERS

F20 Flat Pack (Eutectic Seal)

θ_{JA} = 75°C/WATT
θ_{JC} = 35°C/WATT

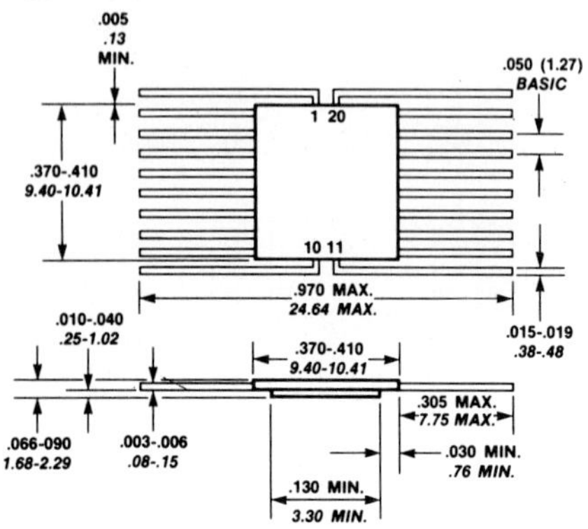

J20 Ceramic DIP

θ_{JA} = 75°C/WATT
θ_{JC} = 35°C/WATT

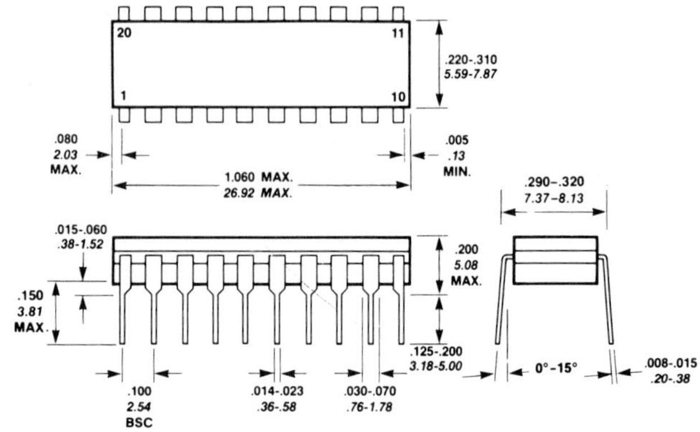

L20 Leadless Chip Carrier

θ_{JA} - 63°C/WATT
θ_{JC} - 35°C/WATT

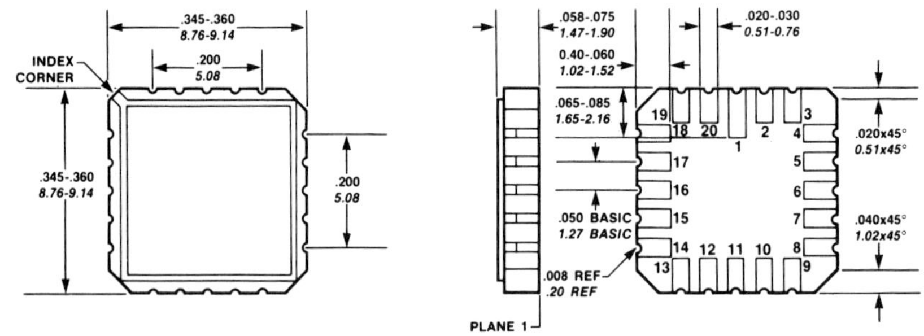

TOP VIEW

BOTTOM VIEW

PLANE 1 IS THE PRIMARY HEAT RADIATING SURFACE

N20 Plastic Kool DIP

θ_{JA} = 75°C/WATT
θ_{JC} = 35°C/WATT

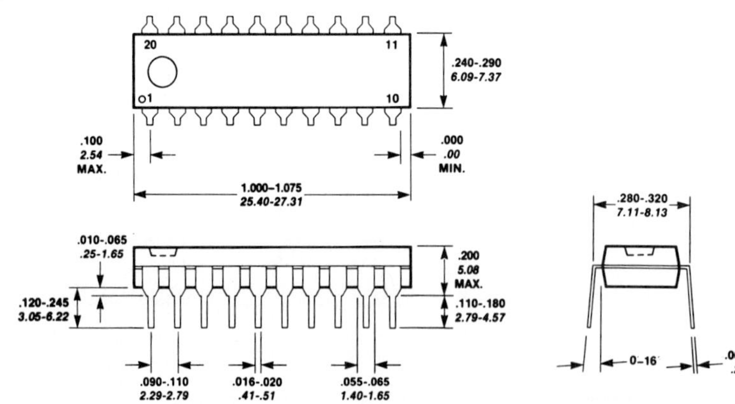

PAL
IMPORTANT,
NOTES

Octal Counter
SN54/74LS461

Features/Benefits

- Octal counter for microprogram-counter, DMA controller and general purpose counting applications
- 8 bits match byte boundaries
- Bus-structured pinout
- 24-pin Skinny DIP® saves space
- 3-state outputs drive bus lines
- Low current PNP inputs reduce loading
- Expandable in 8-bit increments

Ordering Information

PART NUMBER	PACKAGE	TEMPERATURE
SN54LS461	JS	MIL
SN74LS461	NS, JS	COM

Description

The LS461 is an 8-bit synchronous counter with parallel load, clear, and hold capability. Two function select inputs (I_0, I_1) provide one of four operations which occur synchronously on the rising edge of the clock (CLK).

The LOAD operation loads the inputs (D_7–D_0) into the output register (Q_7–Q_0). The CLEAR operation resets the output register to all LOWs. The HOLD operation holds the previous value regardless of clock transitions. The INCREMENT operation adds one to the output register when the carry-in input is TRUE ($\overline{CI}$ = LOW), otherwise the operation is a HOLD. The carry-out ($\overline{CO}$) is TRUE ($\overline{CO}$ = LOW) when the output register (Q_7–Q_0) is all HIGHs, otherwise FALSE ($\overline{CO}$ = HIGH).

The output register (Q_7–Q_0) is enabled when OC is LOW, and disabled (HI-Z) when $\overline{OC}$ is HIGH. The output drivers will sink the 24 mA required for many bus interface standards.

Two or more LS461 octal counters may be cascaded to provide larger counters. The operation codes were chosen such that when I_1 is HIGH, I_0 may be used to select between LOAD and INCREMENT as in a program counter (JUMP/INCREMENT).

Logic Symbol

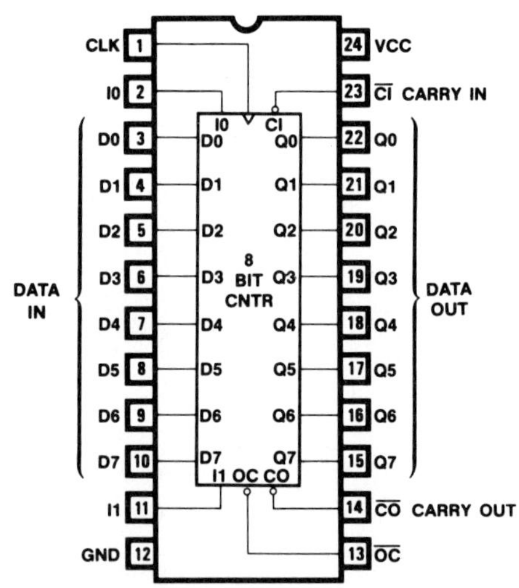

Function Table

$\overline{OC}$	CLK	I_1	I_0	$\overline{CI}$	D_7–D_0	Q_7–Q_0	OPERATION
H	X	X	X	X	X	Z	HI-Z
L	↑	L	L	X	X	L	CLEAR
L	↑	L	H	X	X	Q	HOLD
L	↑	H	L	X	D	D	LOAD
L	↑	H	H	H	X	Q	HOLD
L	↑	H	H	L	X	Q plus 1	INCREMENT

For supplementary information, see appendix, this section.

1165 East Arques Avenue, Sunnyvale, CA 94086 Tel: (408) 739-3535 TWX: 910-339-9229

Monolithic Memories MMI

Logic Diagram

Octal Counter

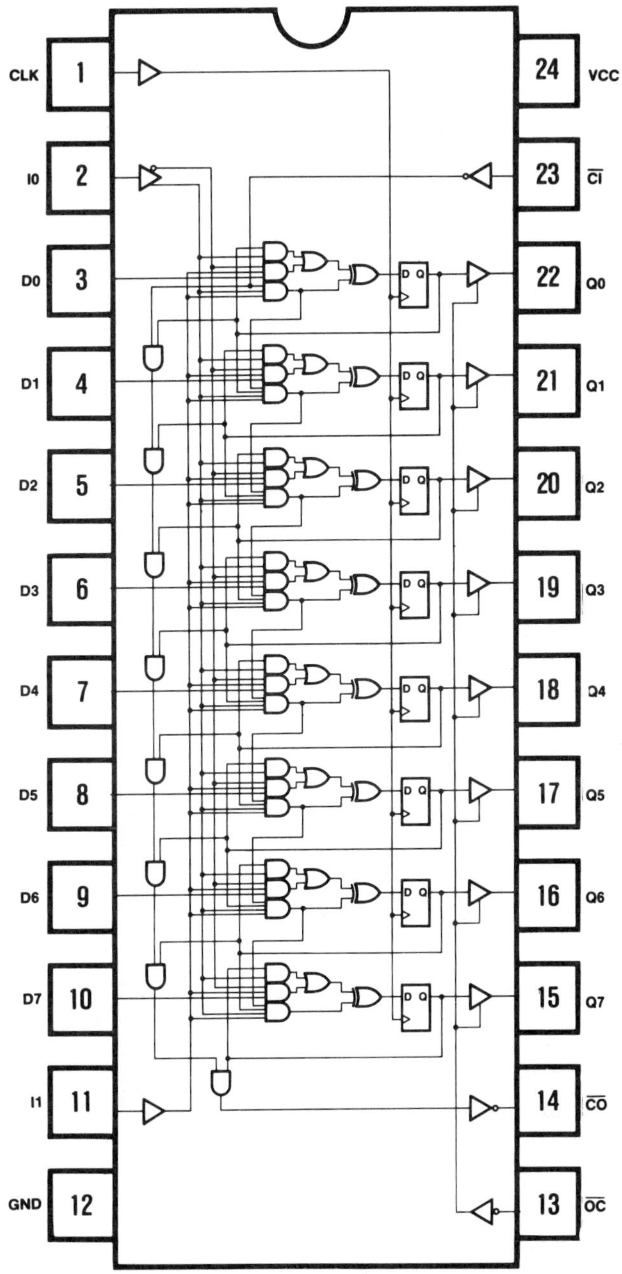

Octal Shift Register
SN54/74LS498

Features/Benefits

- Octal shift register for serial to parallel and parallel to serial applications
- 8 bits match byte boundaries
- Bus-structured pinout
- 24-pin SKINNYDIP™ saves space
- 3-state outputs drive bus lines
- Low current PNP inputs reduce loading
- Expandable in 8-bit increments

Ordering Information

PART NUMBER	PACKAGE	TEMPERATURE
SN54LS498	JS	MIL
SN74LS498	NS, JS	COM

Description

The LS498 is an 8-bit synchronous shift register with parallel load and hold capability. Two function select inputs (I_0, I_1) provide one of four operations which occur synchronously on the rising edge of the clock (CLK).

The LOAD operation loads the input (D_7-D_0) into the output register (Q_7-Q_0). The HOLD operation holds the previous value regardless of clock transitions. The SHIFT LEFT operation shifts the output register, Q, one bit to the left; Q_0 is replaced by LIRO. RILO outputs Q_7.

The SHIFT RIGHT operation shifts the output register, Q, one bit to the right; Q_7 is replaced by RILO. LIRO outputs Q_0.

The output register (Q_7-Q_0) is enabled when $\overline{OC}$ is LOW, and disabled (HI-Z) when $\overline{OC}$ is HIGH. The output drivers will sink the 24 mA required for many bus interface standards.

Two or more LS498 octal shift registers may be cascaded to provide larger shift registers as shown in the application section.

Logic Symbol

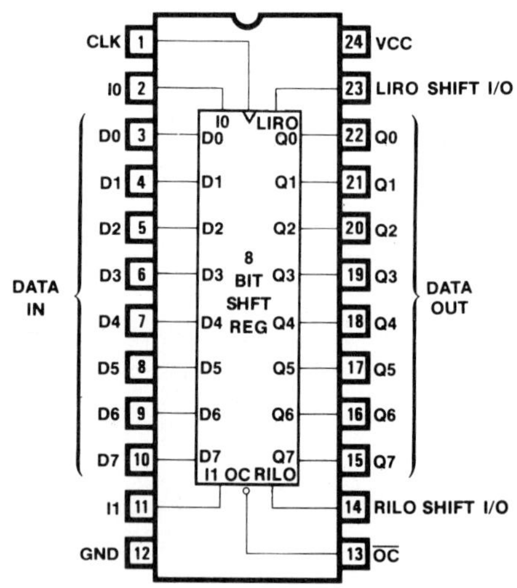

Function Table

$\overline{OC}$	CLK	I_1	I_0	D_7-D_0	Q_7-Q_0	OPERATION
H	X	X	X	X	Z	HI-Z
L	↑	L	L	X	L	HOLD
L	↑	L	H	X	SR(Q)	SHIFT RIGHT
L	↑	H	L	X	SL(Q)	SHIFT LEFT
L	↑	H	H	D	D	LOAD

For supplementary information, see appendix, this section.

Logic Diagram

Octal Shift Register

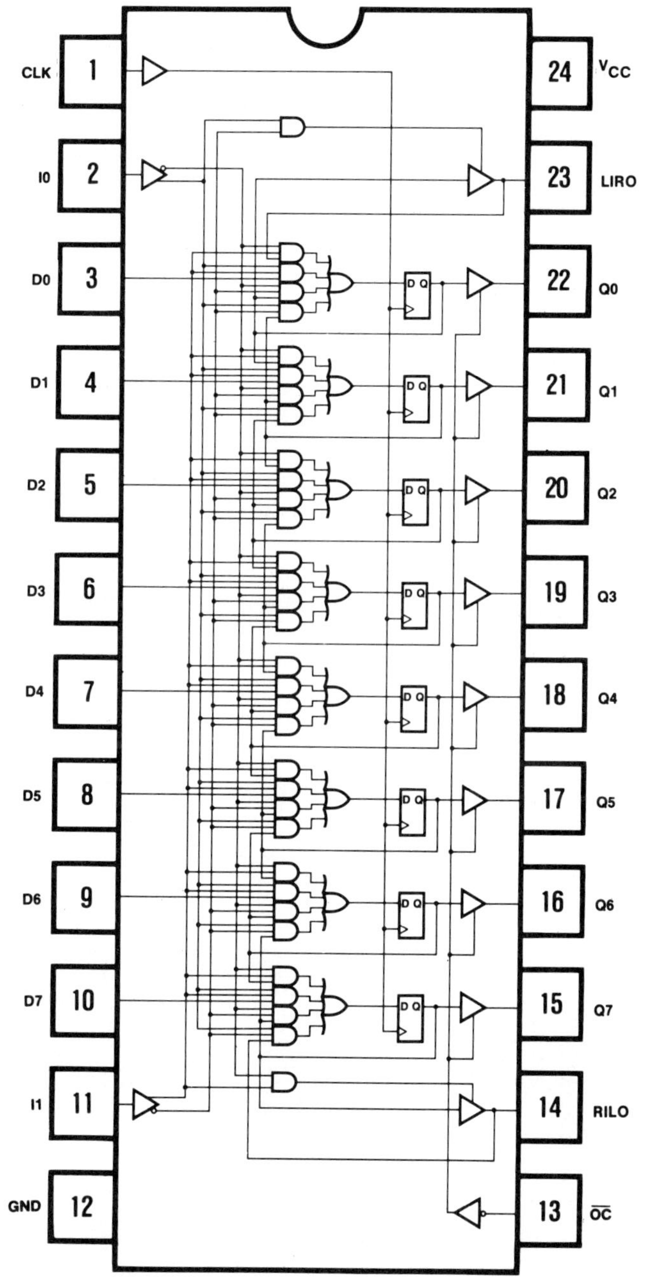

Multifunction Octal Register

SN54/74LS380

Features/Benefits

- Octal Register for general purposes interfacing applications
- 8 bits match byte boundaries
- Bus-structured pinout
- 24-pin SKINNYDIP™ saves space
- 3-state outputs drive bus lines
- Low current PNP inputs reduce loading

Ordering Information

PART NUMBER	PACKAGE	TEMPERATURE
SN54LS380	JS	MIL
SN74LS380	NS, JS	COM

Description

The LS380 is an 8-bit synchronous register with parallel load, load compliment, preset, clear, and hold capacity. Four control inputs ($\overline{LD}$, POL, $\overline{CLR}$, $\overline{PR}$) provide one of four operations which occur synchronously on the rising edge of the clock (CLK). The LS380 combines the features of the LS374, LS377, LS273 and LS534 into a single 300 mil wide package.

The LOAD operation loads the inputs (D_7-D_0) into the output register (Q_7-Q_0), when POL is HIGH, or loads the compliment of the inputs when POL is LOW. The CLEAR operation resets the output register to all LOWs. The PRESET operation presets the output register to all HIGHs. The HOLD operation holds the previous value regardless of clock transitions. CLEAR overrides PRESET, PRESET overrides LOAD, and LOAD overrides HOLD.

The output register (Q_7-Q_0) is enabled when OC is LOW, and disabled (HI-Z) when $\overline{OC}$ is HIGH. The output drivers will sink the 24 mA required for many bus interface standards.

Logic Symbol

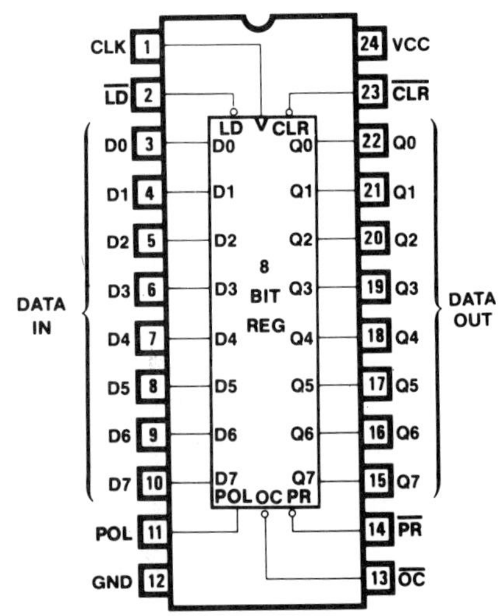

Function Table

$\overline{OC}$	CLK	$\overline{LD}$	POL	$\overline{CLR}$	$\overline{PR}$	D7-D0	Q7-Q0	OPERATION
H	X	X	X	X	X	X	Z	HI-Z
L	↑	X	X	L	X	X	L	CLEAR
L	↑	X	X	H	L	X	H	PRESET
L	↑	H	X	H	H	X	Q	HOLD
L	↑	L	H	H	H	D	D	LOAD true
L	↑	L	L	H	H	D	$\overline{D}$	LOAD comp

For supplementary information, see appendix, this section.

Logic Diagram

Octal Register

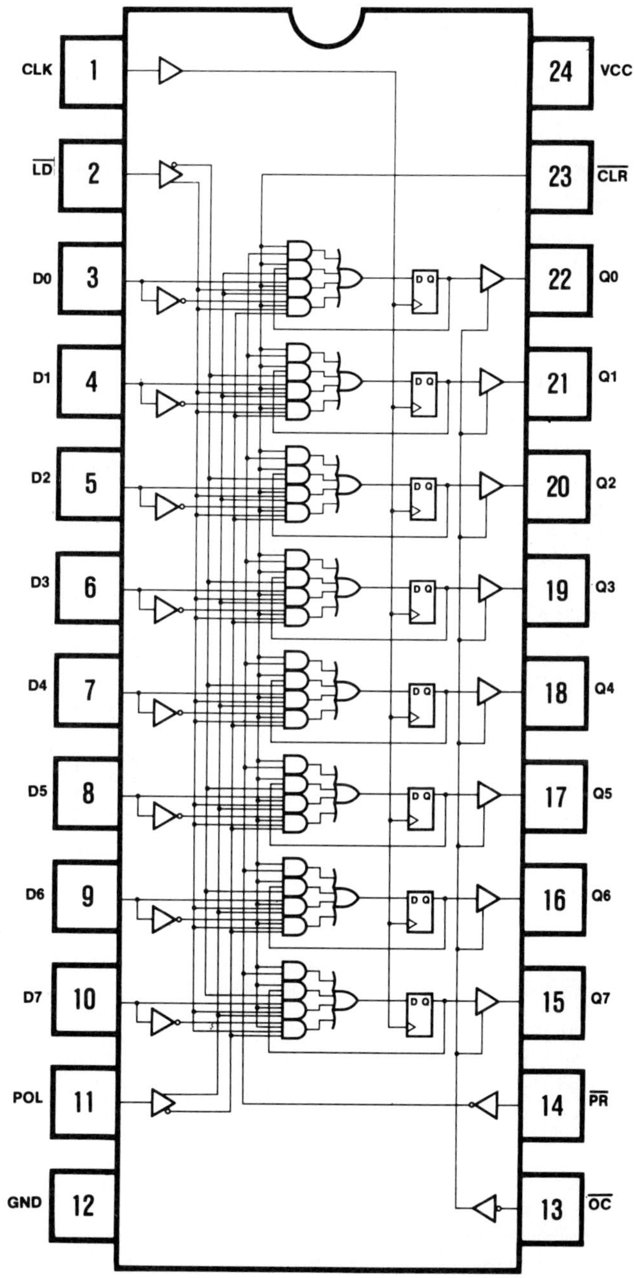

10-Bit Counter
SN54/74LS491

Features/Benefits

- CRT vertical and horizontal timing generation
- Bus-structured pinout
- 24-pin SKINNYDIP™ saves space
- 3-state outputs drive bus lines
- Low current PNP inputs reduce loading

Ordering Information

PART NUMBER	PACKAGE	TEMPERATURE
SN54LS491	JS	MIL
SN74LS491	NS, JS	COM

Description

The ten-bit counter can count up, count down, set, and load 2 LSB's, 2 MSB's and 6 middle bits high or low as a group. All operations are synchronous with the clock. SET overrides LOAD, COUNT and HOLD. LOAD overrides COUNT. COUNT is conditional on CIN, otherwise it holds.

All outputs are enabled when OC is low, otherwise HIGH-Z. The 24 mA I_{OL} outputs are suitable for driving RAM/PROM address lines in video graphics systems.

Logic Symbol

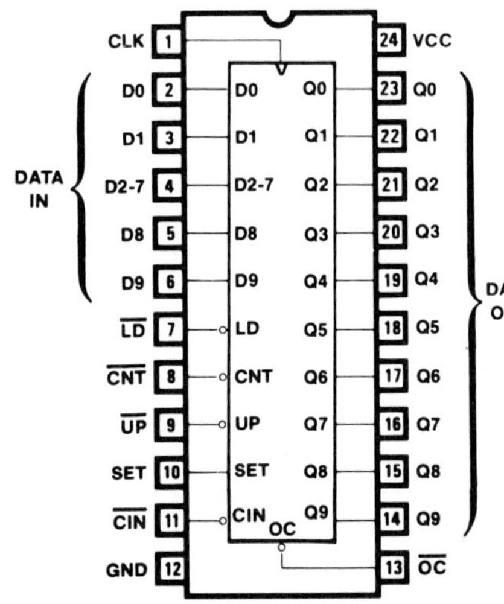

Function Table

$\overline{OC}$	CLK	SET	$\overline{LD}$	$\overline{CNT}$	$\overline{CIN}$	$\overline{UP}$	D9-D0	Q9-Q0	OPERATION
H	X	X	X	X	X	X	X	Z	HI-Z
L	↑	H	X	X	X	X	X	H	Set all HIGH
L	↑	L	L	X	X	X	D	D	LOAD D
L	↑	L	H	H	X	X	X	Q	HOLD
L	↑	L	H	L	H	X	X	Q	HOLD
L	↑	L	H	L	L	L	X	Q plus 1	Count UP
L	↑	L	H	L	L	H	X	Q minus 1	Count DN

For supplementary information see appendix this section.

Logic Diagram

10-Bit Up/Down Counter

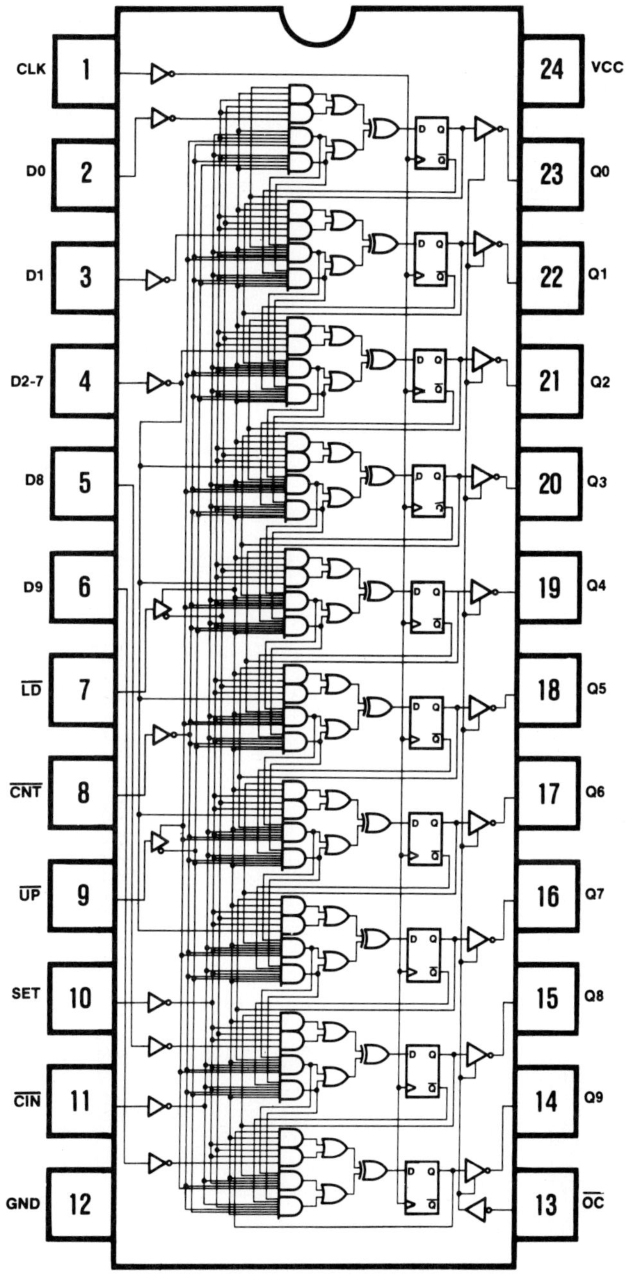

16:1 Mux
SN54/74LS450

Features/Benefits

- 24-pin SKINNYDIP™ saves space
- Similar to 74150 (Fat DIP)
- Low current PNP inputs reduce loading

Ordering Information

PART NUMBER	PACKAGE	TEMPERATURE
SN54LS450	JS	MIL
SN74LS450	NS, JS	COM

Description

The 16:1 Mux selects one of sixteen inputs, E0 through E15, specified by four binary select inputs, A, B, C, and D. The true data is output on Y and the inverted data on W. Propagation delays are the same for both inputs and addresses and are specified for 50 pF loading. Outputs conform to the standard 8 mA LS totem pole drive standard.

Logic Symbol

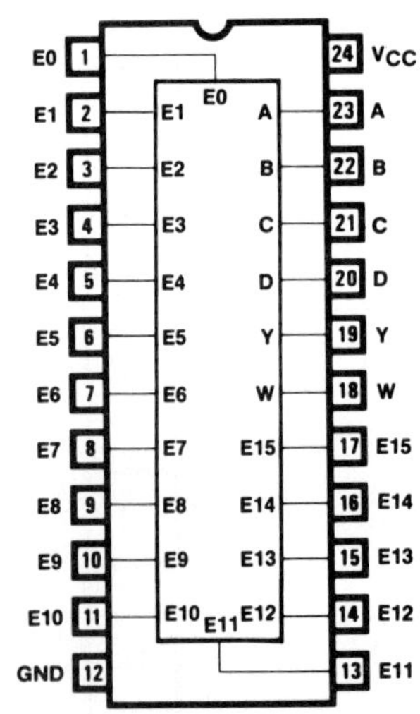

Function Table

INPUT SELECT				OUTPUT	
D	C	B	A	W	Y
L	L	L	L	$\overline{E0}$	E0
L	L	L	H	$\overline{E1}$	E1
L	L	H	L	$\overline{E2}$	E2
L	L	H	H	$\overline{E3}$	E3
L	H	L	L	$\overline{E4}$	E4
L	H	L	H	$\overline{E5}$	E5
L	H	H	L	$\overline{E6}$	E6
L	H	H	H	$\overline{E7}$	E7
H	L	L	L	$\overline{E8}$	E8
H	L	L	H	$\overline{E9}$	E9
H	L	H	L	$\overline{E10}$	E10
H	L	H	H	$\overline{E11}$	E11
H	H	L	L	$\overline{E12}$	E12
H	H	L	H	$\overline{E13}$	E13
H	H	H	L	$\overline{E14}$	E14
H	H	H	H	$\overline{E15}$	E15

For supplementary information, see appendix, this section.

Logic Diagram

16:1 Mux

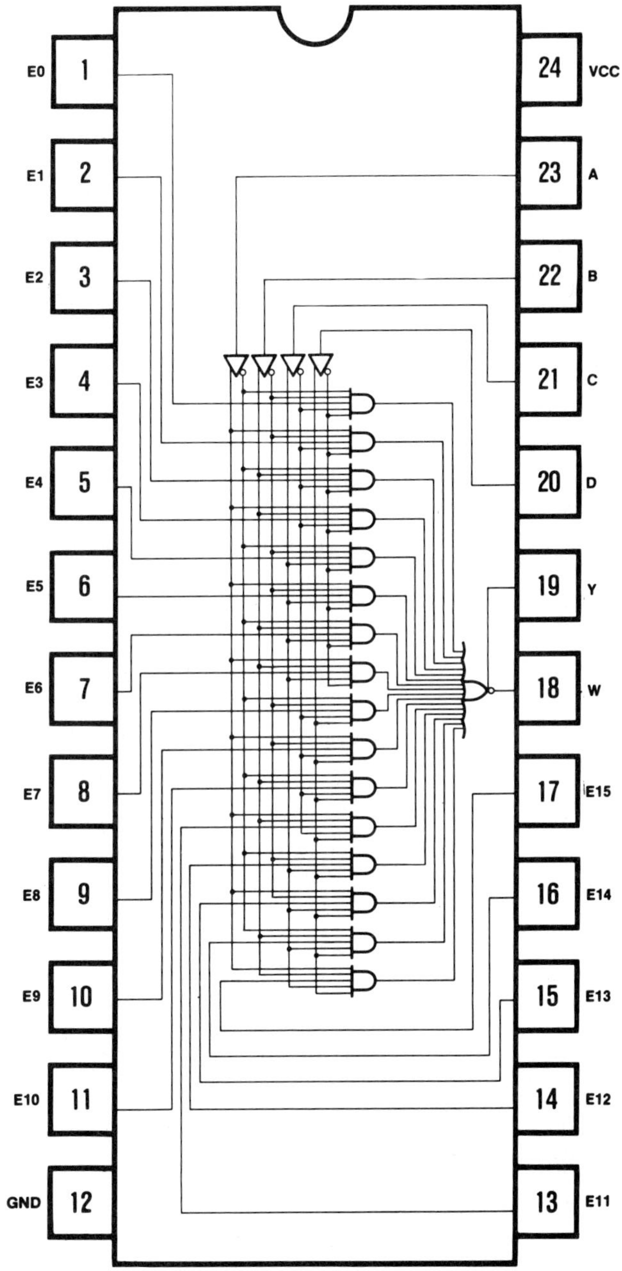

Dual 8:1 Mux
SN54/74LS451

Features/Benefits

- 24-pin SKINNYDIP™ saves space
- Twice the density of 74LS151
- Low current PNP inputs reduce loading

Ordering Information

PART NUMBER	PACKAGE	TEMPERATURE
SN54LS451	JS	MIL
SN74LS451	NS, JS	COM

Description

The dual 8:1 Mux selects one of eight inputs, D0 through D7, specified by three binary select inputs, A, B, and C. The true data is output on Y when strobed by S. Propagation delays are the same for inputs, addresses and strobes and are specified for 50 pF loading. Outputs conform to the standard 8 mA LS totem pole drive standard.

Logic Symbol

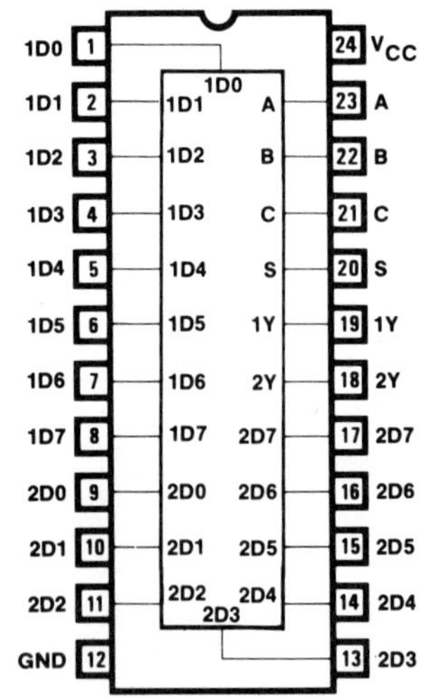

Function Table

INPUTS				OUTPUTS
SELECT			STROBE	Y
C	B	A	S	
X	X	X	H	H
L	L	L	L	D0
L	L	H	L	D1
L	H	L	L	D2
L	H	H	L	D3
H	L	L	L	D4
H	L	H	L	D5
H	H	L	L	D6
H	H	H	L	D7

For supplementary information, see appendix, this section.

Logic Diagram

Dual 8:1 Mux

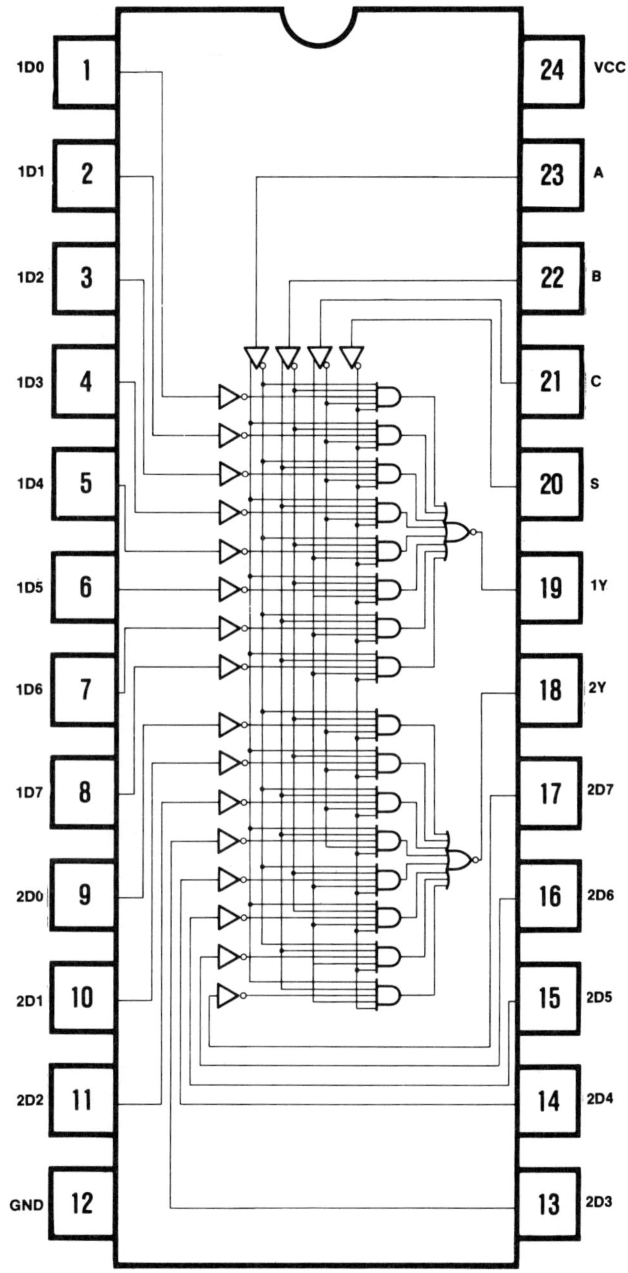

Quad 4:1 Mux
SN54/74LS453

Features/Benefits

- 24-pin SKINNYDIP™ saves space
- Twice the density of 74LS153
- Low current PNP inputs reduce loading

Ordering Information

PART NUMBER	PACKAGE	TEMPERATURE
SN74LS453	JS	MIL
SN54LS453	NS, JS	COM

Description

The quad 4:1 Mux selects one of four inputs, C0 through C3, specified by two binary select inputs, A and B. The true data is output on Y. Propagation delays are the same for inputs and addresses and are specified for 50 pF loading. Outputs conform to the standard 8 mA LS totem pole drive standard.

Logic Symbol

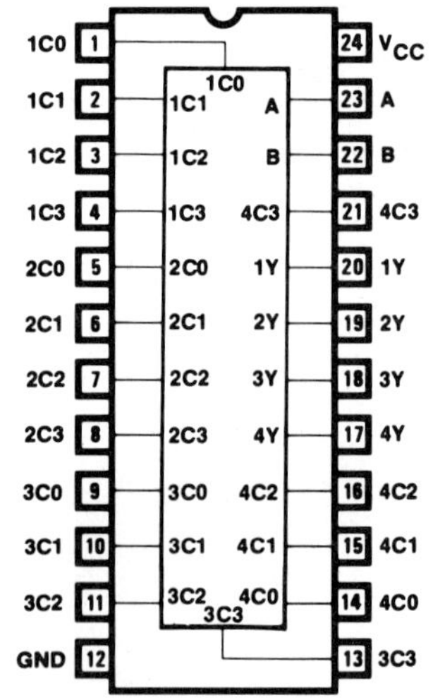

Function Table

INPUT SELECT		OUTPUTS Y
B	A	
L	L	C0
L	H	C1
H	L	C2
H	H	C3

For supplementary information, see appendix, this section.

Logic Diagram

Quad 4:1 Mux

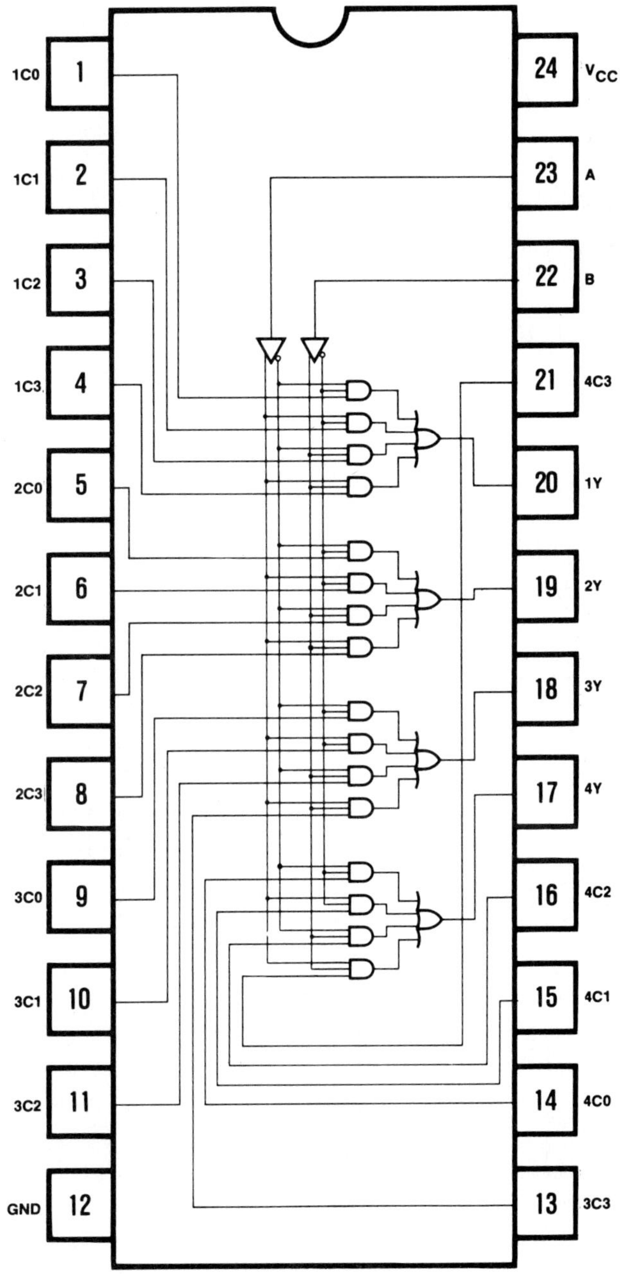

HMSI Appendix

Absolute Maximum Ratings

Supply voltage V_{CC} 7V
Input voltage 5.5V
Off-state output voltage 5.5V
Storage temperature .... –65° to +150°C

Operating Conditions

SYMBOL	PARAMETER		MILITARY MIN	MILITARY TYP	MILITARY MAX	COMMERCIAL MIN	COMMERCIAL TYP	COMMERCIAL MAX	UNIT
V_{CC}	Supply voltage		4.5	5	5.5	4.75	5	5.25	V
t_w	Width of clock	Low	40			35			ns
		High	30			25			
t_{su}	Set up time		60			50			ns
t_h	Hold time		0	–15		0	–15		
T_A	Operating free-air temperature		–55			0		75	°C
T_C	Operating case temperature				125				°C

Electrical Characteristics Over Operating Conditions

SYMBOL	PARAMETER	TEST CONDITIONS		MIN	TYP†	MAX	UNIT
V_{IL}	Low-level input voltage					0.8	V
V_{IH}	High-level input voltage			2			V
V_{IC}	Input clamp voltage	V_{CC} = MIN	I_I = –18mA			–1.5	V
I_{IL}	Low-level input current	V_{CC} = MAX	V_I = 0.4V			0.25	mA
I_{IH}	High-level input current	V_{CC} = MAX	V_I = 2.4V			25	μA
I_I	Maximum input current	V_{CC} = MAX	V_I = 5.5V			1	mA
V_{OL}	Low-level output voltage	V_{CC} = MIN, V_{IL} = 0.8V, V_{IH} = 2V	MIL I_{OL} = 12mA; COM I_{OL} = 24mA			0.5	V
V_{OH}	High-level output voltage	V_{CC} = MIN, V_{IL} = 0.8V, V_{IH} = 2V	MIL I_{OH} = –2mA; COM I_{OH} = –3.2mA	2.4			V
I_{OZL}	Off-state output current	V_{CC} = MAX, V_{IL} = 0.8V, V_{IH} = 2V	V_O = 0.4V			–100	μA
I_{OZH}			V_O = 2.4V			100	μA
I_{OS}	Output short-circuit current*	V_{CC} = 5.0V	V_O = 0V	–30		–130	mA
I_{CC}	Supply current	V_{CC} = MAX			120	180	mA

* No more than one output should be shorted at a time and duration of the short-circuit should not exceed one second.

† All typical values are at V_{CC} = 5V, T_A = 25°C

Switching Characteristics Over Operating Conditions

SYMBOL	PARAMETER	TEST CONDITIONS (See Test Load)	MILITARY MIN	MILITARY TYP	MILITARY MAX	COMMERCIAL MIN	COMMERCIAL TYP	COMMERCIAL MAX	UNIT
f_{MAX}	Maximum clock frequency	C_L = 50 pF, R_1 = 200Ω, R_2 = 390Ω	10.5			12.5			MHz
t_{PD}	$\overline{CI}$ to $\overline{CO}$ delay			35	60		35	50	ns
t_{PD}	Clock to Q			20	35		20	30	ns
t_{PD}	Clock to $\overline{CO}$			55	95		55	80	ns
t_{PZX}	Output enable delay			35	55		35	45	ns
t_{PXZ}	Output disable delay			35	55		35	45	ns

Absolute Maximum Ratings

Supply voltage V_{CC} 7V
Input voltage 5.5V
Off-state output voltage 5.5V
Storage temperature .... −65° to +150°C

Operating Conditions

SYMBOL	PARAMETER		MILITARY MIN	MILITARY TYP	MILITARY MAX	COMMERCIAL MIN	COMMERCIAL TYP	COMMERCIAL MAX	UNIT
V_{CC}	Supply voltage		4.5	5	5.5	4.75	5	5.25	V
t_w	Width of clock	Low	40			35			ns
		High	30			25			
t_{su}	Set up time		60			50			ns
t_h	Hold time		0	−15		0	−15		
T_A	Operating free-air temperature		−55			0		75	°C
T_C	Operating case temperature				125				°C

Electrical Characteristics Over Operating Conditions

SYMBOL	PARAMETER	TEST CONDITIONS			MIN	TYP†	MAX	UNIT
V_{IL}	Low-level input voltage						0.8	V
V_{IH}	High-level input voltage				2			V
V_{IC}	Input clamp voltage	V_{CC} = MIN	I_I = −18mA				−1.5	V
I_{IL}	Low-level input current	V_{CC} = MAX	V_I = 0.4V				0.25	mA
I_{IH}	High-level input current	V_{CC} = MAX	V_I = 2.4V				25	μA
I_I	Maximum input current	V_{CC} = MAX	V_I = 5.5V				1	mA
V_{OL}	Low-level output voltage	V_{CC} = MIN, V_{IL} = 0.8V, V_{IH} = 2V	MIL	I_{OL} = 12mA			0.5	V
			COM	I_{OL} = 24mA				
V_{OH}	High-level output voltage	V_{CC} = MIN, V_{IL} = 0.8V, V_{IH} = 2V	MIL	I_{OH} = −2mA	2.4			V
			COM	I_{OH} = −3.2mA				
I_{OZL}	Off-state output current	V_{CC} = MAX, V_{IL} = 0.8V, V_{IH} = 2V		V_O = 0.4V			−100	μA
I_{OZH}				V_O = 2.4V			100	μA
I_{OS}	Output short-circuit current*	V_{CC} = 5.0V		V_O = 0V	−30		−130	mA
I_{CC}	Supply current	V_{CC} = MAX				120	180	mA

* No more than one output should be shorted at a time and duration of the short-circuit should not exceed one second.

† All typical values are at V_{CC} = 5V, T_A = 25°C

Switching Characteristics Over Operating Conditions

SYMBOL	PARAMETER	TEST CONDITIONS (See Test Load)	MILITARY MIN	MILITARY TYP	MILITARY MAX	COMMERCIAL MIN	COMMERCIAL TYP	COMMERCIAL MAX	UNIT
f_{MAX}	Maximum clock frequency		10.5			12.5			MHz
t_{PD}	I0, I1 to LIRO, RILO	C_L = 50 pF		35	60		35	50	ns
t_{PD}	Clock to Q	R_1 = 200Ω		20	35		20	30	ns
t_{PD}	Clock to LIRO, RILO	R_2 = 390Ω		55	95		55	80	ns
t_{PZX}	Output enable delay			35	55		35	45	ns
t_{PXZ}	Output disable delay			35	55		35	45	ns

Absolute Maximum Ratings

Supply voltage V_{CC} 7V
Input voltage 5.5V
Off-state output voltage 5.5V
Storage temperature .... –65° to +150°C

Operating Conditions

SYMBOL	PARAMETER		MILITARY MIN	MILITARY TYP	MILITARY MAX	COMMERCIAL MIN	COMMERCIAL TYP	COMMERCIAL MAX	UNIT
V_{CC}	Supply voltage		4.5	5	5.5	4.75	5	5.25	V
t_w	Width of clock	High	40			40			ns
		Low	35			35			
t_{su}	Set up time		60			50			ns
t_h	Hold time		0	–15		0	–15		
T_A	Operating free-air temperature		–55			0		75	°C
T_C	Operating case temperature				125				°C

Electrical Characteristics Over Operating Conditions

SYMBOL	PARAMETER	TEST CONDITIONS			MIN	TYP†	MAX	UNIT
V_{IL}	Low-level input voltage						0.8	V
V_{IH}	High-level input voltage				2			V
V_{IC}	Input clamp voltage	V_{CC} = MIN	I_I = –18mA				–1.5	V
I_{IL}	Low-level input current	V_{CC} = MAX	V_I = 0.4V				0.25	mA
I_{IH}	High-level input current	V_{CC} = MAX	V_I = 2.4V				25	µA
I_I	Maximum input current	V_{CC} = MAX	V_I = 5.5V				1	mA
V_{OL}	Low-level output voltage	V_{CC} = MIN, V_{IL} = 0.8V, V_{IH} = 2V	MIL	I_{OL} = 12mA			0.5	V
			COM	I_{OL} = 24mA				
V_{OH}	High-level output voltage	V_{CC} = MIN, V_{IL} = 0.8V, V_{IH} = 2V	MIL	I_{OH} = –2mA	2.4			V
			COM	I_{OH} = –3.2mA				
I_{OZL}	Off-state output current	V_{CC} = MAX, V_{IL} = 0.8V, V_{IH} = 2V		V_O = 0.4V			–100	µA
I_{OZH}				V_O = 2.4V			100	µA
I_{OS}	Output short-circuit current*	V_{CC} = 5.0V		V_O = 0V	–30		–130	mA
I_{CC}	Supply current	V_{CC} = MAX				120	180	mA

* No more than one output should be shorted at a time and duration of the short-circuit should not exceed one second.

† All typical values are at V_{CC} = 5V, T_A = 25°C

Switching Characteristics Over Operating Conditions

SYMBOL	PARAMETER	TEST CONDITIONS (See Test Load)	MILITARY MIN	MILITARY TYP	MILITARY MAX	COMMERCIAL MIN	COMMERCIAL TYP	COMMERCIAL MAX	UNIT
f_{MAX}	Maximum clock frequency	C_L = 50pF, R_1 = 200Ω, R_2 = 390Ω	10.5			12.5			MHz
t_{PD}	Clock to Q			20	35		20	30	ns
t_{PZX}	Output enable delay			35	55		35	45	ns
t_{PXZ}	Output disable delay			35	55		35	45	ns

Absolute Maximum Ratings

Supply voltage V_{CC} 7V
Input voltage 5.5V
Off-state output voltage 5.5V
Storage temperature .... −65° to +150°C

Operating Conditions

SYMBOL	PARAMETER		MILITARY MIN	MILITARY TYP	MILITARY MAX	COMMERCIAL MIN	COMMERCIAL TYP	COMMERCIAL MAX	UNIT
V_{CC}	Supply voltage		4.5	5	5.5	4.75	5	5.25	V
t_w	Width of clock	High	40			40			ns
		Low	35			35			
t_{su}	Set up time		60			50			ns
t_h	Hold time		0	−15		0	−15		
T_A	Operating free-air temperature		−55			0		75	°C
T_C	Operating case temperature				125				°C

Electrical Characteristics Over Operating Conditions

SYMBOL	PARAMETER	TEST CONDITIONS		MIN	TYP†	MAX	UNIT
V_{IL}	Low-level input voltage					0.8	V
V_{IH}	High-level input voltage			2			V
V_{IC}	Input clamp voltage	V_{CC} = MIN	I_I = −18mA			−1.5	V
I_{IL}	Low-level input current	V_{CC} = MAX	V_I = 0.4V			0.25	mA
I_{IH}	High-level input current	V_{CC} = MAX	V_I = 2.4V			25	μA
I_I	Maximum input current	V_{CC} = MAX	V_I = 5.5V			1	mA
V_{OL}	Low-level output voltage	V_{CC} = MIN, V_{IL} = 0.8V, V_{IH} = 2V	MIL I_{OL} = 12mA; COM I_{OL} = 24mA			0.5	V
V_{OH}	High-level output voltage	V_{CC} = MIN, V_{IL} = 0.8V, V_{IH} = 2V	MIL I_{OH} = −2mA; COM I_{OH} = −3.2mA	2.4			V
I_{OZL}	Off-state output current	V_{CC} = MAX, V_{IL} = 0.8V, V_{IH} = 2V	V_O = 0.4V			−100	μA
I_{OZH}			V_O = 2.4V			100	μA
I_{OS}	Output short-circuit current*	V_{CC} = 5.0V	V_O = 0V	−30		−130	mA
I_{CC}	Supply current	V_{CC} = MAX			120	180	mA

* No more than one output should be shorted at a time and duration of the short-circuit should not exceed one second.

† All typical values are at V_{CC} = 5V, T_A = 25°C

Switching Characteristics Over Operating Conditions

SYMBOL	PARAMETER	TEST CONDITIONS (See Test Load)	MILITARY MIN	MILITARY TYP	MILITARY MAX	COMMERCIAL MIN	COMMERCIAL TYP	COMMERCIAL MAX	UNIT
f_{MAX}	Maximum clock frequency	C_L = 50pF, R_1 = 200Ω, R_2 = 390Ω	10.5			12.5			MHz
t_{PD}	Clock to Q			20	35		20	30	ns
t_{PZX}	Output enable delay			35	55		35	45	ns
t_{PXZ}	Output disable delay			35	55		35	45	ns

Absolute Maximum Ratings

Supply voltage V_{CC} 7V
Input voltage 5.5V
Off-state output voltage 5.5V
Storage temperature .... −65° to +150°C

Operating Conditions

SYMBOL	PARAMETER	MILITARY			COMMERCIAL			UNIT
		MIN	NOM	MAX	MIN	NOM	MAX	
V_{CC}	Supply voltage	4.5	5	5.5	4.75	5	5.25	V
T_A	Operating free-air temperature	−55			0		75	°C
T_C	Operating case temperature			125				°C

Electrical Characteristics Over Operating Conditions

SYMBOL	PARAMETER	TEST CONDITIONS			MIN	TYP†	MAX	UNIT
V_{IL}	Low-level input voltage						0.8	V
V_{IH}	High-level input voltage				2			V
V_{IC}	Input clamp voltage	V_{CC} = MIN	I_I = −18mA				−1.5	V
I_{IL}	Low-level input current	V_{CC} = MAX	V_I = 0.4V				0.25	mA
I_{IH}	High-level input current	V_{CC} = MAX	V_I = 2.4V				25	μA
I_I	Maximum input current	V_{CC} = MAX	V_I = 5.5V				1	mA
V_{OL}	Low-level output voltage	V_{CC} = MIN V_{IL} = 0.8V V_{IH} = 2V		I_{OL} = 8mA			0.5	V
V_{OH}	High-level output voltage	V_{CC} = MIN V_{IL} = 0.8V V_{IH} = 2V	MIL COM	I_{OH} = −2mA I_{OH} = −3.2mA	2.4			V
I_{OS}	Output short-circuit current*	V_{CC} = 5.0V		V_O = 0V	−30		−130	mA
I_{CC}	Supply current	V_{CC} = MAX				60	100	mA

* No more than one output should be shorted at a time and duration of the short-circuit should not exceed one second.

† All typical values are at V_{CC} = 5V, T_A = 25°C

Switching Characteristics Over Operating Conditions

SYMBOL	PARAMETER	TEST CONDITIONS (See Test Load)	MILITARY			COMMERCIAL			UNIT
			MIN	TYP	MAX	MIN	TYP	MAX	
t_{PD}	Any input to Y or W	C_L = 50 pF R_1 = 560Ω R_2 = 1.1kΩ		25	45		25	40	ns

Absolute Maximum Ratings

Supply voltage V_{CC} 7V
Input voltage 5.5V
Off-state output voltage 5.5V
Storage temperature .... −65° to +150°C

Operating Conditions

SYMBOL	PARAMETER	MILITARY MIN	MILITARY NOM	MILITARY MAX	COMMERCIAL MIN	COMMERCIAL NOM	COMMERCIAL MAX	UNIT
V_{CC}	Supply voltage	4.5	5	5.5	4.75	5	5.25	V
T_A	Operating free-air temperature	−55			0		75	°C
T_C	Operating case temperature			125				°C

Electrical Characteristics Over Operating Conditions

SYMBOL	PARAMETER	TEST CONDITIONS			MIN	TYP†	MAX	UNIT
V_{IL}	Low-level input voltage						0.8	V
V_{IH}	High-level input voltage				2			V
V_{IC}	Input clamp voltage	V_{CC} = MIN	I_I = −18mA				−1.5	V
I_{IL}	Low-level input current	V_{CC} = MAX	V_I = 0.4V				0.25	mA
I_{IH}	High-level input current	V_{CC} = MAX	V_I = 2.4V				25	μA
I_I	Maximum input current	V_{CC} = MAX	V_I = 5.5V				1	mA
V_{OL}	Low-level output voltage	V_{CC} = MIN, V_{IL} = 0.8V, V_{IH} = 2V		I_{OL} = 8mA			0.5	V
V_{OH}	High-level output voltage	V_{CC} = MIN, V_{IL} = 0.8V, V_{IH} = 2V	MIL	I_{OH} = −2mA	2.4			V
			COM	I_{OH} = −3.2mA				
I_{OS}	Output short-circuit current*	V_{CC} = 5.0V		V_O = 0V	−30		−130	mA
I_{CC}	Supply current	V_{CC} = MAX				60	100	mA

* No more than one output should be shorted at a time and duration of the short-circuit should not exceed one second.

† All typical values are at V_{CC} = 5V, T_A = 25°C

Switching Characteristics Over Operating Conditions

SYMBOL	PARAMETER	TEST CONDITIONS (See Test Load)	MILITARY MIN	MILITARY TYP	MILITARY MAX	COMMERCIAL MIN	COMMERCIAL TYP	COMMERCIAL MAX	UNIT
t_{PD}	Any input to Y	C_L = 50 pF, R_1 = 560Ω, R_2 = 1.1kΩ		25	45		25	40	ns

Absolute Maximum Ratings

Supply voltage V_{CC} 7V
Input voltage 5.5V
Off-state output voltage 5.5V
Storage temperature .... −65° to +150°C

Operating Conditions

SYMBOL	PARAMETER	MILITARY			COMMERCIAL			UNIT
		MIN	NOM	MAX	MIN	NOM	MAX	
V_{CC}	Supply voltage	4.5	5	5.5	4.75	5	5.25	V
T_A	Operating free-air temperature	−55			0		75	°C
T_C	Operating case temperature			125				°C

Electrical Characteristics Over Operating Conditions

SYMBOL	PARAMETER	TEST CONDITIONS		MIN	TYP†	MAX	UNIT
V_{IL}	Low-level input voltage					0.8	V
V_{IH}	High-level input voltage			2			V
V_{IC}	Input clamp voltage	V_{CC} = MIN	I_I = −18mA			−1.5	V
I_{IL}	Low-level input current	V_{CC} = MAX	V_I = 0.4V			0.25	mA
I_{IH}	High-level input current	V_{CC} = MAX	V_I = 2.4V			25	μA
I_I	Maximum input current	V_{CC} = MAX	V_I = 5.5V			1	mA
V_{OL}	Low-level output voltage	V_{CC} = MIN, V_{IL} = 0.8V, V_{IH} = 2V	I_{OL} = 8mA			0.5	V
V_{OH}	High-level output voltage	V_{CC} = MIN, V_{IL} = 0.8V, V_{IH} = 2V	MIL I_{OH} = −2mA; COM I_{OH} = −3.2mA	2.4			V
I_{OS}	Output short-circuit current*	V_{CC} = 5.0V	V_O = 0V	−30		−130	mA
I_{CC}	Supply current	V_{CC} = MAX			60	100	mA

* No more than one output should be shorted at a time and duration of the short-circuit should not exceed one second.

† All typical values are at V_{CC} = 5V, T_A = 25°C

Switching Characteristics Over Operating Conditions

SYMBOL	PARAMETER	TEST CONDITIONS (See Test Load)	MILITARY			COMMERCIAL			UNIT
			MIN	TYP	MAX	MIN	TYP	MAX	
t_{PD}	Any input to Y	C_L = 50 pF, R_1 = 560Ω, R_2 = 1.1kΩ		25	45		25	40	ns